1/87

The Encyclopedia of Religion

The Encyclopedia of Religion

Mircea Eliade

EDITOR IN CHIEF

Volume 4

MACMILLAN PUBLISHING COMPANY
New York

Collier Macmillan Publishers
London

MACMILLAN PUBLISHING COMPANY
866 Third Avenue, New York, NY 10022

Collier Macmillan Canada, Inc.

Library of Congress Catalog Card Number: 86-5432

PRINTED IN THE UNITED STATES OF AMERICA

printing number
1 2 3 4 5 6 7 8 9 10

Library of Congress Cataloging-in-Publication Data

The Encyclopedia of religion.

Includes bibliographies and index.
1. Religion—Dictionaries. I. Eliade, Mircea, 1907–1986. II. Adams, Charles J.
BL31.#46 1986 200′.3′21 86-5432
ISBN 0-02-909480-1 (set)
ISBN 0-02-909730-4 (v. 4)

Acknowledgments of sources, copyrights, and permissions to use previously published materials are gratefully made in a special listing in volume 16.

Abbreviations and Symbols Used in This Work

abbr. abbreviated; abbreviation
abr. abridged; abridgment
AD *anno Domini,* in the year of the (our) Lord
Afrik. Afrikaans
AH *anno Hegirae,* in the year of the Hijrah
Akk. Akkadian
Ala. Alabama
Alb. Albanian
Am. *Amos*
AM *ante meridiem,* before noon
amend. amended; amendment
annot. annotated; annotation
Ap. *Apocalypse*
Apn. *Apocryphon*
app. appendix
Arab. Arabic
'Arakh. *'Arakhin*
Aram. Aramaic
Ariz. Arizona
Ark. Arkansas
Arm. Armenian
art. article (pl., arts.)
AS Anglo-Saxon
Asm. Mos. *Assumption of Moses*
Assyr. Assyrian
A.S.S.R. Autonomous Soviet Socialist Republic
Av. Avestan
'A.Z. *'Avodah zarah*
b. born
Bab. Babylonian
Ban. Bantu
1 Bar. *1 Baruch*
2 Bar. *2 Baruch*
3 Bar. *3 Baruch*
4 Bar. *4 Baruch*
B.B. *Bava' batra'*
BBC British Broadcasting Corporation
BC before Christ
BCE before the common era
B.D. Bachelor of Divinity
Beits. *Beitsah*
Bekh. *Bekhorot*
Beng. Bengali
Ber. *Berakhot*
Berb. Berber
Bik. *Bikkurim*
bk. book (pl., bks.)
B.M. *Bava' metsi'a'*
BP before the present
B.Q. *Bava' qamma'*
Brāh. *Brāhmaṇa*
Bret. Breton
B.T. Babylonian Talmud
Bulg. Bulgarian
Burm. Burmese
c. *circa,* about, approximately
Calif. California
Can. Canaanite
Catal. Catalan
CE of the common era
Celt. Celtic
cf. *confer,* compare
Chald. Chaldean
chap. chapter (pl., chaps.)
Chin. Chinese
C.H.M. Community of the Holy Myrrhbearers
1 Chr. *1 Chronicles*
2 Chr. *2 Chronicles*
Ch. Slav. Church Slavic
cm centimeters
col. column (pl., cols.)
Col. *Colossians*
Colo. Colorado
comp. compiler (pl., comps.)
Conn. Connecticut
cont. continued
Copt. Coptic
1 Cor. *1 Corinthians*
2 Cor. *2 Corinthians*
corr. corrected
C.S.P. Congregatio Sancti Pauli, Congregation of Saint Paul (Paulists)
d. died
D Deuteronomic (source of the Pentateuch)
Dan. Danish
D.B. Divinitatis Baccalaureus, Bachelor of Divinity
D.C. District of Columbia
D.D. Divinitatis Doctor, Doctor of Divinity
Del. Delaware
Dem. *Dema'i*
dim. diminutive
diss. dissertation
Dn. *Daniel*
D.Phil. Doctor of Philosophy
Dt. *Deuteronomy*
Du. Dutch
E Elohist (source of the Pentateuch)
Eccl. *Ecclesiastes*
ed. editor (pl., eds.); edition; edited by
'Eduy. *'Eduyyot*
e.g. *exempli gratia,* for example
Egyp. Egyptian
1 En. *1 Enoch*
2 En. *2 Enoch*
3 En. *3 Enoch*
Eng. English
enl. enlarged
Eph. *Ephesians*
'Eruv. *'Eruvin*
1 Esd. *1 Esdras*
2 Esd. *2 Esdras*
3 Esd. *3 Esdras*
4 Esd. *4 Esdras*
esp. especially
Est. Estonian
Est. *Esther*
et al. *et alii,* and others
etc. *et cetera,* and so forth
Eth. Ethiopic
EV English version
Ex. *Exodus*
exp. expanded
Ez. *Ezekiel*
Ezr. *Ezra*
2 Ezr. *2 Ezra*
4 Ezr. *4 Ezra*
f. feminine; and following (pl., ff.)
fasc. fascicle (pl., fascs.)
fig. figure (pl., figs.)
Finn. Finnish
fl. *floruit,* flourished
Fla. Florida
Fr. French
frag. fragment
ft. feet
Ga. Georgia
Gal. *Galatians*
Gaul. Gaulish
Ger. German
Giṭ. *Giṭṭin*
Gn. *Genesis*
Gr. Greek
Ḥag. *Ḥagigah*
Ḥal. *Ḥallah*
Hau. Hausa
Hb. *Habakkuk*
Heb. Hebrew
Heb. *Hebrews*
Hg. *Haggai*
Hitt. Hittite
Hor. *Horayot*
Hos. *Hosea*
Ḥul. *Ḥullin*
Hung. Hungarian
ibid. *ibidem,* in the same place (as the one immediately preceding)
Icel. Icelandic
i.e. *id est,* that is
IE Indo-European
Ill. Illinois
Ind. Indiana
intro. introduction
Ir. Gael. Irish Gaelic
Iran. Iranian
Is. *Isaiah*
Ital. Italian
J Yahvist (source of the Pentateuch)
Jas. *James*
Jav. Javanese
Jb. *Job*
Jdt. *Judith*
Jer. *Jeremiah*
Jgs. *Judges*
Jl. *Joel*
Jn. *John*
1 Jn. *1 John*
2 Jn. *2 John*
3 Jn. *3 John*
Jon. *Jonah*
Jos. *Joshua*
Jpn. Japanese
JPS Jewish Publication Society translation (1985) of the Hebrew Bible
J.T. Jerusalem Talmud
Jub. *Jubilees*
Kans. Kansas
Kel. *Kelim*

Ker. *Keritot*
Ket. *Ketubbot*
1 Kgs. *1 Kings*
2 Kgs. *2 Kings*
Khois. Khoisan
Kil. *Kil'ayim*
km kilometers
Kor. Korean
Ky. Kentucky
l. line (pl., ll.)
La. Louisiana
Lam. *Lamentations*
Lat. Latin
Latv. Latvian
L. en Th. Licencié en Théologie, Licentiate in Theology
L. ès L. Licencié ès Lettres, Licentiate in Literature
Let. Jer. *Letter of Jeremiah*
lit. literally
Lith. Lithuanian
Lk. *Luke*
LL Late Latin
LL.D. Legum Doctor, Doctor of Laws
Lv. *Leviticus*
m meters
m. masculine
M.A. Master of Arts
Ma'as. *Ma'aserot*
Ma'as. Sh. *Ma'aser sheni*
Mak. *Makkot*
Makh. *Makhshirin*
Mal. *Malachi*
Mar. Marathi
Mass. Massachusetts
1 Mc. *1 Maccabees*
2 Mc. *2 Maccabees*
3 Mc. *3 Maccabees*
4 Mc. *4 Maccabees*
Md. Maryland
M.D. Medicinae Doctor, Doctor of Medicine
ME Middle English
Meg. *Megillah*
Me'il. *Me'ilah*
Men. *Menaḥot*
MHG Middle High German
mi. miles
Mi. *Micah*
Mich. Michigan
Mid. *Middot*
Minn. Minnesota
Miq. *Miqva'ot*
MIran. Middle Iranian
Miss. Mississippi
Mk. *Mark*
Mo. Missouri
Mo'ed Q. *Mo'ed qaṭan*
Mont. Montana
MPers. Middle Persian
MS. *manuscriptum,* manuscript (pl., MSS)
Mt. *Matthew*
MT Masoretic text
n. note
Na. *Nahum*
Nah. Nahuatl
Naz. *Nazir*
N.B. *nota bene*, take careful note
N.C. North Carolina
n.d. no date
N.Dak. North Dakota
NEB New English Bible
Nebr. Nebraska
Ned. *Nedarim*
Neg. *Nega'im*
Neh. *Nehemiah*
Nev. Nevada
N.H. New Hampshire
Nid. *Niddah*
N.J. New Jersey
Nm. *Numbers*
N.Mex. New Mexico
no. number (pl., nos.)
Nor. Norwegian
n.p. no place
n.s. new series
N.Y. New York
Ob. *Obadiah*
O.Cist. Ordo Cisterciencium, Order of Cîteaux (Cistercians)
OCS Old Church Slavonic
OE Old English
O.F.M. Ordo Fratrum Minorum, Order of Friars Minor (Franciscans)
OFr. Old French
Ohal. *Ohalot*
OHG Old High German
OIr. Old Irish
OIran. Old Iranian
Okla. Oklahoma
ON Old Norse
O.P. Ordo Praedicatorum, Order of Preachers (Dominicans)
OPers. Old Persian
op. cit. *opere citato*, in the work cited
OPrus. Old Prussian
Oreg. Oregon
'Orl. *'Orlah*
O.S.B. Ordo Sancti Benedicti, Order of Saint Benedict (Benedictines)
p. page (pl., pp.)
P Priestly (source of the Pentateuch)
Pa. Pennsylvania
Pahl. Pahlavi
Par. *Parah*
para. paragraph (pl., paras.)
Pers. Persian
Pes. *Pesaḥim*
Ph.D. Philosophiae Doctor, Doctor of Philosophy
Phil. *Philippians*
Phlm. *Philemon*
Phoen. Phoenician
pl. plural; plate (pl., pls.)
PM *post meridiem*, after noon
Pol. Polish
pop. population
Port. Portuguese
Prv. *Proverbs*
Ps. *Psalms*
Ps. 151 *Psalm 151*
Ps. Sol. *Psalms of Solomon*
pt. part (pl., pts.)
1 Pt. *1 Peter*
2 Pt. *2 Peter*
Pth. Parthian
Q hypothetical source of the synoptic Gospels
Qid. *Qiddushin*
Qin. *Qinnim*
r. reigned; ruled
Rab. *Rabbah*
rev. revised
R. ha-Sh. *Ro'sh ha-shanah*
R.I. Rhode Island
Rom. Romanian
Rom. *Romans*
R.S.C.J. Societas Sacratissimi Cordis Jesu, Religious of the Sacred Heart
RSV Revised Standard Version of the Bible
Ru. *Ruth*
Rus. Russian
Rv. *Revelation*
Rv. Ezr. *Revelation of Ezra*
San. *Sanhedrin*
S.C. South Carolina
Scot. Gael. Scottish Gaelic
S.Dak. South Dakota
sec. section (pl., secs.)
Sem. Semitic
ser. series
sg. singular
Sg. *Song of Songs*
Sg. of 3 *Prayer of Azariah and the Song of the Three Young Men*
Shab. *Shabbat*
Shav. *Shavu'ot*
Sheq. *Sheqalim*
Sib. Or. *Sibylline Oracles*
Sind. Sindhi
Sinh. Sinhala
Sir. *Ben Sira*
S.J. Societas Jesu, Society of Jesus (Jesuits)
Skt. Sanskrit
1 Sm. *1 Samuel*
2 Sm. *2 Samuel*
Sogd. Sogdian
Soṭ *Soṭah*
sp. species (pl., spp.)
Span. Spanish
sq. square
S.S.R. Soviet Socialist Republic
st. stanza (pl., ss.)
S.T.M. Sacrae Theologiae Magister, Master of Sacred Theology
Suk. *Sukkah*
Sum. Sumerian
supp. supplement; supplementary
Sus. *Susanna*
s.v. *sub verbo*, under the word (pl., s.v.v.)
Swed. Swedish
Syr. Syriac
Syr. Men. *Syriac Menander*
Ta'an. *Ta'anit*
Tam. Tamil
Tam. *Tamid*
Tb. *Tobit*
T.D. *Taishō shinshū daizōkyō*, edited by Takakusu Junjirō et al. (Tokyo, 1922–1934)
Tem. *Temurah*
Tenn. Tennessee
Ter. *Terumot*
Ṭev. Y. *Ṭevul yom*
Tex. Texas
Th.D. Theologicae Doctor, Doctor of Theology
1 Thes. *1 Thessalonians*
2 Thes. *2 Thessalonians*
Thrac. Thracian
Ti. *Titus*
Tib. Tibetan
1 Tm. *1 Timothy*
2 Tm. *2 Timothy*
T. of 12 *Testaments of the Twelve Patriarchs*
Ṭoh. *Ṭohorot*
Tong. Tongan
trans. translator, translators; translated by; translation
Turk. Turkish
Ukr. Ukrainian
Upan. *Upaniṣad*
U.S. United States
U.S.S.R. Union of Soviet Socialist Republics
Uqts. *Uqtsin*
v. verse (pl., vv.)
Va. Virginia
var. variant; variation
Viet. Vietnamese
viz. *videlicet*, namely
vol. volume (pl., vols.)
Vt. Vermont
Wash. Washington
Wel. Welsh
Wis. Wisconsin
Wis. *Wisdom of Solomon*
W.Va. West Virginia
Wyo. Wyoming
Yad. *Yadayim*
Yev. *Yevamot*
Yi. Yiddish
Yor. Yoruba
Zav. *Zavim*
Zec. *Zechariah*
Zep. *Zephaniah*
Zev. *Zevaḥim*

* hypothetical
? uncertain; possibly; perhaps
° degrees
\+ plus
− minus
= equals; is equivalent to
× by; multiplied by
→ yields

(CONTINUED)

CONCENTRATION. *See* Attention *and* Meditation.

CONFESSION OF FAITH. *See* Creeds.

CONFESSION OF SINS. The word *confession* has a twofold meaning that can be partially explained by etymology. The Latin *confiteor,* from which *confession* derives, means specifically "to confess a sin or fault," but also, in a more general sense, "to acknowledge or avow." Thus one may speak both of the sinner who confesses his sins and of the martyr who confesses his faith. Since the confession or witness of a martyr normally took place before a tribunal, it did in fact bear a formal resemblance to the confession of sins. The resemblance should prevent us from separating the two basic meanings of the word *confession* too sharply. Nevertheless, the present article will be concerned solely with an examination of the confession of sins in the strict sense, that is, as utterances concerning sins or offenses that are made in order to escape from these sins and their consequences. Confession in this strict sense normally occurs in a ritualized context that transcends the individuality of the sinner or offender. It must be done before a "recipient" who hears the confession. In many cases, it is performed in the interest not only of the one confessing but also of the community (familial, social, ecclesiastical) to which both the confessing person and the recipient belong.

From the methodological point of view, two approaches to the study of confession can be distinguished. On the other hand, one may view the confession of sins as one of many elements, such as prayer, sacrifice, the priesthood, and so forth, in the phenomenology of religion. These common elements can be recognized within various religions throughout the ages in different cultural areas, though they may have been motivated and shaped quite differently. On the other hand, one may view the partial phenomenological similarities of the different rituals that are conventionally labeled confessions of sins as the products of historical convergences.

In the first approach, the comparative-historical study of confession may transcend the purely phenomenological classification of the different forms and functional interpretations of confession to suggest hypotheses concerning the process of its formation. It may study the relative antiquity of the various subtypes of confession and the particular cultural-historical contexts in which confession originates as a more or less structured institution. This was the approach of Raffaele Pettazzoni, who developed the theory that the confession of sins originated from forms of magic, specifically from the magic of the spoken word. Confession, in this theory, was originally a ritual intended to expel or eliminate a sin by means of its verbal expression. The sin itself could be unconscious and involuntary; it was conceived of as a kind of substance that was charged with destructive or obstructive power. Pettazzoni believed that such rites were well adapted to cultural contexts such as those found in agricultural, matriarchal societies.

This theory, despite Pettazzoni's own qualifications of it, elicited scholarly objections, particularly from scholars belonging to the Viennese cultural-historical school. They pointed out that Pettazzoni's unilinear reconstruction of the history of confession—leading from the magical to the theistic and assigning an ethical character only to the latter, with its stress on the voluntary character of sin and the value of contrition—could in fact mean a return to a farfetched evolutionism.

Moreover, if one explains the similarities observed among the different forms of confession as being the result not of a unilinear evolution but rather of occasional convergences in the history of religions, as in the second approach, one can avoid appealing to such a general theory. In fact, magical and theistic forms of confession, far from being products of a single unilinear evolution, are sometimes found together within a single cultural-historical milieu. Their relative antiquity cannot be determined merely by citing the frequency with which they are mentioned in extant religious documents. To be sure, it is necessary to distinguish between a sin conceived as the infringement of a moral code, emanating from (or at least guaranteed by) a deity, and a sin resulting from the neglect of a taboo, a law not necessarily motivated by the will of a suprahuman, personal agency. A distinction must also be made between voluntary and involuntary transgression, both of moral codes and of mere taboos. But the coexistence of these alternatives in some religions does not necessarily imply that one is chronologically later than the other. Furthermore, the motivation for apparently identical eliminatory or deprecatory ritual gestures may differ according to the context: magical techniques can be used to reinforce theistic motivations, while theistic beliefs sometimes motivate magical practices.

Confession of Sins in Nonliterate Cultures. An interpretation of the confession of sins among nonliterate peoples must consider that there is indeed a tension between theistic conceptions of confession, where the goal is divine forgiveness, and nontheistic conceptions, where the efficacy of confession is intrinsic to the act itself. The Sanpoli and Nespelen (Salish Indians), whom Wilhelm Schmidt ranked among the *Urvölker*, that is, among the people of the greatest possible antiquity, practice a theistic form of confession, accompanied by prayer to the supreme being. The purpose of the confession is the sinner's attainment of heaven and presupposes the positive disposition of the person confessing. By contrast, among the Kikuyu, an agricultural people of East Africa, one finds a nontheistic form of confession. Here the transgression of a taboo or other ceremonial regulation can be eliminated by "vomiting" it, that is, confessing it to the sorcerer.

This distinction between theistic and nontheistic forms of confession, should not be overemphasized, however, important though it is in the history of religions. As already noted, fundamentally identical gestures and expressions may be found in both forms; but they receive particular meaning only from the context of their use.

The study of the content of confession is no less important than the study of its general forms. One of the most typical, perhaps the most typical subject of confession, is a woman's confession of adultery, particularly when the confession is occasioned by the act of childbirth. The recipient of the confession may be a priest, a sorcerer, the husband, or perhaps another woman. The woman making the confession must either enumerate her partners or identify them by name. This requirement may be intended to allow the offending partner to redress his wrong by offering a sacrifice or paying a fine (as among the Luo of Dyur and the Nuer of East Sudan respectively). This requirement reflects the belief that the concrete effects of a wrong action can be eliminated only through an equally concrete confession of each act. Unconfessed adultery possesses an inherently obstructive power that must be removed by means of ritual confession. The Luo, the Nuer, and also the Atcholi of Uganda believe that the destructive power of unconfessed adultery may become manifest through the death of the delivered child. These regulations and beliefs presuppose the ethical value of marriage, a standard that influences the understanding of confession. To explain the negative effects of adultery in the case of the child's death as due to sickness deriving from the material effects of libertinage would be clearly reductive. In New Caledonia, young male initiands are questioned by elders concerning any previous sexual behavior. They must confess cases of illicit sexual relations with women; not doing so, they would cause danger to the society as a whole.

Another typical occasion for making a confession in nonliterate societies is the activity of hunting or fishing. The magical practices associated with these activities are well known. For example, women must observe particular taboos while their husbands are away hunting in order not to compromise the success of the expedition. The husbands themselves, during the days preceding departure, must abstain from various activities, in particular from cohabitation with their wives. Confession is another preparatory practice. Individual members of the hunting or fishing party must confess their sins prior to departure, since the unacknowledged breaking of a taboo or a persistent condition of impurity and culpability would endanger the success of the entire expedition. One who resisted making the required confession would be excluded from participating.

Another peculiarity of confession of sins in nonliterate societies is the fact that the transgression to be confessed need not be voluntary or conscious, particularly a transgression of taboos or of ritual regulations. The same is true of other purificatory rituals. As I shall discuss below in greater detail, the need for confession of sin to be circumstantial and at the same time thorough (i.e., not achieved through generic formulations) led to the construction of long lists of possible sins or offenses. Such lists were to be recited by the one confessing in order to avoid the omission of any committed sin. This clear example of the elaboration of sacral techniques demonstrates how the original need for confession may be eventually overshadowed by the need for completeness. Yet this need to be complete does not essentially contradict the nature of confession, whether theistic or magical. Confession is characterized not by generic utterances of culpability but by the necessity to be concrete and specific, to evoke and destroy the very existence and malignant efficacy of a particular sin.

Another characteristic of confession among preliterate peoples is that it may be associated with the rhythms of the astronomical year as well as with the production cycle. Among the Lotuko of East Sudan, there is a public confession by the warriors at the beginning of the great hunting season. Their confessions are made individually with lowered voice and then repeated by the priest serving the rain god. The reason for this procedure cannot be to avoid exposing the warriors to shame; more probably, the custom is meant symbolically to preserve, to the extent that it is possible, the originally individual character of confession. Other instances of confession on the occasion of annual ceremonies of renewal are found among the Bechuana, the Algonquin, and the Ojibwa.

New Year rituals of confession are clearly eliminatory. Faults and their evil efficacy must not be allowed to extend beyond the close of the expiring year; they must be abolished. Other eliminatory rituals or customs may take place on such occasions, such as throwing away or destroying old and damaged implements. In confession, however, elimination concerns things not exterior to man but interior to him. This remains true whether the interiority of sin is conceived of magically (as a substance, fluid, or influx) or theistically, as a condition of being and a reality reflected in the conscience of the person confessing. Such annual confessions, though remaining fundamentally an act of the individual, also have collective, even cosmic, implications. These are all the more evident when a confession is made by the king as an authorized representative of the collectivity, bound to it by the bonds of "sympathy." This common idea is found in other well-known rites where the very person and life of the king are involved in rituals ensuring the perpetuity of the world and the smooth transition from one season to the next. The king as an individual sinner, as the proper subject of confession, paradoxically becomes the representative of the multitude and acts in the people's interest. Thus, even here, the individual nature of the act of confession is preserved.

Finally, we must note the connection of confession of sins with the ordeal that may be used to test the sincerity of the confessing person. Here two different ritual procedures are intermingled. Evil is not the consequence of a sin that goes unconfessed; it is rather the consequence of a confession that was not sincere. The ethical side of confession becomes paramount; a reference to the elimination of occult sin would be out of place here. This instance makes clear the inadequacy of reducing confession strictly to a material utterance having magic, autonomous effects.

Confession is also found in association with other rituals. Among the Nandi, a solemn form of confession is associated with circumcision. Among the Sulka (New Britain) and the Maya (Yucatán), confession is associated with initiation, and in Chiapas (Mexico) with marriage. In other words, confession may be an element in rites of passage, both individual and seasonal.

Confession is sometimes associated with such ritual and ascetic procedures as fasting, abstinence, and chastity, evidently because of their importance in achieving ritual and/or ethical purity. Confession has also been associated with the scapegoat ritual, but it is preferable, in this instance, to speak not of confession but of the magical or juridical transfer of sin onto an animal destined to be eliminated from the community. Confession as an explicit acknowledgment of sin is quite different; moreover, it requires a recipient, a more or less qualified "hearer" or counterpart. In the confession among primal cultures, there is an efficacy not only in the word that is spoken, but also in the word that is heard. The dialogical context is thus crucial. Both speaker and hearer embody a circle that functions, whether theistically, magically, or both, to consume the sin confessed.

Confession of Sins in Traditional High Cultures and World Religions. We pass now to the significance of confession of sins in traditional high cultures (both past and present), which are mostly polytheistic, and to the world religions.

Mexico and Peru. Confession was practiced in old Mexico in connection with Tlacolteótl, the goddess of impurities. She symbolized the sexual offenses (particularly adultery) that were the main object of confession. The priests of the goddess acted as the recipients of confession, and the confession itself was understood as taking place before the great, omniscient god Tezcatlipoca. The confession was secret and was followed by the imposition of a rather complicated penance, to be performed on the festival day of the goddess. The penance involved drawing blood from the tongue or ear, and it was accompanied by symbolic eliminatory acts, such as casting away wooden sticks that had been in contact with the wound. Extraction of blood was frequent in the religious life of the Mexicans, having an eliminatory and perhaps sacrificial meaning. Another object of confession was intoxication on the sacred drink, *pulque.*

In modern Mexico, confession is practiced by the Huichol at the time of the annual expedition to collect the hikuli, a sacred plant. This expedition requires a condition of purity in the participants, achieved through confession of sexual offenses. For mnemonic purposes, knots corresponding to sins are tied in a rope that is then burned at the end, a typical symbolic form of elimination.

Confession was also practiced in Peru, associated with the bath *(upacuna)* and with other eliminatory or symbolic acts, such as blowing away powders. The recipient of confession was the *ichuri,* who was not a priest but belonged, rather, to a low class of diviners. The typical occasion for confession was sickness, whether of oneself or of one's relatives, and the integrity of the confession could be tested by ordeal. Other occasions included bad weather and times of preparation for festivals. The emperor (the *inca*) and the high priest ordinarily confessed their sins directly to the Sun and to the great god Viracocha, respectively. This fact reduces the value of these examples for the study of the typology of confession, since confession normally has a human recipient. Nevertheless, if this irregularity is attributed to the special status of the emperor, the confession of the *inca* may continue to be looked upon as genuine.

The sickness of the *inca* was an occasion for his subjects to practice confession, not only in homage to the emperor's dignity, but to show the sympathetic connection between the emperor and his people. In China the reverse happened. There, the emperor confessed to the people.

The site of confession in Peru was the peninsula that provided access to the shrine of the Sun, located on a sacred island in Lake Titicaca. A long and detailed list of sins was employed, and some had to be confessed before the high priest. Generally speaking, the practice of confession in Peru did not involve secrecy.

Japan and China. The biannual Shintō ceremony of Oho-harahi resembles a rite of confession, but it is only a recitation of a complete list of possible sins or impurities by the *nakatomi,* a high dignitary, or by other priests. The ceremony is accompanied by such symbolic eliminatory acts as throwing impure objects into running water. Cases of individual confession are attested.

In China, eliminatory rituals were related to the grand conception of the Tao, the universal, heavenly order. A disturbance of this order, whether caused by the emperor or by his people, had serious consequences. It was the emperor's duty to redress the wrong, often through the vicarious performance of penance and a written confession of sins. Individual confession was also practiced in China, particularly in the context of the Taoist tradition, especially in the case of sickness. Sins were written down, perhaps in imitation of the emperor's confession or as a means of reinforcing their expression, and were then thrown into water.

India. In contrast to the political character it acquires in the Inca, Japanese, and Chinese empires, the confession of sins in India belongs to the mainstream of religious speculation and practice. In the Vedas there is an insistence on the purifying properties of fire and water together with faith in Varuṇa, a heavenly and omniscient god. Varuṇa punishes sinners by entangling and binding them in his net. He can also liberate the sinner from these bonds. He is connected with ethical laws, especially with the eternal order of *ṛta,* yet his *modus operandi* is clearly magical, and his jurisdiction extends to involuntary offenses. Nevertheless, the Vedas know nothing of confession proper; they know only of generic declarations of fault. It is in the Brāhmaṇas, which exalt the magical omnipotence of sacrifice, that confession is found, with particular reference to adultery; here confession is accompanied by eliminatory rituals. Brahmanic confession occurs at the summer feast of Varuṇapraghāsa; the name of the god may indicate a partial continuity with the ethical sphere of the Vedic Varuṇa. Starting this ceremony without having first confessed adultery is believed to create an insupportable burden for one's conscience, even in the context of an objective or material conception of sin. The confession of adultery must be complete, including the names or the number of lovers, since otherwise it could cause evil to the confessing woman's relatives. Confession is followed by an eliminatory sacrifice. An important feature of this ritual is its mythic motivation: it was created by the god Prajāpati. Similar motivation exists in the case of the Shintō ritual described above, which is connected with the figure of Susano-o.

In the Sūtra literature, as in classical antiquity, what is alleged to be a confession of sins is actually an individual's public proclamation that he is a sinner, a proclamation that does not involve a specific recipient. It is more a notification, as Pettazzoni rightly noted when he criticized Franz Boas's theory that such a procedure constituted the most ancient form of confession.

Jainism. Confession in Jainism (*alocana* and, more generally, *pratikramaṇa*) is mainly a monastic institution, performed twice daily. The laity make confession before their respective gurus. Jainism combines the elimination of sin with the doctrine of the annihilation of *karman,* conceived of as something substantial. Confession before death is considered important, and an insincere confession can perpetuate the cycle of rebirths.

Buddhism. The Pāṭimokkha of the Buddhist monks is a gradated list of possible sins or transgressions, recited bimonthly at the night services called Uposatha. The participant monks must be in a state of purity; sins must be confessed in an individual and reciprocal form. Similar occasion for confession was the *pavāraṇā* ("invitation"), which occurred during the rainy season, when the monks led a sedentary life. Monks would invite from their fellows statements concerning their (i.e., the inviter's) individual conduct. According to Pettazzoni, both celebrations were originally public confessions, made in response to the reading of the list of sins at the Pāṭimokkha and to the threefold interrogation by the presiding monk. In the classical form of the ritual, however, it was presupposed that the monks had achieved the required state of purity through confession prior to the Pāṭimokkha recitation, so that no one was expected actually to accuse himself of transgression during the ritual. The purpose of repeated interrogation, according to Pettazzoni's interpretation, was to confirm this state of purity formally. However, another explanation is possible. These formal, silent answers, based as they were on previous confessions, were a kind of negative confession designed to reveal sincerity of conscience: a proclamation of purity.

With Buddhism, the objective conception of sin and purification, found in both Jain and Brahmanic conceptions of *karman*, was abolished. *Karman* was now understood to be produced through the subjective element of volition, and, as Pettazzoni noted, there was a corresponding modification of the meaning of confession. With time, however—it would seem—monastic casuistry tended to lower this new moral emphasis in the Buddhist conception of confession.

Western Asia and Greece. It is difficult to assimilate the practices described in some of the epigraphic and literary texts of the religions of antiquity to the category of confession of sins. These texts mention the mere acknowledgment and subsequent public declaration of a sin or other offense by an individual. It is scarcely possible to speak of the confession of sins when the regent of Byblos writes to Amenophis IV that he has confessed his fault to the gods, or when the Hittite king Mursilis confesses a sin before the god of heaven. The same applies to the repeated confessional utterances (*homologein, exomologeisthai*) of the "superstitious man" described by Plutarch, a man continually and scrupulously resorting to purificatory rituals in the sanctuary. Similarly, the Galli of the Magna Mater, when participating in the procession of the goddess, enthusiastically and repeatedly declared the particular misdeeds of their past life, as well as describing the punishment (usually some form of sickness) that the god had inflicted upon them. This repeated evocation of past faults is the exact opposite of a ritual of confession, which is meant to eliminate the dangerous presence of sin once and for all. Nor can the term "confession" be applied to certain texts of Roman poets concerning personal experiences in the context of the cult of Egyptian deities or describing the vicissitudes of mythic or legendary characters: Ovid, *Metamorphoses* 11.129–143 (esp. v. 134, "peccasse fatentem," referring to the sinful King Midas) and *Fasti* 4.305–327 (esp. v. 321, "si tu damnas, meruisse fatebor," referring to the falsely accused Roman matron Claudia Quinta, who introduced the sacred stone of the Magna Mater to Rome in 204 BCE).

None of these records mentions the recipient of an oral confession, a necessary element of any penitential structure or institution. The texts present no more than a free initiative by the concerned sinner. The same is true of writings related to the confession of sins in Greek and Roman Orphism. Vergil (*Aeneid* 6.566–569) speaks of a "confession" in the otherworld, imposed by the judge of souls, Rhadamanthus, on those who persisted in enjoying their bad deeds until the end of their lives without having been purified. This does not necessarily imply an allusion to the neglected confession of sins during life. The same situation is found in Dante's *Commedia* (*Inferno* 5.7–10) where the souls come before Minos, the judge of the dead in the netherworld, and "confess," that is, declare their sins in order to be sent to the appropriate eternal penance. The same holds for Thespesius's episode in Plutarch, where the *homologein* ("acknowledgment of sinfulness") of a sinner in the netherworld is mentioned: a man who had always refused to reveal his sin on earth is condemned to confess it continuously.

The sole testimony of a confession of sins in Greece seems to consist of two anecdotes concerning the mysteries of Samothrace, which are told about two Spartan admirals, Antalkidas and Lysandros, requested by the priest in charge of the ritual of initiation (or perhaps purification) to mention the worst deed they committed in their lives. Possibly the so-called confession inscriptions of Phrygia (also of Lydia and Knidos) are evidence of a genuine confession of sins. Here persons of lower estate confess their transgression of some ritual regulation or their violation of some sacral person or property and dedicate a confessional inscription at the sanctuary as a record of the misdeed. According to Pettazzoni, these inscriptions testify to a particular connection of the Anatolian form of confession with the local great goddess. In another instance, an inscription recording a perjury is placed in the Anatolian sanctuary of Zeus Asbamaios. But these inscriptions are, in fact, testimonies to a popular pattern of behavior rather than to a ritual structure. All in all, it is with good reason that Pettazzoni criticized Richard Reitzenstein's belief that confession of sins was a phenomenon diffused throughout the Greek world.

Southern Arabia, Babylon, Egypt. Some confessional inscriptions have been discovered in southern Arabia, although their chronology is uncertain. They seem similar to the confessional inscriptions of Phrygia, but with a peculiar emphasis on sexual sins.

Babylonian religion recognized several theistic and magical means for eliminating ethical and ritual offenses. For instance, lists of sins were written on tablets and were then destroyed. Nevertheless, a ritual of confession properly so called is far from clearly attested. The same holds for the Babylonian penitential psalms, despite their ritual background. Herodotus attributed to the people of Babylon the custom of placing the sick in the public square so that they might confess their sins publicly; this is nearer to the repetitious declarations of the enthusiastic Galli, mentioned above, than to ritually structured confession. Among other things, there is here no appointed recipient of confession.

More akin to present typology is the negative confession of the king at the beginning of the New Year festival in Babylon, the Akitu festival. True, a negative confession in which the king declares his innocence of a series of offenses against the city and the people is in a sense the opposite of a confession of sins. Yet both establish an immediate connection between the evocation of sin and the annihilation of it and its consequences. The most famous example of a negative confession is found in the Egyptian *Book of Going Forth by Day* (no. 125) where two complete lists of possible sins are used for the examination and weighing of the soul in the afterlife. This kind of totalitarian confession encompasses all kinds of possible sin, whether conscious or unconscious, in order to omit none of them. Although this is not confession in the strict sense, it nevertheless achieves its purpose.

Israelite religion. Strong objections can be raised against the interpretation of many Old Testament texts, including the penitential psalms, as evidence for an institutionalized ritual of the confession of sins within the vast scope of the purification rituals. The same applies to the so-called collective confessions, where the general wording "we have sinned" (corresponding to the "I have sinned" of the former texts) does not properly fit into our typology. As for the scapegoat ritual, I have already remarked that it is not properly a form of confession but rather a religiously valorized transfer of sin for the purpose of expelling it. Although the procedure has an oral, declaratory element, it cannot be assigned to the typology of confession.

Christianity. In the first centuries, the Christian church practiced a canonical penance for sins considered "mortal" or "capital." The penitential act started with the sinner entering the order of the penitents through a confession rendered before the bishop, or at least with the acceptance of the assigned penance. With the gradual introduction of the private form of confession, from the seventh century onward, a new form of the celebration of reconciliation came into practice. The private form of confession necessarily emphasized the "accusation" made by the penitent. The spiritual personality of the priest recipient of private confession was particularly stressed in the tradition of Eastern Christianity.

Zoroastrianism, Mandaean religion, and Manichaeism. From Sasanid times on, Zoroastrianism recognizes a form of the confession of sins, the *patet* ("expiation"), made before a priest or, in his absence, before the sun, the moon, and the divine fire. An annual confession is encouraged, in the month of Mihr (after Mihr, the god Mithra). According to Pettazzoni, Zoroastrian confession was actually derived from Christian confession, but alternative explanations are possible. It resembles the form of confession found in the Manichaean *X˘āstvānīft*, a book preserved in the Uighur language of Central Asia. As for the meaning of confession in Manichaeism, it obviously depended upon the Manichaean concept of sin, which was based on belief in a radical dualism of soul and body. The soul was believed to be not responsible for the actions of the body. Salvation was accordingly attained by means of the soul's complete separation from the body, a separation effected through a knowledge, or gnosis, of the soul's heavenly origin and a series of radical abstentions from bodily activities.

There are three main Manichaean texts used in confession. (1) The *X˘āstvānīft*, mentioned above, consists of a list of sins and is intended for the laity (the "hearers"); it contains the recurrent formula "Man āstār hirzā" ("Forgive my fault"), which was used in the liturgy, read aloud, perhaps, by the priest to the faithful. Also employed were (2) a prayer composed in Chinese and used for communal confession and (3) a form of confession composed in Sogdian and intended for the elite, bearing the title *Manichaean Book of Prayer and Confession.* Possibly this latter text was read during Bema, the annual festival of the Manichaeans.

The Mandaeans, adherents of a gnostic, ethnic religion that survives still in Iraq, recognize a confession for sins that can be repeated no more than two times before the sinner is excommunicated. The Mandaean confession covers both conscious and unconscious faults. It is similar to the Parsi and Manichaean forms of confession.

[*See also* Repentance *and, for a more general discussion,* Purification.]

BIBLIOGRAPHY

For a discussion of the topic by one of its major interpreters, see Raffaele Pettazzoni's *La confessione dei peccati,* 3 vols. (1929–1936; Bologna, 1968). Pettazzoni's *La confession des péchés,* 2 vols. (Paris, 1931–1932), is the enlarged translation by René Monnot of volume 1 of the work mentioned above. For the Viennese school's criticism, see Leopold Walk's "Pettazzoni, Raffaele's 'La Confessione dei peccati,'" *Anthropos* 31 (1936): 969–972, and a series of articles by Michele Schulien, listed in *Etnologia religiosa* (Turin, 1958), p. 286, note 7, by Renato Boccassino. Further studies by Pettazzoni on the theme are found in his *Essays on the History of Religions* (Leiden, 1954): "Confession of Sins and the Classics," pp. 55–67, and "Confession of Sins: An Attempted General Interpretation," pp. 43–54, with further bibliography found on page 54, note 12. P. Wilhelm Schmidt's *Der Ursprung des Gottesidee,* vols. 5, 7, 8 (Münster, 1934, 1940, 1949), discusses the concept among most primitive cultures as well as pastoral cultures (consult the indexes). See Franz Steinleitner's *Die Beicht im Zusammenhange mit der sakralen Rechtspflege in der Antike* (Leipzig, 1913) for the Anatolian confessional inscriptions and related topics. On the confession of sins in other traditions and cultures, see Arthur Darby Nock's *Essays on Religion and the Ancient World,* 2 vols., edited by Zeph Stewart (Cambridge, Mass., 1972), pp. 66 and 427, note 77; Jacques Duchesne-Guillemin's *La religion de l'Iran ancien* (Paris, 1962), pp. 113ff.; and Kurt Rudolph's *Die Mandäer,* vol. 2, *Der Kult* (Göttingen, 1961), pp. 247–254. The last work cited includes an extensive bibliography concerning confession in Zoroastrianism, Manichaeism, and Mandaeism. On doctrine and practice in contemporary Catholicism, see Pope John Paul II's *Reconciliation and Penance* (Washington, D.C., 1984).

Ugo Bianchi

CONFUCIANISM IN JAPAN.

[*This entry is primarily devoted to outlining the historical development of Confucianism in Japan. For a discussion of the origin and growth of the Confucian tradition in its native setting, including an overview of the religious and philosophical content of the tradition, see* Confucian Thought, *especially the article on* Neo-Confucianism.]

The earliest Japanese chronicles tell us that Confucianism was introduced to Japan near the end of the third century CE, when Wani of Paekche (Korea) brought the Confucian *Analects* (Chin., *Lun-yü;* Jpn., *Rongo*) to the court of Emperor Ōjin. Although the actual date of this event may have been a century or more later, it is also likely that continental emigrants familiar with Confucian teachings arrived in Japan prior to the formal introduction of Confucianism.

Japanese Confucianism to 1600. The Confucianism to which the Japanese were first exposed represented more than the humble ethical dicta of Confucius himself. By this time, those doctrines had been overlaid and to some extent obscured by the doctrines of Taoism and Yin-yang dualist speculation, which combined to form a rudimentary cosmology. Prior to the seventh century it is likely that these Confucian teachings remained a virtual monopoly of scribes and literati attached to the Yamato court where they probably assisted with quasi-diplomatic correspondence and record keeping.

Both supporting and being supported by the political forces of centralization in the nascent Japanese state, Confucian teachings first achieved prominence in Japan during the time of Prince Shōtoku (573–621), who served as regent to his aunt, the empress Suiko (592–628). In 604, Prince Shōtoku wrote and promulgated the Seventeen-Article Constitution, which was intended to centralize further the administration of Japan by emphasizing administrative efficiency and harmony among contending factions. The constitution reflected the Confucian cosmology that regarded the universe as a triad composed of heaven, earth, and man, with each element having specific and mutual responsibilities. Again under Confucian influence, the cause of centralization and unification was furthered by the Taika Reforms of 645 and 646, which asserted the Confucian imperial principle of unified rule, and by the introduction of a complex legal and administrative system patterned after the codes of the Chinese T'ang dynasty during the eighth century.

The influence of Confucian principles in government administration declined during the ninth and tenth centuries along with the political power of the imperial court. Confucian advice on how to regulate the state and the affairs of man was secondary to the more superstitious uses to which the Confucian cosmology could be applied. The Korean monk Kwalluk (Jpn., Kanroku) had brought books on geomancy and divination as early as the year 602, and "Confucian" advice on where to build a home or when one might auspiciously marry was more familiar at the popular level than were other Confucian principles. Perhaps disillusioned by this trend, Japanese Confucians of the eleventh and twelfth centuries engaged more in textual analysis and criticism than in original thought or interpretation.

The Neo-Confucian doctrines of Chu Hsi (Jpn., Shuki, more commonly, Shushi; 1130–1200) were introduced to Japan, if the sources are to be believed, soon after Chu Hsi's death. Institutionally, the doctrines were taught in Zen monasteries where such Neo-Confucian practices as "maintaining reverence and sitting quietly" *(jikei seiza)* were regarded as intellectually stimulating variations of what Zen practitioners already knew as "sitting in meditation" *(zazen)*. Though Neo-Confucian doctrines were from time to time favorably received at the imperial and shogunal courts, particularly during the reigns of the emperors Hanazono (r. 1308–1318) and Go-Daigo (r. 1318–1339), and despite the attempts of the Ashikaga Academy to propagate Neo-Confucian teachings, Neo-Confucianism would remain largely in the shadow of its Zen patrons through the sixteenth century. Nonetheless, since Neo-Confucianism originally arose in China as a secular and rational alternative to the teachings of Buddhism, it may have been inevitable that a rupture would eventually occur between the two, and it was out of that rupture that Neo-Confucianism achieved independent status in Japan.

Tokugawa Confucianism (1600–1868). Perhaps the only positive result of the abortive Japanese invasions of Korea in the 1590s was the consequent introduction of new texts from the Confucian tradition into Japan. Fujiwara Seika (1561–1619) was made aware of this new tradition during his study in a Zen monastery. He had his first interview with Tokugawa Ieyasu (1542–1616), the future empire builder, in 1593, a decade before Ieyasu would be granted the title of *shōgun*. Regarding Neo-Confucianism as a possible basis for stable international relations, Ieyasu invited the philosophically eclectic Fujiwara Seika to join his government, but Seika declined and recommended in his stead a young student of his, Hayashi Razan (1583–1657).

Like his teacher, Hayashi Razan had studied Zen but was soon drawn to the orthodox teachings of Chu Hsi. With his appointment to Ieyasu's government, a degree of official attention was conferred on these teachings, and his descendants would serve as official Confucian advisers to the Tokugawa government throughout the period. Known for the quality of their scholarship and their initial fidelity to the teachings of Chu Hsi, Hayashi Razan's descendants succeeded in securing further official recognition for their doctrines. Tokugawa Yoshinao (1600–1650) erected the Seidō (Sages' Hall) near the Hayashi residence in Edo (Tokyo), and the fifth Tokugawa shogun, Tsunayoshi (r. 1690–1709) endowed the Hayashi school, the Shōheikō (School of Prosperous Peace) alongside the Seidō. Nonetheless, after Hayashi Razan the most important Tokugawa Confucians all came from outside the Hayashi family.

The final important champion of fidelity to the teachings of Chu Hsi in Japan was Yamazaki Ansai (1618–1682). His school, the Kimon, had as its goal the popularization of the ethics of Chu Hsi. Like other Neo-Confucians, this school generally took a dim view of human emotions and feelings, regarding them as potentially disruptive to the delicate balance that must lie at the heart of both man and the cosmos.

Another center for seventeenth-century Confucianism was the domain of Mito, where the daimyo, Tokugawa Mitsukuni (1628–1701), began a major historiographical enterprise seeking to reinterpret the Japanese polity in terms of Confucian imperial principles. He was assisted in this venture, titled the *Dainihonshi* (History of Great Japan), by the Chinese Ming loyalist and refugee Chu Shun-shui (Jpn., Shushunsui; 1600–1682).

During the second half of the seventeenth century, Neo-Confucian assumptions and vocabulary penetrated the new popular culture of Japan, but what has been called the "emotionalism" of the Japanese at this time made the puritanical Neo-Confucian stance on emotions and feelings incompatible with the mainstream of Japanese culture. These teachings had dominated long enough, however, to leave a lasting legacy of humanism and rationalism that enriched later Tokugawa thought.

In China, the most compelling Confucian alternative to the orthodox teachings of Chu Hsi were the teachings of the fifteenth-century figure Wang Yang-ming (Jap., Ōyōmei). His teachings, known in Japan as Yōmeigaku, were first propagated by Nakae Tōju (1608–1648), who emphasized the Wang school's teachings on intuition and action. Kumazawa Banzan (1619–1691), a pupil of Tōju, interpreted these activist teachings in terms of their relevance to the samurai class. These teachings would have their greatest impact in Japan during the nineteenth century when such leaders as Sakuma Shōzan (1811–1864) and his disciple Yoshida Shōin (1830–1859) became ideological leaders of the Meiji restoration. Both tried to stow away on one of Commodore Perry's vessels in 1854 but were caught and imprisoned. Sakuma's advocacy of "Eastern ethics and Western science" inspired generations of later reformers. Yoshida went so far as to plan to assassinate a shogunal emissary to the imperial court who was seeking the emperor's approval of a treaty with the United States. His plot was exposed, and he was beheaded in 1859, but he continued to serve as a model for loyalist activism.

In Japan, however, the most intellectually compelling alternative to Neo-Confucian teachings was presented by a succession of schools known collectively as Ancient Learning (Kogaku). Yamaga Sokō (1622–1685), the first proponent of Ancient Learning, argued that if the goal of Confucian exegesis was to find the true message of the sages, then that end might better be served by reading the works of Confucius and Mencius (Meng-tzu) directly rather than by reading the commentary on those works by Chu Hsi or others. Yamaga was drawn to the relevance of Confucian teachings in a military age, and he is regarded as the modern founder of the teachings of Bushidō, the Way of the Warrior. His publication in 1665 of a frontal attack on the orthodox teachings of Chu Hsi resulted in his banishment from Edo during the years 1666–1675. He insisted that Japan, and not China, was the true "central kingdom" and repository of Asian culture.

Itō Jinsai (1627–1705) and his son Itō Tōgai (1670–1736) further developed the fundamentalist assumptions of Ancient Learning. In their school, the Kogidō (School of Ancient Meanings), located in Kyoto, Confucius was revered as the supreme sage of the universe, and the school openly showed disdain for the metaphysical explanations of the Sung and Ming Confucians in China.

The most important Ancient Learning figure, however, was Ogyū Sorai (1666–1728), who located his school, known as the Kobunjigaku (School of Ancient Words and Phrases), in Edo. An ardent Sinophile, Sorai regarded ancient Chinese writings as the repository of intellectual resources for establishing the organization of social institutions, the performance of ancient rituals, and principles of governmental administration. He revolutionized Confucian teachings in East Asia by insisting that the principles of the Confucian way were not *a priori* principles but were, rather, the products of the sages' own inventive wisdom. Sorai thus insisted that aspiration to sagehood was at the least irrelevant to, and at worst destructive of, the polity.

With the decline of the school of Ogyū Sorai during the mid-eighteenth century, Confucianism as a whole began to decline. After Hayashi Razan, the most influential Confucian adviser to the government was Arai Hakuseki (1657–1725), who served as mentor to the sixth shogun, Ienobu, and as adviser to the seventh, Ietsugu, during the years 1709–1715. He was instrumental in revising the Laws Governing Military Households and was known as an able administrator who sought to tighten fiscal policy and management. Known for the high degree of rationalism in his thought, he was also a gifted historian.

Aware of and concerned over the decline of fidelity to the Neo-Confucian teachings in the official *bakufu* (military government) college of the Hayashi family, Matsudaira Sadanobu (1758–1829), head of the Council of Elders *(rōjū)*, promulgated in 1790 the Prohibition of Heterodox Studies *(Kansei igaku no kin)*. This attempt at ideological reform enjoyed some measure of success in the *bakufu* college, the edict had limited effect on the more important regional schools scattered throughout Japan.

Confucianism in Modern Japan. During the mid-nineteenth century, the historical, emperor-centered nationalism of the Mito school came to find points of agreement with the xenophobic, Shintō-influenced patriotism of the nativist (Kokugaku) schools. Spurred into action by the philosophy of Yōmeigaku, Confucian activists took the lead in restructuring the Japanese polity in the Meiji restoration of 1868, in which direct rule was returned to the imperial court. Nonetheless, Confucianism as an independent doctrine declined during the decades immediately following the restoration, in part because Confucian teachings had been identified so strongly with the previous Tokugawa government. Further, most prominent Tokugawa Confucians died during the first twenty-five years of the Meiji period, and only a scant handful had satisfactory successors to carry on the teachings. Still, the Confucian ideals of loyalty, duty, filial piety, and harmony persisted well into this period.

Motoda Eifu (1818–1891), Confucian tutor and adviser to the Meiji emperor, was the last important Japanese Confucian. He regarded Confucianism as a remedy for excessive infatuation with Western methods and served as Confucian lecturer in the Imperial Household Ministry from 1871 to 1891. Concerned over the lack of ethical teachings in the new public school curriculum, he was responsible for issuing in 1890 the Imperial Rescript on Education that introduced Confucian teachings on loyalty and filial piety into the standard curriculum.

Confucianism played a relatively passive role through the end of World War I. By this time the originally Confucian notions of loyalty and filial piety had come to be regarded as native Japanese virtues, and in 1937 these virtues were propounded in a work entitled *Kokutai no hongi* (Essentials of the National Polity) as the cardinal principles of Japanese national morality. Confucianism served Japanese imperialist aims in Korea after its annexation in 1910, in Manchuria after 1932, and in the Japanese-controlled portions of North China after 1937. Japanese militarist rulers in these territories regarded Confucian teachings as one way to emphasize a common cultural heritage in East Asia. They felt that the survival of such teachings in Japan indicated not only that Confucian civilization was superior to Western civilization but that Japanese civilization was the primary form of civilization in East Asia.

After World War II, Confucian teachings were removed from the Japanese curriculum by the occupation authorities, and Confucianism has not yet recovered from this blow. Nonetheless, to the extent that such ideals as harmony and loyalty can be said to belong to

Confucianism, these qualities may be fundamental to Japanese culture and are likely to survive.

[*Many of the thinkers discussed herein are subjects of individual biographical entries.*]

BIBLIOGRAPHY

A most valuable source book of materials on Japanese Confucianism is *Sources of Japanese Tradition,* 2 vols., compiled by Ryusaku Tsunoda, Wm. Theodore de Bary, and Donald Keene (New York, 1958). Also useful, although somewhat dated, is Robert C. Armstrong's *Light from the East: Studies in Japanese Confucianism* (Toronto, 1914). Joseph J. Spae's *Itō Jinsai* (New York, 1967) is helpful both for information on the Ancient Learning school and on early Japanese Confucianism. Robert Bellah's *Tokugawa Religion* (New York, 1957) casts the major themes of Japanese Confucianism into a broader perspective. Kate Nakai's "The Nationalization of Confucianism in Tokugawa Japan," *Harvard Journal of Asiatic Studies* 40 (June 1980): 159–199, provides a lucid account of how continental Confucianism was transformed into Japanese Confucianism. From a methodological point of view, the most stimulating volume available in English is Maruyama Masao's *Studies in the Intellectual History of Tokugawa Japan,* translated by Mikiso Hane (Princeton, 1975). It may be the single most important book on this subject. See also the volume that I have edited, *Confucianism and Tokugawa Culture* (Princeton, 1984). Herman Ooms's *Charismatic Bureaucrat: A Political Biography of Matsudaira Sadanobu, 1758–1829* (Chicago, 1975) is a superb account of this important late Tokugawa figure. Finally, the reader is directed to the only available study of the modern fate of Confucian thought in Japan, *Confucianism in Modern Japan,* 2d ed. (Tokyo, 1973), by Warren W. Smith, Jr.

PETER NOSCO

CONFUCIANISM IN KOREA. [*This entry is primarily devoted to outlining the historical development of Confucianism in Korea. For a discussion of the origin and growth of the Confucian tradition in its native setting, including an overview of the religious and philosophical content of the tradition, see* Confucian Thought, *especially the article on* Neo-Confucianism.]

While Confucianism did not achieve status as a dominant thought system in Korea until the founding of the Yi dynasty (1392–1910), the introduction of the Confucian classics to the peninsula predates the common era. In the seventh century, the Silla government, at first a tribal federation, turned to Confucianism as a tool of centralization. In 651, the Royal Academy was established, in which officials, drawn from the aristocracy, were exposed to the Confucian classics. Furthermore, Confucian precepts found their way into aristocratic codes of behavior, even becoming incorporated into the rules of conduct for the *hwarang,* a knightly class instrumental in the Silla unification of the Korean Peninsula in 668.

Under the Unified Silla (668–935), Confucianism found a more fertile environment. Government examinations were instituted at the Royal Academy in 788 and close relations with T'ang China led late in the dynasty to the rise of a group of scholars who were steeped in Confucian learning there, and who returned to Korea with a Confucian vision of government and a resolve to restore the deteriorating social order. An example is Ch'oe Ch'iwŏn (b. 857), who passed the T'ang government examinations but returned hoping to end anarchic conditions in the provinces. Disillusioned, he died a recluse.

From the inception of the Koryŏ dynasty (918–1392) an expanded role for Confucian doctrine was envisioned. In the celebrated "Ten Injunctions" addressed to his descendants by the dynastic founder, Wang Kŏn (r. 918–943), Buddhism was chosen to govern spiritual matters, geomancy was to be used for prophecy and prognostication, and Confucianism was chosen as the guiding principle in the sociopolitical sphere. Two of the injunctions are direct restatements of traditional Confucian precepts. One declares that the people's livelihood and welfare should be the foremost concern of government while another admonishes the occupant of the throne to heed ministerial advice in fulfilling this task.

In the late tenth century the government was reorganized into a centralized bureaucratic structure. Local officials were appointed by the central government. Among the long term results were the emergence of the civil and military bureaucracy as a social force and the transformation of the Koryŏ polity into an aristocratic-bureaucratic state in which the power of the ruling elite derived from government position rather than an ancestral seat. This change reflected the Confucian rhetoric of government; it conformed to the hierarchical order at whose summit reigned the sovereign as paterfamilias of the state with corresponding responsibilities to and respect from his subject-children.

Under this Confucian system, civil officials served in the capital, where the mode of life included the pursuit of scholarly and literary activities. Educational institutions such as the National Academy, established in 992, and twelve private academies, the first founded by Ch'oe Ch'ung (984–1068) in the eleventh century, arose to serve this group. This early Koryŏ civil elite is often characterized as having been more interested in the literary rather than the philosophical aspect of Confucian studies. This group seems to have accepted the Confucian precepts of civilization with its moral and political implications. The *Samguk sagi* (Historical Record of the Three Kingdoms), the first extant dynastic history in Korea, written by the twelfth-century Confucian scholar Kim Pu-sik, expresses this outlook. The work is an attempt to place Korean history in the context of Confucian civilization. Moral appraisal is the foremost criterion for evaluating the legitimacy of historical states or depicting events or persons.

The military coup of 1170 disrupted this Confucian social order. The Mongols, who invaded Korea in 1231, were instrumental in bringing about the end of military rule in 1259. Koryŏ kings, married to Mongol princesses and devoid of power, spent a great deal of time prior to their accession and after their retirement in the cosmopolitan Yüan capital. Establishments such as that of the scholar-king Ch'ungsŏn (r. 1289, 1308–1313) served as meeting places for Chinese and Korean scholars, and Korean scholars for the first time had first-hand exposure to Sung dynasty (960–1279) Neo-Confucian scholarship, particularly that of the Ch'eng-Chu school, so-called for its putative founders, Ch'eng I (1033–1107) and Chu Hsi (1130–1200). The result was an impressive array of scholars beginning with An Hyang (1243–1306) and Paek Ijŏng (fl. 1300), commonly regarded as having introduced Neo-Confucianism to Korea, and including, by the mid-fourteenth century, such scholars as Yi Saek (1328–1396), Chŏng Mongju (1337–1392), and Yi Sungin (1347–1392). They succeeded in including the Neo-Confucian texts—the Four Books and Five Classics—in the civil service examination and in the curriculum at the Royal College and in reinstituting the royal lecture, complete with Neo-Confucian texts and teacher-officials who lectured to the king-student. [*See* Chinese Religion, *article on* Religious and Philosophical Texts, *and the biographies of Ch'eng I, Ch'eng Hao, and Chu Hsi.*]

Founding of the Yi Neo-Confucian Polity. Neo-Confucianism was posited on a holistic vision of the moral universe in which a unifying moral principle operated in the phenomenal as well as the nonphenomenal world, particularly in the human world. Society should be organized to conform to this moral order and an individual should try to live in accordance with its principles. Commitment to Neo-Confucianism rendered it impossible for its practitioners to concede the religious realm to Buddhism. The founding of the Yi dynasty (1392–1910) was, in this sense, not merely a change in political power. Its founders were all confirmed Neo-Confucians and they sought to create a new sociopolitical order based on their moral vision. Chŏng Tojŏn (1342–1398), the leader of this group, campaigned to discredit Buddhism. Motivated by the Neo-Confucian belief in the centrality of man, Chŏng challenged the Buddhist view that this world, the phenomenal world, was illusion, terming such a view invalid and harmful. His theoretical attack was accompanied by institutional sanctions against the Buddhist establishment, which undermined its special position. Chŏng articulated the new political ideology in the coronation edict he composed for Yi T'aejo (r. 1392–1398). The *raison d'être* of the government was the attainment and maintenance of a Confucian moral order. Thus, it should be staffed with people who understood Confucian moral principles. The legitimacy of the Yi monarchy was based on the claim that it had received from Heaven a mandate to carry out this task.

Beginning with changes in the political structure, the Yi government launched a massive transformation of Korean society that was not fully realized for several centuries. The most conspicuous changes were the adoption of a new system of education, a restructuring of social organization along patrilineal groups, the adoption of Confucian ritual, and the propagation of Confucian ethics through local associations. In order to disseminate Confucian values more widely to the educated class, the Yi government sought to establish a nationwide public school system. Four schools in the capital and one school in each county supposedly would make primary education widely available, while the Royal College in the capital would provide advanced education for qualified students. This departed from Koryŏ practice, in which education was limited to a small elite. Private schools and academies began to appear in the mid-fifteenth century; although government-supported, they became alternatives to government service for renowned scholars. Thus, the relationship between the private academies and the state became ambivalent—mutually supportive but competitive for influence and the opportunity to define orthodoxy.

The civil service examination became the accepted channel of entry to an official career. Almost all high officials passed the *munkwa*, the final stage of the civil service examinations; of the two preliminary examinations, the one in the exposition of classics became more important than the one in literary composition. Nonetheless, the rigid class structure of Korean society precluded the development of the strict meritocracy envisioned by the Yi founders and power still remained confined to a relatively small elite. But the examinations did have the effect of confucianizing the governing elite; by the mid-sixteenth century, Confucian ideology was no longer just a means by which the governing class ruled but rather the system of values by which they were measured. From the king down to the lowest officials, all had to justify their actions and intentions in the context of Confucian rhetoric and ideals. This confucianization of the official class was paralleled by an attempt to disseminate Confucian normative values among the peasantry.

The Development of Confucian Scholarship. By the sixteenth century, Korean scholars turned to the more purely intellectual and speculative aspects of Confucian learning, looking directly to the Ch'eng-Chu school. Despite close ties with Ming dynasty (1368–1644) scholarship, Korean Neo-Confucianism developed independently of contemporary scholarship there. While Korean scholars accepted the authority of the Ch'eng-Chu school, they defined issues in their own way, adding insights and interpretations. The scholars Pak Yŏng (1471–1540), Sŏ Kyŏngdŏk (1489–1546), and Yi Ŏnjŏk (1491–1553) reflect the diversity and independence of the Korean school. [*See the biography of Sŏ Kyŏngdŏk.*] Pak devoted himself to the question of *ihak* (Chin., *li-hsüeh,* "learning of principle"), one of the main themes of Neo-Confucian philosophy. Based on his study of the *Ta-hsüeh* (Great Learning), he asserted that principle and knowledge should be sought entirely within one's self. Later scholars found in this assertion a resemblance to the works of the Ming dynasty thinker Wang Yang-ming (1472–1529) and for this reason found his thinking heterodox. Sŏ Kyŏngdŏk, on the other hand, turned to Chang Tsai's (1020–1077) *t'aehŏ* (Chin., *t'ai-hsü,* "great void"). Speculating on the cosmology of creation, it was natural that he should grant primacy to the role of *ki* (Chin., *ch'i,* "material force"). Primarily interested in observing natural phenomena and unconcerned with the moral implications of the role of principle, he parted from Chu Hsi. Unlike Sŏ, who lived as a recluse and shunned bookish learning, Yi Ŏnjŏk had a long official career and left copious writings. His erudition, his interests in a broad range of topics, and his laborious textual studies set new standards for scholars of future generations. [*See the biographies of Chang Tsai and Wang Yang-ming.*]

It was Yi Hwang (1501–1570), better known by his pen name, T'oegye, who brought Korean Neo-Confucianism to maturity. Working at a time when Wang Yang-ming's thought seemed to be gaining influence in the Korean scholarly community, he devoted himself to defining orthodoxy, to distinguishing "right learning" from deviant thought. The definition of a Korean orthodoxy within the tradition of the Ch'eng-Chu school, one that excluded the ideas of the Wang Yang-ming school, is often attributed to his efforts. T'oegye accepted Chu Hsi's dual theory of principle and material force and the relationship between them. While Chu Hsi acknowledged that principle and material force cannot exist in isolation, he held that principle is prior and material force posterior. The superiority of principle was a defining feature of his philosophy: principle was identified with the Way *(tao)* and the nature *(hsing),* which are permanent and unchanging, while material force was identified with physical entities, which constantly change. But Chu Hsi's position proved somewhat ambiguous. One could ask whether the priority of principle was existential or evaluative, that is, did it exist first or did it just have a superior moral value? Further, in what sense did principle exist prior to material force if it could not manifest itself without material force? Much of T'oegye's work was devoted to this question. He concluded that the priority of principle applied in the realm of ethical values, and that principle exerted a positive ethical influence. He wrote, for instance, that "Good occurs if principle manifests itself and material force follows, while evil occurs if material force veils principle and principle recedes."

Like the Sung Neo-Confucians, Korean scholars including T'oegye were deeply concerned with the problem of human evil. If man's original nature was good, then how can one explain evil? T'oegye again accepted Chu Hsi's concept of human nature based on his dual theory of principle and material force. Principle is immanent in everything in the universe. What individuates one thing from another is material force. Since principle is good, what determines the moral quality of an entity is its material force. Man has an original nature and a physical nature and only when he returns to original nature does he act in accordance with moral principle. What determines the morality of human action is mind. The mind possesses innate knowledge of moral principle and has the cognitive capacity to discern it. Yet, this capacity of mind can be prevented from functioning when it becomes clouded by selfish desire. T'oegye used the terms *tosim* (Chin., *tao-hsing,* "moral mind") and *insim* (Chin., *jen-hsin,* "human mind") to describe the two aspects of mind. The term moral mind described a mind rectified and discerning of moral principle while human mind referred to a mind containing seeds of selfish desire and prone to error. Moral cultivation was necessary to develop mind into a moral state.

Korean scholars seized upon this question of mind and the result was one of the characteristic themes of Korean Neo-Confucian thought. The debate centered around the *sadan* (Chin., *ssu-tuan,* "four beginnings") and the *ch'ilchŏng* (Chin., *ch'i-ch'ing,* "seven emotions"). The Four Beginnings, which appear in *Meng-tzu (Mencius),* are the moral qualities of man that give rise to the original goodness of human nature. The Seven Emotions, mentioned in the *Chung-yung* (Doctrine of the Mean), are human feelings. The questions debated were whether both the Four and the Seven were feelings, how they were related to the moral mind and the human mind, and their relationship to principle and material force. T'oegye took Chŏng Chiun's (1509–1561) position that the Four issued from principle and therefore must be good while the Seven issued from material force and therefore could be either good or evil. The Four were the basis of the moral mind and the Seven the basis of the human mind. Challenged by Ki Taesŭng (1527–1572) in their famous "Four-Seven" debate, T'oegye acknowledged that both involved principle and material force and that both were feelings, but he insisted that their origins were different. The Four are initiated by principle and material force follows them while the Seven are initiated by material force and principle rides on them. In order to posit that the four are initiated by principle, T'oegye had to endow principle with a generative power. Principle does not merely constitute human nature; it guides the mind toward the realization of goodness.

T'oegye later used the same theory to take issue with Wang Yang-ming's theory of the unity of knowledge and action. In his emphasis on innate knowledge, Wang dismissed the need for acquiring knowledge through examination and inquiry. T'oegye argued that this was applicable to the emotional activity of the mind but not to rational thought. [*See the biography of Yi T'oegye.*]

While Yi T'oegye chose to limit himself to what was explicit in Chu Hsi, Yi I (1536–1584), known by his pen name, Yulgok, preferred a more independent and creative approach to scholarship. Taking the formula "obtain truth through one's own effort" as his credo, he regarded adhering too rigidly to previous masters' positions as contrary to the spirit of Neo-Confucian learning. He accepted Chu Hsi's authority, but he was willing to differ with him on specific issues. Yulgok is regarded as having established the school of Material Force in Korea. Yulgok conceded that, at least logically, principle and material force were distinct. What is referred to as the primacy of material force in Yulgok is his theory of the inseparability of principle and material force in both function and manifestation. As principle cannot be expressed without material force and material force has no root without principle, they are interrelated. Thus, to him it was illogical to conceive of them as prior and posterior and he denied that principle has its own generative power. Principle is passive and material force is active and they always manifest themselves together. His belief in their inseparability led him to object to the notion that principle is unchanging and always in a pure state. Departing from Chu Hsi, he held that principle was not a unified entity but that the principle in each thing was distinct, conditioned, and determined by its material force. Hence an individuating principle in a thing is always changing and in varying states of purity.

Yulgok's ideas of the Four Beginnings and the Seven Emotions were also developed along these lines. In a celebrated debate with Sŏng Hon (1535–1598) on the subject, he denied that the Four are associated with principle and the Seven with material force. They both are manifestations of material force that contains principle. The difference is that the Four are "good" manifestations of material force or, more specifically, the Seven themselves manifested as good. Likewise, the "moral mind" and the "human mind" do not rise from different origins but are rather purely descriptive terms referring to different states. In positing that an entity—the Four Beginnings—could be a good manifestation of material force, Yulgok was challenging the dichotomy that made material force the source of evil and principle the source of good. [*See the biography of Yi Yulgok.*]

Yi T'oegye and Yi Yulgok are regarded as the founders respectively of the school of Principle and the school of Material Force. T'oegye's philosophy was developed by the Yŏngnam school while Yulgok's was developed by the Kiho school, which emerged as political as well as scholarly rivals. Continuing refinements in the study of principle and material force and new interpretations of the Four Beginnings and the Seven Emotions constituted the mainstream of Korean Neo-Confucian scholarship. The scholars of the school of Principle emphasized the generative power of principle that T'oegye proposed. Yi Hyŏnil (1627–1704), Yi Sangjŏng (1710–1781), and Yi Chinsang (1811–1878) assigned ever greater roles to principle, endowing it with priority in existential sequence and in function as well. This tendency culminated in Yi Hangno (1792–1868) who identified principle with creative force, divinity, and mind.

The scholars of the school of Material Force correspondingly attributed even greater function to material force. Song Siyŏl (1607–1689), for example, posited that mind, which acts, is material force and the nature, which does not move, is principle. Han Wŏnjin (1682–1750) refined this theory, but Im Sŏngju (1711–1788) went one step further. He declared that since mind and the nature are one then the latter should also be material force. He denied that principle could exist at all without material force. Hence man could not be good because of principle but must be good because his material force is good. This flies in the face of the Ch'eng-Chu school dictum that the (original) nature, being perfectly good, is principle.

As T'oegye emphasized the universality of principle and Yulgok spoke of individuating principle, their successors pushed to extremes in developing these opposing views. Ultimately, this led to the eighteenth-century debate concerning man's relationship to the cosmos. If principle is universal and omnipresent then man is connected to other things through principle sharing the nature. If, however, principle is completely determined by material force then man, who possesses different material force than other things, would not share the same nature. The debate, known as the Nak-Ho debate, began between Yi Kan (1677–1727) and Han Wŏnjin. Yi took the position that men share their natures with other things in the universe while Han maintained that man was separated from other things with respect to original nature. This debate generated an intense discussion, which eventually came to involve much of the Korean scholarly community of the time.

Both the school of Principle and that of Material Force, despite their differing interpretations, were viewed both by themselves and by others as firmly within Ch'eng-Chu orthodoxy, this, even though both schools had views that sometimes departed from the original Ch'eng-Chu teachings. Reinterpreting specific issues within the tradition was one thing, but a direct challenge to orthodoxy was another. Pak Sedang (1629–1703) was termed a heterodox thinker for his work *Sabyŏnnok*, in which he directly opposed Chu Hsi's scholarship and offered his own views. As a result of the fall of the Chinese Ming dynasty to the "barbarian" Ch'ing dynasty (1644–1911), seventeenth century Korean intellectuals became concerned with orthodoxy in an attempt to redefine Korea's role in the Confucian world. Perhaps the conflict between Song Siyŏl and Yun Hyu (1617–1680) indicates this process. Song Siyŏl's position can be characterized by his desire to maintain Chu Hsi orthodoxy intact in Korea. As a follower of Yulgok, his philosophy differed somewhat from that of Chu Hsi, but he maintained an unswerving loyalty and commitment to the supremacy of the Ch'eng-Chu school. [*See the biography of Song Siyŏl.*] Yun Hyu, on the other hand, preferred a wider definition of orthodoxy. He regarded Chu Hsi as a great scholar, but felt that measuring one's scholarship by him or, for that matter, even by Confucius, was too confining and harmful. He wrote his own commentaries on several of the Four Books, for which he was ostracized by Song and his followers as heterodox. [*See the biography of Yun Hyu.*]

The intellectual scene in the eighteenth century was somewhat freer and more diverse. Chŏng Chedu (1649–1736), who received high honors from King Yŏngjo (r. 1724–1776), openly espoused ideas of Wang Yang-ming which had long been suppressed in Korea. This period also witnessed the flowering of the Sirhak ("practical learning") school. Centuries of factional struggle and growing competition for office had left many scholars outside the mainstream of political power. Practical Learning scholars were disaffected intellectuals who wrote treatises on social and economic reform. They fall largely into two groups. Yu Hyŏngwŏn (1622–1673) and Yi Ik (1681–1763) accepted the Confucian vision of an agrarian society presided over by the rule of virtue and urged social improvement through land reform and moral rule. Pak Chiwŏn (1737–1805), Hong Taeyong (1731–1783), and Pak Chega (b. 1750), on the other hand, searched for alternatives. They addressed themselves to such issues as commerce, trade, and technology. Pak Chiwŏn's biting satire of the class system, Hong Taeyong's interest in science as it was expressed in his notion of the moving earth, and Pak Chega's belief in technology founded on a startling theory of a consumer economy clearly departed from the conventional mode of thinking. Chŏng Yagyong (1762–1836), often considered the greatest Practical Learning scholar, encompassed both trends in his reform ideas. His attention to the improvement of local government is well known. While these scholars worked within the Confucian political and value system, they are regarded as precursors of modernization for their critique of contemporary society and their innovative proposals for reform. [*See the biography of Chŏng Yagyong.*]

In the late nineteenth century as Korea came under increasing pressure from the major powers and the Confucian value system itself came under attack, Confucian thinking turned defensive. Confucian scholars committed to preserving the orthodox tradition became conservatives who opposed treaties and modernizing measures. Seeing themselves as the defenders of the only true civilization, they put up real resistance. Ch'oe Ikhyŏn (1833–1906) was a representative scholar of this generation. His fearless memorials objecting to the government's domestic and diplomatic policies resulted in frequent banishment. When Korea became a protectorate of Japan in 1905, he organized what is known as the Righteous Army and fought against Japanese and Korean royal troops. Arrested by the Japanese and imprisoned in Tsushima Island, he died of starvation, considering it unprincipled to accept food from the enemy. The role of Confucianism in Korea's modernization process, however, remains to be examined.

[*See also* Buddhism, *article on* Buddhism in Korea, *and* Korean Religion.]

BIBLIOGRAPHY

Works in Korean. For an overview of the history of Korean Confucianism, see Youn Sa-soon's *Han'guk yuhak yŏn'gu* (Seoul, 1980). Works by the major thinkers include: Ch'oe Ikhyŏn's *Myŏnamjip* (Seoul, 1906); Chŏng Tojŏn's *Sambongjip* (reprint, Seoul, 1961); Chŏng Yagyong's *Chŏng Tasan chŏnsŏ*, 3 vols. (reprint, Seoul, 1960–1961); Hong Taeyong's *Tamhŏnsŏ*, 2 vols. (reprint, Seoul, 1969); Ki Taesŭng's *Kobong munjip* (reprint, Seoul, 1976); Pak Chega's *Pukhagŭi* (Seoul, 1971); Pak Chiwŏn's *Yŏnamchip* (1932; reprint, Seoul, 1966); Pak Sedang's *Sabyŏnnok* (Seoul, 1703); Song Siyŏl's *Songja taejŏn*, 7 vols. (1929; reprint, Seoul, 1971); Yi T'oegye's *T'oegye chŏnsŏ*, 2 vols. (reprint, Seoul, 1958); Yi Yulgok's *Yulgok chŏnsŏ*, 2 vols. (reprint, Seoul, 1961); Yi Ik's *Sŏngho saesŏl*, 2 vols. (reprint, Seoul, 1967); Yi Ŏnjŏk's *Hoejae chŏnsŏ* (reprint, Seoul, 1973); Yu Hyŏngwŏn's *Pan'gye surok* (reprint, Seoul, 1958); and Yun Hyu's *Paekho chŏnsŏ*, 3 vols. (Taegu, 1974).

Works in English. Articles in English include Martina Deuchler's "The Tradition: Women during the Yi Dynasty," in *Virtues in Conflict*, edited by Sandra Matielli (Seoul, 1977), pp. 1–47; Park Chong-hong's "Historical Review of Korean Confucianism," *Korea Journal* 3 (September 1963): 5–11; and Key P. Yang and Gregory Henderson's "An Outline History of Korean Confucianism," *Journal of Asian Studies* 18 (November 1958 and February 1959): 81–101 and 259–276. *The Rise of Neo-Confucianism in Korea*, edited by Wm. Theodore de Bary and me (New York, 1985), contains a number of important essays. See Julia Ching's "Yi Yulgok on the 'Four Beginnings and the Seven Emotions'" (pp. 303–322); Chai-sik Chung's "Chŏng Tojŏn: 'Architect' of Yi Dynasty Government and Ideology" (pp. 59–88); Martina Deuchler's "Reject the False and Uphold the Straight: Attitudes toward Heterodox Thought in Early Yi Korea" (pp. 375–410); Tomoeda Ryūtarō's "Yi T'oegye and Chu Hsi: Differences in Their Theories of Principle and Material Force" (pp. 243–260); and Tu Wei-ming's "Yi T'oegye's Perception of Human Nature: A Preliminary Inquiry into the Four-Seven Debate in Korean Neo-Confucianism" (pp. 261–282).

JaHyun Kim Haboush

CONFUCIAN THOUGHT. [*This entry consists of three articles.* Foundations of the Tradition *discusses the origin and development of Confucianism through the ninth century.* The State Cult *surveys the use of Confucian thought as the ideological foundation of Chinese political institutions.* Neo-Confucianism *treats the history of the Confucian tradition from the tenth to the twentieth centuries. For a discussion of the influence of Confucian thought in the other major cultures of East Asia, see* Confucianism in Korea *and* Confucianism in Japan.]

Foundations of the Tradition

The conquest of the Shang dynasty (1751–1122? BCE) by the Chou (1111–249 BCE) ushered in a period of several hundred years of radical change in Chinese history. Although some scholars believe Chinese feudalism had existed since legendary times, it was during this period that a feudal society rapidly replaced the old tribal system. To consolidate the newly established empire, the duke of Chou (d. 1094) inaugurated a system of definite domains, enfeoffing his relatives and loyal supporters. Rather than claiming divine origin for their power, the Chou rulers legitimized their rule by asserting that the founders of the dynasty were men of moral perfection, that is, sages, whose perfection was sanctioned by Heaven (T'ien). Many poems of the early Chou period glorify the first king, Wen, and claim that the dynasty's founders had received Heaven's mandate and favor because of their virtuous character.

Under the Chou, the conception of divinity shifted from the anthropomorphic, all-powerful Ti, who conferred legitimacy upon the Shang house and administered divine justice at whim, to the impersonal Heaven (T'ien), the source of life and morality. Divination and sacrifice to spiritual beings, particularly ancestors, continued to be important activities. But whereas in the Shang spiritual beings were obeyed because of their power, in the Chou spiritual beings were worshiped for the glorification of the virtue that they embodied. As the records of the oracle bones show, the Shang rulers would undertake no important action without first obtaining the approval of spiritual beings through sacrifice and divination. In the Chou such events were more often than not justified on moral grounds. As the *Book of Rites (Li chi)* states, "The people of Yin [Shang] honor spiritual beings, serve them, and put them ahead of ceremonies. . . . The people of Chou honor ceremonies and highly value the conferring of favors. They serve the spiritual beings and respect them but keep them at a distance. They remain near to man and loyal to him." Despite this significant shift of emphasis, the Chou permitted the Shang house to continue ritual propitiation of Ti. [*See also* T'ien *and* Shang-ti.]

It was also during this period that China underwent the transition from the Bronze Age to the Iron Age. The less expensive and more workable iron became available to a larger sector of the population, including commoners. This led to a greater distribution of wealth and the introduction of new tools, products, trades and trade centers, weapons and war strategy. The nobility's increasing reliance on commoners and artisans occasioned slow but radical changes in the feudal social structure. The emphasis on birthright and inherited status was giving way to the recognition of talent and ability and, by the Spring and Autumn period (722–481 BCE), an individual's merit could occasionally lead to political prominence. At this time the terms *hsien* ("worthy," or man of virtue and ability) and *sheng* ("sage") were often used interchangeably, indicating a growing cultural orientation toward the concept of the perfectibility of man. One account, dating from the seventh century BCE, tells of a slave, an expert on irrigation, who became a high official. According to the *Tso chuan* (Duke Hsiang, twenty-fourth year), during the same period a scholar claimed that immortality did not rest in the survival of *hun* (the spirit of man's intelligence and and power of breathing) and *p'o* (the spirit of man's physical nature) but in one's virtue, accomplishments, and words. It was in this atmosphere that Confucius (551–479 BCE) was born.

Confucius and Confucian Thought. Confucius (the latinized form of the Chinese K'ung Fu-tzu, "Master K'ung") could trace this family heritage to nobility, but by the time of his birth the K'ung family was poor. His father was a minor official, who, at a late age, entered into a third marriage with a woman from the Yen family. After addressing prayers to the holy Mount T'ai the couple was rewarded with a son, whom they named Ch'iu, later styled Chung-ni. Confucius's father died when Confucius was perhaps no more than three years of age. When he was about nineteen, he married a woman from P'in-kuan in the state of Sung. They had a son and a daughter. Without benefit of a regular teacher, Confucius nonetheless managed to become a highly learned man, perhaps the most learned of his age, and had by his twenties begun to attract students. At this time he served as a clerk in his native state, keeping account of grains and animals reserved for religious sacrifices. No doubt the work aroused his interest in religious sacrifices and ceremonies. According to legend, in his thirties or forties he journeyed to the capital of Chou to consult the Taoist philosopher Lao-tzu (then the custodian of archives) on ceremonies. Upon returning to Lu several months later he encountered a steadily worsening political situation. In order to avoid the outbreak of civil hostilities, he fled to the neighboring state of Ch'i, where he was cordially consulted on government. Later, he returned to Lu and attracted more students. In 501 BCE, when he was fifty-one, he was made a magistrate in Lu. In that same year he also became minister of public works. Subsequently, he served Lu as a minister of justice, whose duties included foreign relations.

As a magistrate, Confucius was said to have brought great peace. Accounts of his career record, anecdotally, that during his tenure things left on the highway were returned to their owners and people were able to retire at night without locking their doors. In 498 BCE, when three Lu families grew too powerful and threatened the rule of the duke of Lu, Confucius ordered his pupils to destroy the three cities so there would be no more strong bases for family troops. Traditionally, most Confucians have denied this episode, obviously to avoid any unfavorable reflection on Confucius. Although the record is questionable, the fact that Confucius seemed to have engaged in a power play, perhaps for selfish reasons, has disturbed Confucians. Critics of Confucius, especially those in the People's Republic, have seized upon this event to denounce him as a desperate supporter of autocracy. In any case, his success at home did not sit well with Ch'i. Later in the year, the duke of Ch'i sent the duke of Lu eighty dancing girls. After their arrival, the duke of Lu ceased holding court early in the morning. Convinced that he could no longer influence the duke, Confucius left Lu to travel with some pupils through nine states for almost thirteen years. In most places he was earnestly consulted on the art of government, but he was surrounded in one state, detained in another, and made a target for assassination in a third. Obviously, his radical ideas were a threat to the rulers. At the age of sixty-eight he returned to Lu to continue to teach and perhaps to write.

Tradition holds that Confucius wrote the *Spring and Autumn Annals (Ch'un-ch'iu)* on the basis of records of his native state from the years 722 to 481 BCE (hence the name of the period), as well as the ten commentaries ("ten wings") of the *Book of Changes (I ching)*. He is also credited with having edited the rest of the Six Classics, namely, the *Book of Odes (Shih ching)*, the *Book of History (Shu ching)*, the *Book of Rites (Li chi)*, and the *Book of Music (Yüeh ching)*. Modern scholarship has rejected much of this tradition, though recognizing that he was surely familiar with many poems and documents that later entered into these classics. On the other hand, it is likely that he wrote the *Spring and Autumn Annals* and at least one of the "ten wings." He died at the age of seventy-three, disappointed perhaps in public life but regarded by posterity as surely the greatest sage in Chinese history.

Confucius's conversations with his pupils and his advice to rulers were compiled by his pupils in the *Analects (Lun-yü)* some decades after his death. Other of his teachings were later gathered in the *Great Learning (Ta-hsüeh)* and the *Doctrine of the Mean (Chung-yung)*. Confucius did not talk about strange phenomena, physical exploits, disorders, or spiritual beings. He seldom discussed profit, fate, or even the general virtue of *jen* (humanity, benevolence). His pupils heard little of abstract speculations on human nature or the Way of Heaven. Nonetheless, his modest dicta laid the foundation for Chinese culture and determined the direction of its development. For over two thousand years he exercised a tremendous influence on Chinese life and thought. Korea, Japan, and Vietnam, too, periodically benefited from his teachings. Generally speaking, Confucius taught literature, ways of behavior, loyalty, and faithfulness. He often talked about history, poetry, and the performance of ceremonies. In this he started a tradition of liberal and moral education in China that was to eclipse the utilitarian and professionally oriented tradition that had hitherto dominated Chinese education. What is more important, while education had traditionally been reserved for the nobility, for Confucius education was open to all, without any class distinction. Following tradition, he glorified Heaven *(t'ien)* as great and august. He taught his pupils to know Heaven and to stand in awe of it. Significantly, however, Confucius did not regard Heaven as Ti, the Lord or the divine ruler, but as a supreme spiritual presence, the greatest moral power, and the source of everything. There is no doubt that he radically changed the Chinese concept of Heaven from an anthropomorphic being to a spiritual and moral one. He had a deep sense of Heaven's mandate and said at one point that he knew the mandate of Heaven at fifty. While he did not talk about spiritual beings he was nonetheless extremely serious about ancestors, advocating personal participation in ancestral rites. In matters of religion, his emphasis was on actual demonstration rather than discussion. Consequently, his discourses centered almost entirely around man and his society.

Humanism had been growing in China for several centuries before the time of Confucius, but it was he who brought it to maturity. When asked about spiritual beings, Confucius replied, "If one cannot serve human beings, how can one serve spiritual beings?" When asked about death, his response was: "If you cannot know life, how can you know death?" Confucius declared that "It is man that can make the Way (moral principles) great, and not the Way that can make man great." Here the emphasis on moral practice is unmistakable. Confucius also introduced a new concept of the perfect man, whom he termed a *chün-tzu*. Traditionally, the term *chün-tzu* had designated the ruler's son, that is, a man of high social station. As in any feudal society, in pre-Confucian China moral worth was equated with social worth. In several places in the *Analects* Confucius still used the term to mean the ruler, but in most cases he interpreted it in a completely new sense, namely, that of the morally perfect man, that is, the "superior man." The *chün-tzu* is discussed in the *Analects* 107 times. Confucius said that the superior man is one who is wise, loving, and courageous; who studies the Way and loves people; who stands in awe of Heaven; who understands the mandate of Heaven; who concentrates his effort on fundamentals; who does not seek to gratify his appetite or seek comfort in his dwelling place but is earnest in deeds and careful in speech; who is not a "utensil" that is useful for only a specific function; who does not set his mind for or against anything but follows only what is right; who practices respect, reverence, generosity, and righteousness; who studies extensively but restrains himself with ceremonies; who meets with friends on the basis of culture and helps himself with their friendship. To sharpen his point, he contrasted the superior man with the inferior man. The superior man understands righteousness, he said, whereas the inferior man understands profit. The progress of the superior man is upward while that of the inferior man is downward. The superior man seeks to perfect the good qualities of others; the inferior man does not.

It is clear that the superior man is possessed of many virtues. The greatest virtue that Confucius taught is *jen*, which specifically means benevolence but in a more general sense refers to humanity or what makes man a moral being. This is another new concept advanced by Confucius. Before his time, words like *shan*, meaning "goodness," or *te*, meaning "virtue," were widely employed, but these are terms for specific virtues, not terms for the universal virtue out of which all specific virtues grow. As in the case of *chün-tzu*, pupils asked about *jen* repeatedly. Forty-eight chapters out of 499 in the *Analects* were devoted to reflections on this concept and the term appears no fewer than 105 times in the text. Confucius never defined it, perhaps because he felt the concept of a universal virtue was incapable of definition. In answer to his pupils' many questions, however, he did say that the man of *jen* loves man. He is a man of earnestness, liberality, truthfulness, diligence, and generosity. He is respectful in private life, serious in handling affairs, and loyal in dealing with others. He studies extensively, is steady in his purpose, inquires earnestly, and reflects on things at hand. In short, he is a man of all virtues. Perhaps the all-inclusive meaning of *jen* is best shown in his answer to a pupil who asked what *jen* was. His answer: "To master oneself and to return to propriety (ceremonies) is humanity." Here, both the self and society are embraced, for ceremonies are guidelines for social conduct.

Confucius said that there is "one thread" running through his teachings. As his outstanding pupil, Tseng-tzu (505?–436? BCE), understood it, this one thread refers to loyalty in one's moral nature *(chung)* and treating others like oneself *(shu)*. Commentators on the *Analects* are unanimous that *chung* and *shu* are the two sides of *jen*, for they cover the total moral life, that is, both the individual and society. The Confucian Golden Rule is put in the negative form, "Not to do to others what one does not want done to oneself." But Confucius also described the man of *jen* positively. He said, "The man of *jen*, seeking to establish his character, also seeks to establish the characters of others, and seeking to be prominent (or successful), also seeks to make others prominent (or successful)." In a word, the man of *jen* is a man of total virtue.

Of all the virtues that *jen* generates, filial piety and brotherly respect are the greatest, for it is on these that humanity is founded. Filial piety, of course, is closely related to ritual life. Confucius taught people to serve their parents in life and bury them in death according to rites *(li)*. But for Confucius, what was central to ritual activity was not adherence to fixed, outward forms—although that, too, was important—but rather the inward disposition or sincerity of the celebrant. Rites to him meant not just proper conduct but also proper state of mind.

To rule a state and restrain human behavior by insisting on fixed ethical norms, liturgically expressed, was unusual advice to give rulers in an age in which men were accustomed to ruling by force alone. Confucius said, "If a ruler is to govern his kingdom with the compliance proper to the rule of propriety (rites), what difficulty will he have?" When a duke asked Confucius how the ruler should employ his ministers and how the ministers should serve the ruler, he said, "A ruler should employ his ministers according to the rules of propriety, and ministers should serve their ruler with loyalty." As for the people, he said, "Lead the people with governmental measures and regulate them by law and punishment, and they will avoid wrongdoing but have no sense of honor and shame. Lead them with virtue and regulate them by the rules of propriety and they will have a sense of shame, and, moreover, will set themselves right." This cardinal principle, government by moral behavior instead of by law and punishment, the practice of his time, has remained a basic conviction in the Chinese tradition, even if it is not always put into practice. The ruler, said Confucius, should set himself as an example, and the people will follow him as all stars follow the polestar. If an official makes his own conduct correct he will have no difficulty in conducting the government, but if he does not rectify himself he cannot rectify others. Again, when a ruler's conduct is correct his government is effective without the issuing of orders. If his personal conduct is not correct he may issue orders but they will not be followed. As Confucius told a pupil, "If a superior loves propriety, the people will not dare not to be reverent. If he loves righteousness, the people will not dare not to submit to him. If he loves faithfulness, his people will not dare not to be sincere."

On the surface Confucius's political doctrines seem to center on the ruler, and, to be sure, this perceived emphasis in Confucius's teachings often led to autocracy in later times. However, Confucius gave equal importance to the plight of the ruler's subjects. He said a ruler must be economical in expenditure, love the people, and employ them at the proper seasons; he must enrich the people and educate them. When a pupil asked about government, he replied that there must be sufficiency of food, sufficiency of military equipment, and the confidence of the people; if one or two must be dispensed with, food and military equipment must go first. With Confucius, the aims of statecraft have now shifted to ensuring the welfare of its people. He said that the trouble for a state is not a small population but an uneven one, not poverty but discontent. The ideal state, he declared, is one in which people living inside it are happy and people outside want to come in. Here the central focus on the people is unmistakable. Some have argued that since the will of the people is the most important factor in the state, the Confucian doctrine of government is essentially democratic. It may be going too far to make that claim, but in a period when feudal lords considered both their territory and their people as their possessions, this shift to the people was definitely revolutionary. To assist the rulers in government, Confucius urged them to "raise people of virtue and ability" to high positions. This surely undermined the tradition of governmental positions held by birthright and tended toward government by the people.

Confucius also urged rulers to "rectify names." The "rectification of names" *(cheng-ming)* is in keeping with Confucius's insistence on an ordered, hierarchical, and liturgically formalized notion of human society. To him, duty and title must correspond: a father must behave like a true father and a son must behave like a true son. When the duke of Ch'i asked him about government, he replied, "Let the ruler be a ruler, the minister be a minister, the father be a father, and the son be a son." This doctrine, although entirely social and moral for Confucius, eventually led to the development of a principle of correspondence between substance *(t'i)* and function *(yung)* in Chinese philosophy. Another ethical doctrine that later became formalized as a philosophical notion is that of the "mean" *(chung)*. When commenting on two pupils, he said one went too far and the other not far enough, and that to go too far is the same as not to go far enough. He praised the beginning poems in the *Book of Odes* as "expressive of enjoyment without being licentious, and of grief without being hurtfully excessive." For Confucius this doctrine means nothing more than moderation, but in the *Doctrine of the Mean* it has become a universal principal of harmony and equilibrium. Confucius himself led a life of moderation. He had no fixed limit for the amount of wine he would drink, but he never became confused or disorderly. In his ideas, he was both a conservative and a radical. To him, "Perfect is the virtue that is according to the Mean." [*See also the biography of Confucius.*]

The Second and Third Generations after Confucius. Very little attention has been paid to Confucius's followers from 500 to 350 BCE, but it is impossible to understand how and why Confucianism came to dominate Chinese history and why it unfolded in the directions it did without understanding how Confucius's teachings were developed by his pupils and his pupils' pupils. Their number far exceeded those in other schools and they operated in a far wider territory. They either taught or served in the government, following exactly the example set by Confucius and setting the pattern for the Chinese intelligentsia even to this day.

The *Shih chi* (Historical Records) said Confucius had three thousand pupils, of whom seventy were talented. These were merely round numbers suggesting many, but there can be no doubt Confucius had the largest following of his time. One hundred and twelve of his pupils are known to us by name. They ranged from four to fifty-four years younger than Confucius and came from ten different states, some far in the south. Aside from four of noble birth, the rest came from ordinary society; some were very poor. In the *Analects,* their questions concern chiefly the three major topics of *jen,* the *chün-tzu,* and government, followed by inquiries into rules of propriety and filial piety. In the *Family Sayings of Confucius (K'ung-tzu chia-yü),* the chief topic of discussion is rules of propriety, especially the rites of three-year mourning for parents. Many subjects are dealt with in the *Book of Rites,* in particular, *jen,* filial piety, and rules of propriety. The most representative and therefore most important literature of the second generation is the *Great Learning,* originally a chapter in the *Book of Rites,* generally attributed to his pupil Tseng-tzu. It consists of the sayings of Confucius on the eight steps of "investigation of things," "extension of knowledge," "making the will sincere," "rectifying the mind," "cultivating the person," "regulating the family," "ordering the state," and "bringing peace to the world." The first five steps involve the individual, while the last three involve society. They may be said to represent *jen* in systematic application, emphasizing as they do an absolute connection, expressed as a logical progression, between one's fundamental inward disposition and one's life in society. Bringing peace to the world depends on a correct ordering of the state, which in turn relies upon the proper disposition of the family (fathers acting as fathers, sons as sons, etc.), which itself relies on inward cultivation ultimately founded on the "investigation of things." For, in the words of the *Great Learning,* "If the root (what is fundamental) is in disarray, what issues from it cannot be well ordered."

The third-generation followers are not so well known. Only thirty-three are known to us by name. We do know from various sources, however, that the topics they discussed were filial piety, the goodness of human nature, rites, poetry, *yin* and *yang* (passive and active cosmic forces), the relation of Heaven and man, and the nourishment of the vital power *(ch'i);* the last four were new topics in the Confucian school, or, as it was to be known, the Ju-chia.

The most important literature of this period is the *Doctrine of the Mean,* generally attributed to Confucius's grandson and Tseng-tzu's pupil, Tzu-ssu (492?–431? BCE). This work, again, originally a chapter in the *Book of Rites,* extends Confucius's idea of moderation to the celebration of the equilibrium and harmony of the moral nature, the mind, and the universe. "The Way of the superior man," it says, "functions everywhere and yet is hidden. Men and women of simple intelligence can share its knowledge and yet in its utmost reaches there is something that even the sage does not know." It is so great that nothing in the world can contain it but is so small that nothing in the world can split it. "The operations of Heaven have neither sound nor smell." Such sayings unmistakably lift Confucian thought to the realm of metaphysics, a level Confucius himself had tried to avoid. Here, the themes of human nature and the Way of Heaven are strongly emphasized. The work begins with the discussion of the "mandate of Heaven" *(t'ien-ming),* described as the source of our nature, which we must follow. Implicit in this discussion is the assumption that human nature is good. Confucius had said that life and death depend on Heaven. The *Doctrine of the Mean* added that while life and death are beyond our control, we should cultivate our person and wait for fate to take its course. With reference to spiritual beings, the text says, "How abundant is the display of power of spiritual beings! They form the substance of all things and nothing can be without them." We should be absolutely sincere in sacrificing to them, believing them to be all about us. Thus, filial piety means to serve the dead as they were served while alive. Sincerity, the text continues, is not only the way of man but the way of Heaven as well. The way of perfect sincerity is mysterious but predictable. It underlies all changes and transformations. Only those who are perfectly sincere can fully develop their nature. Those who can do so can then develop the nature of others, can develop the nature of things, and can assist Heaven and earth in the transforming and nourishing process, thus forming a trinity with them. With this text, Confucianism at once becomes religion, metaphysics, and moral social philosophy.

Meng-tzu and Hsün-tzu. The two most prominent followers of Confucius, Meng-tzu (372?–289? BCE) and Hsün-tzu (fl. 298–238 BCE), were contemporaries, but although both traveled extensively they never met. Meng-tzu (whose name was latinized as Mencius) was not aware of Hsün-tzu but Hsün-tzu criticized Meng-tzu. They shared an adoration of Confucius, and both believed that all men are capable of becoming the *chün-tzu*. Both held in high regard the Confucian moral values of humanity and righteousness. Both strongly advocated education, the rectification of names, kingly government (in which taxes are light, punishments are slight, and war is avoided), and the necessity of social distinctions such as that between senior and junior. In short, both were loyal followers of Confucius.

In their own doctrines, however, they proceeded in opposite directions. Confucius had said merely that people were born alike but that practice made them different. His thesis that all men could become superior men, however, argued by implication for the innate goodness of human nature. Meng-tzu's thought begins at this point by categorically affirming the original goodness of our nature. He maintains that man is born with what he termed the "four beginnings," that is, compassion, which is the beginning of humanity, shame and dislike, which is the beginning of righteousness, the feeling of respect and reverence, which is the beginning of propriety, and the feeling of right and wrong, which is the beginning of wisdom. For Meng-tzu, all people possess innate knowledge of the good and an innate ability to do good. Evil is due merely to circumstance and self-neglect. If one should fully develop his nature and recover his "lost mind," he will become a sage. Hsün-tzu attacked Meng-tzu severely, claiming that man's nature is originally evil. Man is born with desires that cannot be fully satisfied. If followed, these desires, together with envy, which is also inborn, inevitably lead to conflict. Virtue is acquired through man's activities, most notably, education, discipline, and rites.

Both Meng-tzu and Hsün-tzu emphasized rules of propriety, but for Meng-tzu rites are expressions of man's sincerity and inner control, whereas for Hsün-tzu they imply external restraint and social control. This led Hsün-tzu to advocate the necessity of laws, whereas Meng-tzu maintained that laws were to be used with regret. Both taught humanity *(jen)* and righteousness *(i)*, but while Meng-tzu usually coupled the two and sharply contrasted righteousness with profit *(li)*, this emphasis was absent in Hsün-tzu. Meng-tzu believed in Heaven, not as an anthropomorphic deity but as the spiritual power we must obey. Heaven always favors the virtuous and controls our destiny. Virtuous government, for instance, is supported by Heaven, while the price of misrule is the loss of this support, that is, of Heaven's mandate to rule. For Hsün-tzu, however, Heaven is simply nature, devoid of ethical principles, impartial to all men, regular and almost mechanical in its operation. Both thinkers promoted the rectification of names, but while Meng-tzu advocated the rectification of names on ethical (i.e., normative) grounds, Hsün-tzu did so on the basis of a logical imperative. For Hsün-tzu, names must indicate actualities, establish distinctions, and discriminate between similarities and differences, the particular and general. To convey best the meanings of things and events in accordance with such distinctions, Hsün-tzu used simple, compound, and general names. His analysis of names led Hsün-tzu to develop a theory of mind and a concomitant epistemology.

Both Meng-tzu and Hsün-tzu promoted kingly government, but for Meng-tzu a kingly government must be humane. In fact, Meng-tzu was the first to use the term "humane government" *(jen-cheng)*. According to him, the ruler must have a mind that "cannot bear" the suffering of the people. Meng-tzu opposed the despot most vigorously; he considered the people the most important element in the state. He went so far as to say that if people were severely oppressed, they would treat the ruler as an enemy, thus suggesting a doctrine of the right to rebel. To Hsün-tzu, a kingly government was one ruled by the most worthy, powerful, and discriminating. The ideal ruler, a sage-king, keeps order through an organized system of laws, regulations, and taxation. Both subscribed to the Confucian doctrine of love for all, but Meng-tzu insisted that the special relationship between son and father must be the foundation of love. Because of this conviction, he bitterly attacked Mo-tzu (fl. 479–438 BCE), who taught universal (i.e. undifferentiated) love, and Yang Chu (440?–360? BCE), who was primarily concerned with self-preservation and hedonism. Meng-tzu contended that Mo-tzu denied the special relationship to parents and that Yang Chu denied the special obligation to the ruler. Hsün-tzu, too, criticized various philosophers. It can readily be seen that Meng-tzu's thought was strongly ethical and religious, while that of Hsün-tzu was strongly psychological and logical.

At the time, Hsün-tzu was probably more influential than Meng-tzu. His pupil Han Fei (d. 233 BCE) carried his ideas of law to a high level and became the most prominent scholar in the Legalist school (Fa-chia). Another of his pupils, Li Ssu (d. 208 BCE), became prime minister during the Ch'in dynasty (221–207 BCE) and implemented the law with liberal rewards and severe punishments. Hsün-tzu's influence extended to the early years of the Han dynasty (206 BCE–220 CE). Meng-tzu's influence was not felt until the T'ang dynasty (618–907), when Han Yü (768–824) placed him in the line of Confucian orthodoxy. By the Sung dynasty (960–1279), however, all Neo-Confucians mentioned Confucius and

Meng-tzu together, with the result that Meng-tzu came to be regarded as the "second sage." In the end, Meng-tzu occupied a key position in the line of Confucian transmission, a lineage from which Hsün-tzu has been excluded. This exclusion is based in part on Hsün-tzu's doctrine of the evil nature of man and in part to his pupils' brutal exercise of power during the Ch'in dynasty. [*See the biographies of Meng-tzu and Hsün-tzu.*]

The Supremacy of Confucianism and Tung Chung-shu. Under the leadership of the Legalists, the Ch'in established the first united Chinese empire and replaced the feudal domains with a system of provinces that is still in existence today. The Ch'in also united and somewhat simplified the Chinese written language, finished the Great Wall, and expanded military power beyond existing Chinese boundaries. To forestall critical opinion, books of the ritual schools were burned in 213 BCE, although those in official archives were retained. Confucians were ousted from office. But in fourteen short years rebellions broke out. The successful rebel, Liu Pang, defeated his rivals, overthrew the Ch'in, and founded the Han dynasty in 206 BCE. In spite of the burning of books, many Confucian works had been hidden in walls or committed to memory. Now the Confucian classics once more came into circulation. Since they required glosses and explanations, Confucian scholars gradually acquired importance and began to replace the Legalists in the government.

Even so, Liu Pang, now the new emperor Kao-tsu, was impatient with Confucian notions of statecraft, as attested by his now famous exchange (dated 196 BCE) with a Confucian scholar by the name of Chia I (201?–169? BCE) who repeatedly extolled the *Book of History* and the *Book of Odes* in the emperor's presence. Kao-tsu finally rebuked the scholar by pointing out, "I have conquered my empire on horseback and I am going to rule my empire on horseback." He was greatly surprised when the scholar said, "Your Majesty, one may conquer an empire on horseback but one may never rule an empire on horseback." That episode may or may not have attracted the emperor to Confucianism, but in his tour around the country the next year, he offered the *ta-chi* ("grand sacrifice") complete with ox, to the tomb of Confucius, the first time any government official had sacrificed to him. Possibly the new emperor was considering adopting Confucianism as the ideology of the new dynasty.

However, although Confucian scholars were slowly gaining influence at court, for the first hundred years of the Han dynasty they played only a secondary role. Those in control of the government were Taoists, chiefly because both the emperors and empresses were devout followers of the new Taoist religion. As a result of the application of the Taoist philosophy of simple government, the reigns of Wen-ti (r. 179–157 BCE) and Ching-ti (156–141 BCE) were times of peace and adequate supply. Still, an extensive empire needed well-educated officials and well-formulated institutions. When Emperor Wu-ti (r. 140–87 BCE) ascended the throne he ordered scholars to appear for personal interviews. Among the hundred-odd scholars summoned to court was Tung Chung-shu (176–104 BCE). In answer to the emperor's questions, he propounded the theory that Heaven (nature) and man are governed by the same principle. When virtue prevails, he said, there will be good omens from Heaven in response. Therefore, if the ruler cultivates his virtue, Heaven will side with him and the people will submit to him. Tung Chung-shu advised the emperor to practice the teachings of Confucius and eliminate whatever trace there was of the harsh rule of Ch'in, abandon the theories of all schools but Confucianism, dismiss all non-Confucian officials, and raise people of virtue and ability to goverment positions. "Nothing outside of the Six Classics and nothing contrary to Confucius's teachings should be allowed," he said, "and only then can the country be settled in one standard." Profoundly impressed, the emperor immediately appointed Tung to be chief minister of a princely state. In 136 BCE, at the recommendation of Tung, Emperor Wu officially promoted the classics and established doctoral chairs for them, thus establishing Confucianism as the state ideology. Later, in 125 BCE, again at Tung's advice, he founded a national university to which fifty of the most talented students in the classics were selected. This institution lasted until the twentieth century.

Tung was a specialist on the *Spring and Autumn Annals* and author of the *Ch'un-ch'iu fan-lu* (Luxuriant Gems of the *Spring and Autumn Annals*), a collection of eighty-two short essays. To him, Confucius did not merely record the events of his native state of Lu but taught in subtle words fundamental principles and natural law. According to Tung, there is correspondence between Heaven and man, not only in general but in exact numerical terms. He said, for example, that man has 360 joints, corresponding to the number of Heaven (the round number of days in a year), and that man's keen sense of hearing and seeing resemble the sun and moon.

While these descriptions are crude, the basic philosophy—that man is a microcosm of the universe—has had a profound effect on Chinese thought. Whatever happens in man, according to this theory, causes a corresponding expression in Heaven and vice versa. Disruptions in the natural order could thus be gleaned from the study of omens and portents, signs of Heaven's mandate; for in the organic universe things are not only related but activate each other. Therefore, man, especially the ruler, must cultivate his own person or else disturb the established harmony in the universe. The correspondence of Heaven and man is not mechanical but dynamic, for all things come from the "origin" (*yüan*, "beginning"), which is the creative power of Heaven and earth. As the king is the beginning (*yüan*, "head") of man, he is entitled to rule. In this connection Tung Chung-shu propounded the doctrine of the Three Bonds, namely, the bonds between ruler and ruled, father and son, and husband and wife. Righteousness and humanity must inform these bonds, lest the natural order be upset and Heaven's mandate lost.

This dynamic interaction of man and the cosmos also serves as a foundation for a theory of history. Just as natural events are subject to cyclical changes, so too do human events undergo regular variations. Tung conceived of history as proceeding in a cycle of three periods, symbolized by the colors black, white, and red. Black represents the formation of things, when the cosmic material force *(ch'i)* starts the process of penetration and transformation, as, for instance, the formation of a seed. White represents the sprouting of the seed; red, the subsequent growth and activity of the plant. Ultimately, red gives way to black, as activity wanes and regeneration begins again. Dynasties too correspond to these same cycles. Hence it was important for the dynasty (in this case, the Han) to be harmonious with the historical cycle and to adjust the royal ceremonials and court dress accordingly. For nowhere was the effect of cyclical time more poignantly felt than in the prospect of dynastic succession attendant upon the loss of Heaven's mandate. But to be correct, the ruler must follow Confucius, for the sage is the only one who can relate the myriad things to the "one" and tie it to the "origin." Perhaps Tung, realizing the growing power of the ruler, wanted to establish the classics as the natural law to which the ruler must obey and make Confucius the bridge between Heaven and man. If Confucius had performed that role, he would have been like Jesus in Western history. [*See* Yin-yang Wu-hsing *and the biography of* Tung Chung-shu.]

In the first century BCE a group of apocryphal texts appeared. Called *wei* ("woof"), in contrast to *ching* ("warp," i.e., the classics), these texts contained portents, charms, and prognostications, many of which were ascribed to Confucius. Confucius himself was depicted in these texts as a divine being. There is the story, for example, that when he was born, he had in his mouth a jade piece on which was carved the message that he was now born to be the "uncrowned king" *(su-wang)*. The implication is that he was the king, without a throne but ordained by Heaven nonetheless. For a hundred years, the effort to deify Confucius continued. Tung did not explicitly support the movement, but his philosophy certainly reinforced it. However, Confucianism was too concerned with human values and its belief in Heaven was too naturalistic to wear a cloak of mystery and superstition for long. The movement died down toward the end of the second century BCE.

Han Confucianism. While Tung Chung-shu was the most outstanding Confucian philosopher in the Han period, he was not typical. Most Han Confucians devoted their attention to the Confucian texts instead of Confucian thought. Since books were out of circulation for decades following the burning of books in 213 BCE, it was natural for scholars to devote their energy to explaining and annotating the words and messages in these works. Consequently, Han Confucians occupied themselves chiefly with textual criticism. Famous commentators like Cheng Hsüan (127–200 CE) did not concern themselves with the doctrines of the classics but only with their literal meanings. What is called Confucian learning (Ju-hsüeh) in the Han is essentially the learning of the Confucian classics and refers principally to their textual annotation.

The only important philosophical theory in the entire Han period was one concerning human nature. The eclectic thinker Yang Hsiung (53 BCE–18 CE) was its principal advocate. In his *Fa-yen* (Model Words), a work in imitation of the Confucian *Analects*, he said that man's nature is a mixture of good and evil and that he who cultivates the good in it will become a good man while he who cultivates the evil in it will become an evil man. There is no elaboration on this simple statement, but it represented a great departure from Meng-tzu. For this reason, Yang Hsiung has been severely criticized by later Confucians. Whether he intended it or not, he directed the attention of the Confucian school to this central problem of human nature, and that in and of itself was a great contribution.

T'ang Confucianism: Han Yü and Li Ao. The central Confucian theme of human nature was strongly reasserted in the T'ang period (618–907) by Han Yü (768–829) and Li Ao (fl. 798). In his famous *Yüan-hsing* (An Inquiry on Human Nature), Han Yü criticized Hsün-tzu's theory of the evil nature of man and Yang Hsiung's theory that man's nature is a mixture of good and evil. He offered his own theory of three grades of human nature, the superior, the medium, and the inferior. According to Han Yü, the superior is good, and good only, because in this grade are practiced the Five Virtues: humanity *(jen)*, righteousness *(i)*, propriety *(li)*, wisdom *(chih)*, and faithfulness *(hsin)*. The medium grade may tend to be either superior or inferior, because in this grade one of the five virtues may be pure. In the inferior grade, one rebels against one of the five virtues and is out of accord with the rest. This theory was meant to refine Meng-tzu's doctrine of original goodness, but inasmuch as the idea of three grades can be found in the classics and was advanced by several thinkers before Han Yü's time, it represents no real advance in Confucian thought. The theory does reaffirm the fundamental Confucian interest in human nature.

Han Yü's friend and possibly his pupil, Li Ao, advocated a principle that he referred to as "recovering one's nature" *(fu-hsing)*, which is highly suggestive of Meng-tzu's injunction to recover one's lost mind. Li Ao's method of having no deliberation or thought may sound Buddhistic, and his recommendation of the fasting of mind *(hsin-chai)* may be derived from Chuang-tzu (369?–286? BCE), but the phrase "having no deliberation or thought" *(wu-ssu wu-lü)* comes from the *Book of Changes* and his "fasting of mind" is essentially the doctrine of "tranquility before the feelings are aroused" as taught in the *Doctrine of the Mean.* Li Ao did say that feelings are evil, thus perpetuating the common opinion of Han Confucians but he added that if one is absolutely sincere, enlightenment will ensue, as the *Doctrine of the Mean* had taught.

The Buddhist and Taoist influence on Li Ao cannot be denied. Han Yü, however, was diametrically opposed to Buddhism and Taoism. In his equally famous essay *Yüan-tao* (An Inquiry on the Way), he strongly attacked Lao-tzu's Way on the grounds that by belittling humanity and righteousness Lao-tzu was actually doing away with them. Consequently, he said, both the Taoists and Buddhists have done away with the importance of human relations and disregarded the process of sustaining and supporting the life of one another. In 819 he petitioned the emperor to refrain from welcoming a relic of the Buddha (allegedly a finger bone) into the palace, claiming that the Buddhist way is barbarian, that moral and cultural achievements in China had been obtained without Buddhism, and that Buddhist monks had deserted the family and the state. The subsequent persecution of Buddhists in 845 may have been motivated chiefly by economic and political factors, but this attack by a celebrated literary giant of the time surely had prepared the way.

In quoting from the *Doctrine of the Mean* and also the *Great Learning*, Han Yü and Li Ao contributed to the prominence of these two chapters in the *Book of Rites* so that eventually they, along with the *Book of Changes*, became basic texts in Neo-Confucianism. Both Han and Li singled out Meng-tzu as the one who transmitted the true doctrine of Confucius to later generations. All in all, they saved Confucianism from possible eclipse by Buddhism and Taoism, determined the direction of future development of Confucianism in Chinese history, and fixed the line of orthodox transmission from Confucius and Meng-tzu. In these respects, Han and Li were truly precursors of Neo-Confucianism.

[*See also* Chinese Philosophy; Chinese Religion, *article on* Religious and Philosophical Texts; Jen and I; Hsin; Li; Tao and Te; *and* Hsiao.]

BIBLIOGRAPHY

Western Sources

Chai, Ch'u, and Winberg Chai, eds. and trans. *The Humanist Way in Ancient China: Essential Works of Confucianism.* New York, 1965.

Chan, Wing-tsit, trans. and comp. *A Source Book in Chinese Philosophy.* Princeton, 1963. See chapters 2–6, 14, and 27.

Chang, Carsun. *The Development of Neo-Confucian Thought.* New York, 1957. See volume 1, chapters 4 and 5.

Creel, H. G. *Confucius and the Chinese Way.* New York, 1960.

Fu, Charles Wei-hsun. "Fingarette and Munro on Early Confucianism: A Methodological Examination." *Philosophy East and West* 28 (April 1978): 181–198.

Fung Yu-lan. *A History of Chinese Philosophy.* 2d ed. Translated by Derk Bodde. Princeton, 1952. See volume 1, chapters 4, 6, and 12.

Liu, Wu-chi. *A Short History of Confucian Philosophy.* Harmondsworth, 1955.

Liu, Wu-chi. *Confucius: His Life and Time.* New York, 1956.

T'ang Chün-i. "Cosmologies in Ancient Chinese Philosophy." *Chinese Studies in Philosophy* 5 (1973): 4–47.

Waley, Arthur. *Three Ways of Thought in Ancient China.* London, 1939.

Chinese and Japanese Sources

Ch'en Ta-ch'i, et al. *K'ung-hsüeh lun-chi.* 2 vols. Taipei, 1957.

Ch'ien Mu. *Chung-kuo ssu-hsiang shih.* Taipei, 1952. See pages 1–85.

Hou Wai-lu. *Chung-kuo ssu-hsiang t'ung-shih.* Peking, 1957. See chapters 1–6, 11, and 15 in volume 1, and chapters 3, 6, and 9 in volume 2.

Kano Naoki. *Chūgoku tetsugakushi.* Tokyo, 1953. See part 1, chapters 1–6; part 3, chapters 2–3; and part 4, chapters 1, 2, and 4.

Liang Ch'i-ch'ao, et al. *Chung-kuo che-hsüeh ssu-hsiang lun-chi: Hsien Ch'in p'ien.* Taipei, 1976. See chapters 1–7, 9–11, and 19.

Lao Ssu-kuang. *Chung-kuo che-hsüeh shih.* Peking, 1981. See volume 1, chapters 1–3 and 6.

Shimizu Nobuyoshi. *Chūgoku shisō shi.* Tokyo, 1947. See part 2, chapters 1–4.

T'ang Chün-i. "Meng, Mo, Chuang, Hsün shuo hsin-shen i." *Hsin-ya hsüeh-pao* 1.2 (1956): 29–31.

T'ang Chün-i. "Hsien Ch'in ssu-hsiang chung." *Hsin-ya hsüeh-pao* 2.2 (1957): 1–32.

T'ang Chün-i. *Chung-kuo che-hsüeh yüan-lun: Yüan-hsing p'ien.* Hong Kong, 1968. See chapters 1 and 2.

T'ang Chün-i. *Chung-kuo che hsüeh yüan-lun: Yüan-tao p'ien.* Hong Kong, 1973. See part 1, chapters 1, 2, 5, 6, 13-15, and 21-25.

WING-TSIT CHAN

Neo-Confucianism

The Confucian movement that began in the Sung dynasty (960–1279) was marked by its wide sphere of interests, including political and educational reforms, the compilation of comprehensive histories, the pursuit of classical scholarship and textual exegesis, the reaffirmation of Confucian morality and ethics, and the study of metaphysics and epistemology. It is the two latter concerns that are perhaps most closely identified with Sung Confucianism. In the West the movement has been called Neo-Confucianism, thus emphasizing its departure from traditional Confucian learning. In Chinese it is generally referred to as *hsing-li-hsüeh* ("learning of nature and principle"), *Sung-Ming li-hsüeh* ("learning of principle in the Sung and Ming dynasties"), or simply *li-hsüeh* ("learning of principle"), thus identifying *li* ("principle") as the central concept of its metaphysical and ethical systems. In the classics *li* meant primarily order or pattern. In the *Meng-tzu* it referred chiefly to moral principles. But in the hands of the Neo-Confucians *li* came to denote a universal principle or law of being. The reinterpretation of this term forms the basis for many related theories, including the "investigation of things" *(ko-wu),* taken from the *Ta-hsüeh* (Great Learning), and the notion of "reverent seriousness" *(ching),* or the disciplined, pure, and alert mind that is a precondition of knowledge.

Sun Fu (922–1057), Hu Yüan (933–1059), and Shih Chieh (1005–1045) are traditionally recognized as the pioneers of the Neo-Confucian movement in the Northern Sung period (960–1126). Their lives exemplify the concerns and spirit of the new scholarship. While they said little about *li* or the investigation of things, they did chart the future course of Confucianism. They were primarily educators, not philosophers: all three taught at private academies, where they emphasized the study of the Confucian classics as a guide to leading a moral and ethical life. In his two decades as a teacher Hu Yüan attracted over one thousand seven hundred disciples, for whom he established two curricula. One treated substance *(t'i),* that is, the study of the classics, the other, function *(yung),* that is, the management of affairs such as mathematics and irrigation. Sun Fu was a specialist on the *Ch'un-ch'iu* (Spring and Autumn Annals). He wrote a book intended to "reveal its subtleties," which to him meant "honoring the king and repelling the barbarians" (i.e., non-Chinese). He attacked the Buddhists and Taoists for what he regarded as their tendency to seek substance at the expense of function and for neglecting Confucianism and its advocacy of humanity and righteousness. Shih Chieh followed Sun Fu in this attack. In his essay *Kuai-shuo* (Strange Doctrines) he also strongly criticized Yang I (974–1020), who was then a famous proponent of flowery composition (i.e., ornamental writing without substance). These three educators also elaborated upon Han Yü's doctrine of an orthodox Confucian transmission. All these trends were resumed by later Neo-Confucians.

The Five Northern Sung Masters. The eleventh century was a period of rapid growth for the Neo-Confucian tradition. Five figures in particular, Shao Yung (1011–1077), Chou Tun-i (1017–1073), Chang Tsai (1020–1077), Ch'eng Hao (1032–1085), and Ch'eng I (1033–1107) contributed to this development. Their work established a Neo-Confucian metaphysics and cosmology based on the selection and redefinition of concepts from the Confucian classics, primarily from the *I ching* (Book of Changes).

The cosmology of Chou Tun-i. Chou Tun-i (given name, Chou Mou-shu; literary name, Chou Lien-hsi) laid the foundation for the Sung dynasty's metaphysical and ethical systems and is generally considered the true founder of Neo-Confucian philosophy. His works include the *T'ung-shu* (Penetrating the *Book of Changes*) in forty "chapters," or short passages, and the *T'ai-chi t'u shuo* (An Explanation of the Diagram of the Great Ultimate). The latter, a short essay of 263 words, has become the most important work in Neo-Confucian literature and invariably heads every Neo-Confucian anthology. Chou indirectly obtained the diagram itself from the Taoist priest Ch'en Tuan (906–989). But whereas the Taoists evidently used the diagram as a guide to winning immortality, Chou Tun-i stripped it entirely of its mystical dimension and used it as the basis for a rational cosmology and moral philosophy.

In his explanation of the diagram Chou develops a theory of creation, maintaining that the *wu-chi* ("ultimate of nonbeing"), that is, reality beyond space and time, is also the *t'ai-chi* ("great ultimate"), reality in its totality. Through its movement, the Great Ultimate generates *yang,* the active cosmic force; through tranquility, it generates *yin,* the passive cosmic force. *Yin* and *yang* alternate, each becoming the "root" of the other. This alternation and transformation gives rise to the *wu-hsing* ("five agents"): metal, wood, water, fire, and earth, which in turn produce the myriad things. Of these, man is the most intelligent. When the five moral principles of man's nature (humanity, righteousness, propriety, wisdom, and faithfulness) become active this activity begets good and evil and the various human affairs. The sage, who is in accord with his nature, settles these affairs through the principles of the "mean" *(chung)*, correctness, humanity, and righteousness. In the twenty-second chapter of the *T'ung-shu* Chou adds that while the two material forces and the Five Agents operate to produce the myriad things, the many are ultimately one and the one is actually differentiated in the many. This same chapter is entitled "Hsing-li-ming," or "Nature, Principle, and Destiny." These three terms became key words in the Neo-Confucian vocabulary, while the postulation of an organic relationship between the one and the many—a significant advance over the cosmology of the *Book of Changes*—became a fundamental concept in subsequent Chinese thought. [*See also* T'ai-chi; Yin-yang Wu-hsing; *and the biography of Chou Tun-i.*]

The numerical cosmology of Shao Yung. Shao Yung, like Chou Tun-i, based much of his thought on the concept of cosmic generation found in the *Book of Changes*. He was most influenced by the passage in the *I ching* that states that the Great Ultimate produces two forces (*yin* and *yang*), which produce four forms (*yin* and *yang* in both major and minor forms), which in turn generate the eight trigrams. These latter ultimately give rise to the myriad things. Reinterpreting this passage, Shao coupled its cosmology to a system of numerology. Underlying universal operations is what he termed "spirit" *(shen)*, from which number arises. Number then produces form and form produces concrete objects. Shao's system takes the number four as the basis for the classification of all phenomena. Thus, there are four heavenly bodies (sun, moon, stars, and zodiacal space), four earthly substances (water, fire, earth, and stone), four kinds of creatures (animals, birds, grass, and plants), four sense organs (eye, ear, nose, and mouth), four ways of transforming the world (by truth, virtue, work, and effort), four kinds of rulers, four kinds of the mandate of Heaven, and so forth. To support his theory of numerical evolution and production Shao expanded this systematic, yet arbitrary, scheme of classification to include a mathematical progression from the number 4 to the number 64 (the number of hexagrams in the *Book of Changes*). He conceived of evolutionary development as opening or expansion and closing or contraction. In this respect, the operations of the universe are dynamic, based on change, and governed by universal principles. In Shao's scheme all phenomena are well organized, definite, numerically predictable, and objectively understandable. In fact, in the quest to understand the universe, his chief methodology is to "view things as things," in other words, to view things from their own perspective and to understand objectively the principles inherent in them.

While Shao Yung shared the Neo-Confucian interest in the nature and destiny of things he did not address the fundamental ethical values of humanity and righteousness. Nor was he concerned with issues of personal cultivation and the nature of a well-ordered state. In many of his charts describing the operations of the universe one can easily see the naturalistic tendencies characteristic of Taoism. His chief work, the *Huang-chih ching-shih* (Supreme Principles Governing the World), did not deal with political affairs but rather with the natural laws governing the world and regulating all existence. In his rare discussion of history he is concerned to demonstrate the numerically determined and cyclical nature of history rather than to explain historical events in order to draw moral lessons. Perhaps it is for these reasons that later Neo-Confucians often excluded him from the mainstream of Neo-Confucian orthodoxy.

Unity and material force in Chang Tsai. Chang Tsai's most important works are the *Cheng-meng* (Correcting Youthful Ignorance), in seventeen chapters, and his short essay, *Hsi-ming* (The Western Inscription). Central to these texts is the concept of material force *(ch'i)*. Chang was considered an expert on the *Book of Changes* and was renowned for his public lectures on it. However, unlike Chou Tun-i and Shao Yung, he departed from the normative interpretation of the passage in the *I ching* that speaks of the Great Ultimate generating the two modes, *yin* and *yang*. To Chang, *yin* and *yang* are but two aspects of the Great Ultimate, which is itself identified with material force. In its original reality or substance, material force is formless and as yet unconsolidated. He called this aspect of material force *t'ai-hsü* ("great vacuity"). In its operation or function, it is called *t'ai-ho* ("great harmony"). As *t'ai-ho*, it functions through *yin* and *yang* in their interaction, rise and fall, integration and disintegration, and tranquility and activity, as is borne out by the way in which day and night, life and death, advance and decline in history, and so forth all proceed in natural harmony. Here, Chang has clearly outlined the theory of substance and function *(t'i-yung)* that later became central to Neo-Confucian thought. Chang further asserts that the Great Vacuity and the Great Harmony are fundamentally one; they are the Way *(tao)*, which is one, clear, and unobstructed. In a very important development for Neo-Confucian metaphysics, Chang reinterpreted the traditional theory of *kuei-shen* (spiritual beings), redefining *kuei* and *shen* as negative and positive spiritual forces, that is, as the contraction and expansion of material force. The spontaneous and natural operation of these two forces is regular, universal, and interrelated. Because he has thus characterized material force, some modern scholars have labeled Chang Tsai a materialist. In so doing, however, they have overlooked the fact that Chang also held that material force is one, clear, and unobstructed, and as such is conceived also as spirit.

With regard to the place of man in the universe Chang writes: "From the Great Vacuity there is Heaven. From the transformation of material force there is the Way. In the unity of the Great Vacuity and material force there is the nature [*hsing*] of man and things; in the unity of the nature and consciousness there is the mind [*hsin*]" (*Cheng-meng* 9). It is clear that in Chang's system the substance of the mind forms a unity with the universe. If one enlarges and directs the mind to encompass all things it will be transformed from a mind limited by subjective perceptions to one that partakes of the universal. The physical nature, which has been made impure by varying endowments of material force, will then be freed from the restrictions of the individual and will enjoy identity with the Great Vacuity and Great Harmony. This doctrine of the transformation of physical nature from evil to good has been hailed as a significant contribution to Neo-Confucian ethics.

Equally influential is Chang's short essay *The Western Inscription*, which he inscribed on a panel in the western window of his study. He begins by claiming that Heaven and Earth are our parents and all things are our brothers, and that we must therefore devote ourselves to filial piety, education of the young, and care for the elderly in order to complete our lives in peace. Here again, we find evidence of Chang's insistence that man forms one body with the universe. Later commentators, beginning with Ch'eng I, posited that in this passage Chang Tsai was addressing the basic Confucian concept of humanity *(jen)*. In its substance, humanity is one (entailing universal love); in its function, it is many (entailing specific moral duties). This, according to Ch'eng I, is an adumbration of his own doctrine that principle is one but its manifestations are many, a doctrine that forms the backbone of Neo-Confucianism as a whole. [*See the biography of Chang Tsai.*]

The Ch'eng brothers' theory of principle. Although the Ch'eng brothers (Ch'eng Hao, honored as Master Ming-tao, and Ch'eng I, honored as Master I-ch'uan) were students of Chou Tun-i and the nephews of Chang Tsai, they neither spoke of the Great Ultimate nor made material force the focal point of their doctrine. Instead, they were the first in the history of Chinese philosophy to base their thought entirely on the concept of principle *(li)*. They conceived of principle as self-evident, self-sufficient, extending everywhere, and governing all things. Principle cannot be augmented or diminished. It is possessed by everyone and everything and is that by which all things exist and can be understood. By claiming that all specific principles are but one universal principle, they bound man and all things into a unity. Most significant is the fact that they were the first to identify the principle inherent in things with *t'ien-li* (the "principle of Heaven"). This is especially true of Ch'eng Hao, for whom, as for all other Neo-Confucians, the principle of Heaven represents natural law; the principle of Heaven is the universal process of production and reproduction. The Ch'engs further equated principle with the mind and with (human) nature *(hsing)*. Indeed, their declaration that "the nature is principle" has come to characterize the entire Neo-Confucian movement.

The Ch'engs followed Meng-tzu's teaching that human nature is originally good. When Ch'eng Hao said that our nature possesses both good and evil, he meant merely that because our endowment of material force is imbalanced and deviates from the Mean there is bound to be both good and evil. He was quick to stipulate that the imbalance is not due to our original nature. While Ch'eng Hao equated principle with the principle of Heaven and stressed the dynamic and creative aspects of the universe, his younger brother, Ch'eng I, strongly emphasized the unity or universality of principle and the diversity of its manifestations. His dictum "Principle is one but its manifestations are many," reminiscent of Chou Tun-i's idea of the relationship between the one and the many, became a standard formula in Neo-Confucianism.

Although the Ch'engs never spoke directly about the relationship between principle and material force, they believed that *li* and *ch'i* are two aspects of all things. Ch'eng I, however, asserted that principle exists above physical form *(hsing-erh-shang)* while material force exists within form *(hsing-erh-hsia)*. The sharpness with which he made this distinction has earned for him the reputation as a dualist. However, he also said that principle can never exist outside of material force. Both brothers understood the operation of *yin* and *yang* as a creative process: Ch'eng Hao described it as production and reproduction; Ch'eng I, as new origination. Both viewed humanity *(jen)* as this creative process. Ch'eng I likened humanity to seeds out of which all things will grow. Not only is humanity foremost among the Five Constant Virtues, but as a seed, it encompasses and gives rise to all other virtues. For Ch'eng Hao humanity is the moral quality by which man identifies himself with Heaven, earth and the myriad things.

Both brothers followed the dictum from the *Book of Changes:* "Seriousness to straighten the internal life and righteousness to square the external life" as a guide to self-cultivation. Ch'eng I's claim that "moral self-cultivation requires seriousness; study rests with the extension of knowledge," stressed both moral or spiritual development and objective, intellectual inquiry. He turned to the authority of the *Great Learning* for support of his theory that the extension of knowledge *(chih-chih)* depends on the investigation of things. According to Ch'eng I, the principles of all things must be investigated. This investigation can be either deductive or inductive, through reading books, examining historical events and personages, or being active in the management of affairs. When one principle is fully understood all principles become clear. Ch'eng Hao emphasized a more internal and subjective approach to self-cultivation, stressing its moral and spiritual aspects. To him, the investigation of things implied correcting the mind and eradicating the evil and selfish tendencies in one's nature. These two approaches to moral self-cultivation, outward investigation and introspective analysis, came to be central (if sometimes contradictory) motifs in the thought of Neo-Confucians throughout the Sung and Ming dynasties.

While the Ch'eng brothers left no written texts of their own hand, their teachings survive in the *I-shu* (Surviving Works), a compendium of their sayings as recorded by disciples. As teachers, both acquired extensive followings, but their outstanding pupils frequently differed in interpretation and emphasis. Many, including Yang Shih (1053–1135) and Hsieh Liang-tso (c. 1050–1120), were criticized by later Neo-Confucians for revealing the influence of Ch'an Buddhism in their interpretation. [*See also* Li; Ch'i; *and the biographies of Ch'eng Hao and Ch'eng I.*]

The Neo-Confucian Synthesis of Chu Hsi. The philosophy of the five Northern Sung masters culminated in the thought of Chu Hsi (1130–1200). While Chu Hsi is generally described as the synthesizer of early Sung Neo-Confucianism, he did not merely gather the essential teachings of his predecessors and organize them into a harmonious whole. Rather, he developed a coherent metaphysical system by selecting and introducing his own innovative elements into such concepts as Chou Tun-i's Great Ultimate, Chang Tsai's material force, and the Ch'eng brothers' principle. Much of Chu's thought was identified with that of the Ch'eng brothers and centered on their concept of principle. Consequently, his school is commonly referred to as either the Ch'eng-Chu school or the school of Principle.

Metaphysics, the Great Ultimate, and principle. It was Chou Tun-i's *Explanation of the Diagram of the Great Ultimate* that provided the metaphysical basis for Chu Hsi's theory of principle. Chu Hsi interpreted the *chi* of *t'ai-chi* as the "ultimate," that point beyond which one can go no further. He defined *t'ai-chi,* or Great Ultimate, as both the sum total of the principles of all discrete phenomena and the highest principle within each of them. He thus extended Ch'eng I's concept of principle beyond the realm of human affairs to include all affairs within the universe. He posited a theory in which principle transcends time and space: there was principle before the existence of the universe and there will be principle after the collapse of the universe. In Chu Hsi's scheme the whole universe is but one principle, the Great Ultimate, one universal whole with which all individual things are endowed. At the same time, however, he emphasized that each phenomenon is endowed with its own defining principle. Thus, it is by their respective principles that a boat travels on the water and a vehicle travels on the road. The Great Ultimate is also the repository for all actualized and potential principles: as new things appear, their principles also appear. In this way, Chu Hsi was able to explain Ch'eng I's formulaic expression, "Principle is one but its manifestations are many." He describes the organic nature of this relationship by likening the Great Ultimate to the moon and its manifestations to the moon's reflection in many rivers. It is not that the moonlight has been broken up and distributed among the reflections, but each reflection is itself the moon in its totality.

Chu Hsi attributed the generative or creative ability to the Great Ultimate rather than to principle or material force. He reaffirmed Chou Tun-i's theory that creation begins with the Great Ultimate. However, unlike Chou, who believed that the Great Ultimate itself could be active or tranquil, Chu Hsi held that the Great Ultimate transcends such limitations of function and thus cannot be subject to either activity or tranquillity. Rather, the Great Ultimate embodies the principles of activity and tranquility. It is out of these principles that the material forces of *yin* and *yang* naturally ensue. The process of creation is dynamic and ever changing. New principles are always forthcoming and the universe is daily renewed.

The foregoing theory of principle and the Great Ultimate allowed Chu Hsi to refute his opponents' charges that the Great Ultimate was no different from the Taoist notions of nonbeing *(wu)* and nothingness *(hsü).* He was able to explain Chou Tun-i's statement that "the Ultimate of Nonbeing is also the Great Ultimate" by invoking the authority of the *Shih ching* (Book of Odes) and the *Chung-yung* (Doctrine of the Mean), both of which claim that Heaven has neither sound nor smell. According to Chu, this does not mean that the Great Ultimate is empty, but rather that it has neither spatial restriction nor physical form.

The relationship between principle and material force. Chu Hsi's greatest contribution to Neo-Confucian thought was his clarification of the relationship between principle and material force and his concomitant explanation of the actualization of phenomena. He adhered to the Ch'eng brothers' saying that "in the universe there has never been material force without principle or principle without material force." But for Chu, despite the fact that principle and material force are merged in each phenomenon and cannot be separated, they are definitely two different things. Principle is incorporeal, one, eternal, unchanging, and indestructible. It constitutes the essence of things, is the reason for creation, and is always good. Principle represents the metaphysical world, or what Ch'eng I referred to as "what exists above form." By contrast, material force is necessary to explain physical form and the production and transformation of things. In Ch'eng I's terms, material force constitutes "what exists within form." It is corporeal, many, transitory, individual, changeable, unequal, and destructible. Material force is the vehicle and material for creation and involves both good and evil.

In opposing principle and material force so diametrically, Chu Hsi drew many queries regarding their priority. This controversy lasted for several centuries in China and Korea. Modern scholars have strongly criticized Chu Hsi for being a dualist and for slighting material force (and therefore the material world). But these critics have overlooked Chu's repeated assertions that principle and material force are intrinsically involved and can never be separated. Principle needs material force to adhere to; material force needs principle for its being. But Chu also said that although neither principle nor material force is ontologically prior, one is obliged to admit that principle enjoys a logical priority by virtue of being the norm according to which material force takes shape. However, this priority is never a temporal one. One cannot say, Chu insisted, that there is principle one day and material force the next.

In order to explain the behavior of principle in its coincidence with material force and its resultant manifestation in all things, Chu Hsi further distinguished three modes of principle: "naturally so" *(tzu-jan)*, "necessarily so" *(pi-jan)*, and "ought to be so" *(tang-jan)*. All principles are naturally so. Being endowed by Heaven, they are not subject to violation or interference. These principles, such as the rotation of the seasons, the growth of plants, and the moral character of man, are individuated, concretized, and specific. This is the aspect of principle that is involved with material and exists within form. Thus, Heaven's endowment of principle in man makes his character naturally humane.

At the same time, all principles are necessarily so. This is the aspect of principle that exists above form and, as such, is transcendent and universal. It, too, is inviolable and unalterable and may be viewed as a moral imperative. Man's endowment from Heaven has the principle of humanity, and thus one cannot help but feel compassion.

The ought-to-be-so mode of principle might be described as the normative or ethical component. As every individual necessarily and naturally has the principle of humanity, there ought to be in him the feeling of compassion.

Chu Hsi's ethics and theory of mind. Chu Hsi's metaphysical speculations on the Great Ultimate, principle, and material force provided the basis for his understanding of man's mind and nature and for his development of a system of ethics and a method for moral self-cultivation. Unifying these elements of his philosophy was the concept of humanity, or *jen,* which had been a central theme in Confucian thought from the time of the *Lun-yü* (Analects). Chu Hsi rejected both Meng-tzu's understanding of humanity as human-heartedness and Han Yü's interpretation of *jen* as universal love. He also criticized as too abstract Ch'eng Hao's insistence that we "know the substance of humanity" and "form one body with Heaven and earth." Instead, he welcomed Ch'eng I's notion that *jen* is the seed from which all other virtues will grow. Reinterpreting the passage in the *Book of Changes* that claims "the great virtue of Heaven and Earth is to give life," Ch'eng I had declared that "the mind *(hsin)* of Heaven [the mind of the Tao] and Earth is to produce things." In his treatise on humanity, Chu Hsi brings this interpretation to bear on the nature of man's mind, defining *jen* as the "character of the mind and the principle of love." Thus, he conceives of *jen* as being derived from Heaven:

"Man and things have received this mind of Heaven and Earth as their [own] mind." This aspect of the mind, which Chu calls the "mind of the Tao" *(tao-hsin)*, embodies principle in its transcendent form and is associated with man's original nature *(pen-hsing)*. It is characterized by humanity and is free from self-interest and selfish desires. The other aspect of the mind, which he called the "human mind" *(jen-hsin)*, is determined by man's imbalanced endowment of material force. Because it is the part of the mind that is bound to material force, the human mind is often characterized by selfish desires and causes man to act out of pure self-interest. Chu Hsi taught that in order for man not to be engulfed by selfishness and evil he must cultivate himself in a manner that rectifies the human mind and develops the mind of Heaven. In order to accomplish the former, Chu offered Confucius's explanation of humanity: "To master one's self and return to propriety is humanity" (*Lun-yü* 12.1). In his commentary on this passage from the *Analects*, Chu interpreted humanity as the perfect virtue of one's mind, which is always associated with the principle of Heaven. Thus, for Chu Hsi, to control selfish desires is to allow one's good moral nature to shine forth. [*See also* Jen and I *and* Hsin.]

Chu Hsi's legacy. Chu Hsi's impact on philosophy, education, and state ideology is unparalleled in Chinese history. Apart from the nine years he served as a local government official and his forty-six days as lecturer to the emperor on the classics, Chu Hsi spent virtually his entire life as a teacher. In 1190 he published the *Analects*, the *Great Learning*, the *Doctrine of the Mean*, and the *Meng-tzu* in a collection he termed the Four Books. From 1313 until 1912 the Four Books and Chu's own commentaries were used as the required texts for public education and as the basis for the questions on the civil service examinations. Chu Hsi compiled the Four Books and wrote the commentaries both to emphasize his concern with daily moral and social affairs and to build a new Confucian orthodoxy. He established an orthodox line of transmission *(tao-t'ung)* that began with the ancient sages, continued through Confucius and Meng-tzu, and then, after a lapse of several hundred years, resumed with the Sung Neo-Confucians Chou Tun-i and the Ch'eng brothers. More than once he hinted that he himself was in the direct line of transmissions, and indeed, the line of transmission from Confucius to Chu Hsi was accepted in China, Korea, and Japan. Related to this question of the orthodox transmission is Chu Hsi's strong personal attachment to Confucius. In his school, he began every morning by offering incense to Confucius and bowing before his portrait. Chu Hsi was an extremely devout man, observing religious rites with care and sincerity. Throughout his life he was exceedingly concerned about the proper performance of ceremonies; the day before he died he was still writing to pupils about the revision of ritual texts. [*See also the biography of Chu Hsi.*]

Alternate Schools of Sung Dynasty Neo-Confucianism. Traditional scholarship speaks of two schools that flourished during the Southern Sung period (1127–1279): the school of Principle *(li-hsüeh)*, whose spokesman was Chu Hsi, and the school of Mind *(hsin-hsüeh)*, associated with Lu Hsiang-shan (Lu Chiu-yüan, 1139–1193). During the Yüan period (1279–1368) the former was deemed orthodox and promoted as the official state ideology; the latter has often and erroneously been tied to the great Ming dynasty Neo-Confucian, Wang Yang-ming (Wang Shou-jen, 1472–1529). Recent scholarship has contended that during this early period of Neo-Confucianism many other schools of thought, the so-called Chekiang school in particular, contributed to the general intellectual dialogue. The leading proponents of this school, whose members are sometimes referred to in the West as utilitarians, were Lü Tsu-ch'ien (1137–1181) and Ch'en Liang (1143–1194), both of whom lived and taught in eastern Chekiang Province. A full account of the Southern Sung would have to include the Hunan school of Hu Hung (1105–1155) and Chang Shih (1133–1180), who advocated the moral neutrality of human nature. These last two schools have been largely ignored due to the general perception that they had little impact on the direction Neo-Confucianism would take in the Yüan and Ming dynasties.

The school of Mind. Chu Hsi's strongest opponent was Lu Hsiang-shan, who conceived of the mind as morally self-sufficient, endowed with the innate knowledge of good and the innate ability to do good. Going beyond Meng-tzu's statement that all things are complete within the self, Lu proclaimed that "the mind is principle." The universe is one's mind, he held, and one's mind is the universe. Consequently, he advocated complete reliance on the mind, self-sufficiency, self-accomplishment, and self-perfection. This view stands in direct opposition to the Ch'eng-Chu thesis that the mind is the function of human nature and that the nature is principle. Lu criticized Chu's theory of human nature, in which the principle of Heaven, which is always good, is contrasted with human desires, which may or may not be good. Lu also refused to accept Chu Hsi's claim that while there is only one mind, a distinction can be made between the human mind and the mind of the Tao.

Lu Hsiang-shan and Chu Hsi were the central figures in two debates held in 1175 at the Goose Lake Monastery in Kiangsi Province. At that time, Lu criticized Chu for paying undue attention to texts, commentaries, and isolated details. In addressing the issue of self-cultivation, Lu accused Chu Hsi of overemphasizing the path of inquiry and study *(tao-wen-hsüeh)* and ignoring the path of honoring the moral nature *(tsun-te-hsing)*. For his part, Chu Hsi attacked Lu for assuming that man could depend solely on his own mind as an objective moral standard. This issue was only implied during these debates, but later it served to place Chu and Lu in opposite camps. In 1181 they corresponded regarding the concept of the Great Ultimate. Lu held that it was a Taoist concept and thus had no place in Neo-Confucian philosophy. Feelings ran high on both sides, with Chu and Lu opposed at every turn. [*See the biography of Lu Hsiang-shan.*]

The Chekiang school. The debate at Goose Lake Monastery was arranged by Lü Tsu-ch'ien, Chu Hsi's good friend and frequent correspondent. Early in 1175 Lü Tsu-ch'ien and Chu Hsi collaborated in the compilation of the first Chinese philosophical anthology, the *Chin-ssu lu* (Reflections on Things at Hand). On many issues, however, they differed radically. While Chu Hsi viewed the classics as sacred texts, Lü looked to the dynastic and comprehensive histories for moral and philosophical lessons. He held that history does not simply gather disjointed facts but is a record of growth and transformation.

Ch'en Liang, another major thinker of the Chekiang school, went even farther in the direction of utilitarianism. He and Chu Hsi carried on a heated debate through their correspondence over the proper manner in which to view history. Ch'en criticized Chu Hsi's discussions on principle and nature as too abstract. He accused Chu of judging historical events from the perspective of an individual's motivation rather than from the outcome of his actions. Ch'en stressed practicality and human effort and regarded success as a virtue. Unlike Chu Hsi, he made no distinction between the principle of Heaven and human desires, between the wise king and the accomplished despot, or between righteousness and profit.

The Hunan school. Hu Hung, the founder of the Hunan school, traced his intellectual heritage back through his father to Yang Shih, a disciple of Ch'eng I. In his work *Chih-yen* (Knowing Words) Hu maintained that the mind is the master of all things and that depending on the way the mind uses nature, nature may become good or evil. He challenged the distinction between the principle of Heaven and human desires, claiming instead that in substance they were the same but in function they differed. Chu Hsi was too young to have met Hu Hung, but he strongly criticized *Knowing Words* for philosophically contradicting the traditional Neo-Confucian doctrine of the original goodness of human nature and for equating evil human desires with the principle of Heaven. Hu Hung's pupil Chang Shih, a very close friend of Chu Hsi, failed in his attempts to bring about a compromise between the two schools, owing largely to Chu's intransigence. Chang Shih did, however, exert some influence on Chu Hsi. Chang's belief, inherited from his teacher, that one must understand the mind before trying to cultivate it, persuaded Chu Hsi to reevaluate his theory of mind and its attendant method of self-cultivation. From his teacher, Li T'ung (1093–1163), Chu had learned that the technique of purifying the mind in quiet sitting must precede an understanding of the mind. In 1167 Chu visited Chang Shih and, under his influence, turned to Ch'eng I's twofold formula for cultivation of mind: "Self-cultivation requires seriousness; the pursuit of learning depends on the extension of knowledge." From this, Chu Hsi developed his theory of mind-cultivation that requires the simultaneous pursuit of moral development and intellectual inquiry.

Neo-Confucianism in the Yüan Dynasty. With the fall of the Sung dynasty in 1179 and the rise of Mongol hegemony over China the spread of the various Neo-Confucian schools virtually came to an end. The only school to survive was that of Chu Hsi. Its survival was due both to its established domination and to a chance set of circumstances. A Confucian scholar, Chao Fu (c. 1206–1299), was captured by the Mongols in Hupei Province, an area of China under the control of the Chin (1115–1234) and hence little influenced by the Neo-Confucian trend in the south. When Chao was sent to the Mongol capital at Yen-ching (modern-day Peking) he took with him several Neo-Confucian texts, most notably, Chu Hsi's commentaries to the Four Books. In Yen-ching, Chao attracted a large following, including the Chinese scholar Hsü Heng (1209–1281). Later, in his capacity as director of the T'ai-hsüeh (the national university), Hsü was able to influence and in effect dominate the intellectual current of China under the Mongols. Hsü Heng vigorously championed the *Hsiao-hsüeh* (Elementary Education), compiled by Chu Hsi in 1189 for the moral edification of the young in their daily conduct. Hsü also advocated use of the Four Books, which he regarded as sacred, and Chu Hsi's commentaries, which he personally copied. It is possible that he promoted the use of these texts because he felt that the Mongols and Central Asians might find the classics too abstruse. Perhaps he felt it simply more prudent to restrict himself to the *Hsiao-hsüeh*, which provided practical examples of proper behavior, and the Four Books, which explained their underlying moral principles. In any event, Hsü shared Chu Hsi's conviction that the Four Books were the direct words of Confucius and Meng-tzu and that the *Hsiao-hsüeh* was the unsurpassed guide to moral conduct. There is no doubt that Hsü-Heng's adoration of Chu Hsi and his commentaries on the Four Books contributed to the imperial edict of 1313 making the Four Books and the Five Classics the basic required texts for the civil service examinations. A decree of the following year reaffirmed Chu Hsi's commentaries as the official interpretations of the Four Books. While many scholars have maintained that the Yüan period was a time of compromise between the Chu Hsi school of Principle and the Lu Hsiang-shan school of Mind, it is not an exaggeration to say that under Hsü Heng's patronage the Ch'eng-Chu school came to monopolize the world of Chinese thought.

Neo-Confucianism in the Ming Dynasty. By the beginning of the Ming dynasty (1368–1644) the philosophy of the Ch'eng-Chu school was the established orthodoxy. Outstanding philosophers of the period—Ts'ao Tuan (1376–1434), Wu Yü-pi (1391–1469), Hsüeh Hsüan (1392–1464), Hu Chu-jen (1434–1484), and others—were all faithful followers of Chu Hsi. However, these thinkers tended to disregard metaphysical speculation on the Great Ultimate, *yin* and *yang*, and the relation of principle to material force and instead turned their attention toward understanding the mind, nature, self-cultivation, and seriousness *(ching)*. These concerns anticipate those of the late Ming dynasty school of Mind.

In his account of Ming dynasty Neo-Confucians, the *Ming-ju hsüeh-an*, the authoritative historian Huang Tsung-hsi (1610–1695) asserted that the new philosophy of the Ming dynasty began with Ch'en Hsien-chang (also known as Ch'en Pai-sha, 1428–1500) and reached its acme with Wang Yang-ming (Wang Shou-jen, 1472–1529). In postulating a connection between these two philosophers Huang was underscoring the commonalities among Ming thinkers. Ch'en's theories of self-cultivation foreshadow the conflict, which was to occupy a dominant position in Ming thought, between honoring the moral nature and following the path of study and inquiry. In his focus on quiet sitting as a dynamic state, Ch'en exemplifies the concerns of those Ming Neo-Confucians who advocated a move away from the excessive study of texts and commentaries that characterized the Ch'eng-Chu school. But however similar their concerns may have been, it is difficult to make a case for a direct connection between Ch'en Pai-sha and Wang Yang-ming. Wang was too young to have met or communicated with Ch'en during the one year (1482) both lived in the capital. Furthermore, in his philosophical discussions Wang neither mentions Ch'en nor demonstrates any familiarity with Ch'en's doctrines.

Wang Yang-ming and the school of Mind. The central thesis of Wang Yang-ming's thought is that principle and mind are one. Outside the mind there is no principle and, conversely, all principles are contained within the mind. Related to this is his concept that the mind is master of the body:

> The master of the body is the mind. What emanates from the mind is the will. The original substance of the will is knowledge, and wherever the will is directed is a thing [event]. For example, when the will is directed toward serving one's parents, then serving one's parents is a 'thing'. . . . Therefore, I say that there are neither principles nor things outside the mind. (*Ch'uan-hsi lu* 6)

These concepts brought Wang into direct opposition to the thought of Chu Hsi. Wang took great exception to Chu's redaction of the *Great Learning*, in which he had emended a chapter so as to expound his theory of the investigation of things and had rearranged the order of the text so as to place the chapter on the extension of knowledge before the chapter on the sincerity of the will. In his own *Ta-hsüeh wen* (Inquiry on the *Great Learning*) Wang also criticizes Chu Hsi for establishing a dualism between "making one's virtue clear" *(ming-te)* and "loving the people" *(ch'in-min)*. The essential point of this work is that, for Wang, all things form a unity *(i-t'i)*.

In general, Wang's critique of Chu Hsi centered on the theory of the investigation of things. He claimed that Chu Hsi divided principle and mind in advocating that one should direct the mind outside to seek principles in external things. Rather than follow Chu's interpretation of *ko-wu* as an investigation *(ko)* of things, Wang revived the interpretation found in the *Meng-tzu*, where *ko* means "rectification." Thus to Wang, *ko-wu* involved rectifying the mind by eliminating incorrectness and removing evil. Wang also asserted that since it is the will of the mind to realize principle, sincerity of the will must precede the investigation of things. To redress these wrongs, in 1518 Wang published the old text of the *Great Learning* as it is found in the *Li chi* (Book of Rites).

Wang's answer to many of the difficulties raised by Chu's thought was a theory of self-cultivation that combined the concept of innate knowledge *(liang-chih)*, derived from the *Meng-tzu*, with the notion of the extension of knowledge *(chih-chih)*, derived from the *Great Learning*. Wang equated nature, knowledge, and the original substance of the mind, which is always good and manifests an innate knowledge of the good. Although Wang never defined innate knowledge, he variously described it as "the original substance of the mind," "the principle of Heaven," "the pure intelligence and clear consciousness of the mind," "the equilibrium before the emotions are aroused," "the spirit of creation," and as "permeating and penetrating all existence." It is man's innate knowledge that gives him his moral sense of right and wrong. Thus, man's mind, in its original substance, understands all principles. To cultivate oneself one need not investigate the principles of things external to the mind; rather, one has only to follow the impulses of one's innate knowledge. If one fully cultivates and extends the innate knowledge, one's nature, which is originally good, will be fully developed and one's actions will be true to his innate sense of the good.

To clarify these points, Wang advanced what is regarded as his most original and significant contribution to Neo-Confucianism: a doctrine of the unity of knowledge and action. Knowledge, which in Wang's thought is limited to moral knowledge, must have its logical expression in action and action must be firmly based in knowledge. "Knowledge in its genuine and earnest aspect is action and action in its intelligent and discriminating aspect is knowledge." To illustrate this, Wang refers to the experience of pain, which one cannot know unless one suffers. (This illustration demonstrates the essentially subjective nature of knowledge in Wang's system.) With respect to moral behavior, Wang said that a man who knows the duties of filial piety will fulfill them, but at the same time, can truly understand those duties only through their fulfillment. This doctrine gave Ming Neo-Confucianism a new dynamic, for it suggests that the extension of innate knowledge is a natural and even irresistible impulse that is true to man's nature. The extension of innate knowlege leads not only to the fulfillment of filial obligations but to love for all beings and the identification of oneself with all things in the universe. This notion is highly reminiscent of Ch'eng Hao's concept that man forms one body with Heaven, earth, and the myriad things.

Wang Yang-ming's legacy. Wang did not live long enough to fully explicate his theory of innate knowledge. His disciples, who dominated China's intellectual world, interpreted it according to their own needs. Some advocated earnest practice, tranquility, or moral restraint, while others went to the extreme of libertinism. To make matters worse, in 1527, two years before his death, Wang told his pupils, "In the original substance of the mind there is no distinction of good and evil. When the will becomes active, however, such distinction exists. The faculty of innate knowledge is to know good and evil. The investigation of things is to do good and remove evil." These "four axioms" aroused bitter opposition among Neo-Confucians, for to say that the original mind is neither good nor evil directly contradicts the Neo-Confucian theory of the original goodness of human nature. In this matter Wang has been misinterpreted and unjustly condemned, for on more than one occasion he insisted that original mind is always good. Perhaps a more adequate interpretation of Wang's pronouncement would emphasize his belief that the mind is so absolutely good that is can have no deliberate intention to be either good or evil. Nevertheless, the misunderstanding was prevalent, and historians came to blame Wang's doctrines and the misbehavior of his pupils for the fall of the Ming dynasty.

Wang's theory of the mind and principle and his criticisms of Chu Hsi have led many scholars to conclude that Wang Yang-ming was reviving Lu Hsiang-shan's school of Mind. Indeed, the alleged connection between the two is reflected in traditional scholarly usage, which refers to their thought as the Lu-Wang school of Neo-Confucianism. Wang, however, showed no particular interest in Lu and claimed that his (Wang's) ideas were drawn directly from Confucius and Meng-tzu. He urged his students and friends not to take part in the controversy, which was thriving at that time, between the followers of Lu and Chu. This older, traditional scholarship, which distinguishes sharply between the school of Mind and the school of Principle, does, however, point to subtle issues differentiating the thought of Chu Hsi and Wang Yang-ming. Wang strongly opposed Chu's division of the human mind and the mind of the Tao. In his contention that "when the mind is rectified it is the moral mind," Wang differed from Chu only in terminology and not in interpretation. His related theory of self-cultivation, however, betrays a radically different approach. Wang did not believe, as Chu did, that it is necessary to study texts extensively in order to understand moral principles. Rather, since the mind contains all possible principles and is, in fact, identified with principle, one need only engage in inner moral and spiritual cultivation. The method he prescribed was the earnest handling of affairs and quiet sitting. Most essential is that man actively seek truth by realizing his innate knowledge and by rectifying his mind of its obscuring selfish desires.

In 1518 Wang published his essay *Chu-tzu wan-nien ting-lun* (Chu Hsi's Final Conclusions Arrived at Late in Life), in which he claimed that Chu had belatedly realized his mistakes. Wang selected passages from Chu's writings to try to prove that Chu had changed his attitude toward self-cultivation from an emphasis on the external search for truth through detailed discussions and commentaries (i.e., the path of inquiry and study) to the cultivation of the mind aimed at fundamentals (i.e., honoring the moral nature). This publication created an intellectual storm that was to last for several centuries. Chu and Wang were pitted as philosophical enemies and the school of Principle and the school of Mind were regarded as irreconcilable rivals. Recent scholarship has tried to amend these misinterpretations by focusing on the continuity within Neo-Confucianism. Scholars are now emphasizing that both Chu and Wang built their philosophies on the concept of principle and that both faithfully followed Confucius and Meng-tzu. While Wang's thought represents a strong challenge to Chu Hsi, it is now seen as a challenge that debates the same fundamental parameters and arises from within the same tradition. [*See the biography of Wang Yang-ming.*]

Neo-Confucianism in the Ch'ing Dynasty. Although Wang Yang-ming's doctrine of innate knowledge dominated the philosophy of the fifteenth and sixteenth centuries, it never entirely eclipsed the teachings of the Ch'eng-Chu school. The Manchu rulers, who conquered China in 1644, reaffirmed the philosophy of the Ch'eng-Chu school as the orthodox teaching. The Four Books and Chu Hsi's commentaries on them were upheld as the required school texts and the basis for the civil service examinations. The general tendency of scholars in the late seventeenth century was either to follow the teachings of Chu Hsi or to attempt a compromise between the perceived rationalism of Chu Hsi and the idealism of Wang Yang-ming. There were, however, outstanding Neo-Confucian scholars like Ku Yen-wu (1613–1682) who began to reevaluate their intellectual heritage. Although Ku was strongly influenced by and inclined toward the philosophy of the Ch'eng-Chu school, he attacked the abstract thinking associated with their theories of the Great Ultimate, the mind, and human nature. In their stead he called for practical and objective learning, the pursuit of empirical knowledge, and involvement in practical affairs. [*See the biography of Ku Yen-wu.*) Among the thinkers who followed Ku Yen-wu, Yen Yüan (1635–1704) and Tai Chen (1723–1777) took the tendency toward practical learning and objective truth even farther.

Yen Yüan rejected the philosophy of both Chu Hsi and Wang Yang-ming. He believed that all the subjects of Sung and Ming speculation—principle, nature, destiny, and the sincerity of the will—could only be found in such practical arts as music, ceremony, agriculture, and military craft. As a teacher, he emphasized mathematics, archery, weight lifting, singing, and so forth, and himself practiced medicine and farming. Yen maintained that there is no principle apart from material force; he insisted that the physical nature endowed with material force is no different from the original nature endowed by Heaven. Because the physical nature is not evil, there is no need to transform it or to repress physical desires. He believed that the investigation of things involved neither the study of principle nor the rectification of the mind, but rather the application of practical experience to the solution of practical problems. While Yen Yüan's thought may appear to be a radical departure from Confucian philosophy, he, in fact, worked from within the tradition. Yen wished to return directly to the works of Confucius and Meng-tzu and called for the revival of ancient methods of land distribution and governmental organization.

Tai Chen, another critic of Chu Hsi, is generally recognized as the greatest thinker of the Ch'ing dynasty. He was a proponent of the new intellectual movement known as "investigations based on evidence" *(k'ao-cheng).* He was a specialist in mathematics, astronomy, water-works, and phonetics and was widely respected as an expert in literary criticism. These pursuits led him to the critical study of the classics as practiced by the Han dynasty Confucians. His objective and critical spirit caused him to reject many aspects of Sung and Ming Neo-Confucianism, in particular, the concept of a universal principle. He complained that philosophers like Chu Hsi and Wang Yang-ming looked upon principle "as though it were a thing." Tai Chen advocated the Han dynasty understanding of principle as an order that is found only in things, by which he meant the daily affairs of men. Principle, he believed, could not be investigated by intellectual speculation, but rather through the objective, critical, and analytical observation of things. He did not follow the Sung Confucians in contrasting the principle of Heaven and human desires as good and evil, respectively. Instead, he held that principle prevails only when feelings are satisfied and that feelings are good as long as they "do not err." In conjunction with this, he postulated the existence of "necessary moral principles," that is, objective and standard principles, that are definite and inherent in concrete things. Tai Chen's insistence on the objective study of things and his emphasis on principle as a systematic arrangement of ordinary daily matters brought a new spirit to the Neo-Confucian tradition. Even allowing for his bitter attack on the Sung thinkers, Tai was still within the Neo-Confucian movement. He relied on the Confucian classics, especially the *Book of Changes;* also prominent in his thought are the concepts of production and reproduction and of humanity. [*See the biography of Tai Chen.*]

The Nineteenth and Early Twentieth Centuries. The nineteenth century was marked by the further diminution of the influence of the Ch'eng-Chu school in the world of Chinese thought. As China was progressively weakened by both the disintegration of Manchu rule and the onslaught of Western imperialism, Confucianism lost favor as the official state ideology. In the face of Western economic and military superiority, Neo-Confucians were forced to reconsider the classic Chinese response to foreign cultures and ideologies. The contemporary slogan "Chinese studies for substance; Western studies for function" expressed the hope of many Chinese for an accommodation with the West that preserved the perennial Confucian views of man and society. *Substance* here refers to Confucian moral principles and institutions; *function*, to Western technology. But this attempt at compromising the East and West did not save either Confucianism or the Ch'ing dynasty. In 1905 the civil service examinations were abolished in favor of a Western system of education. With the establishment of the Republic in 1912, the official sacrifices to Confucius and to Heaven were terminated. Although the classics continued to be taught in public schools they were increasingly subject to denunciation.

During these turbulent times groups of intellectuals continued the effort to reinterpret and reestablish their Confucian heritage. K'ang Yu-wei (1858–1927), an outstanding scholar of the Confucian classics, justified his attempts at institutional reform by recourse to Confucian ideology. Believing that the strength and prosperity of Western nations derived from their having a state religion, K'ang petitioned the emperor to establish Confucianism as the national cult. Although the Draft Constitution Committee of 1913 declined to institute Confucianism as the state religion, it did adopt an article that stated: "In the education of citizens, the doctrines of Confucius shall be regarded as the basis of moral cultivation." In the following year the president, Yüan Shih-k'ai (1858–1916), decreed the resumption of the sacrifices to Heaven and the worship of Confucius. At the same time, however, other groups of intellectuals called for the final defeat of Confucianism. The intellectual renaissance of 1917 declared Confucianism unsuited to modern life. Confucian morality, in particular filial piety, was condemned as "a big factory for the manufacture of obedient subjects." Participants in this movement, who turned to Western philosophy and science for answers to China's problems, asserted that "Confucianism is absolutely inconsistent with republicanism," and raised the cry "Destroy the old curiosity shop of Confucius." [*See the biography of K'ang Yu-wei.*]

For a time it seemed as though Confucianism was doomed. As the revolutionary fervor cooled, however, Chinese intellectuals began to reconsider the role of the tradition in the future of China. Liang Shu-ming (1893–) published a study comparing Chinese and Western civilizations. He championed Confucian moral values and condemned the wholesale adoption of Western institutions as unsuited to the Chinese spirit. During the following twenty years, Fung Yu-lan (1895–) and Hsiung Shih-li (1895–1968) emerged as prominent spokesmen for Confucianism. Fung's *Hsin-li hsüeh* (New Learning of Principle), published in 1939, is a reconstruction of the Ch'eng-Chu school of Neo-Confucianism. This study, firmly grounded in Western philosophy, treats four major metaphysical concepts—principle, material force, the substance of the Way *(tao)*, and the Great Whole—as formal concepts with logical implications. Hsiung's reconstruction of the Idealist school of Neo-Confucianism, published as the *Hsin wei-shih lun* (New Treatise on Consciousness Only), appeared in 1944. In it, he conceived of reality as perpetual transformation and transition in which "original substance" unceasingly arises, resulting in a diversity of manifestations. In Hsiung's assertion that reality and its manifestations (i.e., substance and function) are one his adherence to the philosophy of the Ch'eng-Chu school is obvious. Furthermore, he follows all Neo-Confucians in characterizing the original mind as humanity *(jen)*, that which allows man to form one body with Heaven.

The Status of Confucianism in the Late Twentieth Century. The Communist victory in 1949 and the Cultural Revolution in the 1960s brought a decided end to the attempts to make Confucianism the state ideology and religion. However, scholars never suspended their study of Confucianism; along with members of China's political hierarchy, they have continued to discuss the historical significance and relevancy of Confucianism. Between 1960 and 1962 thirteen conferences were held to debate the status of Confucius and Confucian philosophy. The philosophical and political issues that were discussed included the following questions: Should Confucius' Heaven be understood as physical or spiritual? Is the mandate of Heaven deterministic or subject to human intervention? Was Confucius a subjective idealist, an objective idealist, or a materialist? Did the Confucian concept of humanity aim at the emancipation of slaves? While these questions were never resolved, the discussants agreed that in spite of his limitations, Confucius was a great man and that his teachings are worth preserving in order to facilitate China's acceptance of Marxism.

The Communist attitude toward the Ch'eng-Chu school has been rather more critical. It is not uncommon for scholars in the People's Republic to judge the statements made by Chu Hsi and the Ch'eng brothers out of the context of their general philosophical concerns. They contend, for example, that Chu Hsi's injunction to one student on one occasion that he spend half the day in quiet sitting and half the day studying is a repudiation of the material world. Since the mid-1970s, however, the scholarly community in China has shown signs of weakening their attack on Neo-Confucianism. In 1980 a conference was held to study the philosophy of Chu Hsi and Wang Yang-ming. The participants' appraisal of Neo-Confucianism was objective and fair, and their remarks about Chu and Wang at once favorable and unfavorable. The official party position, affirmed at this session, is that Neo-Confucianism played a major role in Chinese history, albeit one that served a feudal society, and thus is worthy of continued study.

Among the overseas Chinese communities, and also in Hong Kong and Taiwan, there has been a resurgence in scholarly interest in Neo-Confucianism. Credit for this trend must go largely to Ch'ien Mu, whose New Asia College has generated a series of provocative and insightful publications on Neo-Confucianism. While scholarly interest in Neo-Confucianism remains a minor but growing trend, Confucian traditions, institutions, and moral standards have always held significance in the lives of the Chinese residing in Hong Kong, Taiwan, and the overseas communities. In the 1980s one still sees evidence of ancestor worship, sacrifice to Confucius, and family morality founded on filial piety.

Is Neo-Confucianism a Religion? This question, asked by Christian missionaries since the seventeenth century and by Chinese scholars since the nineteenth century, continues to be debated in both Chinese and contemporary Western scholarship. The debate has centered on, and been determined by, several factors. First, Christian missionaries, observing both popular and elite traditions, came to regard the Chinese worship of deities as superstition and the Confucian classics as simply humanistic texts for kingly rule. Second, Chu Hsi's system of metaphysics has long been regarded as a system of rationalism, devoid of religious significance. Third, looking at the institutions of dynastic rule, which legitimized itself in Confucian terms, the bureaucracy, which was recruited through the (Confucian) civil service examinations, and the state cult, which saw the emperor perform sacrifices to Heaven and decree the enshrinement of Neo-Confucian sages in the Temple of Confucius, scholars have concluded that Neo-Confucianism was the basis of a state ideology and polity. Finally, Neo-Confucianism cannot be defined in terms of organized, institutionalized religion—it had no formal clergy, laity, sacred texts, or liturgy. All of these factors have diverted attention from the religious aspects of Neo-Confucianism. Thus, in discussing Neo-Confucianism as a religion, a distinction must be made between the official cult, state ideology, and the practice and goal of Neo-Confucianism.

Neo-Confucian philosophy begins with a religious positivism based on the opening line of the *Doctrine of the Mean*, "What has been mandated from Heaven in man is his nature." The practice of Neo-Confucianism is to cultivate this nature, which is always morally good; the goal of this cultivation, deemed attainable by all men, is sagehood. For the Neo-Confucians, the sage is the exemplar of the perfected moral nature, a living model for the path one must follow to live one's life in accord with Heaven. Thus, the sage is regarded as the embodiment of the principle of Heaven. The focus of the debate concerning self cultivation concerns the proper manner by which man transforms himself from a life that is false to a life that is true, self-transcendent, and in accord with the way of Heaven.

Following the opening line of the *Doctrine of the Mean* it is evident that, for Confucians, Heaven is supreme, the creator of our being. The Confucian notion of a Great Ultimate that generates all things is in itself a theory of creation and genesis. Given the pronouncement that it is "the mind of Heaven and Earth to produce things," materialistic or mechanical interpretations of the nature of Heaven should be ruled out.

Rituals, including funerary, marriage, and mourning rites, and sacrifices to ancestors and to Confucian sages and worthies is another aspect of Neo-Confucian religiosity. Chu Hsi related rites to Heaven, defining them as the "restraint and ornament of the Principle of Heaven." Ceremonies are meant to give beauty and rhythm to the operations of Heaven as manifested in the human realm. Furthermore, rituals are a means through which man unites himself with Heaven. Performed with the proper attitude of reverence and seriousness, rituals are simply another facet of self-cultivation. The Neo-Confucian structure of study, rituals, and self-cultivation has, in the end, the one goal of bringing the ways of Heaven and principle into one's daily life.

[*See also* Chinese Philosophy; Chinese Religion, *article on* Religious and Philosophical Texts; Tao and Te; *and the biography of Meng-tzu.*]

BIBLIOGRAPHY

Western Sources

Chan, Wing-tsit, trans. and comp. *A Source Book in Chinese Philosophy.* Princeton, 1963. See chapters 28–35 and 38.

Chan, Wing-tsit. "Chu Hsi's Completion of Neo-Confucianism." *Sung Studies* ser. 2, no. 1 (1973): 59–90.

Chang, Carsun. *The Development of Neo-Confucian Thought.* 2 vols. New York, 1957–1962.

Ching, Julia. *To Acquire Wisdom: The Way of Wang Yang-ming (1492–1529).* New York, 1976.

Chu Hsi. *Reflections on Things at Hand.* Translated by Wing-tsit Chan. New York, 1967.

de Bary, Wm. Theodore, ed. *Self and Society in Ming Thought.* New York, 1970.

de Bary, Wm. Theodore, ed. *The Unfolding of Neo-Confucianism.* New York, 1975.

Fung Yu-lan. *A History of Chinese Philosophy.* 2d ed. 2 vols. Translated by Derk Bodde. Princeton, 1952–1953. Extensive discussion of Neo-Confucian thought can be found in volume 2.

Graham, A. C. *Two Chinese Philosophers: Ch'êng Ming-tao and Ch'êng Yi-ch'uan.* London, 1958.

Okada Takehiko. "The Chu Hsi and Wang Yang-ming Schools at the end of the Ming and Tokugawa Periods." *Philosophy East and West* 23 (January–April 1973): 139–162.

Tillman, Hoyt C. *Utilitarian Confucianism: Ch'en Liang's Challenge to Chu Hsi.* Cambridge, Mass., 1982.

Wang Shou-jen. *Instructions for Practical Living, and Other Neo-Confucian Writings, by Wang Yang-ming.* Translated and edited by Wing-tsit Chan. New York, 1963.

Chinese and Japanese Sources

Araki Kengo et al., comps. *Yōmeigaku taikei.* 12 vols. Tokyo, 1971–1973.

Ch'ien Mu. *Sung Ming li-hsüeh kai-shu.* Taipei, 1953.

Ch'ien Mu. *Chu-tzu hsin hsüeh-an.* 5 vols. Taipei, 1971.

Chung-kuo che-hsüeh shih tzu-liao hsüan-chi. 6 vols. Edited by the Chung-kuo K'o-hsüeh-yuan Che-hsüeh Yen-chiu So. Peking, 1982. See volume 4.

Hou Wai-lu. *Chung-kuo ssu-hsiang t'ung-shih.* Peking, 1959. See volume 4, chapters 10–15 and 20.

Hu Shih. *Tsai Tung-yüan ti che-hsüeh.* Shanghai, 1912.

Huang Tsung-hsi. *Ming-ju hsüeh-an.* Ssu-pu Pei-yao edition.

Huang Tsung-hsi and Ch'üan Tsu-wang. *Sung Yüan hsüeh-an.* Ssu-pu Pei-yao edition.

Jung Chao-tsu. *Ming-tai ssu-hsiang shih.* Shanghai, 1941.

Kusumoto Masatsugu. *Sō Min jidai jugaku shisō no kenkyū.* Tokyo, 1962.

Liu Shu-hsien. *Chu-tzu che-hsüeh ssu-hsiang ti fa-chan yü wan-ch'eng.* Taipei, 1982.

Lo Kuang. *Chung-kuo che-hsüeh ssu-hsiang shih: Sung-tai p'ien.* Taipei, 1980.

Mo Tsung-san. *Ts'ung Lu Hsiang-shan tao Liu Chi-shan.* Taipei, 1980.

Morohashi Tetsuji, ed. *Shushigaku taikei.* Tokyo, 1974–.

Okada Takehiko. *Sō Min tetsugaku josetsu.* Tokyo, 1970.

Okada Takehiko. *Chūgoku shisō ni okeru rigaku to genjitsu.* Tokyo, 1977.

Tomoeda Ryūtarō. *Shushi no shisō keisei.* Rev. ed. Tokyo, 1979.

WING-TSIT CHAN

The State Cult

The state cult of imperial China was a system of ritual places and the sacrifices performed there whereby successive dynasties intended to legitimize, safeguard, and benefit their rule. It was the means of regularizing and maintaining formal relationships between the ruler of "all that lay beneath Heaven" *(t'ien-hsia)* and the most potent powers of the numinous realm. Formulation and rationalization of the ceremonies appropriate to these purposes were the responsibility—indeed the monopoly—of the *ju* (Confucian scholars), and in this sense the state cult was a product of *ju* thought.

Objects of Worship. Although differing in details from dynasty to dynasty, the state cult preserved in its essentials the ideas of antiquity. Here I shall use the system of the Ch'ing (Manchu) dynasty (1644–1911) as illustrative of the cult. Four classes of spiritual beings worshiped in the state cult may be arbitrarily distinguished: the great powers of nature, the tutelary spirits of political territories, the agricultural god, and souls of the dead.

1. Heaven and earth, which, combined in a single term, signified the universe, were by far the most important of the powers of nature. One of the most ancient titles of emperors was "son of Heaven" *(t'ien-tzu)*, indicating that they owed their legitimacy as rulers to a mandate conferred by the supreme power. Earth, the essential counterpart of Heaven, the producer and sustainer of all life, was hardly less important. These two, along with the emperor's own ancestors, were the objects of the most profound expressions of reverence by the ruler of men. Other natural objects also received personal worship by the emperor, although to a lesser degree: the heavenly bodies, great mountains and rivers, clouds, rain, wind, and thunder.

2. Tutelary spirits of political territories formed a hierarchy from the county, prefectural, and provincial levels up to the empire as a whole. Occupants of these spiritual offices might well be classified under the category of souls of the dead, as they were usually distinguished men appointed to their postmortem duties by the emperor. However, the tutelary god of the whole empire (She) was one of the most ancient and eminent deities and received the personal worship of emperor.

3. The god of grain (Chi) was originally the mythical ancestor of the Chou people who established China's ancient Chou dynasty (c. 1100–256 BCE). The vital nature of his assistance is obvious for an agrarian society such as China. In ancient times the very existence of a state as a political entity was equated with the altars of She and Chi. Indeed, this idea persisted down through the ages; the two deities shared an altar and in the capital received the personal worship of the emperor.

4. "Souls of the dead" is such a broad category as practically to comprehend most of the deities of Chinese religion. Here the term refers to various recipients of worship in the state cult. By far the most important were the ancestors of the emperor. From the beginning of Chinese history and even before that, the ancestral cult was central. The sovereign of the ruling dynasty also paid reverence to the spirits of all the kings and emperors of past "legitimate" dynasties, on the assumption that they were still powerful in the numinous realm. The initiators of the basic arts of mankind were First Farmer (Hsien Nung), First Sericulturalist (Hsien Ts'an), and First Healer (Hsien I). They were given prominence in the state cult along with many other legendary and historical culture heroes. Since the Former Han dynasty (202 BCE–9 CE) the state cult had included worship of the soul of Master K'ung (Confucius). In the Ch'ing period he was elevated to the first rank. Along with Confucius himself, his greatest disciples and advocates through the ages were also worshiped. In the same manner, but to a lesser degree, the state cult exalted many of the great ministers of state and other worthies of history. Sacrifices to souls in any of the above categories were expressions of thanks and supplications for continuing favors. Aside from these benevolent spirits, the state did not neglect the dangers from the spiritual dimension of that great class of malevolent souls who had been deprived of the sacrifices due them by their descendants and who therefore constituted a clear and ever-present danger to the communities of the living. The state cult included propitiatory sacrifices to these bereaved souls.

In addition to these general categories, certain prominent cults of the popular religion were adopted into the state system. During Ch'ing times, these included the cults of Kuan-ti, Wen Ch'ang, the spirit of the North Star, and T'ien-hou.

Organization and Practices. The state religion was under the supervision of the Ministry of Rites *(li pu)*, one of the six major branches of administration, whose antecedents went back to the beginnings of Chinese history. Two important departments in the ministry were the Directorate of Sacrifices *(t'ai ch'ang ssu)* and the Bureau of Astronomy *(ch'in t'ien chien)*. The former made all the arrangements, provided the necessary utensils, and assisted at the performance of the many kinds of imperial sacrifices. The Bureau of Astronomy calculated the calendar and fixed the proper dates for the various sacrifices. Regulations issued by the ministry spelled out every detail of the rituals.

The full pantheon of deities was worshiped in the capital by the emperor or his representatives. In the provinces, the senior officials of administrative regions were responsible for carrying out the state cult in miniature versions of the great services offered by, or on behalf of, the sovereign. Ritual places were prescribed for every county, prefecture, and province. They were to include a *wen miao* ("civil temple, temple of literature," or "temple of culture"), which was dedicated to the soul of Confucius and his most eminent followers; memorial halls to other great men (much less important than the *wen miao*); altars; and officially sanctioned cult temples. The altars were for the gods of territory and of grain, the gods of mountains and rivers, clouds, rain, wind, and thunder, and most important, the god of the walls and moat *(ch'eng-huang-shen)* of the local capital. This last was the spirit counterpart of the magistrate in charge of the area. Included in the spirit magistrate's duties was the control of the bereaved spirits.

Practice of the state cult took the form of sacrifices graded in elaborateness according to the rank of the deity. These sacrifices were feasts to which the spirits were invited. Spread out for their delectation were dishes of meats, grain, vegetables, soups, and liquors, as well as one or more of the major sacrificial animals—pig, sheep, or bull. Which specific dishes were to be offered to specific deities was prescribed in the sacrificial regulations. Participants in the services wore ceremonial gowns and caps and observed the most formal etiquette, as if in the court of a prince. The chief sacrificiant, emperor or official, silently performed the advances and retirings, and the bowings and prostrations before the spirit tablet or image of the deity, guided by the cries of a herald and accompanied by ushers. Incense rose from many sticks placed in the great bronze braziers, music sounded, and a crowd of subordinate officials saluted the deity in concert with the chief sacrificiant. A prayer posted on a board was read, honoring the deity with many flattering titles and attributions of power, soliciting his continued blessings, and inviting him to descend and enjoy the banquet. It is important to understand that the state cult employed no class of ordained priests, but that the officiants of its sacrifices were the scholar-bureaucrats, or *ju*, who performed religious ceremonies as one part of their routine duties.

Confucian Thought and Its Relation to State Cult. The *ju* constituted an ancient class of teachers and ritual specialists. They were state appointees whose job it was to advise on matters of ritual and protocol at the courts of feudal lords and kings and to instruct the children of aristocrats in the various literary and non-literary subjects taught in the schools. Above all, they were specialists in the *li*—correct modes of behavior in all social circumstances or, more narrowly, correct ritual deportment of aristocrats toward one another and toward spiritual beings. In the feudal society of ancient China the *li* were supposed to be sufficient, on the principle of *noblesse oblige*, to keep good order among the elite class. It is understandable why the writings associated with the *ju* devoted much attention to the *li*.

Confucius was by profession a *ju*, and a strong advocate of the view that the *li* were the most suitable means of controlling society. But he also emphasized that something more than ritual correctness was essential, namely, the tireless effort to perfect one's character as a moral being. His truly revolutionary teaching was that true nobility is not a matter of blood but of character, and hence is achievable by any man. Confucius's charismatic personality and his challenging call to ethical greatness strongly influenced first his own students and eventually the whole class of *ju*. Thus the term *ju* came to refer to those who, while seeking professional careers as officials of state, were imbued with the principles of the moral law enunciated by Confucius.

Surviving the crises of many centuries, the Confucian *ju* attained a position of supreme influence in Chinese state and society when their texts and doctrines were adopted as orthodox by the Martial Emperor (Hsiao Wu, r. 140–87 BCE) of the Han dynasty. This act was not so much a declaration of faith on the part of the emperor, as it was recognition of the fact that men molded in the *ju* tradition made the best servants of the state. It was this fact that enabled the *ju* as a class to survive—and usually to dominate—the many different administrations of the empire throughout history. It could not be otherwise, since as a rule it was they who served as officials, tutors of princes, advisors of emperors, and ritual specialists.

The state cult was an expression of the understanding of ancient rulers that the *li* were a basic means of controlling their feudal retainers and great officers as well as the masses. Ritual behavior was paired with ritual music (orchestra, chorus, and rows of costumed dancers or pantomimists) as "gentle" methods of government, ideally sufficient in lieu of forcible edicts and punishments available to the ruler. According to the *ju* texts, the legendary sage-kings had not only used ritual and music as their primary instruments of government, but had themselves devised those rituals and composed that music. Ritual and music reached their most elaborate forms in the system of state sacrifices supposed to have been performed under the supervision of the Ministry of Religion. An idealized description from the early Han period tells us:

> By the Auspicious Rituals they served [i.e., sacrificed to] human souls, celestial spirits, and terrestrial spirits of the [feudal] states [of the empire] . . . by the Inauspicious Rituals they express condolence for sorrowful events in the feudal states of the empire . . . by the Rituals of Entertaining Guests they [unite the feudal lords in] brotherly love . . . by the Military Rituals they [awed] the feudal lords of the empire into cooperation . . . by the Congratulatory Rituals they [united] the myriads of common people in mutual affection.
> (*Chou Li*, "Officials of Spring")

The original state religion during the Western Chou was designed for a confederation of feudal states under the suzerainty of a king. During succeeding centuries the Chou king became a powerless figurehead, and a handful of the states, now swollen to great size by having swallowed up all the others, existed side by side in political independence and bitter rivalry. Each state thereupon devised its own cult system based, of course, upon the practices of the past. With the destruction of these warring states and the unification of China under Ch'in Shih-huang-ti (r. 221–208 BCE), and with the subsequent establishment of the long-lived Han empire (202 BCE–220 CE), still a third version of the state religion came into being, one that served the new polity. Throughout these changes, the necessary models came from the *ju* texts. Even under the dynasties of recent centuries, their ancient form and spirit characterized the state cult.

The peculiarity of the state cult of China was that it represented no living religion at all. While many countries have had religions of the state, these have always been the religions of at least a substantial portion of their people. But in China, after the ancient period, the state cult ossified. It had no real connection with the living religions of Taoism, Buddhism, or Neo-Confucianism, much less the popular religion of the masses. To be sure, the scholar-bureaucrats officiated at its mock-antique ceremonies, which they laid out and regulated in accordance with the prescriptions of their ancient texts. But as far as their own religious or philosophical interests were concerned, the texts that inspired them were not the pre-Confucian explications of *li*, but the writings of Confucius and his major disciples dealing with perennial problems of ethics, self-cultivation, and the quest for personal sageliness or sainthood. It may not be going too far to characterize the state cult of recent dynasties as little more than pageantry, assertions of the legitimacy of the dynasty, devoid of doctrinal content, ritual for the sake of ritual. It is no wonder that with the fall of the Ch'ing in 1911, the state cult vanished instantly, leaving only the grand altars and temples of Peking as architectural monuments to testify that it had ever existed.

[*See also* Chinese Religion, *overview article and article on* Mythic Themes.]

BIBLIOGRAPHY

The history of the state cult is covered in Werner Eichorn's *Die alte chinesische Religion und das Staatskultwesen* (Leiden, 1976); the sacrificial system of antiquity (Western Chou through mid-second century BCE) is treated in detail in Lester J. Bilsky's *The State Religion of Ancient China,* 2 vols. (Taipei, 1975). The victory of the Ju school is the subject of a definitive article by Hu Shih, "The Establishment of Confucianism as a State Religion during the Han Dynasty," *Journal of the North China Branch, Royal Asiatic Society* 60 (1929): 20–41. An authoritative statement regarding the nature of the objects of imperial worship during Ming and Ch'ing times is in James Legge's *The Notions of the Chinese Concerning God and Spirits* (1852; reprint, Taipei, 1971), see especially pages 24–42. The special position of Confucius in state religion is given historical treatment in John K. Shryock's *The Origin and Development of the State Cult of Confucius* (New York and London, 1932). Detailed description of the practices of the last imperial dynasty is given in Edward T. Williams's *China Yesterday and Today* (New York, 1923), see chapter 13. For a vivid picture of the Ch'ing imperial sacrifices by an observer of the still living cult, see Joseph Edkins's "Imperial Worship" in his *Religion in China,* 2d ed. (Boston, 1878), chap. 2; see also the reprint of the 1859 edition, entitled *The Religious Condition of the Chinese* (reprint, Taipei, 1974). For the broadest interpretations of relationships between political power, Confucian thought, and religion, see the fundamental study of C. K. Yang, *Religion in Chinese Society* (Berkeley, 1961).

LAURENCE G. THOMPSON

CONFUCIUS (552?–479 BCE), known in Chinese as K'ung Ch'iu (also styled Chung-ni); preeminent Chinese philosopher and teacher. The name *Confucius* is the Latin rendering of *K'ung Fu-tzu* ("Master K'ung"). Confucius was born in the small feudal state of Lu, near modern Ch'ü-fu (Shantung Province). Little can be established about his life, forebears, or family, although legends, some of very early origin, are abundant and colorful. The biography in Ssu-ma Ch'ien's *Shih chi* (Historical Annals, second century BCE) is unreliable. The *Lun-yü* (Analects), a record of Confucius's conversations with his disciples, likely compiled in the third century BCE, is probably the best source, although here, too, apocryphal materials have crept in. The *Analects* may be supplemented by the *Tso chuan,* a commentary to the *Ch'un-ch'iu* (Spring and Autumn Annals; also third century BCE), and by the *Meng-tzu* (Mencius; second century BCE).

In all these accounts, fact and legend are difficult to separate. The *Tso chuan* makes Confucius a direct descendant of the royal house of the Shang dynasty (c. 1766–1123 BCE), whose heirs were given the ducal fief of the state of Sung by the succeeding Chou dynasty (1111–256 BCE). According to this account, three to five generations prior to the sage's birth, his forebears moved to the neighboring state of Lu. His father is said to have been a soldier and a man of great strength; his mother, to have been a woman much younger and not the first wife. Some accounts make Confucius the issue of an illegitimate union. Tradition has it that at his birth dragons appeared in his house, and a unicorn *(lin)* in the village. These may command as much belief as the description of Confucius that endows him with a forehead like that of the sage-king Yao, shoulders like those of the famous statesman Tzu-ch'an, the eyes of Shun, the neck of Yü, the mouth of Kao-yao, the visage of the Yellow Emperor, and the height of T'ang, founder of the Shang dynasty.

Of Confucius's childhood and youth, we hear little even from legends, except for references to the early loss of his father, followed later in his youth by the death of his mother. His favorite childhood game was reportedly the setting up of sacrificial vessels and the imitation of ritual gestures. He married young; some accounts allege that he later divorced his wife, although that cannot be proved and is unlikely to be true. He is also supposed to have visited the capital of the Chou dynasty (present-day Lo-yang) and to have met Lao-tzu, from whom he sought instruction. But this report as well appears to be unfounded. [*See the biography of Lao-tzu.*]

In the *Analects,* Confucius says that he was of humble status. Perhaps he came from the minor aristocracy, as he received an education—although not from a famous teacher—and also trained in archery and music. He probably belonged to an obscure and impoverished clan. He would say of himself that by age fifteen he had fixed his mind on studying (*Analects* 2.4). As a young man, he held minor offices, first overseeing stores with the task of keeping accounts, and later taking charge of sheep and cattle (*Meng-tzu* 5B.5). Confucius probably served in a junior post at the Lu court, if the *Tso chuan* is correct about his encounter in 525 with the viscount of T'an, a visitor in Lu, of whom he asked instructions regarding the ancient practice of naming offices after birds. At this point Confucius would have been twenty-seven years old.

Confucius lived in an age of great political disorder. The Chou royal house had lost its authority and the many feudal lords were competing for hegemony. He himself was concerned with the problems of restoring order and harmony to society and of keeping alive the ancient virtues of personal integrity and social justice. For him, a good ruler is one who governs by moral persuasion and who loves the people as a father loves his children. Confucius was especially learned in rites and music, finding in them both the inspiration and the means for the achievement of moral rectitude in society. He reflected deeply on the human situation about him in the light of the wisdom of the ancients. By about the age of thirty he felt himself "standing firm" (*Analects* 2.4) on his insights and convictions.

Like others of his time, Confucius viewed service in the government—the opportunity to exert moral suasion on the king—as the proper goal of a gentleman *(chün-tzu).* At about thirty-five, he visited the large neighboring state of Ch'i. He stayed there for about one year and was so enthralled by the *shao* music (attributed to the sage-king Shun) that for three months, he claimed, he did not notice the taste of the meat he ate (*Analects* 7.14). Clearly, he hoped to be of use at the ducal court. The *Analects* (12.11) reports his conversations with Duke Ching of Ch'i about government, and his emphatic belief that a ruler should be a good ruler, the minister a good minister, the father a good father, and the son a good son. The duke decided not to use him (*Analects* 18.3).

In Lu again, Confucius hesitated some time before accepting public office, perhaps because of the complexity of Lu politics. The Chi family, which had usurped power, was itself dominated by its household minister, Yang Hu (or Yang Huo?), and Confucius was reluctant to ingratiate himself with this man (*Analects* 17.1; *Meng-tzu* 3B.7). Perhaps it was at this point that he determined to develop his ideas and to teach disciples. He said of himself that "at forty, I had no more doubts" (*Analects* 2.4). But some time after 502 (*Meng-tzu* 5B.4), at about age fifty, he accepted the office of *ssu-k'ou* (police commissioner?): "At fifty I knew Heaven's decree" (*Analects* 2.4). In 498 he attempted in vain to break the power of the three leading families of Lu and restore power to the duke. Perhaps this failure caused him to leave Lu the following year. The *Analects* (18.4) claims that Confucius left because the head of the Chi family of Lu had been distracted from his duties by dancing girls, while the *Meng-tzu* (6B.6) gives as the reason the fact that the head of Lu had failed to heed his advice. (The *Shih chi* reports that Confucius became prime minister of Lu, but there is reason to question the authenticity of the account.)

After leaving Lu, Confucius traveled for some thirteen years with a small group of disciples. He first visited the state of Wei (*Analects* 13.9). Although Duke Ting of Wei did not have a good reputation, Confucius took office under him, but left his service when the duke asked his advice on military rather than ritual matters (*Analects* 15.1). To avoid assassins sent by an enemy, he had to disguise himself while passing through the state of Sung (*Analects* 7.23; *Meng-tzu* 5A.8). In Ch'en he accepted office under the marquis; but his stay in Ch'en was marred by many difficulties and he was once near starvation (*Analects* 15.2; *Meng-tzu* 7B.18). In 489 he went on to the state of Ts'ai, where he met the governor of She, a visitor from Ch'u. When the governor asked Confucius's disciple Tzu-lu about his master, Confucius offered this description of himself: "[Tell him I am] the kind of man who forgets to eat when trying to solve a problem, who is so full of joy as to forget all worries, and who does not notice the onset of old age" (*Analects* 7.19). He was then about sixty-three years old. He also said of himself: "At sixty, my ears were attuned [to truth]" (*Analects* 2.4).

From Ts'ai, Confucius traveled to Wei via Ch'en and found it in disorder as the deceased duke's son sought to oust the new ruler, his own son, from the ducal throne. Such disputes help us to understand Confucius's insistence on the "rectification of names" *(cheng-ming)*—that fathers should be paternal and sons filial. After extensive travel through states that lay within present-day Shantung and Honan, Confucius returned to Lu around 484. He was given an office, perhaps as a low-ranking counselor (*Analects* 14.21). He also occupied himself with music and poetry, especially the *ya* and the *sung*, which now make up two of the sections of the *Shih ching* (Book of Poetry). During this period he conversed with Duke Ai of Lu and with the head of the Chi family on questions of government and ritual.

It is known that Confucius had at least one son, K'ung Li (Po-yü), and one daughter, whom he married to his disciple Kung-yeh Ch'ang. He also married the daughter of his deceased elder brother to another disciple, Nan Jung (*Analects* 5.1, 11.5). Of his son little is known, except that the father urged him to study poetry and rites (*Analects* 16.13). Although he is popularly portrayed as a severe moralist, the *Analects* show Confucius as fond of classical music and rituals, informal and cheerful at home, affable yet firm, commanding but not forbidding, dignified and yet pleasant, with an ability to laugh at himself. In his old age, he devoted more and more time to his disciples. He also knew that he had reached spiritual maturity: "At seventy I could follow my heart's desires without overstepping the line" (*Analects* 2.4). But his last years were saddened by the successive deaths of his son, his favorite disciple, Yen Hui, and the loyal though flamboyant Tzu-lu.

According to the *Tso chuan*, Confucius died in 479 at the age of seventy-three. While no description exists concerning his last hours, the account of a previous illness shows how Confucius probably faced death. At that time Tzu-lu wanted the disciples to attire themselves like stewards in attendance upon a high dignitary. Confucius rebuked him, saying, "By making this pretence of having stewards when I have none, whom do you think I shall deceive? Shall I deceive Heaven? Besides, is it not better for me to die in the hands of you, my friends, than in the hands of stewards?" (*Analects* 9.12). When Tzu-lu requested permission to pray for him, Confucius replied, "I have already been praying for a long time" (*Analects* 7.35). The word *praying* here has been understood to mean living the life of a just man.

Confucius's political ambitions remained largely unrealized; he is remembered by posterity above all as a teacher, indeed as the greatest moral teacher of East Asia. He is said to have accepted students without regard to their social status or ability to pay. While the *Shih chi* credits him with three thousand disciples, the more conservative number of seventy (or fewer) is more likely. With two known exceptions, most of the disciples were of humble station and modest means. The majority came from Confucius's own state of Lu, although a few were from the neighboring states of Wei, Ch'en, and Ch'i.

The modern scholar Ch'ien Mu divides the disciples into two groups—those who had followed Confucius even before he left Lu for ten years of travel and those who came to him after his return to Lu. The earlier disciples include Tzu-lu, Yen Hui, and Tzu-kung. Tzu-lu was the oldest in age, only some nine years younger than Confucius himself; his valor and rashness stand out in the *Analects*. Yen Hui, the favorite of Confucius, was about thirty years his junior. His early death at about forty caused much sorrow to Confucius. Tzu-kung, about Yen's age, was an enterprising and eloquent diplomat. Tzu-lu perished—in a manner that had been predicted by Confucius—during a rash effort to rescue his master in the state of Wei (480). Tzu-kung served at the Lu court and was leader of the disciples at the time of Confucius's death. He is reported to have stayed on at his master's grave in Ch'ü-fu for three years longer than the mourning period of twenty-seven months prescribed for the death of one's parents, vivid testimony to the depth of his commitment to his teacher.

The later disciples were mostly much younger, sometimes forty years Confucius's junior. Those mentioned in the *Analects* include Tzu-yu, Tzu-hsia, Tzu-chang, Yu-tzu, and Tseng-tzu, who was only about twenty-seven at the time of his master's death. All five men played important roles in spreading Confucius's teachings, but Tseng-tzu, exemplary for his filial piety, is remembered as the principal spiritual heir through whom Confucius's essential message reached later generations.

Traditionally, Confucius has been credited with the editing of the Five (or Six) Classics: the *Shi ching* (Book of Poetry); the *I ching* (Book of Changes), a divination manual with metaphysical accretions; the *Shu ching* (Book of History), a collection of speeches and documents; the *Li chi* (Book of Rites); the *Ch'un-ch'iu* (Spring and Autumn Annals), historical records of the state of Lu during the years 722 to 481, said to have been compiled by Confucius; and the now lost *Yüeh ching* (Book of Music). Modern scholarship does not support these traditional attributions. Although the *Analects* mentions Confucius's knowledge of the *Poetry*, *History*, and *Changes*, there is no evidence that he had a part in editing these texts; nor was it his immediate disciples who, in their study of these texts, started the traditions of transmission for them. Of his relation to antiquity, one can say that Confucius loved the ancients—above all the duke of Chou, to whom the dynasty allegedly owed its rituals and other institutions—and that he read widely in the ancient texts and passed his understanding on to his disciples.

Confucius's place in history derives from his activities as a teacher and from the teachings that he crystallized and transmitted. In an age when only aristocrats had access to formal education he was the first to accept disciples without regard to status. He instructed them—according to each disciple's ability—not only in the rituals, knowledge of which was expected of all gentlemen, but also in the more difficult art of becoming one who is perfectly humane *(jen)*. Although none of his disciples attained high political office, Confucius the teacher wrought a real social change. Because of his teaching, the word *gentlemen* (*chün-tzu*, literally, "ruler's son") came to refer not to social status but to moral character. A new class gradually emerged, that of the *shih* (originally, "officers" or "government counselors"), a class of educated gentry. Those among the *shih* especially distinguished for scholarship and character were known as the *ju* (originally meaning "weaklings"?). Hence the Confucian school is known in Chinese as "the Ju school."

Confucius had a clear sense of his mission: he considered himself a transmitter of the wisdom of the ancients (*Analects* 7.1), to which he nonetheless gave new meaning. His focus was on the human, not just the human as given, but as endowed with the potential to become "perfect." His central doctrine concerns the virtue *jen*, translated variously as goodness, benevolence, humanity, and human-heartedness. Originally, *jen* denoted a particular virtue, the kindness that distinguished the gentleman in his behavior toward his inferiors. Confucius transformed it into a universal virtue, that which makes the perfect human being, the sage. He defined it as loving others, as personal integrity, and as altruism.

Confucius's teachings give primary emphasis to the ethical meaning of human relationships, finding and grounding what is moral in human nature and revealing its openness to the divine. Although he was largely silent on God and the afterlife, his silence did not bespeak disbelief (*Analects* 11.11). His philosophy was clearly grounded in religion, the inherited religions of Shang-ti ("lord on high") or T'ien ("heaven"), the supreme and personal deities of the Shang and Chou periods, respectively. [*See also* Shang-ti *and* T'ien.] He made it clear that it was Heaven that protected and inspired him: "Heaven is the author of the virtue that is in me" (*Analects* 7.23). Confucius believed that human beings are accountable to a supreme being, "He who sins against Heaven has no place left where he may pray" (*Analects* 3.13); nevertheless, he showed a certain scepticism regarding ghosts and spirits (*Analects* 6.20). This marked a rationalistic attitude that became characteristic of the Confucian school, which usually sought to resolve problems by active human involvement rather than by hoping or praying for divine intervention.

Confucius himself was devoted to the civilization of the Chou dynasty, although he might have been a descendant from the more ancient Shang royal house. The reason for this may have derived from the fact that Chinese civilization assumed a definitive shape during the Chou dynasty, or from the special relationship Confucius's native state of Lu enjoyed as a custodian of Chou culture. Its rulers were descended from the duke of Chou, the man who established the institutions of the dynasty and who acted as regent after the death of his brother, the dynasty's founder.

Confucius's emphasis on rituals is significant, as it is ritual that governs human relationships. Rituals have a moral and social function as well as a formal and ceremonial one. The Chinese word *li* refers also to propriety, that is, to proper behavior. Confucius teaches also the importance of having the right inner disposition, without which propriety becomes hypocrisy (*Analects* 15.17).

Confucius's philosophy might appear unstructured to those who cast only a cursory glance at the *Analects*, perhaps because the book was compiled several generations after Confucius's death. But the teachings found in the *Analects*, with all their inner dynamism, assume full coherency only when put into practice. Confucius did not attempt to leave behind a purely rationalistic system of thought. He wanted to help others to live, and by so doing, to improve the quality of their society. In defining as his main concern human society, and in offering moral perfection as the human ideal, Confucius has left behind a legacy that is perennial and universal. On the other hand, his teachings also show certain limitations that derive from his culture, the authoritarian character of government, and the superior social status enjoyed by men, for instance. These limitations do not, however, change the validity of his central insights into human nature and its perfectibility.

[*For an account of the rise and development of the tradition that bears Confucius's name, see* Confucian Thought. *For further discussion of the Confucian classics, see* Chinese Religion, *article on* Religious and Philosophical Texts. *See also* Jen and I *and* Li.]

BIBLIOGRAPHY

For information on Confucius in English, a useful reference work is the *Encyclopaedia Britannica (Macropaedia)* (Chicago, 1982). His life is well summarized in Richard Wilhelm's *Confucius and Confucianism*, translated by George H. Danton and Annina Periam Danton (New York, 1931); in H. G. Creel's *Confucius: The Man and the Myth* (New York, 1949), reprinted under the title *Confucius and the Chinese Way* (New York, 1960); in the introduction to James Legge's translation of the *Analects* (1893; 3d ed., Tokyo, 1913), which is not critical enough of the sources; in the introduction to Arthur Waley's translation, *The Analects of Confucius* (London, 1938), which is definitely better; and in the introduction and appendixes to D. C. Lau's much more recent translation, *Confucius: The Analects* (London, 1979), which is a further improvement. A summary of Confucius's teachings is also given in Liu Wu-chi's *A Short History of Confucian Philosophy* (Harmondsworth, 1955), and in the relevant chapters in Fung Yu-lan's *A History of Chinese Philosophy*, translated by Derk Bodde, vol. 7 (Princeton, 1952). (Volume 2 has excellent chapters on Neo-Confucianism.) My *Confucianism and Christianity* (Tokyo, 1977) is a comparative study from a theological perspective.

Certain Chinese works are indispensable for a study of Confucius's life. Ts'ui Shu's (1740-1816), *Chu-ssu k'ao-hsin lu*, a small work in three *chüan* (with a three *chüan* supplement), offers an excellent critical study. Ch'ien Mu's *Hsien Ch'in chu-tzu hsi-nien*, vol. 1 (Hong Kong, 1956), is immensely useful. Ku Chieh-kang's *Ku-shih-pien*, vol. 2 (Shanghai, 1930–1931), should also be consulted.

There are interesting Japanese studies of Confucius's life. Kaizuka Shigeki's *Koshi* (Tokyo, 1951) has been translated into Chinese (Taipei, 1976); Geoffrey Bownas's English translation, *Confucius* (London, 1956), is also recommended. Morohashi Tetsuji's *Nyoze gamon Koshi den* (Tokyo, 1969) reports both facts and legends while distinguishing between them wherever possible.

Julia Ching

CONGREGATIONALISM.

Congregational churches arose in England in the late sixteenth and seventeenth centuries. In their early days, Congregationalists were also known as Independents. They are most numerous in the United States, England, and Wales, but recently most of them have joined with others to form united churches in several parts of the world.

Among churches, they have stood somewhere between the Presbyterians and the more radical Protestant groups, with a distinctive emphasis on the rights and responsibilities of each properly organized congregation to make its own decisions about its own affairs without recourse to any higher human authority. This, along with an emphasis on freedom of conscience, arose from convictions concerning the sovereignty of God and the priesthood of all believers.

Historical Survey. The "Congregational way" emerged as a major factor in English life during the English Civil War, but its roots lay in Elizabethan Separatism, which produced Congregationalism's first three martyrs, Henry Barrow, John Greenwood, and John Penry. Some of the Separatists settled in Holland, and it was from among these that the *Mayflower* group set out for New England in 1620. During the English Civil War, Congregationalists, then usually called Independents, were particularly prominent in the army, reaching the peak of their influence during the Commonwealth through Oliver Cromwell and such outstanding ministers as John Owen and Hugh Peter. The Restoration of Charles II was a disaster for their cause, and the Act of Uniformity of 1662 was the first of many efforts to suppress them. Most of the two thousand ministers ejected from livings in the Church of England at that time were Presbyterians, but many Independent ministers who did not hold livings also suffered. Persecution was not so severe as to prevent creative work being done, and the major theological works of John Owen, the greatest poems of John Milton, an Independent, and John Bunyan's *Pilgrim's Progress* (although Bunyan's closest affinities were with the Baptists) all appeared after the Restoration. The works of the latter two, along with some of the hymns of Isaac Watts, have become part of the furniture of the English imagination.

The accession of William and Mary in 1688 made life more tolerable for Congregationalists, and, after a threatened setback in the reign of Queen Anne, they played a significant minor part in eighteenth-century England. They were particularly active in education, where the Dissenting Academies were educational pioneers at a time when Oxford and Cambridge languished. The spiritual influence of such leading ministers as Philip Doddridge and Isaac Watts helped prevent Congregationalists from becoming Unitarians, as most Presbyterians did at that time. Congregationalists received a considerable spiritual quickening toward the end of the century through the influence of the Methodist revival. One result was the founding in 1795 of the London Missionary Society, through whose agency churches were established in Africa, India, Madagascar, China, Papua, and the South Sea Islands.

English Congregationalism shared fully in nineteenth-century ecclesiastical prosperity. As members of the emerging lower middle classes crowded into the churches, they became more politically minded. Voluntarism, opposing state support of denominational education, and the Liberation Society, advocating the disestablishment of the Church of England, were influential. The Congregational Union, linking the churches in a national organization, was formed in 1832, and the Colonial (later Commonwealth) Missionary Society for promoting Congregationalism in English-speaking colonies in 1836. Many large new churches were erected, and some ministers, like R. W. Dale of Birmingham, were well-known public figures. Civic disabilities were steadily removed. Mansfield College was founded at Oxford in 1886. Thriving churches in city centers and residential neighborhoods were hives of social, philanthropic, and educational activities, which anticipated many of the services taken over by the state in the twentieth century. The victory of the Liberal party in the 1906 election represented the peak of the political and social influence of Congregationalism. After that, numerical and institutional decline began, hastened by the upheaval of World War I and the increased mobility of population. Although churches were losing much of their popular appeal, the emergence of several distinguished theologians and ecumenical leaders in the interwar period provided evidence of continuing vitality. In 1972 the majority of Congregationalists joined with the Presbyterian Church in England to form the United Reformed Church.

In the rest of Britain, Congregationalists have been strongest in Wales, where the Welsh-speaking churches, known as the Union of Welsh Independents, retain their identity. These churches were transplanted successfully from the countryside to industrial Wales during the industrial revolution and became strong centers of distinctively Welsh life, cherishing their traditions of preaching, hymns, and poetry. The numerically smaller Scottish churches acted as a liberalizing influence in Scottish life and gave much to the wider church through such outstanding figures as Robert Moffat, David Livingstone, George McDonald, and P. T. Forsyth.

It is in the United States that Congregationalism achieved its greatest public influence and numerical strength. The New England experiment has been a major factor in determining the character of the nation. The Separatists of the Plymouth Colony were more radical than the Puritans of Massachusetts Bay, but they had enough in common to form a unified community and to repudiate the more radical views of Roger Williams and Anne Hutchinson. Their statement of faith, the Cambridge Platform of 1648, accepted the theology of the English Presbyterian Westminster Confession of 1646 but laid down a Congregational rather than a Presbyterian polity. In this, it was followed by the English Savoy Declaration of 1658.

The original New Englanders were not sectarian; they worked out an intellectually powerful and consistent system of theology and church and civil government that they strove, with considerable success, to exemplify. John Cotton's *Keyes of the Kingdom of Heaven and the Powers Thereof* (1644) is a classic statement of their view of the church. The very success of the New England settlement made it difficult for succeeding generations to retain the original commitment, and the Half-Way Covenant was devised to find a place for those who were baptized but could not make a strong enough confession of faith—permitting them a form of church membership that did not confer a place at the Lord's Table or in church government. Education was seen as vital from the outset. Harvard College was founded in 1637 to maintain the succession of learned ministers. Yale and others followed later, the precursors of a long succession of distinguished colleges founded under Congregational auspices across the country.

New life came with the Great Awakening, the revival movement begun in 1734, in which Jonathan Edwards, a minister at Northampton, Massachusetts, and one of the greatest American theologians, was prominent. Differences began to emerge at the turn of the century between the two wings of Congregationalism, those who continued to accept the modified Calvinism represented by Edwards and those who were moving toward Unitarianism. Unitarianism became dominant in the Boston area but not in Connecticut, where Congregationalism remained the established church until the early nineteenth century.

Despite the loss to the Unitarians, who took with them many of the most handsome colonial churches, Congregationalism flourished in the nineteenth century and was active in the westward expansion of the nation. It adopted in 1801 a Plan of Union with the Presbyterians, who were concentrated chiefly in the Middle Atlantic states, for joint home missionary activity. One factor in the ultimate breakdown of this agreement was the growing theological liberalism of Congregationalism. Horace Bushnell was a representative theologian who challenged the traditional substitutionary view of the atonement and whose influential book *Christian Nurture* (1847) questioned the need for the classic conversion experience. The so-called Kansas City Creed of 1913 summed up this liberalism, which represented a break with the Calvinist past. This liberalism continues to prevail, although substantially modified after World War II by the influence of neoorthodoxy.

The mainly Congregational American Board of Commissioners for Foreign Missions (1810) promoted missions in China and the Near East. A national Congregational organization was founded in 1871, and its boards of Home Missions and Education have done much to start schools and colleges among the black community in the South. Modern Congregationalism has been exceptionally active in the ecumenical movement. Union with the Christian Churches in the United States was achieved between the wars and with the substantial Evangelical and Reformed Church in 1961, to form the United Church of Christ.

Beliefs and Practices. The beliefs and practices of most Congregationalists have been broadly similar to those of other mainline evangelical Protestant churches of the more liberal kind. The English historian Bernard Manning described them as "decentralized Calvinists," but this fails to allow for their emphasis on the free movement of the Holy Spirit, which gives them some affinity with the Quakers as well as with Presbyterians. In its origin, their notion of the "gathered church" was not a form of secular voluntarism but an attempt, as against Anglican territorialism, to recognize "the crown rights of the Redeemer" and the primacy of the free Spirit's action in gathering together the covenant people of God. Their strong emphasis on this freedom has not only led them to be reluctant to give binding authority to creeds but also served indirectly to promote the rights of minorities of many kinds, especially in England. The long-faced, repressive Puritan of legend is largely a caricature.

Preaching is important in Congregationalism because the word in scripture is thought of as constitutive of the church. The ministry derives its authority from the word, not vice versa. Baptism and the Lord's Supper are the only recognized sacraments, and infant baptism is customary. Traditionally, public prayer has been *ex tempore,* but in this century set forms have been widely used. Hymns are important. The English *Congregational Praise* (1952), with many hymns by Isaac Watts, the greatest Congregational writer of hymns, is an outstanding compilation.

Congregational polity is sometimes charged with promoting spiritual individualism, but this is based on a misunderstanding. It is an attempt to give the most concrete expression to the church as a local visible community. It must be properly organized, with Bible, sacraments, a duly called and trained ministry, and deacons and members in good standing. With these, no body can be more fully the church, because all necessary means of grace are available. Congregationalism has never concluded that this has meant spiritual isolation or indifference to "the communion of the churches with each other." This is shown by the fact that no group of churches has shown a greater readiness to enter schemes of reunion.

One of the most distinctive Congregational institutions is that of the church meeting, a regular gathering at which all church members have the right and responsibility to participate in all decisions. This has not always had the vigor that its place in the polity demands, but strong efforts have been made to revive it in recent times. Women have always been active in Congregational churches, which were among the first of the American and British denominations to admit women to the full-time ministry of the word and sacraments.

Until they merged with other bodies, Congregational churches were linked in associations or unions, at local and national levels, and in an International Congregational Council, to which such related bodies as the Swedish Mission Covenant Church and the Dutch Remonstrant Brotherhood also belonged. In the course of this century, churches in the United States appointed officials called state superintendents, and those in England officials called moderators, to exercise a general ministry to churches over a wide area. When a covenant with the Church of England and the Methodist Church was proposed by the United Reformed Church in England in 1980–1982, it was implied that the moderators should be made into bishops. This was hotly challenged by a substantial minority as a denial of the Reformed understanding of the ministry. The failure of the Church of England to ratify the covenant meant that this particular proposal was abandoned.

Congregational churches have existed chiefly in English-speaking countries and in communities related to them, and they have not been among the larger Christian groups. Their ideas and practices, however, have had a greater influence than their size might suggest. The Congregational tradition continues to exercise influence as one element in the life of larger reunited churches in many lands.

BIBLIOGRAPHY

Williston Walker's *Creeds and Platforms of Congregationalism* (New York, 1893) is a classic sourcebook. Douglas Horton's *Congregationalism: A Study in Church Polity* (London, 1952) and *The United Church of Christ* (New York, 1962) are two works by the most representative American Congregationalist of the twentieth century. Geoffrey F. Nuttall's *Visible Saints: The Congregational Way, 1640–1660* (Oxford, 1957) emphasizes the "spiritualizing" element in Congregationalism, and R. Tudur Jones's *Congregationalism in England, 1662–1962* (London, 1962) is a comprehensive tercentenary history. A fresh view of Congregationalism in the light of the ecumenical movement is presented in my book *Congregationalism: A Re-statement* (New York and London, 1954), and essays on modern Congregationalism can be found in *Kongregationalismus* (Frankfurt, 1973), edited by Norman Goodall as volume 11 of "Die Kirchen der Welt."

DANIEL JENKINS

CONSCIENCE, as commonly understood, is the faculty within us that decides on the moral quality of our thoughts, words, and acts. It makes us conscious of the worth of our deeds and gives rise to a pleasurable feeling if they are good and to a painful one if they are evil.

Origin of the Notion. Three articulations of human experience appear to be at the basis of the Western notion of conscience: the Hebrew scriptures, the writings of Cicero, and the writings of Paul.

1. In the Hebrew scriptures God is presented as someone who knows and evaluates our entire being. Psalm 139 develops the theme:

> O Lord, thou has searched me and known me!
> Thou knowest when I sit down and when I rise up;
> thou discernest my thoughts from afar. . . .
> If I take the wings of the morning
> and dwell in the uttermost parts of the sea,
> even there thy hand shall lead me,
> and thy right hand shall hold me. . . .
> Search me, O God, and know my heart!
> Try me and know my thoughts!
> And see if there be any wicked way in me,
> and lead me in the way everlasting!
> (*Ps.* 139:1–2, 9–10, 23–24)

The pious psalmist is confident that the divine scrutiny will vindicate him. Others, the enemies of Israel, are the wicked ones who will be found wanting. (See also *Job* 34:21–23.)

The idea of divine omniscient scrutiny leads, however, to vigorous self-scrutiny: "the spirit of man is the lamp of the Lord, searching all his innermost parts" (*Prv.* 20:27). The prophet Jeremiah is appalled by what he sees when he looks inside himself:

> The heart is deceitful above all things,
> and desperately corrupt;
> who can understand it?
> "I the Lord search the mind and try the heart,
> to give to every man according to his ways,
> according to the fruit of his doings."
> (*Jer.* 17:9–10)

But, here again, the prophet is confident that God is his refuge (see vv. 17–18). That God, not the self, judges the self is good news: the Strong One who sees me all (in my interiority as well as my outward acts) is a good protector, and I am safe in his hands.

2. Cicero uses *conscientia* in another sense, to refer to an internal moral authority on important issues. Most of the time conscience is consciousness of something, agreeable consciousness of one or many good deeds (*Orationes Philippicae* 1.9; *Res publica* 6.8) or disagreeable consciousness of a trespass (*Tusculanae disputationes* 4.45, where he speaks metaphorically of the bite of conscience). He speaks with zeal of the force of this inner testimony: "Great is the power of conscience, great for bliss or for bane" (*Pro Milone* 61; see also *De natura deorum* 3.85, where it is specified that the workings of conscience unfold without our having to assume divine design). Some passages speak of bad conscience as if it were the internalization of a disapproval voiced by others or by public opinion in general (*In Catilinam* 3.25; *Tusculanae* 4.45). Good conscience, however, is presented as independent of public opinion. (Here, he speaks mainly of his own.) Cicero, for instance, has a good conscience about withdrawing from public life and devoting himself to writing (*Epistulae ad Atticum* 12.28.2) and is determined never to stray from the straight path of conscience. In such cases conscience is referred to without stating what it is consciousness of. While one text stresses to the juror that he should follow his conscience alone but that he should also take comfort from the fact that he is not alone in his judging (*Pro Cluentio* 159), most texts make the good conscience a rather isolated self-approval. A stunning metaphor states that no theater, no audience offers an applause that has more authority than that of conscience (*Tusculanae* 2.64). Finally, we should note that Cicero speaks of conscience in a rhetorical context and with moralizing intent; he inveighs against evil men, commends good ones, and voices his assurance of his own worth.

3. In the New Testament, Paul uses the notion of conscience (Gr., *suneidēsis*) as he finds it in everyday speech and common moral reflections. He puts forward his own unshakable good conscience (*Rom.* 9:1, *2 Cor.* 1:2; see also *Acts* 23:1); he urges respect for the conscience of others, especially when that conscience is weak and judges matters erroneously (*1 Cor.* 8:7, 8:10); he appeals to conscience (*2 Cor.* 4:2); he allows that in evil people conscience is corrupted (*Ti.* 1:15). *Romans* 2:15 launched a momentous new understanding of it: conscience is a witness within all men, including pagans; it states what the law of God requires (it is "the law written in their hearts"), and it accuses all men. So far, Paul speaks of *suneidēsis* very much like Philo (who speaks mainly of *elenchos*, "reproof"). The Jewish philosopher found in all men a "true man" who should be ruler and king, who is a judge and umpire, a silent witness or accuser. Human beings live thus with a court of law inside them, and they should behave in such a way as to keep their internal judge pleased. Philo, like Paul, sees this internal authority as a gift of God, but he also accepts immanent views of it (Wallis, 1975).

But there is in Paul something else that is peculiar to him and was to prove very influential on all subsequent developments. Though he seems to have had a morally rather robust conscience, not haunted by feelings of guilt (Stendahl, 1976), Paul frequently wrote in a manner that revealed a troubled self-consciousness. He feels pain at not being acknowledged for what he is (*Gal.* 1:10); a physical handicap humbles him (*2 Cor.* 12:7). We thus find in his writing a new sort of literary voice: a self-consciousness bruised by despairing self-humiliation. His will is divided; his body does not obey him; his urgent convictions are challenged by adversaries, his life's work nearly overthrown. Under his pen, all this is not trivial autobiographical detail but is made to reflect a cosmic crisis. Paul feels that he and others are caught in the transition between a passing age and a new dispensation. His inner troubles interiorize the death of Christ. Still caught up in the age that is passing, he feels impotent, worthless; but this conviction of despair is considered by him to be a form of suffering through which he—and, he believes, all men—must pass before they can share in new life with the risen Christ (Altizer, 1983). Inner pains are thus inevitable birth pangs. A subtle shift has occurred: the notion that God welcomes a contrite heart (*Ps.* 34:18) is in the process of becoming indistinguishable from the notion that God likes—or requires—a broken heart. In *Romans*, conscience, the accuser, caught up in an eschatological drama, always convicts (3:9, 7:15–20). Good conscience before God means surrender of what men call good conscience. This eschatological turmoil gives to Paul's writings on conscience a ring very different from Philo's serene utterances.

Historical Developments. The church fathers adopt the notion of conscience as an inner voice of divine origin. The assumption is that all human beings have it, and only Christians obey it and thus please God. The firmness of the Christians' conscience enables them to obey God rather than men, live as people who do not belong to this world, and accept martyrdom with joy. Augustine compares conscience to a tribunal in the mind and speaks of it with a tone of restive introspection. He thus confirms the blending, initiated by Paul, of the three notions of divine judgment, moral self-evaluation, and the troubled forays into the hidden recesses of one's heart. A classic passage links the three realities with the Latin *conscientia:*

> "What O Lord could be hidden from you, even if I wanted not to confess it, since the abyss of human conscience is naked before your eyes? I should only be hiding you to me, not me from you. Now that my tears testify how disgusted I am with myself, you only are my light and please me; you are the object of my love and desire. I am ashamed of myself so that I cast myself aside to choose you and want to please myself or you only through you." (*Confessions* 10.2.2)

That God knows the self is a source of comfort that overcomes the intense discomfort the introspective self feels. The misery of self-rejection seems to be the necessary price to be paid before one reaches divine acceptance.

The Middle Ages use the notion of conscience primarily to elaborate a theory of moral judgment. In their systematic construction, the Scholastics use two terms to designate two functions. *Synderesis* (the word probably appears first as an erroneous reading; medieval ignorance of Greek let it become established) is the faculty that knows the moral law; it remained unaffected by the Fall. The Franciscan school makes of it a *potentia affectiva*, namely a disposition of the heart. The Dominicans make of it a sort of cognition; it exists in the reason. *Conscientia* applies the moral law to concrete cases. It is a *habitus* of the practical intellect, say the Franciscans; an act, according to the Dominicans, which applies knowledge to action. To Thomas Aquinas (c. 1225–1274) *synderesis* decides; it always orients us to the good. *Conscientia* controls; we can set it aside. When it functions, *conscientia* is a witness; it says what we have done or not done. It binds or motivates; it says what we should or should not do. Finally, it excuses or accuses; it tells us whether what we have done was well or not well done. While *synderesis* cannot err, *conscientia*, a sort of decree of the mind, is fallible (*Summa theologiae* 1.79.12–13). Conscience now is no longer an occasional voice at important moments, but a concomitant of all morally relevant action.

Medieval theologians also examine whether one is obligated to follow an erroneous conscience. It is allowed that some consciences are invincibly erroneous, that is, their error cannot be overcome by the use of moral diligence or thorough study. Even in these circumstances the self must obey conscience. *Romans* 14:23 is the norm: whatever is not from faith is deemed sinful. One must, however, at all times seek to correct one's conscience by instruction. Thomas Aquinas teaches that to hold in contempt the dictates of an erroneous conscience is a mortal sin and that conscience binds, even when it contradicts the precepts of a superior, if it endures.

This intellectual clarification is accompanied by a system of practical guidance. In 1215, the Fourth Lateran Council made it an obligation for all Christians to confess their sins and receive the sacrament once a year. This came to be known as the tribunal of conscience. A practice was required and an occasion offered: the self had to embark upon intellectual deliberation on its behavior and could obtain expert advice or counsel. Benjamin Nelson (1981) described this system of spiritual direction under a threefold heading: conscience, casuistry, and the cure of souls. The individual, like all men, is obligated by the universal moral law. Like some other men, he has peculiar dilemmas related to his age, his class, his role in life; casuistry studies these cases of conscience and enlightens the individual by drawing upon the experience of those whose lot is comparable. [*See* Casuistry.] Finally, the individual is unlike everyone else; he has his own sorrows and fears; his soul needs to be ministered to in a therapeutic way and comforted. The system reaped behavioral fruit: the lives of Western Christians were progressively ordered in conformity with Christian moral principles. Consciences were slowly educated. Fear of divine judgment loomed large among the motivational forces. While the theologians' *synderesis* and *conscientia* were purely moral principles, the pastoral tribunal of conscience often functioned in an atmosphere of religious anguish: God would be angry if sins were not confessed and corrected. His searching of the hearts was felt to be a perilous affair; sinners were threatened with outright condemnation.

While canon lawyers instituted the tribunal of conscience and while pastors appealed to or pounded on individual consciences, the national monarchies and the royal law of France and England developed in such a way as to give an increasing social relevance to the notion of moral conscience. Frenchmen in the twelfth and thirteenth centuries began to be aware of themselves as one people, living together civilly in a good land under the rule of a just and Christian king. This emergence of national consciousness came simultaneously with urbanization, with an increased practice of prudence and courtesy in social relations (the arts of peace), and with the rise of an ethics of intention, such as that discussed by Abelard (1079–1142). Now new collective representations give expression to a shared will to live together for the sake of peace and to the happy sense of forming together a good society. The sense of the sacred has begun to shift from a largely supernatural realm to the national Christian society that provides a good, secure life. A sacred bond now unites the righteous king and the loyal people. And a man can now encounter people he has never seen before (and with whom no one in his village has ever had dealings) and still have civil relations: strangers are conscious at the outset of belonging to the same people. In England, the old Aristotelian notion of equity is introduced into the royal law: law is said always to aim at justice and to be corrigible whenever principles of equity are violated, for instance, whenever the helpless are dealt with unfairly, or whenever widows and orphans are oppressed. Correction is said to be introduced "for the sake of conscience." In France and in England, society can henceforth be said to have a collective and civil conscience, to be sensitive to the moral demands of common peace and universal justice, to visualize royal power as not simply heroic but merciful as well. (This Western confidence that human beings can collectively govern themselves well is reflected in Calvin's *Institutes* 2.2.13.)

The stage is now set for the great crises and transformations of the sixteenth century. For the first time conscience has become a culturally central, crucial notion among Christians. The three notions of it we originally identified now merge to define the problem: the man of conscience is "spiritual," he lives "before God"; he is also moral and has obligations to his fellow men; he has a rapport with himself and feels condemned or saved. The Protestant Reformation saw itself as a defender of conscience. The word became one of its most militant terms.

The reformers spoke of conscience as being oppressed by the medieval system. While considering itself obliged to obey "the pope's commandments," conscience saw itself weighed down by the burden of bad and illegitimate laws of human origin, which it was impossible to obey. There was anguish in trying to obey and anguish in disobedience because of the nagging sense of fearsome consequences. Luther articulated his own scrupulous monastic experience of anguish over every action and involuntary impulse by indentifying with Paul. He vibrated in unison, he thought, with Paul's and Augustine's autobiographical statements. Conscience and the law jointly accused him and brought him death. (Unlike Paul, Luther was under the yoke of bad law; identifying with Paul, he overlooked the difference in the objective content of the laws.) The monk Luther, however, was not alone. Henry VIII, a Catholic king, was afraid his marriage to Catherine of Aragon was sterile because it had been cursed by God. (Catherine had been engaged to Henry's brother; even though the brother was dead, the marriage was incestuous by canonical if not dynastic rules.) Was his conscience genuinely troubled or was his second marriage expedient or self-indulgent? (It is significant that the issue is still debated.)

In any case, the medieval burden of being trapped by a guilty conscience was thrown off by many who broke their vows or changed their lifestyles. The religious authorities' guiding conscience had ceased to be credible in the eyes of many of the people of God. Most theological reformers also rejected the very principle of trying to please God with deeds (works); no action was conceivable that could give man a joyful conscience before God. Thus the Protestant Reformation also rejected the whole system of the tribunal of conscience. Freed by grace, living in faith, the Christian immediately receives a good conscience from his God. He thus recaptures the sense of the covenant found in the Hebrew scriptures: that God can fathom our hearts and that he alone judges us once again becomes good news. We are not accountable to ecclesiastical authorities, and they should not haunt our consciences and enrich themselves at our expense. Thus with good consciences, redeemed Christians walk straight in the paths of righteousness. Activities of public reform persuade these Christians that they are indeed setting up a more moral order. For its part, the Roman Catholic church maintains the system of casuistry and cure of souls. But in time, with a more saintly clergy, the authority of the spiritual directors is restored. Consciences are again more guided than tyrannized.

It must be seen that the Protestant Reformation fostered a new Western assurance of conscience. Conscience became safe, certain. The system of casuistry was dealing in probabilities, constantly weighing pros and cons, and every authority was liable to be overthrown by other authorities. The civil conscience was also always open to correction. Reading his Bible, the Protestant Christian gained subjective certainty once and for all: he was God's child and his path was straight. (The sixteenth century began many moves toward certainty: the Protestant Reformation gave subjective assurance and the scientific revolution began to give objective certainty: Galileo did not weigh the relative merits of authorities; he knew for sure. See Nelson, 1981.) Luther's conscience is lyrical: he is ultimately safe in God's arms and above pleasing men or worrying about their opinions. All the reformers agree: he who has faith has good conscience. No human forum can accuse him. Conscience has nothing to do with a man's dealing among his fellow men but only with his reception of divine forgiveness. Paul Tillich (1948) coined the term *transmoral conscience* to refer to this notion of man's innerness as it meets God. Calvin is clear: conscience must not be confused with "police." Its business is not with men but with God (*Institutes* 3.19.15–16; 4.10.3). It must be unhappy at first. "It is necessary that conscience drive our misery home to us before we can have some sense of God" (*Institutes* 1.1.1 and 4.19.15–16). While Calvin as an elect does not let others challenge his own conscience, he openly distrusts the conscience of others: "Nothing is more common, just as nothing is easier than to boast of faith and a good conscience" (Neal, 1972). The notion of conscience as a subjective absolute is reinforced by the practice of religious privatism: sins are remitted by private confession to God, without confession to a fellow human being or reparation to the victim. With Calvin, the assurance of conscience among the elect is coupled with a particularly vigorous moral action in the world. The concept that had been used to detach the individual from the world now presides over the conscientious effort to shape the world according to the Christian's moral aspirations. The stage is set for the polemics in which Protestants blame Catholics for the erroneous precepts they impose on conscience, and Catholics blame Protestants for their unbridled "conscientious" energies.

The sixteenth century witnessed also the rise of a fresh, vigorous articulation of conscience in the civil tradition. Surrounded by wars waged for the sake of conscience, the French moralist Montaigne (1533–1592) inaugurated the art of writing for oneself the story of an observant, rigorously honest conscience (Brunschwicg, 1953). Both moral and introspective, this conscience ponders the actions of the self and of others and looks at the relations and roles the self is involved in. Self-critical, open to instruction and correction from those who have experience of the world, this conscience treasures selected friendships and enjoys a measure of self-acceptance. It holds on to the few truths and rare marks of humanity it believes itself to be capable of. The dramas of acceptance and rejection at the hands of the biblical God recede in the background. Front stage belongs to the dramas of human likes and dislikes. Descartes (1596–1650) puts an analysis of conscience at the center of his philosophy. In his case, conscience is troubled or disturbed by the experience of its fallibility and by the idea of the infinite; the goodness of God provides decisive reassurance on both points. In the ambit of French civilization, conscience will henceforth keep these crucial characteristics: it is autonomous, moral, and social, somewhat skeptical, worldly wise, and it has a modest but firm pride.

The authority of conscience receives its fullest religious legitimacy in the theory of inner light common to many seventeenth-century English sects. Instead of being an act of interpretation of a law, this conscience is an absolute and final insight. It is also British philosophy that gave to moral conscience its most ample philosophical underpinnings. The theory of moral sense identifies the consciousness of right and wrong with the voice of an inner moral law (the unwritten, inborn law of which Cicero spoke in *Pro Milone* 10). Inner voices or feelings are described as edicts of one's conscience. L. Butler (1692–1752; *Sermons*) affirms that it has a natural authority; it is the voice of God within us. Conscience has become a faculty of the mind that judges immediately and finally on moral matters. In the Middle Ages conscience was a function: people had more or less of it, and tried more or less to exercise it. With the reformers it was a fact of spiritual life: people had a troubled or a joyful one; it became an individual organ—you have your conscience and I have mine, just as each of us has his own stomach. This conscience was said to be infallible and generally philanthropic. It was also inviolate. No serious conflicts of conscience were foreseen. The stage was set for the good conscience of the West to be applied in colonial expansion. All human beings have conscience, it was thought. Western Christians liberated what they deemed to be inferior races from the fears to which their idolatrous and superstitious consciences were prone; they established liberty of conscience (freedom of religion) wherever they ruled, and they did all this without violating consciences. Being most developed, the Western consciences helped others develop too. Western expansion was optimistically expected to moralize the world.

Modern Conflict between Conscience and Consciousness. Theoreticians declare what conscience always says to the inner man. Conscience may in fact behave according to theory; but also it might not. Or, more commonly, the individual realizes that what conscience pronounces clashes with some other inner state he is aware of at a given moment. Distinctions need to be made among the voices in one's inner debate. Luther translated the medieval *conscientia* with *das Gewissen.* Two centuries later, Christian Wolff (1679–1754), the founder of German philosophy, translated the *conscientia* of the Cartesians with *das Bewusstsein.* In sixteenth-century English, *conscience* can denote authoritative, secure moral conscience or simple, trivial consciousness. (The French language still uses *la conscience* to speak both of the moral rationales the self fully accepts and of fleeting mental events.) With the eighteenth century, the sense of a separation between conscience and consciousness became widespread. While moral beings naively went on believing in their stable, good, unerring conscience, literature (the novel especially) increasingly explored the chasm between conscience and the vagaries of consciousness. The semiblind yet massive good conscience of the modern theoreticians of conscience and their followers could now become manifest. Moralists became aware of time, of the necessary distinction between what is abiding and what is transitory in a man's sense of himself. Conscience then came to be seen as a firm statement that the self utters before others or privately, a plea entered in a public or inner forum. Like consciousness, conscience is an event; but unlike it, it is also a moral discourse, a public claim. Hence, the critical question: is this discourse fully aware of the actualities of the case? Is conscience conscious? (Engelberg, 1972).

Nineteenth-century probings ordinarily shared the conviction that human beings should always be as fully conscious as possible, with actions completely lucid and deliberate. Rousseau (1712–1778) believed he could derive norms for political life from the assumption that politics consists of free, conscious, virtuous interaction among autonomous, independent individuals. (He even believed the whole of social life could consist of such interaction.) Kant (1724–1804) pursued the point with theoretical thoroughness. All moral action proceeds from good will and is conscientious. *Das Gewissen* never errs. It is "the moral faculty of judgment, passing judgment upon itself . . . a state of consciousness which is itself a duty" (*Religion within the Limits of Reason Alone* 4.2.4). With each action, the individual should reflect and proceed only if he is sure that this action obeys the dictates of conscience. The consequence does not escape Hegel (1770–1833): consciences will be in conflict, each vibrating with its assurance, each alone in its certainty of obeying the moral law (Despland, 1975). Far from being a reliable guide, conscience now appears to be potentially immoral arrogance.

The nineteenth century is full of denigrations of conscience. The poet William Blake (1757–1827) is sarcastic: "Conscience in those that have it is unequivocal" ("Annotations to Watson"). Goethe (1749–1832) commends an alternative: Faust heals himself, grows by purging himself of conscience (he does not let himself be crippled by the episode with Marguerite) and ever widening his consciousness. Nietzsche (1844–1900) attempts to show that conscience only imitates ready-made values; the hard human task is to embody knowledge in ourselves, to create conscious values; and consciousness is not given gratis.

But the claims of conscience remain tenacious even in the post-Romantic age. Conscience, however, becomes more tragic, more solitary. Rare are those who see in it the workings of an other-regarding instinct. To Kierkegaard (1813–1855), the inwardness of conscience is demonic: more conscience means more consciousness and deeper despair. Such is also the case in Dostoevskii's *Notes from the Underground* (1864): conscience has become an obsessive inner court; the self is the accuser, the accused, the judge, and the executioner. In a bizarre extension of Paul's and Luther's autobiographical pages, self-consciousness merges into compulsive self-humiliation, with no redemption in sight. Conscience is no longer active knowledge immersed in the social flow of life but purely retrospective, solitary self-condemnation, or entirely fearful anticipation.

More balanced statements of this construction are found in the writings of Coleridge (1772–1834) and Conrad (1857–1924). The poet-critic Coleridge stresses that conscience no longer acts "with the ease and uniformity of instinct"; rather, consciousness is the problem. In *Lord Jim*, Conrad shows us his protagonist haunted by a conscience that prevents his awareness of the good new life he has built for himself, while in *Heart of Darkness* we see Kurtz surrendering conscience and letting his consciousness be flooded by instinctual experience. Without conscience, Kurtz is all awareness and lacks an interpreter; he stands thus naked before horror.

Application of the Notion to the Study of Religious and Ethical Systems. Hindu and Buddhist philosophies have very articulate and complex theories of consciousness. All religious traditions have notions of moral law and moral judgment. All encourage reflectivity and offer conceptual tools and practical techniques for self-evaluation. But the notion of conscience as internal organ is not found outside of Christianity. As commonly understood, it is peculiar to the West. The generalization of the tribunal of conscience, the universal legal requirement for annual confession and penance, is a uniquely Western phenomenon. Westerners seem to have taken on a special burden of responsibility. (This was probably not particularly helpful morally.) I must have a vision of myself—of my vocation, for instance—for which I alone will be accountable. Consider, for instance, the notion of conscience found in the writings of the German existentialist philosopher Heidegger (1889–1979): that there is an objectless call of conscience that summons us, not to be in a particular manner, but to choose in what manner we shall be. The wars against guilty thoughts and the self-condemnatory forays into self-consciousness seem also linked to the unique history of Western man (the gnostic and the celibate monastic episodes being probably particularly influential). Recall that most of the decisive articulations of conscience were autobiographical statements focusing on inner turmoils.

Nineteenth-century founders of the science of religion used the idea of evolution of conscience to bridge the gap between themselves, the Western scholars able and desirous to know all mankind, and the people they studied, whose outlook was perceived as regional, if not primitive. So they wrote about the dawn of conscience in the ancient Near East and about the various stages of conscience reached in non-Christian religions. The moral and religious dignity of man was commonly tied to the functioning of this individual organ. The evolutionary view was self-serving and is now discarded, but it had the merit of affirming a commonality among all mankind.

Articles on conscience in James Hastings's *Encyclopaedia of Religion and Ethics* (vol. 4, 1911) illustrate this stage of scholarship. There is a polemic against the nascent sociological reductionist view that sees in conscience an interiorization of social rules. A lengthy article seeks to establish the Jewish view of conscience. The article is not in the least embarrassed by the fact that rabbinic Judaism has no such notion. (For a respected account of Jewish morality, see Neusner, 1981: the will has some power to affect the world, and its intention should be good.) Attempts to find everywhere notions of conscience comparable to the Western one have now largely been abandoned. Current influential works in the discipline of comparative religious ethics have no recourse to it (Little and Twiss, 1978; Bird, 1981). In contrast, the concept is important in current philosophical ethics (Childress, 1979).

Anthropological and Theological Considerations. Etymology may once again be suggestive. Conscience is "knowledge-with," that is, a shared knowledge of something. The foundational experience is the awareness that somebody else is aware of what I have done; I have been seen, and I know that he knows, and I know that he knows that I know that he knows. There is, for a fleeting moment, a shared awareness between us. There is intelligence in the birth of conscience: the other can be a clever accomplice or an articulate critic. But there is also co-feeling: my action is endorsed or disapproved of. The mutual awareness is not just mental. There is also compassion: he knows how it feels to do what I have done, and I know how it feels to observe this being done. Conscience, then, is not just a matter of sight and scrutiny; there is also sensitivity and heart in it. And if conscience makes us potentially morally liable, it makes us also aware of potential moral support.

After this initial point, conscience becomes an interpretive activity. Thus, I own my act and articulate its meaning, serenely, aggressively, or defensively. But while I interpret, others (the initial fellow-feeler or some third party) also interpret. My interpretation will be happy and secure if it agrees in detail or broadly with a wider community of interpretation. It was the merit of the medieval "domestication" of conscience (Lehmann, 1963) that an authoritative, plausible community was always near. Conscience was the court of first instance to adjudicate the worth of my action, and it was the court of last instance. But there was guidance from intermediate courts, which could function in a human manner, with intellectual stability and a measure of understanding. It was the weakness of the Kantian theory that conscience became the only (first and last) tribunal. (Paul had had the good sense to admit that God, not his conscience, judges him. See *1 Corinthians* 4:4.) Kant prepared the "decline and fall" of conscience: solitary conscience is either hostile to self and cruel, or self-righteous and insensitive to others. Freud (1856–1939) could only spell out the irrelevance and uselessness of this conscience (Lehmann, 1963).

The interpretive activity of conscience must therefore always be an account to the other, to others. De Jaucourt (*Encyclopédie,* 1765) emphasized quite soundly that what is important about conscience is the quality of the reasons it can put forward. Hegel saw quite correctly that, to be moral, an action must be owned and expressed: it must be said that it is from conscience. Accountability before somebody else (the one or those affected, or an ideal observer) is intrinsic to morality; the effort of persuasion directed toward others in their otherness is bound with the aspiration to worth. The self needs to be at least symbolically endorsed by others, to be supported at least in words. It is the utmost hypocrisy to claim that conscience can judge itself with skill and authority. Conscience does not produce a private hell or heaven but a public person. When conscience is alive it evaluates the action of the self as part of a continuing moral action (and interaction and further interaction). It is a diseased conscience that carries out nothing but introspective, retrospective self-appraisal. The healthy conscience lives in the present. (In the moment of conscience, consciousness becomes conscious of its past social unconsciousness, and moves on.) And conscience lives in the presence of another human being or beings. It forges an intention, takes an initiative, faces others with a proposal, issues forth in a public act (Jankélévitch, 1933, 1950). Wise and foolish consciences, happy and unhappy ones, are not immobile, self-enclosed realities. They are stages in conscious histories. Healthy consciences share their stories. Each narrates old stories and listens to old stories: in the process, a new story is shared and action shaped. It takes a story to account for one's conscience, and it takes a shared, ongoing story for conscience to form—and enjoy forming—action.

On the interreligious scene today, it is to be wished that dialogue and encounter shall proceed from conscience. And the notion of conscience may well be—or become—part of the account that each will give to the other of his or her own humanity. Such meeting of consciences cannot occur without the labor of consciousness: each trying to communicate over a period of time what he is aware of.

Any attempt in the West to develop a theologically relevant notion of conscience must overcome two traditional tendencies. First of all, religious conscience should be purged of its tendency to reject the fellowship of men and become absorbed in the private dialogue of the soul with God. Conscience, wrote Luther, is the place where we must live with God as man and wife (*Lectures on Psalms* 3.593.28–29). It must also heal itself of the tendency to assume that God will love us if we hate ourselves. From Augustine on, the notion has persisted that to lay bare before God our innermost hearts, admit we find there utter corruption, and profess to feel pain will miraculously turn a bad conscience into a good one. Such self-serving self-humiliation is either an insincere act or an abject one. Self-torture does not make man morally better. A bad conscience may prevent worse sins, but it never brings joy.

A reconstruction might proceed from the biblical sense that conscience and heart are interchangeable. Conscience is then constituted by the hearing of—or sensitivity to—a call, a commandment. The idea of conscience can be built on what happens in an encounter between persons, rather than on the notion of a moral experience. Such a notion mistakenly assumes that a moral subject is already established, before hearing the claims of the other; one might recall here that Paul told the Corinthians not to advance their own (strong) consciences but to heed the (weaker) consciences of others. What is heard in the depths of the encounter with the widows, the orphans, and the poor of the land is the infinite call of vast human need. Within the compass of being, there are persons who are not beings; that is, they are not beings one should simply adapt oneself to or exercise power on. In each person there is also an infinite with which one can and should talk, in lucid awareness of one's own strength. The primal condition of conscious human freedom is to be unfree because claimed by the presence of a weaker other. He who is conscious of the nature of ordinary human relations has just put food in his mouth and a roof over his head: he has time to think. The mere fact of his respite makes him infinitely liable to those who are still hungry. And the infinite that meets us in other concrete human beings is an infinity of demands that cannot be answered by a mere rule of what is right and sufficient; it is also an infinity of stories that cannot be reduced to one plot. Thus there is in every other being an excess of possibilities over the possibilities that are inherent in me; something new should result from our encounter. Scripture affirms that God meets us in the lowest among our brethren. Only in these meetings are found the birthplace of morality and the voice of God. (See the analyses of Lévinas, presented in Smith, 1983.) Kierkegaard praised the faith that clung to the divine promise and readied itself to disobey the law. In contrast, Emmanuel Lévinas urges us to give up the hope of a warm rapport with God and love the law instead, austerely. This is what God requires; what we (both we the strong and we the weak) most need in order to fulfill God's requirement are some firm exterior rules of justice (Lévinas, 1976, pp. 189–193).

[*For discussion of conscience in the Christian tradition, see* Christian Ethics *and* Theology, *article on* Christian Theology. *For a treatment of the philosophical tradition that lies behind the concept, see* Natural Law. *Other related entries are* Conversion; Morality and Religion; Religious Experience; *and* Sin and Guilt.]

BIBLIOGRAPHY

Altizer, Thomas J. J. "Paul and the Birth of Self-Consciousness." *Journal of the American Academy of Religion* 51 (September 1983): 359–370.

Bird, Frederick. "Paradigms and Parameters for the Comparative Study of Religious and Ideological Ethics." *Journal of Religious Ethics* 9 (Fall 1981): 157–185.

Brunschwicg, Léon. *Le progrès de la conscience dans la philosophie occidentale* (1927). 2d ed. 2 vols. Paris, 1953.

Childress, James F. "Appeals to Conscience." *Ethics* 89 (July 1979): 315–335.

Despland, Michel. "Can Conscience Be Hypocritical? The Contrasting Analyses of Kant and Hegel." *Harvard Theological Review* 68 (July–October 1975): 357–370.

Engelberg, Edward. *The Unknown Distance: From Consciousness to Conscience, Goethe to Camus.* Cambridge, Mass., 1972.

Jankélévitch, Vladimir. *La mauvaise conscience* (1933). Paris, 1982.

Jankélévitch, Vladimir. *L'ironie ou la bonne conscience.* 2d ed. Paris, 1950.

Lehmann, Paul L. *Ethics in a Christian Context.* New York, 1963.

Lévinas, Emmanuel. *Difficile liberté.* 2d ed. Paris, 1976.

Little, David L., and Sumner Twiss, Jr. *Comparative Religious Ethics.* New York, 1978.

Neal, J. R. "Conscience in the Reformation Period." Ph.D. diss., Harvard University, 1972.

Nelson, Benjamin. *On the Roads to Modernity.* Totowa, N.J., 1981.

Neusner, Jacob. *Judaism: The Evidence of the Mishnah.* Chicago, 1981.

Smith, Steven G. *The Argument to the Other: Reason beyond Reason in the Thought of Karl Barth and Emmanuel Lévinas.* Chico, Calif., 1983.

Stendahl, Krister. "Paul and the Introspective Conscience of the West." In *Paul among Jews and Gentiles, and Other Essays.* Philadelphia, 1976.

Tillich, Paul. "The Transmoral Conscience." In *The Protestant Era.* Chicago, 1948.

Wallis, R. T. *The Idea of Conscience in Philo of Alexandria.* Berkeley, 1975.

Michel Despland

CONSCIOUSNESS, STATES OF. Each of the major religions and philosophies of the world speaks, often in symbolic terms, about states of consciousness other than those of our ordinary experience. According to these teachings, we have the potential to experience qualitatively different levels of perception, awareness, and orientation toward ourselves, others, and the universe. The first two of these distinct realms of existence—ordinary sleep and ordinary waking consciousness—constitute the "normal" human condition, our customary experience. "Higher" states of being correlate with finer, more subtle levels of reality.

Transformation to higher states of consciousness may result from adherence to the ideas, methods, and prescribed meditations of an authentic religious discipline, whereby consciousness is refined, converted, and realigned from "the coarse to the fine." The higher, or superior, states are characterized by enhanced faculties of attention, thought, feeling, and sensation. A new type of seeing becomes prominent, and perception, awareness, and experience conform more adequately and fully to the various levels of reality and truth in the universe.

In this view, higher states of consciousness are not the same as mood changes or any other phenomena—no matter how unusual or exciting—evoked through normal thought and feeling. According to the great traditions of mysticism and esoteric religions, the honing of rational thought and intense emotions can never, by itself, produce a superior consciousness. These faculties are inherently limited, and without spiritual development they serve only the egoistic aspect of human nature.

Superior states of consciousness, on the other hand, reflect the awakening and development of an exceptional attention and awareness, generating new powers of the self: new feelings, sensitivities, and cognitions. These are regarded as authentic intelligence, or "the wisdom of the heart." It is said that this development provides unmediated contacts with reality, allowing for the comprehension and experiencing of life's meaning, value, and purpose in relation to man's impersonal or transcendent nature.

The distinction between qualitatively different states of experience and fluctuations within one state can be made clear by analogy to water, ice, and mist. Whether blue, black, red, or clear, whether a drop, a quart, a gallon, or an ocean, whether in a quiet lake or in a raging river, water is water. Its molecular arrangement remains unchanged. Ice, however, is structurally different from water. Water vapor, too, represents an entirely different structural state. Its molecules move more quickly, and it is less dense and lighter. The transformation from ice to water to mist may be said to correspond to man's potential transmutation from a coarse to a finer (more ethereal) state of being.

The idea that man has access to higher realms of consciousness and reality is prevalent in all esoteric contemplative traditions. In Plato's remarkable allegory of the cave, the ordinary human condition is portrayed as existence in a cave, where shackled prisoners with limited vision—able to look only at the wall in front of them—mistake shadows and echoes for reality. Liberation, the ascent into the real world, is arduous and requires loosening the chains, turning around, and being able to overcome the initial confusion and persist. The prisoner must become realigned so that he can control his dark fears and shadowy thoughts and so escape from the cave. Once he is out of the cave, complete vision is possible through the liberation of the higher mind *(nous)*. Higher consciousness meets reality, thereby apprehending the laws of the universal order—the True, the Beautiful, and the Good.

This train of thought, positing a hierarchy of human development that corresponds to accurate perceptions and experiences of reality, can be found in teachings from both the East and the West. The Hindu tradition, for example, speaks of four states of consciousness. The first *(jāgrat)* is the habitual waking consciousness and is analogous to that experienced by Plato's shackled prisoner. The second *(svapna)* occurs when one experiences reality as the product of one's subjective projections rather than as random, inexplicable, and either indifferent or cruel in its circumstances. *Svapna* conforms to the experience of the unchained prisoner seeking escape. The third state *(suṣupti)* is one of "divine wisdom"—clearly the purview of the liberated person. The fourth *(turīya)* is, fittingly, ineffable.

The idea of levels of self-awareness is evident in the Middle East. The Ṣūfī teacher Javad Nurbakhsh, shaykh of the Nimatullahi order, delineates four stages of development: (1) self becoming emptied; (2) self becoming illuminated; (3) self becoming adorned; (4) self having passed away *(fanā')*. Through a spiritual training revolving around an exceptional master-pupil relationship, an initiate on the path *(ṭarīqah)* may penetrate the sufferings, confusions, and convolutions inherent in egoism—represented by life in the Platonic cave—and pass beyond them to bliss, truth, and communion with God.

In the West, the great fourteenth-century Christian contemplative Meister Eckhart affirms a transcendent state in which man, who is always in the presence of God, experiences the kingdom of heaven within. Heaven, portrayed as an inner experience, can be attained in this life when the mind becomes uncluttered and allows God to enter the soul. This requires a diligence and attention wherein energy is not squandered on the outward person but is reserved for the inner person, the transformed being who knows God.

For the past several hundred years the concept of states of consciousness has been explored by psychologists. In many instances this study has been from another perspective than that of religious spirituality. No study of this subject would be complete without consideration of modern psychology's confrontation with states of consciousness, from William James and Franz Anton Mesmer to the present day.

William James. James (1842–1910) is the most noted modern psychologist to have seriously investigated altered states of consciousness and the influence of states of consciousness on the perception of reality. In *The Varieties of Religious Experience* (1902), James discusses mystical states that, although inaccessible to the purely rational mind, impart exceptional meaning and understanding. The enhanced powers of cognition exhibited in such states suggest that human beings possess faculties beyond those of the ordinary mind for attaining certainty and wisdom:

> One conclusion was forced upon my mind at that time, and my impression of its truth has ever since remained unshaken. It is that our normal waking consciousness, rational consciousness as we call it, is but one special type of consciousness, whilst all about it, parted from it by the filmiest of screens, there lie potential forms of consciousness entirely different. . . . No account of the universe in its totality can be final which leaves these other forms of consciousness quite disregarded. How to regard them is the question—for

> they are so discontinuous with ordinary consciousness. . . . At any rate, they forbid a premature closing of our accounts with reality. (James, [1902] 1961, p. 305)

James defines mystical states by demarcating four of their salient qualities. He does this, in part, to rescue the appellation from its disreputable position as the catchall synonym for any unusual, exciting, or weird experience.

The first such quality James terms the "noetic," or cognitive, aspect of the mystical state. This is not the rational, discursive, comparative function of the mind; it is, rather, wisdom—a power of heightened intellectual discernment and relational understanding in which positioning, valuation, and function are apprehended and seemingly disparate facts are properly ranked and organized into meaningful entities.

The second component he characterizes as "ineffability." Because they are ineffable, these transformations in consciousness cannot be verbalized in a manner that does justice to the nuances of the experience.

The third characteristic is "transience." Mystical states usually are short-lived. Having their own distinctive flavor, they appear to be connected and continuous with each other; and those who experience them generally report a new and vivid awareness of being in the present moment.

Fourth, mystical states are characterized by a feeling of "passivity," as if one's personal will were suspended and one had opened oneself to a higher or superior force. The experience is of not quite being oneself; there is another force, power, or "person" operating through one. These four distinctions delineated by James have in recent times attracted the interest of contemporary researchers studying human consciousness.

In *The Principles of Psychology* (1890) James took a different tack and pondered the relationship between the faculty of attention and a developed human mind. James advises that it is what one directs his attention to that determines the merit of one's life. People do not share identical experiences because they direct their attention or interest to different aspects of life's infinite possibilities. This directing of one's attention is the only power within human control and is of paramount importance for James because it determines the significance of one's life: "The faculty of voluntarily bringing back a wandering attention, over and over, is the very root of judgment, character, and will. No one is *compos sui* [master of himself] if he have it not. An education which should improve the faculty would be *the* education *par excellence*" (James, [1890] 1950, vol. 1, p. 424). [*For further discussion, see the biography of James.*]

What is the relationship between altered states of consciousness, the superior intellectual faculties described by James, and the evolution of this power of sustained directed attention? On the whole these questions—so central to the esoteric traditions—do not appear to have interested mainstream psychologists either in James's time or in ours. Yet the question of superior faculties of intellection and states of consciousness was compelling for one of modern psychology's seminal explorers, Franz Anton Mesmer.

Franz Anton Mesmer. A century before William James the notion of disparate states of consciousness became prominent as a result of Franz Anton Mesmer's experimentation with "magnetized states," or hypnotic trances. Mesmer (1734–1815), a remarkable healer of what are today called psychosomatic and hysterical illnesses, was knowledgeable in medicine, psychology, hermeticism, and alchemy. He postulated that people possess two distinct realms of consciousness, the ordinary waking state and an underlying unseen realm. In this invisible realm two related powers seem to be activated. The first is an exchange of rarefied energies, or "fluids," between individuals that allows certain sensitive persons to influence others by their presence; that is, to influence them in more subtle ways than are generally believed operative in human exchanges. The second is a faculty of superior intelligence and will. The recognition of these submerged potentials as put forth by Mesmer and the psychologists who succeeded him has led to investigation into the powers, scope, and subtleties of the conscious and unconscious mind.

In his healing endeavors Mesmer found himself capable of affecting other people by his presence. He was able to transmit a mysterious energy that he named "animal magnetism" to his patients. This force, or energy, balances the fundamental underlying fluid common to everything in existence.

Mesmer discovered this ability to transfer his surplus animal magnetism while treating a woman whose vacillations between episodes of illness and periods of relative calm not only reminded him of the endless oscillations of the tides and the seasons but gave him the idea that these bouts, like the ebbs of the tides, might be essential components of a more complete process. That insight generated his strategy of inducing an "artificial tide" in his patient (with the aid of magnets) to evoke a cathartic ebb or "crisis," a therapeutic convulsion to enhance the body's "fluid" circulation and bring about a cure. The cures he effected in this way persuaded him that the cure of psychosomatic illness was facilitated by circulating this subtle fluid and rebalancing this underlying realm within the patient. Such a realignment seemed to be induced by Mesmer's own magnetism and internal balance, for it was inexplicable by the prevailing theories of the day. The inferences are that one's state of consciousness, balance, or sensitivity may profoundly affect another person and that this balance corresponds to the fundamental order of the universe itself.

In addition, Mesmer and his disciples discovered exceptional human powers that could be elicited in patients during the deep sleep or trance of the "crisis" state. During this artificial somnambulism, or hypnotic state, medically untrained persons displayed outstanding diagnostic and therapeutic powers, interpretive and healing skills liberated only while they were "magnetized."

Along with this curative power there emerged a deep clarity of thought, an impeccable memory of all personal experiences, and an inner visionary faculty connected to the universal order. Not only did Mesmer relate this inner faculty to a property of the universal order, but he also reflected upon the nature of the special sensitivities he discerned in this state of sleep:

> Man's sleep is not a negative state, nor is it simply the absence of wakefulness; modifications of this state have taught me that the faculties of a sleeping man not only are not suspended, but that often they continue to function with more perfection than when he is awake. One can observe that certain persons walk, and conduct their affairs with more planning and with the same reflection, attention, and skill as when they are awake. It is still more surprising to see faculties which are called "intellectual" being used to such an extent that they infinitely surpass those cultivated in the ordinary state. (Mesmer, in Bloch, 1980, p. 112)

Investigations after Mesmer. After Mesmer the inquiry into hypnotic states led many to ponder the nature of human consciousness and the plethora of intriguing phenomena that the mind can generate. This exploration can be said to have taken two directions. In one—generally on the fringe of psychology—the focus was on positing superior states of consciousness to account for the extraordinary powers the mind displayed. In the second, the focus was upon integrating the discovered states into normal consciousness and the structure of the ego.

Postulation of superior states. One result of Mesmer's work was that the "mesmerists" who followed him posited hierarchically arranged levels of consciousness, including states surpassing that of ordinary consciousness. A representative comprehensive system was proposed by Carl Kluge, who in 1811 speculated about six levels of the hypnotic state:

> (1) Waking state . . . ; (2) Half-sleep . . . ; (3) "Inner darkness," that is, sleep proper and insensitivity; (4) "Inner clarity," that is, consciousness within one's own body, extrasensory perception . . . ; (5) "Self-contemplation": the subject's ability to perceive with great accuracy the interior of his own body and that of those with whom he is put into rapport; (6) "Universal clarity": the removal of veils of time and space and the subject perceives things hidden in the past, the future, or at a remote distance. (quoted in Ellenberger, 1970, p. 78)

Another result of research in the domain of hypnosis has been the speculation by some psychologists that normal consciousness itself might be merely one aspect of the human mind and that there might exist other states as different from normal consciousness as is this subconscious state. The hypnotic trance had revealed subconscious "autonomous entities." In some cases, these "subpersonalities" exhibited fragmentary constrictive protective behaviors and clearly represented inferior states of being. In other cases, they exhibited astonishing capacities of independence, alertness, awareness, organization, and intelligence and thus raised questions about whether these types of powers might portend an untapped superior realm of consciousness.

For example, one perplexing subentity uncovered during hypnosis is Ernest Hilgard's "hidden observer," a latent witness that is apparently aware of and able to communicate all that happens when called upon by the hypnotist, despite the apparent unresponsiveness of the more "conscious" parts of the subjects. The scope and limits of such a covert omniscient power are not clear, nor are the conditions under which such an enduring awareness is possible for an unsleeping, nonhypnotized conscious human being.

Integration theorists. In contrast to these theorists of superior states of consciousness, most mainstream psychologists, Janet and Freud for example, assumed that the consciousness belonging to a developed normal ego was the highest state available to man. Therefore they neither investigated nor posited qualitatively higher states; they focused instead on purging the "inferior" states to achieve the level of freedom attainable for habitual consciousness, a freedom determined through their therapeutic encounters. The aim here was to integrate the subentities or fragments of the psyche into a restored and enhanced normal consciousness. The pathological motives associated with these unconscious fragments, behaviors, and experiences, which were taken as representative of inferior states, were not differentiated from nonpathological motives, values, and behaviors. The question of the nature or value of these latter unconscious forces—that is, whether they originate from supraconsciousness rather than subconsciousness—was denied or ignored. All unconscious elements came to be treated as of equal value; they were to be integrated into and understood by the governor of normal consciousness, the ego. These psychologists analyzed and synthesized the insights they gleaned from their contacts with various neurotic patients into theories of the human mind, and from this pastiche they forged their view of the unconscious, of consciousness, and of man himself.

Pierre Janet. The study of hysteria and other "neuroses," such as dissociations and somnambulisms, brought Janet (1859–1947) into contact with a hidden realm of the mind that he called "the subconscious." In such works (discussed in Ellenberger, 1970) as *L'automatisme psychologique* (1889) and *L'état mental des hysteriques* (1911), Janet postulated that man can be controlled by either his conscious or subconscious mind: the psychologically strong are conscious, the psychologically weak are "unconscious."

The separation of subconscious from conscious awareness creates a psychologically debilitated person (exemplified by the dissociated personalities and amnesiacs Janet treated) who is compelled to live in a distorted corner of reality. This nonintegrated person becomes enslaved by the impulses and fears housed in this submerged domain and succumbs to its cunning power to constrict and obfuscate reality into piecemeal fragments. The subconscious absorbs the very fragments it has manufactured, and these fragments are, in turn, present for the next event, creating still further splintered replacements for reality. This process condemns its victims to a life of intellectual distortion and other neurotic symptoms.

Optimal human functioning, according to Janet, is the rule of the conscious mind over the subconscious. It is the sublimation and integration of the subconscious into ordinary consciousness. He calls the apex of his "hierarchy of the mind" a "grand synthesis," which he counterposes against the automatic actions or motor discharges of "psychological automatism," that which is relegated to the lowest rung of his system.

Man's freedom, possible only for the exceptional individual who is in control of his subconscious and capable of directing his attention to the immediate present, lies in his ability to perceive reality accurately and influence it intentionally and appropriately. Indeed, this ability to experience and affect reality is the result of the integration of consciousness and the development of a sustained attention to the present moment, which alone can attain truth in man's inner and outer world. Few people, Janet says, possess such attention.

Sigmund Freud. Freud (1856–1939) instructed the modern Western world to "make conscious the unconscious" for the realization of the modicum of freedom he perceived to be allotted to man. The task Freud set was for the rational mind and ego to illuminate and control the underlying emotions, the impulses and fears that, residing in the deep recesses of the unconscious, are at the root of our existence. Such insight into the emotions by the mind allows us to choose the best possible way of life, one free from pathologies and other enfeebling circumstances. It was this vision of the human potential for consciousness—expressed in his famous dictum "Where id was there shall ego be"—that situated Freud as the father of modern psychology. Inspired by his own work in psychoanalysis, Freud touched upon another approach to the meaning of states of consciousness.

Consciousness, for Freud, is the ego's awareness and mediation of the unconscious. This awareness allows the ego realistically to ration a portion of the sexual force (libido) for sexual activity and love and productively to sublimate the remainder for meaningful work. In some mysterious manner, unexplained by Freud, such a healthy ego could also perceive a close approximation of reality through its principal faculty for acquiring knowledge: reason. Reason for Freud created science, which is man's instrument of salvation. Reason can bring us as close to truth as is humanly possible. Presumably, the more conscious the person the better the scientist he would be.

In *Civilization and Its Discontents* (1930), Freud is inclined to identify the mystical experience as merely one more self-deception to which man, in his desperation and naiveté, falls prey. There Freud writes of a friend who is opposed to his idea that religion is a crutch allowing psychologically weak people, enfeebled because of their ignorance of scientific truths, to project a father figure, in the form of God, onto the universe. The solace provided by this wishful thinking assuages their fears in the face of a terrifying and unintelligible world. Freud's friend responds by saying that Freud has ignored some exceptional feelings that authenticate the mystical experience. These feelings are of "eternity" and of something "oceanic."

In Freud's dismissal of this mystical state, with its reputed component of a superior sensitivity, he presents a valuable criterion for validation: one's own experience. Freud confesses that he cannot discover this "oceanic" feeling in himself, suggesting that one's personal experience can serve as a standard to measure veracity. In this instance, however, Freud overlooks the question—of paramount importance to him at other times—regarding the nature or quality of personal experience: that is, whether one's state of sensitivity or consciousness influences one's perception, understanding, or experience itself.

Even though Freud discounted the mystical state, his

lifework was, in part, a tribute to self-study and the search for understanding and truth. When he speaks about his persistent efforts to help his patients discover the truth about themselves, Freud is suggesting a way of life that he does not acknowledge when he talks about the pathology of man's essential nature. Within Freud's system, the yearnings for ultimate truth and virtue are at best unfulfillable strivings because they fail to conform to the real structure of human nature and the real structure of the universe. According to Freud's theories, genuine human motivation is reserved for pleasure, sex, and security. Any ennobling motivation is, in essence, either a self-deception or a compromise, the transformation or sublimation of these selfish energies that is possible only for a mature adult. Simultaneously, the universe is indifferent to man; it is purposeless and unconscious. There is no intelligence, love, or virtue in the cosmos for man to call upon or to support human aspirations. But that formulation appears to contradict his lifelong attempts, in the face of the derision, censure, and hostility he incurred, to free his patients (and himself) from the tyranny of the unconscious. This liberation of their repressed energies, through listening carefully to his patients with an "evenly-hovering attention," he designated "spiritual guidance in the best sense of the word." Freud's resolve in extricating these energies through the process of self-knowledge offers a taste of another possibility, where seeing what one is confers a new type of meaning, dignity, and virtue on man. [*For further discussion, see the biography of Freud.*]

Transpersonal Psychologies. In the 1960s, transpersonal psychology emerged as a movement devoted in part to the study of alternative states of consciousness. Though by no means representative of the mainstream of psychological research in the West, transpersonal psychologists are intrigued by the possibility that human beings possess transcendent powers of consciousness. Some speculate about the mind's untapped potential for awareness and hold a view of the universe as conscious and purposive. They are convinced that we can be motivated by broader and less selfish impulses than physiological needs and egoistic emotions. For these psychologists, our most important motivations spring from a selflessness that revolves around the pondering of ultimate questions—questions about the meaning, purpose, and value of human life. Often influenced by the recent influx of Eastern psychologies and philosophies into the West, transpersonal psychology seeks to reverse what it considers the disproportionate attention given to man's psychological afflictions at the expense of his great potentialities. This movement may be understood as an attempt to reconnect the science of psychology with the perennial metaphysical teachings of the spiritual traditions.

Abraham Maslow. Maslow (1908–1970) was particularly interested in fully developed or "self-actualized" people who frequently undergo "changes in consciousness" that he called "peak experiences." Believing that people have an inherent inner core that strives for growth (cf. Carl Rogers, Rollo May), Maslow developed a hierarchy of human motivations that seeks to encompass the entire spectrum of man's growth.

The lowest and most basic needs he designated as physiological and safety needs; these are fundamentally personal, selfish, and self-serving. The next stages include aesthetic and cognitive impulses. At the top of Maslow's hierarchy are "beta," or "being," needs. These operate in the self-actualized person who surpasses all personal motivations and strives for the good of humanity by acting from feelings of "wholeness," "justice," "self-sufficiency," and "aliveness," strivings capable of affecting all aspects of life. These fortunate people have thoroughly developed the inner self with which all people are born but that is generally squelched, obfuscated, or distorted by societal and parental conditioning.

Peak experiences are most often the prerogative of Maslow's self-actualized persons. These experiences are held to be transformations of consciousness and perception wherein life is imbued with a sense of impersonality, or "self-transcendence," and meaning. In *Toward a Psychology of Being* (1968), Maslow reports that they are states where vision is whole rather than partial, where perception is based upon reality rather than subjective projection, and where life's meaning and goodness are experienced directly and with certainty. Time appears to be suspended and the experiencer escapes the stress of "becoming." He lives a tension-free life in the calm of "effortless being." Through such self-actualizing development and peak experiences, man lives a completely engaged life.

C. G. Jung. While Jung (1875–1961) does not explicitly talk about states of consciousness, he does touch upon the subject indirectly; he speaks about consciousness, individuation, wholeness, and the development of the "self," or the "modern man." In "The Spiritual Problem of Modern Man" (chap. 10 in *Modern Man in Search of a Soul*, 1955), Jung describes the modern man as the rare, exceptional human being who, completely conscious and having fully integrated the solutions of the past and faced the problems of the future, is free to break with all constraints and live wholly in the present.

For Jung the unconscious consists of three realms. The first and most accessible layer contains man's motivations for personal survival and the repressed material that violates the self-image he can tolerate for himself. The second layer contains the cultural habits and heritage that condition him unawares.

The third and fundamental layer is the collective unconscious. This is a transpersonal primordial realm that contains man's impersonal aspirations, cunning adversaries, and ultimate possibilities. It houses the archetypes, structures rooted in the collective unconscious that extend in diluted form to individual consciousness and that create, organize, and store all psychic potentialities. Sometimes the archetypes are personified by Jung and likened to disparate subpersonages within the individual; however, archetypes cannot be seen directly but can only be inferred through the analysis of experience. [*See* Archetypes.]

The collective unconscious helps Jung account for the plethora of parapsychological phenomena—such as psychokinesis, clairvoyance, and synchronicity—that so captivated him. If man's psychic life is somehow linked to that of all humanity, then reports of apparently inexplicable events such as extrasensory perception are not quite so unintelligible.

True self-study entails complete analysis and integration of aspects of the personal, cultural, and collective unconscious, which brings about wholeness, or individuation. This integration is accomplished through the confrontation with and analysis of individual private dreams and intense experiences, and by the emotional encounter with and analysis of the universal myths, visions, and images that human beings have experienced and shared over the millennia. Only seldom can a human being attain this level of consciousness and thus live open to the present. [*For further discussion, see the biography of Jung.*]

Holistic Health. Holistic health proponents of the 1960s and 1970s have encouraged all kinds of speculation about possible states of human consciousness. In promoting techniques like biofeedback, autogenic training, and progressive relaxation, holistic health practitioners have frequently induced powerful, inexplicable experiences in their clients. These methods, which grew partly out of the attempt to reconnect the troubled "client" to his body—because the human body had virtually been ignored by mainstream psychologists—were simultaneously endeavors to reverse the prevailing mind-body dualism and to cure psychosomatic maladies. At times they have generated new feelings of self-responsibility, self-awareness, and human wholeness. Such novel experiences have spawned an abundance of theories about alternative states of consciousness among the field's principal researchers.

One popular holistic health procedure is biofeedback. Now principally employed as a cure for stress-related psychosomatic disturbances, it was originally touted as "a shortcut to meditation" and a vehicle for transforming consciousness. A method to facilitate the integration of "mind, body, and spirit" by educating people about how to take command of their own health, biofeedback uses electronic devices to amplify weak physiological sensations—like the minuscule changes in the magnitude of muscle tensions—so that people can purportedly control autonomic or "involuntary" body processes ordinarily considered impervious to volitional control.

Two approaches to the alteration or expansion of consciousness ensued from biofeedback. First, investigators attempted to induce "meditative" states in novices by teaching them to mimic the brain-wave patterns of experienced meditators. Many researchers now feel that this endeavor fizzled. Second, investigators discovered that in order for their subjects to profit from biofeedback, these subjects could not force the desired state to occur. They needed to learn to "relax" and allow a "passive attention" to replace their habitual striving. Moreover, the experience of relaxation and passive attention—to everyone's surprise—was sometimes accompanied by healings, the enhancement of cognitive powers, creativity, and feelings of union with a higher source. Sometimes people even experienced a new sense of themselves, their lives, and the universe. This type of experience has been explained in every conceivable manner and associated with every meditative state. One cannot help but feel that the explanations proffered do not do justice to the subtleties of these experiences and that such events do more to raise questions about the nature, meaning, and potentials of human existence than to answer them.

Conclusion. The modern era has witnessed the virtual disappearance of metaphysical ideas about the nature of man and the universe as religious claims to understand the human mind have been eclipsed by the influence of modern psychology. This phenomenon is apparent when one examines the topic "states of consciousness" and sees how unfamiliar and even alien the issues connected to it can appear. Much of the power and allure of modern psychology, and perhaps some of its current fragmentation, is rooted in its encounter with various aspects of the human mind that it has only recently discovered but that have been the focus of many ancient teachings.

Virtually unheard two decades ago, the expression "states of consciousness" has by now entered the vocabularies of many men and women. How this idea will present itself in the years to come; how a subject so intimately wedded to metaphysical and religious concerns will fare in modern culture; and how religion, philosophy, and psychology may meet in their concern over this subject may prove decisively important to all who seek answers to the perennial questions of human life.

[*See also entries on various states of consciousness:* Ecstasy; Enthusiasm; Frenzy; Dreams; Inspiration; Sleep; *and* Visions.]

BIBLIOGRAPHY

Darnton, Robert. *Mesmerism and the End of the Enlightenment in France.* Cambridge, 1968.

Ellenberger, Henri F. *The Discovery of the Unconscious: The History and Evolution of Dynamic Psychiatry.* New York, 1970. A comprehensive reporting of the study of the subconscious and of ego consciousness within modern psychology. Includes substantial material on Franz A. Mesmer and an in-depth study of the work of Pierre Janet.

James, William. *The Principles of Psychology* (1890). 2 vols. New York, 1950. Contains a chapter on the subject of "attention," a subject that has been virtually ignored by modern psychology.

James, William. *The Varieties of Religious Experience: A Study in Human Nature* (1902). New York, 1961. The chapter entitled "Mysticism" opens up many important issues related to the idea of states of consciousness.

Maslow, Abraham. *Toward a Psychology of Being.* 2d ed. New York, 1968. Attempts to speak about the range of human motivations beyond merely personal security needs to include impersonal or "transcendent" motivations.

Mesmer, Franz A. *Mesmerism: A Translation of the Original Scientific and Medical Writings of F. A. Mesmer.* Translated and compiled by George Bloch. Los Altos, Calif., 1980. An extremely valuable set of essays that demonstrates the scale and scope of Mesmer's psychological, metaphysical, and cosmological interests and discoveries.

Needleman, Jacob. *Consciousness and Tradition.* New York, 1982. A compilation of essays, many of which are relevant to the relationship of the spiritual traditions to the subtleties of states of consciousness.

Nurbakhsh, Javad. *Sufism.* Tehran, 1977. A serious presentation of some principal ideas about Sufism, this book contains a discussion of states of awareness.

Prem, Sri Krishna. *The Yoga of the Bhagavat Gita.* London, 1949. One appendix provides a concise delineation of states of consciousness as outlined in Hinduism, while the text provides the sensitive reader with a feeling for the Hindu tradition.

JACOB NEEDLEMAN and REGINA EISENBERG

CONSECRATION. As a cross-cultural concept, consecration refers to the practice of investing particular objects with extraordinary religious significance. The significance of any single instance of consecration depends in good part on the type of object consecrated. Places and buildings are made into habitations for spiritual beings; higher powers enliven icons and food; kings and hierarchs are recognized as maintainers of a higher order on earth. Yet despite the diversity of both consecrated objects and the traditions from which their religious meaning derives, most instances of consecration reveal some basic structural resemblances. First, an act of consecration is at root a creative act. It is a deliberate attempt to alter the environment, to establish in the visible world some definite, concrete means for fruitful interaction with the divine. Second, a consecrated object, now represented as a link to higher reality, is often itself understood to be transformed—purified or empowered, transmuted into divine substance or given over to the divine. And third, as something extraordinary in its environment, a consecrated object is often ritually marked off, delimited from the mundane, everyday world.

Making Places Holy. The power of limits themselves to consecrate holy places is evident in the practical significance of the Theravāda Buddhist concept of *sīmā* ("boundary"). In Theravāda Buddhism monks and laity are represented as two orders in society, each with its own role in the economy of salvation. The monks, through observing their ascetic code, help maintain the cosmic order; the laity should serve the monks. These two roles are played out in different physical spaces, with a boundary between them. Thus, in the villages of modern Thailand, the monastic compound is set clearly apart. Monks may leave the compound for specific monastic duties but not to gossip in the village; villagers should enter the compound to serve the monks. In addition to the definite but sometimes unmarked boundary around the extended monastic compound, the observance hall, where monks are ordained and make group confession, has a marked boundary of its own. This boundary is denoted by stones—called *sīmā* stones—that are installed according to prescribed rites; it is normally respected by laypersons, who must remove their shoes to enter the observance hall. Here, then, ritual consecration expresses a crucial socioreligious division visible in this world.

When interaction with sacred reality is seen to demand traffic between worlds, the consecration of a physical structure on earth may instill in it the presence of an otherworldly being. Sometimes this link between worlds is forged with the help of material traces left by a holy person who has passed beyond the earthly realm. Relics of the Buddha are ideally embedded in the great stupas of ancient India and the pagodas still found in Southeast Asia. In reverencing these structures, built as memorials to the Buddha, devotees revere the Buddha's person. In the consecration of Roman Catholic churches, usually named after saints, installation of the relics of the patron saint plays a part in a larger ceremony through which the building is literally marked out for, and consigned to, the crucified Lord.

Each of the three major parts of the ceremony presents a phase in the building's transformation. The bishop begins by marking off and purifying the church externally, circumambulating it three times and sprinkling its walls with water. He then has the door unlocked and makes the sign of the cross with his staff on the threshold; inside, a cross of ashes is drawn joining the four corners of the church. Through the cross on the door and on the floor during this first phase of the ceremony, Christ the crucified is understood to take possession of the church. The second phase of the ceremony makes the church a suitable dwelling place for the Lord through both negative and positive means: first evil is banished through the sprinkling of specially prepared holy water, and then a solemn prayer for grace and sanctification is offered. The third phase, in which relics are enclosed in the altar, materially links the spiritual focus of the church to the power of a divine intercessor. [*See* Relics.]

Putting Life into the Image of a Deity. In Hindu temples, the central physical repositories of spiritual power are not relics but images. Devotees often see the image as a manifestation of the deity itself. [*See* Images.] In their ritual worship, devotees interact with the deity as a person with whom they attempt to come into intimate terms. In large temples, long-hallowed images are enthroned and revered as sovereigns. At the temple to Śrīnāthjī in Nāthdwāra, Rajasthan, for example, people are allowed to see the image only at the times of day an important personage would be pleased to grant audience. Śrīnāthjī wears clothes suited to the time of day and season and is treated to lavish banquets. Deities in household shrines, on the other hand, are treated more like guests who may only be visiting for a particular festive occasion. In order to perceive the divinity in these household images, the performance of a consecratory rite may be particularly crucial. Grand images at major temples are sometimes understood to have arisen spontaneously: Śrīnāthjī, they say, emerged from Mount Govardhan, sacred to Kṛṣṇa. But a clay image from the bazaar brought into the house for a temporary period must be visibly transformed in order to be seen to embody the deity's person.

The household consecration ceremony performed for Gaṇeśa, the elephant-headed deity, by Hindus of Maharashtra reveals how human beings can put life into divine images. When the image is brought home it is put on an altar, around which designs of powdered chalk have been drawn and ceremonial implements laid out. Special space has thus been demarcated for the deity to be embodied, but the image itself remains lifeless clay. In the ritual's central act *(prāṇapratiṣṭhā)* the worshiper installs vital breath into the image. But to do this the worshiper himself must first take on the aspects of the divine through preliminary consecrations. To align his microcosmic world with the macrocosm, the worshiper makes brief utterances while touching parts of his body and his ritual implements, identifying himself as the primal cosmic being and the implements as cosmic elements. The breath is installed in the deity when, to the accompaniment of a priest's recitation of particular utterances, the worshiper touches the image with a kind of grass understood to be a potent conduit. At the climax of this rite, the worshiper understands both himself and the deity to have a common identity in the cosmic life force. This identity is then invoked in further ritual worship that includes feeding the deity and sprinkling it with water, both important aspects of consecratory ritual in many Indian traditions.

The installation of the image of Gaṇeśa in Maharashtrian homes takes place on the day of his annual festival, which falls in August or September. The consecration of the day itself is thus marked by the visit of Gaṇeśa, which may be extended for some time longer. As long as the image of the deity continues to remain in the house it is offered daily ceremonial hospitality, with flowers, songs, and incense. Both the image and the time remain sanctified. But when Gaṇeśa's visit is over, usually within ten days, the worshiper symbolically closes the image's eyes by brushing them with the same kind of grass he used to enliven it. The breath is then said to leave the clay image, which is immersed in a nearby source of water and dissolves. In separating from each other, both breath and clay return to a state that is both formless and timeless; but through their interpenetration in the enlivened image, the ritual transformation of a material form has helped consecrate a particular time.

One of the most important media through which Hindus interact with a deity like Gaṇeśa is consecrated food. Devotees offer food to the god in hospitality and later eat what are then seen as the deity's leavings. Through eating the deity's leavings, the devotee partakes of his substance and his power. The idea that something of the deity's person inheres in these leavings derives from pervasive Hindu cultural presuppositions. For traditional Hindus see the world as a hierarchy of interpenetrating substances, and food, ingested in the body, is a potent medium for transmitting psychic substance between individuals. Thus, food prepared by people of low spiritual status is degrading to those above, food offered by brahmans and gurus can offer spiritual benefits, and food left over from the plate of the deity is likely to be the most powerful of all. Through contact with a higher being, food is consecrated naturally in Hindu eyes, sometimes without any special ritual at all. In Hindu tradition, communion with the deity through consecrated food takes place without mystery.

Giving Persons Divine Authority. Communion via the sharing of consecrated food in Roman Catholic tradition is deliberately identified as a mystery and requires a consecrator legitimately ordained in the church to be effective. Although the precise meaning of transubstantiation remains an issue of theological speculation, the rite effecting this transformation of bread and wine into the physical substance of Christ—a daily, worldwide occurrence—is fairly simple. The priest, reenacting the role of Jesus at the Last Supper, utters over the offerings a formula taken from the Gospels: "Take, eat; for this is my body." During the act of consecration, the priest is understood to represent Jesus, and for his act to be valid, he must be unambiguously acknowledged by hierarchs recognized as true successors to the apostles. Thus the consecrator himself needs to be consecrated. [*See* Ordination.]

While the rite conferring priesthood for a long time highlighted the priest's sacramental authority, it has always expressed his spiritual inheritance through apostolic succession. As an essential element of the ordination rite, the tradition of instruments—which distinctly expresses sacramental power—is known only from the twelfth century. In this tradition ordinands touch a chalice filled with wine and a paten containing bread (the "instruments") while the bishop utters a formula that bestows on the applicants the power to celebrate Mass. But the tradition of instruments was always accompanied by that of the laying on of hands, which dates from early Christian times, and is accompanied with prayer by a spiritual elder for the personal religious welfare of the ordinand. Now understood to be the only essential rite of ordination for bishops and deacons as well as for priests, the laying on of hands expresses the continuity of saving grace, from senior to junior, through the generations. From the consecration of a bishop as successor to the apostles of Jesus to the transformation of ordinary foodstuffs into the body of Christ, the rituals of consecration in Roman Catholic tradition make the power of a divine personage of the past present in today's world.

In premodern societies, the religious authority of the priest often exists in tension with that of a monarch, who may claim a divine status of his own. The Christian West has known a series of contests and accommodations between papal and royal power, which led in the early Middle Ages to the celebration of royal consecration as a sacrament of the church. God was understood to empower the king through the bishop, and the king, transformed, was given status in the clergy. In ancient India, on the other hand, though clergy performed the consecration of the king, his religious status was of a different order from theirs. From the beginning, rituals of royal consecration in India have closely resembled rituals performed for divinities. In fact the essential part of the ritual, the anointing—*abhiṣeka* in Sanskrit, literally "sprinkling"—seems to have been preeminently a royal ceremony that was later applied to the consecration of divine images. But more than the consecration of images, royal consecrations were also likely to have a visible social and political import. However deified he might sometimes appear, the king was also very much a man subject to the flux of worldly affairs, and his consecration was usually marked by prayers for his popularity, the prosperity of himself and his people, and the extent and stability of his dominion. To maintain all these potentially fleeting goods, the consecration of early Indian kings was ideally repeated annually, a custom that finds parallels in the royal New Year festivals of ancient Mesopotamia and the Chinese imperial sacrifice performed on the winter solstice. The brilliance of the ancient king's reign was usually in practical fact as well as religious belief closely linked to the welfare of his people, and both could use regular, visible signs of renewal.

Personal Consecrations and Renewal. The renewal and repetition of consecration becomes increasingly important in tradition to the extent that consecration is understood to be a human act and a personal one. In Indo-Tibetan Tantra, the consecration of a deity—referred to as *abhiṣeka,* like the royal anointing—expressly ties outer ritual to inward contemplation and is performed as a regular spiritual exercise. In some instances, moreover, the outer ritual may be dispensed with and only the inward consecration remain. As in Roman Catholic practice, the power to perform consecrations in most Buddhist traditions requires a legitimate source: initiations into both the powers of deities and the sanctity of monkhood need to come through a recognized lineage. But the established channels of sacramental authority in Catholicism and Buddhism are oriented in different directions. In the Roman rite, the power to consecrate is bestowed largely for the good of others, not for the personal benefit of the recipient, who as consecrator becomes a public instrument for the distribution of grace in the world. Once given, the power is supposed to be permanent; a force of its own working through the individual consecrator, it is not closely dependent on his spiritual state. In Buddhism, on the other hand, sacraments are more inwardly oriented: in Buddhist Tantra people perform regular consecrations largely for their own spiritual benefit; in Theravāda, the value of the monk for the community lies in his inner purity, and if this cannot be maintained it is thought best for all that he leave the order.

For people in ritual and devotional traditions everywhere, consecration in its most general sense can become a way of life. In the orthodoxies of Hinduism and Judaism all vital acts are ideally carried out according to divinely ordained precepts and are usually attended by ritual or prayers. In this way, rising, eating, sex, and even elimination become consecrated, that is, made part of the sacred world. For ardent devotees, consecration can mean surrender, a giving up of one's person and one's goods to the Lord. Through dedication, the Christian religious attempt to consecrate themselves fully to the service of God; Hindus following the path of the *Bhagavadgītā* give up the fruits of their works to Kṛṣṇa. Entailing an infinite succession of individual acts, consecration as a way of life demands perpetual vigilance, an acting out of the tension between divine absolutes and temporary realities that lies at the heart of consecration's religious meaning.

Conclusion. Deriving from Latin roots that connote an act of bringing particular things "together with" *(com)* the "sacred" *(sacrum)*, the very word *consecration* implies a dichotomy between what is sacred and what is profane. Marking this dichotomy, moreover, is an important aspect of consecratory acts in many religious traditions. But in cross-cultural perspective the concept of consecration also suggests other continuities in the religious thought and practice of diverse peoples. When accompanying the enshrinement of relics of the dead or the initiation of living persons into hallowed spiritual lineages, an act of consecration in the present maintains the efficacy of specific divine sources revealed in the past. The efficacy of the act may also demand a consecration of the consecrators themselves, whose ritual performance presents some of their most exalted religious potentials: while celebrating Mass, the priest already ordained in the church is seen to be most fully representative of Jesus; to enliven an image, the Hindu worshiper is identified with the primordial cosmic person. Finally, the difference between temporary and permanent consecration that emerges from a global perspective highlights the continuing religious problem people face in attempting to establish the divine in the material world: consecrations taken as permanent express the absoluteness of divine presence; those seen as temporary reveal the limits of human effort and the impermanence of material embodiments.

[*See also* Blessing.]

BIBLIOGRAPHY

Most ready material on consecration is to be found in works on specific traditions. Monastic ordinations and the concept of boundary in Theravāda Buddhism are approached through their classical sources by John Holt in *Discipline: The Canonical Buddhism of the Vinayapiṭaka* (New Delhi, 1983) and are examined in contemporary Thai tradition by S. J. Tambiah in *Buddhism and the Spirit Cults in North-east Thailand* (Cambridge, 1970). The meanings of enlivened images in different Hindu traditions are presented in *Gods of Flesh, Gods of Stone,* edited by Joanne Waghorne and Norman Cutler in association with Vasudha Narayan (Chambersburg, Pa., 1985). The work of Paul Courtright on the worship of Gaṇeśa, a description of whose consecration is condensed into an article for the last-mentioned volume, can be found in fuller form in his *Gaṇeśa: Lord of Obstacles, Lord of Beginnings* (New York, 1984). In *Ancient Indian Kingship from the Religious Point of View* (Leiden, 1966), Jan Gonda summarizes accounts of Indian royal consecrations found in divers Sanskrit sources. A detailed account of the rite described in the priestly Śrautasūtras with a valuable socioreligious interpretation is presented by Jan C. Heesterman in *The Ancient Indian Royal Consecration* (The Hague, 1957). On Tantric consecrations, see Alex Wayman's *The Buddhist Tantras* (New York, 1973) for insight into the relationship between ritual worship and contemplation.

A full treatment of ritual consecrations and their historic development in Roman Catholicism is given by Ludwig Eisenhofer and Joseph Lechner in *The Liturgy of the Roman Rite,* translated by A. J. Peeler and E. F. Peeler and edited by H. E. Winstone (Freiburg, 1961). The development and meaning of the Catholic priest's sacramental authority is concisely described by Joseph Lécuyer, C.S.SP., in *What Is a Priest?,* translated by P. J. Hepburne-Scott (New York, 1959). On the relationship between the divine authority of kings and hierarchs in western Europe, the classic account remains Gerd Tellenbach's *Church, State and Christian Society at the Time of the Investiture Contest,* translated by R. F. Bennett (New York, 1959).

DANIEL GOLD

CONSERVATIVE JUDAISM. Conservative Judaism is one of the major religious movements in modern Judaism. Founded in central Europe in the middle of the nineteenth century, it proved attractive, first in Europe and later in the Americas, to those who preferred a Jewish expression that avoided the extremes of ultraliberalism on the one hand and right-wing traditionalism on the other. By affirming the valid claim of Jewish tradition upon modern Jews, Conservative Judaism acquired the allegiance of many Jews who sought to remain psychologically and culturally loyal to their image of the relgion of their predecessors. In addition, by accepting the necessity of coming to grips with the new climate of modernity, the movement placed itself firmly on record as willing to mediate between the claims of the tradition on the one hand and the radically new circumstances of modern Jewish life on the other. In the process, it has required that both its leaders and its rank and file become vitally concerned and knowledgeable about the central values inherent both in the tradition and in modern culture. Today, its academic center and professional training school is the Jewish Theological Seminary of America in New York, and it has several branches around the world: the University of Judaism in Los Angeles, the American Student Center (Neve Schechter) in Jerusalem, and the Seminario Latinamericano in Buenos Aires.

Background and Institutional History. Conservative Judaism originated in the conviction that the earlier Reform Jewish movement had simply gone too far in its efforts to accommodate modern Judaism to the visible models of Christian church society. In 1845, at the (Reform) Rabbinical Conference in Frankfurt am Main, Zacharias Frankel grew concerned about the increasingly radical tenor of the discussions and finally decided that he could not agree with his Reform colleagues' decision that the Hebrew language was only an "advisable," not a "necessary," feature of Jewish worship. He withdrew from the meeting and issued a widely circularized public denunciation of the extremist departures from tradition that had been countenanced by the participants.

While Frankel did not see fit to launch a new movement, he did insist on periodically expounding his new theological approach to modern Judaism, which he named positive-historical Judaism. This approach accepted the "historical" dimension that had been so enthusiastically embraced by the Reformers, and which emphasized the evolutionary character of the change from generation to generation. It also insisted, however, that the "positive" dimensions of Jewish religion and ritual, the ones that offer continuity and recognizability, needed to be afforded greater emphasis than was being granted to them by the radical Reformers.

Frankel's approach to modern Judaism was widely propagated through his *Monatsschrift* journal and received a warm reception in many quarters in central and western European Jewish communities, particularly among scholars and communal leaders. It was not surprising, therefore, that when the first modern Jewish theological seminary was established in Wrocław (Breslau) in 1854, its founders turned to Zacharias Frankel to be its dean in preference to the other major candidate, Abraham Geiger, the leading Reform rabbi of the period. This school attracted some of the great nineteenth-century scholars, including Heinrich Graetz, Isaak Markus Jost, Moritz Steinschneider, and David Hoffmann, and through its graduates it became a powerful traditionalizing influence in central and western European Jewry throughout the nineteenth and twentieth centuries, until it was closed by the Nazis in 1938.

Origins in the United States. In the United States, Conservative Judaism was formally launched in 1886 with the founding of the Jewish Theological Seminary of America, eleven years after the establishment of the (Reform) Hebrew Union College in Cincinnati (1875). The new seminary was organized in direct reaction to the issuance of the Pittsburgh Platform by a representative group of Reform rabbis in 1885, which set forth their ideological commitment to a Judaism of morality and ethics, but one that was devoid of its national and ritual dimensions and that entertained only a God "idea," not a deep-rooted conviction in a "personal" God. In the ensuing reaction, a broad coalition of moderate Reform rabbis (Benjamin Szold, Frederick de Sola Mendes, and Marcus Jastrow) together with several traditionalist rabbis (Sabato Morais, Alexander Kohut, and Henry Pereira Mendes) joined together to establish the new seminary.

These founders of the new seminary had earlier sought to cooperate with the organizers of the Hebrew Union College until it became clear that the young institution had been turned essentially into a training school for Reform rabbis. In their efforts to maintain unity, the traditionalists had followed in the path of Isaac Leeser, the Philadelphia rabbi who had sought since the beginning of his ministry in 1827 to steer a moderate path between the ultraorthodox and the radical reformers. Leeser's mainstream thrusts were exemplified by his monthly publication *The Occident*, by his organization of the Board of Delegates of American Israelites, and by his founding of Maimonides College, the first rabbinical training school in America. Most of his innovations did not survive his death, in 1868, and left the field clear for the Reform leaders, led by Isaac Mayer Wise, as they established the Union of American Hebrew Congregations in 1873 and their Hebrew Union College two years later.

The Jewish Theological Seminary began its classes in 1886 in rooms provided by the Shearith Israel congregation in New York. It was largely staffed and funded by its founding volunteers during its early years and was led by its president, Sabato Morais of Philadelphia. Its initial broad constituency, however, did not long endure; the polarization of American Jewry between the German Jews, who inclined toward Reform, and the recent immigrants from eastern Europe, inclined toward Orthodoxy, made the new seminary's search for a moderate constituency an increasingly difficult task. By the time Sabato Morais died, in 1897, the prospects for the Conservative seminary's survival seemed increasingly dim.

Reorganization of the Jewish Theological Seminary. At that low point, a new and powerful coalition appeared on the seminary's horizon, possessing both the intellectual energy and the material resources necessary to reverse its decline. Organized by Cyrus Adler, librarian of the Smithsonian Institution, this strong cadre of cultured philanthropists included the renowned attorney Louis Marshall, the eminent banker Jacob Schiff, the judge Mayer Sulzberger, and industrialists like Adolph Lewisohn and Daniel and Simon Guggenheim. Adler successfully persuaded them that the Jewish Theological Seminary of America could become a powerful americanizing force for the thousands of Jews who were beginning to arrive from eastern Europe. Through respect for their traditions, it could provide a healthful synthesis of learning and observance, while drawing them into the modernist world ofnew ideas and open horizons. Above all, it could produce rabbis who would combine the wisdom of the Old World with the disciplines and skills of the New World and facilitate the generational transition from Yiddish-speaking immigrant to upstanding American citizen.

The key to the successful reorganization of the seminary in the minds of these philanthropists and community leaders was the appointment of a world-renowned Jewish scholar and personality to oversee the new institution, who could chart appropriate goals and methods for the accomplishment of their ambitious program. The person they sought was Solomon Schechter (1850–1915), then professor at Cambridge University, who had acquired international acclaim with his discovery of the long-lost literature of the Cairo Genizah (a depository for discarded Jewish books) and whose academic and communal pronouncements in England had attracted wide attention. It was expected that Schehter, a product of eastern European piety and learning coupled with western European academic accomplishments, would be able to communicate equally well with the new immigrants and the established Jewish populations in the United States.

After considerable negotiation, Schechter agreed to undertake the new challenge, and Adler, Schiff, and Marshall proceeded with the reorganization of the Jewish Theological Seminary, appropriating the main administrative positions. Schechter arrived in 1902 and as dean proceeded in systematic fashion to develop a curriculum, engage a faculty, establish a library, recruit students, and to implement the type of academic standards for the seminary to which he had become accustomed in the graduate schools with which he had been associated in England and the continent.

Schechter's initial efforts were widely hailed as important contributions to the strengthening of American Jewry, and indeed their influence has been of such long-lasting quality that until the 1970s the seminary was widely referred to as Schechter's seminary. By 1909–10, Schechter had become convinced that the mere excellence of his institution's academic programs was not sufficient to acquire and retain the type of lay support that would be necessary to continue the intellectual and spiritual breakthroughs that would be required to redirect American Jewry. This was particularly so since the organized Reform and Orthodox movements were becoming increasingly defensive and even hostile toward his seminary and its program. He therefore spearheaded the establishment of a consortium of congregations that could lay the framework for a national organization in support of the seminary. After considerable negotiation, the United Synagogue of America was organized in 1913, with Schechter as its first president, and it began pioneering the establishment of organizations and programs that eventually coalesced into the Conservative movement.

Launching the new organization was not an easy task. Many of the ideological issues that would later beset the Conservative movement were discussed emotionally at the founding meeting. Schechter, Adler, and some of their foremost colleagues on the faculty of the seminary preferred to view the new organization as an "Orthodox-Conservative Union" whose major mandate would be to stem the persistent tide toward Reform Judaism. The younger leaders, who were alumni of the seminary, including Mordecai Kaplan, Jacob Kohn, and Herman H. Rubenovitz, tended to prefer a clearly defined "Conservative" federation of congregations. A smaller, fringe group, led by Judah Magnes, insisted that the new organization proclaim itself as a new, third denomination in Jewish life, distinct from Orthodox and Reform. Eventually the alumni position would prevail, but at the founding meeting a temporizing compromise was struck, and the title of the new organization was voted as the United Synagogue of America, modeled on the British organization, whose chief rabbi, Joseph Hertz, was a seminary alumnus and took part in the proceedings.

Upon Schechter's death in 1915, Cyrus Adler succeeded him as president of both the seminary and the United Synagogue of America until his death, in 1940. This era was characterized by the progressive strengthening of the seminary and its affiliated arms, the United Synagogue and the Rabbinical Assembly, and by the establishment of such significant organizations as the Women's League for Conservative Judaism and the National Federation of Jewish Men's Clubs.

Growth of the movement. Adler's successor in 1940 as titular head of the Conservative movement was Louis

Finkelstein, a seminary alumnus who had studied under Schechter and had become a mainstay of the seminary faculty and administration during the Adler era. Finkelstein almost immediately launched a broad-based expansion of the seminary's programs during the wartime and postwar periods, an expansion that was carried forward with vision, energy, effectiveness, and a large measure of success. These efforts coincided with several important developments in the maturation of the American Jewish community, all of which combined to produce a heightened readinenss for the "message" that was being advanced by the seminary. The proliferating suburban congregations in the major metropolitan areas were all seeking a new meaningful structural identity; the virtual disappearance of Europe as a reservoir of new Jewish leadership and ideas compelled the emerging American Jewish leadership to accept far more responsibility; the returning war veterans felt far more at home in America than had their parents, and were better prepared emotionally to experiment and build the types of institutions that would more fully meet their needs. The changing American Jewish community of those traumatic years seemed to be ready for exactly the type of organizational outreach that was coming from the seminary leadership.

The Finkelstein era (1940-1972) was characterized by enormous growth in the number of congregations affiliated with Conservative Judaism, a sharp escalation in the number of programs offered by the institutions of the movement, and greater recognition of the responsibilities that devolved upon the movement in view of its newfound preeminence in American and world Jewish affairs. Having grown from about 200 affiliated congregations in 1940 to some 830 congregations by 1965, the movement had become the largest federation of synagogues in the Diaspora.

To respond properly to its enormously enlarged responsibilities, the Conservative movement proceeded to establish the types of agencies that would seek to adequately serve its new constituency. In 1940 the National Academy for Adult Jewish Studies was founded; in 1947 the first in the network of Ramah summer camps was established; in 1951 the United Synagogue Youth movement was organized; in 1956 the first Solomon Schechter Day School was launched; in 1958 the American Student Center in Jerusalem (Neve Schechter) was dedicated and in 1959 the World Council of Synagogues was initially convened and the Seminario Latinamericano was opened in Buenos Aires.

The phenomenal growth of Conservative Judaism tapered off in the mid-1960s. By then the movement had established a full network of professional and lay organizations designed to enhance its local, national, and international functioning. Its California branch, the University of Judaism, had become a major force in the growth of West Coast Jewry. The Mesorati ("traditional," i.e., Conservative) movement was launched to establish Conservative congregations in Israel. The Cantors Institute, the Teachers Institute, and the seminary's various graduate schools were seeking to meet the perennial shortage of qualified Jewish professionals. The burgeoning Association for Jewish Studies, serving the academic community, was heavily populated by scholars trained in the Conservative Jewish institutions. Prayer books for the Sabbath, festivals, High Holy Days, and weekday services had been published by the United Synagogue and the Rabbinical Assembly. While not departing radically from the form and substance of the traditional prayer books, these "official" publications of the Conservative movement made several highly symbolic changes. They eliminated references to the future restoration of the sacrificial system, sought to inject a more gender-egalitarian tone into the prayers, and eliminated what were seen as anti-gentile passages.

In 1972 Finkelstein announced his retirement. His successor, Gerson D. Cohen, also a seminary alumnus, had served with distinction as a professor of Jewish history at Columbia University and at the seminary. He became chancellor of an institution that was now in the forefront of American Jewish institutional life and titular head of the largest of the Jewish religious movements. The agenda for the new administration included resolving some of the lingering ideological issues that had been brushed aside during the rapid expansion period of Conservative Judaism, consolidating the many activities of the movement, and addressing the capital improvement projects that had become increasingly imperative as the movement had grown.

During the chancellorship of Gerson Cohen (1972–1986), therefore, the attention of the Conservative movement was drawn to the intensified decision making that took place in the Committee on Jewish Law and Standards (on matters involving marriage and divorce, women's right, Sabbath and festival observances, etc.); to the enhancement of relationships between the seminary and its partners in the movement, the Rabbinical Assembly and the United Synagogue, and its associated groups, such as the Women's League for Conservative Judaism, the Educators Assembly, and the Cantors Assembly; and, most strikingly, to the mammoth undertaking of completing the seminary's physical facilities, with the building of its new Boesky Library, which was dedicated in 1983.

A major accomplishment of this period was the expansion of the Conservative movement in Israel. By 1985 there were some forty Mesorati congregations in

Israel, up from the two or three that had been functioning two decades earlier. An additonal highlight was the major decision, laboriously arrived at, to admit women into the seminary's rabbinical school. In 1984, women were admitted for the first time, and in 1985 the seminary ordained its first female rabbi, Amy Eilberg, a woman who previously had achieved considerable advanced credit and training before being admitted.

The election of Ismar Schorsch, then a professor of Jewish history at the seminary, to succeed seminary chancellor Gerson D. Cohen in July 1986, followed a year-long search process and marked the beginning of a new period in the development of the Conservative movement and its central institution. The announced perception of both the search committee and the new chancellor was that the new era was to begin with a period of mending rifts and healing organizational wounds. At this time it was hoped that the women's issue and the related strains in the interpretation of Jewish law would be resolved in a more consiliatory vein, allowing the movement to unite more fully in pursuit of its central mandates.

Major Organizations. Over the course of the century, the Conservative movement spread from the Jewish Theological Seminary of America into a web of religious and social institutions which are herewith described.

The United Synagogue of America. Founded by Solomon Schechter in 1913, the United Synagogue is the national association of Conservative congregations, responsible for the coordination of activities and services of the Conservative movement on behalf of its constituent congregations. Divisions of the the United Synagogue created for this purpose include some of the most important bodics of thc movcmcnt. The Commission on Jewish Education provides for the publication of textbooks, in-service training of educators, guidance on educational policies, and mobilization of the resources of the movement on behalf of afternoon schools and the Solomon Schechter Day Schools. The Department of Youth Activities oversees the development of the broad programs of the United Synagogue Youth movement (USY) with its regional and local chapters, as well as its summer and year-round activities in Israel. The National Academy for Adult Jewish Studies seeks to stimulate the entire movement to intensify its programs in the area of adult Jewish education. The Israel Affairs Committee plans projects to place the Israel dimension more actively on the agenda of the United Synagogue affiliates via periodic news alerts to its constituent congregations and by promoting the organizational development of MERCAZ, the Conservative Zionist membership movement within the World Zionist Organization. In addition, the United Synagogue coordinantes the activities of several professional organizations and their placement services—the Educators Assembly, the Cantors Assembly, and the National Federation of Synagogue Administrators.

The Rabbinical Assembly. The Rabbinical Assembly (RA) is the organization of Conservative rabbis and has a membership of over eleven hundred rabbis. The Rabbinical Assembly has historically served as the religious policy-making body in the Conservative movement; its Committee on Jewish Law and Standards (CJLS) has been recognized as the authoritative forum for the development of Jewish legal precedents for the movement. Its placement director serves as the chief administrator of the Joint Placement Commission for the referral of rabbinical candidates to individual congregations. It has become a major publisher of the liturgical texts used in religious services in Conservative congregations. The annual *Proceedings* of its conventions provide important source material for the historical, ideological, and organizational developments in Conservative Judaism. Its quarterly journal, *Conservative Judaism*, provides a popular and literary forum for the exchange of ideas, innovations, and creative writing.

The Women's League for Conservative Judaism. More than eight hundred synagogue sisterhoods are affiliated with the Conservative movement through the coordinating body of the Women's League. Founded by Mathilde Schechter in 1918, the Women's League has historically proven to be one of the pioneering organizations in Conservative Judaism in the development of social, educational, and philanthropic programs for the entire movement. In addition, the Women's League spearheaded the expansion of the seminary's facilities and the building of the Mathilde Schechter student dormitory, and it continues to provide important support to the seminary's programs through its annual Torah Fund drives.

The National Federation of Jewish Men's Clubs. The four hundred men's clubs affiliated with the Conservative movement plan joint ventures for the advancement of Conservative Judaism. The National Federation of Jewish Men's Clubs is particularly active in the areas of social action, youth activities, and Israeli affairs.

The World Council of Synagogues. The international arm of the Conservative movement, the World Council of Synagogues was established in 1959 to assist in bringing the message of Conservative Judaism to the attention of world Jewry outside the borders of North America. It maintains offices in Jerusalem, Buenos Aires, and New York and meets in convention every two years in Jerusalem.

Conceptual Components of the Movement. Throughout its relatively brief history, the leadership and members of the movement have striven to understand and define the role of Conservative Judaism in its increasingly important place in the Jewish organizational world. A close analysis of the ideological stands taken by its major cultural leaders generally reveals the central concepts that have served to unify the rank and file of the movement's propounders, both in Western Europe and now in the United States, and can therefore be considered central to Conservative Judaism.

Positive-historical Judaism. The philosophical approach of Zacharias Frankel, described above, became the rallying cry of the nascent Conservative movement. As Frankel explained it, and as it was later interpreted by Solomon Schechter, modern Judaism did indeed require an appreciation of the "historical" dimension, which accounted for evolution and changeability in Jewish life, as insisted upon by the Reform leaders. However, what the Reform movement did not adequately appreciate, he felt, was the fact that Judaism's integrity and survival required an enduring commitment to the "positive" dimension—the ritual commandments, personal observances, and communal structures—that had characterized all ages of Jewish history.

How this "positive-historical" balance was to be struck, and just who would be empowered to make the necessary adaptations, was a subject addressed a generation later by Solomon Schechter, writing first in England and then in the United States. In his introduction to *Studies in Judaism: First Series* (rev. ed., Philadelphia, 1945), Schechter speaks of *Catholic Israel,* the collective spirit and body of the Jewish people throughout the world that evolutionarily decides which aspects of the tradition are worthy of perpetuation and which can be safely discarded. More recently, both Conservative leaders and their opponents have noted that contemporary world Jewry is far less observant than the Jewry of Schechter's day and warn that "catholic Israel" is a concept that today would support radical Reform hypotheses. The response of Conservative leaders has been that it is not the general community but rather that of the observant and the learned that comprises the policy-making and guidance-offering body of "catholic Israel" and its evolutionary dimension.

Zionism. Zionism was embraced as a major component of the Conservative Jewish ideology at an early stage of its development. As a result of the encouragement of Solomon Schechter, several of his most active associates (among them Israel Friedlander, Mordecai Kaplan, Henrietta Szold, and Judah Magnes) became pioneers in the development of American Zionism. Ideologically, the founders of the Conservative movement found themselves deeply moved by the Zionism inherent in the Bible and prayer book and not overly affected by the hostility toward secular nationalism that pervaded the religious thinking of both the Reform and Orthodox leadership of the nineteenth and early twentieth centuries. Historically, American Zionists have been able to count upon Conservative Judaism as their most reliable ally in building the strength of their movement.

Revelation. Along with its corollary, the authority of the *halakhah* (Jewish law), revelation has been one of the central ideological issues in the evolution of Conservative Judaism. As a coalition movement of traditionalists and liberals, Conservative Judaism has swung pendulum-fashion, cyclically, in its several generations of existence. Traditionalists, such as Louis Finkelstein, Cyrus Adler, and Abraham Joshua Heschel, have tended to emphasize the literal aspects of the covenant of Sinai and the consequent obligation upon Jews to adhere closely to the classic formulations of Jewish law. Liberals, such as Mordecai Kaplan, Robert Gordis, and Gerson D. Cohen, have stipulated that revelation was more of an evolutionary process and that the evidence of adaptations in tradition and *halakhah* throughout the centuries is sufficient to allow responsibly continued adjustments and innovations. Consequences of this ongoing debate have been the departure of the ultraliberal wing of the movement in 1966 to establish the Reconstructionist Rabbinical College and the debates within the CJLS on issues such as *kashrut,* marriage and divorce, conversion and intermarriage, Sabbath and festival observances, and, most recently, the rights of women.

Religious education. Jewish culture has been spread through education in Hebrew, Jewish history, and religious and literary texts has been at the center of the program of the Conservative movement since its inception. Solomon Schechter founded the Teachers Institute in 1909 and chose Mordecai Kaplan to develop its program, faculty, and horizons. The Rabbinical Assembly has repeatedly convened major conferences to intensify the educational offerings of the Conservative movement, with large measures of success. The United Synagogue has in recent decades been the prime mover in educational advances through its high priority Commission on Jewish Education. The Ramah camps have become one of the most remarkable achievements of the Conservative movement; thousands of elementary and high-school students have savored the educational, recreational, and inspirational atmosphere of these remarkable summer camps. For the past twenty years, a great deal of the movement's educational energy and resources have been invested in the development of the Solomon Schechter Day Schools, with gratifying results both in numbers and in quality education. Educational philosophy, methodology, and textual materials have been among the major mandates of the Melton Research Program in Jewish Education of the Teachers Institute.

Issues and Debates within the Conservative Movement. From its very inception, the Conservative movement has been comprised of a broad coalition of liberal, moderate, and traditional Jewish constituencies. The Rabbinical Assembly until the 1960s routinely alternated its presidential nominations, traditionalist succeeding a liberal and a liberal succeeding a traditionalist; it thus recognized *de facto* its committment to safeguarding the prerogatives of both elements of the movement. It gradually became clear to the centrists that they had been left out of the rotation, and they felt that the movement had become paralyzed by the concessions granted regularly to the right and the left. They thereupon demanded, and received, the right to high office that their preponderant numbers warranted. With their accession, the mood of the Rabbinical Assembly began to change noticeably.

Halakhic revision. The Rabbinical Assembly's Committee on Jewish Law and Standards is generally recognized as the movement's governing body on matters of ritual decision-making. As a result, it has been the focus of some of the major policy controversies that have arisen within the leadership of the movement during the latter half of the twentieth century. Despite considerable frustration and soul-searching, the committee stayed within the limits acceptable to the traditionalists during the 1930s and 1940s, and only in 1950 did it cross the so-called "Halakhic Rubicon," by declaring it acceptable (by majority decision) to drive to the synagogue on the Sabbath, and similarly, to use electricity on the Sabbath.

These symbolically significant decisions were followed by a period of relative quiescence on the part of the CJLS while it negotiated intensively with the seminary Talmud faculty on matters affecting marital and divorce procedure. By 1967, however, under the leadership of its chairman Benjamin Kreitman, it initiated several far-reaching modifications of Jewish ritual practice. The committee approved (religious) court-ordered annulment of marriages in cases where civilly-divorced spouses refused to grant the *geṭ* (divorce document) necessary for religious remarriage. It further liberalized several laws of *kashrut* and granted to congregations the option of eliminating the second day of the three pilgrimage festivals, Sukkot, Passover, and Shavu'ot. The procedural questions raised by these halakhic questions and revisions brought a revamping of the committee's internal regulations in 1970 to keep the Rabbinical Assembly responsive to the new largely centrist thrust. Whether these rabbinical decisions play any decisive role in the daily life and decision-making activities of the Conservative membership and laity remains an open question.

Women's rights. The newly reorganized committee became preoccupied in the 1970s with the unavoidable issue of women's rights. Although in 1955 the committee had approved the right of women to receive *'aliyyot* (the honor of ascending to the pulpit to read from the Torah) its approval had largely been overlooked. It now reaffirmed this right and in 1974 voted to give women the right to be counted toward a *minyan* (religious quorum of ten). The issue of admitting women into the rabbinical program at the seminary was now raised with more frequency and pressure, especially since the Reform and Reconstructionist movements had been ordaining women regularly since the early 1970s. After the seminary faculty, upon the repeated urging of the chancellor, Gerson Cohen, finally agreed in 1984 to accept female students, the Rabbinical Assembly voted to accept its first woman into membership in 1985. It remains to be seen, of course, whether this constitutional acceptance will be accompanied in the near future by a functional and social acceptance of women into the ranks of recognized candidates for major congregational appointments. There remain, in addition, lingering religious issues that have not as yet been resolved, such as the right of women to serve as judges on *batei din* (religious courts), or to serve as witnesses for religious documents, or to serve as *sheliḥei tsibbur*, the congregational leaders who represent the community in worship.

Communal-congregational tensions. The model of the Conservative congregation that evolved during the rise of the movement was that of the "institutional synagogue." The congregation was to undertake any and all functions that were useful in educating Jews, facilitating worship, fostering Jewish sociability, encouraging interfaith activities, promoting youth activities, and so forth. In short, the synagogue, by definition, was to become the central institution in the Jewish community. This mandate, when exercised to its fullest extent, made inevitable a broad variety of tensions between its existing agencies and institutions in the Jewish community. Synagogues became embroiled in "jurisdictional" disputes with groups such as Jewish community centers, communal Hebrew schools, Jewish federations, and Jewish community relations councils. These tensions are more frequently encountered by Conservative congregations than by their Orthodox and Reform counterparts, since the former rarely venture beyond ritual and education, and the latter concentrate most often on social action and liturgical innovation.

The Future of the Movement. Sociological trends seem to indicate that the Conservative movement will not long continue to enjoy the numerical preeminence that it has experienced during the past two decades. Surveys taken by various communities as well as the National Jewish Population Study indicate that the percentage of Jews who identify themselves as Conservative, while still high, has been decreasing for some time. Gerson Cohen suggested in a 1977 address entitled "The Present State of Conservative Judaism" that "what is immediately required, therefore, is a strong emphasis on mass learning within our movement, so that the canard that only Conservative rabbis identify with the principle of 'tradition and change' can finally be put to rest" (*Judaism: A Quarterly* 26, no. 3, Summer 1977: p. 272).

An address entitled "Unity in Diversity" given by Mordecai Kaplan to a United Synagogue convention in the 1950s caught the imagination of its audience. It seemed to capture the essence of the appeal of the Conservative movement to its broad constituency. Conservative Judaism offered modernity to the American born generations seeking to establish themselves in the new suburbs surrounding America's cities in the postwar era; and it offered the flavor of tradition to those whose roots in the Old World, or ties to traditional parents and grandparents, remained of strong concern. Making few demands and simulating an "all things to all men" approach, the movement grew rapidly in the 1950s and 1960s. By the 1970s not only had the Orthodox experienced an upsurge in popularity, but the Reform had begun to introduce far larger measures of traditional material into their liturgical and educational programs. The situation in the 1970s was reminiscent of the haunting analysis made by Israel Goldstein to his colleagues in the Rabbinical Assembly at their 1927 convention: "As Orthodoxy becomes more and more de-ghettoized and Reform becomes more and more Conservatized, what will be left for the Conservative Jew to do? How will he be distinguished from the other two? With both his wings substantially clipped he will surely be in a precarious position" *(Proceedings of the Rabbinical Assembly of America,* 1927, p.35*)*. In the meanwhile, Jews continue to flock to the educational and cultural programs sponsored by the movement, the quality of academia at the seminary and related institutions remains impressive, and both men and women are eagerly entering the Conservative rabbinate.

[*Related entries include* Jewish Thought and Philosophy, *article on* Modern Thought; Judaism, *article on* Judaism in the Western Hemisphere; Zionism; *the biographies of Frankel, Heschel, Kaplan, Schechter, and Szold; and* Reconstructionist Judaism; Reform Judaism; *and* Orthodox Judaism.]

BIBLIOGRAPHY

The standard works on the origins of the Conservative movement are Moshe Davis's *The Emergence of Conservative Judaism* (Philadelphia, 1963), Herbert Parzen's *Architects of Conservative Judaism* (New York, 1964), and my own *Conservative Judaism: A Contemporary History* (New York, 1983). The definitive sociological study of the movement is Marshall Sklare's revised and augmented *Conservative Judaism: An American Religious Movement* (New York, 1972). Conservative views of Jewish tradition can be found in *Tradition and Change* (New York, 1958), an anthology of essays by leading Conservatives edited by Mordecai Waxman, and in a special issue of the magazine *Judaism* 26 (Summer 1977). Conservative approaches to Jewish law are intensively described in Isaac Klein's *A Guide to Jewish Religious Practice* (New York, 1979) and in *Conservative Judaism and Jewish Law,* edited by Seymour Siegel (New York, 1977). Journals published by various arms of the Conservative movement include the following: *Conservative Judaism* (New York, 1945–), published quarterly by the Rabbinical Assembly; *The Outlook* (New York, 1930–), published quarterly by the Women's League for Conservative Judaism: the *Torchlight* (first published as *The Torch* in 1941, renamed in 1977), published quarterly by the National Federation of Jewish Men's Clubs; *The United Synagogue Review* (New York, 1945–), published quarterly by the United Synagogue of America; and *Proceedings of the Rabbinical Assembly* (New York, 1927–), published annually.

Important aspects of Conservative ideology are explored in Simon Greenberg's *A Jewish Philosophy and Pattern of Life* (New York, 1981) and in Elliot N. Dorff's *Conservative Judaism: Our Ancestors to Our Descendants* (New York, 1977). In addition, shorter treatments of Conservative Judaism have been written by Robert Gordis, Simon Greenberg, and Abraham Karp, and there are important chapters on the Conservative movement in large works by Joseph Blau, Arthur Hertzberg, Mordecai Kaplan, Gilbert Rosenthal, and David Rudavsky, among others.

HERBERT ROSENBLUM

CONSTANTINE (272/273–337), known as Constantine the Great, Roman emperor and agent of the christianization of the Roman empire. Born at Naissus, the only son of Helena and Flavius Constantius, Constantine was assured a prominent role in Roman politics when Diocletian, the senior emperor in the Tetrarchy, appointed his father Caesar in 293. Educated in the imperial court at Nicomedia, and permitted to accompany the eastern emperors on provincial tours and military campaigns, he doubtless expected to succeed to his father's position when Diocletian and Maximian abdicated in 305. But Galerius, who may have contrived the abdication and as the new eastern emperor controlled the succession, ignored Constantine—and Maxentius, the son of Maximian—and instead nominated as Caesars his own nephew and the praetorian prefect Severus. Constantine could not challenge this decision immediately, but when his father died at York in July 306, he reasserted the claim, this time backed by the British and Gallic armies, and requested confirmation from the eastern emperor. Galerius resisted, preferring Severus as Constantius's successor, but to avoid a confrontation offered Constantine the lesser rank of Caesar. When Maxentius rebelled at Rome in October 306, however, he refused to grant a similar concession, and for the next seven years civil war disrupted the western half of the empire.

In the end it was Constantine who dislodged the resilient Maxentius from Rome, defeating his army at the Milvian Bridge on 28 October 312. For Lactantius and Eusebius of Caesarea, Christian observers who produced accounts of the event a few years later, this was more than a political triumph. On the eve of the battle, they insisted, Constantine had experienced the vision (or visions) that inspired his conversion to Christianity. Constantine's motives are beyond reconstruction, but it is clear that he believed the victory had been won with divine assistance. Even the inscription on the triumphal arch in Rome erected by the Senate in 315 to mark the event attributed his success to the "prompting of a deity." If the language is ambiguous, perhaps in deference to the sentiments of the pagan majority, Constantine's legislation and activities after 312 attest the evolution of his Christian sympathies.

Whether the "conversion" represented a dramatic break with the pagan past is more problematic. Constantine had never been a persecutor; indeed, in 306 he had ordered the restoration of property in Britain and Gaul that had been confiscated from Christians during the Great Persecution (303–305). Unlike Galerius, who had vigorously persecuted Christians in the East, Constantine was a tolerant pagan, content with the accumulation of heavenly patrons (Sol Invictus, Apollo). In 312 he may well have considered the God of the Christians simply another heavenly patron, demonstrably more powerful than others but not necessarily incompatible. Though he refused to participate after 312 in distinctly pagan ceremonies, Constantine retained the title *pontifex maximus* and evidently did not find the demands of government and religion irreconcilable. Exclusive commitment and a sense of mission, however, would develop over time. Early on he expressed his gratitude and allegiance through special exemptions and benefactions; after 324 he did not hesitate to use his office to condemn pagan beliefs and practices and to promote the christianization of the empire.

Politics accounts in large measure for Constantine's transformation from benefactor to advocate. The conversion did not alienate pagans, for religion had not been an issue in the civil war, and nothing indicates that Licinius, whom Galerius had chosen as co-emperor in 308, objected to Constantine's evident Christian sympathies in 312. At Milan the following year, in fact, the two survivors joined in the publication of Galerius's edict of toleration, drafted just before his death in 311, and ordered the restoration of Christian property in the East. As political rivalry developed over the next few years, however, the religious policies of the emperors diverged, especially after the inconclusive civil war of 316/7. Politics and religion became so entangled that Constantine, using attacks on Christians in the East as pretext, could declare his campaign against Licinius in 324 a crusade against paganism. His victory at Chrysopolis (18 September) simultaneously removed the last challenge to his authority and legitimized his emerging sense of mission.

Denunciations of pagan practices followed immediately, coupled with lavish grants for the construction of churches and preferential treatment of Christian candidates for administrative posts. Constantine also took the lead in efforts to restore order in an increasingly divided church. The Council of Nicaea (325), which three hundred bishops attended, was not his first attempt at ecclesiastical arbitration. A decade earlier he had summoned fractious North African bishops to a council at Arles (314) to decide a disputed election in Carthage and to rule on the orthodoxy of the Numidian bishop Donatus. The latter was condemned, but his partisans (Donatists) continued for the remainder of Constantine's reign to resist the council's decision. The prospects for settlement in 325 were bleaker still. The nature of Christ, not simply a disputed election or the propriety of rebaptism, was the question at issue. Arius, a presbyter of Alexandria in Egypt, had repeatedly argued that Christ was a created being, a view that seemed to deny his divinity. The bishops assembled in Nicaea (Bithynia), responding to the counterarguments of Alexander (bishop of Alexandria) and others, condemned Arianism and adopted a creed (the Nicene Creed) that declared the Father and Son to be of the same essence. This language satisfied the majority in attendance, but it did not silence Arians. By midcentury, in fact, the Arian position, not the Nicene, had been accepted by most of the eastern churches represented at Nicaea and by the successors of Constantine.

Pagans, of course, would not have found much to applaud in all this; their prosperity was determined by Constantine's handling of everyday affairs, not by his performance in church councils. Victories over the northern barbarians, reform of the coinage, rationalization of the bureaucracy—these were the issues that shaped their sense of well-being. That the emperor, especially during the last decade of his reign, was attentive to these concerns is clear, so much so that he can be credited with the refinement and implementation of the reforms introduced by his pagan predecessors. And yet, it is his Christianity that sets him apart. His reputation rests on his skillful manipulation of Christian symbols—the Milvian Bridge, the Council of Nicaea, the foundation of Constantinople (the "second Rome" that served as the principal capital after its dedication in 330). He was both the new Augustus and the thirteenth apostle, the pagan emperor who, after his encounter with the God of the Christians, adopted as his personal mission the christianization of the empire. In pursuit of this objective, he had created by his death in 337 a Christian Roman empire that would endure for a thousand years.

BIBLIOGRAPHY

Barnes, Timothy D. *Constantine and Eusebius.* Cambridge, Mass., 1981.

Barnes, Timothy D. *The New Empire of Diocletian and Constantine.* Cambridge, Mass., 1982.

Dörries, Hermann. *Constantine the Great.* Translated by Roland H. Bainton. New York, 1972.

Jones, A. H. M. *Constantine and the Conversion of Europe.* Rev. ed. New York, 1962.

Momigliano, Arnaldo, ed. *The Conflict between Paganism and Christianity in the Fourth Century.* Oxford, 1963.

JOHN W. EADIE

CONSTANTINIANISM is a policy establishing a particular Christian church as the religion of the state, also known as Caesaropapism. Formulated originally by the Roman emperor Constantine I, the Great (d. 337), it was continued in the Byzantine empire (until 1453), the Frankish kingdom, the Holy Roman Empire (962–1806), and numerous states of Europe, being modified in most states since the Protestant Reformation but persisting in some even today. According to this policy, state and church should form a close alliance so as to achieve mutual objectives. [*See also the biography of Constantine.*]

Constantinianism Conceived. Following his "conversion" in 312, Constantine proceeded by stages to establish Christianity as the sole religion of the empire. From 312 to 320 he tolerated paganism but he elevated the standing of Christianity with increasing vigor. From 320 to 330 he thrust the organization of the church into the foreground and directed a frontal attack on polytheism. From 330 to 337, after moving the capital from Rome to Byzantium, he waged an open war on the old religion.

Constantine, whatever the exact nature of his conversion, believed that the supreme God whom Christians worshiped had given him the victory at the Milvian Bridge and dominion over the empire. He hoped that by doing God's will he would obtain further prosperity for himself and his subjects and feared that if he offended God he would be cast down from power and pull the empire down with him. In a letter to an official charged with responsibility for healing the Donatist schism, the emperor confessed he would feel secure "only when I see all venerating the most holy God in the proper cult of the catholic religion with harmonious brotherhood of worship." This concern for right worship prompted him to seek not merely the establishment of Christianity but the conservation of a united and orthodox Christianity. Bitterly offended by division among Christians, he felt duty-bound to impose unity, first in the Donatist controversy and then in the Arian. To resolve the latter, he summoned a universal council representing the whole church to meet at Nicaea, and presided over it himself. In an opening address he deplored the internecine strife in the church as a disaster greater than war or invasion. During the crucial part of the debate, he himself chaired and took an active part in guiding the proceedings. He used his imperial presence to secure an inclusive formula with which all except ardent Arians could agree, proposing the phrase "of one essence" *(homoousios)* to express the Son's relation to the Father. [*See also* Donatism *and* Arianism.]

Though Constantine's peacemaking efforts within the church turned out rather badly both for his and later generations, he put in motion a program that would eventually secure the triumph of Christianity over its competitors. When his co-emperor Licinius turned sour toward Christianity and backed away from the tolerance guaranteed by the Edict of Milan (313), Constantine initiated against him a virtual crusade culminating in his defeat and death in 324. Thenceforth, as Constantine once remarked in a speech to bishops he was entertaining, he considered himself "a bishop established by God of those outside [the church]." He thought of himself, too, as a "thirteenth apostle." If he did not undertake to promote missionary work outside the empire, he did so within its boundaries. He grew increasingly impatient with the unwillingness of his subjects to accept the Christian faith until finally, in 330, exasperated with the tenacious grip of paganism on old Rome, he established a new Christian capital at Byzantium. Thereafter he held back nothing, razing and looting temples and lavishing public monies on the churches, forcing pagans to return property confiscated from Christians under Licinius, building churches of great splendor in important cities, and enticing soldiers and public officials with lavish favors. His successors, Julian (361–363) excepted, followed suit, and by the time of Justinian (527–565), intolerance toward non-Christians had become a public virtue.

Constantinianism Controverted. Constantinianism was never seriously contested in the Byzantine empire, but it has been in other nations, especially in the West. The so-called Donation of Constantine, a spurious document composed between 752 and 778 in the Carolingian (Frankish) kingdom, inaugurated a long history of debate over relations between church and state with strong advocacy of the superiority of popes to princes by grant of Constantine himself. Charlemagne, king of the Franks from 778 to 814, and his successors operated on the Constantinian model, aiding the church in its evangelism but using it to achieve royal aims and freely interfering in ecclesiastical affairs. Their practice of lay investiture, secular rulers handing symbols of office to the clergy at their installation, however, touched off a fierce battle with the papacy on which compromise was not achieved until 1122. Subsequently, Innocent III during his years as pope (1198–1216) stood Constantinianism on its head by liberal interference in matters of state in the Holy Roman Empire and virtually every nation in Europe. [*See also the biography of Innocent III.*]

The strongest objections to Constantinianism, however, have been voiced by sects that have suffered from its emphasis on uniformity. The ancient Donatists, ruing their request for imperial involvement in ecclesiastical disputes, soon advocated separation of church and state. So too did some medieval sects. The most persistent and consistent voice against Constantinianism, however, has come from the so-called free churches that emerged at the time of the Protestant Reformation in the sixteenth century and after. Many of these, especially Anabaptists and Baptists, have denounced the alliance of church and state that Constantine effected as a "fall" of the church, resulting not only in religious intolerance and persecution but also in an adulteration of Christianity. According to a Hutterite chronicle, this well-intended alliance is how "the disease of craftiness, which creeps about in darkness, and the corruption which perverted at high noon, [was] introduced by violence" and "the Cross was conquered and forged to the sword." In opposition to Constantinianism, the free churches espoused voluntary association in congregations and separation of church and state. "Gathered churches" composed of "regenerate members," and not the state or its magistrates, would, by this plan, exercise discipline in doctrine and behavior over their constituents. Although government has a legitimate role to play, the free churches further stated, it should restrict its activities to the civil realm and leave religion to the churches. God alone is Lord over the human conscience in religious matters.

[*See also* Church and State; Reformation; Anabaptism; *and* Heresy, *article on* Christian Concepts.]

BIBLIOGRAPHY

Constantine's Christian intentions have been the subject of many recent books. Most helpful in interpreting his policy are Andrew Alföldi's *The Conversion of Constantine and Pagan Rome,* translated by Harold Mattingly (Oxford, 1948), and A. H. M. Jones's *Constantine and the Conversion of Europe* (London, 1948). A critical assessment of Constantinianism can be found in Hermann Dörries's *Constantine and Religious Liberty,* translated by Roland H. Bainton (New Haven, 1960).

E. Glenn Hinson

CONSTITUTION OF THE UNITED STATES. *For discussion of First Amendment issues, see* Law and Religion, *article on* Religion and the United States Constitution.

CONTARINI, GASPARO (1483–1542), Venetian statesman, author of philosophical and theological works, proponent of Roman Catholic church reform, and cardinal. Born in Venice on 16 October 1483, he died in Bologna on 24 August 1542. Belonging to an ancient patrician clan, Contarini received a solid education first in Venice and then, from 1501 to 1509, at the University of Padua, where he studied philosophy, mathematics, and theology. In 1511, during a period of inner turmoil and search for personal vocation, he arrived at the conviction that humankind is justified before God by faith, not works. This belief, similar to Martin Luther's, later enabled him to deal sympathetically with Protestantism.

His career in the service of Venice began in 1518. Among its highlights were embassies to Emperor Charles V from 1521 to 1525, and to Pope Clement VII from 1528 to 1530. Dispatches from both missions show the development of Contarini's considerable diplomatic skill. Between 1530 and 1535 he was a member of the Venetian government's inner circle, holding high office almost continuously, including that of the head of the Council of Ten. This period also saw the completion of his best-known work, *De magistratibus et respublica Venetorum,* which contributed to the widespread diffusion of the idea of Venice as a perfectly ordered state.

On 21 May 1535, Pope Paul III appointed Contarini cardinal. He became the center of a group of reformers at the papal court, heading a commission to propose reforms in the church before the calling of a general council. As a member of subsequent commissions for the reform of various curial offices, he was an insistent spokesman for the necessity of removing abuses and clashed with his conservative colleagues. In January 1541, he was chosen as papal legate to the religious colloquy between Catholics and Protestants in Regensburg. In an unsuccessful effort to break down the differences between the two confessions, Contarini proposed a theory of double justification. It was eventually rejected by both sides. He spent the last months of his life as papal legate in Bologna, suspected by intransigents in Rome of having been too accommodating to Protestants and of leaning toward their ideas. Contarini remains perhaps the most attractive personality among Catholic reform thinkers before the Council of Trent.

BIBLIOGRAPHY

Franz Dittrich's *Gasparo Contarini* (Braunsberg, 1885) is still the fullest biography. Contarini's works have been issued under the titles *Gasparis Contarini cardinalis opera* (1571; microfilm reprint, Rome, 1964) and *Regesten und Briefe des Cardinals Gasparo Contarini, 1483–1542,* edited by Franz Dittrich (Braunsberg, 1881). Useful studies include Hubert Jedin's "Gasparo Contarini," in *Dictionnaire d'histoire et de géographie ecclésiastiques,* vol. 13 (Paris, 1956), pp. 772–784; James B. Ross's "The Emergence of Gasparo Contarini: A Bibliographical Essay," *Church History* 41 (1972): 22–46; and Gigliola Fragnito's "Gasparo Contarini," in *Dizionario biografico degli Italiani,* vol. 28 (Rome, 1983), pp. 172–192.

ELISABETH G. GLEASON

CONTEMPLATION. *See* Meditation; *see also* Attention; Prayer; *and* Silence.

CONTRITION. *See* Repentance *and* Confession of Sins.

CONVERSION. The word *conversion,* although primarily a Jewish and Christian term, points to phenomena that are associated with personal and communal metamorphosis. Change pervades religious history and experience, since individuals and groups manifest various intensities and durations of transformation. Virtually all religions have forms of initiation, or rites of passage, along with methods of incorporating outsiders and revitalizing insiders who have in some way lost their original status vis-à-vis the group.

Definitions of conversion abound. Within Judaism and Christianity, conversion indicates a radical call to reject evil and to embrace a relationship with God through faith. Some scholars in the human sciences limit conversion to sudden, radical alterations in people's beliefs, behaviors, and affiliations. To be more inclusive, however, this article will seek to be descriptive rather than normative; in other words, it will explore the varieties of conversion, rather than narrow the topic to a specific theological perspective. Conversion will be viewed as a dynamic, multifaceted process of change. For some, that change will be abrupt and radical; for others, it will be gradual and not inclusive of a person's total life. Thus, this article will include a variety of conversion types, processes, and structures.

Tradition, Transformation, and Transcendence. Most studies of conversion tend to focus on one dimension of conversion to the exclusion of other equally important aspects. To appreciate its diversity and complexity, conversion should be understood in three dimensions: tradition, transformation, and transcendence. Certain fields of scholarship elucidate different dimensions. Obviously, the three dimensions interact and interpenetrate, but for heuristic purposes the threefold division can be illuminating.

Tradition. Tradition encompasses the social and cultural matrix that includes symbols, myths, rituals, worldviews, and institutions. Tradition structures the present circumstances in which people live and ensures connection with the past. [*See* Tradition.] Most religious traditions include beliefs and practices that encourage, shape, and evaluate religious change.

Sociologists examine the social and institutional aspects of traditions in which conversion takes place. They consider social conditions at the time of conversion, important relationships and institutions of potential converts, and characteristics and processes of the religious group to which people convert. Sociologists also focus upon the interaction between individuals and their environmental matrix and on relations between individuals and the expectations of the group in which they are involved.

Anthropologists delineate the ideological and cultural realms of tradition. They consider culture as a manifestation of human creativity and as a powerful force in the shaping and renewal of individuals, groups, and societies. They study phenomena such as rites of passage, rituals, myths, and symbols, which weave the meaningful fabric of the culture. Further, anthropologists examine a culture's symbols and methods for religious change, the cultural impact of conversion, the ways culture impedes or facilitates religious change, and stages of the development of new religious orientations.

Historians collect and integrate the details of concrete particular conversions. Attention to historical particulars complements theoretical models; provides a rich, vast data base; and traces the nature of conversion over time.

Transformation. The second way to understand conversion is through the dimension of transformation. Transformation may be defined as the process of change manifested through alteration in people's thoughts, feelings, and actions. Psychology is the discipline that considers transformation, in both objective and subjective aspects, of the self, consciousness, and experience.

The classic study of conversion, from a psychological perspective, is William James's *The Varieties of Religious Experience.* Following the work of James and other early figures, the typical psychological study of conversion stresses the way in which conversion is often preceded by anguish, turmoil, despair, conflict, guilt, and other such difficulties. Psychological theorists approach conversion from various perspectives: psychoanalysis, behaviorism, humanistic/transpersonal, social, and cognitive psychology.

Psychoanalysts focus on internal emotional dynamics, especially as they reflect on the relationships between parents and children. Behaviorists emphasize a person's behavior and judge the degree of congruence with the immediate social environment, with its rewards and punishments.

Humanistic and transpersonal psychologists stress the way in which conversion gives the individual a richer self-realization. They accent the growth and beneficial consequences resulting from conversion. Conversion is seen as normal for the adolescent and within the bounds of normality for the adult. Finally, social and cognitive psychologists examine the impact of interpersonal and intellectual influences on individuals and groups.

Transcendence. Transcendence refers to the domain of the sacred—the encounter with the holy that, according to many religions, constitutes the source and goal of conversion. Religious people affirm that the divine works within the human situation in order to bring people into relationship with the divine and provide a new sense of meaning and purpose. Theologians consider this dimension absolutely essential to the whole process of human transformation; other factors are subordinated to it.

The disciplines of religious studies concentrate on transcendence by inquiring into the religious expectations, experiences, and worldviews of converts and potential converts. Recently scholars have argued that conversion is a progressive, interactive process that has consequences in the community. Conversion is thus not a single event, but an evolving process in which the totality of life is transformed.

Typology of Conversion. A good theory of conversion requires a heuristic typology that takes into account the diversity and complexity of conversion. The typology proposed in this article seeks to delineate as precisely as possible the range of phenomena that the word *conversion* designates. Conversion studies would be enhanced if scholars specified the precise nature of the religious change being discussed.

Tradition transition. This refers to the movement of an individual or a group from one major religious tradition to another. Moving from one worldview, ritual system, symbolic universe, and lifestyle to another is a complex process that often takes place in a context of cross-cultural contact and conflict. Such movement has taken place throughout history, especially in the eighteenth, nineteenth, and twentieth centuries, when massive numbers have been involved in this type of conversion because of European colonial expansion. Christianity and Islam are religions that have initiated and benefited from massive tradition transition. [*See* Missions.]

Institutional transition. This involves the change of an individual or a group from one community to another within a major tradition. An example is conversion from the Baptist to the Presbyterian church in American Protestantism. The process, which sociologists call "denomination switching," can involve affiliation with a church because of convenience (such as geographical proximity) and/or a significant religious change based upon a profound religious experience.

Affiliation. This is the movement of an individual or a group from no commitment or minimal commitment to involvement with an institution or community of faith. Affiliation has recently been viewed as controversial because of the allegation of manipulative and coercive recruitment strategies used by some new religious movements and some fundamentalist groups. Many converts to new religious movements have little or no religious background, so that few countervailing forces act against the desire to affiliate.

Intensification. This is the revitalized commitment to a faith with which converts have had a previous affiliation, formal or informal. It occurs when nominal members of a religious institution make their belief and commitment a central focus in their lives, or when people deepen and intensify involvement through profound religious experience and/or explosive new insights.

Apostasy/defection. This is the repudiation of a religious tradition or its beliefs by previous members. This change does not involve acceptance of a new religious perspective but often indicates adoption of a nonreligious system of values. Deprogramming, an intensive method sometimes used to get people out of cults, may be seen as a form of forced deconversion or apostasy. Apostasy is included in this typology because the dynamics of leaving a group or of loss of faith constitute an important form of change, both individually and collectively, in the contemporary setting. [*See* Apostasy.]

The above typology focuses on the sociocultural aspects of the religious change process. The types are arranged according to the sociocultural distance between a potential convert and actual conversion. Thus, tradition transition involves major dislocations, whereas intensification requires very little social or institutional movement, being only the deepening of a person's commitment to a tradition. Apostasy, while more complex than any single type, is portrayed as merely one category; it is movement away from involvement in and commitment to a religious orientation.

A Stage Model. A heuristic stage model that seeks to integrate and elucidate the complex processes involved in conversion can be presented here. Although the model has been developed through empirical research and its usefulness thus demonstrated, one should see it not as universal and invariant but as one attempt to organize systematically and lucidly the vast literature on conversion.

Context. The context is the total social, cultural, religious, and personal environment. To clarify its complexities, it is useful to distinguish between the macrocontext and the microcontext.

Macrocontext. This is the cultural and social context of the larger environment. For instance, in the United States and Great Britain the macrocontext combines industrialization, extensive mass communication, and the shrinking of Christianity's traditional hegemony. Such a situation allows people within the culture an enormous, sometimes overwhelming, range of religious options. This cultural pluralism can create alienation and confusion; consequently, people may eagerly choose a new religious option to lessen anxiety, find meaning, and gain a sense of belonging.

Microcontext. This is the more immediate world of the family, ethnic group, religious community, and local neighborhood. These groupings play an important role in the creation of a sense of identity and belonging. Microcontext groups interact with the macrocontext in various ways; some approve and facilitate the larger context, while others reject and seek to alter the macrocontext. The microcontext can counteract the influence of the macrocontext, intentionally or unintentionally. Many believe that some religious groups deliberately isolate themselves from the wider world. The intensity of these groups heightens milieu control, manipulation, and persuasiveness, so that people may be rendered compliant to the wishes of the group, which considers itself in special relationship to the divine.

Crisis. Virtually all students of conversion agree that some kind of crisis precedes conversion. The crisis may be religious, political, psychological, or cultural, or it may be a life situation that opens people to new options. During the crisis, myths, rituals, symbols, goals, and standards cease to function well for the individual or culture, thus creating great disturbance in the individual's life. According to social scientists, who often work on the assumptions of psychopathology, a conversion in this situation can be seen as a coping mechanism.

Revitalization movements often emerge from massive cultural changes that originate in the erosion of a cultural tradition no longer able to sustain meaning or legitimate organizational structures. Thus, revitalization takes place when myths, rituals, and symbols are rediscovered; people are transformed, and energies are mobilized to create new possibilities. [*See* Revival and Renewal.]

Generally, psychologists see individual crises emerging from the context of a destructive family situation, failure of socialization, or some other personal trauma. Whatever the cause, personal deficiencies make people vulnerable and open to change. Some psychologists argue that certain positive needs, desires, or aspirations predispose people to religious change. In addition, research has shown that those from religiously heterogeneous families (families where parents are from different religious groups) are more open to the possibility of religious change.

Quest. Human beings continually engage in the process of world construction in order to create meaning and purpose in life. Some religious traditions would say that spiritual forces are working; others believe that all aspects of life are orchestrated to lead a person to conversion. Recently social scientists have begun to see people as active agents in the creation of meaning and in their selection of religious options. A word that seems to sum up what is meant in many of these orientations is *quest*.

The notion of quest begins with the assumption that people seek to maximize meaning and purpose in life. Under abnormal or crisis situations this active searching becomes more compelling; people look for resources for growth and development in order to "fill the void" and/or enrich life. Quest is an ongoing process, but one that may intensify during times of crisis. [*See* Quests.]

Encounter. The fundamental structure of the encounter, from a social scientific point of view, involves advocates, potential converts, and the setting of the encounter. Many factors influence the outcome of the encounter, but most social scientists believe that congruence or compatibility of ideology, age, sex, education, and so forth is important.

The encounter stage includes not only the affective, intellectual, and cognitive needs of potential converts but also the needs of the advocate (or missionary). Some religions explicitly engage in missionary work, whereas others grow through less formal, less conscious kinds of expansion.

Considerations as to the nature of advocates include: Is conversion central to their mission? What do they understand conversion to be? What is their personal experience of conversion? Often scholars of religious conversion have downplayed the role of the converter and emphasized the predisposition of the convert. It must be remembered that there is a complex interplay between advocate and potential convert.

In the colonial setting missionary advocates generally carried a tremendous amount of power. They were, in one way or another, representatives of the colonial government by virtue of the military support they enjoyed, as well as their language skills, economic superiority, and political influence. In some settings missionaries held great power simply because they provided access to many aspects of the "superior" society.

Charisma often plays an important role in the encounter stage. The discussion of charisma is intricate, being fraught with many conflicts in the academic disciplines. Many converts report that a crucial element in their conversion was their coming into contact with an individual, either a leader or a member of the group, in whom they sensed the ideal, vital embodiment of beliefs. Such a leader or member advocates the belief system and testifies to the transformation in his or her own life and hence becomes a model, guide, and friend. This happens often in movements in which the leader plays a central role in advocating innovative beliefs and a radically different way of life.

The relationship between the charismatic leader and the converts may be a symbiotic one. Followers project onto the leader their intense longings and their deepest needs, and the leader requires the affirmation of the followers to sustain his or her own vision of personal and world transformation. This relationship can have terribly destructive or enormously positive consequences; the cases of Jim Jones, Martin Luther King, Jr., and the Ayatollah Khomeini continue to be debated. Conversion and charisma are reflected in the synergistic relationship between leader and follower.

Potential converts, either as active questers or as passive partners, bring to the encounter certain intellectual, emotional, and practical needs for religious change. Everyone requires an intellectual framework to interpret the world. Groups that provide compelling and comprehensive ideologies are very attractive to people who are cognitively perplexed. Because of the breakdown of family, erosion of community, and geographic mobility, most people feel to some degree the emotional need for a sense of community, a feeling of belonging. Hence groups that gratify this need are very attractive. One of the effects of secularization and the erosion of religious education among the young is the lack of religious methods or techniques for living a religious lifestyle. Thus a group that enunciates concrete, specific methods for prayer, worship, meditation, and so forth draws people to it.

It should also be noted that the indigenous religious orientations and desires of converts play a powerful role in the conversion process. Indeed, some would argue that advocates are catalysts who merely trigger major changes that are, in large part, the responsibility and creative product of the "receptor." The enormous creativity and diversity of African Christianity illustrate the power of converts to take a religious belief system and way of life and modify them to fit their own needs, wishes, and aspirations.

Interaction. If people continue with the group after the encounter, the interaction intensifies. Essentially, potential converts now learn more about the teachings, lifestyle, and expectations of the group. The group provides various opportunities, both formal and informal, for people to be more fully incorporated into the group. The intensity and duration of this phase differs from group to group. Some insist on a very long period of education and socialization. Others are more interested in brief, intense periods during which potential converts are encouraged or required to make a decision.

Another important variable is the degree of control exerted by the group. If the group is affirmative of the wider world, it will tend to have fairly flexible boundaries and less control over communication and social interaction within and outside the group. However, those groups that reject the world and exclude outsiders tend to exert extensive pressures to control communication and social interaction. The amount of control relates in part to the degree to which the macrocontext accepts or rejects the group. If the group is "deviant" vis-à-vis the wider world, it is quite likely that the group will feel compelled to encapsulate itself and repudiate the "evil" world.

Personal relationships are crucial during this phase. Some have theorized that the formation of relationships enables people to experience acceptance, and that such personal affirmation releases energy that gives vitality to the new orientation. Others have theorized that the experience of group acceptance enables people to transcend conflict, enhance self-esteem, and gain a new perspective on life.

One of the most debated areas in conversion research is the nature of the persuasion process. Specifically, many argue that the recruitment methods used by some religious movements are manipulative, a form of "brainwashing." Some researchers report that certain new religious movements seek out vulnerable people and then exert pressure on them through control of environment and communications and allocation of affection and affirmation as rewards for compliant behavior. Rendering people malleable through the manipulation of their deepest needs, wishes, and aspirations is destructive, because vulnerable people are victims of the group's powerful persuasion tactics. Even though one could question the nature and extent of "brainwashing" in the proselytizing religions, it does seem that people are sometimes manipulated. Hence, it is imperative that scholars and advocates of religious conversion candidly explore the ethics of persuasion.

Decision making is another aspect of the interaction phase. Exclusive groups tend to stress the centrality of making an explicit public decision. Groups that stress the importance of rejecting the world often require people to repudiate their old ways of life and start over. At this point people may experience great conflict; potential converts have lived in a certain manner for years and are now asked to alter their life radically. The conflict may be agonizing and prolonged. Autobiographical narratives dramatically reveal the anguish and struggle. But once a decision is made, people feel relief and divine confirmation.

Commitment. The juncture of commitment is often experienced as a profound and clear-cut set of options. In various ways—through preaching, teaching, or mystical experience—potential converts believe that they are confronted with a choice between the way of life and the way of death. The experience of transcendence reveals to people simultaneously the inadequacy of their life, the limitations of the world, and the vast potential of religious transformation.

The symbols of death and rebirth are commonly utilized by religious traditions in their myths, rituals, and symbols. This kind of symbolism is directly linked to the tradition's perception of the human predicament. In other words, religious traditions that tend to denigrate the world and its evil require in the conversion process a radical rejection of the old and a thorough absorption of, and commitment to, the new.

The commitment will be more marked when the group requires public testimony from new converts. People learn new frames of reference from hearing testimonies and gradually begin to reinterpret their life history from these perspectives. Persons actively reexamine and reshape the past through selection, arrangement, and modification of life experience in light of the group's discourse. Scholars report that some religious groups require converts to learn the roles, expectations, and vocabulary in such a way as to give their testimony to the group as both a condition for and result of conversion. Research indicates that what people profess before a group consolidates belief. Through a subtle interplay between speaker and audience, people come to believe what they say. Thus behavior sometimes precedes belief or at least consolidates it.

Public testimony serves a dual purpose. It helps converts solidify commitment through biographical reshaping, and it also confirms and reminds the group of the validity of its worldview and methods. Audience and speaker form a powerful matrix of support and reinforcement.

Consequences. Many contemporary scholars believe that authentic conversion is an ongoing process of transformation. The initial change, while important, is merely the first step in a long process, a pilgrimage. Some write of moral, intellectual, and emotional facets of conversion. Converts may make the initial turning on the basis of one of these dimensions; yet, for conversion to be genuine, converts must change all other aspects of life in order to be totally transformed. Also important in conversion is the process of becoming keenly aware of and committed to the welfare of others in the world, especially in terms of peace and justice. Conversion is not merely personal salvation and comfort, but a reorientation that may lead to compassion, sacrifice, and service.

The nature of the consequences is determined, in part, by the nature, intensity, and duration of the conversion. How many aspects of life are affected by the conversion? How extensive are these changes? The effects of conversion can be described by comparing converts to what they were like prior to the conversion. Beyond such estimates, judgments about converts' progression or regression are fundamental value judgments; any evaluation of conversion derives from a particular viewpoint, never from pure scientific objectivity. Thus one's assumptions about human nature and religion influence what one considers progressive and regressive.

The consequences of conversion may be evaluated from many points of view. For example, does the religious tradition allow for growth and maturation after conversion, or does the group demand that converts remain fixed in some ideal state achieved by the conversion experience itself? To what extent are converts alienated from or reconciled to the wider world? No absolute standards can be used to judge conversion. The norms of the community to which people are converted may be made explicit and used as a standard. Psychological indicators of health and wholeness may be useful as long as one recognizes one's own assumptions.

Conclusion. Conversion is a dynamic, multifaceted process of religious change. The interplay of advocates, converts, and contexts generates various methods, processes, and consequences. Perhaps the underlying theme is the ancient and persistent dream of the metamorphosis of frail humanity into beings who find unity with the divine and the cosmos and in so doing experience joy and redemption. Connection with the sacred, as mediated through human institutions, personal and social relationships, and religious experience, gives people moments of transcendence. These powerful moments sustain hope for some ultimate transformation that will create a new heaven, a new earth, a new humanity.

[*For further discussion of issues concerning conversion, see* New Religions.]

BIBLIOGRAPHY

Aviad, Janet O'Dea. *Return to Judaism: Religious Renewal in Israel.* Chicago, 1983. Aviad, combining sophisticated sociological analysis and appreciative empathy for religious aspirations, gives us a fine study of the contemporary *ba'alei teshuvah* (those who repent and return) movement in Israel. The *ba'alei teshuvah,* European, American, and Israeli young people who have returned to Judaism through enthusiastic discovery and adoption of Orthodox Judaism, are good examples of conversion as intensification.

Beckford, James A. "Accounting for Conversion." *British Journal of Sociology* 29 (1978): 249–262. Beckford, along with Bryan Taylor (see references below), persuasively argues that learning to give one's personal testimony is an integral part of conversion. The group's ideology becomes the person's story and thus shapes his or her memory and autobiography.

Beidelman, T. O. *Colonial Evangelism.* Bloomington, Ind., 1982. This book is one of the best examples of the importance of giving serious consideration to the converters as well as the converts. Beidelman's analysis provides sophisticated and important perspectives on the nature of religious change.

Conn, Walter E., ed. *Conversion: Perspectives on Personal and Social Transformation.* New York, 1978. Conn's work on conversion is a major contribution. He integrates the thought of Jean Piaget, Lawrence Kohlberg, Erik Erikson, James W. Fowler, Robert Kegan, and Bernard J. F. Lonergan in such a way as to provide a precise, extensive exploration of conversion within the developmental life cycle.

Horton, Robin. "African Conversion." *Africa* 41 (1971): 85–108.

Horton, Robin. "On the Rationality of Conversion: Part 1." *Africa* 45 (1975): 219–235.

Horton, Robin. "On the Rationality of Conversion: Part 2." *Africa* 45 (1975): 373–399. Horton's essays are required reading for anyone interested in conversion and religion in Africa.

James, William. *The Varieties of Religious Experience.* New York, 1902. James's Gifford Lectures of 1901 and 1902 remain seminal in the psychology of conversion. Of enduring significance is his phenomenological approach to the richness and complexity of conversion.

Levtzion, Nehemia, ed. *Conversion to Islam.* New York, 1979. This book contains an excellent collection of original articles on islamization. The bibliography is the most complete listing of works on conversion to Islam available.

Lofland, John, and Norman Skonovd. "Conversion Motifs." *Journal for the Scientific Study of Religion* 20 (1981): 373–385. Lofland and Skonovd argue that a typology of conversion is mandatory in order to bring some clarity to the field of conversion studies. Although very different from the typology proposed in the following article, it is an important contribution to the field.

Lofland, John, and Rodney Stark. "Becoming a World-saver: A Theory of Conversion to a Deviant Perspective." *American Sociological Review* 30 (1965): 862–875. This is perhaps the single most influential article ever written on the sociology of conversion.

MacMullen, Ramsay. *Christianizing the Roman Empire, A.D. 100–400.* New Haven, 1984. MacMullen's vast knowledge of classical antiquity is richly demonstrated in this bold and insightful study of conversion. While fully aware of social, political, economic, and psychological motivations, MacMullen vigorously argues for the importance of religious motivation for conversion. MacMullen's book is one of the few that fully appreciate the complexity and diversity of conversion.

Nock, Arthur Darby. *Conversion: The Old and the New in Religion from Alexander the Great to Augustine of Hippo.* Oxford, 1933. This book continues to be a significant source for understanding conversion during antiquity and the rise of Christianity.

Rambo, Lewis R. "Current Research on Religious Conversion." *Religious Studies Review* 8 (April 1982): 146–159. This bibliographical essay contains more than two hundred items on conversion to many different religious groups and includes material from anthropology, sociology, psychology, history, and theology.

Robertson, Roland. *Meaning and Change.* Oxford, 1978. Excellent sociological analysis of conversion is provided in this splendid book.

Sanneh, Lamin O. *West African Christianity: The Religious Impact.* Maryknoll, N.Y., 1983. This book contains one of the most vigorous arguments for the importance of indigenous creativity and vitality in the conversion process.

Sarbin, Theodore R., and Nathan Adler. "Self-Reconstitution Processes: A Preliminary Report." *Psychoanalytic Review* 57 (1970): 599–616. This is one of the best articles in the psychological literature on conversion. The authors delineate factors that they believe characterize all methods of personality change.

Taylor, Bryan. "Conversion and Cognition." *Social Compass* 23 (1976): 5–22.

Taylor, Bryan. "Recollection and Membership: Convert's Talk and the Ratiocination of Commonality." *Sociology* 12 (1978): 316–324. See the comments on Beckford (1978), above.

Tippett, Alan R. "Conversion as a Dynamic Process in Christian Mission." *Missiology* 5 (1977): 203–221. This article, along with Lofland and Stark (1965), provides the basic structure of the stage model.

Wallace, Anthony F. C. "Revitalization Movements." *American Anthropologist* 58 (1956): 264–281. This is a seminal article for the understanding of cultural and religious change.

Lewis R. Rambo

COOMARASWAMY, ANANDA (1877–1947), Sinhala art historian and religious thinker who spent the last three decades of his life in the United States.

Coomaraswamy's work falls into three periods, distinguished less by topic than by purpose and sensibility. From 1903 to 1916, as a young scholar and idealistic author, Coomaraswamy was a well-known proponent of traditional Indian and Sinhala culture and a stirring essayist on behalf of cultural and political independence in both countries, then under British rule. He was also an extraordinarily perspicacious art historian who discovered and restored in historical perspective one of the great schools of Indian painting. In his middle years, from 1917 to 1931, when he was curator of Indian and Muslim art at the Museum of Fine Arts in Boston, he applied his erudition to the production of a series of scholarly books and articles on Asian art; many of these works are still consulted for both fact and interpretation. Unlike the publications of his youth, which show more than a trace of late romantic idealism and a concern for literary finesse, the works of his middle period are scientific in the best sense: directed toward factual knowledge and coolly analytical in approach. In 1932 Coomaraswamy began to combine his early, value-oriented scholarship with the factuality of his middle period; this synthesis led to the masterful works of his old age. In book after book, essay after essay—he was once described as "New England's most prolific author"—Coomaraswamy undertook a scholarly and yet visionary exploration of traditional religious art and culture, primarily of India and medieval Europe. These works, his final contribution, have an eloquence, a force of conviction, and a stunning erudition that make them still, and perhaps classically, a literature to which both scholars and seekers may turn for guidance and inspiration.

Born in Ceylon (present-day Sri Lanka) to a distinguished Hindu legislator and his English wife, Ananda Kentish Coomaraswamy was educated in England. He earned the degree of doctor of science in geology from London University and in 1902 returned to Ceylon as a geologist. There he combined professional work with a growing interest in the indigenous, precolonial culture of the island, which had been weakened by nearly a century of British rule. Deeply influenced by William Morris (1834–1896), the British craftsman, author, and humanitarian socialist, Coomaraswamy toured the island, making observations and taking photographs that became the substance of his first major nongeological publication, *Mediaeval Sinhalese Art* (1908). The book was a pioneering effort to inventory and interpret a traditional and inherently religious art.

Coomaraswamy's geological career gave way to his authentic vocation. Shifting his interest and residence to the larger world of India, where he became an intimate of the family of the poet Rabindranath Tagore (1861–1941) and an active polemicist on behalf of *swadeshi* ("home rule"), Coomaraswamy also engaged in studies of art history that gradually drew near a major discovery. His *Indian Drawings* (1910) and its companion *Indian Drawings, Second Series, Chiefly Rajput* (1912) are primarily portfolios of illustrations and are of limited textual interest, but they mark the beginning of a reversal in British (and Western) opinion of Indian art that was largely due to the efforts of Coomaraswamy and his colleagues, such as the British critic Roger Fry, in the newly founded India Society.

Coomaraswamy's next major publication in the field of art history, *Rajput Painting* (1916; reprint, 1975), formally disclosed to the world the Hindu painting of Rajasthan and the Punjab, now universally admired and widely studied but essentially unknown until Coomaraswamy's research. Confused with contemporaneous Muslim painting, the masterworks of this art lay unrecognized in obscure collections throughout India and had hardly been valued until Coomaraswamy traveled far and wide, built a splendid collection, and for the first time interpreted them in historical and aesthetic terms.

During these predominantly Indian years, broken by sojourns in England, where he maintained a home, Coomaraswamy also published *Myths of the Hindus and Buddhists* (1913) and *Buddha and the Gospel of Buddhism* (1916). The latter is an early and graceful summary of Buddhism for general readers, published in an era that had seen few if any studies of its quality. Essays from this period were collected a few years later for his first American publication, *The Dance of Shiva* (1918; reprint, 1957). Coomaraswamy had recently moved to the United States, and this widely read book established his popular reputation there as an authority on Indian culture.

Accepting a curatorial post at the Boston Museum, which acquired his unique collection of Indian painting, Coomaraswamy now entered his period of rigorous scholarly effort. His work in the 1920s is epitomized by two publications, the multivolume *Catalogue of the Indian Collections in the Museum of Fine Arts, Boston* (1923ff.) and his *History of Indian and Indonesian Art* (1927; reprint, 1972). Both works of exact scholarship in art history were written as a much-needed service to the field he had helped to found.

As noted above, Coomaraswamy's work—and undoubtedly his person—underwent a major transformation in about 1932. While he continued to write art history at nearly his customary pace, he also began to publish studies of the religions, myths, aesthetics, and traditional cultures of India and medieval Europe—indeed, of tradition wherever he encountered it. The art historian ceded some ground to the religious thinker and philosopher; the scientist ceded to the man of conviction, who contrasted the secular, industrialized way of life in the modern world with the traditional order of life in which knowledge is primarily religious and art is visible religion. Although the books and essays of this period were born of a powerful conviction that modern man must remember and allow himself to be moved by the depth and light of tradition, Coomaraswamy's writings were not predominantly polemic in character; for the most part they are encyclopedic works that explore the metaphysics and theology, the iconography and symbols, and the artistic and social forms of the East and West, often on a comparative basis. Coomaraswamy was one of the first erudite practitioners of cross-cultural study and interpretation to be biased—if he was at all—toward the East. His later works initiate the reader unforgettably into both the general structure and the countless details that constitute traditional religious culture in the premodern world. Occasional polemic essays drive home, with wit and passion, the importance that this lesson in ancient things holds for modern man. No brief summary can do justice to his works in this period. It must suffice to say that they blend remarkable scholarship with the dispassionate quality of religious passion known in Indian tradition as *jñāna*. As he once asked in an essay, "Can we imagine a perfected ardor apart from understanding, or a perfected understanding without ardor?"

BIBLIOGRAPHY

The major works from Coomaraswamy's late period include *The Transformation of Nature in Art* (1934; New York, 1956), *Elements of Buddhist Iconography* (1935; New Delhi, 1972), *Why Exhibit Works of Art?* (1943; reprinted as *Christian and Oriental Philosophy of Art*, New York, 1956), *Hinduism and Buddhism* (1943; Westport, Conn., 1971), *Figures of Speech or Figures of Thought* (London, 1946), *Am I My Brother's Keeper?* (New York, 1947), and *Time and Eternity* (Ascona, 1947). A three-volume collection entitled *Coomaraswamy* (vol. 1, *Selected Papers: Traditional Art and Symbolism;* vol. 2, *Selected Papers: Metaphysics;* vol. 3, *His Life and Work*), respectively edited and written by me (Princeton, 1977), gathers additional writings from the late period and explores Coomaraswamy's life and mind, with emphasis on the later years.

ROGER LIPSEY

COPERNICUS, NICOLAUS (1473–1543), Polish cleric and astronomer, known in Polish as Mikolaj Kopernik. Copernicus lost both parents before he was twelve. His uncle, the bishop of Ermland (Varmia, Polish Prussia), saw to his education at the University of Cracow and secured a position for him as canon at the Cathedral of Frauenberg (Frombork). Copernicus studied in Italy at the universities of Bologna, Padua, and Ferrara, receiving doctor's degrees in canon law and medicine while also studying astronomy. Back at Frauenberg in 1503 he served as physician to his uncle and as adminstrator of church property for the province. In 1510 he built a small observatory near the cathedral.

Sometime around 1514 Copernicus sketched his heliocentric astronomy in an unpublished manuscript, the *Commentariolus,* which achieved wide circulation. A Lutheran astronomer named Rheticus was attracted by the new system and became Copernicus's chief disciple. Rheticus's *Narratio prima* of 1540 was the first published account of Copernican astronomy. Its favorable reception influenced Copernicus to publish his detailed technical account, *De revolutionibus orbium caelestium* (On the Revolutions of the Heavenly Spheres), in 1543.

Reportedly, he was shown the published book just hours before he died. *On the Revolutions* set forth an astronomy based upon a rotating earth that revolved yearly around the sun, the center of the universe. It challenged Ptolemaic astronomy, which assumed a central stationary earth around which all celestial bodies revolved. [*See the biography of Ptolemy.*]

To evaluate the religious significance of Copernicus it is essential to see how he transformed astronomy. Hellenistic mathematical astronomy did not attempt a physically true theory of the universe. Its task was to "save the appearances" of the motions of celestial bodies by making them perfectly understandable through circles. Ptolemy was immensely successful in using geometrical devices such as the epicycle, eccentric, and equant. However, the minute yearly inaccuracy of his astronomy added up to an enormous deviation after a millennium. Renaissance astronomers in the humanist tradition attempted to prove that the inaccuracies were due to measurements and methods and not to inaccuracies of the text. The reform of astronomy was made more imperative by the need to reform the ecclesiastical calendar. Nonetheless, the task of astronomy remained the same. The Lutheran theologian Osiander, who prefaced *On the Revolutions* with an unauthorized and anonymous address to the reader, emphasized in this preface the hypothetical nature of astronomy. The heliocentric premise, he wrote, had only the value of a calculating device. Copernicus accepted the assumption that celestial motions had to be described by circles and so he used epicycles and eccentrics as did Ptolemy. Indeed, Copernicus went to lengths to show how his calculations matched Ptolemy's. In this he was the last great Ptolemaic astronomer. But he did not follow Ptolemy in the latter's insistence that mathematical order had no reference to physical order.

Ptolemy's astronomy was a "monster," wrote Copernicus in the dedication of *On the Revolutions,* because Ptolemy's astronomical solutions were not systematic. The world was the product of the "best and most orderly Workman of all" and there ought to be one certain theory of its machinery. As he contemplated astronomical calculations from the perspective of a moving earth, Copernicus discovered something that made astronomy's claim to physical truth unavoidable. The assumption of a moving earth and a central sun provided the reason why the motions of the planets should be of the observed orders, magnitudes, and positions, and not otherwise. Ptolemaic astronomy described these observations as well as Copernican astronomy did, but it could not explain why they were as they were. Copernicus had transformed astronomy into a physical science. In the process he had revealed something universal and fundamental about mankind, and herein lies his central religious significance. Not only can man's mathematical ability "save the appearances" of the physical world through computing devices, it can disclose structures of physical reality even where the appearances are deceiving. That the empirical proof (i.e., stellar parallax) for Copernicus's insight was not produced until the nineteenth century underscores his achievement and significance. The Copernican revolution in astronomy became the paradigmatic manifestation of scientific authority.

The Copernican revolution had two great religious consequences. The first concerned the tension between scientific and religious authority. Even before *On the Revolutions* was published, Martin Luther condemned heliocentric astronomy because of scriptural references to a central stationary earth. By 1616 *On the Revolutions* was on the Index of Forbidden Books of the Catholic church, and the new astronomy was labeled atheistic. (The condemnation compelled the Jesuits in China to preserve Ptolemaic astronomy and impeded the dissemination of Copernican astronomy in the Far East.) Up to the condemnation, the church had no formal cosmological position. It even used calculations based on Copernican astronomy from Erasmus Rheinhold's *Prutenic Tables* (1551) to help reform the calendar in 1582. The previous latitude on cosmological questions reflected something central to Christianity that the confrontation with the new astronomy reemphasized. Christianity was a religion not tied to any view of the universe, a point made in the distant past by Augustine of Hippo (*Confessions,* bk. 5), and in recent times by the theologians Karl Barth and Rudolf Bultmann. The conflict with Copernican astronomy initiated the gradual divestiture of Hellenistic and Hebraic cosmological components that had been taken for granted in Christianity. The process was quite dislocating and is often cited as the most outstanding example of modern secularization. But it was also the reaffirmation of Christianity's independence from cosmological views. History, not the cosmos, is the vehicle of God's revelation. Man's importance lies in being the focus of God's interest, not in occupying the center of the universe.

Second, the problems of Copernican astronomy, which culminated in the laws of Kepler and Newton, led inexorably to the conclusion that the universe was infinite. The perception of man's insignificance in an infinite universe has become one of the decisive experiences of modernity. In the mid-seventeenth century the scientist and mystic Blaise Pascal gave a classical expression of its exhilarating and anxiety-producing aspects in his apology for Christianity, the *Pensées* (1670). He made it clear that the experience had a symbolic value, for it revealed something fundamental about the human condition—what existentialists describe as cosmic *Angst.* Pascal recognized that the two discoveries, the authority of science and the infinite universe, were related. In the *pensée* entitled "Disproportion of Man," he pointed out that in the face of the infinite, man's presumption to know becomes as infinite as its object at the same time that his finite limitations become inescapably evident.

BIBLIOGRAPHY

A thorough biography of Copernicus and an excellent annotated bibliography of Copernican scholarship accompany *Three Copernican Treatises: The Commentariolus of Copernicus, the Letter against Werner, the Narratio prima of Rheticus,* 3d ed., rev., edited and translated by Edward Rosen (New York, 1971). A translation of *De revolutionibus* is included in *Ptolemy, Copernicus, Kepler,* "Great Books of the Western World," vol. 16, edited by Robert Maynard Hutchins (Chicago, 1952). At a glance one can compare Ptolemy's and Copernicus's work and see how carefully Copernicus followed Ptolemy in format and content. A very readable discussion of the technical development of Ptolemaic and Copernican astronomy and their cultural consequences is found in Thomas S. Kuhn's *The Copernican Revolution: Planetary Astronomy in the Development of Western Thought,* rev. ed. (New York, 1959). Discussions of religious, scientific, and cultural factors involved with Copernicus can be found in the articles collected in *The Copernican Achievement,* edited by Robert S. Westman (Berkeley, 1975). The religious consequences of the development of science and the complexity of the problem of secularization is discussed in Enrique Dussel's "From Secularization to Secularism: Science from the Renaissance to the Enlightenment," in *Church History: Sacralization and Secularization,* edited by Roger Aubert (New York, 1969).

MICHAEL A. KERZE

COPTIC CHURCH. The Coptic church is the ancient church of Egypt; the name *Copt* derives from the Greek *Aiguptioi* ("Egyptians"). According to tradition within the church, its founder and first patriarch was Mark the Evangelist, who first preached Christianity in the forties of the first century AD. For several centuries the new faith engendered by Mark's preaching and the old pagan culture mingled with the teachings of both Neoplatonism and gnosticism, amid waves of Roman persecutions. The consummation of the persecutions came under Diocletian, from the beginning of whose reign the Copts began their own calendar of the martyrs in 284 (1 Anno Martyri). This church calendar remains in use to the present day.

Biblical papyri and parchment codices found in Egypt are testimonies of the penetration of the new faith into Egypt long before the end of the age of persecutions. Such papyri as the Chester Beatty papyrus in Dublin, the Bodmer in Geneva, and the Oxyrynchus in Cairo attest to the antiquity of Christianity in Egypt. With the Edict of Milan (313), whereby Constantine made Christianity the official religion of the empire, Alexandria became the seat of Christian theological studies. There, the doctrines of what was an amorphous faith were formulated into a systematic theology.

The Catechetical School of Alexandria. The catechetical school of Alexandria, which began in about 190, was to become a center of Christian scholarship under the leadership of some of the greatest church fathers. Pantaenus (d. 190?), its first head, promoted the Greek alphabet in lieu of the cumbersome demotic to facilitate study of the Gospels. Clement of Alexandria, who succeeded him, advocated the reconciliation of Christian doctrine and the Bible with Greek philosophy.

The school of Alexandria came of age under Origen, perhaps the most prolific author of all time. One of Origen's works, the *Hexapla,* is the first collation of the texts of the Bible in six columns of Greek and Hebrew originals. Origen's exegetical, philosophical, and theological writings had broad influence on the early church. His pupils included such pillars of orthodoxy as the patriarch Heraclas (230–246), who was the first in the annals of Christianity to bear the title of pope, Athanasius, Cyril of Alexandria, Gregory of Nazianzus, Basil of Caesarea, and Jerome. The school of Alexandria proved to be an arena of free religious thinking and scholastic endeavor, paving the way for ecumenical developments in the early church.

Ecumenical Movement. An ecumenical movement intended to combat heresy was inaugurated by Constantine with the Council of Nicaea (325). At this and subsequent councils, orthodoxy was defined for theological questions concerning divine essence and the divinity and humanity of Christ. These councils were preeminently controlled by the authority of Alexandria: Athanasius's doctrine that the Father and Son were of the same essence and Cyril's formula about the unity of Christ's divinity and humanity were upheld.

At the time of the Second Council of Ephesus (449), a change of emperors drew together Rome and Constantinople, greatly affecting the Alexandrian ecclesiastical hegemony. Cyril's nephew, Dioscorus I, who had dominated that council (called a "Robber Council" by the Romans), was summoned to Chalcedon in 451 by the eastern emperor Marcion and forced to defend his views on Christology. Before the arrival of the majority of the Egyptian bishops, the council condemned Dioscorus, who was consequently deposed and exiled.

Henceforth, the place of the Coptic church in the

Christian world was curtailed. Two parallel lines of succession to Mark came to pass. One, Melchite and Byzantine, accepted the doctrines of the Council of Chalcedon; the other, native Coptic and nationalistic, held the so-called monophysite interpretation of Cyril's formula of the nature of Christ. A wave of persecution was begun against the Copts to curb their separatism, with disastrous consequences on the eve of the Arab conquest of Egypt.

Monastic Rule. Though severe social and economic factors must have played a role in accelerating the flight of Copts to the desert, it remains true that monasticism as an institution was initiated principally by Coptic piety. The first or founding stage is associated with Antony (c. 251–356), who fled to the solitude of the eastern desert from his native village of Coma after hearing *Matthew* 19:21 ("Jesus said to him, 'If you would be perfect, go, sell what you possess and give to the poor, and you will have treasure in heaven; and come, follow me.' "). Others followed his example, and a monastic colony arose around his cave in the Red Sea mountains. All practiced a life of austerity and the torture of the flesh to save the soul. Although committed to complete solitude, these men of religion found it spiritually profitable to be within sight of their great mentor for guidance, and physically protective to be within reach of other brothers. These circumstances led to the development of the second stage in monastic evolution, a stage that may be called collective eremiticism.

The third and final stage in the development of cenobitic life must be ascribed to Pachomius (d. 346). Originally a pagan legionary, he was inspired by the goodness of Christian villagers who ministered to the needs of the soldiers and was baptized a Christian. After spiritual training by a hermit, Pachomius developed a community and subsequently an original rule. The rule prescribed communal life in a cenobium and repudiated self-mortification. According to the rule, monks should develop their potential in useful pursuits, both manual and intellectual, while preserving the monastic vow of chastity, poverty, and obedience.

Pachomian monasteries multiplied rapidly during their founder's life, joined by monks from numerous nations—Greeks, Romans, Cappadocians, Libyans, Syrians, Nubians, and Ethiopians. This Pachomian rule gradually took root in Europe, beginning with the preaching of Athanasius at the papal curia of Julius I (337–352). A number of church fathers resided for a time in Pachomian foundations. Among these was Jerome (c. 342–420), who translated the rule of Pachomius into a Latin version, which was probably used by Benedict of Nursia in compiling his rule. Others include Chrysostom (c. 354–407); Basil of Caesarea (c. 329–379), founder of a Byzantine monastic order; John Cassian (c. 365–c. 435), the father of monasticism in Gaul; Palladius (c. 365–425), bishop of Helenopolis in Bithynia, who compiled the lives of the desert fathers in *The Lausiac History;* Rufinus (c. 345–410), the renowned ecclesiastical historian; and Augin, or Eugenius, of Clysma (d. 363?), father of Syrian asceticism. [*See* Monasticism, *article on* Christian Monasticism.]

Missionary Endeavor. Those who lived in Pachomian monasteries and later took Pachomian monasticism to their homelands may be regarded as unchartered ambassadors of Coptic Christianity, but, further, the Copts themselves were active in extensive missionary enterprise. In North Africa, the Copts concentrated on the easternmost part of Libya, called the Pentapolis. They also penetrated Nubia in the upper reaches of the Nile. Archaeological excavations in Nubia and lower Sudan demonstrate the early influence of Coptic Christianity. It is known that Justinian (r. 527–565) issued an order for the conversion of all pagan tribes in the outlying districts of the Byzantine empire including Nubia. This imperial injunction accelerated a process already in progress. Though Justinian aimed at winning Nubia to the Melchite cause, the Copts were able with the connivance of Empress Theodora to send a monophysite bishop to the capital of the Nubian kingdom, where Coptic victory was complete in 559.

The conversion of the kingdom of Ethiopia took place in the fourth century. Two brothers, shipwrecked on their way to India, were taken into the household of the Ethiopian monarch. One served as tutor to the crown prince, who, upon accession to the throne, declared his conversion to Christianity and made it the official religion of the state.

Coptic activities in Asia lack written evidence. However, isolated cases provide instances of missionary work on that continent. Pantaenus was commissioned by the Coptic patriarch Demetrius I (188–230) to preach the gospel in India. On his return, he visited Arabia Felix (modern Yemen). Sometime later, Origen was invited to Bostra (Syria) to arbitrate in doctrinal differences in Arabia. Augin of Clysma was founder of Coptic monastic rule in Mesopotamia, and thus in the Persian empire.

In Europe, Coptic monks followed in the steps of Roman legionaries to preach the gospel in Gaul, Switzerland, and Britain. In catacombs at Marseilles are found remains of sarcophagi with carvings showing the influence of Coptic art motifs. On the island of Saint-Honorat off the Mediterranean coast of Cannes monks continue to practice the rule of Pachomius.

The Swiss mission may be traced to a group of Christian legionaries from Egypt led by Mauritius about the year 285. They were martyred by Maximian (286–305) for refusing to sacrifice to Roman deities and for refusing to kill Christian converts. Mauritius's sister, Varena, is commemorated for healing the sick and baptizing new converts in the region of Zuzrach. Three martyred saints who baptized in defiance of imperial command are the subject of the coat of arms of the present city of Zurich.

The Copts appear to have introduced Christianity to the British Isles. In England, Egyptian monastic rule prevailed until the coming of Augustine of Canterbury in 597, and the powerful Irish Christianity that shaped the civilization of northern Europe may be regarded as the direct descendant of the Coptic church. A record pertaining to seven monks from the area of Lake Mareotis (near Alexandria), who were buried at Disert Uldith (in present-day Donegal County, Ulster), has received substantiation from the archaeological findings of several ampuls with the figure of the Egyptian martyr Menas. The provenance of these ampuls was probably the majestic monastery of Saint Menas (southwest of Alexandria), from where the ampuls with their healing water traversed Europe in the steps of the Roman legionaries.

Christianity and the Arts. It is possible that the Coptic missionaries who traveled through Europe imparted the essence of their native religious chanting to the communities of the Western world. There is a hypothesis that Coptic church music, which is entirely vocal and of which ancient Egyptian music is the progenitor, influenced the development of the Gregorian chant. [*See also* Chanting *and* Music, *article on* Music and Religion in Greece, Rome, and Byzantium.]

Recent discovery of Coptic art has aroused much excitement and interest among historians, archaeologists, and modern artists. Its motifs emerge in stonework, painting, terra-cotta, ivories, and, preeminently, in monochrome and polychrome fabrics. Early Coptic weavers produced scenes of classical antiquity; in the fourth century, these motifs were replaced by Christian themes. They have proved a source of inspiration to modern artists such as Matisse, Derain, Picasso, and the American painter Marsden Hartley.

In the realm of Coptic church architecture, it may be assumed that the genesis of the basilical style in the Christian world can be traced back to ancient Egypt, with Coptic craftsmanship the bridge between the dynastic temple and the modern cathedral. In the beginning, the Copts transformed ancient Egyptian temples into Christian churches. Later, when the Copts started to construct independent chapels of their own, the Coptic architects adopted existing models of these ancestral temples.

The topography of the ancient Egyptian temple comprised three main divisions. First the outer gate flanked with two lofty pylons led into a spacious open court lined with two side rows of columns with narrow stone roofing; this area was devoted to the use of the general public. The second division was the hypostyle, an area filled with columns supporting a massive stone roof, and reserved for the royal family and the aristocracy. The third section at the end of the temple was a dimly lit chamber. This was the inner shrine, where the deity resided, accessible only to the high priest and pharaoh.

The primitive Coptic churches retained this triple division. The innermost area behind the iconostasis was the sanctuary with the altar (*haykal*) in the middle. This was reserved for the priests and deacons officiating at the mystery of the sacrament. Outside the sanctuary, the central part of the church was reserved for the congregation of baptized Christians, while a third outer section reaching the narthex or western entrance of the church was open to unbaptized catechumens. This architectural arrangement suited the Coptic offices, which consisted of three chapters. The first was the liturgy of the catechumens at the end of which they were supposed to withdraw from the church. The second was the liturgy of the faithful attended only by those who were baptized. The third was the anaphora, which was performed after drawing the curtain over the entrance of the sanctuary for the mystery of the sanctification of the body and blood before Holy Communion.

At an unknown date, the disappearance of the distinction between the baptized faithful and the unbaptized catechumens rendered this transverse division of the church meaningless. Instead, a perpendicular triple division of nave and aisles took the place of the earlier transverse sections, originating the basilical style. Evidence for this development lies, for example, in the archaeological remains of Saint Mena's cathedral built by Emperor Arcadius (395–408) west of Alexandria, and the ruins of the magnificent cathedral at Al-Ashmūnein. It would be a mistake, however, to assume that the change was sudden; the irregularity of church forms in Old Cairo proves that the definitive style of the basilica must have had an extended development. [*See* Basilica, Cathedral, and Church.]

From Doctrinal Conflict to Ecumenism. The Council of Chalcedon in 451, with its condemnation of the Coptic patriarch Dioscorus I, and its interpretation of Cyril's formula of the nature and person of Christ contrary to the Coptic profession, led to the cleavage of Christendom into two divergent camps. To this day, Chalcedon is bitterly remembered by the Coptic natives of Egypt, as well as by others (Syrians, Ethiopians, and Armenians). The outcome of Chalcedon was immediately felt in Egypt: the Byzantine emperors who aimed at unity within the church as the sole bearer of cohesion in the empire forcibly imposed that unity on the Egyptian people. Persecution was inaugurated to obliterate all vestiges of separatism. For effective action, the emperor combined the civil, military, and ecclesiastical authority in Egypt in the hands of one man, the prefect Apollinarius, who was governor, army general, and patriarch of Alexandria at one and the same time. Thus he had immense powers to force the Chalcedonian profession of faith on the Copts, who were adamantly opposed to the Greek dictates. In opposition to this military rule of the church, the natives elected their own national patriarch who, pursued by the legionaries of the Melchite patriarch, moved in secret from monastery to monastery. Excessive taxation and horrible torture and humiliation were inflicted upon Egyptians throughout the period from 451 to 641, until the Arab conquest.

The defeat of the Greeks and the surrender of Cyrus, the last prefect-patriarch, to the Arab conquerors has often been ascribed to Coptic connivance; however, the Copts simply took a neutral position toward the contestants. The Arabs promised religious freedom to all the "people of the book," that is, to Christians and the Jews. In fact, after the downfall of the last Greek bastion, Alexandria, the conquerors offered the fugitive Coptic patriarch Benjamin I honorable safe-conduct and possession of the vacated Melchite churches. At the time of the conquest, the Arabs referred to Egypt as Dār al-Qibṭ (Home of the Copts).

Muslim rule created a new barrier between the Christians of the East and those of the West. Internally, the growing Muslim majority generally accorded the Copts a certain status as good neighbors and honest civil servants. In modern times, the Copts were on occasion offered integration with other Christian powers. Peter the Great (1689–1725) offered a merger with the Copts on the condition that they become a Russian protectorate. The Copts, however, systematically chose a life of harmony with their Muslim compatriots.

When the French expedition of 1798–1802 entered Egypt, the Copts began to establish a measure of communication with Western Christendom. Soon after, with the emergence of democracy and the enfranchisement of the Egyptians, the Copts emerged from their closed communities.

The Church of England proposed a merger with the Copts, which drew a negative response. Yet growing openness to previously distrusted Western sects and creeds in a climate of ecumenism has led to a gradual rapprochement that has ended the old Chalcedonian feud. Perhaps the most significant demonstration of the rebirth of interaction between East and West is Coptic participation in the World Council of Churches meeting that convened in 1954 in Illinois. Since then, the Copts have been active in the council.

Several factors have aided the survival of this ancient form of Christianity. The Copts have developed a profound spirituality, greatly strengthened by the history of martyrs who suffered for their faith. Further, the integrity of the church has been preserved by a conception of racial purity: the Copts regard themselves as the true descendants of the ancient Egyptians. Thus Coptism, initially a way of worship, has become a way of life and a symbol of an old culture. Numbering more than thirty million worldwide, including some seven million native Egyptians, Copts are bearers of a torch that they are determined to hand on to posterity.

[*See also the biographies of Christian thinkers mentioned herein.*]

BIBLIOGRAPHY

This bibliography includes a brief selection of general books in English. For further and fuller reference to original sources and to special studies, see Winifred Kammerer's *A Coptic Bibliography* (1950; reprint, New York, 1969) and also the footnotes and bibliography of my *History of Eastern Christianity* (1968; reprint, Millwood, N.Y., 1980).

Burmester, O. H. E. *The Egyptian or Coptic Church*. Cairo, 1967.

Butcher, Edith L. *The Story of the Church of Egypt* (1897). 2 vols. New York, 1975.

Butler, Alfred J. *The Ancient Coptic Churches of Egypt* (1884). 2 vols. Oxford, 1970.

Duchesne, Louis. *Early History of the Christian Church, from Its Foundation to the Fourth Century*. 3 vols. Translated from the fourth French edition. London, 1950–1951.

Fortescue, Adrian. *The Lesser Eastern Churches* (1913). New York, 1972.

Fowler, Montague. *Christian Egypt: Past, Present, and Future*. London, 1901.

Groves, Charles P. *The Planting of Christianity in Africa* (1948–1958). 4 vols. London, 1964.

Hardy, Edward R. *Christian Egypt: Church and People*. Oxford, 1952.

Kidd, Beresford J. *The Churches of Eastern Christendom, from A.D. 451 to the Present Time*. London, 1927.

MacKean, William H. *Christian Monasticism in Egypt to the Close of the Fourth Century*. New York, 1920.

Masri, Iris Habib el. *The Story of the Copts*. Cairo, 1978.

Meinardus, Otto F. A. *Christian Egypt: Ancient and Modern*. Cairo, 1965.

Neale, John Mason. *A History of the Holy Eastern Church: The Patriarchate of Alexandria*. 2 vols. London, 1847.

Waddell, Helen J., trans. *The Desert Fathers*. London, 1936.

Wakin, Edward. *A Lonely Minority: The Modern History of Egypt's Copts; The Challenge of Survival for Four Million Christians*. New York, 1963.

Westerman, William Linn, et al. *Coptic Egypt*. Brooklyn, N.Y., 1944.

Worrell, William H. *A Short Account of the Copts*. Ann Arbor, 1945.

A. S. Atiya

CORBIN, HENRY (1903–1978), French writer, philosopher, and Iranologist. After early training in music and philosophy, Corbin eventually attained the *diplôme des études supérieures de philosophie* of the University of Paris in 1927. From 1925 he began the study of Near Eastern languages and received the diploma in Arabic, Persian, and Turkish in 1929 when he was already employed as a librarian working with oriental manuscripts in the Bibliothèque Nationale. In 1930 he made the first of several journeys to Germany and established contacts there with leading thinkers. For almost a year (1935–1936) he was attached to the French Institute in Berlin. Much of Corbin's early publication consisted of translations from German or reviews of German works. In 1931 he met Martin Heidegger and became the first to translate Heidegger into French. The translation appeared in 1939 as *Qu'est-ce que la métaphysique?* The early writings also evidenced other interests, ranging from the spiritual tradition of the Reformation to contemporary Protestant theology and the hermeneutics of Martin Luther.

The determinative event for Corbin's career was his meeting Louis Massignon in the Bibliothèque Nationale in the autumn of 1929, for it was Massignon's presentation of a lithographed edition of *Ḥikmat-al Ishrāq* of Shihāb al-Dīn Yaḥyā Suhrawardī that first made Corbin acquainted with the work of this great Iranian philosopher. Corbin saw the presentation as a symbolic act, the transmission of wisdom from master to disciple. He followed Massignon's courses in the university and in 1954 was appointed as his replacement in the chair of Islam and the religions of Arabia at the École Pratique des Hautes Études. Corbin published the first of his numerous works on Suhrawardī in 1933 and in the same year married Stella Leenhardt, who was his helper as well as companion through the succeeding years.

In 1939 Corbin was seconded from the Bibliothèque Nationale to the French Institute in Istanbul where he intended to spend six months. Because of World War II, however, six years were to elapse before he returned to France. During this long period Corbin explored the numerous and rich libraries of Turkey and laid the foundation for his later studies in Iranian philosophy. The most basic development of these years was his discovery of the corpus of Suhrawardī's works. The first volume of the first of his editions of Suhrawardī, *Opera metaphysica et mystica* (1945), containing three treatises of the master, was prepared in Istanbul and published there.

Corbin paid his first visit to Iran in the autumn of 1945, even before returning to France. The visit brought him into contact with Iranian scholars who became his collaborators in later years, but, more important, it planted the seeds from which sprang the department of Iranology of the new Institut Franco-Iranien in Tehran. In 1946 he was appointed head of the department of Iranology, a post that he held until retirement in 1973. The enduring fruit of Corbin's work in Tehran is the monumental "Bibliothèque iranienne," founded in 1949, a series of text editions, translations, and studies offering unparalleled resources for the analysis of Iranian and Islamic philosophy. From his appointment as professor in Paris in 1954 onward, it was Corbin's custom to pass each autumn in Iran and to return to Paris for his teaching in the winter and spring. From 1949 also began his association with the annual Eranos conferences, which he attended faithfully; many of Corbin's more important writings were contributions to the Eranos meetings and first appeared in the pages of the *Eranos Jahrbuch*.

Corbin's scholarly work may be classified into five principal categories: first is his contribution to knowledge of the philosophy of Suhrawardī. Not only did he publish and study the long-neglected works of the Iranian thinker, but he adopted the latter's philosophy of light as his own. Suhrawardī had professed his purpose to be the resurrection of the ancient Iranian philosophy of light, and Corbin shared that purpose. He was most interested in Suhrawardī's angelology, which presented the gradations of reality in the cosmos in terms of hierarchies of angels. The angelology provided a link between the thought of ancient Iran and Twelver Shīʿī gnosis, enabling Corbin to hold there to be a distinct Irano-Islamic philosophy. The scholarly attention that Suhrawardī receives today is largely due to Corbin's influence.

The second focus of Corbin's work was Shiism. He did important studies on the Ismāʿīlīyah, but greater attention went to the Twelvers, whose mystical and philosophical aspects in particular he explored. Here also he was a pioneer in his work on imamology, studying the *aḥādīth* of the Twelver imams, and in his work on such groups as the Shaykhīyah. He was the first to describe the so-called School of Isfahan, a group of thinkers responsible for the revival of Iranian philosophy in Safavid times and whose principal thinker was Mullā Ṣadra (Ṣadr al-Dīn al-Shīrāzī). Corbin believed Twelver

Shiism to be the complete or integral Islam since it was concerned with the esoteric as well as the exoteric aspect of the prophetic revelations, as other branches of Islam were not.

Corbin is also responsible for redirecting the study of Islamic philosophy as a whole. In his *Histoire de la philosophie islamique* (1964), he disputed the common view that philosophy among the Muslims came to an end after Ibn Rushd, demonstrating rather that a lively philosophical activity persisted in Iran and, indeed, continues to our own day.

Sufism also attracted Corbin's interest, his principal contribution being the study of *L'imagination créatrice dans la soufisme d'ibn ʿArabī* (1958). Again rejecting the common opinion, Corbin did not believe Sufism to be the unique vehicle of spirituality in Islam. He found an even more significant spirituality among the Twelver Shīʿah, one that refused the approach of the Ṣūfī orders but was, nonetheless, deeply and genuinely mystical. In genetic terms he thought Shiism to be the origin of all other mysticism in Islam. In this light Sufism appears as a kind of truncated Shiism, possessed of Shiism's spirituality but lacking its essential basis, the doctrine of the imams.

Finally, Corbin was concerned with a broad spiritual philosophy of contemporary relevance. He was primarily a philosopher, and his Iranian and Ṣūfī studies, though they have a historical aspect, were attempts to answer questions that he thought to have been raised for all men at all times. His purpose was not merely to describe a spiritual philosophy but to advocate it. The central concept of this philosophy was the *mundus imaginalis* or imaginal world, where the soul has its life, and which is known through visions and dreams. He discerned a strong bond and parallelism between the spirituality of the West exemplified in such as Jakob Boehme, the stories of the Grail, or Emanuel Swedenborg, and that of Iran, and he called for a universal spiritual chivalry *(javānmardī)* that would preserve mankind's ancient spiritual heritage, its inner life, against the corrosion of modernity, secularism, and historicism.

[*See also* Images, *article on* The Imaginal.]

BIBLIOGRAPHY

A number of Corbin's books are available in English translation. These include *Avicenna and the Visionary Recital* (New York, 1960), *Creative Imagination in the Sufism of Ibn ʿArabi* (Princeton, 1969), *Cyclical Time and Ismīʿīlī Gnosis* (London, 1983), *The Man of Light in Iranian Sufism* (Boulder, 1978), and *Spiritual Body and Celestial Earth: From Mazdaen Iran to Shiite Iran* (Princeton, 1977).

Biographical notes and bibliographies of Corbin's works are to be found in *Les Cahiers de l'Herne*, in the number entitled *Henry Corbin*, edited by Christian Jambet (Paris, 1981), and in *Mélanges offerts à Henry Corbin*, edited by Seyyed Hossein Nasr (Tehran, 1977). Both volumes also contain appreciations of his work by scholars and associates.

CHARLES J. ADAMS

CORDOVERO, MOSHEH (1522–1570), Jewish mystic of Safad. Mosheh Cordovero is among the most prominent individuals in the history of Qabbalah, or Jewish mysticism. The likelihood is that Cordovero was born in Safad, a small Galilean city north of Tiberias in Israel where an important renaissance of Jewish mysticism occurred in the sixteenth century. From his name it appears that his family was Spanish in origin.

Cordovero studied rabbinic law with the outstanding legal authority Yosef Karo (1488–1575), but it is in the sphere of Qabbalah that he attained widespread fame as a teacher and author. His master in qabbalistic studies was his brother-in-law Shelomoh Alkabets. It appears, however, that a reversal of roles took place and pupil became teacher. Cordovero quickly succeeded in becoming the principal master of esoteric studies in Safad. His disciples included most of the great mystics of that city: Eliyyahu de Vidas, Avraham Galante, Ḥayyim Vital, Avraham ben Eliʿezer ha-Levi Berukhim, Elʿazar Azikri, Shemuʾel Gallico, and, for a short while, Isaac Luria.

Cordovero was a highly prolific writer; his most important works include *Pardes rimmonim, Ellimah rabbati,* and *Or yaqar,* a massive commentary on the classic text of thirteenth-century Qabbalah, the *Zohar.* Cordovero's major literary contribution was his construction of a highly systematic synthesis of qabbalistic ideas: he may be considered the foremost systematizer of qabbalistic thinking.

At the same time, however, Cordovero addressed creatively the theoretical problems raised by qabbalistic theology and speculation. For example, one central theoretical issue in the qabbalistic system concerns the nature of the relationship between the aspect of the godhead that is utterly concealed and beyond human comprehension, Ein Sof ("the infinite"), and the ten qualities of divine being that emanate from within the depths of Ein Sof, known as the *sefirot* ("divine radiances"). Are the *sefirot* of the same "substance" as Ein Sof, which is, after all, the source of their existence, or are they separate and differentiated from Ein Sof? Cordovero offered a compromise: the *sefirot* should be conceived as both separate from Ein Sof as well as possessing substantive identification with it. Whereas from the divine point of view Ein Sof embraces all reality, from the human perspective the *sefirot* are perceived as lower stages, constituting a secondary reality that has an existence separate from Ein Sof.

Besides being a subtle and master theoretician of Qabbalah, Mosheh Cordovero was a spiritual mentor, as evidenced by the rules of piety that he established for his disciples. Testimony is also preserved concerning his experiences of automatic speech, which he had when he and Alkabets would wander among the gravesites of departed teachers. It was on these occasions that he and Alkabets would, in the manner of sudden motor automatism, utter qabbalistic mysteries and words of esoteric knowledge.

BIBLIOGRAPHY

A valuable full-length study of Mosheh Cordovero's speculative system is Yosef Ben Shlomo's *Torat ha-Elohut shel R. Mosheh Cordovero* (Jerusalem, 1965). Useful information on Cordovero can be found in Gershom Scholem's *Kabbalah* (New York, 1974), especially pages 401–404. An essay on Cordovero's doctrine of evil is Kalman Bland's "Neoplatonic and Gnostic Themes in R. Moses Cordovero's Doctrine of Evil," *Bulletin of the Institute of Jewish Studies* 3 (1975): 103–130. An excellent translation of a short but influential ethical treatise written by Cordovero is *The Palm Tree of Deborah,* translated and edited by Louis Jacobs (1960; New York, 1974). Cordovero's rules of mystical piety and ethics are found in my own *Safed Spirituality: Rules of Mystical Piety, The Beginning of Wisdom* (New York, 1984).

LAWRENCE FINE

COSMIC LAW. The term *cosmic law* designates the principle or set of principles believed to represent the most generalized nature of the order of things in the universe. In the realm of human behavior, the concept is used to refer to reality, truth, and right or to human rights and justice—and, by extension, to the entire range of social and moral norms on which society is established.

Properly understood, the concept of cosmic law embraces two axiological dimensions: (1) a conceptual or ideational aspect, in which it serves as a cognitive representation of universal order, and (2) an applicative or practical aspect, in which it serves as a basis of normative judgments and moral actions. According to the useful distinction of Clifford Geertz, cosmic law functions within a cultural framework both as a model of the structural and componental organization of the universe and as a model for the organization of human life in ways that are commensurate with the actual nature of the universe.

For those cultures that have developed such a notion the principle of cosmic law serves as the indispensable and immutable basis for the maintenance of a universal system or of a sense of cosmic order. Confidence in the existence of a principle of order in the universe at large is, in turn, reflected in a common belief that individual events within society are not random (hence meaningless) occurrences but parts of larger meaningful patterns that extend through time. Furthermore, it is this confidence—that the entire universe is established upon and governed by a principle of natural and moral order—that enables human beings, individually and collectively, to deal effectively with intellectual, moral, and spiritual life crises.

Examples of the concept of cosmic law include the following: *ṛta* and, later, *dharma* in the Indian tradition; *dharma* (Pali, *dhamma*) in Buddhism; *tao* or *t'ien-ming* in Confucianism and Taoism; *maat* in ancient Egyptian religion; *moira, dikē, logos,* or *heimarmenē* in the Greco-Roman tradition; *ḥaqq, qismah, sharī'ah, fiṭrah,* or *khalq* in Islam, and, in the terminology of Western philosophy from Hugo Grotius (1583–1645) on, *jus naturale,* or natural law.

Hinduism. Hindus developed a concept of cosmic law during the earliest stage of their religious history and the idea has served as the central basis for the development of the entire tradition up to the present day.

Two terms have usually been used to refer to cosmic law, namely *ṛta* and *dharma.* In the Vedic literature *ṛta* designates cosmic order, the law governing the natural world, or simply the course of things. Derivative uses include such related meanings as established order or divine law; reality or truth; what is fitting, proper, or right; or, by extension, righteousness. *Dharma,* the post-Vedic term that supplanted *ṛta,* is derived from *dhā* ("to establish, create, or support"). Hence the term refers to what is established and firm, with regard to both the natural order and the socio-moral order (i.e., law, ordinance, customary observances, duty, right, justice, or virtue). When interpreted as referring to the general principle of human behavior, the term is a virtual equivalent of "religion."

Viewed synoptically, the terms *ṛta* and *dharma* appear to have been used historically to articulate three categories of meaning: (1) the law governing the natural order—hence, natural law or universal order; (2) the normative principles on which the moral and social orders are established and by which the ethical quality of human actions *(karman)* is to be determined and evaluated; and (3) the body of injunctions and prohibitions governing religious life, primarily the performance of the myriad of sacramental rites incumbent upon the males of the three upper castes. Indeed, the native Indian term for the religious tradition that the West calls "Hinduism" is *sanātanadharma* ("eternal law"). Given these three layers of significance, *dharma* might be described as the nature of the universe (its basic immutable order, constitution, and operations), or as the principles that form the ritual and ethical basis of human actions (especially, the performance of moral and religious duties), actions that, when performed according to the general laws governing the universe, reflect or embody those laws concretely. [*See* Dharma.]

In the Vedas (c. 1200–1000 BCE), *ṛta* refers to the undeviating law of the universe, a cosmic entity that preceded the gods and supersedes them in power and authority. [*See* Ṛta.] This law is the embodiment of reality and truth *(satya)* and is established upon and maintained by the performance of sacramental rites (*vrata*s). The term *dhātā* is applied to a creator who produces *ṛta* from his spiritual fervor *(tapas)* and from that, the sun, moon, heaven and earth, and so forth. By and large, *ṛta* is understood to be a transpersonal universal law that is supervised and protected by various deities (especially Mitra and Varuṇa) and that human beings support through offerings of prayers, hymns, and oblations.

The Upaniṣads (c. 800 BCE–200 CE), in keeping with the general tendency within this tradition toward the "internalization" of the sacrifice, tend to identify *dharma* with the essence of the human soul or self *(ātman)*. A distinction is made between two systems of ethics, which in turn reflect two different views of the universe, namely, the active life of the worldly being *(pravṛtti)*, which embraces the performance of all ritual and ethical duties prescribed by the sacred texts *(smṛti)*, and the contemplative life *(nivṛtti)* of the ascetic or the renouncer *(yogin, saṃnyāsin)*, a spiritual discipline that is epitomized in the quest for final liberation *(mokṣa)* from ignorance and rebirth.

According to the great lawgiver Manu (c. second century BCE?), *dharma* is the foundation or the essence of the entire system of social, moral, and religious principles governing human life and "obedience to caste rules is the very essence of *dharma*." Hence, the proper knowledge of cosmic law dictates the terms of the organization of human life: the four social classes (*varṇa*s), the four goals (*artha*s), and the four stages (*āśrama*s).

Commensurate with its function as the grand synthesis of most, if not all, the diverse social, political, moral, and spiritual strands of the tradition that preceded it, the *Mahābhārata* perpetuates the view of *dharma* as the designation of both the eternal and unalterable foundation of the universe and the moral basis of social life. It is declared to be the regulating and directing principle that assists in the avoidance of unnecessary conflict and excessive self-indulgence. Yudhiṣṭhira, the hero of the great epic, is addressed as the "son of cosmic (or moral) law" (Dharmapūtra) and the protector and preserver of that law. Kings, whose primary concern is to promote the material welfare of the realm, are expected to be executors and regents of the *dharma*. Righteous rulers such as Rāma are believed to be embodiments of *dharma*. It is from *dharma* that both profit *(artha)* and desire *(kāma)* flow. Hence, one should live in such a way that *dharma* is upheld and maintained, for "*dharma* alone is eternal, everything else is transitory." Hence, within the social realm, where there is conflict between righteousness and material gain or pleasure, the former should prevail. Only in this way can the cosmic law be protected from corruption and decay.

The *Bhagavadgītā*, the syncretistic text *par excellence* in classical Hinduism, reiterates the belief that all beneficial and meritorious human action is performed in strict compliance with *dharma*, at both the macro- and microcosmic levels. The truly innovative teaching in the *Gītā* is the assertion that the normative social order was created by God (Kṛṣṇa) and hence arose from the divine nature. Since God is understood to be both the efficient and material cause of the universe, then the divine nature is manifested in and through *dharma*, considered under the rubrics of cosmic law and social or moral order. (This idea represents a reversal of the Vedic idea that the gods were offspring of *ṛta*.) Hence, Kṛṣṇa urges each individual to follow a calling appropriate to his birth, moral constitution, and social station or caste position (3.35; 18.47–48), to perform actions according to the dictates of his own inner nature *(svadharma)* with a desire to serve God (18.54–58) and thereby to uphold and maintain *dharma* (which is itself a cosmic projection of the divine nature) and, in the end, achieve perfection (18.45–48). In fact, it is Kṛṣṇa himself who, by coming into the world, reestablishes the eternal *dharma* whenever it is in a state of decline (4.7–8). *Dharma*, then, is instituted and ordained by God and is maintained by him through the virtuous and self-abnegating actions of humans (3.19, 3.25).

Śaṅkara (c. 800 CE), the outstanding spokesman for Advaita Vedānta, believed that *dharma*, including all of a person's duties and rights, is transcended in the moment of enlightenment *(prajñā)* and liberation *(mokṣa)*. At the same time, quite paradoxically, the liberated being is also released from bondage to rebirth and from the moral obligations to which all lesser mortals are subject.

According to Mohandas Gandhi, true morality is not obedience to codes of social custom and morality but rather the discovery of the right path for oneself and adherence to it, by means of which the cosmic basis of the Absolute (God or *brahman*), which is the source of the unity of all creatures, is manifested concretely in human society. Thus is one of the most ancient and influential of all Hindu convictions expressed in modern garb.

Buddhism. Many aspects of the various Hindu concepts of *dharma* are shared by Buddhism but qualified by numerous innovative factors required by the uniqueness of the teaching of the Buddha and the historic development of the Buddhist community. Likewise, various Buddhist texts impute to the Sanskrit term *dharma* (Pali, *dhamma*) a number of different meanings appropriate to a given context. There is general consensus throughout the tradition, however, that *dharma* signifies both the cosmic law that regulates the workings of the universe (including the whole and all of its parts) and the moral law or the law of righteousness.

Dharma designates, first, the whole of the teachings of the Buddha, both those that he delivered in the first sermon in the Deer Park following his enlightenment (i.e., the Four Noble Truths and the Eightfold Path) and all the other doctrines attributed to him throughout the rest of his lifetime. By means of this initial instruction, the Buddha set in motion the Wheel of the Law (cosmic and moral), which supports and directs the operations of all finite entities, up to and including the universe itself. The purpose of the teachings is, first, to present to all humanity a complete and accurate representation of the nature of the world and, second, to promote the crossing of the waters of existence (ignorance, suffering, and rebirth) to the perfect state of liberation *(nirvāṇa)*. As the set of doctrines delivered by the Buddha, the Dharma is to be viewed as the true way, or the way of truth, or, better still, simply truth and hence the way of righteousness.

Secondly, *dharma* is nothing more or less than reality reflected in the Buddha Dharma. As a philosophical or metaphysical term, *dharma* is used in singular form to refer to ultimate, eternal, and unconditioned reality and in the plural form to designate the plethora of subtle factors or conditions that constitute finite things and states of being. Hence there is nothing within the universe or beyond that is not embraced by this term. The word includes all aspects of reality: eternal and temporal, infinite and finite, conditioned and unconditioned, good and evil. As the appellation for the whole of reality, *dharma* is manifested in the *dharma*s, or fundamental constituents of the universe. According to the Sarvāstivāda school only the *dharma*s are real, and every combination of them is a mere name covering a plurality of separate but interdependent elements. According to the Mahāyānists, even the *dharma*s are empty and hence unreal. They, like all compounded objects, are subject to the eternal law of change and decay. The Mahāyānists came to identify the causally interrelated *dharma*s with the one and only Dharma and thence dispense with the usage of *dharma*s altogether. Interpreted as ultimate and unconditional reality, the Dharma is symbolized in the concepts of the eternal body *(dharmakāya)* of the Buddha and the *dharmadhātu*, the Absolute, both elementary factors constituting the ever-changing world. Viewed *sub species aeternitatis*, it is the pure, auspicious, and deathless realm of *nirvāṇa* or the sphere of the knowledge of the eternal Buddhas (*bodhisattva*s, *tathāgata*s). In the "formless form," *dharma* is extremely subtle, imperceptible to the senses, inconceivable to the mind, and beyond the scope of all speech. The supreme *dharma* is *nirvāṇa*, the very nature of things or "suchness" *(tathatā)* and hence objective truth or sheer factuality. It is epitomized in the doctrines of the three marks of all existence (impermanence, unsatisfactoriness, and no-selfhood), causation *(pratītyasamutpāda)*, and emptiness *(śūnyatā)*.

Finally, *dharma* is to be construed as the moral law, the law of righteousness, the system of right conduct, or the path of virtue. This moral law undergirds and informs the body of moral precepts *(śīla)* that the Buddha delivered first to his disciples and then to all humanity; a system of moral and spiritual development, which, if cultivated to the fullest extent of human capabilities will lead to *nirvāṇa*. This path of virtue is real and true (or reality and truth) by virtue of the fact that it is coterminous with the universal law, the way things are. The realization of *nirvāṇa* is nothing more than seeing things as they really are and living with that knowledge without compromise or qualification. As an early Buddhist text commented with characteristic succinctness, "Never can hatred be appeased by hatred . . . but only by nonhatred. This is an everlasting *dhamma*" (*Dhammapada* 5).

China. In China, as in India, the idea of cosmic law has been used to designate both the natural law that supports and directs the operations of the universe and the moral and social order that governs the affairs and destinies of human beings. The generic term most commonly used in both Confucianism and Taoism is *tao*, a word meaning road or path, and, by extension, way of conduct, system of morality, or the right way of moral action. [*See* Tao and Te.]

Confucius (551–479 BCE) did not employ the word in a mystical or metaphysical sense as did the later Taoists. Rather, he used the term to refer to the ethical path that all human beings should follow. If one followed it faithfully, one could expect to achieve a state of happiness here and now. The Tao included both the ethical code of the individual and the form and style of government that should produce the greatest happiness for the greatest number of people. Confucius declared, "If a man hear the Tao in the morning, he may die in the evening without regret."

For Confucius, therefore, the Tao is the way of action informed by principles of justice and what is appropriate. Knowing the Tao means finding one's proper path and following it. Fundamentally, for Confucius the Tao suggested simply the way or the principle of the "ancients," superior in every way to the teachings of the "moderns" because of the closer proximity of the former to the mandate of Heaven *(t'ien-ming)*.

With closer analysis, it becomes apparent that Confucius employed *tao* in two ways, quite similar to the use of *dharmas* by the Buddhists. As a single and singular universal law, the Tao governs the production and transformation of all things. Its generational activities are articulated succinctly in the aphorism "One *yang* and one *yin*, this is the Tao." In its pluralistic and multifaceted manifestation, the Tao is a myriad of *tao* principles that determine the definitive essences of various classes of objects—that is, the wetness of wet things, the finitude of finite things, the sovereignty of sovereigns, and so forth. The concept is somewhat similar in function to Plato's concept of the ideas and various other Western thinkers' notions of universals.

In combination, these two modes of manifestation of *tao* cover the production and dissolution of everything, within both the concrete and individual and the general and universal realms of being.

The other major development of the concept of the Tao in ancient Chinese culture appears in the writings attributed to two semilegendary figures representing the tradition of Taoism, Lao-tzu (fl. sixth century BCE) and Chuang-tzu (fl. fifth century BCE). In the writing known as *Tao-te ching* (The Way and Its Power), *tao* is employed to indicate the Path or Way in a metaphysical or mystical sense. As such, the Tao is cosmic law or the principle of the natural order. It is the transcendent Absolute, the totality of all things, the primal stuff of the universe, and the source of all being. As the governor and regulator of life of all entities, animate and inanimate, the Tao is the undivided unity in which all contradictions and distinctions of existence are ultimately resolved. It is indescribable, beyond the limits of thought and words, both known and knowable only through mystical knowledge or intuitive insight and achieved through contemplative quietude. In a life of the Tao strife, conflict, and coercion would be absent and every moment would be lived in a state of natural spontaneity.

The ideal ruler is one who "rules the kingdom as one would cook a small fish" (i.e., gingerly, with a tender touch). He pursues a path of extreme laissez-faire rulership. As uninvolved as possible in the affairs of his subjects and still able to promote their general welfare, he shows his people the way leading back to a state of innocence, simplicity, and harmony with the Tao. He is a living embodiment of the virtue of nonaction or noncoercive action *(wu-wei)*.

The *Tao-te ching* declares that the *tao* that can be named or described is not the eternal Tao. The real Tao is nameless, eternal, immutable, and infinite in magnitude but not contained within an existing entity. It is a perfect unity, but it is manifested in the multiplicity of phenomena that constitute the realm of "a hundred thousand things." It is the mother of all things, the mystery at the heart of all mysteries, empty yet full, fathomless yet in harmony with all light, formless form, born before heaven and earth, and the extremely subtle, indeed imperceptible basis for perfect peace and harmony.

Again, the ideal life lived in adherence to the Tao is one of utter simplicity, quietude, and poise, most likely attainable only in isolated rural areas. Such a life would approximate that state of existence that preceded the arising of the distinction between good and evil—before the advent of morality, which serves only to confuse human beings' inborn knowledge of the right Way and thereby to lead them astray.

In the words of Chuang-tzu, "when the self and the other lose their opposition, then we have the very essence of Tao. Only the essence of Tao may occupy the center of the circle and respond, therefrom, to the endless opinions coming from all directions."

Ancient Greece and Rome. Confusion reigned in ancient Greece as to the precise identity of the root cause of all events of whatever nature. Among the numerous candidates for this office were fate *(moira)*, destiny *(heimarmenē)*, natural law *(dikē)*, a cosmic source of all existing entities *(phusis)*, chance or universal randomness *(tuchē)*, the decrees of heaven or the gods, universal reason *(logos)*, the wandering stars, the four elements in varying combinations, or, finally, the decisions of the individual which set events moving in a given direction with ineluctable determination.

Many Greek writers from Homer onward, but especially the poets and dramatists, accounted for the course of human events by appealing to the notion of blind inexorable fate or invincible necessity. Some writers declare that even the gods are subservient to the ironclad dictates of fate.

The belief that the course of human affairs is directed by the pleasure of a god or the gods is dramatically epitomized in Homer's image of the two urns that rest on Zeus's threshold, one containing evils and the other blessings (*Iliad* 24.527). By combining the ingredients from the two urns, Zeus creates fluctuations in a person's fortunes—now success and happiness, now failure and sorrow.

The playwright Euripides (c. 484–406 BCE), who was first and foremost a humanist, traces the causes and conditions of human events, not to blind fate or to chance, nor to the willful actions of the gods, but to the character of the individual who suffers and endures the arrows of misfortune. For example, Herakles is safe from the missiles of both fate and the gods so long as he fulfills his destiny.

According to Heraclitus (fl. c. 503 BCE), all things occur according to the decrees of fate *(kath' heimarmenan)* and the essence of fate is universal reason *(logos)*. [*See* Logos.] While Plato appears to assume throughout his writings that human existence is influenced by a preestablished rule of destiny, he is not consistent in identifying the nature of the principle or agency behind this order, whether personal or impersonal, divine or human. In the *Laws* (4.709A), he declares that "God governs all things and that chance or opportunity cooperate with Him in the governance of human affairs" (Jowett).

Socrates and Plato took a stand against the Sophists by attempting to demonstrate that a law *(nomos)* of development and control, harmony and proportion is operative in the nature *(phusis)* of humanity. In addition, this law of human nature functions within the framework of the entire universe. In light of this fact, they defined the *summum bonum* of human life as the alignment of man's aspirations with an ideal order that rests upon the all-embracing structure of the universe.

Cicero (106–43 BCE) stands nearly alone during the Hellenistic period in his denial of the absolute dominion of fate and his adherence to a belief in the existence of a modicum of human freedom in nature *(phusis)* and to a belief in chance *(tuchē)* as a sufficient explanation for any and all occurrences within the human and natural orders (*Fate* 3). The Greco-Roman period was a time that witnessed the spread of the "mystery religions," which promised adherents personal salvation and liberation from the ruthless decrees of blind fate. It was also at this time that the belief in *nemesis* (dispensation of justice) and *tuchē* (chance or fortune) was widespread, a time when human suffering was attributed to demons and when magic and astrology flourished.

The Stoics defined the ideal human life as one that is pursued in strict adherence to a sense of duty and informed by the requirements of human reason. Following directives from both Plato and Aristotle, Stoic thinkers such as Cicero, Epictetus, and Marcus Aurelius believed that authentic duty is established in the nature of things—in the eternal, rational order *(logos)* of the universe. While they recognized, after Heraclitus, that the entire universe is caught up in a continual state of fluctuation, they believed that everything is reciprocally interconnected with each part cooperating with all the others to form a single, well-ordered, and rationally intelligent cosmos. In the words of Marcus Aurelius: "There is but one universe made up of all things and one God immanent in all things and . . . one Law, one Reason common to all intelligent creatures, and one Truth . . . perfecting the living creatures that have the same origin and share the same reason" (*Meditations* 6.15, 7.9). The Stoic idea of cosmic order established on universal reason would leave a notable imprint upon the early Christian writers (see especially the belief expressed in the *Gospel of John* and the *Letter to the Romans* that Jesus, the Christ, is the Logos, or eternal Word of God).

Judaism, Christianity, and Islam. The three religions that belong to the so-called Semitic family of traditions can, for present purposes, be treated as a unit and in brief scope. While a belief in the reality of fate or necessity is present within each of the three traditions, an overriding confidence is placed in a single personal God who is believed to be the causal basis for order and law in the universe. This God is a conscious and purposeful God who created the universe at the beginning of time and is continuing to govern it according to his divine will from now until the end of the world. His purposes are revealed in sacred scripture (the Torah, the Bible, and the Qu'rān, respectively), which in turn certifies the belief that God is the sovereign ruler over the universe, the source of both life and order, in this life and in eternity.

The notion of blind fate or ruthless necessity, then, is replaced by that of divine providence and predestination. Christian theologians such as Augustine and Thomas Aquinas attempt to reconcile human freedom with the providential ordering of the universe by the will of God. In the writings of Luther and Calvin, predestination and the providential will of God are accorded the same decisive role as was fate in the views of the ancients. The tendency in all three traditions to assign to God's will an inflexible determinative role in causing events in time and space has been counterbalanced by the notion that God's will for humanity and the world is realized in and through the exercise of human choice.

Conclusion. Many of the questions concerning chaos and cosmos, order and disorder, and disorder within order, questions that have puzzled the minds of the best thinkers in the past, both East and West, are still with us today. Although the form and the content of such questions have been redefined according to the demands of the many new academic disciplines and aesthetic styles of modern times (especially those of biology and physics), the same questions present their case in the court of the human mind and demand a judgment: "Is the universe established upon a foundation of a principle of sovereign and dependable order? If so, is that principle of order knowable and can it be grasped and defined by the human mind? Are human actions caused, conditioned, or influenced to a significant degree by such a law of universal regularity? If so, then where is the place of human freedom within the cosmic scheme of things?"

In our time, the question of the very existence of a principle of cosmic order and the identity of the signs of its operation within the natural and human realms has come to the fore with a vengeance. Beginning with the revolutionary discoveries of Einstein, Bohr, and Heisenberg in physics and that of Darwin in biology and botany, the debate over the existence and nature of cosmic law has been fired up to an impressive level of incandescence. The current debate over the reality of cosmic law resembles a contrapuntal exchange between two opposing perspectives. The "blessed rage for order" is epitomized in Einstein's famous declaration that "God does not shoot dice with the universe." The persistence of doubt and skepticism has, perhaps, been expressed most dramatically by John Wheeler, who said that there may be no such thing as a "glittering central mechanism of the universe." Regardless of whether one or the other viewpoint is vindicated in years to come or even whether questions about cosmic order are ultimately laid to rest by the discovery of a principle of absolute certainty, a significant clue to the nature of the universe and of *Homo sapiens* is represented in the very persistence with which the human mind raises and struggles with these questions.

[*Related ideas are discussed in* Nature; Fate; *and* Natural Law; *for the mythic contest between cosmic law and its opposite principle, see* Chaos.]

BIBLIOGRAPHY

Hinduism

O'Flaherty, Wendy Doniger, and J. Duncan M. Derrett, eds. *The Concept of Duty in South Asia.* New Delhi, 1978. A useful collection of essays concerning the notions of personal and collective obligations in Hinduism, Buddhism, and Islam from the period of the Vedas to the present. Many informative discussions of the relationship between Dharma (cosmic law) and *svadharma* (personal duty).

Kane, P. V. *History of the Dharmaśāstra (Ancient and Medieval Religious and Civil Law).* 5 vols. in 7. Poona, 1930–1962. A comprehensive history of the concepts of Dharma as natural law and social order and the duties incumbent upon everyone belonging to the three upper castes. An awesome accomplishment by an erudite scholar.

Buddhism

Conze, Edward. *Buddhist Thought in India.* Ann Arbor, 1962. An informative history of Buddhist philosophy in India in both the Theravāda and Mahāyāna traditions by one of the most learned of all recent Western scholars of Buddhism.

de Bary, Wm. Theodore, et al., comps. *Sources of Indian Tradition.* New York, 1958. A valuable collection of original sources on Hinduism, Buddhism, and Islam from the Vedic period to the present. Numerous selections pertinent to the subject of *dharma.*

Stcherbatsky, Theodore. *The Central Conception of Buddhism and the Meaning of the Word Dharma* (1923). 4th ed. Delhi, 1970. A detailed analysis of the core ideas informing Buddhist thought as expounded in the *Abhidharmakośa;* extensive discussions of *dharma.*

China and Japan

de Bary, Wm. Theodore, et al., comps. *Sources of Japanese Tradition.* New York, 1958. A rich and wide-ranging collection of original documents from each of the major segments of the Japanese tradition—Shintō, Amida, Zen Buddhism, Neo-Confucianism, and so on.

de Bary, Wm. Theodore, et al., comps. *Sources of Chinese Tradition.* New York, 1960. Contains a wealth of materials from the indigenous Chinese sources, drawn from Confucian, Neo-Confucian, Taoist, and Buddhist traditions, among others. Includes considerable amount of material on the Tao and related concepts.

Fung Yu-lan. *A Short History of Chinese Philosophy.* Edited by Derk Bodde. New York, 1948. An excellent one-volume account of the development of Chinese thought from earliest times to the present. Extensive treatment of the Tao, *li, ch'i,* and related concepts.

Waley, Arthur, ed. and trans. *The Way and Its Power.* London, 1934. English translation of the entire *Tao-te ching,* accompanied by a lengthy expository and analytical introduction (137 pp.).

Waley, Arthur, trans. *The Analects of Confucius.* London, 1938. A translation of the primary text of Confucianism, with lengthy introduction.

Greek and Roman

Cornford, Francis M. *From Religion to Philosophy: A Study of the Origins of Western Speculations.* London, 1912. A most informative introduction to Greek religious and philosophical ideas. On the topic of cosmic law, see especially chapters 1 and 2.

Greene, William Chase. *Moira: Fate, Good and Evil in Greek Thought.* Cambridge, Mass., 1944. A competent and highly readable account of the development of the ideas of fate, destiny, necessity, and chance in Classical Greek literature. See especially chapter 1 and appendix 4 for additional readings.

Harrison, Jane E. *Themis: A Study of the Social Origins of Greek Religion* (1912). Cambridge, 1927. A somewhat dated but still dependable and useful study of the primitive sources of Greek religion that served as the matrix for the development of the Homeric and Olympian religion.

Jaeger, Werner. *Paideia: The Ideals of Greek Culture.* 3 vols. Oxford, 1939–1944. An authoritative and comprehensive study of the whole of Classical Greek culture.

J. BRUCE LONG

COSMOGONY. The word *cosmogony* is derived from the combination of two Greek terms, *kosmos* and *genesis. Kosmos* refers to the order of the universe and/or the universe as an order. *Genesis* means the coming into being or the process or substantial change in the process, a birth. Cosmogony thus has to do with myths, stories, or theories regarding the birth or creation of the universe as an order or the description of the original order of the universe. One type of narrative portraying meanings and description of the creation of the universe is the cosmogonic myth. These myths, which are present in almost all traditional cultures, usually depict an imaginative religious space and time that exist prior to the universe as a normal habitation for human beings. The beings who are the actors in this primordial time are divine, superhuman, and supernatural, for they exist prior to the order of the universe as known by the present generation of human beings.

Cosmogonic myths in their narrative form give a rhetorical, stylistic, and imaginative portrayal of the meaning of the creation of the world. These myths set forth a tonality and stylistics for the modes of perception, the organizing principles, and provide the basis for all creative activities in the cultural life. While these myths are always specific to the cultures in which they are found, it is possible to classify them in various ways. One may classify them according to the cultural-historical strata in which they appear; thus, one might place together myths from hunter-gatherer cultures, or from early Neolithic cultures, agricultural societies, and so on. Myths may also be classified in terms of specific religions or cultural-geographical areas (e.g., ancient Near Eastern myths, Hindu myths, etc.), or in terms of linguistic groups (e.g., Indo-European myths).

Myths may be classified further according to the symbolic structures and relationships portrayed and narrated in the myths. In the cosmogonic myth the symbols give expression to the religious imagination of the creation of the world. As the prototypical story of founding and creation, the cosmogonic myth provides a model that is recapitulated in the creation and founding of all other human modes of existence. [*See* Culture Heroes.] In this sense, it expresses, to use Bronislaw Malinowski's phrase, a charter for conduct for other aspects of the culture. As such some creation myths find extended expression in ritual actions that dramatize certain symbolic meanings expressed in the myth. Myths should not, however, be thought of simply as the theoretical or theological dimension of a ritual. Even when analogous meanings are portrayed in myth and ritual, these meanings may arise from different modes of human consciousness. There are mythic meanings that may arise from ritual activity. R. R. Marett, the English anthropologist, surmised that myths might have arisen as attempts to give order to the dynamic rhythms and experiences of life that first found expression as ritual activities. Pierre Bourdieu, the French ethnologist, has refined interpretations of this kind by making a distinction between two types of theories. There is a theory that is the result of speculative human thought and there is another kind of theory that arises out of practical activity. Myth as theory may be of either type, but in each case the myth is a distinctive expression of a narrative that states a paradigmatic truth; this is especially true in the cosmogonic myth.

Creation myths are etiological insofar as they tell how the world came into existence, but what is important in the etiology of the creation myth is the basis for the explanation, that is, the basis of the explanation is in the founding or creation of the world itself. In other etiological stories the ultimate cause is not of primary importance.

Types of Cosmogonic Myths. Cosmogonic myths may be classified into the following types according to their symbolic structures: (1) creation from nothing; (2) from chaos; (3) from a cosmic egg; (4) from world parents; (5) through a process of emergence; and (6) through the agency of an earth diver. Cosmogonic myths are seldom limited to any one of these classifications; several symbolic typological forms may be present in one myth. For example, in the *Viṣṇu Purāṇa,* the creation myth shows how Viṣṇu evolves from the primordial reality of *prakṛti;* how Viṣṇu as a boar dives into the waters to bring up earth for the creation (earth diver); how the creation is produced from austerities and meditation; how creation results from the churning of the primordial ocean. There is in addition the symbolism of the cosmic egg as a meaning of the creation. The classification of myths into these types is thus meant not to be a stricture of limitations but rather to emphasize a dominant motif in the myth.

Creation from nothing. Though the type of cosmogonic myth recounting creation from nothing is usually identified with the monotheistic religions of the Semitic traditions, it is a more pervasive structure. However, its identification with these religions opens up a fruitful line of study. It is clear that the monotheistic religions—Judaism, Christianity, and Islam—presuppose a religious history prior to their coming into being: for Judaism, the western Semitic tradition as expressed in Mesopotamia; for Christianity, the Hebrew tradition; and, finally, for Islam, the traditions of Hebrews and Christians.

Given this history, it is legitimate to raise the issue of the relationship of prior empirical cultural history as a background to the religious imagination of creation *de novo*, or creation from nothing, in these traditions. The facticity of the Near Eastern religions enables us to more easily recognize the issue of the prehistory of those cultures in which this kind of myth appears. As a matter of fact, the very powerful symbolism of a deity who creates from nothing is a symbolic *tour de force* against the impacted empirical cultural histories as the basis for a new founding and ordering of the world and the human community. The power of the deity in myths of this type establishes the cosmos as unrelated to, and discontinuous from, all other structures prior to the statement of the creation of the cosmos and the human condition as enunciated in the myth. To the extent that older structures are present they are reintegrated within the new mode of creation.

Thus in the Egyptian myth of Khepri, it is stated, "I spat out what was Shu, and I sputtered out what was Tefnut." In the Hebrew myth the action is just as direct: "And God said, 'Let there be light'; and there was light" (*Gn.* 1:3). In the Polynesian myth, one of the names of the creator god is Io-matua-te-kora, which means "Io, the parentless"; this deity has no parents, brothers, or sisters. The deity exists in the void in himself and by himself; the autonomous and self-created nature of the deity appears out of the void or out of nothingness, which are understood to be potent realities. Thus in a Tuomotuan myth it is stated that "Kiho mused all potential things whatever, and caused his thought to be evoked." The notion of nothingness as a creative potency is related to the mode of creation as a conscious, deliberate act; it is either stated explicitly or defined by the style of the narrative. The deliberate process of the creation signifies willful volition and the fact that the creation is brought forth as a form of perfection from a supreme being.

The creator deity in myths of this kind is often symbolized by the sky or sky deities. In such cases the sky symbolism shows that the deity who creates from nothing is not contingent to the world although the created order is contingent to the deity. Ultimately, the creation from nothing emphasizes that the creation is not a mere ordering or even founding but has come forth as a powerful religio-magical evocation from a powerful supreme being.

Creation from chaos. Some creation myths describe how the creation arises out of a prior matter or stuff that is either negative or confused. [*See* Chaos.] The chaotic condition may be variously depicted as water, a monster, or as the qualities of coldness, sterility, quiescence, repression, and restraint. In any case, the situation of chaos inhibits creation.

In a number of Near Eastern and Indian myths, chaos is in the form of a serpentlike monster. [*See* Dragons.] Mary Wakeman has classified such myths into two types, a space model and a time model. In the space model the monster is a withholder of water, sun, and fertility. The monster is repressive and acts as a tyrant in relation to its subjects. The monster prevents vital forces and energies from finding expression in a created order. The restraint and repressive nature of the monster does not allow the place and space for a created order to come forth. Chaos is thus defined as a holding back of the orders and energies of creation; this is a situation of primordial confusion and indeterminacy. It is clear, however, that there is power and potency in this confused situation. The repressive and restraining nature of chaos is equally the expression of an inertia in the face of a definitive order; chaos in this sense defines a stasis.

In the time model all the potencies are similarly contained within a primordial chaos. There is no change, no movement, and no differentiation. Conversely, some myths portray the chaos as a constant state of flux in which everything changes so fast that no distinguishable ordered form is possible. In the time model of myths of chaos, the drama shows how the forces and potencies of creation are energized to move and also how the constant flux is reduced to a measured movement in which the tendency to dissipation is balanced by a force of cohesion and integration, and this tendency is complemented by the deployment and expansion of the order. Human existence is seen as a mean between these extremes; thus the meaning of ordered human time appears from the regulation of this original chaos.

In some myths of this type the chaos is never completely overcome. While order may emerge from the chaos in the forms of space and time, vestiges of the chaos remain and the created order is always in danger of slipping back into chaos or chaos appears as the destiny of the cosmos when it has exhausted the meaning of its time and space.

Creation from a cosmic egg. In many myths involving creation from chaos there is also the symbolism of a cosmic egg or an ovoid shape out of which creation or the first created being emerges. [*See also* Egg.] Myths of this kind are found in Polynesia, Africa, India, Japan, and Greece. The egg is obviously a symbol of fertility. In egg myths the potency for creation is contained within the form of the egg. The incubation of the egg implies a time-ordered creation and a specific determination regarding the created order.

Hermann Baumann has suggested that one motif of the egg symbolism has to do with the statement and resolution of the problem of sexual antagonism, and has its origin in megalithic cultural circles. For Baumann there is, first of all, an early stage in megalithic cultures in which the meaning of creation is expressed in the form of a sky father and earth mother as sexually differentiated deities; there is another stage in which the parents are separated and may reside within the egg as twins. A third stage portrays the meaning of sexuality as abstract principles such as *yin* and *yang* in China. In this stage the gods possess these abstract principles as attributes. In the final stage there is the attempt to recover the antagonism of sexual differentiation and to resolve it. This is the myth of androgyny. [*See* Androgynes.]

The symbolism of the egg also connotes a state of primordial perfection out of which the created order proceeds. In a Dogon myth from West Africa, the god Amma created a world egg as the first order of creation. Within the egg twins were incubating. In time these twins were supposed to come forth as androgynous beings, indicating perfection on the level of sexuality. Other aspects of the created order were correlated with this mode of perfection. For example, instead of the dualism of day/night, the world was to be in perpetual twilight, and instead of either wet or dry, the world was supposed to be damp, and the twins were supposed to be amphibious. Due to a mishap this perfection was not attained and thus the created order as we know it is a compromise alternating between the dualism of day and night, wet and dry, land beings and water beings, male and female sexes. A philosophical statement of this myth of dualism stated in terms of androgyny is found in Plato's *Symposium* (190–192).

World-parent myths. In some myths creation is the result of the reproductive powers of primordial world parents. The birth of offspring from the world parents is often portrayed as an indifferent or unconscious activity. Even the sexual embrace of the world parents is without passion or intent. The sexual embrace does not appear as the result of a desire or an intention; it is simply the way things are. In this way the sexual embrace of the world parents is like the twins contained within the world egg, and the embrace itself recapitulates an original androgyny. As a matter of fact, the Dogon myth states that the male and female in sexual embrace is an imitation of the original androgynous archetype. In myths of this kind there is a reluctance on the part of the primordial couple to separate from this embrace. The embrace has no beginning or climax; it is perpetual and the world parents are indifferent or unaware of the offspring produced from this embrace.

In world-parent myths the world parents are, in most cases, the second phase of the primordial ordering. Prior to the appearance of the world parents there is a chaotic or indeterminate phase. For example, in *Enuma elish,* the Babylonian creation myth, it is stated that waters commingled as a single body in a state of indeterminacy; the Polynesian myth of Rangi and Papa speaks of a darkness resting over everything. In a similar fashion, in the Egyptian myth of Seb and Nut primeval chaotic waters precede the coming into being of the world parents. From this point of view, the world parents are part of the ordering of the cosmos, a specific stage of its coming into being as a habitat for the human community.

The offspring of the world parents tend to be aliens to their parents. The close embrace of the parents allows no space and thus no reality for their mode of being. The world parents are for the most part indifferent to the needs and desires of their offspring. A tension comes about because of this alienation and the offspring become the agents of the separation of the world parents. In some cases the agent of separation is another deity or one of the offspring, but in most cases the separation marks the beginning of a community and a discourse among the offspring. In *Enuma elish* this community and discourse have to do with a battle between the offspring and the world parents. The same sequence takes place in the Polynesian myth of "the children of heaven and earth." In cases of this sort the community of offspring are the archetypal models for the human community.

The separation of the world parents is a rupture in the order of creation. In *Enuma elish* the mother's body is made into the earth that human beings now inhabit. This is similar to a theme in the Dogon world-egg myth, where one of the twins leaves the egg before maturity, tearing the yolk of the egg off with him; this yolk becomes the earth. Amma must then sacrifice the other twin to make the earth habitable for human beings. In other versions of this type of myth the separation comes about when a woman who is pounding grain needs more room for her pestle and pushes the world parents apart so that she can have more room for her work.

The agents of separation in the world-parent myths are the cultural heroes who make space for the specific tasks of the human community. They bring light where there was darkness, and they set forth a certain meaning and destiny for the human community. The symbolism of light in the form of the sun is prominent in these myths, for it refers to human knowledge and the destiny of the human community. The separation of the world parents presages the human community as a distinct mode of being, but the price of this separation is the remembrance of the tragic rupture between the parents and the offspring as a necessary condition for the human mode of being.

Emergence myths. The emergence myths describe the creation of the cosmos in the symbolism of gestation and birth. The most prominent symbol in myths of this kind is that of the earth as a mother. The earth is depicted as the source of all powers and potencies. Within this womb of the earth are all the seeds and eggs of the world; they exist in embryonic form within the earth. The emergence of the forms of the world from the womb describes a process whereby the maturation of the forms within the earth take place before appearing on the face of the earth. The movement through the layers and strata of the earth is a gradual and cumulative one; at each stage some new forms are added to the growing embryos. The process is also one of integration and harmony, which has an ethical and logical meaning, for the meaning of the ethical is understood in terms of the harmonious relationship among all the forms of the created order. The capacity for the ethical is acquired during the process of the emergence upward through the strata of the earth.

In emergence myths hardly any prominence is given to the meaning of the male principle as father. The myths of this kind emphasize the earth as womb and mother, the container of all powers and potential realities. When the maturation is complete and humans emerge from the earth they are exposed to the light for the first time. The light at the last emergence is the symbol of the sun, which is the male ordering principle, but the basic formation of humans has taken place within the bowels of the earth.

Earth-diver myths. In earth-diver myths water constitutes the primordial stuff of the beginning. Water, in its undifferentiated indeterminacy, covers everything in the manner of a chaos. A culture hero, usually an animal, dives into the primordial waters in an attempt to bring up a particle of sand, mud, or earth, any substantial form of matter out of which a more stable mode of order might be established. Several animals make the attempt and fail; finally, one of the animals succeeds in bringing up a piece of earth, mud, or sand. Upon coming to the surface of the water the bit of matter, which is usually so minuscule that it is lodged under the animal's fingernails, expands to great proportions, thus constituting the landmass of the world on which all beings reside.

Some myths of this kind tell the story of the antagonism between two creative primordial beings. In some of the myths, which bear certain Christian elements, God and Satan have created the primordial waters. God sends Satan to dive into the waters to bring back a piece of earth. After several attempts Satan brings back a small portion of earth, which expands into the world. But after this landmass is created, God does not know how to make further determinations of directions, valleys, mountains, and so on. Satan seems to have this knowledge and muses to himself how stupid God is, for he does not know how to order the landmass. God sends a bee over to eavesdrop on Satan's musings. The bee overhears Satan giving the proper knowledge as he muses to himself; he flies back and gives this knowledge to God, who then orders the world in its proper proportions. In another version, it is a human being who dives into the waters to bring up earth. He brings up earth and gives it to God, but he secretly hides a piece of earth in his mouth, thinking that he will make a world on his own. When God orders the earth to expand, the hidden earth in the mouth of the human also begins to expand and the human must expose his secret. God then orders him to give him that piece of earth, and out of it God makes the swamps and boggy places of the earth.

Earth-diver myths are widespread, but there is a preponderance of them in the aboriginal cultures of North America. In these cultures the myths are part of the trickster-transformer-culture hero cycle of myths. This type of cultural figure is somewhat unique to myths of this kind. In these myths the antagonism and tensions between the creator deity and a culture hero in the form of an animal or a human being is made clear. The antagonism is not a direct one of confrontation as in the separation motif in the world-parent myths; it is subtle, indirect, and subdued, but nevertheless intense. There is obviously a desire on the part of the culture hero to create a different world in a different mode from that of the creator deity.

The American folklorist Alan Dundes interprets this meaning in a psychoanalytical manner. He interprets the diving into the waters to bring up a piece of substantial matter according to Freud's suggestion that what is ejected from the body as waste is at the same time experienced as a source of value and the basis for a new creative order. Insofar as the trickster-transformer-hero exhibits male characteristics, Dundes speculates that this is an expression of birth envy on the part of the male. The waters, which can be seen as a symbol of the primordial womb, are potent but cannot give birth; it is only through the earth diver that the necessary form of matter is brought to the surface as a basis for the creation. But once brought to the surface there is still an antagonism or a distrust between the creator deity and the earth diver.

Mac Linscott Ricketts, a historian of religions, interprets these motifs as a new and paradoxical meaning of sacrality. The trickster-transformer-hero is for him the religious symbol of the human being who is independent of the gods and their power. It expresses the desire to know on the part of the human, and this desire for knowledge does not follow the pattern of archetypal participation in the sacredness of that which has been created in primordial times by the gods. The trickster-transformer-hero figure represents for Ricketts the rejection of the ways of the gods as a mode of life and knowledge; his way is a kind of "primitive humanism," wherein knowledge is sought through experiments that reveal the foolishness and the humorous, even comical nature of the human being who attempts to know apart from the sacred power and forms of the creator deities.

Ideograms, Themes, and Structures. Rudolf Otto, in his classic work *The Idea of the Holy,* speaks of ideograms as modes of expression that lie somewhere between experience and concept. It is possible to discern from the cosmogonic myths such orderings of meaning that will color more systematic thought concerning the meaning of the creation of the world.

Primordiality. The primordial has to do with the problem of the basic stuff out of which the creation has emerged. In one sense what is before the creation may always be understood as chaos, for the only modes of order are those that are forthcoming in the created order itself. However, the meaning of this primordial order expresses in symbolic terms the intention of the creation. The primordial order may be spoken of in neutral terms or as alien and inimical or it may, as in the emergence myths, connote a nurturing womb.

Mircea Eliade has spoken of two meanings of primordiality; one is the original primordiality, which may be seen in the symbols of water, earth, darkness, or nothingness. The other mode of primordiality is the first mode of ordering in the creation; this may be through a world egg, world parents, a creator deity, and so forth. It is at this stage that a specific meaning and direction is given to the creation of a world for human habitation, for this is the stage at which cultural heroes appear.

Ruptures. Ruptures and discontinuities are present at several points in cosmogonic myths. There is first of all the rupture between the primordial stuff and the first mode of ordering. In some cases this discontinuity is stated as the word of power of a powerful deity whose very power breaks through the inertia of the first primordiality. In other cases a new form simply appears, as in a world egg that appears upon the waters. The other stage of rupture is occasioned by the desire of the embryonic and prehuman forms, which are the result of this first stage of ordering, to exist. These are the offspring of the world parents, or the twins who are maturing in the egg, or the earth diver who does not wish to be subject to the imitation of deities and divine models for existence.

In the world-parent and egg myths the impatience of the offspring and the twins leads to tragic results, for in both cases there is a tearing, killing, and violation of the primordial order for the sake of existence. This tragic element explains the finitude of the human community and introduces death as a cosmogonic structure of human existence. It furthermore qualifies the perfection of the primordial order, for with the coming of human existence the meaning of the primordial order itself is changed.

This is turn raises the issue of the mutual contingency of the human order and the primordial order. While a case for mutual contingency and dependence could be made for a myth such as *Enuma elish,* the Egyptian myth of Khepri with its powerful evocation of creation from the power of the deity does not lend itself to any mode of dependence of the creator upon the creation. The aseity of the deity and the relationship of the deity to the created order thus becomes a meaning that receives theoretical and practical forms in most communities.

Dualisms. What is the meaning of the distinction between the two modes of primordiality, and which possesses the greater qualitative power? Is the first ordered form of the primordial time an absolute victory and advance over the primordial chaos? This is an initial issue of dualism in cosmogonic myths. There is also the dualism of the structure of the first order and the offspring of that order. There is the dualism of partners in the creation. In the Dogon myth there is ostensibly a good twin and a malevolent one, and the human condition is constituted by a mixture of both of them.

The human condition is thus riddled with ordinary and qualitative dualisms—that of night and day, wet and dry, male and female, and so on. Are these the marks of finitude of lesser beings or does the human condition represent the original intention of creation? These dualism are also between the nonhuman creators, as in the case of God and Satan in the earth-diver myths. How can these dualisms be handled on the human level? Are they to be harmonized and alternated, or do they represent fundamental differences and orientations in the cosmos?

Ethics. The ethical has to do with the proper, appropriate, and right conduct of a community. It is obvious that such behavior must be based upon some principles, and those principles in one way or another presuppose an explicit or implicit understanding of the nature of the world in which one lives. Cosmogonic myths are narrative statements of the origin of the various worlds of humankind. The origin of the world is often the basis for the principles that define the resources, possibilities, limitations, and validities of the meaning of human existence for the human community. There is not, however, a one-to-one relationship between the structures and themes of cosmogonic myths and the ethics of a community.

The cosmogonic myths, more often than not, serve as background and context for thinking about the issue of ethics. It is not only those elements of the cosmogonic myth that may lead to explicit philosophical and ethical principles that are important. Equally important are the style and rhythms of these stories of the ordering of the world that are a basis for reflection and creative thinking in a community. There may be similar structures in the cosmogonic myths of different communities, but these similar structures may very well lead to quite different ethical reflections and modes of behavior. The philosopher of religion Paul Ricoeur has put forth the notion that the "symbol gives itself to thought." By this he means to set forth a basis for religious and ethical thought within a religious community. Thought can arise as a reflection upon a tradition of thought within a community, but thought may also arise out of that which is not understood as simply a part of the traditional thought of the community. The symbol and the myth define a more archaic mode of presentation, expression, and style that engenders thought within a community. There may be some cosmogonic myths that are inimical to ethical reflection or that set forth ethical options that are to be rejected by the community, as well as cosmogonic symbols that appear to be neutral or indifferent as far as ethical reflection is concerned. This does not mean that such myths and symbols cannot constitute part of the ethical reflection of the community, for the myths do not simply present principles that are to be carried out in behavior. The relationship between symbol and myth on the one hand, and modes of thought, behavior, and conduct, on the other, is a much more problematic one.

Cosmogonic myths form the horizons of meaning in cultures where they still have their original power and efficacy. In this way the meaning of thought and behavior is shaped by them. It is instructive to understand the term *shaped* in an aesthetic sense, as something being created within the context of certain resources of materials that are suggested by the cosmogonic myth, for it is necessary for ethical thought and moral conduct not only to be right but to be appropriate, to fulfill aesthetic concerns, and to fulfill some of the possibilities adumbrated as possible orders for the world.

BIBLIOGRAPHY

For a general discussion of cosmogony within the framework of cosmogonic myths, see Charles H. Long's *Alpha: The Myths of Creation* (New York, 1963) and Barbara C. Sproul's *Primal Myths: Creating the World* (San Francisco, 1979). For ancient Near Eastern myths of creation, see *Ancient Near Eastern Texts relating to the Old Testament*, edited by J. B. Pritchard (Princeton, 1950); Theodor H. Gaster's *Thespis: Ritual, Myth, and Drama in the Ancient Near East*, 2d rev. ed. (Garden City, N.Y., 1961); Hermann Gunkel's *The Legends of Genesis* (Chicago, 1901); Mary K. Wakeman's *God's Battle with the Monster* (Leiden, 1973); *Before Philosophy: The Intellectual Adventure of Ancient Man*, by Henri Frankfort, Henriette A. Frankfort, John A. Wilson, and Thorkild Jacobsen (Harmondsworth, 1963); and Henri Frankfort's *Kingship and the Gods* (Chicago, 1948).

For a general philosophical and comparative study of ancient Near Eastern and Greek cosmogonies, see Paul Ricoeur's *The Symbolism of Evil* (New York, 1967). Langdon Gilkey's *Religion and the Scientific Future* (New York, 1970) deals with ancient cosmogonic themes in light of contemporary philosophy and Christian theology.

W. K. C. Guthrie's *In the Beginning: Some Greek Views on the Origins of Life and the Early State of Man* (London, 1957) is one of the best introductions to Greek cosmogonic thought. Louis Gernet's essays in his *The Anthropology of Ancient Greece*, translated by John Hamilton and Blaise Nagy (Baltimore, 1981), relates certain cosmogonic notions to law, social institutions, and the beginnings of Greek philosophy. The origins of the Greek style of thinking within ancient Greece and its basis for Western thought are explored in Richard B. Onians's *The Origins of European Thought* (Cambridge, 1954) and in Bruno Snell's *The Discovery of Mind* (New York, 1960).

For the trickster figure in cosmogonic myths, see the following works: Daniel G. Brinton's *The Myths of the New World: A Treatise on the Symbolism and Mythology of the Red Races of America* (New York, 1868); Mac Linscott Ricketts's "The North American Indian Trickster," *History of Religions* 5 (Winter 1966): 327–350; Robert D. Pelton's *The Trickster in West Africa* (Berkeley, 1980); and Stanley Walens's *Feasting with Cannibals: An Essay on Kwakiutl Cosmology* (Princeton, 1981). See also *The Trickster: A Study in American Indian Mythology*, edited by Paul Radin (New York, 1956).

The most thorough discussion of the distribution and meaning of the egg as a symbol in cosmogony is Anna-Britta Hellbom's article "The Creation Egg," *Ethnos* 28 (1963): 63–105. For earth-diver myths, see Alan Dundes's "Earth-Diver: Creation of the Mythopoeic Male," in his *Sacred Narrative* (Berkeley, 1984). This anthology of interpretive essays on cosmogonic myths also contains Mircea Eliade's "Cosmogonic Myth and Sacred History," Franz Kiichi Numazawa's "The Cultural Background of Myths of the Separation of Sky and Earth," and

Anna Birgitta Rooth's "The Creation Myth of North American Indians."

For a general survey of Indo-European creation myths, see Bruce Lincoln's "The Indo-European Myth of Creation," *History of Religions* 15 (1975): 121–145. In this article Lincoln describes and compares the structures of the Puruṣa myth of *Ṛgveda* 10.90, the *Bundahishn* of the Zoroastrian Avesta, the *Prose Edda* of Germanic mythology, and the creation myth of the *Śatapatha Brāhmana*. Hans H. Penner's article analyzes in detail the creation myth in the *Viṣṇu Purāna* in "Cosmogony as Myth in the Vishnu Purana," *History of Religions* 5 (Winter 1966): 283–299. Since the creation myth sets forth the origin of all modes and forms of life, the origin of death and evil are often narrated in the cosmogony. Wendy Doniger O'Flaherty's *The Origins of Evil in Hindu Mythology* (Berkeley, 1976) discusses this meaning in Hindu myths; Hans Abrahamsson's *The Origin of Death* (Uppsala, 1951) classifies a wide variety of myths of death in Africa.

Most speculative, philosophical, and theological works of religious cultural traditions proceed from a theme or structure in the culture's cosmogonic or cosmological tradition. Charles Hartshorne and William L. Reese's *Philosophers Speak of God* (Chicago, 1953) is an example of this type of discussion in the Western tradition. A group of essays discussing the relationship of cosmogony to ethics can be found in *Cosmogony and Ethical Order*, edited by Robin Lovin and Frank E. Reynolds (Chicago, 1985). C. F. von Weizsäcker's *The Relevance of Science: Creation and Cosmogony* (Chicago) is still the best introduction to the relationship of religious mythical cosmogonies and those of modern physics.

CHARLES H. LONG

COSMOLOGY. [*This entry consists of three articles that deal with mythic views of the universe:*

An Overview
Hindu and Jain Cosmologies
Buddhist Cosmology

The first article is a general discussion of cosmologies in various religious traditions. It is followed by specific treatments of cosmology in Hindu and Jain as well as Buddhist traditions.]

An Overview

Cosmology is the term for the study of cosmic views in general and also for the specific view or collection of images concerning the universe held in a religion or cultural tradition. The twofold meaning of the term is reminiscent of the double meaning of *mythology*, which is at the same time the study of myths and the dominant or representative assemblage of myths in a given tradition. However, the double usage of the term *cosmology* is still wider in one respect: quite explicitly, it relates also to inquiries in the natural sciences. It is customary in the natural sciences to associate the term primarily with the first meaning given; more specifically, these sciences reserve *cosmology* for the scientific study of the universe considered as a whole. Thus, it is the most encompassing task of astronomy and is distinct from, even if presupposed by, sciences with a comparatively more limited object, such as physics or geology.

Images of the World as Subjects for Historians. For historians, including historians of religion, the study of cosmology surveys and tries to classify and understand the significance of mythical images and religious conceptions concerning the cosmos and the origin and structure of the universe. The variety of images held, historically and globally, leads to one central question: what is the relationship between man's view of the world and the validity or authority of his tradition? Hence the two meanings of *cosmology* noted above do not present an ambiguity: the study of the structure of the universe and the history of cosmological imagery are interrelated and inseparable. In contrast, the natural scientist, in his study of cosmology, does not usually need to concern himself with images of the world held in past civilizations and in regions distant from the centers of modern scientific learning. For the historian of religions, however, the opposite is true: the cosmic views held by modern scientists cannot be ignored, for they are but the latest in a long series of views and are thus as worthy of consideration as those, for instance, of the tribes of central Australia or the Hindus of India.

The history of religions is the only discipline seeking to relate two branches of learning that have been kept apart for a considerable time; that is, the humanities (including history) and the natural sciences. With respect to images and theories of the universe, the borderline between science and myth has fluctuated throughout history. The significance of religious and historical studies in cosmology is largely due to this fluctuation, because the investigations of the historian of religion must overstep the boundaries that normally divide basic disciplines of study (i.e., specialized disciplines precisely delineated and separated from each other in objective and method) and can thereby illuminate features and themes or provide insights that in any given specialization can hardly be surmised.

In most instances, as we shall see, every aspect of a culture or religion seems to presuppose a view of the cosmos. Nevertheless, even this generalization should be made with some caution. It is true that in the case of the modern natural sciences there is no doubt about the pervasiveness of an implicit worldview, even though many of the details of this view may be open to debate. However, in the study of religious images of the world the presupposition of a cosmic view does not necessarily apply. The sacred and the phenomenal world are related, but they are by no means identical. Certainly, notions of "the sacred" vary widely from one tradition to another, yet in every tradition one notion or configuration of "the sacred" is prominent and forms the *sine qua non* of the religion concerned and constitutes the vantage point for our understanding of it. The same is not true of images of the cosmos, for in certain traditions these are of mere secondary importance (as in Christianity and Buddhism). A hierophany (a manifestation of the sacred) can lead to an image of the cosmos, but images of the cosmos do not necessarily take on a sacred significance.

Cosmology and Worldview. It follows from what has been said so far that the terms *cosmology* and *worldview (Weltanschauung),* though related, cannot often be used interchangeably. *Worldview* is the term for a more general, less precisely delineated, but commonly accepted set of ideas (an "ideology") concerning life and world. *Cosmology* refers to more consciously entertained images, doctrines, and scientific views concerning the universe. In religious traditions, the natural place to look for cosmology is the myths of creation or birth of the world (cosmogony), whereas questionnaires might be the best means to arrive at a dominant worldview. The philosopher Immanuel Kant (1724–1804) introduced the term *Weltanschauung,* but he used it as a synonym for *cosmology* or *image of the world.* The vaguer term now most generally used is to a large extent the result of philosophical discussions and disagreements that have taken place for the most part outside of theological circles. The general meaning of the term in common use today is a generally sensed answer to a question concerning the meaning of life that is felt rather than expressed. Its lack of articulation distinguishes it from cosmology. No wonder that much discord has continued to exist among philosophers on the meaning and definition of *worldview,* although it has been accepted as a philosophical concept (e.g., by Karl Jaspers). It is easy to see that a worldview, precisely to the extent that it is held uncritically, can be a remnant of an earlier cosmology.

The relationship between scientific views of the universe and worldview and the influence of the former on the latter are strikingly exemplified in developments of the twentieth century. Discoveries in astronomy, the popularization of unimaginable distances in space, and the beginning of space travel have contributed to a new anxiety.

Man has become a conspicuously lonesome creature in the universe. Typically, in science fiction literature, space travelers risk the danger of literally getting lost in space. This anxiety is part of a widespread worldview. It is tied to a new cosmology produced by scientific discoveries. A relation to traditional religious systems might seem completely absent, if it were not for the accompanying fully conscious realization that man's central place in the cosmos has faded. Thus the anxiety concerns precisely the cardinal point in all traditional religious imageries: the world is man's world.

Classification of Cosmologies. Cosmic worldviews may be examined from two distinct perspectives: in terms of geographical location or in terms of culturally evolved themes.

Geography. The most obvious grouping of cosmic views is given according to the continents of the earth, the various regions within them, and their ethnic and linguistic divisions. Although it is necessary as a first step and appeals to our thirst for empirical knowledge, this method is most valuable in showing the extreme difficulty of making generalizations and is useful in demonstrating the impossibility of finding helpful answers to a number of elementary questions. For instance, the continent of Africa seems relatively poorly endowed with myths in general and with developed articulations of cosmic views in particular; the lack of solar and lunar myths is especially striking. At the same time, however, one observes in Africa a variety of traditions and a great dissimilarity in historical influences and levels of culture. Moreover, in African traditions there are few pure cosmologies, in the sense of myths explicitly dealing with the origin and structure of the universe, when compared to Oceanic traditions. However, this is counterbalanced by a pronounced significance given to man's acts in the world from its inception. The choices made by man as reflected in his acts obviously concern the world, even if the cosmos itself is not described in its origin and structure with the poetic beauty characteristic of, for instance, many Indonesian myths.

A geographic compilation of cosmic views leads to a very natural and necessary first conclusion: man, or humanity, is a central theme in all traditional cosmologies. Whether poetic visions of primordial mountains and oceans or a preoccupation with the risks or failures in human acts prevail, we may indeed say that the world of man is the theme of all traditional mythology, including the narratives and the symbolism that refer expressly to "nature," "the universe," "the cosmos," or "the earth." This basic conclusion must indeed be drawn; it eliminates much unnecessary confusion on cosmological and cosmogonic myths as supposed steps toward satisfying man's scientific curiosity or cravings for establishing causes.

Cultural themes. Any worldwide survey of cosmological views must consider a crucial factor: the variety of cultural levels on which views of the cosmos have developed. At first glance, this variety may seem only to increase the almost overwhelming abundance and perplexity of the material to be studied; but in the end it provides the only sturdy vantage point for a thematic classification on which some scholarly agreement might exist. This is not to say that the various livelihoods (hunting-gathering, tilling the soil, livestock raising) are presented as ironclad systems in myths. Yet to quite an extent, views of the cosmos are in harmony with the social order in a tribe or tradition, and as a rule reflect the prevailing mode of production (and may shed light on the legal customs of the society as well).

The generating earth. Even though no unambiguous examples of matriarchy have been found, there are many examples of female cosmic principles and deities. [*See* Goddess Worship.] In certain very early agricultural societies, as in prehistoric eastern Europe, it seems most likely that supreme goddesses to some extent mirrored the importance of women in society. There is, however, much more at stake than a mere projection of society. There are indications that a mother deity functioned at one time as the sole generative principle, giving birth without the participation of a male counterpart. It is not necessary to think of the peoples holding such ideas as ignorant concerning impregnation; obviously, such ignorance, wherever it existed, could not be the point of the cosmogony. Evidence of the imageries of a sole maternal figure comes from well-developed early and classical cultures, including those of the Greeks, the Egyptians, the Hittites, and the Japanese. The earth, constituting "the whole place" in which man found himself, evidently was conceived as the center or foundation of the cosmos. A Sanskrit word for earth, *pṛthivī*, is feminine and literally means "the one who is wide." Taking all evidence together, it is advisable to be cautious in speaking without further qualification of motherhood as the cause of all these imageries. Less sociopsychologically, but not less concretely, the preoccupation with the fact and act of generating seems central in all examples of the *generatrix* ("she who brings forth"). In the settled, archaic society of the Zuni, but also among many other Indians of the New World, myths tell us of people emerging from the earth in very early, mythical times. Here the subject of originating is much more emphatically presented in the tradition than is the principle of motherhood.

The predominant significance of the earth in a number of traditions is commonly referrred to with the adjective *chthonic*. It is derived from the Greek word *chthōn* ("earth"), and it was first used by classicists to describe the quality of many deities in Greece, whether female (such as Gaia and Semele) or male (such as Ploutos, identified with Hades). Gaia (from "earth") is the equivalent of Tellus in Roman mythology, and Ploutos, called Pluto by the Romans, is the provider of wealth that comes from the earth. Gaia is regarded as the oldest of the deities in Greek tradition, arising by her own power out of chaos. In many cosmogonic myths in the ancient Mediterranean world the theme of the spontaneity of life and life arising from death is repeated and elaborated. Its variations are not limited to the classicial civilizations in the Mediterranean but occur wherever agricultural life exists. [*See* Earth.]

Divine male fashioner. Many nonliterate traditions know of a primordial celestial god who created the world and who withdrew after having accomplished that act. [*See* Deus Otiosus.] The great monotheistic systems (those of ancient Israel, Judaism, Christianity, Islam, as well as Zoroastrianism) that also speak of a supreme creator are very different; they brought into existence monotheism properly so called, not the idea of someone who merely creates. Their monotheism is the result of their fight against polytheism of one type or another; it is a matter of a revolution in the development of religion. [*See* Monotheism.] Not by chance are they historically rooted in pastoral traditions and in civilizations far more extensive than those of early hunters and gatherers. Here the father is the undisputed head of the family. The world is governed strictly by the creator; the biblical god, Yahveh, sets the course for the celestial bodies. However, societies of a pronounced patriarchal type with a monotheistic religion are relative latecomers in history, and their diversity is striking. One would hesitate to emphasize similarities between them beyond a few general lines linking cosmic structure, social structure, and their type of deity. The paterfamilias (father and head of the household) in Roman religion may focus the attention on a striking feature, yet brings to mind the complexity of an ideologically pastoral, agriculturally based, advanced urban society. Also, it reminds us that the most typical examples of monotheism (as in Israel and Islam) are not an inevitable product of one homogeneous sociocultural development. After all, Rome did not itself yield to monotheism until Christianity's gradual conquest in the third, fourth, and fifth centuries CE.

World parents. Enlarging upon the themes of the earth's generative power and a supreme fashioner is the theme of the world parents. The primordial union out of which all there is was born is often that of sky and earth, that is, the primal pair of parents. Iconographically the pair is often depicted as if in shorthand form through a square or rectangle (the earth) and a circle (the sky). [*See* Maṇḍalas.] We should bear in mind that here also we are not confronted merely with inadequate scientific knowledge and fanciful illusions concerning the structure of the universe but with fundamental issues in a lasting religious quest. In addition to the immediate world of man there exists the sky, at the same time undeniably there and yet unreachable; it is the first image of what in philosophy will come to be called "transcendence." Out of the opposites of earth and sky the world (and one may want to call it more precisely "the human world") is born.

Pointing to the theme of the world parents as an expression of the mystery of all creation is far from exhausting the subject. This theme occurs with infinite variations. In ancient Egypt, for instance, the earth and the sky are male and female respectively, unlike the vast majority of traditions. In the ancient Near East, the primordial pair, Tiamat and Apsu, in their relationship exist distinct from and prior to the establishment of sky and earth; they are portrayed as a series of opposities, one of which is the opposition of the primeval salt water and fresh water oceans that were crucial to Babylonian existence. The two form the beginning of the god's life and the beginning of organization necessary for the world that is yet to come. Hence, the pair of deities is both theogonic and cosmogonic. [*See* Hieros Gamos.]

Other motifs. Several other themes that deal with the origin of the world and its structure may be related with certainty to the specific cultural environments in which they are narrated. Nevertheless, they cross cultural boundaries or occur with modifications that can be expected by cultural anthropologists and historians. However, with chthonic creativity and the world parents, it is not necessary here to think in terms of diffusion from one point of the globe to another; on the basis of observation and experience one may conclude that independent origins are not uncommon and in fact are often more likely. Among the notable exceptions are the variations within the cosmos of conflicting dualisms that are observable in many areas of the world and that are attributable directly or indirectly to Iranian or Manichaean influences. [*See* Dualism.]

A number of archaic hunters' traditions know of an earth diver, a creature that descends to the bottom of the primordial ocean to pick up the earth from which the dry land is to be fashioned on the surface of the water. (The theme occurs, for example, in North America among the Huron.) In some regions, the motif appears with the addition of a character, often divine, who orders the earth diver to descend and fetch the required particles of earth. Finally—and here the striking example of a historically traceable influence comes in—the theme recurs with an earth diver who attempts to keep the earth to himself, or who sets himself up in opposition to the divine creator. There is no doubt that a dualism of Iranian (Zoroastrian) or Manichaean origin is making itself felt here. In the new versions, the earth, in the end, is the product of both the good maker and the "helper," who turns out to be a satanic figure. Thus the existence of evil is acknowledged, but the (good) god is not held responsible for it. Such a dualistic cosmogonic procedure is described in various ways in eastern European and Siberian traditions.

Again, caution is in order in making generalizations, for it goes without saying that the opposition of "good" and "evil" is not alien to any human society, even though in some cases we can infer specific historical influences. Of general importance is the realization, first, that all myths are subject to historical changes, even if we have not yet succeeded in tracing these changes in detail; and second, that a cosmogonic myth of any thematic type is not necessarily wiped out or replaced but can be merely modified when a great religious system is superimposed on a civilization. In the example of the earth diver, we can see how first a dualistic change came about, no doubt from outside, and yet the new, dualistic version continued its life after Christianity had gained ascendancy in eastern Europe.

Themes that in all probability were created independently in various traditions may be mentioned: the world egg; the cosmic tree; creation *ex nihilo*; creation from chaos; and creation from sacrifice. Each of these usually occurs in conjunction with other themes. The tree of the world and of life occurs in one form or another from the ancient Germanic and Celtic peoples to ancient Babylonia and to classical and modern Java. This symbolism, perhaps even more than the others, allows for interpretations of the cosmos at large (the macrocosm) and the "world" of a person's body and existence (the microcosm). Many traditions elaborate on such double application (e.g., *Bhagavadgītā* 15).

The imagery of the world egg occurs also in many places (in Africa, Polynesia, Japan, and India, for instance) that are far apart and cannot be expected to have been in contact in such a way as to explain the similarity. The power of the imagery must be sought in the imagery itself. Just as water is always and everywhere given as a basic ingredient expressive of perfect potentiality because it takes on any form given to it, having no form of its own (hence symbolically interchangeable with chaos), and plays an essential role at birth, the egg is given as a cosmogonic image precisely because it represents a form that contains all there is "in principle" and produces life. [*See* Egg.] The creation out of nothing, well known from the traditional Christian interpretation of *Genesis* 1, occurs unambiguously and articulately in a Tuamotuan tradition (Polynesia).

Sacrifice as an act resulting in the creation of the world is especially well developed in early India (Vedism and Brahmanism).

Common characteristics of religious cosmologies. When symbolism and mythology depict cosmogony and cosmology, the view is confirmed that the cosmos is always the world of man and is not an external object of inquiry. We may add that an ethical concern, which by itself has no evident part in the study of nature or of astronomy, is very much in evidence in religious views of the world. The behavior required of man is often described and always implied in the account of the world's structure.

Even if certain features do not make an obvious ethical impression on most Western readers, they nevertheless may tell us something concerning the rules that govern human behavior. Sacrificial or headhunting techniques are given within the structure of the cosmos. The renewal of the world celebrated in the Babylonian New Year festival is a cosmological event that has little, if anything, in common with modern scientific researches, most obviously so because it implies a renewal that must be observed in human existence. We may also think of the teachings concerning many births and rebirths in Hinduism, Jainism, and Buddhism; they fit in traditions that speak of world cycles, successions of worlds, and multiple worlds. Finally, the intimate relationship of the macrocosm and the microcosm, which is widely attested, is a striking formal link between various views of the cosmos.

Do Science and Religion View the Cosmos Differently? Contrary to popular opinion, it is not often necessary to ponder conflicts between science and religion. It is more to the point to think of differences in questions asked and in subject matter. Pre-Islamic Indian literary sources are almost unanimous with respect to the conception of the continents of the earth. They depict the continents geometrically rather than empirically, and India itself occurs in the center of the world's map. The idea of many long ages and periods with truly astronomical numbers and the concept of many worlds existing both in succession and simultaneously are pan-Indian. As indicated, the center is and remains man and his quest for liberation. This does not at all mean that the large figures of years given in the Purāṇas are figments of the imagination or betray a disregard for science. Quite the reverse is true, in spite of earlier fashions in scholarship that disparaged India's talent for science (a tradition fostered by some eminent Sanskritists). On this score scholarship has been set right by recent investigations in the history of science, in the forefront of which is the work of David Pingree.

On a wider scale a comparable correction has been made with respect to the generally held opinion that prehistoric man and, in his wake, members of every nonliterate tradition were wanting in intellectual power capable of raising scientific questions. This correction has been made through the work of Alexander Marshack, who persuasively interpreted prehistoric data as records of precise astronomic observations. None of this suggests oppositions between religion and science; such oppositions are in fact a very recent phenomenon in history and are restricted to very few sciences and only to specific religious traditions. It is certainly impossible on the basis of the cumulative evidence to regard religious and mythical views of the cosmos merely as precursors to science or as preliminary, inadequate endeavors that are discarded with the development of science. Moreover, not only from the point of view of the historian of religions, but also from that of the historian of science, no single moment in history can ever be established to pinpoint the supposed fundamental change from myth to science. In fact no such moment exists.

The relationship between clearly recognizable religious views and scientific views is complex, but much clarity can be gained by looking critically at the sort of questions that are asked, the nature of the assumptions the questioner makes under the influence of his own culture, or the intellectual habits of his age.

One tradition, fundamentalism, though largely limited to the history of American Protestantism, illuminates the study of the problem of science and religion with regard to cosmology. Fundamentalism is rooted in America's frontier experience and in rural life, yet ideologically it has had an emotional impact on urban communities and educational institutions. The public evil of religious illiteracy is the root cause of most questionable ideas concerning religion and science. Taking biblical statements about the cosmos literally, fundamentalists build up a "supernaturalism" that does not replace naturalism so much as it is superimposed on it, while the religious character of religious accounts is obscured in the process. In a bizarre legal procedure in 1981–1982, a group of fundamentalists known as "creationists" tried to provide educational institutions with the right to spend equal time on "creation science" (based on biblical statements about the physical universe) alongside the teaching of generally accepted modern scientific inquiries. The assumption is that religious accounts can be viewed for their factual, that is, verifiable and inferential accuracy. The question of the religious intention is not raised, because the "creation scientist" postulates a factuality that is positivistic in nature (in the sense of Auguste Comte, the French philosopher, 1798–1857, and after the manner of Herbert Spencer, the English social philosopher, 1820–1903, for whom "religion" covered everything not yet figured out by science).

Rather than holding ideas of this sort up for ridicule, serious scholars (such as C. F. von Weizsäcker and L. B. Gilkey) have used them to show more clearly the weakness of ideas shared in the widest intellectual circles. We cannot ignore the modern intellectual problem of creating a dichotomy where our documents show a unity or seem to indicate no more than aspects of the same thing. The contrast between modern science and traditional religious ideas concerning the world and cosmogony has occupied the minds of many Westerners, especially since the eighteenth century. This contrast has blurred the intention of world images given in religious traditions.

It would not be appropriate to allow a conflict generated by the French Enlightenment and repeated and modified since then in Western intellectual history to distort our perception of all religious symbolism concerning the world. Instead, it is necessary to see religion and science together in their development, and to realize that every attempt to view religious cosmologies side by side with modern scientific cosmologies fails if the cardinal point mentioned before is missed: the former are man-centered, while the latter is only man-observed and man-calculated. This distinction, with which modern man should be familiar, is nevertheless not a division, and few ages and communities have found it necessary to make the distinction into a special subject for discourse or emphasis.

The ancient Babylonians thought of the earth as the center of the universe and conceived of it as a mountain, hollow underneath and supported by the ocean, while the vault of heaven kept the waters above from those below; the "waters above" explained the phenomenon of rain. Roughly the same cosmic scheme occurs throughout the entire ancient Near East and returns in the creation account in the *Book of Genesis*. One may think also of Thales of Miletus (c. 600 BCE), the Ionian "natural philosopher," who is famous for positing water as the primal substance of the universe. If, however, this schematization strikes us as scientifically most primitive, we should remember that such a scheme was in fact never presented in any tradition; it is only the summary that the modern mind, the product of an average education, draws from far more complex mythologies. Although we can choose to study the development of the natural sciences in isolation, the documents of the exact sciences, available from the ancient Babylonians (the period of the Hammurabi dynasty, 1800–1600 BCE) and the ancient Egyptians on, are recorded not only in mathematical signs, as one might expect, but are also surrounded by mythological images. Mythological images simultaneously absorb and appropriate scientific discoveries, calendrical calculations, and established views of the world, stars, and planets as their symbols. We have no option but to distinguish the two sciences, yet we must recognize the fact that our documents make no separation and establish no contrast. Various scholars, for example Mircea Eliade and Werner Müller, have stressed the cosmic character of all archaic religious traditions. It is of great importance, however, to add that the history of science points to the interwovenness of science (notably astronomy and physics) and religion.

Epistemological considerations are not separable from socioreligious traditions and cannot be kept for long from the work of a modern scientist. Basic definitions functioning in scientific research are not central in scientific education, yet typically "normal," consensus-bound research ultimately results in revolution. The process of change in religion is quite analogous. As a rule, renowned mystics, prophets, and great reformers have followed their tradition so persistently as to arrive willy-nilly at a change that in some cases amounted to a rebirth or total overhaul of a tradition (e.g., the great reformers in Christianity; Nāgārjuna in Buddhism; the great *bhakti* philosophers, and especially Rāmānuja, in Hinduism; al-Ghazālī in Islam). Any such great change is reflected in the image of the world.

The breakdown of the classical, Aristotelian world image, shaken by Copernicus, Tycho, Brahe, Galileo, Johannes Kepler, and Isaac Newton, is principally due to René Descartes, the initiator of philosophy in modern Western history. The world, instead of being man's environment and being accessible to him through the senses, now becomes definitely an object of rational inquiry of a new, truly objective character of which man is no longer the unquestionable center. The conflict between Galileo and the church is well known and has been given so much attention as to obscure the structures of both science and religion. This conflict is limited to only one science (astronomy) and only one religion (Christianity) in a particular phase of each. Other sciences, such as the science of music or the science of crystals, have never found themselves in a comparable predicament with Christianity. It stands to reason that a religion such as Buddhism, in which the subject of the world's creation and the earth's central position in it has no significant part at all, could not be expected to provoke comparable polemics between astronomers and defenders of the religious tradition.

Two final points must be made to complete the subject of the distinctive place of religion with respect to cosmology. In the first place, we cannot meaningfully speak of an absolute break between religion and the sciences after Copernicus and Descartes. From Gottfried Leibniz to Pierre Teilhard de Chardin, C. F. von Weizsäcker, and Karl Jaspers, writers, scientists, and theologians have dealt with the unity and meaning of the world, a world designed to be religiously and scientifically comprehensible. In the second place, a point of significance, complementary to the first one, is that if we can speak of the cosmos under two aspects in the religious documents we have, the religious view, wherever it does come to the fore, tends to show a certain priority. This is not only true in the temporal sense that the historical development shows us religious assumptions concerning the world before the first recognizable scientific strides are taken, but also in terms of relative importance. Karl Barth has rightly emphasized (in part in opposition to theories by the New Testament theologian Rudolf Bultmann) that the histories of Israel and of the church have unfolded under the impact of various dominant views of the cosmos without being disturbed by them; characteristically, in the entire history of the church, no creed ever made the structure of the universe an item worthy of concern. *Mutatis mutandis,* the same holds true for other religious traditions as well. Even though in archaic traditions the sacred can be expressed primarily through cosmic forms, the sacred supersedes the cosmic in all religions.

[*For further treatment of cosmological myths, see* Cosmogony; Eschatology; *and* Ages of the World. *For a discussion of philosophical views of the cosmos and the nature of reality, see* Metaphysics.]

BIBLIOGRAPHY

For African creation accounts, the most helpful work is Herman Baumann's *Schöpfung und Urzeit des Menschen im Mythus der afrikanischen Völker* (Berlin, 1936). Jean Bayet's *Histoire politique et psychologique de la religion Romaine,* 2d ed. (Paris, 1969), has a special eye for the interwovenness of human orientations and conceptions of the world throughout Roman history. Hendrik Bergema's *De boom des levens in schrift en historie* (Hilversum, Netherlands, 1938) is the most extensive collection of tree symbolisms in religious traditions. A sociological attempt to show that human beings by nature orient themselves toward a more encompassing world than that of their observable social and psychological reality is made by Peter L. Berger and Thomas Luckmann in *The Social Construction of Reality* (Garden City, N.Y., 1966). Edvard Jan Dijksterhuis's *The Mechanization of the World Picture* (Oxford, 1961) is the classic study of philosophies and discussions leading to the birth of science in modern history. Mircea Eliade's *Cosmos and History: The Myth of the Eternal Return* (New York, 1954), *Myth and Reality* (New York, 1963), and *Patterns in Comparative Religion* (New York, 1958) offer the most comprehensive religio-historical studies of cosmic symbolism, especially in archaic societies, with special emphasis on cosmogony as the fundamental myth in any tradition, and on the significance of world renewal. Eliade's *Australian Religions: An Introduction* (Ithaca, N.Y., 1973) elaborates on these and other themes in the particular compass of some culturally most archaic tribal traditions. Adolf E. Jensen's *Myth and Cult among Primitive Peoples* (Chicago, 1963) is especially concerned with the relationship between cosmic views and human behavior. Willibald Kirfel's *Die Kosmographie der Inder* (Bonn, 1920) treats views of the world among Hindus, Buddhists, and Jains.

The most influential works in the history of science to open our eyes to the wider philosophical and religious context of the origins of modern science are by Alexandre Koyré: *Entretiens sur Descartes* (New York, 1944) and *From the Closed World to the Infinite Universe* (Baltimore, 1957). *Mythologies of the Ancient World,* edited by Samuel Noah Kramer (Garden City, N.Y., 1961), ranges from the ancient Near East to ancient Mexico and to India, China, and Japan, their mythologies, including their cosmic views. The best observations made within the context of Vedic and Brahmanic ritual concerning the cosmos are available in Herta Krick's *Das Ritual der Feuergründung* (Vienna, 1982). W. Brede Kristensen's *Het leven uit de dood* (Haarlem, 1926) is the unsurpassed study on the relation of cosmogonies to the spontaneity of life as a central issue in ancient Egyptian and Greek religion. Including all periods and many civilizations, yet with most relevance to cosmogonies in nonliterate traditions, one of the best collections is Charles H. Long's *Alpha: The Myths of Creation* (New York, 1963).

Alexander Marshack's *The Roots of Civilization* (New York, 1972) was the first work to break down artificial barriers between religion and scientific views of the universe on the basis of prehistoric data. Jacques Merleau-Ponty and Bruno Morando's *The Rebirth of Cosmology* (New York, 1976), is a detailed reflection on the limits of modern astronomy. A collection of studies on cosmos and myth in seventeen different nonliterate traditions, plus one playful attempt at a structural analysis of the *Book of Genesis* as myth by Edmund Leach are collected in *Myth and Cosmos,* edited by John Middleton (Garden City, N.Y., 1967). Marijan Molé's *Culte, mythe et cosmologie dans l'Iran ancien* (Paris, 1963) presents a full discussion of ancient Iranian cosmology, with elaborate textual documentation. Werner Müller's *Die heilige Stadt: Roma quadrata, himlisches Jerusalem und die Mythe vom Weltnabel* (Stuttgart, 1961) discusses the tenacity of cosmic views forming the model of city planning; with lengthy bibliography. Teachings concerning the cosmos and its hierarchy, with special attention to microcosmic views are given in Seyyed Hossein Nasr's *An Introduction to Islamic Cosmological Doctrines* (Cambridge, 1964). Joseph Needham's *Science and Civilisation in China,* vol. 2 (Princeton, 1956), is the best study available on any civilization that illuminates the rise of science, cosmology, views of nature within the course of religious traditions and change. Otto Neugebauer wrote the classic work on *The Exact Sciences in Antiquity,* 2d ed. (New York, 1969). Martin P. Nilsson's *Geschichte der griechischen Religion,* 3d ed., 2 vols. (Munich, 1967–1971), is indispensable for the study of religious complexities within which cosmic views in Greece arose and changed. F. S. C. Northrop's *Man, Nature and God* (New York, 1962) deals with the problem of cosmology, science, and nature within a world that is religiously, culturally, and philosophically diverse, yet has no option but to come to terms with its unity.

The best available text on astronomy from classical India is *The Yavanajātaka of Sphujidhvaja*, 2 vols., edited and translated, with commentary, by David Pingree (Cambridge, 1978). For the problem of monotheism and the origin of the cosmos, see Raffaele Pettazzoni's *Essays on the History of Religions* (Leiden, 1954) and *The All-Knowing God* (London, 1956). Don K. Price's "Endless Frontier or Bureaucratic Morass?" and Robert L. Sinsheimer's "The Presumptions of Science," both in *Daedalus* 107 (Spring 1978), present indirect but eloquent arguments for the necessity of a more significant framework for science than science itself can provide. *Ancient Near Eastern Texts relating to the Old Testament*, 3d ed. with supp., edited by James B. Pritchard (Princeton, 1969), is a large collection of myths, laws, and epic texts in which cosmological ideas are embedded. Dualistic views characteristic of Manichaeism are described in Henri-Charles Puech's "Le manichéisme," in *Histoire des religions*, vol. 2, edited by Puech (Paris, 1972). C. F. von Weizsäcker's *The History of Nature* (Chicago, 1949), is a balanced and thoughtful account of the modern natural sciences between philosophy and religion and is of abiding interest. *Studies of A. J. Wensinck* (New York, 1978) interpret a number of cosmological symbols in Mesopotamian, ancient West Semitic, and Arabic traditions.

KEES W. BOLLE

Hindu and Jain Cosmologies

Cosmological speculation concerned with cosmogony, various realms of the universe, and the elements as keys to philosophical doctrines is prominent throughout Indian texts of all periods. In a simplified way, we may say that the Vedas are concerned with fire, the Upaniṣads with water, Sāṃkhya philosophy (an adjunct of Yoga) with breath or wind, and the *bhakti* (devotional) traditions with earth. As Hinduism evolved through the Vedic, Upaniṣadic, Sāṃkhya, and Bhakti periods, it became increasingly concerned with the systematic presentation of cosmological themes. Time was introduced as the principle that organizes the drama of salvation and acts as the medium for divine and human events. The Jains and the Ājīvikas also produced significant bodies of cosmological speculation; these share certain affinities, among which are the absence of divine agencies and an emphasis on the more controlling aspects of time. The deterministic vision of the Ājīvikas eliminates the role of human action as well.

Hinduism

The cosmological formulations of Hinduism differ dramatically from period to period even while drawing on common imagery. Reflections on being and nonbeing become speculations concerning the reality of the world and the soul, and examinations of the structure of the cosmos came to integrate the role of human actions with those of the deity in determining the ultimate destiny of beings.

Vedic Period. The Vedas and Brāhmaṇas, the earliest Hindu sacred writings, are replete with cosmological imagery. At the oldest levels, the mythology of the Vedas speaks of the cosmos as Father Sky (Dyaus Pitṛ) and Mother Earth (Pṛthivī). Elsewhere, the cosmos is said to consist of three realms: *bhūr* (earth), *bhuvaḥ* (air), and *svar* (sky or heaven). The Agnicayana, or ritual building of the Vedic fire altar, is described in the *Śatapatha Brāhmaṇa* as a symbolic construction of the cosmos for ritual purposes. [*See* Maṇḍalas, *article on* Hindu Maṇḍalas, *and* Vedism and Brahmanism.]

Two explicitly philosophical hymns are frequently cited to illustrate the level of philosophical refinement in these ancient texts. The first (*Ṛgveda* 10. 129.1–7) describes the cosmogony:

> Then even nothingness was not, nor existence.
> There was no air then, nor the heavens beyond it.
> What covered it? Where was it? In whose keeping?
> Was there then cosmic water, in depths unfathomed?
> Then there were neither death nor immortality,
> nor was there then the torch of night and day.
> The One breathed windlessly and self-sustaining.
> There was that One then, and there was no other.
> At first there was only darkness wrapped in darkness.
> All this was only unillumined water.
> That One which came to be, enclosed in nothing.
> Arose at last, born of the power of heat.
> In the beginning desire descended on it—
> that was the primal seed, born of the mind.
> The sages who have searched their hearts with wisdom
> know that which is, is kin to that which is not.
> And they have stretched their cord across the void,
> and know what was above, and what below.
> Seminal powers made fertile mighty forces.
> Below was strength, and over it was impulse.
> But, after all, who knows, and who can say
> whence it all came, and how creation happened?
> The gods themselves are later than creation,
> so who knows truly whence it has arisen?
> Whence all creation had its origin,
> he, whether he fashioned it or whether he did not,
> He, who surveys it all from highest heaven,
> he knows—or maybe even he does not know.
> (quoted in Basham, 1954, pp. 247–248)

The second (*Ṛgveda* 10.90) portrays the universe as a cosmic man *(puruṣa)*. It is this imagery that seems to be reintegrated in the later *bhakti* materials, which see the universe as the body of the deity and apparently bring together the cosmic *puruṣa* with the *puruṣa* understood as the individual soul of Sāṃkhya philosophy.

Upaniṣadic Period. The Upaniṣadic literature provides a systematic presentation of the doctrines of *karman* and transmigration, expands the hierarchy of Vedic worlds from three to seven, and introduces certain cosmographic themes, including speculation involving the imagery of water. The individual self *(ātman)* is likened to a river that loses its identity as it flows into the great self *(brahman),* represented by the ocean.

Cosmography. Compared with later materials, the cosmographies of the Upaniṣads are not highly developed. They do, however, provide a hint of things to come. For example, the *Bṛhadāraṇyaka Upaniṣad* (3.3.2) states: "This inhabited world, of a truth, is as broad as thirty-two days [i.e., days' journeys] of the sun-god's chariot. The earth, which is twice as wide, surrounds it on all sides. Then there is an interspace as broad as the edge of a razor or the wing of a mosquito." (*The Thirteen Principal Upaniṣads,* trans. Robert E. Hume, 2d rev. ed., New York, 1931, p. 111). Among other things, we find here a numerology, namely, the progression from one to sixty-four, derived either arithmetically or geometrically, that functions as a recurring theme within the cosmological materials.

The sun and moon are of interest primarily as they concern the journey of the soul to other worlds. At death, the soul is said to leave the funeral pyre and to take, depending on its *karman,* one of two paths: the path of the gods *(devayāna)* or that of the fathers *(pitṛyāna)* (see *Bṛhadāraṇyaka Upaniṣad* 6.2.16, *Chāndogya Upaniṣad* 4.15.5).

If the *devayāna* is taken, the soul enters the flames created by the burning of the corpse. It then proceeds into the day, then into the bright half of the month (waxing of the moon), the bright half of the year (ascending movement of the sun through the signs of the zodiac), the year, the sun, the moon, the lightning, and finally into *brahman* and liberation.

If it follows the *pitṛyāna,* which leads to its eventual rebirth, the soul enters the smoke rather than the flame, then continues into the night, the dark half of the month (waning of the moon), the dark half of the year (descending movement of the sun through the signs of the zodiac), the world of the fathers, the *ākāśa* ("space"), and finally into the moon "as long as a remnant (of good works) yet exists." Return from the moon results in rebirth according to a variety of principles.

Vertical cosmology. The three levels of the Vedic universe are now expanded into seven realms. These include, from lowest to highest, *bhūr, bhuvaḥ, svar, mahas, janas, tapas,* and *satyam.* Astronomical conceptions of the various heavenly bodies are of limited interest in the Upaniṣads.

Sāṃkhya. In its strictest sense the term *sāṃkhya* means "enumeration," but it is frequently rendered as "cosmology." Sāṃkhya describes how the universe evolved from *prakṛti* (primordial, undifferentiated matter, regarded as feminine) by becoming entangled with *puruṣa* (individual soul, regarded as masculine). This differentiation results in an enumeration of twenty-four evolutes, which include the senses and the elements. The earth element *(kṣiti)* is the last of the evolutes.

As a philosophical companion to the practice of yoga, Sāṃkhya provides a model whereby the yogin gradually extricates the soul from the evolutes of *prakṛti.* In the end the soul realizes its eternal nature and is no longer subject to death and transmigration. Although it embraces *karman* and transmigration, Sāṃkhya espouses no sense of time as an agent in itself or as something that embraces all beings.

While the evolutes of *prakṛti* do constitute a cosmology in some sense, their basis in the individual soul means that they do not constitute a world in the sense of a support for all beings. There is, however, at least one attempt—in the *Yogabhāṣya*—to represent the Sāṃkhya enumeration of elements in terms of a hierarchical universe of the sort generally regarded as a cosmological system. Here the lower evolutes represent the hells and the high evolutes constitute the heavens. In this manner, the soul, through the practice of yoga, detaches itself from the lower elements, beginning with the earth. After suppressing them, it moves gradually to the higher realms and finally, upon its last departure from *prakṛti,* dissolves the world. [*See* Sāṃkhya.]

Bhakti Period. Cosmological speculation abounded during all of the earlier periods of Hinduism, but it was never presented so systematically or accorded such a central place as during the period in which the *bhakti,* or devotional traditions, dominated Hinduism. According to the *bhakti* cosmologies, the world supports all beings. All beings form part of the body of the deity, and time—also an aspect of the deity—is an agent that moves the beings toward their final state. This world is often described as existing for the sake of progeny, and its gods must frequently prevent it from "sinking" under the weight of all the beings.

Mahābhārata. Although the *Mahābhārata* is not a cosmological treatise *per se,* it does contain at least two sections that are explicitly cosmological. The *Bhīṣmāparva* (sections 4–12), for example, presents a fully developed cosmograph, characteristic of the *bhakti* traditions, although it differs in important details from that of the Purāṇas. Themes concerning the nature of time and its division into *kalpa*s and *yuga*s appear in the *Śān-*

tiparvan (12.224). Similar outlines are also given in the *Manusmṛti* (1.64–86).

The Epics and Purāṇas contain explicit and implicit teachings on the doctrine of *avatāras*, or "descents." [*See* Avatāra.] These *avatāras* appear at various points when time has lost its power to fight the demons and to restore the Dharma. As early as in the *Bhagavadgītā* of the *Mahābhārata*, Kṛṣṇa apparently refers to the notion of time and to the integration of the doctrine of descents (*avatāras*) with the descending ages (*yugas*). [*See* Bhagavadgītā.] He states:

> For the protection of the good,
> And for the destruction of the evil-doers,
> To make a firm footing for the right,
> I come into being in age after age [*yuge yuge*].
> (*Bhagavadgītā* 4.8)

Purāṇas. Cosmology seems to be at the very heart of the Puranic vision. The Purāṇas ("that which is ancient") have been characterized as having five marks *(pañcalakṣaṇa)*, among them creation *(sarga)* and secondary creation *(pratisarga)*, which include the various destructions *(pralaya)*. [*See* Purāṇas.]

Cosmograph. The *bhakti* cosmograph is described in a number of writings, including the *Viṣṇu Purāṇa*, a text generally considered to date from the fourth century CE. The cosmograph consists of the flat disk of the earth, which is itself composed of a series of circles. These circles are understood to be seven concentric islands that double in size as one moves from the center to the perimeter. The islands are separated from each other by a series of oceans, each of which has the width of the island it encircles. In the center of the innermost island, Jambudvīpa, stands the great golden mountain known as Mount Meru, which is conical in shape and points downward. Mountain ranges, running in straight, parallel lines from east to west, further divide Jambudvīpa into a series of nine *varṣas*, or regions.

The northernmost *varṣa* is Uttarakuru, whose name may refer to the Kurukṣetra, the scene of the central battle in the *Mahābhārata*. To the south are Hiranmaya and Ramyaka. Jambudvīpa is divided through the center and from east to west into Ketumāla, Ilavṛta, and Bhadrāśya. South of these are Harivarṣa, Kimpuruṣa, and Bharata. Most of the existing secondary literature assumes that Bharata is the same region occupied by modern-day India because Indians still call their country Bharata. Bharata's primary attribute, however, is its designation as a *karmabhūmi*, or realm where actions are subject to the laws of *karman*. As a result, salvation can be achieved in this region alone. Bharata is subdivided into nine sections, and the Alakanandā River, which is the southern branch of the celestial Ganges, divides here into seven branches. One additional characteristic of Bharata: it is here alone that rain falls.

The full series of seven islands, then, begins with Jambudvīpa, whose diameter is 100,000 *yojanas*. (A *yojana* has been defined variously as the equivalent of 2.5, 4, 5, or 9 English miles, although its etymological link to *yoga* and *yuga* suggests a metaphysical significance as well). Jambudvīpa forms an actual circle whose radius measures 50,000 *yojanas*; the remaining islands are more accurately described as ring shaped. Proceeding outward from Jambudvīpa, which is at the center, the islands are Plakṣadvīpa (with a width of 200,000 *yojanas*), Śālmaladvīpa (400,000), Kuśadvīpa (800,000), Krauñcadvīpa (1,600,000), and Śākadvīpa (3,200,000). The seventh and outermost island is Puṣkaradvīpa, whose width equals 6,400,000 *yojanas*. All the islands derive their names from the trees and plants that grow on them.

Various systems of mountains characterize these islands as well. As noted, Jambudvīpa is divided into seven *varṣas* by a series of parallel mountain ranges. In the center of the island, the mountains surrounding Mount Meru create two additional *varṣas* for a total of nine *varṣas* in Jambudvīpa. Each of the five intermediate islands is divided into seven *varṣas* by seven radial mountains, the names of which change from island to island. The inner (Dhātakīvarṣa) and outer (Mahāvīravarṣa) halves of the outermost island, Puṣkaradvīpa, are delineated by the ring mountain known as Mānassottara.

The oceans that separate these islands from one another, which have the same diameter or width as the island they surround, are known as Lavaṇoda (Salt Ocean, 100,000 *yojanas*), Ikṣura (Ocean of Molasses, 200,000), Suroda (Ocean of Wine, 400,000), Ghṛtoda (Ocean of Ghee, 800,000), Dadhyoda (Ocean of Curds, 1,600,000), Kṣīroda (Ocean of Milk, 3,200,000), and Svādūdaka (Freshwater Ocean, 6,400,000). This last ocean circulates beyond Puṣkaradvīpa and separates it from the golden realm, which constitutes the end of the universe *(lokasaṃsthiti)*. The golden realm contains an additional ring mountain, known as the Lokāloka Mountain, which divides the world from the nonworld; beyond it, the sun does not shine. Between Lokāloka Mountain and the shell *(aṇḍakaṭāha)* of the egg of Brahmā *(brahmāṇḍa)*, which envelops the universe in its entirety, is a region of perpetual darkness. Although the texts are not clear, it appears that only the unmixed elements (earth, wind, air, and fire) exist here. The entire diameter of this universe is said to equal 500,000,000 *yojanas*.

The stars and the other heavenly bodies are located

above the surface of the earth. According to a variety of sources, the stars move around Mount Meru in a circular manner, using the North Star (Dhruva) as their pivot. Below them lies the flat disk of the "earth." The sun, moon, and planets move about in chariots drawn by horses. Together with the stars, they are attached to the North Star by "bands of air" that allow them to travel in their proper orbits.

The Hindu cosmograph, with its conical center, Mount Meru, and the chariot of the sun and disk of stars circulating above the disk of concentric islands and oceans, may be based on a projection of the celestial sphere onto a flat surface. In such an analysis, the circle of the sun is the mythographic expression of the circle of the ecliptic. Mount Meru represents the projection of the celestial Tropic of Cancer, while the Mānassottara Mountain represents the projection of the Tropic of Capricorn. The prominence of the North Star (Dhruva), the conspicuous absence of the south polar star, and stories about the exile of Agastya (Canopus) to the Southern Hemisphere to preserve the cosmograph all support the idea that the Hindu cosmograph is a northern, planispheric projection of the sort used to construct such instruments as the astrolabe.

Vertical cosmology. The vertical cosmology of the *Viṣṇu Purāṇa* divides the universe into the seven realms of the Upaniṣads—*bhūrloka, bhuvaḥloka, svarloka, mahasloka, janasloka, tapasloka,* and *satyamloka*—although with considerable additional elaboration. The *bhūrloka* contains the cosmograph of the seven islands outlined above, including Bharata, which is the only *karmabhūmi,* or land of works. It also contains the seven Patalas (netherworlds)—Atala, Vitala, Nitala, Gabhastimat, Mahātala, Sutala, and Pātāla (the lowest). Below these are some twenty-eight hells.

The *bhuvaḥloka* is the realm of the sun, which moves through its annual course in its chariot. Above this is the *svarloka* (heaven), containing, from lowest to highest, the Moon, its twenty-seven or twenty-eight Nakṣatras (mansions of the moon), Mercury (Buddha), Venus (Śukra), Mars (Angāraka), Jupiter (Bṛhaspati), Saturn (Śani), the Seven Ṛṣis (Great Bear), and Dhruva (North Star).

These three realms—*bhurloka, bhuvaḥloka,* and *svarloka*—are collectively known as *kṛtika,* meaning that they are transitory or made. They are described as the region of the consequences of works and are said to be renewed with every *kalpa.* It is in these realms that the fruits of *karman* acquired in Bharata manifest themselves and that souls are reborn to enjoy these fruits. These are the enjoyment realms *(bhogabhūmi),* as opposed to the *karmabhūmi* of Bharata.

Above the *svarloka* is the *mahasloka,* which is considered a mixed realm because it is deserted by beings at the end of a *kalpa* but is not destroyed. Finally, the three highest realms—*janasloka, tapasloka,* and *satyamloka*—are described as *akṛitika.* They perish only at the end of the life of Brahmā.

Chronology. The *bhakti* traditions divide time into such components as *yugas, caturyugas, kalpas,* and days and nights of Brahmā. It provides an extraordinarily thorough analysis of these components. Together with doctrines concerning the various destructions (*pralayas*), they are the glue that holds this cosmology together and provides it with a coherent drama of salvation. Indeed, the *Viṣṇu Purāṇa* asserts that it is time that constitutes the body of the deity.

Hindu divisions of time are as follows. Fifteen twinklings of the eye make a *kāśṭhā;* thirty *kāśṭhās,* one *kalā;* and thirty *kalās,* one *muhūrtta.* Thirty *muhūrttas* constitute a day and night of mortals; thirty such days make a month, which is divided into two halves (waxing and waning). Six months form an *ayana,* and two *ayanas* compose a year. The southern *ayana* is a night and the northern a day of the gods. Twelve thousand divine years, each comprising 360 such days, constitute the period of the four *yugas (caturyuga).* The *kṛtayuga* consists of four thousand divine years; the *tretāyuga* of three thousand; the *dvāparayuga* of two thousand, and the *kaliyuga* of one thousand. The period that precedes a *yuga* is called a *sandhyā;* it lasts for as many hundred years as there are thousands in the *yuga.* The *sandhyānsa,* at the end of the *yuga,* is of similar duration. Together the four *yugas* constitute a *kalpa.* A thousand *kalpas* is a day of Brahmā, and fourteen Manus reign within that term during a period known as a *manvantara.* At the end of a day of Brahmā, the universe is consumed by fire and its dissolution occurs. Brahmā then sleeps for a night of equal duration, at the end of which he creates anew. Three hundred sixty such days and nights constitutes a year of Brahmā and one hundred such years equal his entire life *(mahākalpa).* One *parārddha,* or half his life, has expired.

Puranic divisions of time are apparently based on Babylonian speculations. The astronomical sciences *(jyotiḥśāstra)* encouraged actual efforts to calculate the number of revolutions of the planets during the *yugas, kalpas,* and *mahākalpas,* as well as efforts to assign dates to the grand conjunctions of the middle planets at Aries. The date 18/19 February 3101 BCE, Thursday/Friday is frequently cited in these traditions as marking the beginning of the *kaliyuga.* The *Paitāmahāsiddhānta* (early fifth century), found in the *Viṣṇudharmottara Purāṇa* (2.166–174), is the earliest astronomical text of this genre and is the basis of the Brāhmapakṣa, which together with the Āryapakṣa and the Ārdharātrikapakṣa constitute the three formative schools of Indian astronomy. All other schools are based on them.

Time and its destructions (pralaya). The various *pralayas* epitomize the agency of time by moving the soul—and, indeed, the universe—from its current state to its eventual salvation and beatitude. The Purāṇas distinguish four types of dissolution, each reversing the process of creation at different levels. These include (1) *nitya-pralaya,* or physical death of the individual caught in the cycle of transmigration; (2) *ātyantika-pralaya,* or spiritual liberation *(mokṣa),* which puts an end to transmigration; (3) *prākṛta-pralaya,* or dissolution of the elements at the end of the life of Brahmā; and (4) *naimittika-pralaya,* or occasional dissolution associated with the cycles of *yugas* and descents of *avatāras*.

Jainism

One of the great heterodox traditions emerging during the fifth century BCE, Jainism developed a tradition of cosmological speculation that is without peer. All beings are subordinate to time, although acts and pursuit of the religious vocation affect destiny.

Cosmography. The cosmograph is situated in the middle tier of the Jain universe, and it is here that all human activity takes place and that the Jain religion flourishes. This middle world is arranged into countless *(asaṃkhyāta)* concentric rings of land (*dvīpas*). These rings surround a central island, and each is separated by various oceans.

As in the Hindu cosmograph, the central island, which is 100,000 *yojanas* in diameter, is known as Jambudvīpa after the Jambu tree that stands atop Mount Meru (Mandara), located at the center of the island. Mount Meru measures 100,000 *yojanas* from top to bottom. It has a truncated cone, whose point faces upward, and is said to have one thousand *yojanas* beneath the surface of the earth. Jambudvīpa consists of seven *varṣas*: Bharata, Haimavata, Ramyaka, Videha, Hari, Hairaṇyaka, and Airāvata. These are separated from each other by six mountain ranges running east to west. Bharata, Airāvata, and half of Videha are *karmabhūmis*, or realms of action, in which liberation can be obtained. The remaining continents are *bhogabhūmis*, or realms of enjoyment. The capital cities of both Bharata and Airāvata are designated Ayodhyā, which is also the name of Rāmā's capital in the *Rāmāyaṇa*. From Bharata or Airāvata to Videha, the width of the lands and mountains that border them increases in the series 1, 2, 4, 8, 16, 32, 64. Actual representations of Jambudvīpa ignore these dimensions.

The first ring continent surrounding Jambudvīpa is Dhātakīkhanda. It is twice the diameter of Jambudvīpa and has an identical arrangement of *varṣas*. It contains radial mountains running toward Mandara and mountain ranges at the north and south that divide its eastern and western halves, each identical with Jambudvīpa and each containing a Mount Meru (Mandara) due east and west of the same mountain in Jambudvīpa. The height of these mountains is eighty-five thousand *yojanas*, with one thousand *yojanas* beneath the earth. Dhātakīkhanda is separated from Jambudvīpa by the Lavaṇa Sea, which is twice the width of Jambudvīpa.

Next is Puṣkaravara, which is again double the size of Dhātakīkhanda. Puṣkaravara is separated from Dhātakīkhanda by the thick, black waters of the Kāloya Sea. Like Dhātakīkhanda, its northern and southern halves are delineated by mountains, and each area has its own Mount Meru. Puṣkaravara is divided into inner and outer halves by the Mānassottara Mountain, represented as summits in each of the cardinal directions. Only the interior half is inhabitable by human beings. Moreover, all human institutions, including chronology *(samaya),* end here.

From 790 to 900 *yojanas* above the surface of Jambudvīpa are the chariots of the gods of light (*jyotiṣas*). These include the stars, suns, moons, constellations, and planets, whose numbers increase from one island to the next. Just as the cosmograph seems divided in half from top to bottom (i.e., north to south), so are there two suns controlling day and night in Jambudvīpa as well as multiple suns circulating around the other island-continents. The moons circulate in 15 spiral orbits about Mount Meru—5 above Jambudvīpa and 10 above Lavaṇa. Similarly, of the 183 orbits of the sun, 65 are above Jambudvīpa, and the remaining 118 are above Lavaṇa.

Vertical Cosmology. The Jain universe *(loka* or *loka-ākāśa)* is conceived as a three-dimensional structure. Just beyond the boundaries of this structure are three atmospheric layers *(valaya):* those of humid air *(ghana-ambu),* dense air *(ghana-vāta),* and rarefied air *(tanu-vāta).* Finally there is the *aloka-ākāśa,* the empty space in which no world, atmosphere, motion, or anything else is to be found.

The hierarchy, or realms, within the *loka-ākāśa* is divided into four parts:

1. The lower world *(adhi-loka)* is the home of the infernal beings *(nāraki),* as well as certain demons, titans, and so on. These regions consist of seven tiers *(bhūmi),* each darker than the one above: *ratna-prabhā, śarkarā-prabhā, vālukā-prabhā, paṅka-prabhā, dhūma-prabhā, tamah-prabhā,* and *mahāt-mah-prabhā.*
2. The middle, or terrestrial, world *(madhya-loka)* consists of innumerable concentric island-continents

(dvīpa-samudra) with Jambudvīpa in the center. This is the abode of humans *(manuṣya)* and animals *(tiryañca)*. Human beings are not found beyond the middle of the third continent.

3. In the higher, or celestial, world *(ūrdhva-loka)* are found the abodes of heavenly beings (*vaimānikadeva,* or gods endowed with celestial vehicles). These gods fall into two categories: those born in *kalpa* heavens *(kalpopapanna)* and those born beyond them *(kalpātīta)*. The former are ordinary beings who may or may not have entered the holy path of insight *(samyak-darśana);* the latter are invariably endowed with this insight and are destined to attain *mokṣa,* or liberation, within two or three births after returning to human existence. The *kalpopapanna* beings reside in one of sixteen realms; the *kalpātīta* have fourteen. The highest of the *kalpātīta* realms is the Sarvārthasiddhi. Beings born here are said to be in their penultimate existence; they will be reborn as human beings and will attain *mokṣa* in that life.
4. *Siddha-loka* is the permanent abode of the liberated souls (*siddhas*). Shaped like an open umbrella, this region appears crescent shaped when viewed from the side. It lies beyond the celestial realms at the apex of the universe.

Chronology. Jain doctrines of time assert that *karmabhūmi* areas are subject to an endless temporal cycle. This is ascending *(utsarpiṇī)* on the one hand and descending *(avasarpiṇī)* on the other. Each is divided into six epochs, similar but different from the Puranic *yugas*.

These epochs include, in the order in which they occur during an *avasarpiṇī, suṣamā-suṣamā* (extremely happy), whose duration is said to be 4×10^{14} *sāgaropamā* (one *sāgaropamā* is equal to $8{,}400{,}000 \times 10^{19}$) years; *suṣama* (happy), with a duration of 3×10^{14} *sāgaropamā* years; *suṣamā-duṣamā* (more happy than unhappy), with a duration of 2×10^{14} *sāgaropamā years; duṣamā-suṣamā* (more unhappy than happy), with a duration of 1×10^{14} *sāgaropamā* less 42,000 common years; *duṣamā* (unhappy) with a duration of 21,000 common years; and *duṣamā-duṣamā* (very unhappy), also with a duration of 21,000 common years. The order is reversed in an *utsarpiṇī,* and one follows another in unbroken succession.

The length of human life varies with the length of the epoch. It is only during the third and fourth epochs, when there is neither an extremity of happiness nor of unhappiness, that *mokṣa* can be attained.

Tīrthaṃkaras. The Jains assert the appearance of twenty-four *tīrthaṃkaras* (those who make it possible to ford the stream) in each half cycle in the *karmabhūmis*. This belief is similar to that found in the Hindu doctrines of *avatāras*. At the present time, we are in an *avasarpiṇī,* whose first *tīrthaṃkara* was Ṛṣabha. The twenty-fourth is the historical founder of Jainism, Mahāvīra. Seventy-five years and eight and one-half months after the birth of Mahāvīra, the fifth *(duṣamā)* era of the current aeon began. [*See* Jainism.]

The Ājīvikas

The Ājīvika tradition emerged at the time of Mahāvīra and Gautama, the founders of Jainism and Buddhism, respectively, but is now extinct. Its ideas relating to determinism *(niyati)* and to transmigration illuminate central aspects of Indian cosmologies.

Determinism. The Ājīvika leader Gośāla (Makkhali Gosāla) embraced the principle of *niyati* as that which controlled every action and left no room for volition. "If with a sharp discus a man reduces all the life on earth to a single heap, he commits no sin. Likewise, if a man go down the north bank of the Ganges giving alms and sacrifices, he acquires no merit" (Basham, 1951, p. 13). *Karman* was not denied, but it was believed unaffected by virtuous conduct. Since free will was illusory, all change and time became illusory as well. This concept can be explained by means of the following logic. If all future events are rigidly determined they can in some sense be considered to exist already. Thus, the future exists in the present, and both future and present exist in the past.

Transmigration. In addition to his concept of determination, Gośāla developed an intricate cosmology for the Ājīvikas. It held that there are 8,400,000 *mahākappas* through which all must travel before they can reach salvation. During this time the soul must be reborn in each of 1,406,600 chief sorts of wombs, or *yoni-pamukha*. Of these, the human births must include all of the six classes of men. Also required are 4,900 births as an Ājīvika, 4,900 as a wandering mendicant, 4,900 as a serpent, 7 as a goblin, and 7 in a lake in which the soul takes refuge before the end of its journey. As the soul approaches the end of its long, cosmic journey, it has 707 dreams of psychic significance and then enters its final 21 births. At the end of these births it finally passes into *nirvāṇa*. In order that the world not be depleted of souls as one after another attains liberation, certain souls return from the liberated state. These souls are called (in Pali sources) *bodhisattas*.

Duration of a Mahākappa. In describing the duration of the cycles to which the soul is subject, Gośāla is said to have used the following metaphor. The bed of the Ganges is 250 *yojanas* in length, half a *yojana* in width, and 500 *dhanus* in depth. If one grain of sand were removed from the riverbed every one hundred years, the total time required for the removal of all the sand would be one *sara.* Three hundred thousand *saras* of this duration equal one *mahākappa.* [*See* Ājīvikas *and the biography of Gośāla.*]

BIBLIOGRAPHY

Basham, A. L. *History and Doctrine of the Ājīvikas: A Vanished Indian Religion.* London, 1951.

Basham, A. L. *The Wonder That Was India.* London, 1954.

Biardeau, Madeleine. *Études de mythologies hindoue,* vol. 1, *Cosmogonies purāṇiques.* Paris, 1981.

Caillat, Colette, and Ravi Kumar. *La cosmology jaína.* Paris, 1981.

Dasgupta, Surendranath. *Yoga as Philosophy and Religion* (1924). Reprint, Calcutta, 1973.

Deussen, Paul. *The Philosophy of the Upanishads.* Translated by A. S. Geden. London, 1906; 2d ed., New York, 1966.

Gombrich, Richard F. "Ancient Indian Cosmology." In *Ancient Cosmologies,* edited by Carmen Blacker and Michael Loewe, pp. 110–142. London, 1975.

Hiltebeitel, Alf. *The Ritual of Battle: Krishna in the Mahābhārata.* Ithaca, N.Y., 1976.

Jaini, Padmanabh S. *The Jaina Path of Purification.* Berkeley, 1979.

Kirfel, Willibald. *Die Kosmographie der Inder.* Bonn, 1920.

Kloetzli, W. Randolph. "Maps of Time—Mythologies of Descent: Scientific Instruments and the Purāṇic Cosmograph," *History of Religions* 25 (November 1985): 116–147.

O'Flaherty, Wendy Doniger, ed. *Karma and Rebirth in Classical Indian Traditions.* Berkeley, 1980.

Pingree, David. "History of Mathematical Astronomy in India." In *Dictionary of Scientific Biography,* edited by Charles C. Gillespie, vol. 15, supp. 1, pp. 533–633. New York, 1978.

Schubring, Walther. *The Doctrine of the Jainas.* Delhi, 1962.

Wilson, H. H., trans. and ed. *The Vishnu Purāṇa* (1840). 2d ed. Calcutta, 1961.

W. Randolph Kloetzli

Buddhist Cosmology

There is no single system of Buddhist cosmology. Virtually every theological tendency within the Buddhist tradition addressed the cosmological sciences from its special perspective—seeing the universe as the stage for a drama of salvation cast in terms of its own particular philosophical and theological predilections. Buddhist systems are related not only to other Indian systems, for example, Hindu, Jain, Ājīvika, and so forth, but to Hellenistic speculations as well.

The single-world system that is particularly prominent in the oldest Buddhist texts pictures the cosmos as a flat disk with heavens and meditation realms above and hells below. Although the oldest tradition apparently limited its interest to a single-world system, a grandiose cosmic structure developed on the perimeter of this single universe. Traces of themes associated with multiple-world systems appear in texts of the Pali canon. A ten-thousand-world system is mentioned in the Jātakas, though with little elaboration, and in a more systematic way in Buddhaghosa's *Visuddhimagga* (sec. 414ff.). These and other similar cosmologies are variants of the *sāhasra* cosmology, or "cosmology of thousands." They focus on themes of cosmic time and belong to the Hīnayāna schools of Buddhism.

The cosmology of the Mahāyāna, characterized by innumerable world systems distributed throughout the ten regions of space, can be characterized as an *asaṃkhyeya* cosmology, or "cosmology of innumerables." Although certain of these world systems lack the presence of a Buddha, most are Buddha fields (*buddhakṣetras*) where a fully and perfectly enlightened Tathāgata resides and teaches the law for the benefit of countless beings. Generally speaking, there are three types of *buddhakṣetras*: "pure" *(viśuddha),* "impure" *(aviśuddha),* and "mixed" *(miśraka).* Sukhāvatī is the best known among the Pure Lands, although in some texts it is clearly subordinated to others. Sahā is the most important of the Impure Lands—although from another perspective, Sahā may be considered a "mixed" land, alternately ornamented (pure) and unornamented (impure). Located in the region of the south, Sahā is our universe and is the field of the Buddha Śākyamuni.

At the core of each of these cosmologies is a drama of salvation. It is this drama of salvation, implicit in all the Buddhist cosmologies, that allows for the integration of the scientific and theological bases of these cosmologies, represented in images of motion and light. More specifically, these cosmologies transform the astronomical themes of motion and light into the mythophilosophic themes of journey and soul. The seemingly fantastic numbers characteristic of these cosmologies are grounded in the power of mathematics that allows the astronomers to measure the motions of the heavens and enables the faithful to comprehend the theological and mystical implications of these measurements.

Single-World System. The basic outlines of the single-world system are generally agreed upon throughout a broad spectrum of Buddhism and are a prominent feature of the Pali texts as well as the Buddhist Sanskrit literature. Buddhist text designate it as the *cakravāla,* after the mountain of iron that surrounds it. Single, circular world systems are prominent in the Puranic and Jain cosmologies as well and have a wide dispersion throughout the classical world in general. This article ignores variations of detail in the Buddhist texts and is restricted to the extensive and systematic testimony of Vasubandhu's *Abhidharmakośa* (hereafter *Kośa*), a Sautrāntika work composed in the fourth or fifth century of the common era.

The cakravāla. The *cakravāla* is represented as a disk ringed with a series of seven circular, golden mountain ranges, arranged concentrically with Mount Meru at the center and the *cakravāla* wall of iron at the perimeter. Proceeding outward from the center, the mountains are known as Meru, Yugandhara, Īṣadhāra, Khadirika, Sudarśana, Aśvakarṇa, Vinataka, Nimindhara, and Cakravāla. Mount Meru has a height of eighty thousand *yojanas* and penetrates the waters in equal measure; each of the mountain ranges is half the height and depth of the preceding range. The waters of various seas *(sītā)* fill the regions between the mountain ranges.

The landmasses are situated in the great ocean *(mahāsamudra)* that flows within the area bounded by Nimindhara and Cakravāla. The four landmasses, located at the points of the compass, are spoken of as "islands" *(dvīpa)* and are named Pūrvavideha (in the east), Jambudvīpa (in the south—named after the Jambu tree that is found there), Aparagodānīya (in the west), and Uttarakuru (in the north). The names of these islands are suggestive of theological directions as well: for example, Videha is the name of disembodied deities and suggests the goal of yoga, which is to liberate the soul from its bondage to the body; the Jambu tree is suggestive of the fruits of the path of Buddhism, Godānīya of Kṛṣṇa's heaven, the Go-loka, and Uttarakuru of the Kurukṣetra, the "field of the Kurus," on which was fought the great battle of the *Mahābhārata*.

All of these entities rest on a layer of golden earth *(kāñcanamayībhūmi)*, and all of the mountains except the *cakravāla* are composed of excrescences of this golden earth. While the islands are not similarly composed, the *vajrāsana* ("diamond throne") situated in the middle of Jambudvīpa is said to rest on the golden earth. The golden earth of the *cakravāla* rests on a circle of water *(ābmaṇḍala)*; a layer of wind *(vāyumaṇḍala)* supports the water and in turn rests on empty space *(ākāśa)*.

The four islands of the *cakravāla* are distinguished from each other in a number of ways, particularly with regard to their size and shape and the life span of their inhabitants. Uttarakuru is square, measuring 2,000 *yojanas* on a side, and life there has a duration of 1,000 years. (A *yojana* has been defined variously as the equivalent of 2.5, 4, 5, or 9 English miles, although its etymological link to *yoga* and *yuga* suggests a metaphysical significance as well.) Godānīya is shaped like a full moon measuring 7,500 *yojanas* around with a diameter of 2,500 *yojanas*, and life there lasts 500 years. Pūrvavideha has the shape of a half moon with three sides said to be 2,000 *yojanas* in length and a fourth that is 350 *yojanas* in length. Duration of life there is equal to 250 years. Jambudvīpa, too, measures 2,000 *yojanas* on three sides, but its fourth side is only 3.5 *yojanas* long. It is said to be shaped like a chariot. (In addition to the four main islands, the *Kośa* recognizes eight intermediate islands, two of which are similar in shape to each of the four main islands, although they are only one-tenth the size. The shape of the faces of the inhabitants of each of the islands is said to resemble the shape of the island.)

Jambudvīpa provides an important exception to the superhuman and unchanging durations of life found in the other islands. The length of human life in Jambudvīpa varies; at the beginning of the *kalpa* it is incalculable, but eventually it diminishes to only ten years and continues to fluctuate throughout the *kalpa*. Because of these irregular life expectancies, the inhabitants of Jambudvīpa are particularly aware of the workings of *karman*. Moreover, it is only in Jambudvīpa during a time of declining life spans that a Buddha will appear. Another distinguishing feature of Jambudvīpa is that all the hells are situated beneath this island. The *Kośa* distinguishes eight hot hells and eight cold hells, although other systems are attested.

A series of heavens is arrayed above the *cakravāla* in three great divisions: (1) those heavens in the "realm of desire" *(kāmadhātu)* corresponding to the six classes of the "gods of desire" *(kāmadeva)*; (2) the seventeen heavens belonging to the "realm of form" *(rūpadhātu)*, grouped into four classes of "meditation realms" *(dhyāna)*; and (3) the four "infinities" of the "realm of nonform" *(ārūpyadhātu)*. For the names of all the heavens and other divisions in schematic form, see figure 1. The significance of these divisions is uncertain except for the fact that they form a schematic representation of Buddhist philosophy and doctrine related to meditation. Nevertheless, several of the heavens have characteristics worth noting. The ruler of the Trāyastriṃśa is Indra, or Śakra, whose abode rests atop Mount Meru. The Tuṣita is distinguished by the fact that it is here that the *bodhisattva* is born immediately prior to being born as a Buddha in Jambudvīpa. The duration of life in the Tuṣita corresponds to the ages in which a Buddha appears. The uppermost heaven is the Akaniṣṭha; the fourth infinity is designated *bhavāgra* ("pinnacle of being").

Associated drama. In its simplest form, the drama of the single-world system depends on the fact that the universe is limited and continuous. The monk travels through all the realms of the universe in the course of his meditations, eventually getting beyond it—detaching himself from it—to take possession of an individual *nirvāṇa* and achieve the state of *arhat*. For the most part, neither the presence of a Buddha nor the divisions of cosmic time are central to this drama.

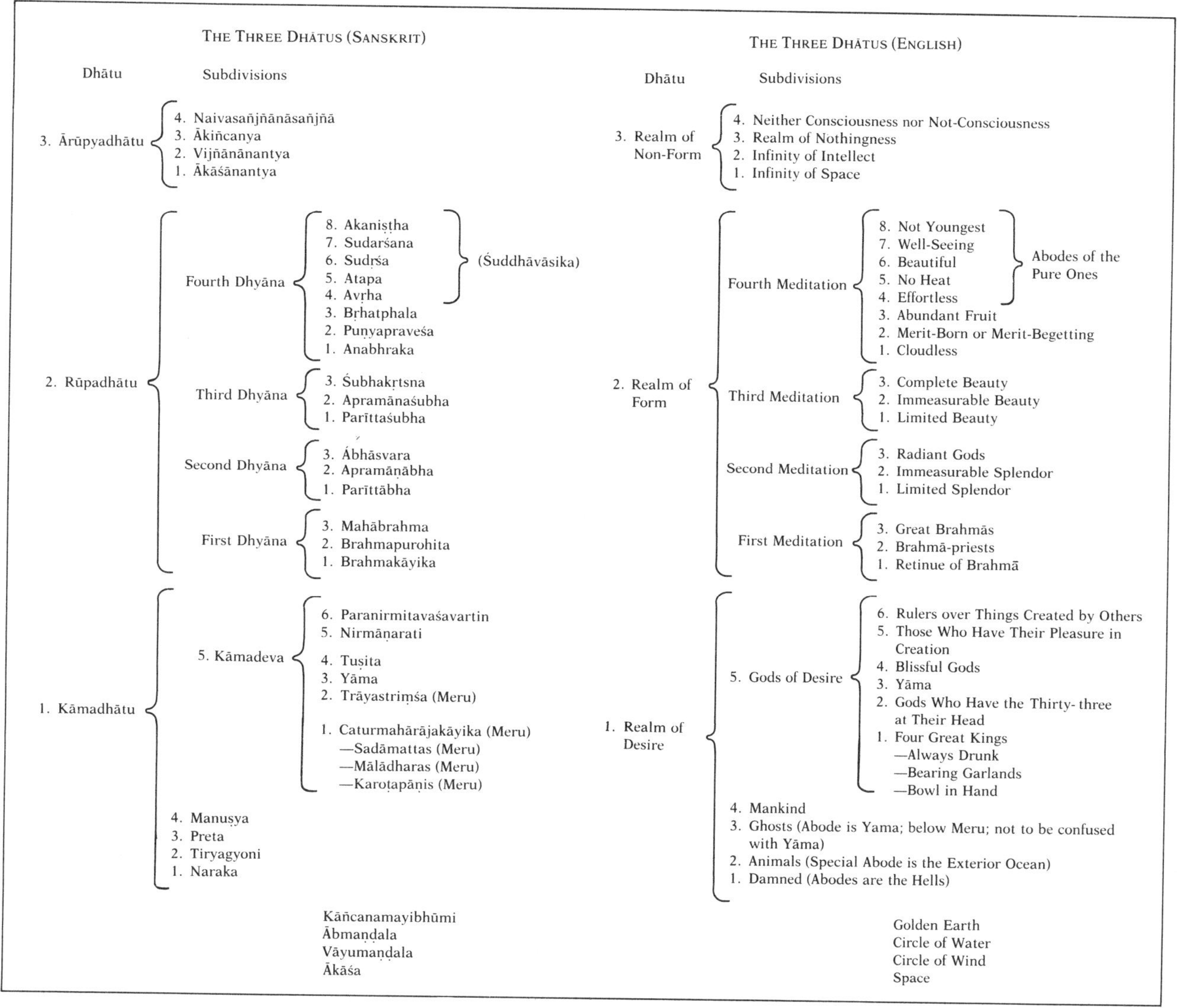

Figure 1. *The Single-World System*

Cosmology of Thousands. There exist countless variations within this general heading, but the combination of thousands of worlds and the superimposition of one cosmic level upon another is a fundamental characteristic of the *sāhasra* cosmology. A second characteristic is the ultimate unity of these various combinations of worlds in the realm of a single Buddha, a single *buddhakṣetra* (Buddha field), or another similarly unifying entity.

The *Majjhima Nikāya* (3.101) describes a division of the *brahmaloka* into multiples of thousands of worlds, making a distinction between a *sahasso-brahmā* governing a *sahassī lokadhātu,* and equivalent realms governed by a *dvisahasso-brahmā,* a *trisahasso-brahmā,* a *catussahasso-brahmā,* a *pancassahasso-brahmā,* and a *satasahasso-brahmā,* gods that rule over worlds numbering between 1,000 and $1{,}000^{100}$.

Another example from the Pali texts is found at *Aṅguttara Nikāya* 1.227, which describes (1) a system of one thousand universes, *sahassī chūḷanikā lokadhātu* ("small chiliocosm"); (2) a system of one million universes, *dvisahassī majjhimikā lokadhātu* ("middle chiliocosm"), embracing one thousand "small chiliocosms"; and (3) a system of one billion universes, *tisahassī mahāsahassī lokadhātu* ("great chiliocosm"), embracing one thousand "middle chiliocosms." The *Kośa* (vol. 3, pp. 138–141) describes the *trisāhasramahāsāhasralokadhātu* in virtually identical terms.

From this description it appears that a *trisāhasramahāsāhasralokadhātu (tisahassī mahāsahassī lokadhātu)* consists of one billion universes like the one in which we live, each consisting of four islands, a *cakravāla* wall, seven concentric ring mountains, a sun, a moon, and a Mount Meru. This arrangement of thousands of worlds is the most representative expression of the *sāhasra* cosmology and emerges as the formulaic expression of a *buddhakṣetra*. Even Mahāyāna texts that recognize the existence of innumerable *buddhakṣetras* acknowledge the fact that each is a *trisāhasramahāsāhasralokadhātu*.

Interpretation of the meaning of the *trisāhasramahāsāhasralokadhātu* remains problematic. However, it is closely associated with speculations on the great division of cosmic time. Because of this association, it is reasonable to assume a connection between the thousands of the *sāhasra* cosmology and the manner in which astronomers measured the movements of the planets, multiplying the fractional measurements of their observations by thousands of years to determine the beginning and end of the world, that is, that time when all planets were (will be) in a straight line. Based on these associations, we may regard the universe as "ever-measuring," constantly productive of the divisions of time grounded in the powers of discrimination.

This association with measurements of time is strengthened by the parallels between the *sāhasra* cosmology and the cosmologies of the Hindu Purāṇas, since the "thousands of worlds" (i.e., one billion) of the *sāhasra* cosmology exactly equal the divisions of time of the Puranic cosmos—if one leaves out references to days and nights and counts only years. The Puranic *yugas* consist of ten divine years, each equal to one thousand human years, for a total of ten thousand years in a *mahāyuga*. One thousand *mahāyugas* are the equivalent of a *kalpa*, which is also a "day of Brahmā," and one hundred years of such days equal the life of Brahmā or a *mahākalpa*. (The full reckoning is: 10 × 1000 × 1000 × 100 = 1,000,000,000.) The *trisāhasramahāsāhasralokadhātu* apparently spatializes the temporal divisions of Hindu cosmology.

Associated drama. In contrast to the drama of the single-world system, the manner whereby salvation occurs within the structures of the *sāhasra* cosmology is inextricably related to the divisions of cosmic time and the appearance of a Buddha.

The largest division of time, corresponding to the duration of the universe, is a *mahākalpa*. A *mahākalpa* in turn consists of four "moments" (*kalpas*), each of which contains twenty *antarakalpas*. Thus, the *mahākalpa* consists of (1) a *kalpa* of creation *(vivartakalpa)*, which extends from the birth of the primordial wind to the production of the first being that inhabits the hells; (2) a *kalpa* that consists of the duration of the creation *(vivartasthāyikalpa)*, which begins with the appearance of the first being in the hells; (3) a *kalpa* of dissolution *(saṃvartakalpa)*, commencing with the moment when beings cease to be reborn in the hells and ending with the moment when the "receptacle world" (i.e., the world inhabited by sentient beings) is destroyed; and (4) a *kalpa* during which the world remains dissolved *(saṃvartasthāyikalpa)* and during which nothing remains but space *(ākāśa)* where the world was. Each of the four *kalpas* are sometimes designated *asaṃkhyeya* ("incalculable") *kalpas*.

The twenty small or "intermediate" *kalpas* (*antarakalpas*) are characterized as follows: In a period of creation, the receptacle world *(bhājanaloka)* is created during the first *antarakalpa;* beings appear during the remaining nineteen. A reverse process occurs during a period of destruction. At the end of a period of creation, humankind has a life that is infinite in duration. During the first *antarakalpa* of the creation, it diminishes *(apakarṣa)* to ten years. Each of the next eighteen *antarakalpas* consists of an augmentation *(utkarṣa)* of life span from ten years up to eighty thousand years and a subsequent diminution back down to ten years again. The twentieth *antarakalpa* consists solely of augmentation up to eighty thousand years.

While not specifically mentioned in the *Kośa*, it should be noted that messianic traditions within Buddhism focus on the figure of Maitreya, the future and last Buddha of our age, who will provide a new *dharma* ("teaching") to replace the degenerated teaching of Śākyamuni. This will occur when the duration of life has reached eighty thousand years.

When all beings have disappeared from the inferior realms and are reunited in a meditation realm, presumably through the power of meditation and possibly the attainment of *nirvāṇa*, the "destructions" (*saṃvartānis*) take place. The agents of the destructions are the "great elements" and are of three kinds: those by fire, those by water, and those by wind. The second meditation realm *(dhyāna)* is the limit *(sīmā)* of the destruction by fire; everything lower is burned and scorched. The third *dhyāna* is the limit of the destruction by water; everything lower is decomposed or dissolved. The fourth *dhyāna* is the limit of the destruction by wind; everything below it is scattered. There is no destruction by earth because the receptacle world consists of earth. The destructions succeed one another in the following sequence: Seven destructions by fire are followed by a destruction by water; this cycle of eight destructions is repeated a total of seven times. Then follow seven more destructions by fire and a final destruction by wind. Thus there are seven times eight, or fifty-six destructions by fire, seven by water, and a final (sixty-fourth) destruction by wind.

While the soteriological drama associated with this cosmology is framed by the speculations on cosmic time, the drama proper divides itself into four discrete "moments." The first is that of the progress of the *śrāvaka,* or one who has undertaken the religious vocation toward becoming an *arhat.* Second is the exercise of miraculous powers. Third is the career of the *bodhisattva,* who makes a vow in the presence of a Buddha to pursue Buddhahood rather than pass into the extinction of *nirvāṇa.* The fourth moment in the drama is the appearance of a Buddha.

The progress of the *śrāvaka* toward the state of *arhat* consists of a series of practices, teachings, and meditations designated in a general way as "the path." Briefly stated, the *śrāvaka* on the way to arhatship masters a path that consists of sixteen "moments" of the four Holy Truths *(abhisamaya)* and 182 moments of the stages of meditation *(bhāvanāmārga)* including taking possession of the "four fruits" of the path: *srotāpanna* ("stream winner"), *sakṛdāgāmin* ("once-returner"), *anāgāmin* ("nonreturner"), and *arhat.*

Following the exercise of certain miraculous powers obtained as a result of meditation, and having made a vow to become a Buddha, the *bodhisattva* then perfects the various virtues (*pāramitā*s) during three *asaṃkhyeya*s of *mahākalpa*s. After countless rebirths among the excellent destinies, the *bodhisattva* is born in the Tuṣita Heaven, during which time he develops the acts that are productive of the thirty-two marks of a great and almost certainly cosmic person *(mahāpuruṣa).* During the course of one hundred supplementary cosmic ages *(kalpaśate śeṣe),* he exhibits in Jambudvīpa the marks of a *mahāpuruṣa.* This he does only in the presence of a Buddha.

The final stage in the drama involves the appearance of a Buddha. While there is considerable doctrinal disagreement on many points relating to this subject, it is generally agreed that a Buddha only appears during a period when the length of human life is declining and when it is between eighty thousand and one hundred (sometimes, eighty) years. Lifespans greater than this are too long to afford beings awareness of the impermanent nature of things; less than this and life is too brief and the five corruptions (*kaṣāya*s) too powerful for the teaching to be mastered. Since the Buddha is clearly of a different order from the *arhat,* and since both are necessarily in possession of *nirvāṇa,* we must conclude that the *nirvāṇa* of the Buddha is of a different order from that of the *arhat.*

Since it is more important to provide a general means of interpreting these systems than to provide ever greater detail, I suggest the following. The single-world system in isolation serves as an aid to monastic meditation in much the same way as Sāṃkhya philosophy serves as a cosmological framework for the practice of yoga. Time (motion) and the cosmos are essentially contained within the body of the individual in its unliberated mode. Time and space are the products of the movements of the primordial matter *(prakṛti)* agitated by the presence of a soul.

As a corollary, there is little need for the great divisions of time—*kalpa*s, *yuga*s, *mahākalpa*s, and so forth. Where these appear, time (and the cosmos) have been incorporated into the body of the deity. While arhatship or the attainment of the individual *nirvāṇa* is the essential drama of the single-world system in the Pali texts, the Sarvāstivādin texts establish a drama involving the relationship between the individual *nirvāṇa (arhat)* and the *nirvāṇa* of the Buddha as a cosmic figure whose body contains the elements of time. This suggestion is supported in part by the fact that the Pali Abhidhamma recognizes a single unconditioned *dharma* and a single *nirvāṇa,* whereas the Sarvāstivādin literature recognizes three unconditioned *dharma*s, including space and two types of *nirvāṇa.*

Alternative dramas. Along with three classes of saints—*arhat, bodhisattva,* and Buddha—the *Kośa* recognizes a fourth class of saint known as the *pratyekabuddha,* or person who achieves enlightenment in isolation. The grouping of four is noteworthy for its transformation in the *Saddharmapuṇḍarīka Sūtra* (Lotus Sutra).

The *Lotus Sutra* describes a "path" to salvation known as the *ekayāna,* or "single path." By means of "devices" *(upāya),* the cosmic Buddha projects three paths—those pursued by the *arhat,* the *pratyekabuddha* and the *bodhisattva*—to suit the differing spiritual capacities of creatures. While these three goals are pursued independently by beings according to their sensibilities, it is after having achieved these various provisional *nirvāṇa*s that the true *nirvāṇa* is bestowed upon them by the Buddha.

There are additional continuities between this drama and that found in the Pure Land traditions. There the faithful are admonished to think at the moment of death of the Buddha Amitābha ("infinite light"), whose field, Sukhāvatī (the Land of Bliss), lies in the west. In so doing, they will be reborn there in what will be their last birth; to live lives without interruption and to hear the *dharma* preached perfectly and thence to obtain final *nirvāṇa.* I shall simply note that Sukhāvatī is the realm of *sukha* ("bliss"), set over against this world of *duḥkha* ("suffering"). The fundamental tenet of the Hīnayāna, of course, is that all existence is suffering *(duḥkha).* The *sukha* world is therefore the visionary representation of all duality and of all striving. It is thus an accommodation to the sensibilities of all creatures and in some ways a provisional *nirvāṇa.* From Sukhāvatī the second stage of the drama unfolds, which is the *ekayāna,* or the *nirvāṇa* granted as a result of the *nirvāṇa* of the Buddha.

With the same thought in mind, but using the stick rather than the carrot, the Japanese monk Genshin (942–1017) compiled extensive and horrible descriptions of the hells associated with the single-world system in order to turn people's minds toward rebirth in Sukhāvatī lest they remain in the realm of *duḥkha* and become subject to its worst torments.

The T'ien-t'ai school of Chinese Buddhism utilizes the *trisāhasramahāsāhasralokadhātu* in another way, basing its interpretation on the second chapter of the *Lotus Sutra.* Here we are told that it represents the three thousand worlds used as a model for the interpenetrating nature of all reality. These three thousand worlds are also known as *dharmas* and are organized in the following manner. There are ten realms of existence—those of the Buddhas, *bodhisattvas, pratyekabuddhas,* direct disciples of the Buddha (*śrāvakas*), heavenly beings, spirits, human beings, departed beings, beasts, and depraved men. Each of these shares the characteristics of the others, thus making one hundred realms. Each of these in turn is characterized by ten "thusnesses" or "such-likenesses" through which the true state is manifested in phenomena. This makes one thousand realms of existence. Each realm is further constituted by the three divisions of living beings, space, and the (five) aggregates (*skandhas*) that constitute *dharmas,* thus making a total of three thousand realms of existence or aspects of reality. Because the interpenetration of these three thousand realms *(trisāhasramahāsāhasralokadhātu)* is immanent in a single instant of thought, all beings have the Buddha nature in them and can thus be saved.

While comparison of these variations in drama with that of the *sāhasra* cosmology is useful, they are better understood in the context of another set of general cosmological structures known as the *asaṃkhyeya* cosmology.

Cosmology of Innumerables. The *asaṃkhyeya* cosmology belongs to the Mahāyāna and is characterized by the "innumerable" *(asaṃkhyeya)* Buddhas and *buddhakṣetras* filling the ten regions of space in place of the single *buddhakṣetra* of the Hīnayāna.

Images of space. While the *sāhasra* cosmology was dominated by the temporal categories of the *kalpa,* the *asaṃkhyeya* cosmology is dominated by spatial categories and images. The emphasis on spatial imagery is carried to the point where the Māhayāna can argue that time does not exist. Just as the appearance of the Buddhas in the *sāhasra* cosmology was linked to the passage of time, the Buddhas are now associated with the directions or points of space and are referred to as the "Buddhas of the ten regions" *(daśadigbuddha).* As a result, the appearance of a Buddha in this cosmology is not a rare event. Instead, it is repeatedly stated that the Buddhas are "as numerous as the sands of the Ganges."

Associated drama. A new drama is expressed in a mytheme that finds wide currency in Mahāyāna texts. It revolves around the "great concentrations" of the Buddha Śākyamuni in his cosmic form and the manner in which the concentrations result in the exercise of miraculous powers, most notably the issuance of rays of light from the body of the Buddha. While the mytheme varies from text to text, it is analyzed with scholastic thoroughness in the *Mahāprajñāpāramitā Śāstra* (chaps. 14–15), a text traditionally attributed to Nāgārjuna. The essential tenets of this drama may be summarized as follows.

The Buddha enters into a concentration in which are contained all the concentrations. Departing therefrom he practices a variety of magical powers, the most notable of which is the issuance of rays of light from his body. Touched by these rays of light, all beings become intent upon enlightenment and are prepared to hear the great sermon of the cosmic Buddha; the world is transformed into a Pure Land, and beings are either able to see and hear the *dharma* being preached in other Buddha fields or are transported to one of those fields where they can hear the *dharma* without obstacle, distraction, or interruption. The Buddha utilizes the magical powers gained through concentration for the welfare of all beings. The power of the rays of light is so great that it is likened to the destruction of the universe by fire at the end of a *kalpa.* As a result of his extinction in concentration, the Buddha exercises miraculous powers that benefit all beings in accordance with their sensibilities. Just as the Hindu cosmologies explore the multivalence of the term *pralaya* (death/destruction of the universe/liberation) the Buddhist cosmologies explore the multiple meanings of *nirvāṇa.*

In the last analysis, it is the *nirvāṇa* of the cosmic Buddha that alone results in salvation, not the *nirvāṇas* of individuals. According to the *Lotus Sutra,* "he does not teach a particular Nirvāṇa for each being; he causes all beings to reach complete Nirvāṇa by means of the complete Nirvāṇa of the Tathāgata" (Kern, 1965, p. 81).

The drama of the *sāhasra* cosmology and that of the *asaṃkhyeya* cosmology can be contrasted on many points. The journey of the *sāhasra* cosmology is one that moves arduously and laboriously through each of the abodes of the cosmography and extends indefinitely in time. The journey of the *asaṃkhyeya* cosmology on the other hand occurs in an instant, transporting the individual to one of the many worlds separated from each other by the void of infinite space. In the former, Buddhas are rare and quiescent, in the latter, numerous and active. Just as the Hindu cosmologies play with a juxtaposition of the term *puruṣa* in its two meanings of multiple individual souls on the one hand and a single, all-encompassing soul on the other, the Buddhist cosmologies are concerned with individual and cosmic *nirvāṇas*.

It may be argued that all of Buddhist cosmological speculation falls into one of these two traditions. Those that accept time as the fundamental cosmological reality belong to the Hīnayāna. Those that embrace metaphors of space belong to the Mahāyāna. It is also likely that the *cakravāla* cosmology and the Pure Land cosmologies actually constitute shorthands or simplifications of these two great traditions, the one for the benefit of the monastic vocation, and the other for the benefit of the devotional traditions of the Mahāyāna.

[*See also* Soteriology, *article on* Buddhist Soteriology; Celestial Buddhas and Bodhisattvas; *and* Pure and Impure Lands.]

BIBLIOGRAPHY

Texts and Translations

Abhidharmakośa, translated by Louis de La Vallée Poussin as *L'Abhidharmakośa de Vasubandhu*, 6 vols. (1923–1931; reprint, Brussels, 1971).

Mahāprajñāpāramitā Śāstra, translated by Étienne Lamotte as *Le traité de la grande vertu de sagesse de Nāgārjuna*, 5 vols. (Louvain, 1949–1980).

Ōjōyōshū, translated by August Karl Reischauer as "Genshin's Ojo Yoshu: Collected Essays on Birth into Paradise," *Transactions of the Asiatic Society of Japan*, 2d ser., 7 (1930): 16–97.

Saddharmapuṇḍarīka Sūtra, translated by Hendrik Kern as *Saddharma-Puṇḍarīka; or the Lotus of the True Law* (1884; reprint, Delhi, 1965). The Chinese version of this text was translated by Leon Hurvitz as *Scripture of the Lotus Blossom of the Fine Dharma (Lotus Sutra)* (New York, 1976).

Sukhāvatīvyūha Sūtra, translated by F. Max Müller and edited by E. B. Cowell in *Buddhist Mahāyāna Texts*, "Sacred Books of the East," vol. 49 (1894; reprint, New York, 1969).

Traibhūmikathā, translated by Frank E. Reynolds and Mani Reynolds as *Three Worlds according to King Ruang* (Berkeley, 1982).

Visuddhimagga, by Buddhaghosa, translated by Bhikkhu Ñyāṇamoli as *The Path of Purification*, 2d ed. (Colombo, 1964).

Other Works of Interest

Andrews, Allan A. *The Teachings Essential for Rebirth: A Study of Genshin's Ōjōyōshū*. Tokyo, 1973.

Basham, A. L. *History and Doctrine of the Ājīvikas: A Vanished Indian Religion*. London, 1951.

"Butsudō." In *Hôbôgirin: Dictionnarie encyclopédique du bouddhisme d'après les sources chinoises et japonaise*, 4 vols., edited by Paul Demiéville. Tokyo, 1929–1931.

Hurvitz, Leon. *Chih-I*. "Mélanges chinoises et bouddhiques," vol. 12. Brussels, 1962.

Kirfel, Willibald. *Die Kosmographie der Inder* (1920). Reprint, Bonn, 1967.

Kloetzli, W. Randolph. *Buddhist Cosmology: From Single World System to Pure Land; Science and Theology in the Images of Motion and Light*. Delhi, 1983.

Lamotte, Étienne. *The Teaching of Vimalakīrti (Vimalakīrtinirdeśa)*. Translated from French by Sara Boin. London, 1976. See especially "Note 1: The *buddhakṣetra*."

La Vallée Poussin, Louis de. "Cosmogony and Cosmology (Buddhist)." In *Encyclopaedia of Religion and Ethics*, edited by James Hastings, vol. 4. Edinburgh, 1911. A lucid and highly detailed discussion of Hīnayāna cosmology.

W. RANDOLPH KLOETZLI

COSTUMES. *See* Masks.

COUNCIL OF TRENT. *See* Trent, Council of.

COUNCILS. [*This entry consists of two articles,* Buddhist Councils *and* Christian Councils, *treating the role of conciliar assemblies in the history of these two traditions.*]

Buddhist Councils

Accounts considering the final events in the life of Siddhārtha Gautama, the historical Buddha, are often quick to point out that his last injunctions to his community include exhortations to remember that all compounded things are impermanent and to work diligently for the attainment of salvation. What these accounts sometimes fail to emphasize is that the Buddha also enjoined the community to appoint no successor in his stead. The Buddha was explicit in arguing that his teaching (Dharma) and disciplinary training (Vinaya) would provide sufficient guidance for the attainment of *nirvāṇa*. He further granted the community authority to abolish all lesser and minor precepts of conduct, although he failed to identify precisely which precepts he deemed minor and lesser. In the absence of an appointed or hereditary successor to leadership of the Buddhist community, and with an obvious uncertainty as to which disciplinary rules were to be retained, much confusion could be expected in the days and years following the leader's demise. To combat the anticipated disorientation, it was suggested that a council be convened whose purpose would be to solidify basic Buddhist doctrine and discipline. In this way, the transition from the ministry of the Buddha's charismatic leadership to one of a newly established social identity was softened and advanced. Further, convocation of this first Buddhist council helped to establish a precedent upon which future Buddhist communities could draw for sanction in resolving disputes.

Council Literature. Literature on these various Buddhist councils derives from both primary and secondary sources. Initially, we look to the canonical sources, and this avenue of inquiry yields fruitful results. Appended to the Vinaya Piṭaka, or disciplinary portion, of each Buddhist school's canon is a section devoted to a considertion of the Buddha's death and the first two Buddhist councils. Noncanonical sources also unearth a mine of useful material. In this regard, we can consult such texts as the Pali *Dīpavaṃsa*, as well as the *Samayabhedoparacanacakra* of Vasumitra, the *Nikāyabhedavibhaṅgavyākhyāna* of Bhavya, the *Mahāprajñāpāramita Śāstra*, (often wrongly attributed to Nāgārjuna), Chi-tsang's *San-lun hsüan-i* (based on an earlier work of Paramārtha), the *Mahāvibhāṣā Śāstra*, the *Śāriputraparipṛcchā Sūtra*, and others. There is also a wealth of secondary material in Western languages, for which the reader is referred to the appended bibliography.

Major Indian Councils. Current buddhological research enables us to document no fewer than five Indian Buddhist councils, each of which must be described in order to unearth its import for the history of the tradition. (These and other councils are arranged in tabular form in table 1.)

The First Council: Rājagṛha. The first Indian Buddhist council was allegedly held during the rainy season immediately following the Buddha's death in, according to the most popular reckoning, 483 BCE. [*For other datings of the death of the Buddha,* see Buddha.] It was held in the capital city of King Bimbisāra, ruler of Magadha and a chief royal patron of the Buddha and the Buddhist community. With food and shelter provided, Rājagṛha proved to be an ideal site for the Buddhists' deliberations. Most accounts tell us that a leading Buddhist monk of the time, Kāśyapa, was selected to convene the council and charged with the task of inviting an appropriate assemblage of monks. There are, however, some indications that the Buddha's first enlightened disciple, Ājñāta Kauṇḍinya, was chosen to preside, thus raising a later scholarly debate as to whether personal merit or seniority was the basis for leadership selection. In any case, as the records recount the story, five hundred monks, all having attained the status of *arhats* (Pali, *arahants*; "enlightened ones"), were selected to participate in the council proceedings. The plan for the enactment of the council was to have the president of the event question first Upāli, a disciple known for his mastery of the disciplinary materials, on Vinaya, and then Ānanda, allegedly the Buddha's most beloved disciple, on the various sermons of the Buddha. Our sources recount, however, that at the time of his selection Ānanda was not yet enlightened. (This fact in and of itself casts some doubt on the accuracy of the account.) In due course, however, Ānanda is reported to have attained *nirvāṇa*, thus enabling him to participate in the expected fashion.

During Kāśyapa's questioning of Ānanda, reference was made to the Buddha's suggestion that the lesser and minor precepts be abolished. With the community in a quandry as to the best course of action, Kāśyapa decided to leave all disciplinary rules intact, lest the community fall into disrepute in such matters. After the recitation of the doctrinal and disciplinary materials,

TABLE 1. *Major Buddhist Councils*

LOCATION	DATE	PRINCIPAL PARTICIPANTS	RELIGIOUS ISSUE(S)
Rājagṛha	483 BCE	500 *arhats*, Kāśyapa, Upāli, Ānanda	Recitation of Dharma and Vinaya
Vaiśālī	383 BCE	700 monks, Yaśas, Vṛjiputraka monks	Controversy over ten illicit practices
Pāṭaliputra	367/346 BCE	future Sthaviras, future Mahāsāṃghikas	Uncertain; possibly laxity, Mahādeva's theses, text expansion
Pāṭaliputra	247 BCE	King Aśoka, Moggaliputtatissa	Debate on orthodoxy, composition of *Kathāvatthu*
Anurādhapura	25 BCE	King Vaṭṭagāmaṇī, Mahāvihāra monks	Finalization of Threefold Canon (Tipiṭaka) in Pali
Gandhāra or Kashmir	c. 100 CE	King Kaniṣka, Vasumitra, 499 scholars	Doctrinal debates, composition of *Mahāvibhāṣā*
Lhasa	792–794 CE	Kamalaśīla, Hva-shan (Mahāyāna)	Debate on sudden versus gradual enlightenment
Mandalay	1871 CE	King Mindon Min	Revision of Pali texts
Rangoon	1954 CE	U Nu, monks from Buddhist Asia	Recitation of Tipiṭaka

other issues of business were entertained and various penalties imposed on individuals who had acted incorrectly. As the convocation prepared to adjourn, a traveling monk, Purāṇa, arrived in Rājagṛha and was invited to join the proceedings. He declined, noting that he chose to remember the Dharma and Vinaya precisely as spoken by the Buddha. In so noting, further suspicion is thrown on the authority and impact of the council. Finally, the council concluded, referring to itself as the *vinayasaṃgīti*, or "chanting of the Vinaya."

We can distinguish at least three major functions for this first council at Rājagṛha. In the first place, there is the practical concern. The council established authority for the fledgling religious community in the absence of its founder, and solidarity was enhanced as well. There was also a secondary concern to begin the post-Buddha period with communal purity confirmed. The meting out of formal penalties assured such a condition. Third, there is the obvious mythic function. A formal religious event effected a renewal of the cosmic and social order, thus providing an auspicious beginning for the religious organization's new mission. Furthermore, in the recitation of the Dharma and the Vinaya (in nothing like their later forms, however), an infant Buddhist canon was established.

The general consensus of scholarship devoted to the first council almost uniformly concludes that the canonical accounts are at best greatly exaggerated and at worst pure fiction. On a small scale, it may be safe to assume that several of the Buddha's intimates gathered after his death to consider their future plight in the Indian religious climate, but the authenticity of the dramatic event presented in the canon is highly questionable.

The Second Council: Vaiśālī. One hundred years pass before we get any further information on the historical development of the Buddhist community. The occasion for this new look into the ongoing progress of the still-infant Buddhist religion was a council held in the town of Vaiśālī. The various Vinaya accounts record that a Buddhist monk named Yaśas wandered into Vaiśālī and observed the resident monks, or *bhikṣus* (formally identified as the Vṛjiputraka *bhikṣus*), engaged in ten practices that seemed to conflict with Yaṣas's understanding of injunctions made explicit in the Vinaya. Yaṣas, the tale has it, formally protested indulgence in these ten apparently illicit practices, but was rejected by the community of monks and sentenced to a penalty known as the *pratisaṃharaṇīya-karma*. This punishment required that he beg the pardon of the monks he had offended by his accusation and obtain their forgiveness. Although initially intending to comply with the penalty, Yaṣas eventually changed his mind, resolving to convince the local laity that the Vṛjiputraka monks were at fault. Upon learning of Yaṣas's renewed attack on their conduct, the resident monks further punished this young agitator with the *utkṣepaṇīya-karma*, literally banishing him from the community.

Undaunted by the formal act of banishment, Yaśas journeyed to Kauśāmbī, seeking the support of a learned monk known as Saṃbhūta Śāṇavāsin. Another well-respected monk, Revata, also decided to come to Yaśas's support on the issue of the ten practices. All the while, the Vṛjiputraka *bhikṣus* were gathering supporters to their side as well. The conflict was brought to a conclusion in the convocation of a formal council in Vaiśālī. Revata was selected to preside over the proceedings. Sarvagāmin, an elder monk who had had the Buddha's direct disciple Ānanda as his *upādhyāya*, or teacher, was questioned on each of the ten points. One by one, Sarvagāmin rejected each point on the basis of various scriptures. With the ten practices condemned and concord renewed, the council concluded, again referring to itself as the "recital of the Vinaya" *(vinayasaṃgīti)* or as the "recital of the seven hundred," the number of monks who attended the gathering.

Of course it is necessary to consider just what these ten illicit practices were and why this particular event seems to have had so great an impact on the early Buddhist community. The ten points include (1) preserving salt in a horn; (2) taking food when the shadow is beyond two fingers wide; (3) after finishing one meal, going to another town for another meal; (4) holding several confession ceremonies within the same monastic boundary; (5) confirming a monastic act in an incomplete assembly; (6) carrying out an act improperly and justifying it by its habitual performance in this way; (7) after eating, drinking unchurned milk that is somewhere between the states of milk and curd; (8) drinking unfermented wine; (9) using a mat without a border; and (10) accepting gold and silver. Although there is considerable scholarly disagreement concerning the meaning and implications of these practices, it is abundantly clear that each of the ten points was fully rejected by the Vinaya of each Buddhist *nikāya*, or school. Based on such scriptural certainty, then, is it possible to make any sense out of these points and their implications for Buddhist history?

Although a reconciliation was effected by the council of Vaiśālī, the very occasion of the council suggests forcefully that there were significant tensions and disagreements already operative in the Buddhist community. That it was divided by various factions must be assumed. If we wish to make general statements, we may summarize the various differences that were emerging as reflecting (1) rigorist versus laxist tendencies; (2) monastic versus lay emphases; and (3) sacred versus secular concern in the community.

Virtually all scholars conclude that the council of Vaiśālī was a historical event. Almost all sources place the event one hundred years after the Buddha's *nirvāṇa* (although two sources cite 110 years) at the Vālukārāma Monastery in Vaiśālī. Wilhelm Geiger and others have suggested that the council of Vaiśālī is the beginning point of Buddhist sectarianism, the point at which the *saṃgha* split into the Sthavira and Mahāsāṃghika schools. This premise, however, has been persuasively rejected by Marcel Hofinger, André Bareau, myself, and others. Thus, at the conclusion of the council of Vaiśālī, the Buddhist community remained bound together, albeit in a rather tenuous and uncertain union.

Pāṭaliputra I: the noncanonical council. By the time of the consecration of King Aśoka (c. 270 BCE), the Buddhist sectarian movement was already well advanced. Attempts to locate the beginnings of Buddhist sectarianism in the scriptures have continually failed. Nonetheless, through the painstaking efforts of Bareau, it has been possible to reconstruct the evidence of a council from which the Buddhist sectarian movement had its birth. By using primarily noncanonical sources, Bareau has been able to conclude that another council followed that of Vaiśālī by less than half a century, and it is this event that must be considered here.

In the study of this new council, only one issue can be found about which all the texts concur: that it was held in Pāṭaliputra. Both the date of the council and the occasion for its convocation are troublesome. Four possible dates appear in the various texts: 100 AN (i.e., after the *nirvāṇa* of the Buddha), 116 AN, 137 AN, and 160 AN. Bareau dismisses the extreme dates as "manifestly aberrant," and initially concludes that the event must have occurred either in 137 AN or 116 AN. According to Bareau, the former date would locate the council under the reign of King Mahāpadma the Nandin, while the latter would place the proceedings in the reign of Kālāśoka. Bareau prefers the former figure, assuming that it would take thirty-seven years or so for the cause of the council to develop fully: namely, disciplinary laxity and five disparaging theses about *arhats* promulgated by an apparently renegade monk named Mahādeva. In other words, Bareau feels quite certain as to the cause of the convocation, and infers the date from the cause.

As to the specifics of the council, Bareau tells us that by the reign of Mahāpadma the Nandin, the Buddhist community had divided itself into two camps, one lax in discipline and supporting the tenets of Mahādeva, the other rigorous and strongly opposed to him. Unable to resolve their dispute internally, the Buddhists approached King Mahāpadma and asked him to mediate the dispute. The king assembled the two groups in his capital of Pāṭaliputra, but being incompetent in religious matters, decided to put the matter to a simple vote. The "laxist" party was apparently in the majority and withdrew, calling itself the Mahāsāṃghikas, or "Great Assembly." The minority party referred to itself as the Sthaviras, or "Elders." Each group then began to develop its own cannon and religious community.

Virtually all the early sources in Buddhist literature conclude that the council described above was a historical event. Further, they consider this initial council of Pāṭaliputra to be the true starting point of the sectarian movement in Buddhism. Recently, however, Bareau's conclusions as to the date and cause of the council have been questioned. Janice J. Nattier and I have suggested that the council took place in 116 AN, under the reign of Kālāśoka, and that disciplinary laxity and Mahādeva's theses had nothing at all to do with the schism (1977). Based on a reevaluation of Bareau's sources and a consideration of the *Śāriputraparipṛcchā Sūtra*, Nattier and I argue that the chief issue of the council, and the resulting sectarian split, was unwarranted Vinaya expansion on the part of the future Sthaviras. We are unable, at this time, to ascertain which hypothesis, if either, is correct. Nevertheless, it is clear that the sectarian movement in Buddhism emerged sometime in the century following the Vaiśālī council; by 200 BCE more than a dozen sects were evident in the Buddhist community.

Pāṭaliputra II: the third canonical council. No king has been more important for the early history of Buddhism in its native land than Aśoka. Although the traditional Buddhist legends tend to conflict somewhat with the picture of Aśoka revealed by his numerous rock edicts and inscriptions, it has generally been concluded that Aśoka was a pious ruler, sympathetic to the many Buddhists in his domain. [*See the biography of Aśoka.*] By utilizing materials in the Pali *Dīpavaṃsa, Mahāvaṃsa, Mahābodhivaṃsa,* and *Samantapāsādikā,* we can construct a fairly accurate account of the events leading up to the third Buddhist council, and of the council itself.

The *Mahāvaṃsa* (v. 280) indicates that the close of the council was in the seventeenth year of Aśoka's reign. The *Dīpavaṃsa* notes the date as 236 AN, or 247 BCE. Apparently, "heretics" had been entering the Buddhist community for some time, undermining the Dharma, and therefore weakening the entire social and religious structure of the *saṃgha*. In order to remedy the situation, Aśoka chose a famous monk, Moggaliputtatissa, to preside over a huge assembly of a thousand monks, who were to determine and restore orthodoxy. Under Tissa's guidance the offending viewpoints were rejected; eventually it was concluded that the Buddha was a *vibhajyavādin*, or "distinctionist." The viewpoints under discussion were recorded in a now well-known Abhidharma text, the *Kathāvatthu*. [*See the biography of Moggaliputtatissa.*]

There is no question that this council was a historical event. It is curious, however, that it is mentioned only in the Pali accounts, lending weight to the supposition that the council may have been only a "party meeting" of the Vibhajyavāda sect. It is now well known that this sect was the parent of the Theravāda *nikāya*. Other possibilities for the function of the council include the separation of the Sarvāstivādin group (the heretical faction under this interpretation) from the Sthavira proper.

The Council of Kaniṣka. Near the end of the first century CE, Kaniṣka became the ruling monarch of the great Kushan dynasty. He tried hard to emulate Aśoka's example of ruling in accord with the Buddhist Dharma, and championed the Sarvāstivādin school of Buddhism. From his capitals of Puruṣapura and Mathurā, he wielded much power in the Buddhist world. Near the end of his reign, about 100 CE, Kaniṣka sponsored a council, probably in Gandhāra (but possibly in Kashmir), to consider the doctrines of the Sarvāstivādin school.

Following the suggestion of the Sarvāstivādin scholar Pārśva, invitations were sent to all the learned Buddhists of the time, from whom 499 were finally chosen to attend the conference. Great debates were held on various aspects of Buddhist doctrine, and expecially on the Abhidharma. The venerable scholar Vasumitra was president of the council, assisted by Aśvaghoṣa. A new Vinaya was committed to writing at the conference, and a great commentary, known as the *Mahāvibhāṣā*, on the Abhidharma text of the *Jñānaprasthāna* was compiled. There is no question but that the position this council occupies in the history of the Sarvāstivāda *nikāya* is analogous to that of the council convened by Aśoka nearly four centuries earlier for the history of the Theravāda *nikāya*.

No collective meeting in Indian Buddhism ever attained the importance of the five heretofore considered. All of the other major convocations were to take place outside of the Buddhist homeland.

Other Ancient Councils. Recognizing the impact the Indian Buddhist councils have had on the continued growth of the religion in its native land, councils have periodically met in other Buddhist countries as well. Of course Aśoka was renowned for exporting Buddhism through a series of missionary endeavors, with Sri Lanka at the forefront of his enterprise. Equally, within several centuries of the close of King Kaniṣka's reign in India, Buddhism had spread into Central Asia, China, and Tibet. It is no surprise then, that Sri Lanka and Tibet were the sites of other ancient Buddhist councils.

The fourth Theravādin council. Records indicate that Aśoka's son Mahinda, a Buddhist monk, was sent to Sri Lanka to propagate the religion. Upon receiving Mahinda's teaching, King Devānaṃpiyatissa became a lay disciple and established a Buddhist monastery, called the Mahāvihāra, in his capital city of Anurādhapura. A branch of the Bodhi Tree was exported to Sri Lanka, and an ordination lineage was started for monks and nuns. [*See the biography of Devānaṃpiyatissa.*]

During the first century the Buddhist order was threatened by invading Tamils from South India and King Vaṭṭagāmaṇī was forced into exile for fourteen years (43–29 BCE). After reassuming the throne, the king found his land threatened by famine and the religious tradition split by schismatic rumblings. To combat rising religious unrest, it was decided to convene a conference in the capital city (in 25 BCE), in the by then old and famous Mahāvihāra. The prime function of the proceedings was to write down the scriptural texts of the Theravādin school of Buddhism in the Pali language. Thus the formal Tipiṭaka ("three baskets," i.e., the Buddhist canon) was established, providing an institutionalized basis for the continued growth and development of the Theravāda tradition. In addition, the Mahāvihāra community had an apparently orthodox, authoritative textual ground from which to refute their rivals in the Mahāyāna-leaning community of the Abhayagiri Monastery. Eventually, the Pali scriptures compiled at this council found their way into all the Theravādin countries of South and Southeast Asia. [*See* Theravāda.]

The Lhasa council in Tibet. By the middle of the seventh century of the common era Tibet had an unusual political and religious relationship to India and China. King Sroṅ-btsan-sgam-po of Tibet seems to have been married to both Nepalese and Chinese wives, and there was a clear influx of Buddhist ideas from each of these countries. After the great monastery at Bsam-yas was completed in 787, a Sarvāstivādin ordination lineage was established, and the institution became a lively place for the discussion of a wide variety of religious viewpoints.

Although King Khri-sroṅ-lde-btsan (r. 759–797?) was able to undermine the claims to state religion of the indigenous Bon religion, his reign was further aggravated by internal disputes among the Buddhists in his kingdom. Not only did the Tantric tradition advanced by Padmasambhava conflict with older Indian ideas maintained by Śāntirakṣita, but a Chinese monk (generally called Hva-shang, or simply Mahāyāna) argued against Śāntirakṣita as well.

As a resolution to the problem, it was suggested that a council be held at court (in 792–794 CE), with the king in attendance. To present the traditional Buddhist viewpoint, Śāntirakṣita's pupil Kamalaśīla was invited to Tibet. Mahāyāna argued the Chinese position. Two chief issues were considered. First, the Chinese monk argued that Buddhahood was attained suddenly, intuitively, while the Indian monk maintained that the path to enlightenment was gradual. Second, the Indian representative argued, as a corollary to the prior point, for the positive value of meritorious action, while Mahāyāna offered a radical opposition. In a lively debate, the Chinese position was clearly defeated (so say the prevailing accounts of the Indian faction), establishing the efficacy of the Indian standpoint for Tibetan Buddhism. The Chinese were forced in no uncertain terms to leave the country, as is reported through both a Chinese source in the Tun-huang manuscripts and the works of Kamalaśīla (preserved in Sanskrit and Tibetan), but the memory of this monumental debate persisted in the minds of many Tibetan Buddhists for generations. [*See the biographies of Śāntirakṣita and Kamalaśīla.*]

Modern Councils. In the millennium between 800 and 1800 CE little mention was made of Buddhist councils. To be sure, there were numerous proceedings of local import in the various Buddhist countries, but it was not until the latter half of the nineteenth century that another council took place of major impact for the entire Buddhist world.

The fifth Theravādin council. In the Buddhist culture of Southeast Asia it is not at all unusual for royal monarchs to be religious scholars, with prior training from within the Buddhist monastic order. Rama IV of Thailand, for instance, developed extensive scholarship in the Pali texts during his twenty-seven years as a monk. It was in this tradition that King Mindon Min of Burma (r. 1852-1877) convened the fifth Theravādin council in Mandalay in 1871. The purpose of the council was explicit: to revise the Pali texts. To insure the survival of the new scriptures the king had all the texts entombed in stupas, thus preserving the 729 marble tablets upon which the texts were inscribed.

The sixth Theravādin council. In 1954, nearly one hundred years after the Mandalay council, the sixth Theravādin council was convened in Rangoon, Burma, by the prime minister, U Nu. The fact that the twenty-five hundredth anniversary of the Buddha's death was approaching made the notion of a council even more auspicious. The basic function of this sixth council was to recite and confirm the entire Pali canon. Nearly two years of preparations were made prior to its inauguration on 17 May 1954.

U Nu delivered the initial address, charging the twenty-five hundred monks in attendance to work diligently at reciting and editing these important scriptural resources. For two years recitation proceeded, culminating with closure on the twenty-five hundredth anniversary of the Buddha's death (according to Burmese reckoning). The council, in addition to having tremendous religious significance, was a national festival in Burma, and established solidarity among all Theravāda Buddhists there and throughout Asia.

The World Fellowship of Buddhists. In an attempt to carry on the spirit demonstrated by the various Buddhist councils, the World Fellowship of Buddhists was established in 1950 as an expression of true religious ecumenism. The Fellowship has exercised its lofty intention through a series of conferences in various Buddhist countries. These conferences have sometimes expressed political as well as religious concerns, but they nonetheless reflect a spirit of cooperation that is thoroughly consistent with the very first Buddhist conclave, held in the rainy season following the Buddha's death in 483 BCE.

BIBLIOGRAPHY

The best general, comprehensive work on the issue of Indian Buddhist councils is André Bareau's *Les premiers conciles bouddhiques* (Paris, 1955). Much of this material, and the work of other researchers, is summarized in Charles S. Prebish's "A Review of Scholarship on the Buddhist Councils," *Journal of Asian Studies* 33 (February 1974: 239–254. A useful study of the Rājagṛha council is presented in Jean Przyluski's *Le concile de Rājagṛha* (Paris, 1926–1928). An equally valuable resource for the Vaiśālī council is Marcel Hofinger's *Étude sur la concile de Vaiśālī* (Louvain, 1946). The Vaiśālī council is also discussed in Paul Demiéville's "À propos du concile de Vaiśālī, "*T'oung pao* 40 (1951): 239–296, and Nalinaksha Dutt's "The Second Buddhist Council," *Indian Historical Quarterly* 35 (March 1959: 45–56. For a somewhat dated but still important viewpoint, consult Louis de La Vallée Poussin's "The Buddhist Councils," *Indian Antiquary* 37 (1908): 1–18, 81–106. The most recent and controversial material on Indian Buddhist councils is presented in Janice J. Natier and Charles S. Prebish's "Mahāsāṃghika Origins: The Beginnings of Buddhist Sectarianism," *History of Religions* 16 (February 1977): 237–272. For non-Indian councils, Demiéville's *Le concile de Lhasa* (Paris, 1952) effectively covers the Tibetan materials. Donald Smith's *Religion and Politics in Burma* (Princeton, 1965) is helpful for Theravādin proceedings, and *Buddhism in the Modern World*, edited by Heinrich Dumoulin and John Maraldo (New York, 1976), offers a constructive overview.

CHARLES S. PREBISH

Christian Councils

Since the beginning of Christian history, designated leaders of Christian communities have from time to time gathered to make authoritative decisions on common teaching and practice. Such gatherings are usually called councils or synods (from the Greek *sunodos,* "a coming together"). Although these two terms are sometimes used synonymously, especially in Greek-Christian literature, *synod* normally designates the gathering of representatives from a local church or a single denomination, as distinct from *council,* which usually means a meeting at which representation is intended to be universal. Although only seven such meetings, all held in Greek cities in Asia Minor between the fourth and eighth centuries, are recognized by most Christian churches today as worldwide, or "ecumenical," councils (from the Greek *oikoumenē,* "the inhabited world") and as classically authoritative in their articulation of Christian faith and church order, the conciliar pattern of decision making has remained a constant feature in the life of most churches. The Roman Catholic church, in fact, has traditionally regarded fourteen later councils, most of them Western gatherings held under papal auspices, as also ecumenical and normative. Christian councils have varied greatly in size, procedure, composition, and the way in which they have been convoked and ratified. The only criterion for determining their authority and importance is the practical norm of "reception": that a council's decisions are subsequently accepted by a church or a group of churches as valid and binding.

Councils in the Early Church. Precedents for early Christian conciliar practice lay in the Jewish Sanhedrin, or national council of priests and elders, which regulated the religious affairs, as well as some secular matters, of postexilic Israel until the destruction of Jerusalem in AD 70, and in the collegial bodies of priests and leading citizens that ruled most local cults in the Hellenistic and Roman world. [*See* Sanhedrin.] The first recorded gathering of Christian leaders to rule in a doctrinal and disciplinary dispute was the "council" of apostles and elders held in AD 48 or 49 and described in *Acts of the Apostles* 15:6–29. That council decided not to require full observance of the Mosaic law from gentile converts. As the Christian church established itself in other regions of the Greco-Roman world, special meetings of the bishops in a particular province or region were occasionally called to deal with disputed issues, such as the prophetic Montanist movement (Asia Minor, c. 170), the date of the celebration of Easter (Asia Minor, Palestine, Gaul, and Rome, c. 190), the readmission to Christian communion of those who had "lapsed" in persecution (Rome, c. 230–250; Carthage, c. 240–250), or the scandalous behavior of Paul of Samosata, bishop of Antioch (Antioch, 264–268).

During the late second and third centuries, episcopal synods probably met regularly in most regions, although the evidence is fragmentary. As the end of the illegal status of the Christian churches drew near, however, their leaders became bolder in organizing such meetings. A synod of Spanish bishops held in Elvira, near Granada, some time in the first decade of the fourth century enacted eighty-one canons on church discipline that remained widely influential, particularly on the indissolubility of marriage and clerical celibacy. Another local synod, at Arles in southern Gaul (August 314), called to consider the response of Catholics to the schismatic Donatist church in Africa, ruled against rebaptizing Donatists who wished to enter the Catholic church.

Early Ecumenical Councils. The first attempt to gather a body of bishops representing the whole Christian world was the council called by the emperor Constantine I at Nicaea, in northwest Asia Minor, in the summer of 325 (19 June–25 August). The Council of Nicaea is still recognized as the first ecumenical Christian council and as the model for later authoritative gatherings. With the style and procedure of the Roman senate likely in mind, Constantine commissioned the 318 bishops who had assembled near his residence in Nicaea, including several representatives from the Latin church of the West, to settle the controversy raised by Arius's denial of the eternity and full divinity of Jesus. In asserting that Jesus, as Son of God, is "begotten, not made" and "of the same substance as the Father," the council's creedal formula laid the groundwork for the classical development of Christian trinitarian theology in the half century that followed. [*See* Creeds, *article on* Christian Creeds.] The Nicene council also excommunicated Arius and his followers, determined a unified way of reckoning the date of Easter, and issued twenty disciplinary decrees or canons, mainly regulating the appointment and jurisdiction of bishops. Although the emperor's influence was strongly felt at Nicaea, it was the bishops themselves—under the leadership of Constantine's adviser, Bishop Hosius of Cordova, and of the young Alexandrian priest Athanasius—who formulated common theological and practical decisions. The bishops of the whole Christian world were now publicly recognized as the senate of the church.

After more than fifty years of sharp controversy over the reception and interpretation of the Nicene formula, a period that saw the proliferation of local synods and the production of many new creeds, the emperor Theodosius I convoked a meeting of some 150 Greek-speaking bishops at Constantinople in 381 (May–July) for what later was recognized as the second ecumenical council (Constantinople I). In addition to confirming Nicaea's insistence on the full divinity of Jesus as Son, this council condemned those who denied that the Holy Spirit is a distinct individual within the trinitarian mystery of God. An expanded version of the Nicene Creed, probably professed by the patriarch-elect Nectarius during the council before his installation in the see of Constantinople, was taken by the Council of Chalcedon (451) to be the official creed of the whole gathering and is still used as the standard profession of faith in many Christian liturgies (the "Niceno-Constantinopolitan Creed"). This council also enacted four disciplinary canons, including one that accorded second place in ecclesiastical honor, after that of "old Rome," to the new imperial capital, Constantinople. That provision was to become a cause of contention between the Eastern and Western churches.

As a result of a bitter dispute between Nestorius, bishop of Constantinople, and Cyril, bishop of Alexandria, over the proper way of conceiving the relationship of the divine and human aspects of Jesus, the emperor Theodosius II summoned a meeting of bishops at Ephesus on the coast of Asia Minor, in the summer of 431, to resolve the issue, and more particularly to judge the propriety of calling Mary "Mother of God" *(theotokos)*, as Cyril insisted on doing. Representatives of the opposing groups could not agree to meet, and the would-be council ended abortively in mutual excommunication. Later (April 433) Cyril came to an agreement with the more moderate of Nestorius's supporters to excommunicate Nestorius and to accept the title *theotokos* as valid, but also to recognize that in Jesus two distinct natures—the human and the divine—are united without confusion in a single individual. On the basis of this agreement, the meeting of Cyril's party at Ephesus in 431 later came to be regarded as the third ecumenical council, and the dossier assembled there by Cyril's supporters was used as a classical anthology of christological documents.

The fullest articulation of the early church's understanding of the person of Christ was made at a council held at Chalcedon, across the Bosporus from Constantinople, in the fall of 451 (October–November). In response to continuing controversy over whether the humanity of Jesus constituted a distinct and operative reality or "nature" after the incarnation of the Word, the emperor Marcian convoked this meeting of over 350 bishops (including three legates from Pope Leo I and two North African bishops) and forced it to formulate a doctrinal statement on Christ that accommodated a variety of theological traditions. The chief inspiration of the document, however, was the balanced "two-nature" Christology articulated by Leo in his letter to Bishop Flavian of Constantinople in 449. The council also enacted twenty-eight disciplinary canons, the last of which confirmed the second rank of the see of Constantinople and awarded it jurisdictional primacy in Asia Minor and northeastern Greece. This meeting, regarded as the fourth ecumenical council, is the first for which we possess detailed minutes as well as final documents.

Chalcedon's formulation of the Christian understanding of Christ proved to be only a new beginning for controversy. After more than a century of recriminations, especially in the East, the emperor Justinian I convoked another meeting at Constantinople (Constantinople II) in the year 553 (5 May–2 June) and persuaded the 168 bishops present to reformulate the Christology of Chalcedon in terms that more clearly emphasized the centrality of Jesus' divine identity. They also condemned the speculative theology of Origen (third century) and his followers, as well as that of the chief opponents of Cyril of Alexandria from the previous century. The Roman bishop, Vigilius I, was present in Constantinople during the council but refused to attend, suspecting—along with most Western bishops—that it was being forced to weaken the stated faith of Chalcedon in the interests of political unity. In February 554, however, he agreed to accept the decisions of Constantinople II, a step that resulted in decades of controversy in Italy and Africa. This synod has generally been accepted since then as the fifth ecumenical council.

In the century that followed, Greek theologians continued to look for ways of reconciling the monophysites, Christians who had broken from the official church after Chalcedon by emphasizing the dynamic unity of the two-natured Christ as a divine person. One such attempt, favored by several seventh-century Byzantine patriarchs and emperors, was the ascription to Christ of a single divine will and "activity," or range of behavior. Led by the exiled Greek monk Maximos the Confessor, a local Roman synod of October 649 rejected this new Christology as a subtle weakening of the integral affirmation of Jesus' humanity. This condemnation was confirmed by a small gathering of mainly Eastern bishops in the rotunda of the imperial palace in Constantinople between 7 November 680 and 16 September 681, a synod subsequently recognized as the sixth ecumenical council (Constantinople III).

Ten years later, the emperor Justinian II summoned another gathering of bishops in the same rotunda to discuss disciplinary issues and formulate practical canons that would supplement the authoritative theological decisions of Constantinople II and III. Hence its customary titles, the "Quinisext" (fifth-and-sixth) synod or the synod "in the rotunda" (Gr., *en trullō*), also known as the Trullan synod. The membership of this meeting was also entirely Greek, and a number of its canons explicitly rejected Western practices. Although this gathering is not regarded as ecumenical, its legislation became one of the main sources of Orthodox canon law and was also frequently cited by Western medieval canonists.

The main theological controversy in the eighth- and ninth-century Eastern church was no longer directly over the person of Christ, but over the related issue of the legitimacy of using and venerating images in the context of worshiping a transcendent God. In 726, Emperor Leo III began the policy of removing and destroying the images in churches (iconoclasm), and his successor, Constantine V, convoked a synod of 338 bishops in Constantinople in 754 to ratify this practice, excommunicating those who defended the use of images, including the theologian and monk John of Damascus. [*See* Iconoclasm.] In 787 (24 September–7 October), however, the empress Irene convoked another synod at Nicaea (Nicaea II), attended by some 350 Greek bishops and two papal representatives. This synod reversed the decision of the year 754 and affirmed the legitimacy of venerating images and of asking for the intercession of the saints, while insisting also that worship, in the strict sense, is due to God alone. A resurgence of iconoclastic influence in the early ninth century delayed full acceptance of this council's decrees in the East, while the rivalry of the emperor Charlemagne and the poor Latin translation of the acts of Nicaea II that reached his court led to resistance in the West and even to condemnation of the council's decisions at a synod of 350 bishops at Frankfurt in June 794. However, Nicaea II was recognized as the seventh ecumenical council at the Council of Constantinople (869–870), a recognition that was endorsed for the West by Pope John VIII in 880. It is the last of the ancient councils recognized as authoritative by virtually all Christian churches.

Medieval Councils. After the death of Theophilos, the last iconoclastic emperor, in 842, controversy in mid-ninth-century Constantinople over the manner of reinstating the veneration of images led to the forced abdication of the patriarch Ignatius in 858 and to the appointment of the learned civil servant Photios, a layman, as his successor. A local synod of 861, attended by two representatives of Pope Nicholas I, confirmed Photios's elevation and declared that the election of Ignatius had been uncanonical; the pope, however, was persuaded by Ignatius's followers to break communion with Photios two years later. Tension between Rome and Constantinople grew, both over the role of the pope as a source of legitimation and a court of appeal for Eastern bishops and over competing missionary activities of the two churches in Bulgaria. A synod summoned by the Greek emperor Michael in 867 condemned Roman incursions in the East, as well as the Roman church's introduction of the word *filioque* into the creed; it asked the Frankish emperor Louis II to depose Pope Nicholas. Another council in Constantinople, summoned by the new Greek emperor, Basil I, in 869–870, deposed Photios in an effort to win the pope's support, but Photios became patriarch again after Ignatius's death in 877 and was recognized by the pope in a council of reunion held in Constantinople in 879–880. This last meeting annulled the decisions of the council of 869–870, but Western canonists in the twelfth century included the earlier gathering among the ecumenical councils, as Constantinople IV, because its twenty-second canon, forbidding the appointment of bishops by laypeople, provided a precedent for their own case against lay investiture. None of the Photian councils is recognized as ecumenical by other churches.

After the synod of 879–880, Eastern and Western bishops ceased to meet over common concerns for almost four centuries. Local and regional synods, however, continued to play an important role in civil and ecclesiastical life. In Constantinople, the "residentiary synod" (Gr., *sunodos endēmousa*) of the patriarch functioned as the administrative cabinet of the Byzantine communion. Synods in North Africa in the early fifth century (especially at Carthage in 418) and in southern Gaul in the early sixth century (especially at Orange in 529) made important formulations of the Western church's doctrine of grace. And provincial synods, attended by both bishops and secular lords, became an increasingly important instrument of government in the Frankish kingdoms of the sixth and seventh centuries. In Visigothic Spain, eighteen synods were held at Toledo between 589 and 702, dealing with both church and civil discipline and with the doctrinal issue of later Arianism. The Celtic and Roman traditions of church order in Britain were unified by the Synod of Whitby in Northumbria in 664. For the Carolingian empire, national synods were an important instrument for fostering political and doctrinal unity.

It was only in the time of the "Gregorian reform," however, in the eleventh and twelfth centuries, that the popes, as part of their program of strengthening the power and independence of the ordained clergy in ruling the church, thought again of convoking councils with a more than regional representation. Gregory VII, in his canonical summary known as *Dictates of the Pope,* insisted that only the bishop of Rome has the right to convoke an ecumenical council—a principle preserved ever since by Western canon law. Corresponding to his vision of the papacy as the active center of a universal and politically independent church, Gregory and his successors began to invite bishops and abbots from other parts of Europe to participate in Roman synods and also took the lead in mobilizing European forces to regain the Christian holy places in Palestine from Muslim occupation.

Three twelfth-century Roman synods—the Lateran councils of 1123, 1139, and 1179—demonstrated the concern of the popes at this period to assert the independence of the hierarchy from lay control by enacting a variety of measures that insured the moral and social integrity of the clergy. The council of 1179 also condemned the emerging Catharist or Albigensian heresy (a Western form of gnosticism), regulated the activities of monastic and military orders, and established the lasting rule that a pope must be elected by a two-thirds majority of the senior Roman clergy, who were known as "cardinals." These three Lateran synods, increasingly international in membership and deliberately modeled on the councils of the early church, were and are regarded as ecumenical councils by the Roman Catholic church. Far more important, however, was the Fourth Lateran Council, convoked in 1215 (11–30 November) by Innocent III. Innocent invited not only all bishops and heads of religious orders from the Western church, but also bishops of the Armenian, Maronite, and Greek churches. Only Latin bishops attended, however, and the council's seventy canons included a strong assertion of papal primacy and a complaint against the Greek church for rebaptizing Latin converts. The meeting—recognized in the West as the twelfth ecumenical council—not only continued the disciplinary reforms of its three predecessors but also issued doctrinal statements on the Trinity and the sacraments (introducing the word *transubstantiation* into official church vocabulary), forbade secret marriages, and instituted the requirement of annual confession for adult Catholics.

Continued conflict between the popes and the Hohenstaufen emperors led Innocent IV to convoke a council of some 150 bishops at Lyons in June and July 1245. Besides calling for renewed efforts to reconquer the holy places, this synod excommunicated the German emperor Frederick II, absolving his subjects from the moral duty of obeying him. Western canonists regard this synod as the thirteenth ecumenical council. Gregory X summoned a second council at Lyons in the summer of 1274 (5 May–17 July), in the hope of restoring communion between the Eastern and Western churches, a bond broken by mutual anathemas in 1054. The Greek emperor, Michael VIII Palaeologus, who had recaptured Constantinople from Latin occupiers in 1261, accepted the invitation to attend, hoping to prevent further Western attacks on his capital. Delegates of the Mongol khan also attended, as did some two hundred bishops and the nonvoting representatives of most Western rulers. Thomas Aquinas, invited to participate as a theological expert, died en route to Lyons. The Greek delegation participated in the papal Eucharist on 29 June, the Feast of Saints Peter and Paul, and agreed to a formal reunion of the churches on 6 July, raising no objection to the traditionally disputed Western doctrines of the procession of the Holy Spirit, purgatory, and papal primacy, or to the new Western understanding of seven sacraments. The council is regarded in the West as the fourteenth ecumenical council. In 1283, however, a synod in Constantinople repudiated the union and deposed the patriarch, John Beccus, who had agreed to it at Lyons. Michael Palaeologus, who had never succeeded in winning Greek support for the council, was excommunicated by Pope Martin IV in 1281, and his own church even denied him a Christian burial on his death in 1282.

In the face of the increasing attempts of Philip IV ("the Fair") of France to control the church, Clement V—the first pope to reside at Avignon—summoned a council to meet in the independent French town of Vienne in 1311–1312 (16 October–6 May). Eager to acquire the wealth of the Knights Templars, Philip had exerted strong pressure on the pope, even before the council, to suppress the military order on allegations of venality, heresy, and immoral practices. The council found no grounds to support these charges, but Clement suppressed the Templars by a bull of March 1312. The council also discussed plans for a new crusade, issued regulations for the growing number of new religious orders, and condemned the strict interpretation of the poverty of Jesus being advanced by the Spiritual Franciscans. Attended by 132 bishops and 38 abbots, all from western Europe, the Council of Vienne was the first to prepare documents in subcommissions and to delegate a standing committee to finish drafting documents still incomplete at the council's dissolution. Western canonists consider it the fifteenth ecumenical council.

In the Greek church a series of local synods in Constantinople (c. 1340) took up the controversy between Gregory Palamas, a monk of Mount Athos, and the Calabrian monk Barlaam about the value of hesychastic prayer (contemplative prayer prepared for by repetition of a mantra) and the possibility of experiencing the presence of God in this life. A synod in July 1351 recognized as orthodox Palamas's doctrine that God's "energies" or activities, if not God's essence, can be experienced in a quasi-visual way by a soul purified through constant prayer, a teaching that has been of central importance for Orthodox monasticism ever since.

In the West, the years of the Avignon papacy (1308–1378) saw continued centralization of papal authority, as well as increasing opposition to papal rule by the German emperors, independent cities, and certain charismatic and millenarian groups within the church. With the beginning of the Great Western Schism in 1378, in which two rival popes claimed the church's obedience, support began to grow among canonists and theologians for a more corporate system of church government, by which the pope would be understood as an executive appointed by and held accountable to the whole church, represented in a carefully appointed general council. This "conciliarist" theory, first proposed in practical terms by William Durandus of Mende at the time of the Council of Vienne, was seen by a number of prominent theologians in the last decades of the fourteenth century as the only way to end the schism. In 1409, a council at Pisa attempted to put conciliarism into practice by deposing both rival popes and electing a new one (John XXIII). The result, however, was simply that three claimants now vied for the Roman see. In 1414, the emperor Sigismund allied with John XXIII to convoke another council at Constance to resolve the issue (5 November 1414–22 April 1418). Following the representative system of the medieval universities, the voting members of the council—who included over 325 bishops, 29 cardinals, more than 100 abbots, several princes, and several hundred doctors of theology—decided to divide into four blocks, or "nations," each of which would have one corporate vote in the council's final decisions. These "nations" were the Germans (including eastern Europeans), the French, the English (including the Irish and Scots), and the Italians; from July 1415 the cardinals at the council were allowed to vote as a fifth unit, and a Spanish "nation" was added in October 1416. Debate was conducted within the "nations," and the whole council was managed by a joint steering committee, in which each "nation," as well as the cardinals, was represented. The council's decree, *Sacrosancta,* enacted on 6 April 1415, declared that the gathering was a general council of the church and that it therefore had supreme authority of itself, despite the absence of John XXIII, who had fled two weeks earlier. The council then condemned the reformist teachings of English theologian John Wyclif (1330?–1384) and his Bohemian disciple Jan Hus, the latter of whom was publicly burned in Constance on 6 July 1415. The decree *Frequens* (5 October 1417) stipulated that another council was to meet five years after the dissolution of the gathering at Constance, followed by a third council seven years later and by subsequent councils at ten-year intervals. Having devised these limitations on papal power, the council appointed a joint conclave of cardinals and delegates from the "nations," who elected Martin V on 11 November 1417. After further measures for structural reform, the council adjourned in April 1418. Although Martin had previously rejected some aspects of conciliar theory (including the idea of appeal to a further council) and never formally endorsed *Sacrosancta* or *Frequens,* he did declare, at the closing session, that he would observe what the whole council had declared on matters of faith.

After an abortive attempt to summon a council at Pavia in 1423, in accordance with the decrees of Constance, Martin convoked another meeting at Basel in 1430. Eugenius IV, who succeeded Martin in March 1431, hoped once again to effect a reunion with the Greek church and believed that an Italian setting would be more appropriate for that purpose. As relations with the delegates at Basel grew more strained, Eugenius ordered the council transferred to Ferrara in September 1437, although most of the members refused to go and remained in Basel as a rival assembly until 1448. The Greek delegation arrived in Ferrara in March 1438, and after preliminary discussions the council was moved to Florence in January 1439, where the city had offered to underwrite its costs. Led by Bessarion, metropolitan of Nicaea, the Greek delegation recognized the legitimacy of the Latin doctrines of the procession of the Spirit, purgatory, and papal primacy without prejudice to the validity of the Greek tradition, which differed on these points. A decree of union between the churches was signed on 6 July 1439. Subsequent decrees of union were signed with the Armenian church (22 November 1439) and with the Copts and Ethiopians (4 February 1442). The date of closure of the council is uncertain. It is regarded by the Western church as the seventeenth ecumenical council. In Byzantium, however, strong opposition led by Mark Eugenikos, metropolitan of Ephesus, who had also been a delegate to the council, was voiced against the union. A synod in Constantinople in 1484 officially repudiated the Florentine decree in the name of the Greek church.

Age of Reformation. Conciliarism had died as a practical force in the Roman church with the end of the Council of Basel. The Renaissance papacy continued to grow in power and wealth, although throughout Europe the demand for "reform in head and members" continued to grow as well. Faced with the attempt of Louis XII of France to convoke the antipapal reform synod at Pisa in 1511, Julius II summoned a Roman council (the Fifth Lateran Council) on 5 May 1512, which continued under his successor, Leo X, until 16 March 1517. Aside from a few decrees aimed at correcting financial abuse and encouraging popular preaching, this council—recognized as ecumenical by the Western church—achieved little.

The wave of institutional and theological reform set in motion by Martin Luther in the 1520s brought new pressure to bear on the popes to convoke a council to deal seriously with "Protestant" issues. Paul III called a council at Mantua in 1537, for which Luther prepared the theses that were later accepted by German Protestants as a kind of manifesto and known as the Smalcaldic Articles. This meeting was transferred to Vicenza in the same year and then suspended in 1539. After several delays, it was reconvened at the Alpine town of Trent, in imperial territory, on 13 December 1545. Rejecting the conciliar structure agreed on at Constance and Basel, the Council of Trent allowed only cardinals, bishops, and heads of religious orders voice and vote in its full sessions. During its first period (December 1545–March 1547), the council discussed the relation of scripture and tradition, the canon of scriptural books, the doctrines of original sin and justification, and various proposed reforms in church administration. Transferred to Bologna (papal territory) in 1547, to escape the plague, the council continued to discuss the Eucharist and the other sacraments, but Paul III agreed not to let it formulate final decisions until it could return to Trent, where Protestants could participate more freely. A second set of sessions was held in Trent from 1 May 1551 until 28 April 1552, in which documents on these topics were finished. After a ten-year hiatus due largely to continued warfare among the German principalities, Pius IV reconvoked the council on 18 January 1562 for a third and final period, during which documents were issued on the sacrificial character of the Mass, on Holy Orders and the education of the clergy, on the sacramental nature of marriage, and on purgatory, as well as numerous disciplinary decrees. The Council of Trent, recognized by Roman Catholics as a nineteenth ecumenical council, was closed on 4 December 1563. Its decrees laid the foundation for the doctrines and practice of the Roman church for the next four centuries. [*See* Trent, Council of.]

The sixteenth and seventeenth centuries, an age of rapid, often violent change in religious and civil institutions throughout western Europe as well as a time of bitter theological controversy, also witnessed a number of gatherings within and between the new Protestant communities. At the Synod of Dort in the Netherlands (13 November 1618–9 May 1619), representatives of the Reformed churches affirmed, against the theories of the Leiden professor Jacobus Arminius, a strict Calvinist doctrine of the predestination of both the saved and the damned, the total depravity of unredeemed humanity, and the limited scope of Jesus' atoning death. In 1643, the English Parliament commissioned a group of Calvinist divines to revise the Thirty-nine Articles of the Church of England along Puritan lines and to draw up a Puritan confession of faith for the British Isles. On 4 December 1646, this Westminster Assembly completed its document, known as the Westminster Confession. It comprised thirty-three articles, largely based on the teaching of Dort and the covenant theology of English Puritanism. Accepted by the Church of Scotland in 1647, it became the chief confessional document of Scottish Presbyterianism. Protestant theology also made its influence felt in the Eastern churches at this time. Synods at Constantinople in 1638 and 1641 condemned the writings of the Western-educated Byzantine patriarch Cyril I (d. 1638) for their Calvinist teaching, and this condemnation was repeated at Orthodox synods in Jassy (Iași, Romania) in 1642 and Bethlehem in 1672.

The Modern Era. The Roman Catholic church showed little interest in large-scale conciliar gatherings during the seventeenth and eighteenth centuries. A regional synod held in Pistoia in Tuscany in September 1786, under the leadership of Bishop Scipione Ricci, demanded a variety of administrative and pastoral reforms in the church but was rejected by Roman authorities as antipapal and Jansenist in inspiration. Eighty-five propositions taken from its documents were condemned by Pius VII on 28 August 1794. As the spirit of political revolution and scientific positivism swept through European culture in the mid-nineteenth century, however, Catholic interest in a general council that would confront these attacks on religious tradition and give confident expression to the church's teaching again grew. Pius IX appointed a commission to prepare for such a council in 1865 and opened it solemnly—as the First Vatican Council—on 8 December 1869. The 774 bishops who attended from around the world discussed prepared drafts on faith and revelation, authority in the church, reform of the Curia Romana, and other subjects. On 24 April 1870, the constitution *Dei filius* was approved. It affirmed the compatibility of faith and reason and the necessity of supernatural revelation (contained both in scripture and in the church's oral tradition) for a full knowledge of God. After prolonged debate on the opportuneness of a conciliar statement on papal primacy and infallibility, a constitution on the church, *Pastor aeternus*, was approved on 18 July, declaring the "immediate, universal jurisdiction" of the pope over all Christians and affirming that when he acts solemnly as spokesman for the universal church in doctrinal matters, the pope "possesses that infallibility with which the divine Redeemer wanted his Church to be endowed in articulating its teaching of faith and morality." Because of the outbreak of the Franco-Prussian War, the French troops that had been protecting the Papal State were withdrawn that same summer, and on 20 September Piedmontese troops occupied Rome. With most of the delegates gone, Pius IX suspended the council on 20 October 1870, despite the unfinished state of its agenda. Although a number of subsequent interpretations of *Pastor aeternus*, recognized approvingly by Pius IX himself, stressed that papal infallibility, as the council had envisaged it, was simply a special, highly restricted exercise of the assurance of faith in which the whole church believed itself to share, the effect of the council's decrees was to widen the gulf between the Roman church and the other churches, as well as to emphasize Catholicism's critical attitude toward secular values. Vatican I is recognized in the Roman Catholic church as the twentieth ecumenical council. [*See* Vatican Councils, *article on* Vatican I.]

In the twentieth century, by contrast with much of previous Christian history, the conciliar principle has come to be used increasingly as a means for fostering unity between Christian groups and mutual understanding between Christians and nonbelievers. The modern ecumenical movement began, on the institutional level, with the World Missionary Conference, a meeting of Protestant missionary groups, at Edinburgh in 1910. Two other cooperative bodies within Protestantism— Life and Work, founded in 1925 to foster common social and political action, and Faith and Order, established in 1927 to discuss doctrinal and liturgical issues—agreed in 1938 to form a World Council of Churches. Delayed by World War II, the constitutive assembly of the council was held in Amsterdam in 1948; the International Missionary Council joined it in 1961. Not a jurisdictional or legislative body, the World Council seeks to facilitate common action and dialogue in faith among all Christian churches with ten thousand members or more and to be an intermediate step toward a more formal Christian unity. [*See* Ecumenical Movement.]

Although it is not yet a full member of the World Council of Churches, the Roman Catholic church took its own decisive step toward Christian unity in the documents and reforms of the Second Vatican Council (11 October 1962–8 December 1965), which it recognizes as the twenty-first ecumenical council. [*See* Vatican Councils, *article on* Vatican II.] Conceived by John XXIII in January of 1959 as a way of leading the Catholic church toward spiritual renewal, toward greater cooperation with other Christian churches and other religions, and toward a more open attitude to contemporary culture, the council was attended by between 2,100 and 2,400 bishops and heads of religious orders from within the Roman communion, as well as by invited observers from other Christian churches and religious bodies. Vatican II produced sixteen documents on a wide range of pastoral, institutional, and theological issues. Affirming the ancient principle of the collegial responsibility of bishops for the governance of the whole church, in union with the pope, the Constitution on the Church (*Lumen gentium*) opened new possibilities for conciliar government in the Catholic tradition, a step that has led to the regular convening of a worldwide synod of bishops in the years since the council. Vatican II's call for liturgical reform, its stress on the centrality of the scriptures to Christian doctrine and practice, and its recognition of the validity of modern methods of biblical criticism have lessened some of the centuries-old differences between Protestants and Catholics and have given a model for practical reform to other churches. The council's declaration on religious freedom (*Dignitatis humanae*), as well as its decrees on ecumenism, on the Eastern churches, and on relations with Jews and other non-Christians, have greatly altered official Catholic attitudes toward people of other faiths. Its Constitution on the Church in the Modern World (*Gaudium et spes*) expressed, in addition, a positive, welcoming attitude toward the potentialities and aspirations of modern society that invites Roman Catholics to move beyond the defensiveness of the nineteenth century. Although much clearly remains to be accomplished, the revolution in Roman Catholic thought and practice since Vatican II and the continued growth of both the World Council and of individual dialogues between churches, suggest that Christian councils may in the future both become genuinely ecumenical once again and lead to the unity in plurality that is essential to the Christian ideal of community.

BIBLIOGRAPHY

A convenient one-volume edition of the decrees of the twenty-one councils recognized as ecumenical by the Roman Catholic church, in their Latin or Greek original, is *Conciliorum oecumenicorum decreta*, 3d ed., edited by Giuseppe Alberigo and others (Bologna, 1972). The most complete collection of Christian synodal and conciliar documents is the *Sacrorum conciliorum nova, et amplissima collectio*, begun in 1759 by the Italian canonist Giovanni Domenico Mansi and continued through Vatican I by Louis Petit and Jean-Baptiste Martin, 57 vols. (1759–1798; reprint in 53 vols., Paris, 1901–1927); the text is often defective, however, and modern critical editions exist of the documents of most major councils.

The most complete history of the Christian councils is still Karl-Joseph von Hefele and Josef Hergenröther's *Conciliengeschichte*, 10 vols. (Freiburg, 1855–1890), especially in its expanded French translation, *Histoire des conciles d'après les documents originaux,* 11 vols., by Henri Leclerq and others (Paris, 1907–1952); the first part of the German original, dealing with the seven ecumenical councils of the early church, has also been translated into English by William R. Clark as *A History of the Christian Councils,* 5 vols. (Edinburgh, 1871–1896). An excellent recent series of monographs on all the councils up to Vatican I, edited by Gervais Dumeige, is "Histoire des conciles oecumeniques" (Paris, 1962–1973). Outstanding studies of individual councils include: on Constantinople I, Adolf Martin Ritter's *Das Konzil von Konstantinopel und sein Symbol* (Göttingen, 1965); on Chalcedon, Robert V. Sellers's *The Council of Chalcedon: A Historical and Doctrinal Survey* (London, 1953); on Constance, Louise R. Loomis, John H. Mundy, and Kennerly M. Woody's *The Council of Constance: The Unification of the Church* (New York, 1961), a translation of the main diaries and documents of the council, with thorough introduction; on Florence, Joseph Gill's *The Council of Florence* (Cambridge, 1959); on Trent, Hubert Jedin's *Geschichte des Konzils von Trient,* 4 vols. (Freiburg, 1949–1975), a monumental work of scholarship, of which the first two volumes have been translated into English by Ernest Graf as *A History of the Council of Trent* (London, 1957–1961), and Remigius Bäumer's *Concilium Tridentinum* (Darmstadt, 1979), a useful collection of historical essays; on Vatican I, Theodor Granderath and Konrad Kirch's *Geschichte des Vatikanischen Konzils,* 3 vols. (Freiburg, 1903–1906); on Vatican II, Giovanni Caprile's *Il Concilio Vaticano II,* 5 vols. (Rome, 1966–1969), the best general history of the council to date, Henri Fesquet's *The Drama of Vatican II* (New York, 1967), a lively diary of the council, *Vatican II: An Interfaith Appraisal,* edited by John H. Miller (Notre Dame, 1966), a useful symposium by representatives of different faiths, and *Commentary on the Documents of Vatican II,* edited by Herbert Vorgrimler, 5 vols. (New York, 1968–1969).

Good brief histories of Christian councils include Edward I. Watkin's *The Church in Council* (London and New York, 1960), Francis Dvornik's *The Ecumenical Councils* (New York, 1961), and Philip Hughes's *The Church in Crisis: A History of the General Councils* (New York, 1961). A useful collection of essays on the history and theology of councils, by Protestant scholars, is Hans-Jochen Margull's *The Councils of the Church* (Philadelphia, 1966). No comprehensive history of local synods exists, but there is a full bibliographical survey of publications on individual meetings: Jakub T. Sawicki's *Bibliographia synodorum particularium* (Vatican City, 1967).

On the history of the theory of councils, the most thorough surveys are those of Hermann-Josef Sieben, *Die Konzilsidee der alten Kirche* (Paderborn, 1979), *Die Konzilsidee des lateinischen Mittelalters* (Paderborn, 1983), and *Traktate und Theorien zum Konzil: Vom Beginn des grossen Schismas bis zum Vorabend der Reformation, 1378–1521* (Frankfurt, 1983). The classic study of the origins of conciliarism is Brian Tierney's *Foundations of Conciliar Theory* (Cambridge, 1955); an excellent recent work on conciliarism in the period before Constance is Giuseppe Alberigo's *Chiesa conciliare: Identità e significato del conciliarismo* (Brescia, 1981).

BRIAN E. DALEY, S.J.

COUVADE is the name given to various ritual acts performed by a husband during his wife's pregnancy, delivery, and postpartum period. In their most extreme form, couvade customs are said to involve the male's mimicking of or experience of pregnancy symptoms and labor pains, followed by his postpartum recovery. Meanwhile, the woman's actual physical experience is given minimal attention, and she continues her regular activities with little interruption. This extreme form of couvade seems to be more hypothetical than actual. The term *couvade* is more generally used to refer to symbolic behaviors engaged in by men during and immediately after their wives' pregnancies and deliveries.

Since in most, if not all, societies men's activities are affected to some extent by their wives' pregnancies and deliveries, it might seem reasonable to conclude that some form of couvade is universal. However, that usage would make the term so broad that some other term would then be needed to refer to the more specific and more demanding practices engaged in by men in certain tribal societies. One of the most recent discussions of couvade suggests that the term not be used to refer to activities such as giving a birth feast or helping the wife with daily chores during pregnancy. It is suggested that a mild form of couvade is involved when the husband keeps food taboos during the pregnancy or postpartum period. A more intensive form of couvade would involve behavior changes in the postpartum period, such as work taboos and restrictions, or staying close to home for varying lengths of time. The most intensive form of couvade involves ritual seclusion of the husband during pregnancy or the postpartum period, sometimes with his wife and sometimes in his own household or the men's house.

These kinds of behaviors are fairly widespread among small-scale societies, with a concentration of such practices in South American and Caribbean societies. However, theoretical discussions of couvade also rely on reports of the practice among the Ainu (the aboriginal tribal inhabitants of Japan) and among some Pacific Island groups.

A condensed summary of couvade among the Kurtachi, a people of the Pacific Islands, provides a specific example of couvade. During delivery, husband and wife are secluded in separate huts. This seclusion continues for six days, during which the man keeps food taboos, ignores his normal subsistence chores, and does not handle sharp tools. After three days he is allowed to see the child, and gives it medicine to make it strong. On the sixth day he ends his couvade by again entering the wife's seclusion hut, this time carrying a large knife with which he pretends to slash the infant.

Couvade among the Black Carib has also been studied

and analyzed somewhat extensively. Their couvade observances vary in length from two days to a full year, with three months being the most typical duration. Various work taboos are considered an important part of couvade, as is a taboo on sexual intercourse, both marital and extramarital. However, food taboos play almost no part in Black Carib couvade.

A superficial approach to couvade would involve rather commonsense interpretations. Many men practicing couvade customs might be likely to see these practices as helping to protect the infant from harm, and ethnographers studying couvade could well see these practices as promoting the bonding of the father with his infant. Within a psychoanalytic framework the institution of couvade might be considered an expression of womb envy, of men's attempt to participate more directly in, or even to usurp, the essential birth-giving task of females. However, the need to protect young infants, to promote the bonding of fathers with their infants, and to defuse cross-gender envy of males, who unconsciously long for more direct participation in the birth process, exists in all societies. Yet only some societies practice couvade as defined and described by most anthropologists. Thus most recent students of couvade seek the rationale of couvade in other, less universal, factors.

By and large, these analysts find the rationale of couvade in specific features of a lifestyle's social structure. One hypothesis regarding couvade has made more refined use of psychoanalytic analysis. Proponents of this hypothesis have suggested that couvade can result from "low male salience," a combination of factors especially involving arrangements in which the mother sleeps with her children while the father sleeps elsewhere, or is absent altogether. It is hypothesized that the absence of significant contact with the father and the absence of other male role models, combined with such intense contact with the mother, promotes a cross-gender identity that encourages the male to engage in vicarious childbirth observances. Advocates of this explanation of couvade also stress that although other societies may also exhibit "low male salience," they do not have strongly institutionalized couvade. These societies, it is claimed, cope with "low male salience" by means of rigorous and demanding male puberty initiation ceremonies. Through these rigorous initiations, young males are supposedly swayed from any cross-gender identification and take on a kind of masculine identity that relieves them of tendencies toward couvade. It has been pointed out that few if any societies practice both intensive couvade and intensive male puberty rituals.

Alternative theories of couvade stress other causal factors that explain the presence of couvade in some but not all societies. It is claimed that in societies with weak fraternal interest groups a man has no reliable legal or economic means to claim paternity rights to a woman's children. He cannot rely on a loyal kin group to back up his claims to the child, nor can he refer to large economic exchanges or binding legal agreements made prior to the marriage and childbirth. Therefore, he engages in a ritual behavior to establish his claims over the child, and this ritual show gains for him a communal consensus regarding his paternity claims. According to this hypothesis, couvade is a form of ritual bargaining rather than a magico-religious attempt to influence biological processes or a ritual expression of unconscious psychodynamics. However, it would also seem that such political expressions cannot occur without some religious or psychological predisposition toward them.

Couvade seems best explained by looking to varying hypotheses rather than by focusing on only one factor as the sole rationale for these practices. It may be worthwhile to recognize the impulse toward couvade as universal, even though that impulse does not always result in the specific practices associated with "the couvade." Males are universally interested in the genesis, birth, and survival of infants whom they perceive as important. Thus, in varying degrees, males in all societies could be expected to experience some pregnancy symptoms or observe some pregnancy taboos, become involved in the childbirth process, and engage in special behaviors in the immediate postpartum period. Although the term *couvade* refers to specific male childbirth practices in some societies, the institution itself is the expression of a universal impulse rather than a strange practice limited to some small-scale societies.

[*See also* Birth.]

BIBLIOGRAPHY

Theoretical discussions of couvade stressing psychodynamics are found in Robert L. Munroe, Ruth H. Munroe, and John W. M. Whiting's "The Couvade: A Psychological Analysis," *Ethos* 1 (Spring 1973): 30–74, and Ruth H. Munroe and Robert L. Monroe's *Cross-Cultural Human Development* (Monterey, Calif., 1975). Couvade as a political ritual to establish paternity rights is discussed in Karen Ericksen Paige and Jeffery M. Paige's *The Politics of Reproductive Ritual* (Berkeley, 1981). All these theoretical papers cite more descriptive literature concerning couvade. A typical ethnographic account of couvade is found in Allan R. Holmberg's *Nomads of the Long Bow: The Siriono of Eastern Bolivia* (Garden City, N.Y., 1969).

RITA M. GROSS

COVENANT. A central idea in the Hebrew scriptures (Old Testament) is that a covenant, a formal sworn agreement, exists between God and certain individuals or the whole chosen people, Israel. Not content with thinking of God as revealed in nature, or under metaphors from family life (as father or mother), Israel sought to capture and express the stability of the deity's relation to men under this figure from political or legal experience. Aspects of ancient Israel's covenant notions were revived by the Essene covenanters, the people of the Dead Sea Scrolls, and, in much revised form, in early Christianity. The idea of a covenant was not, however, prominent in subsequent Christian theology until after the Reformation of the sixteenth century, when Old Testament ideas were deliberately exploited in some varieties of Protestant theology, and eventually had even wider influence.

The common Hebrew word for covenant (also "treaty" or "alliance") is *berit;* the usual equivalent in the ancient Greek translation (Septuagint) is *diathēkē,* which is carried over into the Greek New Testament. The etymology of *berit* is uncertain and in any case not important for understanding the associated concepts. In fact, one of the most important principles to grasp is that this same word refers to two very different conceptions of a relationship with God, almost contradictory in their intentions, and that Old Testament terms, literary forms, modes of address, or ways of thinking and acting may be related to the concept of a covenant even when the term *berit* is absent.

Scholarly description of Old Testament thought has always assigned some importance to covenant, and the well-known theology of Eichrodt made this concept the central organizing principle. The following, however, describes a more recent phase of inquiry, in which ancient Near Eastern secular prototypes for Israel's religious covenants have been more vigorously and fruitfully exploited.

The Covenant of Grant in the Old Testament. One type of Old Testament covenant is an unconditional divine gift to some man or men. The divine promise to Noah (*Gn.* 9:8–17) after the Flood is called a covenant, and the rainbow is the "sign of the covenant." Examination of the story shows that the deity alone undertakes obligations; Noah and his descendants are not bound in any way. The significant word *remember* is used of God; God will remember what he has promised.

The covenant with David and his line is similar in intent (*2 Sm.* 7). David is said to have been assured that God would continue his line forever. God would keep this promise even if David's sons proved disobedient. One formulation of this covenant is "I will be his father, and he will be my son." The political language of the ancient Near East drew on family terminology: *father* and *son* might refer to the greater and lesser partners to an agreement. Here this terminology is adopted into the religious vocabulary.

The covenant with Abraham, of which we have accounts in *Genesis* 15 and 17 (thus from the "J" and "P" sources of the Pentateuch), is also a one-sided divine grant. Abraham is assured of divine choice and eternal possession of the land of Canaan without being made to assume any corresponding obligation. To be sure, at this point circumcision is enjoined, but this is hardly on a scale with the task undertaken by God, and indeed circumcision is called the "sign of the covenant" (*Gn.* 17:11)—a reminder to God like Noah's rainbow. The curious ceremony in the "covenant between the parts" (*Gn.* 15) illustrates vividly the one-sided nature of these covenants of grant, and Israelite concreteness in thinking of them. Ancient solemn agreements involved an oath, the promiser invoking a curse on himself if he should be untrue. Sometimes this curse was symbolized or enacted, most often by cutting up an animal and touching it or passing between the parts, hence the common Hebrew idiom "to cut (i.e., make) a covenant." In *Genesis* 15 the deity or symbols of the deity are said to pass between the parts, a dramatic expression of the unbreakable unilateral divine commitment.

The secular model on which Israel drew in fashioning such a concept of covenant was apparently the royal grant, as Moshe Weinfeld has argued; the function and terminology of such grants in human society resemble the setting and form of the covenant of grant in the religious economy. Such covenants were not unique to Israel; a Phoenician inscription from Syria (seventh century BCE) refers to a covenant with Asherah, a prominent Canaanite goddess.

As described above, the covenant of grant obviously functioned as a kind of charter myth, validating and guaranteeing forever some desirable state of affairs. On another view, it emphasized spontaneous divine grace, an aspect of Old Testament thought correctly perceived by Paul. It is not to be supposed that there is absolutely no mutuality in these covenants. On the contrary, Noah, Abraham, and David are all good men, and it is expected that they will continue to walk with God. Even so, the only explicit obligation here is on God, and his is the only oath.

The Covenant of Obligation in the Old Testament. The other main conception of a covenant between God and Israel pointed in the opposite direction: the deity undertook no specific obligation, but the human partners swore to abide by certain stipulations, the penalty for disobedience being calamitous curses on the community and ultimately its exile. This conception of the religious covenant, which was at times a social and political reality, not just an idea, called for allegiance to a single God and observance of important mutual obligations in the society (respect for life, property, justice, etc.) and thus was a powerful force for national union, an operative principle rather than a theological abstraction.

The covenant of obligation followed a different secular model from that which lay behind the covenant of grant. In 1931, Viktor Korošec published an analysis of ancient Hittite international treaties from the viewpoint of the history of law. These treaties are written in either Akkadian or Hittite and come from several centuries before the formation of the Israelite state in the thirteenth century BCE. Typically they contain five main parts: (1) a preamble giving the title of the great king who is granting the treaty; (2) a historical prologue, describing past relations between the greater and lesser kings, emphasizing the kindness of the great king and intended to lay the basis for obedience to the terms of the pact; (3) the stipulations, obligations on the vassal; (4) a list of the gods who witness the treaty and who will enforce it; (5) blessings for obedience and curses for disobedience. These Hittite treaties have remained central to discussion of Old Testament covenant because they are the richest body of such texts, but it is not argued that the Hittites had some special relation to Israel; there is reason to believe that a somewhat similar treaty form was in widespread use among various peoples during the second millennium BCE, preservation of the Hittite examples being by chance. There are extant treaties earlier than the Hittite treaties, and an important number of first-millennium treaties from the Aramaeans and the Assyrians; also, Hannibal of Carthage in 215 BCE concluded an alliance with Philip V of Macedon in a form preserving important elements of Near Eastern treaty terminology.

This rich body of materials has been vigorously exploited in recent scholarly attempts to elucidate the complex of ideas that makes up the Israelite conception of a covenant of obligation, Mendenhall's study of 1954 being the earliest. In his view, the Israelite covenant is similar to these early Near Eastern treaties in major emphases and intent: God gives the covenant—as at Sinai (*Ex.* 20) or Shechem (*Jos.* 24)—based on his past gracious actions, but without himself swearing to any performance. The human partners are bound to specific obligations toward him and one another (the Decalogue), transgression of which will bring awful retribution.

Along with this general resemblance go parallels in detail. The position and function of the history of relations between the partners (as in *Jos.* 24) are very similar to the role of history in the secular model. Blessings and curses associated with the covenant are abundantly present, especially in *Leviticus* 26 and *Deuteronomy* 28, and some of these curses show very close verbal resemblances to maledictions in Assyrian treaties. It is not surprising that there are no divine witnesses to Israel's covenant with her god, but the notion of witnesses is there in vestigial form: the people themselves have that role in *Joshua* 24, and in *Deuteronomy* and in prophetic texts heaven and earth, mountains and hills are called to witness (e.g., *Dt.* 32:1, *Is.* 1:2, *Mi.* 6:2); such deified elements of the universe are often invoked in Hittite treaties along with named gods.

Pursuit of these covenant formulations in Israel has led into other areas as well. The love of God, it has been plausibly argued, is a covenant idea related to the language of treaties. Love for God that can be commanded and that consists in walking in God's ways and cleaving to him (*Dt.* 11:22) is a transformation of the "love" for the overlord expected of a treaty partner. "Knowledge" of God at least sometimes in the Old Testament represents not an intellectual or mystical act, but an attitude of submission and loyalty; this use of the term *knowledge* is illuminated by terminology associated with treaty relations; thus *Amos* 3:2, "You only have I known of all the families of the earth; therefore I will punish you for all your iniquities." The prophets often pronounce doom in forms reminiscent of treaty curses. For example, "I will make them eat the flesh of their sons and the flesh of their daughters" (*Jer.* 19:9) has close parallels in Assyrian treaties. Perhaps such resemblances indicate a deliberate covenant stance by the prophets: as Israel has broken the covenant, so she shall bear the prescribed consequences. Rather often the prophets depict God as entering on a "lawsuit" with his erring people; form and vocabulary of such passages (e.g., *Dt.* 32, *Is.* 1:2–3, *Mi.* 6:1–8) have led to identification of them as "covenant lawsuits."

On this line of thought, the covenant of obligation was central and pervasive in Israel's thought. By it, divine grace and mortal obligation were set in place, and loyalty to God and care for one's neighbor were tied together. "The covenant form itself furnished at least the nucleus about which the historical traditions crystallized in early Israel. It was the source of the 'feeling for history' which is such an enigma in Israelite literature . . . what we now call 'history' and 'law' were bound up into an organic unit from the very beginnings of Israel itself" (Mendenhall, 1954, p. 70).

Recent emphasis on the covenant of obligation and on the relevance of ancient treaties has come in for spirited criticism. No one will deny that Israel assigned *some* importance to a divine-human covenant. Critics have questioned the validity or significance of specific parallels in treaties and have asserted that the covenant was a later idea. To the first objection, while there is need for testing of details and especially for recognizing considerable variety in the treaties themselves, it seems that what is called for is a refining and nuancing in the use of treaty materials, not an abandonment of this approach altogether, which would mean ignoring many unmistakable resemblances and leave us without a plausible secular prototype for this aspect of Israel's religious thought. The word *covenant (berit)* is rare in the earliest (eighth-century) prophets. It becomes common along with associated vocabulary and ideas only in the seventh-century Deuteronomic writings; some of the most striking parallels to the treaties come from this century. Hence, it is argued, the covenant idea is late in Israel and so not possibly constitutive of her society or theology in the formative period. But these facts may be viewed otherwise: the paucity of references to covenant in the eighth-century prophets may indicate a turning away from an older idea, while the Deuteronomic usage may display the adaptation of an older conception to changes in the secular sphere, just as Paul's use of *diathēkē* reflects Hellenistic legal use of the term, although the idea is, of course, much older. At present, nothing seems to forbid the supposition that covenant was an old religious idea in Israel, but the biblical evidence is such that no unanimity on such a matter exists or is likely to develop.

Blending of Old Testament Covenant Ideas in the Priestly Writer. Although two separate and nearly opposite conceptions of the covenant prevailed in ancient Israel, they did not remain apart. The late (sixth-century BCE?) priestly writer provides the most impressive and influential example of an arrangement of contrasting covenants and use of them to structure history. Human history from creation through the time of Moses is divided into eras by the covenants (of grant) with Noah, and then Abraham; finally comes the Sinai covenant (of obligation), for which a separate Hebrew term (*'edut*) is used. This discrimination underlies that of Paul (*Gal.* 3) and ultimately much dispensationalism.

Covenant at Qumran and in the New Testament. The nearly contemporary writings of the Qumran community, the people of the Dead Sea Scrolls, and the New Testament reveal contrasting uses of covenant ideas: the former amounts to a repristination of Old Testament practices, with a basic change in orientation, while the latter displays some theological and polemical use of the term but in effect abandons the idea and associated social forms in favor of others.

The Essenes styled themselves "those who entered the new covenant in the land of Damascus" (C D [Damascus Document] VI 19), and the community bound themselves to the Law of Moses by a formal ceremony of oaths involving blessing and cursing, much in the old style. But while the Israelite covenant of obligation was thought of as given by God, at his initiative, the Essene covenant is the result of human determination. Blessing and curse now lie respectively on those within and those outside of the community; they are no longer possibilities confronting those bound to the covenant.

There is no clear evidence that entry into a covenant and associated ideas played anything like the same role in early Christianity. The word *covenant* in various phrases was used in connection with the Eucharist (*Mt.* 26:26–29, *Mk.* 16:22–25, *Lk.* 22:15–20, *1 Cor.* 11:23–25), but though some elements of this phrase may go back to Jesus himself, the intent is not clear, and no formal covenant ceremony, such as that found among the Essenes, is suggested. The later development of the Eucharist is not in the direction of a revival and imitation of Old Testament covenant ideas and forms.

The writer of the letter to the Hebrews uses the term *covenant* rather often, and views Jesus as the "mediator of a new covenant" *(diathēkē)*, but the covenant concept is not fundamental to his view of the new faith. The reverse is closer to the truth: "covenant" is one Old Testament idea, along with the concepts of priesthood, sanctuary, and so on, whose sense is illumined by Christ.

Paul's employment of *covenant* is rather similar, with a sharp polemical point. The covenant of grace (grant) is older than the Sinai covenant and thus superior in force (*Gal.* 3); the superiority of the new covenant in Christ, which continues the Abrahamic covenant, is argued in *2 Corinthians* 3. Paul uses the Greek *diathēkē* for "covenant," following the usage of the ancient Greek translation of the Old Testament (Septuagint). In secular Greek usage, *diathēkē* mostly meant "last will" or "testament," a sense never borne by the Hebrew *berit.* Paul exploits the Greek sense to make the point that a covenant (testament), such as that with Abraham, is unchangeable. In so doing he illustrates the extent to which *covenant* has become a word remote from the way the community defines its identity.

Covenant in Christian Theology and Church History. Although the Christian church ultimately retained the Old Testament as sacred scripture and thus assured continued acquaintance with covenant ideas, the interests of its theologians and the forms of its polity led away from any profound concern with the ancient Israelite covenant. This state of affairs endured until the Reformation of the sixteenth century opened the door to a search for new forms of common life and a renewed interest in the Old Testament, especially on the part of Calvin and his followers. The best known, though not the earliest, of the "covenant theologians" was John

Koch (Cocceius; 1603–1669), whose teaching of a sequence of divine covenants was especially appealing within Calvinism as grounding human salvation in an arbitrary divine act. The Scottish national covenants of the seventeenth century were an early expression of biblical covenant ideas in the political as well as religious sphere, and influenced the development of English Protestantism. The Puritan movement in England and America drew liberally on biblical covenant ideas.

[*For discussion of broadly related topics, see* Binding *and* Election. *For further discussion of God's covenant with the people of Israel, see* Israelite Religion *and* Judaism, *overview article.*]

BIBLIOGRAPHY

Eichrodt, Walther. *Theology of the Old Testament* (1933–1939). 2 vols. London, 1961–1967. Organizes Old Testament thought around the idea of a covenant.

Hillers, Delbert R. *Covenant: The History of a Biblical Idea.* Baltimore, 1969. A popular survey of the biblical usage of *covenant;* follows Mendenhall.

McCarthy, Dennis J. *Old Testament Covenant: A Survey of Current Opinions.* Richmond, 1972. A survey drawing on the author's lengthy technical study, *Treaty and Covenant,* 2d ed. (Rome, 1978).

Mendenhall, George. *Law and Covenant in Israel and the Ancient Near East.* Pittsburgh, 1955. Reprinted from "Ancient Oriental and Biblical Law," *Biblical Archaeologist* 17 (1954): 26–47. The succinct pioneer study that initiated much of the modern discussion of treaty and covenant.

Pritchard, James B. *Ancient Near Eastern Texts.* 3d ed. Princeton, 1969. Contains translations of some important treaty texts.

Weinfeld, Moshe. *Deuteronomy and the Deuteronomic School.* Oxford, 1972. Long portions are devoted to the relation of Deuteronomy to contemporary treaty forms.

DELBERT R. HILLERS

COWS. *See* Cattle.

CRANMER, THOMAS (1489–1556), archbishop of Canterbury (1533–1556), a principal figure in the reformation of the Church of England. Born of a gentry family in Nottinghamshire, Cranmer entered Jesus College, Cambridge, at the age of fourteen. After taking his B.A. (1511) and M.A. (1515), he became a fellow of the college. His marriage to a gentlewoman named Joan cost him the fellowship, but it was restored when Joan, with her baby, died in childbirth.

After his ordination (before 1520), he was appointed one of twelve university preachers and, on obtaining his B.D. (1521) and D.D. (1526), a university examiner in divinity. Cranmer kept aloof from other Cambridge scholars who met frequently to discuss Luther's writings. Instead, he privately tested these writings by his own independent study of the Bible and early church fathers.

Cranmer left Cambridge in 1529 to serve the cause of King Henry VIII's annulment of his marriage to Queen Catherine. During an embassy to Emperor Charles V in 1532 he became acquainted with several Lutheran leaders, among them Andreas Osiander at Nuremberg, whose niece Margaret he secretly married. She bore him a daughter and a son. Few were privy to this marriage until the next reign.

When Archbishop William Warham died in 1532, Henry decided that Cranmer would succeed him at Canterbury. The king was convinced that Cranmer would be dutiful not for any personal convenience, much less ambition, but from his sincere (and somewhat extreme) belief that scripture taught obedience to the divine right of kings and princes. This conviction explains many compromises and vacillations in Cranmer's life. Privately he would advise and admonish Henry and plead for mercy for the king's victims, but he would never openly disobey him.

In January 1533, Henry's secret marriage to Anne Boleyn, already pregnant, made the annulment issue urgent. Although Pope Clement VII suspected Henry's intentions, he consented to Cranmer's consecration, which took place on 30 March. Both before and twice during the rite Cranmer read a protestation that his oath of obedience to the pope did not bind him if it was against the law of God, the laws and prerogatives of the Crown, or the reformation of the church.

Within a few weeks, Cranmer pronounced the marriage to Catherine null and that to Anne valid. In July the pope issued but did not publish excommunications of Henry, Anne, and Cranmer. Any hope of reconciliation ended when the Act of Supremacy (1534) declared the king and his successors "the only supreme head in earth of the Church of England."

Cranmer supported but did not initiate the major reforms of Henry's reign: the dissolution of all monastic and religious houses between 1536 and 1539 (carried out more because of the Crown's greed for their vast properties than for the sake of any principle) and the official authorization in 1539 of the English "Great Bible," for which Cranmer wrote a notable preface in 1540.

The stringent Act of Six Articles (1539) closed the door to any reforms in doctrine or practice. Cranmer spoke against it in the House of Lords, but he voted for it because the king willed it. By now Cranmer was commonly believed to be a Lutheran. In 1543 the privy council voted to arrest him as a heretic, but Henry intervened and saved him. Until Henry's death Cranmer worked quietly on projects of liturgical reform, but of these only the *English Litany* of 1544 was authorized.

Reformers dominated the privy council of King Edward VI (1547–1553), Henry's precocious young son, who was educated by Protestant tutors. Among the councillors committed to religious reform were the young king's uncle the duke of Somerset and Lord Protector, and Cranmer, his godfather. Cranmer soon published a *Book of Homilies,* one part to be read every Sunday, and translated a Lutheran catechism by Justus Jonas. Clerical celibacy was abolished. Communion including both bread and wine was ordered, for which Cranmer prepared *The Order of the Communion* (1548), a vernacular devotion for the people's Communion at Mass.

At Pentecost 1549 *The Book of Common Prayer* came into use under an act of uniformity. The book's reforming principles were derived from Lutheran sources; but its Catholic heritage was preserved by Cranmer's skillful adaptation and translation of liturgical forms and prayers from Latin service books. The daily offices were reduced to two, matins and evensong, with one chapter from both the Old and New Testaments read at each. The Holy Communion eliminated all sacrificial references except "praise and thanksgiving" and forbade any elevation of the consecrated elements. The prayer book was not popular, however, with either conservatives or radical reformers.

After Somerset's fall from power, the duke of Northumberland became Lord Protector. He was more interested in the church properties he acquired than in the radical reforms he promoted. In 1550 Cranmer published *The Form and Manner* for ordaining bishops, priests, and deacons, based on the Latin *Pontifical* and a work of Martin Bucer, and also his principal theological work, *A Defence of the True and Catholike Doctrine of the Sacrament of the Body and Bloud of Our Saviour Christ.*

A revised prayer book was issued in 1552 under an act of uniformity. Most of the old vestments and ceremonies were abolished, and the Communion service was rearranged and conformed to the Swiss reformers' doctrine. All images, crosses, rood screens, and other ornaments were smashed, removed, or sold; and a wooden "holy Table" replaced all altars.

While Edward lay dying, Northumberland plotted to place his cousin Lady Jane Grey (granddaughter of King Henry VII) on the throne. Cranmer strongly opposed this until Edward commanded him to submit. But the coup was short-lived. Mary I, the elder daughter of Henry VIII, was acclaimed queen. Many reformers fled to the continent, and Cranmer sent his family back to Germany.

An ardent Roman Catholic, Mary persuaded Parliament to revoke all reforms of Edward's reign. Cranmer was arrested, tried, and condemned as a traitor; but Mary had other plans. When Cardinal Reginald Pole, papal legate and archbishop-designate of Canterbury, arrived in 1554, he absolved the kingdom and restored papal authority. The burning of heretics then began.

Under pressure, Cranmer wrote several recantations, but to no avail. On the day of his degradation and burning, 21 March 1556, he publicly recanted all his recantations, hastened to the stake, thrust his fist into the fire crying "This hand has offended," and soon collapsed. His monument lives in *The Book of Common Prayer,* often amended and enriched, which is used in the worship of all churches of the Anglican communion.

BIBLIOGRAPHY

The principal collections of Cranmer's writings can be found in *The Remains of Thomas Cranmer, D.D., Archbishop of Canterbury,* 4 vols., edited by Henry Jenkyns (Oxford, 1833), and the two volumes edited by John Edmund Cox for the Parker Society, *Writings and Disputations of Thomas Cranmer, Archbishop of Canterbury, Martyr, 1556, Relative to the Sacrament of the Lord's Supper* (Cambridge, 1844) and *Miscellaneous Writings and Letters of Thomas Cranmer, Archbishop of Canterbury, Martyr, 1556* (Cambridge, 1846).

Many other sources and later assessments of Cranmer are evaluated in the biography by Jasper Ridley, *Thomas Cranmer* (Oxford, 1962), with full bibliography and index of names. On the controversies over Cranmer's doctrine of the Eucharist, with much bibliographical detail, see Peter Brooks's *Thomas Cranmer's Doctrine of the Eucharist: An Essay in Historical Development* (London, 1965). A learned, fair, and readable account of the background of Cranmer's work can be found in W. K. Jordan's *Edward VI: The Young King* (Cambridge, Mass., 1968) and *Edward VI: The Threshold of Power* (Cambridge, Mass., 1970).

Massey H. Shepherd, Jr.

CREATION MYTHS. *See* Cosmogony.

CREEDS. [*This entry consists of three articles: an overview, a treatment of Christian creeds, and a discussion of Islamic creedal statements, or* 'aqīdahs.]

An Overview

A creed is a confession of faith; put into concise form, endowed with authority, and intended for general use in religious rites, a creed summarizes the essential beliefs of a particular religion. The notion of creed comes from the Christian thought world, and it is not possible to identify in other religions the exact parallel, in form and function, of what Christians call a creed. However, approximate parallels may be noted.

According to the definition given above, there are three Christian creeds: the Apostles', the Nicene, and the Athanasian. Here is the text of the shortest and, as far as its sources are concerned, the oldest of the three, the Apostles' Creed, as found in the Anglican *Book of Common Prayer* (1945):

> I believe in God the Father Almighty, Maker of heaven and earth:
>
> And in Jesus Christ his only Son our Lord: Who was conceived by the Holy Ghost, Born of the Virgin Mary: Suffered under Pontius Pilate, Was crucified, dead, and buried: He descended into hell; The third day he rose again from the dead: He ascended into heaven, And sitteth on the right hand of God the Father Almighty: From thence he shall come to judge the quick and the dead.
>
> I believe in the Holy Ghost: The Holy Catholic Church: The Communion of Saints: The Forgiveness of sins: The Resurrection of the body: And the Life everlasting. Amen.

The three Christian creeds are authoritative in large segments of the church, although Eastern Orthodoxy considers only the Nicene Creed as completely authoritative. Certain branches of Protestantism (those that emphasize freedom from traditional rites, a rational approach to religion, or the autonomy of individual religious experience) ignore creeds altogether.

In Judaism, a formula taken from *Deuteronomy* 6:4 and called the Shema' (from the first word, meaning "Hear!") is the expression of monotheistic faith:

> Hear, O Israel: The Lord our God is one God.

Recited liturgically, the Shema' includes, in addition, *Deuteronomy* 6:5–9, 11:13–21, and *Numbers* 15:37–41.

In the *Yasna*, the chief liturgical work of the Avesta (the sacred writings of the Zoroastrian religion), are found several short confessions of faith, summarizing in various wordings the principal beliefs of that religion. One of these (*Yasna* 12:1) is:

> I drive the *daēvas* hence; I confess as a Mazdā-worshiper of the order of Zarathushtra, estranged from the *daēvas*, devoted to the love of the Lord, a praiser of the Bountiful Immortals; and to Ahura Mazdā, the good and endowed with good possessions, I attribute all things good, to the holy One, the resplendent, to the glorious, whose are all things whatsoever which are good.

In Hinduism, the widely used Gāyatrī Mantra, based on *Ṛgveda* 3.62.10, corresponds in some ways to the definition of creed:

> Oṃ [the supreme power]! O earth! O air! O heavens! Let us meditate on the resplendent glory of Savitṛ [the sun god] that it may awaken our thoughts.

This formula is more precisely an invocation of the gods, but implicit in it is a confession of faith. The recitation of a creed functions as prayer in other religions as well.

Buddhism's Triple Refuge is a profession of faith in the wisdom of the Buddha, in the truth of his teaching, and in the significance of the community:

> I take refuge in the Buddha;
> I take refuge in the Dharma [doctrine];
> I take refuge in the Saṃgha [community of believers].

In Islam, the creed is recited as a twofold witness:

> I witness that there is no god but God
> and that Muḥammad is the Messenger of God.

In Sikhism, the opening words of Japji, the guru Nānak's prayer, are expressive of basic Sikh doctrine and are universally recited by that religious community:

> There is but one God whose name is true, the Creator, devoid of fear and enmity, immortal, unborn, self-existent; by the favor of the Guru.
>
> The True One was in the beginning;
> The True One was in the primal age.
> The True One is now also, O Nānak;
> The True One also shall be.

Functions of Creeds. Creeds function in different ways: (1) as the basis for membership in a religious community, whether accompanying a rite of initiation (Christian baptism) or constituting one of the elements of religious distinctiveness (Buddhism, Islam, Judaism, Sikhism); (2) as a test of orthodoxy, in formal opposition to heresy (Christianity); (3) as a type of prayer used in private or public worship (Hinduism, Zoroastrianism, Christianity; in Alsace, Lutherans are invited in their liturgy to "pray the creed"); (4) as a basis for religious instruction; (5) as a corporate or individual response in faith to divine revelation leading to conduct of commitment (Jews call their creed "the acceptance of the yoke of the kingdom of heaven"); (6) as an expression of self-understanding by the religious community; (7) as an assertion and confirmation of the unity of the community (Islam, Christianity, Judaism); or (8) as a witness to the world, expressing the core of belief (Judaism, Islam, Christianity).

Sources of Authority. Only in Christianity has the authority of creeds been legislated formally by conciliar action. The creed of Islam draws its authority from the fact that its elements are found in the Qur'ān, and from its express wording in the *ḥadīth,* or from reports of the prophet Muḥammad where he affirms that the creed is one of the five pillars upon which Islam is built. The Shema' of Judaism is an exact quotation from the Bible. In other religions, the formulas functioning as creeds base their authority on communal unanimity.

Terms Designating Creeds. Besides the word *creed*—not strictly a name in its origin, since it is derived from the Latin verb *credo* ("I believe"), with which the Apostles' Creed and the Nicene Creed open—Christians use the phrase "symbol of the faith" to designate a creed.

In Islam, the creed is called the Shahādah, meaning "witness." Sikhs refer to their creed as the Mul Mantra or "root formula." In the Avesta, the term *fravarāne* is used for "confession of faith."

Extension of the Definition. Sometimes the definition of creed is broadened to include longer, more detailed statements of doctrine. These are more precisely called "articles of faith" or "confessions of faith" in Christianity and *'aqīdah*s in Islam. Examples of such doctrinal treatises are likewise seen in Judaism, attributed to such great scholars as Philo Judaeus, Josephus Flavius, and Moses Maimonides. Contrary to the strict definition of creed given above, articles of faith are not recited orally in liturgical settings, and their authority has been limited to certain segments of a religious community.

The advent of Protestantism in sixteenth-century Christendom prompted the preparation and use of several important confessions of faith that distinguish one denomination from another. Examples are the Augsburg Confession of Lutheranism (1530) and the Westminster Confession of the Reformed tradition (1646).

Islamic *'aqīdah*s have often served to emphasize controverted points of doctrine and practice or to attack heretical tendencies, so they do not necessarily deal with the full range of doctrine. Such statements of faith emerged from the five schools of Sunnī jurisprudence that predominate in the Muslim world today, as well as from schools of thought that have disappeared, and from theologians, legal scholars, mystics, and philosophers, both ancient and modern.

BIBLIOGRAPHY

The article "Creeds and Articles" in the *Encyclopaedia of Religion and Ethics,* vol. 4, edited by James Hastings (Edinburgh, 1911), is not so much an overview of the subject as a series of unconnected descriptions of beliefs in the various religions, with quotations from original sources. The overall nature of creeds is much more clearly set forth in the article "Bekenntnis" by Gustav Mensching et al., in *Die Religion in Geschichte und Gegenwart,* 3d ed., vol. 1, edited by Kurt Galling (Tübingen, 1957). Most of the article is devoted to Christian creeds, and this rightfully, since the notion of creed is most specifically a Christian phenomenon.

The exhaustive and still irreplaceable source of information about Christian creeds is Philip Schaff's *The Creeds of Christendom, with a History and Critical Notes,* 3 vols., 6th ed. (1919; reprint, Grand Rapids, Mich., 1983). A more accessible work, containing a good introduction on the nature and function of creeds, is *Creeds of the Church: A Reader in Christian Doctrine from the Bible to the Present,* 3d ed., edited by John H. Leith (Atlanta, 1982). J. N. D. Kelly, in *Early Christian Creeds,* 3d ed. (New York, 1972), gives a fine study of the origins and development of creed making in Christendom. The entry by Louis Jacobs, "Shema, Reading of," in *Encyclopaedia Judaica,* vol. 14 (Jerusalem, 1972), describes the historical background, liturgical function, and theological meaning of the Jewish creedal formula.

A. J. Wensinck's *The Muslim Creed: Its Genesis and Historical Development* (New York, 1965) deals with the subject in a broad way, analyzing the content of several ancient *'aqīdah*s. Some attention is given to the significance and function of the Shahādah.

Perceptive remarks on the general nature of creeds, strictly defined as a special type of holy word, can be found in Gerardus van der Leeuw's *Religion in Essence and Manifestation,* vol. 2 (1938; reprint, Gloucester, Mass., 1967), pp. 441–443.

R. MARSTON SPEIGHT

Christian Creeds

Christian usage tends to apply the word *creed* preeminently to the Apostles', Nicene, and Athanasian creeds (the so-called ecumenical symbols), to use *dogma* for specific ecclesiastical pronouncements, and to use *confession of faith* for the comprehensive manifestos of the Protestant Reformation. But the terminology remains fluid, and *creed* may be taken in a broad, generic sense to include any official codification of a belief, or the beliefs, of a religious community. Distinctions must then be made among the Christian creeds with respect to their functions, their degree of comprehensiveness, their authority, and their several authorizing bodies.

The various churches differ markedly on the status claimed for their respective pronouncements. Creeds may be invested with the authority of divine revelation. But at the opposite end of the scale, the entire notion of a normative, as distinct from a purely descriptive, statement of belief has often been rejected outright as a threat to the unique authority of scripture, the freedom of faith, or new communications from the Holy Spirit. Since the late nineteenth century, there has also been a tendency to disparage creeds on the ground that they occasion discord in the church and misrepresent the nature of Christian belief.

The greatest number of Christian creeds date from the Reformation era: they were byproducts of the division of the Western church, serving to legitimate the several groups that claimed to be, or to belong to, the true or catholic church. For precisely this reason, the sixteenth-century confessions asserted their continuity with the past; many of them expressly reaffirmed the three ecumenical symbols, and some endorsed as well the pronouncements of the ecumenical councils. But there was, and is, no unanimity on which creeds and which councils may legitimately be classed as ecumenical.

The themes to be considered are, accordingly, the nature and authority of Christian creeds in general, the ecumenical creeds and councils, the Lutheran and Reformed confessions, other creeds of the Reformation era, and Christian creeds in the modern world.

Nature and Authority of Christian Creeds. It is often assumed that a creed is a catalog of authorized beliefs designed as a test of orthodoxy. But the history of the origin and use of Christian creeds proves that such an interpretation is too narrow. A useful clue to this complex history may perhaps be taken from one possible meaning of the word "symbol," by which the Apostles' Creed was known from the earliest times. Tyrannius Rufinus (c. 345–410) thought the creed was so termed because it was intended as a kind of password or means of identification (Lat., *symbolum*). The basic creedal function that underlies all the others is to establish the identity of a community or to identify oneself with it.

Types of creed. The several types of Christian creeds are generated by the diverse situations that demand the affirmation, or the reaffirmation, of identity. The roots of Christian creeds, so understood, must be sought in biblical faith—in the self-understanding of the people of God. A clear prototype of the earliest Christian creeds is to be found in such Old Testament declarations as *Deuteronomy* 26:1–11, which may be described as a historical credo or confession of faith for liturgical use. In content, it is a grateful recital of the redemptive deeds of God—the deliverance from bondage and the gift of the Promised Land—by which the people of Israel were, and still are, constituted. And it is expressly designed as a liturgical formula for the sanctuary—to accompany the presentation of an offering to the Lord. Similarly, the core of the early Christian creeds was recital of the so-called Christ-kerygma, the deeds of God in Jesus Christ understood as continuous with the Old Testament story. (Compare the second article of the Apostles' Creed with, e.g., *1 Corinthians* 15:3–7 and *Acts* 13:16–41.) And the Christian creeds too had their original place in a liturgical rather than a legal setting: they celebrated the identity of the church as the community called into being by the crucified and risen Lord. From the earliest times there was a close connection between creed and baptism, and in most of the historic liturgies of the churches, in both East and West, a creed has been recited or sung as part of the eucharistic service.

It would be a mistake, however, to link Christian creeds exclusively with liturgy (the forms prescribed for corporate worship) or with any particular element in it, such as baptism or the Eucharist. Creeds also served the church's educational needs. Here, too, the Old Testament appears to offer a prototype: in *Deuteronomy* 6:20–25 there is a historical credo without a liturgical context, and the recital of God's marvelous deeds is simply for the instruction of the young, lest future generations forget the events that brought the people into existence. Early Christian creeds likewise found their place not only in the worship but also in the instruction of the church, including catechetical instruction before baptism.

Besides the constant requirements of worship and education, periodic divisions within a church and threats from outside have provided special occasions for the development and use of creedal formulas. Indeed, it is sometimes said that creeds and confessions are most properly born in times of crisis. Although this too is an oversimplification (like the notion that creeds are tests of orthodoxy), it is certainly true that defense against the peril of false belief—in the form of heresy, persecution by another church, or paganism—has been one stimulus to creed-making throughout Christian history. And it must be added that not only the desire to exclude competing beliefs but also the desire to overcome divisions has produced creeds, in which previous recriminations are laid aside in a new sense of unity.

The diverse uses of Christian creeds are reflected in the traditional nomenclature. An affirmation of communal identity having symbolic authority might be called "creed," "confession," "articles of faith," "canons," "decree," "catechism," "declaration," "covenant," "consensus," "platform," "apology," and so on. But in practice, function and title do not invariably coincide, and many creeds have been put to more than one use.

Authority of creeds. The status of creeds in the Roman church is closely bound up with the Roman Catholic understanding of the church, its magisterium and its infallibility. Though degrees of authoritative statement are differentiated, the highest ecclesiastical pronouncements have a juridical character and are binding on the church's members: to deviate openly and obstinately from any truth of the catholic faith is heresy. The tendency of Rome to accumulate dogmas is not approved by the Eastern Orthodox churches, but they invest the Nicene Creed and the pronouncements of their seven ecumenical councils with much the same authority that Rome accords its more abundant dogmatic norms. By contrast, the status of creeds in Protestantism is not uniform, and in view of the Protestant appeal to the sole authority of scripture, it is often seen as a problem.

The followers of Martin Luther (1483–1546) wanted a common form of doctrine to which all the evangelical churches could be expected to subscribe. Their Formula of Concord (1577) drew an explicit parallel between the authoritative ancient symbols and their own Augsburg Confession (1530), "the symbol of our time." This raised questions about the relationship of the Augsburg Confession and other Lutheran symbols to the authority of scripture. The Formula drew a line between the word of God and postapostolic witness to it, but allegiance to the symbols presupposed that they were no more than summaries of scriptural truth required by the threat of false teaching. An identity of content was claimed between scripture as the *norma normans* and the Lutheran confessions as the *norma normata,* so that an actual critique of the Lutheran church's doctrine would appear to be, in principle, as hard to undertake from within as Luther found it to launch a critique of the Roman church's doctrine. Irreformability of the Lutheran church's dogmatic standpoint was implied in the assertion "We do not intend, either in this [the Formula of Concord] or in subsequent doctrinal statements, to depart from the aforementioned [Augsburg] Confession or to set up a different and new confession." Some of the Lutheran churches regard their *Book of Concord* (1580) as a now-closed collection of symbolic books: no subsequent statement, after 1580, could attain symbolic status. Others, however, never endorsed the Formula of Concord or, with it, the *Book of Concord.*

It is sometimes asserted that the authority of confessions is weaker in the Reformed church than in the Lutheran. But the historical evidence is ambivalent. On the one hand, the absence of a single preeminent confession and a closed symbolic collection among the Reformed does appear to invite continuous revision of their confessional stand. To this extent, an admission of reformability is tacitly built into Reformed confessionalism; and the authors of Reformed confessions have sometimes expressly disowned any exclusive claim for their particular terminology, or have invited correction if in any respect they should be found to have departed from the word of God. On the other hand, subscription to the prevailing local creed or creeds has commonly been demanded of pastors and sometimes of schoolteachers—or even of entire populations (as happened in Geneva in 1537). The history of the Westminster Confession (1647), the principal creed of the English-speaking Reformed (the "Presbyterians"), is particularly instructive. The Westminster Divines seem not to have wanted it to become the rule of faith and practice rather than a "help," but that is exactly how the Scots used it north of the border, and Scottish influence became paramount. The Presbyterian appetite for heresy trials presupposed that the Westminster Confession had a legal status not unlike that accorded by the Roman church to Roman Catholic dogmas.

An unmistakable shift can be observed within Protestantism when one moves from the Lutheran and Reformed churches to what may be broadly, if loosely, called the "free church" tradition. For instance, in their Savoy Declaration (1658) the Congregationalists adapted the Westminster Confession to their own use but they expressly disavowed any intention to bind consciences, since that would belie the very name and nature of confessions of faith and turn them into exactions and impositions of faith. Since 1970, Congregationalists have belonged to the World Alliance of Reformed Churches. But Congregationalism has generally, if not always, affirmed a descriptive rather than a normative view of creeds. They "declare, for general information, what is commonly believed among" Congregationalists (English Declaration, 1833). In this manner the agony of heresy hunts is avoided, but the more strictly confessional churches are likely to argue that the basic creedal function of preserving the community's identity is here in peril of being surrendered.

Churches that renounce the use of creeds altogether may differ from the confessional churches in little more than the refusal to commit their beliefs to formal, written definitions; they may in practice be just as intolerant of any deviations from the approved language of the community. If we set aside unwritten creeds, however, we may perhaps conclude that there are three types of Protestant attitude to formulas of belief: a closed confessionalism that requires allegiance to a past symbol or a completed collection of symbols, an open confessionalism that calls for the drafting of present symbols of belief, and a purely descriptive confessionalism that denies to "human formularies" any binding or symbolic authority at all. While these three types appeared among the Lutherans, the Reformed, and the Congregationalists, respectively, they cannot be simply identified as denominational positions. All three communions have had a complex history of subscription controversies. And the three types do not exhaust the options. The Anglican communion, for example, understands itself largely as a worshiping community, and its leaders often point to *The Book of Common Prayer* (1662) and the historic episcopate rather than the Thirty-nine Articles (1563–1571) as the pledge of corporate identity.

Ecumenical Creeds and Ecumenical Councils. In the New Testament, faith, confession, and salvation are inseparable (*Mt.* 10:32, *Rom.* 10:10). The simplest formula of Christian confession is the assertion that Jesus is Christ (*Mk.* 8:29) or Lord (*Rom.* 10:9, *1 Cor.* 12:3), and the Western text of *Acts* 8:37 evidently reflects early use of a similar formula ("Jesus Christ is the Son of God"; cf. *Mt.* 16:16) in connection with baptism. But it was the conviction of the early Christians that Jesus himself enjoined baptism in the triadic name of Father, Son, and Holy Spirit (*Mt.* 28:19), and summaries of Christian belief emerged, known as "rules of faith" but fluid in their wording, as the Christ-kerygma came to be incorporated into a triadic framework. Similar to them in basic structure, only more fixed in wording, two major families of creed developed, culminating in the Apostles' Creed in the West and the Nicene Creed in the East.

The Apostles' Creed. The legend that the twelve apostles themselves jointly composed the creed named after them, each in turn contributing one clause, was not seriously doubted before the critical labors of Lorenzo Valla (c. 1405–1457) and Reginald Pecock (c. 1393–c. 1461). In its present wording, the Apostles' Creed makes its first verifiable appearance in the West no earlier than the eighth century, in a treatise by the monk Pirminius (or Priminius, d. 753), and it has remained strictly a Western creed. But a long history certainly brought it to its final form. It is generally agreed that the historical roots of the Apostles' Creed are in the ancient baptismal confession of the Roman church, the "Old Roman Creed" (R), which Archbishop James Ussher (1581–1656) first attempted to reconstruct from Marcellus (d. around 374) and Rufinus.

More recent scholarship suggests that the earliest version of R was a Greek creed in interrogative form ("Do you believe . . . ?") and that it dates back to about AD 200, when Greek was still in use in the Roman church. Behind it there probably lies a still earlier trinitarian confession, also of the interrogative type but without the Christ-kerygma. It may simply have asked the candidate for baptism: "Do you believe in God, the Father, Almighty? And in Christ Jesus, his only Son, our Lord? And in the Holy Ghost, the holy church, the resurrection of the body?" (Another explanation of the term "symbol" is that the triple interrogation was understood to be symbolic of the Trinity.) The insertion of the Christ-kerygma into this presumed early-Roman baptismal confession may have been encouraged by the need to refute docetism, the denial of Jesus' humanity. The received text of the Apostles' Creed makes the point cumulatively: Jesus was conceived, was born, suffered, "was crucified, dead, and buried." Finally, the shift to the declarative form ("I believe . . ."), which required recital from memory, perhaps was made initially in catechetical preparation for baptism, then carried over into the baptismal rite itself.

The Nicene Creed. Until modern times, it was traditionally assumed that the so-called Nicene Creed was the creed promulgated by the Council of Nicaea (325), as revised and endorsed by the Council of Constantinople (381). Especially since the researches of Eduard Schwartz (1858–1940), the tradition has been generally abandoned, but much scholarly disagreement remains. Perhaps tradition was right in linking the Nicene Creed with the Council of Constantinople; hence modern scholarship designates it "the Niceno-Constantinopolitan Creed" (C). But it does not seem to have been a mere revision of the creed promulgated at Nicaea (N); rather, the two creeds must be said to belong to a common Eastern type, as does the creed of Caesarea, which was once supposed to have been adopted at Nicaea as the first draft of N.

The Eastern creeds are distinguished from R by their greater interest in the preexistence of Christ before the incarnation: they place the Christ-kerygma in a cosmic setting. Hans Lietzmann (1875–1942) thought it was possible to reconstruct an Eastern or "Oriental" prototype (O) analogous to R, but it remains uncertain whether O, or something like it, actually existed as the model for other Eastern creeds. In any case, N advances beyond O in the attempt to exclude Arianism: it affirms that the Son of God was "God from God . . . of the same substance [*homoousion*] as the Father" and concludes with anathemas against the Arian watchwords (that there was a time when the Son was not, etc.). C, in turn, advances beyond N in affirming, against the Macedonian heresy, the equality of the Holy Spirit with the Father and the Son, although the technical term *homoousios* is not used of the Spirit as well. Some time in the sixth or seventh century, the word *filioque* was inserted into the Latin text of C, so that the Holy Spirit was said to proceed from the Father *and the Son.* The insertion became a bone of contention between Rome and the Eastern churches, which firmly rejected it.

The Nicene Creed (C) came to be used liturgically in the Eastern church in both baptism and the Eucharist; in the West it was adopted as the eucharistic confession. The creed of Nicaea (N), by contrast, was designed not for instruction or worship but as a test of orthodoxy, which could be invoked even against a bishop of the church. In this respect, the Council of Nicaea marked a new stage in creedal history: its creed was the first to be promulgated by an ecumenical council with a claim to universal authority throughout the entire church.

The Athanasian Creed. The so-called Creed of Saint Athanasius (also known as the Quicunque Vult, from its opening words in Latin) was probably composed in southern France during or after the post-Nicene debates on the incarnation. After the Council of Nicaea, theological interest shifted from the eternal relations of Father, Son, and Spirit within the divine Trinity to the relationship between the divine and human natures of the incarnate Son. Arianism, now officially condemned, was succeeded by the Apollinarian, Nestorian, and Eutychian heresies. While the provenance of the Athanasian Creed can be inferred from the evidence of its earliest use and influence, the date assigned to it depends chiefly on the answer to the question which of the three christological heresies it was intended to oppose. It was indeed argued by Daniel Waterland (1683–1740) that even its statements on the doctrine of the Trinity require a date no earlier than 420, because they reflect the language of Augustine's (354–430) trinitarian speculations. In any case, the christological statements almost certainly allude not only to Apollinarianism but also to Nestorianism, possibly to Eutychianism; and the three heresies were condemned respectively at the councils of Constantinople (381), Ephesus (431), and Chalcedon (451). The attribution of the creed to Athanasius, who died in 373, is clearly impossible and was already discredited in the seventeenth century by Gerhard Jan Voss (1577–1649). Alternative suggestions have been made; perhaps the most persuasive case points to Lérins, the island abbey opposite Cannes, as "the cradle of the creed" (J. N. D. Kelly), and someone close to Vincent of Lérins (d. around 450) and Caesarius of Arles (d. 542) as its author.

The first part of the Athanasian Creed presents the doctrine of the Trinity, and the second part places the Christ-kerygma in the protective setting of propositions against the christological heresies. Although the creed came to be sung regularly in the West, it most likely originated not as a hymn but as a form of instruction for clergy; and its technical, metaphysical, and threatening style has gradually reduced its liturgical use. In the East it was unknown until the twelfth century and never won very high regard. The Chalcedonian definition, though never added to the number of the ecumenical symbols, actually enjoys wider authority as a defense against christological heresy because of its association with an ecumenical council.

Recognition of the creeds and councils. Most of the major churches recognize the ecumenical creeds and councils insofar as they present fundamental Christian beliefs about God and Christ. But only the Nicene Creed can fully claim the rank of ecumenical symbol, and it is unfortunate that its significance is tarnished by debate over the *filioque* insertion. Ecumenical status is assigned by the Eastern Orthodox church to seven councils: two of Nicaea (325, 787), three of Constantinople (381, 553, 680), Ephesus, and Chalcedon. The Roman church claims ecumenical rank also for its own synods, the last of which, Vatican II (1962–1965), was counted the twenty-first ecumenical council; and Rome considers the decrees of an ecumenical council to be "an infallible witness to the Catholic rule of faith." Protestants tend to single out the first four "general councils" as especially worthy of reverence, but deny that their decrees are in principle infallible; rather, they are to be tested by the word of God.

Lutheran and Reformed Confessions. The Protestant confessions of the Reformation era were intended to restore to the church its true image and identity, which, it was widely agreed, had been obscured by the errors and abuses of the later Middle Ages. The heart of the Reformation creeds is the rediscovery of the gospel as, in Luther's memorable phrase, "the real treasure of the church." The church, Luther held, is the creation of the gospel; it is the word of God in Jesus Christ that makes the church the church. And he believed that the church's confession of the divinity of Christ was fatally impaired wherever this gospel was displaced or misconstrued.

Lutheran confessions. Of the ten symbols included in the Lutheran *Book of Concord,* the first three are the ecumenical creeds; the rest, in chronological order of publication, are Luther's Large and Small Catechisms (1529), the Augsburg Confession, Philipp Melanchthon's (1497–1560) *Apology for the Augsburg Confession* (1531), Luther's Smalcald Articles (1537), Melanchthon's *Treatise on the Power and Primacy of the Pope* (1537), and the Formula of Concord. Among the distinctively Lutheran symbols, all German in origin, the Augsburg Confession holds a special place. Lutheranism was granted legal recognition by the Peace of Augsburg (1555) as "the religion of the Augsburg Confession." The spread of Lutheranism beyond Germany always meant adoption of this confession, and the Formula of Concord itself claimed to be simply the correct and final explanation of it in response to certain inner-Lutheran controversies.

The confession was presented to Emperor Charles V on 25 June 1530 at the Diet of Augsburg (whence the name by which it is familiarly known). Although earlier documents by other hands lay behind it, in its final form its principal author was Melanchthon, whose ecclesiastical strategy it reflects. According to the Formula of Concord, the Augsburg Confession "distinguishes our reformed churches from the papacy and from other condemned sects and heresies." But that by no means conveys the author's intention. He was certainly eager to disown the Zwinglians and the Anabaptists, but precisely in order to confirm the essential Lutheran agreement with Rome. The confession (or "apology," as it was initially called) set out to accomplish two goals: to defend the catholicity of Lutheran doctrine and to justify the innovations in Lutheran practice. Part one (arts. 1–21), the confession of faith proper, contains a summary of the doctrines taught in the Lutheran churches. It claims to present the faith of the catholic church, not of a particular Lutheran church, and it insists that there can be no disagreement with Rome if Rome's teaching, too, conforms to antiquity. The contention is not over articles of faith but over a few usages, and these are taken up in part two (arts. 22–28), which lies outside the confession of faith in the strict sense.

Melanchthon's design required the suppression of several controversial issues, including the authority of scripture, papal primacy, and the priesthood of all believers. How well he succeeded is open to question, but it is significant that in 1980, when the 450th anniversary of his confession was celebrated, there were widespread discussions between Roman Catholic and Lutheran theologians on the possibility that Rome might recognize the Augsburg Confession as a catholic confession. Still, it is undeniable that the confession bears a distinctively Lutheran stamp precisely in the regulative place it assigns to the gospel, understood as the message of justification through faith without any merits of our own. It is this "chief article" that provides one implicit definition of an "abuse" for part two of the confession: any usage implying that grace can be earned is an abuse (art. 15). The same chief article constitutes the actual core of part one, shaping the doctrines of church, ministry, and sacraments as well as the Lutheran understanding of the Christian life, neighborly love, and the earthly callings.

It is not surprising that the Roman Catholic critics of the confession, while they welcomed the affirmation of the real presence in the Eucharist (art. 10), found uncatholic the pivotal notion that the sacraments in general are testimonies of God's good will for the purpose of arousing faith, that is, the faith through which we are justified (art. 13). Sacraments are thereby interpreted (or reinterpreted) as functions of the word of God, forms of the gospel proclamation; and the entire medieval conception of the church and its ministry is transformed accordingly. This was one strictly doctrinal issue that lay behind the Lutheran charge, in part two of the confession (art. 24), that it is an abuse to celebrate the Mass as a sacrifice for sin. It would be unfair to conclude (as has sometimes been done) that Melanchthon was devious or naive. The point, rather, is that his concern was to reaffirm the gospel of grace without letting the Lutheran reform rend the unity of the catholic church.

The Reformed confessions. Unlike the Lutherans, the Reformed churches of the sixteenth and seventeenth centuries were not held together by a single confession of faith. Though they often acknowledged one another's confessions—sometimes even the Lutheran Augsburg Confession—in general each national or regional church drew up its own standard or standards of belief. The most comprehensive collection of Reformed creeds (E. F. K. Müller, 1903) contains fifty-eight items, and the editor remarks that the number could be doubled without achieving completeness. Other individual collections have appeared from time to time, but none has ever acquired, or could have acquired, ecclesiastical endorsement as the Reformed "Book of Concord." It was a new departure—and the act of only one branch of the Reformed family—when the United Presbyterian Church in the United States of America in 1967 authorized its *Book of Confessions,* a selection of Reformed creeds of international origin. In the 1983 edition, the *Book of Confessions* of what had become the Presbyterian Church (U.S.A.) included six documents from the Reformation era (along with the Nicene and Apostles' creeds and two twentieth-century confessions): the Scots Confession (1560), the Heidelberg Catechism (1563), the Second Helvetic Confession (1566), the Westminster Confession (rev. ed., 1958), and the two Westminster Catechisms (1647). None of these six creeds stands very close to John Calvin (1509–1564), an omission that could be remedied with the French (Gallican) Confession of 1559, perhaps the outstanding Reformed creed of the declarative type. Originally conceived as an apology of the persecuted French Protestants to the king of France, the confession was not a creed for theologians only but a confession of the church, and it came to be printed inside the Bibles and Psalters of the French Reformed congregations.

Dogmatic uniformity is hardly to be expected throughout the total Reformed *corpus confessionum,* and no one confession can be taken as regulative for them all. But they were first and foremost, like other Protestant confessions, "evangelical"—that is, reaffirmations of the gospel of Christ, or (what for them was the same thing) of the lordship of Christ, as alone constitutive of the church's identity. This is particularly clear in the documents from the early years. The very first Reformed confession, the Sixty-seven Articles

(1523) of Ulrich Zwingli (1484–1531), sounds the characteristic note in its opening assertions (cf. Ten Theses of Bern, 1528; Lausanne Articles, 1536). In subsequent confessions the primacy of the gospel comes to be set in a more systematic framework, but it is still affirmed, either within the confessions (e.g., First Helvetic Confession, 1536, art. 12; cf. art. 5) or in preambles to them (e.g., the French and Scots confessions), and serves as the constant norm for sifting out truth from error in the prevailing beliefs and practices of the church.

The dogma of double predestination, sometimes imagined to be the center of Reformed or Calvinistic theology, is not emphasized in the sixteenth-century confessions; in some (e.g., the First Helvetic Confession and the Heidelberg Catechism) it is not even mentioned. If one looks for a distinctively Reformed emphasis, it might more plausibly be located in the concern for the order, discipline, and worship of the church. The "parity of presbyters" (i.e., the equality of all ordained clergy in rank) and the need for elders to assist the pastors in maintaining discipline are expressly included in some of the confessions—apparently as matters of faith. But here too the fundamental principle is the sole lordship of Christ, the only universal bishop of the church, the ever-present and life-giving head of the body, who needs no "vicar" (French Confession, arts. 29–30; Scots Confession, chap. 16; Belgic Confession [1561], art. 31; Second Helvetic Confession, chap. 17; etc.). And the same line of thinking prevents Zwingli's memorialist conception of the Lord's Supper, which occasioned the breach with Lutheranism, from intruding into the major Reformed confessions. In the Lord's Supper the living and present Lord feeds and strengthens his people "with the substance of his body and of his blood" (French Confession, art. 36; cf. Scots Confession, chap. 21, Second Helvetic Confession, chap. 21, and so on).

Other Creeds of the Reformation Era. Besides the Lutherans and the Reformed, other non-Roman churches in the West produced statements of belief during the Reformation era. The Church of England had its Thirty-nine Articles, the Unitarians their Racovian Catechism (1605), the Mennonites their Dordrecht Confession (1632); the Congregationalists, the Baptists, and even the Quakers continued to add to the confessional literature of the earlier Reformation. But none of these groups has invested its statements with the doctrinal authority the Lutherans and the Reformed accord to theirs; most of them would say that their confessions are for instruction, not for subscription. Sometimes the new statements borrowed freely from the old. Already in the sixteenth century the Thirty-nine Articles were largely derived from continental Protestantism, and in the following century the Congregationalists and the Baptists (both "Particular" and "General" Baptists) made their own recensions of the Presbyterian Westminster Confession, as John Wesley (1703–1791) was later to make a Methodist recension of the Anglican articles (the Twenty-five Articles of 1784).

Eastern Orthodox churches. The Eastern churches remained aloof, as far as possible, from the Reformation crisis, judging it to be an internal problem of the Western church. Some exchange did take place, however, and it generated more or less official Orthodox responses to Protestantism. Most important among them was the Confession of Dosítheos, issued by the Synod of Jerusalem (1672) to combat the Calvinizing opinions advanced by, or attributed to, Cyril I (Kyrillos Loukaris, 1572–1638), former patriarch of Constantinople. It is generally assumed that the patriarch of Jerusalem, Dosítheos (1641–1707), was the principal author of the confession, which constitutes chapter 6 of the synod's decrees. He avoided Roman Catholic doctrines and practices that Orthodoxy does not accept (papal supremacy, the celibacy of all clergy, withholding the cup from the laity) and took essentially the same stand as Rome against the Protestant views of authority and justification. The Calvinist doctrine of the Eucharist is opposed (decree 17) not only by affirming a propitiatory sacrifice but also by borrowing the Latin idea of transubstantiation.

In addition to promulgating its own confession, the Synod of Jerusalem endorsed the earlier replies of Jeremias II (c. 1530–1595), patriarch of Constantinople, to overtures from the Lutheran theologians of Tübingen. The replies (published in 1584) rejected the distinctive doctrines of the Augsburg Confession on everything except the marriage of priests. The synod also gave its sanction to a catechism drafted (c. 1640) partly in opposition to the Calvinizers by Petr Moghila (1596–1647), metropolitan of Kiev, which was probably the most influential witness to the Orthodox faith of the Greek and Russian churches until superseded in 1839 by the Catechism of Filaret (1782–1867), metropolitan of Moscow. But neither Filaret's catechism nor the documents promulgated or endorsed by the Synod of Jerusalem have the same authority in Eastern Orthodoxy as the Nicene Creed, which commended itself all the more because it was safe from the conflict in the Western church. Insofar as the Eastern church faced the Reformation at all, it has usually considered its responses to be strictly contextual; use of the Latin dogma of transubstantiation, for example, in the Confession of Dosítheos did not make it an Orthodox dogma.

The Roman Catholic church. The Roman church, by contrast, produced its most comprehensive standard of belief (until that time) precisely in response to the Protestant Reformation. In 1545, fifteen years after the Diet of Augsburg, the long-hoped-for council that was to settle the religious questions was finally convened at Trent. Its last session took place in 1563, eighteen years later. The Orthodox and the Protestants were not represented, but Trent is considered by the church of Rome to be the nineteenth ecumenical council. (The Lutherans were invited, and delegates from Saxony and Württemberg did appear briefly in the spring of 1552, but they could be received only as errant children of the church, which had condemned Luther three decades before.) The canons and decrees of the Council of Trent were published in their entirety in 1564. Not all twenty-five sessions produced decrees on doctrine. Those that did were mainly interested in three matters of faith: authority, justification, and the sacraments.

After adopting the Nicene Creed as its confession of faith and shield against heresies (sess. 3), the council proceeded to specify the two witnesses to which it would appeal in confirming dogmas and restoring morals in the church: scripture and unwritten traditions (sess. 4). The express concern of Trent, like that of the Protestants, was for "the purity of the gospel." But there could be no question of appealing to the gospel against the traditions or teaching of the church. For the truths of the gospel, according to Trent, are contained both in scripture and in the unwritten traditions handed down from the apostles; both are to be received with the same devout reverence. And the scriptures themselves are not to be interpreted by anyone's private judgment contrary to the sense that holy mother church has held and holds.

It did not follow that the Roman church wished to stand behind the practices and beliefs that the Protestant confessions had judged to be violations of the gospel. Trent did reject the Lutheran protest in principle, and it could not accept the Lutheran inventory of abuses without discrimination. But in its decrees on reform the council inaugurated a Catholic reformation, which dealt extensively with many of the alleged abuses, eradicating some and purging others. And in its decrees on doctrine it defined positions that cannot be simply identified with positions the Lutherans and the Reformed had attacked. In particular, the decree on justification (sess. 6), which took seven months to complete, seems to deny forthrightly the very opinion against which the Lutherans had most vehemently protested: that the grace of justification can be merited (chap. 8). Trent's denial of merit before justification has been the subject of divided interpretation among twentieth-century historians, and in any case other confessional differences concerning justification, or possible differences, certainly remain, but the dividing lines are not as sharp as sixteenth-century polemics made them out to be. The same holds true for sacramental theology.

Among the controverted sacramental issues, none ranks higher in importance than the debate over the sacrificial character of the Mass. Both the Lutheran confessions (e.g., Augsburg Confession, art. 24) and the Reformed confessions (e.g., Scots Confession, art. 22) presumed that in the Roman Mass the priest was credited with sacrificing Christ to appease God. The Mass, they alleged, therefore detracted from Christ's self-sacrifice on the cross and violated the heart of the gospel—that grace is not obtained through human works. The language of the Tridentine response (sess. 22) is neither uniform nor wholly transparent. But no competition between cross and altar is implied. The once-for-all offering on the cross is said to be "represented" in the Mass and its benefits applied to daily sins, "so far is the latter from derogating in any way from the former" (chaps. 1–2). And though the sacrifice of the Mass is carried out "by the church through the priests," the decree adds: ". . . the same now offering by the ministry of priests who then offered himself on the cross" (chaps. 1–2).

Confessional legacy of the Reformation. The Tridentine decrees must be seen in relation to subsequent dogmatic pronouncements of the Roman Catholic church, especially the constitutions of the First and Second Vatican Councils (1869–1870; 1962–1965). But the confessional legacy of the Reformation era appears less totally and irrevocably divisive than might be supposed. Just as the Reformed confessions did not perpetuate the Zwinglian sacramental views that the Lutherans found so offensive, so also the Tridentine decrees did not simply immortalize the errors and abuses with which the Protestants charged the late medieval church. And a more irenic age would have to ask, in turn, how just were the Tridentine anathemas hurled against the Protestants.

Christian Creeds in the Modern World. Although the Reformation era may be singled out as the most productive period of Christian creed-making, dogmas have continued to be defined and confessions drafted down to the present time. The Roman church's dogmas of the Immaculate Conception (1854), papal infallibility (1870), and the Assumption of the Virgin Mary (1950) were important developments of traditional Roman Catholic beliefs about Mary and the papacy. Other creedal statements have been self-conscious attempts to rethink confessional positions in the modern world. But it is also during the last three centuries that the very idea of a creed has become most precarious.

Modern anticreedalism. The problem of what may be termed "anticreedalism" has naturally made itself felt more especially in Protestantism. From the first, even the most staunchly confessional of the Protestant churches, the Lutheran, was not entirely of one mind about its symbolic books. Distinctions were made between one confession and another, and not all the Lutheran bodies adopted the Formula of Concord. Moreover, in the non-Lutheran churches there was a tendency to contrast all human formularies much more sharply with the divinely inspired scriptures. Modern anticreedalism, however, has other roots besides biblicism. Most important is the drift toward a less dogmatic variety of Christian religion. With roots in sixteenth-century humanism and antitrinitarianism and in seventeenth-century Arminianism, aversion to distinctively Christian dogmas flourished in English Deism and was nurtured by the theologians of the German Enlightenment. In the course of the eighteenth century, Protestant orthodoxy, already weakened by Pietism, retreated before enlightened disdain for inherited superstitions and dogmatic particularism. Friedrich Schleiermacher (1768–1834) tried to deal more sympathetically with the old creeds as authentic, though reformable, deliverances of the Christian consciousness. But the resurgence of Lutheran confessionalism in the early nineteenth century was directed against Schleiermacher as well as against the rationalists, and it was carried by German immigrants to the New World.

By the end of the nineteenth century, the beleaguered antidogmatic line in Protestant theology found new resources in the work of Ritschlian church historian Adolf von Harnack (1851–1930), who argued with massive erudition that Christian orthodoxy arose as a corruption of the gospel by Hellenic metaphysics and intellectualism. Dogmas, as he put it, are "a work of the Greek spirit on the soil of the gospel"; by them, confidence in the Father God of Jesus is transformed into intellectual assent to metaphysical propositions about the inner life of the godhead and the two natures of the incarnate Son. From this standpoint, Harnack considered himself free to subject even the Apostles' Creed to detailed criticism and to oppose its continued use as a legal ordinance.

Strictly speaking, Harnack and the liberal Protestants who rallied around him did not want to abolish the Apostles' Creed, or creeds in general. Harnack in fact made a classic case for what we have termed "open confessionalism." While he deplored what he saw as the "catholicizing" of Lutheranism, he judged the opposite demand for a totally undogmatic Christianity to be a mistake. The church's task, he believed, was not to dispense with creeds but to add a new creed to the old. "Upon the path of the old Creeds we must remain," he wrote. "Satisfied with them we cannot be. The entanglements of history divide us from them."

The objection is sometimes made that such a program, despite the disavowals, abrogates the entire notion of a creed: a temporary dogma is no dogma at all, and adoption of a new confession is tacit denial of the old. But in the centuries that separate the Reformation from the present, another danger, more surely fatal to the life of a confessing church, has become increasingly clear: an old creed may be retained only as a sacred relic, a token of outward conformity, to be invoked on rare occasions for some shibboleth that it conveniently enshrines—and not as the living confession of a church. And there is a growing readiness among Christians of every communion, even among those who do not object either to creeds in principle or to the specific dogmas of the traditional creeds, to admit that every confession of faith is conditioned by the circumstances of its historical origin, and none is therefore likely to serve as the sufficient confession of another day. This admission has made it easier in practice for the churches to reappraise the historic creeds of other traditions, while accepting the responsibility to add to their own.

Modern creeds. Four twentieth-century documents represent the continued activity of Christian creed-making in the modern world. Two of them address specific political and social crises by reaffirming, sharpening, and applying elements already present in the confessional tradition: the lordship of Christ (the original Christian confession), and reconciliation through Christ, respectively. The Barmen Declaration (1934) was adopted by a synod of representatives from the Lutheran, Reformed, and United churches in Germany to address the crisis of National Socialism. Largely inspired by Karl Barth (1886–1968), it was the response of the Confessing church to the so-called German Christians. Its six terse affirmations and corresponding condemnations asserted the sole lordship of Jesus Christ, the one word of God, over every area of life against the encroachments of the Nazi state and its *Führer*. Broader in scope, but still a declaration rather than a comprehensive confession of faith, the Confession of 1967 was adopted by the United Presbyterian Church in the U.S.A. to reaffirm the message of reconciliation and bring it to bear on four urgent social issues: racial discrimination, international conflict, enslaving poverty, and alienation between the sexes.

The opening message (1962) of the Second Vatican Council also singled out two issues as especially urgent: peace between peoples and social justice. But the council's sixteen dogmatic constitutions, decrees, and declarations are not a response to a particular crisis or to critical issues; they are a broad and detailed attempt at an "updating" *(aggiornamento)* of the Roman church's entire stand in the twentieth century—her self-understanding and her relationships with other Christian groups, the non-Christian religions, and the whole human community. They call for all Christians and men of goodwill to join the Catholic church in "building up a more just and brotherly city in the world." In issuing this call, the council made up for an omission in the work of Trent and for what many Roman Catholics perceive as one-sidedness in the work of the First Vatican Council.

The Council of Trent did not undertake to define the nature of the church at all; differences among the fathers themselves made any such venture impolitic. The First Vatican Council, on the other hand, which Rome counts as the twentieth ecumenical council, did produce a Constitution on the Church of Christ (1870), but it was concerned exclusively with the primacy of the pope and with his infallibility when he defines a doctrine concerning faith or morals. Vatican II, especially in its Dogmatic Constitution on the Church (*Lumen gentium*, 1964), presents a much fuller doctrine of the church, in biblical rather than juridical language. The hierarchical structure of the church and the primacy of the pope are reaffirmed. But Vatican II places a stronger emphasis than Vatican I on the regular and collective, or "collegial," office of all the bishops in communion with the pope, and it takes "the church" to mean the whole body of the Lord, the people of God, laity as well as clergy. All the faithful in their several ways share in the priestly, prophetic, and kingly functions of Christ. By her relationship with Christ, the church is a kind of sacrament—that is, a sign and instrument—of union with God and the unity of all mankind. Not only the Catholic faithful but all who believe in Christ are in some way united with this people of God in the Holy Spirit, who is operative among them too with his sanctifying power.

Finally, the Lima Document on Baptism, Eucharist, and Ministry (1982), which approaches the creedal type of a union statement, may serve as a useful indication of the consensus and dissensus between the inherited confessional positions at the present time. Ecumenical dialogue has repeatedly shown the possibility of agreement on traditionally divisive issues, including the doctrines of justification and the sacraments. The Lima Document, produced for the Commission on Faith and Order of the World Council of Churches by representatives of all the major confessional traditions (including Roman Catholics, who have no official participation in the World Council itself), faces some of the most divisive issues of all. Its main text establishes a large measure of agreement, mainly by appeal to the common biblical heritage, and the additional commentaries indicate the differences that either have been overcome or are still in need of further discussion. Even on two of the most intractable differences—between infant and believer baptism, and between episcopal and nonepiscopal ministry—the way is pointed out toward mutual recognition as a step in the direction of greater unity of doctrine, order, and practice. It has thus become a dominant concern of modern Christian creed-making, not only to meet the political, social, and intellectual problems of the day but also to reverse the tendency of the sixteenth- and seventeenth-century creeds toward inflexibility and separation.

[*See also* Councils, *article on* Christian Councils, *and* Theology, *article on* Christian Theology. *Aspects of various Christian creeds are also discussed in articles on particular churches and in biographies of their leaders.*]

BIBLIOGRAPHY

Despite its age (it was first published in 1877), the best resource for the study of Christian creeds and confessions is still Philip Schaff's monumental *Bibliotheca Symbolica Ecclesiae Universalis: The Creeds of Christendom, with a History and Critical Notes*, 6th ed., 3 vols. (New York, 1931), which has been reissued (Grand Rapids, Mich., 1983). *The Faith of Christendom: A Source Book of Creeds and Confessions*, edited by myself (Cleveland, 1963), is a modest introduction to symbolics (the study of creeds) through analysis of the ecumenical creeds and six documents from the Reformation period. *Creeds of the Churches: A Reader in Christian Doctrine, from the Bible to the Present*, edited by John H. Leith, first published the same year (1963), includes many more documents with shorter historical introductions, and the third, revised edition (Atlanta, 1982) contains important additions from the intervening two decades. All three of these general works provide further bibliographical guidance.

The standard English work on the ecumenical symbols is J. N. D. Kelly's *Early Christian Creeds*, 3d ed. (New York, 1972). Kelly is also the editor and translator of Rufinus's *A Commentary on the Apostles' Creed*, "Ancient Christian Writers," vol. 20 (Westminster, Md., 1955), and he has published a separate study of the third of the ecumenical symbols (barely mentioned in *Early Christian Creeds*), *The Athanasian Creed* (New York, 1964).

The best English edition of the Lutheran confessions is *The Book of Concord: The Confessions of the Evangelical Lutheran Church*, translated and edited by Theodore G. Tappert and others (Philadelphia, 1959). A useful collection of Reformed creeds in English is *Reformed Confessions of the Sixteenth Century*, edited by Arthur C. Cochrane (Philadelphia, 1966). The seventeenth-century Westminster standards are included in *The Constitution of the Presbyterian Church (U.S.A.)*, part 1,

Book of Confessions (New York, 1983). For free-church creeds, see Williston Walker's *The Creeds and Platforms of Congregationalism* (1893; reprint, Boston, 1960); W. J. McGlothlin's *Baptist Confessions of Faith* (Philadelphia, 1911); and William L. Lumpkin's *Baptist Confessions of Faith* (Chicago, 1959). An able commentary on the *Book of Concord* is Edmund Schlink's *Theology of the Lutheran Confessions* (Philadelphia, 1961). Nothing comparable is available in English on Reformed creeds, but a useful symposium, occasioned by the proposal for the new Presbyterian Confession of 1967 and published as an issue of *McCormick Quarterly* (vol. 19, no. 2, January 1966), provides extensive guidance on the corpus, theological character, and function of the Reformed confessions.

For the reasons indicated, one cannot point to any collection of Eastern Orthodox symbols. A translation of the Confession of Dosítheos was given in *The Acts and Decrees of the Synod of Jerusalem*, translated and edited by J. N. W. B. Robertson (London, 1899), and is reproduced in both Leith's and my work. An English version of the Catechism of Filaret will be found in Schaff. The Roman Catholic church, by contrast, has a semiofficial collection of authorized symbols, including the doctrinal decrees of Trent, in Heinrich Denzinger's *Enchiridion symbolorum*, translated from the thirtieth edition by Roy J. Deferrari as *The Sources of Catholic Dogma* (Saint Louis, 1957). The most important guide to Trent is Hubert Jedin's history, *Geschichte des Konzils von Trient*, 4 vols. in 5 (Freiburg, 1959–1975). The translation by Ernest Graf, *A History of the Council of Trent* (Saint Louis, 1957–), is unfortunately still incomplete.

Harnack's position on the modern use of creeds is succinctly outlined in his somewhat neglected writing, *Thoughts on the Present Position of Protestantism* (London, 1899). Reappraisal of creeds across the confessional divide may be illustrated from the discussions of the Augsburg Confession as a catholic document in *The Role of the Augsburg Confession: Catholic and Lutheran Views*, edited by Joseph A. Burgess (Philadelphia, 1980), and *Augsburgisches Bekenntnis im ökumenischen Kontext*, edited by Harding Meyer (Stuttgart, 1980). The Barmen Declaration will be found in Cochrane, Leith, and the Presbyterian *Book of Confessions*. For the complete text of the Confession of 1967, see the *Book of Confessions* or *Reformed Witness Today: A Collection of Confessions and Statements of Faith Issued by Reformed Churches*, edited by Lukas Vischer (Bern, 1982). Denzinger-Deferrari includes the Marian dogmas of 1854 and 1950 and the dogmatic constitutions of Vatican I, but does not reach Vatican II, for which see *The Documents of Vatican II*, edited by Walter M. Abbott (New York, 1966). Leith reproduces the Lima Document in his third edition.

B. A. GERRISH

Islamic Creeds

An *ʿaqīdah* is an Islamic creed or creedal statement; the plural, *ʿaqāʾid* ("articles of belief"), is used in a similar sense. Since there is no Islamic body corresponding to the Christian ecumenical councils, Islamic creeds do not have the official status of the Christian creeds and thus are not used liturgically. What might be regarded as an exception to these assertions is the Shahādah, or confession of faith ("There is no deity except God; Muḥammad is the messenger of God"), which is universally accepted by Muslims and is repeated in the formal worship or prayers *(ṣalāt)*. The Shahādah is not generally regarded as an *ʿaqīdah*, however, though it might be considered the basis of all later creeds. The terms *ʿaqīdah* and *ʿaqāʾid* are applied to works of greatly varying length, ranging from those with fewer than a dozen lines to voluminous theological treatises.

The Development of the Islamic Creeds. Although they hold no ecumenical councils, the Sunnīs, who are the great majority of all Muslims, have come to a large measure of agreement about the articles of belief through informal consensus. Each legal/theological school, and notably the Ḥanafī and Ḥanbalī schools, has developed creeds which the school has accepted and often attributed to its founder, even when the composition might date from several centuries later. The various subdivisions of Shīʿī Islam have also produced their creedal statements, as have some of the minor sects.

The process by which the Sunnī creed was elaborated is similar to that in Christianity, namely through argument against the views of some believers which were felt to be heretical by the main body of believers. Among the views excluded by the Sunnīs were the Shīʿī belief that the prophet Muḥammad had designated ʿAlī to succeed him and that each of the following (Shīʿī) imams had been similarly designated by his predecessor, the Khārijī belief that a person who commits a grave sin is thereby excluded from the community, and the Muʿtazilī belief that human acts are independent of God's control.

The Main Doctrines of the Sunnī Islamic Creed. The following are the main articles of belief accepted by Sunnīs, though the wording does not follow any specific creed. The order is roughly that of the Ḥanafī creed (found in Wensinck, 1932); comments have been added.

1. God is one and unique in the sense that there is no deity other than God; he has neither partner nor associate, and neither begets nor is begotten. This is the first clause in the Shahādah and also appears in the Qurʾān, though not in the earliest portions. *Allāh* is the Arabic word for God, used also by Arabic-speaking Christians, but some of Muḥammad's contemporaries recognized Allāh as a "high god" alongside other deities. It is against such people, and polytheists in general, that this article emphasizes the uniqueness of God, which became one of the distinctive features of Islam.

2. He has been from all eternity and will be to all eternity with all his names and attributes. These attributes may be essential or active (attributes pertaining to activity): among the former are life, power (or omnipotence), knowledge (or omniscience), speech, hearing, sight, and will; and among the latter, creating, sustaining (with food), giving life, and raising (from the dead). All these attributes are eternal; they are not God and yet not other than God. The Qur'ān frequently applies names to God, such as the Merciful, the Forgiving, the Creator, the Knowing. Ninety-nine such "beautiful names" are commonly recognized and used in devotions. The theologians held that God possesses the qualities or attributes *(ṣifāt)* corresponding to these names, as the quality of mercy corresponds to "the Merciful." The seven essential attributes listed above were much discussed by theologians in the third and fourth centuries AH (ninth and tenth centuries CE). Some, especially the Muʿtazilah, held that the attributes are not distinct from God's essence, so that, for example, he might be said to know by his essence; others held that the attributes have a hypostatic character (not unlike the three hypostases of the Christian Trinity), so that it is by his knowledge rather than his essence that God knows. The latter view, which made allowance for the special position of the Qur'ān as God's attribute of speech, came to be the standard Sunnī position and was accepted by the Ashʿarīyah, the Māturīdīyah, and others. With regard to the active attributes, the Ashʿarīyah held that these are not eternal, since, for example, God cannot be creator until he has created. The Māturīdīyah, on the other hand, held that these names and attributes apply to God eternally. There was also some discussion, especially in later times, when there was greater familiarity with philosophical ideas, as to whether existence, eternity, and the like were to be regarded as attributes. [*See* Attributes of God, *article on* Islamic Concepts.]

3. *God created the world and all that is in it; he did not create things from any preexisting thing.* God's creation of the world *ex nihilo* is always implied in the creeds, although it is not always stated explicitly.

4. *God is unlike all created things: he is neither body nor substance nor accident (of a substance); he has no spatial limit or position.* Nevertheless, as the Qur'ān indicates, he has two hands, two eyes, and a face, and he is seated on the throne. The otherness and, in this sense, transcendence of God are clearly expressed in the Qur'ān ("No thing is like him" [42:11]), and this point received much emphasis in later times. It was a serious problem for the theologians to reconcile this otherness of God with the anthropomorphisms in the Qur'ān, which include not merely such terms as *hands* and *face,* but also most of the names and attributes. Some of those who insisted on the otherness and incorporeality of God, like the Muʿtazilah, held that the anthropomorphic terms were to be understood metaphorically, and they called those who understood them literally *mushabbihah* ("those who make [God] resemble [humanity]"). Most Sunnī theologians, following Aḥmad ibn Ḥanbal, said they were to be accepted *bi-lā kayf,* or "amodally" (literally "without [asking] how [they were to be understood]"), that is, neither literally nor metaphorically. Some later Ashʿarī theologians allowed metaphorical interpretation, within limits however.

5. *The Qur'ān, as it is written down, remembered, and recited, is the speech of God and uncreated. Our writing and reciting of it, however, are created.* This matter was the subject of violent discussions in the ninth century. In the so-called inquisition *(miḥnah)* begun by Caliph al-Ma'mūn around 833, prominent jurists and other officials were obliged to state publicly that they believed the Qur'ān to be the created speech of God. Among those who refused to make the profession was Aḥmad ibn Ḥanbal, and for a time he was the main defender of the uncreatedness of the Qur'ān. The point at issue seems to have been that, if the Qur'ān is created, God could have created it otherwise, and so it is not unthinkable that the caliph, if regarded as inspired by God, could alter its rules. On the other hand, if it is uncreated, it expresses something of God's being and cannot be humanly altered; this implies that the final decision about the application of Qur'anic rules to practical matters is in the hands, not of the caliph, but of the accredited interpreters of the Qur'ān, namely the *'ulamā',* or religious scholars. The Shīʿah, who believe their imams are inspired, still hold the Qur'ān to be created, but since the end of the inquisition around 850, the Sunnīs have adhered firmly to the doctrine of the uncreatedness of the Qur'ān.

6. *God's will is supreme, and he controls all mundane events. No good or evil comes about on earth except as God wills, but although he wills all events, good and evil, he does not command or approve what is evil. Actions are good or bad, not in themselves, but because God commands or forbids them; he could, if he so willed, change what is good and bad. Human acts are created by God and "acquired" by the individual.* Belief in the absolute sovereignty of God (for which there are precedents in the Bible and in pre-Islamic Arabia) enabled Muslims to face life with assurance, knowing that no disaster could happen to them unless God willed it. The Muʿtazilī assertion of human free will was seen to threaten God's sovereignty, and so many Sunnī theologians tried to find a way of reconciling God's omnipotence with human freedom. The Muʿtazilah and their opponents agreed that when a people acted, it was through a "power" or "ability" which God created in them, but while the Muʿtazilah held that this was a "power" to do either the act or its opposite and was created before the act, the others insisted that it was the "power" to do only the act in question and was created in the moment of acting. Many Sunnī theologians, especially the Ash'arīyah, further held that while God created the act, the human agents only "acquired" *(kasaba)* it, meaning that they somehow "made it theirs" or had it "credited" to them as their act. The Mu'tazilah had shown that if the act was not the individuals' act and was sinful, God could not justly punish them for it. Most Sunnīs held that whether people were believers or unbelievers depended on their own acts and not on God. At the same time they thought that God could, in his goodness, help people to belief, yet also in his justice lead them astray or abandon them, in the sense of withdrawing guidance from them, but ultimately such treatment followed on sins by the people in question.

7. *God will judge all human beings on the Last Day after they have been raised from the dead. Among the realities of the Last Day are the balance* (mīzān), *the bridge* (ṣirāṭ), and the pool or basin (ḥawḍ). *Before the Last Day sinners will be exposed to the punishment of the tomb.* God's judgment on the Last Day is prominent in the Qur'ān and is implied in all creeds even when not explicitly stated. A balance to weigh a person's good deeds against bad deeds is spoken of in the Qur'ān, but there are no clear references there to the pool from which Muḥammad quenches the thirst of the believers or to the knife-edge bridge over Hell from which evildoers fall down: these are popular eschatological conceptions which have found their way into some creeds, as is also the belief in a punishment in the tomb *('adhāb al-qabr).*

8. *Muḥammad and other prophets are permitted to intercede with God on the Last Day for sinful members of their communities.* Although the Mu'tazilah held that the Qur'anic references to intercession did not justify this belief, it came to be generally accepted.

9. *Paradise and Hell are already created, and will never cease to exist.* This was a denial of some sectarian views attributed to the Jahmīyah and others.

10. *God will be seen by the believers in Paradise.* This is asserted in the Qur'ān, but it is difficult to understand literally since God is incorporeal. It was eventually held to be true "amodally" *(bi-lā kayf).*

11. *God has sent messengers* (rusul) *and prophets* (anbiyā') *to human communities with his revelations. Prophets are preserved* (ma'ṣūm) *from sin by God; Muḥammad is the seal of the prophets.* Prophets are sometimes said to be very numerous, reaching as many as 120,000, although only a small number, sometimes 313, are messengers. According to the Māturīdīyah, prophets are preserved from all sins; according to the Ash'arīyah, only from grave sins. The phrase "seal of the prophets" is now always taken to mean "last of the prophets," but originally it may have meant the one who, like a seal, confirmed previous prophets.

12. *The most excellent of the community after Muḥammad is Abū Bakr, then 'Umar, then 'Uthmān, then 'Alī.* This apparently nontheological assertion is a denial of the Shī'ī view that 'Alī was most excellent after Muḥammad, and thus it is an essential element of Sunnism. It was agreed upon only after much discussion, especially regarding the place of 'Uthmān because of criticisms of his conduct.

13. *Faith* (īmān) *consists in assenting with the heart, confessing with the tongue, and performing works; it may increase or decrease.* This is the Ash'arī and Ḥanbalī understanding of faith, or what makes a person a believer. The Māturīdīyah and other Ḥanafīyah, on the other hand, exclude performing works from the definition and then insist that faith can neither increase nor decrease.

14. *A believer who commits a grave sin does not thereby cease to be a believer.* This is directed against the Khārijīs, who held that the grave sinner is excluded from the community of believers. Sunnīs generally came to hold that a grave sinner of the community might be punished in Hell for a time, but would eventually go to Paradise through the intercession of Muḥammad.

Shī'ī Beliefs. Whereas for Sunnī Muslims true doctrine is what is asserted in the Qur'ān and *ḥadīth* as interpreted by accredited *'ulamā',* for Shī'ī Muslims authority in matters of doctrine rests with the divinely inspired imam. There are three main subdivisions of the Shī'ah, namely the Imāmīyah (Twelvers), the Ismā'īlīyah (Seveners), and the Zaydīyah. All believe that 'Alī was the rightful imam, or leader of the Muslims in succession to Muḥammad, and was followed by his sons, Ḥasan and Ḥusayn, and that thereafter each imam designated his successor, usually a son. The Twelvers, with their center in Iran, hold that in 874 the twelfth imam went into occultation *(ghaybah),* but is still alive and will return as the Mahdi at an appropriate moment to set things right in the world. The Ismā'īlīyah accept the first six Twelver imams, but hold that the seventh was a son of the sixth named Ismā'īl, and that the series of imams continues until today. The present Aga Khan is the imam of the best-known subsection of the Ismā'īlīyah. The original Zaydī view was that the rightful imam was a descendant of Ḥasan or Ḥusayn who claimed the imamate and made good his claim by the sword. The Shī'ah in general reject the twelfth of the articles presented above and also hold that the Qur'ān is created, but they accept most of the rest of the creed, although the Zaydīyah, and to a lesser extent the Twelver Shī'ah, tend to the position of the Mu'tazilah. The strength of the Twelver *'ulamā'* in Iran today is in part due to the fact that they represent the Hidden Imam.

[*See also* Polemics, *articles on* Christian-Muslim Polemics *and* Muslim-Jewish Polemics, *and entries on the individual sects, theological groupings, and historical figures mentioned herein.*]

BIBLIOGRAPHY

The only book devoted to the topic is the pioneer work of A. J. Wensinck, *The Muslim Creed: Its Genesis and Historical Development* (1932; reprint, New York, 1965). This is built around translations of three Ḥanafī creeds and includes long scholarly commentaries on them. Much more is now known about later developments of the creeds, and it should be noted that Wensinck was not clearly aware of the differences between the Ḥanafīyah (including the Māturīdīyah) and the Ash'arīyah, as seen in article 13 above. Creeds by al-Ash'arī, al-Ghazālī, Abū Ḥafṣ al-Nasafī, and al-Faḍālī are translated by D. B. Macdonald in his *Development of Muslim Theology, Jurisprudence and Constitutional Theory* (1903; reprint, New York, 1965), but otherwise the book is somewhat out of date. Two versions of al-Ash'arī's creed are translated and edited by Richard J. McCarthy in *The Theory of al-Ash'arī* (Beirut, 1953).

For the development of dogma, there is a brief account in Wensinck's book; I have given a much fuller account of the early period in *The Formative Period of Islamic Thought* (Edinburgh, 1973), and I present a survey up to the present in my *Islamic Philosophy and Theology*, 2d rev. ed. (Edinburgh, 1984).

For the beliefs of the Twelver Shī'ah, the creed by Ibn Bābawayhi (d. 991) is contained in *A Shi'ite Creed*, translated by A. A. Fyzee (London, 1942); that of 'Allāmah al-Ḥillī (d. 1326) appears in *Al-Bābu'l-Ḥādī 'Ashar, a Treatise on the Principles of Shī'ite Theology*, translated by William Miller (London, 1928). A modern work is *A Shi'ite Anthology*, edited by William C. Chittick (Albany, N.Y., 1981). For the Ismā'īlīyah there is a summary of a long creed from about 1200 in *A Creed of the Fatimids* by Vladimir A. Ivanov (Bombay, 1936). The most important work on the Zaydīyah is Wilferd Madelung's *Der Imam al-Qāsim ibn Ibrāhīm und die Glaubenslehre der Zaiditen* (Berlin, 1965).

W. Montgomery Watt

CREMATION. *See* Funeral Rites.

CRESCAS, ḤASDAI (c. 1340–1410?), Spanish rabbi, philosopher, natural scientist; author of the anti-Aristotelian Hebrew classic, *Or Adonai* (The Light of the Lord). Son of a distinguished family of scholars and merchants, Crescas was raised in Barcelona, studying there under the renowned Talmudist and homilist Nissim ben Re'uven. He served as rabbi in Barcelona and from 1387 was an adviser to the king and queen of Aragon, Joan I and Violant. In 1389, Crescas assumed the post of rabbi of Saragossa, and the next year he was recognized by the throne as judge of all the Jews of Aragon. Following the anti-Jewish mob riots of 1391, in which thousands of Spanish Jews—including his only son—were murdered and more than a hundred thousand were converted to Christianity, he devoted himself to the physical and spiritual reconstruction of the Jewish communities of Aragon and of Spain as a whole. His *Epistle to the Jewish Community of Avignon* (translated from the Hebrew in Kobler, 1952), dated 20 Heshvan 5152 (19 October 1391), is a terse chronicle of the massacres that may have been written as background for entreaties to the papal court. The *Epistle* bears somber biblical allusions: the great Jewish communities of Spain are desolated Jerusalems (allusions are made to *Lamentations* 2:2, 2:4, 2:7, 5:4); Crescas's son is an Isaac sacrificed upon the altar (allusions are made to *Genesis* 22:2, 22:7–8). His *Refutation of the Dogmas of the Christians* (1397–1398), written in Catalan but surviving only in the Hebrew translation of Yosef ibn Shem Ṭov *(Biṭṭul 'iqqarei ha-Notsrim,* 1451; Frankfurt, 1860; Kearny, N.J., 1904), was intended to combat christianizing literature aimed at Jews and *conversos.* It is a nonrhetorical logical critique of ten basic elements of Christianity: original sin, salvation, the Trinity, the incarnation, the virgin birth, transubstantiation, baptism, the messiahship of Jesus, the New Testament, and demons. Even his profound philosophical treatise, *The Light of the Lord* (1410; Ferrara, 1555; Vienna, 1859–1860; Johannesburg, 1861; and modern photoeditions), written in Hebrew, was to some extent a response to the troubles of his times. Its assault on Aristotelianism was in part motivated by the belief that Aristotelian philosophy was weakening the commitment of Jewish intellectuals to Judaism and thus facilitating their apostasy.

The Light of the Lord, a counterblast to Maimonides' *Guide of the Perplexed,* was planned as the philosophical first part of a two-part work. The unwritten second part was to have been an analytic codification of rabbinic law and was intended to supersede Maimonides' rabbinic masterwork, the *Mishneh Torah* (Code of Law). The *Light* is divided into four books. Book 1 discusses three roots *(shorashim)* of the Torah: God's existence, his unity, and his incorporeality. (In grouping these three principles together, Crescas followed Maimonides; cf., e.g., *Guide of the Perplexed,* intro. to part 2.) Book 2 discusses six fundaments *(pinnot)* of the Torah: God's knowledge, providence, and power; prophecy; human choice; and the purposefulness of the Torah. The fundaments are concepts that follow necessarily (i.e., analytically) from Crescas's definition of the Torah as "the product of a voluntary action from the Commander, Who is the initiator of the action, to the commanded, who is the receiver of the action" (*Light* 2, intro.). Book 3 discusses eleven nonfundamental obligatory beliefs of the Torah: God's creation of the world, the immortality of the soul, reward and punishment, resurrection of the dead, the eternality of the Torah, the uniqueness of Moses' prophecy, the efficacy of the Urim and Tummim, the coming of the messiah, the efficacy of prayer, the spiritual value of repentance, and the special providential nature of the High Holy Days and the festivals. Book 4 examines thirteen nonobligatory beliefs held by sundry groups of Jews; for example, the Jewish Aristotelian proposition that God is the Intellect and the qabbalistic doctrine of metempsychosis *(gilgul)*.

The *Light* is best known for its revolutionary logico-conceptual critique of Aristotelian physics (e.g., theories of space, time, motion, the vacuum, infinity), important parts of which were translated into Latin in Gianfrancesco Pico della Mirandola's *Examen vanitatis doctrinae gentium* (1520). In place of Aristotle's closed world, Crescas suggested that both space and time are infinite extensions *in actu* in which many worlds—an infinite number?—are continuously being created by the infinitely good, infinitely loving God. Crescas rejected Maimonides' Aristotelian proofs of God, but did offer a short metaphysical proof of his own: whether causes and effects are finite or infinite, there must be a cause of the whole of them; for if all are effects, they would have merely possible (i.e., contingent) existence, and thus they must have something that determines their existence over their nonexistence, and this is the first cause or God (*Light* 1.3.2, quoted in Spinoza, *Epistle* 12). Such rationalistic reflection, Crescas held, can incline one toward belief in the true God of religion, but only revelation can establish that belief firmly. In a celebrated discussion of human choice (*Light* 2.5), Crescas upheld the determinist view that the notion of human choice coheres with both divine omniscience and strict physical causality. In his theologically significant discussion of teleology (*Light* 2.6), he argued that love is the purpose of man, the Torah, the created universe, and God. Against the Aristotelians, he maintained that love is not intellectual, that the immortal essence of the human soul is not intellect, and that God is to be understood not as passionless Intellect but as joyfully loving.

Crescas's own highly original philosophy emerges out of his radical critique of Aristotle and of Aristotelians such as Maimonides, Ibn Rushd (Averroës), and Levi ben Gershom (Gersonides) and is argued in their vocabulary. In some areas, it is significantly influenced by Ibn Sīnā. Its spirit, however, recalls Abū Ḥamid al-Ghasālī, Yehudah ha-Levi, and Nissim ben Re'uven. It is also colored by Qabbalah. Its precise relationship to Latin and Catalan writers is a subject for speculation.

Among Crescas's students was the well-known philosophical popularizer Yosef Albo, who in his Hebrew *Sefer ha-'iqqarim* (Book of Roots; 1425) adapted and simplified some of his master's teachings. Crescas's *Light of the Lord* had an appreciable influence on later Jewish philosophers, notably Judah Abravanel (c. 1460–1521) and Barukh Spinoza (1632–1677).

[*For further discussion of Crescas's thought, see* Jewish Thought and Philosophy, *article on* Premodern Philosophy.]

BIBLIOGRAPHY

For Crescas's life, see Yitzhak Baer's *A History of the Jews in Christian Spain*, 2 vols. (Philadelphia, 1961–1966). Crescas's critique of Aristotelian physics is the subject of Harry A. Wolfson's monumental *Crescas' Critique of Aristotle* (Cambridge, Mass., 1929); the volume includes Hebrew texts from the *Light* with facing English translation. Shlomo Pines explored the connection between Crescas's science and that of Nicole d'Oresme and other Latin authors in "Scholasticism after Thomas Aquinas and the Teachings of Hasdai Crescas and His Predecessors," *Proceedings of the Israel Academy of Sciences and Humanities* 1 (1967), n.p. On Crescas's critique of Christianity, see Daniel J. Lasker's *Jewish Philosophical Polemics against Christianity in the Middle Ages* (New York, 1977). On his influence on Spinoza, see Wolfson's *The Philosophy of Spinoza*, 2 vols. (Cambridge, Mass., 1934). Crescas's *Epistle to the Jewish Community of Avignon* is found in English translation in Franz Kobler's *Letters of Jews through the Ages* (London, 1952), pp. 272–275.

WARREN ZEV HARVEY

CREUZER, G. F. (1771–1858), German Romantic mythologist. Educated at Marburg and then Jena, Georg Friedrich Creuzer was appointed professor of philology at Marburg in 1802, and in 1804 professor of philology and ancient history at Heidelberg, where he taught for almost forty-five years. Creuzer's major work was *Symbolik und Mythologie der alten Völker, besonders der Griechen* (1810–1812).

Creuzer argued that ancient Greek religion derived from a spiritually pure and noble monotheism carried from India by wandering priests. But this high monotheism needed to be adapted to the crude, native polytheism. There thus arose an exoteric and popular teaching for the vulgar many, one that spoke of many gods, and an esoteric teaching for the initiated and refined worshiper. Creuzer claimed that this esoteric tradition informed Eleusinian and Samothracian mysteries,

Orphism and Pythagoreanism, and Neoplatonism. His book quickly became famous and was both admired and criticized. There was much speculation on the part of German Romantics—often extravagant or fantastic—about India as the homeland of all true religion and wisdom. Creuzer seemed to give solid historical support to this enthusiasm for the East and its synthesis with Greece. But because Creuzer's work claimed to be accurate history, it also became the chief target of scholarly attacks on the excesses and defects of the Romantic mythologists. This quarrel between "romanticists" and "rationalists" is a major episode in early nineteenth-century history of religion. Creuzer's data and methods were rebutted, from various positions, by such famous scholars as Gottfried Hermann (1819), Karl Otfried Müller (1825), Christian Lobeck (1829), and Ludwig Preller (1854). One result of this controversy was that "rationalistic" and philological study of myth often disdained "romantic" enthusiasm and speculation about myth as a living religious force.

Creuzer's views on myth also met opposition in the Romantic camp. He firmly distinguished between myth and symbol. Divine meaning shone forth first of all in the symbol. The first interpretations here (as by Indic sages) took the form of images or pictographs, so as to preserve the symbol's union of spirit and matter. Only later, and on a lower level, came the narrated stories found in myth. Creuzer suggests these are concessions to popular taste. For Creuzer, the symbol embodies monotheism; myths are the vehicles of polytheism. One general criticism is summed up in the judgment of the German idealist philosopher and mythologist Friedrich Schelling, who suggests Creuzer simply reduced myth to allegory, and did so because he reproduced in Romantic terms the old Christian charge that polytheistic myth only plagiarized (and confused) the original monotheistic revelation.

BIBLIOGRAPHY

No English translation of Creuzer's *Symbolik* exists. There is a French translation by Joseph D. Guigniaut under the title *Religions de l'antiquité considérées principalement dans leurs formes symboliques et mythologiques*, 4 vols. (Paris, 1825–1841). For the controversy over Creuzer's *Symbolik*, see Ernst Howald's *Der Kampf um Creuzers Symbolik* (Tübingen, 1926), which contains excellent selections and commentary. Henri Pinard de la Boullaye's *L'étude comparée des religions*, 4th ed., vol. 1 (Paris, 1929), pp. 261–268, discusses Creuzer as a religious historian. In *The Rise of Modern Mythology, 1680–1860* (Bloomington, Ind., 1972), Robert Richardson and I discuss Creuzer as mythologist, with translated selections.

BURTON FELDMAN

CROSS.

The cross is a sign formed by the meeting of two lines intersecting at a center from which four directions depart. The cruciform sign is used in artistic and scientific expression—in mathematics, architecture, geography, and cosmology. It also occupies an important position in culture in a more general sense and, especially, in religion. Sources from remotest antiquity in Egypt, Crete, Mesopotamia, India, and China show that this sign is an important symbol in the life of *homo religiosus*. It should first be studied within the specific context of diverse civilizations before being submitted to an interpretation reflecting several paths of knowledge. The first such path would begin with spatial and temporal conceptions of the cosmos: four cardinal points, four directions departing from a center, the compass rose, the *axis mundi*, time versus eternity. A second hermeneutic path is to be derived from numerical symbolism, which is connected, moreover, to the preceding path since the number four constitutes the figure of the cross. [*See* Quaternity.] A third approach is based upon the cruciform shapes that strike the eye in the course of human activities: the appearance of the human body with its arms outstretched; activities of tilling and navigation; the view of a tree planted in the earth or used as a pillar in the construction of a building. Finally, a fourth approach to the hermeneutics of cross symbolism is based on a specific theophany, linked to a historic event and a doctrine of salvation: the crucifixion of Jesus of Nazareth and the Christian doctrine of redemption.

Non-Christian Crosses. On statues of Assyrian kings preserved in the British Museum, the cross can be seen hanging from a necklace, whether as jewelry or as a religious sign. In Mesopotamia the cross with four equal arms is the sign for heaven and the god Anu. A cross of four equal branches found in a chapel at Knossos has been considered a symbol of the sovereign divinity of heaven. The cross appears as a decoration on the walls of many Cretan sanctuaries. Thus the cross is present in the ancient cultures of Asia, Europe, North Africa, and America. In sub-Saharan African art, cruciform motifs are numerous in diverse cultures. Such universality asks for an explanation. What does the cross mean in the life of *homo religiosus?*

History. The sign of life in ancient Egypt was the ankh, in Coptic *onech*. It is formed by a loop elongated downward, to which a tau is attached (see figure 1). Adopted by the Coptic Christians, this sign became the *crux ansata* or ansate cross of the Christian communities in Egypt. The ankh appears in relief on temple walls, on tombs, and in inscriptions. It is customarily placed in a god's or goddess's hand. In representations

FIGURE 1. *Six Types of Cross*

expressing life, the divinity holds it under the pharaoh's nose as if wishing to make him inhale its vital forces. On reliefs from the Tell al-'Amarna era, the rays of the sun—the god Aton—are directed at the king and queen and terminate in hands distributing the ankh. This sign is also found on ceramics, metals, and amulets, apparently as a protective sign against adverse forces.

Much discussion has been devoted to the meaning of the ankh as a hieroglyph used to designate life. Egyptologists agree in regarding it as the symbol of life as opposed to death—earthly life and life after death. The ankh is also a particular property of the gods to whom life preeminently belongs as a divine attribute. The divinity communicates life to the pharaoh, hence the representation of the pharaoh holding the ankh in his hand or receiving lustral water, symbolized by life signs and poured on his head from a pitcher held by divine hands. The inscriptions often reproduce the god's salutation to the king: "I give you all of life." The sign of life held under the pharaoh's nose shows the link between life and breath perceived by the Egyptians. As Alexandre Moret notes in *Le Nil,* one of King Djeser's cylinders from the third dynasty shows the falcon, Horus, and the ankh with an inscription saying, "Let him give all life, strength, and stability [to the king]." From the time of the Old Kingdom on, the ankh was reproduced on amulets. Under the New Kingdom the sign began to appear on libation vessels, and especially in illustrations of funeral scenes. Artists multiplied it in vignettes in the *Book of Going Forth by Day,* where it is placed on the knees of Re (Hunefer Papyrus and Ani Papyrus), set on the sarcophagus, equipped with arms that hold up the solar disk, and finally placed at the fingertips of Anubis as he leads the deceased toward the weighing of the soul and in the hand of Horus as he conducts the deceased toward Osiris.

Although the meaning of the ankh as a symbol of life is clear, the question of its origin has given rise to numerous hypotheses. The first interpreter, Athanase Kircher (seventeenth century), considered it a mystical *tau.* In the eighteenth century it was thought of as a key for regulating the floods of the Nile. This interpretation was picked up again by Josef Strzygowski in 1904 *(Koptische Kunst).* Egyptologists like Flinders Petrie and A. Wiedemann see it as originating with an article of clothing: a belt circling the waist and knotted in front of the body, which leaves the two ends dangling. This interpretation, shared by other Egyptologists, relates the ankh to the knot of Isis, an amulet somewhat similar in its figuration. Another interpretation alludes to the sandal strap (B. Gunn, Adolf Erman, H. Schäfer). None of these hypotheses has yet been accepted as definitive. Maria Cramer (1955) inclines toward the association with the belt and the knot. One thing is certain, the ankh is the sign of life considered as a force and a power present everywhere, but originating in the divine. Christianity adopted this ansate cross because of these significations.

The gammadion is a Greek cross with its ends bent at right angles: four gammas attach to a common base, all pointing either clockwise, to the right, or counterclockwise, to the left. In India, it is an ancient solar symbol and is the emblem of the god Viṣṇu, representing the cosmic wheel spinning on an axis. When the branches point to the right, the cross is called a swastika (see figure 1) or, in Sanskrit, a *svastika.* The *svastika* is emblematic of the masculine principle. When the branches point counterclockwise, toward the left, the sign is called a *sauvastika* and represents the feminine principle. In astronomy this form designates the sun during fall and winter; it is the less common form of the swastika. When the branches of either of these forms are rounded instead of forming right angles, the figure is called by the general term *tetraskelion.*

The swastika is found as early as the pre-Vedic civilization of the Indus Valley. At Mohenjo-Daro it is found on seals and pottery (Marshall, 1973). From the Vedic era in India to the present time, the swastika has been a sacred sign, engraved on the walls of temples and painted on houses. In the *Rāmāyaṇa* it marks the ships departing for Lanka. It is found on coins and monuments. Today Hindus still trace it on their account books and their doorsteps. Thus the antiquity and permanence of this sign in India deserves our attention.

In the Buddhist tradition, this sign marks the Buddha's feet—indeed, his footprints, as can be seen on the bas-reliefs of Amarāvatī. It often frames Buddhist inscriptions by being placed at the beginning and end of the text. Even today, Tibetan Buddhists use it as a clothing decoration or a funeral ornament. With Buddhism, the swastika passed into the iconography of China and Japan through statues of the Buddha and *bodhisattvas*. China adopted the sign as an ideogram designating plurality, abundance, prosperity, and long life. It also designates the number ten thousand, that is, the totality of living beings and their manifestation.

The swastika also appears in the Elamite area, dating from the same epoch as the civilization of Mohenjo-Daro. Jan de Vries believed that from Elam the sign spread into Mesopotamia and the Hittite world. An evaluation, however, of its influence and impact on the civilization of the Indus has yet to be determined (Casal, 1969). The swastika did in fact experience great diffusion throughout the areas of Aryan migration. Heinrich Schliemann found numerous examples among the debris of cities on the Hisserlik plateau near the site of ancient Troy. In the Caucasus this sign is found on arms and jewels dating back to the Bronze Age. Documented in the Hittite world, it also appears on ancient vases from Cyprus, Rhodes, and Athens. Here we are dealing with the diffusion group of Troy (I, II, IV) and the Danube region, followed by the post-Mycenaean phase, which exercised its influence on the Mediterranean world. The swastika spread into Macedonia, central Europe, and Italy, where it has been found on urns (Capanna di Corneto, Bolsena, Vetulonia, Capua), in the mosaics of Pompeii, on Italo-Greek vases, and on coins. Thus its existence has been traced back to the Etruscans. We find it on jewels, arms, and inscriptions among the Celts, in Gaul, and among the Germanic peoples. In Scandinavia the swastika was already known during the Bronze Age, as shown both by cave inscriptions like those of Bohuslän in Sweden and by diverse objects. Its actual expansion into the Germanic Scandinavian world dates from the Iron Age. The sign is related to the god Thor's hammer. It finally enters the arsenal of magic rites devoted to driving out demoniacal powers. At the time of the conversion to Christianity, the Germanic swastika was replaced by the Christian cross. Hitler reappropriated it as an Aryan cultic sign and a symbol of anti-Semitism: from 1933 to 1945 he made it the symbol of Nazism.

Numerous discussions concerning the swastika's significance have yet to be resolved conclusively. Specialists in Aryan thought have maintained that it represented the sacred fire in the form of a living flame (Eugène Burnouf), the union of the four castes in India (Fred Pincott), or the path of the sun (Max Müller, Eugène Goblet d'Alviella). The latter interpretation seems confirmed by the presence of the swastika in Mesoamerica, where it is clearly a solar and cosmic symbol. The discovery of the swastika in the civilization of Mohenjo-Daro is perhaps a clue permitting us to specify its area of origin in the Indo-European world. Furthermore, its connections with the god Viṣṇu can direct our interpretation. Viṣṇu symbolizes everlasting life and has the power to hold together the cosmos. This god has measured the world in three steps—earth, air, and sky—that represent the positions of the sun in the morning, at noon, and at night. Shown with four arms and four hands, Viṣṇu expresses the immanence of the divine in the cosmos. The number four symbolizes divine dominion over the directions in space as well as the four social classes, the four stages of Aryan life, and the four Vedas. In each of his hands Viṣṇu holds a cosmic symbol: the conch, a symbol of the five elements; the disk, a symbol of the sun; the arc and the lotus, symbolizing the changeable universe; and the club, a symbol of primordial knowledge (*Gopāla-uttara-tapanīya Upaniṣad* 55–57). If it is confirmed that the cult of Viṣṇu took over the fertility cults of the pre-Vedic era, the swastika could have been adopted as a symbol of universal life that the god Viṣṇu is in charge of maintaining. In the swastika we would have a meaning analogous to that of the ankh in Egypt: fullness of life. As an emblem of the Buddha, the swastika stands for the wheel of the law. In Roman art, artists have more than once represented Christ against a swastika determining his posture as well as his gestures and the folds of his garments—a remarkable symbolism of "creative turbulence around which are layered the creative hierarchies emanating from it" (Champeaux and Sterckx, 1966, p. 25).

The ancient civilizations of Peru have left us valuable information on the role of the cross in solar cults. A recent discovery has just been added to the Peruvian solar crosses already known for several centuries: a cross of huge dimensions cut into the rocky surface of the bank of the river Pantiacollo. Decorative motifs used as models in basket making show solar crosses similar to the swastika. Flornoy's discovery on the banks of the Urcubamba, the "river of happiness," reveals a representation of the man of light; a human silhouette, its arms outstretched, crowned by a sun shooting out its rays; at the intersection of two lines forming the cross is the heart. The symbolism becomes even more expressive when it involves a divinity shown under a cruciform symbol, as in the solar portico of Tiahuanaco. Located at the center of a crown formed by ears of maize, which is the solar plant, the divinity holds a scepter in each hand, extending his arms to form a cross while seeming to have the whole solar crown as a scepter. A ritual ceramic vase from Nazca is decorated with a figure having before its eyes a cross occupying a place analogous to the star found on similar vases. At Chancay, a mummy's winding-sheet has an elaborate cruciform decoration accompanied by nature and animal motifs; in this context the allusion to life is obvious. Similar iconography is found in the Inca traditions of Peru several centuries prior to the Spanish conquest; here the cross is used in the ancestor cult and in purification ceremonies, and it is commonly engraved at the heart of a stylized flower (Wedemeyer, 1970, pp. 366–375).

On a mountain in northern Peru, at an altitude of 3,200 meters, early in the twentieth century, Julio Tello discovered the temple complex of Chavín de Huantar, dating from two centuries before the common era. Under the ruins of the visible complex exist diverse galleries, the most important of which is cruciform, centered on the four cardinal points. An idol stands at the center of the four arms of the cross, which also forms "the sanctuary of the spear." The divinity is shown in the form of an obelisk. Other vestiges of a cruciform arrangement centered on an obelisk have been found among the ruins. The shrine was very likely conceived as being the center of the world, where the idol rejoins heaven. A ritual ceramic allows us to define the significance of the cross in the civilization of Chavín. The sacrificial vase has the shape of a puma, the animal symbolizing the sun god. In the decoration covering his body there are many crosses worked into the decorative motif (Wedemeyer, 1970, pp. 375–378).

At the time of the conquest of Mexico, the Spaniards discovered many figurations of the cross in temples and manuscripts, which greatly facilitated the acceptance of the Christian cross by the native Mexicans. In the civilization of Teotihuacán, the god Quetzalcoatl, or "plumed serpent," is found everywhere. Identified with the morning and evening star, he is the god of vegetation and plenty, a god of many shapes that the Aztec also identified with the wind. The god Quetzalcoatl inaugurates the age of the Fifth Sun, which is the present age. In temple decorations in Teotihuacán, a frequent motif is the quincunx, made up of five points with the fifth point marking the center. This figure provided the cross called the cross of Quetzalcoatl, of which we have many examples: on Quetzalcoatl's clothes at Teotihuacán and elsewhere; on the Aztec braziers and incense burners; at La Venta, instead of the solar eagle's eye; in the fire ceremony described by the Codex Borbonicus; and on the headgear of the god of fire at Veracruz (Séjourné, 1982, pp. 90–96).

For the ancient Mexicans, the world was built on a cross—the crossroads joining east to west and south to north. Thus the cross becomes a symbol of world unity. At Palenque there are many representations of the cross. One of these is a tree crowned by a bird. Another is the Latin cross with two worshipers in front of it; the god Quetzalcoatl sits enthroned on top of the cross. Furthermore, the bas-reliefs of the Maya civilization have given us many models of the cross. In manuscripts, the center and the four cardinal points are sometimes marked by stylized trees with a bird. The Codex Magliabecchi shows Quetzalcoatl with the characteristics of the wind god carrying a shield decorated with a large cross.

Symbolism of non-Christian crosses. The extraordinary dissemination of the cross throughout many different parts of the world prior to Christianity and outside its influence is explained by the multivalence and density of its symbolic signification. It is a primordial symbol related to three other basic symbols: the center, the circle, and the square (Champeaux and Sterckx, 1966). By the intersection of its two straight lines, which coincides with the center, it opens this center up to the outside, it divides the circle into four parts, it engenders the square. In the symbolism of the cross, we will limit ourselves to four essential elements: the tree, the number four, weaving, and navigation.

In the eyes of primordial man, the tree represents a power. [*See* Trees.] It evokes verticality. It achieves communication between the three levels of the cosmos: subterranean space, earth, and sky. It provides one with an access to the invisible, as exemplified by the shaman's stake, Jacob's ladder, the central column of a house or temple, the pole of a Voodoo sanctuary, and the tree symbolizing Mount Meru in India. In many cultures a particular species or a single tree is designated: the oak of the Celts and the Gauls; the oak of Zeus at Dodona, of the Capitoline Jupiter, of Abraham at Sichem and at Hebron; the ash of the Greeks in Hesiod; the date palm of the Mesopotamians; the fig tree in India; the Siberian birch; the Chinese *chien-mu* tree; and the cedar of Lebanon.

Mircea Eliade (1949, pp. 230–231) has classified the principal meanings of the tree into seven groups: (1) the rock-tree-altar microcosm present in the most archaic stages of religious life (Australia, China, India, Phoenicia, the Aegean); (2) the tree as image of the cosmos (Mesopotamia, India, Scandinavia); (3) the tree as cosmic theophany (Mesopotamia, India, the Aegean); (4) the tree as symbol of life in relation to the mother goddess and water (India, the Near East); (5) the tree as center of the world (Altaic peoples, Scandinavians, American Indians); (6) the mystical tree in human life, like the sacrificial stake in India and Jacob's ladder; and (7) the tree as symbol of the renewal of life. Such a wealth of meanings shows a symbolic system encompassing the essential functions of *homo religiosus:* life, ascension toward the invisible, meditation, enlightenment, fertility. The symbolism of the cross draws widely on this multivalence.

In its association with water and the altar, the tree is linked to center symbolism, as in the Australian totemic centers, in India, at Mohenjo-Daro, in Greece, in the Minoan world, and among the Canaanites and the Hebrews. Tree, water, and altar make up a microcosm, a sacred space around the tree representing the *axis mundi.* These are perhaps humanity's most ancient holy places, maintained in great religions like Hinduism, in the cults of the ancient Near East (*Jer.* 17:1–3), and in the religious customs of Buddhism (the Buddhist *caitya*). Associated with water as a sign of life, and with rock, which represents duration, the tree manifests the sacred strength of the cosmos and of life.

Aryan thought in particular has emphasized the symbol of the cosmic tree. India readily represents the cosmos as a giant tree. The *Kaṭha Upaniṣad* (6.1) shows it as an eternal fig tree with its roots in the air and its branches turned downward to the earth. The same figure of the tree is found in the *Maitri Upaniṣad* (6.4): *brahman* is a fig tree with its three roots pointed to the sky and its branches extending toward earth. The *Bhagavadgītā* (15.1–3) compares the cosmos to a giant tree, an imperishable *aśvattha,* roots skyward and branches turned toward the earth, its leaves being the hymns of the Veda. For the ancient Scandinavians, Yggdrasill, an *askr* (ash, yew, or oak), is the world's axis or support. Its three roots plunge into the realms of gods, giants, and men respectively. It is the beam of Mimir, Odin's adviser. It is also Larad, the tree protecting the family, a sign of fertility. Inhabited by the weaving Norns, it is the tree of destiny. The three springs at its roots make it the tree of all life, knowledge, and destiny. It binds the universe in a coherent whole.

Orientation is a basic need in the life of *homo religiosus.* This need explains the importance of center symbolism. [*See* Center of the World.] The cosmic tree is a symbol of absolute reality: the tree of earthly paradise, the shaman's tree, the tree against which the Aryan temple is built, the tree of gnosis (knowledge). It is where the divinity lives. The tree Kiskanu of Babylonian cosmology extends toward the ocean, sustaining the world. It is the dwelling place of the fertility goddess Ea. In Vedic India the *yūpa*—the sacrificial stake fashioned by the priest after the ritual cutting down of the tree—becomes the road permitting access from the earth to the sky, linking the three cosmic regions. Thanks to this stake, the sacrificer climbs to heaven and conquers immortality. Likewise, the shaman climbs up a post cut with seven or nine notches; he announces that he is climbing heavenward, to the seven or nine heavens. It is by way of the tree, the *axis mundi,* that heaven descends toward man. It is at the foot of a fig tree that the Buddha received enlightenment. Sun and moon descend in the shape of birds, by means of the Siberian larch. In China the *chien-mu* tree is placed in the center of the world with nine branches and nine roots that touch the nine springs and the nine heavens; by means of it the sovereigns, mediators between heaven and earth, ascend and descend. In Egypt the *djed* column, representing a tree stripped of branches, plays an essential role in the cult of Osiris and in religious life.

The number four is the number symbolizing the totality of space and time. It is linked to the symbolism of the center that marks the meeting of four directions and the transcendence of them. Four is also linked to the symbol of the cosmic tree. The tree and the notion of quaternity are the essential elements in a symbolism of completeness that plays a primordial role in the life of *homo religiosus.* [*See* Numbers.]

For example, like other native peoples of pre-Columbian America, the ancient Mexicans attached a great importance to spatial directions. The Codex Fejévary-Mayer, which probably originated in the region of Teotitlán, gives us an artistic elaboration of Aztec and Maya cosmological thought. At the beginning, the illuminator represents the four cardinal regions of the earth by trees shaped like crosses and crowned by birds. The tree of the eastern red region emerges from an image of the sun and is crowned by a quetzal bird. The western tree, whose color is blue, is spiny and emerges from a dragon; it is crowned by a hummingbird. The green southern tree arises from the jaws of the earth and is crowned by a parrot. The yellow northern tree, emerges from a bowl; the eagle sits enthroned on top of it. This document symbolizes the cardinal directions and the visible universe. The tree and the number four are united in the same symbolic system (Alexander, 1953).

The number four has various cosmological aspects: four cardinal points, four winds, four lunar phases, four seasons, and the four rivers at the beginning of the world. According to Hartley B. Alexander (1953), the number four is basic to the mind of North American Indians. There are four parts of the terrestrial world and four divisions of time (day, night, moon, year). There are four parts of a plant: root, stem, flower, fruit. To the four celestial beings—sky, sun, moon, stars—correspond four kinds of animals: those that crawl, those that fly, quadrupeds, and bipeds. Among the Dakota, the four masculine virtues of courage, endurance, generosity, and honor correspond to the four feminine virtues of ability, hospitality, fidelity, and fertility. The Indian mystery Wakantanka is fourfold: God the chief, God the spirit, God the creator, God the doer. Alexander observes that the religious philosophy of the Dakota and of all the peoples of the Plains is reminiscent of the Pythagorean tetrad, a numerical symbol of the world order.

Jacques Soustelle has shown that for the ancient Mexicans the cardinal points merged with space and the four directions. There are four quarters of the universe, linked to four time periods (*L'univers des Azteques,* Paris, 1979, pp. 136–140). The fifth direction in space is the center, where the other directions cross and where up meets down. The Codex Borgia designates the center by a multi-colored tree crowned by a quetzal. The Mexicans distinguish four winds. Four colors characterize the directions of space. The center is the synthesis and meeting place of the four colors, as among the Pueblo. The four primary gods are each designated by one of these colors. (These concepts relating to the cardinal points and colors are identical in China.) The world is built on a cross, on crossroads that lead from east to west and from north to south. [*See also* Crossroads.] In manuscripts, the center and the four cardinal points are shown by stylized trees. Space and time are linked; to be precise, each time connects with a predetermined space. In this cosmological outlook, natural phenomena and human deeds are all immersed in space-time. For the Dogon of Mali, four is the symbol of creation. The Luba of the Kasai River region imagine the world divided into four planes on the branches of a vertical cross oriented from west to east.

The Vedas are divided into four parts. The *Chāndogya Upaniṣad* (4.5) distributes the Brahmanic teachings into quarters, making them correspond to the four realms of the universe: spaces, worlds, lights, senses. In India there are four classes: the three Aryan classes *(brāhmaṇa, kṣatriya, vaiśya)* and the *śūdra* class. The three Aryan classes are invited to pass through four *āśrama*s, stages of life: *brahmacarya* (student), *gṛhastha* (householder), *vānaprastha* (forest dweller), *saṃnyāsa* (ascetic renunciant).

This idea of wholeness and universality symbolized by the number four is also found in the biblical texts. Out of the Garden of Eden ran a river that divided into four branches (*Gn.* 2:10–15). The twelve tribes of Israel form four camps around the meeting tent. In Ezekiel's vision, there are four animals in the center, each having four faces and four wings (*Ez.* 1:5–6). *Revelation* appropriates this number as characterizing the universe in its totality: four angels, four corners of the earth, and four winds (*Rv.* 7:1). It also speaks of four living beings (*Rv.* 4:6–8).

The Cross and Human Activity. The symbolism of the cross is also found in one of the oldest activities of *homo faber:* weaving. [*See* Webs and Nets.] From the very beginning, the technique of weaving requires the crossing of two threads at a center. The warp represents the basic element; between its taut threads passes the woof. The meeting place of each thread of the warp with each thread of the woof forms a cross: a vertical line, a horizontal line, and a meeting in the center. Thrown into space and time, primeval man instinctively felt the need to transform chaos into cosmos. Hence the importance of the tree, of the symbolism of the center, the symbolism of the four directions, myth, and ritual. Primeval man also needed to clothe himself. Through weaving he responded to this need, which was as pressing as the need for food. Through weaving, a labor of immediate usefulness to life, the hands of men and women become familiar with the cruciform symbolic system discerned in the cosmos.

It is not surprising, then, to find the vocabulary of weaving applied to many different human activities. In India the thread lends its symbolic meaning to literature. The Sanskrit word *sūtra* means "thread," but it also designates a chapter of a book, which is made up of a series of *sūtra*s. The word *tantra* also designates the thread, especially the woof of a material.

Weaving symbolism also appears in the concept of the world and fate. The *Muṇḍaka Upaniṣad* (2.5) designates *brahman* as that upon which worlds are woven like a warp and woof, while the *Bṛhadāraṇyaka Upaniṣad* (3.8.7) tells of the present, past, and future being woven in the sky and on earth while located between the two. Cloth, thread, and the profession of weaving are symbols of fate. Many of the spinning goddesses of the ancient Near East and the Indo-European world are goddesses of fate: Moirai, Parcae, and Norns. In northern Africa, in the mountainous massifs, each house has its rudimentary loom: two wooden beams supported by two uprights. The upper beam is called the beam of heaven, whereas the bottom one represents earth. These four logs symbolize the universe (Jean Servier, *L'homme et l'invisible,* 1980, pp. 65–66).

All these elements show that in the work of weaving *homo faber* was able to relate the symbolic system of his profession to the four directions and the symbolism of the center. Weaving, cross, and cosmos are inseparable.

Symbolism of the cross also figures in the art of navigation. Since the earliest times, navigation has occupied a very important place in the lives of individuals and nations. The need to build boats capable of braving the sea for purposes of travel, trade, war, and exploration became apparent very early. Among mythologies and literatures dedicated to the nautical art, Greek and Latin documents have given us the most interesting items. [*See* Boats.] There we find a number of descriptions revealing the symbolic system of the cross, beginning with the image of the mast and the yard that crosses it (Ovid, Pliny the Elder, Vergil, Lucian, Plutarch).

Both the merchant ship and the warship bore a mast that Latin authors called the *malus* or the *arbor*. The main mast—often the only mast—was cut in one piece from a tree. Upon its strength depended the successful outcome of the voyage or battle. This mast always impressed the imagination of the ancients, as seen in Homer's *Odyssey*. This mast is simultaneously a symbol of the tree and the center. The yard crossing the mast is designated by a word pregnant with meaning: *antenna* in Latin, *keraia* in Greek. The mast and the yard are the signs of a good ship. Their shape reproduces the cross, which thereby becomes the symbol of force, security, and victory.

The symbolism of the nautical cross strongly impressed the psychology of ancient man. The view of masts on the horizon sometimes evoked fear, sometimes joy and hope, depending on whether they were the masts of enemies, pirates, or saviors. If lightning strikes the mast, or if the storm tears away the yard, disaster is near. Mast and yard are life or death, safety or accident, spared lives or shipwreck. In myths they are invested with a sacred character and become emblematic of man's great voyage of life and destiny.

A symbolism such as this could not fail to have great repercussions on man's religious thought and behavior. The nautical cross, seen within the complex symbolism of the tree, the number four, the center, and the *axis mundi*, provides us with an important contribution in our understanding of the cross in the life and art of peoples before the impact of specifically Christian iconography. Taking as a basis the symbolic, psychological, and ethical meaning of the mast and the yard, the church fathers integrated them into their theology of the cross (Rahner, 1964, pp. 362–375).

The Christian Cross. For Christians, the cross is a sign evoking a historical event basic to the history of salvation: the crucifixion and death of Jesus at Calvary.

History. The crucifixion of Jesus, attested by the first generation of Christians, lies at the heart of the Fathers' theology and early church teachings. However, the image of a god abandoned to a shameful punishment and nailed on a cross was not likely to arouse enthusiasm. On the contrary, such an image created serious difficulties in the eyes of pagans, who were unable to resolve the apparent contradiction of a crucified god who in so dying became a savior. Unable to understand this doctrine, some Christians separated from the church and, following the Gnostics, imagined a death in appearance only according to docetic teachings. In their eyes, expiating sin by a *servile supplicium* seemed a contradiction in itself.

Early Christianity. For Christians ever since the apostolic age, the unfathomable mystery of the crucifixion is an object of faith (*1 Tm.* 3:16, *1 Cor.* 2:7). The church itself is a great mystery in which the cross is the decisive event for salvation and is linked to the mystery of creation. In pagan eyes, the human death of Jesus and his crucifixion are pure madness. The apologist Justin Martyr gives us echoes of this pagan reaction that accused Christians of madness for daring to place a crucified man on the same level as the creator of the world (*1 Apology* 13). A certain Palatine graffito leaves us with a proof of this reaction. On a tau-shaped cross a figure is fastened, his arms outstretched, his head—an ass's head—turned toward another figure in adoration before him. Under this illustration is inscribed: "Alexander adores his god." In the second century, Christians engraved three forms of the cross in the catacombs (see figure 1): the Greek cross, the Latin cross, and the *tau*, which is the shape of the torture instrument to which Origen and Tertullian allude. The catacombs also give us another representation of the cross, taken from a nautical object, the anchor. The examples found show the horizontal bar placed in the middle of the vertical bar, or even a fish stretched out on the stem of the anchor—two symbolic representations that Christians had no difficulty understanding. The patristic texts bear witness to the familiarity Christians had with the cross and its representations. Tertullian calls the Christians *crucis religiosi* (*Apology* 16.6). For Clement of Alexandria (*Stromateis* 6), the cross is *tou kuriakou sēmeiou tupon*, "the sign *par excellence* of the Lord." Archaeological documentation gives us diverse cruciform symbols (see figure 1): the decussate cross, or cross of Saint Andrew; the patibulary cross (the *tau*); the capital cross, called the Latin cross; the Greek or quadrate cross; the *florida* cross, covered with ornaments; the ankh or ansate cross, the sign of life used in ancient Egypt and taken up by the Christians; and the gammadion cross, used also in the Aryan world.

The age of Constantine. With the Edict of Milan, display of the cross as a symbol of the crucifixion is no longer subject to the discretion of Christians living in a hostile pagan world. Two events mark this turning point: (1) the adoption of the labarum, or chrism traced on shields and banners; and (2) the discovery of the true cross at Jerusalem. According to Eusebius of Caesarea, Constantine, who consistently showed respect for the cross, had many reproductions made of it (*Life of Constantine* 1.40; *Church History* 9.8). The emperor had images in his own likeness made with the cross in his hand. From the year 314, the scaffold for execution was no longer designated by the word *crux*, but by *patibulum*. Constantine finally abolished crucifixion as a sentence. The cross was placed at the pinnacle of basilicas, on the emperor's diadem and scepter, on coins, and on the doorsteps of Jewish dwellings. However, the enthusiasm for the cross and its reproductions did not eliminate Christian reserve in regard to the scene of the crucifixion. Sarcophagi of the fourth and fifth centuries show that artists tried to combine the crucifixion and the resurrection of Jesus in the same symbolic scene. In the fifth century, images of Christ carrying his cross or stretched out on the cross begin to appear. The most significant document in this evolution is the crucifixion panel on the door of Santa Sabina in Rome dating from the sixth century. There the artist has shown Christ on the cross between two thieves.

Thus under Constantine the church experienced a profound alteration in its attitude toward reproductions of the cross. Jeweled and flowered crosses, stational crosses, ansate crosses, and crosses wreathed in greenery proliferated. The discovery of the wood of the Savior's cross, together with the worship and honor rendered to the cross, rapidly transformed the former reticence into conspicuous public devotion. Yet for all this, reservations about the crucifixion scene were not abolished. The ampullae from the treasury at Monza in Lombardy serve as valuable evidence for this twofold attitude.

The Eastern church. The theological discussions of the fifth century ended in the councils of Ephesus (431) and Chalcedon (451), which condemned Nestorianism and monophysitism. In Syria and Egypt, the monophysites affirmed their doctrine by removing the figure of Jesus from the cross. They represented the cross bare or ornamented. Thus the apparent incompatibility between Christ's divinity and his crucifixion, which had formerly made the pagans, the gnostics, and the Docetists recoil, was reintroduced in a subtler form. The sculptures of certain schools of Syria and many fabrics coming from the same provenance as Coptic articles show the care taken by the monophysites to separate the figure of the crucified from the crucifix, since the crucifixion of the God-man implied the recognition of the union of two natures.

The decisions of the councils were to have a noticeable impact on Christian art. The defenders of orthodoxy—joined by the Nestorians, who insisted on the human nature of Christ—began to reproduce the scene of Calvary. They affirmed that Jesus had actually suffered for man's salvation, because he had a true human nature subject to suffering and death. Also, in the sixth century, the cross and the crucifix make their appearance on the altars of Eastern churches and in Syrian monasteries. With the help of theological discussions, Eastern artists and monks introduced the crucifixion into religious art.

The Western church. Western Christianity remained diffident concerning the scene of Calvary as a subject of realistic representation. In the sixth century at Narbonne, the faithful were scandalized by the representation of the naked crucified Jesus. At Ravenna, the basilicas of Sant' Appollinare in Classe and San Vitale and the Orthodox baptistery develop the whole system of biblical symbols except the crucifixion. It is the same at Hagia Sophia in Constantinople. Toward the end of the seventh century, the crucifix acquired a place in the art and piety of the faithful. In 692 the Trullan Council of Constantinople, in its eleventh canon, asked that the church truly commit itself to the fullness of the Covenant by replacing the ancient lamb with Christ in his human form, by contemplating the sublimity of the Word through his humility, and by gazing at Jesus dying for our salvation. Thus the crucifixion asserted itself in both the East and the West. Often Christ was shown dressed in a long tunic, the colobium. By the eighth century, the crucifixion decorated all monuments in the East and the West.

The Coptic church. The copious documentation at our disposal shows that representation of the cross depends on theological thought and the diverse conditions of Christian existence, resulting in extraordinary variety and richness. We are acquainted with Latin, Greek, Merovingian, Lombard, Celtic, and Egyptian crosses. The ansate cross of the Christians in Egypt deserves special mention. This cross is found on Christian funeral stelae at Erment, at Akhmīm, in the Faiyūm region, at Luxor, at Isna, and at Idfu. We see them on Coptic fabrics. Other examples are furnished by mural iconography at El Bagauât, Bawīt, Dar-al-Genadlah, Dar-al-Medinah, Dar-al-Bahari, and Dar-aba-Hennes (Cramer, 1955). More than once, the ankh of Ptolemaic and pharaonic Egypt is reproduced facing the Greek cross and the labarum. Archaeological documents reveal an obvious intention to preserve the ankh throughout the transformation of a pagan temple into a Christian church. The explanation of this gesture is given by three Christian historians: Socrates Scholasticus (c. 450), Sozomen (c. 443), and Rufinus (c. 410). Speaking of the demolition of the temple of Serapis, they note the discovery of sacred signs engraved on the rocks that are similar to the sign of the cross. A discussion arose between Christians and pagans, each group wishing to relate these signs to its own religion. Pagans converted to Christianity who still understood the meaning of the hieroglyphs explained that the ankh is the sign of life to come. Thus, among the Copts, the ancient pharaonic sign has become the symbol of the cross and of the *vita ventura.* The numerous archaeological and iconographic documents at our disposal attest to this practice and allow us to date it from the fourth to the ninth century.

Christian symbolism of the cross. Against the mysteries of pagan religions, the church fathers set the Christian mystery. In their eyes, the salvation decree proclaimed by God was revealed in the crucifixion of Christ. For Christians, Christ's death on the cross marked the end of Judaism as well as radical separation from pagan cults. They later vigorously opposed the various gnostic theories that refused to see history unfolding within the context of salvation through Christ and his achievement in the world. The Fathers quoted Paul (*Eph.* 1:10) to emphasize that in the crucifixion of Jesus creation was completed and a new world begun. They stressed the reality of the events related by the evangelists: agony, blood, human death, the heart wounded, the cross made of two pieces joined in the center. From the simplicity of the elements, shocking to both Jews and pagans, they developed an understanding of the great mystery of the cross (see *1 Cor.* 1:24–25, 2:8).

Greek thought was familiar to the church fathers in the first centuries. They saw in the cross the cosmic symbolism described by Pythagorean wisdom and developed in the works of Plato (*Timaeus* 36b–c). The two great circles of the world that intersect, forming a prone Greek *chi* around which turns the celestial arch, became for the Christians the cross of heaven. Hanging from the cross, the Logos—creator of the world—contains the cosmos. Thus, in the eyes of Justin Martyr (*1 Apology* 60.1) the celestial *chi* of Plato symbolizes the cross. For Irenaeus (*Against Heresies* 5.18.3), the sign of the cross is the totality and the visible manifestation of the cosmic future: the four dimensions of the cosmos are reproduced by the cross. The Logos of God, creator of the world, becomes man: all creation bears his imprint, he directs and orders all. Hanging on the cross, he epitomizes the cosmos. To those who had come to be baptized on the spot where Jesus died, Cyril of Jerusalem says that Golgotha is the center around which the cosmos circles; thus the symbolism of the center receives a true Christian consecration (*Catacheses* 13.18). Gregory of Nyssa exalts the cross as a cosmic seal stamped on both the heavens and the earth.

The Latin Christians soon moved in the same direction. At the end of the third century, precisely when pagan mysticism and the solar cults were reaching their apogee, Hippolytus of Rome celebrated the cross by reviving the entire range of ancient symbolic associations (*Paschal Homily* 6). For him, the cross was a tree rising from the earth to the sky, a point of support and repose, a cosmic pole. We find analogous suggestions in Lactantius: on the cross Christ opens his arms, embracing the earth's circle and bringing men together from sunrise to sunset (*Divinae institutiones* 4.26, 4.36). For Firmicus Maternus, the cross of Jesus maintains the motions of the heavens, reinforces the foundations of the earth, and leads men toward life (*De errore profanarum religionum* 27.3). This theme of the cosmic cross had great repercussions in the lives of Christians and in church theology. As proof of this we have Tertullian (*Apology* 16.6) and Minucius Felix (*Octavius* 29.6–7). The mystery of the cross marks all creation: the human body, the flight of birds, agriculture, and the Christian in prayer with arms outstretched. This symbol makes it possible to understand the graffiti of the catacombs, the orants, and all the simplicity of Christian primitive art. The cosmic symbolism that recaptitulates the basic facts of the world is also applied to Christ's return at the end of the world. The cross will be the great luminous sign preceding the transfigured Christ (*Didachē,* 16.6). The last day of the world will completely reveal the mystery of the cross (Rahner, 1954, pp. 61–74).

Christian symbolism of the cross is linked to the mystery of creation as well as to the mystery of redemption. If, as just noted, the church fathers reinterpreted ancient cosmic symbolism, they also reinterpreted images from the Hebrew scriptures (Old Testament). On the day of Christ's crucifixion, the curtain of the Temple was torn revealing in all its fullness the mystery of God hidden within the Ark of the Covenant.

In the writings of the Fathers, each reference to wood in the Old Testament becomes a symbol of the cross. One tree in particular, however, symbolizes the mystery of Golgotha: the Tree of Life planted near the four rivers in the midst of Paradise (*Gn.* 2:9), which is mentioned in *Revelation* (22:14). This tree prefigures the mystery of the cross, for in its place, and in the place of the first Adam, we now have the new Adam whose tree of salvation is erected toward the sky, embracing the cosmos and making the baptismal spring of life flow at its feet. This symbolism of tree and water, taken from *Genesis* and applied to the event at Golgotha, has had extraordinary repercussions. It has inspired the baptismal theology of both the Eastern and Western church fathers from Justin to Augustine, through Ephraem Syrus, Irenaeus, and Gregory of Nyssa. The artists responsible for decorating Roman baptisteries have brought it to life in stone and metal. This symbolism, indentified by Augustine as the *sacramentum ligni* ("sacrament of wood"), provides a fertile theme throughout the centuries for artists and poets, preachers, and storytellers.

We are able to witness its continuity during the Middle Ages in numerous representations of Adam's skull at the foot of the cross. It takes root in Pauline meditations on the connection between Adam and Christ (*1 Cor.* 15:45–49). At the beginning of the third century, in a lyrical flight of rare beauty Hippolytus of Rome sings the praise of that biblical and cosmic tree: tall as the sky, immortal in its growth, cornerstone of the world, and gathering all men unto itself (*Paschal Homily* 6).

In the eyes of the church fathers, the cross is prefigured throughout the Old Testament, which already contains the mystery of the Logos. The Fathers discern annunciatory symbols in it. Justin Martyr does not hesitate to say that the Old Testament reveals the mystery of the cross in all its power (*Dialogue with Trypho* 91.1); he supports this by citing numerous passages referring to the cross or to the future crucifixion of the Savior (*1 Apology* 31.7, 32.4, 35.2–7, 55.4, 60.3–5). He insists on the value and necessity of symbolic language in the foretelling of that prophecy, for it is thanks to this symbolic language that the cross will no longer be perceived as shameful (ibid., 55.1). Other patristic documents echo this theme of the cross's shamefulness, important during the first Christian centuries (Tertullian, *Against Marcion* 3.18). The apologists and the Fathers especially stress the prophetic aspect of wood as mentioned in the Old Testament. All wood in the Old Testament becomes a harbinger of the instrument of salvation: Noah's Ark (*Gn.* 6:14–16); the oak of Mamre (*Gn.* 18: 1); the wood for Isaac's burnt offering; Jacob's ladder; Moses' rod (*Ex.* 4:2–5, 14:16, 17:5–6). Gregory T. Armstrong (1979) has made a partial but impressive enumeration of Old Testament passages used by the Fathers as prophecies of Christ's cross (pp. 34–38).

An examination of these texts clearly shows that during the first centuries Christians understood the biblical mystery of the cross as connected to both the mystery of creation and the mystery of redemption. The profundity of that understanding of the two testaments remained alive until the Middle Ages, as is shown by Romanesque art and Gothic mysticism. In another connection, as soon as the church was free from persecution, theologians began to associate diverse aspects of the cruciform emblems of pagan religions with the Christian cross. A valuable testimony to this new orientation in the fourth century is a treatise by Firmicus Maternus, *De errore profanarum religionum*, written around 346. Challenging the pagans on the subject of the *symbola profanae religionis* (21.1), the author casts blame on the god with two horns, without specifying whether he means Dionysos in the shape of a bull or the god Pan, who belongs to the world of Bacchus and Adonis. He claims that ornament of glory, the horn, for the Christians, for "cornua nihil aliud nisi venerandum signum Crucis monstrant" (21.4). For Firmicus Maternus, the horn raised vertically holds up the sky and holds down the earth; east and west are joined by fastening the other horn in the center. It is the symbol of the cross sustaining the world and thus the symbol of Christ who, by extending his arms, sustains the heavens and the earth. The author sees the forerunner of the event in the prophet Habakkuk (*Hb.* 3:3–5), and in Moses' gesture during prayer (*Ex.* 17:9–12). Thus Firmicus Maternus conjoins three symbolic systems: the cosmic, the pagan, and the biblical.

From the second century on, this symbol system is taken up and developed by Christian thinkers. Justin Martyr devotes all of the fifty-fifth chapter of his first Apology to this symbolism. To show the pagans that the cross is the sign of Christ's strength and power, he asks them to consider a series of objects that come before their eyes: "Could one cut through the sea if that trophy was not raised intact on the ship in the shape of a sail? Is work possible without the cross? Can pioneers or manual laborers work without instruments bearing that shape?" (55.2). He then enumerates several signs that suggest the power of the cross: the human body, its arms outstretched; the banners and trophies that go before armies, and statues of emperors (55.6–7). Justin emphasizes the figure of the trophy shaped by the mast and by the yard on which the sail is hung, because it permits him to elaborate his argument. Just as the mast and the sail are indispensable to the security of sailors and passengers, so only the cross of Christ that they symbolize is capable of granting salvation. Justin similarly perceives the *vexilla* and *tropaia* that led the troops into battle in the same way.

Several decades later, Tertullian also takes up these images. In the famous sixteenth chapter of his *Apology*, where he attacks pagan representations of Christ depicted with an ass's head, he explains the Christian worship of the cross. In his refutation of pagan accusations, he notes that banners and ensigns also bear the shape of a cross. This text can be found again, expanded, in *To the Nations* (1.12.1–16). Tertullian's use of the word *siphara* shows that in his mind the images of the banner and the ensign are connected to the mast and yard of the ship. Hippolytus of Rome further develops these nautical symbols in his text *De Antichristo* 59. The church sails the sea of the world bearing the sign of victory, the Lord's cross. The white sail is the spirit. A ladder leads to the top of the mast and beyond, that is to say, right up to heaven. The topsails are the apostles, prophets, and martyrs. As Hugo Rahner (1964) has admirably shown, the nautical symbolism of the cross has known an extraordinary development in patristic theology.

Conclusion. Several conclusions can be drawn from this brief survey. It must first be stated that copious documentation referring to the cross is available to the historian of religions. The cross is everywhere: in pre-Vedic civilization; in the Elamite world and Mesopotamian iconography; in the vast area of Aryan migrations and the cultures to which they gave birth; in China; in pre-Columbian and American Indian civilizations; among nonliterate peoples who are our own contemporaries. Such universality shows that we are dealing with a basic phenomenon in the life of *homo religiosus*, the explanation of which necessitates reflection on several levels: the symbolism of the tree seen as *axis mundi;* man's need for orientation in his attempts to transform chaos into cosmos; the symbols of the number four and the center; and diverse cruciform images that appear to man in his basic activities. The cross shows that *homo religiosus* is also *homo symbolicus*. When the historian of religions examines the documents referring to the cross in the life of *homo christianus*, he is obliged to enlarge his hermeneutic field. It is because of a historical event—the death of Jesus of Nazareth crucified at Golgotha—that the cross is endowed with transcendent significance. The entire ancient symbol system is assumed, but it is now placed within the context of a new vision of history framed by the theology of creation and redemption. In the eyes of the Christian, the cross is considered inseparable from the mystery of the divine Logos. Hence it takes on a cosmic dimension, a biblical dimension, and a soteriological dimension.

BIBLIOGRAPHY

Alexander, Hartley B. *The World's Rim: Great Mysteries of the North American Indians.* Lincoln, Nebr., 1953.

Andresen, Carl, and Günter Klein, eds. *Theologia Crucis, Signum Crucis: Festschrift für Erich Dinkler zum 70. Geburtstag.* Tübingen, 1979.

Armstrong, Gregory T. "The Cross in the Old Testament according to Athanasius, Cyril of Jerusalem and the Cappadocian Fathers." In *Theologia Crucis, Signum Crucis: Festschrift für Erich Dinkler zum 70. Geburtstag*, edited by Carl Andresen and Günter Klein, pp. 17–38. Tübingen, 1979.

Blake, Willson W. *The Cross, Ancient and Modern.* New York, 1888.

Bousset, Wilhelm. "Die Seele der Welt bei Plato und das Kreuz Christi." *Zeitschrift für neutestamentliche Wissenschaft* 14 (1913): 273–285.

Casal, Jean-Marie. *La civilisation de l'Indus et ses énigmes: De la Mésopotamie à l'Inde.* Paris, 1969.

Champdor, Albert. *Le livre des morts: Papyrus d'Ani, de Hunefer, d'Anhai du British Museum.* Paris, 1963. Translated by Faubion Bowers as *The Book of the Dead* (New York, 1966).

Champeaux, Gérard de, and Sébastien Sterckx. *Introduction au monde des symboles.* Paris, 1966.

Chevalier, Jean, and Alain Gheerbrant, eds. *Dictionnaire des symboles.* Paris, 1982.

Cramer, Maria. *Das altägyptische Lebenszeichen im christlichen (koptischen) Ägypten.* Wiesbaden, 1955.

Dölger, Franz Joseph. "Beiträge zur Geschichte des Kreuzzeichens." *Jahrbuch für Antike und Christentum* 1 (1958): 5–19, 2 (1959): 15–29, 3 (1960): 5–16, 4 (1961): 5–17, and 5 (1962): 5–22.

Eliade, Mircea. *Traité d'histoire des religions.* Paris, 1949.

Eliade, Mircea. *Images and Symbols: Studies in Religious Symbolism.* New York, 1961.

Erler, Martin. *Das Symbol des Lebens im alten Aegypten.* Munich, 1968.

Goblet d'Alviella, Eugène F. A. "Archéologie de la croix." In *Croyances, rites, institutions,* vol. 1, pp. 63–81. Paris, 1911.

Goblet d'Alviella, Eugène F. A. *La migration des symboles.* Paris, 1891.

Guénon, René. *Le symbolisme de la croix.* Paris, 1957. Translated by Angus Macnab as *Symbolism of the Cross* (London, 1958).

Kennedy, Charles A. "Early Christians and the Anchor." *Biblical Archaeologist* 38 (1975): 115–124.

Korvin-Krasinski, Cyrill von. "Vorchristliche matriarchalische Einflüsse in der Gestaltung ältester koptischer und armenischer Kreuze." *Symbolon: Jahrbuch für Symbolforschung* (Cologne) 3 (1977): 37–73.

Laliberté, Norman, and Edward N. West. *The History of the Cross.* New York, 1960.

Leclercq, Henri. "Croix et crucifis." In *Dictionnaire d'archéologie chrétienne et de liturgie,* edited by Fernand Cabrol, vol. 3, pp. 3045–3144. Paris, 1914. A probing study of the history of the Christian representation of the cross.

Marshall, John, ed. *Mohenjo-Daro and the Indus Civilization.* 3 vols. Delhi, 1973.

Mortillet, Gabriel de. *Le signe de la croix avant le christianisme.* Paris, 1866.

Porter, Arthur K. *The Crosses and Culture of Ireland.* New Haven, 1931.

Rahner, Hugo. *Mythes grecs et mystères chrétien.* Paris, 1954.

Rahner, Hugo. *Symbole der Kirche: Die Ekklesiologie der Väter.* Salzburg, 1964.

Rech, Photina. *Inbild des Kosmos: Eine Symbolik der Schöpfung.* 2 vols. Salzburg, 1966.

Schneider Berrenberg, Rüdiger. *Kreuz, Kruzifix: Eine Bibliographie.* Munich, 1973. Contains more than two thousand headings (iconography, art history, archaeology, theology, philology, and folklore).

Séjourné, Laurette. *La pensée des anciens Mexicains.* Paris, 1982.

Stählin, Wilhelm. "Das Kreuzeszeichen." In *Deine Sprache verrät dich.* Kassel, 1974.

Stierlin, Henri. *L'art des Astèques et ses origines.* Paris, 1982.

Streit, Jakob. *Sonne und Kreuz: Irland zwischen Megalithkultur und frühem Christentum.* Stuttgart, 1977.

Wedemeyer, Inge von. "Das Zeichen des Kreuzes im Alten Peru." *Antaios* (Stuttgart) 12 (1970): 366–379.

JULIEN RIES
Translated from French by Kristine Anderson

CROSSROADS in religion belong to the general phenomenon of sacred places and are a specific instance of the sacrality of roads. Wherever two or more roads intersect—forming a T or a fork or, most significantly, a junction of two roads at right angles to form a cross—there religious people often feel that the divine has intersected with the mundane. The nature of this divine presence may be positive but is very often negative. Most often, however, the divinity associated with a crossroads is paradoxically both good and evil: it seems that the meeting of different roads attracts and then expresses very well the meeting of opposites within the god.

Buddhist pilgrims travel with pleasure to a crossroads, for it is there that they are likely to find a reliquary structure containing precious remains of the cremated body of the Buddha. The Lord himself stated in the *Mahāparinibbāna Sutta* that the remains of all great beings should be treated alike: "At the four crossroads a stupa should be erected to the Tathāgata" (5.26–28). Expectations were different for a pious Greek or Roman who came to a meeting of three roads, for that was the domain of the goddess Hekate, whose name, Vergil says, "is howled by night at the city crossroads" (*Aeneid* 4.609). Associated with death as well as with darkness, Hekate could be propitiated by the burial of the body of a criminal at her favorite place. This helps to explain the English custom, prevalent until modern times, of burying suicides and criminals at a meeting of roads. The execution of criminals there probably gave rise to the phrase "dirty work at the crossroads."

The folk deity Dōsojin of Japan and the Olympian Hermes of ancient Greece are gods of boundaries and of roads, but also of crossroads. They are both commonly represented by phallic images that express uneasily, even for their worshipers, the unexpected union of spirit and nature. Dōsojin may be found at the crossroads in the shape of an upright stone phallus or—capturing the god's ambivalence—a pair of phalli or a male and female holding hands. Hermes' quadrangular stone pillars are topped by the god's head and fronted by his erect penis. Located at the juncture of roads, these herms were supposed to guide and protect travelers, but might just as easily bring them grief. As the Homeric *Hymn to Hermes* puts it, "And even though he helps a few people, he cheats an endless number." Something similar must be said of the Vedic god Rudra, whose "favorite haunt," according to the *Śatapatha Brāhmaṇa* (2.6.2.8), is the crossroads. Rudra is fierce but must be addressed as "Śiva" (Auspicious One) if he is to heal the wounds that he himself inflicts. Rudra is not himself phallic, but he provides a name and an ambivalent character for the later Hindu deity Śiva, whose chief image is the phallus. Thus, we can understand the ancient advice to an Indian bridegroom traveling with his bride: "On the way, he should address crossroads. . . . 'May no waylayers meet us' " (*Gṛhyasūtra of Gobhila* 2.4.2). In so doing, he is calling to Rudra for help, yet asking him to stay away.

Crossroads also appear, with a different level of meaning, in the boyhood vision of Black Elk, the Oglala Lakota holy man, described in his life story, *Black Elk Speaks* (Lincoln, Nebr., 1932). Looking down from a high place, he saw the earth and two roads crossing, a red one and a black. These roads symbolized the good times and the troubled times that his people must necessarily experience; yet the crossing of them provided a center where there bloomed a "holy stick" by which his people would flourish. It was this image that provided Black Elk himself with a center and an orientation for the rest of his life.

BIBLIOGRAPHY

After consulting the sources given and the standard scholarship for each religion mentioned, one might read the two essays on "Cross-roads" by J. A. MacCulloch and Richard Wünsch in the *Encyclopaedia of Religion and Ethics,* edited by James Hastings, vol. 4 (Edinburgh, 1911). For accounts of crossroads rites, see James G. Frazer's *The Golden Bough,* 3d ed., rev. & enl., 12 vols. (London, 1911–1915).

GEORGE R. ELDER

CROWN. The significance of the crown lies chiefly in its place on top of the head, where it marks the bearer's relationship to what is above, to what is transcendent. At the same time the crown represents the joining of what is above to what is below, the divine and the human, the celestial and the terrestrial. The crown symbolizes access to rank and to superior force, and therefore to dignity, royalty, and power.

From a very early time crowns were associated with the sun, especially with its rays. On a third-century bas-relief from the Roman city of Virunum the sun is shown receiving his radiant crown from Mithra, who has beat him in a wrestling match. In alchemy the spirits of the planets receive their light in the form of crowns from their king, the sun. In the ancient religions of Mexico and Egypt, the king in his divine aspect is the sun.

The crown's meaning can also be discovered in its circular shape, which signifies perfection and eternity. The material of the crown may represent the divinity with which its wearer is associated or even assimilated. Thus, the laurel wreath often related its wearer to Apollo, while oak leaves were emblems of Zeus. At the end of the harvest in Europe celebrants have traditionally worn wreaths of ears of grain.

During a Tibetan ceremony that seeks to eliminate the spirits of the dead, the priest wears a crown that guarantees the cosmic worth of the sacrifice by bringing together symbolically the five Buddhas and the material universe, as well as the four cardinal points with their center. In the West the Crown of Charlemagne, made for Otto I, founder of the Holy Roman Empire, is octagonal in shape, recalling the walls of Rome and the ramparts of heaven.

Crowns, often in the form of wreaths, have been awarded to victors in war or contests where the honored hero is identified with a divine patron of the contest or with a warrior god. Another religious dimension is added when—as in Mithraism and Christianity—the souls of the elect are crowned like athletes or soldiers as victors over death.

In some religious sacrifices the sacrificer wears a crown; in others the victims, even animal victims, do the same. The dead may also be crowned: in Egypt both the mummy and the statue that represented the deceased were crowned for the triumphant entry into the next life. In Christianity the crowning of martyrs is often pictured: the wearer of the crown is always related through it to a greater transcendent power.

Objects, as well as persons, can be crowned. Holy scriptures, icons, pictures, and statues are frequently honored and dedicated with crowns. Crowns sometimes assume significance independent of the crowned. Among the Yoruba of West Africa sheep were occasionally sacrificed to the crown, which had magical powers. In ancient Egypt a crown or diadem representing the highest sovereignty could execute the king's secret purpose or inflict vengeance. In one version of the legend of Ariadne and Theseus, a crown of light guides Theseus through the labyrinth after he has killed the Minotaur.

BIBLIOGRAPHY

The image of the crown appears extensively in most religious literature, but no single source begins to explore the whole range of material with both examples and interpretation. G. F. Hill's long essay, "Crowns," in the *Encyclopaedia of Religion and Ethics*, edited by James Hastings, vol. 4 (Edinburgh, 1911), describes mostly Western history and tradition and says relatively little about the religious symbolism of the crown. Nonetheless, the article is good background material. J. E. Cirlot, in *A Dictionary of Symbols*, 2d ed. (New York, 1971), and Jean Chevalier and Alain Gheerbrant, in their *Dictionnaire des symboles* (Paris, 1982), have written interesting discussions without pretending to cover the subject.

ELAINE MAGALIS

CRUSADES.

[*This entry, in two parts, discusses the Crusades first from the Christian point of view, then from the Muslim.*]

Christian Perspective

Crusades were military expeditions against various enemies of the church; the term refers particularly to the medieval campaigns aimed at liberating the Holy Land from the Muslims. The word *crusade* (Span., *cruzada;* Fr., *croisade*) derives from the Latin *crux* (cross); the Latin term *cruciata* does not occur before the thirteenth century. It recalls the ceremony of "taking the cross" (*Mt.* 10:38), the public act of committing oneself to participate in a crusade. Crusaders wore a red cloth cross sewn to their cloaks as a sign of their status. In modern times the word *crusade* is used metaphorically to designate evangelistic efforts at promoting all kinds of religious or moral causes.

Roots and Causes. While the roots of the movement were complex, a major religious impulse came with the fusion of pilgrimage and holy war. The Crusades continued the old tradition of pilgrimage to the Holy Land that was often undertaken in fulfillment of a vow or as a penance; its earlier designations were *via, iter,* or *peregrinatio.* Attractive for pilgrims were not only the holy places themselves but their relics, above all the Holy Sepulcher, to which the emperor Heraclius had restored the True Cross in AD 627. The finding of the Holy Lance at Antioch (June 1098) revitalized the First Crusade. In the Christian *terra sancta* mythology the name of Jerusalem ("vision of peace") evoked the image of the heavenly city, the goal of the Christian life (cf. *Gal.* 4:26, *Heb.* 12:22, *Rv.* 21:10–27). As "navel of the world" Jerusalem also figured in apocalyptic expectation; according to the Tiburtine Sibyl, the last battles would be fought and the last emperor hand over his rule to Christ in Jerusalem.

During the twelfth century armed pilgrimages began to be regarded as just wars fought in defense of the Holy Land against its illegitimate occupation by the Muslim infidel. The notion of a just war as revenge for an injury done to Christ had been invoked in the fight against Muslims in Spain and Sicily and, even earlier, in the Carolingian expeditions against pagans and Saracens. In 878, Pope John VIII offered spiritual incentives to those who would arm themselves against his foes in Italy. Gregory VII (1073–1085) envisaged a *militia Christi* for the fight against all enemies of God and thought already of sending an army to the East. An additional factor was the expectation of religious benefits. In the popular perception, the Crusade indulgence offered nothing less than full remission of sins and a sure promise of heaven. In a feudal society of warriors, crusading for God's sake under the banner of Saint Michael ranked as the ultimate fulfillment of the ideal of Christian knighthood.

Among the political causes of the Crusades, the appeals for help from the Byzantine emperors were prominent. The year 1071 saw the defeat of the Byzantine army at Manzikert in Asia Minor. Jerusalem fell to the Seljuk Turks in 1077. There is no clear evidence that these events led to increased harassment of Christian pilgrims. Nevertheless, they caused great alarm and spurred papal offers of assistance. Moreover, in dealing with the fighting spirit of the aristocracy, reform movements such as the Cluniac and the Gregorian were promoting the "Peace of God" (protection of unarmed persons) and the "Truce of God" (*treuga Dei*, suspension of all fighting during specified times). In this situation, participation in holy warfare provided an outlet for the martial vigor of Christian knights.

Campaigns. Any attempt at systematizing the Crusades remains arbitrary. Nevertheless, for clarity's sake, we shall follow the customary numbering of the main expeditions.

First Crusade (1096–1099). Urban II's call for participation in an expedition to the East at the Council of Clermont on 27 November 1095 met with an enthusiastic response. He himself declared the acclamation "God wills it!" to be the divinely inspired battle cry for the Crusaders. Thousands took the cross, especially French, Norman, and Flemish knights. Several bands of badly armed pilgrims from France and Germany, most of them poor and inexperienced, set out for Constantinople even before the army gathered. Some started by massacring Jews on their way through Germany. Many died in Hungary, and the remnants perished in Anatolia. The main force, under the papal legate Bishop Adhémar of Le Puy and an illustrious baronial leadership (including Godfrey of Bouillon, Baldwin II of Flanders, Raymond IV of Toulouse, Robert II of Normandy, and Bohemond I of Taranto), assembled at Constantinople (December 1096 to May 1097) and set out on a long, arduous march through Asia Minor. After costly victories at Nicaea and Dorylaeum (June–July 1097) and enormous hardships, the Crusaders captured Antioch (3 June 1098) and finally Jerusalem (15 July 1099), consolidating their victory by the defeat of a Fatimid army at Ascalon (12 August 1099). A side expedition under Baldwin had already taken Edessa to the north (6 February 1098). Only Nicaea was returned to the Byzantine emperor, and four Crusader states were organized along the Syro-Palestinian coast: the counties of Edessa and Tripoli, the principality of Antioch, and the kingdom of Jerusalem. Measured against the original goal, the First Crusade was the only successful one. Its territorial gains, protected by inland ridges and a system of fortresses along the coast, formed the basis that future Crusades sought to defend against mounting Muslim pressure. Constant quarrels among the leaders and rival interests of the major European powers, however, prevented any effective cooperation and success.

Second Crusade (1147–1149). The preaching of the Second Crusade had its immediate cause in the loss of Edessa to the Muslims of Syria (1144). Moved by the preaching of Bernard of Clairvaux, Louis VII of France and Conrad III of Germany led separate armies through Asia Minor. The losses suffered by the troops were disheartening. Furthermore, rather than aiming at Edessa, the remnant joined the Palestinian knights in an unsuccessful siege of Damascus (July 1148), which had been at peace with the kingdom of Jerusalem. This diversion worsened the plight of Edessa, Antioch, and Tripoli. Even at home the crusade was soon recognized as a disaster.

Third Crusade (1189–1192). At the initiative of the archbishop of Tyre, the Third Crusade responded to the defeat of the Palestinian knights at Ḥiṭṭīn in Galilee (4 July 1187) and the resulting loss of Jerusalem to the sultan, Saladin. The leadership included Frederick I Barbarossa, Philip II Augustus of France, and Richard I ("the Lionhearted") of England. But Frederick accidentally drowned during the march, and the crusading effort disintegrated through attrition, quarreling, and lack of cooperation. Only Acre was recaptured (July 1191) and some ports secured, mainly through the initiative of Richard, who also took Cyprus from the Byzantines and finally negotiated a three-year truce with Saladin (September 1192).

Fourth Crusade (1202–1204). Pope Innocent III (1198–1216) made the reorganization of the crusade under papal auspices one of the priorities of his pontificate. A first appeal went out on 15 August 1198. The response was slow, and the fervor aroused by the preaching of Fulk of Neuilly did not reach beyond France and Italy. The leaders contracted for transportation with the doge of Venice, Dandolo, but lack of funds forced a diversion from the original plan to attack the Muslims in Egypt. At the request of the Venetians, the Crusaders first attacked the Christian city of Zara in Dalmatia (November 1202) and then sailed on to Constantinople, where they hoped to enthrone Alexios, an exiled Byzantine pretender to the crown, and to receive the material assistance they needed. When these plans failed, the Crusaders laid siege to the city and finally stormed it (12 April 1204). Byzantium was looted for its treasure of relics, art, and gold, and was made the residence of a Latin emperor, with Baldwin IX of Flanders as the first incumbent. A Byzantine army recaptured the city almost casually in 1261.

The Fourth Crusade was followed by the legendary Children's Crusade of 1212. A group consisting mostly of young people under the leadership of a boy named Nicholas tried to cross the Alps and find passage to the Holy Land. All trace of them was lost even before they reached the Mediterranean ports. Crusade preaching, religious fervor, and respect for children as instruments of God's power contributed to the phenomenon. Later sources confuse this crusade with a French movement led by a shepherd boy, Stephen of Cloyes, who wanted to deliver a heavenly letter to the king.

Fifth Crusade (1217–1221). In connection with his call for the Fourth Lateran Council in 1215, Innocent III tried to stir up new interest in the crusade. In the Levant, Acre had become the center of Christian activity. From there an expedition under baronial and clerical leadership (Cardinal Pelagius) attempted to strike at the heart of Ayyubid power in Egypt (May 1218). The harbor city of Damietta was forced to surrender (5 November 1219), but further hopes were dashed by the defeat at al-Mansūra on the way to Cairo (24 July 1221). A stunning novelty was the expedition of Emperor Frederick II of Hohenstaufen (the so-called Sixth Crusade, 1228–1229). Frederick sailed to Cyprus and Acre (June 1228), secretly negotiated a ten-year truce that included the return of Jerusalem, Bethlehem, and Lydda to the Christians, and crowned himself king of Jerusalem (18 March 1229), although he had been excommunicated by Gregory IX for his failure to act on a Crusade vow earlier. The Holy City was retaken by Muslim allies in 1244 after an expedition of Count Thibaut IV of Champagne had failed to secure the diplomatic gain (1239–1240).

Seventh and Eighth Crusades. Two crusades of the thirteenth century are connected with the name of Louis IX (Saint Louis) of France. In fulfillment of a vow, Louis sailed to Cyprus with a splendid host of fifteen thousand men and attacked Egypt (Seventh Crusade, 1248–1254). Damietta was occupied again (June 1249) but had to be returned together with a huge ransom when the king and his army were routed and taken captive on their slow march south (6 April 1250). Louis took up residence in Acre for four years, attempting to strengthen the Crusader states by, for example, working toward an alliance with the Mongol khan. Another expedition against the sultan of Tunis (Eighth Crusade, 1270–1272) also ended in failure. The king died in North Africa (25 August 1270), and the Muslims succeeded in buying off the Crusaders. In the meantime, all of Palestine as well as Antioch was lost to the Mamluk sultan, Baybars. The last Christian bastion on the Syrian coast, Acre, was stormed by the sultan in 1291.

The fourteenth and fifteenth centuries saw several papal attempts to revive the crusade or support expeditions to the East. In 1365, King Peter I of Cyprus captured Alexandria; this victory was widely hailed but inconsequential. Soon the fight against the Ottoman Turks turned into a defense of Christian lands, especially after Muslim victories over the Serbs, the Hungarians (Nicopolis, 1396), and a last Crusader army under John Hunyadi and Julian Cardinal Cesarini (Varna, 1444). The fall of Constantinople in May 1453 led to a serious initiative on the part of Pius II, who wished to go on the crusade in person. He died on the way to joining the fleet at Ancona (July 1464).

Other Crusades. During the medieval period crusades were also used against internal foes in the West. The granting of Crusade indulgences for the fight against the Moors in Spain beginning with Alexander II (1072) and a crusade to convert the Slavic Wends in northern Germany (1147) set the precedent. These actions were followed by savage crusades against Albigensian heretics in southern France (1209–1229), northern German peasants (1232–1234), and the Hussites (1421–1435), by wars of conversion against the pagan Prussians in the Baltic region (after 1236), and similar expeditions. A different development came with the "political" crusades to protect the papal lands in Italy against the Hohenstaufens. Gregory IX proclaimed the crusade against Frederick II in 1240; Innocent IV followed in 1245; and the French Angevins took Sicily (1261–1264) with full Crusaders' privileges granted by Urban IV.

Characteristics. From the beginning, the movement depended on the initiative of the papacy; as a result, the latter's claims to universal leadership were strengthened. Urban II preached the crusade himself, as did other popes. Generally, however, this task was delegated to bishops, papal legates, and specially commissioned Crusade preachers. Few examples of this preaching are known. We have, however, a manual for Crusade preachers written around 1250 by the Dominican master general, Humbert of Romans. A crusade was announced through papal bulls, the first of these having been issued by Eugenius III (1 December 1145). They normally included exhortation, narration (of the situation in the East), and the enumeration of privileges. The last point was of particular importance. Canon law specified the Crusader's rewards: plenary indulgence, legal advantages such as protection of family and property and the right to be judged in ecclesiastical courts, and financial incentives like exemption from certain taxes and interest payments or the right to sell and mortgage property. Violations were subject to severe punishment, including excommunication, which also applied to those who failed to act on a crusading vow.

Originally, participants expected to pay their own way and to provision their vassals. As enthusiasm faded, the financing of a crusade became more complicated. Apart from using current income, popes from the mid-twelfth century on authorized special Crusade taxes of 1 to 10 percent on ecclesiastical income for up to five years; taxing rights or a share of the ecclesiastical tithe could be granted also to secular leaders. In 1187, Pope Gregory VIII began granting Crusade indulgences for persons assisting the effort at home, who soon came to include the wives of Crusaders.

A consequence of the growing financial involvement of the popes was the wish to have more direct control of the goals and operations. While Urban II still discouraged participation of the clergy, in practice the situation soon changed. Many clerics joined the expeditions, and papal legates regularly accompanied the armies. Conflicts over authority and leadership were inevitable. Yet the popes had to be flexible. No crusade could be conducted without popular support. The early enthusiasm probably was the expression of a genuine religious sentiment, often in response to charismatic preachers such as Peter of Amiens, Bernard of Clairvaux, Fulk of Neuilly, and Jacques of Vitry. But after the initial success and the later shock over the failure of the Second Crusade, a revival of the original zeal became more difficult despite increased incentives and propaganda efforts. From the middle of the twelfth century on, critical voices were heard, including imperial publicists, Rutebeuf, Roger Bacon, and William of Tripoli. Papal opinion polls (Gregory X, 1272; Nicholas IV, 1292) elicited many answers. As in the isolated event of Francis of Assisi's visit to Sultan al-Kamīl during the Fifth Crusade (spring and summer 1219), the need for a fundamental shift from military intervention to peaceful mission efforts was often stressed, leading to missionary initiatives in the late Middle Ages, especially from the mendicant orders.

Outcome. The results of the Crusades are difficult to assess. In terms of religion, the failures nourished doubts about God's will, church authority, and the role of the papacy. Religious fervor yielded to apathy, cynicism, and legalism. On the other hand, the Crusades stimulated religious enthusiasm on a large scale and gave Christendom a unifying cause that lasted for centuries. They inspired a great literature of tracts, chronicles, letters, heroic tales, and poetry, not only in Latin but in the vernaculars. Ignorance of Islam was replaced by a measure of knowledge, respect, and occasionally tolerance. An emphasis on informed apologetics (for instance those of Thomas Aquinas and Ramón Lull) and on Eastern languages (canon 11 of the Council of Vienne, 1311) as a prerequisite for mission was characteristic of the later Middle Ages.

Politically, the Crusades brought few lasting changes. The Crusader states and the Latin empire remained episodes. Their precarious status forced new diplomatic contacts with Eastern powers but also strengthened the Muslim conviction that holy war *(jihād)* could be carried farther west. In this sense the Crusades led directly to the Turkish wars of later centuries, during which Ottoman expansion threatened even central Europe.

The effect of the Crusades on relations with Byzantium was primarily negative. The Crusades needed Byzantine support as much as Byzantium needed Western armies. But what started as an effort to help Eastern Christians ended in mutual mistrust and enmity (for example, the Crusades against the Byzantines in 1237, 1261, and 1282). The shrewd moves of Byzantine diplomacy created the image of the "treacherous Greeks" among Crusaders, while the sack of Constantinople left the indelible impression of Western barbarity on the Greek mind. Thus, the "unions" of Eastern churches with the West (at the councils of Lyons, 1274, and Florence, 1439) had no support at home.

One novelty with an impact on European politics was the military orders founded in the East. The Templars' financial deals with the French crown led to their ruthless suppression (1307–1312); the Hospitalers' odyssey took them to the island of Rhodes (1309–1322) and to Malta (after 1530). The Teutonic Knights found a new task in the Baltic states, and several chivalrous orders in Spain and Portugal were to influence Iberian politics for centuries.

The Crusades imposed huge burdens on clergy and laity; at times the papacy was unable to support any other cause. Yet they also furthered the growth of a money economy, banking, and new methods of taxation. The widening of the geographic horizon prepared Europe for the age of discovery. Urban culture, especially in Italian city-states such as Genoa, Pisa, and Venice, received strong impulses through trade with the East. In the West, Islamic science, philosophy, and medicine deeply influenced intellectual life.

BIBLIOGRAPHY

Many general bibliographies on the Middle Ages feature sections on the Crusades. Two specialized bibliographies provide a thorough introduction to sources and literature: A. S. Atiya's

The Crusade: Historiography and Bibliography (1962; reprint, Westport, Conn., 1976) and Hans Eberhard Mayer's *Bibliographie zur Geschichte der Kreuzzüge* (Hanover, 1960) with its supplement, *Literaturberichte über Neuerscheinungen zur ausserdeutschen Geschichte und zu den Kreuzzügen,* "Historische Zeitschrift, Sonderheft," vol. 3 (Munich, 1969).

The most comprehensive treatment of the Crusades in English is found in the excellent volumes of *A History of the Crusades,* under the general editorship of Kenneth M. Setton, with Marshall W. Baldwin, Robert Wolff, and especially Harry W. Hazard as editors (vols. 1–2, Philadelphia, 1955–1962; new edition and continuation, vols. 1–5, Madison, Wis., 1969–1984). Steven Runciman's *A History of the Crusades,* 3 vols. (Cambridge, 1951–1954), presents another comprehensive, though somewhat idiosyncratic, approach. The best short introduction is Hans Eberhard Mayer's *The Crusades* (Oxford, 1972).

Carl Erdmann's classic book on the roots of the movement is now available in English: *The Origin of the Idea of Crusade* (Princeton, 1977). Still the most thorough investigation of the religious aspects is Paul Alphandéry's *La Chrétienté et l'idée de croisade,* 2 vols. (Paris, 1954–1959). Benjamin Z. Kedar's *Crusade and Mission: European Approaches toward the Muslims* (Princeton, 1984) stresses the interaction of the two main strategies toward Islam.

Much recent attention has focused on canonical and legal aspects. Major studies are James A. Brundage's *Medieval Canon Law and the Crusader* (Madison, Wis., 1969); Maureen Purcell's *Papal Crusading Policy,* "Studies in the History of Christian Thought," no. 11 (Leiden, 1975); and Joshua Prawer's *Crusader Institutions* (Oxford, 1980). A standard work on critical voices is Palmer A. Throop's *Criticism of the Crusade: A Study of Public Opinion and Crusade Propaganda* (1940; reprint, Philadelphia, 1975).

KARLFRIED FROEHLICH

Muslim Perspective

The Muslims of Syria, who were the first to receive the assault of the Crusaders, thought the invaders were Rum, the Byzantines. Accordingly, they regarded the invasion as still another Byzantine incursion into Islamic territory, and, in fact, one inspired by previous Muslim victories in Byzantine domains. It was only when the Muslims realized that the invaders did not originate in Byzantium that they began referring to them as Franks, although never as Crusaders, a term for which there was no Arabic equivalent until modern times. Even a century later, the Arab historian Ibn al-Athīr (1160–1233) characterized that first invasion as a part of the general expansion of the Frankish empire that had begun with their conquests in Muslim Spain, Sicily, and North Africa a decade before the campaign in Syria. Nevertheless, the establishment of Frankish kingdoms in Islamic territory, the periodic reinforcement of troops from Europe, and the recurrence of invasion all contributed to a growing Muslim consciousness of the nature of the Frankish threat in Syria and Palestine.

This consciousness was reflected in the development of propaganda in Arabic designed to support the mobilization of Muslim forces against the infidel troops. The second half of the twelfth century saw the emergence of both a major Muslim leader and a literature to abet his efforts. The leader was Nūr al-Dīn (1118–1174), who succeeded in forging the political unity of the Muslims of northern Syria and upper Mesopotamia, thereby providing the basis of a military force strong enough to confront the Franks. Fatimid Egypt was brought under the control of Nūr al-Dīn's lieutenant, Ṣalāḥ al-Dīn, known to the West as Saladin (1138–1193). The literature consisted of poetry, *jihād* ("holy war") tracts, and books extolling the merits of Jerusalem and Palestine. Cumulatively, these works celebrated a Muslim warrior for the faith *(mujāhid)* who would unite the believers in a *jihād* to drive the soldiers of the Cross from the holy places. After the death of Nūr al-Dīn, Ṣalāḥ al-Dīn was able to build on the former's political and military accomplishments and exploit the fervor engendered for a Muslim hero as a means of achieving spectacular success against the Crusaders. Although no single Muslim leader of equal stature emerged under the Ayyubid or Mamluk dynasties that followed, literary support for prosecution of war against the Franks flourished until the very end, when the fall of Acre and the remaining Crusader fortifications on the coast was celebrated as a great victory for Islam, the culmination of a century-old struggle.

It should be emphasized, however, that with few exceptions active support for a concerted Muslim campaign against the Franks was limited to the areas threatened with occupation, namely Syria, Palestine, and Egypt. Various attempts to enlist the help of the Abbasid caliph of Baghdad were futile, partly, no doubt, because the institution of the caliphate was by this time virtually defunct. Even Ṣalāḥ al-Dīn, who was assiduous in seeking caliphal sanction for his activities, never received more than symbolic recognition from a reluctant caliph.

It should also be pointed out that war against the Franks was never total, that Muslim rulers often felt no compunctions about allying themselves with Crusader princes in order to gain their own ends, and that the call for *jihād* was muted when it was expedient, as in 1229 when the Ayyubid ruler al-Malik al-Kāmil (d. 1238) ceded Jerusalem to Holy Roman Emperor Frederick II. Ṣalāḥ al-Dīn himself did not hesitate to strengthen Egyptian ties with the Italian commercial cities in order to obtain the materials he needed from Europe for his campaigns.

With the exception of their fortresses and churches, the Franks left few traces in Muslim territory or consciousness. Although the Muslims looted columns and at least one portal from Crusader structures and incorporated them into their mosques as trophies of victory, Islamic architecture developed independently. Nor is there any evidence of significant influence of Crusader minor arts on Islamic counterparts or, for that matter, of substantial Crusader influence on any aspect of Islamic cultural and intellectual life. There are indications, certainly, in the memoirs of the Syrian knight Usāmah ibn Munqidh (1095–1188) and the Spanish traveler Ibn Jubayr (1145–1217) that Muslims observed their Frankish neighbors with interest, interacted with them on occasion, and even approved of some aspects of their behavior—their treatment of peasants, for example. But the Muslims apparently made no effort to imitate the Franks. While it is sometimes claimed that the Crusaders contributed to the persecution of Christians in Muslim territory, the evidence for this is by no means consistent. There are clear signs that the Muslims in Egypt could and did distinguish between the Copts and the Franks and treated each accordingly. Probably the main Crusader legacy to the Arab Muslims should be sought in the field of commerce. There is little doubt that the activities of European merchants in eastern Mediterranean ports continued to be tolerated, even encouraged, by the Muslim conquerors and thus kept commercial contacts between East and West alive. However, recent Arabic historiography depicts the Crusaders as precursors of modern European infiltrations of the Arab world.

BIBLIOGRAPHY

A detailed study of the Muslim response to the Crusades is Emmanuel Sivan's *L'Islam et la croisade: Idéologie et propagande dans les réactions musulmanes aux croisades* (Paris, 1968), which, though it focuses on the ideological reaction, relates it to political and military events as well. For a different perspective on some of the material discussed by Sivan, see Hadia Dajani-Shakeel's "Jihād in Twelfth-Century Arabic Poetry: A Moral and Religious Force to Counter the Crusades," *Muslim World* 66 (April 1976): 96–113. See also Amin Maalouf's *The Crusades through Arab Eyes* (London, 1984).

Attitudes of contemporary Arab Muslims toward the Crusades can be studied firsthand in *Arab Historians of the Crusades,* edited by Francesco Gabrieli and translated from the Italian by E. J. Costello (Berkeley, 1969), and in Usāmah ibn Munqidh's *Memoirs of an Arab-Syrian Gentleman or an Arab Knight in the Crusades,* translated by Philip K. Hitti (1927; reprint, Beirut, 1964). For a comparative study of Muslim and Christian concepts of holy war see Albrecht Noth's *Heiliger Krieg und Heiliger Kampf im Islam und Christentum* (Bonn, 1966).

DONALD P. LITTLE

CÚ CHULAINN. *See* Táin Bó Cuailnge; *see also* Celtic Religion.

CULT. *See* Community; New Religions; *and* Religious Communities, *article on* Religion, Community, and Society.

CULT OF SAINTS.

[*This entry discusses Christian traditions and practices associated with saints. For related discussions in broader religious context, see* Sainthood; Pilgrimage; Relics; *and* Shrines.]

The cult of saints in the early Christian church began with the commemoration and veneration of the victims of persecution. The earliest forms of this veneration were part of the traditional funerary *memoria* of the dead. The inclusion of the names of martyrs in the liturgies of early Christian communities and the earliest celebrations of the anniversaries of martyrs, often observed at their tombs, rapidly gave rise to specific cults that went far beyond mere commemoration of the dead. The practice of petitions addressed to martyrs on behalf of the living arose out of the belief in the communion of saints, the resurrection of the body, and the high status accorded those who had died for the faith, and who, through their remains, remained physically present among the living. The acceptance of the intercessory role of the martyrs can be seen as early as the *Passion of Saint Perpetua* (early third century). [*See* Persecution, *article on* Christian Experience.]

Although the martyr epitomized the ideal type of saint for centuries, the end of the period of persecution (early fourth century) brought with it a new concept of sanctity: namely, that those persons who lived lives of constant self-martyrdom and extraordinary virtue—had there been persecutions they too would have been martyrs—were also worthy of veneration. Increasingly, first in Syria but then throughout Christendom, persons living lives of extraordinary asceticism were venerated as *sancti* (holy persons). *Sancti* were thought capable of exerting hidden supernatural powers through miracles and, as an extension of this, powers within human society. Thus, *sancti* functioned as mediators among local groups and between local communities and regional and central powers. The sort of human and supernatural patronage that these individuals provided was thought to continue at the site of their tombs after they had died. The bodies were preserved and honored as pledges (Lat., *pignora*) of their continued interest in the living. The sorts of veneration accorded to them—vows, petitions for cures and other miracles, incubation at their tombs, and offerings of goods and specie to the clerics who had charge of their tombs—closely resembled the practices associated with pre-Christian pagan cults, such as that of Asklepios. [*See* Asklepios.]

The initial cult of saints was focused on their tombs, but the increasing demand for cult objects in the fourth century led, in the eastern part of the empire, to the practice of moving bodies of saints to new locations, although such translations and the practice of dismembering bodies and distributing the various parts as relics were against Roman law. Along with the veneration of saints through their corporeal remains, a cult of saints focusing on their images, or icons, developed in the East. This cult, apparently encouraged by emperors as an extension and reinforcement of the secular cult of the emperor's image, survived the violent iconoclastic attacks of the seventh and eighth centuries and became a major aspect of Eastern Christianity. [*See* Icons *and* Iconoclasm.]

In the West, the cult of saints was more conservative and, throughout the eighth century, continued to focus on the tombs of martyrs and early confessors. Nevertheless, objects that had been in physical proximity to saints' tombs were distributed as relics, particularly by the bishops of Rome, who gained much of their prestige from controlling large quantities of remains of Roman martyrs. Relics of the saints played a major role in the christianization of the West because the relics were offered to new converts to replace their pagan gods. The locations where bodies or relics were found became primary sites for contact between the human and divine worlds and formed the basis for the reorganization of sacred geography. While the classical world had emphasized the sacrality of urban space and considered extraurban cemeteries unclean, the Christian cult of martyrs and saints gave priority to the suburban cemeteries at the expense of the city.

Churchmen such as Pope Gregory the Great (d. 604) and the bishop Gregory of Tours (d. 594), both of whom sought to establish indigenous Christian traditions, attempted to anchor the cult of saints within the control of the hierarchy by deemphasizing living saints, who were, after all, difficult to regulate, in favor of the dead and by writing lives of Western martyrs and confessors. In these lives and in early medieval hagiography (literature dealing with saints)—which included not only *passiones* ("accounts of martyrdom") but *vitae* ("lives"), *libri miraculorum* ("books of miracles"), and *translations* ("accounts of translations")—saints were largely presented as members of social elites elected before birth as instruments of divine power. The social roles of such saints were severely limited: aside from the early martyrs, the men were normally bishops or monks and the women were almost without exception members of religious orders who had spent their lives in the cloister. The saints' lives and the promotion of their cults, particularly those of Merovingian saints written in the seventh century, were often closely related to the efforts of aristocratic relatives to establish a sacred heritage on which to base their claims of lordship. Thus saints were presented less a models of the Christian life than as evidence of supernatural power.

Threats to Rome by the Lombards in the mid-eighth century led popes to translate the remains of many martyrs into the city from the undefended catacombs. The Franco-papal political and cultural alliances of the following century resulted in an unprecedented number of translations—both sanctioned and illicit—of saints from Rome, Spain, and Gaul to the northern and eastern territories of the Frankish empire.

The demand for the remains of the saints for the purpose of promoting Christianity was enormously important in the subsequent development of medieval religion. In the ninth through eleventh centuries Roman martyrs and local saints, who were often deemed responsible for the evangelization of specific regions, were the focus of much of religious life. Veneration centered on the tombs of the saints, usually buried under the sanctuary of a church. Access to these tombs was controlled by the clergy of the church, frequently monks or canons, who were responsible for the celebration of the liturgy of the saints and direction of the cult. The importance of saints as miracle workers, patrons, and protectors of the region in which their remains were found resulted in the advent of pilgrimages made on principal feast days as well as at other times in the fulfillment of individual vows. The need to accommodate numbers of pilgrims without disrupting the regular liturgical life of the church led to the development of the characteristic pilgrimage church, with its raised crypt and wide ambulatories allowing the faithful to reach the saint's tomb or shrine without disturbing the liturgical life of the community.

During the tenth century the popularity of three-dimensional images of saints began to increase, particularly in the south of France. These statues, which were not unknown earlier and probably developed from statue reliquaries, became increasingly important during the twelfth century, when expanded contact with the Near East and improved internal communication and centralization contributed to the growth of the cults of more international saints, particularly the Virgin and the apostles of Christ. Although relics of the saints maintained their importance, miraculous statues and paintings, particularly in Italy during the later Middle Ages, became the focus of devotions.

Some saints' cults, such as those of the martyrs in

Rome, the cult of Saint James in Compostela, and the cult of Saint Foy (Faith) in Conques, became international in their appeal. Most cults, however, were primarily local and regional. Consequently, competition between cults of different saints and between different cult locations for the same saint could be fierce. Beginning in the twelfth century devotion to exclusively local saints gave way to more individual or group choices of patrons as both laity and religious chose specific patrons for their activities and organizations. Devotion to particular patrons became an integral aspect of solidarity and identity in religious orders and communities, lay fraternities, craft and trade guilds, communes, and nascent states. In addition, specific saints became identified with specific types of miracles and thus were sought for specialized assistance.

The competition among cults, as well as the concern of secular and religious authorities over the proper identification and recognition of saints, led in the course of the later Middle Ages to an increasingly formal means of authentication of saints. Prior to the ninth century the process had been extremely informal: the existence of a popular cult among the faithful was usually seen as proof of sanctity. Starting in the ninth century, however, church synods insisted that no new or previously unknown saints could be venerated unless their sanctity was proved by the authenticity of their lives and miracles. The determination of authenticity was the responsibility of the local bishop; recognition meant the inclusion of the saint's name and feast day (usually the traditional anniversary of his or her death) in the liturgical calendar of the diocese. As of the tenth century local groups increasingly sought the inclusion of the saint's feast in the Roman calendar as well, and in time this led to the customary request that the pope recognize the saint's cult with a solemn canonization. With the growth of papal centralization, this practice became more formalized, and from the time of the pontificate of Innocent III (1198–1216), the right of canonization has been reserved to the pope. This did not, however, change the primary role of the faithful in the development of the actual cult. On the contrary, the role of the faithful was of the utmost importance: without an existing cult and evidence of post mortem miracles, no individual, no matter how exemplary his or her life, could be canonized. Because of the enormous expense, political negotiations, and investment of time necessary to effect a papal canonization, very few of the hundreds of persons who were the objects of cults were ever actually canonized, and those who were tended to be members of princely or aristocratic families or important religious orders who could organize, finance, and sustain the canonization process.

The intervention of the papacy in the recognition of saints as well as the social and economic transformations of the later Middle Ages prompted a change in the popular image of saints. From the thirteenth century on, more emphasis was placed on the quality of life of the individual as an imitation of the life of Christ than on miracles. The spectrum of social backgrounds from which the venerated men and women came was also greatly broadened. Under the influence of mendicant spirituality there were more saints from the bourgeoisie, more women who had active roles outside the cloister, and more laity who were seen to have achieved sanctity.

Throughout the late Middle Ages there existed a broad consensus on both the existence of a sort of sensorial code by which one could recognize special servants of God and on a belief in the saint's ability to intervene in all areas of human need. However, from the twelfth century on, a widening gulf separated the mental structures of the laity and the majority of the clergy from the university-trained elite. In the later Middle Ages three groups of persons developed who were accorded sanctity based both on geography and social position. According to André Vauchez (1981), the popular saints were the first group. Venerated primarily in rural areas—generally in northern Europe—they were the closest to the archaic type of saint: persons who, regardless of life and piety, met violent and undeserved deaths. The second group, local saints, varied according to region. In northern Europe they were, as in the early Middle Ages, persons of high rank whose bodies produced miracles. In the Mediterranean world, the local saints were most often persons who had renounced a normal existence for voluntary asceticism, poverty, and chastity. The third group of saints most closely resembled the type of saints whose cults were promoted by the official church.

The official teaching concerning the communion of the saints, the efficacy of the saints as intercessors and, thus, the validity of the cult of saints, has always insisted that whereas saints may be the object of veneration (Gr., *dulia*), they must never be the object of adoration (Gr., *latria*). Since the virtues of the saints are the virtues of Christ, praise of the saints, prayers to them, and veneration of their relics are all ultimately directed to Christ. The reality of several of the specific cults of saints, however, was often at great variance with this official position, and throughout the Middle Ages orthodox reformers occasionally objected to excesses or deviations from the official stance. From the late twelfth century on, radical reformers, such as Pierre Valdès, founder of the Waldensians, went still further by rejecting the intercessory role of saints, thereby denying the validity of the cult. Sixteenth-century reformers, especially John Calvin, were even more forceful in rejecting the mediatory role of saints and condemning the cult of relics and images as idolatry. Despite these oppositions, the cult of saints, especially that of the Virgin, has continued to play an important role within the Catholic tradition, particularly in southern Europe and in Latin America, where the cult of Christian saints has merged with indigenous and African cults in a process similar to that which took place in Europe in late antiquity.

[*For further discussion, see* Popular Christian Religiosity *and* Pilgrimage, *articles on* Roman Catholic Pilgrimage in Europe, Roman Catholic Pilgrimage in the New World, *and* Eastern Christian Pilgrimage.]

BIBLIOGRAPHY

Peter Brown's *The Cult of the Saints: Its Rise and Function in Latin Christianity* (Chicago, 1981) is a brief, interpretative introduction to the cult of saints in late antiquity. More specialized are his articles on saints and holy men in his *Society and the Holy in Late Antiquity* (Berkeley, 1982). Ernst Kitzinger's "The Cult of Images in the Age before Iconoclasm," *Dumbarton Oaks Papers* 8 (1954): 83–150, reprinted in his *The Art of Byzantium and the Medieval West* (Bloomington, Ind., 1976), pp. 90–156, remains a fundamental introduction to the development of the cult of icons by a leading art historian. In František Graus's *Volk, Herrscher und Heiliger im Reich der Merowinger: Studien zur Hagiographie der Merowingerzeit* (Prague, 1965), the important Czech historian provides a classic study of the place of saints and hagiography in early medieval society. For the later, Carolingian, period, Joseph-Claude Poulin's *L'idéal de sainteté dans l'Aquitaine carolingienne d'après les sources hagiographiques, 750-950* (Quebec, 1975) examines the changing values of society as reflected in the cult of saints.

Three recent studies have examined the cult of saints in the later Middle Ages in relation to changing social forms and spiritual values. Michael Goodich's *Vita Perfecta: The Ideal of Sainthood in the Thirteenth Century* (Stuttgart, 1982) presents a computer-assisted prosopographical analysis of thirteenth-century saints as an ideal cultural type. Donald Weinstein and Rudolph M. Bell, in their *Saints and Society: The Two Worlds of Western Christendom, 1000-1700* (Chicago, 1982), examine saints between 1000 and 1700 in order to understand the transformation of late medieval and early modern piety. The most important of the three is that of André Vauchez, *La sainteté en Occident au derniers siècles du Moyen-Âge d'après les proces de canonisation et les documents hagiographiques* (Rome, 1981). This magisterial examination of the cult of saints in the later Middle Ages is essential for understanding the interplay of social, religious, political, and cultural factors in the cult of saints.

A number of recent anthologies have collected important articles on saints from specialized journals. The most significant of these are *Agiografia altomedievale*, edited by Sofia Boesch Gajano (Bologna, 1976), and *Saints and Their Cults: Studies in Religious Sociology, Folklore and History*, edited by Stephen Wilson (Cambridge, 1983). The latter is particularly valuable for its rich annotated bibliography on all aspects of saints and hagiography both Christian and non-Christian.

PATRICK J. GEARY

CULTS OF AFFLICTION. *See* Affliction, *article on* African Cults of Affliction.

CULTURE CIRCLES. *See* Kulturkreiselehre.

CULTURE HEROES. The culture hero is a mythical being found in the religious traditions of many archaic societies. Although he sometimes assists the supreme being in the creation of the world, his most important activity occurs after creation, when he makes the world habitable and safe for mankind. He establishes institutions for humans, brings them cultural goods, and instructs them in the arts of civilization. Thus, he introduces culture to human beings. [*See* Cosmogony.]

The culture hero, unlike the supreme being, is neither omniscient nor omnipotent. In some cases, his behavior resembles that of a clown or buffoon; in the myths of many North American Indian tribes he appears as the trickster. Various scholars have referred to the culture hero as transformer, demiurge, culture bringer, *héros civilisateur*, and, most frequently, *Heilbringer*.

History of Scholarship. The German historian Kurt Breysig first introduced the term *Heilbringer* in 1905. Since then, the idea of the culture hero has been interpreted in various ways. Early interpretations emphasized the place of the culture hero in the evolution of the idea of a supreme being. Breysig, for example, saw the culture hero as belonging to a stage of religious development that was not only earlier than, but also inferior to, mankind's awareness of a personal supreme being. The German ethnologist Paul Ehrenreich, in developing his theory of "nature mythology," interpreted the myths about culture heroes as attempts by primitive man to understand his natural surroundings. Ehrenreich saw in the culture hero the embodiment of the structure and rhythms of natural phenomena, for example, the rising and setting of the sun, the waxing and waning of the moon, and the movement of the stars and constellations. On the other hand, Wilhelm Schmidt, an ethnologist and historian of religions, was the chief proponent of the doctrine of primitive monotheism *(Urmonotheismus)*. Theorizing that even early man believed in a supreme being, he contended that the *Heilbringer* was never a genuine creator and that the form appeared in archaic societies after, not before, the idea of the supreme being.

The interpretations of Breysig, Ehrenreich, and Schmidt have been rejected by later students of culture and historians of religions, who, having access to more and different ethnological data, have recognized the autonomy and complexity of the culture hero. Scholars such as Hermann Baumann, Adolf E. Jensen, Mircea Eliade, Otto Zerries, Raffaele Pettazzoni, and Harry Tegnaeus have made significant contributions to a new appreciation and understanding of the culture hero. Rather than pursue an evolutionary approach, these scholars have examined the relation between the details of the myths and the historical and cultural realities of the archaic societies—their economic activity, their political and social institutions, and their attitude toward space, time, and mortality.

Characteristic Activities. In many of the myths that tell of his exploits, the culture hero is portrayed as setting the stage for human survival. The myth of the Jicarilla Apaches of the southwestern United States tells how the culture hero Jonayaiuin saved mankind by destroying huge monsters that were killing people. By removing this threat of annihilation, the culture hero made the world fit for human habitation. The Malecite Indians of northern Maine tell that long ago a monster, Aglabem, withheld all the water in the world, causing people to die of thirst. Their culture hero, referred to as "a great man," killed Aglabem and released the waters by felling a huge tree. This tree became the Saint John River; its branches, the tributaries of the river; its leaves, the ponds and lakes at the heads of the streams. To the tellers of this myth, the shape of the landscape is evidence that the culture hero made the world fit for human life.

In various ways, the culture hero creates distinctions between men and animals. The Tupian peoples of the Amazon basin in eastern Brazil believe that Korupira, a deity who is referred to as "lord of the beasts," protects wild game against human hunters. Korupira has the power to close the forest to hunters and punish those who kill his animals needlessly. [*See also* Lord of the Animals.] The Mbuti, hunters and gatherers who inhabit the rain forest of Zaire, are one of many groups who credit their culture hero with bringing them fire. The Mbuti hero, Tore, stole fire, much to the chagrin of the neighboring chimpanzees, and gave it to mankind. From that time on, man has enjoyed the use of fire while chimpanzees have lived in the forest without it. In the stories of numerous societies, the culture hero introduced humans to speech and manners, established the social differences between males and females, and instituted the laws of society.

The culture hero is also perceived as making economic life possible for humans. According to the myths of the San (Bushmen), a hunting and gathering people living in South Africa and Namibia, the culture hero Kaang created all wild game and gave the animals their colors, names, and characteristics. He taught the San how to make bows, poisoned arrows, traps, and snares, and he instructed them in hunting techniques. Tudava, the culture hero of the Trobriand Islanders, not only taught the Trobrianders how to build canoes and to fish but introduced them to the cultivation of yams and taros, the first root crops. Nyikang, the culture hero and first king of the Shilluk, pastoral nomads of East Africa, is said to have been the son of a cow. He released the waters and provided grazing land for the Shilluk's cattle. Among the Dogon people of Mali, West Africa, the twin culture heroes known as Nommo are credited with bringing the first millet seeds from heaven to earth and with teaching the arts of blacksmithing and pottery.

In numerous myths, the culture hero is connected with the origin of death. [*See* Death.] In a story told by the Khoi (Hottentots) of South Africa, the moon sends an insect to tell men that after they die they will come back to life, as the moon does. The culture hero, Hare, overtakes the insect and volunteers to carry the message. However, Hare delivers the opposite message to men, saying that they will perish forever.

Through the adventures in which he ensures human survival, institutes the difference between humans and animals, introduces mankind to social and economic activity, and originates human mortality, the culture hero saves mankind from chaos. He orders and arranges the world, introducing mankind to the possibilities of human creativity.

Birth of the Culture Hero. The culture hero is able to perform these feats because he is imbued with power; he comes from another world. His divine origin is revealed in his parentage and in the supernatural nature of his birth. Tudava, the culture hero of the Trobriand Islanders, was said to have been born of a mother who became pregnant while sleeping in a cave, when her vagina was pierced by water dripping from a stalactite. The mother of Manabozho, the culture hero of the Menomini tribe of North America, was made pregnant by the wind. The mother of the culture hero of the Dinka of East Africa came to earth already pregnant. Among several African peoples, the culture hero was born from the knee or thigh of a man or woman. Regardless of the way the culture hero is born, his origin is not of this world.

Disappearance and Transmutation. After setting the world in order for humankind, the culture hero usually disappears. Sometimes he is killed while conquering monsters; frequently he returns from whence he came—into the sky or earth. In the myths of several peoples, the culture hero is transformed into the moon or stars or constellations. In other instances, particularly among the Australian tribes, he disappears into the earth at a specific spot, which is marked by a stone, a plant, or a body of water. Such a place, imbued as it is with power, becomes the site of the tribe's initiation and increase ceremonies.

One of the dramatic myths of the disappearance and transformation of a culture hero is that of the people on the island of Ceram in Indonesia, reported by the German ethnologist Adolf E. Jensen. The principal culture hero, Hainuwele, who in this case was a maiden, was murdered by other beings in mythical times. Their punishment, imposed by Hainuwele's sister, was that they were forced to consume the body of their victim. Then the body of Hainuwele was transformed into useful root crops, which before that time had not existed. Her sister became mistress of the underworld. This primeval murder signaled the end of mythical time and the beginning of the historical world.

The events leading up to the murder and transformation of Hainuwele established the institution of cannibalism among the people of Ceram. It also established the initiation ceremony: the young men must kill, imitating the primordial murder of Hainuwele as part of their rite of passage to manhood. Further consequences of this murder were the cultivation of root crops, the delineation of the people into separate clans, the establishment of cult houses, the separation of humans from ghosts and spirits, and the establishment of rules governing entrance to the mythical land of the afterlife. Jensen's research demonstrated the significance of the murdered culture hero among those peoples who practice root crop cultivation.

In the mythology of the Cheyenne of North America, maize originated from the murdered body of their culture hero. The transmutation of the culture hero into food, however, is not limited to the myths of agricultural societies. The Central Inuit (Eskimo) tell of Sedna, a female culture hero, who was murdered by her father. Different sea animals emerged from parts of her mutilated body—whales from her fingers, whale bones from her fingernails, and seals from the second joints of her fingers. As in the case of Hainuwele's sister, Sedna became the mistress of the underworld.

Various Manifestations. The culture hero often appears as twins, who usually symbolize opposites. [*See* Twins.] They may be of different sexes. Frequently the elder is the hero while the younger is depicted as foolish and inept. The twin heroes of the Iroquois of North America are brothers who have different fathers: one, who represents good, is the son of the sun, while his brother, who represents evil, is the son of the waters.

While Hainuwele, Sedna, and many other culture heroes are anthropomorphic, the culture heroes of many societies are theriomorphic. [*See* Animals.] In Oceania, the culture hero is frequently a snake; in South America he is often a jaguar. In many tribes of North America and Africa, the culture hero appears as an animal or insect and has the characteristics of a trickster. Ananse the spider, the culture hero of many of the peoples of West Africa, is popularly known as "the foolish one"; the southern African San's culture hero, Praying Mantis, is seen as a mischievous trickster. Among North American tribes, the coyote, the hare, the mink, the chipmunk, and the crow are common forms of the trickster.

In many instances, the activities of the trickster parallel those of other culture heroes: he destroys monsters, creates animals, and introduces men to various forms of technology and social institutions. However, his adventures are also marked by failures and stumblings, deceptions and lies, awkwardness and crudity. He is often portrayed as oversexed, gluttonous, and amoral. The trickster continually violates the institutions and prohibitions he has established. He can be alternately gracious and cruel, truthful and mendacious. [*See* Tricksters.]

The American anthropologist Paul Radin (1956) interprets the figure of the trickster and his adventures as symbolic of mankind's development from an undifferentiated psyche to a differentiated and individual one. The adventures of the trickster, Radin contends, are symbolic of the movement from a state of asociality or nonsociality to one of sociality, from isolation to being a part of the community. The trickster not only creates or modifies the physical and social environment of mankind; by his violation of the social rules and the contempt he exhibits toward sacred objects, he creates a kind of internal space for mankind. He legitimates rebellion and disobedience by constantly challenging the status quo of the cosmos.

The phenomenon of the culture hero is very complex. Although the hero usually appears as male, some cultures have a culture heroine. In some societies, the hero is the object of a cult; in others he is not. Sometimes he appears as the offspring of the supreme being and assists in creation; in other instances, he is the supreme being's adversary. His visible form ranges from human to animal, from insect to heavenly body.

Having completed his task on earth, the culture hero disappears; sometimes he ascends to the sky or descends to the underworld. Occasionally he is transformed into a natural phenomenon such as the stars or the moon, while in some religious traditions his parting accounts for shapes in the landscape.

In spite of the multifarious forms and adventures of

the culture hero as he appears in different cultures, he clearly discloses one characteristic: his mode of being reveals the sacrality of cultural and social institutions and activities that constitute the context of ordinary life for mankind. Participation in these activities by the people of archaic societies provides meaning and value to their lives and enables them to live in a sacred cosmos.

BIBLIOGRAPHY

A general discussion of the culture hero can be found in the chapter entitled "Mythische Urzeitwesen und Heilbringer" in Ferdinand Hermann's *Symbolik in den Religionen der Naturvölker* (Stuttgart, 1961), pp. 98–109. This book also contains an excellent bibliography. Two good books on the culture hero in Africa are Hermann Baumann's *Schöpfung und Urzeit des Menschen im Mythus der afrikanischen Völker* (Berlin, 1936) and Harry Tegnaeus's *Le héros civilisateur* (Stockholm, 1950). Otto Zerries's *Wild- und Buschgeister in Sudamerika* (Weisbaden, 1954) is an exhaustive study of the culture hero in the myths of hunting and gathering cultures in South America. The role of the culture hero among archaic cultivators is discussed in Adolf E. Jensen's *Myth and Cult among Primitive Peoples* (Chicago, 1963). This book also treats the relation of the culture hero to the supreme being. The pioneering work on the trickster figure among North American Indians in Paul Radin's *The Trickster: A Study in American Indian Mythology* (New York, 1956). A readable and enlightening critique of Radin's position can be found in Mac Linscott Ricketts's "The North American Indian Trickster," *History of Religions* 5 (Winter 1966): 327–350. Robert D. Pelton, in *The Trickster in West Africa: A Study of Mythic Irony and Sacred Delight* (Berkeley, 1980) extends the study of the trickster to the peoples of Africa and applies methods of literary criticism in his analysis.

JEROME H. LONG

CULTUS. *See* Worship and Cultic Life; *see also* Ritual.

CUMONT, FRANZ (1868–1947), Belgian historian of religions, philologist, archaeologist, and epigraphist. Franz-Valéry-Marie Cumont studied at Ghent, Bonn, Berlin, Vienna, Rome, and Paris, and was professor of classical philology at the University of Ghent. He left that position in 1912 when he was refused the chair of history of religions by the minister of public education. From then on, being a man of independent means, he lived as a private scholar in Rome and Paris. His first major study, *Textes et monuments figurés relatifs aux mystères de Mithra* (1894–1899; an abridged version was translated into English as *The Mysteries of Mithra* and published in 1910), remained the standard work on Mithraism for more than half a century. He then went successively to Asia Minor, Syria, and Mesopotamia, and his hope of solving the problem of the origin of the Mithra mysteries was frustrated. The Mithraeum at Dura-Europos, on the Euphrates, was discovered after he had ceased working there.

Cumont's reconstruction of the Mithra mysteries is now generally considered biased: whenever a feature of Mithraism was found both in the religion of ancient Iran and in that of Greece or Rome, he never hesitated to plump for the Iranian origin. This position has been repeatedly challenged, with some measure of success.

He remained interested in ancient Iran almost to the end of his life, but never took the trouble to learn its languages. Although engrossed in the problem of Eastern influences in Greece and Rome, which he perhaps exaggerated, he remained a classicist. Cumont's lectures, given as a guest professor at the Collège de France, formed the basis for his *Les religions orientales dans le paganisme romain* (1906), which went through four editions; it was translated as *The Oriental Religions in Roman Paganism* (1911). This work contains lectures on cults from Asia Minor, Egypt, Syria, and Iran, and concludes with a lecture on astrology and magic. The Phrygian goddess Cybele, portrayed with her partner Attis, was introduced to the Romans as Magna Mater in 204 BCE. The mysteries of Isis and Serapis (the latter a Ptolemaic creation) came to Rome from Egypt and gained the favor of the common people despite opposition from the political and religious officials. The cults of Atargatis and other Semitic deities came from Syria and brought to Rome the theological doctrines of the Chaldeans. Though Mithra was originally an Iranian god, Cumont recognized the fact that the cult of Mithra probably developed under Hellenistic influence in either Asia Minor or Rome. These religious cults, Cumont believed, paved the way for the adoption of Christianity.

With the Hellenist Joseph Bidez, Cumont published *Les mages héllenisés* (1938), a critical edition of and abundant commentary on texts (mostly in Greek) that were issued in antiquity under the authority of "Zarathushtra" or some other so-called magus. The title of the book, however, is misleading, for the very existence of hellenized magi remains doubtful: many if not all of those works were written by Greeks, Romans, and others, who were not magi.

In his work *Recherches sur le symbolisme funéraire des Romains* (1942) Cumont argued that though a small proportion of the funerary art was supposed to represent literally the afterlife in the netherworld, the atmosphere, or the moon, most of this art was allegorical. Cumont examines how the Greek myths—such as the stories of Phaethon, of Marsyas's challenge of Apollo, of the union of Ares and Aphrodite, and of the Muses—

came to be used, through philosophical interpretation, as themes for the sculpture that decorated the sarcophagi of the upper classes. Some of these figures depict the dead as eternally sleeping or banqueting, others allude to the former labors of the deceased on earth as peasants, hunters, or soldiers.

A book Cumont published in the United States in 1922, *After Life in Roman Paganism*, was considerably changed when it was posthumously published in French under the title *Lux Perpetua* (1949). In this work, Cumont traces the development of the idea of the soul. According to ancient popular belief, a dead person survived in the tomb or as a shadow in the netherworld and could return to earth as a ghost to haunt the living. Belief in celestial immortality, although probably based on the simple association of earthly fires with the fire of heavenly lights, appeared to Cumont to have been borrowed from Irano-Chaldean magi by Greek philosophers. This belief, owing to Pythagorean, Platonic, and Stoic influences, gradually spread from the cultivated elite to the general populace. However, at this point, the soul was still not conceived of as nonmaterial; rather, it was believed to be a subtle fluid or vapor. It was not until the rise of Neoplatonism that the opinion arose, which prevailed in Christianity, that the soul was distinct from the conditions of space and time and reached, after death, beyond the limits of the world into eternity. Cumont's work on this subject continues to be the standard text.

In 1935 Cumont was elected president of the International Congress for the History of Religions held in Brussels, and in 1947 he bequeathed his rich library to the Academia Belgica in Rome.

BIBLIOGRAPHY

Biographical sketches of Cumont can be found in *Biographie nationale* 39, supp. 11 (1978): 211–222, and in *Nationaal Biographisch Woordenboek* 1 (1964). 361–366, written by F. de Ruyt and G. Sanders, respectively. A summary of Cumont's work appears in an article by Julien Ries in the *Dictionnaire des religions* (Paris, 1984), pp. 362–363.

JACQUES DUCHESNE-GUILLEMIN

CUNA RELIGION.

There are perhaps forty thousand Cuna Indians today, living mostly in the San Blas Reserve on Panama's Atlantic coast, with small groups along the interior Bayano and Chucanaque rivers and in three villages in Colombia. The Cuna survived the traumatic but ephemeral Spanish conquest of the Darien Isthmus (modern-day Isthmus of Panama) after 1510. They are thus one of the few remnants of the flourishing pre-Colombian chieftaincies of the circum-Caribbean. The Cuna maintained their autonomy partly by allying themselves with the buccaneers who harassed the Spaniards.

Cult Organization. Institutionally, Cuna religion is organized in both communal and shamanic cults. The communal cult is maintained by the village chiefs *(sailakana),* who chant from oral mythological texts known as Pap Ikar ("god's way") some three nights a week to the assembled village. Official interpreters *(arkarana)* explain the arcane language of the chants, using homilies on contemporary morality. Female puberty feasts are collective rites sponsored by each village once a year.

The shamanic cult is not conducted communally, save for the rite of village exorcism that occurs during epidemics or other collective dangers. Shamans (*nele*s) are credited with clairvoyance, through trance or dreams, into the four layers of the underworld. *Nele*s, who may be male or female, are born to their role and are discovered by midwives through signs in their afterbirth. A born *nele* must nurture the gift and be apprenticed to an adult *nele.*

Other experts are not clairvoyants. All know a sacred text, *ikar* ("path" or "way"). These texts invoke spiritual helpers, such as stick dolls *(suar nuchu)* or magical stones *(akwanusu),* as allies in combating evil, meddlesome spirits, who usually have captured the patient's soul and who hold it in their stronghold at the fourth level of the underworld. In addition, there are herbalists *(inatuleti)* who know native plant medicines and brief incantations. Usually these specialists go to work only after a *nele* has clairvoyantly diagnosed the patient.

The various curing, exorcism, female puberty, and funerary texts are all recited verbatim as learned from an authoritative master. Not so with the texts of the chiefly God's Way. Chiefs are free to render myths as they see fit, or even to recount events from recent history. Some of their chants are not narratives, but complicated poetic metaphors.

Cosmogony and Mythic Themes. Cuna cosmogony, as disclosed in God's Way, posits an original creation by God, who sends the first man, Wako, to earth. In a primordial paradise, Wako finds the earth to be his mother, and the rivers, the sun, the moon, and the stars to be his brothers. The trees are young women. Wako lives here blissfully until God calls him back. (This image of a primordial paradise resembles the childhood of a male Cuna in a matrilocal household belonging to his mother and composed of his brothers and sisters, the type of household that exists before marriage disperses the brothers to other households and brings in outsiders to marry the sisters. Thus Wako does not have to grow up.)

Wako is merely the first of many human sons or emissaries whom God sends to earth. Most of their descendants become corrupt, necessitating more emissaries to correct them. When this fails, God repeatedly visits catastrophic punishments upon mankind and the cycle begins again. This is not quite a creation cycle since mankind is never destroyed and created anew. Rather, emissary prophets attempt to correct wayward peoples. They succeed with some, for a time; others degenerate into evil spirits and—later—"animal people."

After Wako, God sends Piler, together with his wife, to found the human race. Piler's grandchildren become vainglorious and quarrelsome. After two successive groups of emissary teachers fail to correct them, God upturns the world, banishing Piler's descendants to the fourth layer of the underworld, where they remain as *ponikan* ("evil ones") ready to wreak illness upon mankind.

The next great emissary prophet is Mako, sent to correct the obstreperous *ponikan* who are making their way through tunnels up from the underworld. Like Piler, Mako is given a wife by God. Both he and his wife are called back to God unblemished. Their three morally ambiguous children, who are neither exemplarily good nor particularly evil, start the major cycle of Cuna mythology: that of Tat Ipelele ("grandfather lord shaman"; also, the personified sun).

Ipelele and his six siblings are born of an incestuous union between two of Mako's children. Forced by their crime to flee, Ipelele's father becomes the Moon, while Ipelele's mother takes refuge with Frogwoman. Frogwoman's animal sons devour Ipelele's mother, and Frogwoman raises the children as her own. Ipelele discovers the secret of his birth and journeys to the underworld to find the herbal medicines that will revive his mother. Able to restore her only temporarily, Ipelele then devotes his life to heroic struggles against the descendants of Piler, as well as against other enemies.

Ipelele marries the daughters of evil chiefs to learn their secrets. He gives his sister to Wind in order to make an ally of him. He discovers the powers inherent in tobacco, hot pepper smoke, and cacao incense to make the *ponikan* drunk and helpless during feasts he offers them. He turns many of them into "animal people," animal spirits with their own strongholds at the fourth layer of the underworld. He finds allies in magical stones and stick spirits (from the balsa tree), which are the magical allies of shamans today. At one point, he even defeats the *ponikan* in battle, leaving the battlefield strewn with their corpses. Finally, Ipelele is called back to heaven to become the Sun, riding each day in a giant canoe steered by his helmsman servant and accompanied by his sister.

After Ipelele's ascent, the cycle of emissary preachers, human corruption, and catastrophic punishment (by fire, wind, darkness, and flood) is repeated four more times. After the final flood comes the beginning of the present epoch. Here the great tribal culture hero, Ipeorkun ("lord gold kuna") arrives among the Cuna, who are at this time corrupt, ignorant, and little different from the "animal people" who surround them.

Mythic Origin of Cuna Culture. Now there is a reversal of the usual theme. Instead of the descendants of a prophet lord becoming corrupt, the Cuna (like Ipelele before them) discover their true identity as *olotule* ("golden people") and shed the filthy ways of the animal people. Ipeorkun, like Mako, is not a warrior but is rather a teacher who reveals the particulars of Cuna culture: female puberty ceremonies; bodily cleanliness and, closely associated with it, purity; "correct" (Cuna) kin terms; terms for parts of the body; how to use the magical spirit allies of the shamans and the texts that control them; how to mourn properly; how to build proper houses; how to sleep in hammocks; and, finally, the texts of God's Way. His sister teaches women the arts of cleanliness and sewing. Ipeorkun—like Wako, Mako, and Ipelele—is called to God.

After Ipeorkun come the eight Ipelerkan ("lord shamans") to continue his teachings. They grow vainglorious and corrupt, now in specifically Cuna ways. For instance, one of them who knows the female puberty text keeps the young initiates for himself. The eight Ipelerkan are corrected by a young son of one of them, Nele Kwani, who foresees a drought (another punishment from God) and bests them all in a contest of magical powers.

Although the Cuna are a horticultural people whose staple is the banana in various forms, and whose cash crop is the coconut, neither crop is sacralized or commemorated in any myths yet collected. Cacao, tobacco, balsa wood, and magical stones, all supernatural allies in the struggle against evil, are, however, richly attested in the Ipelele cycle of narratives.

Cosmology. Cuna cosmology, with its four levels above and four below the earth, is continuously revealed by the *nele*s, who mystically journey through the cosmos, often forging alliances with evil spirits to learn their secrets. In the underworld are the strongholds of the kings of the spiritual allies. Heaven itself, revealed by the *nele*s through a chant that recounts the adventures of a soul brought back from the dead, is a stronghold at the fourth layer above. Its golden buildings not only evoke the ancient chiefly strongholds of nearby Colombia, but today heaven also includes skyscrapers, automobiles, and telescopes, which permit souls to gaze upon the living, the underworld, and the United States (located, by implication, somewhere near the underworld). Souls who arrive at God's golden house do so only after having been physically punished for their earthly sins as they journey through the underworld.

God and Morality. The image of God, called Pap ("father") or Diosaila (from the Spanish *Dios* and the Cuna *saila,* "chief"), is that of a stern and distant paternal figure. He is never directly personified, unlike his sons and emissaries. His morality is consistent with the good and harmonious management of a matrilocal extended household and of a community made up of a number of such households. That morality, preached weekly in the local assemblies, enjoins a man to be hard-working, productive, and cooperative, and a woman to be fertile, clean, industrious, and nurturant. Women must avoid gossip, and men, quarrels. Minor conflicts must be dealt with promptly by wise, paternal chiefs, and punishment meted out swiftly—often in the form of verbal admonishments—after which all is forgiven and forgotten. To do otherwise raises the specter of backsliding into the evil ways of the "animal people."

Mythology and Cultural Survival. Armed with this religion, the Cuna were an insuperable foe to the Spaniards, whom the Cuna associated with the *ponikan,* and whom they correctly identified as the source of illnesses. Just as the *ponikan* steal men's souls, so did the Spaniards capture their bodies and enslave them. The Cuna borrowed their mythological strategy for dealing with the *ponikan* and applied it to the Spaniards. Just as *nele*s ally themselves mystically with friendly spirits, get the *ponikan* drunk magically, and confine them to their proper strongholds, so too did the Cuna form alliances with the Atlantic enemies of Spain, feast the Spaniards, and keep them at arm's length. In 1925, the strategy was played out exactly. The great tribal chief Nele Kantule, who was also a shaman, formed an alliance with an American adventurer and organized an uprising against the Panamanian administration, which took place during Carnival. The plotters fell upon unsuspecting, drunken guardsmen and killed them. The United States imposed on Panama a treaty favorable to the Indians.

Cuna mythology is kept open-ended and vital through the *nele*s and through the chiefs who incorporate recent history into their chants. The dominant ritual is the recitation of texts. Prayer and sacrifice are not practiced.

Cuna religion continues to be practiced vigorously despite the incursions of Christian missionaries and public health clinics. One community, however, has already appointed "singing chiefs" for a traditional congress house separate from the "administrative chiefs" who conduct secular affairs. It is possible that this development contains the seeds of a Cuna church or ecclesiastical cult separate from the civil government. Such a church could very well be the outcome of continuing acculturation and urbanization.

BIBLIOGRAPHY

The single most important source for Cuna mythology is Norman MacPherson Chapin's *Pab Igala: Historias de la tradición Cuna* (Panama City, 1970). This comprehensive set of texts is arranged in a sequence that Chapin's chiefly informants agree is correct. The current edition is mimeographed, but a print edition is planned. There has been no such compilation of curing, puberty, or funerary texts. The text for childbirth appears in Nils M. Homer and S. Henry Wassen's *The Complete Mu-Igala in Picture Writing* (Göteberg, 1953). This is the subject of a celebrated essay by Claude Lévi-Strauss, "The Effectiveness of Symbols," in *Structural Anthropology* (New York, 1963). Chapin has corrected Lévi-Strauss's ethnographic errors in "Muu Ikala: Cuna Birth Ceremony," in *Ritual and Symbol in Native Central America,* edited by Phillip Young and James Howe (Eugene, Oreg., 1976). This volume also contains Howe's cogent "Smoking Out the Spirits: A Cuna Exorcism," pp. 69–76. The best study of curing is Chapin's "Curing among the San Blas Cuna" (Ph.D. diss., University of Arizona, 1983).

Unfortunately, recent work has shown the texts of Erland Nordenskiöld's 1920s expedition to the Cuna to be garbled. His *An Historical and Ethnological Survey of the Cuna Indians,* written in collaboration with Ruben Pérez and edited by S. Henry Wassen (Göteberg, 1938), should be read only in connection with other works cited here.

James Howe, Joel Sherzer, and Norman MacPherson Chapin have published *Cantos y oraciones del Congreso Cuna* (Panama City, 1979) in a beautiful edition that presents a number of texts and excellent sociolinguistic and ethnological analyses. Sherzer expounds the different styles used in reciting Cuna sacred texts in "*Namakke, sunmakke, kormakke:* Three Types of Cuna Speech Event," in *Explorations in the Ethnography of Speaking,* edited by Richard Bauman and Joel Sherzer (New York, 1974).

The female puberty ceremony is described, without symbolic analysis and without the major sacred texts, in Arnulfo Prestán Simón's *El uso de la chicha y la sociedad Kuna* (Mexico City, 1975). The continuing open-endedness or *productivité* of Cuna sacred texts is explained in Dina Sherzer and Joel Sherzer's "Literature in San Blas: Discovering the Cuna *Ikala,*" *Semiotica* 6 (1972): 182–199. I have explicated the application of this mystical strategy to practical diplomacy in "Lore and Life: Cuna Indian Pageants, Exorcism, and Diplomacy in the Twentieth Century," *Ethnohistory* 30 (1983): 93–106. My "Basilicas and King Posts: A Proxemic and Symbolic Event Analysis of Competing Public Architecture among the San Blas Cuna," *American Ethnologist* 8 (1981): 259–277, explicates the peculiarly rectangular Cuna house construction both in mythological and symbolic terms. Finally, the single best ethnographic study of the Cuna is James Howe's "Village Political Organization among the San Blas Cuna" (Ph.D. diss., University of Pennsylvania, 1974).

Alexander Moore

CURES. *See* Diseases and Cures.

CURSING. Religious cursing is an activity closely related to blessing: the same people are usually empowered to do both, and the forms given to curses and blessings are frequently parallel. [*See also* Blessing.] Curses express disapproval or displeasure, but the manner in which they are pronounced ranges from spontaneous, explosive rage to the carefully considered rendering of an adverse judgment. While virtually anyone can utter a curse, some religious traditions look favorably only upon certain curses and regard unauthorized curses as magical and sacrilegious. Deities and holy persons, and others with a temporary aura gained through such conditions as great suffering or advanced age—in short, those who have the power to invoke blessings—are the very ones who can legitimately call down misfortune, including death or destruction, upon people or things.

Curses are found, sometimes prominently, in cultures throughout the world and throughout history. The central drama of the Christian tradition begins with the curse of God the creator upon the first man, Adam, for his disobedience, and through Adam upon all mankind; its climax comes with the redemptive death of Jesus, which liberated mankind from that curse and thus rendered eternal salvation possible for those who believe.

In the Hebrew scriptures, God frequently strikes down enemies and punishes the disobedient with curses. The great leaders and prophets also exercise such powers, and the Psalms are dense with curses. In the Qur'ān God is similarly relentless in cursing unbelievers and wrongdoers. The message of the New Testament in this regard, though, is mixed. Peter sent Ananias and Sapphira to abrupt deaths by the force of his words (*Acts* 5:5–10), and Paul readily cursed those who believed or taught differently from the way he did (*1 Cor.* 16:22; *Gal.* 1:8). Jesus cursed the barren fig tree (*Mt.* 21:19; *Mk.* 11:13–14), but he taught his followers to love their enemies (*Mt.* 5:44), a revolutionary change in attitude summed up by Paul: "Call down blessings on your persecutors—blessings, not curses" (*Rom.* 12:14).

The sages of the ancient Vedic tradition were storehouses of verbal power, greatly to be feared by enemies, and even by those who interrupted them in prayer. Such sages were a necessary component in the entourage of any political or military leader. Every Celtic king, too, had his druids who, with their verses, could "rhyme to death" his enemies. The conversion of the Irish to Christianity is of particular interest in this light, since it marks the first advance of Christianity beyond the borders of the Roman empire. Although Saint Patrick (c. 389–c. 461) was a Briton, and thus of Celtic origin, he had assimilated Roman culture thoroughly, as witnessed by his classical Latin writings. Starting about two and one half centuries after his death, accounts of his life portray him as a deft wielder of blessings and curses: he blesses those who convert and curses those who do not; he transforms the fields of a thief from arable land into salt marsh; he engages in a cursing contest with druids at Tara, and causes one of them to fly into the air and fall head first, smashing his skull to pieces. The Patrick of legend is thus clothed in the mantle of the ancient druids; this was also the case with the other leading Irish saints.

Religious curses can serve several purposes, most notable among them the harassment of enemies; the enforcement of law, doctrinal discipline, and proper behavior; instruction in morals; and the protection of sacred places and objects. A few examples will suffice: When the Romans trapped the Welsh tribesmen they were pursuing on the island of Anglesey in 60 CE, they saw, according to Tacitus, a dense array of armed warriors, surrounded by druids with their hands stretched up toward heaven, pouring forth imprecations. The Roman soldiers seemed at first paralyzed with fear, but their officers encouraged them to advance and led them to a thorough triumph (*Annals* 14.30). [*See* Magic, *article on* Magic in Greco-Roman Antiquity.]

Standards of Muslim behavior call for the cursing of enemies. For example, the model of behavior for Muslims condemned to be slain in captivity was set at Mecca by Muḥammad's companion Khubayb, who, just before his execution, called out, "O God, count their number and slay them one by one, and let none of them remain alive."

Specific techniques for dealing with enemies are found in the various religious traditions influenced by Tantrism. Initiates learn, among other things, the power of destruction, the power of driving away, the power of paralyzing, and the power of causing dissension. The rites prescribe for these certain times (the dark fortnight of the moon) as well as precise *mantras* (sacred words) and *mudrās* (sacred gestures).

There were gods who used curses against their human enemies, as in the story of the Danish king Hadding, who unwittingly killed a god who was disguised as a beast. The gods thereupon sent a woman to curse him soundly for this sacrilege: "Whether you walk in fields or spread canvas over the seas, you shall suffer the hate of the gods, and wherever you go you shall see the elements oppose you." The images that follow include strong winds that toss his ship about, storms that destroy his dwelling, and freezing temperatures that kill his herd. Only by making sacrifices to the gods was Hadding able to assuage their anger.

To enforce the law, Moses resorted to curses. Once he had transmitted God's commandments to the people of Israel, he directed two groups of them to assemble on two hills, one to bless those who observed these commandments and the other to curse those who did not. A lengthy litany of curses followed (*Dt.* 27–28). In the case of a challenge to his authority by a faction of 250 powerful men led by Korah, Dathan, and Abiron, Moses asked God to authenticate his mission. The sign of divine approval, he specified, would be the opening up of the earth under these rebels. "Hardly had Moses spoken when the ground beneath them split; the earth opened its mouth and swallowed them and their houses" (*Nm.* 16:1–35).

The discipline of the faith of Islam is also maintained, in part, by curses; according to the Qur'ān, "Those who reject the faith, and die rejecting it, on them is God's curse and the curse of angels and of all mankind" (2:161).

To enforce law and morality in Tanzania, the senior kinsmen among the Nyakyusa murmur (the word is that for the buzzing of a hive of bees) to bring on fever in some person considered a wrongdoer. This terrible murmuring is called "the breath of men." The onset of illness in the alleged wrongdoer must be followed by the men "speaking out," that is, admitting their anger, confessing that they are responsible for the illness, and expressing good will (a wish for the wrongdoer's return to health).

Curses also have a place in moral instruction. To cite an Irish example, Brigit of Kildare (460–528), according to a late medieval legend, taught a lesson on almsgiving to a woman who brought her a basket of apples. Lepers approached Brigit at just that moment to beg for food, and Brigit instructed the woman to give them the apples. But the woman refused, insisting that she had brought the apples for Brigit and her sisters, not for some lepers. Brigit cursed the apples in the woman's barn (they disappeared) and all the trees in her orchard (they were henceforth barren).

The preventive curse is a standard device for protecting sacred places and objects as well as deeds or agreements between persons. There is a virtually universal desire for the peaceful repose of the deceased; this stems from a widespread respect for ancestors (who, if not placated, can usually return to haunt the living), and, in some cases, from the practice of placing objects of great material value in tombs. In the ancient Near East, curses were usually placed on a tomb to warn against such violations as changing an inscription or opening, looting, misusing, or reusing the tomb itself. A common, thoughtful variant warned that there was neither silver nor bronze in the tomb; but this was still accompanied by a malediction against the life and posterity of the violator.

In Egypt a disturber of tombs was promised the chance to contend with crocodiles and serpents. Many of the figures on the facades of Hindu and Buddhist temples are silent but eloquent curses against disturbers of the sacred peace. At the royal abbey of Saint-Denis, just north of Paris, Abbot Suger (1081–1151) adorned the main altar with gold panels, gold candlesticks, and numerous precious gems. On one side he had inscribed a record of his own generous benefaction; on the other he caused to be written: "If any impious person should despoil this excellent altar, may he perish, deservedly damned, in the company of Judas." Valuable books, too, before the time of Gutenberg, commonly bore curses that promised injury, death, obliteration from human memory, or other such punishments to those imprudent enough to steal or in any way harm them. And many thousands of deeds recording transfers of property, usually in the form of gifts to religious institutions, conclude with clauses that curse potential violators of the terms set forth.

In western Europe, where such spiritual sanctions were in use between the ninth and twelfth centuries (a period when juridical institutions functioned poorly in many areas), a service called the Clamor (meaning "appeal [for justice]") or Malediction came into the standard liturgical repertory. Such a service was for use in times of trouble; it was to be held on a feast day, and a member of the religious community was required to explain in everyday language to the faithful assembled just exactly what was disturbing the community. Amid the reciting of psalms and prayers, there was intoned a lengthy litany of curses, based principally upon those found in *Deuteronomy* and the *Book of Psalms*, and directed against the malefactor or malefactors disturbing the peace. In one variant of the Clamor, the saint's relics were removed from the altar and placed on a piece of rough cloth on the floor; with the relics thus "humiliated," and a liturgical strike thereby initiated, community pressure was brought upon malefactors to restore right order in the sanctuary. While the Clamor of late antiquity was a complaint or appeal made by a plaintiff before a judge, the liturgical Clamor of the post-Carolingian period (ninth to twelfth centuries) was performed by clerics at an altar, before the duly constituted authorities of their time, namely God and the local patron saint. In its vestigial forms, this service changed from being specific and occasional to general and regular; it appeared finally as the Ash Wednesday Service of Commination in *The Book of Common Prayer*.

Such formal recitations of curses can be seen in other contexts as well: in the maledictions read in synagogues against Jewish Christians (Jews who became followers of Jesus without repudiating their Judaism) during the earliest Christian centuries; in the prayers of Ṣūfī Muslims against their political opponents; and in the utterance of "poison songs" directed against enemies by Sri Lankan Buddhist monks. They are found virtually everywhere that communities have rites of separation or exclusion. Such rites in turn can usually be followed by complementary ceremonies for deactivating the curses; these constitute a clear indication of a belief in the force and independent vitality that curses contain. At the conclusion of a dispute among the Tiv of northern Nigeria, all show acceptance of the settlement by "blowing out the curse." The group forms a ring, and a gourd filled with water is passed around; participants take water in their mouths and then blow it out in as fine a spray as possible. If anyone has reservations about the settlement, but participates nonetheless, the curse will rebound upon him.

Ceremonies for withdrawing curses and reintegrating the accursed give yet another insight into the use and value of curses. While it is in the nature of the horror that curses engender that what they propose be total and irremediable (not only death but no proper burial; exposure of the corpse to beasts and vultures), curses in fact seem frequently to function as instruments of negotiation. It is in reading accounts of cases in which curses are used, rather than just formulaic texts themselves, that one discovers the pattern of perceived injustice, pronouncing of curses, willingness to negotiate, settlement, and joyous reintegration of the disrupted community. Where courts of law backed up by a powerful state are absent, the society, which is of course not shown thereby to be lawless, is likely to have various other mechanisms for resolving disputes; curses frequently occur among such mechanisms.

In terms of linguistic analysis, cursing can be considered a "speech act," since a curse is simultaneously a verbal utterance and a deed performed. In order for the curse to be effective, and, in the same way, in order for the utterance to qualify as a given speech act, certain conditions must be met, such as that there be the proper actors, time, place, verbal formulas, and gestures. What is "proper" is defined by the community; it is a matter of generally held beliefs, including confidence in the efficacy of duly performed blessings and curses. Thus a bishop's saying "I anathematize you" in the proper circumstances is deemed authentic, while a lay person's saying the same thing is not.

An utterance using an active, indicative, present-tense verb and the first-person pronoun, such as "I anathematize you," is the simplest and most explicit form of a speech act of cursing. But curses are often expressed in the subjunctive mood and the passive voice, and the agent is not always specified ("May he be cursed," "May he be killed"); they are often in the form of petitions to others to intervene ("May the saints strike him dead"). Still, the speaker in such cases has done something—not the terrible deed mentioned in the curse but the utterance of the curse itself. And the person addressed has not yet been afflicted by the deed mentioned but has immediately become accursed. In the case of a provisional curse ("If anyone should disturb this tomb, may he suffer such-and-such"), the speech act is not complete upon utterance because of the lack of one of the necessary conditions, namely the presence of a malefactor. The moment a person commits the anticipated offense, thus becoming the malefactor, the lone missing condition is met, the malefactor is cursed, and the speech act is accomplished.

The value of curses should in the final analysis be seen in relation to power, for they are all, some way, instruments of the weak. Those who have physical, military, or juridical power tend to use such power; they use it to maintain their vision of order. The aged, the sick, the pregnant, the orphaned, the outcast all lack such power, and yet they have ipso facto some special power of the word. Religious or spiritual authority is, by its nature, not military or physical. Religious authorities, while often hardly defenseless or outcast and, indeed, while usually allied with military forces, nonetheless wield their peculiar kind of authority through the manipulation of words and gestures. In military encounters, it is not likely that the more powerful forces bother to curse the weaker; at Anglesey we would not have expected the Romans to curse the Welsh. When the mighty do utter their most terrible curses, they are no longer so mighty, as when Oedipus—blind, exiled, about to die—found cursing his only remaining weapon against Creon and Polynices.

Finally, a curse ascribed to Saint Maedoc of Ferns (d. 626) itself contains the ultimate lesson about religious cursing: "Woe to that person," it warns, "whose neighbor is an angry saint."

BIBLIOGRAPHY

Curses are mentioned in countless ethnographic, historical, and religious studies, but only a very few of these—and they are mainly articles—are devoted entirely to this subject. The only extensive bibliography is woven through a lengthy German encyclopedia article whose range is the Mediterranean region in the ancient and early Christian periods; see Wolfgang Speyer's "Fluch," in *Reallexikon für Antike und Christentum*, vol. 7 (Stuttgart, 1969). A brief but well-informed and suggestive section on cursing is found in Keith Thomas's *Religion and the Decline of Magic: Studies in Popular Beliefs in Sixteenth and Seventeenth Century England* (New York, 1971), pp. 502–512. On the Vedic sages, see Heinrich Zimmer's *Philosophies of India,* edited by Joseph Campbell (New York, 1951), pp. 48–83. Ethnographic material on the use of curses by Tamils is found in Carl Diehl's *Instrument and Purpose: Studies on Rites and Rituals in South India* (Lund, 1956). On the druids, see Fred Norris Robinson's "Satirists and Enchanters in Early Irish Literature," in *Studies in the History of Religion Presented to Crawford Howell Toy,* edited by David G. Lyon and George Foot Moore (New York, 1912), pp. 95–130. For the Irish saints, see Kathleen Hughes's *The Church in Early Irish Society* (Ithaca, N.Y., 1966) and *Early Christian Ireland: Introduction to the Sources* (Ithaca, N.Y., 1972), pp. 217–247, on hagiography. On the ceremony of the Clamor, see my article "La morphologie des malédictions monastiques," *Annales: Économies, sociétés, civilisations* 34 (January–February 1979): 43–60. Patrick Geary treats the "Humiliation of Saints," in *Saints and Their Cults: Studies in Religious Sociology, Folklore and History,* edited by Stephen Wilson (Cambridge, 1983), pp. 123–140. The English philosopher J. L. Austin developed the theory of speech acts (or performative utterances); see his Harvard lectures entitled *How to Do Things with Words* (1962; 2d ed., Cambridge, Mass., 1975). There is a considerable body of literature deriving from Austin's work, although little of it refers to curses. One notable discussion of the theory as it relates to ritual language is Benjamin Ray's "'Performative Utterances' in African rituals," *History of Religions* 13 (August 1973): 16–35.

LESTER K. LITTLE

CUSANUS. *See* Nicholas of Cusa.

CUSHITE RELIGION. *See* Kushite Religion.

CYBELE is a goddess, probably of Oriental origin, known in the Greek world from approximately the seventh century BCE. She is probably identical with the goddess addressed as "Earth, mother of all" by Homeric *Hymn 30,* which is usually thought to date from the seventh century BCE (see also *Hymn 14*). She was sung by Pindar in association with Pan (*Pythian Odes* 3). She became known in Rome as Magna Mater ("great mother [of the gods]") when her cult was imported to the city at the end of the third century BCE. But she was also known to the Romans under the name of Cybele (with such variants as Cybebe, Cybelis, and, at Locri in Italy, Qybala). The name is obviously parallel to that of the goddess Kubaba of Carchemish, who in the second millenium BCE was also worshiped in the Assyrian trade post of Canis in Cappadocia and was known in Ugarit.

Cybele was adopted as goddess by the Phrygians, who established her central cult in Pessinus. From Phrygia the cult probably passed to Sardis, capital of the kingdom of Lydia, and to Hellenic cities of Asia Minor and Europe. In the Hellenistic period Ilium (Troy) and Pergamum were centers of her cult. Relations between the temple-state of Pessinus and the kings of Pergamum are documented in the second century BCE. According to Herodotus (4.76), the Scythian Anacharsis introduced the cult of the Great Mother from Cyzicus to Scythia and lost his life in the process. At least in the Hellenistic period, and probably even earlier, the cult of Cybele in Greece had mysteric elements (see Arnobius, *Against the Pagans* 5.5).

Cybele is often represented standing or sitting between two lions or two leopards. This type of image is already recognizable in an isolated terra-cotta found at Çatal Hüyük, near the site of the ancient city of Iconium in Phrygia (now at the Museum of Anatolian Civilizations in Ankara), that has been dated circa 6000 BCE. The goddess is also represented with a lion on her lap or accompanied by two musicians. She was often associated with mountains and caves and was supposed to protect from illness, and generally to help, mothers and children. Oracles and divination were connected with her. In Greek she was not always easily distinguishable from analogous goddesses (such as Rhea, Demeter, Gaia, Themis).

In several places, the cult of Cybele was combined with that of Attis. According to a prestigious version of the myth (Ovid, *Fasti* 4. 223ff.), Attis had been loved by Cybele and had been unfaithful to her. In a fit of insanity he castrated himself and died. The resurrection of Attis is explicitly affirmed by Firmicus Maternus in the third book of *De errore profanarum religionum* in the fourth century CE; it is doubtful, however, whether the resurrection played a part in the actual cult. In several, but not necessarily all, places where Cybele and Attis were associated, devotees known as Galli emasculated themselves and fulfilled special, but subordinate, functions in the cult. They contributed much to the dancing, the healing, and the divining. Some of the Galli lived as itinerant beggars.

In Athens the cult of Cybele was introduced among contrasts in the fifth century BCE. For a while the archives of the Athenian state were placed in the temple of the goddess, which was called the Metroon. The cult statue of this temple was attributed to Phidias or to his pupil Agoracritus. It is doubtful whether Attis was introduced along with Cybele into Athens in the fifth century, but in the Athenian harbor of the Piraeus he was apparently associated with her at least from the third century BCE.

The cult of the Magna Mater was imported to Rome from Pessinus via Pergamum (details uncertain) in 204 BCE, toward the end of the Second Punic War. This step was taken by the Roman government in a time of religious agitation and following pronouncements from the

Sibylline Books. It was approved by Apollo's oracle at Delphi and connected with the Trojan origins of Rome. Members of the most prominent gentes (such as the Cornelians, the Valerians, and the Claudians) patronized the transfer. Cybele was given a temple on the Palatine—an exceptional honor for a foreign cult—which was dedicated in 191 BCE. An annual festival called the Megalesia (4–10 April), which included theatrical performances, was instituted. Banquets that amounted to aristocratic dinner parties were also connected with this festival. Cicero (*On Old Age* 13.45) presents the severe Cato, who had been a *quaestor iust* in 204, as taking part in these aristocratic entertainments.

From Rome and Italy the cult of the Magna Mater spread to the provinces. Although supported by aristocratic groups, the cult met with opposition. It implied the reception of a black stone, a meteorite, as the chief cultic object (though there was also a female cult image). It had orgiastic features and encouraged mendicancy. It associated the cult of Cybele with that of Attis, though the earliest sources (including Ovid in the *Fasti*) are reticent on this point. A great many images of Attis, found by Italian archaeologists in the precincts of the temple of the Palatine, date from the second and first centuries BCE. Even more important, castrated Galli soon appeared as followers of Cybele in Rome. In the organization of the cult, they seem to have been subordinate to a priest and a priestess who originally came from Phrygia but who later must have been chosen in Rome. According to an obscure passage of Dionysius of Halicarnassus (*Roman Antiquities* 2.19.5), which is indicative for the first century BCE, the Roman Senate prohibited the participation of Roman citizens in certain ceremonies of the cult of Cybele.

The cult was certainly reformed, perhaps more than once, in the first centuries of the empire, but again the details are obscure. Roman citizens appear as priests of Cybele during the empire; a Roman citizen, as Archigallus, appears to control the cult in Rome, and other Archigalli are found in control of temples of Cybele elsewhere in Italy and in the provinces. Fraternities or corporations—such as the Dendrophori ("tree bearers") and the Cannophori ("reed bearers")—assisted in the ceremonies; the Dendrophori became an influential fraternity in the cities. The liturgical language of the cult seems to have been Greek. The role of Attis in the cult became greater. His part in the cult may have been officially recognized for the first time by the emperor Claudius, according to information contained in Johannes Laurentius Lydus's *De mensibus* (4.59), written in the sixth century CE. The so-called calendar of Philocalus, which dates from the middle of the fourth century, mentions five days of festivities in March in honor of Attis, followed on March 27 by the ceremonial washing of the black stone in the Almo, a little river outside Rome. We also know that, at least in Italy and Gaul, the cult of Cybele was placed under the supervision of the Roman priestly corporation of the Quindecemviri Sacris Faciundis.

The increased participation of Attis in the cult seems to have helped give the whole cult a more mysteric form with promises of salvation for the initiated. The ritual of the *taurobolium* came to be associated with this cult at least from the second century CE and was frequently performed as an explicit homage to the emperor. At least in the fourth century CE, the *taurobolium* was definitely a baptism performed with the blood of a sacrificed bull and is described as such about 400 CE by Prudentius in his *Peristephanon* (10.1006–1050), although he describes the ritual as the baptism of a priest. In the fourth century the cult of Cybele and Attis attracted the emperor Julian, who wrote an oration in honor of Cybele, and was conspicuously displayed by that part of Roman aristocracy that had not been converted to Christianity. It is, however, noteworthy that the association of the *taurobolium* with homage to the emperor disappeared in the same century. Nonetheless, in the fifth century the philosopher Proclus wrote a book, now lost, on Cybele.

BIBLIOGRAPHY

General Works

Bömer, Franz. "Kybele in Rom." *Mitteilungen des Römischen Archäologischen Instituts* (Römische Abteilungen) 71 (1964): 130–150.

Graillot, Henri. *Le culte de Cybèle, Mère des dieux, à Rome et dans l'Empire romain.* Paris, 1912. A fundamental work.

Nilsson, Martin P. *Geschichte der griechischen Religion* (1941–1950). 2 vols. 3d ed. Munich, 1967–1974. See volume 1, pages 725–727, and volume 2 (2d ed., 1961), pages 640–657.

Thomas, Garth. "Magna Mater and Attis." In *Aufstieg und Niedergang der römischen Welt,* vol. 2.17.3, pp. 1500–1535. Berlin and New York, 1984.

Vermaseren, Maarten J. *Cybele and Attis: The Myth and the Cult.* Translated by A. M. H. Lemmers. London, 1977.

Vermaseren, Maarten J. *Corpus cultus Cybelae Attidisque.* 4 vols. to date. Leiden, 1977–1982.

Special Studies

Bremmer, Jan. "The Legend of Cybele's Arrival in Rome." In *Studies in Hellenistic Religions,* edited by Maarten J. Vermaseren, pp. 9–22. Leiden, 1979.

Carcopino, J. "Attideia." *Mélanges d'archéologie et d'histoire, École de Rome* 40 (1923): 135–159, 237–324.

Duthoy, Robert. *The Taurobolium.* Leiden, 1969.

Gérard, J. "Legende et politique autour de la Mère des dieux." *Revue études Latines* 58 (1981): 153–175.

Lambrechts, Pierre. *Attis: Van herdersknaap tot god.* Brussels, 1962.

Romanelli, P. "Lo scavo al tempio della Magna Mater sul Palatino." *Monumenti antichi dell'Accademia Nazionale dei Lincei* 46 (1963): 201–330.

Romanelli, P. "Magna Mater e Attis sul Palatino." In *Hommage à Jean Bayet*, pp. 619–629. Brussels, 1964.

Arnaldo Momigliano

CYCLADIC RELIGION. *See* Aegean Religions.

CYPRIAN (c. 205–258), also known as Thascius Caecilius Cyprianus; bishop of Carthage. According to his own testimony, Cyprian was raised in Carthage, where he was born probably in the first decade of the third century. Scion of a noble pagan family, he had the opportunity to become well trained in literature and rhetoric. Because he was a successful rhetorician, he acquired fame and friends in the ranks of high society.

Cyprian was already mature when in 246, attracted by the purity of Christian ethics, he was initiated into the Christian faith by the presbyter Caecilius, whose name he adopted. He found theological guidance in the works of Tertullian, whom he called "the teacher," even though he did not follow him in his extreme views.

Within a short period of time Cyprian had acquired such authority that in 248, after the death of Donatus, bishop of Carthage, he was elected his successor "by the voice of the people and the verdict of God." [*See* Donatism.] A year later the persecutions under Emperor Decius began. While the pagan mob cried, "Give Cyprian to the lion," he found refuge outside the city, whence he administered the church with the assistance of a committee of vicars.

The persecution badly disrupted the unity of the North African church. The edict of Decius invited all Christians either to sacrifice to the idols, whereupon they would receive a *libellus* ("certificate"), or to suffer martyrdom. Large groups of Christians everywhere became martyrs to the faith, but others (the *sacrificati*) offered some kind of sacrifice, while yet others (the *libellatici*) managed to obtain false documents stating that they had offered sacrifice. When these *lapsi*, or "backsliders," expressed the desire to return to the church, Cyprian instructed his clergy to grant full communion to the sick, but to give only pastoral care to the others until peace came, when a decision could be reached on how to receive the *lapsi*.

Cyprian found opposition to his policy, however, from a group of tolerant Christians under the layman, later deacon, Felicissimus, who advocated the immediate acceptance of all backsliders without restriction. They were backed by those presbyters who were displeased by Cyprian's election to the episcopate, as well as by numerous confessors, who promptly gave letters of recommendation to backsliders.

When he returned to his see fourteen months after he left, Cyprian convoked a synod that established in concert with Rome the fundamental principles for receiving the backsliders. The *sacrificati* should undergo penance of varying length, while the *libellatici* would be received immediately. However, there was a reaction on the part of the rigorists as well. Cyprian did not succeed in preventing a double schism, which resulted from the election of two new bishops as his rivals, Fortunatus and Maximus.

A new crisis, threatened during the reign of Gallus (252) by an outbreak of the plague, was averted by the self-sacrificing attitude of the Christians toward the victims of the misfortune, both Christian and pagan. In the period that followed, Cyprian carried out fruitful pastoral, social, and interchurch activities.

The validity of the baptism of heretics, an old problem exacerbated by the extension of the influence of Novatian, a leading presbyter in Rome, was to vex the church anew. How should the returning heretics be received? Cyprian, in accordance with the custom of the African church, and on the basis of his own ecclesiological persuasions, thought that no sacrament had any validity if performed outside the canonical church. Consequently, all heretics who returned would have to be rebaptized. His opinion was confirmed by three successive synods in 255 and 256. Pope Stephen, maintaining that acceptance should be made only by the laying on of hands, broke relations with Cyprian.

Under Valerian a new edict was issued against the Christians. Cyprian, not wishing to hide this time, was arrested, exiled to a place north of Carthage, and finally condemned to death. On hearing the decision, he said only "Deo gratias." He was beheaded on 14 September 258.

Though the Christian stage of Cyprian's life was short and troubled, he became one of the great writers of the church. He certainly did not possess the force and depth of Tertullian, whose terms and topics he borrowed extensively, but he showed greater understanding and moderation than the latter. His works are the product and proof of his practical interests and they reflect all the major issues and personalities of the day. Three ancient lists cite the titles of his writings, mostly short treatises and letters.

A friend of Cyprian's, Donatus, had difficulty in breaking away from old pagan customs. In *To Donatus*, Cyprian says that he himself also feared that he would find difficulty after his turn toward Christianity but that the water of regeneration had made him a new man. *To Quirinius*, later called *Testimonia*, is a collection of biblical passages with short comments for the training of new Christians. *On the Ornaments of Virgins* was written at the beginning of Cyprian's episcopate to praise the virtue of virginity and stress the need for modesty in dress. Cyprian issued *On the Lapsed* when he returned to his see in 251. In it he expresses his sorrow for the victims of the persecution and draws principles on the basis of which the problem of the backsliders should be solved.

On the Unity of the Catholic Church was written in 251, in face of the apparent danger of a split in the church, to stress that the church of Christ is one and that those who split it bring about an evil worse than the persecution. *On the Lord's Prayer,* written in 252, presents an edifying allegorical interpretation of the Lord's Prayer. The two treatises *To Demetrianus* and *On Morality* answer questions about suffering. The first is an answer to the accusations that arose during the plague, namely that Christian refusal to worship Roman deities was responsible for the present evils. Responsibility for these evils, states Cyprian, is to be found in the moral disorder of pagan society. *On Morality* was written during the same period to answer the question of why Christians endure the same evils as the pagans—dying prematurely from the plague and from hunger. Cyprian reasons that natural laws, established by the divine will, have universal bearing. Moreover, death is not a punishment for Christians: what travelers do not long to return to their homeland? Heaven is the home of Christians.

Other treatises cover almsgiving, baptism, jealousy, and envy, or are meant to enhearten Christians facing persecution. A number of other short treatises, mostly from the third century, have been falsely attributed to Cyprian.

The letters of Cyprian, some of them small treatises in themselves, are also important. Most refer to the problems of his episcopate: the consequences of persecution under Decius, the problem of the backsliders, the Novatian schism, and the question of the baptism of heretics. Popes Cornelius, Lucius, and Stephen, and the bishop of Caesarea in Cappadocia, are his most eminent correspondents.

A man of action, Cyprian was concerned exclusively with practical questions as aspects of the great problem of the church. "We struggle for the honor and the unity of the Church," he declares (*Letters* 73.11). His insistence that there is only one leader of the faith and his fear of the separatist movements within the church led him to stress the element of unity. He insisted that on a high level the church is one, because its founder is one, but simultaneously it is also universal. The one church is diffused into the universal through the multiplicity of bishops. The Petrine chair, the *cathedra,* is the one church; the sees of the local bishops constitute the universal church.

The fourth chapter of Cyprian's *On the Unity* examines unity on a second level, the unity of the body of bishops. The interpretation of this text, preserved in two recensions, has presented problems for theological research. The longer recension, because it is favorable to papal primacy, was once considered by many to be an interpolation. After the research of Othmar Perler, Maurice Bévenot, and others, however, both recensions are regarded as genuine. The long text stresses that "primacy was given to Peter" by Christ and that "those who abandon the chair of Peter cannot belong to the church." The mistake of earlier historians was that they identified the chair of Peter with the see of Rome. It appears that Cyprian was already aware of such a misunderstanding, and for this reason he removed those expressions and gave the text the short form. What Cyprian wished to say was that in the famous verse of *Matthew* 16:18, "Upon this rock [*petra*] I will build my Church," the rock and chair of Peter is the faith, and since the faith is one, the see is also one. In this one see all the apostles take part, as well as their successors. "Episcopatus unus est" ("The episcopate is one"), and the particular bishops are coparticipants in it. Further, the bishops are closely joined by the law of personal love and concord, and also through their common origin (*Letters* 43.5; 69.3). Therefore the important problems of the church can be solved only by a common decision of the bishops in synod.

On the local level, every church constitutes a unity achieved through the bond of the bishop, the clergy, and the laity. The faithful must be united with the bishop in the sense understood by Ignatius of Antioch; and he who is not one with the bishop is not even with the church. But the unity must operate reciprocally. Cyprian never acted without consultation with his clergy and people.

There are definite consequences of this kind of unity for the process of salvation. The church is the bride of Christ, pure and incorrupt; therefore, "no one can have God as Father, if he does not have the Church as mother" (*On the Unity* 6). In opposition to Tertullian, Cyprian insisted that the Holy Spirit is active only within the church: "Salus extra ecclesiam non est" ("There is no salvation outside the church," *Letters* 73.21). The church is the ark of Noah, whose passengers were the only ones saved from the great flood. The sacraments of the church, especially baptism, eucharist, penance, and ordination, are valid only within the framework of the canonical ecclesiastical life.

Cyprian's feast is celebrated in the Western church on 16 September, while in the Eastern church it is celebrated on 2 October, and in the Anglican on 26 September; the confusion occurs because of an Antiochian magician of the same name who converted to Christianity. At the time of Augustine, there were already three churches dedicated to Cyprian's name. His relics were transferred to Lyons under Charlemagne and were later deposited at Moissac in southern France.

The dissemination of Cyprian's writings in the Middle Ages shows that he was more honored than any other Latin church writer, except for the four great doctors of the Western church. He is one of the principal founders of Latin theology. Augustine was profoundly influenced by his views; the Council of Ephesus (431) used demonstrative passages from his works; the *Gelasian Decree* put him at the head of its list of orthodox bishops; and the *Decretum* of Gratian gave official weight to his treatise *On Unity,* which was widely used during the investiture controversy.

BIBLIOGRAPHY

Works by Cyprian. The works of Cyprian were edited for the first time by Johannes Andreae in *Cypriannus opera* (Rome, 1471). This edition is unsatisfactory, as is that of Étienne Baluze and S. Mauri, *Sancti Caecilii Cypriani* (Paris, 1726), reprinted in *Patrologia Latina,* vol. 4, edited by J.-P. Migne (Paris, 1865). A critical edition, *S. Thasci Caecilii Cypriani Opera omnia,* 3 vols., "Corpus Scriptorum Ecclesiasticorum Latinorum," 3.1–3 (1868–1871), has been edited by Wilhelm Hertel. Robert Weber, Maurice Bévenot, Manib Simonetti, and Claudio Moreschini have edited the excellent *Sancti Cypriani episcopi opera,* 2 vols., "Corpus Christianorum, seria Latina," 3, 3A (Turnhout, Belgium, 1972–1976). The works of Cyprian have been translated by Robert E. Wallis in *Saint Cyprian: Writings,* 2 vols., "Ante-Nicene Christian Library," vols. 8, 13 (Edinburgh, 1868–1869).

Works about Cyprian. The comprehensive studies of Edward White Benson, *Cyprian: His Life, His Times, His Work* (London and New York, 1897), and Paul Monceaux, *Histoire littéraire de l'Afrique chrétienne,* vol. 2, *Saint Cyprien et son temps* (Paris, 1902), are still valuable, as is also the discussion of Cyprian's doctrine by Adehémar d'Alès, *La théologie de S. Cyprien,* 2d ed. (Paris, 1922). The recent study of Michael M. Sage gives a complete and good picture of his personality, times, and activity. The studies of Ulrich Wickert, *Sacramentum unitatis, Ein Beitrag zum Verständnis der Kirche bei Cyprian* (Berlin, 1971), Peter Hinchliff's *Cyprian of Carthage and the Unity of the Christian Church* (London, 1974), Charles Saumagne's *Saint Cyprien, évêque de Carthage, "pape" d'Afrique, 248–258: Contribution à l'étude des "persécutions" de Dèce et de Valérien* (Paris, 1975), and Michael A. Fahey's *Cyprian and the Bible: A Study in Third-Century Exegesis* (Tübingen, 1971) present particular aspects of Cyprian's activity. Hugo Koch has presented his research, which sheds new light on the evaluation of Cyprian's ecclesiology, in two writings, *Cyprianische Untersuchungen* (Bonn, 1926) and *Cathedra Petri: Neue Untersuchungen über die Anfänge der Primatslehre* (Giessen, 1930). Maurice Bévenot published, besides a number of small articles, a large work, *The Tradition of Manuscripts: A Study in the Transmission of Saint Cyprian Treatises* (Oxford, 1961).

PANAGIOTIS C. CHRISTOU
Translated from Greek by Philip M. McGhee

CYRIL I (1570/2–1638), surnamed Loukaris, known also as Cyril Lucar; Greek Orthodox patriarch of Constantinople. Next to Gennadios Scholarios, the first patriarch after the fall of Constantinople, Cyril was the most brilliant and influential head of the Greek church during the period of Turkish rule. Living at a time of intense conflict, when both Rome and the Protestants were seeking to bring Greek Orthodoxy under their control, Cyril strongly favored the Protestant side.

He was born at Candia (modern-day Heraklion) in Crete, then under Venetian sovereignty, and was given the baptismal name of Constantine. He studied at Venice under the celebrated Greek scholar Maximos Margounios, and then at the University of Padua. At his ordination (c. 1593) to the diaconate in Constantinople by Meletios Pegas, patriarch of Alexandria, who was probably his relative, Loukaris took the new name of Cyril. In 1594 he was sent to Poland to strengthen the Orthodox resistance against Roman Catholic propaganda and to help with education. In 1596, when the Synod of Brest-Litovsk ratified the union of the Orthodox church in Poland with the Roman Catholic church, Cyril took part in the countersynod held in Brest by those Orthodox who opposed the union. He stayed in Poland until 1598 and went for a second visit in 1600–1601. Returning in 1601 to Constantinople, Cyril was ordained priest, and in Egypt that autumn he was elected patriarch of Alexandria succeeding Pegas, an office he held until 1620, residing much of the time in Constantinople.

While in Poland, although siding with the antiunionist party, Cyril maintained friendly relations with leading Roman Catholics; in his early sermons (1599–1600) he draws on Catholic apologists such as Roberto Bellarmino and makes use of Latin scholastic categories, accepting among other things the doctrine of the Immaculate Conception. As late as 1608 he wrote to Paul V in terms implying a recognition of papal primacy. During his time as patriarch of Alexandria, however, Cyril came to feel increasing sympathy with Protestantism, particularly in its Calvinist form. His Protestant contacts were chiefly Dutch: he formed a close friendship with Cornelius van Haag (or Haga), Dutch ambassador at Constantinople; corresponded with the theologian Jan Uytenbogaert; and met David Le Leu de Wilhem. He also exchanged letters with George Abbot, archbishop of Canterbury, and in 1617 he sent a young Greek monk, Metrophanes Kritopoulos (1589–1639), to study at Oxford. Kritopoulos remained in England until 1624, later becoming patriarch of Alexandria (1636–1639).

In 1620 Cyril was elected patriarch of Constantinople (he had been patriarch briefly in 1612). He remained on the ecumenical throne until his death in 1638, though with some interruptions: he was deposed, reinstated in 1630, deposed a third time and restored in 1633, deposed and again reinstated in 1634, deposed in 1635 and not restored until 1637, thus serving altogether no fewer than seven different periods in office. The frequency with which he was ejected is an indication of the extreme instability of the ecumenical patriarchate at this time, subject as it was to constant interference from the Turkish authorities, and with its bishops deeply divided by internal strife. Throughout his years as patriarch, Cyril was the center of a bitter conflict between the anti-Roman and pro-Roman factions in the holy synod; behind this conflict lay the wider struggle between different states of western Europe for influence within the Ottoman empire. Cyril's opponents in the synod, the chief among them being Cyril (Kontaris) of Beroea, himself on several occasions patriarch, were supported by the Propaganda Fide in Rome and by the Jesuits in Constantinople, as well as by the French and Austrian ambassadors; on his side, Cyril relied upon the assistance of the Dutch and English embassies. He enjoyed the friendship of Thomas Roe, English ambassador during 1621–1628, through whom he donated the Codex Alexandrinus in 1628 to King Charles I of England. He also became close friends with Antoine Léger, chaplain at the Dutch embassy from 1628.

As patriarch, Cyril struggled to raise standards of education. In particular he opened a printing press at Constantinople in 1627, but this functioned for only a few months before it was closed by the Turks in 1628. He commissioned a translation of the New Testament into modern Greek, which was eventually published at Geneva in 1638. But he is chiefly remembered for his *Confession of Faith,* first published at Geneva in 1629. This work is openly Calvinist in its teaching, and many have denied its authenticity; yet, even if it was drafted by one of Cyril's Protestant friends, such as Léger, Cyril himself appended his signature to it and accepted it as his own.

Cyril's life came to a tragic end on 27 June 1638. He was arrested on an accusation of inciting the Don Cossacks to attack the Ottoman domains. After a few days in prison he was taken out to sea in a small boat and strangled. A man of vision and energy, and endowed with an able intellect, in calmer times Cyril might have succeeded in effecting a theological rapprochement between East and West, as well as in raising cultural and educational standards within the ecumenical patriarchate. As it was, his great gifts of leadership were largely wasted in an unremitting and futile struggle for power.

Cyril's *Confession of Faith* expresses to a considerable degree a reformed rather than an Orthodox viewpoint. He states that "the authority of scripture is higher than that of the church," since scripture alone, being divinely inspired, cannot err (sec. 2); and he denies the infallibility of the church (sec. 12). He adopts the standard Calvinist teaching on predestination and election (sec. 3) and insists on justification by faith alone, without works (sec. 13). He holds that there are only two "sacraments of the gospel," baptism and the Eucharist (sec. 15), and he dismisses "the vainly invented doctrine of transubstantiation," arguing that the faithful receive the body of Christ "not by crushing it with their physical teeth, but by perceiving it through the sense and feeling of the soul" (sec. 17). He rejects the doctrine of purgatory, denying that there can be change or progress after death (sec. 18), and he repudiates the veneration of icons (answer 4).

Cyril's *Confession* is the most far-reaching attempt ever made by an Eastern church leader to bring Orthodox teaching into line with Protestantism. It is hard to determine whether he was seeking merely to please his Calvinist supporters, or whether he was expressing his own deepest convictions in the hope of inspiring some sort of reformation within the Orthodox church. In fact the *Confession* found little favor and was condemned by no fewer than six Orthodox councils in the half century following Cyril's death (Constantinople, 1638, 1642; Jassy, 1642; Constantinople, 1672; Jerusalem, 1672; and Constantinople, 1691). The most significant of these condemnations was at the Jerusalem Council of 1672; this council ratified the *Confession* composed by Patriarch Dositheos of Jerusalem, which rebutted Cyril's *Confession* point by point. Even though Dositheos was influenced by Latin theology, his deviation from mainstream Orthodoxy was far less radical than Cyril's. The influence of Cyril's *Confession* was in this way largely negative, serving to push the Greek church in an anti-Protestant direction; but, if only by way of reaction, it also served to clarify seventeenth-century Orthodox thinking about the church, the sacraments, and the state of the departed.

BIBLIOGRAPHY

The Greek text of *The Eastern Confession of the Christian Faith* may be found in part 1 of Ernest Julius Kimmel's *Monumenta fidei ecclesiae orientalis* (Jena, 1850), pp. 24–44. It has been translated into English and edited by James N. W. B. Robertson in *The Acts and Decrees of the Synod of Jerusalem* (London, 1899), pp. 185–215; another translation is George A. Hadjiantoniou's *Protestant Patriarch: The Life of Cyril Lucaris, 1572–1638, Patriarch of Constantinople* (Richmond, 1961), pp. 141–145. Some of Cyril's earlier sermons have been edited by Keetje Rozemond in *Sermons, 1598–1602* (Leiden, 1974). Cyril's correspondence may be found in *Monumens authentiques de la religion des Grecs, et de la fausseté de plusieurs confessions de foi des chrétiens orientaux,* edited by Jean Aymon (The Hague, 1708), pp. 1–200; also, in Émile Legrand's *Bibliographie hellénique, ou Description raisonnée des ouvrages publiés par des*

Grecs au dix-septième siècle, vol. 4, *Notices bibliographiques* (Paris, 1896), pp. 175–521.

Source material on Cyril's career is to be found in Thomas Smith's *Collectanea de Cyrillo Lucario, patriarcha Constantinopolitano* (London, 1707) and in *The Negotiations of Sir Thomas Roe* (London, 1740). Among modern studies, the most scholarly are in Greek: see especially Chrysostom Papadopoulos's *Kurillos Loukaris,* rev. ed. (Athens, 1939) and Ioannis N. Karmiris's *Orthodoxia kai Protestantismos* (Athens, 1937), pp. 177–275. The work of Hadjiantoniou, cited above, is a readable but partisan account by a Greek evangelical. There is a briefer but more balanced treatment in Steven Runciman's *The Great Church in Captivity: A Study of the Patriarchate of Constantinople from the Eve of the Turkish Conquest to the Greek War of Independence* (Cambridge, 1968), pp. 259–288. On the political background, see Gunnar Hering's *Ökumenisches Patriarchat und europäische Politik, 1620–1638* (Wiesbaden, 1968).

KALLISTOS WARE

CYRIL AND METHODIUS. Cyril, also known as Constantine (c. 826–869), and Methodius (c. 815–844) were called the "apostles to the Slavs" because of their religious and cultural contributions to the people of the Danube basin (in modern-day eastern Czechoslovakia and western Hungary) and later to all Slavic-speaking people. Constantine (who took the name Cyril only in the last months of his life) and Methodius were born into a prominent Christian family in Thessalonica, Greece. The brothers learned Greek and probably also Slavic, since many Slavic people had migrated south into their area of Macedonia. After their father's death, Constantine moved to Constantinople. Then only fourteen, he was cared for by the family of a high government official. He later attended the imperial university and benefited from studying with the leading teachers in the region, including Photius, the future patriarch of Constantinople (858–867, 877–888). He became librarian of Hagia Sophia, the leading church in the East, and later professor of philosophy at the imperial university. He also participated in religious debates with church leaders and Muslim scholars.

Methodius, meanwhile, had been awarded the governorship of a Slavic-speaking district. After some years as governor, however, he withdrew into a Greek monastery in Bithynia (in Asia Minor), where Constantine joined him in 855. In 860, the patriarch sent Constantine and Methodius on a mission to the Khazars, a people occuping the territory northeast of the Black Sea, who had asked that the Christian message be explained to them. The result of their visit was that two hundred Khazars requested baptism. This success led to another, more important mission shortly thereafter.

In 862, Rastislav, duke of Greater Moravia (modern-day eastern Czechoslovakia and western Hungary), sent a request for help to the emperor in Constantinople, Michael III. Rastislav's Slavic-speaking subjects had already been widely evangelized by missionaries from western Europe, that is, from the East Frankish kingdom (modern-day West Germany and Austria). The Slavic peoples, however, had no written language and no strong cultural or church leadership, and Rastislav perceived a danger in the political and ecclesiastical influence of the neighboring Germanic tribes. He hoped that aid from Constantinople would enable Moravia to remain politically and religiously autonomous.

Recognizing the importance of the request, the Byzantine emperor and the patriarch, Photius, agreed to send Methodius and Constantine. In the months before their journey, Constantine prepared for the mission by developing a written language for the Slavs. He formed the alphabet from Hebrew and Greek letters (in its final form, this alphabet, the Cyrillic, is still used in modern Russian and in a number of other modern Slavic languages). Using this alphabet, Constantine translated the Gospels and later the epistles of Paul and the *Book of Psalms* into Slavic.

In late 863, the brothers began the mission. They sailed around Greece and up the Adriatic to Venice, then traveled overland to Moravia, where they were warmly welcomed. Their work included training a native clergy, instructing them in the newly written Slavic language, and translating liturgical textbooks. The latinized clergy in the area vigorously opposed the Slavic liturgy; they held to a "trilingualist" theory that only Latin, Greek, and Hebrew were acceptable for worship. To win papal support for their innovations, the brothers journeyed to Rome in 867. The also took along some trainees for ordination. On the way, they spent several months south of the Danube in Pannonia (modern-day western Hungary), where another Slavic chieftain, Kocel (ruled 861–874), welcomed the brothers and entrusted to them a group of young men for training.

When the brothers reached Rome, Pope Adrian II welcomed them and granted full approval to their Slavic liturgy. After some months, and while still in Rome, Constantine became seriously ill. The brothers had been staying in a Greek monastery, and during his illness Constantine took a vow to remain a monk and at that point assumed the name Cyril. In less than two months, at the age of about forty-two, he died.

With papal encouragement, Methodius returned to work with the Slavic princes of Pannonia, Moravia, and the area around Nitra (in modern-day eastern Czechoslovakia). Wishing to gain jurisdiction over the areas, Adrian II sent letters with Methodius approving the Slavic liturgy. The princes welcomed Methodius back, and in 869 the pope ordained him archbishop of Pannonia and Moravia, with his cathedral at Sirmium (near present-day Belgrade, Yugoslavia). Opposition to this appointment came from the neighboring Frankish (Bavarian) bishops, Hermanrich of Passau, Adalwin of Salzburg, and Anno of Fresing, all of whom had long worked for Frankish ecclesiastical and political influence in the area. In 870, with the help of Svatopluk, the ruler of Nitra, Bishop Hermanrich contrived to arrest Methodius and imprison him in a monastery in Swabia (southwestern Germany). In 873, Pope John VIII ordered his release, reinstalled him in his former diocese, and reaffirmed, with slight reservations, papal support for the Slavic liturgy.

The work of Methodius among the Slavs seems to have prospered, but opposition continued from the Frankish clergy and from Svatopluk, the new ruler in Moravia. Accused of heresy, Methodius successfully defended himself and won from John VIII a bull that praised his orthodoxy, reaffirmed the independence of his diocese, and expressly authorized the Mass in Slavic. During the last years of his life, Methodius continued to meet opposition. Nevertheless, with the help of two disciples, he completed the translation of the Bible into Slavic and codified both the civil and the ecclesiastical law. After Methodius's death in 884, his disciples were expelled by their Frankish opponents but found refuge in southern Poland, Bulgaria, and Bo hemia (modern-day western Czechoslovakia). Through them the work of Constantine-Cyril and Methodius continued, contributing substantially to the growth of the Greek church and Slavic Christian culture in eastern Europe.

BIBLIOGRAPHY

A detailed study with notes, maps, and bibliography is Francis Dvornik's *Byzantine Missions among the Slavs: SS Constantine-Cyril and Methodius* (New Brunswick, N.J., 1970).

H. McKENNIE GOODPASTURE

CYRIL OF ALEXANDRIA (c. 375–444), church father, theologian, and saint. Cyril succeeded his uncle Theophilus as bishop of Alexandria in 412. His aggressive nature involved him in a series of polemics against heretics. His rhetorical skills were sometimes stronger than his theological judgment, and he was often forgetful of evangelical moderation. In the early days of his studies in the humanities and in religion, he had not been trained to distinguish between the authentic treatises of Athanasius, his most admired predecessor, and those by Apollinarius, listed under Athanasius's name in the episcopal library of Alexandria. Thus he mistakenly urged a form of Christology best expressed by Apollinarius's phrase, which he believed to be Athanasian: "the unique incarnate nature of God the Logos."

Cyril's most famous controversy was with Nestorius, his colleague in the imperial metropolis of Constantinople. A monk from Antioch, made bishop of Constantinople by Emperor Theodosius II in 428, Nestorius preached against Arian and Apollinaristic factions in the monasteries surrounding the capital. Both groups called Mary *theotokos* (Mother of God) in claiming that the Logos incarnate was born, grew up, and suffered. Nestorius became suspicious of this epithet and preferred Mother of Christ. Denounced to Cyril, who ignored the local circumstances and was eager to interfere in the debates at Constantinople, Nestorius was accused by his powerful Alexandrian rival of dividing Christ into two beings, a mere man and the Logos. An exchange of several letters between January and June 430 did not help. Nestorius, with an obvious lack of needed theological acumen, was unaware of the coming storm. Cyril gained strength speedily, and now without diplomatic maneuvers, he garnered the full support of the Roman bishop Celestine and the ear of the emperor. The latter called for a general council in Ephesus, at Pentecost, on 7 June 431. Before numerous Eastern bishops, led by John of Antioch, could arrive—they were moderate supporters of Nestorius and opposed to the passionate initiatives of Cyril—Nestorius was condemned as a heretic and deposed, on 22 June. It took Cyril two years to become reconciled with his Eastern colleagues. Nestorius was sent into a bitter exile in Petra, and later to the Great Oasis in southern Libya. His supporters were all sent to work camps as prisoners.

The literary and theological legacy of Cyril focuses on his christological system and on biblical exegesis. In the wake of anti-Nestorian polemics, he demonstrated a strong opposition to the Antiochene school of scriptural hermeneutics. The main teachers and actual founders of this school were Diodorus, bishop of Tarsus from 378 to around 394, and Theodore, bishop of Mopsuestia from 392 to 428. They were accused by Cyril of having paved the way for Nestorianism, and were condemned by the imperial court. Most of their invaluable biblical commentaries were destroyed.

Cyril's commentaries include an interpretation of christological evidences taken by him from the Pentateuch. These are known as *Glaphura,* which includes extensive interpretations of *Isaiah* and the Minor Prophets, as well as commentaries on *John, Luke, Matthew,* and the Pauline letters. In his exegesis he uses the traditional Alexandrian method, laying out the literal, typological, and moral teaching of scripture. His knowledge of different Greek versions and of the Hebrew text of the Old Testament was complemented by his familiarity with allegorical and etymological techniques of interpretation. His dogmatic works on trinitarian theology popularized the notion of one divine substance in three persons. The main contribution of Cyril in the christological debate was to prepare a clearer notion of the interrelated properties of God and man in the unity of Christ, the so-called *communicatio idiomatum.*

Through the centuries (in both the East and the West), Cyril has been regarded as one of the main defenders of imperial orthodoxy as it was transmitted into the Middle Ages.

[*See also* Nestorianism *and the biography of* Nestorius.]

BIBLIOGRAPHY

Grillmeier, Aloys. *Christ in the Christian Tradition.* 2d ed., rev. Atlanta, 1975.

Kerrigan, Alexander. *Saint Cyril of Alexandria, Interpreter of the Old Testament.* Rome, 1952.

Scipioni, Luigi I. *Nestorio e il concilio di Efeso: Storia, Dogma, Critica.* Studia Patristica Mediolanensia, vol. 1. Milan, 1974.

CHARLES KANNENGIESSER, S.J.

CYRIL OF JERUSALEM (313–386), ecumenical doctor and father of the church. Born in or around Jerusalem, Cyril was ordained presbyter in 343 by Bishop Maximus II, whom he succeeded at the beginning of 348. Although seemingly indifferent to dogmatic subtleties, Cyril could not remain outside the climate of his time. He was acknowledged by the Arians because he avoided the term *homoousios* ("of the same substance"), but he disappointed them at the beginning of his episcopate by placing himself among the adherents of the Nicene dogma. This fact was one reason for his break with Acacius, the Arian metropolitan of Caesarea who had ordained him. A second reason for this rupture was the ambiguity of the seventh canon of the Council of Nicaea (325), which ordered that the bishop of Jerusalem be honored according to ancient custom but be subject to the metropolitan of Caesarea.

Acacius, a favorite of the Arian emperor Constantius, succeeded in banishing Cyril from his see (357), and, although he was recalled by the Council of Seleucia in 359, Cyril had to endure further banishments lasting many years. Having returned under the reign of Julian, he was not personally affected by the emperor's plans to degrade Christianity and promote paganism by all means possible. However, banishment under Valens kept Cyril far from his flock for eleven years. After returning to his see in 378, he remained undisturbed in his work until his death (386).

Cyril's chief work was his *Catecheses,* a collection of twenty-four instructions, delivered in the Church of the Resurrection before and after Easter 348. Their aim was to initiate the catechumens in the fundamental doctrines of Christian faith and life and to explain the main sacraments of the church to the newly baptized.

The collection contains three types of instruction. One preliminary teaching (the *Procatechesis*), which emphasizes the importance of the last stage of instruction, draws the new tasks of the catechumens and points out the need for their preparation for baptism. Next, eighteen catecheses to the *phōtizomenoi* (those who had reached the stage of awaiting baptism at the coming of Easter) deal with the subjects of repentance and baptism, describe the basic doctrines of Christianity and the rules of life, and offer a theologically edifying interpretation of the creed. Finally, five mystagogical catecheses to the newly baptized give a detailed interpretation of the sacraments of baptism, confirmation, and the Eucharist. Some manuscripts ascribe this third section to Cyril's successor, John of Jerusalem.

These instructions seem to have been delivered impromptu, as is noted in some manuscripts. However, their style is clear, vivacious, and cordial. Their mode of instruction is based on sound pedagogical principles; the author repeats a number of times the essential elements so that they may be consolidated in the minds of the hearers. The work has been translated into many languages, both ancient and modern.

Of the homilies of Cyril only one has been preserved; it deals with the cure of the paralytic (*Jn.* 5:5). A letter addressed to Emperor Constantius reports the miraculous apparition of a cross of light above Calvary on 7 May 351. Some other unimportant texts, including an anaphora, have been falsely attributed to him.

As an adherent of the Council of Nicaea, Cyril declared that he neither separated the persons of the Trinity nor confused them. He does not, however, use the critical term *homoousios.* This omission certainly is not owing to his insistence on the necessity of biblical language in doctrine, since the term *homoeos* ("like"), which he does use to define the relation of the Son to the Father, is also nonscriptural. Neither can it be attributed to a semi-Arian tendency, since his struggle against Arianism would therefore go unexplained. It may be ascribed to his fear of a deviation toward Sabellianism, a fear that possessed many adherents of the Nicene Creed. Indeed, Cyril said, "We should not either say there was a time when the Son was not, or put our faith in the doctrine of *huiopatoria* (that is, the Father and the Son are the same person); let us not deviate either to the left or to the right" (*Catecheses* 11.16). He might have been compelled to use the term later on as an indispensable weapon in the struggle against Arianism, but we have no such evidence.

Cyril characterizes the sacrament of baptism in two ways: first, according to the Pauline presentation, as a tomb from which the baptized are resurrected, dying and rising together with Christ; and second, according to the Johannine presentation, as mother of the new spiritual birth. In the eucharistic doctrine he emphasizes clearly the real presence of Christ in the elements: "in the *tupos* of bread" the body of Christ exists, and "in the *tupos* of wine" the blood of Christ exists. Therefore, the faithful, receiving both of these, become "co-bodily and co-bloodily" of Christ. Christ, who at Cana changed water into wine, would have no difficulty in changing wine into blood. Yet Cyril does not mention the words of institution in the Eucharist, probably because they are too sacred for such mention.

After his death Cyril was not often cited, but gradually, as knowledge of his theology spread, his major writings were widely used by theologians, who came to consider them one of the more valid sources for Orthodox theologizing. In 1893 Cyril was proclaimed a doctor of the church by Pope Leo XIII. His feast is celebrated in both the Eastern and the Western church on 18 March.

BIBLIOGRAPHY

Dionysius Kleopas has edited the *Procatechesis* and the *Catecheses* in two volumes (Jerusalem, 1867–1868). A popular edition is F. L. Cross's *St. Cyril of Jerusalem's Lectures on the Christian Sacraments: The Procatechesis and the Five Mystagogical Catecheses* (London, 1951). William Telfer has translated the texts with introduction in *Cyril of Jerusalem and Nemesius of Emesu* (London, 1955).

Several studies treat particular aspects of Cyril's activity and teaching. W. J. Swaans attributes the five mystagogical pieces to John of Jerusalem in "À propos de 'Catéchèses mystagogique,' attribuées à S. Cyrille de Jerusalem," *Muséon* 55 (1942): 1–42. Jacob H. Greenlee treats the biblical sources in his *The Gospel Text of Cyril of Jerusalem* (Copenhagen, 1955). The educational methods of Cyril are treated in Demetrios Moraitis's *Cyril of Jerusalem as a Catechete and Pedagogue* (in Greek; Thessaloniki, 1949); in Elias Voulgazakis's *The Catechesis of Cyril of Jerusalem* (Thessaloniki, 1977), a very important work in modern Greek; and in Antoine Paulin's *Saint Cyrille de Jerusalem Catéchète* (Paris, 1959). Some aspects of Cyril's theological teaching are examined by Basilius Niederberger in *Die Logosidee des hl. Cyrillus von Jerusalem* (Paderborn, 1923); by Hugh M. Riley in *Christian Initiation: A Comparative Study of the Interpretation of the Baptismal Liturgy in the Mystagogical Writings of Cyril of Jerusalem, John Chrysostom, Theodore of Mopsuestia and Ambrose of Milan,* "Studies in Christian Antiquity," no. 17 (Washington, D.C., 1974); and by Edward Yarnold in *The Awe-Inspiring Rites of Initiation: Baptismal Homilies of the Fourth Century* (Slough, England, 1972).

PANAGIOTIS C. CHRISTOU

CYRUS II (c. 585–c. 529 BCE), called Cyrus the Great; builder and ruler of the Persian empire from 559 BCE until his death. A king of the Achaemenid dynasty, Cyrus (OPers., Kurush) combined great ambition, shrewd calculation, and military expertise to establish the largest empire in world history. From his base in Anshan he conquered neighboring Media in alliance with the Babylonian king Nabonidus in 550, overtook Lydia in Asia Minor in 547, defeated resisting areas in the Greek mainland, then returned to Persia and drove his armies eastward as far as India. With his power thus increased, he conquered Babylonia and proclaimed himself king of all Mesopotamia—indeed, of the world—in 539.

Nabonidus had alienated the Babylonian priesthood through his extraordinary devotion to the moon cult. Capitalizing on Nabonidus's heresy, Cyrus achieved popularity in Babylon by restoring the cult of its chief god, Marduk, and by reestablishing the shrines and proper worship of other gods in their former locations. In a proclamation composed in Babylonian, Cyrus asserts that Marduk delivered his lands to the conqueror and that Bel (Enlil) and Nabu, the local Babylonian gods, love his rule. The Hebrew scriptures preserve two versions of an edict by Cyrus in which the conqueror attributes his victories to the Israelite god, "YHVH God of Heaven" who "commanded me to build him a temple in Jerusalem" (*Ezr.* 1:1–3, 6:3–5). The Judeans living in exile in Babylonia saw Cyrus as their liberator because he permitted them in 538 to return to their homeland in Judaea and to rebuild the Temple, which had been destroyed by Babylonia in 587/6. A prophet of the Judean exile, the so-called Second Isaiah, portrayed Cyrus as the "shepherd" chosen by the Lord to subjugate nations and reestablish the Jerusalem Temple (*Is.* 44:28, 45:1ff.; cf. *Is.* 41:1ff.).

Subsequent Jewish traditions tend to play down Cyrus's personal rectitude while seeing him as an instrument of God (B.T., *Meg.* 12a). Christian exegetes have often regarded Cyrus as a prefiguration of the Messiah.

BIBLIOGRAPHY

For the history of Cyrus's conquest and reign, see Albert Ten Eyck Olmstead's *History of the Persian Empire: Achaemenid Period* (Chicago, 1948), pp. 34–58. His Babylonian proclamation is translated by A. Leo Oppenheim in *Ancient Near Eastern Texts relating to the Old Testament,* 3d ed. with suppl., edited by J. B. Pritchard (Princeton, 1969), pp. 315–316, and a good analysis of this text, with bibliography in the notes, is Amélie Kuhrt's "The Cyrus Cylinder and Achaemenid Imperial Policy," *Journal for the Study of the Old Testament* 25 (February 1983): 83–97. The Hebrew and Aramaic edicts of Cyrus are analyzed by Elias J. Bickerman in "The Edict of Cyrus in Ezra 1," *Journal of Biblical Literature* 65 (1946): 249–275. The most comprehensive explanation of Cyrus's policies is Hayim Tadmor's "Hareqa' ha-hisṭori le-hatsharat Koresh," in *'Oz le-David,* edited by Menahem Haran et al. (Jerusalem, 1964), pp. 450–473.

EDWARD L. GREENSTEIN

DACIAN RIDERS. The so-called Dacian Riders were associated with a mystery religion of the Getae and the Dacians, peoples of Thracian stock who lived in ancient Dacia (roughly equivalent to modern-day Romania). The cult of the Dacian, or Danubian, Riders began to spread among Roman soldiers soon after 106 CE, when Dacia was conquered by Trajan and made a province of the Roman empire. Traces of the cult have been found as far away as the Roman provinces of Gaul and Britain.

Numerous reliefs and gems depicting the Dacian Riders are extant. Of the 232 items catalogued by Dumitru Tudor (1969–1976), 60 were found in Dacia, 24 in Moesia Superior, 34 in Moesia Inferior, 47 in Pannonia Inferior, and 25 in Pannonia Superior. Most of the Dacian reliefs are made of marble. They were copied on a large scale in lead, a very expensive material whose use can be explained only by the magical purposes for which the images of the Dacian Riders were intended. Of the 90 lead copies extant, 44 were found in Pannonia Inferior.

The most ancient reliefs show only one horseman, whose iconography was influenced by that of the Thracian Rider. [*See* Thracian Rider.] Later monuments show two riders at either side of a goddess whose principal symbolic attribute is a fish. Of the 31 pieces belonging to the one-horseman type, 18 were found in Dacia. The two-horseman type belongs to the later period of this cult, which flourished in the third century CE and declined in the fourth.

Besides the two horsemen and the goddess with a fish, the iconography of the monuments includes prostrated characters, attendants, and various symbols, such as the sun, the moon, stars, and numerous animals (including the ram, dog, lion, eagle, peacock, raven, cock, snake, and sometimes even the bull). Scholarly identifications of the goddess are widely divergent. The two horsemen have been identified with the Dioscuri by some scholars and with the Cabiri brothers by others. The Greek iconography of the Dioscuri has had a particular impact on that of the Dacian Riders, but all these scholarly hypotheses are more or less fanciful.

It is likely that certain beliefs and practices, borrowed especially from Mithraism, were added to a local Dacian cult and that these borrowings changed the cult into a mystery religion. Although the myth of the Danubian Riders remains unknown, it is safe to state that it was based on some Dacian beliefs not shared by the Thracians south of the Danube. The two horsemen and the goddess were probably supposed to establish a link between three cosmic layers (heaven, earth, and underworld), as the partition of the reliefs into three registers seems to suggest.

Only three degrees of initiation were present in the mysteries of the Dacian Riders: Aries ("ram"), Miles ("soldier"), and Leo ("lion"). The first two were placed under the influence of the planet Mars, the last one under the influence of the sun. If we interpret the numerous animals depicted in the reliefs of the Danubian Riders as astrological entities, then we may surmise that the symbolism of this mystery religion was fairly complicated. Inscriptions are unusually scarce in number, short (especially those on gems), and indecipherable. Initiates in the mysteries identified their grade by badges and seals; for example, a gem of unknown provenance bears as its inscription the single word *leon.*

In all probability, sacrifice of a ram played an important part in these mysteries.

BIBLIOGRAPHY

On the Dacian Riders, see the excellent work of Dumitru Tudor, *Corpus monumentorum religionis equitum Danuvinorum,* 2 vols. (Leiden, 1969–1976). Volume 1, *The Monuments,* translated by Eve Harris and John R. Harris, is a detailed catalog; volume 2, *The Analysis and Interpretation of the Monuments,* translated by Christopher Holme, is a thorough survey of scholarly theories concerning the mysteries.

IOAN PETRU CULIANU and CICERONE POGHIRC

DACO-GETIC RELIGION. *See* Geto-Dacian Religion.

DAGAN was a god first of Syria-Mesopotamia, later of the Canaanites to the west, and finally of the Philistines. Although Dagan (called Dagon in the Bible) has a certain notoriety because of the Old Testament passage (*Jgs.* 16) in which Samson brings down the Philistine temple of Dagon at Gaza, actually very little is known about either his origins or his exact nature.

By most evidence Dagan was a pre-Sumerian, pre-Semitic god worshiped in the middle Euphrates region, an area that entered the Sumerian sphere of influence at an early date. There were important shrines of Dagan at Tuttul, Mari, and Terqa, all within present-day Syria. With the emergence of the empire of Akkad under Sargon (c. 2300 BCE), Dagan was adopted as an Akkadian national god. Cuneiform sources indicate that Sargon visited the shrine of Dagan at Tuttul. During the following period of neo-Sumerian renaissance (Ur III, c. 2100–2000 BCE), Dagan's name is found on seals alongside that of his consort, Shalash, a goddess of perhaps Hurrian origin. She may be the same as Shala, the consort of the Babylonian weather god Adad. In the Isin-Larsa period (c. 2000–1900 BCE) two kings of Isin bear names with the element *dagan,* Idindagan ("Dagan has given") and Ishmedagan ("Dagan has heard").

Dagan seems to have enjoyed the most popularity during the "Mari Age" of the late seventeenth century BCE. At Mari alone, an Amorite city, more than fifty different personal names compounded with *dagan* have been found. Unfortunately, the epithets of Dagan used in these names offer little clue as to the precise nature of the god, since they are epithets used of many other gods and there is no common theme.

No doubt Dagan had a significant function among the Canaanites, but few sources provide real evidence of his role. There was a temple of Dagan at Ugarit, and he was included in Ugaritic offering-lists. Baal is called "son of Dagan," a rather ambiguous title since Baal is also called "son of El." Finally, within Canaanite territory were several towns named Bet-Dagan ("temple of Dagan").

Dagan was the chief god of the Philistines, who surely borrowed his cult from the Canaanites. He had major temples at Gaza (the Samson story, *Judges* 16) and at Ashdod (the Philistines steal the Ark, *1 Samuel* 5; they place Saul's head in Dagon's temple, *1 Chronicles* 10).

Early authors who assumed *Dagan* to be a Semitic name analyzed it either as *dag on* ("fish of sadness") or as a derivation from the word for grain, *dagan.* Most scholars now see the name as non-Semitic, and suggest that the word for grain is derived from the name of the god, not vice versa. This association, however, as well as the occasional links between Dagan and weather, do indicate that Dagan was most likely a god of good weather and agricultural fertility.

BIBLIOGRAPHY

Secondary sources are few indeed. Seriously outdated but still useful is Frank J. Montalbano's "Canaanite Dagon: Origin, Nature," *Catholic Biblical Quarterly* 13 (October 1951): 381–397. There are many references in Edward E. Hindson's *The Philistines and the Old Testament* (Grand Rapids, Mich., 1971). For onomastics, see Herbert B. Huffmon's *Amorite Personal Names in the Mari Texts* (Baltimore, 1965).

WILLIAM J. FULCO, S.J.

DAGHDHA, an Irish deity associated with war and druidry, has four names or surnames in Irish mythology: Daghdha ("good god"), Eochaid (**ivo-katu-s,* "who does combat with yew," an allusion to the magical and warlike uses of this wood), Ollathir ("powerful father"), and Ruadh Rofhess ("the red one of great knowledge"). He corresponds to the Gaulish Jupiter as defined by Caesar in the *Gallic Wars* (6:17): "Louem imperium caelestium tenere" ("Jupiter rules the empire of the heavens"). He forms a couple with Oghma (Gaulish Ogmios), who is the "champion" and the "binding" god, to make an equivalence to an archaic sovereign divinity, the dual Mitra-Varuṇa of the *Ṛgveda.*

Daghdha is the druid god, the god of contracts, of friendship, of all that is intelligible, regulated, and ordered. He is the lord of the climate and of chronological time, of the elements (air, water, land, and fire); a wise god and a warrior god, he is also one of the lords of the otherworld. In the cycle of Édaín his daughter is Brighid (the Gaulish "Minerva") and his principal son Oenghus ("only choice"), otherwise known as Mac ind Óg ("young son"), born of his adulterous affairs with

Boann (*bo vinda, "white cow"), the wife of his brother Elcmhaire (another name for Oghma). (Boann is also the eponym of the Boínne, the mythological river.) In another tale, the *Battle of Magh Tuiredh,* he has three or four disagreeable mishaps, but it is he who, along with Lugh and Oghma, organizes the victorious war of the Tuatha Dé Danann against the Fomhoire. But in this war he does not do battle: he is happy to couple with his wife, Morríghan ("great queen"), the goddess of war.

The Irish scribes, transcribing their mythology much later, made of him a king of Ireland, most often by the name of Eochaidh. The texts portray him as a formidable druid, who is also a warrior. His principle attributes are the caldron of plenty and of resurrection; the club that kills with one blow (in this world) and revives with another (in the otherworld); and the harp that contains all tunes.

His residence is the Bruigh na Boínne, or "hostel of the Boínne," located in the protohistoric tumulus of Newgrange, but a brief tale recounts how his son Oenghus, or Mac ind Óg, dispossessed him of it by means of a juridical ruse: having no domain of his own, Mac ind Óg asks his father to grant him the use of Bruigh na Boínne for a night and a day. But when the time has expired and Daghdha returns, Mac ind Óg refuses to leave, alleging that a night and a day are the symbol of eternity. This quarrel between father and son, the young and the old, symbolizes—as with Juventus and Terminus in Rome—the ambiguous and difficult relations of time (Oenghus, god of youth) and eternity (Daghdha, who suspends the march of time).

BIBLIOGRAPHY

Guyonvarc'h, Christian-J., and Françoise Le Roux. *Textes mythologiques irlandais,* vol. 1. Rennes, 1980.

Le Roux, Françoise. "Le dieu-druide et le druide divin: Recherches sur la fonction sacerdotale celtique." *Ogam* 12 (1960): 349–382.

FRANÇOISE LE ROUX AND CHRISTIAN-J. GUYONVARC'H
Translated from French by Erica Meltzer

DAHOMEAN RELIGION. *See* Fon and Ewe Religion.

DAINAS. In Baltic cultures, the songs known in Latvian as *dainas* and in Lithuanian as *dainos* deal with two fundamental cycles, the life cycle of humans and the festival cycle of the agricultural seasons. Although they are often referred to by the common designation *folk song,* this modern term is misleading, for the *dainas,* with their trochaic and dactylic meters, differ from the folk songs known to European scholars. The original Lithuanian *dainos* have to a great extent disappeared because of the influence of the European folk song, but Latvian *dainas* have survived in great numbers. About sixty thousand (not including variants) have been collected and published by scholars. Their content reveals that they were an integral part of daily agrarian life among Baltic peoples; as such, they bear directly on Baltic religion.

Regarding the etymology of the term, Suniti Kumar Chatterji has pointed out that

> the Baltic word *daina* had unquestionably its Aryan [Indo-Iranian] equivalent, etymologically and semantically, which is perfectly permissible. . . . An Indo-European root **dhi-, *dhy-ei, *dhei-,* meaning 'to think, to ponder over, to give thought to', appears to be the source of the Vedic *dhēnā* and the Avestian *daēnā.* An Indo-European form **dhainā* as the sourceword can very easily and quite correctly be postulated. (Chatterji, 1968, pp. 69–70)

From the age of Vedic literature words derived from this source word deal with the following notions: speech, voice, praise, prayer, panegyric, and song. The Pahlavi *dēn* ("religion") developed into the Avestan *daēna,* which, in turn, appears in modern Arabic as *dīn,* meaning "religion," specifically, orthodox Islam. These etymological derivations and semantic relationships suggest that *dhainā* is an ancient Baltic word that has retained the meaning of "song" through the years.

Life Cycle. *Dainas* figure prominently in an individual's life cycle at three major points: birth, marriage, and death. Each of these events determines not only the content but also the form of the *dainas.*

1. In songs dealing with childbirth, the mother figure appears not only as the one who bears the child but also as the one who rears it and determines its fate. These *dainas* are characterized by their deep emotionality. This is particularly true of *dainas* dealing with the fate of foster children. *Dainas* sung directly after the birth of a child during the cultic feast *(pirtīžas)* in the sauna, the traditional place of birthing, have a special significance because of their cultic character. These *dainas* are devoted to the goddess of fate, Laima.

2. *Dainas* dealing with love, the selection of a partner, and marriage are rather different from those associated with birth. They are imbued with joy and contain erotic and sexual elements intended to chafe and mock others. Some of the songs are so caustic that the seventeenth-century bishop Paul Einhorn, having heard the wedding songs of Latvian peasants, failed to comprehend their deep religious and cultic character. He wrote in dismay in his *Historie lettice* in 1649: "Afterwards such improper, brazen, and flippant songs were sung without interruption, day and night, that even the devil himself could not have devised and put forth anything more improper and lewd." Yet such fertility *dainas* belong to the very old family cult.

3. The third group of life-cycle *dainas,* those dealing with death, are rich in content, representing the individual's preparation for death. Their cultic character becomes evident in songs that describe the bearing of the casket from the home to the cemetery, which was the site of the cultic feast. There a particular type of *daina* was sung to guarantee that the dead person would have a favorable relationship with the ruler of the grave and the realm of death, occasionally referred to as Kapu Māte ("grave mother").

Festival Cycle. The second cycle includes *dainas* that describe the agricultural work routine and festivals. In their sequence they mirror the yearly cycle, including its holidays. The most important holidays are the summer and winter solstices. The commencement and conclusion of particular work phases also have an important place in the cycle. In the spring, when planting began, bread and meat were plowed into the first furrow. Similarly, the leading of the first cattle to pasture and the first horses to night watch were also observed as special events. All of these occasions were associated with sacral feasts under the leadership of the paterfamilias. Appropriate *dainas* were an integral part of these rituals. The commencement as well as the conclusion of certain jobs was observed, especially during the fall harvest. This was a time of relative abundance, and therefore the feasts were especially lavish.

Religious Dimensions. Both of these cycles mirror the framework of the Baltic peasant's life, which consisted of both hard work and joyous festivity, represented by work *dainas* and festival *dainas.* The peasants, in close harmony with nature, performed their tasks with songs that helped them to adhere to the rhythm of work. Festival *dainas,* whether of the first or second cycle, introduce another ancient element inherent in the name *dainas* itself: that of dance. The verb *dainot* really means "to sing and move rhythmically in a group," that is, "to dance" in the broadest sense of the word.

The great majority of *dainas* are songs describing various chores that have no specific religious content. Many describe nature, using explicit personifications of and metaphors for natural phenomena. A significant number of songs, however, do have a religious dimension, which can be explained by the significance of religion in Baltic daily life. Man's place in nature and his dependence on it forced him to ponder the basis of his existence and to determine his relationship with the forces of nature. The *dainas* are the clearest proof of this close relationship. Furthermore, because the source material relating to the religious life of the Baltic peoples is limited, the *dainas* represent an irreplaceable source for the reconstruction of this religious framework.

BIBLIOGRAPHY

Barons, Krišjānis. *Latwju dainas.* 2d ed. 6 vols. in 8. Riga, 1922. An academic complete-text edition with variants of Latvian *dainas.*

Chatterji, Suniti Kumar. *Balts and Aryans.* Simla, India, 1968.

Greble, Vilma. "Tautas dziesmas." In *Latviešu literatūras vēsture,* vol. 1, pp. 22–158. Riga, 1959. Historical survey of the different editions of *dainas* and a short introduction to the main problems.

Jonval, Michel. *Les chansons mythologiques lettonnes.* Paris, 1929. A selection of religious *dainas* concerning the pre-Christian Latvian deities.

Katzenelenbogen, Uriah. *The Daina.* Chicago, 1935. The only edition of *dainas* in English, with a brief introductory survey of their ethnological value.

Lietuvių tautosaka, vol. 1, *Dainos.* Vilnius, 1962. A complete-text edition of Lithuanian *dainos* with a Marxist ideological introduction.

HARALDS BIEZAIS

DAIVAS. The Iranian term *daiva* originally signified "god," as is shown in several occurrences of the word in the Avesta (Av., *daēva;* OPers., *daiva;* MPers., Pahl., *dēv*). Like the Vedic *deva* or the Latin *deus, daiva* may be related to the Indo-European root meaning "shine, be bright." In Zoroastrian Iran, however, *daiva* had a negative sense. Other terms were used to refer to divine beings, such as *baga* ("one who distributes"), *ahura* ("lord"), and *yazata* ("one worthy of worship"), while *daiva* was used to designate malefic or demonic powers. For that reason one speaks of a "demonization" of the *daiva* as a phenomenon characteristic of Zoroastrianism.

In all probability *daiva* acquired a negative value in the Iranian world because of the condemnation by Zarathushtra (Zoroaster) of traditional religion. The prophet of Ahura Mazdā propounded a faith and a doctrine of monotheistic inspiration, and the gods of ancient polytheism were repudiated as illusions or chimeras.

Later, after Zoroastrianism had reached a compromise with the older religious sensibility and with the various forms of polytheism that had spread throughout the Iranian world in the first millennium BCE, the *daivas* were condemned not because they were considered, as Zarathushtra had seen them, the fruit of ignorance and superstition but because they were thought to be real demonic beings. The significance of *daiva* thus changed from "god" to "demon." In this later form of the religion, Indra, Saurva, and Nānhaithya—who had prominent positions in the Indian pantheon as Indra, Śarva, and Nāsatya—became archdemons. They were opposed, respectively, by the Amesha Spentas Asha, Khshathra Vairya, and Ārmaiti.

The Zoroastrian pandemonium is particularly rich. Among the most important *daivas* are Aēshma ("wrath, fury"), known throughout the Zoroastrian tradition; Apaosha ("dearth"), fought by Tishtrya, the *yazata* of the star Sirius; Astō-vīdhātu ("dismembering of skeleton"); Būshyąstā ("sloth"); and Nasu ("corpse"), the demon of decay.

Zarathushtra's condemnation of the *daivas*, intended as the rejection of the gods of polytheism, always remained, if only with the modification explained above, a characteristic feature of Zoroastrianism. In all its subsequent historical manifestations—as, for example, in an inscription of Xerxes at Persepolis—we can recognize traces, even if partly distorted, of Zarathushtra's original teaching.

BIBLIOGRAPHY

Benveniste, Émile. "Hommes et dieux dans l'Avesta." In *Festschrift für Wilhelm Eilers*, pp. 144–147. Wiesbaden, 1967.

Bianchi, Ugo. "L'inscription 'des daivas' et le zoroastrisme des Achéménides." *Revue de l'historie des religions* 192 (1977): 3–30.

Boyce, Mary. *A History of Zoroastrianism*, vol. 1. Leiden, 1975.

Burrow, T. "The Proto-Indoaryans." *Journal of the Royal Asiatic Society* (1973): 123–140.

Duchesne-Guillemin, Jacques. *Ormazd et Ahriman*. Paris, 1953.

Gershevitch, Ilya. "Die Sonne das Beste." In *Mithraic Studies*, edited by John R. Hinnells, vol. 1, pp. 68–81. Manchester, 1975.

Gnoli, Gherardo. *Zoroaster's Time and Homeland*. Naples, 1980.

Gray, Louis H. *The Foundations of the Iranian Religions*. Bombay, 1930.

Henning, W. B. "A Sogdian God." *Bulletin of the School of Oriental and African Studies* 28 (1965): 242–254.

Lommel, Herman. *Die Religionn Zarathustras nach dem Awesta dargestellt*. Tübingen, 1930.

Molé, Marijan. *Culte, mythe et cosmologie dans l'Iran ancien*. Paris, 1963.

Nöldeke, Theodor. "Der Weisse Dēv von Māzandarān." *Archiv für Religionswissenschaft* 18 (1915): 597–600.

Widengren, Geo. *Stand und Aufgaben der iranischen Religionsgeschichte*. Leiden, 1955.

GHERARDO GNOLI
Translated from Italian by Roger DeGaris

DAKHMA. The Iranian term *dakhma*, which probably originally signified "tomb," seems to be derived from the Indo-European root **dhm̥bh*, "bury" (Hoffman, 1965), and not from *dag*, "burn," as some scholars have proposed. It is occasionally used in the Avesta with a negative meaning, insofar as the burial of bodies was condemned: the funeral rites adopted by the Zoroastrian community (and which were already practiced in priestly circles in the Achaemenid period, as we know from Herodotus) were designed to avoid scrupulously any contamination of the earth, fire, and water and can be traced to earlier practices widespread among the nomads of Central Asia. These—as we learn from the *Vendidad*—prescribed that corpses, considered impure, be exposed to vultures so that the bones could be cleansed of flesh. Once they were purified of humors and putrefying flesh, the bones were placed in special ossuaries. According to Strabo, the exposure of corpses was also practiced in eastern Iran during the Parthian period.

Later, *dakhma* became the technical term for the "towers of silence," the buildings used for the rites of exposure of the corpses, whether in Zoroastrian communities in Iran or in Parsi communities of India. The modern translation "towers of silence" seems to have been used for the first time by R. Z. Murphy, Oriental translator for the British government at Bombay (Modi, 1937).

The *dakhma*, which continues to be used today, although in more limited forms, is a circular tower, constructed of stone and often located on a hill. An iron door opens onto a large platform consisting of three concentric circles. The first and largest is for the bodies of men; the second, in the middle, is for those of women; and the third is for those of children. After the corpse has been exposed and reduced to a skeleton, the bones are put in a large, deep hole at the center of the *dakhma*.

Zoroastrian ritual attaches great importance to funerals, which are consequently very detailed and complex, as well as meticulous in their purificatory practices. Equally complex are the rites for the consecration of the *dakhma*, which consist of ceremonies for the excavation of the site, for the foundation, and for the consecration itself.

BIBLIOGRAPHY

Boyce, Mary. "An Old Village *Dakhma* of Iran." In *Mémorial Jean de Menasce*, edited by Philippe Gignoux and A. Tafazzoli, pp. 3–9. Louvain, 1974.

Boyce, Mary. *A History of Zoroastrianism*, vol. 1. Leiden, 1975.

Boyce, Mary. *A Persian Stronghold of Zoroastrianism*. Oxford, 1977.

Boyce, Mary. *Zoroastrians: Their Religious Beliefs and Practices*. London, 1979.

Duchesne-Guillemin, Jacques. *La religion de l'Iran ancien*. Paris, 1962.

Hoffmann, Karl. "Av. daxma-." *Zeitschrift für vergleichende Sprachforschung aus dem Gebiete der indogermanischen Sprache* 89 (1965): 238.

Modi, Jivanji Jamshedji. *The Religious Ceremonies and Customs of the Parsees.* 2d ed. Bombay, 1937.

GHERARDO GNOLI
Translated from Italian by Roger DeGaris

DALAI LAMA, title of the spiritual and formerly political leader of the Tibetan people, is a combination of the Mongolian *dalai* ("ocean"), signifying profound knowledge, and the Tibetan *blama* ("religious teacher"). The title dates from 1578 CE, when it was conferred by Altan Khan of the Mongols upon Bsod-nams-rgya-mtsho (1543–1588), third hierarch of the Dge-lugs-pa school of Tibetan Buddhism, commonly called the Yellow Hat sect. The title was applied posthumously to the two preceding hierarchs, Dge-'dun-grub-pa (1391–1475), founder of Bkra-śis-lhun-po (Tashilhunpo) monastery near Shigatse in Gtsaṅ province, and Dge-'dun-rgya-mtsho (1475–1542), founder of the Dalai Lama's residence in 'Bras-spuṅs monastery near Lhasa in Dbus province. After 1578 the title was given to each of the successive reincarnations of the Dalai Lama. The present Dalai Lama is fourteenth in the lineage.

Incarnation (Tib., *sprul sku*), the manifestation of some aspect of the absolute Buddhahood in human form, is an ancient doctrine and one common to various schools of Mahāyāna Buddhism, but the concept of the reincarnation *(yaṅ srid)* of a lama is unique to Tibetan Buddhism. The concept emerged in the fourteenth century in the hierarchic lineage of the Black Hat Karma-pa and was soon adopted by the other Tibetan schools.

From the inception of the institution, traditional procedures for discovering the rebirth of a Dalai Lama, similar to those used for other reincarnate lamas, were followed. Indicative statements made by the previous Dalai Lama during his lifetime, significant auguries surrounding his death and afterward, and meditative visions by special lamas were recorded and interpreted as guides to finding his rebirth. In time, but no sooner than nine months after the death of the previous Dalai Lama, the people began to expect reports of an exceptional male child born in accordance with various omens. Such a child, usually two or three years old when discovered, was subjected to tests to determine physical fitness, intelligence, and the ability to remember events and objects from his previous existence. If more than one likely candidate was found, the final selection was made by drawing a name from a golden urn. Once the true reincarnation was determined, he was enthroned in the Potala palace as the Dalai Lama. The monastic education of a Dalai Lama, directed by learned tutors of the Dge-lugs-pa school, occupied his time for years. When he attained his majority, at about eighteen years of age, he assumed the religio-political power of the office of Dalai Lama.

In the beginning, the religious power of the Dalai Lama was limited to the monastic members and lay patrons of the reformed Yellow Hat school. By the middle of the sixteenth century, religio-political power in Tibet was unevenly divided between the Red Hat Karma-pa, supported by the lay king of Gtsaṅ, and the Yellow Hat Dge-lugs-pa, patronized by lay princes of Dbus. The third hierarch of the Yellow Hat school was subsequently invited to Mongolia by Altan Khan, who gave him the title Dalai Lama. When the Dalai Lama died in Mongolia, his reincarnation was discovered to be none other than the great-grandson of Altan Khan himself. The fourth Dalai Lama, Yon-tan-rgya-mtsho (1589–1617), is the only one in the lineage ethnically not a Tibetan. Escorted from Mongolia to Lhasa, he was enthroned in the Dalai Lama's residence in 'Bras-spuṅs monastery. Recognition of this Mongol prince as the reincarnation of the Dalai Lama thereafter bound the Mongols by faith to the Yellow Hat school, and in time they were to protect it militarily from its enemies.

The power struggle in Tibet between the Red Hat Karma-pa and the Yellow Hat Dge-lugs-pa continued to escalate in favor of the Red Hats and the lay king of Gtsaṅ. Finally in 1642, at the invitation of the fifth Dalai Lama, Ṅag-dbaṅ-rgya-mtsho (1617–1682), Gu-śrī Khan of the Mongols led troops into Tibet, defeated the Red Hat opposition, and executed the lay king of Gtsaṅ. In effect Gu-śrī Khan had conquered Tibet, but true to his faith, he presented the country to the fifth Dalai Lama as a religious gift. Thus the Dalai Lama became the religious and political head of Tibet. Since he was a monk, a civil administrator was appointed to handle the day-to-day affairs of state.

After the enthronement of this Dalai Lama, a prophetic scripture was discovered. It revealed that the reincarnate Dalai Lama was also an incarnation of the Bodhisattva of Compassion, Avalokiteśvara (Tib., Spyan-ras-gzigs), traditionally regarded as the patron *bodhisattva* of Tibet. The relationship between the noumenal Avalokiteśvara and the phenomenal Dalai Lama was attested by symbolism. According to Buddhist doctrine, the mystical abode of Avalokiteśvara is a mountain called the Potala; so the fifth Dalai Lama ordered a massive fortress, also called the Potala, to be built on a mountain in the Lhasa area. Begun in 1645, the Potala at Lhasa served as the palace of the Dalai Lama for over three hundred years.

The most common Tibetan prayer is the six-syllable "Oṃ maṇi padme hūṃ." Printed on prayer flags, contained in prayer wheels, carved repeatedly in wood and stone, and chanted daily by Tibetan Buddhists, this is the vocative mantra in Sanskrit of Avalokiteśvara. In view of his relationship to the Dalai Lama, the six-syllable mantra symbolically serves at once as an invocation to both the noumenal and phenomenal manifestations of the Bodhisattva of Compassion. Because of the belief that the Dalai Lama is an incarnation of Avalokiteśvara as well as a reincarnation of his predecessor, he is frequently, but incorrectly, called the "God-King" of Tibet in Western writings.

The fifth Dalai Lama was a learned scholar and the author of many texts, including a history of Tibet. During the forty years he was head of state, the Mongols helped to protect his newly established government and to expand its territorial control. In recognition of the important role he played in religio-political history, he is referred to in Tibetan literature as the Great Fifth.

The death of the fifth Dalai Lama was kept secret for fifteen years by the civil administrator for political reasons. His reincarnation, Tshaṅs-dbyaṅs-rgya-mtsho (1683–1706), was discovered in due course but was not officially acknowledged as the next Dalai Lama until 1697. Unlike the monastic training of his predecessors, who had been publicly enthroned and tutored as children, that of the sixth Dalai Lama was not only kept secret but was apparently less than strict. Already in his teens when enthroned in the Potala, he soon gained notoriety for his addiction to wine, women, and song. Censure caused him to renounce his vows as a monk in 1702, but he remained in the Potala as the Dalai Lama. Finally in 1706, he was deposed by Lha-bzaṅ Khan, a great-grandson of Gu-śrī Khan, and deported to China; he died enroute. The sixth Dalai Lama is perhaps best remembered for sixty-two four-line verses, commonly referred to as his "love songs." A recurring theme in his poetry is the psychophysiological conflict between his monastic obligations as the Dalai Lama and his passion for mundane pleasures.

After the deposition and death of the sixth Dalai Lama, Lha-bzaṅ Khan became undisputed ruler of Tibet. He enthroned a puppet in the Potala, but the Tibetan people refused to accept him as the Dalai Lama. Instead, a boy born in eastern Tibet was recognized as the true reincarnation. Owing to the unstable situation in Lhasa, the seventh Dalai Lama, Bskal-bzaṅ-rgya-mtsho (1708–1757), was taken to Kumbum monastery in the Kokonor region for safekeeping. In 1717 Mongols from Dzungaria, in support of the seventh Dalai Lama, invaded Tibet and killed Lha-bzaṅ Khan. The puppet Dalai Lama was deposed and later deported to China. The seventh Dalai Lama was escorted to Lhasa by a Manchu imperial army and enthroned in the Potala in 1720.

A significant change was made in 1721 in the structure of the Tibetan government. The office of the civil administrator, which had concentrated political power in one pair of hands, was abolished and replaced with a council of four ministers collectively responsible for the secular branch of the dyadic hierocracy.

The death of the seventh Dalai Lama in 1757 led to the creation of a new government position. The office of the Dalai Lama had become institutionalized by then, and there was no question but that his reincarnation would succeed to his position of ruling power. Thus, the death of a Dalai Lama meant an interregnum of some twenty years, during which his reincarnation had to be discovered and educated, and his majority attained before he would resume power. During that period, another reincarnate lama of the Dge-lugs-pa school was appointed regent to rule Tibet on behalf of the minor Dalai Lama. Reluctance of successive regents and their supporters to hand over power each time a Dalai Lama reached his majority is blamed, perhaps unjustly, for the fact that the eighth Dalai Lama ruled only for a few years, the ninth and tenth died young without assuming power, and the eleventh and twelth Dalai Lamas ruled only for short periods before their death.

The thirteenth Dalai Lama, Thub-bstan-rgya-mtsho (1876–1933), assumed full power in 1895. He survived an attempt on his life by his former regent, who purportedly resorted to witchcraft in hopes of furthering his political ambitions. During his long reign as head of state, the thirteenth Dalai Lama was forced to flee to Mongolia in 1904 to escape British troops invading from India. He spent years traveling in Mongolia and China. Not long after his return to Lhasa, he was again forced to flee early in 1910, this time to India to avoid the invading Chinese forces. The Chinese revolution of 1911 that overthrew the Manchu dynasty and established the Republic of China also marked the end of Manchu domination of Tibetan affairs. The Manchu imperial garrison at Lhasa, which had been set up early in the eighteenth century, was deported to a man by the Tibetan government. From 1913 until his death in 1933, the thirteenth Dalai Lama was the head of an independent government. Living in exile in British India motivated the thirteenth Dalai Lama to implement various reforms in Tibet to improve the welfare of his people. His importance in Tibetan history can be compared with that of the Great Fifth Dalai Lama in the seventeenth century.

The fourteenth and present Dalai Lama, Bstan-'dzin-rgya-mtsho, was born in 1935 of Tibetan parentage in the Chinghai province of China. Two other likely candidates were also found; but the one from Chinghai successfully passed all the tests, the omens were in mystical agreement, and he was confirmed as the true reincarnation by the State Oracle of Tibet himself. The Chinghai candidate was duly enthroned in the Potala at Lhasa in 1940. During the next decade, half of which was taken up by World War II in Asia, the young Dalai Lama was educated and prepared for the time he would assume his role as religio-political ruler of Tibet.

The invasion of eastern Tibet late in 1950 by forces of the People's Republic of China precipitated the empowerment of the fourteenth Dalai Lama when he was just fifteen years old. He was escorted to a village near the Indian border to avoid capture by the Chinese. In 1951, an agreement was reached between the Tibetan government and the Peking regime, and the Dalai Lama subsequently returned to Lhasa.

In 1956, the Dalai Lama and the Panchen Lama, the high-ranking reincarnate lama of the Yellow Hat monastery of Bkra-śis-lhun-po, were invited to India to attend the Buddha Jayanti, a great celebration marking the twenty-five-hundredth anniversary of the birth of the Buddha. After the Dalai Lama returned to Tibet, however, the constrained political situation there continued to deteriorate, and in March 1959 the Tibetan populace revolted against the Chinese regime in Lhasa. The Dalai Lama fled to India. That month the Chinese abolished the traditional Tibetan government, ending over three hundred years of hierocratic rule by the Dalai Lama, incarnation of Avalokiteśvara, Bodhisattva of Compassion.

The present Dalai Lama continues to live in exile in India. He has traveled internationally, visiting various Asian countries as well as continental Europe, the United Kingdom, and the United States. The leaders of two great religious traditions met when the fourteenth Dalai Lama of Tibetan Buddhism was welcomed in the Vatican by Paul VI in 1973 and by John Paul II in 1979.

[*For further discussion of the development of the Dge-lugs-pa school, see* Dge-lugs-pa.]

BIBLIOGRAPHY

The only book dealing with the first thirteen Dalai Lamas in some detail remains Günther Schulemann's *Die Geschichte der Dalailamas,* 2d ed. (Leipzig, 1959). Charles A. Bell's *Portrait of the Dalai Lama* (London, 1946) is a biographical sketch based on the author's personal friendship with the thirteenth Dalai Lama, but part 2 of the book explains what a Dalai Lama is and how he is discovered and educated. A scholarly listing, but with basic dates and data only, of all fourteen Dalai Lamas, as well as the regents who successively served them, can be found in Luciano Petech's "The Dalai-Lamas and Regents of Tibet: A Chronological Study," *T'oung pao* (Leiden) 47 (1959): 368–394.

English translations of three books by the fourteenth Dalai Lama, Tenzin Gyatso, are recommended. His autobiography, *My Land and My People* (New York, 1962), is an interesting narrative of his selection, education, and experiences. *The Opening of the Wisdom-Eye and the History of the Advancement of Buddhadharma in Tibet* (Bangkok, 1968) and *The Buddhism of Tibet and the Key to the Middle Way* (New York, 1975) provide lucid expositions of the fundamental philosophical teachings of Tibetan Buddhism that must be mastered by a Dalai Lama.

Also recommended are David L. Snellgrove and Hugh E. Richardson's *A Cultural History of Tibet* (New York, 1968), Rolf A. Stein's *Tibetan Civilization* (Stanford, Calif., 1972), and Tsepon W. D. Shakabpa's *Tibet: A Political History* (New Haven, 1967). Each of these works contains an excellent bibliography.

TURRELL V. WYLIE

DAMASCENE, JOHN. *See* John of Damascus.

DAMIAN, PETER (1007–1072), also known as Pier Damiani; Italian author, monk, cardinal, doctor of the church, and Christian saint. Born in Ravenna, Damian acquired his training in the liberal arts, his superior command of Latin, and his knowledge of Roman law at Ravenna, Faenza, and Parma, where an urban culture survived. Ravenna, capital of Romagna and the old Byzantine exarchate, regained importance through the Ottonian revival. Throughout his lifetime, Damian retained ties with Ravenna's civil and clerical circles.

In 1035, when already a priest and teacher, he changed careers to join the disciples of the extreme ascetic Romuald (d. 1027) in the wilderness at Fonte Avellana, a hermitage near Monte Catria in the Marches. Damian is reticent about his conversion, but it is known that it was not sudden. *Vita Romualdi,* Damian's first datable work (1042), is as valuable for its view of eremitical life as the apex of Benedictine observance as it is as a source for the life of Damian's revered mentor. Chosen prior in 1043, Damian turned the colony into a stable community with a written rule, a library, and a temporal base, and saw it grow into a widespread congregation.

Damian's conviction that his pursuit of evangelical perfection did not exempt him from public service helped him cope with an important challenge of his day, namely the reform of the church, appeals for which mounted from outside monasteries, from Emperor Henry III, from Archdeacon Hildebrand (later Pope Gregory VII), and from others. A rare insight into the mystery of the church as the union of every member in Christ complemented his strong support of its hierarchical structure in the Roman tradition. His collaboration with the popes began under Leo IX (1049–1054) and was closest with the moderate Alexander II (1061–1073). Damian became cardinal bishop of Ostia in 1057, carrying out delicate missions in Italy, France, and Germany. After reconciling the archbishop of Ravenna with the Roman see, he died at Faenza, where his cult began.

The flow of writings from Damian's pen, matching his tireless activity in the church, includes 175 letters, small tracts, some 50 sermons, saints' lives, prayers, hymns, and poems. His efforts at reform, based on the norms of church law, reflect the issues of his times: clerical immorality *(Liber Gomorrhianus),* theological problems raised by traffic in church offices *(Liber gratissimus),* and political-ecclesiastical strife *(Disceptatio synodalis).* Of lasting interest are the fruits of his beloved solitude: his ideal of Christian virtue and fidelity to duty in all walks of society, and his spiritual counsel, scriptural comments, and meditations. He was steeped in the Bible and drew on the church fathers, especially Augustine, whose works he procured for Fonte Avellana. Still prized in the twelfth century, his writings were eclipsed by the intellectualism of the Scholastic age, but Dante's praise assured Damian recognition outside the church as well (*Paradiso* 21.106–111). Thanks to excellent transmission of the manuscripts, Damian's corpus was secured for the modern age in the *Editio princeps* of Costantino Gaetani (four volumes, Rome, 1606–1640). Scholarship has shifted from its earlier selectivity to a consideration of Damian's whole legacy and of the man himself, as evidenced in the studies published in 1972 for the ninth centennial of his death. Perhaps the major significance of Peter Damian for Western religion lies in the fact that he, like the Camaldolese and Carthusians, gave new life and form to the strain of contemplative life and asceticism stemming from the Desert Fathers of Egypt.

BIBLIOGRAPHY

The collected works are available in *Patrologia Latina,* edited by J.-P. Migne, vols. 144 and 145, (Paris, 1853). Single items have modern editions, and an edition of the letters is in preparation for the "Monumenta Germaniae Historica" series. The only anthology in English is *Saint Peter Damian: Selected Writings on the Spiritual Life,* translated with an introduction by Patricia McNulty (London, 1959). Both Owen J. Blum's *Saint Peter Damian: His Teachings on the Spiritual Life* (Washington, D.C., 1947) and my own *Saint Peter Damiani and His Canonical Sources: A Preliminary Study in the Antecedents of the Gregorian Reform* (Toronto, 1956) have ample bibliographies. An expert portrayal is Jean Leclercq's *Saint Pierre Damien: Ermite et homme d'église* (Rome, 1960). Two important collections of new studies are *San Pier Damiano: Nel IX centenario della morte, 1072–1972,* 4 vols. (Cesena, 1972–1978); and *San Pier Damiani: Atti del convegno di studi nel IX centenario della morte* (Faenza, 1973).

J. JOSEPH RYAN

DANCE. [*To explore the role of dance in religion, and vice versa, this entry consists of three articles:*

Dance and Religion
Popular and Folk Dance
Theatrical and Liturgical Dance

The first article provides a typology of religious dance, drawing on examples from various religions and cultures. The second explores the religious dimensions of dance that thrive in changing cultural settings in the Middle East, Europe, and the Western Hemisphere. The third investigates the persistence of religion in choreographed dance and surveys examples of the reiteration in modern Western dance of motifs drawn from various religious traditions.]

Dance and Religion

Dance is part of many systems of belief about the universe that deal with the nature and mystery of human existence and involve feelings, thoughts, and actions. Why, how, and to what ends do humans dance in religious practice?

From a comparative worldwide perspective, dance may be seen as human behavior composed—from the dancer's point of view—of purposeful, intentionally rhythmical, and culturally patterned sequences of nonverbal body movements. These are different from ordinary motor activities; they have inherent and "aesthetic" values, that is, appropriateness and competency. According to historical and anthropological research, people dance in order to fulfill a range of intentions and functions that change over time. They dance to explain religion, create and recreate social roles, to worship or honor, conduct supernatural beneficence, effect change, embody or merge with the supernatural through inner or external transformations, and reveal divinity through dance creation.

The power of dance in religious practice lies in its multisensory, emotional, and symbolic capacity to communicate. It can create moods and a sense of situation in attention-riveting patterns by framing, prolonging, or discontinuing communication. Dance is a vehicle that incorporates inchoate ideas in visible human form and modifies inner experience as well as social action. The efficacy of dance in contributing to the construction of a worldview and affecting human behavior depends upon the beliefs of the participants (performers and spectators), particularly their faith in their ability to affect the world around them.

Dance may also be meaningful in itself in terms of sensory sensitivity and perception: the sight of performers moving in time and space, the sounds of physical movements, the odors of physical exertion, the feeling of kinesthetic activity or empathy, and the sensations of contact with other bodies or the dancer's environment. Meaning may also lie in the expectation that within a particular dance style a particular dance element—rhythm, effort, spatial pattern, or use of the body—will be recognized, repeated, or followed by a different element at some specified point in the dance. Alternatively, meaning may be found in novelty, surprise, incongruity, ambiguity, and altered states of conciousness.

More like poetry than prose, dance may also have cognitive, languagelike references beyond the dance form itself. Meaning may be conveyed through various devices such as metaphor (a dance in place of another expression that it resembles to suggest a likeness between the two), metonym (a dance connected with a larger whole), concretization (mimetic presentation), stylization (somewhat arbitrary religious gestures or movements that are the result of convention), and icon (a dancer enacting some of a god's characteristics and being regarded or treated as that god). Meaning may also be in the spheres of the dance event that include nondance activity: the human body in special action, the whole dance performance, performance segments as they unfold as in a narrative, specific movements or style reflecting religious values, the intermeshing of dance with other communication media such as music, the presence of a dancer conveying a supernatural aura or energy.

We have no way of knowing the origins of religious dance. Rock art verifies its antiquity, however, and many peoples have explanatory myths. The Dogon of Mali, for example, say that God's son the jackal danced and traced out the world and its future; the first attested dance was one of divination that told secrets in dust. A spirit later taught people to dance. Hindus of India believe that Śiva danced the world into being and later conveyed the art of dancing to humans.

A popularly held psychological and theological theory found in numerous histories of dance suggests that dance evolved instrumentally to cope with unknown happenings in the human environment. Spontaneous movement—an outlet for the emotional tension endemic in the perpetual struggle for existence in a baffling environment—developed into patterned, symbolic movements for the individual and group. When a desired situation occurred following an instrumentally intended dance (for example, rain followed a danced request), the dance was assumed to have causative power and sacred association. Over time, style, structure, and meaning in dance changed through the perception of supernatural revelation, individual or group initiative, and contacts with other people.

Acceptance of Dance as Religious Practice. Views of mind and body, especially concerning emotion and sexuality, affect dance in religion (as well as in other aspects of life). Whereas various arts use the body as an accessory to create sounds or visual objects, dance is manifest directly through the body and evokes bodily associations. Christian, Muslim, and Hindu beliefs and practices illustrate significantly different perspectives about dance and religion.

Christianity's love-hate relationship with the body and acceptance of a mind/body dichotomy—which the rationalism of sixteenth-century Europe intensified—has led to both positive and negative attitudes toward dance. Recognizing Christ as fleshly, Christianity views the human body as a temple housing the Holy Spirit, and it calls its church the "body of Christ." Paul said, "Glorify Christ in your bodies." From the second century, Christians (e.g., Theodoret of Cyrrhus, Clement of Alexandria) described dance as an imitation of the perpetual dance of angels, the blessed and righteous expressing physically their desire to enter heaven. Christianity built upon the Hebrew tradition of demonstrating through pious dance that no part of the individual was unaffected by the love of God. Yet Christianity also scorned flesh as a root of evil to be transcended, even mortified. Misunderstanding Paul's view of flesh, by which he meant to refer to the individual acting selfishly, led to negative attitudes toward the body in general that he did not share. Christianity's rejection of the body reflects an inability to come to terms with the passing of time and with death.

Although the Greeks, Hebrews, and Christians took part in ancient fertility and sustenance dances, some of these dances took the form of unrestrained, sensual rites. This perceived debasement of religion led to the periodic proscription of dance and penalties against dancers. Legends of Salome's sensuous dance, for which she received John the Baptist's head in reward (she either obeyed her revengeful mother in requesting this or expressed her anger about John's not reciprocating her sexual interest in him), have kept alive negative associations with dance. Some Christians hold any glorification of the body, including dancing, anathema: outspoken enemies of physicality with an ascetic dislike of eroticism, which could undermine faith and unsettle the hierarchic status quo, they preach the ideal of the Virgin. Western philosophy and Victorian prudishness have not, however, affected the Eastern Orthodox church to the extent of eliminating dance in worship.

Because the nineteenth- and twentieth-century European industrializing nations that imperialistically dominated the world economy were largely Christian, this religion has had a worldwide stifling impact on dance.

Europeans recognized that non-European dance intertwined with indigenous religions and moralities. Even though these dances often had themes and origins comparable to those of European folk dances, colonialists considered indigenous dances to be the manifestation of savage heathenism and thus antagonistic to the "true faith"; therefore they frequently sought to eliminate them. The British influence, for example, contributed to the demise of Hindu temple dancing without succeeding in spreading Christianity. However, even when proscribed or out of fashion, dance rises phoenixlike in new religious transformation. Black slaves in the United States, members of Nigerian Yoruba Assemblies of God, and a number of white Christian groups have all included in their worship what appears to be dance—but under a different name, such as "play," "the shout," or "feeling the Lord."

As former European colonies in Africa, Latin America, and Asia regained independence, they frequently reevaluated and renewed their devalued dances. Moreover, counterreactions in the twentieth-century West to claims of the separation of mind from body have led to a renaissance of dance as religious practice in that cultural milieu, too. When Westerners developed more accepting attitudes about the body, and biblical scholarship on dance increased after the 1960s, a sacred dance movement gave impetus to the reappearance of Christian congregational, choir, and solo dancing.

Islam generally disapproves of dancing as a frivolous distraction from contemplating the wisdom of the Prophet. Its religious leaders look upon dancing with contempt.

The sacred and secular, the ritualistic and playful, and the spiritual and sexual do not everywhere have the dichotomous character so common in Muslim and in industrial societies where specialization and separation are hallmarks. For example Hinduism generally merges the sacred and the sexual in a felicitous union. As religion is about mystery, potential danger, hope of heaven, and ecstasy, so too are sexual love and its ramifications. Rather than considering carnal love a phenomenon to be "overcome" as in some Christian denominations, a strand of Hinduism accepts sexual congress as a phase of the soul's migration. Through the path of devotion *(bhakti)*, a surrender to the erotic self-oblivion of becoming one, a man and a woman momentarily glimpse spiritually and symbolically the desired absolute union with divinity. This is a microcosm of divine creation that reveals the hidden truth of the universe. The dance conveys this vision of life in telling the stories of the anthropomorphic gods. Hinduism has a pantheon of deities and is really a medley of hundreds of belief systems that share commonalities, as do Christian denominations. The supreme, all-powerful God is manifest in a trio of divinities: Brahmā, Viṣṇu (who appears in the incarnation of Kṛṣṇa, of amorous nature and exploits), and Śiva (Lord of the Dance, who created the universe, which he destroys and regenerates through dance). Śiva's rhythms determine those of the world. The classic Indian sacred treatise on dance, the *Nāṭya Śāstra*, describes dance as an offering and demonstration of love to God, a cleansing of sin, a path of salvation, a partaking of the cosmic control of the world, and an expression of God within oneself.

Typology of Sacred Dance Practice. Dance is frequently an element of the process by which meanings are exchanged through symbols related to the supernatural world of ancestors, spirits, and gods. In this respect, from the perspectives of various religions and the functionalist, structuralist, and feminist theories that view religion as part of the larger social system, there appear to be nine categories of dance, neither exhaustive nor mutually exclusive. The specific dances referred to in the discussion below are from different times and cultures, removed from their rich historical and social contexts; they are chosen to illustrate kinds, or classes, of beliefs and acts.

Explaining religion. Dance is part of ritual constructions of reality communicated to people so that they may understand the world and operate in it. The lore of sacred and profane belief, often intertwined, is told and retold in dance.

In early Christendom, dancing began as metaphor and metonym for the mysteries of faith. During the first part of the Middle Ages, dancing accompanied Christian church festivals and processionals in which relics of saints or martyrs were carried to call attention to their life histories. Later, in the twelfth, thirteenth, and forteenth centuries, dance was an accepted liturgical art form in mystery and miracle plays. Elaborate dramatic presentations flourished in the Renaissance, but then printed tracts, pamphlets and books, and other promotions of the ascendance of the mind began to erode the importance of dance as a medium of religious expression. The Jesuits sponsored ballet as honorable relaxation in the seventeenth and eighteenth centuries until its suppression for being veiled political commentary.

The Spanish Franciscans used dance dramas, especially those depicting the struggle of the church against its foes, to explain the Christian faith to the illiterate New World Indians they hoped to convert. Pageants of Moors and Christians were common. Appropriating indigenous Indian dances, the Franciscans suffused them with Christian meaning. Similarly, Muslims in East Africa at the end of the nineteenth century used indigenous attachment to the old Yao initiation dances to gradually introduce another dance that was regarded as an initiation into Islam.

Contemporary Western theatrical dance performances in churches, public theaters, film, and television perpetuate the tradition of dance explaining religion. Choreographers present biblical scenes, incidents, and concepts in addition to religious philosophy, characters, events, and processes. Of course, all religious dance may have an entertaining element.

Creating and re-creating social roles. Often used as a means to legitimize social organization, religion may employ dance as its agent to convey attitudes about the conduct of social life at the same time that it fulfills other purposes and functions. An example comes from Hinduism, which has a rich ancient history in the arts and religion. Although both male and female royalty in early India may have been well versed in dancing, the *Nāṭya Śāstra* is the scripture of a male sage, Bhārata Muni, who upon receiving instruction from the gods later handed it down through his sons. He thought danced enactments of myths and legends would give people guidance in their lives. His treatise says that dancing is symbolic.

Male brahmans (members of the priestly class) taught dance to males who performed only as young boys *(gotipuas)*, to males who performed in all-male companies *(kathakali)*, and to women dedicated to serving in the temples *(devadāsīs)*. A dancer usually performs both male and female roles and movement styles for the deities in private devotions and at religious festivals involving the larger community.

Some common religious dance themes are about male-female relations. In the allegories of Rādhā (loveliest of the milkmaids) and Kṛṣṇa (the eternal lover dancing in the heart of every man), for example, their illicit love becomes a spiritual freedom, a type of salvation, and a surrender of all that the strict Indian social conventional world values.

Human analogies explain Hindu divinity; conversely, the tales of the gods—more powerful versions of men and women, with the same virtues and vices—provide sanctified models for human actions as well as fantasies with vicarious thrills related to cultural sexual taboos. Danced enactments of legends send messages that it is acceptable for men to lustfully wander outside of marriage, whereas, in contrast women are supposed to be faithful to their husbands, forgive them, and bear their children in spite of the pain, risk of death, and agony from high infant mortality.

In the West Sepik District of Papua New Guinea, the Umeda people convey gender status through the annual Ida dance, a ritual for sago palm fertility and a celebration of survival in the face of physical and mystical dangers. Although the sexual division of labor is supposedly complementary, in this dance cultural creativity of men is pitted against the biological creativity of women, and female culture is opposed and ultimately conquered by male culture.

The myths and metaphors of religious codes present basic propositions concerning expected behavior between leaders and followers besides relations between the sexes. Such codes are danced for all to see. The Indian *kathakali* (in which feminine-looking boys learn to dance female roles) draws upon the physical training techniques from Kerala's military tradition. This powerful and spectacular drama staged as a public ritual for the entire community has been claimed to be a reaction to foreign aggression and a reaffirmation of the priestly and warrior social status, as well as an affirmation of masculine pride in matrilineal and matrilocal society.

Dance in pre-Conquest Mexico was devoted to deities and agricultural success; its performance, as well as its representation in artifacts, appears to have served contemporary sociopolitical designs: to create, reflect, and reinforce social stratification and a centralized integrated political organization encompassing diverse, geographically dispersed ethnic groups. Nobles, priests, and commoners, old and young, male and female, each had distinct dances and spatial levels for performing at the pyramid temple.

Worship or honor. At regularly scheduled seasonal times, at critical junctures, or just spontaneously, dances are part of rituals that revere; that greet as a token of fellowship, hospitality, and respect; that thank, entreat, placate, or offer penitence to deities, ancestors, and other supernatural entities. Not only may dance be a remedial vehicle to propitiate or beseech, it may also be prophylactic—gods may be honored to preclude disaster.

Dance is a means of religious concentration as well as of corporeal merging with the infinite God. The Jews dance to praise their God in sublime adoration and to express joy for his beneficence. The Hebrew scriptures refer to "rejoicing with the whole being" as well as to specific dances performed for traditional festivals. The God-given mind and body are returned to God through dance. As a result of the destruction of the Temple in 70 CE, Jews generally eliminated dance and song from regular worship until such a time as they could return from the Diaspora and rebuild the Temple. The Talmud, ancient rabbinic writings that constitute religious authority for traditional Judaism, describes dancing as the principal function of the angels and commands dancing at weddings for brides, grooms, and their wedding guests. Procreation is God's will, weddings a step toward its fulfillment, and dancing a thanksgiving symbolizing fruitfulness. Even in exile there could be dancing, because out of the wedding might be born the Messiah who would restore the people to the Land of Israel.

In Christianity the Catholic church allowed dances created for special occasions such as the canonization of cardinals or commemoration of their birthdays. Throughout Latin America devotional dances are part of a pilgramage and processional fiesta system that fuses Indian and Catholic tenets. The dance training and production preparation are often undertaken as part of a religious vow to a powerful saint, the Virgin, or a Christ figure. The Mormons believe that when engaged in by the pure of heart, dance (excluding the embracing-couple position of Western social dance) prepares the individual and community for prayer meetings or other religious activity; devotion and recreation unite the individual with God. Brigham Young, who led the Mormon migration from Illinois to Utah, discovered that dance was a means to strengthen group morale and solidarity through providing emotional and physical release from hardship.

In Orissa, India, the custom of small boys dancing dressed as girls has coexisted with a female dance tradition since the fifteenth century. The *sakhi-bhāva* cult believes that since Kṛṣṇa is male, the most effective way of showing devotion is as a female, like the milkmaids (*gopīs*) who dance their love for Kṛṣṇa.

The Gogo of Tanzania dance the Cidwanga as a sign of reverence in the annual ritual for good rains and fertility. Groups in Nigeria provide many illustrations. The Kalabari believe that human beings make the gods great. Fervent worship adds to a deity's capacity to aid the worshipers, and just as surely, the cutting off of worship will render them impotent or at the least cause them to break off contact with erstwhile worshipers. Among the Efik, the worshipers of the sea deity Ndem briskly dance in a circle at the deity's shrine to express metaphorically the affective intensity of a wish, for example, a wish for a child or a safe journey. The brisker the dance, the more likely Ndem is to grant requests.

Because among the Ubakala dance honors and propitiates the respected living, it is not surprising that the spirits of the departed and other supernatural entities are also honored in this way. Some deities, such as the Yoruba Ṣango, love to be entertained and can be best placated with good dancing. Like the human creatures they basically are, the ancestors of the Fon of Dahomey (or the other spiritual entities who are given anthroposocial attributes) are believed to love display and ceremony. Thus both living and spiritual entities are believed to watch a dance performance, and both categories of spectators may even join the dancers, the latter often doing so through possession. Supernatural beings are sometimes honored to ensure that they do not mar festivals.

Conducting supernatural beneficence. Dance may be the vehicle through which an individual, as self or other (masked or possessed), becomes a conduit of extraordinary power. Among the Ganda of central Uganda, parents of twins, having demonstrated their extraordinary fertility and the direct intervention of the god Mukasa, would dance in the gardens of their friends to transmit human fertility supernaturally to the vegetation. Yoruba mothers of twins dance with their offspring and promise to bless all those who are generous with alms. Here, the motional, dynamic rhythm, and spatial patterns of dance transfer desired qualities to objects or individuals.

The men and women of Tanzania's Sandawe people dance by moonlight in the erotic Phek'umo rites to promote fertility. Identifying with the moon, a supreme being believed to be both beneficial and destructive, they adopt stylized signs or moon stances; they also embrace tightly and mimic the act of sexual intercourse. The dance, metaphorically at least, conducts supernatural beneficence.

Because dance movement is metonymical with life movement, dance parody of sorcerer-caused disease and death affects the ascendance of life spirits and health forces. Thus the Tiv of Nigeria parody dropsy and elephantiasis through dance.

The Sun Dance of the hunting peoples of the Great Plains of North America was an elaborate annual pageant performed during full summer when scattered tribal bands could unite in a season of plenty. Representatives danced to renew the earth, pray for fertility or revenge for a murdered relative, and transfer medicine. The typical Sun Dance involved a week of intense activity culminating in dramatic climactic rites. Male dancers participated in accord with personal vows made previously for success in warfare or healing of a loved one. Each dancer strove to attain personal power. Dancers were pierced through the breast or shoulder muscles and tethered with thongs to the central pole of a ceremonial lodge altar. Staring at the sun, they danced without pause, pulling back until the flesh gave way. [*For further discussion, see* Sun Dance.]

Effecting change. Dance may be used as a medium to reverse a debilitating condition caused by the supernatural or to prepare an individual or group to reach a religiously defined ideal state. This includes status transformation in rites of passage, death, curing, and prevention, as well as rites to reverse political domination.

The United Society of Believers in Christ's Second Appearing, commonly called Shakers because of their dramatic practice of vigorous dancing, believed that the day of judgment was imminent. Numbering about six thousand members in nineteen communities at its peak, the group held that salvation would come through confessing and forsaking fleshly practices. Notwithstanding their professed attitudes toward the body, the first adherents were seized by an involuntary ecstasy that led them to run about a meeting room, jump, shake, whirl, and reel in a spontaneous manner to shake off doubts, loosen sins and faults, and mortify lust in order to purify the spirit. In repentance they turned away from preoccupation with self to shake off their bondage to a troubled past. This permitted concentration on new feelings and intent.

Dancing for the Shakers, who believed in the dualism of spirit versus body, appears to be a canalization of feeling in the context of men and women living together in celibacy, austerity, humility, and hard manual labor. Shaker dance involved a sequence of movements, designed to shake off sin, that paralleled the sexual experience of energy buildup to climax and then relaxation. Individualistic impulsive movements evolved into ordered, well-rehearsed patterns. Shaking the hand palm downward discarded the carnal; turning palms upward petitioned eternal life.

For Buddhist Sherpa lamas, laymen, and young boys in Nepal, dancing is a means by which they resolve the necessity of simultaneously affirming and denying the value of worldly existence. The spring Dumje ceremony purges the forces of repression and guilt that oppose the erotic impulses so that life may continue. The young boys' highly lascivious *tek-tek* masked dances represent sexuality as well as the children who are its desired fruits.

Dance mediates between childhood and adult status in the Chisungu, the girls' initiation ceremony of the Bemba of Zambia. The women conducting the ceremony believe that they are causing supernatural changes to take place as each initiate is "danced" from one group with its status and roles to another. Among the Wan of the Ivory Coast, a man must dance a female initiate on his shoulders. During the initiation to an ancestral cult, the Fang of Gabon carry religious statues from their usual place and make them dance like puppets to vitalize them.

Another form of status change occurs at death. The Ubakala of Nigeria perform the dance dramas Nkwa Uko and Nkwa Ese to escort a deceased aged and respected woman and man, respectively, to become ancestors residing among the spirits, later to return in a new incarnation. These forms are similar to the dances in the Christian tradition that enable one to enter heaven.

Among the Dogon, death creates disorder. But through the symbolism and orderliness of dance, humans metaphorically restore order to the disordered world. Symbolically spatializing things never seen, the Dogon represent heaven on earth. So, too, at the time of death, the mask dance helps to mitigate the psychic distress and spiritual fear of the dead.

The funeral dance of the Nyakyusa in Tanzania begins with a passionate expression of anger and grief and gradually becomes a fertility dance. In this way dancing mediates the passionate and quarrelsome emotions felt over a death and the acceptance of it.

Dances related to death were common in medieval Europe, a largely preliterate society dominated by the Christian church. It interpreted an economically harsh and morally complex world that was fought over by God and the Devil. Part of a convivial attempt to deny the finality of death, dances also had other manifestations and functions. In the so-called Dance of Death, a performer would beckon people to the world beyond in a reaction to the epidemic Black Death (1347–1373), a bubonic plague outbreak in Italy, Spain, France, Germany, and England. Evolving with the image of the skeletal figure seen as our future self, the dance was a mockery of the pretenses of the rich and a vision of social equality. The dance emphasized the terrors of death to frighten sinners into repentance. Hallucinogenic and clonic cramp symptoms of bread and grain ergot poisoning, called Saint Anthony's Fire, led some of its sickly victims to move involuntarily in dancelike movements. Such people were believed to be possessed. Other victims sought relief from pain through ecstatic dancing, considered to be of curative value and efficacious in warding off death. Dances were also connected with wakes for the dead and the rebirth of the soul to everlasting life. Dancing at the graves of family, friends, and martyrs was believed to comfort the dead and encourage resurrection as well as protect against the dead as demons.

Among the Gogo, dance metaphorically effects a supernatural change through role reversal in a curative and preventative rite. When men fail in their ritual responsibility for controlling human and animal fertility, disorder reigns. Then women become the only active agents in rituals addressed to righting the wrong. Dressed as men, they dance violently with spears to drive away contamination.

The Hamadsha, a Moroccan Ṣūfī brotherhood, performs the *ḥaḍrah*, an ecstatic dance, in order to cure an individual who has been struck or possessed by a devil. They seek a good relationship with a *jinnī* ("spirit"), usually ʿĀ'ishah. In the course of the dance, people become entranced and slash at their heads in imitation of

Sīdī ʿAlī's servant, who did so when he learned of his master's death. A flow of blood is believed to calm the spirit. The Hamadsha women fall into trance more readily and dance with more abandon than the men.

Dance was an integral part of many American Indian religious revivals and reaffirmations in response to historical, economic, and political situations they wanted to change. The Northern Paiute and peoples of the northwest Plateau believed that ceremonies involving group dancing, a visible index of ethnic and political alliances and action, would bring about periodic world renewal. The Indians thought certain group dances had the power to end the deprivation that resulted from defeat at the hands of whites and bring about the return of Indian prosperity. The Ghost Dance religion incorporated Christian teachings of the millennium and the second coming of Christ in order to attract acculturated Indians. [*See* Ghost Dance.]

The Mexican dance groups, known as *concheros, danza Chicimeca, danza Azteca,* and *danza de la conquista,* originated in the states of Querétaro and Guanajuato as a response to the Spanish Conquest in the sixteenth century. The groups may also be seen as "crisis cults," syncretistic attempts to create prideful cultural identity and new forms of social integration. Participants, at the low end of the socioeconomic scale and heavily represented in the laborer and shoeshine occupations, adopt the nomenclature of the Spanish military hierarchy and perform dances reenacting the Conquest that were derived from Spanish representations of the Moors and Christians. The warlike dances involve women, the aged, and children as well as men.

Embodying the supernatural in inner transformation: personal possession. Dance may serve as an activating agent for giving oneself temporarily to a supernatural being or force. This process is usually accompanied by a devout state and is often aided by autosuggestion or autointoxication, further reinforced by audience encouragement. The dance itself is often characterized by a particular type of musical accompaniment and repetitive, rapid turning or frenzied movement. A possessed devotee may achieve a consciousness of identity or a ritual connection with the supernatural iconically, metonymically, metaphorically, or experientially and cross the threshold into another order of existence.

A supernatural possessor may manifest itself through the dancer's performance of identifiable and specific patterns and conventional signs. In this way it communicates to the entire group that it is present and enacting its particular supernatural role in the lives of humans. Thus fear of the supernatural entity's indifference is allayed. Possession may alter somatic states and cause a dancer's collapse. The specific characteristics of possession are culturally determined, and even children may play at possession.

There are four types of personal possession. Diviners, cult members, medicine men, and shamans are among those who participate in the first type, "invited" spirit mediumship possession dances. Numerous African religions and their offshoots in Haitian Voodoo and Brazilian Macumba, as well as other faiths, involve the belief that humans can contact supernatural entities and influence them to act on a person's behalf. Thus the worshiper takes the initiative and lends his or her body to the tutelary spirit when there is an indication that the spirit wishes to communicate with the living or when the devotee desires a meeting. As a sensorimotor sign, the dance may indicate the deity's presence or a leader's legitimacy; as a signal, it may be a marker for specific activities; as a metonym, it may be part of the universe; and as a metaphor, it may refer to human self-extension or social conflict.

The Kalabari believe a possessed dancer brings the god as guest into the village. Dancing the gods is considered an admirable achievement. Masquerade dancers may become possessed, and in some cases the performer is expected to await possession before dancing. In possession dances the ability of Water People gods to materialize as pythons is accented as they metamorphose from acting like men to writhing on the ground and slithering about the house rafters as the great snakes do. The *oru seki* ("spirit") dancing occurs in the ritual to solicit a special benefit or to appease a spirit whose rules for human behavior have been infringed. Possession of the invoker, an iconic sign in the midst of the congregation, assures the spirit's presence, power, and acceptance of the invocation and offerings.

Among the Ga of Ghana, it is through a medium, whose state of possession is induced by dance, that the god signifies its presence and delivers messages prophesying the coming year's events and suggesting how to cope with them. Possession legitimizes leadership among the Fanti of Ghana. Because the deities love to dance, the priests assemble drummers, become possessed, and then speak with the power and authority of the deity. The Korean shaman attains knowledge and power in the role of religious leader through trance possession induced by dancing.

Possession may be a mechanism for individuals to transact social relationships more favorably. Healing practices often mediate the natural, social, and supernatural. In Sinhala healing rites, an exorcist attempts to sever the relationship between a patient and malign demons and ghosts. The exorcist's performance of various dance sequences progressively builds up emotional tension and generates power that can entrance both the healer and the patient. Their bodies become the demonic spirit's vehicle, constitute evidence of its control, and convince spectators of the need, as the healer prescribes, for a change in social relations that will exorcise the demonic spirit and transform the patient from illness to a state of health.

A second kind of possession dance, known as "invasion," also often a metaphor and signal of social pathology or personal maladjustment, indicates that a supernatural being has overwhelmed an individual, causing some form of malaise, illness, or personal or group misfortune. Dance becomes a medium to exorcise and appease the being, thus freeing the possessed individual and ameliorating his or her irksome ascribed status or difficult situation. Meeting the wishes of a spirit as part of exorcism frequently imposes obligations on those related to the possessed.

The *vimbuza* healing dance of the Chewa and Tumbuka societies in Malawi is a socially sanctioned means of expressing those feelings and tensions that if otherwise broadcast would disrupt family or community relationships. The dance is medicine for the *vimbuza* disease; which causes terrifying dreams or visions, the eating of unusual meat, or the uttering of a specific groan.

A third kind of possession, called "consecration," involves initiation and the impersonation of a deity, during which time the dancer becomes deified. In India the audience worships the young performers in the Rāmalīlās who play Kṛṣṇa, Rādhā, Rāma, and other mythic heroes in the same way they would revere icons. Performers of the Tibetan sacred masked dance, or *'cham,* are viewed as sacred beings.

Not only may individuals be possessed by supernatural entities but they may also experience "essence possession," the fourth type, by a religious or supernatural potency, an impersonal supernatural. Among the Lango of Uganda, *jok* is liberated or generated in dancing. Similarly, among the !Kung San of Namibia, dance activates *n/um,* that potency from which medicine men derive their power to protect the people from sickness and death. The medicine dancer may go into trance and communicate with spirits without being possessed by them. The ceremonial curing dance may be called for in crisis situations, or the dance may occur spontaneously; it is redressive and prophylactic.

Merging with the supernatural toward enlightenment or self-detachment. Illustrations of another form of inner transformation through dance come from Turkey or Tibet. In Turkey the followers of the thirteenth-century poet-philosopher Mawlānā Jalāl al-Dīn Rūmī, founder of one of Islam's principal mystic orders, perform whirling dances. Men with immobile faces revolve in long white shirts with covered arms outstretched, slowly at first and then faster until they reach a spiritual trance. These men, the dervishes (the word refers to a person on the threshold of enlightenment), strive to detach themselves from earth and divest themselves of ties to self in order to unite with a nonpersonified God. This process occurs through revolving movement and repeated chanting that vibrates energy centers of the body in order to raise the individual to higher spheres. [*For discussion of Islamic conceptions of enlightenment, see* Darwīsh.]

The Tibetan Buddhist dance ritual called Ling Dro Dechen Rolmo permits imaging the divine. The dancer's circular path and turning movement aid the participants toward enlightenment by providing a means to realize that the deity is a reflection of one's own mind.

Embodying the supernatural in external transformation: masquerade. Sacred masquerade dances, part of a people's intercourse with the spirit world, make social and personal contributions through symbolic actions that are similar to those made through dances that explain religion, create and re-create social roles, worship and honor, conduct supernatural beneficence, effect change, and involve possession. The Midimu masked dancing of the Yao, Makua, and Makonde of Tanzania and Mozambique helps to explain religion by marking the presence of the supernatural (dead ancestors) in the affairs of the living. In effect, ancestors return from the dead to rejoice on the occasion of an initiate's return from the training camp. The Dogon's masked-society dancing patterns depict their conception of the world, its progress and order, and its continuity and oneness with the total universe. Thus dance is here a model of the belief system. Participants in the Nyau society of Chewa-speaking peoples dance a reenactment of the primal coexistence of men, animals, and spirits in friendship, and their subsequent division by fire. The people believe that underneath their masks the dancers have undergone transformation into spirits.

Social roles are emphasized when the Yoruba's Gẹlẹdẹ society masquerade figures appear annually at the start of the new agricultural year to dance in the marketplace and through the streets. They honor and propitiate the female *oriṣa* ("spirits") and their representatives, living and ancestral, for the mothers are the gods of society and their children its members. All animal life comes from a mother's body. Although both men and women belong to the Gẹlẹdẹ cult (to seek protection and blessings and assuage their fear of death), only men dance, with masks portraying the appropriate sex roles of each character. Mothers have both positive (calm, creative, protective) and negative, or witch, dimensions (unmitigated evil affecting fertility, childbirth, and the functioning of men's sexual organs). The mothers possess powerful *aṣẹ* ("vital, mystical power"). A man can have *aṣẹ* most fully when he is spiritually united with an *oriṣa*. When men symbolically externalize the vital life forces in dance, they may be asserting their virility and freedom in the presence of the powerful mothers and, in addition, recognizing and honoring their powers in order to appease them to ensure that they utilize their *aṣẹ* for male benefit.

Among the Nafana people of the Ivory Coast, masked dancing occurs almost nightly during the lunar month of the year. The dancing is intended to worship and to effect change. Living in the masks, the Bedu spirits bless and purify the village dwellings and their occupants and metaphorically absorb evil and misfortune, which they remove from the community so that the new year begins afresh.

The masked (antelope headdress) dance of the Bamana of Mali represents Chi Wara, the god of agriculture, a supernatural being, half animal, half man, who first taught men how to cultivate the soil. Chi Wara's public presence is an invocation of its blessings. In a concretized form that makes appeals more understandable to the young, animal masked dances remind humans that they have some animal characteristics as participants respond to the dancers positively and negatively. In this way the masked dancing presents human foibles at a distance for examination without threat to individuals, thus helping to effect change.

Masked dancing can be a metaphor for both normative and innovative behavior. Under religious auspices the dancer is freed from the everyday restrictions on etiquette and thus able to present secular messages and critiques. Presented by the unmasked, these messages might produce social frictions or hostilities rather than positive change.

Among the Nsukka Igbo of Nigeria, the council of elders employed masked dancers representing an *omabe* spirit cult whenever there was difficulty in enforcing law and order. In Zambia, Wiko Makishi masqueraders, believed to be resurrected ancestors and other supernatural beings, patrol the vicinities of the boys' initiation lodges to ward off intruders, women, and non-Wiko.

A Chewa man residing with his wife and mother-in-law often resorts to the male masked Nyau dancer to mediate between himself and a mother-in-law whose constant demands on him he resents. When the dancer dons the mask of the Chirombo ("beast"), he directs obscene language against her. No action may be taken against him, for in his mask he enjoys the immunity of the Chirombo. Afterward the mother-in-law often reduces her demands.

Socially sanctioned ritual abuse with ribald and lewd movements and gestures in a highly charged atmosphere is permitted in the Bedu masked dance mentioned above. There appear to be humor and an underlying feeling that these acts are socially acceptable and that through them participants will be purged of whatever negative emotions they may harbor.

The masked dancer may be an iconic sign, revered and experienced as a veritable apparition of the being he represents, even when people know that a man made the mask and is wearing it. Because the Angolan Chokwe mask and its wearer are a spiritual whole, both in life and death, when a dancer dies, his mask is buried with him.

Revelation of divinity through dance creation. Within a Protestant Christian view, artistic self-expression is analogized to the creative self-expression of God as creator. Dancing a set piece is considered a reflection of the unknowable God's immanence irrespective of the performer's intention. The dancer is to dance as God is to creation. The language of movement is God given, and both the progression of a dancer's training and the perfection of performance reveal God's achievement. Within the Franciscan view, God is present in good works and in the creative force of the arts. Through dance rituals in Latin America, performers become one with creation. When an individual dances with expertise—individuality, agility, and dexterity—the Gola of Liberia consider this to be a sign of a *jina*'s gift of love given in a dream.

Dance appears to be part of a cultural code or logical model enabling humans to order experience, account for its chaos, express isomorphic properties between opposing entities, and explain realities. Dance and religion merge in a configuration that encompasses sensory experience, cognition, diffused and focused emotions, and personal and social conflicts. People dance to explain religion, convey sanctified models for social organization, revere the divine, conduct supernatural beneficence, effect change, embody the supernatural through internal or external transformation, merge with the divine toward enlightenment, and reveal divinity through creating dance. Permeated with religious tradition, dance continually changes.

In many parts of the world that have, to a large extent, become modernized and secularized, participants in nonsacred theatrical dance often choose to explain religion, create and re-create social roles, honor the divine, and infuse their dances with elements drawn from religions throughout the world. Many folk dances associated with religious holidays or events have been transformed into theatrical productions and into performances (by dancers other than the "folk") for recreational purposes.

[*For further discussion of many of the dances and rituals treated herein, see various articles on dance and dance drama under* Drama *and separate entries on particular religious traditions.*]

BIBLIOGRAPHY

Adams, Doug. *Congregational Dancing in Christian Worship.* Rev. ed. Austin, 1980. Biblical, historical, and theological perspectives provide the context for a discussion of dance principles and practices.

Amoss, Pamela. *Coast Salish Spirit Dancing: The Survival of an Ancestral Religion.* Seattle, 1978. A probing of the reasons for this revival within its new context.

Andrews, Edward Deming. *The Gift to Be Simple.* New York, 1940. A description of the history, songs, music, and dances of the Shakers.

Coomaraswamy, Ananda K. *The Dance of Shiva: Fourteen Indian Essays.* New Delhi, 1971. Reprint edition of *The Dance of Shiva* (New York, 1957). A discussion of dancing milkmaids as a metaphor of human souls.

Cuisinier, Jeanne. *La danse sacrée en Indochine et Indonesie.* Paris, 1951.

Drewal, Henry John, and Margaret T. Drewal. *Gẹ̀lẹ̀dẹ́: Art and Female Power among the Yoruba.* Bloomington, Ind., 1983. A description of masked dancing.

Fallon, Dennis J., and Mary Jane Wolbers, eds. *Focus on Dance X: Religion and Dance.* Reston, Va., 1982. Twenty-two articles primarily in the area of Western culture.

Felice, Phillipe de. *L'enchantement des danses, et la magie du verbe.* Paris, 1957.

Fergusson, Erna. *Dancing Gods: Indian Ceremonials of New Mexico and Arizona.* New York, 1931. A descriptive presentation.

Friedlander, Ira. *The Whirling Dervishes: Being an Account of the Sufi Order Known as the Mevlevis and Its Founder the Poet and Mystic Mevlana Jalalu'ddin Rumi.* New York, 1975. Includes numerous photographs and bibliography.

Gell, Alfred. *Metamorphosis of the Cassowaries: Umeda Society, Language, and Ritual.* London, 1975. A descriptive analysis of ritual dances.

Granet, Marcel. *Danses et legendes de la Chine ancienne.* 2 vols. Paris, 1926.

Griaule, Marcel. *Conversations with Ogotemmêli: An Introduction to Dogon Religious Ideas.* London, 1965. A Dogon elder's account of his people's cosmology.

Hanna, Judith Lynne. *To Dance Is Human: A Theory of Nonverbal Communication.* Austin, 1979. A theory based on contemporary knowledge that explains how dance works and how it can be studied. Extensive bibliography.

Hanna, Judith Lynne. *The Performer-Audience Connection: Emotion to Metaphor in Dance and Society.* Austin, 1983. Discussion of religious attitudes that shape performance expectations, focusing on two forms of Hindu dance and a black spiritual.

Kapferer, Bruce. *A Celebration of Demons.* Bloomington, Ind., 1983. A descriptive analysis of the role of dance gesture and style in ritual healing among the Sinhalese.

Leeuw, Gerardus van der. *Sacred and Profane Beauty.* New York, 1963. Commentary on the secularization of dance, believed to be the original art.

McKean, Philip F. "From Purity to Pollution? The Balinese Ketjak (Monkey Dance) as Symbolic Form in Transition." In *The Imagination of Reality: Essays in Southeast Asian Coherence Systems,* edited by A. L. Becker and Aram A. Yengoyan, pp. 293–302. Norwood, N.J., 1979.

Oesterly, W. O. E. *The Sacred Dance.* Cambridge, 1923. An estimate of the role of sacred dance among the peoples of antiquity and non-Western cultures.

Sendrey, Alfred. *Music in Ancient Israel.* New York, 1969. Chapter 8 is about dance, verbs that express the act of dancing, and the functions of dance.

Taylor, Margaret F. *A Time to Dance: Symbolic Movement in Worship.* Philadelphia, 1967. An overview of dance in the history of the Christian church and its reawakened use in the twentieth century.

Wood, W. Raymond, and Margot P. Liberty, eds. *Anthropology on the Great Plains.* Lincoln, Nebr., 1980. Articles with bibliographies on the Sun Dance and Ghost Dance religion.

Zoete, Beryl de. *Dance and Magic Drama in Ceylon.* London, 1957.

JUDITH LYNNE HANNA

Popular and Folk Dance

Dance and religion have been intertwined in various ways through the centuries. The attitudes toward dance expressed in ancient Greek writings and the Bible are part of a philosophical legacy that has been influential throughout the intellectual and cultural history of the Western world. The ancient Greeks believed that dance was supreme among the arts, indeed that it was fundamentally inseparable from music and poetry. In the *Laws,* Plato writes that all creatures are prompted to express emotions through body movements, and he notes that such instinctive response is transformed into dance by virtue of a gift from the gods: rhythmic and harmonic order. Other Greeks held the general belief that dance was originally transmitted directly from the gods to humans, and consequently that all dancing is a spiritual endeavor. Whatever the origin of dance, classical historians maintain that religious rituals were indeed the source of many Greek dances, though dancing was not confined to rituals or occasions of formal worship. Dance was also an integral part of Greek social life, as recreation and as a means of solemnizing events or experiences. The spiritual nature of dance was apparently considered so all-encompassing that the Greeks made no rigid distinction between religious dancing and secular dancing.

The Hebrew scriptures contain numerous references to the dance activities of the Israelites in biblical times. Dancing was an expression of joy in all realms of life, a celebration of mental and corporeal fulfillment as well as a personal declaration of spiritual devotion. Modern scholars have debated whether dance was a part of actual religious rituals or formal worship in the Jewish faith. Some believe that there was no role for dancing in the Temple or in performances of the religious officiants during services and ceremonies. Even so, dance clearly played a significant part in the public festivals that accompanied the holy days. For example, the pilgrimages associated with seasonal festivals were sanctified by dancing, singing, and the playing of musical instruments such as the harp. Also, the triumphs of the Jewish people over their oppressors were celebrated in victory parades with dancing and special songs.

By the dawn of the Christian era, two major factors affected the status of dance in the philosophy of the church establishment. The first was the tangible and immediate heritage of attitudes toward dancing found among the Jewish people; the second was the active dance traditions of the various pagan cults that were now converting to Christianity. The Christian community shared with the Jews the fundamental belief that dance was a means of expressing reverence to God. The angels danced in heavenly joy, and mortals danced to celebrate their faith. Many ancient pre-Christian customs found in European cultures were preserved (e.g., the practice of dancing at burial grounds) and coexisted alongside the new rites of the church. Other dance customs were actually integrated into Christian religious ceremonies. Religious dances performed by the clergy included the ring dance and the processionals that formed part of the various saints' festivals. Other dances were performed only by members of the congregation, including ribbon dances, ring dances accompanied by songs and hand-clapping, and processionals. Over the centuries as Christianity spread, local enthusiasm for dancing remained strong, and church officials were compelled to limit the types of religious events in which dancing was acceptable. Regional church authorities forbade dancing in the house of the Lord: dancing would be permissible (to varying degrees) only in the religious observances that took place in public festivals outside the church structure itself. The fact that such restrictions were issued repeatedly indicates that they were not always obeyed, nor were they always enforceable in local communities.

The continued strength and tenacity of dance customs in the face of the declining approval of church authorities suggest the depth of the fundamental Western belief in the spiritual nature of dance. In *Religious Dances* (1952), Louis Backman provides a chronicle of historical references that illustrates individual dance forms and activities and their relationship to the Christian church in various regions. The interconnection of dance and religion, however, must be considered in a context that extends beyond the confines of official, formalized religion. The very definitions of folk dance and popular dance have developed from a spectrum of cultural beliefs that ranges from the organized religious establishment to the vernacular spirituality that animates everyday life.

Folk Dance and Popular Dance. Although the terms *folk dance* and *popular dance* did not enter common use until the early twentieth century, the dance phenomena they describe have existed for centuries. Rather than referring to particular dance choreography, *folk dance* and *popular dance* refer to the dancing found in certain social strata of European society in a certain period of history.

As Peter Burke notes in *Popular Culture in Early Modern Europe* (1978), by the sixteenth century European society was sufficiently stratified to be able to distinguish between the culture of the common people and the culture of the elite. The elite were a minority who had access to formal scholastic training; they were the innovators and primary beneficiaries of such intellectual movements as the Renaissance and the Enlightenment. The rest of society went about everyday life, molding and adapting time-worn traditions and values to accommodate the inevitable shifts demanded by social and economic change. It cannot be assumed, however, that the common people were a homogeneous group, or that the elite educated minority did not participate in popular culture. Burke illuminates the complexity of these issues, noting the diversity of the common people: there were poorer peasants and richer peasants, freemen and serfs, uneducated laborers and literate merchants, rural dwellers and urban dwellers, religious sects and regional subcultures. The elite took part in a broad range of popular culture outside the boundaries of their intellectual pursuits, if simply because they were surrounded by that culture.

By the late eighteenth century factors such as dramatic population shifts, the radical expansion of commercial capitalism, and the advent of industrialization contributed to the disruption of traditional community life in many parts of Western Europe and the subsequent demise of many popular traditions. In the same period, a new intellectual movement took root in which the folk or rural peasants became increasingly idealized in the eyes of the elite, and "folk culture" became a national treasure embodying the survivals of the uncorrupted national past. In the nineteenth century the anthropologist E. B. Tylor pointed to folklore, especially old customs and beliefs, as providing evidence of the historical development of primitive culture into civilized society. Folklore materials were seen as the vestiges of primitive culture, somehow preserved by the folk memory in the midst of an otherwise relatively civilized society.

This argument was supported further by comparing folklore to parallel cultural elements found in existing primitive societies. Seemingly irrational folk beliefs or antiquated folk customs were explained on the basis of their full-fledged primitive counterparts; the original function and meaning of the folklore survivals were considered equivalent to those of the related primitive practices, even when the forms or contexts of performance differed greatly. Many scholars believed that primitive religion was the ultimate source of folklore because religion played such a prominent role in primitive life. [*For further discussion, see* Folklore *and* Folk Religion.]

If folklore was what remained of ancient pagan religion, then it might follow that folk dance was what remained of ancient religious ritual. Yet it is curious that the genre of folk dance was neglected in the heyday of naming and documenting folk cultural genres in the nineteenth century. There is no doubt that the folk were dancing, but most scholars mention dancing only in passing, generally in reference to seasonal or religious festivals or the celebration of rites of passage. This puzzle still remains to be explored fully, but two factors can be suggested as important elements in this regard.

The first factor is that as a cultural commodity vying for scholarly attention, dance was of comparatively low status. The young fields of folklore and anthropology were intent on establishing themselves as scientific pursuits, and toward that end researchers were concerned with the task of generating texts. Dance was not a literary genre that could be recorded in words, and unlike music it did not have associated with it a common form of notation. To be sure, scholars did not hesitate to describe folk customs and celebrations in written accounts that were often illustrated with drawings and, later, photographs. The first studies of the late nineteenth century that discussed dance in any detail used that type of descriptive narrative: they presented dance customs, complete with notes on costumes, other related material paraphernalia such as swords, ribbons, sticks, or bells, unusual dramatic characters such as a man or woman impersonator or a hobbyhorse, and the social event of which the dance activity was a part. Yet very little explicit or technical description was included of the actual dance forms or styles themselves. It seems that, while writing about dance customs was certainly possible, the difficulty of rendering dance into documentary evidence hardly encouraged early scholars to invest their intellectual enthusiasm in such an elusive genre.

The second factor in the scholarly neglect of folk dance is that it was indeed believed to manifest the remnants of ancient religious ritual. This is ironic because that type of connection with primitive culture would generally have been considered a favorable quality in the evolutionary school of thought that considered folklore to be descended from ancient religion. In the case of dance, however, it may have contributed to some intellectual discomfort. By the nineteenth century, dance style was socially stratified, although the choreographic forms danced in the elite ballrooms were not dissimilar to those danced in peasant villages. The elite were responsible for infusing these dance forms with an educated and refined style of performance appropriate to their social class, for the physical abandon and overt emotionalism displayed in much peasant dancing would have been judged quite improper, even uncivilized, by the upper classes. The contemporary observations of European missionaries and travelers of wild, impassioned dancing in primitive societies served as a graphic comparison to dancing in folk communities in Europe and may have intensified the elite's sense of a debasing impropriety of folk dance. More so than any other folk performance genre, dance may have seemed a bit threatening—too primitive and too close to home; for it could be argued that the only thing separating the dancing of the elite themselves from the blatantly uncivilized dancing of the folk was a fine line of decorum. In addition, scholars were well aware of the fact that the Christian clergy had long believed that dance and dance customs (which nineteenth-century scholars would have equated with folk dance) were the survivals of pagan religious rituals. For centuries, throughout Europe, the church had been waging campaigns to cleanse Christian ritual of any taints of paganism, of which dance was one of the most insidious elements. Whatever their intellectual creeds, nineteenth-century scholars in Europe and America were good Christian gentlemen and ladies, and there can be little doubt that the official religious prejudice against dancing influenced scholarly perceptions. It is possible that this Christian heritage contributed to a sense of discomfort with folk dance material, which in turn further discouraged researchers from working in that field.

In the last decade of the nineteenth century, dance began to be considered with some seriousness. James G.

Frazer included dance as one of the myriad customs examined in his comparative treatise on magic and religion, *The Golden Bough* (1890). The development of the open-air folklife museum in Scandinavia with its focus on traditional folkways gave impetus to the founding of the Friends of Swedish Folk Dance in 1893. This was one of the first organizations of its kind, dedicated to the preservation and perpetuation of regional folk dances. Lilly Grove, in her history of dancing (London, 1895), included whole chapters on national dances and dance customs. English folklore journals published essays on seasonal festivities that discussed rustic examples such as maypole dancing and morris dancing. The year 1903, in saw E. K. Chamber's *The Mediaeval Stage* (London), one of the earliest uses of the terms *folk dance* and *Volkstanz* in a scholarly study, signalling a subtle shift in intellectual attitudes: dance was finally included in the rank of folk-compound genres, and a whole group of dance forms and customs associated with the romantic notion of the folk became "folk dance."

Throughout the early twentieth century, the concept of the folk dance was codified through the collecting and publishing of dance materials and through work in the now growing fields of folklore studies and dance education. To differentiate certain important features of dance culture, particularly the origin and transmission of dance forms and styles and the contexts of dance performance, the term *popular dance* began to be used. *Folk dance* referred to dances whose origins were obscured in ancient customs and ceremonies that derived from primitive religious ritual. Folk dances were passed on from one generation to the next and were performed as part of traditional folk community festivals. Though popular dances might be adopted into the folk repertoire and performed in traditional contexts, they were not native to the folk community. Popular dances originated from an external source, such as a foreign culture or a professional dance instructor. Popular dances were transmitted through a broader variety of social relationships than would generally have been included in the traditional folk learning process; that is, people learned from non-community members, from strangers, or from dance teachers. Popular dances were most often performed during recreational events organized for the purpose of social dancing, often in a public setting such as a dance hall. Folk dance was believed to be a pure expression of national identity, whereas popular dance was a commodity in the aesthetic marketplace of a heterogeneous, multicultural society.

The development of the concepts of folk dance and popular dance is critical to a larger understanding of dance and religion. The very definition of folk dance is inextricably tied to Western ideas about the history of religion and human culture. In the end, however, the definitions of folk dance and popular dance have to do not so much with types of dance activity as with the progression of intellectual judgments about social and economic class. According to the nineteenth-century models on which they are based, folk dance is the dance performed by the folk, and popular dance is the dance performed by the working class, or bourgeoisie. These intellectual constructions are so romantically idealized and oversimplified, however, that they do not reflect the cultural reality of the time. Even if nineteenth-century peasants had been the pristine, homogeneous group the folk were supposed to be, there was constant interaction between folk and popular culture. Popular dances did circulate among rural peasant communities and in some cases were regarded as having more prestige than older traditional forms because they were new, different, innovative, or exotic. Likewise, the dancing of the new working class was full of deeply embedded traditional elements: a foreign or popular dance form would be performed in the traditional, regional body movement style of the performer, reflecting traditional concepts of the body; a laborer who paid an admission fee to enter a public dance hall would pursue social interaction with members of the opposite sex and different age groups according to traditional—and commonly shared—rules. Perhaps most importantly, the new popular dances were evaluated and accepted on the basis of how well they satisfied current fashions, but those fashions were at least partially rooted in a folk aesthetic. The complexity of the historical interrelations between folk dance and popular dance and the disparity between intellectual ideals and cultural reality must be considered seriously.

Fundamental beliefs about dance as a form of expresion run deep in Western culture and have influenced the intellectual fashions of every age. Whatever the criteria used to delimit folk dance and popular dance, it is in the meaning of dance in vernacular culture that the relationship between dance and religion can be explored most profitably. Vernacular dance, then, refers to dancing that is integral to the everyday life and beliefs of a given group of people, irrespective of whether that dancing might also be classified as folk or popular. Religion must also be contemplated in terms of everyday culture, ranging from the dogma of the official religious establishment to the traditional beliefs and practices that embody spirituality.

Vernacular Dance, Spirituality, and Religion. There are three general categories of dance as it relates to religion and spiritual values: religious dance, ceremonial dance, and social dance. Each of those categories can be distinguished on the basis of context, belief, and—to a lesser extent—form. *Religious dance* is dance performed as part of religious worship, often taking place in the church or sanctuary. It is believed to be devotion incarnate, more than just a symbol or gesture of piety. Common forms of religious dance include the processional, circle, and solo individual dance. In performance the dancer seeks to express reverence and to interact directly with the divine.

Ceremonial dance is a much broader category and includes dancing that is part of a whole spectrum of celebratory events, from the religious to the secular. Religious events such as saints' festivals and secular events such as civic parades frame a continuum of events that manifest many types and degrees of spiritual belief. Celebrations such as Carnival, certain rites of passage, and seasonal festivities embody an ambiguous spirituality that lies somewhere between the sacred and the secular, or perhaps encompasses elements of both. [*See* Carnival.] Ceremonial dance is believed to transcend the realm of everyday life, reaching toward a higher spiritual power, be it a deity, luck, or art. Of any category, ceremonial dance embraces the largest variety of dance forms including processionals, circle and line dances, various set formations, couple dances, and solo dancing.

Social dance, finally, refers to dancing that is performed for recreation, generally as part of events that are oriented around leisure activity and social interaction. Social dance is believed to be the expression of the individual or a social relationship and does not refer directly to any religious or spiritual concept, except in one sense. In that dancing is considered artistic performance, it attends to the immanent spirituality of art as a vehicle of power and meaning. The forms of social dance include various group and couple formations and solo individual dancing.

These three categories of dance—religious, ceremonial, and social—are somewhat fluid. Changes in one factor or another can result in a shift in category for a given dance. For example, with a change in context, social dance can become ceremonial dance; with a change in belief, ceremonial dance can become religious dance (this is what occurs in many cases when a dancer becomes "possessed" by a spirit or deity.) Thus it is clear that dance cannot be considered an inanimate cultural object. Its significance must be assessed in performance as it is actively employed in a social process. Following is a sampling of dance customs found in different cultures in Europe, the Middle East, and the New World, illustrating primarily examples of religious and ceremonial dance.

Europe. The religious revival movement of Hasidism developed in Europe in the eighteenth century. In reaction to the Jewish orthodoxy of the time, Hasidism emphasized the individual expression of devotion that was within the means of every man and woman and not limited to those educated few who were privileged to study the Torah. Dance became a primary mode of religious expression, and as Hasidism spread through eastern European Jewish communities, ecstatic dancing became an identifying marker of Hasidic worship. In fact, critics of the revival sometimes mocked or ridiculed the exaggerated dance style when voicing disapproval of religious extremism. Hasidic dance is religious dance in the fullest sense; it is a means of inspired communication with God. Not only is dance and ritual movement a revered element of religious services but dancing infuses the spirit of religious devotion into numerous other festivities and celebrations. A prominent form of Hasidic dance is solo improvisation, which sometimes consists of little more than simple shuffling steps or weight shifts, various distinctive body postures, and gestures of the arms and hands, which are often raised above the head. Specific dance steps are not required, and any decorous movement performed with a spiritual intent can be acceptable. Group and couple formations are also common, though men and women are strictly segregated in all aspects of religious worship, including dance. Couple forms include simple variations of linking elbows and turning, and of forward and back patterns; group forms include complex set dances in square and circle formations. The Ḥasidim have apparently never hesitated to adopt dance forms from surrounding gentile cultures, and this process continues in Hasidic communities today.

One end of the spectrum of ceremonial dance, that which is associated with the religious or sacred, is found in the Romanian ritual Căluş. For approximately one week beginning on Whitsunday, the villagers of southern Romania observe Rusalii, a period when the spirits of the dead are believed to return to be among the living. Also during this period, evil forces are believed to be unusually threatening, and various types of behavior are restricted or forbidden in efforts to ward off the illness caused by being "possessed by Rusalii." Such an illness can only be cured through the ritual Căluş. In addition to the general healing and protective properties of Căluş, the ritual is also seen as a source of good luck and fertility. Handerkerchiefs or small articles of clothing are sometimes attached to the dancers' costumes in hopes that they will be imbued with this luck, which is then brought back to the owner of the object. Likewise, threads from the dancers' costumes are throught to be charmed, and spectators often pluck them in hopes of deriving some magical benefit. Căluş involves a complex of performance genres, material culture, and beliefs, and it is believed they work together to effect some modicum of human control over nature and the supernatural.

In Căluş, women of the community sing long, emotional laments in the traditional manner to maintain contact between the dead and the living. All the dancing, however, is performed only by a select group of men, the Căluşari. These men are all highly skilled dancers and must take an oath not to reveal the secrets of Căluş and to obey certain behavioral interdictions. Dancing is a primary vehicle of ritual magic and healing and is performed with great seriousness and sense of responsibility. The Căluşari visit each house in the village, dancing in the courtyard to a group of eager spectators. The performance includes exhibition dances that are done only by the Căluşari and a final group dance in which the villagers dance with the Căluşari. The exhibition dances are of two types, one consisting of simple walking figures done in circle formation, the second being a combination of complicated steps, jumps, and acrobatic leaps that demand virtuosic skill from each dancer. In Căluş, dancing is an act of magic, an inexorable part of the healing ritual and beliefs about supernatural forces.

The Tuscan *veglia* offers an example of dancing that straddles the boundary between social and ceremonial dance. The *veglia* is the traditional evening social gathering that is held regularly through the winter season. This custom lingers on to this day in some areas but was common throughout Tuscany until a general decline that began in the 1970s. At the *veglia,* family and friends gather around the kitchen hearth in rural homes, and amid general socializing and merriment, the performance of traditional narratives unfolds. Through storytelling, children are instructed in the moral values of the community, young unmarried couples court each other with the singing of love songs, and the elders reflect on their experiences by exchanging tales of insight, happiness, and woe. Though the *veglia* is primarily a social occasion, it also has ceremonial qualities: it is a seasonal event; it is only open to people who have a certain relationship to the host family; there are prescribed rules for social intercourse between age groups; and there is a particular sequence that is appropriate for the performance of certain artistic genres. The *veglia* is a time of heightened social interaction defined by a community reverence for traditional values and a group negotiation of the boundaries of artistic performance.

Though dancing takes place throughout the year except during Lent, Carnival season is especially devoted to dance events. The "Carnival *veglia*" is often organized by the young unmarried men, who arrange for a suitable location, hire a musician, and provide refreshments. They then invite young women to the dance, who always come accompanied by a chaperon. At other times, the dance *veglia* is hosted by a given household, in which case one's attendance is dependent on being acquainted with the family and garnering an invitation. In either case, the dance *veglia* is specifically an event for the young to socialize. Every year during Carnival, the landlords hold a dance party to which people of all social classes are invited. Peasants and landowners dance together as equals, temporarily nullifying class differences.

There are also two instances when the dance *veglia* is held in a public hall. In one case, the young men arrange for a dance party to be held on a Sunday afternoon following the religious service. This dance is semisecretive in that it is not announced formally in the community, thereby allowing the young women to attend without the knowledge of their mothers and chaperons. A public hall is also the setting for the special dance parties that are held on the three most important days of the Carnival period. These are organized by private social clubs whose members are confined to representatives of the families from a given village. The young people dress in elaborate finery, the men in dark suits with white gloves, the women in special outfits that are supposed to have never been seen before. The proceedings of the dance event are directed by the *caposala,* who is a well-known and respected man from the community. The *caposala* formally presides over the various and sundry forms of social interaction. He coordinates the sequence of dances, dance and courting games, and dancing competitions, and he serves as a matchmaker, employing both overt and covert methods to bring certain young couples together to dance and enforcing the etiquette that demands that no favoritism be shown in choosing dancing partners so that all the young women have at least one dance with each young man. He also maintains peaceful social equilibrium, settling any dispute and expelling troublesome participants. These dance *veglie* often last until dawn, although the party held on the final night of Carnival ends promptly at midnight, which marks the beginning of Lent. The last part of the Carnival season was, in years past, distinguished by the appearance of two costumed characters. The first of these masked men, dressed in fancy black formal attire, was the incarnation of Carnival itself, and he arrived just in time to dance the last dance of the evening. The second man entered at midnight, cloaked in a long gray coat decorated with smoked herrings; he was the embodiment of Lent, and he brought the festivities to a ceremonious end.

The dance forms performed at a *veglia* are always the

same and are always danced in a particular sequence. The first dance is a polka, followed by a mazurka, a waltz, and a quadrille. The quadrille was considered the climax to the dance sequence, as it involved a variety of complicated steps and patterns and allowed the greatest opportunity for flirting during the changing of partners. Recently, other couple dances have been inserted after the waltz, such as the tango and the one-step. All of these forms are popular dances, and though they are all based on folk dance forms to varying degrees, none is specifically native to Tuscany. Despite the fact that these dances have been, at some point in history, imported into the Tuscan countryside from some foreign source, they have been unabashedly adopted into the community repertoire and through generations of performance have become thoroughly naturalized. The dancing that takes place at a *veglia* is social dancing in the most straightforward sense: young men and women dance together to be with each other, confirming and expanding an everyday relationship. It can also be considered ceremonial dancing by virtue of its central role in the *veglia,* transforming everyday life and social interaction into festivity and artistic performance.

Middle East. The Middle East is the birthplace of three of the world's major religions—Judaism, Christianity, and Islam—and home to a variety of regional cultures and linguistic groups. Though all three religions and their subdenominations are found in the Middle East today, Islam predominates. In *The Middle East* (1976), anthropologist John Gulick distinguishes between the "great tradition" and "little tradition" in Islamic religion. The "great tradition" refers to the tenets of official religion based on the sacred written texts. The "little traditon" refers to the belief systems surrounding the veneration of saints, the control of evil spirits, and other spiritual endeavors. The beliefs and customs of the little tradition are not specified in the official religious texts and are, in fact, frowned upon by some religious functionaries. They are, nonetheless, an integral part of everyday religious prescriptions of devotion. It is in this little tradition of vernacular spirituality that we find dance customs related to religious life. There are few studies that discuss dancing in Muslim and Jewish communities, and virtually none that examine Christian settlements. Even these limited materials, however, suggest some cultural consistency or interrelationship between customs, and possibly dance forms, found among different religious groups in the Middle East. It remains for future research to explore fully the implications of ethnicity, religion, and regionality on artistic performance.

The "little tradition" of many Muslim communities includes a type of ceremonial dancing that plays a key role in a ritual process of exorcism known as the *zār.* Though found in several Middle Eastern countries, the *zār* appears to be most well known and vital in the Nile region, particularly in Egypt. The spirit that must be exorcised in the *zār* ceremony is also known as *zār.* The *zār* ceremony is performed to cure an individual of spirit possession. Though anyone is potentially vulnerable to possession, women are the most commonly afflicted. It is believed that pure spirits are ever present, wandering around the earth. These spirits demand respect, and humans are required to observe rules of spiritual etiquette, such as giving thanks or asking permission for certain actions. Pure spirits can impose good or evil upon human beings, but it is believed that committing some infraction or allowing a breach in deferential protocol will provoke a spirit to possess an individual and wreak punishment. Such possession can manifest itself in a variety of physical and mental symptoms, such as chronic aches and pains in certain body parts, general indolence, allergies, rheumatism, epileptic fits, and different feminine complaints, including barrenness.

The *zār* ceremony requires the services of two important ceremonial functionaries, as well as an ensemble of musicians. One role is that of the *shaykhah,* who is a spiritual intermediary. Through consultations, divination, and the prescription of different types of ritual behavior, the *shaykhah* ascertains what is needed to appease and expel the spirit. The second role is that of the *munshidah,* who is a singer versed in the specialized traditional repertoire of *zār* songs. The *munshidah* sings different songs throughout the ceremony, entreating the spirit to make itself known and interact with the *shaykhah.* Both the *shaykhah* and *munshidah* are generally hereditary roles passed on from mother to daughter.

The *zār* ceremony itself can last anywhere from one to several days, depending on the wealth of the possessed woman who has come for help. The "patient" must follow the advice of the *shaykhah* to wear special garments and ornaments or to consume certain foods and drinks. The patient provides whatever offerings the *shaykhah* determines are necessary, generally a combination of a few fowl and pieces of gold or silver jewelry. At sunset, a large circular table is covered with an elaborate meal, accompanied by chants and special songs. At two o'clock the following morning, the animals are ritually slaughtered according to Islamic custom, and the possessed woman is smeared with the warm blood. The next day the *zār* ceremony continues as the *shaykhah* guides the patient through various rituals while the *munshidah* sings the appropriate songs.

The emotional climax of the ceremony is reached

when the possessed woman starts to dance. Individual spirits are associated with distinctive rhythmic patterns, and as the musicians play a particular beat the possesed woman will be drawn to dance. The dancing is frenzied and ecstatic, and the dancer speaks in the voice of her possessing spirit. The spirit makes demands that the *shaykhah* must then interpret and satisfy. The dancing continues and the excitement builds as the musicians, *munshidah,* and *shaykhah* encourage the dancer, who will dance until she is thoroughly exhausted. The dance is always a solo improvisational form, consisting of torso bending and swaying, head and arm gestures, and some simple stepping and floor patterns. The dancing performed in the *zār* ceremony is considered a vehicle for the spirit to express itself and a critical cathartic element in the process of exorcism.

Yemenite Jewish culture provides a vibrant example of the range of dance activity in the religious and spiritual life of a community. Jewish communities in Yemen were among the most isolated in the Middle East, and many ancient customs were preserved as an ongoing part of daily life. For example, religious dancing was an integral part of the observation of certain holidays, such as Simḥat Torah. In celebration of the yearly cycle of reading the Torah, the congregation sang special verses of the *pizmon,* which are religious texts sung only in the synagogue. Along with their joyous, exuberant singing, the congregation danced around with the Torah scrolls, carrying them from the central desk of the synagogue, where they were placed for reading, back to the ark, where they were stored. The dancing consisted of simple walking steps without much elaboration or stylization, but the dancing was considered an expression of devotion to Jewish religious law as written in the Torah.

There was also ceremonial dancing in Yemenite Jewish communities. Celebrations and rites of passage such as circumcisions or the two weeks of preparations and festivities that accompanied a wedding were commemorated with dancing and singing. Traditionally, men and women danced separately, each to the singing of special dance songs and the playing of a drum. The dance songs sung by the men had fixed religious texts in Hebrew, Aramaic, or literary Arabic and were performed by two singers who sat apart from the dancers. The women sang songs about everyday life, including the importance of the event being celebrated at the time. Their song texts were sung in local Yemenite Arabic dialect and were performed by the women as they danced. Though the women's songs were less overtly religious, the dancing of both men and women was considered a means of rejoicing and of honoring the celebrants.

New World. Among the European cultures in the New World, the religious sect known as Shakers offers a unique example of religious dancing in community worship. The Shakers originated in England in the mid-eighteenth century and settled in America shortly before the Revolution. [*See* Shakers.] They held that the second appearance of Christ was imminent and that true believers must follow certain tenets in order to transcend wordly existence and achieve everlasting life. The foundations of Shaker faith were observed through keeping apart from the world at large, the two sexes living separately and remaining celibate, sharing all property in common, diligently pursuing craftwork with their hands, and worshiping with joyful abandon. The early Shakers were overcome with ecstasy in their worship and were given to fervent and eclectic displays of divine inspiration including speaking in tongues, whirling or shaking, singing song fragments, shouting, and jumping.

As the sect grew and developed, their deranged array of spiritual responses was institutionalized into orderly forms of song and dance. Though the expression of their religious zeal was largely disposed to tidy devotional exercises, the Shaker's faith was no less impassioned. Dancing was considered a spiritual gift, or the "work of God," which they were most happy to receive. Devotinal dancing was also believed to function as a means of expelling and pacifying carnal desires, thereby allowing a pure bodily manifestation of faith. There were instances of individuals dancing by themselves while receiving the spirit, but most Shaker dancing was performed in large groups consisting of all the able-bodied Believers. Men and women formed separate lines or circles and danced a variety of floor patterns and simple figures. There were dances in square and circle formations as well as processionals and sacred marches. Many of the dance patterns were said to have originated in spiritual visions and dreams received by the Shakers and were imputed with specific symbolic meanings illustrating Shaker beliefs.

The population of the New World is a panoply of different cultural groups, with a broad spectrum of religious beliefs and customs. Over the centuries different cultures have come into contact, influencing each other to varying degrees. Rather than dissolving into a homogeneous mass, however, distinct aspects from different cultural traditions were reblended into new creole forms. These creole cultures, languages, or performance traditions often contain elements that can be easily identified and traced to specific Old World origins, but the new incarnation is not an exact replica of the original. In all cases, there has been change, development, and adaption to suit new conditions and social contexts.

One of the most dramatic examples of this reblending process is found in Afro-American culture. The historical circumstances of the slave trade threw together Africans from several different national territories in west Africa, including at least five major cultural groups. The intermingling of different African traditions and beliefs has yielded an array of new Afro-American forms, which have also intermingled with other non-African traditions according to regional and historical conditions.

The Voodoo religion practiced in Haiti is one instance of this intermingling of African and non-African traditions. It incorporates a synthesis of different African beliefs and rituals that further interface with Roman Catholic practice and symbolism. Voodoo is based on a complex mythology that relates major gods to lesser divinities. These spirits are called *lwa*, a Kréyol term, and they include ancestor spirits, gods and goddesses of nature, a trickster, a god of creativity, and a supreme god who presides over all the others. Every spirit has an individual personality and is associated with certain domains of everyday life or spiritual well-being. To ensure the goodwill of the *lwa* and be taken under their protection, a person must be initiated into the spiritual society. A priest or priestess, known as *hungan*, coordinates the ceremonies and rites that take place in their sanctuary and tends to community needs requiring divination, exorcism, and healing. [*See* Voodoo.]

Voodoo ceremonies and dances are generally performed in a covered shed that has a post standing in the center of the floor space. This center post is considered the means by which the spirits descend into the peristyle. Though the spirits communicate with initiates through symbolic dreams and vision, they commonly possess people and make their will known. Each spirit expresses itself through a distincitve repertoire of speech mannerisms, body movements, special dances, and a predilection for certain objects, such as a hat, bottle, or stick. It is said that a spirit "mounts" its "horse" when a person becomes possessed; the person is a vehicle for the spirit, an expressive body through which the spirit interacts with the crowd and other spirits. Possession behavior is regarded as tangible evidence of a spirit's personality and temperament, and watching the possessed during Voodoo ceremonies is believed to be an important way for potential initiates to learn about the spirits.

Dancing and possession are closely interrelated. Three dances are performed to honor each spirit, accompanied by songs and the playing of a drum ensemble. Rhythm acts as a kind of supernatural intermediary and entices the spirits themselves to dance. Each spirit has its own particular dances through which it reveals its power and aesthetic agility. Dancing is considered a ritual act on several levels. In one sense, dancing is held to be a gift, performed by initiates as an offering to please the spirits. In another sense, dancing is believed to be a means of divine communication by which a spirit imparts its essence or intentions to a devotee. On yet another level, dancing is transcendental, in that aesthetic fulfillment has spiritual significance. Both humans and spirits dance, seeking to achieve greater spiritual power through artistic performance. The dancing in Voodoo worship that is associated with possession is undeniably religious dancing, as it is the actual practice of religious belief and devotions.

BIBLIOGRAPHY

A well-rounded and detailed study discussing the nature of dance in Greek civilization is Lillian B. Lawler's *The Dance in Ancient Greece* (London, 1964). This book also outlines the important Greek philosophical tenets that have influenced Western ideas about dance. A good historical study of literary references to dancing and Christianity, especially focusing on the dance epidemics, is Eugène Louis Backman's *Religious Dances in the Christian Church and in Popular Medicine,* translated by E. Classen (London, 1952). An excellent introduction to the history of popular culture and folk culture is Peter Burke's *Popular Culture in Early Modern Europe* (New York, 1978). This book also has a very useful bibliography.

The classic work that epitomizes the nineteenth-century study of comparative religion and ideas of cultural evolution is James G. Frazer's *The Golden Bough*, 3d ed., rev. & enl., 12 vols. (London, 1911–1915). Though his source materials are quite uneven, Frazer includes a multitude of references to dance-related customs. A further elaboration of evolutionary ideas is found in Curt Sachs's *World History of the Dance,* translated by Bessie Schönberg (New York, 1937). While this book has been used as a standard text for many years and offers interesting examples of dance customs, it ignores twentieth-century developments in the study of human culture and restates outdated nineteenth-century philosophy. One of the few examinations of dance by a historian of religions can be found in Gerardus van der Leeuw's *Sacred and Profane Beauty* (New York, 1963).

Additional source material on the history of folk dance, popular dance, and vernacular dance is discussed in my article "Folkdance," in the *International Encyclopedia of Dance* (New York, forthcoming). One of the first works to develop the concept of vernacular dance is Marshall Stearns and Jean Stearns's *Jazz Dance: The Story of American Vernacular Dance* (New York, 1964). A varied collection of short essays is *The Chasidic Dance,* edited by Fred Berk (New York, 1975). Of particular interest in that collection is the article by Jill Gellerman, "With Body and Soul: The Dance of the Chasidim" (pp. 16–21), which recounts the contemporary practices of Hasidic communities in Brooklyn, New York. A recent monograph that offers detailed description and analysis based on first-hand observations is Gail Kligman's *Căluş: Symbolic Transformation in Romanian Ritual* (Chicago, 1981). A delightful account of traditional social life, which includes a collection of song and narrative texts, is Alessandro Falassi's *Folklore by the Fireside: Text and Context of the Tuscan Veglia* (Austin, 1980). A good introduction to the culture of the Middle East written from an anthropological perspective is John Gulick's *The Middle East* (Pacific Palisades, Calif., 1976). This book contains useful annotated bibliographies after each chapter.

There are very few sources on dance in the Middle East, but a good overview is found in Lois Ibsen al-Faruqi's "Dance as an Expression of Islamic Culture," *Dance Research Journal* 10 (Spring–Summer 1978): 6–13. Two short studies that contain interesting history and illustrations are Metin And's "Dances of Anatolian Turkey," *Dance Perspectives* 3 (1959): 5–76, and Morroe Berger's "The Arab Danse du Ventre," *Dance Perspectives* 10 (1961): 4–67. Two longer studies that offer detailed descriptions and contextual information based on contemporary observations are Magda Ahmed Abdfel Ghaffar Saleh's *A Documentation of the Ethnic Dance Traditions of the Arab Republic of Egypt*, 2 vols., Ph.D. diss., New York University (Ann Arbor, 1979), and Shalom Staub's *The Yemenite Jewish Dance*, M.A. thesis, Wesleyan University (Ann Arbor, 1978).

The classic work on the Shaker sect remains Edward Deming Andrew's *The Gift to Be Simple: Songs, Dances, and Rituals of the American Shakers* (New York, 1940). A revealing examination of Afro-American art and the process of creolization, much of which is in relation to religion, can be found in Robert Farris Thompson's *Flash of the Spirit: African and Afro-American Art and Philosophy* (New York, 1981). A classic study in the field of Afro-American religion remains Alfred Métraux's *Voodoo in Haiti* (New York, 1959).

LEEELLEN FRIEDLAND

Theatrical and Liturgical Dance

A distinction often drawn between dance in the West (the Euramerican tradition) and dance in the rest of the world is that the latter is closely tied to religion, while dance in the West, especially theatrical dance, has developed outside religious institutions and often in opposition to them. Most of the major Asian dance-drama forms originated in religious contexts, involve religious themes, and, especially in the past, were often performed by religious practitioners. Outside Europe and Asia, dancing intended for presentation to an audience has been rare until recently and has usually taken place in a religious context. Divine possession has often been a vehicle for quasi-theatrical performance.

A dichotomy can also be discovered between the history of Western dance on the one hand and that of Western music, visual arts, and architecture on the other. While religion provided a legitimate context and a source of patronage for the growth of other European arts, this was not the case for dance. For the most part, the church not only did not support dance, it vehemently opposed it.

Yet, such broad generalizations about the divorce of dance from religion tend to obscure recognition of how influential religion has in fact been. While direct religious intent has been relatively rare, it has been strong in some periods and for some choreographers. A few have been motivated to express their religious conviction in dance, and others have sought in dance the wellsprings of spirituality. These choreographers have often found inspiration in non-Western religions where the connection between the spirit and the body is often a key principle. Whereas in earlier centuries myth and ritual were used as plot devices or as political metaphors, often in recent decades the choreography has explored the deeper dimensions of their symbolism.

Religious content has entered Western theatrical dance in a variety of ways, including (1) the use of biblical or folkloric religious themes; (2) the depiction of characters, rituals, and myths of non-Judeo-Christian religions or of unorthodox sects; (3) the influence of religious philosophies; (4) explorations of the concept of ritual or the stylizations of specific rituals; (5) the enactment of myths or the probing of mythic symbolism; (6) the use of general religious concepts or central characters, events, or processes, such as Death, Creation, and the Devil; (7) plots involving supernatural characters and stories; (8) the theme of religiously motivated sexual repression; (9) the use of religion as a device for exploring cultural identity; (10) explorations of altered states of consciousness as often occurs in sacred dance; and (11) settings of the Mass as theatrical works. In addition, many dance plots presuppose a knowledge of Judeo-Christian ethics, symbolism, ritual, and history in order to be understood fully. Religion has also indirectly affected theatrical dance history by its varying attitudes toward dance, which have included suppressing, supporting, and ignoring it.

Conflicting attitudes toward the human body and, by extension, toward dancing have characterized all three of the major monotheistic religions in the West—Judaism, Christianity, and Islam. Although the negative view has generally won out, alternative models and solutions constantly challenge any overwhelming orthodoxy. Biblical literature, for instance, provides both favorable and unfavorable pictures. On the one hand, there is the model of King David's joyous dance before the Ark of the Covenant (*2 Sm.* 6:14–16); on the other hand, there are the Israelites' idolatrous dance around the Golden Calf (*Ex.* 32:19) and Salome's allegedly lascivious dance before King Herod (*Mt.* 14:6, *Mk.* 6:22). Contradictory, too, are possible interpretations of the words of the apostle Paul. For instance, his statement that the "body is a temple of the Holy Spirit" (*1 Cor.* 6:19) has been interpreted as indicating the appropriateness of using the body in dance as a vehicle of worship and also as justification for condemning dance as a defilement of the "temple." Ambiguity about the relation of body and soul has plagued Jews, Christians, and Muslims alike, and has militated against the acceptance of dancing.

Interestingly, some heterodoxies in monotheistic religions have incorporated dance as a major focus of expression—the gnostic sects of early Christianity, the Ṣūfīs in Islam, the Ḥasidim of Judaism, and the Shakers of American Christianity. The Mormons are unusual in their embrace of dancing as both a social and theatrical experience.

There has been more interrelationship between religion and theatrical dance in the twentieth century, in quantity as well as in diversity of expression, than at any other time. With organized religions in general neither condemning nor supporting dance, perhaps dance has been freer to adopt religious themes without political ties or negative consequences. Perhaps the apparent secularization of society has rendered religious themes more neutral raw material. On the other hand, the growing popularity of dance has made this medium of expression more acceptable in religious contexts. In addition, while primarily growing up outside of religious institutions, theatrical dance in the twentieth century has returned to the church and synagogue in the burgeoning liturgical or sacred dance movement.

Early Christianity through the Middle Ages. The strongest evidence that there was dancing connected with religion in the early Christian church is the persistent condemnation of dance chronicled in the writings of over six hundred years of church councils. At this time, dancing was particularly associated with ceremonies at the shrines of martyrs.

The disdain of the church for dancing stemmed in part from the state of dancing at the time. Much of the refinement of Greek and Roman dance and theater had degenerated into generally bawdy mime and acrobatic shows, or else the dancing had become associated with pagan rituals. The church even refused baptism to performers. A growing asceticism further divorced Christianity from dance. In addition, certain heretical movements incorporated dance into their liturgy, further fueling orthodoxy's condemnation of it. For instance, the gnostic sects enacted the "Round Dance of the Cross" from the *Acts of John* as an actual sacred ritual dance that enabled the participants to identify with Christ and to transcend human suffering. Such lines as the following have become a rallying point for other religious sects that wish to recognize sacred dance: "To the universe belongs the dancer. Whoever does not dance does not know what happens" (*Acts of John* 95:16–17).

Condemnation of dancing continued into the later Middle Ages. However, the inherent theatricality of the Christian liturgy, as well as of the biblical literature, could not be ignored. Dramatic performances were often elaborate, sometimes involving processionals and dancing. Dance roles tended to be comic or grotesque character parts. Starting around the twelfth century through about the fifteenth century, plays were associated with Easter and Christmas. Corpus Christi festivals involved dancing, often by guild members or under government sponsorship. Los Seises, a ritual dance performed by boy choristers, was initiated in Seville and is still performed today. The Pelota of Auxerre is thought to have been a complex dance in which the clergy passed a ball among themselves along the stations of a labyrinth. Dances moving along the paths of labyrinths on the floors of cathedrals, such as the one at Chartres, were also integrated into the liturgy.

Dancing in both a recreational and performance context took place mostly outside the church, often in conjunction with local saint days and religious festivals. Christmas was particularly enlivened by popular dancing often involving mumming, a practice that still accompanies this holiday in parts of the United Kingdom and in North and South America. The Feast of Fools provided the opportunity for burlesques of the established church. Many of the celebrations on these holidays had pagan roots, providing further reason for official condemnation.

The miracle, mystery, and morality plays of the Middle Ages were performed in the churchyards and contained some of the beginnings of professional dance. The dancing parts tended to be fools, shepherds, and demons. The Devil was often blamed for inventing dancing, and it is the Devil who was one of the most danced characters. Minstrels, jongleurs, and other traveling performers of this period often included acrobatics, mime, and dancing in their performances. Pageants included *tableaux vivants* depicting biblical scenes. While generally not dance per se, they involved the communication of meaning through postures and movement rather than through words. The Dance of Death was a pervasive visual and literary symbol.

Social dancing was practiced in the feudal manors of the Middle Ages, and performances including dancing began to enter the courts toward the end of the period. However, it was in the courts of Renaissance Europe that the roots of theatrical dancing emerged, roots not directly linked to religion, but affected by religious ideas in indirect ways.

Renaissance. With the rediscovery of classical antiquity during the Renaissance came a desire to discover the relationship between Greek philosophy and dance. Renaissance courtiers viewed dance as a medium that could express cosmological, moral, and political principles. Aristotelian ethical theory, Plato's mystical geometry, and Neoplatonist ideas of love were exemplified in dance. While dance in the Renaissance was for the most part composed of simple patterns of stepping, there was also an emphasis on elaborate spatial formations. Much like the members of a contemporary marching band at a football game, the performers constantly created floor patterns that they skillfully transmuted to other patterns. To the Renaissance dancer and spectator, the geometrical figures that were formed had symbolic significance: the dissolution of the patterns revealed the mutability of nature, but underlying these shapes and changes was a grand unifying order emanating from God. The patterns of the dancing were interpreted in different ways. For example, in cosmological terms, they might reveal the harmony of nature as in the cycles of the heavenly bodies; in moral terms, they might exemplify order and virtue and the resolution of extremes; and in political terms they might demonstrate the court's control over these cosmic patterns. It was felt that dancing helped create order within the individual's soul and thereby could promote order and peace in political affairs as well. Dance linked the political, moral, and cosmological orders in an inseparable cycle. Dance did not just portray ritual, it was felt to affect the cosmic and mundane realms of existence.

The dance-plays had primarily mythological themes. The best-documented ballet of this period, *Le ballet comique de la reine* (1581), related the triumph of Minerva (Wisdom) and Jupiter (Virtue) over the evil Circe. The king is seen as her ultimate conqueror, restoring the cosmos to peace. Another important later work has a historical theme relating to Christianity. In *Le deliverance de Renaud* (1617), the Christian crusader Renaud is seduced away from battle by the enchantress Armide. Subsequently, the Christians lose, but Armide's powers fail and Renaud is able to escape and liberate Jerusalem. The plot was interpreted as an allegory for the king freeing France from chaos.

Thus although in European history dance has often been associated with immorality, the Renaissance also offered an alternative interpretation: the conception of dance as virtue. There are examples of this attitude in antiquity, in the writings of Plato and Cicero, for instance, but a fuller development of this theme blossomed in the sixteenth century with the developing concept of the gentleman. Sir Thomas Elyot's *Boke Named the Governour* (1531) and Sir John Davies's poem *Orchestra* (1594), among other works, reveal this perspective. Adapting the concept of correspondences, they discovered the symbolic relationship between dance and particular virtues or states of being. Elyot associated dance with prudence, reason, and order. Particular dance movements were analyzed for their moral symbolism. Davies saw the correspondence between dance and chastity and marriage in contradistinction to the usual correlation between dance and lust. Both authors describe couple dancing in terms of a model of cosmic harmony. Dance was elevated to the status of an ethical ideal. Political concepts were couched in mythological themes that were revealed in dance.

During the Renaissance, *Tanzhausen* were important institutions in the Jewish ghettos of northern Europe. They fostered many choreographers, then called "dance masters," who traveled throughout Europe, often arranging dances at various courts. The best-documented Jewish dance master was, however, a product of the court tradition of southern Europe: Guglielmo Ebreo (William the Jew of Pisaro) is the author of one of the earliest extant dance manuals, dating from the mid-fifteenth century.

In the later Renaissance and early Baroque period in Italy, ballet developed in conjunction with the growth of opera. Monteverdi's *Il combattimento di Tancredi e Clorinda* (1624) featured a duel between the Christian crusader Tancredi and the disguised Muslim maiden Clorinda whom he loved. He kills her, and as she lies dying she asks for baptism. The same theme has been treated by others, most notably by the American choreographer William Dollar in his 1949 ballet *The Duel.*

With the rise of Protestantism, the opposition to dancing grew and was taken to extremes in Calvinist contexts. Although the Puritan condemnation of dance was not so vehement or all-encompassing as often painted, it was strong enough to squelch much social dancing and to thwart theatrical dancing in America and in some strongly Calvinist countries in Europe.

The objection was especially strong to "mixed" or couple dancing and to women appearing on the stage. Such ambivalance toward dance persists to the present and was dramatically represented until well into the twentieth century in the United States in the so-called blue laws, which prohibited dancing and similar activities on Sunday. From the eighteenth century into the twentieth, dance performances often had to be billed as lectures or sacred concerts. Puritanical repression of the body and dancing has been a theme in several twentieth-century choreographies, especially in the works of Martha Graham.

Baroque and Pre-Romantic Periods. It is in the French court of Louis XIV (r. 1643–1714), called the Sun King, that theatrical dance germinated. In numerous court pageants the king himself was the star dancer, and his favorite role was Apollo, the personification of the sun. The subject matter of court ballets continued to be mythological or pastoral, and the message was still a political one. Professional dancers began to appear, and with the establishment of the Paris Opéra, ballet finally left the confines of the court. With the evolution of the proscenium stage, the figure-based style of the Renaissance with its attendant symbolism was no longer viable; the frontal view of the body was the focus. The ballet vocabulary rapidly expanded in this context. The aesthetic still had a moral overtone; *complaisance,* an air of refined constraint, was the ideal.

Religious institutions were also directly involved in the ballet of the Baroque period in the form of the performances regularly produced by the Jesuit colleges. These colleges were not seminaries, but rather institutions of higher secular education. Unlike most other orders, the Jesuits embraced dance as *divertissements honnêtes.* They performed plays at different times throughout the year, but the principal event was during graduation. They generally staged a five-act tragedy with a biblical, classical, or national theme. A four-act ballet was performed between the acts of the play. The ballets were sometimes loosely connected to the play, but they did not deal overtly with religious themes, favoring the Greek mythological or allegorical plots prevalent also in the court and opera ballets. They were performed in the colleges throughout Europe by the students and were immensely popular. They served as a welcome relief from the heaviness of the often obscure Latin rhetoric of the plays. In Paris the students were joined by the most famous dancers of the Paris Opéra, and the ballets were choreographed by the same preeminent dance masters, such as Pierre Beauchamps and Louis Pécour, who created the masterpieces of the secular theater.

The ballets were often veiled social and political commentaries couched in mythological terms. Themes ranged from "Crowns," a depiction of methods of royal succession, to "The History of Dance," an apologia for dance, to "The Empire of Fate," a critique of the doctrine of predestination promoted by the Jansenists, a group that was ultimately to cause the downfall of the Jesuits in the mid-eighteenth century. Dancing was compatible with the Christian humanist, this-worldly orientation of the Jesuit order. Their ballets differed from their secularly sponsored counterparts in having no female performers or romantic plots and in always having a moral point.

Dance also developed in England, where choreographer-scholars like John Weaver (1673–1760) debated the significance of the dance. The French choreographer Jean-Georges Noverre (1727–1810) shared similar concerns with Weaver, and both were instrumental in the development of *ballet d'action,* which led into another phase of dance history, the pre-Romantic. The characters were still mythological or pastoral, but rather than being merely allegorical symbols, they often displayed emotions and showed some sense of characterization. Important ballets of this period were the mythologically based *The Loves of Mars and Venus* (1717) of Weaver and Noverre's *Medea and Jason* (1763). It was the Age of Reason, and theatrical dance also emulated these ideals.

The French Revolution affected the development of ballet in several ways. For one, it dispersed many of its aristocratic dancers to other countries, including the United States, where theatrical dancing ran up against Puritan disdain. At this time, too, a different energy was at work outside the Opéra in the boulevard theaters of Paris. Catering to the middle class, they featured comic, acrobatic movements, themes from exotic lands and medieval times, grand visual spectacles, and sometimes characters drawn from life rather than from mythology or antiquity. The boulevard theater also discovered the potential for spectacle in biblical themes, producing such ballets and pantomimes as *Samson, Suzanne et les vieillards, Daniel,* and *David et Goliath* during the period from 1816 to 1838. Many of the production techniques and themes of this Theater of Marvels were adopted and refined at the Opéra.

One curiosity of this period was the highly popular, somewhat sacrilegious, political satire *The Ballet of the Pope* (1797) by Dominique Le Fevre, performed at La Scala in Milan. The choreographer danced the role of Pope Pius VI, who engaged in most unpopelike behavior. An important work of this period was Salvatore Viganò's *La vestale* (1818), which told the story of the forbidden love of a Roman Vestal Virgin, ending in the dual murder of the two would-be lovers. Pierre Gardel's *L'enfant prodigue* (1812) was perhaps the first of a long succession of interpretations of this story.

The Romantic Ballet. With the rise of romanticism in the arts, another type of religious theme entered ballet. The beginnings of the Romantic ballet are commonly traced to the 1831 opera *Robert le diable* in which Marie Taglioni, the dancer who was to become the quintessential ethereal ballerina, led a group of the spirits of nuns in a supernatural scene. The development of ballet technique, especially the beginning of *pointe* work, created a mechanism to promote the otherworldly ideals of romanticism. *La sylphide* (1832) and *Giselle* (1841), versions of which are still widely performed, are considered the epitomes of romanticism in ballet. Both exist in a context of the depiction of otherworldly spirits and the desire to escape from this-wordly reality. Because of the Romantic emphasis on emotionalism, subjectivity, malaise, and the attraction to ungovernable forces, this aesthetic trend has often been labeled as un-Christian. Yet a pervasive theme is the contrasting of these uncontrolled states with the tranquility and harmony of nature and Christian values.

Overtly religious themes were rare, but Christian ethics were pervasive. The conflict between Christian values and the supernatural or wild unknown was displayed in many guises. The Romantic litterateur Théophile Gautier characterized the two leading ballerinas of his day, Marie Taglioni and Fanny Elssler, respectively, as a Christian and a pagan dancer, referring to the virginal ethereality of the former and the voluptuous passion of the latter. The roles available to the Romantic ballerina in this era also reflected this kind of dichotomy: supernatural wood and water nymphs alternated with female bandits, gypsies, and exotic temptresses. Plots often contrasted the two.

In *Giselle*, the peasant girl is betrayed by an aristocratic suitor, goes mad, and dies, joining the ranks of avenging *wili*s, spirits who dance men to death. At one point, Giselle protects her lover by shielding him against the cross on her tomb. Thus, religious symbolism often entered the ballet in incidental or subtle ways. The Devil also showed up in many Romantic ballets—for example, *Le Diable boiteux* (1836) and *Le violin du Diable* (1849).

Another variation of the Romantic ballet thrived in Denmark under the choreographer Auguste Bournonville (1805–1879). His ballets also reveal the fascination with the supernatural and the exotic, but Bournonville emphasized the optimistic and harmonic aspects of the Romantic spirit, for the most part eschewing the darker emotionalism of the Romantic ballets in France, England, and Russia. Contemporary Danish dance critic Erik Aschengreen noted: "Bournonville's ballets rest on the idea of spiritual aspiration, with poetry and beauty as important qualities and with Christianity as the conqueror of all dissonances" (Aschengreen, 1979, p. 111).

While rarely dealing with religious subject matter per se, Bournonville's ballets are suffused with Christian values and symbolism. His ballets contrast social harmony with uncontrolled forces outside society. Christian symbols often are the devices that effect the triumph of human values over the danger of the irrational. He often uses two women (or one woman in two transformations) as a device for contrasting the rational and irrational, Christian and pagan. A striking example of this is in his extant ballet *A Folk Tale* (1854). This is the story of the human baby Hilda who was snatched from her cradle and replaced by the troll baby Birthe. Each grows up unaware of the truth. Birthe struggles to conform to the human world, but bursts of temper and uncontrolled and vulgar movements reveal her troll nature. Hilda, on the other hand, instinctively bows to church bells in the distance and fashions herself a cross from sticks. Her calm nature soothes the chaos around her. The ballet ends happily with each character acknowledging the rightness of remaining true to one's nature. A wedding, the sanctioning of love by the church, ends this ballet, as in many other Romantic works. In *Napoli* (1842) and *The Flower Festival in Genzano* (1858), the heroine invokes the aid of the Madonna. In *Napoli*, for instance, the heroine is saved from her transformation into a sea nymph by an amulet of the Virgin Mary.

The theme of another ballet, *Arcona* (1875), is overtly Christian—a chronicle of the christianization of the Slavs in Denmark. The heroine is about to be initiated into the pagan religion when she sees the cross worn by a Danish prisoner. Bournonville's libretto states: "No sooner has Hella hung the cross around her neck . . . than her whole being is suffused with a religious feeling hitherto unknown to her" (McAndrews, 1982–1983, p. 330). She proceeds to free the Christian prisoner. In Bournonville's *La sylphide* (1836), which is still his most widely performed work, the hero's rejection of home to quest after the sylphide results in his losing everything, an example of how the choreographer contrasted the virtues of the Christian home with the disruptive forces of the nonsocial.

Classical Ballet. The Romantic ballet began to decline in Europe and the United States, and the values changed to promote spectacles that were often merely vehicles for flaunting women's legs. Ballet became more the province of the music hall. However, the evolution of ballet continued in Russia, where the great classical ballets *Swan Lake* (1895), *The Nutcracker* (1892), and *Sleeping Beauty* (1890) were choreographed. The themes were primarily fairy tales or exotic spectacles, but the choreographic quality of the works of Marius Petipa (1818–1910) and Lev Ivanov (1834–1901) elevated the genre. Few ballets from this period are extant, but it seems that very few had more than a gloss of religious significance. Thus, Petipa's *La bayadère* (1877) continues a tradition of depicting Hindu priests and temple dancers, and his *La fille du pharon* (1862) depicts his notion of Egyptian religion. Ironically, Ivanov's *The Nutcracker,* and the many versions of this work rechoreographed by others, has become almost synonymous with Christmas. It takes place at a Christmas party, but it has no Christian significance per se although it involves religious phenomena such as magical transformation. It is probably performed by more companies in more performances all over the world than any other work and might be said to be a symbol of the secular Christmas.

Delsarte. During the nineteenth century, another trend with religious overtones was developing that was to have profound impact on the growth of twentieth-century dance. François Delsarte (1811–1871) developed a system for analyzing and explaining the source of expression in movement, especially as it relates to singing, acting, and oratory. In the United States, a primary application was to dance. Underlying his quasi-scientific categorization of movement possibilities and their meanings are two basic laws. The Law of Correspondence states, "To each spiritual function responds a function of the body; to each grand function of the body corresponds a spiritual act." The Law of Trinity led him to divide all nature, and therefore movement too, into a series of triads. For instance, he presented the following series:

Life	Soul	Mind
Physical	Emotional	Mental
Ease	Coordination	Precision
Motion	Space	Time
Energy	Love	Wisdom

There were three corresponding zones of the body: limbs (or lower torso), torso (or upper torso), and head. Each body part could be further subdivided into three areas, each of which replicated the physical, emotional, and mental layering. Thus, which body part one used, in conjunction with which other parts, in what section of space determined the expressive message of the movement. Outgrowths of Delsarte's work were the art of statue-posing, in which the performers created *tableaux vivants* according to Delsartean principles; aesthetic gymnastics, a form of physical fitness for Victorian women; and pantomiming of poetry. These forms of performance were precursors of modern dance.

To some followers of Delsarte, the system was "the basis of a new religious education, destined to perfect the children of men . . . and redeem the earth" (quoted in Ruyter, 1979, p. 20). An underlying idea was that since man was made in the likeness of God, then his movements must inherently reveal God. The three great precursors of twentieth-century dance—Isadora Duncan, Ruth St. Denis, and Ted Shawn—were explicitly influenced by Delsartean philosophy, and through their teachings Delsarte indirectly affected the first generation of modern dancers.

Early Twentieth-Century Modern Dance. Isadora Duncan (1878–1927) is usually credited with pioneering the break with the past and ushering in a twentieth-century dance form. She discarded what she felt was the artifice and vulgarity of the theatrical dance that surrounded her and looked to an idealized conception of Greek spirit embodied in dance. She found her models also in nature, as in the curves and flow of waves and shells. She drew on Delsartean principles and philosophy, but she also developed her own ideas, which were impregnated with religion and politics. Through dance she believed that one could liberate not only the body but also the soul. One could become united with nature, and nature was sacred. She wrote: "This is the highest expression of religion in the dance: that a human body should no longer seem human but become transmuted into the movements of the stars" (quoted in Pruett, 1982, p. 57).

She found inspiration in the writings of the philosopher Friedrich Nietzsche, often quoting his statement: "Let that day be called lost on which I have not danced" (Duncan, 1928, p. 77). She was fascinated by his distinction between the Apollonian and the Dionysian. She wanted the audience to experience her work as more than entertainment, as participation in her "invocation."

She searched for inspiration in Greek antiquity. She contemplated the Parthenon and sought a dance form that would be worthy of this temple. When she found it, she exclaimed, "And then I knew I had found my dance, and it was a Prayer" (Duncan, 1928, p. 65). Her dancing was composed of simple runs, skips, and walks, often accompanied by gestures pregnant with meaning. Although one of her best-known pieces was *Ave Maria* (1914), her dances rarely had overtly religious themes.

The next major figures of twentieth-century dance were Ruth St. Denis (1879–1968) and Ted Shawn (1891–1972), her husband. Out of Denishawn, their school and company, came the three most influential pioneers of modern dance: Martha Graham, Doris Humphrey, and Charles Weidman. Not only were St. Denis and Shawn seminal in the development of modern dance but they were also the most directly involved in exploring the relationship between religion and dance in their choreography and in their teachings—and both pioneered the return of dance to the church.

St. Denis (born Ruth Dennis) ransacked the world's dances searching not only for visually exciting forms but insight into the use of dance in religion that was so prevalent outside the West. While the religious intent of her choreography was so often buried in the spectacle of her performances in the vaudeville circuit, her writings and teachings emphasized spiritual intent. In her later years, she was able to fulfill some of her dreams to create religious theatrical dancing, becoming the first major choreographer to develop liturgical dance.

In St. Denis's biography, appropriately titled *Divine Dancer,* a distinction between her own and Duncan's views on dance in relation to religion is succinctly phrased as follows: "[Duncan and St. Denis] followed the polar paths of mysticism: one, seeking the Self in the Universe; the other, seeking the Universe in the Self. St. Denis . . . probed toward an unseen center, cultivating an interior space. Duncan . . . created an expanding consciousness that seemed to consume the cosmos" (Shelton, 1981, p. 97).

From childhood St. Denis had been exposed to various forms of spiritual philosophy, from "American Transcendentalism to Swedenborgian mysticism of her parents' Eagleswood colony, to her explorations of Christian Science and, ultimately, the Vedanta" (Shelton, 1981, p. 93). Her dance was deeply influenced by Delsartean principles both in the techniques of movement and in her belief in the correspondence between the physical and the metaphysical. She believed that "the Creative Dancer is always striving to give expression to Divine Intelligence" (quoted in Cohen, 1974, p. 134) and that "dancing is a living mantra" (quoted in Shelton, 1981, p. 244).

As early as St. Denis's first concert, she choreographed works based on Eastern religions. In *Radha* (1906) she was a goddess surrounded by worshiping priests. She danced a solo built on each of the five senses, culminating in a final dance in which she renounced all sensuality, ending in the yogic Lotus Position, lost in *samādhi* (meditative trance). Her costume featured a bare midriff, and even more daring, she danced in bare feet. Other of her signature works were *Incense* (1906), in which she performed a *pūjā* ritual, and *The Yogi* (1908), based on a passage from the *Bhagavadgītā,* which was a very austere unfolding of a few simple gestures revealing a yogin's spiritual state. She also danced *White Jade,* in which she portrayed Kuanyin, the Chinese goddess of mercy, and in other dances she took the roles of various goddesses (Isis, Ishtar, et al.) and biblical heroines. In her later years, she danced Madonnas. She presented pageants in churches and theaters dancing the role of the Virgin in *Masque of Mary* (1934), *Ballet of Christmas Hymns,* and *Healing.* In the *Blue Madonna of St. Mark's* she portrayed Mary's life from the birth of Christ to the crucifixion. She was eighty years old at its premiere. In the "He Is Risen" section of *Resurrection,* she danced Mary Magdelen. She formed the Society of Spiritual Acts, a Christian Science discussion group for which she choreographed dances based on religious themes. Out of this grew her Rhythmic Choir, which performed in churches.

Edward (Ted) Shawn had studied to be a Methodist minister but found dance instead. He described the basis for the Shawn–St. Denis relationship as follows: "She, pursuing the dance upstream to its source, found there religion, and I, pursuing religion upstream, found the dance was the first and finest means of religious expression, and so we have wedded artistically and humanly ever since" (Shawn, 1926, p. 12). In a taped interview he explained his calling as follows: "I feel my whole life as a dancer has been a ministry . . . because it includes in it every attribute of God; it has lightness and rhythm and proportion and expressiveness . . . the only way you can describe God is to describe him in the terms of a great dancer." He often quoted Nietzsche's comment, "I could not believe in a God who did not know how to dance." He was more directly Christian in his intent and choice of themes, while St. Denis was immersed in Eastern religions and mystical philosophy.

Among his many works were *Brothers Bernard, Lawrence, and Masseo: Three Varieties of Religious Experience; O Brother Sun and Sister Moon,* a study of Francis of Assisi; *Dance of the Redeemed,* inspired by religious visual arts such as William Blake's illustrations for the *Book of Job;* and *Mevlevi Dervish.* He often incorporated the dancing of the Doxology into his concerts.

The religious import of St. Denis's dances was usually lost to the audience, which saw only exotic spectacle. Realizing this, Shawn and later St. Denis turned to explicit Christian themes and contexts. As early as 1917, Shawn choreographed an entire church service held in the Scottish Rite Temple of San Francisco. (In 1921 the same work was censured by the local clergy and the commissioner of public safety of Shreveport, Louisiana.)

An accompanist and composer for Denishawn was to become a major force in shaping American modern dance choreography. Louis Horst (1884–1964) became mentor to at least two generations of modern dancers. He developed a systematic method for composing dances, using musical composition as a guide to teach dancers about form and style. One of his choreographic devices was based on "modern dance forms," that is, stylistic models garnered from the arts of an era and translated into dance. What he called Primitivism embraced two styles, Earth Primitive and Air Primitive. Both were characterized by awkward asymmetrical movements, the former revealing a sense of vitality, the latter of awe. The Archaic style was conceived of as ritualistic, and the movement style was based on Egyptian and Greek bas-reliefs. Medievalism had two aspects, religious and secular. It included the symbolism of denial of the flesh as revealed in off-balance, distorted postures. The ecstasy of saints and the exuberance of courtly love and minstrelsy were the essence of secular life. In Horst's outline, the nineteenth and twentieth centuries were characterized by Introspection/Expression, Cerebralism, Jazz, Americana, and Impressionism. Primitivism, the Archaic, and Medievalism took clues from visual arts and music, and all had religious connotations. Those themes have been repeated throughout twentieth-century modern dance and ballet, whether or not directly as a result of Horst's teaching. Stylized gestures have often been used to evoke an archaic context, as in Nijinksy's *L'après-midi d'un faune* (1912), which predates Horst, and in Paul Taylor's *Profiles* (1979). The stylization of religious ecstasy has characterized the many versions of *The Rite of Spring*. Horst worked with almost all the early modern dancers, but he had an especially close collaboration with Martha Graham.

Doris Humphrey and Martha Graham. Nurtured by "Miss Ruth's" spiritual lectures and later influence by Horst's methodology and theories of movement style, the two great pioneers of American modern dance, Martha Graham (b. 1894) and Doris Humphrey (1895–1958), brought to their independent careers Delsartean principles and religious themes. During the early period of modern dance, in the late 1920s and the 1930s, ritual was a common theme. Two classics are Graham's *Primitive Mysteries* (1931) and Humphrey's *The Shakers* (1931). The former was inspired by the rituals of the Native American Christians of the southwestern United States. It is an abstraction of the passion play as seen through the experience of the Virgin Mary. The three sections—"Hymn to the Virgin" (adoration), "Crucifixus" (Virgin's grief), and "Hosannah" (exaltation)—are punctuated at the beginnings and ends by processions of the Virgin and her attendants, composed of weighted, solemn steppings. Processions are a frequent device in Graham's works, and they lend to virtually any theme a ritualistic quality. In the same year, *The Shakers* depicted the essence of the dance ritual of the American religious sect, the Shakers, who used dance and song as their primary modes of worship. Both works created fictitious rituals based on actual sources.

Religious themes per se were not common in Humphrey's choreography or that of her colleague Charles Weidman (1901–1975). Their choreography was, however, religious in the wider sense of showing a concern for the fundamental issues of human life. For instance, Humphrey described her *New Dance* (1935) trilogy as having the theme of the relationship of man to man. To her, *New Dance* represented "the world as it should be, where each person has a clear and harmonious relationship to his fellow beings" (quoted in Cohen, 1972, p. 137). It conveys its message without overt narrative; it is through the organization and disorganization of group relationships that the theme is developed.

Humphrey's *Passacaglia and Fugue in C Minor* (1938) is a plotless work to Bach's music. However, she found in the music religious import that colored the dance. For instance, in a program note she points out that the "minor melody . . . seems to say 'How can a man be saved and be content in a world of infinite despair?' " (quoted in Cohen, 1972, p. 149). Dancing to Bach was highly controversial. Even his secular music has been interpreted as being suffused with spirituality. One of Humphrey's earliest pieces was to Bach's so-called *Air for the G String* (1929), which consists of a group of women with a leader who basically walk, pose, dip, and sway in sumptuous draperies inspired by the paintings of Fra Angelico. Although there is no plot or context, the costumery, music, and the rapturous poses (often in Gothic sway as in sculptures of the Madonna), suggest a pious ritual. Humphrey later defended her use of Bach, especially in the context of World War II, by stating: "Now is the time for me to tell of the nobility that the human spirit is capable of" (quoted in Cohen, 1972, p. 243). Choreographers continue to use Bach as a means of lending a spiritual aura to their works. In later years Weidman choreographed *Christmas Oratorio* (1961), *Easter Oratorio* (1967), and *Bach's St. Matthew's Passion* (1973).

It is impossible to look at Martha Graham's towering sixty-year career without considering the role of religion. Her work can be seen as falling into several periods. Her earliest works were stark, ascetic, often ritualistic pieces. She later turned to more narrative works, exploring facets of female psychology and aspects of Americana. In the 1940s she began her epic treatment of mythological and biblical themes, which has continued for forty more years. Almost all her early works are lost, but some of their titles are suggestive: *Figure of a Saint, Resurrection, Vision of the Apocalypse, Heretic,* all choreographed in 1929, stand out among other titles.

El penitente (1940), inspired by the Spanish-Indian flagellant sects of the American Southwest, is the depiction of Christ's journey to Calvary as performed by a troup of touring players. *Appalachian Spring* (1944) is the story of a wedding in the nineteenth-century frontier. The figure of the Revivalist who weds the couple is a crystallization of one aspect of American religion. The ambivalence about physical enjoyment (whether in the sexual connotations of marriage or in the abandonment of dance and play) is expressed in the Revivalist's movements. He dances a tormented solo of self-condemnation characterized by crawling on his knees, breast beating, and fervent praying. The moralistic dilemma of ambivalence toward sexuality is explored in many of Graham's works, especially in her treatment of women, such as in her *American Provincials: Act of Piety, Act of Judgment* and the *Scarlet Letter.* In Graham's *Letter to the World* (1940), the poet Emily Dickinson battles repression as personified in an ancestress figure. Graham's family was staunchly Presbyterian, and her father had objected to dancing for moral reasons.

Graham's *Dark Meadow* (1946) is a ritual of rebirth and procreation with strong erotic overtones and pervasive Jungian and Freudian symbolism. Archetypal characters, such as She of the Ground (representing the female principle), dance a myth of rebirth. There are allusions to the worship of phallic monuments and to sacrifice in the name of fertility. Her monumental works based on Greek mythology include *Cave of the Heart* (1946), retelling the Medea legend; *Night Journey* (1947), the Oedipus story through the experience of Jocasta; the full length *Clytemnestra* (1958); and *Cortege of Eagles* (1967), the story of Hecuba; and lesser-known works, such as *Phaedra* (1962), *Circe* (1963), and *Andromache's Lament* (1982). Other biblical works include *Herodiade,* the Salome story as seen through the psyche of her mother; *Judith* (1950) and *Legend of Judith* (1962); *Gospel of Eve* (1950); *Embattled Garden* (1958), a major retelling of the Adam-Eve-Lilith myth; and *Lucifer* (1975). A major historical work, *Seraphic Dialogue* (1955), is based on the story of Joan of Arc. The characters are Saint Michael, Saint Catherine, Saint Margaret, and Joan at the moment of canonization. Joan recalls the three facets of her life as the Maid, the Warrior, and the Martyr.

Graham uses religious themes as a device for probing psychological dimensions. She treats mythology as the psychology of another age and seeks to reveal the "inner landscapes" of the human psyche in her dance. Even in her less frequent plotless works there are religious reverberations. *Diversion of Angels* (1948) is a rare lyrical and joyful work for four couples and three solo women, yet at the end the soloist in white is crowned with the splayed fingers of a symbol of benediction. The title of *Acrobats of God* (1960), derived from the name of a group of early church fathers who lived in the desert, alludes to a comparison of the ascetic spiritual life of the Desert Fathers to the arduous training of dancers. Both works celebrate the dancer, and their titles may reveal Graham's conception of their superhuman quality. In the last section of the abstract *Acts of Light* (1981), the "Ritual of the Sun" is evoked by the stylization of a technique class.

Other first-generation American modern dance choreographers. Two other pioneers were Lester Horton (1906–1953) and Helen Tamiris (1905–1966). Very few of their works survive. Horton often used themes from other cultures that were inherently religious: *Siva-Siva* (1929), *Voodoo Ceremonial* (1932), *Sun Ritual* (1935), and *Pentecost* (1935) are examples of works utilizing such themes. His three best-known works all have religious themes: *Salomé* (several versions from 1934 to 1950), *Le sacre du printemps* (1937), and *The Beloved* (1948). *The Beloved* is still in active repertory. Although it is not expressly religious, it is an example of the theme of sexual repression implicitly derived from religious beliefs. It is a duet for a husband and wife. The man, outwardly a symbol of rectitude, proceeds to manipulate and then to strangle his wife, who presumably is guilty of a sexual transgression.

Tamiris (born Becker) choreographed many works of social protest. She is best known for her *Negro Spirituals.* This is a suite of dances (solos and group pieces) to which she added over a period of fifteen years beginning in 1928. She is credited as the first to use black spirituals. *Negro Spirituals* is set to music representing a gamut of moods. Partially pantomimic in degrees of abstraction, each piece is a distillation of a theme. The crucifixion section, for instance, was inspired by the visual imagery of medieval religious paintings. Her goal was to reveal the human side of suffering, oppression, and joy. Ted Shawn also choreographed *Negro Spirituals* in 1933, and the theme became very popular among black choreographers beginning with Alvin Ailey's *Revelations* (1960).

Central European modern dance. In Europe, another approach to modern dance developed. The foremost figure there was Rudolf Laban (1879–1958), better remembered today for his theoretical work (now called Laban Movement Analysis) and the development of a dance notation system (Labanotation or Kinetography Laban), than for his choreography, which has been lost. Laban believed in the spiritual source of movement and felt that dance was a means of attuning to the harmony of the universe. He had been impressed in his youth by the dancing of Muslim dervishes and sought to find and understand the link between movement and spirituality. He developed the idea of "movement choirs," communal dancing of lay dancers, as an expression of the festive spirit of humanity. His stage choreography often dealt with cosmic themes. For example, *The Swinging*

Temple was a choreodrama of all types of dancing from primordial rhythms through priestly processions, to ecstatic, comic, and combative dances. His writings and the scenarios for many of his dance works have a strain of mysticism, a search for the divine power of movement, whereas the system for the analysis of movement that developed from his theories is known for its objectivity.

Laban's two most famous students were Mary Wigman (1886–1973) and Kurt Jooss (1901–1979). Wigman is considered the principal dancer-choreographer of central European modern dance. While not concerned with themes from any specific religion, her work in general grapples with spirituality and the larger issues of life. Many of her works deal with death or the cycle of nature. Her signature work was the solo *Witch Dance* (1914, rechoreographed in 1926), which probes the demonic side of human nature. Many of her works revolved around the darker, grotesque aspects of life, themes that seem to have been appropriate to Germany between the two world wars, her most productive period.

Jooss is best known for *The Green Table* (1932), an antiwar ballet still widely performed. In this work, he draws on the medieval image of death as the Grim Reaper, placing the work in a religious historical context.

The European tradition of modern dance was established in America by Wigman's student Hanya Holm (b. 1898). Her works of the 1930s often made social and political statements but can also be seen as having an underlying moral message. Her masterwork, *Trend* (1937), was nonliterary, but its theme was the discovery of the meaning of life.

At the same time that Laban was beginning his experimentation, there were several others in Europe exploring the relationship between movement and spirituality in the context of new religions. Among these were Rudolf Steiner (1861–1925) and G. I. Gurdjieff (1877?–1949). Steiner developed a comprehensive religious and philosophical system called Anthroposophy, which encompassed a movement and dance system called Eurythmy. In this practice, specific gestures and floor patterns are correlated with specific sounds and spiritual functions. Performing the movements thereby promotes physical and spiritual health. Structured choreography to works of classical music is one form of expressing this philosophy. Gurdjieff, influenced by Sufism, developed dancelike movement exercises designed to effect certain mystical states. The work of Steiner and Gurdjieff was part of a tradition that centered on the belief that mystical knowledge could be manifested in physical behavior and that the altered states of consciousness generated by movement could put one in touch with the underlying patterns of the universe. [*See* Anthroposophy *and the biographies of Steiner and Gurdjieff.*]

Second Generation of American Modern Dance. Humphrey's closest protégé was José Limón. Several of his major works were based on religious themes. He often drew on his Mexican and Native American heritage. *La Malinche* (1949) is a form of the passion play as performed by a troupe of traveling Mexican peasants. *The Visitation* (1952) is based on the Annunication; *The Apostate* (1959) captures a battle between Christianity and paganism; and *There Is a Time* (1956) is a danced version of *Ecclesiastes* 2. Limón's *Psalm* (1967) includes the theme of the Jews under Hitler, and *The Unsung* (1970) deals with the spirituality of Native Americans. In *The Traitor* (1954) he retells the story of Jesus and Judas, casting Judas as a symbol of modern man. *Missa brevis* (1958), first performed in a bombed-out church in Budapest, is a dance of pain and an affirmation of faith. At certain points, women dancers are carried like the statues of the Madonna in Mexican religious processions.

The choreography of Alwin Nikolais, a student of Holm, rebels against the emotionalism of the first generation of modern dance. He turns instead to portraying the moving body as just one element of a multimedia theater. He has often been criticized for dehumanizing the dancer, but he interprets his work in a religio-philosophical manner; he sees man as a "fellow traveller . . . rather than the god from which all things flowed. . . . He lost his domination but instead became kinsman to the universe" (quoted in Siegel, 1971, p. 11). His pieces often are glimpses into the ritualistic lives of what seem to be alien tribes of people whose activities make profound comments on human existence. His *Tower* (1965), for example, details the building of a metaphorical Tower of Babel to which each dancer contributes a piece only to have the whole monument topple at the end.

Erick Hawkins is among those choreographers who worked with Graham. His choreography is notable as a rejection of her aesthetic and technique. He has been inspired by Zen philosophy and feels that an audience should be brought to enlightenment. His goal has been to develop a technique that would be harmonious with nature, gentle and free of tension. His choreography is often ritualistic and deals with the human relation to nature and the oneness of body and soul. The mood of his works is often meditative with poetic resonances. In *Plains Daybreak* (1983), for example, masked dancers represent the essences of animals during a mythical time near the beginning of creation. *Lords of Persia* (1965) is a portrayal of an ancient game of polo stylized as sacred ritual.

Paul Taylor has produced a wide range of works that frequently make comments on the human condition and social relationships. Sometimes his works involve religious themes. One of his most enduring works is *Three Epitaphs* (1960), in which dancers covered in black appear as figures whose postures and gestures convey both humor and pathos. The title of this work and the accompaniment of early New Orleans jazz funeral music provide an ironic commentary to the antic interactions of these creatures. His *Churchyard* (1969) is a dance of piety transformed into wild eroticism; *Runes* (1975) creates a prehistoric ritual of sacrifice and regeneration.

Merce Cunningham made a radical break with the past. He creates plotless works in which movements, music, and decor are conceived of as separate elements. Pure movement is the primary content of his works, and therefore religious themes are irrelevant. However, underlying Cunningham's choreography is a philosophy based on Zen Buddhism. Like his principal musical collaborator, John Cage, Cunningham often composes according to chance principles; for instance, throwing the *I ching* (casting lots) determines the order in which movement phrases will be combined. Such an indeterminate method of choreography helps him to feel liberated from becoming attached to his possessions, which are his choreographic creations.

Postmodern Dance. Cunningham signaled the beginning of a reconception of dance. The idea that theatrical dance was marked by storytelling, emotional expression, and a fixed relationship to music and decor was shattered by his work. Many choreographers in the next generation of modern dance have been called "post-Cunningham" or postmodern. One of the more prominent characteristics of this trend in dance has been the focus on movement for movement's sake. Dances were often composed of everyday movements danced by untrained performers. They wished to return dance to the people, rather than reserving it for the virtuosic performer. Religious themes would not seem relevant to plotless works that aimed to expose the nature of movement rather than the nature of human and spiritual existence. Yet, a major stream of postmodern dance has been the exploration of the concept of ritual. Many choreographers shared the aims of the experimental theater of the 1960s and 1970s, especially the idea that dance and theatrical performances could be rituals for both performers and audience. A goal was to provide a transformative experience, a function of many religious rituals. The means of effecting these changes in physical and mental states were also modeled on a conception of ritual that often emphasized symbolism, manipulations of time and space, repetititons, nonlinear development of actions, and a highly formal structure. Some aimed at the creation of a feeling of community; others reached for a spiritual experience, a feeling of holism or integration with the universe. They were concerned with experiencing dance as a metaphor for life. [*See* Drama, *article on* Performance and Ritual.]

Anna Halprin has been a pioneer in this area. She explored the use of trance, the expression of communal feeling through dance, and the healing nature of movement. Deborah Hay created a series of Circle Dances based on simple movements to be performed in a group with no spectators. She was influenced by *t'ai-chi ch'üan* and Taoist philosophy. The goal of these dance experiences was to understand the inner self, the power of the group, and the individual's connection to the cosmos. Meditation as well as ecstatic movements have characterized these ritualistic dances.

Meredith Monk, on the other hand, creates multimedia theatrical works that are often ritualistic in character. She creates layers of evocative imagery and archetypal characters and transforms ordinary speech into chants and spectacular sounds. Her *Vessel* (1971) dealt with Joan of Arc. Many of her other works, such as *Quarry* (1976) and *Education of the Girlchild* (1972), have presented themes of human life and history in a ritual structure.

Twentieth-Century Ballet. While modern dance grew out of a desire for self-expression, ballet traditionally has been concerned with telling stories. The twentieth century saw the development of plotless (or abstract) works that inherently give limited scope for interior states or religious themes. Yet, ballet also expanded its expressive powers in such a way as to become a vehicle for religious ideas as well.

The first major break with nineteenth-century ballet in both form and content was Sergei Diaghilev's Ballets Russes. This company produced a few biblical works: *Salomé* (1913), *The Legend of Joseph* (1914), and *Prodigal Son* (1929). *Le dieu bleu* (1912) was based on the Hindu god Kṛṣṇa. The most remarkable religious work was also perhaps the most revolutionary ballet in dance history—*Le sacre du printemps* (1913), choreographed by the great dancer Vaslav Nijinsky. The dance and its music by Igor Stravinsky caused a riot at the premiere, and the ballet was performed only a few times. It drew on a mythic history of Old Russia, but its pounding rhythms, ecstatic dancing, circular floor patterns, and sacrificial dance of death became a model for many other rituals in twentieth-century dance. There have been many other rechoreographings of the Stravinsky music, including Léonide Massine's 1930 reworking for Diaghilev (in which the Chosen Maiden was danced by Martha Graham, who fifty-four years later was to choreograph her own *Rite of Spring*). Other notable examples were by Horton, Wigman, ballet choreographer Maurice Béjart, German Expressionist modern-dance choreographer Pina Bausch, and Paul Taylor, who transformed the ritual into a gangster play within a play.

Two of the last works that Diaghilev produced were *Apollon musagète* (1928) and *Prodigal Son* (1929), both choreographed by George Balanchine, who was to become the most influential ballet choreographer in the United States, if not the world. Though Balanchine is known primarily for his plotless works, these two early ballets with religious themes are counted among his greatest, and both are performed in many companies around the world. *Apollon musagète,* now titled *Apollo,* retells the birth of the god and his coming of age under the tutelage of three of the Muses. In *Prodigal Son,* Balanchine drew on motifs from his native Russia, including visual imagery from religious icons, especially the two-dimensional quality, and certain gestures and liturgical movements from the Russian Orthodox church, such as beating the chest and back.

Other Balanchine works of some religious significance include his *Nutcracker* (1954), *Noah and the Flood* (1962), and his Greek mythological masterpiece, *Orpheus* (1948). His *Don Quixote* (1965) also has much religious imagery. Despite the relative lack of religious themes in his choreography, religion was very important in Balanchine's personal life. One of the last works he created incorporated much religious symbolism and has been interpreted as his comment on death. In 1981, he choreographed the last movement of Tchaikovsky's *Pathétique* Symphony as a ballet of the same name. A dance of grief is followed by a procession composed of angels with enormous wings, hooded figures, and monks who prostrate themselves in the form of a cross. A child extinguishes a candle to the final notes of the symphony.

Another choreographer for the Ballets Russes was Léonide Massine. Although he is best known for his character ballets, he also choreographed several ambitious but short-lived works based on religious themes. *Seventh Symphony* (1938), set to Beethoven's Seventh Symphony, was a chronicle of the world from its creation to its destruction; *Noblissima visione* (1938) was the story of Saint Francis of Assisi; and *Laudes evangelii* (1952) was the translation into dance of a fourteenth-century text depicting eight episodes from the life of Christ.

Frederick Ashton has been the principal choreographer in Great Britain. Like British ballet in general, his works tend to be literary, although he occasionally has used religious themes. An early Ashton work was the choreography for the Virgil Thomson–Gertrude Stein opera *Four Saints in Three Acts* (1934). His *Dante Sonata* (1940), based on the *Inferno* of Dante's *Commedia,* was a reaction to World War II. It was conceived as a battle between the Children of Light and the Children of Darkness. *The Wise Virgins* (1940) was also an antiwar ballet. Performed to Bach cantatas and chorale preludes, it created visual images reminiscent of Baroque art. The work had a devout atmosphere. He also occasionally used mythical themes, as in *Cupid and Psyche, Leda, Mercury, Mars and Venus,* and *Daphnis and Chloe.* His *The Quest* (1943) was the story of Saint George; his *Tiresias* (1951) depicted a Cretan athletic ritual.

Other choreographers in England include Ninette de Valois, founder of the Royal Ballet. One of her most successful works was *Job, a Masque for Dancing* (1931) based on William Blake's drawings. As an example of Western ambivalence toward the relationship between religion and dance, censors prohibited the depiction of God in this work, leading de Valois to create a character called Job's Spiritual Self. *Miracle in the Gorbals* (1944) by Robert Helpmann was a morality play in dance in which Christ comes to the slums of Glasgow, revives a suicide, and in turn is murdered by the crowd.

Antony Tudor is known for his psychologically motivated ballets, and few of his works are religious in content. His *Shadowplay* (1967), which depicts a wild boy as lord of the jungle, however, was influenced by Zen Buddhism. Underlying his masterwork *Pillar of Fire* (1942) is the theme of religiously induced sexual repression. His *Dark Elegies* (1937) is a ritualization of grief.

In the twentieth century, mythic characters are often used to create a psychological dimension. Tudor's *Undertow* (1945), for example, is a contemporary murder story, but the characters have mythological names, and his *Judgment of Paris* (1938) is set in a Paris bar where Juno, Minerva, and Venus are tawdry showgirls.

The American John Butler, who choreographs in both the ballet and modern dance idioms, has produced a large opus of religious works. He was the principal choreographer for the American religious television series *Lamp unto My Feet* in the 1960s. One of his major works is *Carmina burana* (1959), which is set to thirteenth-century poems discovered at a Benedictine monastery. The monks and nuns of the dance temporarily discard the discipline of their order to engage in the passions of secular life and to experience the wheel of fate.

Robert Joffrey and Gerald Arpino, choreographing for the Joffrey Ballet, have created several works based on religious themes. Joffrey's *Astarte* (1967), which has been called the first psychedelic ballet, is a contemporary depiction of the Akkadian Ishtar, moon goddess of love and fertility who was called Astarte by the Greeks, though audiences are often unaware of this theme. Set to loud electronic rock music, flashing lights, and projected film, the dance evokes the atmosphere of an après-discotheque seduction. The man strips to his briefs, the goddess lets down her hair, and an erotic *pas de deux* of power and submission takes place in a hallucinatory sequence. It was the first multimedia rock ballet to receive widespread attention, and it ushered in a new trend in ballet, enticing new audiences into the theater. Arpino's *Sacred Grove on Mount Tamalpais* (1972) is a paean to the "flower children" of the 1960s, an innocent romp of renewal depicting a wedding ceremony and the birth of a son who promises to be a kind of prophet to the celebrants. His *Trinity* (1969) is a three-part contemporary ritual of young people employing some popular dance movements set to a rock orchestration of Gregorian chant and other sacred music styles. In the third section, "Saturday," the dancers carry lighted candles. A male soloist dances to a rock version of the hymn "Ite, missa est" that concludes the Latin Mass. The final image is of the stage, empty except for the pattern of votive candles on the floor.

Contemporary European choreographers have been more attracted to religious themes than their American counterparts. John Neumeier, mainly choreographing for the Hamburg Ballet, created the four-hour *Saint Matthew's Passion* (1981) set to Bach's work. The story is conveyed through *tableaux vivants* interspersed with dancing commenting on the deeper aspects of the drama. Neumeier's *Mahler's Third Symphony* has a theme of redemption and incorporates Mahler's idea of the quest for divine love.

The Czech Jiri Kylian, working primarily for the Nederlands Dans Theater, has offered *Psalm Symphony* (1978), based on Psalms 39, 40, and 150, among other works. Further examples include John Cranko's *Kyrie eleison* (1968) and Kenneth Macmillan's *Requiem* (1976). Maurice Béjart, choreographer for his Belgian company, Ballet of the Twentieth Century, is known for tackling grand epic themes. Several of his works have themes with religious connotations. In his *Nijinsky—Clown of God* (1971), the Ballets Russes is cast as Nijinsky's Paradise with Diaghilev as its overseeing God. His *Bhakti* (1968) draws on Hindu mythology, and his *Notre Faust* (1975) is one of several dance treatments of this work over the centuries.

Contemporary ballet has incorporated many movements and much of the sensibility of modern dance. It often does not use *pointe* work but may reserve this kind of movement to portray particular ideas. A ballerina on *pointe* sometimes is cast in a higher spiritual mode. For instance, in Ashton's *Illuminations* (1950), Sacred Love dances on *pointe*, while Profane Love has one bare foot; in Neumeier's *Mahler's Third Symphony*, the figure of idealized love dances on *pointe* while most of the other dancers do not.

Biblical Themes. The flexibility of interpretation inherent in biblical literature has been an inspiration for many different treatments that range from literal interpretations to the probing of universal psychological truths to political and social commentary. Several characters and episodes have been particularly appealing. These include: the theme of creation, the garden of Eden, the story of Cain and Abel, Noah and the Flood, Job, David and Goliath, Joseph, Samson and Delilah, Salome, the Prodigal Son, the Wise and Foolish Virgins; and the many biblical heroines, including Miriam, Jephthah's Daughter, Esther, Deborah, Judith, Ruth, the Virgin Mary, and Mary Magdalene. The life of Christ and interpretations of various psalms have also been frequently choreographed themes. One of the more popular subjects has been the story of Adam and Eve. Treatments of this theme indicate some of the range of interpretations of biblical stories. Graham's *Embattled Garden* (1958) introduces Lilith into the domestic routine of the Garden of Eden, whereas Butler's *After Eden* (1966) and Limón's *The Exiles* (1950) both deal with the fate of Adam and Eve after the expulsion, while Roland Petit's *Paradise Lost* (1967) featured a pop interpretation with Adam plunging into a backdrop of a huge lipsticked mouth at the end of the dance. The story has been treated with awe and wonder and irony, and as tragedy and comedy.

The *Book of Genesis* has provided a source of comedic ballets. *Billy Sunday* (1946), choreographed by Ruth Page, is the retelling of these familiar stories as they might have been explained by the baseball-player-turned-preacher Billy Sunday, who used the vernacular and often employed baseball analogies in his exuberant evangelical addresses. In this work Bathsheba does a striptease behind a screen fashioned from a scarf, and Joseph's seducer is the contemporary Mrs. Potiphar. Page emphasizes those stories that portray women betraying men. Taylor's *American Genesis* (1973) recasts the stories as episodes in American history, using bits of Americana—such as minstrel-show techniques—as ironic commentary on both United States history and the biblical stories themselves.

Other ways in which biblical stories have served as a means of social commentary include interpreting the story of Joseph as a message about overcoming political oppression and the story of Esther as a metaphor for Nazism's "final solution." Jooss's *Prodigal Son* found his downfall not in the pursuit of decadent living but in the quest for power, a poignant theme for Germany in 1931.

Religious Themes and Cultural Identity. Modern dance, built on a philosophy of the expression of emotions and personal identity, has provided a vehicle for the exploration of ethnic and religious identity through dance. This has been true, in particular, for Jewish, Afro-American, and Asian choreographers.

Jewish history, ritual, and music have inspired several twentieth-century works in both modern dance and ballet. Several topics have been particularly popular: Jewish village life of tsarist Russia and eastern Europe, the Holocaust, Hasidism, Sefardic Judaism, and Jewish folk tales. Some works employ movement qualities and steps associated with dances from Jewish communities or with prayer movements, while others use Jewish themes or music without any particular ethnic movement style.

The second generation of modern dancers were particularly drawn to social and political themes. This period of growth also coincided with World War II and the attendant Holocaust, providing thematic material for powerful dances. Many of the works of Pearl Lang have Jewish themes. Perhaps her best-known work is *The Possessed* (1975), based on the dybbuk legend. She also choreographed dances using Hasidic themes, biblical stories, and poems composed by Holocaust victims. Her *Tailor's Megillah* is the retelling of Esther's story in a tailor's shop.

Anna Sokolow created the solo *Kaddish* (1946); *Dreams* (1961), an abstract enactment of the horrors of the Nazi concentration camps; and *The Holy Place* (1977), based on Psalm 137 and dealing with the theme of the Jews in exile. The first part of *The Exile* (1939) is set in ancient times, the second deals with persecution, culminating in Nazism. She created both *The Bride,* in which a shy Jewess faces a wedding to an unknown groom, and *Mexican Retablo,* in which she danced a Madonna.

Tamiris choreographed *Memoir* (1957), depicting themes of Jewish life. Holm offered *Tragic Exodus* (1939) and *They Too Are Exiles* (1940), which dealt with the dispossession and persecution of all peoples, but at that time, reference to the Jews in Hitler's Germany was all too apparent. Sophie Maslow choreographed *The Village I Knew* (1950) as an evocation of Jewish life in tsarist Russia.

In ballet, Eliot Feld has contributed *Tzaddik* (1974), a representation of a scholar's intensely emotional introduction of two students into the world of religious study. His *Sephardic Song* (1974) was influenced by traditional Sefardic music. Jerome Robbins choreographed *The Dybbuk Variations* (1974), an abstract version of this story. Robbins is also well known for his staging and choreography of the musical-theater work *Fiddler on the Roof* (1964), which drew on many dance forms and images of turn-of-the-century Jewish life in Russia.

Israel has a very active theatrical dance culture. Many choreographers there naturally turn to Jewish and biblical themes. One of the more prominent companies, the Inbal Dance Theatre, whose principal choreographer is Sara Levi-Tanai, draws on the dances and rituals of the Jewish minorities of the Middle East, especially the Yemenites. Some examples of works by Israeli choreographers include Levi-Tanai's *Psalm of David* (1964), which features the story of Avishag, the girl brought to the aging David; Margalit Oved's *The Mothers of Israel,* choreographed for Ze'eva Cohen, draws on the image of the biblical Sarah, Rebecca, Rachel, and Leah; the Bat-Dor Company performs Domy Reiter-Soffer's *I Shall Sing to Thee in the Valley of the Dead My Beloved* (1971), which tells the history of Israel through the story of King David's loves; Rina Schoenfeld choreographed *Jephthah's Daugher* for the Batsheva Company; and the Russian dancer Rina Nikova founded the Biblical Ballet of Israel.

Afro-Americans have also drawn on dance as a vehicle for the expression of cultural identity. Religious practices and music are a major component of this identity and have formed the basis for many ballet and modern dance works. *Revelations,* a work by Alvin Ailey, was one of the first of these works, and it has also proved to be the most popular and enduring. It is a suite of dances to black hymns and gospel music, each section revealing the theme or spirit of the song—from the solemn abstraction of "I've Been 'Buked" to the rousing church service of the finale. The audience is often whipped into an enthusiastic hand-clapping and foot-stomping participation that is akin to the atmosphere of many black churches. In this way, *Revelations* has introduced to the Western theater a different model for the role of the spectator at a ballet performance. Some of the other religiously inspired Ailey works include *Three Black Kings* (1976) and the often humorous *Mary Lou's Mass* (1971), in which biblical stories are reenacted.

Many African and Afro-American choreographers also draw on African religious practices. Katherine Dunham, Pearl Primus, and Asadata Dafora were among the first to do this. Dunham's *Rites of Passage* (1941) depicted a fertility ritual, and *Shango,* a Voodoo rite. Primus's *Fanga* (1949) created a ritual in an African context.

Asian religious themes have often been popular in Western dance history. In the past, Eastern themes tended to be used as a device for creating exotic spectacle. St. Denis promoted a form of Orientalism that adopted the color and sensuality of Asian dance but also attempted to expose its spiritual import. Cunningham, Hawkins, and Tudor have been influenced by Zen Buddhism. Starting in the 1960s, but especially in the 1970s and 1980s, there has been an explicit attempt to create a dance form that assimilates Eastern and Western dance and that especially captures the spiritual quality of Asian dance. Asian and Asian-American choreographers have been particularly active in adopting Eastern techniques and themes to the modern dance context, often emphasizing the creation of ritual. Kei Takei and the duo Eiko and Koma are particularly noteworthy for their use of Japanese rituals and movement qualities, and Mel Wong is known for his synthesis of Chinese culture and American modern dance.

The discovery of Asian religions in the context of the "hippie," drug-influenced 1960s led to works such as Béjart's *Bhakti,* a ballet about love as manifested in the relationships between Rāma and Sītā, Kṛṣṇa and Rādhā, and Śiva and Śakti. In the 1970s and 1980s, there has been a growing interest in Ṣūfī dancing, and choreographers have adopted spinning techniques, as in the work of Laura Dean, and have explored the mystical symbolism of Muslim faith.

Modern dance also took root in Japan, where a unique synthesis of American and central European Expressionist modern dance, Japanese *nō,* and *kabuki* combines with a post–World War II sensibility. An avant-garde trend called *butoh,* a word referring to an ancient dance, exists in the shadow of Hiroshima and Nagasaki and lends itself to the creation of ritualistic theatrical probings of primordial and postapocalyptic images.

Sacred or Liturgical Dance. Dance has returned to the church and synagogue in the twentieth century. With St. Denis and Shawn as its foremost pioneers, the sacred dance or liturgical dance movement has grown rapidly. Another early experiment with ritual dancing in the church took place at Saint Mark's-in-the-Bowerie Church in New York, beginning in the 1920s. Choreographed by the rector of the church, William Norman Guthrie, the dance, depicting the Annunication, was performed by six barefooted women robed in flowing white material probably dancing in the Duncanesque style of the avant-garde of the time. For this scandalous act, Saint Mark's was suspended from the Episcopal church. The ritual dance was performed annually for many years and continued to cause controversy.

Contemporary sacred dance covers a range of ways in which movement can be incorporated into the liturgy. These include (1) rhythmic or dance choirs, analogous to singing choirs, (2) performances based on religious themes or stories by lay or professional dancers, which the congregation watches, (3) congregational dancing in which everyone participates, (4) dancing based on ritual dances of other cultures, (5) charismatic dancing, (6) danced individual prayers, and (7) dance with therapeutic intent (spiritual healing through dance). Aims of sacred dance include promoting the affirmation of the body, offering dance to God, creating a sense of community, finding the festive nature of life and religion, and integrating body and soul. Leaders in the sacred dance movement have been, among others, Margaret Fiske Taylor, Douglas Adams, Mary Jane Wolbers, Judith Rock, and Carla de Sola. Exponents of liturgical dance have also been unusually prolific writers. In the United States, the Sacred Dance Guild was formed in the late 1950s, and the movement grew rapidly in the 1960s and 1970s in many countries, fed by other related trends: the reemergence of exuberant social dancing, the growth of alternative religions and religious practices, and the rise of dance therapy. While the sacred dance movement is mainly a Christian movement, there is also a growing following in Judaism. A central controversy within the movement is whether to emphasize the liturgical aspect or the aesthetic aspect, whether sacred dance should be performed by the laity with a communal, participatory focus or whether it should be performed by professionals with an aesthetic goal. Ironically, the success of theatrical dance in America, despite the opposition of religious orthodoxies, has led to the addition of a new (or rediscovered) dimension of religious practice—the expressive power of dance.

[*For discussion of broadly related topics in the history of religions, see* Circumambulation; Labyrinth; *and* Procession.]

BIBLIOGRAPHY

There has been very little written about religion and theatrical dance. Aside from a few isolated articles or books on particular topics, most information must be gleaned from general books on dance. There are, however, a few anthologies that cover aspects of this topic. In 1979, an International Seminar on the Bible in Dance was held in Israel. The papers from the conference were not published as a group, but the manuscripts are available at the Dance Collection, New York Public Library at Lincoln Center, and elsewhere. Papers of special interest to this topic are those on Limón, Graham, *The Prodigal Son, Billy Sunday,* labyrinths, and biblical dance on television. In conjunction with this event, Giora Manor published an extensive study of the use of biblical themes in ballet and modern dance, *The Gospel according to Dance* (New York, 1980). *Worship and Dance,* edited by J. G. Davies (Birmingham, 1975), is particularly useful for information on dance in the church, both historically and as part of the contemporary liturgical dance movement. *Focus on Dance X: Religion and Dance,* edited by Dennis J. Fallon and Mary Jane Wolbers (Reston, Va., 1982), includes Lynn Matluck Brooks's "The Catholic Church and

Dance in the Middle Ages," Diane Milhan Pruett's "Duncan's Perception of Dance in Religion," and Georganna Balif Arrington's "Dance in Mormonism: The Dancingest Denomination." A thought-provoking article by Douglas Adams and Judith Rock, "Biblical Criteria in Modern Dance: Modern Dance as Prophetic Form," also delivered at the seminar in Israel, is an application to dance of Paul Tillich's four categories of the relation between religion and visual arts. About half the articles in this volume are devoted to the liturgical dance movement. The journal *Parabola*'s issue on "Sacred Dance," vol. 4, no. 2 (May 1979), contains articles on the dance of Jesus by Elaine H. Pagels and on labyrinths by Rosemary Jeanes. Jamake Highwater's *Dance: Rituals of Experience* (New York, 1978) is a personal view on the importance of reaffirming the ritual nature of dance; his book includes a discussion of which contemporary theatrical choreographers create works that fulfill his conception of ritual.

Most information about religion and theatrical dance must be pieced together from a general history of Western dance. A basic introduction to this topic is Jack Anderson's *Dance* (New York, 1979). A more detailed, although somewhat out-of-date book is Lincoln Kirstein's *Dance: A Short History of Classical Theatrical Dancing* (New York, 1935). Marcia B. Siegel's *The Shapes of Change* (Boston, 1979) analyzes some of the important works of American dance including *Negro Spirituals, Shakers, Revelations,* and several of Graham's works. A brief description and listing of dances by major modern dance choreographers can be found in Don McDonagh's *The Complete Guide to Modern Dance* (Garden City, N.Y., 1976). Anthologies of primary sources include *Dance as a Theatre Art,* edited by Selma Jeanne Cohen (New York, 1974), and, for theoretical essays, *What Is Dance?,* edited by Roger Copeland and Marshall Cohen (New York, 1983). One of several books of synopses of ballet librettos is *101 Stories of the Great Ballets* by George Balanchine and Francis Mason (Garden City, N.Y., 1975).

For dance in the early Christian church and in the medieval European tradition, see Eugène Louis Backman's *Religious Dances in the Christian Church and in Popular Medicine* (London, 1952). For later attitudes held about dance by the Christian church, see *The Mathers on Dancing,* edited by Joseph E. Marks III (Brooklyn, N.Y., 1975), which contains an extensive bibliography of antidance literature from 1685 to 1963. On the Renaissance, see James Miller's "The Philosophical Background of Renaissance Dance," *York Dance Review* 5 (Spring 1976), and Roy Strong's *Splendour at Court* (London, 1973).

For the Baroque, see Shirley Wynne's "Complaisance, an Eighteenth-Century Cool," *Dance Scope* 5 (Fall 1970): 22–35, and Wendy Hilton's *Dance of Court and Theater: The French Noble Style, 1690–1725* (Princeton, 1971). On the Jesuit theater, see Régine Astier's "Pierre Beauchamps and the Ballets de Collège," *Dance Chronicle* 6, no. 2 (1983): 138–151. for pre-Romantic ballet, the principal history is Marian Hannah Winter's *The Pre-Romantic Ballet* (Brooklyn, N.Y., 1975). Ivor Guest has written extensively on the Romantic ballet; his books include *The Romantic Ballet in Paris,* 2d rev. ed. (London, 1980), and *The Romantic Ballet in England* (Middletown, Conn., 1972). On Bournonville, see his autobiography, *My Theater Life,* translated by Patricia N. McAndrew (Middletown, Conn., 1979), and Erik Ashengreen's "Bournonville: Yesterday, Today and Tomorrow," *Dance Chronicle* 3, no. 2 (1979): 102–151. His librettos have been translated by McAndrews in various issues of *Dance Chronicle* (1980–1983).

On Delsarte and his impact, see Nancy Lee Ruyter's *Reformers and Visionaries: The Americanization of the Art of Dance* (New York, 1979), which also contains an extensive bibliography of primary sources, and Ted Shawn's *Every Little Movement* (Pittsfield, Mass., 1984). Duncan's own writings in *The Art of the Dance* (New York, 1928) reveal her thoughts on religion and dance. Suzanne Shelton's *Divine Dancer* (Garden City, N.Y., 1981) gives an excellent analysis of St. Denis's beliefs and choreography. Some of Shawn's ideas are in *The American Ballet* (New York, 1926). On Humphrey, see Selma Jeanne Cohen's *Doris Humphrey: An Artist First* (Middletown, Conn., 1972) and my "The Translation of a Culture into Choreography: A Study of Doris Humphrey's *The Shakers,* Based on Labananalysis," *Dance Research Annual* 9 (1978): 93–110. *The Notebooks of Martha Graham* (New York, 1973) provides unique perspective on the development of her choreographic ideas. For information on Laban, see his autobiography, *A Life for Dance,* translated by Lisa Ullmann (New York, 1975). On Wigman, see her *The Language of Dance,* translated by Walter Sorell (Middletown, Conn., 1966). For information on Steiner and Gurdjieff, see the "Occult and Bizarre" issue of *Drama Review* 22 (June 1978).

For the second generation of modern dance, Margaret Lloyd's *The Borzoi Book of Modern Dance* (New York, 1949) is the most detailed. Hawkin's ideas are explained in *Erick Hawkins: Theory and Training,* edited by Richard Lorber (New York, 1979). Nikolais discusses his work in "nik: a documentary," edited by Marcia B. Siegel, *Dance Perspectives* 48 (Winter 1971). For an overview of the Ballets Russes, see John Percival's *The World of Diaghilev* (New York, 1971). For Balanchine, see among others, *Choreography by George Balanchine: A Catalogue of Works,* edited by Harvey Simmonds (New York, 1983), and Marilyn Hunt's "*The Prodigal Son*'s Russian Roots: Avant-Garde and Icons," *Dance Chronicle* 5, no. 1 (1982): 24–49. Post-modern dance is introduced in Sally Banes's *Terpsichore in Sneakers* (Boston, 1980). Anna Halprin's *Movement Ritual* (San Francisco, 1979) is an example of one of the outgrowths of this movement.

On the sacred dance movement, see Carlynn Reed's *And We Have Danced: A History of the Sacred Dance Guild and Sacred Dance, 1958–1978* (Austin, 1978), which contains a useful bibliography.

SUZANNE YOUNGERMAN

DAN FODIO, USUMAN (AH 1168–1232, 1754/5–1817 CE), renowned Fulbe Islamic teacher and shaykh. Shehu (Hausa for *shaykh*) Usuman dan Fodio was born in the Hausa kingdom of Gobir, in the north of the present-day state of Sokoto, Nigeria. He came of a line of Muslim scholars of the Fulbe clan Torodbe that had been established in the area since about 854/1450. They worked as scribes, teachers, and in other literate roles and contributed over several generations to the dissemination of Sunnī Islam among the inhabitants of Gobir. As a result, the Gobir royals were superficially won over to Islam. Nonetheless, authority in Gobir still rested on customary norms, not the Islamic *sharī'ah,* at the end of the eighteenth century CE. This caused mounting frustration among these Muslim literates and resulted in the emergence of an Islamic reform movement that reached its peak at that time. The Shehu Usuman became widely accepted in Gobir and neighboring kingdoms as its leader.

The Shehu Usuman spent his early manhood as a teacher and preacher of Islam in Gobir and the nearby kingdoms of Zamfara, Katsina, and Kebbi. He appears to have had no initial intention of pursuing reform by force, but the prolonged resistance of the Gobir chiefs and courtiers to demands for stricter adherence to Islam built up tension. After several violent incidents, organized warfare broke out between the Gobir forces and the Shehu's followers in 1219/1804. For the Muslim reformers this was *jihād,* war against unbelievers.

The campaigns in Gobir ended in 1223/1808, when the Gobir dynasty collapsed and was replaced by a polity organized along Islamic lines that the reformers described as a "caliphate" (Arab., *khalīfah*). The Shehu remained its titular head until his death in 1232/1817, when he was succeeded by his son, Muhammadu Bello. Elsewhere in the Hausa kingdoms and even as far south as Yorubaland and the Nupe kingdom other *jihād*s, led by the Shehu's "flag bearers," or military commanders, continued until brought to a halt by the colonial occupations of the late nineteenth and early twentieth centuries.

The Shehu was not only a war leader but also a scholar and poet in the classical Arabic tradition. Best known among his verse works is his panegyric to the prophet Muḥammad, *Al-dālīyah (The Ode Rhyming in Dāl),* that helped to spread the prophet's Ṣūfī cult and was seminal to a genre of Hausa prophetic panegyric (Hau., *madahu*) among the generations that followed him.

His Arabic prose works are numerous (see Last, 1967). Their main thrust is against all manifestations of indigenous, non-Islamic Hausa culture—song, music, ornate dress, architecture, social mores, and so on—and an insistence that these be replaced by Islamic alternatives. His works also influenced his society, and posterity, by disseminating the ideas of the Qādirī order of Ṣūfīs, to which he was deeply committed, especially as regards the cult of the *awliyā' (Arab.; sg., walī,* "one near" to Allāh). Indeed, the Shehu's own charisma stems largely from his reputation as a *walī.*

The immediate political consequences of the *jihād* were to overthrow the discrete Hausa principalities based on traditional, unwritten customary codes and to substitute the unified Islamic system of the caliphate governed by the revealed and written *sharī'ah.* More long-term cultural and religious consequences were to displace, to some extent, indigenous African notions about cosmology and replace them with the Islamic celestial architecture, to challenge African cyclical explanations of life and death with the finality of the Islamic doctrine of divine punishment and reward, and to enhance the status of Arabic literacy in Hausa society.

The Shehu is still a much revered personality among Hausa Muslims, having become something of a symbol of Hausa Muslim nationalism. However, the Ṣūfī aspects of his teaching are now less emphasized than in the past, perhaps because the Wahhābī doctrine has become more influential in West Africa.

BIBLIOGRAPHY

The bibliography on the Fulbe *jihād* is extensive, and the student is advised to consult lists in Murray Last's *The Sokoto Caliphate* (London, 1967). The following will also be found useful in the first instance: my edition and translation of *Tazyīn al-waraqāt* (Ibadan, 1963), an account of the Shehu's life and the *jihād* from the Muslim reformers' own viewpoint; my *The Sword of Truth* (New York, 1973), a study of the life and times of the Shehu based on the Arabic and Hausa sources; my *The Development of Islam in West Africa,* (New York, 1984), which places the Fulbe reform movement in the wider West African context; and *Bayān wujūb al-hijrah 'alā al-'ibād,* edited and translated by F. H. el-Masri (Khartoum and Oxford, 1978), the edited Arabic text and English translation of one of the Shehu's major works with an excellent critical introduction. There are also many articles in learned journals that deal with aspects of the Shehu's life and writings. These are conveniently listed in Hiskett (1973 and 1984) and Last (1967).

MERVYN HISKETT

DANIEL, or, in Hebrew, Daniyye'l; hero of the biblical book that bears his name. Daniel is presented as a Jew in the Babylonian exile who achieved notoriety in the royal court for his dream interpretations and cryptography and for his salvation from death in a lion's pit. He also appears in the last chapters of the book as the revealer of divine mysteries and of the timetables of Israel's restoration to national-religious autonomy. As a practitioner of oneiromancy in the court, described in *Daniel* 1–6 (written in the third person), Daniel performs his interpretations alone, while as a visionary-apocalyptist, in *Daniel* 7–12 (written in the first person), he is in need of an angel to help him decode his visions and mysteries of the future. It is likely that the name Daniel is pseudonymous, a deliberate allusion to a wise and righteous man known from Ugaritic legend and earlier biblical tradition (*Ez.* 14:4, 28:3).

The authorship of the book is complicated not only by the diverse narrative voices and content but by its language: *Daniel* 1:1–2:4a and 8–12 are written in Hebrew, whereas *Daniel* 2:4b–7:28 is in Aramaic. The language division parallels the subject division (*Daniel* 1–6 concerns legends and dream interpretations; 7–12 concerns apocalyptic visions and interpretations of older prophecies). The overall chronological scheme as well as internal thematic balances (*Daniel* 2–7 is chiliastically related) suggest an attempt at redactional unity. After the prefatory tale emphasizing the life in court and the loyalty of Daniel and some youths to their ancestral religion, a chronological ordering is discernible: a sequence from King Nebuchadrezzar to Darius is reported (*Dn.* 2–6), followed by a second royal sequence beginning with Belshazzar and concluding with Cyrus II (*Dn.* 7–12). Much of this royal dating and even some of the tales are problematic: for example, *Daniel* 4 speaks of Nebuchadrezzar's transformation into a beast, a story that is reported in the Qumran scrolls of Nabonidus; Belshazzar is portrayed as the last king of Babylon, although he was never king; and Darius is called a Mede who conquered Babylon and is placed before Cyrus II of Persia, although no such Darius is known (the Medes followed the Persians, and *Darius* is the name of several Persian kings). Presumably the episodes of *Daniel* 2–6, depicting a series of monarchical reversals, episodes of ritual observances, and reports of miraculous deliverances were collected in the Seleucid period (late fourth to mid-second century BCE) in order to reinvigorate waning Jewish hopes in divine providence and encourage steadfast faith.

The visions of *Daniel* 7–12, reporting events from the reign of Belshazzar to that of Cyrus II (but actually predicting the overthrow of Seleucid rule in Palestine), were collected and published during the reign of Antiochus IV prior to the Maccabean Revolt, for it was then (beginning in 168 BCE) that the Jews were put to the test concerning their allegiance to Judaism and their ancestral traditions, and many refused to desecrate the statutes of Moses and endured a martyr's death for their resolute trust in divine dominion. All of the visions of Daniel dramatize this dominion in different ways: for example, via images of the enthronement of a God of judgment, with a "son of man" invested with rule (this figure was interpreted by Jews as Michael the archangel and by Christians as Christ), in chapter 7; via zodiacal images of cosmic beasts with bizarre manifestations, as in chapter 8; or via complex reinterpretations of ancient prophecies, especially those of *Jeremiah* 25:9–11, as found in *Daniel* 9–12.

The imagery of the four beasts in chapter 7 (paralleled by the image of four metals in chapter 2), representing four kingdoms to be overthrown by a fifth monarchy of divine origin, is one of the enduring images of the book: it survived as a prototype of Jewish and Christian historical and apocalyptic schemes to the end of the Middle Ages. The role and power of this imagery in the fifteenth- and sixteenth-century work of the exegete Isaac Abravanel, the scientist Isaac Newton, and the philosopher Jean Bodin and among the Fifth Monarchy Men of seventeenth-century England, for example, is abiding testimony to the use of this ancient topos in organizing the chiliastic imagination of diverse thinkers and groups. The schema is still used to this day by various groups predicting the apocalyptic advent.

The encouragement in the face of religious persecution that is found and propagandized in *Daniel* 11–12 contains a remarkable reinterpretation of *Isaiah* 52:13–53:12, regarding the suffering servant of God not as all Israel but as the select faithful. Neither the opening stories about Daniel and the youths nor the final martyrological allusions advocate violence or revolt; they rather advocate a stance of piety, civil disobedience, and trustful resignation. Victory for the faithful is in the hands of the archangel Michael, and the martyrs will be resurrected and granted astral immortality. Presumably the circles behind the book were not the same as the Maccabean fighters and may reflect some proto-Pharisaic group of *ḥasidim,* or pietists. The themes of resistance to oppression, freedom of worship, preservation of monotheistic integrity, the overthrow of historical dominions, and the acknowledgment of the God of heaven recur throughout the book and have served as a token of trust for the faithful in their darkest hour.

BIBLIOGRAPHY

Bickerman, Elias J. *Four Strange Books of the Bible: Jonah, Daniel, Koheleth, Esther.* New York, 1967. See pages 53–138.

Braverman, Jay. *Jerome's Commentary on Daniel.* Washington, D.C., 1978.

Hartman, Louis F., and Alexander A. Di Lella. *Book of Daniel.* Anchor Bible, vol. 23. Garden City, N.Y., 1978.

MICHAEL FISHBANE

DANTE ALIGHIERI (1265–1321), Italian poet, theologian, and philosopher. Dante offered in his *Commedia* a "sacred poem" of enormous erudition and aesthetic power, which more than any other work of Christian literature merits the appellation conferred on it by a mid-sixteenth-century edition: "divine." After producing the *Vita nuova* in 1295, Dante entered the volatile world of Florentine politics, which, however unjustly, subsequently led to his banishment from the city in 1302. In exile for the remainder of his life, he wrote the *Convivio,* the *De vulgari eloquentia,* and the *De monarchia* in the following decade, works that together reveal a commonality of themes: an admiration for the Latin classics, a dedication to the study of philosophy, and a commitment to the revival of the Roman imperial ideal. These concerns are all transfigured in the long and elaborate course of the *Commedia (Inferno, Purgatorio, Paradiso),* which represents an encyclopedic synthesis of late medieval thought subsumed within an overarching theological vision. The poem is at once profoundly traditional in its religious ordering of human experience and an innovation of substance and form that suggests an utterly new mentality at work. It can be seen both as an attempt to exorcise what would shortly become the spirit of the Renaissance and yet also as a brilliant precursor of it.

Dante came of age in Florence at a time when the papacy was embroiled with the Holy Roman Empire over temporal jurisdiction in Italy. Widespread corruption in the church, as well as within the powerful mendicant orders of the Franciscans and the Dominicans, seemed to give rise to many individualistic and charismatic expressions of piety that, while passionately Catholic, nonetheless found themselves alienated from the established religious institutions and hierarchies. It is in this context that a devout layman like Dante, discovering himself a mere "party of one," could dare to arrogate to himself the quasi-biblical role of prophet. He became a voice crying in the wilderness, instructing the powers of church and state in their true responsibilities at the same time that he was attempting to woo the ordinary reader (in a daring use of the vernacular for so ambitious a poetic work) into a full conversion of the heart.

Whatever the poet's personal upbringing may have given him, we know that he studied for an extended period "in the schools of the religious orders and at the disputations of the philosophers" (*Convivio* 2.12). At Santa Croce he would have been exposed to the wealth of Franciscan piety, while at Santa Maria Novella the Dominican Remigio de' Girolami expounded the theology of Thomas Aquinas with special regard for the Aristotelian philosophy that subtends it. In such an intellectual atmosphere Dante found validated what was to be one of the most impressive characteristics of his own work: the massive appropriation of pagan and classical writers for Christian reflection and use.

In assessing Dante's relation to medieval theology and religious thought it is commonplace to emphasize the formative influence of "the Philosopher" (Aristotle) and the "Angelic Doctor" (Thomas); that is, to stress his strong debt to Scholasticism. It must be remembered, however, that the poet everywhere shows himself to be an independent and eclectic thinker, whose imaginative meditation on the Christian faith leads him far and wide: to the systematics of Peter Lombard, the Platonism of Bonaventure, the mysticism of Bernard of Clairvaux and the Victorines, the biblical exegesis (as well as the retrospective confessional mode) of Augustine. Thus, while we may well speak of Dante as standing at the crossroads of medieval religious thought, the intersection is one that he personally constructed rather than discovered ready-made. The synthesis of the *Commedia* is idiosyncratically his own.

As a propagator of the Christian religion Dante must, of course, be assessed by the achievement of his great poem, with its account of the state of the soul after death portrayed in the course of a journey undertaken by the poet himself (lasting from Good Friday 1300 to the Wednesday of Easter Week) through the realms of damnation, purgation, and beatitude. Granted this extraordinary experience through the intercession of his deceased love, Beatrice, the pilgrim-poet is led step by step through a process of conversion by a series of guides and mediators: the pagan poet Vergil, Beatrice herself, and the churchman-mystic-crusader Bernard. But in its larger aspect, the poem is itself an invitation to conversion: to the individual reader, to rediscover the Gospels' "true way"; to the church, to recover its spiritual mission; and to the state, to exercise its divinely ordained mandate to foster temporal well-being.

There are other transformations as well. Hell is portrayed not as a place of arbitrary horror, but as the eternal living out of the soul's self-choice, whereby punishments not only fit but express the crimes of sin. Dante also brings Purgatory aboveground and into the sun, turning the traditional place of torturous penance into more of a hospital or school than a prison house. No less striking is the presentation of Beatrice, at once the earthly lover praised in the youthful pages of the *Vita nuova* and the Christ-event for Dante: a woman in whom we see human eros accorded an unprecedented place in the scheme of human salvation. But perhaps most significant of all—and most singularly responsible for the *Commedia*'s immense and enduring popularity—is Dante's superb representation of the self: ineradicable even in death; more vivid than the theological context in which it is eternally envisioned; more subtly and realistically portrayed than in any other work of medieval literature. The poem's itinerary leads us along the paths of theology to a vision of God, but its hundred cantos offer an investigation of human nature and culture that grounds the reader's attention in the complex realities of earth.

BIBLIOGRAPHY

The quantity of secondary material on Dante written in English alone is staggering. Carole Slade's extensive and somewhat annotated bibliography in *Approaches to Teaching Dante's Divine Comedy* (New York, 1982) gives a fine sense of the whole range. Among those works that deal sensitively with Dante's relation to Christian belief and tradition, one needs to accord special tribute to the critical oeuvre of Charles S. Singleton, who has exerted a powerful influence on American studies of Dante by underscoring the importance of the poem's theological assumptions. In addition to Singleton's translation and commentary (Princeton, 1970–1975), there are his earlier works: *An Essay on the Vita Nuova* (Cambridge, 1949), *Dante Studies 1: Commedia, Elements of Structure,* 2d ed. (Baltimore, 1977), and *Dante Studies 2: Journey to Beatrice,* 2d ed. (Baltimore, 1977). Charles Williams's *The Figure of Beatrice* (London, 1958) gives a coherent theological reading of all of Dante's works, whose point of view informs not only Dorothy Sayers's commentary and notes (Harmondsworth, 1951–1967) but her *Introductory Papers on Dante* (New York, 1954) and *Further Papers on Dante* (New York, 1957). There are also brilliant insights into the religious ethos of the *Commedia* in Erich Auerbach's *Dante: Poet of the Secular World* (Chicago, 1961) as well as in an important chapter of his *Mimesis* (Princeton, 1953). Robert Hollander's *Allegory in Dante's Commedia* (Princeton, 1969) and *Studies in Dante* (Ravenna, 1980) deal masterfully with the poet's claim to write an "allegory of the theologians" (and therefore in the manner of scripture itself). John Freccero's many brilliant essays on the *Commedia,* collected under the title *The Poetry of Conversion* (Cambridge, Mass., 1986), stress the poet's debt to Augustine's *Confessions* and the Christian Neoplatonic tradition. The latter connection is explored in Joseph Anthony Mazzeo's *Structure and Thought in the Paradiso* (Ithaca, N.Y., 1958). Finally, William Anderson's *Dante the Maker* (Boston, 1980) takes seriously the visionary origin of the *Commedia* and therefore forces us to examine again the literal level of the poem and its bid to be believed as a genuine vision of God.

PETER S. HAWKINS

DARKNESS. *See* Light and Darkness.

DARŚANAS. *For discussions of the six orthodox systems of Indian philosophy, see* Nyāya; Vaiśeṣika; Sāṃkhya; Yoga; Mīmāṃsā; *and* Vedānta.

DARWIN, CHARLES. *See* Evolution; *see also* Science and Religion.

DARWĪSH. The Persian word *darwīsh,* from the Pahlavi *driyosh,* is most likely derived from the term *darvīza,* meaning "poverty," "neediness," "begging," and so forth. The word *darwīsh* has entered the other Islamic languages, such as Turkish and Urdu, and is even found in classical Arabic sources. It has become an English word in the form of *dervish.* In all these cases, including the original Persian, it is related primarily to spiritual poverty, equivalent to the possession of "Muhammadan poverty" *(al-faqr al-muḥammadī).* Hence the term *darwīsh* referring to a person who possesses this "poverty" is the same as the Arabic term *faqīr* used in Sufism for Muhammadan poverty. Within Ṣūfī circles, these words are used interchangeably, along with *mutaṣawwif,* "practitioner" of Sufism.

The term *darwīsh* appears in Persian literature as early as the tenth century and in such early Persian Ṣūfī texts as the works of Khwājah ʿAbd Allāh Anṣārī of Herat, where it carries the basic meaning referred to above but encompasses such variations as "ascetic," "hermit," and "wandering Ṣūfī" *(qalandar).* Later it also became an honorific title bestowed upon certain Ṣufīs such as Darwīsh Khusraw, the leader of the Nuqṭawīyah school at the time of Shah ʿAbbās I. Throughout the history of Sufism, the state of being a *darwīsh,* or *darwīshī,* has been held in great honor and respect, as seen from the famous *ghazal* of Ḥāfiẓ that begins with the verse

> Rawḍiy-i khuld-i barīn khalwat-i darwīshānast
> Māyiy-i muḥtashimī khidmat-i darwīshānast
>
> The sublime eternal Paradise is the spiritual retreat of the dervishes;
> The essence of grandeur is the service of the dervishes.

There is, however, a secondary meaning associated with *darwīsh* that carries negative connotations, interpreting simplicity of life, limitation of material needs, reliance upon God for sustenance, and other aspects of Muhammadan poverty or Sufism as laziness, lackadaisicalness, indifference to cleanliness, neglect of duties toward oneself and society, and other injunctions emphasized by the *sharīʿah,* or Muslim law. This negative aspect of the term increased with the decay of certain Ṣūfī orders during the past two or three centuries and also with the attempt by some people to pass themselves off as *darwīsh* without any involvement with Sufism at all. Nonetheless, the association with spiritual poverty, self-discipline, and the basic virtues of humility, charity, and veracity remains the primary meaning of the word.

BIBLIOGRAPHY

Arberry, A. J. *Sufism: An Account of the Mystics of Islam* (1950). Reprint, London, 1979.

Birge, John K. *The Bektashi Order of Dervishes* (1937). Reprint, New York, 1982.

Keddie, Nikki R., ed. *Scholars, Saints, and Sufis: Muslim Religious Institutions in the Middle East since 1500.* Berkeley, 1972.

Nicholson, Reynold A. *The Mystics of Islam* (1914). Reprint, London, 1963.

Schimmel, Annemarie. *Mystical Dimensions of Islam.* Chapel Hill, N.C., 1975.

SEYYED HOSSEIN NASR

DASAM GRANTH. The compilation of the writings of Gobind Singh, the tenth Sikh *gurū*, is known as the *Dasam Granth* (The Book of the Tenth [Gurū]). This text is regarded as the second scripture of the Sikhs, the first being the *Ādi Granth*, its primacy acknowledged by the tenth *gurū* himself. According to Kesar Singh Chhibber (in his *Bansāvalī Nāmā*), the *Dasam Granth* was compiled in 1698 CE under the supervision of Gobind Singh, who refused to include his own compositions in the *Ādi Granth*, saying, "The real *Granth* is the *Ādi Granth;* mine is only a poetic pastime." During the battles of the tenth *gurū* with the hill chiefs and the Mughal armies, this book of the tenth *gurū* seems to have been lost. Copies of various portions of the text were widely dispersed when Bhāī Manī Singh began the compilation of the *Dasam Granth.* He collected the scattered fragments of the *gurūs* compositions and prepared the *Daswen Pātśah kā Granth* (The Book of the Tenth Gurū).

After the execution of Bhāī Manī Singh, the abovementioned compilation was examined by learned Sikhs at Talwandī Sābo (later named Damdamā) in Patiala state, in the present-day state of Punjab. Several of them objected to the inclusion of the Persian tales entitled *Hikāyāt* and the stories depicting the wiles and vagaries of women entitled *Charitropākhyān* or *Triā Charittar,* on the grounds that they ought not be placed side by side with the religious compositions of the *gurū.* The savants wished to omit them from the volume. With the arrival of Sardār Mehtāb Singh of Mīrankot at Damdamā, the matter was deferred pending the success or failure of his impending mission. One Massā Ranghar, a Muslim official, is said to have forcibly occupied the Harī Mandir (Golden Temple), where he profaned it by allowing drinking and the dancing of courtesans. Sardār Mehtāb Singh had taken a vow to kill Massā. Finally, a wager was set in order to end the controversy. It was decided that if Massā were killed, the volume would remain as it was, but should the mission fail, the objectionable compositions would be omitted. Since Sardār Mehtāb Singh was successful in his mission, the *Granth* compiled by Bhāī Manī Singh was allowed to remain intact. Though the controversy subsided for some time, it did not end completely. Scholars have subsequently raised doubts about the authenticity and authorship of some of the portions of the *Granth.*

Besides the volume prepared by Bhāī Manī Singh in 1713, some other important recensions of the *Granth* are also available. The original compilation of Bhāī Manī Singh remains in the possession of the family of Raja Gulab Singh Sethi, in New Delhi. One compilation of the *Granth,* known as *Bābā Dīp Singh wālī Bīr,* is at Damdamā. Another recension is housed at Gurdwārā Motī Bāgh, Patiala. A version known as *Bhāī Sukhā Singh wālī Khās Bīr* is in Patna. Another volume is in the Dīwan Khānā, Sangrur. In these different versions, there are a few scattered additions and alterations, but the major compositions are the same.

The compilation of Bhāī Manī Singh includes *Jāp Sāhib, Bachittar Nātak, Śastar Nām Mālā, Gyān Prabodh, Akāl Ustat, Vār Durgā Kī, Charitropākhyān, Hikāyāt,* and *Zafar Nāmā. Jāp Sāhib* is the morning prayer of the Sikhs and is recited along with *Japu* of Gurū Nānak, which is the first composition in the *Ādi Granth. Bachittar Nātak* includes not only the autobiography of the tenth *gurū* but also *Chandī Charittar* (parts 1 and 2), *Chaubīs Avatār, Brahmā Avatār, Rudra Avatār,* and *Śabad Hazāre* ("nine hymns" in the *rāga* mode), as well as thirty-three *svayyās* ("stanzas"). The *Chandī Charittar* is based upon the *Durgā Saptaśatī* of the *Mārkaṇḍeya Purāṇa,* a poem depicting the battles between the goddess Durgā and the demons. *Chaubīs Avatār* contains a description of the feats of the twenty-four incarnations of Viṣṇu, *Brahmā Avatār* narrates the stories of the nine incarnations of Brahmā, and *Rudra Avatār,* of the two incarnations of Śiva. A description of the feats of Mehdī Mīr is appended to *Chaubīs Avatār. Śastar Nām Mālā* is a eulogy of armaments. *Gyān Prabodh* is an incomplete poem depicting *dharma* (duty) in various forms. *Akāl Ustat* is a poetic fragment on the same theme. It also contains a eulogy of *brahman* and an attack on hypocrisy and pretension. The same can be said about *Śabad Hazāre* and the thirty-three *svayyās.* The *Charitropākhyan* contains the stories regarding the deceitful ways of women. All the above-mentioned compositions have been written in Braj Bhāṣā (Eastern Hindi) and in various stanza forms. *Vār Durgā Kī,* also called *Vār Bhagautī Jī Kī,* is a heroic poem of fifty-five stanzas in Punjabi. *Zafar Nāmā* (Epistle of Victory) is the letter written by the *gurū* to Aurangzeb, the emperor of India, in Persian verse.

The narrative poetry of the *Dasam Granth,* aside from the *Hikāyāt* and *Charitropākhyan* sections, is mostly Puranic in content. Several portions, such as *Kṛṣṇa Avatār* and *Rāma Avatār,* have been recognized as specimens of great medieval Hindi poetry. In addition to the tenth *gurū*'s masterful command of diction and versification, the heroic element is apparent throughout the compositions. At times there is an adept commingling of Hindi vocabulary with Persian and Arabic words. The Puranic lore in the tenth *gurū*'s poetry did not necessarily emanate from his beliefs; it stands as a powerful poetic exercise in itself.

[*For further discussion of the compilation of the* Dasam Granth, *see the biography of Singh. See also* Ādi Granth *and* Sikhism.]

BIBLIOGRAPHY

Āshtā, Dharampāl. *The Poetry of Dasam Granth.* Delhi, 1959.

Banerjee, Indūbūshan. *Evolution of the Khālsā.* Calcutta, 1936.

Macauliffe, Max A. *The Sikh Religion: Its Gurus, Sacred Writings, and Authors,* vol 5. Oxford, 1909.

Sehgal, Kumārī Prasinnī. *Gurū Govind Singh aur unkā kāvya.* Lucknow, 1965.

SURINDAR SINGH KOHLI

DAVID, second king of Israel and Judah (c. 1000–960 BCE) and founder of a dynasty that continued until the end of the Judean monarchy. David was the youngest son of Jesse from Bethlehem in Judah.

David's Place in the History of Israel. David is regarded by both tradition and modern scholarship as the greatest ruler of the combined states of Israel and Judah. He was able to free them from the control of the Philistines and to gain a measure of domination over some of the neighboring states (Edom, Moab, Ammon) and some of the Aramaean states of Syria. At the same time he established treaty relations with Tyre and Hamath. He also extended the territories of Judah and Israel to include a number of major Canaanite cities and took Jerusalem by conquest. It became his capital and remained the ruling center of Judah until the end of the monarchy.

There are no references to David in any historical source outside the Bible. One contemporary ruler, Hiram of Tyre, mentioned in *2 Samuel* 5:11, is known from other historical sources, but the correlation of the chronologies of the two kings remains problematic.

The assessment of David's career is based upon sources in *1 Samuel* 16 through *1 Kings* 2. Some of these that mention his military activities reflect annalistic or formal documents. These are now embedded within two literary works often regarded as nearly contemporary with David and an important witness to the events: the story of David's rise to power (*1 Sm.* 16 through *2 Sm.* 2:7, *2 Sm.* 5), and the court history, or succession story (*2 Sm.* 2:8–4:12, 6:16, 6:20–23; *2 Sm.* 9–20; *1 Kgs.* 1–2). It remains less clear how *2 Samuel* 6–8 relates to either of these works or how they all fit into the larger history of the monarchy. The materials in *2 Samuel* 21–24 are supplemental additions that do not belong to the other sources.

There are, however, two serious questions about this literary analysis. First, the identification of a distinct literary work, the story of David's rise to power, may be doubted, since it may be viewed as a continuation of earlier materials in *Samuel* and as having strong ties to the rest of the so-called Deuteronomist's history of the monarchy—in which case it would be a work of the exilic period. Second, the court history was not originally part of this history but constitutes a later addition with quite a different perspective. If these two views can be sustained, then both works are comparatively late, and great caution must be exercised in using them as historical sources for the time of David.

David in the Tradition of Israel. Whatever their historical value might be, the literary works within *1 Samuel* 16 through *1 Kings* 2 establish David's place within the Israelite-Jewish tradition. Two quite different views of David's character and his significance for later Israel are given in these works.

Rise to power. David's introduction is directly linked to God's rejection of Saul, so that he immediately appears as the "one after God's own heart" to replace Saul. Shortly after David enters Saul's service as personal armor bearer, musician, and successful military leader, Saul becomes jealous and turns against David. While Saul's son Jonathan, his daughter Michal, his servants, and all the people grow to love David, Saul grows to hate him and makes various attempts on his life so that David flees. David establishes a band of followers in Judah and becomes a vassal of the Philistines. Saul, demented, cruel, and forsaken by God, ultimately dies on the battlefield with his sons. David, after offering a lament for Saul and Jonathan, is made king at Hebron, first by Judah and subsequently by Israel. David then captures Jerusalem and wages successful warfare against the Philistines. All of this comes to David because "God is with him." Throughout the entire account, David is viewed as one who can do no wrong. Heroic and magnanimous, he is the obvious replacement for Saul.

The dynastic promise. Once the land is at peace, David is able to bring the Ark to Jerusalem (*2 Sm.* 6) and build himself a palace (*2 Sm.* 5:11). He then proposes a plan to Nathan the prophet to build a temple for the Ark, and this leads to a dynastic promise by God through the prophet (*2 Sm.* 7). Although some have argued that this promise is based upon a special document of the early monarchy, it seems preferable to regard it as the thematic center of the larger Deuteronomic history of the monarchy and its ideology of kingship.

The dynastic promise is the real climax to the account of David's rise to kingship. With David a new era begins in two respects. God promises David an eternal dynasty but assigns the task of building the Temple—a permanent abode—to his son Solomon. God will be "a father" to the king, and he will be God's "son." He may be disciplined for disobedience to God's laws, but the dynasty will remain in perpetuity.

David as the "servant of Yahveh" who is completely obedient to God becomes the model for all future kings, especially those of Judah. Not only is his obedience rewarded with an immediate heir, but it is said to merit the perpetuation of his dynasty even if some future kings are disobedient to God's laws.

This dynastic promise also becomes the basis for the hope of a restoration of the monarchy after the destruction of the state in 587/6 BCE and ultimately leads to messianism—the belief that a son of David will arise and restore the fortunes of Israel and usher in the final reign of God.

Court history. The so-called court history, or succession story, variously regarded as a unique piece of early history writing, a historical novel, and a work of royal propaganda, is a literary masterpiece of realistic narrative. Some view it as written in support of Solomon, while others understand it as anti-Solomonic. If this work is an early source used by the historian of *Samuel* and *Kings,* then it is not clear how he could have been reconciled to such a pejorative view of David, since the rest of the history so completely idealizes him.

The court history, in fact, was a later addition to the history that seeks to counter the idealized view of David by suggesting that he gained the throne from a son of Saul under doubtful circumstances and that the divine promise to David was constantly used by David, Solomon, and others to legitimize very questionable behavior. The "sure house" of David is characterized by endless turmoil, and Solomon finally succeeds David after a palace intrigue. David himself commits adultery and murder. One of his sons, Amnon, rapes his sister Tamar and is avenged by his brother Absalom. After an exile Absalom returns to lead a revolt against his father that finally ends in Absalom's death. This is followed by yet another revolt between north and south.

This pejorative view of David's monarchy and the dynastic promise did not suppress the royal ideology or its evolution into messianism. At most it "humanized" David and gave added appeal to the tradition as a whole.

David in the Books of Chronicles. The historian of *1* and *2 Chronicles* sees in David the real founder of the Jewish state, a state dominated by the Temple and an elaborate priestly hierarchy (*1 Chr.* 10–29). The Chronicler's source for David was the history in *Samuel* and *Kings* modified by his perception of the state, which was based upon his own times in the Hellenistic period. He presents David as immediately coming to the throne over all Israel after the death of Saul. There is no account of his struggle with Saul or of his warfare with Saul's son, Ishbosheth. The whole of the court history has been excised as too derogatory. In its place David becomes the real founder of the Temple, laying all the plans, providing for all the workmanship and the materials, and even establishing the whole hierarchy of priestly and Temple officials. Of particular importance for later tradition is the association of David with the Temple music, which did much to identify him as the "sweet singer of Israel." In this history David is completely idealized, and the time of David is an anachronistic legitimation for the ecclesiastical state that developed in the time of the Second Temple.

David and the Psalms. David is directly mentioned in only a few psalms (78, 89, and 132), those that make reference to the dynastic promise, all of which are dependent upon *Samuel* and *Kings.* In the Hebrew scriptures the superscriptions, which are all late, and which modern scholarship considers secondary additions, attribute seventy-three psalms to David. This continues the tradition of David's association with the sacred music of the Temple. But in a number of instances the individual laments (e.g., *Ps.* 51) are associated with particular events in David's life. Thus the psalms that were originally anonymous become increasingly associated with the figure of David.

David in Prophecy. While the royal ideology had at most a minor place in preexilic prophecy, it was only in late prophecy and in exilic and postexilic editing of prophetic books that the dynastic promise to David plays a major role in visions of the future (*Is.* 9:5–6 [Eng. version 6–7], 11:1–10, 61:1–7; *Jer.* 33:14–26; *Ez.* 34:23–24; *Am.* 9:11ff.; *Mi.* 5:1–3 [EV 2–4]; *Zec.* 12:7–9). Hope is expressed for the restoration of the Davidic dynasty and times of prosperity. In their most elaborate form these prophecies predict an "anointed one" (the Messiah) who would manifest all the idealized attributes of royalty, liberate Israel from its enemies, and bring in the reign of Yahveh.

David in Rabbinic Judaism, Christianity, and Islam. The most important development in the Davidic tradition in postbiblical Judaism was the regarding of David as the author of the Psalter, or at least as author of most of the psalms within it. This meant that David, as the composer of Israel's sacred hymns and prayers, was a model of Jewish piety. In the psalms David speaks not only for himself but for all Israel. His praise represents the spiritual life of the worshiping community, and in his prayers he supplicates God for Israel in all time to come. Furthermore, a number of the psalms have as their theme the glorification of the Law (Torah) and the ardent devotion of the psalmist to the study of the Law day and night (*Ps.* 1, 19, 119). Consequently, David was viewed as a great authority on the Law, and his words and example could often be invoked to settle a point at issue in the discussions of legal matters *(halakhah)* (B.T., *Ber.* 4a; B.T., *Yev.* 78b–79a). Since the Psalter came to be regarded as holy writ, David was also considered a prophet through whom God spoke and gave his revelation to Israel.

Some elements in the Davidic tradition gave the rabbis difficulty, most notably David's sin of adultery with Bathsheba. Some attempted to exonerate him, but those who found him guilty of wrongdoing saw a divine purpose in the events, namely that David was to be an example of contrition and repentance to give hope and encouragement to Israel when it sinned (*Midrash Tehillim* 40.2, 51.1, 51.3). Another problem was the tradition that David was descended from Ruth the Moabite (*Ru.* 4:17), since this would make him ineligible for participation in the congregation of Israel. As a compensation, every attempt was made to enhance David's genealogical line and give him the strongest possible pedigree. The dynastic promise to David represented the future hope of Israel, but many rabbis were concerned that it not be used for political or ideological manipulation by messianic adventurers. At the same time the liturgical tradition continued to embody the hope in a restoration of the kingdom of David in the age to come.

Christianity, as reflected in the New Testament, also recognized David as author of the psalms, as an example of piety, and as a prophet of divine revelation; but the emphasis was clearly on the messianic aspects of the tradition. Since Jesus was identified as the Messiah, he received the title "son of David," although he repudiated the political connotation of such a designation. Matthew and Luke, in their birth stories, connect Jesus with Bethlehem, the city of David, and supply genealogies that trace his lineage back to David. David as prophet also bears witness in the psalms to Jesus as the Messiah (*Acts* 2:25–37).

Islam's tradition about David is slight. The Qur'ān knows of a few episodes in David's life, such as the victory over Goliath, but this and other stories are confused with those of other biblical figures (2:252). The Qur'ān also recognizes that God gave *Psalms* to David as a divine book in much the same way as Moses and Muḥammad received their revelations (17:56).

BIBLIOGRAPHY

Treatments of the historical periods of David's reign may be found in John Bright's *A History of Israel,* 3d ed. (Philadelphia, 1981); the contribution by J. Alberto Soggin, "The Davidic-Solomonic Kingdom," in *Israelite and Judaean History,* edited by John H. Hayes and J. Maxwell Miller (Philadelphia, 1977); and those by Benjamin Mazar and David N. Freedman in *The World History of the Jewish People,* vol. 4, pt. 1, edited by Abraham Malamat (Jerusalem, 1979), pp. 76–125.

The standard treatment on the story of David's rise to power is Jakob H. Grønbaek's *Die Geschichte vom Aufstieg Davids, 1 SAM. 15–2 SAM. 5: Tradition und Komposition,* "Acta Theologica Danica," vol. 10 (Copenhagen, 1971). The classic work on the so-called succession story is Leonhard Rost's *Die Überlieferung von der Thronnachfolge Davids,* "Beiträge zur Wissenschaft vom Alten und Neuen Testament," vol. 3, no. 6 (Stuttgart, 1926), translated by Michael D. Rutter and David M. Gunn as *The Succession to the Throne of David* (Sheffield, 1982). Building upon this study was the important essay by Gerhard von Rad, "Der Anfang der Geschichtsschreibung im Alten Israel," *Archiv für Kulturgeschichte* 32 (Weimar, 1944): 1–42, translated by E. W. Trueman Dicken as "The Beginning of Historical Writing in Ancient Israel," in Gerhard von Rad's *The Problem of the Hexateuch and Other Essays* (Edinburgh, 1966), pp. 166–204. See also the studies by Roger N. Whybray, *The Succession Narrative* (London, 1968), and David M. Gunn, *The Story of King David: Genre and Interpretation* (Sheffield, 1982). A more detailed treatment of my own views may be found in chapter 8 of my *In Search of History: Historiography in the Ancient World and the Origins of Biblical History* (New Haven, 1983).

For a more detailed treatment of the Jewish and Christian traditions with bibliography, see the article "David" in *Theologische Realenzyklopädie,* vol. 8 (New York, 1981).

JOHN VAN SETERS

DA'WAH. The Arabic term *da'wah* (lit., "call, invitation, summoning") is used especially in the sense of the religious outreach or mission to exhort people to embrace Islam as the true religion. The Arabic root *d'w* occurs frequently in the Qur'ān, where it can also mean calling upon God in prayer (as in *du'ā'*). The Qur'ān contains many imperatives to spread Islam, as in surah 16:125–126:

> Call [*ud'u*] thou to the way of thy Lord with wisdom and good admonition, and dispute with them in the better way. Surely thy Lord knows very well those who have gone astray from his way, and he knows very well those who are guided. And if you chastise, chastise even as you have been chastised; and yet assuredly if you are patient, better it is for

those patient. And be patient; yet it is thy patience only with the help of God.

Da'wah can also mean simply an invitation to a mundane affair, such as a meal, or propaganda for a political or sectarian cause. A specialized meaning of *da'wah* has been the quasi-magical practice of spell and incantation through invocation of the names of God and his good angels and *jinn,* in pursuit of personal goals such as healing, success in love or war, avoidance of evil, and other things. This occult practice became highly elaborated and included astrology, a magical alphabet, numerology, and alchemy.

During the early centuries of Islamic history, *da'wah* often had strong political orientations when used to mean a summons to support a claimant to Islamic rule. New movements would spread their ideologies of Islamic statehood through highly organized and disciplined networks of information and indoctrination. The most forceful and long-lived *da'wah* enterprise was the Shīʿī sect known as the Ismāʿīlīyah, which insisted that the true Muslim community should be ruled by a politico-religious leader descended from the family of Muḥammad through the line of Ismāʿīl Jaʿfar al-Ṣādiq (d. 756 CE), one of the great Shīʿī imams. The Ismāʿīlīyah developed *da'wah* into a comprehensive political theology aimed at their ultimate dominance of the Muslims. The movement inducted converts into a fanatically devoted community that observed a hierarchy of degrees of membership, marked by initiation into ascending levels of esoteric knowledge. The leaders at each level were called *dāʿīs,* "summoners," who exercised authority by regions in which they preached and taught the doctrines of the movement. The *dāʿīs* were considered by the Ismāʿīlīyah to be the representatives of the imam. In some cases, the head *dāʿī* was the highest religious leader of a country, a sort of Shīʿī "bishop." More often, the *dāʿīs* functioned in an underground manner, spreading their doctrines in territories not under Ismāʿīlī rule. As well as preaching and propaganda, advanced theology and philosophy were major activities of the *dāʿīs.*

In the modern period, *da'wah* most often refers to Islamic missionary activities, which are increasingly characterized by long-range planning, skillful exploitation of the media, establishment of study centers and mosques, and earnest, urgent preaching and efforts at persuasion.

Da'wah as mission should never be spread by force (surah 2:256). If the hearers refuse to embrace Islam, then they should be left alone, at least for a time. But a committed Muslim should not give up the task of *da'wah.* If nothing else succeeds, the silent example of a devout Muslim may be used by God as a means to someone's voluntary conversion.

In the strong Islamic revival of the late twentieth century, *da'wah* has a less specifically political and a more marked spiritual and moral emphasis than in earlier times. The *ummah,* the Muslim community, is believed to transcend national political entities, and the *sharīʿah,* the sacred law, is said to make claims on Muslims even when it is not embodied as the actual legal code (except in certain countries). *Da'wah,* then, is the cutting edge of Islam and as such is directed at fellow believers as well as at the multitudes outside the *ummah* who nevertheless possess the God-given *fiṭrah* (surah 30:30), or "inherent character," also to be intentional Muslims and thus vicegerents (*khulafāʾ*; s.g., *khalīfah,* "caliph") of God on earth (2:30). From North Africa to Indonesia, and beyond, Muslim individuals and organizations are strenuously dedicated to missionary activities, utilizing the media and other advanced means of communication and "market research." *Da'wah* faculties are prominent in Muslim training schools and universities, and the hope is that the strong obligation to spread Islam will be felt by Muslims at all levels of society. *Da'wah,* as well as migration, is responsible for the significant recent growth of Muslim populations in Western countries.

[*See also* Shiism, *article on* Ismāʿīlīyah.]

BIBLIOGRAPHY

Maurice Canard's article "Da'wa," in *The Encyclopaedia of Islam,* new ed. (Leiden, 1960–), offers a detailed analysis with extensive source citations, although it does not treat modern Islamic mission. A provocative collection of exploratory essays and discussions is *Christian Mission and Islamic Da'wah: Proceedings of the Chambésy Dialogue Consultation,* edited by Khurshid Ahmad and David Kerr (London and Ann Arbor, Mich., 1982), first published as a special issue of the *International Review of Mission* 65 (October 1976). For an introduction to *da'wah* as occult spell and incantation, see the article "Da'wah" in Thomas Patrick Hughes's *A Dictionary of Islam,* 2d ed. (London, 1896). A standard survey of Shīʿī sectarian concepts and practices of *da'wah* as propaganda is Bernard Lewis's *The Origins of Ismāʿīlism* (1940; reprint, New York, 1975).

FREDERICK MATHEWSON DENNY

DAY, DOROTHY (1897–1980), personalist revolutionary, journalist, and lecturer. Between 1933, when she brought out the first penny-a-copy issue of the *Catholic Worker,* and 1980, when she died, Dorothy Day became, in the opinion of many, America's foremost Roman Catholic voice calling for peace and a profound change in the major institutional forms of the contemporary world. She opposed what she regarded as the enslaving colossus of the modern state and the technological giantism to which it was a partner. Fundamental to her ideas of social reordering was her insistence on the personal transformation of value based on the primary reality of spirit rather than the spirit of acquisitiveness. For her, this meant taking her directions from church tradition, the papal encyclicals, and her literal reading of the Gospels. She used these sources to justify her absolute pacifism and her communitarian ideas on social reconstruction.

For Day, the ultimate and transfiguring value was love, a subject that was the theme of her best writing. The exercise of a sacrificial love was at the heart of her personalist revolt against the enlarging domain over life of institutional forms. The world would be renewed by persons who loved and not by state management. In her own case she chose to wage her revolution by establishing "houses of hospitality" in the destitute areas of lower Manhattan in New York City, by promoting communitarian farms, and by an immense writing and speaking regimen that left few Catholic parishes or schools untouched by her ideas by the time of her death.

She was born the third in a family of five children in Brooklyn on 8 November 1897, the daughter of Grace Satterlee and John Day. An opening in journalism for John Day took the family to San Francisco in 1903, but the earthquake there, three years later, forced a removal to Chicago. In 1915 the family moved to New York where Dorothy, having finished two years at the University of Illinois, began her own life in journalism as a reporter for the Socialist *Call.*

For the next five years she dabbled in radical causes, moving from one cheap flat to another, mostly in the lower New York area. In 1919 she left a hospital nurse's training program to live with a flamboyant journalist, Lionel Moise. The affair ended with her having an abortion, a circumstance that filled her with such grief that she was brought to the brink of suicide. Later, living in a fisherman's shack on Staten Island as the common-law wife of Forster Batterham, she bore a daughter, Tamar Therese. Out of gratitude for her daughter and a mystical rapture she felt in living on such close terms with nature, she turned to God and was subsequently baptized a Catholic. In 1932 she met the French itinerant philosopher, Peter Maurin, and after some months of tutelage she acquired from him the idea of "the correlation of the spiritual with the material." This was the beginning point of her vision of social recreation.

Her personality was remarkably forceful and engaging, but she could be given to moments of authoritarian harshness. After a series of retreats during World War II, the unremitting struggle of her life was to grow in sanctity. In her later years the impression she gave was of one who had achieved a rare level of holiness. She died on 29 November 1980 and was buried at Jamestown, Long Island, not far from the site of her conversion.

BIBLIOGRAPHY

Dorothy Day wrote five books, all of which, from various perspectives, are autobiographical. The best and most comprehensive is *The Long Loneliness* (New York, 1952). A full-length biography is my *Dorothy Day* (New York, 1982), based on personal acquaintance with Day and for which I had access to all of her personal manuscript materials. An excellent edition of Day's writings is Robert Ellsberg's *By Little and Little: The Selected Writings of Dorothy Day* (New York, 1983).

William D. Miller

DAYANANDA SARASVATI (1824–1883), leading Hindu reformer and founder of the Ārya Samāj, known by the westernized form of his religious name, Dayānanda Sarasvatī. What is known of Dayananda's early years comes from two autobiographical statements made after he founded the Ārya Samāj in 1875. Although he refused to reveal his family and personal names or place of birth in order to preserve his freedom as a *saṃnyāsin* ("renunciant"), these statements allow a reconstruction of his life before he became a public figure.

Dayananda claimed to have spent his childhood in a small town—from his description, most likely Tankara—in the princely state of Morvi in northern Kathiawar, now in Gujarat's Rajkot District. His father was a high-caste brahman landowner and revenue collector and a devout worshiper of Śiva. Dayananda received Vedic initiation at eight and began to study Sanskrit and the Vedas. Although his father preferred that he become a devotee of Śiva, an experience in the local Śiva temple undermined Dayananda's faith that the temple icon was God, and turned him away from Śaiva ritual practice involving images. The deaths of a sister and a beloved uncle a few years later made him realize the instability of worldly life, and when, around 1845, he learned that his family had secretly arranged his marriage, he fled to become a homeless wanderer.

The young mendicant studied the monistic philosophy of the Upaniṣads with several teachers before being initiated into an order of *saṃnyāsin*s as Dayananda Sarasvati in 1847. He lived as an itinerant yogin for the next thirteen years, but in 1860 he settled in Mathura to study with the Sanskrit grammarian Vrijānanda (1779–1868). Vrijānanda, whom Dayananda accepted as his guru, aided Dayananda in perfecting his Sanskrit and also convinced him that the only truthful texts were those composed by the *ṛṣis* ("seers") before the *Mahābhārata,* since, he taught, all later works contained false sectarian doctrines. Dayananda committed himself to spreading this message when he left his guru in 1863, though it took him most of his life to decide which individual texts were true and which were false.

Between 1863 and 1873, Dayananda spent most of his time in small towns along the Ganges River in what is now western Uttar Pradesh meeting representatives of various Hindu communities and debating sectarian pandits. These experiences confirmed his early doubts about image worship and led him to reject all of the Hindu sectarian traditions—not only Vaiṣṇavism, to which he had an early aversion, but eventually even worship of the formless Śiva. In place of sectarianism and the related religious and caste restrictions, he argued with growing conviction for a united Hinduism based on the monotheism and morality of the Vedas.

Throughout this period Dayananda continued to dress as a yogin in loincloth and ashes and debated only in Sanskrit; thus his message was restricted mainly to those orthodox upper-caste Hindus who were most solidly opposed to his views. Early in 1873, however, he spent four months in Calcutta as the guest of the Brāhmo Samāj leader Debendranath Tagore, met the great Brāhmo spokesman Keshab Chandra Sen, and discussed religious issues with these and other westernized Hindu intellectuals. Dayananda saw firsthand the influence of the Brāhmo organization, learned the value of educational programs, public lectures, and publications in effecting change, and accepted from Sen some valuable advice to improve his own reception: abandon the loincloth and the elitist Sanskrit in favor of street clothes and Hindi.

Dayananda left Calcutta with an unchanged message but a broader perspective and a new style, lecturing and writing in Hindi and seeking a receptive audience for his message. He found the first such audience in Bombay, where he founded the Ārya Samāj ("society of honorable ones") on 10 April 1875. His major breakthrough, however, came two years later in the Punjab, where a rising class of merchants and professionals was seeking a defense of Hinduism against Christian missionary activity. A chapter of the Ārya Samāj was founded in Lahore in 1877, and this soon became the headquarters for a rapidly expanding movement in the Punjab and western Uttar Pradesh.

Dayananda left control of the Ārya Samāj in the hands of local chapters and spent his last years perfecting his message. He completed the revision of his major doctrinal statement, *Satyārth prakāś,* shortly before his death on 30 October 1883. With final conviction, he declared that the Vedic hymns revealed to the *ṛṣis* were the sole authority for truth, and he reaffirmed his faith in the one eternal God whose revelation thus made salvation possible for all the world.

[*See also* Ārya Samāj.]

BIBLIOGRAPHY

Dayananda's longest autobiographical statement appeared in *The Theosophist* in three installments in 1879–1880. This statement has been supplemented by an excerpt from one of his lectures in Poona in 1875 and published with explanatory notes, a doctrinal statement, and a chronology of his life in *Autobiography of Swami Dayanand Saraswati,* edited by K. C. Yadav (New Delhi, 1976). The best scholarly study of Dayananda's life and thought is J. T. F. Jordens's *Dayānanda Sarasvatī, His Life and Ideas* (Delhi, 1978). A more focused analysis of the central element in Dayananda's belief system is provided by Arvind Sharma's "Svami Dayananda Sarasvati and Vedic Authority," in *Religion in Modern India,* edited by Robert D. Baird (New Delhi, 1981), pp. 179–196. The standard account of Dayananda's life by one of his followers is Har Bilas Sarda's *Life of Dayanand Saraswati, World Leader,* 2d ed. (Ajmer, 1968).

THOMAS J. HOPKINS

DAY OF ATONEMENT. *See* Ro'sh ha-Shanah and Yom Kippur.

DAZHBOG was the pre-Christian sun god of the East and South Slavs. The name *Dazhbog* (Old Russian, *Dazh'bog"*) is first mentioned in the Kievan pantheon, listed in the Russian *Primary Chronicle* (c. 1111 CE). His connection with the sun is clearly stated in the *Malalas Chronicle* of 1114: "Tsar Sun is the son of Svarog, and his name is Dazhbog." (Svarog, the creator of the sun, is identified in Greek translation with the smith Hephaistos. Like his Lithuanian counterpart, the heavenly smith Kalvelis, whose achievement is described in the *Volynian Chronicle* of 1252, Svarog probably hammered the sun into shape and placed it in the sky. For the chroniclers, he was identical with Helios.) The importance of this god is attested in the thirteenth-century Old Russian epic *Slovo o polku Igoreve,* where the phrase "grandchildren of Dazhbog" is used to refer to the Russian people.

Dazhbog seems to have been one of the various manifestations of the Indo-European god of the "shining sky" or "heavenly light." In the Kievan pantheon his name appears next to that of Khors, another sun deity (cf. Persian *khursīd,* "sun"), and he was identified with the Greek god Apollo by early Russian translators. Dazhbog is possibly an analogue of the northwestern Slavic deity Svarozhich (Svarožiči, Zuariscici; "son of

Svarog"), who was worshiped in the temple at Radigast (Rethra), near Feldberg, in present-day northern Germany. There, as noted in 1014 by Thietmar, bishop of Merseburg, were a number of carved idols dressed in armor and helmets, each dedicated to some aspect of the god. The most important one was that of Svarozhich.

In Roman Jakobson's view, Dazhbog, like the Vedic Bhaga, is "the giver of wealth," and the name of Dazhbog's immediate neighbor in the Kievan pantheon, Stribog, means literally—like that of Bhaga's partner Aṃśa—"the apportioner of wealth" (see Jakobson, 1972). The name *Dazhbog* is a compound of *dazh'* (the imperative form of *dati,* "to give") and *bog"* ("god"). Both Slavs and Iranians eliminated the Proto-Indo-European name for the "god of heavenly light," **diēus,* and assigned the general meaning of "god" to a term that originally signified both wealth and its giver, *bog"*. The origin of the name *Dazhbog* may go back to the period of close Slavic-Iranian contacts, not later than the Scythian-Sarmatian period.

In Serbian folk beliefs, Dabog (i.e., Dazhbog) is an adversary of the Christian God: "Dabog is tsar on earth, and the Lord God is in heaven." Dabog is also known as "the silver tsar"; in mining areas as Dajboi, a demon; and as Daba or Dabo, the devil.

BIBLIOGRAPHY

Čajkanović, Veselin. *O srpskom vrhovnom bogu.* Posebna izdanja, Srpska Kraljevska Akademija, vol. 132. Belgrade, 1941.

Dickenmann, E. "Serbokroatisch *Dabog.*" *Zeitschrift für slavische Philologie* (Leipzig) 20 (1950): 323–346.

Jagić, V. "Mythologische Skizzen: 2, Daždbog, Dažbog-Dabog." *Archiv für slavische Philologie* (Leipzig) 5 (1881): 1–14.

Jakobson, Roman. "Slavic Mythology." In *Funk and Wagnalls Standard Dictionary of Folklore, Mythology, and Legend* (1949–1950), edited by Maria Leach, vol. 2, 1025–1028. Reprint, 2 vols. in 1, New York, 1972.

MARIJA GIMBUTAS

DEA DIA was a Roman agricultural divinity. The name is an emphatic doublet, meaning literally "the deity goddess." Roman cult encompassed a wide variety of divine entities, each with a narrowly circumscribed but essential function in the agricultural life of the community. Thus the godhead Semo functioned in the sphere of sowing and had a counterpart in deities such as Seia, Segetia, and Tutilina, who presided over aspects of the growing cycle. Dea Dia performed her divine function between the periods of sowing and harvesting and was thus the power that brought the crop from germination to maturation. This is evident in both the date and the ritual of her festival. Her feast was always held in May, about a month before the beginning of harvest in central Italy. Its exact date was announced in January, after the season of sowing. The ritual at her festival employed green ears from the current crop together with dried ears of grain from the previous year's crop.

Dea Dia's worship was in the hands of a priesthood of twelve, the Fratres Arvales (Arval Brothers), and she possessed a shrine in a grove outside Rome at the fifth milestone on the Via Campana. The diety, her cult, and her priesthood go back very early in Roman history but underwent a major renovation by Augustus (31 BCE–14 CE). In its new form the priesthood consisted of twelve members chosen by cooptation from the most distinguished families. The reigning emperor was always a member. The reorganization was one element in Augustus's policy of directing enthusiasm for his person and policies into traditional religious channels. Under the empire the Fratres Arvales offered sacrifices not only to Dea Dia but to a wide variety of divinities to secure the health and prosperity of the emperor and his family. Records of these dedications and sacrifices were inscribed on marble, and numerous fragments have been preserved. These records, extending from 21 BCE to 241 CE, provide a source of major importance for traditional Roman religion in the imperial age. The cult and its priesthood are documented as late as 304 CE.

[*See also* Arval Brothers.]

BIBLIOGRAPHY

The records of the Fratres Arvales are available in two Latin editions: *Acta Fratrum Arvalium,* edited by Wilhelm Henzen (Berlin, 1874), and *Acta Fratrum Arvalium,* edited by Aelius Pasoli (Bologna, 1950). Some of the records can be found in translation in Frederick C. Grant's *Ancient Roman Religion* (New York, 1957), pp. 233–238, and in *Roman Civilization,* vol. 2, edited by Naphtali Lewis and Meyer Reinhold (New York, 1955), pp. 254–257. A survey with bibliography is offered by Eckart Olshausen in "Über die römischen Ackerbrüder: Geschichte eines Kultes," in *Aufstieg und Niedergang der römischen Welt,* vol. 2.16.7 (Berlin and New York, 1978), pp. 820–832. A more detailed study of the problems posed by the character and cult of Dea Dia is offered by Ileana Chirassi in her article "Dea Dia e Fratres Arvales," *Studi e materiali di storia delle religioni* 39 (1968): 191–291.

J. RUFUS FEARS

DEAD SEA SCROLLS. The manuscripts unearthed between 1947 and 1956 in the Judean desert, in caves along the coast of the Dead Sea, have come to be known collectively as the Dead Sea Scrolls. The main body of materials comes from Qumran, near the northern end of the Dead Sea, 8.5 miles (13.7 km) south of Jericho. Other texts, including the Masada scrolls and the Bar Kokhba texts, are occasionally also referred to as Dead Sea Scrolls, but this article will pertain only to the Qumran scrolls themselves. These scrolls constituted the library of a sect of Jews in the Greco-Roman period that has been identified by most scholars as the Essenes.

Discovery. In the second half of the nineteenth century, Hebrew manuscripts discovered in the *genizah* ("storehouse") of the Ben Ezra synagogue in Cairo began circulating in Europe. Much of this collection, known as the Cairo Genizah, was acquired for the University of Cambridge by Solomon Schechter in 1896. Among these texts was a strange composition, known as the *Zadokite Fragments* or the *Damascus Document,* that outlined the life and teachings of a Jewish sect. Eventually, this same text was found at Qumran.

There, in 1947, a young bedouin entered what is now designated Cave I and found a group of pottery jars containing leather scrolls wrapped in linen cloths. These scrolls, the first finds, were sold to Athanasius Samuel, the Syrian metropolitan of Jerusalem, and to Eliezer Sukenik, a professor representing the Hebrew University of Jerusalem. The scrolls in the possession of the Syrian metropolitan were purchased in 1954 by Yigael Yadin, Sukenik's son, on behalf of the Hebrew University.

Scientific exploration of the cave in 1949 by G. Lankester Harding and Roland de Vaux uncovered additional fragments and many broken jars. From 1951 on, a steady stream of manuscripts has been provided by bedouin and archaeologists. Some of these manuscripts are held in the Archaeological (Rockefeller) Museum in East Jerusalem. Many are displayed in the beautiful Shrine of the Book, a part of the Israel Museum built especially for the display and preservation of the scrolls.

Dating. From the beginning, the dating of the scrolls was a matter of controversy. Some saw the new texts as documents of the medieval Jewish sect of the Karaites. Others believed they dated from the Roman period, and some even thought they were of Christian origin.

Of primary importance for dating the scrolls was the excavation of the building complex immediately below the caves on the plateau. In the view of most scholars, those who lived in the complex copied many of the scrolls and were part of the sect described in some of the texts. Numismatic evidence has shown that the complex flourished from circa 135 BCE to 68 CE, interrupted only by the earthquake of 31 BCE.

Similar conclusions resulted from carbon dating of the cloth wrappings in which the scrolls were found. Study of the paleography (the form of the Hebrew letters) in which the texts are written has also supported a similar dating. It is certain, then, that the scrolls once constituted the library of a sect that occupied the Qumran area from after the Maccabean Revolt of 166–164 BCE until the great revolt against Rome of 66–74 CE.

The Scrolls. The many scrolls that were found in the Qumran caves can be divided into three main categories: biblical manuscripts, apocryphal compositions, and sectarian documents.

Fragments of every book of the Hebrew scriptures have been unearthed at Qumran, with the sole exception of the *Book of Esther.* Among the more important biblical scrolls are the two *Isaiah* scrolls (one is complete) and the fragments of *Leviticus* and *Samuel* (dated to the third century BCE). William Albright and Frank Moore Cross have detected three recensional traditions among the scrolls at Qumran: (1) a Palestinian, from which the Samaritan Pentateuch is ultimately descended, (2) an Alexandrian, upon which the Septuagint (the Greek translation of the Bible) is based, and (3) a Babylonian, which serves as the basis of the Masoretic (received and authoritative) text fixed by rabbis in the late first century CE.

The apocryphal and pseudepigraphical writings were known until recently only in Greek and Latin translation. The Cairo Genizah yielded Hebrew and Aramaic fragments of medieval recensions. Among the important fragments found at Qumran are *Ben Sira, Jubilees,* Aramaic fragments of the *Enoch* books, the *Testament of Levi,* and additions to *Daniel.*

By far the most interesting materials are the writings of the sect that inhabited Qumran. The *pesharim* are the sect's biblical commentaries, which seek to show how the present premessianic age is the fulfillment of the words of the prophets. Prominent among these texts are the *pesharim* to *Habakkuk, Nahum,* and *Psalms,* and the *florilegia,* which are chains of verses and comments. The commentaries allow us a glimpse of the sect's self-image and allude to actual historical figures who lived at the time during which Qumran was occupied.

The *Damascus Document* describes the history of the sect and its attitudes toward its enemies. It also contains a series of legal tracts dealing with various topics of Jewish law, including the Sabbath, courts and testimony, relations with non-Jews, oaths and vows, and so forth.

Admission into the sect, the conduct of daily affairs, and the penalties for violating the sect's laws are the subjects of the *Manual of Discipline.* This text makes clear the role of ritual purity and impurity in defining membership in the sect as well as detailing the annual mustering ceremony of covenant renewal. Appended to it are the *Rule of the Community,* which describes the community in the End of Days, and the *Rule of Benedictions,* which contains praises of the sect's leaders.

The *Thanksgiving Scroll* contains a series of poems describing the "anthropology" and theology of the sect. Many scholars see its author as the "teacher of righteousness" (or "correct teacher") who led the sect in its early years.

The *Scroll of the War of the Sons of Light against the Sons of Darkness* describes the eschatological war. The sect and the angels fight against the nations and the evildoers of Israel for forty years, thereby ushering in the End of Days. This scroll is notable for its information on the art of warfare in the Greco-Roman period.

Unique is the *Temple Scroll,* which is an idealized description of the Jerusalem Temple, its cult, and other aspects of Jewish law. This text is the subject of debate as to whether it is actually a sectarian scroll or simply part of the sect's library.

Numerous smaller texts throw light on mysticism, prayer, and sectarian law. As of 1986, many of these texts have not yet been published or are still awaiting thorough study.

The Sect and Its Beliefs. The Qumran sect saw itself as the sole possessor of the correct interpretation of the Bible, the exegesis of which was the key to the discovery of God's word in the present premessianic age. Like other apocalyptic movements of the day, the sect believed that the messianic era was about to dawn. Only those who had lived according to sectarian ways and had been predestined to share in the End of Days would fight the final battle against the forces of evil. In order to prepare for the coming age, the sect lived a life of purity and holiness at its center on the shore of the Dead Sea.

According to the sect's own description of its history, it had come into existence when its earliest members, apparently Zadokite priests, decided to separate themselves from the corrupt Judaism of Jerusalem and left to set up a refuge at Qumran. The sect was organized along rigid lines. There was an elaborate initiation procedure, lasting several years, during which members were progressively received at the ritually pure banquets of the sect. All legal decisions of the sect were made by the sectarian assembly, and its own system of courts dealt with violations and punishments of the sectarian interpretation of Jewish law. New laws were derived by ongoing inspired biblical exegesis.

Annual covenant renewal ceremonies took place in which the members of the sect were called to assemble in order of their status. Similar mustering was part of the sect's preparations for the eschatological battle. The Qumran sect believed that in the End of Days, two messiahs would appear, a Davidic messiah who was to be the temporal authority, and a priestly messiah of Aaron, who was to take charge of the restored sacrificial cult. They were both to preside over a great messianic banquet. Meals of the sect were periodically eaten in ritual purity in imitation of this final banquet.

The sect maintained a strictly solar calendar rather than the solar-lunar calendar utilized by the rest of the Jewish community. The sect was further distinguished by its principle of communal use of property. Although private ownership was maintained, members of the sect could freely use each other's possessions. The scrolls themselves refute the widespread view that the sectarians of Qumran were celibate.

Identification of the Sect. Dominant scholarly opinion has identified the Dead Sea sect as the Essenes described in the writings of Philo Judaeus and Josephus Flavius of the first century CE. Indeed, there are many similarities between this group and the sect described by the scrolls.

In many details, however, the Dead Sea Scrolls do not agree with these accounts of the Essenes. Josephus himself calls the Essenes a "philosophy" and makes clear that it was composed of various groups. If, indeed, the Dead Sea community was an Essene sect, perhaps it represented an offshoot of the Essenes who themselves differ in many ways from those described by Philo and Josephus. A further difficulty stems from the fact that the word *essene* never appears in the scrolls and that it is of unknown meaning and etymology. [*See* Essenes.]

Scholars have noted as well the points of similarity between the Qumran writings and aspects of the Pharisaic tradition. Louis Ginzberg has called the authors of these texts "an unknown Jewish sect." Indeed, many groups and sects dotted the spiritual and political landscape of Judaea in the Greco-Roman period, and the Dead Sea sect, previously unknown from any other sources, may have been one of these groups.

Qumran and the History of Religions. The Dead Sea Scrolls have illuminated the background of the emergence of rabbinic Judaism and of Christianity. In the years leading up to the great revolt of 66–74, Judaism was moving toward a consensus that would carry it through the Middle Ages. As Talmudic Judaism emerged from the ashes of the destruction, other groups, like the Dead Sea sect, fell by the wayside. Nonetheless, the scrolls allow us an important glimpse into the nature of Jewish law, theology, and eschatology as understood by one of these sects.

The scrolls show us that Jews in the Second Temple period were engaged in a vibrant religious life based on study of the scriptures, interpretation of Jewish law, practice of ritual purity, and messianic aspirations.

Some Jewish practices known from later texts, such as phylacteries, thrice-daily prayer, and blessings before and after meals, were regularly practiced. Rituals were seen as a preparation for the soon-to-dawn End of Days that would usher in a life of purity and perfection.

The scrolls, therefore, have shown us that Jewish life and law were already considerably developed in this period. Although we cannot see a linear development between the Judaism of the scrolls and that of the later rabbis, since the rabbis were heirs to the tradition of the Pharisees, we can still derive great advantage from the scrolls in our understanding of the early history of Jewish law. Here, for the first time, we have a fully developed system of postbiblical law and ritual.

The Dead Sea sect, and, for that matter, all the known Jewish sects from the Second Temple period, were strict adherents to Jewish law as they interpreted it. At the same time, with their emphasis on the apocalyptic visions of the prophets, the sects provide us an understanding of the emerging Christian claims of messiahship for Jesus. Only against the background of the Dead Sea Scrolls can the worldview of early Christianity be understood.

The contribution of the biblical scrolls to our understanding of the history of the biblical text and versions is profound. We now know of the fluid state of the Hebrew scriptures in the last years of the Second Temple. With the help of the biblical scrolls from Masada and the Bar Kokhba caves, we can now understand the role of local texts, the sources of the different ancient translations of the Bible, and the process of standardization of the scriptures that resulted in the Masoretic text.

In the years spanned by the Dead Sea Scrolls, the text of the Hebrew scriptures was coming into its final form, the background of the New Testament was in evidence, and the great traditions that would constitute rabbinic Judaism were taking shape. The scrolls have opened a small window on these developments the analysis of which will reshape our knowledge of this crucial, formative period in the history of Western religion.

BIBLIOGRAPHY

An excellent introduction is Yigael Yadin's *The Message of the Scrolls* (New York, 1957). The archaeological aspect is discussed thoroughly in Roland de Vaux's Schweich Lectures of 1959, *Archaeology and the Dead Sea Scrolls* (London, 1973). Important scholarly studies are Frank Moore Cross's *The Ancient Library of Qumrān and Modern Biblical Studies*, rev. ed. (Garden City, N.Y., 1961), and Géza Vermès's *The Dead Sea Scrolls: Qumran in Perspective* (Philadelphia, 1981). The theology of the Qumran sect is studied in Helmer Ringgren's *The Faith of Qumran*, translated by Emilie T. Sander (Philadelphia, 1963). On the relationship to Christianity, see Matthew Black's *The Scrolls and Christian Origins* (London, 1961) and William S. LaSor's *The Dead Sea Scrolls and the New Testament* (Grand Rapids, Mich., 1972). Two studies of the importance of the scrolls for the history of Jewish law are my books *The Halakhah at Qumran* (Leiden, 1975) and *Sectarian Law in the Dead Sea Scrolls* (Chico, Calif., 1983).

LAWRENCE H. SCHIFFMAN

DEATH. The statement that there is no life without death and no death without life is as banal as it is true. Its truth is self-evident; its banality arises from the fact that life and death can be—and, as a rule, are—defined as mutually exclusive states of being, which turns the statement into a truism. The widespread belief in the continuity of life after death does not diminish the validity of this definition, because life after death is conceived of as a mode of being essentially distinct from life on earth, the life between birth and death. [*See* Afterlife.] This is true also when life after death is thought of as a replica of life on earth, for the replica can never be exact.

Given the inevitability and definitiveness of death, it is not surprising that in all cultures, so far as our knowledge goes, the idea of dying has captured the thoughts and imagination of human beings. Indeed, during certain periods, such as the European Middle Ages, as demonstrated not only by the church but also by art and literature, this is true to a high degree. In a relatively small number of religions—among which are three of the most important in world history: Buddhism, Christianity, and Islam—preoccupation with death has led to the conviction that life after death (that is, eternal life, which no longer is subject to the restrictions of time and even is the real life as compared with human existence on earth) must be considered as far greater in importance than life on earth. This tradition still colors to a high degree the mental outlook and moral judgment of countless millions in modern times. Yet from the point of view of history and anthropology the regarding of death as more important than life is far from common. The majority of religions firmly accent life here and now.

It is true that in a few cultures, the Indian ones among them, both life and death can be relativized. Even then, however, life and death are considered different modes of being. We must keep in mind also that immortality, eternal life in the strict sense of Christianity and Islam, is not a common concept. A great many cultures believe that life after death, too, may come to an end.

In a great number of cultures there seems to exist a connection, if not direct then, in any case, indirect, between the first coming of death into this world and the origin of both the countless imperfections that are part of the world of man and, more especially, evil. In her thorough study entitled *The Origins of Evil in Hindu Mythology,* Wendy Doniger O'Flaherty writes, "The Hindu mythologies of evil and of death are closely related." On the same page she remarks further, "The myths of death and evil share the same recurrent motifs and often offer the same solutions to the different problems posed" (O'Flaherty, 1976, p. 212).

Put differently, the original perfect order of the entire cosmos, as perceived by a great number of cultures, excludes disorder and death, and death is thought to result once the order has been broken down or invalidated. As has been noted by many scholars, the coming of evil and of death is often closely connected with the appearance of sexual desire and hunger. In any case, death seems to be something whose existence requires explanation. According to the general belief, and practically all cultures conceive it in this manner, the appearance of death is the worst and most basic break in the original normality of human life as it was meant to be in principle.

Although many individuals die in peace, willing resignation in the face of death is rare as a motif in mythology. A myth from the Ivory Coast tells of the time when death was unknown and of its first coming. When Death approached, everyone fled into the bush except one old man who could no longer walk, and he asked his young grandson to make him a mat to lie upon. When Death came the child was still busy working on the mat, and so they both died.

The Origin of Death. In 1886 Andrew Lang presented a classification of myths about the origin of death, and in 1917 Franz Boas published an article on these myths among the North American Indians. Hermann Baumann in 1936 and Hans Abrahamsson in 1951 presented classifications of the African myths about the origin of death, including maps that show the geographic division of the several motifs found on this continent. Because such classifications according to specific motifs result in a long list, even when just a single continent is treated, I have opted for a more systematic classification. Although death can be personified as the god of death, as is the case in a great number of religions, for purposes of classification this makes little or no difference. As can be expected, a number of myths combine the characteristics of more than one motif, and where examples of this occur I have classified them according to what I consider to be the main motif.

An analysis of the reasons given for the coming of death into this world, according to the classification system that I have adopted, shows a number of types:

1. Death is considered the natural destination of man, or, at least, it is considered to be in accordance with the primordial will of the gods and as such is to be accepted, if not without demur then without the necessity of further explanation. Death forms, as it were, an indispensable part of the divine administration (or the divine economy) and is simply acknowledged as such.
2. The death of a god or some other mythic being has given rise to the existence of death in the human world as well, and so it is not in any respect due to the behavior of man.
3. Human death is the result of conflict among divine beings.
4. Death is the result of man being cheated by a god or some other mythic being, or of the carelessness or stupidity of such a being.
5. Death is the result of some human shortcoming, sometimes a rather futile one in our eyes. It remains somewhat doubtful, however, whether in strict terms this impression of futility is justified and to what degree it is due to imperfect understanding, insufficient knowledge of the culture in question, or incomplete reporting by our sources.
6. Death is the result of a wrong judgment or a wrong choice made by man.
7. Death results from some kind of guilt, usually, but not exclusively, human guilt. Yet the question of guilt can be difficult to decide. In certain cases there is only a sin of omission, which can also be seen as a simple case of human shortcoming, of being at fault, at most a venial sin. There may be—to show the difficulty—more than one argument given for the origin of death, such as, for example, curiosity and disobedience. Curiosity in itself is a minor shortcoming, if it is one at all, but when it leads to disobedience it becomes decisively important; according to the various myths, disobedience is the actual sin that deserves death. In my discussion of this reason for the coming of death, I shall mainly treat sins of commission. Apart, then, from a number of cases in which the question of whether we can actually speak of human guilt must be left as a matter of opinion, the three main reasons given in which this point is clear are disobedience, sexual offense, and killing.
8. Man dies because he himself has desired death.

A few myths pose such specialized and detailed problems that they cannot be treated satisfactorily within the scope of a general introductory article. This holds, for example, for some myths current in South Asian religious traditions.

Death as a natural or god-willed designation. While modern scientific understanding teaches us that individual organic life is finite not only by necessity but even in essence, all the possibilities envisaged by religious thinking involve the belief that death is an interruption of natural life, that it is, in fact, unnatural. The unwillingness of many nonliterate peoples to accept the possibility of a "natural" death shows this clearly. Originally, so the myth frequently runs, man was destined for a paradisiacal existence until some untoward occurrence changed that destiny.

Similar is the conviction that death is the ordained and god-willed destiny of man, as is the case in a number of religions. Death as a rule remains the enemy of man. The Lugbara of East Africa, although they believe that practically all matters of importance are in the hands of the ancestors, consider death an act of God. In various parts of Indonesia we find the belief that human beings are somehow identical with the cattle of the gods. Whenever the gods in heaven slaughter an animal, a man on earth dies.

The Luba of the southeastern Kongo region tell a mythical story of an old woman who had lost all her loved ones and remained alone on earth. She could not understand why this had to happen to her and so left her home in order to find God and ask him the reason for her sad fate. She had a long and weary journey, but in the end she found God and was able to pose her question. She had to be content, however, with the same answer Job received when he complained to God that he did not understand why he, the example of faith and piety, should be so sorely plagued: God then answered that he is mighty and cannot be called to account by man. So, too, the old Luba woman had to console herself with the knowledge that her fate had been willed by God.

In Greece also we find this resignation in the face of death. In a famous passage of the *Iliad* (5.146–149), Homer compares the generations of humans to the leaves on a tree: when the season of winter storms begins, leaves fall from the tree, and, in the same way, one human generation must make way for the next.

The classic, often-quoted example of this theme occurs in the Babylonian *Epic of Gilgamesh*, where, after the sudden death of his friend Enkidu, Gilgamesh roamed the world in search of the secret of eternal life but, in the end, without success. Gilgamesh did discover the herb of life, whose name means "as an old man, man becomes young again." Yet even though after countless difficulties and dangers he succeeded in acquiring the small plant, which grew on the far side of the waters of death and made man young again, he lost it to a snake while returning to the world of the living. The snake stole the herb while Gilgamesh slept, and since then snakes have no longer died but have simply changed their skin. This motif of the snake is found in a number of variations in many cultures all over the world.

Gilgamesh was obliged to accept the conviction of man's mortality and to abide by the will of the gods, who had decided on that mortality. The Gilgamesh epic phrases it thus:

> Gilgamesh, where are you roaming?
> You shall not find the life you search after!
> When the gods created mankind,
> they destined death for man,
> but life they kept firmly in their own hands.

Although ancient Egypt knew no myth to explain the origin of death, the texts make it clear that death was seen as a negative element, an abnormality that unfortunately is inherent in creation. One of the Pyramid Texts states clearly that no death existed in primeval time, before the gods, the world, and mankind were made. The Egyptians were consequent: the created gods—who were distinguished from the primeval ones, the creator-gods themselves—were also mortal, at least ultimately.

A myth from Tahiti tells of the gods Hina and Tefatou and their disagreement over the fate of man. Hina proposed that man should rise again after his death, but Tefatou answered that because the earth and all plants must die, man should share the same destiny. Hina had to be content with the moon, which "dies" and yet rises again.

The concept of death as resulting from the will and power of a god may lead to religious problems. The tribes of Patagonia (South America), now practically extinct, believed that death was the work of the supreme god Waitaunewa, but they did not accept this belief meekly and passively. On the contrary, when one of their loved ones died they not only wailed but also protested: they accused the god of murder and avenged themselves by killing the animals that belonged to him. In this context it must be mentioned that the problems of death and of all suffering in the world are closely connected with theodicy, as is the problem of the origin of evil.

Death as the result of a divine death. There is a concept that man dies because a god or some other mythical being died first, and in this no question of fault or guilt is ascribed to human beings. The German anthropologist Adolf E. Jensen (1963) has given the name *dema* to a class of mythical beings who, by their deeds in a primeval time, originated human life and culture as we know it now; their deeds, however, ended with their own death. Some myths relate that the *dema* were murdered, but others say that they suffered a voluntary death. The life and death of the dema provide the divine paradigm for human experience, for man follows the pattern set by these mythical originators. There is a parallel between divine and human fate: because a god once died, human beings, too, are now subject to death. There are also examples of this theme that are not connected with the concept of *dema* gods. In a myth of the Shuswap Indians of North America, for example, we are told that the son of a heavenly chief died for reasons unknown. His was the first death, but since then all human beings have had to die.

Death as the result of a divine conflict. Human death may also be seen as resulting from a conflict between gods. A myth from the island of Ceram in eastern Indonesia relates an argument between a stone and a banana regarding the way in which man should be created. The stone killed the banana, but on the next day the children of the banana were ready to continue the fight. In the end the stone fell into an abyss and admitted defeat, but with one condition: man would be as the bananas wanted him to be, but he must die just as a banana does.

The Shilluk of the upper Nile have a tradition that explains the origin of death in terms of a quarrel between the god Nyikang and his brother Duwat. In an election for a new king Duwat was chosen and Nyikang passed over. To avenge himself Nyikang stole part of the regalia and departed with his supporters. Duwat went in pursuit of his brother but failed to overtake him. Seeing this, he threw his digging stick after Nyikang and said, "Take this stick to bury your people!" And in this way death came into the world.

A myth from the Musarongo of the lower Kongo region also tells about divine conflict that ended in death for mankind. The Dogon of Mali tell of a quarrel between the gods in which the penis of the god Ogo was crushed. This led first to the death of the god himself and then to the death of man as well. The Blackfeet Indians of North America tell about a time when an Old Man and an Old Woman disagreed on every occasion. The man wanted the best for human beings and intended to give them life, but the woman had other plans and, as always, had the last word. A well-known variation of this pattern is found in the myths in which the quarreling beings are twins.

Another variant of the quarrel between gods is the conflict between the Sun (or some other divinity) and the Moon concerning human life. In these stories Sun and Moon are, of course, mythical beings. A number of these myths can be found in Africa, each one connecting the destiny of man with that of the Moon. This type of myth can also be found all over the world, however, because speculation about the connection of the moon's phases with human life and death is nearly universal. [*See* Moon.] A myth from the Fiji Islands in the South Pacific acquaints us with the story of two gods, Moon and Rat, who quarrel about the fate of man. Moon wants man to grow old, disappear, and then be young again, after his own example, but Rat insists that men should die as rats do, and his voice prevails.

A myth from the Caroline Islands in the western Pacific states that in the beginning the life and death of man ran parallel to the phases of the moon, but then an evil spirit succeeded somehow in contriving that man should die and never wake up again. The Numfor of Sarera Bay (formerly Geelvink Bay) in Indonesia relate a myth that very much resembles the one from the Carolines. This myth recounts how a werewolf succeeded in cheating man and thus seducing him into disobedience, and in this manner men lost their power of rejuvenation.

Death as the result of a god's cheating or carelessness. Death sometimes is attributed to divine cheating. Here, of course, the well-known mythical figure of the trickster looms up. According to the myths of the Indian tribes of central California, Sedit, the trickster, personified by the coyote, brings death into the world through his intrigues. Hence the Maidu tell how he destroyed the hill on top of which was a lake with the water of life, which could have prevented mankind from dying. Numerous North American Indian myths describe Coyote or another trickster as the bringer of death. The trickster combines creative and destructive characteristics. As the divine figure who introduces disorder and chaos into an ordered world, he, like the creator himself, is an indispensable part of the cosmos, which is conceived of as a totality in which mutually opposed elements are united. [*See* Tricksters.]

In West Indian Voodoo religion Gèdè is the god of death as well as the trickster. Maya Deren, in her fascinating book on Voodoo, *Divine Horsemen: The Living Gods of Haiti* (London, 1953), calls Gèdè "corpse and phallus; king and clown." He is the lord of darkness and the lord of crossroads. He reminds every man that death will give way to no one, not even to the richest, most powerful, and most illustrious men. The combination of the trickster and the god of death is apt, for the cruelest joke of the gods is that they have ordered creation in such a way that not only the possibility but even the inevitability of death is built into it, so that every human being must eventually die.

In another myth of the Dogon we are told that the first human beings, the Andumbulu, did not die but instead were transformed into snakes. One day the god Amma offered to sell a cow to a young woman. The woman asked the price, and the god told her that the price was death. The woman bought the cow and shortly afterward her husband died. She remonstrated with the god, but he reminded her of the price that he had asked and she had agreed to pay. Amma refused to cancel the agreement and take the cow back, and so death came into this world.

In other cases we find reports that death resulted from the carelessness or stupidity of some mythical being. This type of myth is called "the message that failed" (Baumann, 1936). The messenger is often a snake or a lizard, both animals that change their skin. The basic idea here is the belief that the supreme deity intended to give man eternal life but some subordinate god inadvertently spoiled his intentions. The Wute of East Africa explain the origin of death in the following manner: God sent a chameleon to man with the message that mankind would live eternally. The chameleon, however, was in no hurry. First it stopped and bought itself a splendid headdress, and then it ambled on at its leisure. After two weeks it finally arrived at its destination. In the meantime the snake had learned of the gift that was meant for man and had gone to man and pretended that it had been sent to convey the message that mankind would be subject to death without resurrection. As punishment both the snake and the chameleon were cursed by God: now men will readily kill them. The message itself, however, could not be reversed, and man was fated to die.

A myth of the Ashanti of Ghana tells of the paradise in which man first lived. This happy state came to an end when a few women objected to God's presence while they ground corn for food. God then retired from the world and went to heaven. He remained benevolently inclined toward man, however, and sent a goat to tell him that he need not fear death, because it meant only that he would live on in heaven. The goat was in no hurry and took time off to have a good meal. God saw this, and so he sent a sheep with the same message, but the sheep instead told man that death would mean the definitive end of existence. Shortly thereafter the first death occurred, and God instructed mankind on how to bury the dead. In a myth of the San of southern Africa the messenger is a hare, which many cultures consider a lunar animal.

A myth from the island of New Britain in the western Pacific belongs to a type more frequently found in Melanesia. It ascribes the coming of death to the stupidity of a messenger, rightly called To Purgo ("stupid one"), who is the wise and benevolent god's twin. Without any malice To Purgo confuses his message and pronounces death for man and everlasting life for the snake. In a myth of the Annamese of Southeast Asia the messenger's mistake is not involuntary: he changes the message because the snakes threaten him.

A myth from central Africa provides a typical example of how man's "deathlessness" was lost because of levity and lack of care. God gave a toad an earthen jar and instructed the creature to be very careful of it because it contained death. The toad met a frog hopping cheerfully along and the frog wanted to take over the job of carrying the jar. The toad hesitated but in the end gave in. The frog hopped off happily juggling the jar and then dropped it. The jar broke, and death got out.

Death as the result of human shortcoming. In another category, death may be seen as having its origins in human nature. That is, it is believed to result from a human shortcoming. This shortcoming, however, can hardly qualify as human guilt. A myth from the Solomon Islands (with parallels from other islands of Melanesia) tells that originally both man and snakes changed their skin as they grew old and, thus reborn, became young again and again. But once a woman left her baby in the care of her mother while she went out to work. The old woman played with the child until it fell asleep and then she went out to the river to bathe and change her skin. The baby woke up after the grandmother had returned and so did not recognize her, for she appeared in the shape of a comely young woman. The child then howled and yelled and remained inconsolable. Finally, furious and desperate, the grandmother returned to the river and put on her old skin. But, so she told the child, from then on all human beings would grow old, and only snakes would preserve the capacity of renewing themselves by sloughing off their skin.

In Africa we find a type of myth that explains the coming of death into the world by saying that during the night God proclaimed to all men the news of life without death, but because they slept on without troubling themselves about this divine revelation they missed the proclamation of their own eternal life. This myth presupposes a certain connection between sleep and death. This connection is, of course, widely recognized and remarked on, but only here and there is it related to the problem of the origin of death. The Greeks held the notion that Sleep (Morpheus) and Death (Thanatos) were brothers, and this motif is known elsewhere as well. A myth from the Ekoi of the Cross River region of West Africa tells that once upon a time God asked the people whether they knew what it meant to die, and they all answered in the negative. God told them to gather in the palaver house of the village, and every few hours he put the same question to them, until they were quite overcome by sleep. Then he told them that they had learned what death is, for death and sleep are similar.

Another motif in this category is that which Hans Abrahamsson calls "discord in the first family." The Lotuko of Uganda tell about a family quarrel that led to death as the irrevocable end of human life. Once upon a time a child died, and the mother implored the supreme god to bring her baby to life again. The god granted her request, but the child's father, for reasons that are not clear, was dissatisfied and killed the child; and this second death proved decisive. Then, according to the myth, the supreme god said, "For the future, whenever a Lotuko dies, he must remain dead."

A myth from the Lake Sentani region of Indonesia reports that the first human beings were unable to understand the language that their father used to tell them the secret of eternal life. This man had died but came to life again the next day. He tried to communicate with the snakes and other animals that now are able to shed their skin. These understood him well enough, but once he told the secret he himself forgot it; and so he had to die once more and this time remain dead forever.

One of the most interesting motifs associated with the appearance of death on earth is the notion that death punishes man for having made death into an occasion for pageantry and merriment. The illogic of this idea is avoided in a number of myths by assuming that it was the death of an animal that occasioned such sport. The Bena Kanioka of the middle Kongo region consider the first death the result of a human transgression. It could have remained an isolated occurrence, however, if man had not made the burial an occasion for feasting and merrymaking. To punish man, death was made permanent. A related motif occurs in a myth from upper Burma: in the beginning of time, when death was still unknown, an old man played a practical joke on the sun god by pretending to be dead. The sun god became angry when he discovered this joke and turned the pretended death into a real one, thus inaugurating death. Here again we see that levity in the face of any death is punished by the appearance or persistence of death in the world of man.

Death as the outcome of a wrong choice. Death can be viewed as the outcome of a wrong choice made by human beings themselves. The Holoholo, a subtribe of the Luba, say that God gave man the chance to choose between two nuts, one in each of his hands; one symbolized life and the other, death. Man, or, in this case, woman, chose the wrong hand, and so death became the destiny of all mankind, while the snake, which was also present at this scene, received the gift of unrestricted renewal of life.

A myth of the Toraja of Sulawesi (formerly Celebes) tells another story of a wrong choice. One day God dropped a stone down from heaven onto the earth as a gift for mankind, but man did not know what to do with this unlikely present and, clearly and openly showing a lack of appreciation, rejected it. Shortly afterward God presented man with the banana, and this he welcomed. Man, however, had not understood the implication of this choice, that is, that he had turned down the offer of life without death, the stone's mode of being, and had accepted instead the manner of existence in which death and birth alternate. The banana tree is widely known as a symbol of death and renewal, because its cuttings grow into new trees, and the pruned tree forms new shoots.

The motif that James G. Frazer, in *The Golden Bough* (1890), his classic study in the history of religion, called "the fatal bundle or the fatal box" belongs in this subdivision to some degree; partly, too, it belongs with the stories of death resulting from disobedience. The Ṅgala of the upper Kongo region explain the coming of death in a myth that tells how God offered a man working in the forest two bundles, a large one that contained a number of useful and pretty things such as knives and beads, and a small one that contained everlasting life. The man dared not decide on the spot which bundle to take, and so he went to the village to ask advice. In the meantime a few women came along, and God offered them the same choice. They unpacked the large bundle and found mirrors with which they could admire themselves and cloth from which they could make dresses, and so they chose the large bundle. In this way man failed to qualify for eternal life and was subject to death.

Death as the result of human guilt. As can be expected, a great number of myths cite human guilt as the cause of death. The anthropologist Paul Radin must have been mistaken when he wrote that nowhere except in the Bible has man been held responsible for the origin of death. This guilt, it is true, can be conceived of in a variety of ways. In Africa, among the Yoruba of Nigeria and the Lobi of Burkina Faso, for example, we find myths in which human death follows on general moral decadence.

The Tamanaco, a now-extinct tribe of the Orinoco River region of South America, told a myth of how in the beginning the earth was created by two divine brothers. One of them, Amalivaca, once lived for a time among men. Before he left them to return to the world of the gods, he announced that he would take off his skin, and he instructed them to do the same whenever they wanted to become young again. One woman, however, seemed to doubt the value of this advice. So the god became angry and told her that she would die; and because of her lack of belief in the words of the god, death came into this world. Three variations on the theme of death caused by guilt can be identified.

Disobedience. A common motif is the belief that death was caused by man's disobeying God. There may be subsidiary motivations present, as, for example, curiosity or carelessness, but disobedience remains the primary point.

The best-known example of the coming of death as a punishment for disobedience is, of course, the biblical myth of Adam and Eve in Paradise as told in the *Book of Genesis*. Some deduce from this story that God had originally intended to give Adam and Eve everlasting life, although this is not expressly mentioned.

Genesis 2:16–18 states without any ambiguity: "You may eat from every tree in the garden, but not from the tree of knowledge of good and evil; for on the day that you eat from it, you will certainly die." Eve was tempted by the serpent and ate the forbidden fruit. She found it good and gave some to Adam, who accepted it willingly. God, as could not be otherwise expected, detected their disobedience and cursed all three: the serpent, Eve, and Adam. Strangely enough, however, and here an ambiguous element appears, death is not expressly named in the formulas of cursing that God uses, but is indicated only in symbolic metaphor: "You shall gain your bread by the sweat of your brow until you return to the ground; for from it you were taken. Dust you are, to dust you shall return" (*Gn.* 3:19).

Only after God had made tunics of skin for Adam and Eve to wear did he reflect on the necessity of chasing the first human beings from the Garden of Eden lest they eat from the tree of life as well: "The man has become like one of us, knowing good and evil; what if he now reaches out his hand and takes fruit from the tree of life also, eats it and lives forever?" (*Gn.* 3:28). The inconsistencies, which are rarely absent from myth, make the *Genesis* story rather enigmatic after all. In God's first proclamation the tree of life is not forbidden, although its existence is mentioned. So we must judge that it was a matter of chance that man did not eat from the tree of life, which was not forbidden, before his disobedience regarding the other special tree led to the judgment pronounced in *Genesis* 3:14–19. However, God's pronouncement that man must certainly die on the day that he eats the forbidden fruit of the knowledge of good and evil is shown up as a rather hollow threat. God, in spite of his threatening words, has to take special measures to prevent man from living on in eternity. This short analysis of the creation myth in *Genesis* shows that the connection between human disobedience and the origin of death is at best rather loose and must lead us to doubt whether the best-known example of death's origin as the result of disobedience is really the best one.

Medieval theologians speculated extensively as to exactly which sin led to the Fall, for disobedience as such is not one of the seven mortal sins. Some medieval theologians ascribed the fall of man to pride *(superbia)* or lust *(luxuria)*. In Buddhism, also, lust and death are closely connected. O'Flaherty writes, "Lust and death are combined in the devil" (O'Flaherty, 1976, p. 213).

Among the Carib of Guyana a myth can be found that tells how the creator-god Purá wanted to give eternal life to man, but because man disobeyed the god's instructions on how to attain this goal, all men became subject to death. Among the Lamba of Zambia is a myth that tells how man received a number of small bundles from God. The messengers to whom the bundles were given were forbidden to inspect them: they had to be handed unopened to the "chief on earth." The messengers, overcome by curiosity, failed to obey and opened the bundles, one of which contained death. The Ekoi tell that God commanded man never to kill and eat a white sheep. Man disobeyed God and was punished by the coming of death for all men.

We also find the notion that death is the punishment for premature burial. The Kongo of the lower Kongo region know a myth about how the creator-god Nzambi ordered man not to bury a child who had died because the child would return to life in three days. But the parents did not believe him, and they disobeyed, and so death became irrevocable. This theme recurs in a myth from the Fiji Islands. And the Dogon have a myth that tells how death originated from the learning of a forbidden language.

The motif of the forbidden fruit is not restricted to the Bible. The Efe, a Pygmy group of central Africa, tell that the creator designated the fruit of one tree as forbidden. It happened, however, that a pregnant woman once experienced an irresistible desire to eat the forbidden fruit, and she prevailed upon her husband to pick it for her. The result was that God sent death into the world as punishment for their disobedience. Although this myth slightly resembles the biblical one, it is probably not derived from missionary sources, either Christian or Muslim. Important details of the biblical story are absent: the tree of knowledge, for example, is not mentioned. Various other details differ as well, such as that of the woman's pregnancy. Moreover, numerous versions of this myth can be found in Africa.

Another variant of the theme of disobedience is the Pandora motif, usually called the "box" of Pandora, although the Greek poet Hesiod, who tells this story in his epic *Works and Days* (80–105), speaks of a jar. Pandora received the jar from Zeus, who strictly forbade her to open it. She disobeyed him, and all kinds of misfortune and evils escaped into the world when she removed the lid. The only positive thing in the jar was hope. Although death is not expressly mentioned in this case, the myth of Pandora clearly belongs to the type called "death in a bundle or box."

Sexual offense. The guilt that brings about death may be a sexual offense committed by man, but this transgression may also be projected back into the world of the gods. Thus, according to a myth of the Dogon, death came into existence as a result of primordial incest committed by the god Ogo.

In Africa we find a myth that tells about God forbidding the first human beings to copulate. When they disobeyed this injunction, death came into existence. A myth from the Nupe of Nigeria relates that God first created the tortoise, then man, and then stone. To the tortoise and man he gave the gift of life, but not so to stone. At this time death did not yet exist, and so the tortoise and man became very old and then young again. They were not content with this state of affairs, however, and went to God to ask him for a child. God told them that they could have children but that then they would have to die. He asked them whether they still wanted children, since they knew that having them would bring about their death. Nevertheless, both creatures insisted that they wanted children. Thus it happened: they begot children, and when the children were born, the fathers died.

A myth from the Baiga of central India connects the beginning of death with the first human copulation. A Baiga man and woman had congress in the forest, a thing unknown before. The earth started to tremble, and they died immediately. Since then, death has formed part of human life. And the Tucano Indians of Colombia ascribe the first death to lasciviousness.

Killing. The first death is also ascribed to a killing, often considered a murder. In many cases a mythical being is killed in the primeval time related in myth. A myth from the Mentawai Islands, near Sumatra, relates that the first human beings came forth from a bamboo plant and immediately fled into the bush. There they lived a miserable existence until the god Siakau took pity on them and taught and helped them. Later the god changed himself into an iguana, a sacred animal on these islands, and in this shape he was accidentally killed by two of the four original human beings. They had not recognized Siakau in his new shape and had wrongly accused him of destroying their gardens. Their punishment was instant death. The other two persons fled, but death had entered the world forever.

Among the Arawak of Guyana we encounter a myth about the creator-god. Once when he visited earth to see how his creatures were faring, man, who was wicked, attempted to murder him. Consequently the god deprived mankind of the gift of eternal life and instead bestowed it on snakes and similar creatures, which since then have been able to change their skin. The Algonquin Indians of North America tell about a conflict that occurred at the beginning of time, during which the aquatic animals drowned a wolf, the little brother of the culture hero Mänäbush. In this manner death was brought into the world.

In a number of cultures we find the belief that there was once a time when human life knew neither death nor birth: life went on forever, and procreation and birth were unknown. Then some disturbance happened, some transgression, usually a killing, was committed, and this occurrence changed the situation and introduced a new mode of life in which birth and death alternated. A good example is the story of Hainuwele ("maiden") in a myth from Ceram, as told by Jensen (1939). In short, this myth relates how the people envied Hainuwele because she was luckier and richer than all others. During a communal gathering the dancers formed a spiral and forced Hainuwele to the center, where they had dug a deep hole. The girl was pushed into the hole while loud singing drowned her cries for help. The grave was filled in with earth and stamped down by the dancers. This primeval murder marked the beginning of the alternation of death and birth.

Death as a desire of man. The last category of myth we must consider recounts how man desired death because he did not want to prolong a life that had become burdensome. Abrahamsson (1951) has drawn attention to African myths of this type, according to which man, plagued by disease or suffering from the indignities of old age and, thus, weary of life, wants to die and so calls out for death to come to him. A myth of the Mum of Cameroon relates that God could not understand why so many men became cold and stiff, but Death (here personified) showed him how the old and miserable people cried out for release from this existence. The Ngala tell that man asked for death because there was so much evil and unhappiness in the world. The Nuba of the upper Nile connect the death wish with the fact of overpopulation.

One myth, probably African but the clearest version of which is known from Morocco and put in Muslim terms, tells the story of a virgin who had lived for five hundred years. Moses happened to find her anklets, taken off before her death, and prayed to God to be allowed to see the dead girl. God granted his request and caused the girl to rise from her grave. In a conversation with Moses she said that she had lived far too long and had grown tired of living. Then Moses beseeched God to let man die sooner. Although this myth does not treat the introduction of death on earth, it clearly shows how weariness of life may become a reason for wishing to die; and in mythical terms this nearly always means a reason for the first appearance of death.

Conclusion. As can be expected, still other motifs related to the origin of death are mentioned in mythology. Myths from India connect the coming of death with the overpopulation of the earth and the resulting starvation. In contrast with the Nuba myth mentioned above, this Indian myth has the gods deciding to send death. A myth from the inhabitants of the Sarera Bay region relates how the god Tefafu, after several false starts, finally succeeded in creating perfect human beings. The god, however, became envious of his own creatures and decided to destroy them by a great flood. He spared only two, a brother and sister. He wanted them to marry, and when they demurred at committing incest, he told them falsely that it was all right. The new generation of mankind, born from this incestuous marriage, was no longer perfect; it was evil and subject to both disease and death. So Tefafu was satisfied and went to sleep.

As to the question of the age of the myths on the origin of death, a general answer, in my opinion, cannot be given, and even a restricted one remains full of uncertainties. Baumann (1936) has tried to date these myths in accordance with the *Kulturkreiselehre,* but as this theory no longer commands much authority, the results gathered in this manner must remain doubtful.

We can assume with a modicum of certainty that, given the primary importance of death for all human beings, the search for its origin originated in a very early phase of human culture; but it is impossible to put even a tentative and approximate date on that time when man first considered death as an unnatural break in life, an inexplicable abnormality, for which an explanation was needed.

[*For cross-cultural discussions of mythical views of death and the afterlife, see* Underworld *and* Otherworld.]

BIBLIOGRAPHY

Abrahamsson, Hans. *The Origin of Death: Studies in African Mythology.* Uppsala, 1951. Authoritative treatment of the African myths on the origin of death.

Baumann, Hermann. *Schöpfung und Urzeit des Menschen im Mythus der afrikanischen Völker.* Berlin, 1936. One chapter treats the origin of death.

Bendann, Effie. *Death Customs* (1930). Reprint, London, 1969. A general introduction.

Boas, Franz. "The Origin of Death." *Journal of American Folk-Lore* 30 (1917): 486–491. First special treatment of the Amerindian myths on the origin of death.

Dangel, R. "Mythen vom Ursprung des Todes bei den Indianern Nordamerikas." *Mitteilungen der anthropologischen Gesellschaft in Wien* 58 (1928): 341–374. Treats the Amerindian myths on the origin of death.

Jensen, Adolf E. *Hainuwele: Volkserzählungen von der Molukken-Insel Ceram.* Frankfurt, 1939. The myth of Hainuwele.

Jensen, Adolf E. *Myth and Cult among Primitive Peoples.* Chicago, 1963. Among other things, contains a thorough treatment of the *dema.*

Lang, Andrew. *La mythologie.* Paris, 1886. First classification of myths on the origin of death.

Muensterberger, Warner, *Ethnologische Studien an indonesischen Schöpfungsmythen.* The Hague, 1939. Contains material on the origin of death.

O'Flaherty, Wendy Doniger. *The Origins of Evil in Hindu Mythology.* Berkeley, 1976. Also treats the origin of death.

Preuss, Konrad Theodor. *Tod und Unsterblichkeit im Glauben der Naturvölker.* Tübingen, 1930. Still a useful introduction, although dated in regard to theory.

TH. P. VAN BAAREN

DECALOGUE. *See* Ten Commandments.

DE CHARDIN, PIERRE TEILHARD. *See* Teilhard de Chardin, Pierre.

DEFILEMENT. *See* Purification *and* Taboo.

DE GROOT, J. J. M. *See* Groot, J. J. M. de.

DEIFICATION

DEIFICATION. The Latin term *deificatio* does not appear until late in the Roman era, and then first in Christian literature, particularly in the controversies involving the Nestorians, who blamed the orthodox for "deifying" the body of Christ. In current usage, the English term *deification* is equivalent to *apotheosis.* In light of history, however, *apotheosis* might be reserved to refer to the consecration of heros, of political personages, of Hellenistic sovereigns and, notably, of Roman emperors. [*See* Apotheosis.] In this article the subject will be the deification of individuals or of things generally through means that correspond to certain general tendencies of Greco-Roman paganism.

Pythagoreanism and Cathartic Deification. Since death makes the radical difference between men and gods, the problem of deification is indeed that of immortalization. [*See* Immortality.] In the Classical epoch, the Greeks attributed the power of immortalizing *(athanatizein)* to the Getae and to the Thracians through a kind of shamanism that may have involved Zalmoxis. No evidence exists of the ritual patterns of these practices, but they must have been based on a doctrine of the soul and on the existence of spiritual elites. Zalmoxis was regarded as a *daimōn* and as a disciple of Pythagoras. The connection is significant, since belief in metempsychosis is sometimes attributed to the Thracians. [*See* Thracian Religion.]

To belief in metempsychosis is tied the first explicit formulation of a deification of persons through asceticism and the satisfaction of penalties consequent upon the pleasures of previous lives. It is found in the writings of the Pythagorean philosopher Empedocles (frag. 145–146): a soul is a kind of "demon" that is bound to the cycle of reincarnation in expiation for its faults. At the end of purifying reincarnations, after having been "prophets, cantors, physicians . . . ," these fallen and ransomed "demons" are "reborn as gods": they become the "table companions of the immortals." The last two verses of the Pythagorean *Golden Verses* (70f.) offer hope of a state like that of an immortal god for the sage "who, having left his body behind, goes forward into the free ether." Hierocles would explain this deifying liberation of the soul as the "highest aim of the hieratic and sacred craft," that is, of philosophy. Deification, then, consists of restoring the personal *daimōn* to its authentic status as an immortal god. It is the goal of a spiritual asceticism confirmed by various means of testing. [*See* Soul, *article on* Greek and Hellenistic Concepts.]

The same teaching is implicit in Plato, notably in the *Phaedo* (69c, 114c), where the philosopher is talking not expressly about a deification, but rather about a sojourn among the gods. It is also seemingly implicit in the inscriptions engraved upon the noted golden tablets of Thurii (fourth to third century BCE) and of Rome (second century CE). These assure the deceased that he will be a god by virtue of his heavenly ancestry, his divine race, and the sentence that he has served. Caecilia Secundina "became divine according to the law," that is, by the law that governs reincarnations (*Orphicorum fragmenta* 32g.4). The deceased in one of these tablets states expressly that he has escaped at last the "circle of sorrows," an image that elsewhere is applied to the cycle of rebirths. Whether these tablets bear inscribed fragments of an Orphic "book of the dead," of a *missa pro defunctis,* or of a Pythagorean *hieros logos* ("sacred teaching"), their formulary promises a posthumous deification.

The same point of view is declared on the new tablet of Hipponium: the soul of the deceased woman will take "the sacred path along which the other initiates and Bacchants walk unto glory." The reference is to Orphic Bacchants. It is significant that Orphic vegetarianism expresses the desire to live not as men but as gods. This asceticism had the aim of purifying man from his Titanic components by liberating the Bacchus within him. A liberation of this sort coincides, as it does in Empedocles and Plato, with the escape from the "circle of genesis." The Orphic-Pythagorean deification thus presupposes a persevering action directed toward oneself, a cathartic and mystic tension. When Hippolytus (*Philosophumena* 6.9.25) attributes to Pythagoras the statement that souls "become immortal, once they are detached from their bodies"; this does not mean that physical death liberates them automatically, but that immortality is the reward for continual effort at personal purification. This conviction is based upon a dualist anthropology.

The Mysteries and Initiatory Deification. Orphic-Pythagorean ideas were disseminated with variations (especially involving metempsychosis) by advocates of Platonism and Neoplatonism. Ever since the Classical epoch, the Orphic mystics, as well as various wandering charlatans, had promised, through the use of specialized formulas, not a religious purification, but only an ethical purification in the spirit of the philosophers. Later, during the Hellenistic age, the multiplication and success of mystery religions popularized a new form of deification.

These cults—centered on deities who were regarded as having lived and suffered among men—put into question the radical distinction between cursed mortals and blessed immortals. Insofar as they made their initiates relive in a liturgical way the trials of the gods who had died and revived (Osiris) or were reborn (Attis), the mystery religions connected their devotees with an adventure that ended with victory over death. Indeed, the initiation that, at first, was regarded as giving the candidates some assurance of a kind of privileged status in the beyond (Eleusis) tended also to safeguard them against bad luck, and even to deify them by a form of ritual identification with Dionysos, Attis, or Osiris. The Dionysian mysteries made a Bacchus of the initiate; the consecration of the initiate by means of the winnowing basket and the phallus regenerated him by immunizing him against death and infernal demons. Dionysos was held to have returned from the nether regions along with his mother Semele, and to have been "reborn." His myth provided a model for the rebirth of any initiate, to whom the same immortality was promised (Turcan, 1966, pp. 396ff., 436ff., 466ff.). This regeneration required the (figurative) death of the initiate, who was subjected to a rite of katabasis. The initiate was seen as undergoing the same trials of initiation that had turned Dionysos into a true Bacchus (ibid., pp. 406ff.). The Neoplatonists compared the restoration of the soul (purified and reintegrated in God) to the awakening of Dionysos Liknites (ibid., p. 401). The initiation of the cult of Isis offers many comparisons. The neophyte had to die to his previous life, and the ritual involved a descent into hell, with some kind of mystical or hallucinatory journey through the cosmos. Yet as recompense the initiate was defied, adorned "ad instar Solis" ("as a likeness of the Sun," that is, Osiris-Helios), and held up to the faithful as an idol. The benevolence of Isis, who judged someone to be worthy, made the neophyte into a new Osiris. The funeral rites of mummification in ancient Egypt had the same purpose. Yet in figuratively anticipating the initiate's death, the mysteries of Isis during the Roman epoch in some way democratized apotheosis, in that in its beginnings only pharaohs were the beneficiaries.

The mysteries of Cybele likewise promised a regeneration to their adherents and an elevation *(epanodos)* toward the gods. Just as in the initiation of the cult of Isis, the initiate is thought of as dying like Attis, in order to share in the love of Cybele in a blessed *hieros gamos.* The Galli, by castrating themselves, identified with Attis. To avoid this personal bodily sacrifice, use was made of the *taurobolium,* the ritual sacrifice of a bull. The function and meaning of the *taurobolium* are debated (R. Duthoy, *The Taurobolium: Its Evolution and Terminology,* Leiden, 1969). Yet the fact remains that the beneficiary of the *taurobolium* was factitiously identified with the victim by drenching himself in the victim's blood, thereby becoming an Attis that those present could worship. Just like the initiate of Isis, the initiate of Attis was "reborn" through the *taurobolium: in aeternum renatus.* Whatever the rites or mysteries, the resting with a divine nature was thought of as a regeneration (Nilsson, 1974, p. 653). This feature is also seen in Hermetic deification.

Hermetism and Gnostic Deification. Comparing astrology with an initiation, Vettius Valens (second century CE) identifies contemplation of the stars with a kind of mystical union with God: the knowledge of the heavens "divinizes" the man who possesses it, as if the subject came to merge with the object. This is even more true of the knowledge of God when, in the imperial epoch, philosophy becomes theosophy. In the *Corpus Hermeticum,* this idea recurs frequently, "for this is the blessed end of those who have the knowledge: they become God" (*Corpus Hermeticum* 1.26). The good choice—that of divine things—"deifies man" (ibid., 4.7). We are "divinized" by the birth into spiritual life that constitutes gnosis. *Asclepius* 41 gives thanks to the supreme God, that he has deigned to "consecrate for eternity," that is, to deify men in the flesh. This affirmation seems to conflict with that in *Corpus Hermeticum* 10.6, where it is denied that the soul can be divinized while in a body.

Indeed, Hermetic gnosis supposes a complete regeneration. It is the new man enlightened and reborn in God who becomes a god by dying to physical life and by becoming alien to the world even in this life. Regeneration consists of the substitution of ten good "powers" (including "the knowledge of God") for twelve evil "powers" attributable to the zodiac. The disciple then identifies himself with the cosmic eternity, Aion, and he is then divinized. This is the very recommendation that Nous makes to Hermes: "Become Aion, and you will understand God" (ibid., 11.20). Here again it is a matter of restoring the soul to its original state: "You are born a god and a child of the One," declares Hermes to Tat (ibid., 13.14).

Similarly, the gnostic systems derived from Christian inspiration, whatever the variations in their myths and their soteriology, envision only the final restoration of the spirit to its original divine state. Finally, the idea that by knowing oneself one learns to know God and to be known by him so as to be "deified," or "generated into immortality," is expressed by orthodox Christians (Hippolytus, *Philosophumena* 10.34). In contrast with Hermes Trismegistos, Hippolytus promises the Christian a body that will be as immortal and incorruptible as the soul itself. But, like the Hermetist, the Christian must also die to the old man and to the profane life.

Magical and Theurgic Deification. Certain procedures of deification are comparable to Hermetic gnosis, at least insofar as they are presented as "formulas for immortality" that feature magical concepts. This is true in the case of the so-called Mithraic liturgy (end of the third century CE), where the name of Mithra appears as only one of those associated at that time with the sun. The ritual involves prayers and a journey of the spirit that in some way anticipates the posthumous ascension of the soul unto Helios and the heavenly Aion, both invoked for the occasion. As in Hermetism, the *apathanatismos* asserts that a subject is regenerated by the very object of his theosophical quest, but this is conditional to the exact application of a formula. Other magical texts insist upon the importance of knowledge revealed by the god or gods: "We thank you for . . . having divinized us through the knowledge of your being," states one papyrus. Following the death of the magus, Aion carries away his breath *(pneuma)* by way of rescuing it from Hades, "as befits a god." The neophyte is "reborn" and freed from fate, as was the initiate of Isis. Neoplatonic theurgy would give its approval to pagan magic, and Psellus could believe that it was capable of making gods of men.

The magus could also deify animals by ritually mummifying them in accordance with traditional Egyptian practices. Further, he could deify idols through telestic action and theurgy. In this sense, *Asclepius* 23 affirms that man is the creator of gods. It was precisely for this reason that Christians reproached pagans: the very idea that men could make gods! The most frequently denounced example of idolatrous fiction is that of Serapis who, according to Origen (*Against Celsus* 5.38), owed his existence "to the profane mysteries and to the practices of sorcerers invoking demons." Indeed, telestic action consists of causing divine influence to enter into idols, to "animate" them or to illuminate them through the magical process known as *phōtagōgia.* This consecration of statues employing magical formulas played a great role in late paganism. [*See* Theurgy.]

Funerary and Iconographic Deification. The adornment of tombs displays the concern for deifying individuals by analogy or through iconography. This tendency was first evident in Rome among the class of freedmen who sought thus to insure themselves some kind of moral promotion. Their cippi or stelae represent, from the first century CE, Herakles, Hermes, Dionysos, and Artemis portrayed after the image of the deceased man or woman. The epitaphs, the architecture of the tombs, and the literary tradition confirm the intention to identify the dead with gods, goddesses, and heros. When the use of sarcophagi began to prevail at the time of the Antonines, sepulchral imagery manifested even more clearly the same concerns that are evident among higher social circles; emperors and empresses provided the example. This style of funerery deification consisted either of featuring the deceased's medallion portrait *(imago elipeata)* as being carried by the gods (Tritons, Centaurs, Victories, Erotes) or of giving the sculpted god, goddess, or hero the same features as the dead man or woman, who could then be seen as Dionysos, Ariadne, Mars, Hercules, Endymion, or Selene. Imagery of predatory animals (eagles, griffins) or gods (Dioscuri, Pluto) also implies a deification by analogy. Finally, sarcophagi with figures of the Muses, or with scenes of teaching, of battle, or of hunting, heroize the deceased through association with the depicted qualities of gallantry or erudition.

Thus, in the Hellenistic and Roman world, philosophy, theosophy, magic, mystery religions, and the cult of the dead all aspired to the same goal (one that on principle was excluded in Classical Greek religion): for the individual person to become or become again a god.

BIBLIOGRAPHY

Bianchi, Ugo. *The Greek Mysteries.* Leiden, 1976.

Bianchi, Ugo, and Maarten J. Vermaseren, eds. *La soteriologia dei culti orientali nell 'Impero Romano.* Leiden, 1982.

Dieterich, Albrecht. *Eine Mithrasliturgie.* 3d ed. Leipzig, 1923.

Dodds, E. R. *The Greeks and the Irrational.* Berkeley, 1951.

Festugière, A.-J. *La révélation d'Hermès Trismégiste,* vols. 3 and 4. Paris, 1953–1954.

Festugière, A.-J. *Hermétisme et mystique païenne.* Paris, 1967.

Festugière, A.-J. *Études de religion grecque et hellénistique.* Paris, 1972.

Festugière, A.-J. *L'idéal religieux des Grecs et l'evangile.* 2d ed. Paris, 1981.

Jonas, Hans. *The Gnostic Religion.* 2d ed., rev. Boston, 1963.

Nilsson, Martin P. *Geschichte des griechischen Religion,* vol. 2, *Die hellenistische und römische Zeit.* 3d rev. ed. Munich, 1974.

Reitzenstein, Richard. *The Hellenistic Mystery Religions.* Translated by John E. Steely. Pittsburgh, 1978.

Rohde, Erwin. *Psyche: The Cult of Souls and Belief in Immortality among the Greeks* (1925). Translated by W. B. Hillis. London, 1950.

Schilling, Robert. "La déification à Rome: Tradition latine et interférence grecque." *Revue des études latines* 58 (1980): 137ff.

Turcan, Robert. *Les sarcophages romains à représentations dionysiaques.* Paris, 1966.

Wrede, Henning. *Consecratio in formam deorum: Vergöttlichte Privatpersonen in der römischen Kaiserzeit.* Mainz am Rhein, 1981.

Zuntz, Günther. *Persephone: Three Essays on Religion and Thought in Magna Graecia.* Oxford, 1971.

ROBERT TURCAN
Translated from French by Paul C. Duggan

DEISM

DEISM. The term *deism* was originally equivalent to *theism,* differing only in etymology: *theism* based on the Greek word for god *(theos),* and *deism* on the Latin *(deus).* [*See* Theism.] In the seventeenth and eighteenth centuries, however, *deism* came to signify one or another form of rationalistic theological unorthodoxy. Often used pejoratively, it was also sometimes worn as a badge of honor. The first known use of the term occurs in the *Instruction chrétienne* (1564) of the Calvinist theologian Pierre Viret: "I have heard he is of that band who call themselves 'Deists,' a wholly new word which they would oppose to 'Atheist.'"

In its principal meaning, *deism* signifies the belief in a single God and in a religious practice founded solely on natural reason rather than on supernatural revelation. Thus Viret characterizes deists as "those who profess belief in God as creator of heaven and earth, but reject Jesus Christ and his doctrines." John Dryden's preface to his poem *Religio Laici* (1682) defines *deism* as "the opinion of those that acknowledge one God, without the reception of any revealed religion." The currency of the term in the eighteenth century was undoubtedly enhanced by the article on Viret in Pierre Bayle's *Dictionnaire historique et critique* (1697).

Like most epithets of controversy, *deism* was used in a number of senses other than its principal one. It was often used as a vague term of abuse with no determinate meaning at all. Among the chief subordinate or deviant senses of the term are (1) belief in a supreme being lacking in all attributes of personality (such as intellect and will); (2) belief in a God, but denial of any divine providential care for the world; (3) belief in a God, but denial of any future life; (4) belief in a God, but rejection of all other articles of religious faith (so defined by Samuel Johnson in his *Dictionary*, 1755).

Some Deists completely rejected all revealed and ecclesiastical religion, adopted anticlerical attitudes, challenged the scriptural canon, questioned the credibility of miracle narratives, or even rejected the New Testament as fabrication and imposture. Thus Edward Stillingfleet, bishop of Worcester, described the addressee of his polemical *Letter to a Deist* (1677) as "a particular person who owned the Being and Providence of God, but expressed mean esteem of the Scriptures and the Christian Religion." Yet a number of influential seventeenth- and eighteenth-century British thinkers described themselves as "Christian Deists" on the grounds that they accepted both the Christian religion based on supernatural revelation and a Deistic religion based solely on natural reason, consistent with Christianity but independent of any revealed authority.

Thus, even the principal sense of *deism*, which refers to belief in God without belief in supernatural revelation, is inherently imprecise. No sharp dividing line can be drawn between Christian or revelationist Deists and Deists who recognized no revelation. The former often accepted Christian revelation precisely because it accords with natural or rational religion and sometimes advocated allegorical readings of scripture in order to secure this agreement, while the latter often disavowed any "mean esteem" of Christian scriptures and expressed admiration for the inspiring way in which the truths of natural religion were presented in them. Further, there is no sharp line separating Christian Deists and orthodox Christian theologians (such as Thomas Aquinas or Duns Scotus) who maintain that some parts of Christian doctrine can be known by natural reason.

Deism was most prominent in England, the only place where it approached the status of a movement. Among its best-known representatives were Lord Herbert of Cherbury (1583–1624), author of *De veritate* (1624); his disciple Charles Blount (1654–1693); John Toland (1670–1722), author of *Christianity Not Mysterious* (1696); Anthony Collins (1676–1729); and Matthew Tindal (1657–1733), author of *Christianity as Old as the Creation* (1730), often described as "the Deist's Bible." The powerful influence of English Deism is attested by the sizable number of attacks on it by the orthodox, including not only Stillingfleet, but also Richard Bentley, Charles Leslie, Samuel Clarke, and (most famously) Joseph Butler in his *Analogy of Religion* (1736). Deism also met with vicious persecution in England, where blasphemy was punishable by forfeiture of civil rights, fines, and even imprisonment. At least two prominent Deists were imprisoned for expressing their blasphemous opinions: Thomas Woolston (1670–1731) was sent to prison in 1729 and died there; Peter Annet was fined, pilloried, and imprisoned to hard labor in 1764 at age seventy.

Deism is generally associated with British religious thought. However, a number of major continental religious thinkers of the late sixteenth, seventeenth, and eighteenth centuries clearly qualify as Deists under the principal meaning of the term. They include Giordano Bruno (1548–1600) and Lucilio Vanini (1584–1619), both burned as heretics for rejecting ecclesiastical authority and scriptural revelation; Barukh Spinoza (1632–1677); François-Marie Arouet (Voltaire; 1694–1778); Jean-Jacques Rousseau (1712–1778); Hermann Samuel Reimarus (1694–1768); Gotthold Ephraim Lessing (1729–1781); Moses Mendelssohn (1729–1786); and Immanuel Kant (1724–1781). (Both Voltaire and Kant, however, repudiated the label "Deist" and always described themselves as "Theists.") There were outspoken Deists among the founding fathers of the United States of America, notably Benjamin Franklin (1706–1790), Thomas Paine (1737–1809), and Thomas Jefferson (1743–1826). [*See the biographies of Bruno, Kant, Lessing, Mendelssohn, Reimarus, Rousseau, and Spinoza.*]

Deism appears to be exclusively a seventeenth- and eighteenth-century phenomenon, but this is partly an illusion. There are special reasons why the term *deism* attained currency then but did not survive longer. The rise of modern science did not immediately initiate warfare of science with religion, but it did initiate warfare within religion, between the orthodox who held fast to tradition, authority, and the supernatural, and the freethinkers, who sought a religion that harmonized with nature and reason. A term was needed by the orthodox to distinguish the freethinkers from themselves, and by the religious freethinkers to distinguish themselves from mere atheists. *Deism* served both needs. The term has fallen into disuse in the past two centuries, however, perhaps chiefly because in nineteenth- and twentieth-century philosophical and religious thought the distinctions between reason and tradition, nature and supernature, have lost the sharpness they had for thinkers of the seventeenth and eighteenth centuries. Greater tolerance of diversity of opinion within Christian society has also lessened the need for an epithet whose principal function was to scourge independent thinkers. Deism itself has also become a less popular position, owing to the increasing tendency of rationalists to become simple unbelievers rather than to settle for compromises and half-measures. Yet deism—in fact, if not in name—still survives in all religious communities and individuals whose convictions arise from autonomous thinking rather than from the submission of reason to ecclesiastical or scriptural authorities.

[*See also* Enlightenment, The, *and* Doubt and Belief.]

BIBLIOGRAPHY

An excellent nineteenth-century account of British Deism is to be found in Leslie Stephen's *History of English Thought in the Eighteenth Century,* vol. 1 (1876; reprint, New York, 1963). A detailed account of Deistic thinkers is presented by J. M. Robertson in *A History of Freethought, Ancient and Modern,* vol. 2, *To the Period of the French Revolution,* 4th ed. (London, 1936). For the social background of Deism, see W. K. Jordan's *Development of Religious Toleration in England,* 4 vols. (1932–1940; reprint, Gloucester, Mass., 1965). Two very good studies of aspects of Deism are Norman L. Torrey's *Voltaire and the English Deists* (1930; reprint, Hamden, Conn., 1967) and Ernest C. Mossner's *Bishop Butler and the Age of Reason* (New York, 1936). Perhaps the two most classic works on religion by thinkers identified above as Deists are Barukh Spinoza's *Tractatus theologico-politicus* (1670), translated by R. H. M. Elwes in *Chief Works,* vol. 1 (1883; reprint, New York, 1955), and Immanuel Kant's *Religion within the Limits of Reason Alone* (1793), translated by Theodore M. Greene and Hoyt H. Hudson (LaSalle, Ill., 1960).

ALLEN W. WOOD

DEITY. As a symbol, deity represents the human struggle at its highest; it represents man's effort to discover his identity in confrontation with the limits of his universe. Deity is the symbol of what transcends the human being and the symbol of what lies hidden most deeply within him. While other creatures merely accept their environments as a given, man exists as such only when he realizes both his solidarity with the universe and his distinction from it. In his journey toward self-identity man encounters deity. In a cross-cultural context, deity symbolizes the transcendence of all the limitations of human consciousness and the movement of the human spirit toward self-identity through its encounter with the ultimate. Deity symbolizes man's knowledge that he is not alone nor the ultimate master of his fate. And yet this knowledge, dim though it may be, associates man with this same deity. Deity both transcends and envelops man; it is inseparable from man's awareness of his own identity and yet is always elusive, hidden, and for some, seemingly nonexistent.

The Polysemy of the Word. *Deity* is a word with a diversity of meanings. It is an ambiguous and often polemical word. The different interpretations that it has been given show that it is also a relative word.

Ambiguity. The word *deity* is ambiguous. It is not a proper name. It is not even a common name, since its possible referents are hardly homogeneous. It is the product of many and heterogeneous abstractions. Most names referring to divine beings or the divine were originally common names singled out in a peculiar way. [*See* Gods and Goddesses.] What was general became specific, concrete, and, like a single being, evocative of emotion. Thus *Allāh* probably comes from *al-illah,* that is, "the God." *Njinyi* or *Nnui,* the name for God among the Bamum of Cameroon, means "he who is everywhere"—and thus is at once concrete and elusive. *Yahveh* means "he who is" (or "he who shall be"), which becomes being *par excellence* for Christian Scholasticism. *Śiva* means "auspicious, benign, kind"—what for the Śaivas represents the highest symbol of the deity stripped of any attribute.

In short, there are gods called Allāh, Nnui, Yahveh, Śiva; but there is no god called Deity. One worships Viṣṇu, or even the Buddha, but one does not worship deity as such. One may worship only a particular deity. We often speak of "major" and "minor" deities in religious traditions. The word *deity,* in short, has a higher degree of abstractness than does the word *God.*

In Western antiquity, in the Middle Ages, and up to the present, *deity* in its adjectival or pronominal form is a word applied to creatures and used without theological misgivings. Works and persons are called "divine" and "deities" because they share in deity in a way in which they would not be said to share in God. Spiritual writers or popular heroes are called "divines" in many languages. The word simply denotes a character of (divine) excellence, which can be shared by many creatures.

The word *god* was also originally a common name, but soon became the proper name of the one God of the theists (and also of the atheists, for many atheists are merely anti-theists; both live within the mythic horizon of the one personal God, accepting or rejecting it). [*See* God.] By extension scholars speak of the African gods, discuss the nature of a supreme god, and the like.

At any rate, *deity* is not identical with *god.* One does not believe in deity in the individualized sense in which one may believe in God. Yet one may accept that there is something referred to by the word *deity.* The referent will always retain a certain mystery and show certain features of freedom, infinity, immanence, transcendence, or the like. For others, this mysterious entity becomes the highest example of superstition, primitivism, unevolved consciousness, and a pretense for exploiting others under the menace of an awesome and imaginary power. The ambiguity of the word is great.

Polemical usage. At the same time *deity* is also a polemical word. It has sometimes stood against some conceptions of God without rejecting the divine altogether. The philosophical Deism of the last centuries in Europe, which developed a concept of the divine more congenial to the natural sciences emerging at the time than to the idea of a personal god, could serve as an example. The deity of the Deists was to substitute for and correct the *theos* of the theists without discarding the belief in the existence of some supreme being or first cause. Yet this polemic was not new to the eighteenth century. The prolific Greek writer-priest at Delphi, Plutarch of Chaeronea (c. 46–c. 119 CE), our first source for the word *theotēs,* uses it in his polemic against the mythological interpretations of historical heroes as they appeared in the work of Euhemerus of Messina (fl. 300 BCE). In the New Testament this word, in the only passage in which it appears (*Col.* 2:9), is translated by the old Latin *deitas,* whereas the Vulgate uses the more current *divinitas*—a word unknown before Cicero (106–143 BCE). In the *Letter to the Romans* 1:20 we find the word *theiotēs* derived from the adjective *theios* and also translated as *divinitas* in the Vulgate.

Deity is not only polemical in regard to a personal conception of God. It is polemical also as a symbol of the political use of the divine. We should not forget the wars of religion, the attempted legitimation of power and use of violence in the name of God, gods, and divinity, nor the justification of so many ideologies by slogans such as "In God we trust" or "Gott mit uns." Deity has been all too often the cause of strife and war, sometimes under the guise of peace.

Relativity. From the perspective of a sociology of knowledge, the modern use of the word *deity* could be interpreted as the Western effort to open up a broader horizon than that of a monotheistic God but without breaking continuity with tradition. *God* was a common name. It became a proper name: the Abrahamic God. And it was then that this *God* came to designate the one God, which Muslims or Christians wanted to propagate around the world. All others were "mere" gods or, at most, inappropriate names for the true God. It is interesting to see how Western scholarship today tries to disentangle itself from its monolithic and colonial mentality. Is the word *deity* the last bulwark of this attitude?

We may draw two opposing conclusions from the paradoxical fact that this word denotes both the most communicable and the most exclusive aspects of the "divine" reality: everything that is shares a divine character, and nothing—no thing—that is can be said to embody or exhaust the divine, not even the totality of those things that are. In sum: the word says everything, every thing, and nothing, no thing. One legitimate conclusion from this ambiguity may be that one should avoid the word altogether or speak of deities in the plural as special superhuman (divine) entities.

There is another possible conclusion, however. Precisely because of its polysemic nature, this word may become a fundamental category for the study and understanding of religion. The subject matter of religion would then be related to deity, and not just to God or to gods. Polysemy does not need to mean confusion. It means a richness of meanings, a variety of senses. *Deity* could then become a true word, that is, a symbol not yet eroded by habit, rather than a univocal concept.

I should now try to describe the field of the symbol "deity" and study its structure. Regarding its field I shall analyze the means of approach to this symbol in its broadest aspect. Then, I shall examine the structure of deity by analyzing the different avenues, contexts, and perspectives under which deity has been studied. I shall then mention the structure of human consciousness when referring to deity. I shall further briefly compare deity with other equally broad categories in order to get a more accurate picture, and finally I shall try to summarize my findings.

An Approach to Deity. This article does not deal primarily with the concept of God as it is generally understood in the Western world, and therefore it is not necessary to discuss, for instance, atheism or the nature of God. Further, this essay's cross-cultural perspective requires that the viewpoints of other cultures be integrated with our own instead of simply reported. Still we are engaged in what is predominantly a Western activity: taking a perspective from one tradition (as betrayed by the very use of the word *deity*) and expanding it in order to achieve a more universal viewpoint.

Linguistic background. Johann Gottlieb Fichte (1762–1814) provides us with a caution: "Deity appears only in the highest performance of thinking." We must keep in mind at the very outset that discourse about deity is unique, because the locus of deity is beyond both the things of the senses and the things of the intellect. Yet the way to deity belongs to the dynamism of our intellect. This is expressed in the first sentence of the *Brahma Sūtra:* "Athāto brahmajijñāsā" ("Now therefore the desire to know *brahman*"). The text refers to the "desiderative knowledge" or the "knowing desire" *(jijñāsā),* which arises out of an existential situation *(atha).* It liberates us from the weight of selfishness *(ahaṃkāra),* permitting us to soar in the search for deity. The process follows both an existential and an intellectual path, with no separation between pure and practical reason. Deity is as much at the beginning as at the end of the human quest—and also in between. The search requires purity of mind, strength of will, and a change of life.

While speaking of deity we have already had occasion to refer to God, and we now introduce *brahman.* Do all these words designate the same "thing"? Or have they at least the same meaning?

Brahman is certainly not the one true and living God of the Abrahamic traditions. Nor can it be said that Shang-ti or *kami* are the same as *brahman.* And yet they are not totally unrelated. Can we affirm that all those names refer to deity as a broad category? Is *deity* perhaps the common name for God, the godhead, the divine, *brahman, mana,* and so forth?

To begin with, it must be stressed that *brahman* and God, for instance, are not the same. The one is passive and does not need to care, it is at the bottom of everything and is the very condition of possibility for all that there is. The other is active and provident; it is above everything, personal, the creator of all that is. But they are not so different as to make the translation of the one by the other totally inaccurate. The Christian Scholastics, while affirming the ineffability of divine names, did not deny that some names are more applicable than others. We shall call *brahman* and God homeomorphic equivalents, because they perform corresponding yet different functions in their respective systems.

It is tempting to use the word *deity* as an abstract noun for all such homeomorphic equivalents. *Deity* would then refer to God, *kami, brahman,* Zeus, Rudra, T'ien, the Tao, El, Baal, Urdr, Re, Kālī, and so on. This enterprise is relatively simple as long as we remain within more or less homologous cultures, making it easier to find common properties like infinity, omniscience, goodness, immutability, omnipotence, simplicity, unity, and so on. But when we attempt to include such properties as futurity, nothingness, or illusion, we find that these attributes are not at all common and are incompatible with the previous ones. In point of fact there is no common structure other than the purely formal one of being a vague something different from and perhaps superior to human beings, and sometimes only apparently so. Deity would then be a purely formal concept with no significant content whatsoever.

We may note the tendency, especially common to the West, to universalize what is familiar, as in the following sentences: "The Christian God is an absolute value for all; modern technology is fit for the entire world; the natural sciences are universally valid; truth is universal." We shall have to avoid such pretension if we are to take other cultures as seriously as we take Western cultures. The word *deity* cannot encompass all that other traditions have said about what in one group of cultures can be rendered by *deity.* Were we to use the term *brahman* or *kami* instead of *deity,* our meaning would change. The context being different, the results would also be different. Thus we must be careful in making extrapolations and avoid generalizations that are not warranted by the self-understanding of the different cultures of the world.

With these preliminary warnings in mind, we may now examine the distinction between God and deity. This distinction was known to medieval Christianity and was given clear expression by Meister Eckhart in his distinction between the godhead and God. The godhead, or deity, is as far from God as heaven is from earth. Deity is here the inner and passive aspect of the divine mystery and is related to the *deus absconditus* that was much commented upon during the patristic period. God, on the other hand, would be the outer and active aspect of the same mystery. Be this as it may, however, we will use the word *deity,* in distinction to *godhead,* to mean not just God's essence (as in Thomas Aquinas) or the "God beyond God" or the ground of God (as in Eckhart), but simply that divine dimension elusively present everywhere, which only our highest thinking performance can glimpse and which is the goal of our existential human quest.

Deity, then, not only may denote God or gods as substantial beings but also may be used as a generic name connoting all those forces, energies, entities, ideas, powers, and the like that come from "above" or "beyond" the human realm. In this sense *deity* represents the element of reality that belongs neither to the material world nor to the merely human realm but is above or beyond the sensible and intellectual order. *Deity* may thus stand for one of the three dimensions of reality that practically all human traditions reveal. First, there is the realm of heaven: the gods, the superhuman powers, the supraintelligible. Then there is the realm of the human: consciousness, ethics, life, mind, the intelligible, and so forth. And finally, the realm of the earth: the cosmic, the material, the spatiotemporal reality, the sensible, and so on.

We cannot proceed further in the study of the human approach to deity until we examine the nature of the "thing" we are trying to investigate. It is irrelevant now whether the world of deity is the paradigm of the human world, in which case the latter would be only a shadow of the real, or whether on the other hand the divine universe is only a projection of the unfulfilled desires of humans. The fact remains that the human experience crystallized in language witnesses to the existence of such a divine world, be it populated by *daimones* or by *theoi,* by *devas, elohim,* spirits of all types, the one God, or by nobody. Have we a common name to designate that universe? Can we say that this is the world of deity? For this we need a historical interlude.

Historical background. How have human beings come to the notion of deity? For some scholars this notion has been the result of an inference of some type of causal thinking. Deity is then a supreme being or beings, of a celestial or other type. The human question about the origin of life, the world, and the like triggers the search for a cause that then will be "located" in whatever place appears to be more appropriate for the dwelling of a supreme being or beings, whether in the heavens or in the earth. Others would see the origin of deity not so much in the intellectual quest as in the existential anxiety of the human being facing the elemental mysteries of life and nature. Still others have seen the search for deity as based neither on causal thinking, nor on anxious feeling, but on simple awareness.

For others deity is the disclosure of a supreme being through its own initiative, which explains why man has come to the idea of deity. If such a supreme being exists, even if its "revelation" is progressive and related to the intellectual development of the peoples concerned, it is always from that power that the first step comes.

Contemporary discussions are the aftermath of that great controversy of past decades about the origin of the idea of God, a controversy that resulted from the conflict of the emerging theory of evolution with traditional beliefs in God. Wilhelm Schmidt (1868–1954), rejecting the evolutionary scheme, searched for traces of a primitive revelation of a "primordial monotheism" among primitive peoples. Schmidt was elaborating the insights of Andrew Lang (1844–1912), who had argued for the existence of a belief in supreme beings among archaic peoples, in opposition to the then pervasive theory of primitive animism, represented by E. B. Tylor (1832–1917). Finally, atheistic movements—scientific, dialectical, or historical—will make of deity a superfluous hypothesis, an artificial tool for the subjection of humans, an undue extrapolation of our present ignorance, a mere illusion to console us in the midst of our impotencies. [*See* Evolutionism.]

It seems fair to say that the most universal, primordial human experience is neither monotheistic, nonatheistic, nor polytheistic but rather a deep-rooted belief in a divine world, a world populated by different kinds of superhuman beings or forces. Whether those beings are one or many, whether they represent a polytheistic hierarchy or an *Urmonotheismus*, is not the most important point. What is most important is that these beliefs express a human experience that says that man is not alone in the universe and that the sensible world is not all there is to reality. [*See* Otherworld.] This is made clear not only by innumerable oral traditions and written texts in nearly every culture but also by the existence of a veritable jungle of names for the divine. All human languages have an enormous treasure of words denoting the super- or extrahuman realm. It belongs to a second moment of human reflection to try to put order into that world, to assign to it its degree of reality, to decide what kind of hierarchy reigns there, and to elucidate the relationship of that world with the human world and the rest of the universe. One does not prove the existence of deity in a primordial civilization. The gods are simply there.

The Structure of Deity. Historical investigation is only a part of the question about deity. How people have come to this idea is less important than the structure of the idea itself. This structure is not an "objective" datum, however. It is in part a function of human interest. We have here an example of how any human enterprise is motivated and conditioned by human interests and prevailing myth. Because deity has no detectable referent outside human consciousness, its structure depends in part on one's opinions about it and on those of any human consciousness for which the notion makes sense. In other words, what deity *is* is inseparable from what people have believed it to be.

We must try then to make sense of the ideas and experiences humankind has had on the subject. For this we must attempt to understand the context in which the problem has been put. This leads us to distinguish between the methods that can be employed to elucidate the question and the horizons within which the problem of deity is set. The main methods are theological, anthropological, and philosophical. These methods are all interrelated, and distinguishing them is really a question of emphasis. The possible horizons of the problem consist of the presuppositions that we make about what we are looking for when we set about asking about deity and its origins. Horizons are a function of our universe and of the myths we live by. I shall distinguish three such horizons. Combining these with the methods just mentioned would give nine different sets of notions about deity. Brevity requires, however, that I do not develop these nine representations of the divine. I will describe only the three fundamental horizons that predetermine the question of deity.

Horizons. In order to understand what kind of deity we are talking about, it is essential to reflect on the horizon of the question. Is the deity to be conceived as absolute consciousness? As a supreme being? As the perfect, ideal individual? Or as the creator of the world? In short, where do we situate the divine? Where is the locus of deity? The horizons are, of course, dependent on the culture of any given time or place. Viewed structurally, however, the function of deity always seems to provide an ultimate point of reference. We may situate this point outside the universe or at its center, in the depths of man (in his mind or heart), or simply nowhere. Cosmology, anthropology, and ontology offer us the three main horizons.

Meta-cosmological. The human being in ancient times lived facing the world. The main concern was the universe as a human habitat. Man's vision is directed toward things in heaven and on earth. The horizon of deity is precisely this universe, but not just as one thing among others. The locus is meta-cosmological.

Deity is here related to the world. Certainly, it may be identified as immanent to the world, or more probably transcendent to it, but deity is the deity of the world, and the world is the deity's world. What type of function or functions deity is supposed to perform and what kind of relation it has with the world are left to the different cosmologies and traditions. In any case, deity is a kind of pole to the world, a prime mover that sets the world into motion, sustains it, directs it, and even creates it.

A temporal metaphor can be used to say the same thing. In this case, the deity is represented as the beginning, present before the big bang, or at the end of the evolution of the physical universe, as the omega point. Or the deity may be both alpha and omega, at the beginning and at the end of the universe.

The most common name for this deity is "God," whether this be Varuṇa, "supreme lord, ruling the spheres" (*Ṛgveda* 1.25.20), or Yahveh who "made heaven and earth" (*Gn.* 1:1). This God is "that from which truly all beings are born, by which when born they live, and into which they all return" (*Taittirīya Upaniṣad* 3.1). This God is the *pantokratōr* of many traditions, Eastern and Western. Even the *deus otiosus* belongs to this group. Deity is here a meta-cosmological category. Its most salient feature is its infinity. The world we experience is contingent, and all things are transient, finite. Only the deity is infinite. [*See* Transcendence and Immanence.]

Meta-anthropological. At a certain moment in history the main interest of man was no longer nature or the world outside, above and mysterious, but man himself. Man's visions were directed toward the inner recesses of the human spirit: the feelings, the mind. The locus of deity is here the human realm, but not just a human field made wider. It has to be deeper as well. The locus is meta-anthropological.

Here deity is seen as the symbol for the perfection of the human being. The notion of deity does not come so much as the fruit of reflection on the cosmos or as an experience of its numinous character as it does from anthropological self-awareness. Deity is the fullness of the human heart, the real destiny of man, the leader of the people, the beloved of the mystics, the lord of history, the full realization of what we really are. This deity does not need to be anthropomorphic, although it may present some such traits. [*See* Anthropomorphism.] Deity is here *ātman-brahman*, the fully divinized man, the Christ, the *puruṣa*, or even the symbol of justice, peace, and a happy society. Here deity may be considered immanent or transcendent, identified with or distinguishable from man, but its functions are related to the human being. It is a living, loving, or menacing deity, inspiring, caring, punishing, rewarding, and forgiving. In this deity all pilgrimage ends, all longing disappears, all thoughts recoil, and all sin is blotted out. The deity is a meta-anthropological category.

The vexed problem of divine personality belongs here, as do psychological analyses of human belief in deity. The most salient feature of this horizon, however, is the attribute of freedom. The deity is here freedom itself, liberating man from his often painful limitations. Modern theologies of liberation belong here, as does the notion of a god acting in history.

Meta-ontological. We are told that the culmination of man's development is self-awareness. The power of reflection makes *Homo sapiens* the superior being that he believes himself to be. The locus of the deity here cannot be just a superman or a ground of the world. It has to be a superbeing. The locus is meta-ontological.

Man is proud of the human power of abstraction. Deity is here not only beyond the physical world but also outside any natural realm, including that of the human world, the intellect, the desires, and the will. Deity is totally above and beyond nature, including human nature. The transcendence or otherness of deity is here so absolute that it transcends itself, and thus it can no longer be called transcendence. Deity does not exist; it is meta-ontological, beyond being. It is not even nonbeing. The apophatism is absolute. The deity neither is nor exists, nor is it thinkable or speakable. Silence is the only proper attitude toward it, not because we are incapable of speaking about it, but because silence is what befits it. [*See* Silence.] This silence neither hides nor reveals. It is silence because it says nothing, there being nothing to say. Possible names for this deity are *śūnyatā*, Neither Being nor Nonbeing, Huperon, and so on. Deity is here a meta-ontological reality. Seen from below, as it were, it belongs to the unthinkable. Seen from within, it belongs to the unthought. To think about it would be idolatry.

Here we encounter the problem of the nothingness of deity, the radical apophatism developed in many traditions. [*See* Śūnyam and Śūnyatā.] The most salient feature here is immanence and transcendence, the two belonging together. Deity is the immanence and transcendence inserted in the heart of every being.

We should hasten to add that these three horizons are not mutually exclusive. Many a thinker in many a tradition has tried to elaborate a conception of deity embracing all three. Within Hinduism, for instance, *nirguṇa brahman* would correspond to the third type, *saguṇa brahman* to the first, and *īśvara* might be the personal deity of the devotee. Similarly, the Christian Scholastic tradition would like to combine God, the prime mover (the first type), with the personal God of the believers (the second type), and that of the mystics (the third type). How far all three can be reduced to an intelligible unity is a philosophical and theological problem that different traditions try to solve in different ways.

The morphological traits of deity may be summarized according to these three horizons, suggesting a threefold structure for deity. The ultimate experience of the meta-ontological deity is the character of the "I." Deity is the ultimate "I," the final subject of activity. "Who am I?" The "I" who can respond to this question without further questioning is the ultimate "I," the deity.

The meta-anthropological deity represents the experience of the "thou." In the human urge toward the deity this latter appears as the ultimate "thou" with whom dialogue and human relations can be established.

The deity as the ultimate cause and prime mover of the world is the "he, she, or it" that only an inference discloses. One speaks of this deity always in the third person.

Methods. We may now turn to the different methods used in the attempt to understand deity. Whatever deity may be, it is neither a sensible nor an intelligible thing. The deity is neither a visible thing nor a mere thought. Modern hermeneutics speaks of "pre-understanding" as a necessary condition of understanding, of a "hermeneutical circle" that is needed in all interpretation. Within the realm of sensible or intelligible objects we may be able to ascertain what pre-understanding is. We acquire an idea of the whole, which we may modify while investigating the parts. It is on the basis of this pre-understanding that a given method is applied to understanding an object. But how can this be done in the case of deity? If every method implies a proleptic jump into the alleged object, a coming back to our starting point, and a methodical process afterward, it is difficult to see how such a method can be applied in our attempt to understand deity. We do not know in which direction we should make the first jump nor with what instruments to approach it—unless we start from the received tradition or with an authentic mystical experience. This amounts to saying that we renounce finding a method of searching for deity and replace it by methods of research, interpreting the opinions of people about it. We know, further, that if we start with some "instruments," the results will greatly depend on the nature of those instruments. We can then neither jump (if we don't know the direction) nor come back (if the subject matter is beyond the senses and the intellect). In a word, the method for seeking the deity is *sui generis*—if indeed there is a method at all.

How do we come to a pre-understanding of deity? We may receive it from tradition. In the case of a direct mystical experience there is not a pre-understanding but an immediate insight that the mystic afterward explicates in terms of the culture in which he or she lives, and so ultimately it comes to the same thing. The mystic needs a post-understanding, as it were, in terms of his or her time and culture, which amounts to an initial pre-understanding for all the others. The pre-understanding of deity is, therefore, a traditional datum. Now, there are three main attitudes toward this datum. If one accepts it as a starting point and proceeds to a critical effort at understanding it, this is the *theological method.* [*See* Theology.] The theologian tries to clarify something from within. If one tries to bracket one's personal beliefs and attempts to decipher the immense variety of opinions throughout the ages regarding the idea of deity, this is the *phenomenological method.* The datum is then the sediment of the history of human consciousness. Finally, if one reflects on one's own experience, enriched as much as possible by the thoughts of others, this is the *philosophical method.* [*See* Study of Religion.]

These methods are not mutually exclusive, and all three play a role in the human quest for deity. All are required and they imply each other. We distinguish between them for heuristic reasons only. Each one presents divisions and subdivisions. Sociology, psychology, anthropology, and so forth are among the important disciplines within these three approaches, each with its own particular methods.

We refer to methods in the plural, for there is not one single theological, phenomenological, or philosophical method. Each of these approaches presents a variety of methods. What we describe here is only a general pattern of methods, which acquire a proper physiognomy when applied to particular cases.

Theological. The theological method begins with an accepted datum: there exists a world of the gods, the world of deity. We will therefore have to clarify and eventually justify the *raison d'être* of such a world, but we do not necessarily have to prove its existence. In short, the origin of the idea of deity is the deity itself—whatever this deity may be. This forms the core of the so-called ontological argument and of any religious enterprise that wants to clarify the nature of deity. Deity could not be known if it did not exist. The theological problem here consists of determining what kind of existence this is. When Thomas Aquinas, for instance, ends each one of his five proofs for the existence of God by saying "and that is what all call God," he shows his theological method of clarifying the existence of something that we already call God. The deity was already there, certainly, as an idea, but also as a reality that hardly anyone doubted, although its rationality had to be demonstrated and its existence verified as real and not merely apparent. Theological proofs thus presuppose faith and only prove that such faith is rational. They are a form of *fides quaerens intellectum* ("faith seeking understanding").

We have already indicated that each combination of method and horizon yields a distinct picture of deity. In fact, theological methods have been mainly combined with the cosmological and the ontological horizons. They have been less conversant with the anthropological one, and this explains the uneasiness in theological circles when dealing with the emerging sciences of man, like psychology and sociology. The theological dialogues with Freud, Jung, and Weber are typical examples. There are serious studies on the psychology and sociology of religion, but little attention has been given to the psychology and sociology of deity from a theological perspective. Hans Urs von Balthasar's work on a theology of aesthetics is a notable exception.

Phenomenological. The phenomenological method could also be described as morphological, or even historical, since it is used in the new science of religions, often called the history of religions. On the whole there is a consensus regarding the phenomenological method, as the study of peoples' beliefs drawn from their own self-understanding, as reflected in the critical consciousness of the scholar. Here is the place for a typology of the conceptions of deity. This method is important today, in a world in which people of different religions mingle in the concerns of daily life, that is, in the stresses of technological civilization.

Use of the phenomenological method uncovers an immense variety of types of deity. We find the so-called animistic conception of deity as an all-pervading and living force animating everything that there is. We find so-called polytheism, the presence of many "gods" as supernatural entities with different powers and functions. We find so-called deism as the belief in a supreme being, probably a creator, who is afterward passive in relation to his creation, a notion that excludes any kind of specially revealed god. We find monotheism of the type of the Abrahamic religions, religions of a living, provident, and creator god. We find the various theisms that modify the exclusiveness of the monotheistic model, and pantheism, the identification of the deity with the universe. We also find all sorts of atheisms, as reactions to theism and especially to monotheism. And of course we find a number of distinctions and qualifications of these broad notions that are intended to respond to the demands of reason or answer difficulties raised by particular or collective experiences.

These types, and the changes that they have undergone through the ages, have been the subject of many useful and comprehensive studies by well-known scholars like Mircea Eliade, Gerardus van der Leeuw, Geo Widengren, Kurt Goldammer, W. Bede Kristensen, and Friedrich Heiler. With the possible exception of Widengren, none of these authors uses the notion of God as a major religious category. Even Widengren, who emphatically wants to distinguish religion from magic, while affirming that "faith in God constitutes the intimate essence of religion," has a very large idea of what God means. All the others recognize that there is a particular sphere that is at the center of religious life.

Philosophical. The philosophical method proceeds differently, although, in ways, not totally disconnected from those of the previous ones. Pascal's famous *mémorial,* which was found stitched in his coat after his death, "The God of Abraham, the God of Isaac, the God of Jacob, not of philosophers and scholars," has since served in the West to emphasize this difference. Without entering into the discussion of whether the "living God" is the *actus purus* or whether one can fall in love with the prime mover, the quintessence of the philosophical method consists in the willingness to question everything. The philosophical method is that of the radical question, be it the question of salvation, *mokṣa,* happiness, or whatever form in which it may be conceived. It is within this framework that the question of deity appears. Here in a cloud either of knowledge or of unknowing, in a science of good and evil, lies the philosophical locus of deity. This locus is the ultimate question, even if there is no final answer.

When this ultimate locus is considered to be being, the question of deity turns out to be what Heidegger calls an "onto-theology," a reflection on the being of beings. Here, the philosophical method meets the historical controversy. Is deity the highest being or is it being as such? In the latter case it cannot be a supreme being. The ontological difference is not the theological one. The history of religions puts the same question by simply asking how the supreme being is related to the entire reality. This polarity between being and supreme being permeates most of the conceptions about deity. We could phrase it as the polarity between the deity of the intellectuals (being) and the deity of the people (supreme being). A more academic way of saying it is this: deity may appear as a result of a thinking reflection (discovering being) or an existential attitude (requiring a supreme being). For the former, deity is the subsisting being, source of being, the foundation, the being "being" in all beings. For the latter, deity is the supreme being, the lord, the divine person, the ultimate in the pyramid of reality. The former conception will have to clarify the relation between deity as a ground of being and an undetermined and general *ens commune.* The latter will have to define the relation between deity as *esse subsistens* and the rest of beings that the deity creates, rules, and directs.

Is deity being *(Sein, sat, esse)* or the supreme being *(höchstes Seiendes, paramātman, ens realissimum)*? One can think about the first, but one cannot worship it. One can adore the second and trust in it, but this God cannot be reasoned about; it is corroded by thinking.

If the philosophical locus of the deity is the ultimate question, we may find as many conceptions of deity as there are ultimate questions. Thus the many and varied answers. The diversity of religions can also be explained from this perspective. Religions give different answers to ultimate questions, and the questions themselves are different. But philosophical reflection may ask still further: what is it that prompts man to ask the ultimate question, whatever this question may be? Why is man an asking being, ever thirsty for questions?

In a word, the issue of the deity has to do with the peculiarity of man as a questioning animal. "God acts without a why and does not know any why," says Meister Eckhart. What prompts man to question is ultimately the consciousness of not being realized, of not knowing, of being finite. This consciousness can be expressed as the anthropological discovery that man is imperfect, still in the making; the cosmological observation that the universe is moving, that is, also still becoming; or the ontological thought of nothingness lurking over being. In sum, the problem of becoming emerges here as the theological problem *par excellence.* If becoming is possible, it is because being is still "being." What covers this gap between being and becoming (encompassing or not encompassing the two) is the locus of the deity: it keeps open the flow of being.

The Texture of Human Consciousness of Deity. The different perspectives on the human approach to deity that we have found end in a healthy pluralism: reality is itself pluralistic. We cannot, of course, encompass this plurality in a unified scheme of intelligibility on a universal scale. Yet if we keep in mind our particular situation in time and place and its various viewpoints and prejudices, we may venture some further valid considerations.

Our point of departure is the lost innocence of our present situation. Whatever deity may be, whatever peoples of other epochs have felt, thought, or believed about deity, even if they have told us that it was the deity itself who spoke to them, it remains always the conviction of contemporary man that all relation to deity takes place in and through human consciousness. This in no way weakens the reality or the objectivity of deity. It only affirms that human consciousness is always a fellow traveler in this journey. If we want to reach a consensus regarding the many opinions on the nature of deity, we shall have to fall back upon the texture of our consciousness, even while accepting that deity may be much more than an act or content of consciousness and that this consciousness may vary with time and place and even be shaped by the power of deity.

In view of the many opinions about deity we have to rely upon the one factor that is common to them all, namely the human consciousness that uses the word *deity* or its homeomorphic equivalents. Deity has this one constitutive feature: it is disclosed to us in an act of consciousness, an act of consciousness that, in spite of having a transcendent intentionality, has no verifiable referent outside of consciousness. The reference of the word *deity,* in fact, is neither visible nor intelligible, and yet every culture in the world witnesses to the fact that men constantly speak about a "something" that transcends all other parameters. We have then to rely on the cultural documents of the past and the present that witness to this *tertium* we call *deity.*

We rely on the fact that people have meant something when using this word or its equivalents. The analysis of deity is based therefore not on the empirical presence of the object nor on the immediate evidence of thought but on tradition in its precise and etymological meaning, that is, on some cultural good that is being transmitted to us. One exception seems to be the case of mystics, who say that they have directly experienced this extra-empirical and supra-intellectual reality. Yet the moment that the mystics speak they have to fall back upon their consciousness. The thought and speech of the divine belong to that unique field of human consciousness whose contents are disclosed in the very experience that has them and nowhere else. This explains the elusive character of the divine and also accounts for the fact that the question is more important than the answer.

Deity is visible only in its alleged manifestations—

and there is no way to make visible the manifesting power beyond what is manifested. Nicholas of Cusa says pointedly that God is the invisibility of the visible world, just as the world is the appearance of the invisible God.

Nor is deity intelligible. It would cease to be divine if we could grasp its meaning as something belonging to the human or worldly sphere. The divine is not subject to observation, nor can there be a science of the divine. Thus Meister Eckhart says that we must transcend not only the things of the imagination but even those of the understanding.

Long before Śaṅkara, the Indian world made crucial the distinction between appearance and reality and recognized that the latter transcends both the senses and the mind. The short *Kena Upsaniṣad* is perhaps one of the best scriptural texts to underline the transcendence and immanence of the deity:

> That which cannot be expressed by words
> but by which the word is expressed . . .
> That which cannot be thought by the mind,
> but that by which, they say, the mind is thought . . .
> That which cannot be seen by the eye,
> but that by which the eyes have sight. . . .
>
> . . .
>
> It is not understood by those who understand;
> it is understood by those who do not understand.
> (1.5ff, 2.3)

In sum, of the divine there is only *logos* ("word"): *theologia*. But it is a *logos* irreducible to *nous;* that is, it is a word only revealed in the experience itself. This does not allow us to conclude that the divine is just a subjective state of experience. All things are related to states of experience, but of all others we have a communicable referent; we can get at the *res nominis,* that is, at the thing named. This is not the case with the divine. The *res nominis* is in the *ratio nominis,* that is, in the meaning of the name itself. And this is what has made theological and religious disputes so uncompromisingly serious. The names of God are all we have. Considering names as mere labels of things (as in nominalism) is the proper procedure of modern science, but this method is not adequate if applied to deity. Without the names we have no way of reaching the referent.

The names of deity are also different from abstract names like justice and beauty. We may infer the meaning of justice by observing a certain pattern of behavior among people and acquire some sense of beauty by contrasting some of our experiences with similar ones of other people. Both human behavior and sensible objects fall in the category of commonly shared experiences. In other words, the referent in all these cases is verifiable outside of consciousness although not independent of it. This is not the case with deity. We cannot verify it as an object outside the field of our own consciousness, nor can we compare our states of consciousness as we can in the case of other abstract concepts. In this latter case we can point to the things or acts reflecting, revealing, or somehow defining the meaning we give to such words. In the case of deity we can certainly infer the idea people have of it from what they say and do, but there is one difference: a dimension of transcendence, of ineffability, inadequacy, ultimacy, or uniqueness, which necessarily leaves a gap between the manifested and its source. This is the reason why some traditions have postulated a special "seventh" sense related to the divine, which is neither reducible to the five senses nor to the "sixth" sense of the intellect.

Now, to affirm that all the names of deity mean ultimately the same thing assumes at the start that "our" name is the real one. We make of our conception of it, expressed in the name we give it, the pattern for all other conceptions. The name we give it would then name the "thing" that is supposed to have other names as well. This is not the case. Not everybody is looking for the same thing, either the ultimate cause, the ground of being, or absolute nothingness, if any of these is what we mean by deity. Much less are the worshipers of Kālī ready to give up their practice and worship Allāh, or true Christians ready to deny Christ and adore Caesar. Deity is not a Kantian "thing in itself." Words matter. The conception we have of deity is certainly not identical with its reality. But it is our way of access to it, which we cannot deny without betraying ourselves. Martyrdom for the sake of a name is a human fact not reducible to sheer fanaticism.

The name we give it, or the name anyone else gives it, does not exhaust the nature of deity. Strictly speaking we do not name it. We only refer to him, her, or it. Or we simply believe, call, pray, shout, dance, or whatever. Deity is not an object of naming but of invocation. Deity is what we appeal to, implore, and worship precisely because it is beyond our apprehending faculties.

In the Greek tradition *theos* is a predicative name. Things are divine, and a particular entity is godly. *Theos* is an attribute. God is not a concept but a name. But when the name loses its power no amount of conceptualization can give it back.

There has been a shift in the idea of deity from the predicate to the subject. This is a great revolution. In the West this could be said to represent the genius of the Abrahamic traditions. While many traditions say that light, love, or goodness is God, that is, divine ("Truth is God" was a slogan of Mohandas Gandhi), the New Testament reverses the sentence and affirms that God is light, love, or goodness. Something similar could be said of the great Upaniṣadic revolution: in the Upaniṣads we witness the passage of the god of the third person (the Vedic gods) to the god of the first person (*aham brahman,* "I am *brahman*") by means of the second person (*tat tvam asi,* "that thou art"). The revelation of the "I" dawns in the very realization of the aspirant to liberation; the "I" is not a third person (he, she, it, or even they). The language of the deity cannot be the third person. The deity has to be the first person. It is only the real "I" when it says "I," or rather when "I" says "I," and more exactly when I say "I". This is what is called realization—the realization of the I (by the I). Only the I can say "I".

At any rate the divine is so linked to our state of consciousness that there is no way of deciding what ontic status it has outside the ontological statement. Or, rather, the deity has no ontic status. An ontological statement has an accepted currency only with people who share in the same myth, one in which a particular form of the divine is taken for granted.

The claim to universality is the temptation of any complex and sophisticated culture. This aspiration to universality is built into human nature. But we often fail to recognize that we cannot make a claim for universality in our own terms, which are far from being universal. [*See* Truth.]

Meaningful talk about the divine is thus restricted to those belonging to the same mythical sphere. Others will hear but not really understand. Each culture or subculture has a myth in which their particular form of the divine is possible and talked about. In this sense it cannot be generalized. It is restricted to those of the same faith, to the initiated. Properly speaking, we do not know what we are talking about when we refer to the divine. We are already taking it for granted, which is the function of any myth, that is, to offer the unquestioned horizon of intelligibility where our words are meaningful.

And yet the world of deity is an ever-recurrent world in the history of mankind. What do all these traditions refer to? If asked, believers might answer that the divine is not just a purely subjective state of consciousness; most will assert that they refer to the highest realm of reality, a realm so high that it is beyond the reach of human powers. And yet they continue to speak of it. It belongs to their myth. The myth is the locus of belief. It is only when pressed by those outside their group that they concede that there is no possibility of showing any referent in the world of common human experience. At most they may point to an homeomorphic experience if they have found a language of communication.

What is, then, the content of such an experience of deity? We have said that the content of the experience is inseparable from the experience itself, so that it cannot be "shown" outside the experience: the divine is neither sensible nor intelligible. Is there something else? Common sense and historical evidence say that of course there is something else, since everybody seems to speak about the divine in one form or another. The critical mind will say that it makes no sense to speak about something that we cannot think. That is why many a philosopher feels more comfortable calling the content of that experience nothingness. All theology ends by being apophatic.

From these considerations we may infer that there is something in human consciousness that points to something beyond, and yet we are unable to "locate" it outside that consciousness. God has been described as a "transcending center of intention" (John E. Smith). No wonder that many thinkers in both the East and West then identify deity with consciousness in its highest form. Others defend a sort of transcendental dynamism of human consciousness toward a superior and perfect form of consciousness, which they then call divine. Still others affirm that it is only a pathological growth of our own consciousness, triggered perhaps by fear of the unknown or fostered by religious priestcraft for the sake of power. Finally, while recognizing both the divine immanence of human consciousness and the human intentionality toward a divine transcendent consciousness, some do not dare to consider deity as the all-encompassing reality but only as a dimension of it. Reality is primary to consciousness. Consciousness is always consciousness *of,* of reality, of being, even of itself. This last is the *noēsis noēseōs* of Aristotle, the absolute reflection of Hegel, and the *svayamprakāśa* ("self-illumination") of Vedānta. Now pure consciousness cannot be of anything, not even of itself. This is what lets Vedānta say that *brahman* is not even conscious of being *brahman.* It is Īśvara, the Lord, who is the full consciousness of *brahman.* Something similar could be said of the Father, the *plenitudo fontalis* of the Christian Trinity.

The Deity between God and the Sacred. Having tried to present the problematic of deity in its broadest aspect, we may ask whether speaking of "the divine" is not preferable to speaking of "deity." It may better describe what we are looking for, namely a super- or meta-category that can serve to express the religious phenomenon in its universality. In fact, *deity,* because its grammatical form is substantive, suggests a certain kind of substantialization that is inappropriate for many religious traditions, which we could call the *nāstikās* or *anātmavādins* (such as the Buddhists who say that there is no God because there is no substance). Thus, in spite of some modern efforts at adaptation, the

Buddhist world, for one, feels uncomfortable with the word *deity*—although not, of course, with deities.

There is another category of similar generality that has often been presented as the center of the religious traditions of humankind. Every religion, we are told, deals with the sacred. [*See* Sacred and the Profane, The.] It was Nathan Söderblom who, in 1913, described the notion of holiness as even more essential than the notion of God. For Söderblom, there is no real religion without a distinction between the holy and the profane. Mircea Eliade is today the most important spokesman for the centrality of the sacred as the religious phenomenon *par excellence*. But, we may ask, if the sacred is the central category of religion, what is the place and role of deity?

There is a danger in wanting to reduce the immense jungle of man's religious experience, as crystallized in the different religions of the world, to a single category or even to a single set of categories. Even if this were possible, its only purpose would be to give a panoramic and coherent picture of the whole. But what cannot be universalized is precisely the perspective of the observer. Let us assume that the sacred is a convincing category for understanding and describing religious phenomena. It would still be true that it is only a suitable category for us—that is, a very special class of readers in time and space. If our parameters of understanding change, then the perspective must also vary. In short, we cannot universalize our perspective, and a "global perspective" is obviously a contradiction in terms. There is thus room for more than one attempt to focus the religious experience of man. Let me try then to point out the locus of deity in the panorama of human religious experience and distinguish it from the sacred.

One feature seems to permeate all the varied meanings of deity: personality. Deity does not need to be a substance nor a person in the modern sense of the word. But on the other hand, *deity* does not denote merely a character of things, as does the word *sacred*. Deity is a source of action, an active element, a spontaneous factor: it is free. Its actions cannot be anticipated; it has initiative. We cannot deal with deity as with an object that we can imprison in the web of our thoughts. Deity has a mysterious quality of being able to act and not just react, to take the lead, even if in a purely passive way.

We should distinguish between personality and person on the one hand and person and substance on the other. We may recall that the concept of person in the West was developed not as a meditation on man but as a theological problem. To speak of the personality of deity is no more an anthropomorphism than is speaking of God as a supreme being, which some would call an anthropomorphism simply because man is also a being. Here the polemical aspect of the notion of deity comes to the fore. Almost everyone will admit that there is a third dimension in reality, since man and the world, as they are experienced by us, do not exhaust that other pole that is neither man nor the world as we experience them now. But not everyone is prepared to admit that this third pole has personality, that is, that it is endowed with freedom, is a source of action, has an identity, and is relationship.

In this sense, the concept of deity is not just the idea that there is a third pole in reality. Nor is it identical with the concept of God. It stands between the sacred and God. It shares with the former its immanence and with the latter its personality (in the sense we have indicated). But while the concept of God seems to imply a certain substance, the idea of deity does not need to present this characteristic. It says only that this third dimension is not a mere mental hypothesis, a piece of mental equipment necessary for making sense of reality or merely something to fill in the gaps in our understanding. The notion of deity affirms boldly that this other dimension is real, that is, active, free, efficacious, and powerful on its own account. But it does not make it independent of the two other poles and thus not even independent of our conceptions of it. In a word, deity connotes the highest form of life.

Conclusion. This cross-cultural approach to the mystery of deity has one liberating consequence. It liberates us from the many aporias that, for centuries, have tortured the human mind as it attempts to consider God as the supreme being. Among these are the questions: is it personal or impersonal? If almighty, how can it condone evil? If infinite, what is the place of finite beings? If absolutely free, why can it not make two and two equal five? If omniscient, what about human freedom? Subtle theological and philosophical answers have been put forward. But the answers could be made simpler by cutting the Gordian knot of a universal theory about God and rediscovering the divine as a true dimension of reality.

Whether the word *deity* means a plurality of divine beings, absolute consciousness, perfect happiness, the supreme being, a divine character of beings, or being as such, thought about deity has no referent. At the same time it seems to be one of the most unvarying and powerful factors in human life throughout ages and across cultures. Words referring to deity or its homeomorphic equivalents are unique. Philosophy avers that the intentionality of human consciousness, while pointing outside itself, cannot show in the realm of the sensible or the intelligible the referent of this intentional act. In a word, there is no object that is deity. Either human consciousness transcends itself, or thought about deity is an illusion, albeit a transcendental illusion of historical reality.

We should return now to one of our earlier queries. Is the word *deity* broad enough to include all the types of the mystery we have tried to describe? We know that its original field is the cosmological, but we have also noted that we distinguish it from the name *God* precisely to allow it other horizons.

The word *deity* may partially fulfill this role on one essential condition: that it strip itself of all connotations coming from a single group of civilizations. This amounts to saying that it cannot have any specific content, because any attribute, be it being, nonbeing, goodness, creatorship, fatherhood, or whatever, is meaningful only within a given cultural universe (or a group of them). Deity becomes then an empty symbol to which different cultures attribute different concrete qualifications, positive or negative. *Deity* would then say something only when translated into a particular language.

I am still critical of such an option, however, and would like to propose a compromise that may appear obvious once explained. Were this article to be translated into Chinese, Arabic, or Swahili, what word would we use to convey this idea of deity? Either we would coin a new name or use an old one with the connotations of the particular language. So we can say that for the English language *deity* may be a convenient name to use to transcend the provincial limits of certain groups of cultures such as the one that thinks, for instance, that Buddhism was not a religion and Confucianism only a philosophy because they do not accept the Abrahamic idea of God. But we should not elevate the word *deity* as the name for that meta-category. It is only a pointer toward the last horizon of human consciousness and the utmost limit of human powers of thinking, imagining, and being. Now, an abstract name like *the Ultimate* or a metaphor like *horizon* are equally dependent on particular cultural systems or ways of thinking. Perhaps the word *mystery* is more adequate, in spite of its Hellenic flavor. Or should we say *brahman, kami, numen . . .?*

At any rate we should insist that this does not mean that all those quests search for the same thing but in different places. The quest is different in each case, and so are the ways or methods involved. We leave open the question (ultimately as a pseudo-question) whether we use different methods because we look for different things or whether we find different answers because we use different methods. Both possibilities are intrinsically related, and their relation does not lie on the level of the *logos* but on the level of the *mythos,* as we have suggested. All our ways and means, all our quests and perspectives already belong not only to the searching but also to what is sought. Deity is not independent of our own search for it. If we radically destroy all the ways to the peak, the entire mountain will collapse. The slopes of the mountain also make the mountain.

Scholars may debate whether humankind is or is not monotheistic, whether a personal god is a universal truth or there actually is a creator, whether the so-called atheists are right in denouncing anthropomorphisms and dogmatisms of all sorts, whether there is a divine origin of this universe or a glorious or catastrophical *parousia.* One thing seems to emerge as a cultural universal and a historical invariant: besides the world and man there is a third pole, a hidden dimension, another element that has received and is still receiving the most varied names, each name being a witness of its power and of the impotence of human beings to reduce everything to a common denominator.

The human being both individually and as a species is not alone. Man is not alone not only because he has an earth under his feet but also because he has a heaven above his head. There is something else, something more than what meets the eye or comes into the range of the mental. There is something more, a plus that humans cannot adequately name but that haunts them nevertheless. This plus is freedom and infinity. Deity stands for all that is un-finished (in-finite) and thus allows for fulfillment in one sense or another. Man needs—and discovers—an opening, a way out of the strictures of the exclusively empirical or ideological affairs of daily life. The idea of deity can provide such an opening, provided that it can be kept free of any particular content. It would then become a symbol for the emerging myth of a human race that can no longer afford to transform cultural discrepancies into a cosmic tragedy.

[*See also* Theism.]

BIBLIOGRAPHY

Balthasar, Hans Urs von. *Herrlichkeit.* Einsiedeln, 1961. A treatment of the topic from the perspective of a theology of aesthetics.

Balthasar, Hans Urs von. *Theodramatik.* Einsiedeln, 1978.

Castelli, Enrico, ed. *L'analyse du langage théologique: Le nom de Dieu.* Paris, 1969. Offers a philosophical perspective.

Eliade, Mircea. *A History of Religious Ideas,* vol. 1, *From the Stone Age to the Eleusinian Mysteries.* Chicago, 1978.

Gilson, Étienne. *God and Philosophy.* New Haven, 1941.

Heidegger, Martin. *Holzwege.* Frankfurt, 1950. Offers distinctions between concepts of God, deity, the sacred, and salvation.

James, E. O. *The Concept of Deity.* London, 1950. A historical treatment.

Kumarappa, Bharatan. *The Hindu Conception of the Deity as Culminating in Rāmānuja.* London, 1934.

Owen, H. P. *Concepts of Deity.* New York, 1971.

Panikkar, Raimundo. *The Unknown Christ of Hinduism.* Rev. & enl. ed. New York, 1981. See pages 97–155.

Panikkar, Raimundo. *Il silenzio di Dio: La risposta del Buddha.* Rome, 1985. An analysis of the Buddhist idea of the emptiness of deity.

Pettazzoni, Raffaele. "The Supreme Being: Phenomenological Structure and Historical Development." In *The History of Religions: Essays in Methodology,* edited by Mircea Eliade and Joseph M. Kitagawa. Chicago, 1959.

Pöll, Wilhelm. *Das religiöse Erlebnis und seine Strukturen.* Munich, 1974. See the chapter entitled "Der göttlich-heilige Pol." A positive analysis of the divine/sacred from a psychological perspective.

Schmidt, Wilhelm. *Der Ursprung der Gottesidee: Eine historisch-kritische und positive Studie.* 12 vols. Munster, 1912–1955. A response to the evolutionary hypothesis concerning the concept of deity.

RAIMUNDO PANIKKAR

DE LAS CASAS, BARTOLOMÉ. *See* Las Casas, Bartolomé de.

DE LA VALLÉE POUSSIN, LOUIS. *See* La Vallée Poussin, Louis de.

DELAWARE PROPHET. *See* Neolin.

DELITZSCH, FRIEDRICH (1850–1922), German Assyriologist. Friedrich Conrad Gerhard Delitzsch was the son of the Old Testament scholar Franz Delitzsch (1813–1890). Both were men of extremely high linguistic ability, but in other respects they formed a striking contrast. The father was pious and conservative in theology, and although he was interested in Christian missions to the Jews, he was warmly appreciative of Judaism; the son became iconoclastic and contemptuous toward traditional doctrine and hostile to the entire dependence of Christianity upon Judaism.

The leading figure in the Assyriology of his time, Friedrich Delitzsch placed grammar and lexicography of the languages of ancient Mesopotamia on a sound and exact basis. In the area of biblical scholarship, his *Die Lese- und Schreibfehler im Alten Testament* (1920) provided an exhaustive classification of ways in which copying errors, such as writing one consonant in place of another, may have affected the text of the Hebrew Bible. His main influence on religious studies came with the "Babel-Bible" controversy. Advances in Assyriology had already made a difference to scholarship but had hardly affected the general public. Delitzsch's two lectures "Babel und Bibel" were delivered, in 1902, before the German Oriental Society and were attended by Kaiser Wilhelm II, who took an active interest in these matters. In the past, the Bible had been considered the oldest book: it was believed to reach back to the beginnings of the world. Now Assyriology presented new knowledge, knowledge that went back to an epoch much earlier than that of which the Bible had known. The similarity between the Babylonian and the biblical worlds was enormous. But this meant that the Old Testament material was not unique and could not count as pure revelation. The Babylonian material confirmed the antiquity of the biblical material but put in question its finality. In fact the Old Testament rose little above the religious and ethical level of Mesopotamian civilization.

By relativizing the authority of many elements within the Bible, the new discoveries made room for a conception of religion that was more in accord with "reason." Delitzsch insisted on the spiritual and universal nature of God as discerned, he thought, by the German Reformation. In this light, what Delitzsch considered the limited, parochial, and sometimes immoral world of the Old Testament could not continue to have authority. These ideas met with a storm of opposition. In his later work *Die grosse Täuschung* (The Great Deception; 1921), Delitzsch continued in the same vein but became more extreme. The Old Testament was a collection of fragments which had some literary and cultural value but had no relevance for Christianity. Christianity had as close a relation to paganism, Delitzsch claimed, as it had to Judaism, and he emphasized to an almost hysterical degree the "defects," "inaccuracies," and "immoralities" of the Old Testament.

Delitzsch was facing real problems in the existence of common ground between the Bible and its antecedent religious environment and of religious differences between some strata of the Bible and others. But the controversial stand he took was rooted more in modern ideological conflicts than in a dispassionate study of the ancient religions. His use of ancient evidence was often exaggerated and distorted, as when he argued that Jesus, being a Galilean, was not of Jewish blood and when he asserted that Jesus' teaching was "anti-Jewish." Similarly, Delitzsch's conception of Christianity draws from only a very narrow strand in the Christian tradition. As history of religion, his assessment of the data was intemperate, and his outbursts had the effect of retarding rather than advancing the cool assessment of the problems that Assyriological discovery had created for the relationship between Bible and religion.

BIBLIOGRAPHY

Delitzsch's controversial lectures were published in German as two books under the same title, *Babel und Bibel* (Leipzig, 1902–1903); the English edition, *Babel and Bible* (Chicago, 1903), contains not only the lectures but a selection from the comments they engendered, including those of Kaiser Wilhelm II and of Adolf von Harnack, along with replies by Delitzsch. *Die grosse Täuschung* (Stuttgart, 1921) appears never to have been published in English.

JAMES BARR

DELPHI. The Delphic oracle was the most important oracle of ancient Greece. Archaeological excavations at Delphi have shown that the temple of Apollo, which was the center of the oracular activities, was not built before 750 BCE. It was a time of extensive Greek colonization, and one in which the oracle, for obscure reasons, managed to play an important role. This activity may well have been the decisive factor in establishing Delphi almost immediately as an authoritative oracle, and Homer's *Iliad*, most commonly dated to the eighth century BCE, already mentions the wealth of its votive offerings. Its geographical location, far from powerful Greek city-states, undoubtedly helped its rise to fame; for none of the consulting states had to fear that its rich presents would foster the development of a rival state. On the other hand, Delphi was not so remotely situated as the oracle of Dodona (in northwestern Greece), its older rival. The Delphic oracle's fame was highest in the Archaic period, when even kings from Lydia and Cyrene came for consultation.

Earlier studies went so far as to stress the role of Delphi in supporting new moral and religious values such as requiring purification following a murder, but the evidence for such Delphic initiatives is actually very slight. It is indeed hard to see why Delphi, unlike all other oracles, should try to influence its clients beyond their immediate needs. The famous sayings "Nothing in excess" and "Know thyself," which in the sixth century were fitted into the wall of the Delphic temple, reflect existing ideas rather than new ones. Both sayings exhort man to remain within his human limits—a common idea in Archaic Greek literature. It seems therefore more likely that the oracle, through its central position in Greek society, functioned as a sounding board that could amplify current religious conceptions and preoccupations.

The ritual of consulting the oracle was relatively simple. After making various sacrifices, consultants of the oracle had to enter the temple of Apollo where they presented their questions, orally or written on a tablet, to the priestess of Apollo, the Pythia. She was an older woman, whose age made it socially acceptable for her to mix in the company of men such as priests and ambassadors. At the same time, she was dressed as a girl; the conception of the Pythia as the bride of Apollo was at least hinted at in Delphic mythology. The priestess made her utterances seated on a tripod and holding a spray of laurel, but unfortunately we are not informed about the exact process whereby she arrived at her oracles. Later reports, both ancient and modern, mention prophetic vapors emerging from a chasm below the priestess, but this has been disproved by modern archaeological findings. Such reports were evidently rationalizing explanations of the Pythia's skill in giving oracles. Her voice was supposed to change when she responded to the inquiries, which seems to indicate an altered state of consciousness. At the "séance," special "prophets" were present who translated the Pythia's utterances into acceptable prose or hexameters. It is not known to what extent the consultants could influence the outcome of the oracle, but it seems clear that the opinion of powerful clients was regularly taken into consideration. The grateful consultants dedicated votive offerings to the god, and in the highly competitive Greek society the exhibition of these offerings encouraged a kind of potlatch in dedications: at the end of the fifth century, there were nearly thirty special buildings in which Greek cities displayed their dedications.

Many of the inquiries and the oracle's corresponding answers have been preserved, although a number of these answers are demonstrably forgeries—products of hindsight. Greek cities as well as individuals sought the oracle's advice on a wide range of religious, political, and private matters. The evidence shows that in general the oracle helped to decide between various alternatives rather than to predict the future; recourse to the oracle must often have been a convenient way of avoiding the risk of being blamed for the wrong decision.

Delphi's prestige remained high until the fourth century BCE, when it was looted and, perhaps more fatal, when Alexander the Great moved the center of the Greek world to the East. The rulers of the warring factions after Alexander's death (c. 323 BCE) had no time for embassies to Delphi. Although on a much lower level, the oracle continued functioning in Roman times when the prolific author Plutarch (c. 45–120 CE) was one of its priests; his two treatises *The Oracles at Delphi No Longer Given in Verse* and *The Obsolescence of Oracles* are a mine of information on Delphi's rich mythology and ritual. In the fourth century CE, Delphi still attracted the attention of Roman emperors, but the prohibition of all pagan cults in 392 by the Christian emperor Theodosius I also meant the end of this age-old institution.

[*See also* Oracles.]

BIBLIOGRAPHY

The best survey of the history of the oracle, together with a collection of all the extant oracles, is H. W. Parke and D. E. W. Wormell's *The Delphic Oracle*, 2 vols. (Oxford, 1956). The oracles are translated and discussed, if in a sometimes too skeptical way, by Joseph Fontenrose in *The Delphic Oracle* (Berkeley, 1978). Georges Roux's *Delphes: Son oracle et ses dieux* (Paris, 1976) is the best modern account of the Delphic complex and its ritual. Simon Price's "Delphi and Divination," in *Greek Religion and Society*, edited by P. E. Easterling and J. V. Muir (Cambridge, 1985), is a good account of Delphi within the context of the Greek belief in oracles. R. C. T. Parker's "Greek States and Greek Oracles," in *Crux: Studies Presented to G. E. M. de Ste.-Croix* (Exeter, 1985), analyses the questions Greek states posed and the answers they received.

JAN BREMMER

DELUGE, THE. *See* Flood, The.

DEMETER AND PERSEPHONE. Demeter, goddess of the grain, and her daughter Persephone, goddess of spring and of the underworld, were prominent figures in the mythology and cultic life of ancient Greece. Demeter, a daughter of Kronos and Rhea, was swallowed by her father and later liberated by her youngest brother, Zeus. Although she was an important member of the Olympian pantheon, her real focus was on earth, not on Olympus. She was originally a fertility goddess who in Classical times was associated primarily with that which grows to human benefit, the grain. After lying with Iasion in a thrice-plowed grainfield, she gives birth to a son, Ploutos, god of wealth, a clear reference to abundant harvests.

With Zeus as father, she also gives birth to a daughter, Persephone. When this child becomes a maiden, Hades, god of the underworld, falls in love with her and receives Zeus's approval of his wish to marry her. Both are sure, however, that Demeter will not give her consent; so one day, while Persephone is gathering flowers in the company of friends, Hades appears and snatches her away. Demeter, distraught by the abduction, wanders over the earth so grief-stricken that she appears age-old, so inattentive to her ordinary responsibilities that no crops grow and the human race is threatened with starvation. Unable to appease her in any other way, Zeus gives in and orders Hades to release the maiden. The reunion between mother and daughter is a joyous one, but because Persephone had eaten several pomegranate seeds while in the underworld, she is required to spend a third of each year there. (Some traditions assert that Persephone's action was the result of a deliberate trick of Hades'; others lay the responsibility on Persephone herself.) The Homeric hymn that relates this myth of the grief and loss inherent in maternal devotion (which is clearly also an allegory about the seed that sprouts in the spring after a winter of dormancy) is appropriately titled *Hymn to Demeter*.

All other accounts of Persephone, also known as Kore ("maiden"), represent her as the dread goddess of the underworld. Often, indeed, she seems to be more directly involved with the fate of the souls of the dead than is Hades himself. She is never reported as absent from her shade-filled realm, and some traditions imply that she has always lived there. Nor are there any indications that she is held there against her will. The idea that underworld existence is to be resisted is a Demetrian one, an upper-world presumption.

The two goddesses are linked not only in myth but also in ritual. The Eleusinian mysteries were known as the Cult of the Two Goddesses. (A strictly women's ritual, the Thesmophoria was dedicated to Demeter alone and provided an occasion for participation in her grief.) The Eleusinian cult was open to men as well as to women and involved an esoteric initiation whose secret remains unknown. But we do know that the focus was on Persephone, the ineffable "She" whose name might not be spoken, and that the rites protected one from the fear of death: "Thrice happy are those of mortals, who having seen these rites depart for Hades; for to them alone is it granted to have found life there" (Sophocles).

[*See also* Eleusinian Mysteries; Thesmophoria; *and, more generally,* Greek Religion. *For discussion of related mythic figures, see* Baubo; Hades; *and* Hekate.]

BIBLIOGRAPHY

The Homeric *Hymn to Demeter* tells the story of the abduction of Persephone and of Demeter's grief in great and beautiful detail; these events are retold in Euripides' *Helen* and in Ovid's *Metamorphoses*. Information about the rites is available in Pausanias. Károly Kerényi's *Eleusis: Archetypal Images of Mother and Daughter* (New York, 1967) and George E. Mylonas's *Eleusisa and the Eleusinian Mysteries* (Princeton, 1961) are helpful modern sources.

CHRISTINE DOWNING

DEMIÉVILLE, PAUL (1894–1979), French Sinologist and Buddhologist. Demiéville was born in Lausanne, Switzerland, and completed undergraduate studies at Bern in 1911. He subsequently studied in Munich, London, Edinburgh, and Paris, finishing work for a doctorate in music at the University of Paris in 1914. He began his study of Chinese the following year at King's College in London, but he returned to Paris to study first at the École Nationale des Langues Orientales and then at the Collège de France, where he worked with Édouard Chavannes. Demiéville graduated from the École des Langues Orientales in 1918, having mastered not only Chinese but Japanese and Sanskrit as well. In 1920 he moved to Hanoi, and from 1924 to 1926 he taught Sanskrit and Western philosophy at the University of Amoy. From 1926 to 1930 he lived in Japan, where he edited the first four volumes (1929–1931) of the encyclopedic dictionary of Buddhism *Hôbôgirin,* compiled under the direction of Sylvain Lévi and Takakusu Junjirō. (The dictionary resumed publication in the 1960s.)

In 1931, Demiéville returned to France to become professor of Chinese at the École Nationale des Langues Orientales, a post he held until 1945, at which time he became director of studies at the École Pratique des Hautes Études, teaching courses in Buddhist philology. In 1946 he succeeded Henri Maspero to the chair of Chinese language and civilization at the Collège de France, the position he held until his retirement in 1964.

Demiéville was a corresponding member of the British Academy, the Association for Asian Studies, and the School of Oriental and African Studies in London and was an honorary member of Tōyō Bunko and of the Académie du Japon. He was awarded honorary doctorates by the universities of Louvain and Rome, and he was elected a member of the Académie des Inscriptions et Belles-Lettres in 1951. He served as codirector of the journal *T'oung pao* (Leiden) from 1945 to 1976.

Demiéville was a prolific writer, publishing 179 studies (books and articles) and 104 book reviews. His works are characterized by philological precision and a thorough examination of the sources. They are models of scholarship. He wrote on Chinese language, art, literature, archaeology, history, philosophy, and religion. But he is best known for his work on Buddhism in China, the school of Ch'an (Zen) in the T'ang dynasty in particular, and for his work on the Buddhist materials found at Tun-huang.

BIBLIOGRAPHY

Book-length studies by Demiéville include the following: *Les versions chinoises du Milindapañha* (Hanoi, 1924); *Le Concile de Lhasa: Une controverse sur le Quiétisme entre bouddhistes de l'Inde et de la Chine au huitième siècle de l'ère chrétienne* (Paris, 1952); and *Entretiens de Lin-tsi,* translated and edited by Demiéville (Paris, 1972). Demiéville was the author of numerous articles, the most important of which are reprinted in two volumes: *Choix d'études sinologiques* (Leiden, 1973) and *Choix d'études bouddhiques* (Leiden, 1973). Both of these volumes contain extensive bibliographies, which are updated in Yves Hervouet's obituary for Demiéville, published in *T'oung pao* 65 (1979): 1–12.

ROBERT G. HENRICKS

DEMIURGE. The Greek term *dēmiourgos* (together with its variants) is derived from the words *dēmos* ("people") and *ergon* ("work") and thus has the basic meaning of "one who works for the people," an artisan or a professional. This etymological base subsequently developed in two directions. On the one hand, *dēmiourgos* came to refer to a magistrate; on the other, it became a name for the original creator of the world, in the specific sense of an ordainer or arranger, someone who as an artist fashions the world out of preexisting matter in accord with a preexisting model. It is this second meaning that is of primary concern here.

The term *dēmiourgos* occurs only twice in Homer, each time in the *Odyssey*. At 17.383 it refers to a professional man such as a soothsayer, physician, carpenter, or inspired poet. At 19.135 it refers to a herald, "one who performs a public function" *(kērukon hoi dēmioergoi easin)*. Here the development of the later meaning, that of "magistrate," is already perceptible. Sophocles uses the term in its original sense when he calls Hades "the savage artisan of Hector's girdle" (*Ajax* 1035). Similarly, Aristophanes links the *dēmiourgoi* ("artisans") with other categories of workers (*Peace* 297) and uses the term *dēmiourgikōs* ("in the style of an artisan, a specialized worker") to refer to Hermes, the versatile god of inventions (*Peace* 429). At one place *dēmiourgos* possibly takes on the specialized sense of "potter" (*Knights* 650), which suggests the future evolution of the word in the sense of "(cosmic) molder." The same term is used in its original meaning by Herodotus (7.31), whereas Thucydides uses it in the sense of "magistrate" (5.47.9; cf. 1.56). The pre-Socratic philosophers use the term *dēmiourgiai* in its original meaning (see, for instance, Philolaos, frag. 11t), whereas in the doxography of these philosophers, the term may refer to a molder or a former, in the sense of a cosmogonic agent (as in Empedocles).

Plato uses the term *dēmiourgos* to refer both to an artisan and to an original arranger of the world. Meaning "artisan" or "craftsman," the term occurs in *Laches*

185e and 195b and in *Charmides* 162e, 164a–b, 171c, 173c, 174e, and 175a. The last two cases include the sense of something that affects or causes; compare *Sophist* 219c, *Philebus* 55d, and *Laws* 829d, where the suggestion is of performers of noble deeds. See also *Gorgias* 452a, 453a–e, and 454a, where rhetoric and arithmetic "produce" persuasion, as do the arts in general. Compare, however, the term used as "creator of phantoms," that is, the opposite of a real creator, in *Republic* 340e, 346c, 599a–d, and 601b; *Apology* 22d and 23e; *Alcibiades 1* 131a and 140b–c; *Gorgias* 447d and 455b; and *Euthydemus* 280c. Note particularly *Republic* 389d and 415a, which quote Homer's *Odyssey* 17.383. In the context of the theory of the three categories of citizens in the *polis*, see *Republic* 597d; *Phaedrus* 248e; and *Sophist* 219c (cf. *Statesman* 280c). See also *Critias* 110c and 112b and *Laws* 746c and 921b.

Closely associated with the meaning "artisan" is the meaning "professional man" or "specialist," which appears in Homer. In this sense the term occurs in *Laches* 195d and *Charmides* 164b (cf. *Philebus* 55d and *Sophist* 229d); *Protagoras* 312b and 322b (*dēmiourgikē technē*, "the professional art" or "skill in handiwork," the gift of Prometheus to mankind, as opposed to the more spiritual or ethical *politikē technē*, the "political art," which is the gift of Zeus); *Cratylus* 389a, where the legislator is the most rare among the "specialists" or "experts" (cf. 428e and *Laws* 921d, respectively, referring to specialists in the arts of instruction and of war); *Euthydemus* 301c and *Phaedo* 86c, where it is a question of artists (cf. also the *Symposium* 186d, among others; *Republic* 401c; and *Sophist* 236a, where it refers to the sculptors of statues); and *Hippias Maior* 290b, where Phidias is mentioned as "a good craftsman knowing the beautiful" (here we are close to the meaning of a molder of the universe inspired by an invisible model). Finally, see *Republic* 596b, where a craftsman "fixes his eyes on the idea or form."

Dēmiourgos in the sense of a divine artisan or creator of the world is found in the *Timaeus*, *Statesman*, *Philebus*, *Republic*, *Sophist*, and *Laws*. It is the *Timaeus*, however, that provides us with the most complete description of the Demiurge. In fact, in the *Timaeus* nearly every occurrence of the noun *dēmiourgos* and the verb *dēmiourgeō* refers to the divine molder of the universe. The only exception to this is 24a, where the reference is to an ordinary artisan. The *Timaeus* presents the role of the Demiurge as essential to both the world and man, since it is responsible for their correspondence as microcosm and macrocosm. Although this theme of the microcosm and macrocosm has led some scholars to posit the survival of (reconstructed) ancient Indo-Iranian speculations on an alleged myth of a primordial man *(makranthrōpos)* in the *Timaeus*, a myth that would express a kind of pantheistic unity of God and world, such a survival is unlikely. In fact, in Plato's *Timaeus* the role of the Demiurge is incompatible with an essentially monistic conception of the world as a gigantic organism. Rather, this text is informed by Plato's fundamental dualism, a dualism that describes an ontological reality while at the same time providing a principle of philosophical hermeneutics.

Plato distinguishes two realms. On the one hand there is the ideal world, the world of the Ideas, the models of all reality. Opposite this stands the sensible world, which comes into being through the activity of the Demiurge, who projects the efficacy of the ideal models that he contemplates into the receptive *chōra* ("receptacle"). Clearly the Demiurge is here to be distinguished both from the Ideas, including the supreme idea, the idea of the Good, and from the soul of the world, the soul that the Demiurge introduces into the "body" of the world in order to animate it.

Plato refers to the Demiurge as a cause or principle *(aitia)* of the world, a term that he also applies to the world of Ideas in its relation to the sensible world. Even the *chōra* itself, the receptacle that preexists the molding activity of the Demiurge, is called an *aitia*, although due to its inferior ontological status it is sometimes referred to inaccurately in translation as "prime matter," in relation to the Demiurge and the world of Ideas.

The molding and animating activity of the Demiurge is an ordering activity that opposes the primordial chaotic disorder of the elements, progressively reducing their disorderly movement. The world is said to be generated by the Demiurge, who is also termed its "maker and father" (*poiētēs kai patēr*, *Timaeus* 28; cf. 41 and "maker and father," *dēmiourgos kai patēr*, at *Statesman* 273; at *Republic* 597d the painter is not *dēmiourgos kai poiētēs*). The Demiurge is also described as "the most perfect of causes," while the world is described as "the most beautiful of generated beings" (*Timaeus* 29). The model that inspires the maker is eternal, always the same, uniform and ungenerated. The Demiurge itself is said to be difficult to know; knowledge of it is impossible to divulge (*Timaeus* 28). Nevertheless, despite these difficulties, the role of the Demiurge does not seem to be in doubt. The beauty of the world sustains the belief that the activity of the Demiurge is beneficent, inspired by an eternal model. As we shall see, this belief stands in marked contrast to the ignorance and the *modus operandi* attributed to the demiurge in gnostic systems. Plato's Demiurge, being good and without envy *(phthonos)*, excludes as much as possible every imperfection from the world.

The role of the Demiurge in fashioning the world is primarily one of providing order. He takes the visible, preexistent mass that moves without measure and order *(kinoumenon plēmmelōs kai ataktōs)* and orders it, placing intellect within the soul of the world and the soul within the world's body, so that the world as a whole might be truly a living being, having a soul and an intellect, and born through the providence of God (29–30). The fashioning of man is somewhat more complex. The Demiurge provides man only with the higher, immortal part of his soul. The soul's inferior, mortal part, as well as the human body, are the creation of the inferior gods. Once brought into being, the Demiurge locates the souls among the stars and notifies them of the "laws of fate" *(nomous tous heimarmenous)*. All souls begin as equals, each enjoying the same original conditions. Their individual destinies are to be determined by either their observance or neglect of piety and righteousness. The just soul is destined to return to its star, while the others are subjected to the law of metensomatosis, according to which a first reincarnation would be in the form of a woman, to be followed by rebirth in the form of an animal, if the soul should persist in its evil (here Plato is heir to the Orphics). Only submission to reason can insure the soul's return to its star. Plato adds that the Demiurge "dictated to them all these laws in order to be in the subsequent times innocent of the evil *(kakia)* of each of them," which can mean either that the Demiurge is innocent of moral evil or, more probably, that it is not responsible for evil souls. It is only after the establishment of this original justice by the Demiurge that the lower gods create for every individual the remaining part of the soul and the body.

Plato discusses the Demiurge in other dialogues as well, although these discussions are not always consistent with the doctrine presented in the *Timaeus* concerning the creation of man. Further discussions may be found at *Statesman* 270, 273 and 308; *Philebus* 27 (cf. 26 and 39); *Republic* 507, 530 (cf. 596 and *Sophist* 234a–b); and *Laws* 902.

The development that leads from the Demiurge of Plato to the demiurge of the gnostics is a long one. As a transitional figure we may mention the Middle Platonist Numenius, who to an extent foreshadowed the pessimistic outlook of the later gnostics. The demiurge of Numenius, which he called the Second God, was an ambivalent figure torn between the possibilities of contemplating the ideal world or, alternatively, directing his attention downward toward the sensible world. A quite different development of the Platonic Demiurge is found in Philo of Alexandria. Philo employs the narrative of the *Timaeus* when he introduces the notion that in creating man God had not worked alone but had been assisted by other heavenly agents. This introduction of demiurgic intermediaries was intended to keep God separate from human evil.

Coming to the gnostics, we encounter the notion of an inferior demiurge, a notion more or less common to the various gnostic schools, sects, and religions, with their anticosmic attitudes, and in clear-cut opposition to the far more positive Platonic notion. This opposition was noticed by the founder of Neoplatonism, Plotinus (third century CE), who wrote a treatise "against those who say that the Demiurge of the world is bad and that the world is bad," namely the gnostics (*Enneads* 2.9). It is true that the gnostic demiurge continues to function as the fashioner of the world and as an intermediary presence. But there is an immense difference: the gnostic demiurge itself belongs to this inferior world, the world of ignorance that holds the spiritual soul in bondage. It is accordingly inferior to the human soul, which, when enlightened by *gnosis*, realizes its consubstantiality with the divine *pneuma*, or spirit. The inferiority of the demiurge is sometimes reflected in its name, as when it is called Saklas ("foolish one").

More precise characterization of the demiurge varies considerably according to the different gnostic schools and sects. On the one hand, there is the monstrous, almost demonic figure of the lion-headed demiurge Ialdabaoth found in the gnostic *Apocryphon of John* and the ignorant, "psychic" (i.e., nonspiritual) Ialdabaoth of the Valentinians. The latter was assigned a role in the preliminary education of man and was destined to be taken up at the end of time into the heavenly realm known as Ogdoad. Significantly, this latter realm was not included in the higher, divine realm of the *plērōma*. On the other hand, among some followers of Basilides one finds the demiurge Sabaoth, who was conceived of as just and who cooperated with the pneumatic or spiritual beings, though he always remained unassimilable to them and was presented as the son of the evil, dethroned Ialdabaoth.

Common to all these gnostic demiurges, however, whether in the Valentinian or Sethian currents, is a complete lack of spiritual or pneumatic nature: they are essentially inferior. In addition, they are often described in terms originally applied to the creator god of the Hebrew scriptures, a god debased in the gnostic ideology. This explains the popularity of Hebrew or pseudo-Hebrew names for the demiurge, such as Ialdabaoth.

The demiurge is also found in other gnostic groups and religions. We may mention the ambivalent demiurge of the Mandaeans, Ptahil, and the demiurge of the Manichaeans, the Spiritus Vivens ("living spirit"), who was an evocation of the Father of Light and was believed to have fashioned the world from the dark, demonic substance of slaughtered demons.

[*See also* Archetypes *and* Gnosticism.]

BIBLIOGRAPHY

Boyancé, Pierre. "Dieu cosmique et dualisme: Les archontes et Platon." In *The Origins of Gnosticism,* 2d ed., edited by Ugo Bianchi, pp. 340-356. Leiden, 1970.

Bréhier, Émile. *The Philosophy of Plotinus.* Translated by Joseph Thomas. Chicago, 1958.

Dodd, C. H. *The Bible and the Greeks* (1935). London, 1964.

Dodds, E. R., et al. *Les sources de Plotin.* Geneva, 1960.

Elsas, Christoph. *Neuplatonische und gnostische Weltablehnung in der Schule Plotins.* Berlin, 1975.

Festugière, A.-J. *La révélation d'Hermès Trismégiste.* 4 vols. Paris, 1950–1954.

Guthrie, W. K. C., et al. *Recherches sur la tradition platonicienne.* Vérone, 1957.

Horst, P. W. van der, and Jaap Mansfeld, eds. and trans. *An Alexandrian Platonist against Dualism: Alexander of Lycopolis' Treatise "Critique of the Doctrines of Manichaeus."* Leiden, 1974.

Jonas, Hans. *The Gnostic Religion.* 2d ed., rev. Boston, 1963.

Merlan, Philip. *From Platonism to Neoplatonism.* 2d ed., rev. The Hague, 1960.

Pétrement, Simone. *Le dualisme chez Platon, les gnostiques et les manichéens.* Paris, 1946.

Places, Édouard des. *Pindare et Platon.* Paris, 1949.

Robinson, T. M. *Plato's Psychology.* Toronto, 1970.

Rose, H. J., et al. *La notion du divin depuis Homère jusqu'à Platon.* Geneva, 1954.

Simon, Marcel. "Eléments gnostiques chez Philon." In *The Origins of Gnosticism,* 2d ed., edited by Ugo Bianchi, pp. 359-376. Leiden, 1970.

UGO BIANCHI

DEMONS. [*This entry consists of two articles:* An Overview *and* Psychological Perspectives. *The first article discusses the origins and development of the term and presents a survey of demons, or spirits, in various religious traditions. It is followed by an essay on the meaning of demons from the point of view of analytical psychology.*]

An Overview

Demons are spirits or spiritual beings, numinous powers both benevolent and malevolent in nature. In Classical Greek culture, *daimōn* may refer to a lesser divinity, a deified hero, a tutelary or protective spirit, an attendant, ministering, or indwelling spirit, or in some cases the genius of a place (e.g., the portal, the hearth, the cattle pen). In Greek mythology, *daimones* are superhuman in that their natures are superior to that of humans, but they are not supernatural because, like humans, their natures are created by God (both evil and good spirits, demons and devils as well as angels).

The original Greek term *daimōn,* from which the English word *demon* is derived through late medieval Latin, designates a semidivine being (normally regarded as beneficial to humans) whose nature is intermediate between human and god. Homer employs the term as virtually synonymous with *theos,* meaning "a god," except that *theos* refers to the personality of a god and *daimōn* to the nature of divine activity. In Hesiod, *daimones* are identified with the souls of those who died during the Golden Age.

In the late Greco-Roman period, the term *daimōn* (along with its adjectival derivative, *daimonios*), like the Latin *genius,* was commonly employed in reference to lesser spirits or demigods, especially patron or guardian spirits that protect the homestead, family, and property of the suppliant. Still later, the word *daimonium* (transliterated into Latin as *daemonium*) was assigned to evil spirits that torment human beings, cause them physical and mental harm, inflict them with mental infirmities, and lead them into evil ways.

In the Septuagint, the earliest Greek version of the Pentateuch (from around the third century BCE), the New Testament, and many early Christian writings (especially those of Irenaeus and Ignatius of Antioch), the Greek *daimonion* (the neuter form of *daimonios*) was used to describe a thing of demonic nature and was assigned generally to all species of evil spirits. In the Vulgate, the terms *daemon* and *daemonium* referred to idols or the gods of the heathen as well as to the evil or unclean spirits by whom demoniacs were possessed. Not only is the belief in evil spirits a well-nigh universal religious phenomenon; the veneration of such invisible beings is a common feature of popular or folk religion in all societies, including those that support advanced or complex religious systems.

Tribal Cultures. The belief in evil spirits or demonic powers of a variety of species is common among all the peoples of the world from the earliest times about which we have any knowledge. Some modern theorists on the nature of religion, such as E. B. Tylor, have conjectured that the belief in demons represents only the shadowy side of the belief in spirit beings generally, a belief that some hold to form the basis of all more advanced religious systems the world over.

Among tribal peoples in various geographic locales, it is commonly held that evil spirits or demons are nothing more than the spirits of deceased ancestors who are hostile and malevolent to living humans. In order to neutralize, if not destroy, the vicious powers of such creatures, elaborate rites of ancestor worship and exorcism have been developed in cultures ranging from the simplest primal societies in Australia and Tierra del Fuego at the southernmost tip of South America to the most advanced, including Hinduism, Buddhism, Christianity, and Islam.

Another category of demons in nonliterate cultures assumes a nonanthropomorphic guise—usually that of animals, birds, or sea creatures. This development stems quite probably from the hunting stage of culture, when many societies represented human beings as existing in close, often symbiotic relationships with a variety of animals.

Hinduism. It is safe to say that from the earliest times in India, Hinduism has been informed by a higher mythology of the gods and the great demons and a lower mythology of the smaller and baser spiritual beings that are closer to the human scene than are the divinities of the sun, moon, and stars.

In the Vedas, the most ancient scriptures of Hinduism, the class of demonic beings is divided between the lower deities who, though not fully divine, are largely benevolent to humanity and are localized in the sky (the highest heaven or the high regions of the sky) and the demonic and fiendish hosts who inhabit the earth, caves, and subterranean caverns; these latter demons strike human beings and animals with diseases, poverty, and death and haunt the spirits of mortals even after death.

In the first category, there are the *ṛbhu*s, Indra's associates who fashioned the god's steeds and who aid mortals in gaining victory; the *apsaras,* celestial water nymphs who live in the water and in trees, are wives of the *gandharva*s, and who later become maidens of great beauty with the power to strike men with the madness of romantic passion; and the *gandharvas,* masculine embodiments of celestial light, protectors of the *soma,* or elixir, husbands of the *apsara*s, and later on divine musicians who accompany the dances of their female consorts.

The second category of demonic beings, dark and sinister in nature, includes the following: the *asura*s, adversaries of the gods (of Indra, in particular), closely associated with darkness and death (especially the drought that withholds the monsoon rains), and hostile to all living beings; the *paṇi*s, Indra's enemies who stole the cows of the invading Aryans; Vṛtra, the chief among demonic powers, archenemy of Indra, a celestial serpentine fiend who constricted the monsoon clouds with the coils of its body; and the *rākṣasa*s, terrestrial demons or goblins, adversaries of mankind, who assume the forms of numerous fiendish animals (e.g., wild dogs, vultures, serpents) as well as of deformed human beings and who consume the flesh and drink the blood of corpses.

The pages of the Hindu epics *(Mahābhārata* and *Rāmāyaṇa)* are littered with images of semidivine, angelic, and demonic creatures of a dizzying variety. There are, first of all, the *locii spiritii*, sprites of rivers, mountains, trees, groves, and numerous species of vegetation. Then, there is a diverse array of animal divinities who embody demonic powers (both beneficial and detrimental to humans). These divinities bestow life, health, and wealth; they also withhold the same. The most common theriomorphic manifestations of demonic beings are the ape, elephant, tiger, numerous types of divine and demonic birds (among the auspicious birds are the parrot, goose, turtledove, and owl; among the inauspicious are the heron, hawk, vulture, crow, and pigeon), and most especially, serpentlike beings (*nāgas*) who live underground, guard the gates leading to the divine treasury, and stand as sources of both wisdom and death.

In addition, the canvas of Hindu mythology is populated with an impressive variety of other superhuman creatures, among which are *preta*s, ghosts or spirits of deceased ancestors; *pitṛ*s, the spirits of the fathers; *bhūta*s, spirits per se that are generally associated with ghosts, ghouls, and goblins in cremation grounds, with a predominant tendency toward evil; and *rākṣasas*, *yātudhāna*s, and *piśāca*s, a triad of spirits, not precisely evil but not sufficiently divine to be regarded as gods. These last three possess red eyes, gray smokelike bodies, fierce, bloodstained teeth, and terrifying claws; they inflict humans with disease and death, and they eat the flesh of corpses. Finally, there is that great company of the "ungodly," the *asura*s, demonic creatures *par excellence*, sons of Diti and Dānu, chief opponents of the Ādityas (gods) and major supporters of all human beings who perpetuate evil, injustice, and death.

Buddhism. At the level of popular religion, Buddhism inherited many of the formulaic features as well as the *dramatis personae* of the demonology of Hinduism. In Buddhism, sentient beings are divided into six types: gods, humans, *asura*s, animals, hungry ghosts (*preta*s), and denizens of hell. In both traditions, beings are subject to rebirth in all of these forms as they undergo the vicissitudes of karmically determined existence.

In Buddhism, the archfiend is Māra, conceived to be either an antigod *(asura)* or a member of the lower order of gods *(deva)*. Māra confronts Gautama on the night preceding his enlightenment with a series of temptations (hedonistic pleasure, power, and wealth, as well as threats of physical destruction) to prevent him from gaining the power of omniscience. Māra's ghoulish retinue is depicted in literature and iconography as possessing the same physical features characteristic of demons elsewhere: deformed bodies, hideous facial features, and multiple eyes and limbs. All Māra's demons are engaged in terrifying and malevolent activities.

Whereas the worship of evil spirits and demonic forces occupies a minor status in the teachings of the Buddha and the earliest strata of the Buddhist tradition, the fact remains that the masses continued the ancient customs of spirit worship as a necessary and integral part of their religious lives. References to demons in the earliest texts are few in number and quite unsystematic in their treatment. Citations of belief in spirits of all kinds are more numerous in the birth stories (Jātakas) of the Buddha; however the term *yakṣa* (Pali, *yakkha*) is used more frequently than *bhūta*, the more customary term in the later literature.

In its simplest form, the Buddha's message is composed of the doctrines of the Four Noble Truths and the Eightfold Path along with a wealth of psychological and ethical instructions for the disciple seeking salvation. Although the Buddha did not deny the existence of good and evil spirits, he viewed them as he did the *devas*—as existent and active throughout the universe but as impotent to affect a person's search for liberation, whether for good or ill. Indeed, it might be argued that the primary objective of the Buddha *dharma* is to free the person from moral and psychological servitude to the kinds of mental states in which one feels either threatened or blessed by invisible beings.

That is to say, demons (*bhūtas*, *pretas*, *piśācas*) of both the benevolent and malevolent variety, rightly understood, are to be viewed as nothing more than the personifications of correlative mental states. Such beings are products of a mental process through which positive and negative, confident and fearful, human emotions are projected onto the external landscape of the cosmos and objectified.

It follows from this that the *arhat*, or perfected being (i.e., the Buddhist saint), has conquered his passions, including both desire *(tṛṣṇā)* and fear *(bhaya)*, and has become a fully enlightened and liberated being. As a consequence, he no longer lives in subjection to the fear of forces or life circumstances that cause pain. It can, therefore, be said of the *arhat* (and of the *bodhisattva* in Mahāyāna) that he has slain the demons, as well as the benevolent spirits. Although he recognizes that such beings exist, they no longer exercise the least degree of influence over his life and thoughts.

On the other hand, the Sūtras (Pali, Suttas) represent the unenlightened mortal as one who is "possessed" by the demons of craving and fear. The modern psychological equivalent of this state is that of neurosis or psychosis. Hence, only the Buddha himself and the perfected beings can be judged to be perfectly sane. All other beings suffer from one or another form of psychosis, types of mental and emotional disequilibrium that are fed by the twin evils of desire and fear. It is the mutually conflicting activities of these two self-destructive emotions that cause mental illness (in modern Western terminology) or the horrifying presence of evil spirits (in folkloristic terminology).

The deities in Mahāyāna (especially in the Vajrayāna tradition of Tibet, Nepal, China, and Japan), like the Hindu gods and goddesses (especially Śiva and Pārvatī), manifest their divine powers in both benevolent and malevolent modes, striking the devotee now with faith, now with fear and dread. In Mahāyāna Buddhist countries throughout Asia, the learned tradition holds that both kind and fearsome deities are to be regarded quintessentially as imagistic projections of corresponding human emotions and mental states. The "imaginary" deities simply evaporate into the void with the experience of enlightenment.

Judaism. In its demonology as in other areas of its theology, Judaism inherited a number of concepts and names of individual demons (e.g., Bel and Leviathan) from its Mesopotamian and Canaanite predecessors. In the earlier books of the Hebrew scriptures, before the Babylonian exile in 587/6 BCE, the belief in demons and evil spirits plays a marginal role in the life of Israel. While these books do not deny the existence of demonic powers, such beings are placed under the suzerainty of the absolute will of Yahveh (*Dt.* 4:35). It was only after the biblical writers came under the influence of foreign ideas, especially the Persian dualistic systems of Zoroastrianism and Zurvanism, that we find a clear separation of powers and personages into good and evil sectors and the solidification of the concept of evil spirits into a distinct company of malicious beings. In rabbinic Judaism, the demons appear prominently only in the *aggadah* (folkloristic rabbinic thought), rarely, if at all, in the *halakhah* (learned tradition).

In the Hebrew scriptures, all spiritual beings, both benign and malevolent, are controlled by the power of God (*2 Sm.* 24:16–17). Even Satan himself is conceived of as a servant or messenger of God, commissioned to test men's loyalty to God (*Jb.* 1:6–12, 2:1–7) or to prosecute them for transgressions before the divine tribunal (*Zec.* 3:1–2). However, the imprint of popular Israelite religion upon the biblical literature is attested to by the occurrence of such entities as *shedim* (evil spirits, *Dt.* 32:17), which orthodox writers related to the pagan gods *se'irim* (*Lv.* 17:7) or *lilit* (*Is.* 34:14). These pagan gods traditionally have been depicted as satyrs, as were the *sa'ir* ("hairy ones," *Is.* 13:21).

Two other noteworthy demonic figures are 'Aza'zel (*Lv.* 16:8), a demon of the desert places to whom the scapegoat was sent on the Day of Atonement, and Lilith (from *lilit*), a demoness who according to postbiblical Jewish legend attacks children and was the first wife of Adam.

In the later books of the Hebrew scriptures and in subsequent apocryphal and popularistic literature (especially that of the mystical tradition of Qabbalah), the amorphous and shadowy demons were more clearly delineated, with many of the more prominent demons receiving personal names and singular functions. Part angelic, part human, they live in desolate places separated from inhabited areas, plying their ghoulish craft at night. Regarded as "unclean spirits," they visit humans with physical and financial disasters and lure them into evil ways that are contrary to God's law (*Jub.* 7:27).

There are many differing theories in the aggadic literary tradition concerning the origin of demons. Some writers speculate that they were created by God at twilight on the eve of the first Sabbath (*Avot* 5.9). Others conjecture that they are the offspring of Adam through Lilith. Still others say that they are the descendants of the fallen angels who engaged in sexual intercourse with women ("the sons of God saw that the daughters of men were fair: and they took to wife such of them as they chose," *Gn.* 6:1–4), or that they themselves are fallen angels who fell as the result of their rebellion against God under the leadership of Satan.

The general nature of the conception of demons in classical Judaism perhaps can best be exemplified by the figure of Leviathan. The name itself in Hebrew means "that which gathers itself together in folds." In the Ethiopic *Apocalypse of Enoch* the seven-headed primordial female sea monster (cf. Hydra in Greek mythology) or crocodile inhabits the subterranean waters or the sea. This creature perpetuates evil deeds and is perhaps the Hebrew equivalent of the Babylonian Tiamat or the Canaanite Lotan. Leviathan also is closely associated with Behemoth, a demonic spirit of the desert (*Jb.* 40:15, *1 En.* 60:8) as well as Rahab (*Is.* 51:9, *Jb.* 9:13, *Ps.* 89:10).

Despite the dramatic increase in the importance granted to demons in medieval Judaism and the prominent position given them in the qabbalistic literature, the belief in demons, though never rejected out of hand, has always been a peripheral part of mainline Orthodox Judaism.

Although unmentioned in either the Talmud or the qabbalistic literature, a demonic figure unique to Judaism appeared in popular Jewish tradition from the seventeenth century onward. The dybbuk (Heb., *dibbuq*, "attachment") is a disembodied ancestral spirit, condemned to wander the earth because of sins committed during his or her lifetime, who takes up residence in the body of a living being and leads that person astray. The demon can be exorcised only by means of special religious rites.

Christianity. Demonology in the New Testament is a complex amalgamation of historical patterns from other, neighboring traditions that preceded (e.g., Judaism, Manichaeism, Greco-Roman thought, gnosticism, and the Hebrew apocryphal and apocalyptic traditions) enriched by the emergence of novel concepts unique to Palestine during the first decades of the Christian era.

The general framework for the growth of the Christian concepts of demons was largely inherited from Jewish apocalyptic literature of the second and first centuries BCE. According to *1 Enoch* 6, the angels or offspring of heaven cohabited with the irresistible daughters of men (cf. *Gn.* 6:1–4) and produced a race of giants who in turn gave birth to a bevy of evil spirits. Because the primary motive for this illicit congress was the satisfaction of sexual desire, lawlessness and warfare spread throughout the world. At this stage, mention is made of numerous devils, but it was left to the New Testament writers to synthesize this company of evil spirits into a single satanic figure who served as the leader of the demonic troops or fallen angels.

It was also at this same time that Satan came to be identified with the serpent in the Garden of Eden who provoked the fall of mankind through the sins of the first couple and, as a result, was himself expelled from heaven.

Jesus, the gospel writers, and the apostle Paul seem to have adopted wholesale the Jewish understanding of the nature and activities of evil spirits. Throughout the New Testament, demonic spirits are regarded as sources of both physical and psychological infirmities (including epilepsy and insanity; see *Mt.* 12:28, *Lk.* 11:20).

In keeping with his general theological orientation, Paul represents Satan and the evil powers as operating within a cosmic theater—in the air (*Eph.* 2:2), on the earth, and in the underworld. He also pictures Satan as the personified ruler over the kingdom of evil as well as the force to be embodied in the Antichrist who is expected to precede the second coming of Christ at the end of the world.

The *Book of Revelation* contains a rich and complicated demonology informed by Jewish apocalyptic, Babylonian, and Persian sources. The book dwells primarily upon the final struggle between the forces of good and evil in the Battle of Armageddon and the ultimate triumph of the forces of God.

The belief in demons and the employment of spiritual and magical practices to control or exorcise them has had a varied history in Christianity through the centuries. From the twelfth century onward, demons were represented pictographically in painting and sculpture as gruesome and horrifying creatures responsible for every kind of misfortune, from such natural disasters as floods, earthquakes, and droughts to warfare, individual suffering, and death. The Fourth Lateran Council in 1215 declared that "Satan and other evil spirits were created good by nature, by God, but they became evil by their own actions." It further stated that at the end of time, once Satan and his forces have been defeated by God, the angels and believers would inherit eternal life in Christ. The demons and unbelievers, on the other hand, would go to "eternal punishment along with Satan."

The fifteenth and sixteenth centuries witnessed the cresting of demonological beliefs and practices. Europe (and later, America) was rife with the practice of witchcraft and sorcery. Witch trials were the order of the day. In consonance with the times, satanic cults and "black masses" were rampant. The dramatic rise of demon worship during this period in European history might be viewed as the last gasp of a set of native European practices that had preceded the rise of Christianity by centuries; this ancient religious orientation has declined steadily in both popular and learned circles from the time of the Enlightenment to the present.

Islam. From the time of the Qur'ān onward, the universe was populated with a diverse array of good and evil spirits exercising direct and formative influence upon the affairs of humanity. One group of such beings, known as *jinn*, possess ethereal or luminescent bodies and are intelligent and invisible. Proud, rebellious creatures in both the human and animal kingdoms, the *jinn* were created from unsmoking fire. They are related in a rather amorphous manner to both the *shayṭāns* and to the personage Shayṭān (Satan) as well as to a figure addressed as Iblīs (a personal name of the devil).

While the *jinn* appear in a majority of orthodox Muslim writings as shadowy, ephemeral creatures who, at most, make life difficult for humans, the *shayṭāns* actively assist Iblīs in maintaining his position of rebellion against God. They are aggressively involved in leading from God's law those persons who are already inclined to go astray. Orthodox Muslim writers debated questions pertaining to the existence, the nature, and the status of the *jinn* and formulated an elaborate system for the grading of the various angelic orders. Other writers, such as Ibn Khaldūn, flatly denied their existence.

In pre-Islamic Arabia, the *jinn* were believed to be sinister spirits of the desert, identified with the forces of nature hostile to human life. By the time of Muḥammad, they were little more than shadowy, impersonal godlings. There are stories of romantic liaisons and even marriages between *jinn* and human beings. Also, the establishment of intimate relationships between *jinn* and saints was the theme of perennial interest in the writings of the Schoolmen and the popular narratives of oral storytellers.

According to Islamic literature, Iblīs appeared at the beginning of the world as an angel who staunchly refused to bow down before Adam. Iblīs himself was composed of elemental fire. Hence, he regarded as insulting the demand that he pay reverence to a being composed of earth. He therefore rose up in rebellion against God. As a consequence of his recalcitrant spirit, he was banished from Paradise and cursed forever. He persuaded God to postpone his punishment until after the Day of Judgment at the end of time. God granted him a stay of punishment and the latitude to lead all people in the world who were not God's loyal followers astray. In time, he came to be addressed as Satan.

There is a dilemma concerning Iblīs, one that is at the heart of the Islamic tradition. The dilemma arises because Iblīs is both an angel (surah 2:34) and "one among the *jinn*" (18:50). The line of distinction between the two orders of supernatural beings was never worked out carefully by the Muslim commentators. The traditional writings *(ḥadīth)* embellished upon the Qur'anic account of Iblīs in an attempt to resolve this dilemma. According to the Arabic historian al-Ṭabarī (c. 839–923 CE), the *jinn* originally inhabited the earth and fell into bloodthirsty battles with one another. God sent Iblīs as his emissary, along with an army of angelic hosts, to put a stop to the conflict. Iblīs drove the *jinn* into the mountains; in time, he came to be identified as their leader. Elsewhere, Iblīs is presented as a rebellious *jinnī* who was captured and brought to heaven to be punished. All the traditional accounts agree on one matter: Iblīs believed that he was superior to all the other angels and to mankind. This belief created within him an overweening pride that drove him to rebel against the sovereignty of his creator and lord and ultimately brought down upon himself God's complete condemnation. On the Day of Judgment, God will cast both Shayṭān and his hosts into the pit filled with hellfire (26:94ff.), where they will suffer forever in flames that burn but are never extinguished.

For their part, the *jinn* play a far more prominent and unambiguously positive role in the folklore of various Islamic societies than in the high or learned tradition. The *jinn* are linked primarily with the practice of the magical arts, both white and black. The frequent intrusion of *jinn* of various sorts into the lives of human beings, sometimes to disastrous effect, occupies an important place in the imaginative literature of both the learned writer and the popular storyteller *(qaṣṣāṣ)*.

In spite of a continuing, identifiable relationship between the folkloristic views of the *jinn* and those in the learned tradition, the Islamic elements are often subsumed under motifs and sentiments coming from various folk traditions (e.g., Egyptian, Syrian, Turkish).

In an attempt to make the teachings of Muḥammad and the learned scholiasts more understandable to the masses, Islamic theologians themselves have developed elaborate systems of angelology and demonology, with various orders of each assigned to reasonably well established statuses within the hierarchical structure.

A Modern Assessment. Up until fairly recent times, the demonology of the Middle Ages in Europe has served as the model for the Western conception of evil and for those persons who adhere to evil ways. However, with the emergence of a more complicated and rationalistic cosmology (and the consequential dissolution of the idea of the three-storied universe as a result of the growth of these scientific cosmologies), the belief among educated people in supernatural beings of all sorts (both good and evil) has steadily declined over the past two and one-half centuries.

Natural disasters such as earthquakes, floods, and plagues, which previously were credited to the malicious activities of demonic powers, are now explained on a purely naturalistic basis. Likewise, all manner of human misfortune and suffering, ranging from physical illness to mental disorder, are assigned purely empirical causes.

With the spread of scientific and technological values and the propagation throughout the world of the idea of universal education based largely upon modern Western values, belief in heaven and hell and a postmortem existence in a realm apart from this one has receded progressively from the central core of beliefs of many religions throughout the world. On the other hand, belief in the existence of evil forces has far from disappeared altogether. Images of evil powers and the demonic have played a pervasive role in the contemporary arts, though largely in demythologized and depersonalized forms.

C. G. Jung, founder of the school of analytical psychology, offered an unsettling judgment concerning the presence of evil forces that he believed are, even now, at work within the human psyche:

> The daemonism of nature, which man had apparently triumphed over, he has unwittingly swallowed into himself and so become the devil's marionette. . . . When these products [demonic factors in the psyche] were dubbed unreal and illusory, their sources were in no way blocked up or rendered inoperative. On the contrary, after it became impossible for the daemons to inhabit the rocks, woods, mountains, and rivers, they used human beings as much more dangerous dwelling places.
>
> (*Collected Works*, Princeton, 1955, vol. 18, pp. 593–594)

One is perhaps justified in concluding—from this and other, related testimonies to the religious crisis that defines our contemporary world—that the "death" of God and of Satan may be one of the formative events in modern culture. Nonetheless, the ancient urge to achieve a fuller knowledge of the nature of good and evil and their respective roles in the human drama persist, with an urgent demand for intelligent reflection and insightful judgment.

[*For discussion of specific kinds of demons, see* Angels; Devils; Fairies; Ghosts; *and* Monsters.]

BIBLIOGRAPHY

The entry "Demons and Spirits" in the *Encyclopaedia of Religion and Ethics*, edited by James Hastings, vol. 4 (Edinburgh, 1911), is a series of twenty articles pertaining to demonology in various cultures and is still worth consulting. Also valuable as a general reference is the *Larousse World Mythology*, edited by Pierre Grimal and translated by Patricia Beardsworth (New York, 1965). Gustav Davidson's *Dictionary of Angels, Including the Fallen Angels* (New York, 1967) is a mine of information. In additon to these general references, the following works can be recommended as sources of information on demons in various religious traditions.

Tribal Religions. Ronald M. Berndt and Catherine H. Berndt, *The World of the First Australians*, 2d ed. (Sydney, 1977). Verrier Elwin, ed. and trans., *Tribal Myths of Orissa* (New York, 1954). E. B. Tylor, *Primitive Culture*, vol. 1, *Religion in Primitive Culture* (1871; reprint, New York, 1970).

Judaism. Edward Langton, *Essentials of Demonology: A Study of Jewish and Christian Doctrines, Its Origin and Development* (London, 1949). "Demonology," in *The Encyclopedia of the Jewish Religion*, edited by R. J. Zwi Werblowsky and Geoffrey Wigoder (New York, 1966).

Christianity. John Hick, *Evil and the Love of God*, 2d ed. (London, 1977). Edward Langton, *Essentials of Demonology* (London, 1949). Eric Maple, *The Dark World of Witches* (London, 1962). Jeffrey B. Russell, *The Devil: Perceptions of Evil from Antiquity to Primitive Christianity* (Ithaca, N.Y., 1977).

Islam. D. Miguel Asín Palacios, *Islam and the Divine Comedy*, translated by Harold Sunderland (London, 1926). Jane I. Smith and Yvonne Haddad, *The Islamic Understanding of Death and Resurrection* (Albany, N.Y., 1981). A. S. Tritton, "Shaiṭān," in *The Encylopaedia of Islam* (Leiden, 1913–1938). Petrus Voorhoeve, "Djinn," and A. J. Wensinck, "Iblīs," in *The Encyclopaedia of Islam*, new ed. (Leiden, 1960–).

Hinduism. W. Norman Brown, "The Rigvedic Equivalent for Hell," *Journal of the American Oriental Society* 61 (June 1941):

76–80. Ananda K. Coomaraswamy, "Angel and Titan: An Essay on Vedic Ontology," *Journal of the American Oriental Society* 55 (1935): 373–419.

Buddhism. James W. Boyd, *Satan and Māra: Christian and Buddhist Symbols of Evil* (Leiden, 1975). Bimala Churn Law, *The Buddhist Conception of Spirits*, 2d ed. (London, 1936). Melford E. Spiro, *Buddhism and Society: A Great Tradition and Its Burmese Vicissitudes*, 2d ed. (Berkeley, 1982). W. G. Weeraratne et al., "Bhūta," in *Encyclopaedia of Buddhism*, edited by G. P. Malalasekera (Colombo, 1971).

J. BRUCE LONG

Psychological Perspectives

The experience of the demon as a supernatural being that can affect human life for good or for bad is found all over the world. Modern depth psychology provides us with a fuller understanding of the nature of this phenomenon. Even in modern civilization where there is no longer the belief in demons, demons continue to play an important role. The existence of demons is a fact. The question of central importance is "How does consciousness interpret this fact?"

The interpretation depends upon the development of consciousness and the awareness of the multiple forces that determine human personality and experience. A more advanced stage of consciousness can look back at the preceding stage and describe it. For the present stage of consciousness, however, there exists no outside objective and critical standpoint from which to observe it. C. G. Jung has distinguished five different stages in the development of consciousness (also referred to as stages of the relation between object and subject). I would like to discuss the attitude toward the existence of demons at each of these five stages with reference first to cultures in which the stage of consciousness dominates and then to cultures of modern Western civilization.

Examples of each of these five stages can be found in human psychology side by side with the more advanced stages. There is no civilization in which consciousness belongs only and exclusively to one stage alone, because different psychological faculties will be developed to a different degree at any one time. Even though the main function may become advanced and rational, the inferior function remains archaic and closely aligned with the unconscious psyche.

The Myth of the Cosmic Man: Archaic Mentality. The unconscious psyche is the original mind of man, his primeval mentality, with which he still functions through his instincts. All persons function in this archaic way when unconscious; that is, to be unconscious in psychological terms is to be governed simply by the unconscious forces of instinct. Mankind has survived for hundreds of thousands of years supported by this primordial mentality, living in a state of identity with the environment called by Lucien Lévy-Bruhl "the participation mystique." The fact that mankind survived the Stone Age points to the value of this instinctive behavior.

The consciousness of these early stages of mankind and of today's hunters and gatherers resembles that of early childhood. At this stage man lives undifferentiated from his surroundings. This does not mean that he cannot differentiate between himself and the objects around him, but rather that for him these objects are alive: they have soul and behave like animated beings. In the words of C. G. Jung, the individual lives as though he were immersed "in a stream of events in which outer and inner worlds are not differentiated, or are differentiated very indistinctly."

For archaic man, the whole world reflects his psyche, or his psyche is just as much outside as inside, because as long as a psychic content is unconscious, it will appear in both realms. This stage of consciousness is mirrored in the myth of the cosmic man, a giant who pervades the entire universe; examples are the Indian Puruṣa or the Scandinavian Ymir. The psyche of archaic man is everywhere. All of the objects in the universe of archaic man lead their own purposeful lives, influencing or even dominating him. He feels inferior to these powers of nature and worships or propitiates them. Religion and magic are at his disposal in order to deal with these powers. Because his own ego is ill defined, it is easily transformed into an animal or possessed by one of the surrounding powers, by a spirit or a demon, or transformed into an animal. Possession belongs to this mentality, and one can be exorcised as easily as possessed. [*See* Spirit Possession.]

By worshiping these powers, human beings acknowledge their reality and importance, and they are kept in the awareness of the entire community. Only when something escapes our attention and is thus neglected are we in danger of being possessed by it.

Possession—when our actions are determined by some psychic (or spiritual) force that overwhelms the ego—is by no means a phenomenon restricted to primitive societies, nor is it limited to those in our present civilization whom we call possessed. On the contrary, it is a universal experience. Whenever an unconscious power takes over the ego, possession occurs. Archaic man is threatened by all the demons and spirits around him, but at the same time he is wrapped also in the protection of the symbolic mother; that is, he is protected by powers that look out for him and provide him with sustenance so that he does not have to worry about himself. For example, when the Kusase people hear a certain tree in the village ask for a new dress and for new offerings, they are not surprised since this happens from time to time. In the context of their world, this is a common event and demands no explanation.

The idea of an all-pervading power in nature *(mana, manitou, orenda, wakanda)* forms part of this animistic view of existence. And magic is the primitive technology that seeks to manage this power. But the religious attitude is already prominent at this stage in the person of the shaman, rainmaker, or weathermaker, who is a specialist in dealing with spiritual powers. Furthermore, the power becomes embodied in certain sacred persons such as the chief, warrior, or blacksmith, as well as in sacred objects such as swords, stones, and medicine.

In modern Western civilization this archaic attitude still survives. Not only fairy tales and legends but also the words of poets reflect this attitude. And whenever an emotion lays hold of us, we fall back into such archaic behavior; for example, we kick the corner that "hit us," or we swear at the car that refuses to budge. We treat things as if they had a will of their own. This indicates that we believe that things share our human nature: the lime tree in the famous folk song bears all the feelings of love and the sorrow of farewell that men and women experience beneath its branches. We find ourselves feeling attached to objects as well as to persons, and when either fails to act according to our expectations, we experience strong emotion, because we identify with them to a certain extent.

If we look closely at our fears, we may detect the old demons and spirits in modern disguise: irrational fear of cancer or of atomic energy, idiosyncrasy, fear of war and power. We do not trust our modern consciousness to be able to handle these mighty things; there might be a demon in them that would make a fool of us. And we still worship the body of Christ in the host or the represented person in icons. In Switzerland, mountain climbing was avoided for a long time because of the belief in a divine numen living on top of the mountain. Old names point to this fact, such as the Vrenelisgärtli of Glärnisch, or "garden of Venus." Many names of parcels of land or of rivers also refer to the ancient spirits of nature that formerly lived in these places. Most vegetation rites in May and on midsummer's night recall the spirits of grain. Many Europeans still put a fir tree with colored ribbons on a newly built house in order to appease the spirits who will enter and dwell there. In Greek religion, the spirits of nature are personified as nymphs, dryads, and satyrs as well as in the form of the god Pan and numerous other local deities. Many of the sanctuaries of the Virgin Mary found in the woods, in a grotto, or by a well have inherited the site from pagan spirits. In the beginning of the common era, Christian churches were built on the site of earlier temples, sometimes with the stones of the earlier temples, because the power of the numen was already present there. Modern exorcists continue to banish ghosts in places that have been haunted for ages.

The Sacrifice of the Cosmic Man: Projection. In the myth of the cosmic man, the giant is sacrificed by the gods or by the wise men of old. This sacrifice symbolizes the cultural moment when the archaic mentality is sacrificed in favor of a different level of consciousness. This moment seems to correspond to the great Neolithic revolution of mankind, the transition from a life of hunting and gathering foods (living off the gifts of nature, the symbolic mother) to the life in which both plants and animals were domesticated. In agriculture and the herding of animals, mankind assumed some responsibility for husbanding natural resources and providing a steady food supply for himself. At this point he becomes separate from his environment; for the first time there occurs a split between man as subject and nature as object. Differentiation from the environment is one of the most difficult tasks for mankind. Psychic development (individuation) depends upon the ongoing continuation of this process. However, the individual is constantly threatened by demons, threatened, that is, by forces that are unconscious. The mythical combat between the hero and the dragon mirrors this dangerous situation.

Therefore it is consciousness that, in effect, creates the cosmos, for in the differentiation of consciousness the world comes into being as a realm separate from man. From this stage onward we can properly speak of a projection whenever there is any doubt as to whether or not a phenomenon does, in fact, belong to the outer world in which we seem to experience it. For example, when a schizophrenic of our civilization hears the voice of the devil, it is correct to interpret the voice as a projection of something that exists within him rather than something existing in the world.

Usually a demon is understood to be a supernatural being of a nature intermediate between that of gods and men. In the writings of Homer, the word for "demon," *daimōn*, can still refer to a god or, in a rather vague sense, to a divine efficacy. In a famous passage of Plato's *Symposium*, Diotima describes Eros as a "great spirit [*daimōn*], and like all spirits a being intermediate between the divine and the mortal" (202e). Psychologically speaking, this corresponds to the complex of the collective unconscious as defined by C. G. Jung. The complex, which is a necessary and normal component of the psyche, is intermediate between the ego and the archetype, having both a personal and an impersonal aspect. Whereas the archetypes are inborn dispositions, the complex comes into being through experiences in the individual life.

At this stage of consciousness, for example, the warrior is no longer believed to be generally demonic, but rather he becomes the berserker who fights with a mad frenzy only when he is possessed by the god Odin. Mediumship and possession attributed to specific gods or spirits are regular phenomena at this stage of consciousness. At this level, every disease is explained as the result of a spirit or demon. They are primitive forms of what we call mental disorders or *Geisteskrankheit* ("spirit-illness"). In psychological terms, a complex, also called a partial personality, takes over the ego.

The shaman is the master of spirits, the one who has overcome his own states of possession. Demons are far from being only noxious. In spirit-mediumship the spirits mediate the power of divination, providing information about the future and about matters removed from ordinary perception. They mediate between the spirit world and men and convey to their society the beneficial power of the gods. Everyone may have his own guiding spirit that controls to some effect his behavior. Mediumship may be experienced as a vocation whereby a spirit chooses a specific person as its vehicle. Our word *inspiration* means that a spirit is whispering wisdom into the ear of the inspired. When the world as a whole is no longer believed to be alive, it remains, nevertheless, filled with spirits and demons. One must be careful lest one be tripped up by a demon unnoticed. Spirit possession can even be contagious, especially during adolescence.

Spirits, particularly those of dead ancestors, may have control over the fertility of the earth, because they are believed to live in the earth under the ground or above the rain clouds. Passing by a cemetery one must take care not to be bewitched by a lurking ghost, the spirit of an ancestor that might cause illness or even death. (Psychologically, this appears to be the same fear that one experiences today when passing by a graveyard late at night.) Furthermore, a young girl has to be careful when she walks by a pond lest one of the unborn souls lurking there might jump into her womb and make her pregnant. The ghosts of the dead are especially hungry and desirous of blood or meat, food that must be provided through sacrifices. The great power of a mighty man continues to hold sway even after his death. In the vicinity of the grave of a shaykh there is a palm tree and a conical stone; barren women may silently step over the stone seven times and eat dates from the tree in order to become pregnant.

A regressive appearance of demons and spirits occurs when the high gods become remote. This often happens when a new civilization overlays an older one, whether by historical change or by conquest. The conquerors impose their social and administrative systems upon the conquered people, but they are themselves unconsciously infected by the spiritual culture of the latter. Some conquering tribes believe that the vanquished tribe survives in spirit form. In the new religious system the high gods become demons and spirits. As high gods they had received a cult and were represented in the collective consciousness, but in the new system they sink into relative unconsciousness. The Greek magical papyri are full of ancient high gods and goddesses, among them both Hekate and Hermes. Hellenistic syncretism absorbed many gods of the Mediterranean culture. In early Christianity the pagan gods became demons or spirits. The medieval iconography of the Devil, for example, depicts the Greek god Pan, who in ancient times was first a spirit of nature and the god of shepherds and finally became god of the universe. (In Greek *pan* means "all.") Plutarch relates the story of the death of the great Pan, according to which some sailors learn of the event and bring the tale to an island, whereupon a great lamentation ensues. This story marks the end of the archaic worship of nature, an end that resulted from the rise of Christianity. Our modern dilemma deriving from the pollution of nature demonstrates the practical value in the worship of ancient nature spirits, which served to render the superhuman quality of nature conscious to mankind, forming a consciousness that has been lost up to our present time. Today, natural science is searching again for the mysteries of nature, albeit with a rationalistic attitude.

Moral Differentiation: Belief in a World of Good and Evil Demons. In the ancient story of Jacob's fight with the angel at the Jabbok River (*Gn.* 32:24) Yahveh is a deadly but not evil power. In the tale of Job from a later period, Satan ("the adversary") is one of the sons of God and represents the partial separation of an inner opposition generated by God himself. Similar is the history of the *deva/daēva* common to both prehistoric India and Iran. Originally the term was a neutral one referring to the celestial, daytime sky. After further development in India the term *deva* came to signify the high gods. In Iran, however, *daēva* acquired the meaning of "demon" in the evil sense.

Moral differentiation splits the world further into the opposites of night and day, earth and sky, left and right, good and evil. The collective consciousness is always in danger of identifying with one of a pair of opposites, abandoning the second to the demonic powers of the unconscious. Such an attitude gave rise, for example, to the Black Mass. Neglected aspects of the psyche are not simply repressed and forgotten, they become more and more powerful in the unconscious psyche and more disturbing to the conscious personality. A worldview that fails to acknowledge and experience the original unity of the opposites is in danger of an invasion from the neglected or rejected side. Psychologically, every optimistic or exclusively good attitude calls forth a reaction from its opposite. The more one-sided the conscious attitude, the larger grows the demonic counterworld.

The Enlightenment: Denial of the Existence of Demons. Modern literature on demons is written for the most part from the standpoint of rationalism and attempts to explain demons as superstitious phenomena of a primitive mentality. The psychoanalytic approach developed by Sigmund Freud toward religious phenomena in general shares this attitude. It is a necessary transitional stage in the development of consciousness for man to ask "Who creates the demons?" and to answer "It is I!" In fact, man cannot help assuming responsibility for the products of his own imagination. They have arisen in him, and therefore he is their creator. Thus man identifies with his consciousness and explains all unconscious phenomena as derivative of that consciousness.

But in our time we can observe a certain counterreaction to this one-sided view in the form of irrational reactions: the new religions; the parapsychology enthusiasts; drug-based religion and fascination with science fiction among the youth; the "worship" of the natural wisdom of animals by some modern scientists; and the popularity of modern myths such as J. R. R. Tolkien's *Lord of the Rings.*

Objectivity of the Psyche: Unus Mundus. Modern analytical psychology attributes to demons a reality of their own, recognizing the important role they play in the psychology of man. Because the *Auseinandersetzung* (Ger., "coming to terms") with the world of demons and spirits in the individuation process is so important, Jung specified a method called active imagination in which the figures of the unconscious are regarded as autonomous living entities of the psyche. Using this method it is possible to approach the archaic mentality from a position of conscious responsibility, acknowledging the unconscious and its personifications (demons, spirits, ghosts, fairies, angels, and so on) and seeking to find the appropriate way to respond to them. For these personifications may become conscious to the ego, but they are not created by it. The ego is obligated to take the unconscious realities into consideration. (This process recalls the Latin *relegere,* "to gather up again.") Spirits and demons must be allowed to arise as inner figures so that the ego can come to terms with them.

Sometimes one central spirit becomes the leading principle. This figure is called the archetype of the Anthropos, or the Self in human form (the unconscious principle of personality). Often the Anthropos is experienced as an inner guide, as, for example, Poimandres ("shepherd of men"), Agathos Daimon ("good spirit"), and Hermes-Thoth in antiquity; Mercurius in alchemy; and Khidr in Islam. The *daimōn* of Socrates was a figure or a voice of a similar kind who forbade him certain things. A later variation is the guardian spirit who mediated between the spirit world and man, bringing dreams and foretelling the future.

The contemporary notion of spirits affects our understanding of mental illness as well as the psychic side of physical illness. Lauri Honko has studied the belief in so-called sickness projectiles, and he demonstrates the appearance of this belief in numerous cultures. For example, the German expression for lumbago is *Hexenschuss,* which means literally "the witch's shot."

The projection plays an important role in the transference of complexes from one person to another. Unconscious complexes are always projected onto other persons whom they may harm. Emotions are energy-laden phenomena that also affect other people. Typically, the gods of love (Eros, Cupid, Amor, Kāma) are armed with a bow and arrow, indicating that projections are sent by the divine principle or demon. But Job's plague, too, was caused by the arrows of Yahveh (*Job* 6:4), and the Vedic god Rudra sends death and illness with his arrows (*Ṛgveda* 7.46). A demon can be either a pathological complex or a new, creative impulse; both issue forth in connection with an archetype and embody a value that can destroy or save the individual person.

Further, the reality that analytical psychology attributes to demons provides insight into the parapsychological meaning of ghosts. The autonomy of the complex, together with the concept of synchronicity (the meaningful coincidence of events), provides tools with which we can understand, though not explain, the psychology of apparitions. French and English literature on this topic is extensive and points to a common belief in locally bound spirits, the *genius loci,* often depicted as a snake. In Roman families the genius was also a spirit of fertility. Modern parapsychology takes into account the psychological conditions that give rise to the appearance of apparitions. Beyond any doubt there are some people who are simply more aware of or sensitive to such phenomena; they are often said to possess second sight. Nevertheless, such occurrences are not uncommon for the less sensitive.

There is little doubt of the existence of the phenomena that have been called demons, angels, spirits, ghosts, and so on. But since these are experiences of a psychic nature, they can never be known except by means of such inner images.

BIBLIOGRAPHY

The most important work for this topic from the standpoint of analytical psychology is Marie-Louise von Franz's *Projection and Re-Collection in Jungian Psychology* (La Salle, Ill., 1980). Recent encyclopedic works mostly treat the topic historically and geographically. I mention here only the more recent and extensive ones. Lutz Röhrich gives a concise survey of demons in legends and fairy tales, including a psychological section, under "Dämon," in *Enzyklopädie des Märchens,* vol. 3 (Berlin, 1979). Material from the standpoint of the history of Christianity is collected in Otto Böcher's article "Dämonen," in *Theologische Realenzyklopädie,* vol. 8 (Berlin, 1981); articles include extensive bibliographies, with mention of Judaism. Even more comprehensive is the article "Geister (Dämonen)," with extensive bibliography, by Carsten Colpe and others in *Reallexikon für Antike und Christentum,* vol. 9 (Stuttgart, 1976). The standard reference for the Bible and Judaism is Werner Foerster's article "Demon," in the *Theological Dictionary of the New Testament* (1935), translated by Geoffrey W. Bromiley (Grand Rapids, Mich., 1964), which also gives the meaning of the term in folklore. Andres's article "Daimon," in *Pauly's Real-encyclopädie der classischen Altertumwissenschaft,* supp. 3 (Stuttgart, 1918), is still useful for Greek material. The church fathers' standpoint is found in G. W. H. Lampe's *A Patristic Greek Lexicon* (Oxford, 1978), pp. 327–331. The *New Catholic Encyclopedia* (New York, 1967) gives a very short survey, as does Bernhard Kötting's article "Dämon," in *Lexikon für Theologie und Kirche,* vol. 3 (Freiburg, 1959). The articles under "Démon," in the *Dictionnaire de spiritualité, ascétique et mystique: Doctrine et histoire,* vol. 3 (Paris, 1957), give very interesting material not found elsewhere.

The classical survey of ancient authors is Julius Tambornino's *De antiquorum daemonismo,* "Religionsgeschichtliche Versuche und Vorarbeiten," vol. 7 (Giessen, 1909). Another classical work is *The Devils and Evil Spirits of Babylonia,* 2 vols., translated by Reginald C. Thompson, which consists of Babylonian and Assyrian incantations against the demons, ghouls, vampires, hobgoblins, ghosts, and kindred evil spirits that attack mankind (London, 1903–1904). The entry in the *Encyclopaedia of Religion and Ethics,* edited by James Hastings, vol. 4 (Edinburgh, 1911), summarizes the material in an extensive and comprehensive way; the introductory article by Louis H. Gray is the most useful.

No important recent works dealing with the subject in a scientific way exist. An outdated, although still useful, book is *Demonology and Devil-Lore,* 3d ed., rev. & enl., 2 vols. (London, 1889), by Moncure D. Conway. Ilmari Manninen's *Die daemonistischen Krankheiten im finnischen Volksaberglauben* (Helsinki, 1922) and Lauri Honko's *Krankheitsprojektile: Untersuchung über eine urtümliche Krankheitserklärung* (Helsinki, 1959) are high-quality standard collections of material related to this topic.

The iconography of demons and spirits is very enlightening, but unfortunately Herbert Schade's article "Dämonen," in *Lexikon der Christlichen Ikonographie,* vol. 1 (Freiburg, 1968), is too short. One needs to refer to Enrico Castelli's *Il demoniaco nell' arte: Il significato filosofico del demoniaco nell' arte* (Milan, 1952), Heinz Mode's *Fabulous Beasts and Demons* (London, 1975), or Jurgis Baltrušaitis's *Réveils et prodiges: Le gothique fantastique* (Paris, 1960). A classical work with pictures is Edward Langton's *Essentials of Demonology: A Study of Jewish and Christian Doctrine, Its Origin and Development* (London, 1949).

Important for our topic is the profound work of Dieter Harmening, *Superstitio: Ueberlieferungs- und theoriegeschichtliche Untersuchungen zur Kirchlich- theologischen Aberglaubensliteratur des Mittelalters* (Berlin, 1979), as well as Wilhelm Dupré's *Religion in Primitive Cultures: A Study in Ethnophilosophy,* "Religion and Reason," vol. 9 (Paris, 1975). An exhaustive collection of material and history of ideas can be found in Karl R. H. Frick's *Die Erleuchteten* (Graz, 1973), *Licht und Finsternis* (Graz, 1975), and *Das Reich Satans* (Graz, 1982).

ALFRED RIBI

DENOMINATIONALISM. [*This entry discusses Protestant denominationalism. For discussion, in transreligional perspective, of various views of religious diversification, see* Schism; Sect; *and* Religious Pluralism.]

Denominationalism is one of the least understood aspects of Protestantism. In both popular usage and dictionary definition, *denominationalism* is commonly equated with *sectarianism.* This is a strange reversal in meaning, for in origin and intention the concept of denominationalism was the opposite of sectarianism.

The fact that few Protestants take offense when their church is called a denomination is evidence of a lingering awareness that the term has a positive connotation quite different from the negative implication of *sectarianism.* A sect by definition is exclusive. It claims the authority of Christ for itself alone, whereas the word *denomination* was adopted as a neutral and nonjudgmental term that implied that the group referred to was but one member, denominated by a particular name, of a larger group to which other Protestant denominations belonged. It was an inclusive term conveying the notion of mutual respect and recognition. Albert Barnes, minister of the First Presbyterian Church of Philadelphia (1830–1867), summarized the meaning of denominationalism when he said that the spirit it fostered

> is opposed to all bigotry and uncharitableness; to all attempts to "unchurch" others; to teaching that they worship in conventicles, that they are dissenters, or that they are left to the uncovenanted mercies of God. . . . The Church of Christ is not under the Episcopal form, or the Baptist, the Methodist, the Presbyterian, or the Congregational form exclusively; all are, to all intents and purposes, to be recognized as parts of the one holy catholic Church.

Denominationalism, in origin, was related to religious toleration and religious freedom. The latter were political and constitutional responses to religious diversity and were designed to enable a religiously diverse people to live together in peace. Denominationalism, on the other hand, was a response to problems created by the division of adherents of a single religious tradition into separate and competing ecclesiastical bodies. They shared a common faith but were divided by issues of church government and worship. Denominationalism took toleration and, later, religious freedom for granted, accepted arguments put forward in their defense, and then moved beyond the goal of peace among competing groups to a quest for unity in the midst of the acknowledged differences of those who shared a common faith. To this end, both an ideology and a system of relationships were devised that would permit members of the several Protestant denominations to acknowledge the unity that transcended their divisions and thus encourage them to maintain friendly coexistence and to engage in concerted action to promote shared concerns and forward common ends. It is interesting that a similar ideology and rationale for mutual respect and cooperative activity, utilizing the equally neutral term *sector* for *denomination,* was adopted by Jacob Neusner, noted professor of Judaic studies at Brown University, to explicate the unity that exists within a divided Judaism. (See his *Sectors of American Judaism,* 1975, pp. 259–277.)

Denomination as a nonjudgmental term in Protestantism was brought into vogue in the eighteenth century by leaders of the Evangelical Revival in Great Britain and of the parallel Great Awakening in North America. John Wesley was representative of British leadership when he declared: "I . . . refuse to be distinguished from other men by any but the common principles of Christianity. . . . I renounce and detest all other marks of distinction. But from real Christians, of whatever *denomination,* I earnestly desire not to be distinguished at all. . . . Dost thou love and fear God? It is enough! I give thee the right hand of fellowship." Gilbert Tennant, based in New Jersey but itinerating throughout the colonies, was even more precise in defining what the word implied: "All societies who profess Christianity and retain the fundamental principles thereof, notwithstanding their different denominations and diversity of sentiments in smaller things, are in reality but one Church of Christ, but several branches (more or less pure in minuter points) of one visible kingdom of the Messiah."

Although the revivalists made current coin of the term, it had been used as early as 1688 by Samuel Willard, minister of Old South Church in Boston, in a lecture later published as part of his *Compleat Body of Divinity,* in which he commented: "Through our knowing *but in part,* it is come to pass that professors of Christianity have been of diverse opinions in many things and their difference hath occasioned several *denominations,* but while they agree in the *foundation* they may be saved." Moreover, the denominational concept was implicit in the participation of Increase and Cotton Mather in 1717 in the ordination of a Baptist minister. And it was equally implicit at about the same time in the acceptance by Harvard College of funds from Thomas Hollis, a Baptist, for the endowment of a professorship of divinity and for a scholarship fund that would be available to Baptist as well as to other ministerial students. Such incipient manifestations of a irenic denominational temper were precipitated by policies of James II and then by the perceived consequences of the Glorious Revolution of 1688 and the Act of Toleration of 1689. Still, the creative moment in forging the concept of denominationalism antedated the crisis of the years following 1688–1689 by almost half a century.

Seventeenth-Century Origin. Usually a movement or a theology is born before it is named. This was true of denominationalism. The denominational understanding of the church had been hammered out by non-Separatist Puritan preachers prior to and during the sessions of the Westminster Assembly of Divines, a body of clergymen summoned in 1643 during the English Civil War to advise the "Long Parliament" in the shaping of a religious settlement. The problem that stymied the Parliament and the Westminster Assembly was the splintering and fragmenting of a triumphant Puritanism. Puritans of several hues had united to bring down rule by "lordly prelates" in the church, but, having done this, they were unable to agree on an alternate policy. A solution to this problem was proposed by non-Separatist Independents (Anglicans of a congregational persuasion) both within and outside the assembly. Those who were members of the Westminster Assembly were called the Dissenting Brethren.

The non-Separatist Independents were indebted to the Protestant reformers of the sixteenth century for their basic insights. They recalled repeated cautions against sanctifying churchly forms. The true church, the reformers had insisted, is not an institution, although it finds institutional expression in the world. Calvin was more confident than Luther that external ecclesiastical arrangements could be deduced from the Bible; still, he had a word of caution for those "who are not satisfied unless the church can always be pointed out with the finger." This, he said in the preface to the *Institutes,* cannot be done in any final sense. The whole question of the boundaries of the church must be left to God, "since he alone 'knoweth them that are his.'" The reformers acted upon this insight only to a limited degree, but they did recognize as true churches, more or less adequate in external form, those possessing an essentially common faith, whether they were Lutheran churches as in various political units of Germany and Scandinavia, Reformed churches as in other political divisions of Europe, or an Anglican church as in England. The new element introduced in mid-seventeenth-century England was the application of this understanding to a situation where divisions were within a geographical area rather than between geographical areas.

As the fragmentation of Puritanism increased after 1640, the moderates associated with the Dissenting Brethren became increasingly aware of "the danger of rending and dividing the godly Protestant party" at its moment of triumph when there was "an absolute necessity of their nearest union." Not only did divisions threaten the achievement of reforms desired by all the godly, they constituted a denial of the spirit of Christianity itself. "We are wrangling, devising, plotting, working against one another," said Jeremiah Burroughes, their most eloquent spokesman in the Assembly, whereas "love and unity are Christ's badge." It was an unhappy fact that "we are divided notwithstanding we are all convinced of the evil of our divisions." The problem was to find a way to peace and unity when Christians did not all agree. "If we stay for peace and love till we come to the unity of faith in all things," Burroughes confessed, "we must stay for ought I know till we come to another world."

With this dilemma in mind, seventeenth-century Independents elaborated a series of principles as a basis on which Christians could be united notwithstanding their differences.

First, so long as people live "in this muddy world" and "deceitfulness" lurks within the human heart, it is inevitable that there shall be differences of opinion even among the godly.

Second, even when differing convictions do not involve fundamentals, they cannot be lightly regarded. Those who fear God must first be persuaded themselves before they can accept the judgment of others.

Third, differences must be approached with humility and a degree of tentativeness. No one put this more vividly than Thomas Hooker of Connecticut, as his contribution to the ongoing discussion in England. "The sum is, we doubt not what we practice, but it's beyond all doubt that all men are liars and we are in the number of those poor feeble men; either we do or may err, though we do not know it; what we have learned we do profess and yet profess still to live that we may learn."

Fourth, as a corollary to human fallibility, Burroughes contended that "God hath a hand in these divisions to bring forth further light. Sparks are beaten out by the flints striking together." How can people know that they are right, asked another, until they "by discussing, praying, reading, meditating, find that out?"

Fifth, "though our differences are sad enough," they do not make us of "different religions." While "godly people are divided in their opinions and ways . . . they are united in Christ." Nor does the mere fact of separation constitute schism. It is schismatic only when it is not "loving and peaceable," only when it is "uncharitable, unjust, rash, violent."

Burroughes gave several illustrations of what he had in mind. Both Scots and refugees from abroad, he noted, had been permitted to have their own churches in England without being regarded as schismatics. This also had been true of Independents when they were in exile on the continent. Furthermore, persons of sufficient means in England had the liberty of "choosing pastors" by "choosing houses," moving from a parish where in good conscience they could not enjoy the means of grace to another parish where they could. When they did so, no cry of schism was raised. Should the same liberty be denied the less affluent who could not afford to move their dwelling from one side of the street to the other? Were they to be condemned as schismatics when their richer brethren were not?

What Burroughes and others were pleading for was a recognition that, although Christians may walk in different "ways" of outward obedience, they are still united in Christ and may work together for common ends of "godliness." They did, in fact, unite in defense of "the good old cause" of religious toleration. Many (those of Episcopal persuasion as well as Presbyterians, Congregationalists, and Baptists) did participate in Oliver Cromwell's "voluntary national establishment" during the 1650s. Later there were the "Heads of Agreement" of 1690, the joint petition to Queen Anne in 1702 from those who came to be called the "three old denominations," and the establishment in 1732 of a formal representative committee, known as "the Dissenting Deputies," to protect and expand the rights of the dissenting churches and their members.

Denominationalism in the United States. The denominational concept of the church was accepted in New England from the beginning. "We do not go to New England as Separatists from the Church of England," said Francis Higginson, "though we cannot but separate from the corruptions of it." As did their brethren at home, they adopted the neutral term *way* when explaining points of distinction from other orthodox Protestants (e.g., John Cotton, *The Way of the New England Churches Cleared*, 1648). Moreover, the elders of the Massachusetts Bay Colony expressed the same willingness to learn from others when responding to an inquiry concerning their practice. "We see as much cause to suspect the integrity of our own hearts as yours; and so much the more as being more privy to the deceitfulness of our own hearts than to yours . . . which causeth us with great reverence to accept and receive what further light God may be pleased to impart unto us by you. But as we have believed, so have we hitherto practiced." They were upset, however, when dissidents challenged their attempt to fashion a new Zion in the American wilderness, since there was ample room for dissidents to establish their own communities. Banishment was the response, but as John Cotton explained, perhaps somewhat blandly, "Banishment in this country is not counted as much a confinement as an enlargement," pointing out that "the jurisdiction (whence a man is banished) is but small, and the country round about it large and fruitful; where a man may make his choice of variety of more pleasant and profitable seats than he leaveth behind him."

Although New Englanders did not always match profession with practice, their understanding of the church was well adapted to the situation in other colonies where religious diversity prevailed and no single group occupied a dominant position. Even North Carolina could be regarded as a southern Pennsylvania in its ethnic composition and religious complexion, and the valley of Virginia and late-blooming Georgia were not greatly different.

Not only was the denominational theory of the church popularized by leaders of the Great Awakening, since 1690 it had been reinforced by the growing influence of John Locke, who had adopted and set forth, in his *Letter Concerning Toleration*, a view of the churches that he derived from his non-Separatist Puritan antecedents. (See George L. Hunt, *Calvinism and the Political Order*, 1965, pp. 111–113.)

By their acceptance of religious freedom following the American Revolution, most Protestant churches (with their general assemblies, general conventions, general conferences, general councils, or general associations) were committed to voluntarism and became, from a legal point of view, voluntary societies. They were under no legal restraint in dealing with their own internal affairs. Nor were most of them the least inhibited in following the practice developed during the years of the Great Awakening in joining together in efforts to promote concerts of prayer and religious revivals. In addition, in the early decades of the nineteenth century, out of their concern for the whole of society, a host of additional voluntary societies, both denominational and interdenominational, were founded to promote missionary, educational, benevolent, and reform activities. These societies became so ubiquitous that Orestes Brownson complained that "matters have come to such a pass that a peaceable man can hardly venture to eat or drink, to go to bed or get up, to correct his children or kiss his wife" without the guidance and sanction of some society.

This pattern of institutional activity persisted into the twentieth century, with new societies being formed as new needs were perceived to supplement the work of the older societies. Such newer societies were as varied as the Student Volunteer Movement, the League for Industrial Democracy, the Fellowship of Reconciliation, and the Southern Christian Leadership Conference. In addition, Protestant churches became linked by such official agencies as the Foreign Mission Conference of North America.

Countervailing Attitudes in the United States. Not everyone was enamored with denominationalism as an expression of Christian unity. There were manifestations of "high church" sentiment by some groups (e.g., Landmark Baptists) who insisted that they alone represented the true church and refused to recognize or cooperate with those outside their ranks. Others (e.g., Old School Presbyterians) established official boards firmly under church control to carry on work hitherto delegated to voluntary societies. Still others, such as Thomas and Alexander Campbell, sought to fashion a unified movement in which denominational distinctions would disappear. They preempted the name Christian for themselves and called upon others to reject party names and nonbiblical creeds and practices that were a source of division and to unite instead on the basis of biblical names and practices alone. Typical of their point of view was the slogan "Where the Scriptures speak, we speak; and where the Scriptures are silent, we are silent." Although the adherents they gathered were regarded as a denomination by others, they repudiated the name and spoke of themselves as a brotherhood.

A major shift in attitude toward denominationalism began in the late nineteenth century. It grew out of a growing conviction among a few key leaders that unity should find expression in a comprehensive church sufficiently broad in outlook and tolerant in spirit to minimize differences of opinion. Phillips Brooks, pastor of Trinity Church in Boston (1869–1891) and briefly Episcopal bishop of Massachusetts, was one who helped cultivate the temper that led in this direction when he declared that humanity itself, not any organized body of believers, is the instrument through which God effects his purposes. This is the true church where "the great human impulses" lead people to do "Christian work in the spirit of Christ" even when they "studiously" disown him. Broad churchmanship, it was sometimes called, or catholic Christianity.

The roots of this catholic Christianity can also be traced back to seventeenth-century England, to the "latitudinarians" of the decades following 1660. Two streams converged to inform the views of the "men of latitude." One was derived from the Cambridge Platonists, non-Separatist Independents at the university, who, unlike fellow Independents serving as pastors, faced the problem of finding a basis for unity within an institution (the university) rather than between institutions (the churches). After 1660 they joined forces with those influenced by the rationalism of the Enlightenment to fashion a defense of diversity (latitude) within a comprehensive state-established church. Thus they stood in opposition to those who insisted upon a narrowly defined Caroline Christianity (i.e., during the reign of Charles II) as the only true faith of the Church of England. The latitudinarian apologetic initially had little relevance to a situation where religious diversity was widespread and there was no dominant state church. Additional changes in the climate of opinion were necessary before it could become pertinent.

Another impulse leading to unhappiness with the denominational concept was the belief that, from an organizational and administrative point of view, the denominational system was inefficient and financially improvident. John D. Rockefeller, Jr., a Baptist who was deeply devout and devoted to the mission enterprise and whose social concerns had been awakened by men who surrounded his father, is a prime illustration of this second impulse. A careful steward, Rockefeller sought efficiency and economy through consolidation of missionary endeavor and other aspects of Christian activity. He used his influence and his money to make Christian outreach cost-effective by initiating such breathtaking schemes to redeem a global society as the Interchurch World Movement of 1919–1920 and the Laymen's Foreign Mission Inquiry of 1930–1932. In the end he ceased contributing to denominational projects, restricting his stewardship to consolidated efforts.

A third factor bringing denominationalism into disrepute was a by-product of German sociological studies, notably those of Ernst Troeltsch (1865–1923). The key concept was a typology that drew a distinction between "church" and "sect" applicable to countries with a predominant state church. A "denomination," however, was difficult to fit into this scheme, for it was neither "church" nor "sect" in terms of Troeltsch's analysis. Still, his views were intriguing. The most influential attempt to adapt Troeltsch's typology to the American scene was H. Richard Niebuhr's *The Social Sources of Denominationalism* (1929), which in a curious way idealized European state churches because they were institutions into which everyone was born, rich and poor alike.

A scathing indictment of denominationalism preceded Niebuhr's analysis of "the ethical failure of a divided church" and his descriptions of the churches of the disinherited, the middle class, and those produced by nationalism, sectionalism, and the color line. "Denominationalism in the Christian church," he declared,

> is an unacknowledged hypocrisy. It represents the accommodation of Christianity to the caste-system of human society. . . . The division of the churches closely follows the division of men into the castes of national, racial, and economic groups. It draws the color line in the church of God; it fosters the misunderstandings, the self-exaltations, the hatreds of jingoistic nationalism by continuing in the body of Christ the spurious differences of provincial loyalties; it sets the rich and poor apart at the table of the Lord, where the fortunate may enjoy the bounty they have provided while the others feed upon the crusts their poverty affords.

Niebuhr acknowledged the insights he had derived from Troeltsch's typology. "Churches" are natural social groups "akin to the family or the nation" into which people of all classes are born, whereas "sects" are "voluntary associations." Sects compromise the universality of the Christian faith by their surrender to various caste systems. As generations pass, sects become denominations that are inclusive in the sense that people are born into them, with membership being determined by custom and family tradition. But as denominations, these former sects perpetuate in the body of Christ the caste systems of society. The volume closed with a summons to organic unity. Denominations were challenged to transcend their social conditioning and coalesce into a comprehensive church that would express the brotherhood of the Christian gospel.

By 1937 Niebuhr had second thoughts and published *The Kingdom of God in America* as a partial corrective to his earlier volume. He was still aware of the ways in which ethnicity, race, sectionalism, and economic circumstance had led to the formation of separate Christian groups. But this was not the whole story. He had not taken into account that denominationalism in its initial manifestation was the product of a new religious vitality with a dynamic sense of mission that placed primary emphasis on inner Christian experience. While differences of outward form and structure were not deemed unimportant and although there were competing claims as to their relative adequacy to express and advance the claims of Christ, stress was upon changed lives and a shared mission that encouraged cooperative activities and a not unfriendly coexistence. Slowly, however, the differing patterns took on greater importance as they became institutionalized. Here the problem was not compromise with caste systems but the process by which institutions over a long period of time begin to regard their own perpetuation as an end in itself. The earlier Puritan and the later evangelical sense of mission that provided the denominations with their reason for existence and bound them together in common causes began to fade. Becoming self-satisfied and self-congratulatory, they made peace with the world. This acculturation won from Niebuhr a stinging rebuke: "A God without wrath brought men without sin into a kingdom without judgment through the ministrations of a Christ without a cross." Niebuhr's summons was a call for renewal, for the recovery of a sense of mission that must precede and accompany any movement toward unity. Only a renewal that translated the love of God into love of brother would be powerful enough to overcome the walls of partition—institutional, ethnic, racial, sectional, economic—that fragmented the body of Christ.

The strictures of *The Kingdom of God in America* did little to mitigate the negative connotation evoked by the term *denominationalism* as a result of its being equated with sectarianism. Niebuhr's earlier *Social Sources of Denominationalism* continued for more than half a century to be his most influential book. Many Protestants seemed oblivious to his second thoughts. Instead of responding to the summons for renewal as a prerequisite for unity, many had become converts to a twentieth-century version of "latitudinarianism" or "catholic Christianity" that sought a united church that would be ample enough to accommodate the views and opinions of everyone. Instead of seeking renewal as a first step, such leaders opted for the more direct approach of tinkering with institutional arrangements to increase the scope of comprehension, a procedure that did not differ in kind from the preoccupation with institutional concerns that Niebuhr regarded as the nub of the problem.

Since the common core of Protestantism had become so badly eroded, it is possible that *Protestant denominationalism* may no longer be a viable term to indicate anything more than Protestant diversity. Perhaps Sidney Mead, author of numerous perceptive and incisive essays dealing with the shape of Protestantism in America, is right in using the words *church, denomination,* and *sect* as synonyms. There is an overabundance of Protestant denominations in this sense, but only minority segments are linked by a common faith and few of these segments possess a theological concept of denominationalism to express their unity and undergird their cooperative activities.

Recognizing this situation, and conceding that the use of the word *denomination* is likely to persist, Martin E. Marty of the University of Chicago in 1982 made a sensible suggestion. As the Bible justifies the use of the word *church* only for a local congregation or the entire church, the word *denomination* can serve as a useful "in-between" term to designate existing ecclesiastical groupings that have provided "family tone" and clusters of memories and symbols that still can be invoked to sustain Christians in their daily lives. "Denominations," Marty noted, "are an offense only when they undercut the local church or the whole church," but when Christians are faithful to their "particular heritage," without condemning others, they enrich the whole church. Such an observation is not far removed from the spirit of those who initially fashioned the denominational concept of the church.

[*See also* Church, *article on* Church Polity; Anabaptism; Anglicanism; Baptist Churches; Christian Science; Congregationalism; Disciples of Christ; Jehovah's Witnesses; Lutheranism; Mennonites; Methodist Churches; Moravians; Mormonism; Pietism; Presbyterianism, Reformed; Puritanism; Quakers; Salvation Army; Seventh-day Adventism; Shakers; *and* Unitarian Universalist Association.]

BIBLIOGRAPHY

While there are many histories of individual denominations, numerous handbooks or guides with accounts of the different religious bodies (e.g., Arthur C. Piepkorn's *Profiles in Belief,* 7 vols., New York, 1977–), and much discussion of the churches as voluntary associations, bureaucratic structures, and ethnic groupings, surprisingly little attention has been given to the theory and concept of denominationalism itself.

The most important discussions of denominationalism, from a variety of perspectives, have been assembled by Russell E. Richey in *Denominationalism* (Nashville, 1977). Richey includes a chapter from H. Richard Niebuhr's *The Kingdom of God in America* (Chicago and New York, 1937) and calls attention to the importance of Niebuhr's *Social Sources of Denominationalism* (Hamden, Conn., 1929). He includes Sidney E. Mead's essay "Denominationalism: The Shape of Protestantism in America," reprinted from Mead's *The Lively Experiment* (New York, 1963), which contains other pertinent material. Other essays included are by E. Franklin Frazier, Fred J. Hood, Winthrop S. Hudson, Martin E. Marty, Elwyn A. Smith, and Timothy L. Smith. Richey notes that the understanding of Protestant denominationalism presented in this entry represents a fairly general consensus, having been adopted by Sydney E. Ahlstrom in *A Religious History of the American People*

(New Haven, Conn., 1972), pp. 96, 381–382; Robert T. Handy in *A History of the Churches in the United States and Canada* (New York, 1976), p. 112; Winthrop S. Hudson in *Religion in America*, 3d ed. (New York, 1981), pp. 81–82; Martin E. Marty in *Righteous Empire: The Protestant Experience in America* (New York, 1970), p. 69; and *The Westminster Dictionary of Church History* (Philadelphia, 1971), "Denominationalism." For the most theologically informed explication of denominationalism, see Jacob Neusner's "Conservative Judaism in a Divided Community," in *Sectors of American Judaism* (New York, 1975), vol. 2 of his *Understanding American Judaism*.

WINTHROP S. HUDSON

DERVISH. *See* Darwīsh.

DESCARTES, RENÉ (1596–1650), French philosopher. Descartes is held to be the father of modern philosophy and chief architect of the modern approach to the relationship between science and religion. The scholastic tradition, already ably criticized by Descartes's time, was in effect obviated by a new, universal metaphysical construction based on the conceptual apparatus of Descartes. The entire development of European philosophy, in all its diverse tendencies, has been dependent, directly or indirectly, on the Cartesian legacy. If it is true, as Whitehead said, that European philosophy consists of footnotes to Plato, modern European philosophy, in the same sense, consists of footnotes to Descartes.

Born to a noble Roman Catholic family, Descartes was educated in the physics and metaphysics of an Aristotelian and Thomist tradition, and in medicine and law. He joined the Dutch army, and, while in the Netherlands, became interested in mathematics and the new physics. Having traveled in various countries, he returned to France, where he outlined the first version of a new method of thinking based on mathematics *(Rules for the Direction of the Mind)*, but he did not complete or publish it. After settling in the Netherlands, he maintained contact with scholars by letter; Marin Mersenne was his main correspondent. He passed the last year of his life in Sweden at the court of Queen Christina.

Descartes's aim was to use mathematics as a model for developing a fully unified form of human knowledge. He applied this method in his *Treatise on the World*. The trial of Galileo and condemnation of Galileo's *Dialogues* convinced Descartes not to print his own work, which clearly confirmed the heliocentric theory. In 1637 he published several parts of it with a methodological introduction, called *The Discourse on Method*, which was to become one of the greatest texts of modern thought. In 1641 he published his other major work, *Meditations on First Philosophy*, which had previously been sent to a number of scholars, among them Gassendi, Hobbes, and Arnauld; their objections and Descartes's replies were subsequently published with the main text. *The Principles of Philosophy* appeared in 1644 and *The Passions of the Soul* in 1649. Some other works and his voluminous correspondence were published posthumously.

The *Discourse* indicates that for Descartes philosophy was a methodological and conceptual basis for the sciences, to make them useful in the domination of nature. Although the metaphysical problems he discussed in his *Meditations* are not subordinated to this goal, it is clear that Descartes was interested only in matters that could be solved by rational means and that his mental attitude was essentially antihistorical.

Cartesian method demands that we accept as true only what is presented "clearly and distinctly" to our mind, leaving no room for doubt. We should suspend our judgment in all matters where the slightest doubt is possible, including all the truths of common sense, in order to find something that resists all doubts. Sense-perception does not provide us with any indubitable knowledge, since we cannot be *a priori* certain that we are not dreaming or that we are not being deceived by a malicious demon. But my very act of doubting, however far extended, and therefore the fact that I am thinking, cannot itself be doubted. And thus I find at least this one certainty in which I cannot be deceived: I think, and I, the thinker, must exist; no demon could induce me to err on this point. This reasoning, summarized in the famous formula "Cogito ergo sum," can be admitted as the basis of knowledge.

The cogito, accepted as a kind of epistemological absolute, is in Descartes's work an implicit challenge to the authority of tradition and an appeal to look for truth only in the reason of a thinking individual. And it implies that the only object that is directly and indubitably accessible to one's mind is its own activity; wherever else we start, our beliefs will be exposed to doubt.

While I grasp my existence as identical with the awareness of existence, I observe, according to Descartes, that nothing belongs necessarily to my nature except the fact that I think; therefore I may describe myself as a thinking thing, or thinking substance, or immaterial soul. This transition from "I think" to "I am a thinking substance" was strongly criticized by Descartes's contemporaries and later. It gave rise to the question, much debated in the twentieth century, whether or not the "self" or "I" can be described at all in "objective" categories.

Our mind, according to Descartes, has a natural light whereby it is capable of acquiring knowledge on most important issues without relying on sense-perception. We have in our mind a natural idea of God, or a perfect being. Since our mind clearly perceives that it is not perfect itself (of which the fact of doubting is evidence, if indeed evidence is needed), it could not have fabricated this idea, as a more perfect thing cannot be produced by a less perfect; consequently the very presence of this idea is a proof of the actual existence of the perfect being. This psychological argument for God's existence, like the ontological argument in traditional version, which Descartes accepts as well, implies nothing about God's presence and signs in the world. God's first function, in Descartes's construction, is to assure the reliability of human knowledge: being perfect, God cannot deceive us, therefore we can rely both on our commonsense belief in the reality of the material world and on our intellectual intuition. (Many critics pointed out the circularity in this reasoning: acts of intuition are necessary to acquire the certainty of the existence of God, who subsequently appears as a guarantor of the infallibility of those very acts.) We can thus affirm the reality of the material world.

Descartes conceived the material world, or "extension," in strictly mechanistic terms. All processes are explained by the laws of mechanics; living organisms behave according to the same principles that govern artificial automata; there is no specific realm of life. To be sure, human beings are endowed with an immaterial soul, which is the seat of all sensations; animals, having no soul, are no more than mechanisms, and their reactions are just mechanical movements. In human beings, organic (that is, mechanical) processes, should be distinguished from psychological events in the soul. The human organism does not differ from other mechanisms; its death is a physical phenomenon, whereas the separation of the soul is not the cause but the effect of death. The two substances—soul and body—that make up the human being cannot affect each other; therefore the question of how we can realize, in perception, the mechanical impacts of other things on our bodies and cause movements of our body by the sheer act of will becomes difficult to solve; and Descartes's followers, when trying to explain the unity of soul and body and their mutual influence, naturally tended to materialist or occasionalist explanations, none of which conformed to the master's doctrine, which implied both that the soul is absolutely free and capable of dominating the affects, and that the affects are passive states caused by the movement of blood.

Descartes's philosophy almost instantaneously produced new lines of division in European intellectual life. Though attacked, mainly for its rationalist rigor, by both Protestants (the school of Voetius) and Catholics (all Descartes's works were put on the Index of Prohibited Books in 1663), its impact was soon to be felt not only among philosophers, scientists, and physicians, but among theologians as well. In the Netherlands, Coccejus's school tried to apply Descartes's methods in theological investigations; in France, Malebranche and other occasionalists attempted a Catholic assimilation of a somewhat modified Cartesianism. In the Jansenist milieu the influence of Descartes was very strong. By the end of the seventeenth century few orthodox Cartesians remained, but the impact of the doctrine was felt throughout the early French Enlightenment; its general rationalist and determinist approach laid the foundation of eighteenth-century materialism, while its skeptical side and the cogito were crucially important in the rise of modern idealism, starting with Berkeley.

Although there are no reasons to doubt that Descartes himself believed in God and in the immortality of the soul, his philosophy made God absent in the world and thus useless in interpreting it. Descartes was not, strictly speaking, a deist, insofar as, according to him, the force needed to sustain the universe in existence is the same as that needed to create it; yet he contributed decisively to the deist and atheist movements of the subsequent centuries. He was the modern founder of totally secularized thinking. Outstanding twentieth-century Thomists (Gilson, Maritain) saw in Descartes the main author of what they believed to be the aberration of modern intellectual life, of its individualist, idealist, and rationalist tendencies. And the problem of the transition from the cogito to the world and vice versa has remained, thanks to Descartes, one of the crucial issues in modern phenomenology and existential philosophy.

BIBLIOGRAPHY

Works by Descartes

Correspondance. 8 vols. Edited by Charles Adam and Gérard Milhaud. Paris, 1936–1963.

Descartes: Philosophical Writings. Selected, translated, and edited by Elizabeth Anscombe and P. T. Geach. Edinburgh, 1964. Contains a good bibliography.

Œuvres de Descartes. 2d ed. 12 vols. Edited by Charles Adam and Paul Tannery. Paris, 1956–1957.

Philosophical Letters. Translated and edited by Anthony Kenny. Oxford, 1970.

Works about Descartes

Adam, Charles. *Descartes: Sa vie et son œuvre.* Paris, 1937.

Alquié, Ferdinand. *La découverte métaphysique de l'homme chez Descartes.* 2d ed. Paris, 1966.

Doney, Willis, ed. *Descartes: A Collection of Critical Essays.* Garden City, N.Y., 1967.

Gilson, Étienne. *La doctrine cartésienne de la liberté et la théologie.* Paris, 1915.

Gilson, Étienne. *Études sur le rôle de la pensée médiévale dans la formation du système cartésien*. Paris, 1930.
Gouhier, Henri. *La pensée religieuse de Descartes*. Paris, 1924.
Laporte, Jean. *Le rationalisme de Descartes*. 2d ed. Paris, 1950.
Leroy, Maxime. *Descartes, le philosophe au masque*. Paris, 1929.
Mouy, Paul. *Le développement de la physique cartésienne*. Paris, 1934.
Sebba, Gregor. *Bibliographia Cartesiana*. The Hague, 1964.

LESZEK KOLAKOWSKI

DESCENT INTO THE UNDERWORLD. Stories and accounts the world over tell of descents into the underworld. Many traditions include myths and rituals connected with journeys to the other world, journeys undertaken by both human and suprahuman beings. Experiences of such journeys are especially common in the shamanistic traditions, but they are also found in association with various ecstatic religious phenomena within the higher cultures. A visit to the underworld, particularly to the kingdom of the dead, is also one of the central themes in the myths that tell of the deeds of human or divine heroes.

The beliefs concerning descent into an underworld inhabited by the spirits are based in part on a psychological experience in which the soul is believed to leave the body during a state of altered consciousness, such as trance or sleep, or during the visions and hallucinations associated with these states. The actual content of such experiences, however, is determined to a large extent by the cultures and traditional beliefs of the persons undergoing them. They tend to be reinforced by the stories of people who were thought dead but who subsequently recovered. Such stories also conform to cultural models.

The Underworld. Beliefs concerning the descent into the underworld are often connected with the concept of a three-layer cosmos, according to which the human world is located midway between the realm of spirits above and the realm of the dead below, the "underworld." [*See* Underworld.] The underworld itself may also be thought of as divided into layers. In certain Asian and Oceanic cultures, for example, the underworld is believed to be divided into as many as nine layers. The Scandinavians too recognized nine levels of the underworld, the lowest of which they called Niflhel. These cosmic levels are often believed to be connected to one another by a cosmic tree or mountain, which is frequently believed to be located in the north. In Inner and North Asia, India, and northern Europe, it is the "center of the world" that is to be found in the north.

The cosmic tree that connects the levels of the cosmos also acts as a path of communication between them. The Vasyugan Khanty and the Scandinavians, for example, believe that it has its roots in the underworld. In the shamanistic tales of Siberia, the opening leading to the underworld is represented as lying at the foot of the cosmic tree, or at the foot of its counterpart, the shaman's tree. The Altaic Turks, on the other hand, locate this opening at the "center of the cosmos," and describe it as a "smoke hole." Many northerly peoples locate the opening to the different cosmic levels in the North Star that shines at the center of the world.

The Realm of the Dead. In all cultural traditions the most important part of the underworld is the realm of the dead. Most of the traditions describing the descent into the underworld are in fact concerned with visiting the dead. Their realm may be described very differently in different cultures. In the high cultures of the East, and in Central Asia, for instance, it is described as the palace of the prince of death, or as a mighty dwelling place. In ancient Scandinavian folklore, it is a great hall, whereas in the Finnish epic it is a large living room. Among the hunting peoples of Siberia, it is conceived of as a yurt village.

It should be noted that not all conceptions of the abode of the dead locate it in the underworld. In some cases it is located in the west, as a kingdom beyond the horizon. In other cases it is conceived of as a kingdom in the sky. According to Germanic and Inuit (Eskimo) beliefs, this heavenly kingdom was the last abode of persons of high rank or persons who had met a violent death in battle. According to the high religions of the Middle and Far East, it was the abode of the innocent and the godly. In these cases, the underworld realm of the dead represents a place where sinners are punished. Despite all this variety in representation, however, many of the concepts surrounding the realm of the dead are astonishingly similar in all parts of the world.

Beliefs in a local opening and road leading to the underworld are common in the cultures of Europe, Asia, West Africa, Melanesia and Polynesia. On the west side of Rarotonga, in the Cook Islands, for instance, one finds the Black Rock, from which the souls of the dead are thought to set off on their journey to the other world. Volcanoes, such as Etna, or caves, such as that of Lough Derg in Ireland, mark the beginning of the road to Hell or Purgatory, as in medieval Christian literature. One of the universal features of such a road to the underworld is darkness. This is why the Yakut shaman has disks representing the sun and moon sewn onto his clothing, to provide light on the route to the otherworld. The road is also dangerous, fraught with difficulties and preternatural obstacles that only an initiate or a spirit being can overcome. In Finnish folklore, such obstacles include a great eagle, a snake, a fiery pond or waterfall, and a river bristling with swords. Similar obstacles are also found in the mythologies of the Middle East, of classical antiquity, and of the Germanic peoples, and they were also cultivated in the Christian vision literature of the Middle Ages. Traditions familiar in both Asia and Europe tell of a stream surrounding the realm of the dead that must be crossed on a ferry, or by a narrow bridge made dangerous by swords, or speak of a wall surrounding the underworld over which the soul must leap. According to the ancient Germans and the Yakuts of Siberia, the dead had to be equipped either with shoes or a horse to protect them on their difficult journey. Another widespread concept connected with the underworld is that of the beast or dog that guards its gates. Examples include the Greek Kerberos and the Scandinavian Garmr; the Babylonian Nedu, with its lion's head, human hands, and bird's feet; and the Egyptian Ammut, who was the watchdog of the underworld god Osiris and had the body of a lion, the front limbs of a crocodile, and the rear limbs of a hippopotamus.

The Shaman's Journey to the Underworld. A journey to the underworld under the helpful guidance of the spirits is the cornerstone of the classical shamanism of Siberia and Inner Asia, and corresponding practices connected with the activities of a seer or an ecstatic healer can be found in other parts of the world as well: in South and North America, in Oceania, in the folk religion of Indochina, and among the early ethnic religions of Europe. [*See* Shamanism.] One typical feature of this type of otherworldly journey is the use that the shaman makes of ritual techniques intended to induce ecstasy.

Where there is a belief in an underworld, it is not uncommon for people to have chance experiences of descending into it during sleep or trance. In shamanistic cultures, such spontaneous experiences were interpreted as proof that the spirits had selected a candidate for a future shaman. According to a Nentsy myth, a woodcutter once suddenly found himself on the back of a *minryy* bird, from which he next fell through a hole into the underworld. There he wandered from the dwelling of one spirit to another and had to recognze each in turn. He was then cut into pieces and put together again, after which one of the spirits guided him back to the earth's surface. This experience was taken to be the man's initiation as a shaman, particularly in view of the dissection and reassembling of his body by the spirits.

Chance visions, pains, and torments were interpreted as the shaman's sickness and were taken as signs of a person's candidacy as a shaman. While learning to use the drum and sing the shaman's songs, the candidate withdrew from the normal life of the community, fasted, and sought contact with the spirits. A journey to the underworld, experienced through visions and auditions, was a prerequisite for initiation. The central element of this journey was the experience of rebirth. The reports of such initiation visions prove that the initiate's experiences were shaped by the shamanistic tradition of the community in question. The older shamans would interpret the candidate's experiences in such a way as to channel them toward accepted, traditional patterns. During this initiation period the new shaman became familiar with that part of the spirit world to which he would later journey during his séances.

A number of the peoples of Inner Asia and southern Siberia refer to the shaman's journeying to the underworld as "black." This seems to be a reference to the fact that the underworld contained not only the abodes of the dead but also the dwelling places of various disease-causing or otherwise dangerous spirits. In order to be an accomplished shaman, one had to know the roads leading to these places and be able to recognize their inhabitants. This made it all the more important for a candidate to study the topography of the underworld during his initiation period. In the more northerly regions this study was conducted under the guidance of special spirits, usually the zoomorphic spirits of nature.

Ritual Descent. The ritual descent into the underworld takes place during a shamanistic séance, in the course of which the shaman describes in song the stages of his journey. In northern Siberia and the arctic regions in particular, the actual transfer to the other world was thought to coincide with the highest point in the shaman's altered state of consciousness and was indicated by loss of external consciousness. The shaman's soul was then thought to have left his body and to be traveling in the other world, in the form of an animal or accompanied by benevolent spirits.

The visit to the underworld was sometimes portrayed through theatrical means. The journey of the "black" shamans of the Altaic Tatars to Erlik Khan, the lord of the underworld, was expressed not only in song but also by means of mime and movement. The shaman would give a detailed description of the stages of his journey and his meeting with Erlik Khan. First he rode southward, climbed the Mountain of Iron, on whose slopes lay the fading bones of unsuccessful shamans, and then descended through a hole into the underworld. He next crossed the sea of the underworld by an extremely narrow and dangerous bridge and arrived at the dwelling of Erlik Khan. At first the lord of the underworld was angry, but as the shaman offered him drink and sacrifices, he became benevolent and promised to fulfill the shaman's wishes. The shaman then returned to earth riding on a goose.

When descending into the underworld, the shaman tried to solve problems that were thought to be caused by the spirits. The reasons for the journey to the underworld thus depended on the sorts of spirits living there and on the way they were thought to influence human life. If an illness was believed to be caused by a loss of soul, it was the shaman's task to fetch the patient's soul from the malevolent spirits who had stolen it. Other typical reasons for descending into the underworld were to acquire knowledge concerning the future, the weather, lost objects, or persons; to meet the spirits who assisted at a birth; to meet the keepers of the game during a period of famine; to escort the soul of a sacrificial animal to its destination; or to accompany the souls of the dead to the underworld. The initiatory vision of the Nganasani shaman Sereptie Djaruoskin reveals that he knew the roads leading from the foot of the shaman's tree to the spirits responsible for every kind of sickness, to the main guardians of the game, and to the spirits who provide protection at births.

If the soul of a dead person should fail to go to the underworld, but instead keep disturbing the peace of the living, the shaman was called upon to play the role of psychopomp. Indeed, among the Nanay (Goldi), the Altaic Turks, and the Nentsy, escorting the soul of the dead to its new abode was one of the shaman's most important tasks. Following a death the Nanay arranged a festival, during which the shaman caught the wandering spirit and placed it on a cushion specially made for the occasion. A big clan memorial festival was then held, and the shaman would escort the soul of the dead to Buni, the clan's own kingdom of the dead. On the way the shaman and the soul in his keeping were assisted by the spirit Buchu, who knew the way, and the bird Koori, who carried the travelers to the underworld on its back. At the séance during which all this took place, the shaman would give expression to the stages of his journey by dramatic means, giving the instructions to the spirits who assisted him and expressing in song his horror and relief over the difficulties along the way. As described at such séances, the road to Buni included eighteen stages that had special names and generally known features. The most difficult task along the journey was crossing the river separating the living from the dead. The shaman could tell when he had reached his destination from strange footmarks, the sound of dogs barking, and other traditional signs.

The Visions of Ascetics and Mystics. Visions of descending into the underworld are also part of the mystic traditions of the religions of the Middle East, of Hinduism, Buddhism, and Christianity. The visit in question is usually to the kingdom of the dead, and one of its main themes is the observation of the torment awaiting sinners in the other world and the judgment of souls. One of the earliest records of the judgment of the dead is an Egyptian papyrus of the first century CE, telling how Setne Khamuas, a high priest of Memphis, descended to the halls of Amenti under the guidance of his son Si-Osiris.

The ascetic practices known as *gyō*, practiced by Buddhist priests in Japan, sometimes led to states of trance that included visions of journeys to the underworld. Some of the visions were of an initiatory nature and had structural and thematic similarities to the shamans' visions. In the *Nihon ryōiki,* one reads how a priest called Chikō, while feigning to be dead, found himself accompanied by two messengers on the road to the underworld. The road led westward and finally to a golden palace, the door of which was guarded by two terrible beings. Three times the messengers ordered Chikō to clasp a burning hot pillar so that his flesh was burned and only his bones remained. Three times the spirits put him together again and finally sent him back to earth, ordering him to renounce the sin of envy. In addition to such reports of initiatory trials, the Japanese narratives also contain revelations of the sentences passed by the king of the underworld and the horrors awaiting sinners. One type of narrative, which has parallels in the Chinese tradition, tells of a person descending into the underworld in order to save one of his relatives from the torments of Hell.

Such descriptions of the judgment and punishment of sinners could serve as a moral warning to lead a virtuous life. These themes were also present in the Middle East and were particularly popular in the Christian literature of the Middle Ages. [*See* Judgment of the Dead.] The descriptions of journeys in Hell, Purgatory, and Paradise, one prototype of which is found in the *Apocalypse of Peter* (c. 100–150 CE), repeat beliefs in the world of the dead that are familiar from Judaism, the religions of antiquity, and from the ethnic religions. Dante gave artistic expression to such beliefs in his *Commedia.*

The journeys to the underworld made by the heroes Väinämöinen and Lemminkäinen in Finnish epic poetry are thought to have been inspired by Christian vision literature. They nevertheless lack the emphasis on the punishment awaiting sinners that lies at the heart of European vision literature. Väinämöinen descends to the underworld in the role of a sage, to seek knowledge and incantations. In this respect he is reminiscent of a shaman. A similar journey is made by the Scandinavian god Óðinn (Odin), who is described as having ecstatic powers. The episodes describing Lemminkäinen's journey have counterparts in mythical themes familiar in the Middle East.

The Hero's Descent into the Underworld. The journeys to the underworld undertaken by shamans and mystics typically involve visions experienced during trance. There are, however, myths and tales in different parts of the world that tell of journeys to the underworld undertaken by humans or gods without the aid of ecstatic powers. Visiting the underworld was thought to be one of the standard deeds of mythical heroes. The heroes descending into the underworld need not necessarily be human, for we find Ishtar making the journey in the Akkadian myth and Lemminkäinen's mother in the Finnish tradition. The reasons for the descent were many. One of the most popular was the rescue of a relative or loved one who had died young. But the journey could also be undertaken in order to search for immortality, knowledge, or some special favor, to escort the dead to their final resting place, or to receive initiation in the mysteries of the underworld. Here one notices a close parallel to the reasons given for the shaman's journey.

A test of strength between love and death is at the base of the legends and myths in which one left behind in this world follows the beloved or relative "to the land of no return." The best-known representative of this type of narrative is the Orpheus theme, various forms of which are to be found not only in Eurasia but also in North America, Oceania, and Melanesia. In Vergil's version, Orpheus sets off for Hades in search of his wife Eurydice, who has died young. With his songs and his music he is able to relieve the suffering in the underworld and wins the favor of the gods. Eurydice is promised to him on condition that he not turn to look at her on the road up. The impatient Orpheus nevertheless breaks his vow and loses his wife. Greater happiness befalls the heroes of the Polynesians, including the New Zealand Maori, who rescue their loved ones by deceiving the spirits that are trying to prevent their escape. In one Maori narrative, Hutu follows Pane, who has died of love for him, to the underworld. There he entertains the spirits, having them sit on the top of a tree that has been bent over and fastened to the ground by a rope. When Hutu lets go of the rope, the spirits are hurled into the air and he is able to escape with his beloved.

In addition to a spouse or a loved one, the main characters in these tales may also be people who are attached to one another by some other tie. For example, there are stories among the Indians of North America that stress sibling attachment. And among the Tatars of the Sayan steppes, the story is told of Kubaiko, who goes to look for her brother in the kingdom of death ruled by Erlik Khan. After carrying out the superhuman tasks imposed upon her by the princes of death, she receives the body of her brother and brings him back to life with the water of life. The story gives a long description of the state after death and the punishment of sinners. A similar description of Hades is found in the story of Odysseus's journey to the land of the dead.

The related idea of the death and resurrection of a god lies behind certain invigoration rites. There is a myth connected with Akkadian Ishtar and her Sumerian counterpart, Inanna, that describes the descent of the goddess into the underworld to bring her young husband back to life. On her way, Ishtar takes off her clothes and her ornaments as she passes through the gates that lead to Arallu. On reaching her destination she dies, and the earthly vegetation wilts. When the gods sprinkle her with the water of life, she recovers and returns to earth. Tammuz, also mentioned in the poem, is a passive hero whose fate remains obscure. The annual rituals held in honor of him nevertheless contain scenes suggesting that Ishtar descended into the underworld in order to restore him to life, and with him the growth of vegetation.

In some cases a hero penetrates the kingdom of death in order to gain immortality. One of the oldest known examples is the Sumerian myth of Gilgamesh, in which Gilgamesh crosses the waters of death and reaches the land of eternal life. There he finds a plant that preserves youth, but a snake snatches it from him on his return trip and he is forced to accept his mortality. The account of Gilgamesh's journey has been compared to the account of Herakles' visit to Hades. Herakles rises victorious from the underworld, bringing with him the watchdog Kerberos.

The pursuit of immortality is also part of the tradition woven around the Polynesian trickster and culture hero Māui. Māui believed that he could make himself immortal by crawling through the body of his giant grandmother, Hine-nui-te-po. Hine-nui-te-po nevertheless wakes as Māui enters her mouth and, closing her mouth, kills the intruder. This swallowing motif, also found in the story of Jonah and the great fish, is quite common in traditions concerned with initiation, and takes both mythical and ritual forms. It is found in the Finnish folk epic, where the hero and sage Väinämöinen, in search of knowledge, enters the belly of a giant sage who had long been dead.

A further reason for traveling to the underworld may

be to overcome the power of hell and rescue those condemned there, as in the medieval apocryphal tradition concerning Christ's victory over hell. Other reasons include the search for some special object, as in the descent of Psyche, or the mere satisfaction of curiosity. In each case the journey is described as being extremely dangerous and difficult, with its success depending on special conditions: the traveler should not eat any food offered him in the underworld, nor should he look back on the return journey, lest he fall under the power of the spirits giving chase from below.

BIBLIOGRAPHY

Bishop, J. G. "The Hero's Descent to the Underworld." In *The Journey to the Other World,* edited by Hilda R. Ellis Davidson, pp. 109–129. Totowa, N.J., 1975.

Blacker, Carmen. "Other World Journeys in Japan." In *The Journey to the Other World,* edited by Hilda R. Ellis Davidson, pp. 42–47. Totowa, N.J., 1975.

Davidson, Hilda R. Ellis. *The Road to Hel: A Study of the Conception of the Dead in Old Norse Literature* (1942). Reprint, Westport, Conn., 1977.

Eliade, Mircea. *Birth and Rebirth* (1958). Reprint, New York, 1975.

Eliade, Mircea. *Shamanism: Archaic Techniques of Ecstasy.* Rev. & enl. ed. New York, 1964.

Hultkrantz, Åke. *The North American Indian Orpheus Tradition: A Contribution to Comparative Religion.* Stockholm, 1957.

Kuusi, Matti, Keith Bosley, and Michael Branch, eds. and trans. *Finnish Folk Poetry: Epic; An Anthology in Finnish and English.* Helsinki, 1977.

Lopatin, Ivan A. *The Cult of the Dead among the Natives of the Amur Basin.* The Hague, 1960.

MacCulloch, J. A. "Descent to Hades (Ethnic)." In *Encyclopaedia of Religion and Ethics,* edited by James Hastings, vol. 4. Edinburgh, 1911.

MacCulloch, J. A., et al., eds. *The Mythology of All Races.* 13 vols. Boston, 1916–1932.

Popov, A. A. "How Sereptie Djaruoskin of the Nganasani (Tavgi Samoyeds) Became a Shaman." In *Popular Beliefs and Folklore Tradition in Siberia,* edited by Vilmos Diószegi, pp. 137–145. Bloomington, Ind., 1968.

Thompson, Stith. *Motif-Index of Folk Literature.* 2d ed., rev. & enl. 6 vols. Bloomington, Ind., 1955–1958.

ANNA-LEENA SIIKALA
Translated from Finnish by Susan Sinisalo

DESERTS.

In areas of continuous occupation, the presence of the sacred transcends and resolves the stresses produced by the environment. In the desert, mankind, deprived of the support of social solidarity and helplessly confronted by supernatural forces, is beset by anguish and fear.

The Desert and Personal Religious Experience. The first visions of the desert, therefore, are pessimistic. It is the region of the savage beasts and malevolent spirits, of demons of all kinds. In primitive societies it is the place of trials, of initiations. It is the place to which the rejected and the exiled are banished: Cain (*Gn.* 4:11–16), Hagar and Ishmael (*Gn.* 21:9–15), and the scapegoat that was burdened with the sins of Israel (*Lv.* 16:8–10). Particularly characteristic of the most ancient sedentary societies of the Middle East (Haldar, 1950), this conception was long lived. For the prophets of Israel (e.g., *Ez.* 20) and in the accounts of the Exodus, the time in the desert is that of infidelity (*Ex.* 17:7), of the golden calf (*Ex.* 32), and of punishment before the entrance into the Promised Land.

But another, parallel attitude also developed: the desert as apprenticeship and self-knowledge. As a terrain of struggle, the desert leads to the discovery of one's own being and, thereby, to the affirmation of the individual. At a more evolved stage of religious thought, it is the privileged place of divine revelation, of the betrothal of Israel with Yahveh (Gillet, 1949), of the offer of alliance, and of law that brings liberation. After the infidelities in the land of Canaan, it was by means of a return to the desert, the place of love and intimacy with the divine, that reconciliation with Yahveh was achieved (*Hos.* 2:14–16; *Jer.* 2:2–3). The desert thus becomes a refuge from corruption and depravity. Philo Judaeus (d. 45–50 CE) adds to this specifically Jewish conception a theme of Hellenistic mysticism—the romantic yearning of the world-weary city dweller for solitude, for retreat to the desert, where he can find peace. The desert, where the air is pure and light (*On the Contemplative Life* 22–23), assumes for Philo an absolute value. It was for this reason that God gave his laws to his people "in the depths of the desert" (*On the Decalogue* 2). This idea leaves its trace, then, through a whole series of Christian authors, for example, Origen: "John the Baptist, fleeing the tumult of the cities, went into the desert, where the air is purer, the sky more open, and God more intimate" (*Homilies on Luke* 11). It is the point of departure of the entire Christian monastic movement toward settlement in the desert after the fourth century—a movement that to a large extent regains the primitive pessimistic vision in its land of choice, Egypt. [*See* Retreat.]

The desert is where the devil is encountered and where Christ contended with him (Mauser, 1963). Monastic asceticism developed as a struggle in a fearsome place that was the land of demons *par excellence.* But this struggle was victorious. The presence of the pious anchorites integrated the desert into the realm of faith either by transforming it into a city, *desertum civitas* (Athanasius, *Life of Anthony* 14; cf. Chitty, 1966), or by fertilizing it and making it bloom according to the prophecy of *Isaiah* 35:1: *desertum floribus vernans* (Jerome, *Letters* 14). Finally, it was in the desert that the monks would find *hēsuchia*, the serenity of solitude. Christian tradition would thus, in the course of centuries, base the movement toward the solitary life that was to become as essential component of it on the image of the desert as a place of solitude *(ēremia)*. [*See* Eremitism.]

This approbation of solitude, brought to its apogee in Christianity, was to be more or less present in all higher religions in which the ascetic imperative is based on meditation, which is facilitated by life in the desert: Buddhism, particularly in the Tantric forms, Taoism, and Islam. However, in the case of Islam, the acceptance was relatively cautious. For the Muslims, the desert was above all a *thème d'illustration* (Arnaldez, 1975). It is necessary to "realize" the desert of spiritual solitude before the sole existent being, God. But it is dangerous to actually take abode in the desert. It is true that there man can avoid hypocritical ostentation *(ri'ā')* and the artificial social role that destroys authentic sincerity *(ikhlāṣ)*. But he thereby runs the risk of arrogance, of developing the cult of his inner self. This more reserved attitude of Islam in regard to the reality of the desert does not affect the value attributed to the desert as a synonym for solitude and retreat, ending in the solitariness *(infirād)* that culminates in mystical ascension. Both by its nature and its symbols, the desert brings man closer to God.

The Desert in the History of Religions. Does this proximity to the divine lead to the development of a particular religious structure? Ernest Renan thought so. In his *Histoire générale des langues sémitiques* (1885), inspired by the long Christian tradition, he wrote: "The desert is monotheistic. Sublime in its immense uniformity, it first revealed to man the idea of infinity, but not the perception of an unceasingly creative life that a more fertile nature inspired in other races" (p. 6). He later returned to this idea and defined it more precisely in his *Histoire du peuple d'Israël* (vol. 1, 1887, pp. 45, 59). He found the basis for the development of primitive monotheism, which he attributed to the Semitic peoples, to be "the customs of nomadic life," where there is little room for cultic practice and where "philosophical reflection, exercised intensely within a small circle of observation, leads to extremely simple ideas." More than a century after Renan, his idea of the desert as source and origin of Jewish monotheistic thought would again inspire the works of a master of biblical archaeology, William Albright (1964, pp. 154–156).

Actually, this idea is now largely outdated and has been vigorously disputed. All the studies on pre-Islamic Arab religion in particular (Wellhausen, 1897; Ryckmans, 1951; Henninger, 1959) have drawn a picture of it that has little to do with monotheism and that associates with the supreme deity, Allāh, a numerous and varied cortege of deities. The desert is the domain of polymorphous and diffuse ritual. It is, to repeat the expression of the Qur'ān, "associationistic," and the desert bedouin are "the most obdurate in their impiety and hypocrisy" (surah 9:97). [*See* Arabian Religions.]

However, the situation remains ambiguous. Beside and above the other gods was Allāh. He was incontestably a god of the nomads, a provider of rain (Brockelmann, 1922), and one can easily imagine the extreme importance that he assumed for a nomad whose survival depends entirely on the condition of the grazing land. Not only among the Arabs was the god of rain the unique god. It has been possible to reconstruct the special characteristics of the religion of pastoral peoples in general in conjunction with the peculiarities of their social structure and their way of life; such a reconstruction has been made for the first time in an environment very different from the desert, namely, that of the high grassy savannas of East Africa (Meinhof, 1926). The creation of powerful personages, of heroic saviors who are then frequently enrobed in historic myths connected with the origins of the tribe, is an expression of the instability of the pastoral tribe, which assembles or disperses in accordance with the importance of the individuals that direct and guide it within a context of aggressive relationships between groups. This orientation often accompanies that which consists of making the god of rain the unique god, dispenser of all benefices. The herdsman soon breaks free of polytheism. Ancestor worship is unknown to him, and the dead are forgotten. The herdsman is knowledgeable and intrepid, little inclined toward fear and superstition.

One is here indeed on the way to the monotheistic god, but under the impetus of a somewhat different logic. It is not that the desert is monotheistic but rather that the pastoral nomad has the tendency, at least, to become monotheistic. In contrast with the profusion of rituals in the Australian desert traversed by primitive hunters or gatherers is the evolution toward the monotheistic god of the warlike pastoral tribe, herders of large beasts of the African savannas or the bedouin of the deserts of the Old World. This trend toward monotheism is a late development in the cultural history of humanity. Contrary to Wilhelm Schmidt's opinion, this "great god of the herdsmen" is not the legacy of a primitive monotheism. Today we know that the pastoral nomads were, in the main, descendants of the first agrarian civilizations of the Old World, or were at least posterior to them. They constitute, in the world of the deserts and the steppes, a relatively recent cultural development, first in the form of the prebedouin herders of bovines, and then, after the domestication of the horse and the dromedary, in the form of the widespread, aggressive, warlike nomadism of the bedouin type, which in the Middle East does not go back further than the second millennium BCE.

But the appearance of monotheistic tendencies in the tribes of pastoral nomads can be rapid, as is shown by the analysis of neopastoral civilizations of the New World (Planhol, 1975). The Navajo of the Colorado plateaus of North America, whose pastoral mode of life did not emerge until the second half of the eighteenth century, still do not recognize a supreme deity (Reichard, 1950). But among the Goajira of Colombia and Venezuela, whose aggressive, cavalieristic, pastoral life goes back at least two or three centuries, there is a process of elaboration that seems much more advanced. Involved here is the predominance of a demiurgic creator (Maleiwa) and a rain giver (Juya), who are, however, not yet confused with each other, although the first signs of such a confusion are evident (Perrin, 1976). Among the herdsmen of East Africa, such as the Maasai, whose formation of a pastoral system goes back at least a thousand years, pastoral monotheism is well defined.

But, rather than being a true monotheism, it is in fact a monolatry in that it is willing to recognize the existence of other gods, who fulfill the same functions for the benefit of neighboring tribes or peoples; it is a protomonotheism in Baly's sense of the term (1970, pp. 258–259). The moral monotheism (Baly's "absolute" or "transcendent" monotheism) is a much more complex and revolutionary structure (Pettazzoni, 1950), the birth of which implies a break, not a simple evolution. Its occurrence exclusively in the Middle Eastern and Old World cultural environment reflects conditions of conflict. Here the presence of groups of pastoral nomads with still rather primitive monotheistic tendencies certainly played an essential role within the orbit of sedentary, sacerdotal civilizations that were polytheistic but much more highly developed (as Weindl, 1935, demonstrated). These conflicts could not be resolved except by a universalistic aspiration such as that of which the birth of Islam, following that of Judeo-Christian monotheism and Zoroastrian dualism, constitutes the final manifestation (Watt, 1953, 1956; Rodinson, 1961). Although Yahvism, as Nyström (1946) has shown, surpasses and in many particulars contradicts and transcends the bedouin ideal, this ideal is nonetheless necessary to it. [*See also* Monotheism.]

There is, therefore, no "religion of the desert." But, in the historical evolution of humanity in the Old World, the deserts have indeed been the privileged place for the development of the pastoral nomadic cultures that evolved precociously toward monotheism and that constituted an essential component in the genesis of the great monotheistic religions.

BIBLIOGRAPHY

Albright, William F. *History, Archaeology, and Christian Humanism.* New York, 1964.

Arnaldez, Roger. "Le thème du désert dans la mystique musulmane, thème d'inspiration ou thème d'illustration." In *Les mystiques du désert,* pp. 89–96. Gap, France, 1975.

Baly, Denis. "The Geography of Monotheism." In *Translating and Understanding the Old Testament,* edited by Harry Thomas Frank and William L. Reed, pp. 258–278. New York, 1970.

Bartelink, G. J. M. "Les oxymores *desertum civitas* et *desertum floribus vernans.*" *Studia Monastica* 15 (1973): 7–15.

Brockelmann, Carl. "Allah und die Götzen, der Ursprung des islamischen Monotheismus." *Archiv für Religionswissenschaft* 21 (1922): 99–121.

Chitty, Derwas J. *The Desert a City.* Oxford, 1966.

Gillet, Jacques. "Thème de la marche au Désert dans l'Ancien et le Nouveau Testament." *Recherches de science religieuse* 36 (April–June 1949): 161–181.

Guillaumont, Antoine. "La conception du désert chez les moines d'Égypte." In *Les mystiques du désert,* pp. 25–38. Gap, France, 1975.

Haldar, Alfred O. *The Notion of the Desert in Sumero-Accadian and West-Semitic Religions.* Uppsala, 1950.

Henninger, Joseph. "La religion bédouine pré-islamique." In *L'antica societa beduina,* edited by Francesco Gabrieli, pp. 115–140. Rome, 1959.

Mauser, Ulrich W. *Christ in the Wilderness: The Wilderness Theme in the Second Gospel and Its Basis in the Biblical Tradition.* London, 1963.

Meinhof, Carl. "Religionen der Hirtenvölker." In his *Die Religionen der Afrikaner in ihrem Zusammenhang mit dem Wirtschaftsleben,* pp. 71–84. Oslo and Cambridge, Mass., 1926.

Les mystiques du désert dans l'Islam, le judaïsme, et le christianisme. Gap, France, 1975. Papers delivered at a conference of the Association des Amis de Sénanque, 28 July–3 August 1974.

Nyström, Samuel. *Beduinentum und Jahwismus: Eine soziologisch-religionsgeschichtliche Untersuchung zum Alten Testament.* Lund, 1946.

Perrin, Michel. *Le chemin des Indiens morts: Mythes et symboles goajiro.* Paris, 1976.

Pettazzoni, Raffaele. "La formation du monothéisme." *Revue de l'Université de Bruxelles* 2 (1950): 209–219.

Planhol, Xavier de. "Le désert, cadre géographique de l'expérience religieuse." In *Les mystiques du désert,* pp. 5–16. Gap, France, 1975.

Reichard, Gladys A. *Navajo Religion.* 2 vols. New York, 1950.

Rodinson, Maxime. *Mahomet.* Paris, 1961. Translated by Anne Carter as *Mohammed* (New York, 1971).

Ryckmans, Gonzague. *Les religions arabes préislamiques.* 2d ed. Louvain, 1951.

Schmidt, Wilhelm. *Der Ursprung der Gottesidee*, vols. 7–12, *Die Religionen der Hirtenvölker.* Münster, 1940–1955.
Watt, W. Montgomery. *Muhammad at Mecca.* London, 1953.
Watt, W. Montgomery. *Muhammad at Medina.* London, 1956.
Weindl, Theodor. *Monotheismus und Dualismus in Indien, Iran und Palästina als Religion junger, kriegerisch nomadistischer Völker im Gravitations bereich von Völkern alter Kultur.* Vienna, 1935.
Wellhausen, Julius. *Reste arabischen Heidentums.* 2d ed. Berlin, 1897.

XAVIER DE PLANHOL
Translated from French by Roger Norton

DESIRE is one of those important subjects that are seldom discussed under their own names, so that one hardly knows where to go for answers to questions about the nature of desire and its significance for the religious or spiritual life. The term *desire* is only rarely found in the index or tables of contents of books on religion, even when the term figures prominently in the author's description or interpretation of religion. In addition, there is no widely shared consensus about the meaning of the term, so it is put to a variety of uses. There is no standard inventory of experiences, realities, or relations to which the term refers.

In order to clarify the subject of desire and indicate some representative ways in which desire has been religiously and spiritually interpreted, its scope and boundaries will be discussed through a cross-cultural overview. In this context, the varieties of desire and of the experiences, realities, and terms closely associated with desire—and of other terms antithetical to it, terms of contrast through which some of the particular meanings of desire become fixed—will be examined. The dimensions of desire will thus be reflected upon by charting the regions of human experience to which the term *desire* refers.

In a discussion of the term *desire,* three kinds of questions need be considered. First, what is it that is being named? How is desire thought of, imagined, represented to oneself, and located in relation to other phenomena? Second, how does desire enter into human experience? In what circumstances does it become an issue for the religious or spiritual life? Third, how do people deal with desire in their religious or spiritual lives? What are the negative and positive strategies with which religious and spiritual individuals, communities, and traditions have dealt with desire? Where desire has been taken as a threat to the religious life or to spiritual integrity, what strategies have been developed to discipline, train, overcome, transcend, detach from, or eradicate desire? Where desire has been viewed more positively, what strategies have been developed to channel, direct, release, render articulate, or otherwise enlist and incorporate the energies and vitality of desire into the spiritual or religious life? In other words, how have individuals and communities sought to share and pass on what they have learned about desire and how to deal with it?

What is named when speaking of desire? How is it thought about, imagined, represented to oneself, and located in relation to other phenomena—particularly to matters of religious or spiritual importance?

Desire is commonly understood in volitional terms, in which case it is identified with such things as willing, wanting, and wishing, choice and appetite, inspiration and motivation, and even with intention. Desire is also understood in more emotional or affectional rather than volitional terms, in which case it is associated or identified with such things as emotion, feeling, passion, love, eros, (and eroticism), attachment, craving, yearning, greed, and lust. These volitional and affectional vocabularies for interpreting desire are, of course, not incompatible—especially if, as is often the case, the affections are understood as central to or constitutive of the self as willing and loving. Where reason is set over against and valued above either will or emotion, desire will usually be viewed as spiritually problematic.

In discussions of religious ethics, desire will figure more positively in teleological than in deontological ethics. Teleological ethics is likely to involve some consideration of the *telos* (goal or object) of desire—its satisfaction or fulfillment in happiness, well-being, pleasure, ecstacy, and/or union or communion or some other form of participation in the divine or sacred reality. In deontological ethics, on the other hand, desire will be seen in tension or conflict with the governing moral principles of obligation and duty. Yet here, too, reality goes beyond our terms of analysis, as when through the agency of religious rituals duty is sometimes converted into desire. According to anthropologist Victor Turner, sacred symbols have two semantic poles, one abstract and normative, the other physiological and "orectic"—that is, relating to desire or appetite, willing and feeling. The drama of ritual action, he suggests, may cause an exchange of properties between these semantic poles, condensing their many referents into a single cognitive and affective field, the biological referents ennobled and the normative referents charged with emotional significance. By such an exchange of qualities between semantic poles, what is socially necessary is rendered desirable, and duty becomes desire.

There is at least one striking contrast in the cultural and religious treatment of desire between Oriental and Occidental cultures. In Western cultures desire is generally given a more positive place in the vision of human being and well-being. But that affirmation tends to remain at a fairly abstract level, formulated by theologians. At the more pedestrian level of spiritual guidance and of daily life among ordinary people, desire is hedged about with all sorts of constraints. In both East and West, desire is treated in a highly differentiated fashion, but the pattern of differentiation varies significantly. In Asia desires are viewed in the context of the stages of life and are judged and constrained or released and licensed differently, according to the stage of life in question. In the West, desires are viewed more consistently in relation to their objects rather than to the stages of life, and desires are evaluated and graded according to higher and lower, finer and coarser objects of desire.

Desire figures in human experience in many ways and becomes religiously valid or problematic under a variety of circumstances. To illustrate the spiritual importance and power of desire and the complexity of the issues raised by desire, consider two of the greatest religious texts: the *Tao-te ching,* the principal classic of Taoism, a collection of about the fourth century BCE attributed to Lao-tzu, and Augustine's *Confessions,* a Christian classic written near the end of the fourth century CE. The *Tao-te ching* is divided into two books. Book 1 begins and ends on the subject of desire:

> The way that can be spoken of
> Is not the constant way;
> The name that can be named
> Is not the constant name.
> The nameless was the beginning of heaven and earth;
> The named was the mother of the myriad creatures.
> Hence always rid yourself of desires in order to observe its [the way's] secrets;
> But always allow yourself to have desires in order to observe its [the way's] manifestations.
>
> . . .
>
> The way never acts yet nothing is left undone.
> Should lords and princes be able to hold fast to it,
> The myriad creatures will be transformed of their own accord.
> After they are transformed, should desire raise its head,
> I shall press it down with the weight of the nameless uncarved block.
> The nameless uncarved block
> Is but freedom from desire,
> And if I cease to desire and remain still,
> The empire will be at peace of its own accord.
> (*Tao-te ching,* trans. D. C. Lau, Baltimore, 1963, pp. 57, 96)

The ambiguity of desire is recognized, as well as the need to be acquainted with it. But real power and serenity lies in freedom from desire and in the active inactivity that is here identified with the "nameless uncarved block." Desire is presented as a problem rather than a resource for true spirituality.

In contrast, Augustine takes a very different view of desire. Addressing himself to God, he begins the *Confessions* by proclaiming the greatness of God and the desire to praise Him. "Thou movest us to delight in praising Thee; for Thou hast formed us for Thyself, and our hearts are restless till they find rest in Thee." But Augustine goes on to write of other desires that distract him from desire for God—desires for success and adulation, sexual desires, that great complex of desires that he came to identify as belonging to the City of Man in contrast with those of the City of God.

How do people deal with desire in their religious or spiritual lives? For some, desire itself, of whatever sort, is spiritually destructive. The primary—or at any rate initial—aim of their spiritual practice and discipline is to wean themselves from all desire, even the desire for enlightenment, self-transcendence, liberation, salvation, *nirvāṇa,* or mystical union with God. For others, desire is not itself intrinsically problematic but is seen as an essential and even a central mark of our humanity and of our spirituality. The issue for them is the right direction of desire, the right ordering of our various desires toward their appropriate objects, and a true perception of appropriate rank among possible objects of desire.

The experience of desire is often powerful and demanding. We may experience a single powerful desire as all-consuming and overriding all others. Or we may experience conflicting desires and find ourselves wrestling with their competing claims. Even if we have resolved the issues raised by a particular desire or set of desires, we may well find that resolution challenged and upset by the appearance in us of yet new desires, and at some point in this process our response may well be to seek a path away from all desire—a way of apathy, disinterestedness.

Desire invokes, if it does not actually generate, tension and contrast—between the present and the future, the actual and the possible, the real and the ideal—and tends to nourish or express restless dissatisfaction with the former in each of these pairs and to assign higher value to the latter. And yet the disquieting role of desire can be seen as undermining complacency, mobilizing creative energies, and generating new achievements.

Eastern Concepts. A representative range of religious movements and texts will be selectively analyzed to illuminate the issues raised by the religious significance of desire. This examination will be a topical study rather than a chronological survey of historical records. For this reason some of the early religious movements are passed over entirely, and modern movements, texts, and developments have generally not been considered.

In India various sentiments have been recorded to define desire. At both the intellectual-scholarly and the popular levels, the element of desire has been discussed and analyzed.

Hinduism. Among the ancient sacred texts that deal with desire, the *Bhagavadgītā* (the most revered of Hindu texts, composed between the fifth and second centuries BCE) has been generally considered the most important one. In this tradition *kāma* (Skt., "desire") is one of the four basic aims or drives (*puruṣārthas*) that need to be either satisfied, redirected, or transcended in life. The four basic aims are *dharma* (in its narrower meaning of social duty), *artha* (enjoyment of material things), *kāma* (pleasurable experiences generally, but often, as in the context of the *Gītā*, the satisfaction of sensual desire), and *mokṣa* (release, liberation). They are to be realized, transformed, or transcended in such a way as to realize one's personal obligation *(svadharma)* in accordance with one's social station and stage of life. Thus the exact nature of one's response to desire depends upon one's place in the class system *(varṇa)* and one's advancement along the path marked by the four basic stages (*āśramas*) of life—student, householder, forest dweller, and renunciant.

The appropriate measure for the enjoyment or the control of desire and its objects and related passions is also seen in Hinduism in terms of the three *guṇas* (energy fields, or strands), which differently combine to form all things in nature *(prakṛti)*. In ascending order of spiritual health, these three *guṇas* are *tamas, rajas,* and *sattva.* A life in which ignorance, insensibility, and lethargy predominate is *tamas* (dullness), one in which emotion and subjectivity predominate is *rajas* (turbulence), and one in which intelligence and objectivity predominate is *sattva* (dynamic equilibrium).

Fulfillment of one's own *dharma (svadharma),* again, involves some combination of three types of discipline *(yoga),* each of them requiring the sublimation and transcendence of desires, passions, and emotions together with an intensification of (1) action without attachment in *karmayoga,* the *yoga* of work and action, (2) loving devotion to a personal deity in *bhaktiyoga,* and (3) knowledge and wisdom in the most demanding path of *jñānayoga.* The aim is to rise above both *tamas* and *rajas* toward the equilibrium and detachment of *sattva,* knowing neither attraction nor repulsion, neither pleasure nor pain, having passed from both the absence and the turbulence of desire to the renunciation of all desires and aversions into a condition of equilibrium or serenity beyond desire.

In the *Gītā,* desire, anger, and greed are described as "the threefold gate of Hell that leads to the ruin of the soul" (16.21). Arjuna, the protagonist, learns that he must move among the objects of sense "with the senses under control and . . . free from desire and aversion" (2.62) if he would attain "serenity of mind" and that the same is required if he would attain intelligence, concentration, peace, or happiness. "He attains peace into whom all desires flow as waters into the sea, which, though even being filled, is ever motionless" (2.70). Yet it is only particular desires that are to be abandoned, for action without attachment involves "desiring [only] to maintain the order of the world" through one's action (2.71), and Kṛṣṇa, the god, declares: "I am the strength of the strong, which is free from desire and passion," but also "I am the desire in all beings, which is not incompatible with dharma" (7.11).

The *Gītā* is the most important sacred text in a tradition in which desires are ultimately to be overcome in detachment. In the Vedas and the Upaniṣads, desire is given a prominent place in the description of human nature, but then precisely for that reason it is ultimately desire that must be uprooted in order to achieve liberation from bondage to the wheel of existence. Nonetheless, in that same tradition, desires appropriate to the stages of life on the way to liberation are affirmed and even celebrated with imaginative exuberance. *Kāma* (desire, most especially erotic and sensual desire, delight, and pleasure) is often assigned a very positive role in the spiritual life and in the religious vision of reality. At one level of this tradition is the *Kāma Sūtra,* a manual for the enrichment of erotic and sexual pleasure appropriate to the householder stage of life.

At a deeper and broader level of this tradition there is the rich and complex Hindu mythology in which the place of desire in the life of the gods is portrayed. Wendy O'Flaherty, in *Asceticism and Eroticism in the Mythology of Śiva* (London, 1973), has shown, for example, how in the mythology of Śiva, desire and asceticism, chastity and sexuality, quiescence and energy, are variously related and yet in a fashion that affirms even where it does not clarify a profound inner connection between asceticism and eroticism and the power inherent in the transformation of one into the other. The tension is exhibited in part through the conflict between Śiva and Kāma—Śiva, the eternal *brahmacārin* (student), the god whose essence is chastity, and Kāma, the god of desire. But the conflict is also evident within Śiva himself, for he sometimes appears in the ambiguous figure of an erotic ascetic, both yogin and lover, (even a yogin because he is a lover) and is sometimes represented in images with an erect phallus, the ithyphallic yogin. While in Hindu mythology asceticism and eroticism revolve about each other in cycles of alternating ascendancy, chastity building into desire and the fulfillment of desire leading to chastity, the balance of these energies is found ideally through the control and transformation of desire.

Tantrism, a complex of teachings and practices that takes both Hindu and Buddhist forms, develops some of these last themes in a radical direction. Tantric teaching envisages the world as a field of energy generated through the sexual union of masculine and feminine aspects of sacred energy, *śakti.* The mobilization of *kāma,* desire, plays an important part in Tantric practice designed to participate in the restoration of the universe to its original unity with its sacred source. That practice involves the sublimation rather than the conquest or destruction of desire. It includes the ritually controlled performance of sexual union, but without consummation, redirecting the energy spiritually upward rather than physically outward. In emulation of the sacred activity of world-generation, erotic desire and play is thus ritually elevated into a vehicle of meditative discipline and devotion *(bhakti)*—and a means of sharing in the plenitude of sacred power by which the world is sustained. [*See* Tantrism.]

Buddhism. The *Dhammapada,* an early Theravāda Buddhist collection of teachings about the moral life and the path to spiritual perfection, includes much on the subject of desire. Desire is a principal manifestation of the selfish craving, grasping, or blind demandingness (Pali, *taṇhā*) that, according to the Four Noble Truths of Buddhism, is the cause of unhappiness, pain, and sorrow *(duḥkha),* and that can only be destroyed by following the Eightfold Path toward the freedom and joy of *nirvāṇa.* [*See* Four Noble Truths.] The 423 aphorisms of the *Dhammapada* offer guidance for those who would follow that Eightfold Path. Humanity is portrayed as besieged by dangerous and destructive desires on every side. "When the thirty-six streams of desire that run towards pleasures are strong, their powerful waves carry away that man without vision whose imaginings are lustful desires" (339). "The creeper of craving grows everywhere," and one must "cut off its roots by the power of wisdom" (340). Only if you "cut down the forest of desires" and its undergrowth, and not only a particular tree of desire, will you "be free on the path of freedom" (283). Beyond that, if the very "roots of craving are not wholly uprooted" (338) the tree and forest of desires will flourish again. Desire is specifically associated with pleasure, passion, lust, sensuousness, and craving (212–216), and all of these are portrayed as generating sorrow, fear, hatred, bondage, and disharmony. On the other hand, the surrender of all desires leads to the joy, wisdom, and freedom of *nirvāṇa.* "The loss of desires conquers all sorrows" (354). "When desires go, joy comes: the follower of Buddha finds this truth" (187). The true brahman, "leaving behind the desires of the world" (415), "has nothing and desires nothing" (421). "He who has no craving desires, either for this world or for another world, who free from desires is in infinite freedom—him I call a brahman" (410).

In Zen Buddhism, a Japanese religious movement of Chinese origin that emphasizes the direct experience of enlightenment, desire is treated in a somewhat different fashion. A Mahāyāna Buddhist text, popular in the Zen school, the *Laṅkāvatāra Sūtra,* extresses compactly the aim of *dhyāna* (Jpn., *zen,* "meditation, trance"): "The goal of tranquilization is to be reached not by suppressing all mind activity but by getting rid of discriminations and attachments." As discrimination dissolves and distinctions—between self and other, between this and that, even between *saṃsāra* and *nirvāṇa*—are experienced as illusory, desire and attachment fall away as well, and delusion is displaced by enlightenment (Jpn., *satori*).

Zen Buddhism in Japan is most powerfully represented by the Rinzai and Sōtō sects, whose principal discipline is *zazen,* sitting meditation. The Rinzai practice is to concentrate meditation on a *kōan,* a riddle designed to break the grip of the discriminating rational mind, opening the way for *kenshō,* the experience of seeing into one's essential Buddha nature and realizing one's unity with all that is. In Sōtō practice the adherent moves through the unity of body and mind in sitting, to concentrate on the sitting itself, *shikantaza,* "just sitting"—not sitting in order to accomplish some objective but just sitting, letting the activity of the "monkey mind" come and go as it will, letting come what may and letting it go, accepting what comes but not desiring and not holding on, simply letting the mind be emptied of all discriminations and attachments, and in that simplicity of presence actualizing one's undefiled Buddha nature and opening the way to *satori,* enlightenment. In all of this there is no place for desire—except of course, paradoxically, for the desire to break through one's own illusory view of reality and experience the true reality of Buddha nature. That desire, too, is dissolved rather than conquered in the sustained discipline of Zen—a way of just being in accord with the Way, letting go of any desire that the "thatness" (*tathatā,* "suchness") of things be otherwise. The practice of meditation then becomes a model for activity in everyday life, with everything to be done just for what it is, just doing, just being, and not aiming at some desired end.

Taoism. Taoism is an important Chinese movement whose influence extended beyond the sectarian confines of the Taoist church to the arts, literature, and Chinese philosophy in general. Its influence can also be discerned in the formation of the Chinese Ch'an school (known in Japan as Zen) of Mahāyāna Buddhism. As is evident from the passages from the *Tao-te ching* already cited, Taoism recommends freedom from desire as essential to the Way (the Tao) and its power or virtue *(te)*. But it proposes to achieve that freedom, not by disciplined control of desire or even of the mind, nor quite by rising above desire, but rather by going beneath it, by following the wisdom of the valley, of water, in which is to be found the power of the Way. "The highest virtue is like the valley" (41). "Highest good is like water. Because water excels in benefiting the myriad creatures without contending with them and settles where none would like to be, it comes close to the Way" (8). Nature rather than empire provides the models. "The river and the sea" are powerful, and their power endures, because "they excel in taking the lower position" (66). Even the empire will be at peace if the ruler will but say with the sage, "I am free from desire, and the people of themselves become simple like the uncarved block" (57). Abandon desires, simply let them drop. Seek not to control them or the world, but find spiritual health—and, not incidentally, survival—in a life of simplicity, humility, and harmony with nature, the flow of which is only disturbed by desires. In *wuwei*, the action that is no action, lies the power of the Way. "The Way never acts yet nothing is left undone" (37). Do not try to establish harmony, as though it depended upon you, but let go and let harmony reign, as it will do of its own accord. Such is the perspective of Taoism on desire.

Western Conceptions. Turning now from religions of Eastern origin to religions of Middle Eastern and Western origin, we must again be very selective, since there is no hope of even surveying the relevant literature on desire or of describing the many strategies for addressing desires. The principal sources that provide the themes upon which variations have been played are to be found in ancient Israel and in ancient Greece, in the Bible and in Hellenistic cultures. The variations are themselves substantial, although for the most part they share a generally more positive assessment of desire as an ingredient in human nature and as contributing to spiritual fulfillment than is characteristics of the religious movements already examined.

Stoicism. Among the traditions in the West, Stoicism provides a unique perspective. The *Enchiridion* of Epictetus, a Hellenistic philosopher who taught in Rome in the late first century and early second century CE, is the most influential formulation of basic Stoic teachings. Epictetus begins by distinguishing things within our power from things beyond our power. Desire is among the former things, and in a world where there is much that is beyond our power, we can achieve spiritual serenity and freedom only to the extent that we disregard things beyond our control and focus on those things we can control. The basis of such a life is the perception that there is a universal *logos* (reason) and *nomos* (law) at work in all that happens and that if one keeps one's mind in harmony with that universal nature, responding to events according to reason and not emotion, then one's external circumstances will be of little consequence. One can live in simplicity, with moderate desires and expectations, not demanding that events happen as one wishes, but wishing them to happen as they do happen. Stoicism is a religious philosophy of lowered expectations and reflective responsibility in the station to which one is assigned by God. [*See* Logos.]

Old Testament. The Old Testament contains many observations about various desires, ranging from the use of erotic love and desire and pleasure as metaphors for God's relationship to Israel to expressions of God's frustrated desire and longing for a covenant faithfulness on the part of the people of Israel and expressions of comparable desire on their part for intimacy with God, as well as injunctions to detach from or to discipline various desires in accordance with God's commandments and laws. What the Bible has to say directly about desire may fairly be summed up in three passages: the Lord's declaration through the prophet Hosea, "For I desire steadfast love and not sacrifice, the knowledge of God, rather than burnt offerings" (*Hos.* 6:60); the exclamation, "My soul thirsts for God, for the living God" (*Ps.* 42:2); and the saying of Jesus, "For where your treasure is, there will your heart be also" (*Mt.* 6:21).

Early Christianity. Augustine (354–430 CE) gives the most powerful classical formulation of the convergence of Hellenistic and biblical traditions. It is from Augustine that we have the most influential expression of Western religious thought about desire and also the most important expression of what has proved for many to be most problematic about the orientation toward desire. There is in Augustine something of the whole range of Christian attitudes toward desire.

Augustine affirms the basic biblical conviction that everything that is has its origin in God and is essentially good and that by the grace of God the world is being restored from a fallen condition to its proper destiny in God. The appropriate human role in that process is to conform the will to God in a covenant of faith and obedience to God's laws, or, to put the same matter differently, to conform the heart to God in love to God and neighbor. In either case the critical human response is a matter of will or of love more than it is of reason or of knowledge, and desire is central to Augustine's understanding of both will and love—or, more precisely, of willing and loving as different terms for the same activity. So, in the *City of God,* Augustine says: "The right will is . . . well-directed love, and the wrong will is ill-directed love. Love, then, yearning to have what is loved, is desire; and having and enjoying it, is joy; feeling what is opposed to it, is fear; and feeling what is opposed to it, when it has befallen it, is sadness" (14.7). In the *Confessions,* Augustine had said that "the mind can experience four kinds of emotion—desire, joy, fear, and sorrow" (10.14). It is these same four emotions that he here presents as forms of love, with the critical and spiritually constructive role assigned to the affirmative affections of desire and joy.

The way in which Augustine appropriates Hellenistic and especially Platonic ideas into his formulation of Christian thought is illustrated by his also presenting the four classical Greek virtues as forms of love:

> Temperance is love giving itself entirely to that which is loved; fortitude is love readily bearing all things for the sake of the loved object; justice is love serving only the loved object, and therefore ruling rightly; prudence is love distinguishing with sagacity between what hinders it and what helps it. The object of this love is not anything, but only God, the chief good, the highest wisdom, the perfect harmony. So we may express the definition thus: that temperance is love keeping itself entire and incorrupt for God; fortitude is love bearing everything readily for the sake of God; justice is love serving God only, and therefore ruling well all else, as subject to man; prudence is love making a right distinction between what helps it towards God and what might hinder it. (*Morals of the Catholic Church,* chap. 15)

The passage is worth quoting at length in this context, for the second formulation shows clearly that the first formulation is also about four forms of that true virtue that for Augustine is not just any love or all love but specifically the love of God. It is also clear that these forms of love are all manifestations of desire, that is, of that phase in the life of the virtuous lover marked more by yearning for what is loved than by the joy of actually or fully having and enjoying it.

Indeed, for Augustine all of human life is moved by desires. He takes it for granted that "we all certainly desire to live happily" and that without desire we do nothing. The problem is not to uproot or transcend desire, which is an essential mark of our humanity and of our belonging to God. It is right rather to direct desires toward their appropriate objects and to order all objects of desire in accordance with their true relation to God, the *summum bonum,* the source and center of all value and beauty, in whom alone our restless hearts will find the satisfaction of all their deepest desires. It is for Augustine the dynamic of desire that draws the heart toward God, though only an infusion of divine grace is sufficient to turn desire from all lesser goods toward God. Augustine makes a major distinction between desires directed upward, which he calls *caritas,* or love, and those directed downward, which he calls *cupiditas,* or lust. The one tends toward God, the other toward worldly goods. An even sharper contrast is invoked as he distinguishes between the City of God and the City of Man, the heavenly and earthly cities into which all of humanity is divided, the one formed by the desire or "love of God, even to the contempt of self," the other by the "love of self, to the contempt of God" (*City of God,* 14.28). An otherwise Platonic contrast between lower and higher desires and their corresponding hierarchy of objects culminating in God is thus transformed into a more historical contrast culminating in heaven and hell—a contrast and contest between those moved to seek God and respond to God's grace and those moved to seek self and the world.

Three kinds of objections have been raised against Augustine's views related to desire. Mention of them can serve as a shorthand way of indicating some alternatives to Augustine among Christians that cannot be surveyed here. One objection is that even if Augustine is right that all of human life is moved by desires, he is wrong in identifying the love of God with desire, and that he is led into that error by adopting the Platonic idea of love as *eros,* an aspiring love moved by the beauty of its object and the desire to possess and enjoy that object. Anders Nygren, a Lutheran theologian, has been most forceful in claiming that "*agape,* Christian love . . . has nothing to do with desire and longing" (*Agape and Eros,* London, 1932–1939), because it is a love which bestows value rather than being attracted by it. M. C. D'Arcy in *The Mind and Heart of Love* (New York, 1947) and Daniel D. Williams in *The Spirit and the Forms of Love* (New York, 1968) are among those who have challenged Nygren's diametrical opposition between *eros* and *agapē.* [*See* Love.]

A second objection has been that Augustine, and with him Thomas Aquinas and much of Christian orthodoxy, has been led by Greek ideas about the impassibility of God—the idea, for example, that God's perfection includes his being unchanging and self-sufficient—into either denying or distorting the biblical view that God, too, is moved by desire, since desire is the mark of some need, some lack, which would be remedied or satisfied by what is desired. The issue is whether a God who is understood to love and act with a purpose in the world can without contradiction be construed as unchanging, impassible, unmoved by desires such as those that are often attributed to God in the Bible and in the piety of both Jews and Christians.

A third objection has been against Augustine's repudiation of sexual desire and his influence on the long history of the Roman Catholic church's requirement of celibacy for the priesthood and its teaching that sexual pleasure and even the expression of love are at best only secondary ends of sexual intercourse, the primary end of which is said to be conception.

Medieval and Renaissance Christianity. The pivotal role of Augustine is illustrated by the fact that the other three most important theologians of Roman Catholic and Protestant Christianity, Thomas Aquinas (1225–1274), Martin Luther (1483–1546), and John Calvin (1509–1564), are all essentially Augustinian and in most respects do not depart from Augustine's views on desire. Thomas Aquinas, following Aristotle, assigns more importance to the intellect and reason in directing the will than does Augustine and gives a more Aristotelian turn to the ranking and the formation of intellectual and moral virtues in the governance of appetites, passions, and desires by reason. The classical Greek virtues are not presented by him as forms of love but are rather supplemented by the three theological virtues of faith, hope, and charity, through which God's grace makes possible and completes the natural desire of all intelligent creatures for the "vision of God."

On the subject of desire, Luther departs from Augustine principally in connection with his insistence upon the universal priesthood of all believers, the dignity of all callings and not only of the priesthood, and hence the abandonment of celibacy as essential to the priesthood. He also exhibits a certain lustiness of character and a more affirmative attitude toward the expression of sexual desire within the context of married love.

John Calvin departs from Augustine primarily by developing a distinctively political strategy in both church and state for the encouragement and the enforcement of sober, righteous, and godly lives turned from ungodliness and worldly lust. He was at war against what he called "irregular desires" or "inordinate desires of the flesh" (*The Institutes of the Christian Religion* 3.3.2). Such desires are considered sinful "not as they are natural, but because they are inordinate" and are contrasted with "those desires which God implanted so deeply" in human nature "that they cannot be eradicated from it without destroying humanity itself." Desires are to be drawn away from the world and toward God. "Whatever is abstracted from the corrupt love of this life should be added to the desire for a better" one in full communion with God (3.2.4). But Calvin rejected too great an austerity as well as a stoic divestment of all affections, arguing that God's gifts are given for our pleasure and delight as well as for our necessity—though we are to use them as though we used them not, according to the requirements of our calling.

European Enlightenment. Barukh Spinoza (1632–1677 CE), a freethinking but "God-intoxicated" philosopher (as some have called him), developed a religious philosophy akin to Stoicism in its determination to see things from a universal and rational perspective. But he assigns to desire a much more crucial and positive role in human experience than does Epictetus. In his *Ethics* he examines the conditions under which desire can spring from reason, from the knowledge and love of God. In his view, there are but three primary emotions—joy, sorrow, and desire. Of these three, to which all other emotions are related, it is the two affirmative affections of desire and joy that are most important, and of these "desire is the very nature or essence of a person" (3.57). It is the intellectual love of God that gives the mind power over its emotions, and the *Ethics* is an elaborate analysis of how this process culminates in and flows from a condition of blessedness.

Monasticism. Monasticism has been an important strategy for spiritual discipline and the control of desires in most religious traditions. For Buddhism it is the *saṃgha*, the community of monks. For Christians there have been a variety of monastic orders, many of them following variations on the rule drawn up by Benedict of Nursia (480–543), with many desires renounced by the three vows of chastity, poverty, and obedience. The Benedictine rule requires manual labor in part to control desires by diverting energy and employs the image of the "ladder of humility" for the disciplinary steps by which "desires of the flesh" are cut away and displaced by the love of God and a "second nature" that delights in virtue. The *Little Flowers* of Francis of Assisi (thirteenth century), a collection of legends and traditions about the saint, reflects a different pattern of monastic discipline, more severe in its insistence upon poverty and freedom from all compromise with the world, but it also offers a more joyful asceticism, sending monks out of the cloister to delight in the created world and its beauty and to celebrate the realized desire for ecstatic union with Christ.

Mysticism. For the mystics, desire is generally equated with search for the transcendent. The testimony of Francis of Assisi has much in common with religious mysticism around the world, in which the experience as well as the language of desire and joy, of ecstasy and delight, play an important role. For the mystic, the spiritual desires cultivated and realized are of far greater significance than all the abandoned worldly desires. [*See* Mystical Union.] In his *Sayings of Light and Love*, John of the Cross (1542–1591) advises:

"If you desire that devotion be born in your spirit and that the love of God and the desire for divine things increase, cleanse your soul of every desire and attachment and ambition in suchwise that you have no concern about anything." In *The Spiritual Canticle* he notes that "the soul lives where she loves more than in the body she animates," and that "God does not place His grace and love in the soul except according to its desire and love." And in *The Living Flame of Love* he declares to God:

> What you desire me to ask for, I ask for; and what you do not desire, I do not desire, nor can I, nor does it even enter my mind to desire it. . . . Tear then the thin veil of this life and do not let old age cut it naturally, that from now on I may love you with the plenitude and fullness my soul desires forever and ever.

Similiarly, the Ṣūfīs considered spiritual union with the transcendent beloved as the pivotal aspect of all their desires and endeavors. All else in existence was generally regarded as superfluous. The urgent quest for the almightly is thus reflected in the prayers of Rābi'ah al-'Adawīyah (d. 801):

> O God, my whole occupation and all my desire in this world, of all worldly things, is to remember Thee, and in the world to come, is to meet Thee. This is on my side, as I have stated; now do Thou whatsoever Thou wilt.
>
> O God, if I worship Thee for fear of Hell, burn me in Hell, and if I worship Thee in hope of Paradise, exclude me from Paradise; but if I worship Thee for thy own sake, grudge me not Thy everlasting beauty. (quoted in Arberry, 1964, p. 51)

As the prayer indicates, for Rābi'ah all aspects in life were subservient to her intense desire for spiritual elevation and union with God.

BIBLIOGRAPHY

Arberry, A. J. *Muslim Saints and Mystics.* London, 1964.

Nygren, Anders. *Agape and Eros.* 2 vols. London, 1932–1939.

O'Flaherty, Wendy Doniger. *Ascetism and Eroticism in the Mythology of Śiva.* London, 1973.

Turner, Victor. *The Forest of Symbols.* Ithaca, N.Y., 1967.

ROLAND A. DELATTRE

DESTINY. *See* Fate.

DETERMINISM. *See* Free Will and Determinism.

DEUS OTIOSUS.

DEUS OTIOSUS. The Latin term *deus otiosus* (pl., *dei otiosi*), meaning literally "god at leisure" or "god without work," denotes a god who has withdrawn or retired from active life. The paucity of detailed descriptions of these deities, when coupled with their widespread appearance in cultures around the globe, presents a puzzle for the study of religions. Athough the outline of these divine personalities is usually sketchy, they maintain a firm hold on the religious imagination. The study of gods who have retired from their arena of activity has provoked deep reflection on the meaning and function of symbols, especially of divine forms, in religious life.

Celestial Associations. Many African creation myths involving *dei otiosi* recount how the divine sky lay flat on the earth at the beginning of time. Nuba and Dogon myths, for example, describe how the chafing of the sky against the earth stunted human growth and disrupted normal routines of work (R. C. Stevenson, "The Doctrine of God in the Nuba Mountains," in *African Ideas of God,* ed. E. W. Smith, London, 1950, p. 216; Marcel Griaule, *Masques Dogons,* Paris, 1938, p. 48). "In particular, women could not pound their grain without knocking against the sky, and so close relations finally ended when the sky's anger at the annoying blows of the women's pestles caused it to withdraw from the earth" (Dominique Zahan, *The Religion, Spirituality, and Thought of Traditional Africa,* Chicago, 1979, p. 16). In other African societies, such as the Nyarwanda and Rundi of central Africa, the creator god lived with the first people at the beginning of time (or the first people lived in the sky with the god). For one reason or another, the god moved away from the company of his creatures—upstream, downstream, to a mountaintop, or to the sky (R. Bourgeois, *Banyarwanda et Barundi,* Brussels, 1957, vol. 3, pp. 19–25).

Most forms of the *deus otiosus* cluster around the symbolism of the sky. The manifestation of the sacred in the sky and the belief in supreme beings of the sky is most often overwhelmed and replaced by other sacred forms. We do not mean to say that devotion to the beings of the sky was the first and only religious practice of archaic humankind. In the first place, we do not have the data we need to reconstitute the first forms of religious practice and belief in human history. More important, the study of histories that we know more fully indicate the unlikelihood that a belief in a supreme being of the sky would exclude all other religious forms. The point to begin with is that the experience of the sky as a religious reality, in fact as the divine sphere, places emphasis on the religious value of withdrawal and transcendence. The sky itself, as a symbol of sacred being, embraces or constitutes these elemental structures of a *deus otiosus,* withdrawal and transcendence. For this reason, countless other hierophanies can coexist with this sacred manifestation of the remote sky. [*See* Sky.]

For example, Puluga is an omniscient sky-dwelling divinity revered in the Andaman Islands. After a stormy relationship with the first people, Puluga reminded them of his commands and withdrew. Men have never seen him since that time of estrangement at the beginning (Paul Schebesta, *Les Pygmées,* Paris, 1940, pp. 161–163). In a similar way, Temáukel, the eternal and omniscient creator of the Selk'nam of Tierra del Fuego, is called *so'onh-haskan* ("dweller in the sky") and *so'onh kas pémer* ("he who is in the sky"). Temáukel created mythical ancestors who took over the process of creating the world. Once creation was accomplished, he withdrew beyond the stars. For his part he remains indifferent to human affairs. Correspondingly, human beings possess no images of Temáukel or regular cult dedicated to him, and they direct their prayers to him only in cases of dire illness or bad weather (Martin Gusinde, "Das höchste Wesen bei den Selk'nam auf Feuerland," in *Wilhelm Schmidt Festschrift,* Vienna, 1928, pp. 269–274). The Muring people of the east coast of Australia recount in their myths the story of Daramulun, their "father" *(papang)* and "lord" *(biamban).* Daramulun, the true name of this divine being of the sky, is known only to initiates. For a brief time he lived on earth and instituted the rites of initiation. Since his return to the heavens his presence is made known mostly in the sounds of thunder, the eerie groans from the nocturnal jungle, and the through the sound of sacred bullroarer used in initiation rites (A. W. Howitt, *The Native Tribes of South-East Australia,* New York, 1904, pp. 362ff., 466ff.). Similarly, Bunjil, the heavenly supreme being of the Kulin tribes of Australia, created earth, trees, animals, and human beings and then left the world to live in the heaven beyond the "dark heaven" visited by holy men (ibid., p. 490).

Absence of Myth and Cult. The most striking feature of the *deus otiosus* is the absence of an active cult dedicated to the god. Even where there is sporadic and spontaneous devotion, it is remarkable how often there is no regular calendar of seasonal rituals celebrated in honor of the god. Mythic accounts of the *deus otiosus* are scanty. Even those myths that exist are short compared to the dramatic epics of heroes, storm gods, or the divine forms associated with the agricultural cycle. A large number of celestial supreme beings receive no regular worship. Among them we may mention Muladjadi of the Batak of central Sumatra, Petara remembered by the Sea Dyaks of Kalimantan (Borneo), Ndengei of Fijian mythology, and Yelefaz from the island of Yap.

The absence of scheduled cult and the brevity of mythic reference to the *deus otiosus* led scholars to a misconception. At the end of the nineteenth century and beginning of the twentieth (and even today, in some circles), scholars of religion and culture overlooked the importance of this religious form. The *deus otiosus* was seen as an anomalous piece of speculation, as a recent addition to the divine pantheon in response to contact with Christian missionaries, or as an archaic idea that had lost the clarity of its expression and meaning. It did not fit into the schemata that evaluated mythic thinking as infantile, unsubtle, or undeveloped. [*See* Supreme Beings.] Rather than regard the absence of the *deus otiosus* from myth and cult as an inherent feature of its structure, scholars frequently ignored the issue or slighted its value in favor of theories that portrayed tribal peoples as theologically naive or intellectually underdeveloped.

Withdrawal of God. Myths that mention the *deus otiosus* usually face head-on the question of the god's absence from the preoccupations of culture. The narratives themselves describe the withdrawal or substitution of the supreme being. For example, Ọlọrun, the Yoruba divinity whose name means "lord or owner of the sky," turned over the project of creating the world to Ọbatala, one of his sons. When Ọbatala became drunk and mismanaged the creation of humans from clay, Oduduwa, his younger brother, usurped the task of creation. Ọlọrun then permanently absented himself from human history. He does not intervene directly in human affairs, for he delegated the care of human creation to his sons and to the *oriṣa,* a collection of deities each with its own precinct, priesthood, temple, and devotees. Although absent from the unfolding course of human affairs, Ọlọrun remains an essential presence, for he inspires the breath of life into all individuals and allots them their destiny. Furthermore, the Yoruba call upon Ọlọrun in times of desperate calamity (E. Bọlaji Idowu, *Olódùmarè: God in Yoruba Belief,* London, 1962; Peter Morton-Williams, "An Outline of the Cosmology and Cult Organization of the Oyo," *Africa* 34, 1964; Benjamin C. Ray, *African Religions: Symbol, Ritual, and Community,* Englewood Cliffs, N.J., 1976, pp. 49–76, esp. pp. 52ff.).

Myths describe the origins of the status of the *deus otiosus* in cultural life as well as in the religious imagination. On the one hand, the god withdraws on his own initiative after finishing his work of creation or of overseeing its accomplishment. On the other hand, another frequent scenario is the usurpation of the supreme being's sovereignty by a younger and more active god. In the Hittite translations of Hurrian texts made around 1300 BCE, there is an initial episode that describes the struggle for the "kingship of heaven." At first, the god Alalu was king, then the divinity named Anu overpowered him. At the beginning of Anu's reign, Kumarbi, the main protagonist of Hittite myth and the father of the gods, was Anu's servant. After nine years, Kumarbi chased Anu into the sky, tossed him to the ground, and bit off his loins (Hans G. Güterbock, "The Hittite Version of the Hurrian Kumarbi Myths: Oriental Forerunners of Hesiod," *American Journal of Archaeology* 52, 1948, pp. 123–124; and C. Scott Littleton, "The 'Kingship in Heaven' Theme," in *Myth and Law among the Indo-Europeans*, edited by Jaan Puhvel, Berkeley, 1970, pp. 93–100). A parallel in Greek mythology describes the castration of the sky god Ouranos and the forced separation of Heaven (Ouranos) from Earth (Gaia). In Mesopotamian mythology as well, the young gods led by Marduk guarantee that the great gods such as An, Enlil, and Ea lose their supremacy in the cult.

The existence in mythology of this most streamlined and ethereal of divine forms, the *deus otiosus*, teaches a lesson about the dynamics of the religious imagination. The *dei otiosi*, especially those supreme beings of the sky who retire after the creative episode, withdraw from the world in several senses. They withdraw on high and leave their creation behind. They also withdraw to the outer margins of the religious imagination and define the outermost reach of creativity, for they assume the most wispy of images. No doubt, contact with outsiders, especially Christians or Muslims, has often played a role in shaping the contemporary forms of *dei otiosi*. However, such contact does not preclude the existence of an indigenous structure of the *deus otiosus*. In fact, the existence of a myth of an otiose god enabled many cultures to recognize aspects of the foreign supreme being and reconcile them with their own. Far from remaining insignificant, the features of the *deus otiosus* exhibit definite signs, especially of vagueness and sublimity, that demarcate the outer reach of imaginable being.

Symbolic Characteristics. The *deus otiosus* is a limit-image, for before and beyond the *deus otiosus* nothing exists. The Winnebago Indians of Wisconsin admitted, "What there was before our Father Earthmaker came to consciousness, we do not know."

Sublimity. The descriptions of supreme beings who withdraw on high introduce students of religion to the most sublime end of the spectrum of divine forms, for the *deus otiosus* is often the most sublimated of sublime forms. By narrating descriptions of the most remote, transcendent, invisible, or intangible reality, cultures offer themselves and scholars expressions of an experience of being that, by definition, most transcends the senses. The myths of the *deus otiosus* are statements about the nature of creativity itself and about the subtle powers and rarefied capacities of the religious imagination. The Witóto of Colombia offer the following example: in the beginning nothing existed except "mere appearance," which was "something mysterious." Moma, the supreme being, touched this phantasm. Moma calls himself Nainuema, "he who is or possesses what is not present." He is an illusive appearance linked to sacred sounds associated with ritual words and chants. By means of dream, Nainuema held the phantasm against his breast and fell into deep thought, his breath helping him hold onto the illusion with the thread of his dream. Moma plumbed the dream-contained, breath-held phantasm to its bottom and found that it was empty. He fastened the illusion to his dream-thread with a gluey substance and then stamped on the bottom of the illusion until he came to rest on the earth. He made the forests rise by spitting and covered the earth with heaven (Konrad T. Preuss, *Religion und Mythologie der Uitoto*, vol. 1, Göttingen, 1921, pp. 27, 166–168). Such sublime features of the *deus otiosus* have great value for the student of religious forms, for they describe the outer boundaries of imaginable being.

Passivity. The passive character of the *dei otiosi* leaves the gods' personalities vague and ill-defined. The deities often avoid dramatic action and remain inert or aloof. In fact, the creativity of the *dei otiosi* is often described in negative terms. Their omnipresence comes across as a lack of presence in any single or definable place over another. Their omnipotence implies an uninvolvement with any single or specific cosmic operation, such as the growth of crops or the transitions of the human life cycle. Their omniscience implies a certain indifference to, or lack of interest in, any one fact over another. Their immortality implies a certain stasis, immobility, and inability to change. These negative valences are a function of the gods' association with creation at the very beginning. Once creation is accomplished and being has appeared for the first time, the function of a creator is completely exhausted and the god becomes otiose. The divinities and their unique creative powers retire from the active world they have initiated. They remain the ground of all created being and of all creative possibilities and, for that very reason, retire into infinity, beyond the bounded spaces of creation. Once the universe comes into existence, the supreme being's active mode is no longer in need of full manifestation, nor is it desired.

Primordiality. The withdrawal of the *deus otiosus* from the creative scene marks the end of the primordium. Therefore, it may be said that the presence of the *deus otiosus* defines primordiality, a potent condition full of possibilities. *Dei otiosi* have always existed; they bespeak the meaning of eternity and antiquity. The sky, or whatever paradisal place the gods dwelled in, has always been inhabited by supernatural beings. For example, for the Aranda of Australia, the "great father" *(knaritja)* is an eternal youth *(altjira nditja)* who lives in an eternally green countryside covered with flowers and fruits. The Milky Way transects this immortal dwelling place. The great father and his heavenly companions, all equally young, take no interest in the affairs of earth; the great father leaves the management of such affairs to the ancestors. The Aranda great father represents the primordium, the state of being that has no immediate significance, although it has unprecedented ontological bearing. Beatific existence, immortality, anteriority, or static antiquity are unmatched conditions of being. That primordial state was interrupted, and direct contact with it became difficult or impossible. Only a few privileged people, such as mythic heroes or specialists in ecstasy, can revisit a situation that has become irretrievably lost. Primordiality reveals something about the very nature of time and space. It is a quality that cannot be recaptured in terms of the present conditions of the cosmos. The withdrawal of the *deus otiosus* is part of the definition of a primordial world that stands over and against history. Primordiality is the milieu in which reality and eternity can truly manifest themselves. Knowledge of the existence of a *deus otiosus* affirms that even unique modes of being can be apprehended as a species of time.

Transcendence. The fate of the *deus otiosus* in mythic history guarantees that the first state of being becomes something less immediate and pressing. The god withdraws and becomes distant, and, for its part, human history becomes enveloped by the wrappings of symbolic life. For example, in the very beginning of the Makiritare creation cycle, all that existed was sky and eternal light. Shi, the invisible sun, had already created Wanadi, the heavenly creator, by blowing on quartz crystal. During that first period, there was no separation between the sky and the earth; the sky had no door in it as it does now, and Wanadi was bright and shining everywhere. He wished to make houses and place good people in them, and for this reason sent aspects of himself to earth. Attawanadi ("house-Wanadi"), the third aspect of Wanadi, specialized in constructing enclosures. He created the enclosed stratum called earth. Attawanadi made a new, visible sky for the earth so that the real sky could no longer be seen. The *atta*, the house or village of the Makiritare, is an exact replica of the first universe created by Attawanadi. Attawanadi's creation of the house-world achieved symbolic closure. He withdrew from his creation.

Myths of creation involving a *deus otiosus* frequently recount the lifting up of the sky and the installation of that heavenly body, the primordial image of transcendence. The sky becomes the paradigm of distance and difference. [*See* Sky.] As the object of first real separation, the *deus otiosus* and its celestial manifestations betoken the possibility of distance between one kind of being and another; their continued transcendence and absence guarantee the symbolic life they signify. Many myths portray the danger that the sky will fall; that is, they portray the fear of the collapse of symbolic possibilities. If the symbolism of withdrawal of the *deus otiosus*, the reality transcendent above all others, will not stand up to scrutiny and cannot stay removed, then no symbolic distance of any kind can be guaranteed, and representational life fails. In fact, it is only at the end of time that many *dei otiosi* make their return. Attawanadi, for example, will return to the Makiritare when the earth ceases to exist (Marc de Civrieux, *Watunna: An Orinoco Creation Cycle*, ed. and trans. David M. Guss (San Francisco, 1980, pp. 28ff.). The relationship between gods and humans comes into being when the separation of creator from created is acknowledged. "The period of man's 'religiousness' is not at all the 'paradisiac' era when God lived in the 'village' of men but the period following when God had lost his earthly and human qualities in order to live separately from mankind" (Zahan, *The Religion, Spirituality, and Thought of Traditional Africa*, p. 16). The withdrawal of the *deus otiosus* becomes the foundation-stone of religious life: "the African feels deeply that the more inaccessible God seems to be, the greater is his need of him" (ibid., p. 16).

Symbolic life, made possible by the withdrawal of primordial being, offers humankind the freedom of the symbolic condition, a dynamic existence that could never have flourished if the creator had continued to crush or overwhelm his creation with his ponderous presence and immediacy. Mediation, intermediaries, and symbolic distance become indispensable and possible when the god retires from the scene.

Implications for the Study of Religious Symbols. The knowledge of the mythic history of the *dei otiosi*, the story of their creative acts and the transformations they undergo while disappearing into the starry vault or into the forest or downstream, are an indispensable part of culture. Equipped with this knowledge, members of a culture live in awareness of the sacred nature of their environment and of their sociocultural order because they know the mythic history of each one of its forms. The withdrawal of the primordial being, the *deus otiosus*, leaves indelible marks on the physical universe and its organic contents.

For example, the Campas of Peru describe the migration of the sun (Pava) into the sky. He enlisted the aid of the hummingbird Neoronke, who carried one end of the sky-rope to the highest level of the universe. As Pava ascended, transformations occurred that gave nature its present condition. Many primordial beings, which at that time existed in protohuman form, became animals such as the tapir or the mouse. Certain trees and flowers used to demarcate the calendrical year were daughters of Pava. The trees are the clothes that these young women shed when they migrated to heaven with him. When the sky-rope dropped to the earth after the ascent, a number of beings fell from heaven to earth, including the wasp, the porcupine, and the sloth (Gerald Weiss, *Campa Cosmology: The World of a Forest Tribe in South America*, New York, 1975, pp. 219–588; esp. pp. 389–390).

There is no guarantee that the divine form of the *deus otiosus* will remain balanced on the periphery of the religious imagination. In some cases it seems that the god lapses into total oblivion. In other instances, prophets reform and revitalize the concept of the supreme being and reinstate his cult. Where mythic knowledge of the retired god disappears entirely, the deity becomes completely otiose and no longer has religious value. Such was probably the fate of Dyaus, the Indo-European sky god, who eventually was no longer worshiped. No hymns or myths present this oldest Vedic religious form. The name simply designates the "sky" or "day." However, there lingers the memory that the "Sky knows all" (*Atharvaveda* 1.32.4) and that there is the "sky father" (*Atharvaveda* 6.4.3), who is one element of the primordial pair, Dyāvāpṛthivī, "sky and earth" (*Ṛgveda* 1.160). This draws Dyaus into the circle of similarly named Indo-European sky gods for whom we possess mythologies: Greek Zeus Pater, Roman Jupiter, Illyrian Daipatures, Scythian Zeus-Papaios, and Thraco-Phrygian Zeus-Pappos.

The god Mwari of the Shona people of Zimbabwe appears to be an instance of the recovery of the *deus otiosus*. Since the fifteenth century, circumstances have contributed to the revitalization of this remote sky god's cult. The Rozvi royal dynasty patronized the cult in the center of the city of Zimbabwe and the priests of Mwari have become important political figures (Daneel, 1970, pp. 30–35).

The form of the *deus otiosus*, even if it is recalled only in wispy outline, is an essential stimulus to the life of the religious imagination. To one degree or another such a form is implied in every complete corpus of myths. Since every reality appearing in the mythic beginnings of the world is a total and absolute statement of its kind of being, the change and dynamism that undergird human history provoke a total eclipse or disintegration of primordial form. The death, transformation, or withdrawal of supernatural beings into the heights or into the extremes of the cosmos exemplifies the fate of primordial existence as a whole.

BIBLIOGRAPHY

Daneel, M. L. *The God of the Matopo Hills: An Essay on the Mwari Cult in Rhodesia.* The Hague, 1970.

Danquah, J. B. *The Akan Doctrine of God.* 2d ed. London, 1969.

Eliade, Mircea. "The Sky and Sky Gods." In his *Patterns in Comparative Religion*, pp. 38–123. New York, 1958.

Eliade, Mircea. "South American High Gods." *History of Religions* 8 (1968): 338–354 and 10 (1970–1971): 234–266.

Ikenga-Metuh, Emefie. "The Paradox of Transcendence and Immanence of God in African Religions: A Socio-historical Explanation." *Religion* 15 (1985): 373–385.

Lienhardt, Godfrey. *Divinity and Experience.* Oxford, 1961.

Long, Charles H. "The West African High God: History and Religious Experience." *History of Religions* 3 (1964): 328–342.

Pettazzoni, Raffaele. "The Formation of Monotheism." In his *Essyas on the History of Religions*, translated by H. J. Rose. Leiden, 1954.

Pettazzoni, Raffaele. "The Supreme Being: Phenomenological Structure and Historical Development." In *The History of Religions: Essays in Methodology*, edited by Joseph M. Kitagawa and Mircea Eliade, pp. 59–66. Chicago, 1959.

Verger, Pierre. "The Yoruba High God." *Odu* 2 (January 1966): 19–40.

MIRCEA ELIADE and LAWRENCE E. SULLIVAN

DEVĀNAṂPIYATISSA (247–207 BCE), king of Sri Lanka. According to the *Mahāvaṃsa*, Devānaṃpiyatissa was an ally of Aśoka and through Aśoka's influence introduced Buddhism to Sri Lanka. At the outset of his reign, Devānaṃpiyatissa sent envoys to India with gifts for Aśoka. In return, Aśoka sent gifts and implicit support for Devānaṃpiyatissa's kingship. The Sinhala chronicles also relate that the Buddhist elder, Mahinda, who was either the son or the brother of Aśoka, visited Devānaṃpiyatissa to establish the Buddhist tradition in Sri Lanka.

Mahinda is said to have arrived in the island on the full-moon day of Poson (May–June), a day still celebrated in Sri Lanka as the date of the founding of Buddhism there. Devānaṃpiyatissa greeted Mahinda on Missaka Hill, now called Mihintale, and proceeded from there to the site of Anurādhapura. Near the royal pavilion in Mahāmegha Park at Anurādhapura, Mahinda and Devānaṃpiyatissa laid out and subsequently built the monasteries and shrines that came to be the international center for the Theravāda Buddhist tradition. The heart of their complex was the Mahāvihāra, the Great Monastery, which was established 236 years after the Buddha. The king also built the first *stūpa* or *cetiya* in Sri Lanka, the Thūpārāma, to enshrine the collarbone relic of the Buddha.

At the request of the women in Sri Lanka, Devānaṃpiyatissa arranged for Mahinda's sister Saṃghamittā to come from India to ordain women into the Buddhist order of nuns. Saṃghamittā brought with her a branch from the Bodhi Tree under which the Buddha attained enlightenment. The king planted this branch at Anurādhapura, where it remains today as a sacred shrine for Buddhists.

[*See also the biography of Aśoka.*]

BIBLIOGRAPHY

The primary source for this subject is *The Mahāvaṃsa, or, The Great Chronicle of Ceylon*, translated and edited by Wilhelm Geiger (1912; reprint, Colombo, 1950). A reliable secondary source is C. W. Nicholas and Senarat Paranavitana's *A Concise History of Ceylon* (Colombo, 1961).

George D. Bond

DEVĪ. *See* Goddess Worship, *article on* The Hindu Goddess.

DEVILS. The definition and derivation of the term *devil* need to be carefully delineated. This need for care in defining *devil* arises from the fact that the very class of creatures being designated as malign may have been originally benign or may be capable of acting in either a benign or malign way. [*See* Demons.] One species of devils in classical Hinduism consists of the *asuras*, also called *pūrvadevas*, or "those who were formerly gods or benign beings." In Zoroastrianism, the same *asuras*, by contrast, are called *ahuras*, or "lords." In Christianity, Satan, the Prince of Darkness, is regarded as a fallen angel. According to Origen (whose view is considered heresy by orthodox Christians), he will, in time, be reinstated in his "pristine splendor and original rank." There are, however, also classes of intermediate beings whose association with evil is equivocal. In Islam, genies or, more properly, *jinn* provide a useful illustration: "They were vaguely feared, but were not always malevolent" (Watt, 1970, p. 153). [*See* Ahuras *and* ʿĀshūrā.]

Biblical Terminology. The problem is also, in part, etymological. The English word *devil* derives from the Greek *diabolos*, which has the original sense of "accuser" or "traducer" (from *diaballein*, "to slander, traduce," lit., "to throw across"). The Hebrew Bible (Old Testament) uses the word *saṭan* in the sense of "adversary," and it was translated in the third century BCE by Egyptian Jews as *diabolos*. When the Greek Septuagint (Old Testament) was translated into Latin, *diabolos* was rendered as *diabolus* (in the early translations) or as *satan*, in the standard Vulgate text (Robbins, 1959, p. 130). In the New Testament, on the other hand, the name *Satanas* is used to mean not just any adversary, as is often the case in the Old Testament, but *the* adversary of God. Throughout the New Testament, *Satanas* refers to the Devil, and *Revelation* 12:9 describes "the great dragon . . . that ancient serpent, who is called the Devil and Satan." As Robbins points out (p. 130), English translations generally render both the *saṭan* of the Hebrew scriptures and *Satanas* of the New Testament as "Satan." [*See* Satan.]

Thus two different conceptions were fused, and this idea of an evil demigod became the common heritage of Judaic and Christian traditions. The word *devil* as used in the New Testament fuses two elements—the Greek and the Judaic. The Greek element is provided by the inclusion of the sense of *daimōn* ("demon"), which referred to a guardian spirit or a source of inspiration. The description of the Devil as the "prince of the demons" (*Mt.* 9:35) is particularly significant in this respect, for, according to Russell (1977, p. 229), the association of the Devil with the demons is paralleled by his association with the fallen angels (see *Rv.* 12:4, 12:7ff; *Eph.* 2:1–2). However, the Greek Septuagint "used *demon* for the Hebrew words meaning 'vengeful idols' *(schedim)* and 'hairy satyrs' *(seîrim)*. The Vulgate Latinized accordingly and the English authorized version (1613) translated both by 'Devil', while the revised version (1881) substituted 'demon' in Deuteronomy and the Psalms [and] retained 'Devil' in the New Testament." The overall result of these philological developments was that "originally distinct species of spirits were unified by interchangeable translations of Devil, demon, fiend. All these terms devolved on Satan" (Robbins, 1959, p. 131). This explanation should clarify the use of the terms *demon* and *devil* as they are employed here. The word *demon* denotes spirits in general while the word *devil* denotes evil spirits, malign beings viewed as embodiments of evil.

Typology. Several typologies of devils are possible, and consideration may be limited to those that proceed by habitation and function. Psellus (eleventh century CE) distinguishes devils by habitat as fiery, aerial, terrestrial, aqueous, subterranean, and heliophobic. A simpler scheme may be applied in the case of Africa and Oceania, where devils could be associated with animals, waters, forest, and mountains. The former scheme has the merit of being comparable with those of otherworld religions, wherein, however, the site of habitation may not be described in terms of elements but may be located in space. Islam provides a link between the two types. The *jinn* are created out of a single element, fire, but are "associated with deserts, ruins and other eerie places, and might assume such forms as those of animals, serpents, and other creeping things" (Watt, 1970, p. 153). But the *jinn* are not necessarily evil like the devils, or *shayṭāns*, who prompt human beings to evil.

According to one tradition the species (for which we may use "genies" as a convenient westernized rubric) is made up of five orders, namely, *jānn, jinn, shayṭāns*, *ʿifrīts*, and *mārids*. The last are said to be the most powerful and the first the least; *shayṭān* is generally used to signify any evil genius; an *ʿifrīt* is a powerfully evil genius, while a *mārid*, as indicated, is an evil genius of the most powerful class. At this point it should be noted that sources admit to some confusion between *jānn* and *jinn;* while it is held that *jānn* are transformed *jinn*, just as certain apes and swine were transformed men, it is also admitted that the two are often used indiscriminately as names for the whole species, whether good or bad (*jinn* is the more common term, however). As for the characteristics of *jinn*, they are of different shapes, appearing as serpents, scorpions, lions, wolves, jackals, and so on; they are of land, sea, and air; and either have wings that allow them to fly, move like snakes or dogs, or move about like men. Other embodiments of evil in Islam may also be mentioned: *quṭrub, gharrār, siʿlah, shiqq*, and *nasnās*. Of these, the *gharrār* is comparable to the ogre inasmuch as the latter is also a figure of folklore who feeds on human beings.

In the Indic worldview the devils have been provided with a habitation and a name. Jainism provides an example of the many typologies of devils in Indic religions. The seven netherworlds contain the hells, one of which, the Vyantaras, includes demons, goblins, ghosts, and spirits, which are divided into eight ranks—*kinnaras, kimpuruṣas, mahoragas, gandharvas, yakṣas, rākṣasas, bhūtas*, and *piśācas*, all of which are found in Hindu mythology in nearly the same forms (Jacobi, in Hastings, 1911, p. 608).

Anthropological studies of Buddhism, particularly as practiced in Burma (Spiro, 1978) and Thailand (Tambiah, 1970), have led to the identification of devilish beings in Buddhism. Thus it has been noted in the case of Burmese Buddhism that *nats*, witches, ghosts, and demons, though substantively different, share the functional attribute of causing pain (Spiro, p. 40). It is noteworthy that although Hinduism does not acknowledge a specific devil, which Buddhism does in the form of Māra, it acknowledges the existence of devilish beings, who are also functionally differentiated. Hindu lore distinguishes between *asuras*, a class of supernatural beings continually opposed to the gods; *rākṣasas*, demonic beings who roam about at night, disturb the penances of ascetics, and harass and kill people; *piśācas*, who frequent cremation grounds; *vetālas*, or vampires; and *pretas* and *bhūtas*, phantoms of the dead who bother human beings on occasion. Sometimes the word *bhūta* is inclusive of *preta* and *piśāca* (Crooke, in Hastings, 1911, p. 608). The Hindu god Śiva, incidentally, presides over his own *gaṇas*, or malevolent troopers, who include some of the abovementioned creatures and can act in extremely unpleasant ways when incensed.

By contrast, in Islam, the various functions of the one and same class of demons—the *shayṭāns*—may be distinguished: they teach humans magic, lead them to unbelief, try to eavesdrop on heaven, and accompany obstinate unbelievers. An intermediate form of functional differentiation, between the Hindu one, organized by class as well as function, and the Islamic one, where different functions are performed by members of the same class, is provided by Zoroastrianism, where the devil, Angra Mainyu, rallies around his standard Aka Manah ("evil thought"), Indra, Saurva, Nānhaithya, (parallel with three Indian deities who are opposed), Taurvi ("hunger") Zairich ("thirst") and Aēshma ("fury"), so that one finds closely allied devil figures performing several diabolical functions, only some of which have been listed. One of the clearest formulations of devilish functions in Christianity is found in the *Admirable History* (1612) of Sebastien Michaëlis, which is set forth in three sets of hierarchies, each specifying the name of the devil, his function, and his adversary (Robbins, 1959, p. 129).

Another way in which devils could be typologized is by gender differentiation, for female devils are not unknown. In popular Hinduism the Churalin, a demoness regarded as the composite spirit of women who have died in childbirth (Babb, 1975, p. 248), is referred to as identifiable by an inverse foot formation. Islam speaks of beings called *ghūl* in general, though properly speaking it is said to apply only to the female, whose male counterpart is the *gharrār*. She is supposed to lead a solitary existence in the deserts, to waylay travelers and practice cannibalism. The case of the lamia, a vampire or (night-)mare, may also be discussed here. The word serves a dual sense, which may cut across gender differentiation: it could mean a succubus demon or a witch. It was suggested in the fifteenth century in Germany and Czechoslovakia that lamiae were demons in the shape of old women who stole children and roasted them.

Possession. As universal as belief in evil spirits is belief in the phenomenon of possession of the body by these evil spirits. [*See* Spirit Possession.] The history of Christianity records epidemics of possession, and a distinction is drawn between possession and obsession, the former being more grave inasmuch as it involves actual residence by the evil spirit in the body of the possessed.

Exorcism has been associated with Christian evangelization since its inception. This is also true of other religions. Tambiah (1970) clearly distinguishes between possession by benevolent and malevolent spirits *(phī)* in the context of Thailand, and notes how the distinction figures in Buddhist mortuary rites. Although the Thai beliefs about such evil spirits are so free-floating as to resist typologizing, certain kinds of devilish spirits most often cited as attacking people may be mentioned. Spirits of the rice field *(phī rai phī naa)* can attack villagers; so can the spirit that lives on a mountain *(phī pu loob)* but the attack of the *phī paub*, a malevolent disembodied spirit, is to be feared most as it may be hosted by some living being. Its origin is attributed to the transformation of spells into an evil force inside a magical expert, either a man or a woman. The force then acquires an existence of its own and can possess others.

Debate on Origins. Speculation regarding the origin of belief in devils has proceeded along several routes. According to one view, belief in devilish beings may have its roots in the experience of prehistoric man. At this time wild animals of strange shapes and sizes roamed the earth, and it would have been easy for early human beings to assume that nonhuman evil spirits abounded and assumed animal forms. Alongside this explanation may be placed the anthropological view, according to which beliefs in all classes of spiritual beings—benign or malign—are derived from belief in the disembodied spirits of the dead. Considerable controversy surrounds this view, but it may be safe to affirm that among many peoples the hostile spirits of the dead would be identified as devils. Psychological explanations for the origin of devils include the ideas of hallucinations and projection with various degrees of sophistication. As early as 1218, Gervase of Tilbury suggested that belief in lamia or nightmare was simply nocturnal hallucination, and some modern scholars would argue that man manufactures his devils out of his fears. It is often considered self-evident that the "conception of such beings doubtless stems from man's instinctive fear of the unknown, the strange and horrific. It is significant that belief in evil spirits or Devils can exist without the idea of the Devil, i.e. the personification of the principle of evil in a single being" (Brandon, 1970, p. 229). [*See* Demons, *article on* Psychological Perspectives.]

In addition to the historical (i.e., prehistorical); anthropological (i.e., animistic); and psychological (i.e., psychoanalytical) explanations, one must consider also the theological aspect, for what is really involved is an explanation of the problem of evil. How is its existence to be reconciled with belief in a benevolent God? [*See* Theodicy.] Evil creatures that defy God, despite his potential supremacy, may offer the scaffolding for some kind of a theological explanation. Given the existence of evil, one can offer a certain range of justifications: (1) what is perceived as evil is necessary for greater good; (2) evil exists as a necessary part of a good creation; (3) the universe is not perfect but is being perfected, hence the existence of evil; and (4) evil is necessary to retain free will. The existence of devils, as of the Devil, can be reconciled in various ways, as representing the principle of evil either singly or collectively and emerging out of an attempt to come to existential grips with the fact that evil exists. Since most events are caused by an agent, one might assume that evil is also caused by an agent, which may itself be either intrinsically or instrumentally evil.

[*See also* Evil.]

BIBLIOGRAPHY

Still useful are the articles grouped under "Demons and Spirits" in the *Encyclopaedia of Religion and Ethics*, edited by James Hastings, vol. 4 (Edinburgh, 1911); see particularly the pieces by Edward Anwyl (Celtic), William Crooke (Indian), Hermann Jacobi (Jain), Arthur Lloyd (Japanese), P. J. Maclagan (Chinese), V. J. Mansikka (Slavic), Eugen Mogk (Teutonic), L. A. Waddell (Tibetan), and A. V. Williams Jackson (Persian). *A Dictionary of Comparative Religion*, edited by S. G. F. Brandon (London, 1970), also contains a useful entry under "Demons," and *The Encyclopedia of Witchcraft and Demonology* (New York, 1959), by Rossell Hope Robbins, offers much information. In addition to these reference works, the following books provide information on devils in particular cultures and religious systems.

Awn, Peter J. *Satan's Tragedy and Redemption: Iblīs in Sufi Psychology.* Leiden, 1983.

Babb, Lawrence A. *The Divine Hierarchy: Popular Hinduism in Central India.* New York, 1975.

O'Flaherty, Wendy Doniger. *Women, Androgynes, and Other Mythical Beasts.* Chicago, 1980.

Russell, Jeffrey Burton. *The Devil: Perceptions of Evil from Antiquity to Primitive Christianity.* Ithaca, N.Y., 1977.

Spiro, Melford E. *Burmese Supernaturalism.* Exp. ed. Philadelphia, 1978.

Tambiah, Stanley J. *Buddhism and the Spirit Cults in North-East Thailand.* Cambridge, 1970.

Watt, W. Montgomery. *Bell's Introduction to the Qur'ān.* Edinburgh, 1970.

ARVIND SHARMA

DEVOTION. In the religious sphere, devotion is ardent affection, zealous attachment, piety, dedication, reverence, faithfulness, respect, awe, attentiveness, loyalty, fidelity, or love for or to some object, person, spirit, or deity deemed sacred, holy, or venerable. Devotion may also be thought of as action, such as worshiping, praying, and making religious vows.

Devotion is a very common phenomenon in all areas of the world and in most religious traditions. In some traditions, sects, or cults, devotion is the central religious concern or is almost synonymous with religion itself. This is the case, for example, in some versions of Chinese and Japanese Pure Land Buddhism, several Hindu devotional movements, and some Christian movements, such as Pietism. The centrality of devotion seems to be more common in religious traditions in which theistic tendencies are central, although the importance of devotion in Pure Land Buddhism is sufficient evidence to caution against equating devotion with theism.

Objects of Devotion. The extensiveness of devotion in religion becomes evident when the variety of objects of devotion is considered. While deities are usually considered the principal objects of devotion, a great many other things are also given devotion in the world's religions. In many African religions, as well as in such historical traditions as Hinduism and Confucianism, ancestors are important objects of reverence, awe, and devotion. Various people, living and dead, are also objects of devotion or the focus of devotional cults. [*See* Ancestors.] Gurus in Hinduism, saints in Christianity, the *hsien* (immortals) in Taoism, the Sage Kings in Confucianism, imams in Islam, *tīrthaṅkaras* in Jainism, and the Buddhas and *bodhisattvas* in Buddhism are only a few examples of divine personages who receive devotion in the world's religions.

Relics associated with sacred personages are the objects of devotion in many religions. [*See* Relics.] The physical remains of the Buddha were incorporated into stupas, the shrines around which devotional Buddhism began. To this day, parts of the Buddha's physical body are enshrined in temples. A well-known example is the Temple of the Tooth in Kandy, Sri Lanka. In Christianity, particularly in the late medieval period in Europe, there was a lively traffic in relics, which became extremely important in popular piety. Relics were incorporated into church altars and often represented the concrete, objective aspect of the divine around which the church was built. Pieces of the true cross, bones of martyrs, vials of the Virgin Mary's milk, even the foreskin of Jesus, were among the holy relics that were the objects of popular devotion. In contemporary Christianity the Shroud of Turin is probably the best-known example of a holy relic. In other traditions as well, the physical remains of saints are commonly revered, and the burial places of saints, where purported miracles attributed to devotion are not uncommon, often become centers of healing cults.

A great variety of places are also deemed sacred and receive devotion. Rivers in Hinduism and mountains in Shintō are often especially revered; indeed, most religious traditions associate sacredness with specific places. Certain cities, for example, play an important role in the tradition of many religions and are often themselves the centers of pilgrimage and devotion. Vārāṇasi in Hinduism, Jerusalem in Judaism and Christianity, Mecca in Islam, and Ise in Shintō are only a few examples. Sometimes whole geographical areas or countries are the objects of devotion. The Indian subcontinent as a whole for Hindus and Israel for many Jews are objects of devotion.

Devotion often focuses on ritual or cult objects. The Ark of the Covenant in ancient Judaism and the Host in Christianity are well-known examples. Sacred texts are also objects of devotion in some religions. The Torah in Judaism, the *Lotus Sutra* in Nichiren Buddhism, the *Ādi Granth* in Sikhism, and the Qur'ān in Islam are a few examples.

Indeed, the sacred, holy, or divine has revealed itself to, or been apprehended by, humankind in so many different ways and in such a variety of forms that at some point in the religious history of the world almost every conceivable object has received religious devotion.

Types of Devotion. Devotion is of different types and takes place in different physical settings, with different attendant moods, and within different kinds of communities. It is often meditative, emotionally disciplined, and subdued, and consists primarily of the willful directing of one's attention to the object of devotion. This is the nature of devotion, for example, as described in the *Bhagavadgītā*. There, Kṛṣṇa teaches Arjuna to center himself mentally on God in all his actions in order to make his entire life an act of devotion. There is a similar emphasis in most theistic traditions in which the devotee is taught to be attentive to God in all things.

Devotion may also express itself in emotional frenzy and passion. [*See* Frenzy.] Ṣūfī devotion is usually accompanied by music and dance, and much Ṣūfī devotional poetry is intensely passionate. The *Bhāgavata Purāṇa*, a medieval Hindu devotional text, says that true devotion is always accompanied by shivering, the hair standing on end, tears, and sighs of passion. The Hindu saint Caitanya (1486–1533) exemplified this kind of devotion. He was so often overcome by fits of emotional devotion to Kṛṣṇa, in which he would swoon or become ecstatic, that he could barely manage the normal routines of daily life.

The setting of devotion may be quite formal.

Churches, synagogues, temples, and mosques are all places in which people devote their minds and hearts to the divine. In such settings devotion may be highly formalized, even routinized, and under the direction of professional clergy. In its formal expression devotion is often communal or congregational and arises from, or is even dependent upon, the coming together of a group of people for a common devotional purpose. On the other hand, devotion in such formal physical settings may also take the form of a lone individual performing an act of devotion to a special saint.

Devotion may also be highly informal and unstructured. The best examples of this are the lives of famous saints who were great devotees. Francis of Assisi (1182–1226) in Christianity and Caitanya in Hinduism were both characterized by spontaneous outbursts of passionate devotion in nearly any setting.

Devotional communities (groups formed primarily as a result of, or in order to cultivate, devotion) also vary from the highly structured to the very unstructured. Monastic orders in Christianity and the Ṣūfī orders in Islam, in which devotion serves a central role, are examples of highly structured devotional communities. [*See* Monasticism.] The South Indian devotee-saints of Śiva (the Nāyaṉārs) and Viṣṇu (the Āḻvārs), in comparison, were part of unstructured traditions in which individual poet-devotee-saints wandered the countryside or resided at temples and sang devotional hymns to their lord. [*See* Bhakti.] The devotional community may extend no further than an individual saint and his or her admirers, students, followers, or devotees. Such was the case in the early days of Saint Francis's religious life and in the cases of such Hindu saints as Lalleśvarī of Kashmir (fourteenth century) and Mīrā Bāī of Rajasthan (1498–1546).

Characteristics of Devotion. Although the contexts, objects, and moods of devotion vary, there are several characteristics that typify most religious devotion. These involve the emotions, the will, and the mind.

1. The object, person, or deity to whom devotion is directed is regarded with awe and reverence. There is a recognition, often more emotional than mental, that the object is imbued with sacred power. This awe or reverence may assume a passionate intensity, exclusivity, or ardor that overwhelms the devotee.

2. Religious devotion is also characterized by faith. There is conviction, trust, or confidence on the part of the devotee that the object of devotion is real, that the object underlies, overarches, or in some way epitomizes reality. This aspect of devotion is usually associated with the will; it involves commitment, loyalty, often submission, to the object of devotion.

3. Devotion is also characterized by single-mindedness; it often involves mental concentration on its object. Spiritual techniques that aim at focusing and concentrating the mind are often part of religious devotion.

Characteristics of theistic devotion. When religious devotion is theistic in nature it is further typified by the following characteristics.

1. Theistic devotion involves a personal relationship in which the deity is imagined and approached as a person and is expected to respond to his devotees accordingly. In Islam, for example, the term *manājāt,* meaning "intimate converse," is supposed to characterize a person's devotion to God. The attitude the devotee adopts in this personal relationship varies and is often dependent upon how the deity is perceived.

2. One of the most common metaphors used in theistic devotion is that of a love relationship. The love of the devotee may be like that of a servant for the master, child for a parent, friend for a friend, or lover for the beloved. In theistic devotion the mood of love, especially when the relationship is familial, erotic, or romantic, introduces great intimacy, passion, and tenderness into the devotional experience. When devotion is expressed in terms of a love relationship, the deity is usually cast in a very approachable role and is described as reciprocating the devotee's love with a passionate love of his or her own. Many goddesses, for example, are portrayed as mothers who are attentive to and fiercely protective of their devotees/children, while the Lord's Prayer in Christianity describes God as the devotees' father. Throughout theistic devotion, deities assume the roles of loving parent, intimate friend, and impassioned lover in response to the devotee's own devotional role.

3. Theistic devotion is also characterized by expressions or feelings of praise and submission. Both attitudes presuppose that the deity is morally superior to, wiser, and more powerful than the devotee, and usually that the devotee has been created by the deity or is wholly dependent on the deity for his continued existence and well-being. In praise, the deity's qualities of goodness, greatness, and generosity are often mentioned. The deity is praised for bestowing various blessings, particularly the blessing of life, on the devotee, his country or nation, or the world as a whole. Theistic devotion typically expresses itself by praising the deity as the source of all good things and as the embodiment of all good qualities. In Islam, for example, the term *ḥamd,* meaning "thankful praise," often characterizes devotion.

The devotee of a deity often expresses total dependence upon his god by feelings, attitudes, gestures, or acts of submission. In Arabic the word *muslim* means "one who surrenders (to God)," suggesting the centrality of this attitude in Islamic tradition. The Muslim term *'ibādah* ("worship") is often used to characterize devotional observances to God, clearly indicating that the divine-human relationship is like that of a master to a slave *('abd)*. In Śrī Vaiṣṇavism, a Hindu devotional movement, the theme of complete self-surrender *(prapatti)* is central; such submission is held to epitomize *bhakti*, or devotion to God.

The style of submission may depend upon the type of relationship envisioned by the devotee. The submission of a child to its mother, for example, might be quite different from the submission of a slave to his owner. In many traditions the status of the devotee compared to the deity is affirmed to be greatly inferior; men and women are often described as morally weak, sinful, corrupt, and insignificant, and the deity as overwhelmingly superior. In this relationship the proper attitude of the devotee is abasement and submission. A Muslim prayer manual, for example, says: "I beseech Thee with the beseeching of the abased sinner, the petition of one whose neck is bowed before Thee—whose face is in the dust before Thee" (cited in Padwick, 1961, p. 10).

Devotion and Religious Practices. Devotion is often associated with or expressed in the context of several common types of religious practices.

Prayer. Devotion often takes the form of prayer. [*See* Prayer.] In prayer a deity is entreated, supplicated, adored, or praised in a mood of devotional service or attentiveness. In some cases, a mood of devotion is cultivated before the devotee prays in order to ensure sincerity and concentration. In medieval Judaism, for example, some authorities recommended the practice of *kavvanah*, the directing of attention to God, before prayer so that prayer might be undertaken with the proper mental inclination.

Moving and dramatic expressions of devotion are found in poems and hymns that articulate the prayers of devotees to the divine. Hymns are found in many tribal religions and in every theistic religious tradition among the world's historical religions. Hymns, such as those central to Protestant Christianity, are devotional prayer set to music. Collective prayer, common in many religions, is another example of formalized devotion.

Worship. As a formal expression of homage, service, reverence, praise, or petition to a deity, worship is closely related to, or expressive of, devotion. Much worship represents a formal, periodic, structured expression of devotion. The prescribed daily and Friday prayers in Islam, called *ṣalāt*, for example, are essentially devotional in nature. In Hindu *pūjā* ("worship"), which is performed in both temple and domestic settings, and which may be performed by an individual or by large groups, the basic pattern of ritual actions denotes personal attendance upon and service of the deity by the worshipers. The deity is symbolically bathed, fanned, fed, and entertained by the priest or directly by the devotee. It is common in worship to make an offering to the deity, which again is often done in the spirit of devotion. Some forms of worship are primarily occasions for devotees to express together their devotion to their god. This is the case, for example, with Hindu *kīrtana* and *bhajan*, gatherings of devotees at which songs are sung in praise of a deity. The setting is usually informal and the mood warm and emotional. It is not uncommon for devotees to dance and leap in joy while they sing their hymns of praise. Protestant revival meetings also represent a context in which open expression of emotional devotion to God is encouraged and expected of those present.

Pilgrimage. In many religions pilgrimage is a very popular undertaking, and for many pilgrims their journey is an act of devotion. [*See* Pilgrimage.] Undertaking a long trip to a sacred place is a physical prayer. Through the pilgrimage the pilgrim may be making a special appeal to the deity or expressing gratitude for a blessing received from the deity. In Islam a pilgrimage to Mecca is enjoined as one of the fundamental acts of submission incumbent upon all Muslims.

The pilgrim may be making the pilgrimage simply to steep himself in an atmosphere of piety and devotion that is far more intense than in ordinary circumstances. The feeling of community that arises among pilgrims is often strong, and the entire journey, which can last weeks, may turn into a devotional extravaganza with hymns being sung all day long, devotees swooning in fits of ecstasy or possession, and miraculous cures or incidents being reported. The annual pilgrimage to Pandharpur in Maharashtra is an example of a pilgrimage that is an act of mass devotion sustained for weeks, a type of pilgrimage not unusual in Hinduism.

Meditation. Although many kinds of meditation may not involve devotion, devotion often uses meditative techniques. [*See* Meditation.] Meditation usually involves disciplining the mind so that it can focus on something without being distracted by frivolous thoughts or bodily needs and discomforts. [*See* Attention.] For many practitioners the goal is to achieve or maintain attentiveness to a deity. Meditation is used to perfect, deepen, sharpen, or enhance devotion. In such cases meditation and devotion may become synonymous. In Japanese Pure Land Buddhism the term *anjin* (which is sometimes translated as "faith") refers to a meditative calm in which the heart and mind are quieted through concentration on Amida Buddha and his paradise. A particularly common meditative technique used to engender, express, or enhance devotion is the constant repetition of the deity's name or a short prayer to the deity. Ṣūfīs invoke the names of God over and over as part of their *dhikr* (a term meaning recollection that refers to devotional techniques); Eastern Orthodox Christian monks chant the Jesus Prayer ("Lord Jesus have mercy on me a sinner") as often as possible; devotees of Kṛṣṇa chant his names repeatedly. In Pure Land Buddhism, devotees chant a short prayer ("Hail to Amida Buddha") over and over to sharpen and concentrate their faith in Amida.

Asceticism and monasticism. Asceticism and monasticism may be practiced for different reasons, but they are often undertaken in the context of devotion, especially in the theistic and Pure Land Buddhist traditions. The most dramatic example of asceticism in Christianity is that of the Desert Fathers, who sought solitude in the desert in order to develop their attentiveness to God without distractions or hindrances from society or other people. Their asceticism was clearly associated with, and intended to cultivate, devotion. An ascetic strain is also strong in Sufism, a highly devotional expression of Islam, and many of the most important Hindu devotional leaders and saints have been world renouncers. In many cases it is clear that asceticism, or renunciation of the world, has been found not only compatible with devotion but a positive encouragement of it.

The case is similar with monasticism. An isolated, cloistered, highly regimented religious community was for centuries esteemed in Christianity as the best place to devote oneself to God. Life in the monastic community was dominated by regular worship and prayer several times a day and imposed a devotional discipline on the individual. To a great extent, monasticism in Christianity was a systematic attempt to perfect a human being's devotional predilections. As in Christian asceticism, the goal was to become attentive to God at all times, except that in the monastic context this goal was sought with the help of a like-minded community and under the guidelines of a carefully regulated spiritual discipline or rule. In many respects, several Ṣūfī brotherhoods and Pure Land Buddhist monastic communities may also be seen as organized attempts to create the ideal environment for cultivating the devotional sentiment.

Mysticism. For many devotees, particularly in theistic traditions, there is a deep longing to be close to, in the presence of, or absorbed in the deity. [*See* Mystical Union.] This is also the goal of mysticism in theistic traditions, and as such devotion and mysticism are often closely associated. In medieval Jewish mysticism, *devequt*, which is usually translated as "cleaving to God," is considered the highest religious state that can be attained. This state of cleaving to God is synonymous with an intense devotion in which the devotee is completely preoccupied with and absorbed in the divine. In Sufism the term *fanā'* describes a point in the devotee/mystic's spiritual quest in which all feeling of individuality and ego fall away and the Ṣūfī is overwhelmed by God. In Christianity, the idea of union with the divine is expressed by Paul as follows: "It is no longer I who live, but Christ who lives in me" (*Gal.* 2:20). In trying to describe the intimacy of his unmediated experiences of God, John of the Cross (1542–1591), a Christian Spanish mystic, spoke of a river merging with the ocean and of iron heated until it becomes one with the fire. Mystical union, then, represents the ultimate goal of many devotees in several different traditions, and the mystical path is often understood as being the highest path a devotee can embark upon.

Social action and charity. In some religious traditions charitable service to one's fellow human beings is considered the most perfect form of devotion to the divine. [*See* Charity.] In Christianity several movements with a strong devotional bias have emphasized works of charity as central to the devotional life. With the inauguration of active religious orders for men by Francis of Assisi in the thirteenth century, and for women by Mary Ward and Vincent de Paul in the seventeenth century, the focus of the religious life, which had earlier been cloistered, shifted from the cultivation of one's spiritual predilections in isolation from society to serving the poor and needy in the world. Several religious brotherhoods and sisterhoods have been founded in Protestant Christianity that aim at serving the poor, while the Social Gospel movement of the nineteenth century in America represents an attempt to provide theological justification for social involvement as central to the Christian life.

A dramatic modern example of devotion as inextricably associated with social service is the life of Mother Theresa of Calcutta and her Sisters of Charity, who minister to the "poorest of the poor" as a way of life. Mother Theresa has said that she teaches the women who join her order to see Jesus in each person they serve; in serving men and women, they serve Jesus.

The theme of service to human beings being equated with service to God exists in other traditions as well. Mahatma Gandhi, for example, who had a strong devotional bent, was once asked why he did not withdraw from the world in his search for God. He replied that if he thought for one moment that God might be found in a Himalayan cave, he would go there at once, but he was convinced that God could only be found among human beings and in their service.

The Philosophy of Devotion. In the Hindu and Buddhist traditions, in which there are very strong competing paths alongside the devotional path, two kinds of arguments are put forth in defending the excellence of the devotional way. In both traditions it is assumed that the world has entered a final period of moral, religious, and ethical decline (the *kaliyuga* in Hinduism and *mappō* in Japanese Buddhism). In this age, human beings are no longer spiritually capable of undertaking certain religious paths that were popular among people in earlier ages. Asceticism, meditation, monasticism, and religious ceremonialism, in particular, are held to be too demanding for people of the present age, whose spiritual capacities are weak. In this age, devotion is the best way to reach the spiritual goal. It is the best because it is the easiest. It can be practiced by anyone, by monk and peasant, rich and poor, priest and layman, man and woman, young and old. The second argument follows from the first. Why is devotion the easiest path? It is the easiest path because it is the most natural path to human beings. In some Hindu devotional movements, *bhakti* (devotion) is said to represent one's inherent *dharma* (proper way of acting) as opposed to one's inherited *dharma,* which is equated with one's caste, occupation, and social roles. All human beings, according to this logic, have an inner longing to love God, and until they do they remain frustrated, incomplete, lonely, and lost. Devotion is understood as a person's cultivation of this natural urge to serve and love the Creator, who has instilled in human beings at the deepest level a longing to be reunited with their source.

The idea of devotion representing a person's natural inclination is also seen in many Ṣūfī images that speak of one who is not devoted to God as being like a fish out of water, a camel far from a watering hole, a bird separated from its mate. To seek God by means of the mystic way is to return home, to seek the familiar and comfortable, to indulge one's natural longings. A similar idea is expressed in Augustine's (354–430) famous saying to the effect that human beings are restless until they find their rest in God.

In the vision of Francis of Assisi, all creation was brought into being in order to praise the Creator; every species in existence praises God in its own special way. Even inorganic nature celebrates the Creator in some way. For Francis, devotion to God represents the inherent and underlying law of the creation and is apparent everywhere. Similarly, in the writings of some Ṣūfīs the entire creation is said to be pervaded by the presence of God. His divine presence intoxicates all creatures and sets them singing and dancing in ecstatic praise.

Another devotional theme is the idea that one who is truly devoted to a deity makes every action, no matter how apparently insignificant, routine, or frivolous, an act of devotion to the divine. In the *Bhagavadgītā,* when Kṛṣṇa teaches Arjuna how to discipline his actions so that he will not reap the fruits of *karman,* he tells him to dedicate all of his actions to God, to become God's instrument in all that he does (9.27). Similarly, in Hasidic Judaism it is taught that the state of *devequt,* or cleaving to God, should be a person's constant state of mind. In everyday life, even while performing the most mundane acts, a person should cleave to the Lord.

[*For a discussion of the subjective experience of devotion, see* Love, *and for the objective expression of devotion in various religious traditions, see* Worship and Cultic Life.]

BIBLIOGRAPHY

There is a lack of books on devotion as a religious phenomenon. Friedrich Heiler's *Prayer: A Study in the History and Psychology of Religion,* translated by Samuel McComb (London, 1938), seeks to describe a widespread devotional phenomenon in religion, but it focuses primarily on Western religious traditions. There are more and better sources for individual traditions. Abraham Zebi Idelsohn's *Jewish Liturgy and Its Development* (New York, 1967) has sections on devotion in the Jewish tradition. Owen Chadwick's *Western Asceticism* (London, 1958) contains translations of important ascetic texts in the Christian tradition and deals with the exemplary role of the ascetic in Christian piety. David Knowles's *Christian Monasticism* (New York, 1969) is a standard work on the monastic ideal in Christian life. Annemarie Schimmel's *Mystical Dimensions of Islam* (Chapel Hill, N.C., 1975) treats the Ṣūfī traditions in Islam, which are highly devotional in nature. Constance Padwick's *Muslim Devotions: A Study of Prayer-Manuals in Common Use* (London, 1961) surveys popular devotional manuals in Islam. A. K. Ramanujan has translated several devotional hymns of a South Indian Hindu devotee and presented an overview of Hindu devotion in a volume entitled *Hymns for Drowning: Poems for Viṣṇu by Nammāḻvār* (Princeton, 1981). Edward C. Dimock and Denise Levertov have translated several Bengali Hindu devotional hymns in a book entitled *In Praise of Krishna: Songs from the Bengali* (New York, 1967). Alfred Bloom's *Shinran's Gospel of Pure Grace* (Tucson, 1965) and Gendo Nakai's *Shinran and His Religion of Pure Faith* (Kyoto, 1946) deal with devotional Buddhism in Japan.

DAVID KINSLEY

DE VRIES, JAN. *See* Vries, Jan de.

DGE-LUGS-PA. The Dge-lugs-pa order of Tibetan Buddhism was founded in the early fifteenth century by Tsoṅ-kha-pa Blo-bzaṅ-grags-pa (1357–1419) in the area of Lhasa, the capital of Tibet. He established a monastic university on a mountain called Dga'-ldan ("the joyous") in 1409, and his sect was thus originally called Joyous Way (Dga'-ldan-pa'i-lugs); later it came to be called Virtuous Way, Dge-lugs-pa. [*See the biography of Tsoṅ-kha-pa.*] Students built two other large monastic universities in the Lhasa area, 'Bras-spungs (1416) and Se-rwa (1419), and the system gradually spread throughout the country. Within two hundred years the sect had become an important political force, such that around 1640, with the help of the Mongolian potentate Gu-śri Khan, the fifth Dalai Lama (1617–1682) assumed power as head of the government. The lineage of Dalai Lamas maintained this position until the Chinese takeover in 1959. [*See* Dalai Lama.]

The Dge-lugs-pa educational system so captured the imagination of Tibetans that its universities attracted great numbers of men. Dge-lugs-pa gradually became the dominant mode of religious education and the dominant cultural force in an area ranging from the Kalmyk Mongolian lands in Russia near the Caspian Sea through Outer Mongolia, Inner Mongolia, Mongolian Siberia, parts of China, and Tibet. Lhasa, with its large Dge-lugs-pa universities, became the cultural, religious, educational, medical, and astrological capital of Buddhist Inner Asia. Great influence was exercised by a complex system of education, devotion, meditation, and cultism, the pattern for which was set by brilliant Dge-lugs-pa leaders in Lhasa over several centuries.

In Lhasa each monastery had at least two competing faculties and student bodies, which periodically met to debate in intense competition. Factionalism between groups of differing philosophic opinion was highly encouraged; thus there was more intellectual activity within the Dge-lugs-pa order on this level than between Dge-lugs-pa and the other orders of Tibetan Buddhism.

Although the Western study of Dge-lugs-pa education is scarcely more than a half century old, it is possible to piece together a picture of this highly developed program for stimulating the metaphysical imagination. In general, Dge-lugs-pa doctrinal training is classified into two types, Sūtra and Tantra, based on a division of the texts regarded as the Buddha's word. Training in the Sūtra system is further divided into a more "practical" and a more "theoretical" system of study. Both practical and theoretical systems are based on great Indian books and Tibetan texts that consist of either explicit commentaries on those texts or expositions of main themes in them.

The practical system centers on Tsoṅ-kha-pa's *Lam rim chen mo* (Great Exposition of the Stages of the Path) and Indian texts such as Śāntideva's *Bodhicāryāvatāra* (Engaging in the Bodhisattva Deeds). The theoretical system centers either on comparative systems of tenets, both Buddhist and non-Buddhist, or on the "Five Great Books." The large Dge-lugs-pa universities take the latter approach for a curriculum of Sūtra study that begins when the student is around eighteen and continues for twenty to twenty-five years.

To prepare students for study of these texts, the curriculum begins with a class on introductory debate that serves to establish the procedure of combative and probing analysis used throughout the entire course of study. The approach is at once individualistic (as used in the preparation and execution of specific debates) and group-stimulated (in that information and philosophic positions are acquired from fellow debaters in an ongoing network of communication). The preliminary classes further study basic psychology and basic theory of reasoning. Then begins a reading of the first of the Five Great Books: the future Buddha Maitreya's *Abhisamayālaṃkāra* (Ornament for Clear Realization), a rendering of the hidden teaching on the path structure in the *Perfection of Wisdom Sūtras;* this work is usually studied for six or seven years.

The class then passes on to the second Great Book, Candrakīrti's *Madhyamakāvatāra* (Supplement to [Nāgārjuna's] Treatise on the Middle Way), to explore for two years the explicit teaching on the emptiness of inherent existence expounded in the *Perfection of Wisdom Sūtras.* Next is Vasubandhu's *Abhidharmakośa* (Treasury of Knowledge), a compendium of the types and nature of afflicted phenomena *(kliṣṭadharma)* as well as the pure phenomena *(vaiyavadānikadharma)* that act as antidotes to them; this takes two years. The fourth Great Book is Guṇaprabhā's *Vinaya Sūtra* (Aphorisms on Discipline), also studied for two years.

Each year throughout the entire twenty-year program, time is taken out for pursuit of the last of the Great Books, Dharmakīrti's *Pramāṇavarttika* (Commentary on [Dignāga's] Compendium of Valid Cognition), largely epistemological and logical studies. At the end there are several years for review and preliminary rounds of debate in preparation for the national yearly debate competition in Lhasa; the winner becomes a national hero.

Throughout the long course of study reasoned analysis is stressed, but at the same time the student maintains daily practice of Tantric rites revolving around visualization of himself as a deity. He also participates in cultic rites at the university, college, and subdivision levels to appease and satisfy various protector deities associated with those units, and participates in devotional assemblies on a daily basis centered on deities like the savioress Tārā. Because of the long training period in Sūtra studies, this less obvious, yet very strong and even dominant Tantric side of Dge-lugs-pa often goes unnoticed by foreign observers.

After taking a *dge-bśes* degree, a monk can proceed to a Tantric college, the two prime ones being the Tantric

College of Upper Lhasa and the Tantric College of Lower Lhasa. Both have as their main purpose the study, transmission, and practice of the *Guhyasamāja Tantra,* again through the extensive commentaries of Tsoṅ-kha-pa. The distinguishing feature of Tantrism is deity yoga; its practitioners meditate on themselves as having the physical form not of an ordinary person, but of a deity embodying the highest levels of wisdom and compassion.

Underlying this entire program of religious immersal through doctrinal, devotional, ritualistic, and meditational means is a commitment to reason. The harmony of reason with the most profound religious experiences of compassion, wisdom, deity yoga, and manifestation of the fundamental innate mind of clear light is stressed. Meditation is viewed as being of two varieties, stabilizing (or fixating) meditation and analytical meditation, with the latter receiving great stress in Dge-lugs-pa. To develop compassion, reflective reasoning is used to enhance basic feelings that are recognized as part of common experience. To develop wisdom, reflective reasoning is used in an intricately devised process so that the student may penetratively understand the incorrectness of assent to the false appearance of phenomena as if they existed in their own right. The aim is not merely to defeat rival systems but to overcome an innate, unlearned misconception of the nature of phenomena.

Such analytically derived realization of emptiness constitutes the first step in practicing deity yoga in Tantrism. The wisdom consciousness—the realization of emptiness impelled by compassion—is then used as the basis for manifesting as a divine being. The wisdom consciousness itself appears as a deity in an indivisible fusion of wisdom and compassion that is symbolized by a *vajra,* a diamond. Utilizing these continuous divine appearances, stabilizing meditation can then be performed on essential points within the body to induce subtler levels of consciousness that are used to realize the same emptiness of inherent existence. When the most subtle consciousness, the fundamental innate mind of clear light, is actualized, the wind (Skt., *prāṇa;* Tib., *rluṅ*), or energy, associated with this most subtle consciousness is said to be used as the substantial cause for appearing in an *actual* divine body such that one no longer needs the old coarse body. Transformation is literally both mental and physical.

This most subtle mind is the same as the clear light of death that terrifies ordinary beings, who fear they are being annihilated when it manifests. The Dge-lugs-pa system of education is aimed at overcoming this fear of one's own most basic nature; thus it suggests that the sense of otherness that many of the world's cultures associate with profound religious experience of the awesome is based on a misconception about the basic nature of one's own being. Further, it suggests that this fear and sense of otherness can be caused to disappear through an understanding of the actual status of phenomena, which is gained through reasoned investigation brought to the level of a profoundly moving experience. This highly developed view of the compatibility of reason and deep mystic insight, expressed in a system of education and ritual exercise, is a distinctive feature of Dge-lugs-pa.

Since the Dalai Lama's flight from Tibet in 1959, just prior to the takeover of the government by Chinese Communists, a refugee community of Dge-lugs-pas under his leadership (which is not confined to members of the Dge-lugs-pa order) has, in scattered places throughout India, reestablished smaller versions of Lhasa's three main monastic universities (each having two competing colleges as subdivisions) as well as two of the Tantric colleges and the monasteries of the Dalai Lama and Panchen Lama. Thus the Dge-lugs-pa educational system has been reestablished in India and, as of the mid-1980s, involves approximately three thousand monks, of whom about two thirds are children. Clearly this is a feat of considerable achievement by an overall Tibetan refugee population in India and Nepal of one hundred thousand.

[*See also* Buddhism, Schools of, *article on* Tibetan Buddhism.]

BIBLIOGRAPHY

The study of Dge-lugs-pa is in its infancy, but several helpful expositions have emerged. For a historical and political study, see David L. Snellgrove and Hugh E. Richardson's *A Cultural History of Tibet* (1968; reprint, Boulder, Colo., 1980), pp. 177–267. A short biography of Tsoṅ-kha-pa, the founder of Dge-lugs-pa, and scattered samples of his teachings are given in *The Life and Teachings of Tsong Khapa* (Dharamsala, 1982), edited by Robert A. F. Thurman. Tsoṅ-kha-pa's analytic style in which reason dominates over and interprets tradition is evidenced in his *Tantra in Tibet,* translated and edited by me (London, 1977). For a stirring autobiography of a Dge-lugs-pa scholar and lama as well as a description of the course of training and basic teachings of the school, see *The Life and Teaching of Geshé Rabten,* translated and edited by B. Alan Wallace (London, 1980). A sense of how a Dge-lugs-pa scholar's mind probes issues can be gained from Lati Rinbochay's *Mind in Tibetan Buddhism,* edited, translated, and introduced by Elizabeth Napper (London, 1980); in this work the topic of basic psychology is examined in depth. The themes of death, the subtler levels of consciousness, and the mind of clear light, as presented by an eighteenth-century Dge-lugs-pa scholar, Yang-jen-ga-way-lo-drö, is given in Lati Rinbochay and my *Death, Intermediate State, and Rebirth in Tibetan Buddhism* (London, 1979). A contemporary Dge-lugs-pa commentary on a classic Indian text,

Śāntideva's *Bodhicaryāvatāra,* which expands and develops important points, is found in Geshe Kelsang Gyatso's *Meaningful to Behold: View, Meditation and Action in Mahayana Buddhism* (Ulverston, England, 1980). The doctrine of emptiness and its place in the Dge-lugs-pa worldview is presented in considerable detail, drawing from several works of their scholastic tradition, in my work *Meditation on Emptiness* (London, 1983). How the doctrine of emptiness and expression of compassion is practiced in Anuttarayoga Tantra is presented in a detailed and intimate way in Geshe Kelsang Gyatso's *Clear Light of Bliss: Mahamudra Meditation in Vajrayana Buddhism* (London, 1982).

P. JEFFREY HOPKINS

DHARMA. [*This entry consists of two articles.* Hindu Dharma *introduces the term and discusses its various applications in the Brahmanic and Hindu traditions.* Buddhist Dharma and Dharmas *treats the uses of the term specific to that tradition.*]

Hindu Dharma

It is somewhat difficult to find a suitable South Asian word to represent what in English is known as "religion," admittedly a rather vague and encompassing term. Perhaps the most suitable would be the Sanskrit *dharma,* which can be translated in a variety of ways, all of which are pertinent to traditional Indian religious ideas and practices.

Derived from the Sanskrit root *dhṛ,* "sustain, support, uphold," *dharma* has a wide range of meaning: it is the essential foundation of something or of things in general, and thus signifies "truth"; it is that which is established, customary, proper, and therefore means "traditional" or "ceremonial"; it is one's duty, responsibility, imperative, and thereby "moral obligation"; it is that which is right, virtuous, meritorious, and accordingly "ethical"; and it is that which is required, precepted, or permitted through religious authority, and thus "legal."

The aggregate connotation here suggests that in South Asian cultures *dharma* represents "correctness," both in a descriptive sense ("the way things are") and in a prescriptive one ("the way things should be"), and reflects the inextricable connection in the religious thought of India between ontology, ritual ideology, social philosophy, ethics, and canon law.

Types of Dharma. South Asian religious and legal systems have presented a variety of definitions of *dharma* and have seen different modes of its expression in the world and in society. Despite those variations, however, certain notions have remained consistent throughout South Asian history.

Dharma and ṛta in the Vedic period. The oldest sense of the word—which appears as early as the *Ṛgveda* (c. 1200 BCE), usually as *dharman*—signifies cosmic ordinance, often in connection with the sense of natural or divine law. As such, it is closely related conceptually to the Vedic notion of *ṛta,* the universal harmony in which all things in the world have a proper place and function. The two terms differ in meaning in that whereas *ṛta* is an impersonal law, *dharman* characterizes those personal actions that engender or maintain cosmic order. The *Ṛgveda* typically discusses such sustaining actions as those pertaining to the gods, especially Mitra and Varuṇa, who are said to separate the day from night, regulate the seasons, and make the rains fall from the skies.

While the expression *adharma* ("against *dharma*") does not appear until a few centuries later, the germ of the idea lies in the term *anṛta* ("against *ṛta*"), a synonym in the *Ṛgveda* for *asatya,* "untrue," in the sense of "unreal." This suggests the notion that improper action leads to the fall of the universe into unreality, and thus to nonbeing. The implication here is that in classical Vedic literatures *dharma* carries ontological weight: being arises out of proper activity while improper action leads to nonbeing. This ontological aspect leads to the normative notion that, in the Saṃhitā literatures, *dharma* is the system of activity that guides the world in such a way that *ṛta* is not violated. This means that each of the gods has a personality that, although each is different, is intrinsically in harmony with the natural world.

It is important to note further that as early as the *Ṛgveda* this "proper action" is connected to the gods' ritual activity, and, to a lesser extent, their ascetic practices. In *Ṛgveda* 5.63.7, for example, the terms *ṛta* and *dharman* appear together in association with *vrata* ("vow, religious rite"): "You, Mitra and Varuṇa, through the creative powers of the gods, protect the ceremonial vows [*vrata*] with actions which uphold the world [*dharma*]. Through cosmic order [*ṛta*] you rule over the whole universe. You placed the sun in the heavens, like a shining chariot." This suggests that the Vedic poets not only saw an efficacious connection between primordial cosmic order and the gods' power to maintain that order, they also understood that such sustaining power resides at least in part in the performance of ceremonial actions. [*See also* Ṛta.]

Varṇāśramadharma and svadharma. At the time of the composition of the Brāhmaṇas (c. 900–600 BCE) the fundamental laws of the universe were understood to be reflected not only in the gods' actions, but, more importantly, in the human priest's performance of rituals prescribed in those texts and designed to ensure a person's well-being in the world to come. *Dharma* is therefore closely aligned with the South Asian concept of *karman*—the idea that one's actions in the present determine the conditions of one's life in the future. This ideological connection grew firmer through the generations, so that by the second century BCE an important lawbook could typically assert that "those who support *dharma* as it is presented in sacred tradition and in revelation gain fame in this world and incomparable happiness after death" (*Laws of Manu* 2.9).

From this sacerdotal and eschatological stance arises a normative dimension to *dharma* in which the term comes to mean the sum total of one's obligations by which one "fits in" with the natural and particularly the social world. This is especially pertinent in regard to the duties determined by one's social class *(varṇa)* and stage of life *(āśrama)*. Thus, for example, a priest *(brāhmaṇa)* ensures the health of society by securing the goodwill of the gods through various rituals; a king or soldier *(kṣatriya)* protects the people from others; a merchant *(vaiśya)* produces material goods to benefit the people; and a laborer *(śūdra)* works in order that all of the above may function smoothly. Similarly, a student *(brahmacārin)* is to study diligently in order to know the sacred tradition; a householder *(gṛhastha)* ensures the continuation of society by establishing a family; a forest hermit *(vanaprastha)* contributes to the welfare of his ancestors by privately performing ritual oblations; and a renunciant *(saṃnyāsin)* procures his final release from the world through homeless asceticism. [*See also* Saṃnyāsa.] Subsumed as a whole, this system of social obligations is known as *varṇāśramadharma.*

Varṇāśramadharma reflects a temporal dimension in orthodox Hindu normative thought. That is, just as a person gains rights and responsibilities while moving in this life from one *āśrama* to the next, he claims certain privileges and accepts specific obligations according to his present *varṇa,* which is determined by his actions in a previous life. Here, again, we see a close ideological assumption connecting *dharma* and *karman.* [*See also* Karman, *article on* Hindu and Jain Concepts.]

It is important to note that the various obligations incumbent on members of the different *varṇa*s and *āśrama*s mutually support each other, and that an imperfect performance of one's responsibilities harms society—and thus the world—as a whole. Furthermore, these moral obligations inhere within the specific *varṇa*s and *āśrama*s themselves and cannot be assumed by a person of another place in society. As the *Bhagavadgītā* asserts in a well-known teaching: "It is better to perform one's own obligations [*svadharma*] poorly than to do another's well" (*Bhagavadgītā* 3.45, 18.47).

The term *svadharma* (particular responsibilities) in this last passage is not to be understood as referring to one's individual or chosen personal obligations. Rather, *svadharma* describes an impersonal generic ethical category which encapsulates one's duties determined by one's place in society. All farmers therefore have the same *svadharma,* but no farmer has the same *svadharma* as, say, a military officer. *Svadharma* thus embodies the same ethical values as does *varṇāśramadharma,* and the two terms are nearly synonymous. [*See also* Varṇa and Jāti.]

Āpaddharma. Some texts note that at times such as severe economic or natural calamity the norms determined by *varṇa* and *āśrama* may be suspended so that society can survive the stress. For example, a priest may assume in those times the duties of a soldier, or a king may take up the responsibilities of a merchant, but they may do so only for the shortest possible time. Such a "duty determined by emergency" is known as *āpaddharma.* However, at no time—even in moments of severe distress—can a person who is not a priest earn a living by teaching the Veda or by performing Vedic ceremonies.

Sādhāraṇadharma, sāmānyadharma, and sanātanadharma. Most authoritative texts further assert that all people, regardless of their age and occupation, should observe some common moral obligations. A representative list of such responsibilities appears in the *Arthaśāstra,* which notes that everyone must refrain from injuring others and must tell the truth, live purely, practice goodwill, be forgiving, and exercise patience at all times (*Arthaśāstra* 1.3.13). Such rules are known as *sādhāraṇa* ("pertaining to everybody"), *sāmānya* ("common"), or *sanātana* ("eternal") in scope.

Sometimes, however, the obligations derived from *svadharma* directly contradict those imperatives of *sādhāraṇadharma,* and a person trying to make an ethical decision must choose between opposing demands. What happens, for instance, when a priest must offer a blood sacrifice or a soldier must fight and kill the enemy? *Sādhāraṇadharma* admonishes them to practice noninjury to all living beings, yet their respective *svadharma*s command them to kill. What is their moral obligation?

Different religious traditions offered various responses to such a quandary. In general, those based most thoroughly in Brahmanic ideology maintained that in order to support cosmic and social harmony one must follow one's *svadharma* at all times, even in those instances when it means breaking the rules of *sādhāraṇadharma.* Thus, the priest must offer the ritual; the soldier must fight. On the other hand, traditions influenced by the Vedānta, Buddhism, and Jainism taught that the demands of *sādhāraṇadharma* always overrule those of *svadharma*. Here, the priest should refuse to perform the sacrifice, and the soldier should lay down his arms. A third alternative was offered by the ideology of *bhakti*, selfless and loving devotion to a personal and supreme deity, in which all actions are performed in service of God's will. In this case, the priest or the soldier should or should not kill, depending on what God demands of him at the particular moment. The problem here (and it is a problem in theological ethics in general) is: how does one know at any given moment what God wants?

The *bhakti* response to such a question in general affirms a direct comprehension of divine will through a personal experience that may or may not be consistent with the precepts established by orthodox tradition. In terms of canon law, however, the inherently fluid nature of such experience is such that *bhakti* ideology has found little place in traditional modes of decision making. [*See also* Bhakti.]

Authoritative Sources of Dharma. Metaethical quandaries ("how does one know what is right?") appear in legal as well as in theological circles, and therefore questions of authority arose even in systems revolving around the structures of *varṇāśramadharma*. In order to adjudicate such problems, most orthodox traditions affirmed three sources *(mūla)* for ethical and legal decisions: divine revelation, sacred tradition, and the practices of the wise. Some texts add a fourth, namely, conscience. These references are serial in nature, revelation being the most determinative and conscience being the least influential.

Śrūti. According to orthodox thought the primary source for all knowledge, legal and otherwise, lies in the Vedic canon comprised of the Mantra Saṃhitās (liturgical hymns of the *Ṛgveda, Yajurveda, Sāmaveda,* and *Atharvaveda*), ceremonial instructions (Brāhmaṇas), and philosophical treatises (Āraṇyakas and Upaniṣads). Together these texts constitute *śrūti,* revealed eternal truths (literally, "that which is heard"). In all orthodox traditions *śrūti* was the primary source of normative guidance. Nothing could go against the values and doctrines presented in *śrūti* and continue to be considered ethical.

Interpretation of the often apparently unsystematic or imprecise nature of *śrūti* literatures was, however, a complicated task. Accordingly, during the Vedic era the scholar-sage Jaimini began a tradition of interpretation known as the Mīmāṃsā, which centered on the thorough "investigation" *(mīmāṃsā)* into the meaning of Vedic texts in order to discern their normative imperatives. [*See also* Mīmāṃsā.]

Smṛti. Not all questions of *dharma* could be resolved through reference to the timeless *śrūti.* Thus, orthodox philosophers and legalists looked also to those more temporal literatures that were passed through the generations. These texts were known as *smṛti,* "remembered" truths and injunctions. *Smṛti* comprises the six Vedāṅgas ("ancillary texts," collections of aphoristic treatises [*sūtras*] that interpret the Veda), the epics *Mahābhārata* (including the *Bhagavadgītā*) and *Rāmāyāṇa,* and the Purāṇas ("stories of old; sacred myths").

Although all of these texts address concerns relating to *dharma,* the most direct in their evaluations are those of the six Vedāṅgas, one of which is made up of the Kalpasūtras, or teachings on proper activity. The Kalpasūtras address three major concerns, each undertaken by a different literary group: the Śrautasūtras interpret large public rituals; the Gṛhasūtras teach the proper ways to perform domestic ceremonies; and the Dharmasūtras elucidate the obligations of the sacred community. [*See also* Sūtra Literature *and* Vedāṅgas.]

Somewhat later (c. 100 CE) a new genre of literatures known as the Dharmaśāstras began to appear. These are specialized works dealing with specific imperatives and problems in Vedic *dharma.* The most influential of these treatises is probably the *Mānava Dharmaśāstra* (The Laws of Manu), which outlines the various rights and responsibilities inherent in the different *varṇas* and *āśramas* of traditional Vedic society. [*See also* Śāstra Literature.]

Sadācāradharma and siṣṭācāradharma. Most classical texts admit that the example given by the honored members of society serves as a third means by which *dharma* may be discerned. If *śrūti* and *smṛti* both fail to elucidate a problem, then the community may look for guidance in the actions of people who "practice what is right" *(sadācāra),* or who generally "act according to [Vedic] instruction" *(siṣṭācāra).* According to the Dharmaśāstras, such people should be virtuous, learned, slow to anger, free of jealousy, contented, modest, and so on.

"Conscience." The *Laws of Manu* and other Dharmaśāstras teach, finally, that when these three sources of *dharma* fail to enlighten an ethically perplexed person, then he or she has recourse to what is described as "that which satisfies the self" (*ātmanas tuṣṭir; Laws of Manu* 2.6) or "that which pleases the self" (*priyam ātmanaḥ; Laws of Manu* 2.12). The vagaries of this category, however, are such that in legal terms personal feelings carry relatively little weight and are always superseded by *śrūti, smṛti,* and *sadācāra.*

[*For further discussion of* svadharma, *see* Indian Religions, *article on* Mythic Themes. *Many of the Hindu texts mentioned in this article are the subjects of independent entries.*]

BIBLIOGRAPHY

Translations of Representative Primary Texts

Bühler, Georg, trans. *The Sacred Laws of the Āryas.* Sacred Books of the East, vol. 2 (Āpastambha and Gautama Dharmasūtras) and vol. 14 (Baudhāyana and Vasiṣṭha Dharmasūtras), edited by F. Max Müller. Oxford, 1879 and 1882.

Bühler, Georg, trans. *The Laws of Manu* (1886). Sacred Books of the East, vol. 25. Reprint, Delhi, 1964.

Edgerton, Franklin, trans. *Bhagavad-Gītā* (1925). Reprint, Oxford, 1944.

Eggeling, Julius, trans. and ed. *The Śatapatha-Brāhmaṇa.* 5 vols. Sacred Books of the East, vols. 12, 26, 41, 43, 44. Oxford, 1882–1900.

Ghārpure, J. R., trans. *Hindu Law Texts: Yājñavalkya Smṛti, with Commentaries by Vijñāneśvara, Mitra-miśra and Śūlapāṇi.* 7 vols. Bombay, 1936–1942.

Jolly, Julius, trans. *The Institutes of Viṣṇu* (1880). Sacred Books of the East, vol. 7. Reprint, Delhi, 1962. A translation of the *Viṣṇu Dharmasūtra.*

Jolly, Julius, trans. *The Minor Law Books* (1889). Sacred Books of the East, vol. 33. Reprint, Delhi, 1965. A translation of the *Bṛhaspati* and *Nārada Dharmaśāstras.*

Kane, P. V., ed. and trans. *Kātyāyana Dharmasastra.* Poona, 1933.

Keith, Arthur Berriedale, trans. *Rigveda Brāhmaṇas: The Aitareya and Kauṣītakī Brāhmaṇas of the Rigveda* (1920). Harvard Oriental Series, vol. 25. Reprint, Delhi, 1971.

O'Flaherty, Wendy Doniger, ed. and trans. *The Rig Veda: An Anthology.* Harmondsworth, 1982.

Whitney, William Dwight, trans. *Atharva-Veda Saṃhitā.* 2 vols. (1905). Harvard Oriental Series, vols. 7 and 8. Reprint, Delhi, 1962.

Introductions and Critical Studies

Aiyangar, K. V. Rangaswami. *Some Aspects of the Hindu View of Life according to Dharmaśāstra.* Baroda, 1952.

Jayaswal, K. P. *Manu and Yājñavalkya: A Comparison and a Contrast; A Treatise on the Basic Hindu Law.* Calcutta, 1930.

Jolly, Julius. *Recht und Sitte.* Strassburg, 1896. Translated by Batakrishna Ghosh as *Hindu Law and Custom* (1928; reprint, Varanasi, 1975).

Kane, P. V. *History of Dharmaśāstra.* 2d ed. 5 vols. in 7. Poona, 1968–1975.

Lingat, Robert. *Les sources du droit dans le système traditionnel de l'Inde.* Paris, 1967. Translated by J. Duncan M. Derrett as *The Classical Law of India* (Berkeley, 1973).

Mees, Gualtherus H. *Dharma and Society.* The Hague, 1935.

O'Flaherty, Wendy Doniger, and J. Duncan M. Derrett. *The Concept of Duty in South Asia.* New Delhi, 1978.

Sen Gupta, Nares Chandra. *Sources of Law and Society in Ancient India.* Calcutta, 1914.

For a more extensive bibliography, see Ludo Rocher's "Droit hindou ancien," vol. E, part 6 of *Bibliographical Introduction to Legal History and Ethnology*, edited by John Gilissen (Brussels, 1965).

WILLIAM K. MAHONY

Buddhist Dharma and Dharmas

The pan-Indian term *dharma* (from the Sanskrit root *dhṛ,* "to sustain, to hold"; Pali, *dhamma;* Tib., *chos*) has acquired a variety of meanings and interpretations in the course of many centuries of Indian religious thought. Buddhism shares this term and some of its meanings with other Indian religions, but at the same time it has provided a set of unique and exclusive interpretations of its own. *Dharma* can imply many different meanings in various contexts and with reference to different things. Here we shall consider it under two general headings: the first as *dharma* in a general sense, comprising a variety of meanings, and the second as *dharma*(s) in a technical sense, denoting the ultimate constituents or elements of the whole of the existing reality.

General Usages. *Dharma* was and still is employed by all the religious denominations that have originated in India to indicate their religious beliefs and practices. In this sense, *dharma* refers broadly to what we would term "religion." *Dharma* also designates the universal order, the natural law or the uniform norm according to which the whole world *(saṃsāra)* runs its course. Within the Buddhist context this universal order is coordinated in the doctrine of dependent origination *(pratītya-samutpāda).* This rigorous natural law, which controls the sequence of events and the behavior and acts of beings, has no cause or originator. It is beginningless and functions of its own nature. It is said in the *Aṅguttara Nikāya* and the *Saṃyutta Nikāya,* and later rephrased in the *Laṅkāvatāra Sūtra,* that the nature of things is such that the causal law as the inevitable determination of *karman* continues to evolve spontaneously whether or not the *tathāgatas* appear in this world. It is an inherent and all-pervading law that does not depend for its existence on the appearance of the Buddhas, whose mission in this world is merely to reveal it. Śākyamuni Buddha first perceived and understood this fundamental law and then proclaimed and explained it to his followers. The discovery of the nature of *dharma* is compared in some *sūtras* to the discovery of an old and forgotten city. In the Mahāyāna, especially within the context of the doctrine of the three Buddha bodies *(trikāya)* and the reinterpretation of the relationship between *saṃsāra* and *nirvāṇa* as two aspects of the same reality, *dharma* as the universal norm received a wider and deeper interpretation. As a part of the compound *dharmakāya,* it signifies both the immanent and transcendental reality of all beings and appearances. Thus, it clearly denotes the essence of sentient beings as well as the nature of the Buddhas. In the sense of denoting phenomenal existence, it is also referred to as reality *(dharmatā)*, the essence of reality *(dharmadhātu)*, suchness *(tathatā)*, emptiness *(śūnyatā)*, or store-consciousness *(ālaya-vijñāna)*. In the sense of referring to the nature of the Buddhas, it is known as Buddhahood *(buddhatā)*, as the self-nature of the Buddhas *(buddhasvabhāva)*, or as the womb of the Buddhas *(tathāgata-garbha)*.

Dharma as the Buddha's teaching or doctrine as a whole comprises his exposition of the universal order of nature as described above and his proclamation of the path toward deliverance. Thus, when his teaching is meant as a whole system it is the term *dharma* (or *śāsana*) that is employed. When his teachings are referred to or explained from two different angles, that is, when theoretical and practical aspects are differentiated, two terms are employed: *dharma*, as a body of religio-philosophical discourses as contained in the Sūtras, and Vinaya, or monastic discipline, the rules and regulations for the application and practice of *dharma*. The Prātimokṣa (monastic code) contains rules of conduct, each of which is also called *dharma*.

The shortest and yet the clearest exposition of *dharma* as the Buddha's word *(buddhavacana)* is epitomized in Śākyamuni's first sermon, when he "set in motion" (i.e., proclaimed) the wheel (lore) of *dharma:* the Four Noble Truths and Eightfold Noble Path. There is suffering and it has a cause that can be eliminated through the knowledge and practice of the path of *dharma* as summarized by the Eightfold Noble Path: right views, right conduct, and so forth. Another presentation of the same path is articulated within the basic trilogy of monastic practice of cultivating wisdom *(prajñā)*, morality *(śīla)*, and meditation *(dhyāna)*. Through wisdom one acquires a full vision of *dharma*, through morality one purifies all that obscures the vision of *dharma*, and through meditation one matures *dharma* within oneself and indeed transforms oneself into an epitome of *dharma*. [*See also* Four Noble Truths.]

Dharma denotes truth, knowledge, morality, and duty. It is the truth about the state and function of the world, the truth about how to eliminate its evil tendencies, and the truth about its immutable spiritual potentiality. It is knowledge in the sense that once one becomes aware of *dharma* one acquires the knowledge to become free from the bonds of phenomenal existence. It is morality, for it contains a code of moral conduct that conduces to spiritual purification and maturation. It is duty, for whoever professes *dharma* has a duty to comply with its norms and to achieve the goal that it sets forth. In this sense there is only one duty in Buddhism: the ceaseless and constant effort to strive for *nirvāṇa*.

Dharma, together with the Buddha and the *saṃgha*, constitute a "threefold jewel" *(triratna)* before which one makes prostrations and in which one takes refuge. Here *dharma* does not so much represent a body of teachings as it assumes a character of awesomeness, protection, and deliverance wholly appropriate to the Truth. One stands in awe of *dharma* as a self-sustained righteousness whose universal legacy is to protect through its righteousness those who profess it. Soon after his enlightenment, realizing that there is no one more perfect than himself in virtue, wisdom, and meditation under whom he could live in obedience and reverence, Sākyamuni decided that he would live honoring and revering *dharma*, the universal truth he had just realized. As one of the Three Jewels, the Buddha is *dharma*'s embodied personification, revealer, and teacher. The *saṃgha* constitutes a body of *dharma*'s followers among whom *dharma* thrives as the norm of daily life, becoming an inspiration and a path to deliverance. The Three Jewels as conceived in the early period can be paralleled, as a somewhat general comparison, with the later concept of the three Buddha bodies. *Dharma* as *dharmakāya* represents its own sublime and absolute aspect, the Buddha as a *saṃbhogakāya* represents the pure and glorified state of *dharma*, and the *saṃgha* as *nirmāṇakāya* represents *dharma* as discovered and operating within the world.

Technical Usages. The strictly technical meaning of *dharma*s as ultimate elements or principles of existence as systematized in the Abhidharma literature, especially in the Abhidharma works of the Sarvāstivāda school, is not so distinct or rigidly formulated in the four Nikāyas (Āgamas). In the *sūtra*s of the four Nikāyas we find many descriptions of *dharma*s and their various classifications, but their systematization into what we could call "*dharma* theory" took place within the Abhidharma literature. Thus, in the Nikāyas *dharma*s are usually characterized as good or bad with reference to ethical conduct, but receive little attention as coherent metaphysical or epistemological systems. The *Dasuttara Sutta* enumerates some 550 *dharma*s to be cultivated or abandoned. The *Saṅgīti Sutta* gives an even larger number of them, and the *Mahāparinibbāna Suttanta* lists some 1,011 *dharma*s. In this latter work we also find a set of *dharma*s that Śākyamuni ascertained to be for the benefit of living beings. These include the thirty-seven *bodhipakṣya dharma*s that constitute the thirty-seven practices and principles conducive to the attainment of enlightenment.

Rather than providing further examples from the *sūtras* I propose now to concentrate on describing the *dharma* theory of the Sarvāstivāda school. Within its systematized presentation one finds practically all the important aspects of *dharmas* and their role; the variant interpretations of other schools will be mentioned wherever appropriate.

Buddhism makes an emphatic and "dogmatic" statement that a "soul" *(ātman)* as interpreted by non-Buddhist schools in India does not exist. By denying the existence of a soul as a permanent and unifying factor of a human entity it has removed all grounds for asserting the permanency of the human entity or the existence of any indestructible element therein. With reference to the substantiality of physical things it has removed the concept of substance and replaced it by modalities: there is no substance but only the appearances of what we call substances or things. Having removed the notion of substance Buddhism has construed an explanation as to how this world functions. According to this explanation, the universe is seen as a flux of *dharmas*, the smallest elements or principles of which it consists, but this flux is not merely a flux of incoherent motion or change. On the contrary, the world evolves according to the strict law of dependent origination *(pratītya-samutpāda)*.

This universal flux can be conveniently viewed, for the moment, at three simultaneous and interrelated levels. If we take the inanimate world (matter) alone, it flows in accordance with a uniformly homogeneous and natural law of change. Similarly, the organic world (vegetation) flows according to its own uniform evolution of natural life (germination, growth, etc.). The third level is constituted by sentient life. This last one, apart from comprehending the other levels (matter and organic functions), includes a sentient element (consciousness or mind) as well. In general, we can say that it includes material as well as immaterial elements. Such sentient life, in which the material and immaterial elements are tied together, evolves or flows according to the strict law of causality as decreed in the causal nexus of dependent origination. Furthermore, this constant flux of sentient life coordinated by the law of dependent origination has a moral law superimposed upon it: the "law" of *karman*. It is with regard to such a flux that the *dharma* theory attempts to provide an explanation. There is no substance or person but there are *dharmas* (psychophysical elements) that flow according to the law of dependent origination that is set in motion by the law of *karman*. Basically, the *dharma* theory provides an explanation of how the universe functions within the context of a sentient life, in particular a human flux, for it is human life that Buddhism is concerned with. *Dharma* theory constitutes then not so much an explanation of what the universe is as it does an attempt to describe of what it consists and how it functions. Thus, in the detailed enumeration of *dharmas* as basic and infinitesimal elements that constitute the conglomeration of the universe we find an analysis of human life and its destiny. But this analysis is not "Buddhist psychology," as many call it; it is an exposition of both the constant and inevitably coordinated flux of phenomena and the inherent potentiality of bringing this flux to a halt.

I shall now describe some general classifications of *dharmas* (again, after the Sarvāstivāda Abhidharma). *Dharmas* are divided into conditioned *(saṃskṛta)* and unconditioned *(asaṃskṛta)*. The conditioned *dharmas* (seventy-two in all) comprise all the elements of phenomenal existence *(saṃsāra)*. They are called conditioned because by their nature and in their flow they cooperate in and are subject to the law of causality; they conglomerate or cooperate in the production of life *(pṛthagjana)*. The unconditioned elements (three in all) are those that are not subject to the law that governs phenomenal existence. *Dharmas* are also divided into those that are influenced or permeated by negative tendencies or depravities *(āsrava;* in a moral sense, bad *karmas*) and those that are not under the influence of depravities (*anāsrava;* morally, good *karmas*). These are the same *dharmas* as in the previous classification but here they are viewed from two aspects: when they are influenced chiefly by ignorance *(avidyā)* their flux has the tendency to perpetuate itself; when they are under the influence of intuitive wisdom *(prajñā)* they acquire the tendency toward appeasement or tranquillity. By their nature the unconditioned *dharmas* must be classed among the *dharmas* that are not under the influence of depravities. We should recall here that the chief characteristic of *saṃsāra* is motion or unrest, *duḥkha*, and that of *nirvāṇa* is tranquillity, *nirodha*. The *dharmas* can be also divided in relationship to the Four Truths. Here again we have a twofold division. The first two truths (unrest, *duḥkha*, and its cause, *samudaya*) refer to the seventy-two *dharmas* that are permeated by depravities or that are conditioned. The two other truths (rest, *nirodha*, and the means to it, *mārga*) refer to the three unconditioned *dharmas* that are always at rest *(nirodha)* and to the *dharmas* that are on the way *(mārga)* to become extinguished *(nirodha)*.

Having described the general divisions I shall now proceed to list a set of three standard classifications within which individual *dharmas* are distributed. The first classification, which includes the conditioned *dharmas* alone, refers to their grouping as perceived in a sentient life. This classification divides *dharmas* into five aggregates or *skandhas*. Here we have (1) matter or body *(rūpaskandha):* eleven *dharmas*; (2) feelings, sensations, or emotions *(vedanāskandha):* one *dharma;* (3) perceptions *(saṃjñāskandha):* one *dharma;* (4) impulses or will-forces *(saṃskāraskandha):* fifty-eight *dharmas;* (5) consciousness or mind *(vijñānaskandha):* one *dharma.* This division into five *skandhas* not only constitutes an analysis of all phenomena but also serves to prove that there is no soul *(ātman)* in a human entity, for none of the five *skandhas* can be identified with or regarded as a soul.

The second classification divides *dharmas* with reference to the process of cognition. Here we have the six sense organs *(indriya)* and the six sense objects *(viṣaya)* jointy called the "bases" or "foundations" *(āyatana)* of cognition. The six sense organs or internal bases are (1) sense of vision *(cakṣur-indriyāyatana);* (2) sense of hearing *(śrotra-);* (3) sense of smell *(ghrāṇa-);* (4) sense of taste *(jihvā-);* (5) sense of touch *(kāya-);* and (6) consciousness or intellectual faculty *(mana-).* The six sense objects or external bases are (7) color and form *(rūpa-āyatana);* (8) sound *(śabda-);* (9) smell *(gandha-);* (10) taste *(rasa-);* (11) contact *(spraṣṭavya-);* and (12) nonsensuous or immaterial objects *(dharma-).* The first eleven *āyatanas* have one *dharma* each; the immaterial objects comprise sixty-four *dharmas.*

The third classification groups *dharmas* in relationship to the flow *(santāna)* of life that evolves within the threefold world (*kāma-, rūpa-,* and *ārūpya-dhātu*) as described by Buddhist cosmology. This group is divided into eighteen *dhātus,* or elements. It incorporates the previous division into the twelve bases, to which is added a corresponding set of six kinds of consciousness to the intellectual faculty. Thus we have (13) visual consciousness *(cakṣur-vijñānadhātu);* (14) auditory consciousness *(śrotra-);* (15) olfactory consciousness *(ghrāṇa-);* (16) gustatory consciousness *(jihvā-);* (17) tactile consciousness *(kāya-);* and (18) nonsensuous consciousness *(mano-).* Within this group the five sense organs and their five objects contain one *dharma* each (ten *dharmas* in all). Consciousness (no. 6) is divided here into seven *dhātus* (no. 6 plus 13–18). The *dhātu* that represents immaterial objects (no. 12) contains sixty-four *dharmas.* All the eighteen *dhātus* exist in the sensuous world *(kāmadhātu)* or the world in which the mind operates through the sense data. In the world of refined matter *(rūpadhātu),* the objects of smell and taste (nos. 9–10) and the olfactory and gustatory consciousnesses cease to exist. In the world without matter (but frequently interpreted as very subtle matter for we are still within *saṃsāra*) all the *dhātus* cease to exist except for consciousness (no. 6), its immaterial objects (no. 12), and its nonsensuous aspect of cognition (no. 18). (See table 1.)

Now at last we come to enumerate the individual *dharmas.* Within the classification into the five *skandhas,* matter *(rūpa)* contains eleven *dharmas:* five sense organs (*āyatanas* 1–5) and their five corresponding sense objects (*āyatanas* 7–11), plus an additional element to be discussed below. *Āyatana (dhātu)* number 12 (nonsensuous objects) is in this system classified as an immaterial *dharma,* as we shall see, and hence is not considered here.

Matter or body is conceived as consisting of the four primary elements (*mahābhūtas*)—earth, water, fire, and air. Secondary or refined matter (*bhautika,* derived from or related to matter) is represented by the senses and their objects (i.e., sense data). As already mentioned above, there is no substance as such. The four primary elements are talked about in Buddhism, but rightly understood these are taken to refer to properties: hardness (earth), cohesion (water), heat (fire), and motion (wind).

TABLE 1. *The Twelve Āyatanas and the Eighteen Dhātus*

BASES OF COGNITION *(āyatana)*		CONSCIOUSNESS *(vijñāna)*
Receptive Faculties *(indriya)*	Objects *(viṣaya)*	
1. Sense of vision *cakṣur-indriyāyatana**	7. Color and form *rūpa-āyatana*	13. Visual consciousness *cakṣur-vijñānadhātu*
2. Sense of hearing *śrotra-*	8. Sound *śabda-*	14. Auditory consciousness *śrotra-*
3. Sense of smell *ghrāṇa-*	9. Smell *gandha-*	15. Olfactory consciousness *ghrāṇa-*
4. Sense of taste *jihvā-*	10. Taste *rasa-*	16. Gustatory consciousness *jihvā-*
5. Sense of touch *kāya-*	11. Contact, tangibles *spraṣṭavya-*	17. Tactile consciousness *kāya-*
6. Intellect *mana-*	12. Nonsensuous objects *dharma-*	18. Nonsensuous consciousness *mano-*

*When the *āyatanas* are enumerated as *dhātus* they are termed *cakṣur-dhātu, śrotra-dhātu,* etc.

The primary matter (four elements) present in a body sustains the secondary matter (the senses and their objects). Since the Buddhists analyze matter within the context of a sentient life, their description of matter is mainly concerned with discerning how it functions and how it appears, not with what it is, for properly speaking it does not exist. The world is in constant flux, the living life changes from one moment to the next. Consequently, because Buddhists are constrained from speaking in terms of soul or substance, matter is styled as sense data alone. Such a definition of the physical *dharmas* that constitute the sense data (ten *dharmas*) accounts for the component of matter that sustains consciousness, the other component of sentient life. What then is the eleventh *dharma*?

The Sarvāstivāda, viewing the human personality as a threefold aspect of body, speech, and mind, divided *karman* (as it operates within a sentient life) into mental action (*manas*, identified with volition, or *cetanā*) and physical and vocal actions. Mental action was classed as immaterial but physical and vocal actions that proceed from mental action were classed as belonging to matter *(rūpaskandha)*. Furthermore, physical and vocal action was seen as being an (external) "expression" *(vijñapti)*, but when mental action was committed but not externalized its "material" concomitant was seen as "nonexpression" *(avijñapti)*. It is the latter "unexpressed matter" *(avijñaptirūpa)* that constitutes the eleventh *dharma* among the *skandha* division. Although immaterial, it was classed as matter because physical and vocal action with which it was associated was classed as such.

Three *skandhas* (feelings, perceptions, and impulses) contain jointly sixty *dharmas*, which are included as immaterial objects within the two other *(āyatana, dhātu)* classifications (no. 12 in both). The three immutable elements *(asaṃskṛta)* and *avijñapti* are also included among the immaterial *dharmas* of these two latter divisions, thus making a total of sixty-four *dharmas*.

Now I shall describe the sixty *dharmas* that are included in all three classifications *(skandha, āyatana,* and *dhātu)*. They are divided into two main groups: one group comprises forty-six associated *dharmas* or mental *dharmas (caittadharma)*, that arise from or in association with pure consciousness or mind *(citta-saṃprayuktasaṃskāra)*; the second group comprises fourteen unassociated *dharmas*, that is to say, *dharmas* that can be associated neither with matter nor with mind *(rūpa-citta-viprayukta-saṃskāra)*.

The forty-six associated *dharmas* include ten mental *dharmas* that are present in a sentient life *(citta-mahābhūmika)*: (1) feeling, (2) perception, (3) will, (4) contact, (5) desire, (6) comprehension, (7) memory, (8) attention, (9) aspiration, and (10) concentration; ten morally good *(kuśala-mahābhūmika) dharmas* that are present in favorable conditions: (11) faith, (12) courage, (13) equanimity, (14) modesty, (15) aversion to evil, (16) detachment from love, (17) detachment from hatred, (18) nonviolence, (19) dexterity, and (20) perseverence in good; six obscuring *(kleśa-mahābhūmika) dharmas* that enter the stream of a sentient life in unfavorable moments: (21) confusion (ignorance), (22) remissness, (23) mental dullness, (24) lack of faith, (25) indolence, and (26) addiction to pleasure; ten additional obscuring *(upakleśa-bhūmika) dharmas* that may occur at different times: (27) anger, (28) hypocrisy, (29) maliciousness, (30) envy, (31) ill-motivated rivalry, (32) violence, (33) malice, (34) deceit, (35) treachery, and (36) self-gratification; two universally inauspicious *(akuśala-mahabhūmika) dharmas*: (37) irreverence, and (38) willful tolerance of offences; and eight *dharmas* that are called undetermined *(aniyata-bhūmika)* or undifferentiated in the sense that they can have different moral implications: (39) remorse, (40) deliberation, (41) investigation, (42) determination, (43) passion, (44) hatred, (45) pride, and (46) doubt. All forty-six *dharmas* listed above cannot be associated with (or cofunction with) consciousness at the same time on the general principle that their inner inclinations are variously geared toward either good or evil.

The fourteen unassociated *dharmas* are (47) acquisition *(prāpti)*, or the controlling force of an individual flux of life, (48) force *(aprāpti)* that suspends some elements, (49) force of homogeneity of existence, (50) force that leads to trance, (51) force produced by effort to enter trance, (52) force that stops consciousness, thus effecting the highest trance, (53) force that projects life's duration, (54) origination, (55) duration, (56) decay, (57) extinction, (58) force that imparts meaning to words, (59) force that imparts meaning to sentences, and (60) force that imparts meaning to sounds.

Pure consciousness or mind constitutes one *dharma* (fifth *skandha*, sixth *āyatana*). In the division into *dhātus vijñāna* is, as it were, subdivided among seven *dhātus* (no. 6 plus 13–18) where the same consciousness is viewed in relation to the sense organs and immaterial objects.

Adding all the conditioned *dharmas* together yields eleven material *dharmas*, one *dharma* representing consciousness, forty-six associated *dharmas*, and fourteen unassociated *dharmas*—seventy-two in all. These are the *dharmas* into which the whole of phenomenal existence is analyzed and which account for all events that take place within it.

The Sarvāstivāda also enumerate three unconditioned *dharmas*: space *(ākāśa)*, emancipation through discerning knowledge *(pratisaṃkhyānirodha)*, and emancipation through nondiscerning knowledge *(apratisaṃkhyānirodha)*. Thus, the total of *dharmas* both conditioned and unconditioned amounts to seventy-five in the Sarvāstivāda school. (See figure 1.)

The Theravāda tradition enumerates only one unconditioned *dharma (nirvāṇa)* and eighty-one conditioned *dharmas*: four primary elements; four secondary elements; five sense organs; five sense objects; two aspects of sex (male and female); heart as the sustaining element of psychic life; two kinds (bodily and vocal) of *avijñaptirūpa;* a psychic vitality of matter; space; three properties (agility, elasticity, and pliability) of body; three characteristics (origination, duration, and decay) of conditioned *dharmas*; material food; fifty-two mental elements, including twenty-five wholesome, fourteen unwholesome, and thirteen morally neutral elements; and consciousness.

The Sarvāstivāda asserted that all the conditioned *dharmas* are real (they exist for they happen) and that they have the characteristic of coming into existence, lasting for a short period, and disappearing again in order to reappear in a new karmically determined formation. They also maintained that *dharmas* exist in all three times: past, present, and future.

The Lokottaravāda school, a Mahāsāṃghika subsect, treated all the conditioned *dharmas* as unreal and held that only the unconditioned *dharmas* are real. The Prajñaptivāda school, another Mahāsāṃghika group, argued that the twelve *āyatanas* are not real because they are the products of the *skandhas*, which are the only real entities. The Sautrāntikas admitted the existence of thought but rejected the reality of the majority of the associated and all the unassociated *dharmas*, denied the reality of the past and future, and maintained that only the present exists. They also rejected the existence of the unconditioned *dharmas*, considering them mere denominations of absence. The Mādhyamika school rejected the ultimate reality of *dharmas* altogether. The Vijñānavāda school recognized mind as the only reality *(cittamātra)* and treated the whole of phenomenal existence as its illusive projection. [*See* Mā-

FIGURE 1. *Correspondences among Three Dharma Classifications*

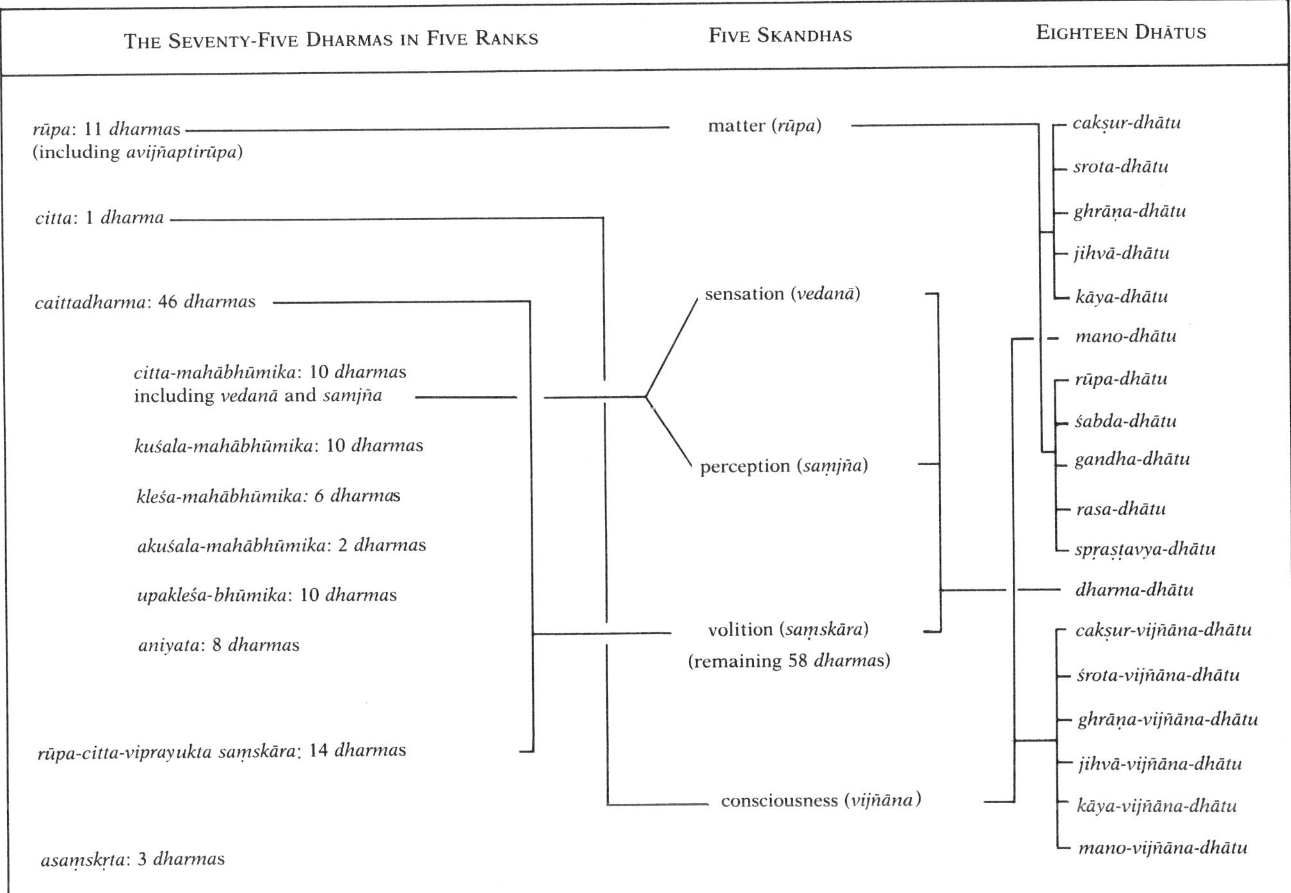

dhyamika *and* Yogācāra.] Finally, a well-known Buddhist formula (*ye dharmā hetuprabhavā*, etc.) expresses the soteriological aspect associated with the analysis of sentient beings in terms of *dharmas*: "Whatever events arise from a cause, the Tathāgata has foretold their cause, and the Great Hermit has also explained their cessation."

[*For further discussion of the Buddhist notion of the person, see* Buddhist Philosophy; Soul, *article on* Buddhist Concepts; Karman, *article on* Buddhist Concepts; *and* Pratītya-samutpāda. *Abhidharma analysis is treated in* Nirvāṇa *and in* Soteriology, *article on* Buddhist Soteriology. *See also* Sarvāstivāda *and* Sautrāntika *for two conflicting views of* dharmas. *For a discussion of* dharma *as truth or law, see also* Cosmic Law.]

BIBLIOGRAPHY

The *dharma* theory of the Sarvāstivādins is systematically set forth in Vasubandhu's *Abhidharmakośa*, translated by Louis de La Vallée Poussin as *L'Abhidharmakośa de Vasubandhu*, 6 vols. (1923–1931; reprint, Brussels, 1971). Theodore Stcherbatsky's *The Central Conception of Buddhism and the Meaning of the Word "Dharma"* (1923; reprint, Delhi, 1970) is a lucid introduction to the topic. For the Theravāda view, see especially *A Buddhist Manual of Psychological Ethics: Dhammasangaṇi*, translated by C. A. F. Rhys Davids (London, 1923), a rendering of the first book of the Theravāda Abhidharma. Ñyāṇatiloka's *Guide through the Abhidhamma Pitaka*, 3d ed., revised and enlarged by Ñyāṇaponika Thera (Colombo, 1957), is the single most useful guide to the study of the Theravāda Abhidhamma. The reader will also find useful A. K. Warder's "Dharmas and Data," *Journal of Indian Philosophy* 1 (1971): 272–295.

TADEUSZ SKORUPSKI

DHARMAKĪRTI (c. 600–660), Buddhist philosopher of South Indian origin, pupil of Īśvarasena, and teacher at Nālandā. Dharmakīrti's thought brings the tradition of Buddhist epistemology and logic as founded by Dignāga (c. 480–540) to its culmination and final accomplishment.

Dharmakīrti's philosophical work consists of seven treatises still extant either in the original Sanskrit or in Tibetan translation. Dharmakīrti's stated intention was to give an explanation of Dignāga's ideas, and tradition accepted his explanation as such. His works, however, surpassed those of the earlier philosopher to become the basis for the study of this tradition by later Indian and Tibetan Buddhists. His first major work, *Pramāṇavārttika* (Commentary on the Means of Valid Cognition), is a verse text in four chapters. The first chapter, "On Inference," was written with a prose commentary, thus constituting his earliest work, and was only later joined with the other chapters, "Establishment of the Means of Valid Cognition," "On Perception," and "On Proof." The *Pramāṇaviniścaya* (Analytical Determination of the Means of Valid Cognition), contains chapters on perception, on inference, and on proof, and is the final formulation of Dharmakīrti's epistemological and logical thought in mixed verse and prose. For its clarity in structure, presentation, argument, and verbal expression, it is a masterpiece of Indian scholarly literature. In what is largely an excerpt of the latter work, the *Nyāyabindu* (A Drop of Logical Argumentation), Dharmakīrti gives a succinct *sūtra*-like formulation of his epistemology.

The *Hetubindu* (A Drop of Logical Reason) examines logical reason, negative cognition, and causality. The *Vādanyāya* (The Rule for Disputations), his last work, attempts to apply the new logical theory to the dialectical practice. Dharmakīrti refuted solipsism in his *Santānāntarasiddhi* (A Proof of Other Mental Continuities) and rejected the reality of relations in *Sambandhaparīkṣā* (Examination of Relation).

Most of Dharmakīrti's thought is devoted to epistemological and logical themes. In its context, this must be understood as an attempt to establish a philosophical foundation of meaningful everyday and Buddhist practice. For Dharmakīrti, valid cognitions can be established only with regard to the Buddha, who—himself a means of valid cognition—can provide the motifs and goals of all human actions that are the frame of judgment necessary to differentiate the validity or invalidity of cognitions. At the same time, perception and inference, the two kinds of valid cognition, can be used to demonstrate that the Buddha is the only conceivable source from which we can derive such advice.

In the field of logic, Dharmakīrti overcomes the formal character of Dignāga's theory, in which only three forms or characteristics of logical reason are formulated as the necessary conditions of logical certainty, by giving an ontological explanation for such certainty. According to this explanation, concepts are related to each other only when they refer to the same real entity or to an entity caused by that referred to by the other concept. The necessary logical relation is thus based on a relation of real identity or of causality. Consequently, only such concepts may be used as logical reasons *(hetu)* that are either "essential properties" *(svabhāva)*, "effect" *(kārya)*, that is, concepts referring to something as the effect of something else, or "non-perception of something perceivable" *(dṛśyānupalabdhi)*.

Dharmakīrti's theory of concepts *(apoha)* explains a concept as the difference from other things that is common to individual entities. Lacking any principle of unity, absolutely different individual entities nonetheless cause the same judgments precisely on account of such experience of them that differs from experience of others. The resultant concept is nothing real, but by recourse to experience and practice there is nevertheless a relation between reality and the false realm of linguistic constructs of varying degrees of reliability. While perception is a direct valid cognition of what is real, inference is an indirect valid cognition, since it is conceptual by nature and must be gained under strict control by means of logical reason *(hetu)*. Concepts that may be used as logical reasons serve to infer other concepts as necessarily true or to remove or correct wrong concepts. One of the most influential results of this new logical theory is a new form of the inference of universal momentary destruction *(kṣaṇikatva)* in which Dharmakīrti derives it from the concept of being *(sattvānumāna)*, thereby offering a new method for establishing the first of the Four Noble Truths, "All is suffering."

[*See also* Buddhist Philosophy.]

BIBLIOGRAPHY

Stcherbatsky, Theodore. *Buddhist Logic* (1930–1932). Reprint, New York, 1962. An introduction to Buddhist logic, including many references to Dharmakīrti.

Steinkellner, Ernst, trans. *Dharmakīrti's Hetubinduḥ*, vol. 2. Vienna, 1967. German translation of the first Indian text on logic as such, including the important proof of momentariness as the essential character of being; also contains an elaborate discussion of causality and a theory of negative cognition.

Steinkellner, Ernst, trans. *Dharmakīrti's Pramāṇaviniścayaḥ*, vol. 2. *Kapitel: Svārthānumānam*. Vienna, 1979. A German translation of the chapter on inference that constitutes the essence of Dharmakīrti's logical thought.

Vetter, Tilmann. *Erkenntnisprobleme bei Dharmakīrti*. Vienna, 1964. A study of Dharmakīrti's theories of cognition, concepts, perception, and being.

Vetter, Tilmann, trans. *Dharmakīrti's Pramāṇaviniścayaḥ*, vol. 1, *Kapitel: Pratyakṣam*. Vienna, 1966. Text and German translation of the chapter on perception, with an investigation of congition in general and the problem of extra-cognitional reality.

Vetter, Tilmann, trans. *Die Lehre des Buddha in Dharmakīrti's Pramāṇavārttika*. Vienna, 1984. German translation of a major part of the second chapter of the *Pramāṇavārttika*. Includes an introductory study of Dharmakīrti's presentation of the essence of Buddhist interpretation of reality and religious practice, providing the motifs, conditions, and purpose of epistemological theory.

ERNST STEINKELLNER

DHARMAPĀLA (530–561), Indian Buddhist thinker associated with the Yogācāra school and founder of a Vijñānavāda ("consciousness only") tradition that was to become highly influential in the scholastic traditions of East Asian Buddhism. His numerous followers include Śīlabhadra, his successor as abbot of Nālandā and teacher of the famous Chinese monk Hsüan-tsang (569–664). It was Hsüan-tsang who introduced Dharmapāla's thought to China, where, under the name of Fa-hsiang ("*dharma* characteristics"), it supplanted the traditions transmitted by Paramārtha (499–569) and Bodhiruci (d. 527) to become the dominant form of Yogācāra there. The Fa-hsiang "school" was introduced to Japan beginning in the late seventh century by the monk Dōshō (629–710), enjoyed three subsequent transmissions, and, as the Hossō school (the Japanese pronunciation of the Chinese *Fa-hsiang*), became perhaps the most eminent of the six scholastic traditions that flouished during the Nara period (710–784).

The eldest son of a minister in Kāñcīpuram, Dharmapāla became a Buddhist monk in his youth. He studied Buddhism at the Nālandā monastic university and later became its head. In several doctrinal debates Dharmapāla defeated philosophers representing both non-Buddhist and Buddhist (especially Hīnayāna) opinion. At twenty-nine, however, realizing that he was not destined to live long, he retired from his post at Nālandā to concentrate on writing. He died two years later. Despite the relative brevity of his career, Dharmapāla wrote a number of works, some of which are preserved in the Chinese canon. These include the *Kuan-so-yüan lun-shih* (T.D. No. 1625), the *Ch'eng wei-shih lun* (T.D. no. 1585), and the *Ta-sheng-kuang po-lun shih-lun* (T.D. no. 1571). The second of these, Hsüan-tsang's translation of the *Vijñāptimātratāsiddhi*, a compilation of ten commentaries on Vasubandhu's *Triṃśika* (Thirty Verses), includes a commentary by Dharmapāla's own hand. More than a mere gloss of the original text of Vasubandhu, however, Dharmarpāla's commentary constitutes an original doctrinal treatise in its own right.

Unlike the Mādhyamika thinkers, who concentrated on the refutation of fallacies without explaining how the magic (i.e., the illusion, in Buddhist terms) of "self" should arise in every living being, Dharmapāla offered an intricate analysis of this process from the Yogācāra point of view. This analysis begins with an interpretation of causality, or "dependent co-origination" *(pratītya-samutpāda)*: every action creates a pattern or potential for future action, just as in legal cases a single decision becomes a precedent for the future. The precedents, karmic residues in this case, are technically referred to as "seeds" *(bīja)*, which are "deposited," as it were, in a "receptacle" or "store" consciousness, from which, under the proper conditions, they manifest themselves at some future time. The process by which actions "deposit" seeds in the subconscious is known as "impression" *(vāsanā);* the actualization of these seeds in the mental life of the being involved is known as "manifestation."

The accumulation of these numerous potentials suggests a division of labor between the storage function, the coordinating function, and the discriminating function. In Yogācāra thought, these functions represent concrete activities of different levels and types of consciousness, usually numbered eight in the system championed by Dharmapāla. The storage function is referred to as *ālaya-vijñāna* ("storehouse consciousness"). It is the *ālaya* that receives the *bījas* deposited by actions and as such functions as a karmic repository in which the continuity of past actions in the stream of an individual's lives is preserved. The coordinating function is called the "cognitive" center *(manas);* it serves to synchronize all the activities of mind so that they function as an integrated whole. It is the *manas* that, turning inward, fails to perceive that the *ālaya* essentially has no existence other than the seeds that it stores, and thus falsely imputes to the *ālaya* the permanence and unity of a self or *ātman.* Such a (false) belief in the existence of a self is traditionally regarded by Buddhists as the very source of suffering. Ordinary sentient beings (as opposed to Buddhas and very highly advanced *bodhisattvas*) are unaware of the actions of these two functions. *Ālaya* and *manas* thus constitute unconscious functions of mind.

The discriminating function is represented by the six types of consciousnesses of which we are all aware: the five senses and the thinking process itself *(mano-vijñāna).* These, like the *manas,* are ultimately the very creations, "evolutes," of the seeds stored in the *ālaya,* which manifest themselves under the proper causal conditions as our psychophysical "selves." What appears in consciousness, under this interpretation, is thus not an external reality but simply the products of previous actions and cognitions thrown into consciousness by the functioning of the *ālaya.* Thus the mind, which should be indivisible, is, in Dharmapāla's view, fundamentally fractured into subjective and objective components: that which is conscious and that which we are conscious of.

The interaction of the three functions, further complicated by the subject-object split, transforms the reality of the illusional existence of living beings. These functions are therefore referred to as the "three sources of transformation." What is usually called "self" is merely the "subject portion" of the *ālaya* as interpreted by the *manas.* Similarly, what is usually called the "external world" is the "object portion," a mere sense of externality. Whether or not there exists a world outside of consciousness is not at issue here: it is the sense of externality that obtains *within* consciousness that is the subject of Dharmapāla's analysis, for deliverance or enlightenment consists in realizing that the "self" and the "real" world are mere reifications, enforced in language, of consciousness.

Yogācāra analysis of reality, a term as ambiguous in Sanskrit as it is in English, thus must take into account the varying ways in which a thing may be construed as real. According to Yogācāra doctrine, a "triple nature" *(trisvabhāva)* is inherent in all things. First, there is the sense in which all things are mere constructs of mind, mental fabrications devoid of reality outside of the consciousness that creates them. This character of things is referred to as *parikalpita-lakṣaṇa* ("imaginary character"). Second, there is the sense in which things are dependently originated, devoid of any independent reality but "real" in the sense that they exist as part of a nexus of events that mutually condition and reinforce each other. This character of things is referred to as *paratantra-lakṣaṇa* ("dependent character"). Finally, things are characterized as "ultimately real" when viewed without the distortions of conceptualization. But what constitutes this "perfected character" *(pariniṣpanna-lakṣaṇa)* is precisely the "emptiness" *(śūnyatā)* of the thing, its *lack* of self-nature *(svabhāva)* or the "ultimate absence of a reality-in-its-own-right." Such a reality is also referred to as "suchness" *(tathatā).* [*See* Tathatā.]

Dharmapāla's *Vijñāptimātratāsiddhi* was the subject of at least three major commentaries (T.D. nos. 1830, 1831, 1832) and a host of subcommentaries. Although Fa-hsiang thought failed to survive the challenges posed by the creation of the new, more fully sinicized, Buddhist traditions of the T'ang period (618–907), its doctrines were kept alive in the wide dissemination of the commentaries to the *Ch'eng wei-shih lun.* In Japan, Hossō thought continues to this day to serve as part of the basic Buddhist training of scholars and clerics alike.

[*See also* Yogācāra; Ālaya-vijñana; *and the biographies of Vasubandhu, Paramārtha, Hsüan-tsang, and K'uei-chi.*]

BIBLIOGRAPHY

Fukaura Seibun. *Yuishikigaki kenkyū.* 2 vols. Kyoto, 1954.

Fukihara Akinobu. *Gohōshū yuishikikō.* Kyoto, 1954.

La Vallée Poussin, Louis de, ed. and trans. *Vijñāptimātratāsiddhi: La Siddhi de Hiuan-tsang.* 2 vols. Paris, 1928–1929.

Nakamura Hajime. "A Brief Survey of Japanese Studies on the Philosophical Schools of the Mahāyāna." *Acta Asiatica* 1 (1960); 67–88.

Radhakrishnan, Sarvepalli. *Indian Philosophy,* vol. 1. 2d ed. London, 1927. Dharmapāla's contributions to Buddhist thought are discussed in the chapter entitled "The Yogācāras."

Sharma, Chandradhar. *A Critical Survey of Indian Philosophy.* Livingston, N.J., 1971. For treatment of Dharmapāla, see chapters entitled "Vijñānavāda" and "Svatantra-Vijñānavāda."

Ueda, Yoshifumi. "Two Main Streams of Thought in Yogācāra Philosophy." *Philosophy East and West* 17 (1967): 155–165.

RICHARD S. Y. CHI

DHIKR (Arab., "remembrance, mention") is an important Islamic concept and practice best known in the West as a form of Ṣūfī ritual. Because it signifies a kind of prayer, the term *dhikr* is usually translated as *invocation,* since it involves the repetition of a name or names of God, often within a set phrase such as "Praise belongs to God." The sources frequently discuss it in conjunction with supplication *(du'ā',* "calling [upon God]"), which normally adds a request to the mention of a name or names; supplication may take the form of a personal prayer in any language, while *dhikr* employs Arabic names drawn from the Qur'ān. Both are fundamentally voluntary and in any case need to be distinguished from the daily prayer *(ṣalāt),* which is incumbent upon all the faithful.

Studies of *dhikr* in Western languages usually emphasize the bodily movements and the techniques for bringing about concentration that are employed by various Ṣūfī groups and thus neglect the centrality of the concept in the Qur'ān, where the term is employed, along with various closely related derivatives, about 270 times. Although techniques have certainly fascinated a number of Islamicists and travelers to the East, they have always been of secondary interest within the Ṣūfī tradition itself. Nor is it necessary to search for outside influence to explain their genesis: perseverance in remembering God—and sincere Islam is nothing if not this—will eventually entail a certain concern with the technical aspects of controlling one's thoughts and attention.

The basic meaning of the term *dhikr* can be brought out by answering three questions:

1. What is the object of remembrance? God, whose nature is defined succinctly by the first *shahādah,* or creedal statement, "Lā ilāha illā Allāh" ("There is no god but God"), and in detail by the whole range of names and attributes *(al-asmā' wa-al-ṣifāt)* mentioned in the Qur'ān.
2. Why should God be remembered? Because human beings are commanded to remember him by his revelations to the prophets and because ultimate human felicity depends upon this remembrance.
3. How can God be remembered? By imitation of the Prophet, who provides the model through his *sunnah* (practice or custom) for all religious and spiritual activity.

In short, to understand the full implications of the term *dhikr* as it is employed in the Qur'ān and the tradition one needs to have a clear grasp of the three "principles of religion" *(uṣūl al-dīn),* namely divine unity, prophecy, and the return to God (in its widest sense, embracing both the "compulsory return" through death and the "voluntary return" through spiritual practice).

Qur'anic Sources. The Qur'ān refers to itself as a remembrance *(dhikr)* or reminder *(dhikrā, tadhkirah)* more than forty times and also alludes to other revelations by the same terms (surahs 10:71, 21:48, 21:105, 40:54). God had to send a long series of prophets—124,000 according to a *ḥadīth*—because Adam's children keep on falling into forgetfulness, the shortcoming of their father (20:110). If the Qur'ān is a remembrance, so also is the human response to it (here the root's fifth verbal form, *tadhakkur,* is often employed). To be human is to remember: to acknowledge and confirm the obvious. "Not equal are the blind and the seeing man, those who have faith and do deeds of righteousness and the wrongdoer. Little do you remember!" (40:58).

The ultimate object of remembrance is God, since nothing else is truly worthy of human devotion, which is to say that "there is no god but God." The Qur'ān employs the term *dhikr Allāh,* "the remembrance of God," twenty-six times in nominal or verbal form. In a number of other instances where the word *ism* ("name") is inserted into this phrase, the emphasis is placed upon the verbal mentioning of the name *Allāh,* for example, when people are commanded to remember/mention God's name before sacrificing animals (5:4, 6:118, and elsewhere), but the command to remember/mention God's name is also a general one: "And remember the name of thy Lord, and devote thyself to him" (73:8; also 2:114, 22:40, 24:36, 76:25, 87:115). In any case the remembrance of God is almost invariably interpreted to coincide with the mentioning of his name, whether vocally or mentally.

Fifteen verses actually command the remembering of God. But beyond obedience to such commands, human beings must remember God because true life—life with God in the next world—depends on it. In Qur'anic terms, "to be forgotten by God" is to burn in the Fire; to be remembered by him is to dwell in Paradise. If we want God to remember us, we must follow the divine command to remember him: "Remember me, and I will remember you" (2:152), since God will forget those who disobey this command. Speaking of the resurrection, God says, "Today we do forget you, even as you forgot the encounter of this your day; and your refuge is the Fire" (45:34; also 20:126, 32:14, 38:26, 59:19). Such verses help explain why the Ṣūfī Ibn ʿAṭāʾ Allāh al-Iskandarī (d. 1309) can say in his well-known treatise on *dhikr,* "All acts of worship will disappear from the servant on the Day of Resurrection, except the remembrance of God" (*Miftāḥ al-falāḥ,* Cairo, 1961, p. 31).

Just as *dhikr* brings about felicity in the next world, so too it provides the way to achieve proximity to God in this world. In contrast to the hearts of the godfearing, the hearts of the unbelievers are "hardened against the remembrance of God" (39:22–23). Note the emphasis through repetition in "Those who have faith, their hearts being at peace in God's remembrance—in God's remembrance are at peace the hearts of those who have faith and do righteous deeds; theirs is blessedness and a fair resort" (13:28). The way to achieve this peace of heart (cf. the "soul at peace with God," 89:27) is to follow the Prophet, one of whose names is Dhikr Allāh: "You have a good example in God's Messenger, for whosoever hopes for God and the Last Day and remembers God frequently" (33:21). The Prophet is the perfect embodiment of God's remembrance; hence, his *sunnah* provides all the details of how to remember God in every act of life. Ibn ʿAṭāʾ Allāh quotes a short *ḥadīth* that epitomizes the pervasive rationale for the love of the Prophet: "He who remembers me has remembered God, and he who loves me has loved God" (*Miftāḥ,* p. 46).

Ḥadīth. The *ḥadīth* literature provides a wealth of material on *dhikr* corroborating the Qurʾanic picture while emphasizing the practice of mentioning or invoking God's names and the benefits it provides beyond the grave. The Prophet calls *dhikr* the best act of worship. Every word a person utters in this life will be counted against him or her in the next life, except "bidding to honor and forbidding dishonor" (surah 3:11, 7:157, and elsewhere) and remembering God. When a companion of Muḥammad complained about Islam's many ordinances and asked for a single practice to which he could cling, the Prophet replied, "Let your tongue remain moist in the remembrance of God." The Prophet reported that God says, "I am with my servant when he remembers me. If he remembers me in himself I remember him in myself, and if he remembers me in an assembly, I remember him in an assembly better than his." Such "assemblies" of God's remembrance are well attested in the Prophet's time and became the model for Ṣūfī gatherings.

The *ḥadīths* make clear that the important formulas of remembrance or invocation are those still heard throughout the Islamic world on every sort of occasion: "There is no god but God," "Praise belongs to God," "Glory be to God," "God is greater," and "There is no power and no strength save in God." Only the last is non-Qurʾanic, while the first, the Shahādah, is said to be the most excellent. The *ḥadīths* also make clear that all of God's names, traditionally said to number ninety-nine, may be employed in invocation and supplication, though certain names, such as *All-Merciful* or *All-Forgiving,* have always been employed far more than others, such as *Avenger* or *Terrible in Retribution.*

The idea that each name of God has a specific characteristic is already well reflected in the *ḥadīth* literature. Thus, for example, many *ḥadīths* allude to "the greatest name of God" *(al-ism al-aʿẓam),* the name "when called by which he answers and when asked by which he gives." Litanies *(awrād, aḥzāb)* composed of divine names, formulas of remembrance, and Qurʾanic verses have been common among Muslims from earliest times. Some of them mention the ninety-nine "most beautiful names"; others, such as *al-jawshan al-kabīr* (quoted from the Prophet in Shīʿī sources, e.g., ʿAbbās Qummī, *Mafātīḥ al-jinān,* Tehran, 1961/2, pp. 179–207), list one thousand names of God.

Ṣūfī Tradition. The Shīʿī *ḥadīth* literature, which includes sayings from all twelve imams as well as from the Prophet, helps to demonstrate that the remembrance of God remained central to Islamic piety in the two centuries following Muḥammad. But while the Qurʾān commands the faithful to remember God, the jurists could not impose remembrance upon the community except in the form of the ritual prayer and other outward acts of worship, since by its nature remembrance is a personal affair related more to the domain of intention than to outward activity. In general, therefore, the Ṣūfīs more than any other group emphasized the importance of the devotional practices. In the words of Khwājah Muḥammad Pārsā (d. 1420), "The root of being a Muslim [*aṣl-i musalmānī*] is 'No god but God,' words that are identical with remembrance." Hence, he says, the soul of the daily prayer and the other ritual practices, such as fasting and pilgrimage, is "the renewal of God's remembrance in the heart" (*Qudsīyah,* ed. Aḥmad Ṭāhirī ʿIrāqī, Tehran, 1975, p. 30). In the same way, the Ṣūfīs considered all Islamic doctrine and theory to be aimed at awakening remembrance in the soul. If on the one hand the Qurʾān commands human beings to remember God, on the other it provides a full justification for the necessity of this remembrance in its teachings about human nature and ultimate felicity, as, for example, in its description of the "trust" given to human beings in preference to all other creatures (33:72).

In commenting on the Qur'anic teachings, the Ṣūfīs in particular demonstrate that remembrance of God implies far more than just the ritual activities that go by this name. Full remembrance means actualizing all the ontological perfections latent within the primordial human nature *(fiṭrah)* by virtue of its being a divine image. These perfections belong ultimately to God, the one true being, and in his case they are referred to as the divine names. Al-Ghazālī and many others speak of human perfection as "assuming the traits of the divine names" *(al-takhalluq bi-al-asmā' al-ilāhīyah);* Ibn al-ʿArabī (d. 1240) even offers this phrase as the definition of Sufism (*Al-futūḥāt al-makkīyah* 2.267.11). Since *Allāh* is the all-comprehensive name *(al-ism al-jāmiʿ),* the referent of all other divine names, the stage of full human perfection is also known as "being like unto Allāh" *(ta'alluh),* or "theomorphism." For Ibn al-ʿArabī and others, the remembrance of the name *Allāh* is the sign of the fully realized human individual to whom reference is made in the prophetic saying, "The Last Hour will not come as long as there remains someone in this world saying, 'Allāh, Allāh!'" (*Futūḥāt* 3.248.17, 3.438.21).

The hallmark of this potential theomorphism is the particular nature of human intelligence, which sets men and women apart from all other creatures. Turning to God—remembrance—actualizes the divine image latent within humans; ultimate felicity is nothing but the remembrance of our own true nature, or the realization of genuine human character traits, the names of God.

Ṣūfī teachings and practice can be summarized by the "best of invocations," the Shahādah: "La ilāha illā Allāh" ("There is no god but God"). The aim is to "annihilate" *(fanā')* all "others" *(aghyār)* and to "subsist" *(baqā')* in the divine. In the words of Ibn ʿAṭā' Allāh, "No one says correctly 'No god but God' unless he negates everything other than God from his soul and heart" (*Miftāḥ,* p. 28). Likewise Najm al-Dīn Rāzī (d. 1256): "When one pursues the *dhikr* and persists in it, the attachment of the spirit to other than God will be gradually severed by the scissors of *lā ilāha,* and the beauty of the monarch of *illā Allāh* will become manifest and emerge from the veil of might" (*The Path of God's Bondsmen,* p. 270). For Rūmī as for many other Ṣūfīs, the fire of love drives the seeker to remember God constantly; only this can effect the final transformation: "Love is that flame which, when it blazes up, burns away everything except the beloved. It drives home the sword of *lā ilāha* in order to slay other than God" (*Mathnavī* 5, vv. 588–590).

Though many authorities agree that "Lā ilāha illā Allāh" is the most excellent invocation, others hold that the "single invocation" *(al-dhikr al-mufrad)*—the mention of only the name *Allāh*—is superior. Ibn al-ʿArabī often quotes approvingly the words of one of his masters, Abū al-ʿAbbās al-ʿUraybī, who held that this invocation is best, since in invoking "no god but God" one could die in the terror of negation, but in invoking Allāh one can only die in the intimacy of affirmation (*Futūḥāt* 1.329.2, 2.110.21, 2.224.34).

Ṣūfī masters employed various names methodically to bring out the spiritual potentialities and shape the character traits of their disciples. Many Ṣūfī works provide information on names that can be appropriately invoked—though never without the permission and inculcation *(talqīn)* of a master—by disciples at different stages of spiritual growth. Works on the "most beautiful names," such as al-Ghazālī's *Al-maqṣad al-asnā* (partially translated by R. Stade, *Ninety-nine Names of God,* Ibadan, 1970), often discuss the moral traits and spiritual attitudes that reflect each of the individual names on the human level. Ibn ʿAṭā' Allāh devotes several pages to the properties of various names and their influence on disciples at different stages of the path. He points out, for example, that the name *Independent (al-Ghanī)* is useful for a disciple who seeks disengagement *(tajrīd)* from phenomena but is unable to achieve it (*Miftāḥ,* p. 35). Nonetheless, those who invoke the name *Allāh* should not be interested in specific benefits but should exemplify the attitude expressed in the famous prayer of the woman saint Rābiʿah al-ʿAdawīyah (eighth century): "O God, if I worship thee for fear of Hell, burn me in Hell, and if I worship thee in hope of Paradise, exclude me from Paradise; but if I worship thee for thy own sake, grudge me not thy everlasting beauty" (A. J. Arberry, *Muslim Saints and Mystics,* London, 1966, p. 51).

Some Ṣūfīs wrote of transcending *dhikr,* since in the last analysis it is an attribute of the seeker and is therefore "other than God," a veil concealing God from sight (al-Kalābādhī, *The Doctrine of the Sufis,* p. 107). Ibn al-ʿArabī explains that there can be no invocation after the veil has been lifted and contemplation *(mushāhadah)* takes place, for "invocation disappears in the theophany of the invoked" (*Futūḥāt* 2.245.21). According to al-Nūrī (d. 907), true invocation is "the annihilation of the invoker in the invoked" (Rūzbihān, *Mashrab al-arwāḥ,* ed. Nazif H. Hoca, Istanbul, 1974, p. 139). Ibn al-ʿArabī's foremost disciple, Ṣadr al-Dīn al-Qūnawī (d. 1274) writes that the Ṣūfī must gradually abandon all invocation, both outward and inward, until total emptiness is achieved (*Al-risālah al-hādiyah al-murshidīyah,* MS; cf. M. Valsan, "L'épître sur l'orientation parfaite," *Études traditionnelles* 67, 1966, pp. 241–268). But the final word for most seekers remains with Ibn al-ʿArabī: "Invocation is more excellent than abandoning it, for one can only abandon it during contemplation, and that cannot be achieved in an absolute sense" (*Futūḥāt* 2.229.24).

Many classifications of types of *dhikr* can be found in Ṣūfī works. Some of these refer to the depth of concentration achieved by the disciple, such as invocation of the tongue, of the heart, of the innermost mystery. Another common classification distinguishes between loud or public and silent or private *dhikr.* The former was usually performed in groups according to various ritual forms that took shape within the different Ṣūfī orders. Sessions of public invocation range from the reserved to the ecstatic; some groups, such as the Mawlawīyah, or "whirling dervishes," considered music and dance aids to concentration, while others banned anything but sober recitation. Most Ṣūfīs would probably agree that public sessions are really a secondary form of Ṣūfī practice, since the individual's progress on the path, to the extent it does not derive totally from God's grace, depends upon his or her own efforts. Thus Saʿdī (d. 1292) is not speaking metaphorically when he says at the beginning of his famous *Gulistān:* "Every breath taken in replenishes life, and once let out gives joy to the soul. So each breath contains two blessings, and each blessing requires thanksgiving." It is the silent and persevering remembrance of God with each breath or each heartbeat, always within the context of the prophetic *sunnah,* that takes the seeker to the ultimate goal.

[*For further discussion of the "most beautiful names" of God, see* Attributes of God, *article on* Islamic Concepts. *See also* Shahādah *and* Worship and Cultic Life, *article on* Muslim Worship.]

BIBLIOGRAPHY

For a representative sampling of the *ḥadīth* literature, see al-Khaṭīb al-Tabrīzī's *Mishkāt al-maṣābīḥ,* 4 vols., translated by John Robson (Lahore, 1963–1965), pp. 476–492. Shīʿī sources provide more of the same in far more detail, for example, Majlisī's *Biḥār al-anwār* (1956–1972; reprint, Beirut, 1983), vol. 90, pp. 148–285. Al-Ghazālī brings together Qur'ān, *ḥadīths,* the sayings of the pious, and the views of contemporary theologians and Ṣūfīs in the chapter on *dhikr* and supplication in his *Iḥyā' 'ulūm al-dīn,* 5 vols. (Cairo, 1932), translated by K. Nakamura as *Ghazali on Prayer* (Tokyo, 1973).

For *dhikr* in the Ṣūfī tradition, see Louis Gardet's entry in *The Encyclopaedia of Islam,* new ed. (Leiden, 1960–), and J. Spencer Trimingham's *The Sufi Orders in Islam* (New York, 1971), pp. 194–217, both of which deal mainly with techniques. A far more insightful treatment is provided by Annemarie Schimmel's *Mystical Dimensions of Islam* (Chapel Hill, 1975), pp. 167–178. Among translated texts a brief overview of the views of the early Ṣūfīs is provided by al-Kalābādhī's *The Doctrine of the Sufis,* translated by A. J. Arberry (Lahore, 1966), pp. 105–108, while a comprehensive explanation of its significance is given by Najm al-Dīn Rāzī's *The Path of God's Bondsmen from Origin to Return,* translated by Hamid Algar (Delmar, N.Y., 1982), pp. 268–285. For a description of various forms of *dhikr* within the context of contemporary Egyptian Sufism, see Michael Gilsenan's *Saint and Sufi in Modern Egypt* (Oxford, 1973), pp. 156–187.

WILLIAM C. CHITTICK

DIALOGUE OF RELIGIONS. Etymologically, the word *dialogue* (Gr., *dialogos*) means simply "conversation," although in Western intellectual history its dominant meaning has been "a piece of written work cast in the form of a conversation." In the history of religions, "conversations" about the meaning of beliefs, rituals, and ethics have no doubt been taking place, though informally and unrecorded, from the very beginning, or at least from the first encounter of divergent belief systems. However, the phrase *dialogue of religions* has become common in various religious traditions only in the second half of the twentieth century.

Written dialogues on religion and on philosophical subjects have a long history. The most celebrated Western examples are no doubt the dialogues of Plato, and particularly those in which the teaching methods of Socrates are presented on a question-and-answer basis. Within many religious traditions, dialogues between teachers and their pupils were recorded as a means of communicating and deepening insights. But in virtually all such cases the neophyte occupied a position of submission to the teacher, whose authority derived from what he had learned orally from his mentor and proved in practice. This type of dialogue is especially marked in the Indian traditions, Hindu and Buddhist alike. A relationship of faith and trust is set up between master and disciple, whereupon the disciple receives instruction, often in response to respectful questioning. Many of the Upaniṣads are cast in dialogue form, as is the *Bhagavadgītā* and a portion of the Buddhist Pali canon. The Judeo-Christian tradition likewise contains much instruction in dialogue form: the Law (Torah) is interpreted orally by rabbis to the circle of their disciples, whereas the teachings of Jesus are often placed in the context of conversations and instruction sessions within the company of followers. It is hardly possible in any of these instances to speak of a dialogue between equals, since the disciple or pupil comes seeking the insights that only that particular teacher can provide. In the Socratic dialogue the pupil is made to play a more active role, certainly, but the presence of the master is what guarantees that insights will emerge.

Artificial or imaginative dialogues on religious and metaphysical subjects also occur frequently in Western literature, following the pattern established in classical antiquity. An early medieval example of the genre was the Icelander Snorri Sturluson's *Prose Edda* (early thirteenth century), in which Gangleri asks three informants about the contents of Norse mythology. Later examples are very numerous, and include works as diverse as David Hume's *Dialogues concerning Natural Religion* (1779), R. A. Vaughan's *Hours with the Mystics* (1856), and Ninian Smart's *A Dialogue of Religions* (1960). This type of dialogue relates closely to the conventions of the theater and the novel, which may serve a similar purpose and of which this type of dialogue is a didactic offshoot. Less artificial were attempts to record the conversations and informal statements of *literati* and religious leaders—Martin Luther's *Tischreden* (*Table Talk,* 1566), Boswell's *Life of Johnson* (1791), *Dialogues of Alfred North Whitehead* (1954), and, from India, *The Gospel of Sri Ramakrishna* (1897).

Imaginative dialogue has also served the cause of interreligious controversy—for example, by convincing an imaginary opponent of the error of his ways. An early missionary example was K. M. Banerjea's *Dialogues on Hindu Philosophy* (1861), which set Indian traditions against one another in the interests of Christianity. This apologetic method was, however, short-lived.

Common to the older forms of didactic or controversial dialogue was the assumption that religious truth is to be arrived at rationally, by reasonable discourse and the weighing of evidence and proofs. Doubtless there were cases in which this actually happened. In the eighteenth and nineteenth centuries, contacts between religious traditions increased rapidly, and along with them actual (as opposed to imaginary) conversational encounters between believers. How often these followed an ideally rational course must remain a moot point: one suspects they seldom did so. But since during this same period the Western countries were politically and economically dominant, and the Christian missionary enterprise was experiencing its greatest successes, conversations usually involved Christians, and were seldom between equal partners. Where other traditions were concerned, for instance in confrontations between Hindus and Muslims in India, there could be a level of mutual suspicion that prevented constructive conversations from taking place at all. The West was, however, becoming steadily better informed on matters concerning other religious traditions, while the rapid onset of theological liberalism was modifying the terms in which Western religion was expressed. Before World War I, the dominant concepts were "sympathy" and "fulfillment," and although innumerable conversations took place, no one applied to them the word *dialogue.*

Apologetics and controversy aside, in the late nineteenth century began a serious attempt to bring the religious leaders of the world together in a spirit of reconciliation, concentrating on what united them rather than what kept them apart. The pioneer assembly was the World's Parliament of Religions, held in Chicago in 1893; its original impulse came from Swedenborgians, yet it gathered under the banner of a common theism. The parliament at least attracted delegates from every major tradition, and although it dismayed the orthodox of many creeds (especially within evangelical Christianity), it established many important contacts. It also marked the beginning of the modern Hindu "mission" to the West in the person of Swami Vivekananda, who taught, following Ramakrishna, the equal value of all religions as pathways to the Real. This view was strongly supported in theory by organizations like the Theosophical Society (founded in 1875) and Bāhā'i. A Chicago "continuation committee" was formed, though no further full-scale parliaments were ever held. The Chicago spirit survived, however, in an International Council of Unitarian and Other Liberal Religious Thinkers and Workers, which worked between 1901 and 1913. Its aims were to introduce believers to one another, to emphasize the "universal elements" in all religions, and to work for the "moral uplift of the world." World War I brought these efforts to a temporary halt, but after the war, when internationalism was held to be one safeguard against further conflict, various interfaith movements emerged, culminating in the World Fellowship of Faiths (1929).

Eight years earlier, Rudolf Otto had instituted his Religiöser Menschheitsbund (Interreligious League) with the same end in view—the lessening of international tensions through the banding together of believers. These moral objectives were accepted on the liberal wing of Christianity, coming to expression at the Jerusalem conference of the International Missionary Council in 1928, and classically in the liberal manifesto edited by W. E. Hocking, *Re-Thinking Missions* (1932). In general, however, Christians were uneasy about interfaith cooperation. Hindus adjusted to it more easily, and in the person of Sarvepalli Radhakrishnan gained an international spokesman of great force and clarity. Radhakrishnan held that the comparative study of religion made exclusive claims on the part of any individual tradition impossible, and that behind all empirical forms of religion there is "the same intention, the same striving, the same faith" (Radhakrishnan, *East and West in Religion,* London, 1933, p. 19).

Between the wars, world congresses and fellowships of faiths continued to meet regularly, even under the lengthening shadow of various forms of totalitarianism. Mention might also be made of the Oxford Group Movement (subsequently retitled Moral Re-Armament), which was basically Christian but which was more concerned with moral than with theological issues: it enjoyed its heyday in the late 1930s, and attracted many non-Christians. On another level, the *philosophia perennis* proclaimed by Coomaraswamy, Schuon, and Guénon gained followers from various traditions, Eastern as well as Western. This, however, was less a meeting place of religious traditions than a means by which they might be transcended. In the area of scholarship, although the study of religion on a multicultural basis undoubtedly did increase mutual respect among the traditions and further dialogue between them, few individual scholars were prepared to pronounce on the issue. One exception was Friedrich Heiler of Marburg, who stated at an international conference in Tokyo in 1958 that "a new era will dawn upon mankind when the religions will rise to true tolerance and co-operation on behalf of mankind. To assist in preparing the way for this era is one of the finest hopes of the scientific study of religion" (quoted in Sharpe, 1975, p. 272). Other scholars, however, regarded this ideal as less than "scientific."

Parliaments, congresses, and conferences continued to bring together religious leaders in a spirit of irenic idealism, on the pattern of the League of Nations. Yet there was an increasing sense of the threat to religion being posed by the European totalitarian regimes, as well as by materialism, and frequent calls were made for the world's religious leaders to band their people together to meet these pressures. What the leaders could not guarantee to do, however, was change the religious configurations of the world. Local situations were still, during the interwar years, dominated by local concerns. Within the Christian churches, there were several notable moves in the direction of increasing visible unity—among Methodists in Britain, Presbyterians in Scotland, Protestant churches in Canada and South India—but relatively little could be done on the interfaith level.

The notion of dialogue in its modern sense entered the world of religion during the confused and confusing years after World War I, and was closely connected with the philosophy of existentialism. Its first and most widely read manifesto was Martin Buber's *I and Thou* (1923), which urged that human beings should cease to look upon one another merely as objects ("I–It") and approach one another directly and with mutual acceptance as fellow humans ("I–Thou"). Buber was Jewish and therefore well acquainted with racial, religious, and economic oppression. But such forms of oppression might emerge whenever and wherever negative value judgments were applied by a dominant group to their (supposed) inferiors. The only cure was the recognition of common humanity, and the personal discourse—or dialogue—of individuals, whatever their beliefs, on that level.

Although Buber and the other existentialists were widely read, and although, as we have seen, many interfaith initiatives were begun between the wars, the application of the term *dialogue* to the relation between religious traditions did not become common until the years after World War II. By that time the political and religious patterns of the world had begun to change more and more rapidly. Western political imperialism was being rapidly dismantled; former colonies were becoming independent almost daily, with a consequent questioning of the values of the colonial period, religious values not excepted; but at the same time Christianity was an important factor in the lives of the new nations, and needed to find a new role, independent of the former governing powers. The newly independent nations were seldom other than partly Christian. India became officially "secular," while having a massive Hindu majority, and Pakistan was created as a Muslim state, for Hindu-Muslim dialogue on the subcontinent had been a marked failure. Elsewhere in the world, whether official ideology was Muslim, Buddhist, Jewish (in the sole case of Israel), or "secular," Christianity was in almost all cases thrust on to the defensive. In the Western countries themselves the Christian pattern underwent a progressive polarization between conservative and liberal views, with liberals in particular suffering greatly from postcolonial guilt on the one hand and an uncertainty as to ultimate religious values on the other.

It was in this atmosphere that the word *dialogue* began to emerge as the only workable term with which to describe the proper attitude of one group of believers over against another. It should be remembered, however, that during the time of its greatest popularity, between the mid-1960s and the mid-1970s, the word was used almost exclusively by the liberal wing of Christianity (both Catholic and Protestant) in the West, and by similarly liberal Christians in developing nations of the "third world." Conservatives found the term unacceptable, since it implicitly placed religious traditions on a par with one another, or at least was less than explicit when it came to affirming the claims of Christianity. In the non-Western world, too, there were those who suspected that the new emphasis on dialogue was no more than a subtler and more insidious form of missionary apologetics.

An important symbolical breakthrough was achieved by the Second Vatican Council (1962–1965) of the Roman Catholic church, which spoke in several documents about dialogue, the church for instance urging "her sons . . . prudently and lovingly, through dialogue and collaboration with the followers of other religions," to "acknowledge, preserve, and promote the spiritual and moral goods found among these men, as well as the values in their society and culture" (*Nostra aetate* 2). Similarly, the disciples of Christ "can learn by sincere and patient dialogue what treasures a bountiful God has distributed among the nations of the earth" (*Ad gentes* 2.11). Statements of this kind had the effect of liberating Catholics from previous restrictions on fellowship with non-Catholics, and of releasing a flood of "dialogue literature," in the production of which Protestants were soon to share.

But not all this literature saw the nature and purpose of dialogue in the same light. In addition, much of it suffered in that it was not actually emerging from discussions between believers belonging to different traditions, but remained on the level of theorizing *about* dialogue. Various types of activity seemed to be capable of being contained beneath the "dialogue" canopy.

1. *Discursive dialogue* (previously "debate" or "discussion") involves meeting, listening, and discussion on the level of mutual competent intellectual inquiry. As such it was neither very new nor very remarkable, though it had always been fairly uncommon. As an intellectual activity, it could only ever be profitable among equally equipped partners, since it presupposes the willingness of both to listen, as well as speak.

2. *Human ("Buberian") dialogue* rests on the existential foundations previously described, and assumes that it is possible for human beings to meet purely and simply as human beings, irrespective of the beliefs that separate them. The great drawback to this approach is its individualism. Although suitable enough among intellectuals in the semisecular West, it leaves out of consideration the extent to which the individual is shaped by the community of which he or she, depending on its support and adhering to its values, is part. To bypass the community is often simply impossible, and although this approach rests on high ideals, it may prove to be little more than a theoretical stance.

3. *Secular dialogue* stresses that where there are tasks to be performed in the world, believers in different creeds may share in a program of joint action, without regard to their respective convictions. In the theological climate of the 1960s and 1970s, dialogue very frequently appeared to be pointed in this direction. It simply bypassed the belief question in the interests of practicalities. "Desacralization turns the eyes of men to the world, to time and history, and the realities of history are often more manageable for purposes of dialogue than the supramundane things of an ethereal world" (Jai Singh, 1967, pp. 43–44).

4. *Spiritual dialogue* has been advocated chiefly by those who have been trained in the contemplative and monastic traditions, and who have learned to set high value upon Eastern (or other) spirituality, while not wishing to lessen their hold upon their own. Its locus is not debate and discussion, but prayer and meditation, and in recent years it has given rise to a considerable number of ashrams and meditation centers in East and West alike. In theoretical terms, it rests on a monistic theology similar in many ways to Vedānta; in practical terms, it often concedes to the East a level of attainment in matters of spirituality superior to that of the West, and is prepared to use non-Christian scriptures, liturgies, and techniques alongside those that are specifically Christian. Often it will stress the importance of *theologia negativa,* negate the primacy of logic and conceptual knowledge, and rely on experience, intuition, and contemplation. In this respect it was a typical product of the 1960s.

Since about the mid-1970s, the term *dialogue* has been somewhat less used than during the previous decade, partly on account of changing fashions, partly in response to socioeconomic pressures. There is little real evidence that the stated goals of dialogue (at least as formulated by Christians) were ever reached, and in any case, each new generation has had to take up the task of meeting other believers afresh. But at least the "dialogue period" helped to banish some of the impatience and the inaccuracies of the past, although doubtless creating fresh problems of its own. While it taught many Christians the importance of sympathy and seriousness in interreligious discourse, it failed to engage the attention of most other traditions on anything but a superficial level. As such, what has often been called a "dialogue of religions" and set forth as a practical activity, has remained on the level of theory and ideals. Actual encounters of believers there will always be. They will undoubtedly remain haphazard, unpredictable, sometimes violent, and always determined by local conditions.

[*See* Truth *for a treatment of the ways in which the members of different religious traditions regard the exclusivity or inclusivity of particular religious beliefs. See also* Apologetics *for a discussion of the ways in which members of different traditions have defended their beliefs. The entry* Religious Pluralism *looks at the confrontation between peoples of varying religious traditions in terms of the theory that the great world religions constitute different ways of conceiving, experiencing, and responding to the same ultimate divine reality.*]

BIBLIOGRAPHY

Jai Singh, Herbert, ed. *Inter-religious Dialogue.* Bangalore, 1967.

Klostermaier, Klaus Konrad. *Hindu and Christian in Vrindaban.* Translated by Antonia Fonseca. London, 1969.

Klostermaier, Klaus Konrad. "Hindu-Christian Dialogue: Its Religious and Cultural Implications." *Studies in Religion* 1 (1971): 83–97.

Sharpe, Eric J. "The Goals of Inter-religious Dialogue." In *Truth and Dialogue in World Religions: Conflicting Truth-Claims,* edited by John Hick, pp. 77–95. Philadelphia, 1974.

Sharpe, Eric J. *Comparative Religion: A History.* London, 1975. See the discussion on pages 251–266.

Sharpe, Eric J. *Faith Meets Faith: Some Christian Attitudes to Hinduism in the Nineteenth and Twentieth Centuries.* London, 1977.

ERIC J. SHARPE

DIAMOND. The diamond, first of all, participates in the hierophany of stones signifying in religious consciousness that which is hard, rugged, and unchanging. Above all, stone *is.* Like all precious stones, the diamond also partakes of the general symbolism of treasures and riches, which in religious terms represent moral and intellectual knowledge.

As a symbol the diamond, as the hardest of all stones, has a wide range of meanings, among them indestructibility, constancy, the unyielding, and dominance. Because of its brilliance it also signifies unconquerable light, excellence, frankness, joy, life, and purity.

In Greek the word for "diamond" is derived from *adamas,* meaning "invincible, unconquerable." In some places, and especially on Greek emblems, it indicated the irradiant mystic center, a meaning discovered in the most obscure examples as well as in the most prominent. Jean Chevalier and Alain Gheerbrant (1982) point out that the German word *Eckstein* ("cornerstone") also refers to the diamond in a deck of cards. The cornerstone is one of many symbols for the center. In a more obvious example, Plato likens the axis of the world to a diamond.

Until the nineteenth century, diamonds were found almost entirely in India. On the subcontinent the word *vajra* meant both "lightning" and "diamond." Thus, the *vajra* of the god Śiva has a double aspect as thunderbolt and diamond scepter. *Vajra* also belongs to the god Agni as a spiritual power and to Indra as a temporal power. As a diamond *vajra* is adamantine and depicts spiritual power, but as thunderbolt and lightning it also represents both destruction and fertilization, death-dealing and life-giving powers, the alternating and complementary forces of the universe.

The symbol of the *vajra* is important in Buddhism as well, where it symbolizes the power of the Buddha's teaching (the Dharma) to overcome the deluding passions of sentient beings. The Diamond Throne or Seat is the place of enlightenment. Situated at the foot of the Bodhi Tree, it is the unchangeable axis or center of the world.

In Tantric Buddhism *vajra* represents immutable, unalterable spiritual power. Symbolizing clarity and light, it also refers to the indeterminate character and ultimate emptiness of the Buddha nature. Mircea Eliade cites a Tantric text that makes a clear identification between *śūnyatā* ("voidness") and *vajra.* The Ch'an patriarch Hui-neng is said to have declared that neither that which is waxing nor that which is waning is the diamond.

In the traditional mineralogy of the Indian subcontinent, the diamond represents perfection. Stones and metals were thought to grow within the earth's womb, each with its own lethargic pace and rhythm. The crystal was unripe (Hindi, *kacchā*) and constituted a state of intermediate maturation. The diamond was the epitome of maturity and ripeness (Hindi, *pakkā*). The crystal is not hard; the diamond is. The Indian alchemist, associating the diamond with immortality, identified it with the philosophers' stone.

Similarly, in Tibetan iconography the diamond scepter signifies the adamantine or immutable world, which is also potential or nonmanifest. The bell or *tilpa* refers to the phenomenal world, which is manifest and changing. The diamond scepter is the active principle; the bell is the passive. The former is wisdom and the latter, human reason.

The diamond has also been linked with the supreme female divinity, who is usually associated with the earth. In Tibet the earth goddess Tārā has a human incarnation, the Diamond Sow. She is also traditionally regarded as the consort of or feminine counterpart to the *bodhisattva* Avalokiteśvara. In the transition from tarot cards to modern playing cards, diamonds replaced the ancient suit of pentacles, which had been symbols of Mother Earth (Tārā) and of the earth as feminine.

The characteristics of hardness and durability have lent themselves to other meanings. In the Old Testament the diamond could symbolize hardness of the heart and forehead (*Jer.* 17:1). In Rome it was believed that the stone promoted harmony, and that it guarded health and vitality if worn on the left hand, close to the heart. This belief probably informed its character as an emblem of reconciliation in the Middle Ages and as a sign of betrothal in the modern world.

In some places the diamond's brilliance and lucidity made it a symbol for Christ. In Hebrew culture the sixth stone of the high priest's breastplate, a diamond, was said to become dark or light according to the guilt or innocence of an accused person.

Mircea Eliade (1958) has related diamonds to "snake stones," which in many cultures are thought to have fallen from the heads of snakes or dragons. In ancient India, and later in the Hellenistic and Arab worlds, it was believed that the stones were poisonous if anyone touched them with their lips, because they had once been in a snake's throat. The notion that precious stones came from snake spittle has been found in areas ranging from China to Great Britain.

Pliny the Elder (23–79 CE) described the *dracontia*, or dracontites, that were to be found in the brains of dragons. Philostratus the Lemnian (170–245 CE) reported that the eyes of some dragons were stones of blinding brilliance imbued with magical powers. Sorcerers, he relates, after they have worshiped reptiles, cut off their heads and take out the precious stones.

Given such beliefs, it is not surprising that the diamond has a reputation as a remedy for snakebite. Indeed, Pliny describes it as a universal talisman, rendering poisons and every malady harmless and causing evil spirits and bad dreams to depart. In occidental Europe, the diamond has been thought to chase away savage beasts, phantoms, sorcerers, and the terrors of the night. In Russia, its purity and lucidity have made it a charm to impede lust and to strengthen the resolve of the chaste.

BIBLIOGRAPHY

Jean Chevalier and Alain Gheerbrant, in *Dictionnaire des symboles* (Paris, 1982), have written an interesting and often provocative essay on the diamond. Mircea Eliade, in *Patterns in Comparative Religion* (New York, 1958), primarily discusses the diamond as a magical object. His description of the significance of stones in the same book is also helpful. Berthold Laufer's book *The Diamond: A Study in Chinese and Hellenistic Folklore* (Chicago, 1915) is one of the few sources that include substantial material on the diamond as a symbol rather than a physical object.

ELAINE MAGALIS

DIANA, the Roman moon goddess, reveals her identity through her name, which like *Iuppiter* is formed from the root **dyeu* and means "the shining one." Opinions differ only over the process by which the word was formed: some hold that *Diana* stems from the adjective *dius*, "luminous" (Paulus-Festus, ed. Lindsay, 1913, p. 65 L.), while others trace it to the locative *diu*, "by day." The original aspect of Diana was that she embodied the light of night as opposed to the light of day. (In this sense she contrasts as well with Dea Dia, the divinity of good weather, invoked in the month of May by the Arval Brothers.) Cicero (*De natura deorum* 2.68–69) correctly commented, "It is thought that Diana is identical with the moon; . . . she is called Diana because at night she provides, so to speak, the day."

The definition of her lunar nature is confirmed by the liturgical calendar: throughout Italy, the anniversary of her cult fell on 13 August, the ides that at one time coincided with the brightest day of the month (Statius, *Silvae* 3.1.59–60), when the full moon would follow daylight. (By the same logic, the anniversary of the Capitoline temple of Jupiter fell on the ides of September.) Also on 13 August ceremonies were performed at the most ancient site of Latin worship: the grove of Aricia (Nemus Aricinum) near Lake Nemi, which was also called "Diana's mirror," Speculum Dianae.

The same date marked the anniversary of the Aventine temple of Diana (Aedes Dianae in Aventino). Rome had constructed it within its walls yet outside the religious and ritual boundary known as the *pomerium* once it had taken over the direction of the federal Latin worship (Varro, *De lingua Latina* 5.43). Diana's quality of *lucifera* ("light-bringing"; Martial, 10.70.7) was also attested by the rite. Even during the time of Ovid (*Fasti* 3.270), women would carry torches from Rome to Aricia: one "would bear the light to the goddess," as Propertius expressed it (2.32.9–10), as if they wanted to stimulate her essential function through sympathetic magic.

There is a problem in dating the Roman sanctuary. Tradition (Festus, op. cit., p. 460 L.) attributes its dedication to the king Servius Tullius by pointing out that the day is commonly called the *dies servorum*, "slaves' day." Festus explains this appellation through a play on words, especially referring to Servius Tullius, born a *servus* ("slave"). This suggests another explanation: the establishment of Diana's cult on the Aventine could have resulted from the defeat inflicted by Rome on the Latins at the battle of Lake Regillus (496 BCE), at which point the Latins were reduced *en masse* to the status of slaves. Be that as it may, 13 August was the feast of slaves under the patronage of Diana of the Aventine (Plutarch, *Quaestiones Romanae* 100).

On the same day, women had the custom of washing their hair (Plutarch, *Questiones Romanae*), which implies that the participation of women in Diana's worship must have gone beyond their role as torchbearers. This in turn raises the question of syncretic contamination of the goddess by Artemis. Diana underwent Hellenic influence quite early. She was joined with Hercules in the first *lectisternium* in 399 BCE, which was intended to halt an epidemic (Livy, 5.13.6). It is probable that the Latin names stand for homologous Greek divinities. Herakles was qualified to intervene in the situation by reason of being the *alexikakos* ("he who drives away illnesses"), a trait known to the Latins (Varro, *De lingua Latina* 7.82). Similarly Artemis, who was not originally a lunar goddess, was viewed at first as the protectress of female life. At the *lectisternium* of 217 BCE Diana was again present, this time associated with her mythological brother Apollo.

The early commingling with Artemis can explain those aspects of Diana that contrast with her virginal nature. Strabo (4.1.5) relates that the cultic statue on the Aventine displayed the same traits as the Artemis of Marseilles, which in turn was identical with the Artemis of Ephesus. At Aricia, votive objects have been discovered that take the form of vulvas and phalluses. Syncretism progressively altered the Latin goddess to the point of conferring various features of the Greek goddess upon her beyond her lunar function; thus she became a midwife like Artemis Locheia, a huntress-goddess, and, as Diana Trivia, a goddess of crossroads, after the example of Hekate Trioditis. By the time of Augustus, the absorption of Diana by Artemis was virtually complete, as can be seen in the *Carmen saeculare* of Horace. Yet an ancient custom persisted at the Grove of Aricia that marked a sharp contrast: the priest of the place, called the *rex nemorensis,* exercised his office only until slain in hand-to-hand combat by a stronger opponent (Servius, *Ad Aeneidem* 6.136). This custom, which attracted only fugitive slaves, survived into the full imperial era (Suetonius, *Caligula* 35.6) as a relic of long-vanished prehistory.

BIBLIOGRAPHY

Alföldi, András. *Early Rome and the Latins.* Ann Arbor, 1965. See pages 85–100 on the sanctuary of the Aventine.

Dumézil, Georges. *La religion romaine archaïque.* 2d ed. Paris, 1974. See pages 409–413. This work has been translated from the first edition by Philip Krapp as *Archaic Roman Religion,* 2 vols. (Chicago, 1970).

Ernout, A., and A. Meillet. *Dictionnaire étymologique de la langue latine.* 4th ed. Paris, 1967. Derives *Diana* from the adjective *dius,* "luminous."

Leumann, Manu, Johann Baptist Hofmann, and Anton Szantyr. *Lateinische Grammatik,* vol. 1. 5th ed. Munich, 1977. See pages 357–358 on the derivation of *Diana* from the locative *diu,* "by day."

Schilling, Robert. *Rites, cultes, dieux de Rome.* Paris, 1979. See pages 366–370 on Dea Dia and pages 371–388 on "Diane latine."

Wissowa, Georg. *Religion und Kultus der Römer.* 2d ed. Munich, 1912. See pages 247–252.

ROBERT SCHILLING
Translated from French by Paul C. Duggan

DIETARY LAWS. *For discussion of Jewish dietary laws, see* Kashrut.

DIETERICH, ALBRECHT (1866–1908), German philologist and historian of Greco-Roman religions. Born in Bad Hersfeld (in the Hesse region of Germany), Albrecht Dieterich completed his secondary studies in the school where his father (who wanted Dieterich to become a theologian) was a member of the faculty. At the University of Leipzig in 1885–1886, Dieterich studied the New Testament and church history; he also took an interest in the philosophy of religion in general and enrolled in courses in classical philology (taught by Georg Curtius, Otto Crusius, and Otto Ribbeck). He pursued higher studies at the University of Bonn from 1886 to 1888, where the teaching of Hermann Usener (whose daughter he later married) had decisive influence upon his scientific orientation. He also studied under Franz Bücheler, who introduced him to funerary epigraphy, and under Reinhard Kekulé, who taught him to appreciate iconography.

Dieterich consolidated the bases of his philological training at Usener's urging, who had him write a dissertation on Aeschylus. He then worked on an edition (with comments) of the magical papyrus J 384 of Leiden; it was submitted to a competition sponsered by Bücheler and won the prize (the text was published in the *Jahrbücher für klassische Philologie,* supp. vol. 16, 1888). In this work Dieterich showed his concern for historical and linguistic comprehension of the papyrus's strange elements (that at first glance appear irrational) by paying attention to how these elements manifest the marginal strains of Greco-Roman religion (e.g., Orphism, Hermetism, and gnosticism). Having obtained his doctoral degree in 1888, he passed his state examination in 1889 with his dissertation addressing the question, "What do we know about the theism or pantheism of Plato?" In 1891 he qualified as a doctor of philosophy at the University of Marburg with his work *De hymnis Orphicis capitula quinque,* in which the problems of literary and religious history are treated together. (The hypothesis that he advanced in this book—that of an Alexandrian elaboration of some "Orphic hymns"—is no longer supported, but nevertheless it is still generally agreed that certain aspects of Orphism in Ptolemaic Egypt deserve attention.)

He had at first planned to edit another magical papyrus of Leiden (J 395) as part of his doctoral work; it was instead published as an appendix to his *Abraxas* (1891). This book, written in homage to Usener, displayed Dieterich's remarkable mastery over hermetic and gnostic literature. He applied himself in *Abraxas* to uncovering in this literature elements of Stoic, Orphic, astrological, Egyptian, and Judaic origin. Yet for all that he did not neglect Classical Greek literature (especially Aeschylus and Aristophanes). He wrote the article "Aischylos" for the *Real-Encyclopädie* (1893); in this article the religious sense of tragic grandeur surpasses the level of purely verbal and bibliographical erudition. The origins of Christianity were part of his concern as well. His study of the *Apocalypse of Peter,* a text discovered in a tomb in Akhmīm, Egypt, led to the publication of *Nekyia* (1893), an in-depth study of the Greek tradition of descent *(katabasis)* into the underworld and of Judeo-Christian apocalyptic tradition. It stressed the importance of popular beliefs and of beliefs of popular origin at the periphery of official cults or of Classical paganism.

During 1894 and 1895, a long Mediterranean voyage took him to Greece, Asia Minor, Naples and Pompeii, Sicily, and finally Rome. He thus made direct contact with the objects of his studies: the countrysides, the representational monuments, the common people's way of life, and the ever-living folklore in rustic festivals. The paintings of Campania (commented upon by August Mau) and Italian theater inspired Dieterich's book *Pulcinella* (1897), a perspicacious study of the history of comic characters from classical antiquity extending into the present. His visit to the Lateran Museum resulted in his publication in 1896 of a commentary on the epitaph of Aberkios (a bishop of Hierapolis, Phrygia) in which he proposed a pagan interpretation, which generated both enthusiastic support (e.g., from Salomon Reinach) and sharp criticism (e.g., from Franz Cumont).

In 1895 he became an auxiliary professor of philology at the University of Giessen, and then became in 1897 a full professor there, succeeding Edvard Schwartz. His teaching on Greek and Latin literature made reference to iconography as well as to popular mythology. Greatly impressed by Erwin Rohde's *Psyché* (1890–1894) and Wilhelm Mannhardt's *Wald- und Feldkulte* (1875–1877), he became fascinated with ethnography and collaborated in the projects of the Hessische Vereinigung für Volkskunde. In this activity he always insisted upon the necessity of providing a philological basis for comparisons. He held conferences at Frankfurt on the rites of birth and death that served as a prelude for his book *Mutter Erde* (1905).

Dieterich was interested in the magical aspect of literature manifested in the mysticism of signs, in demonology, and in all the aberrant and disturbing fringes of Greco-Roman paganism, which until then were somewhat neglected by classical philologists. In a similar way, Oriental religions also concerned him. In a letter written in 1897, he argued that the Egyptian deity Sarapis was a syncretic god foreshadowing a kind of henotheism that would pave the way for Christian monotheism. Hugo Hepding, with his book *Attis* (1903), inaugurated the series "Religionsgeschichtliche Versuche und Vorarbeiten," which Dieterich, along with Richard Wünsch, edited until Dieterich's death. The same year saw the publication of Dieterich's *Eine Mithrasliturgie,* an expansion of an article he had published in 1902 ("Die Religion des Mithras" in the journal *Bonner Jahrbücher*); the topic was the famous papyrus in the National Papyrus Library in Paris (Supplementum Graecum 574) that contains the "formula for immortality." Although Dieterich's description of this text as a Mithraic liturgy is no longer generally accepted, his commentary does display prodigious erudition.

Dieterich moved to the University of Heidelberg in 1903, succeeding Otto Crusius as professor of classical philology. There he dedicated himself mainly to the history of religions. Beginning in 1904, his editing (at first with Thomas Achelis but from 1905 to 1908 alone) of the journal *Archiv für Religionswissenschaft* occupied the greater part of his time. This, however, did not prevent him from writing a *magnum opus* that he had been nurturing for some time: *Mutter Erde: Ein Versuch über Volksreligion* (1905). In it he defends the thesis that rites of birth and death can be explained as functions of a fundamental belief, a primitive and universal given in the history of religions. His idea enjoyed considerable success. It was answered with justified criticisms (for example, by Olaf Pettersson in his book *Mother Earth,* Lund, 1967); yet the work still has merit, and any criticisms of it ought to be nuanced (see my review of Pettersson's book in *Revue de l'histoire des religions* 175, 1969, pp. 69–71). Significantly, *Mutter Erde* was dedicated to Usener on the occasion of his seventieth birthday. In the same year (1905), a supplement to *Archiv für Religionswissenschaft* was also dedicated to Usener; in it, a piece entitled "Sonnentag" by Dieterich drew a relationship between a Heidelberg custom and the ancient and modern feasts of Palm Sunday. He was planning one work on popular religion and another on the origins of Christianity.

Dieterich died of a cerebral apoplexy shortly after beginning a course of lectures at Heidelberg; he was fully active and in the prime of his career. His students (notably Friedrich Pfister, Eugen Fehrle, and Otto Weinreich) bear the clear stamp of his teaching. He contributed to a greater understanding of Greco-Roman paganism by opening classical philology to the exegesis of obscure texts from late antiquity; he also contributed to the comparative study of religions and to the study of popular traditions without ever losing sight of the great Hellenic literary tradition.

BIBLIOGRAPHY

Dietrich's published works include the following.

De hymnis orphicis capitula quinque. Marburg, 1891.

Abraxas: Studien zur Religionsgeschichte des spätern Altertums. Leipzig, 1891.

Nekyia: Beiträge zur Erklärung der neuentdeckten Petrusapokalypse. Leipzig, 1893.

Die Grabinschrift des Aberkios. Leipzig, 1896.

Pulcinella pompjanische Wandbilder und römische Satyrspiele. Leipzig, 1897.

Eine Mithrasliturgie (1903). 3d ed. Edited by Otto Weinreich. Leipzig, 1923.

Mutter Erde: Ein Versuch über Volksreligion (1905). 3d ed. Leipzig, 1925.

Kleine Schriften. Edited by Richard Wünsch. Leipzig, 1911. Includes detailed biographical information on Dieterich.

ROBERT TURCAN
Translated from French by Paul C. Duggan

DIFFUSIONISM. *See* Evolutionism *and* Kulturkreiselehre.

DIGNĀGA (c. 480–540 CE), founder of the Buddhist school of epistemology and logic in India. Born near Kāñcī in South India, Dignāga first belonged to the Vātsīputrīya school of Hīnayāna Buddhism, but unconvinced of the adequacy of its doctrine, he left the school. Some source materials record that he became a pupil of Vasubandhu, a renowned scholar of Buddhist philosophy, but his direct relationship to Vasubandhu may be questioned: a passage in one of Dignāga's works indicates an uncertainty concerning the authorship of a book traditionally attributed to Vasubandhu. Dignāga stayed for some time in Nālandā, then the center of Buddhist learning, and obtained mastery of the Vijñānavāda philosophy and of logic. His latter years were spent in Orissa.

Dignāga composed many philosophical treatises. Most are no longer extant in Sanskrit, but a certain number of them are available in Tibetan or Chinese translation. The important ones are (1) *Prajñāpāramitā-piṇḍārtha-saṃgraha,* a summary of the *Prajñāparamitā Sūtra* from the Yogācāra standpoint; (2) *Traikālya-parīkṣā,* a treatise on the concept of time consisting of verses taken from Bhartṛhari's *Vākyapadīya* with a slight but significant modification: it is intended to set forth the Yogācāra view that phenomenal existences are produced by the consciousness *(vijñāna);* (3) *Abhidharmakośa-marma-dīpa,* an abridgment of Vasubandhu's book treating the dogmatics of the Hīnayāna schools; (4) *Hastavāla-prakaraṇa,* an examination of the Sautrāntika concepts of ultimate reality *(paramārtha-sat)* and empirical reality *(saṃvṛti-sat);* (5) **Upādāya-prajñapti-prakaraṇa,* a clear explanation of the Sautrāntika concept of empirical reality, arguing at the conclusion from the Yogācāra viewpoint that empirical reality is a product of the consciousness; (6) *Ālambana-parīkṣā,* an examination of the object of cognition; (7) *Hetucakraḍamaru;* (8) *Nyāyamukha;* (9) *Hetumukha* (not extant except for a few fragments); and (10) *Pramāṇa-samuccaya.* These last four works treat logic and epistemology.

Dignāga was a proponent of the Yogācāra doctrine insofar as he maintained that phenomenal existence was fabricated by the consciousness. However, the notion of the *ālaya-vijñāna* ("receptacle consciousness"), a central Yogācāra doctrine, is not mentioned in any of his works. He belonged to that school of the Yogācāras that did not recognize the *ālaya-vijñāna* and the "I-consciousness" *(manas)* separately from the six kinds of ordinary sense consciousness: visual, auditory, olfactory, gustatory, tactile, and discriminative. In some of his works he evinces an interest in Sautrāntika doctrine, and in fact, Dignāga's epistemological theories as expounded in the *Pramāṇasamuccaya* were made acceptable for both the Sautrāntikas and the Yogācāras.

Among the treatises concerning the Yogācāra philosophy, the *Ālambana-parīkṣā* is most important. In this work Dignāga repudiates the realists by arguing that a cognition cannot take for its object a thing in the external world, whether it is an individual atom or an aggregate of atoms. His discussions are similar to those presented by Vasubandhu in his *Viṃśatikā-vijñaptimātratāsiddhi.* However, the originality of Dignāga lies in his insistence that an object of cognition *(ālambana)* must fulfill two necessary conditions: first, the object must be the cause *(kāraṇa)* of a cognition, and second, it must possess the same form *(ākāra)* as that which appears in the cognition. To satisfy these two conditions the object must be a real entity *(dravya-sat)* and possess a gross form *(sthūlākāra).* With these two conditions in view Dignāga examined and rejected the realist theories and drew the conclusion that the object of cognition is nothing other than the form of an object that appears in the cognition.

Dignāga's major contribution in the field of logic is the invention of the "wheel of reasons" *(hetucakra)*, which shows nine possible relations between a logical reason *(hetu)* and what is to be proven *(sādhya)*, and enables one to distinguish a valid reason from invalid ones. The *hetucakra* was first presented in the *Hetucakraḍamaru*, and later incorporated in the *Nyāyamukha*, a work treating the dialectic on the model of Vasubandhu's *Vādavidhi*, and in the *Pramāṇasamuccaya*, a systematic exposition of the theory of knowledge.

The *Pramāṇasamuccaya* is the most important of Dignāga's works, for it is the synthesis of the doctrines expounded by him in different treatises. It comprises six chapters focusing on, respectively, (1) perception *(pratyakṣa)*, (2) inference *(svārthānumāna)*, (3) syllogism *(parārthānumāna)*, (4) proper and improper examples in syllogism *(dṛṣṭānta-dṛṣṭāntābhāsa)*, (5) "differentiation from others" *(anyāpoha)* as the meaning of a word, and (6) futile rejoinder *(jāti)*. In the first chapter, Dignāga makes a radical distinction between the two means of cognition, namely, perception, which apprehends the particular *(svalakṣaṇa)* with no conceptual construction *(kalpanā)*, and inference, which apprehends the universal *(sāmānyalakṣaṇa)* produced through conceptual construction. The doctrines that invited attack from opponents, such as that of the identity between the means *(pramāṇa)* and the result *(pramāṇaphala)* of cognition and that of "self-awareness" *(svasaṃvitti)* of cognition, are advocated in this chapter. Chapters 2, 3, 4, and 6 deal with logical problems. In these chapters Dignāga discusses in full detail such topics as the distinction between inference for oneself *(svārthānumāna)* and inference for others *(parārthānumāna)*, the three characteristics *(trirūpa)* of an inferential mark *(liṅga)*, the object of inference *(anumeya)*, the "wheel of reasons" *(hetucakra)*, and the concomitance in agreement *(anavaya)* and in difference *(vyatireka)* between inferential mark and example, and establishes the system of three-membered syllogism. The fifth chapter is devoted to the elucidation of the *apoha* doctrine, that is, the doctrine that the function of a word consists in the "differentiation (of an object) from other things" *(anyāpoha)* and not in the direct reference to a real entity. This doctrine also aroused controversy among the scholars of the different philosophical schools.

Dignāga had a great influence on the scholars of both Brahmanic and Buddhist schools. Uddyotakara (c. sixth century) of the Nyāya school, Kumārila Bhaṭṭa (c. seventh century) of the Mīmāṃsā school, and Mallavādin (c. sixth century) of the Jain school made vehement attacks on his doctrines as presented in the *Pramāṇasamuccaya*. Praśastapāda (c. sixth century), a Vaiśeṣika philosopher, was much indebted to Dignāga for the formulation of his theory of inference. Among Buddhist scholars, Dharmakīrti (c. 600–660) wrote an elaborate commentary on the *Pramāṇasamuccaya*, the *Pramāṇavārttika*, in which he fully developed the ideas formulated by Dignāga. Soon this work took the place of the *Pramāṇasamuccaya* in academic circles, and was studied both by Buddhists and by members of rival schools.

[*See also* Yogācāra; Indian Philosophies; *and the biographies of Vasubandhu and Dharmakīrti.*]

BIBLIOGRAPHY

Frauwallner, Erich. "Dignāga, sein Werk und seine Entwicklung." *Wiener Zeitschrift für die Kunde Süd- und Ostasiens* 3 (1959): 83–164. On the basis of the careful examination of Dignāga's works, the author proposes a chronological order for them and sketches the development of Dignāga's thought. The Sanskrit or Tibetan texts of some short treatises are appended.

Hattori Masaaki, trans. *Dignāga, On Perception, Being the Pratyakṣapariccheda of Dignāga's Pramāṇasamuccaya.* Cambridge, Mass., 1968. An annotated English translation of chapter 1 of the *Pramāṇasamuccaya*, based on the Sanskrit fragments and the Tibetan versions. In the annotation references are made to the philosophical arguments of the rival schools and Dignāga's followers. Transliterated texts of two Tibetan versions are printed on facing pages.

Kitagawa Hidenori. *Indo koten ronrigaku no kenkyū: Jinna no taikei.* Tokyo, 1965. A lucid exposition of Dignāga's system of logic (part 1) and a Japanese translation of the main portions of the *Pramāṇasamuccaya*, chapters 2, 3, 4, and 6, with explanations based on Jinendrabuddhi's commentary (part 2). Appendix A consists of an annotated English translation of Dharmakīrti's *Saṃtānāntarasiddhi*, and an abridged English translation of Dignāga's *Ch'ü yin chia she lun (*Upādāyaprajñapti-prakaraṇa)*. Appendix B presents two Tibetan texts of the *Pramāṇasamuccaya*.

HATTORI MASAAKI

DIHLAWĪ, SHĀH WALĪ ALLĀH. *See* Walī Allāh, Shāh.

DILTHEY, WILHELM (1833–1911), German philosopher of history and intellectual historian. Dilthey was born in Biebrich am Rhein, where his father, a liberal Calvinist theologian, was court chaplain to the duke of Nassau. Following graduation at the head of his *Gymnasium* class in nearby Wiesbaden, he enrolled at Heidelberg in 1852 to study theology. After only a year, however, he left for Berlin and there began to concentrate on history and philosophy, studying with some of the greatest representatives of German historical scholarship: Leopold von Ranke, Theodor Mommsen, Jakob Grimm, August Boeckh, Franz Bopp, and Karl Ritter. In philosophy, his principal mentor was the Aristotelian F. A. Trendelenburg. Dilthey's interest in the German theologian and philosopher Friedrich Schleiermacher also stems from this Berlin period. In 1860, his essay on Schleiermacher's hermeneutics was awarded two prizes by the Schleiermacher Society and was followed by a commission to complete an edition of Schleiermacher's correspondence and write his biography. Dilthey defended his doctoral dissertation on Schleiermacher's moral principles in 1864. In the same year he presented a monograph on the analysis of moral consciousness that served as his *Habilitationsschrift,* the thesis that qualified him for university teaching. After a brief period of teaching at Berlin, he was called to Basel in 1867, and then to Kiel in 1868.

In 1870, Dilthey published the initial volume of his *Leben Schleiermachers* (Life of Schleiermacher), the first of several ambitious projects that would remain unfinished. In 1871, he accepted a chair at Breslau, where his main efforts were devoted to the problem of the nature and methods of the human sciences. In 1883, he published the first part of his major philosophical work, *Einleitung in die Geisteswissenschaften* (Introduction to the Human Sciences). In 1883, Dilthey also returned to Berlin to succeed Hermann Lotze in the chair that had once been occupied by Hegel. Election to the Prussian Academy of the Sciences followed in 1897. In 1900, he gave up his seminars, and in 1907 he retired from teaching altogether in order to develop more systematically the philosophical ideas put forward in the *Einleitung.* Dilthey died while on a working holiday in the Austrian Tyrol in 1911.

Dilthey's research on Schleiermacher and his account of the process of understanding the activity of a religious thinker constituted an important component of his work on the theory and practice of intellectual history. Yet his major contribution to religious studies lies in his theory of the human studies and its implications for the scientific investigation of religion.

Dilthey's theory of the human studies may be understood as an attempt to establish the idea that these disciplines have a distinctive subject matter and method that differentiate them from the natural sciences. The difference in subject matter is not grounded in two different modes of being but is, rather, based on two different ways of experiencing the world. Each is empirical, and each has its own definitive scientific objectivity and validity. The distinctive subject matter of the natural sciences is the world as given in the abstractions of sense perception and structured by reference to causal laws. The distinctive subject matter of the human sciences is the world as the person actually experiences it: the historically constituted ensemble of meanings and values that are the objects of his practical projects and interests. Because the artifacts of this historical world are all expressions of the human spirit, or *Geist,* the human sciences are the *Geisteswissenschaften,* the disciplines that investigate expressions of the human spirit.

Verstehen, or understanding, the distinctive method of these disciplines, is a consequence of the attitude that defines their subject matter. Because the actions and artifacts that express the human spirit are meaningful entities, a kind of knowledge is possible in the human sciences that cannot be reduced to explanation, or knowledge of the nomological structure of natural phenomena. *Verstehen* identifies the meaningful content of expressions of the spirit and the structures in which they are implicated. Much of Dilthey's work in the philosophy of the human sciences was concerned with the elucidation of this process of understanding and its distinctive epistemological quality, which he called the hermeneutic circle. An interpretation of the Romantic movement, for example, presupposes prior knowledge of which persons, actions, and artifacts fall within it. However, the latter are identifiable only on the basis of a general criterion that defines the features of romanticism. Thus knowledge of the whole rests on knowledge of the parts, which in turn presupposes knowledge of the whole.

The main aim of Dilthey's philosophical work was to develop a critique of historical reason that would resolve the question of how knowledge in the human sciences is possible. Dilthey struggled with this enterprise for more than forty years in the attempt to identify a basic or foundational science for the human sciences. In his writings of the 1880s and the early 1890s, he seems to have envisaged a descriptive, analytical, and phenomenological psychology as this foundation. Beginning in 1895, however, he stressed hermeneutics, or the theory of interpretation, as the basis for a valid theory of knowledge on which the human sciences can be grounded. Nevertheless, in his last works Dilthey retained intact many of the psychological theses of his earlier writings; moreover, the hermeneutic doctrines of his later work are also present in his earlier writings. As a result, the relationship between psychology and hermeneutics in the development of Dilthey's thought remains one of the most controverted issues among scholars who have attempted to understand his project of a critique of historical reason.

BIBLIOGRAPHY

The standard edition of Dilthey's works is the *Gesammelte Schriften*, 2d ed. (Stuttgart, 1957–), of which eighteen volumes, prepared by various editors, have appeared to date, with more to follow. Also being published is a six-volume English edition of selected works by Dilthey. Under the general editorship of Rudolf A. Makkreel and Frithjof Rodi, two volumes have so far been issued: *Poetry and Experience* (Princeton, 1984) and *Introduction to the Human Sciences* (Princeton, 1985). Major works on Dilthey in English include Makkreel's *Dilthey: Philosopher of the Human Studies* (Princeton, 1975), Michael Ermarth's *Wilhelm Dilthey: The Critique of Historical Reason* (Chicago, 1978), H. P. Rickman's *Wilhelm Dilthey: Pioneer of the Human Studies* (Berkeley, 1979), and Theodore Plantinga's *Historical Understanding in the Thought of Wilhelm Dilthey* (Toronto, 1980). For extant English translations of Dilthey's works, see Plantinga's bibliography. Since 1983 there has also been a scholarly journal devoted to Dilthey's work, with some articles in English and current bibliography: *Dilthey-Jahrbuch für Philosophie und Geschichte der Geisteswissenschaften* (Göttingen).

GUY OAKES

DINKA RELIGION. *See* Nuer and Dinka Religion.

DIOLA RELIGION. Numbering some four hundred thousand people, the Diola inhabit the well-watered coastal plain between the Gambia and São Domingo rivers of Senegambia and Guinea-Bissau. They are sedentary wet-rice farmers and usually described as a stateless people, governed by village councils. Despite a common ethnic label the various Diola subgroups speak distinct dialects and have somewhat divergent religious beliefs and political organizations.

The past two centuries of Diola religious history have been characterized by the increasing interaction of Diola religion with Islam and Christianity. While Muslims and Christians have been in contact with the Diola at least since the sixteenth century, few conversions occurred before the late nineteenth century. On the north shore of the Casamance River, where contact with Islam was both earliest and most violent, many Diola have embraced Islam and, to a lesser extent, Christianity. However, the growth of these new religions had to await the firm establishment of colonial rule and the growth of commerce in peanuts before gaining dominance over the traditional religion. On the south shore the vast majority of the population resisted the advance of Islam and Christianity until after World War II. While Christianity has made substantial inroads since that time, Diola religion remains dominant. This may partly result from the south's escape from the devastation of the Mandinka invasions and its slower integration into the colonial economy. A major factor, however, was the ability of south shore religion to adapt to rapidly changing conditions in the nineteenth and twentieth centuries. Innovations in ritual structures, the creation of new cults, and the emergence of Diola prophets have all contributed to the vitality of Diola traditional religion. This study will focus on south shore Diola religion.

Adherents of Diola religion believe in a creator god and in a number of lesser spirits whose powers originate with the supreme being but who are more accessible to the religious community. A study of Diola ritual might suggest that the supreme being, variously known as Ata-Emit or Emitai, was a remote high god whose name was rarely invoked in prayer, who had no shrines, and who was not a moral force in community life. The lesser spirits, variously known as *ukine* or *sinaati*, dominate ritual life. By examining the history of various cults and other religious beliefs, it becomes clear that Emitai is an active force in Diola life as a provider of life itself, as a source of spiritual aid in a time of crisis, and as the creator of the various cults. His name is derived from *emit*, meaning both "sky" and "year," thus indicating a strong relationship with the heavens and the order of an agricultural year. Furthermore, *Emitai ehlahl*, which means "it is raining," indicates Emitai's crucial role in the disbursement of that life-giving resource.

Emitai is seen as the creator of the world and all its inhabitants and as the source of human knowledge of farming, ironworking, and healing. He established a set of duties and interdictions to which he holds people accountable. At the time of death, Emitai decides whether a person has lived morally enough to become an ancestor or whether, if the individual concerned disregarded Emitai's interdictions, he will become a phantom wanderer or, ambivalently, a village dweller in a land to the south. All fates are temporary; the dead are eventually reincarnated.

Emitai communicates with people through dreams and visions and endows some of them with powers to communicate with him and with lesser spirits. While lesser spirits receive the bulk of ritual attention, prayers are ultimately received by Emitai. In times of crisis or when people feel they have exhausted other means, Emitai is prayed to directly. This is especially true during droughts when a ritual known as Nyakul Emit is performed. Rituals are conducted at all the village shrines, and prayers are offered directly to the supreme being: "Ata-Emit, is it true that this year's rice is destined to wither in the rice paddies? . . . The misfortune will be so large that we will not have the strength to speak. Give us water, give us life."

In Diola religion, the lesser spirits provide specific ways for individuals, families, and communities to resolve recurrent problems and to sustain a religious community. Thus there are shrines associated with rain, women's fertility, farming, hunting, fishing, war, ironworking, healing, family welfare, and village councils. These cults were introduced in a variety of ways. Some are said to have existed since the time of the first ancestors, that is, beyond the memory of Diola historians. Others were borrowed from the Bainounk, a people who were conquered by the Diola but who still retain a spiritual authority as the first inhabitants of the region. Still others were introduced by people who had spiritual powers, who were said to be able to travel up to Emitai or make contact with spirits through dreams or visions. Others were learned about from neighboring Diola or from other neighboring peoples. Such shrines were installed by elders from the outside community who also initiated a local group of shrine elders. The large number of shrines helps to ensure that one path can resolve any particular problem, and it allows a broad access to religious authority. Most people eventually become shrine elders. The shrines themselves contain ritual objects associated with spirits but not the spirits themselves. These objects help to summon the spirits and focus the attention of the worshipers.

While the preceding description represents broad continuities in Diola religion since 1700, environmental disruption, political and economic changes, and prophetic leaders have all influenced Diola religion. Droughts and epidemics have created spiritual challenges that have led to the formation of new cults and changes in ritual structure. Diola participation in the slave trade generated new sources of community vulnerability as well as new sources of social stratification, each of which had religious consequences. Men who gained wealth from the ransom or sale of captives often invested their wealth in the acquisition of priestly offices, thereby changing the role of priests and the ability of the less fortunate to gain religious authority. A new series of cults stressing lavish sacrifices to gain ritual authority became increasingly important to the Diola in the eighteenth century.

During World War II a Diola woman named Alinesitoué had a series of visions of Emitai. It was a time of severe drought and increasing French military conscription and confiscation of rice and cattle. Alinesitoué revealed that Emitai had given her a series of shrines that would help procure rain but whose ritual offices would be open to all, regardless of wealth, age, or sex. She advocated a renewed commitment to community, a stripping away of social and religious hierarchies, and a reaffirmation of many customs that had fallen into disuse. She taught that Emitai was deeply involved in the lives of the Diola and that they could expect his assistance if they followed his ways. Alinesitoué's teachings enabled the Diola to meet the crisis generated by the French occupation and a renewed Christian mission challenge. They allowed the Diola to adapt to their increasing integration into the rapidly changing order of a colonial and independent Senegal with the support of a vital Diola religion.

BIBLIOGRAPHY

The major ethnographic study of the Diola, with extensive discussion of religious issues, is Louis-Vincent Thomas's *Les Diola,* 2 vols. (Dakar, 1958). Thomas has also written a vast number of articles on Diola ritual, concepts of death, initiation, and so on. J. David Sapir has written a number of articles on Diola symbolic thought, of which "Kujamama: Symbolic Separation among the Diola-Fogny," *American Anthropologist* 72 (December 1970): 1330–1348, is the most important. On the relationship between religious beliefs and legal and economic change, see Francis G. Snyder's *Capitalism and Legal Change: An African Transformation* (New York, 1981). Historical approaches to Diola religion include Jean Girard's *Genèse du pouvoir charismatique en Basse Casamance (Sénégal)* (Dakar, 1969) and my "Belief and Value Change among the Diola-Esulalu in Eighteenth and Nineteenth Century Senegambia" (Ph.D. diss., Yale University, 1986). There are also two important studies of the influence of Islam among the Diola: Frances Anne Leary's "Islam, Politics and Colonialism: A Political History of Islam in the Casamance Region of Senegal, 1850–1914" (Ph.D. diss., Northwestern University, 1970) and Peter Allen Mark's "Economic and Religious Change among the Diola of Boulouf (Casamance), 1890–1940" (Ph.D. diss., Yale University, 1976).

ROBERT M. BAUM

DIONYSIUS THE AREOPAGITE (c. AD 500), Christian mystical theologian, also known as Pseudo-Dionysius. In the early sixth century, a set of treatises and letters appeared under the name of Dionysius the Areopagite, whom Paul had converted in Athens (*Acts* 17:34). At a synod in Constantinople in 533, the writings were used to support the monophysite position, but their authenticity was challenged. Nevertheless, the works soon came to be accepted as both apostolic and orthodox, and assumed nearly canonical status and authority in Eastern and Western Christendom.

Hilduin first translated the works into Latin (c. 832), and mistakenly identified Dionysius the Areopagite with Denis, the first bishop of Paris and patron saint of France. Though Abelard challenged this last identification, not until the Renaissance did Lorenzo Valla and Erasmus again question the authenticity of the writings' apostolic claims. These claims were decisively overturned in 1895, when two scholars, Joseph Stiglmayr and Hugo Koch, documented the dependence of the Dionysian corpus on Proclus, the fifth-century Neoplatonic philosopher. The works were thus composed in the late fifth or early sixth century. Despite many scholarly attempts to identify their author, he remains hidden behind his influential pseudonym. Dionysius's treatises are *Divine Names, Celestial Hierarchy, Ecclesiastical Hierarchy,* and *Mystical Theology.* The titles indicate Dionysius's principal concerns: religious language, hierarchy, and spirituality.

Divine Names poses the problems of religious knowledge and language by contrasting divine transcendence and theophany. In itself the divine nature is beyond being *(huperousios),* yet God becomes manifest in all being as its cause. God is both utterly transcendent and present in all things. This paradox underlies Dionysius's affirmative and negative theology. Affirmative theology focuses on divine causality and knows God through God's self-manifestations. It traces the causal procession from God's unity, through the divine ideas, or forms, to celestial hierarchy and thence to the sensible world; as it follows this descent, affirmative theology discovers an increasing variety of divine names, from "good" and "one" to "ancient of days," "sun," and "rock." Conversely, negative theology retraces the procession of beings in a return that moves from the sensible world, through the intelligences and forms, and to divine unity. Thus Dionysius emphasizes the dissimilarities in sensible symbols and the limits of all intelligible divine names. His work *Mystical Theology* negates all language about God because divinity cannot be known in its transcendence. For Dionysius, therefore, God is both nameless and praised in all names.

In *Celestial Hierarchy* Dionysius defines hierarchy as "a sacred order, activity and knowledge" that seeks "as far as possible [an] assimilation and union with God" (3.1–2). Its order is defined by each rank's capacity for assimilation to God, and its activity is purification, illumination, and perfection as it receives and communicates divine knowledge.

The celestial hierarchy consists of nine ranks of angelic intelligences, arranged in groups of three: (1) seraphim, cherubim, thrones; (2) dominations, virtues, powers; and (3) principalities, archangels, angels. The first triad is immediately united to God, whose light and knowledge it communicates to the lower ranks. In its turn the third triad presides over the human hierarchies. The ecclesiastical hierarchy stands between the celestial hierarchy and the hierarchy of the Mosaic law, which it supersedes (*Ecclesiastical Hierarchy* 5.2). Within the church there are six ranks in two triads: (1) bishops, priests, and ministers or deacons; and (2) monks, the "holy people of God," and those being purified (e.g., penitents and those awaiting baptism). Dionysius again stresses the activities of perfecting, illuminating, and purifying, but his focus here is symbolic and sacramental. Baptism is the sacrament of initiation and illumination, and the eucharistic liturgy exemplifies both the christological mystery and the perfecting "communion and union with the One" (*Ecclesiastical Hierarchy* 3.1). Contemplation *(theōria)* of the sacraments' hidden meanings purifies and illumines the understanding, and produces an intellectual insight akin to that of the celestial hierarchy.

The brief treatise *Mystical Theology* both completes and transcends the schemes of the divine names and of the hierarchies. It emphasizes the divine nature's radical transcendence, and it envisions mystical union in terms of unknowing *(agnōsia).* The concluding chapters present negative theology's ascending motion by stripping away the sensible and intelligible names of God. Dionysius then denies that God can be named adequately even in negative terms, because God is prior to all affirmation and negation. In itself the divine nature remains beyond all the contrasts that arise in its causal self-disclosure—and thus beyond all knowledge and speech. For Dionysius, mystical theology is an austere, intellectual ascent to union with God, and because divinity is essentially unknowable, this union occurs in the cloud and darkness of unknowing. This assimilation to God also completes the task of hierarchy. It is the perfection that the intellect seeks in symbols, sacraments, and intelligible divine names. Yet mystical theology accomplishes this ecstatically, by going out from intellect and hierarchy to their hidden source in the divine nature itself. In this way mystical theology completes the return to the God "beyond being."

The Dionysian writings are the product of a thoroughly hellenized Christian mind. Their reliance on Proclus and Damascius continues and even exaggerates the Greek patristic use of Platonic and Neoplatonic thought to interpret Christian faith. Dionysius was drawn into the mainstream of Byzantine theology by Maximos the Confessor, John of Scythopolis, and John of Damascus. Dionysius's major impact, however, came in the medieval West, where he was an immensely authoritative but alien figure. As the only Greek father to be fully and widely welcomed in the West, Dionysius influenced the whole range of Latin theology and spirituality. His account of the angelic hierarchy became standard, and his treatment of liturgy and the sacraments enriched the symbolic thinking of the Middle Ages. The Dionysian corpus became a major source for speculative thinkers, including John Scottus Eriugena, Albertus Magnus, Thomas Aquinas, and Nicholas of Cusa. Perhaps most important was the influence of

Dionysius on mystical theology, evident in the Victorines, the Rhineland and English mystics, and in John of the Cross. Even while these Western thinkers were transforming his doctrine in their schools and monasteries, they consistently revered him as the "divine Dionysius." Although Dionysius's influence waned with the increasing suspicion concerning his identity, he still speaks powerfully on the issues of religious knowledge, language, and symbolism and their inherent limits.

BIBLIOGRAPHY

The standard edition of the extant works of Dionysius remains that of Balthasar Cordier (Antwerp, 1634), published in volume 3 of J.-P. Migne's *Patrologia Graeca* (1857; reprint, Turnhout, 1977). Gunther Heil has prepared a new edition of *La hiérarchie céleste* with a French translation by Maurice de Gandillac and an introduction by René Roques (Paris, 1970). The Dionysian corpus is available in English translations: John D. Jones's *Pseudo-Dionysius Areopagite: The Divine Names and Mystical Theology* (Milwaukee, 1980); *Mystical Theology and the Celestial Hierarchies*, 2d ed. (Fintry, England, 1965); Thomas L. Campbell's *The Ecclesiastical Hierarchy* (Lanham, Md., 1981; from a Ph.D. diss., 1955); and Ronald F. Hathaway's translation of Dionysius's letters in his study *Hierarchy and Order in the Letters of Pseudo-Dionysius* (The Hague, 1969). An excellent survey of Dionysius and his influence is the series of articles by René Roques and others under "Denys l'Aréopagite," in the *Dictionnaire de spiritualité*, vol. 3 (Paris, 1957), edited by Charles Baumgartner. Other studies include Denys Rutledge's *Cosmic Theology: The Ecclesiastical Hierarchy of Pseudo-Denys* (Staten Island, N.Y., 1965); Bernhard Brons's *Gott und die Seienden* (Göttingen, 1976); and Jan Vanneste's "Is the Mysticism of Pseudo-Dionysius Genuine?," *International Philosophical Quarterly* 3 (1963): 286–306.

DONALD F. DUCLOW

DIONYSOS is included in the pantheons of the majority of Greek cities and is present at such very early festivals as the Apaturia, the festival of the phratries, and the Anthesteria, that of new wine and the assembly of the dead. The youngest of the Olympian gods, he is somewhat insecure about his divine identity because he was conceived in the womb of a mortal woman, Semele. His semidivine status may account for his consistent interest in mortals and wine drinkers. As the god of masks, Dionysos appears in many forms, but he most loves to disguise himself as a god of the city, posing as a political deity and expressing absolute power. He appears in this form at Teos, where the city and the territory are consecrated to him and where he has a magnificent temple. In the town of Heraia in Arcadia, one of the two Dionysian temples is reserved for Dionysos the Citizen (Dionysos Polites). In Patras, where he is promoted to the rank of tyrant and given the title of Aisymnetes, he is the magistrate in charge of giving every person his rightful share. His political career begins in the seventh century on the island of Lesbos. Here he appears alongside Zeus and Hera in the common sanctuary as the god who is an "eater of raw flesh" (Alcaeus, *Fragment* 129). Thus the keystone of this political and religious edifice is Dionysos's subversive character, expressed in his rejection of the sacrificial system of eating food that is cooked according to the proper order (roasted then boiled) in favor of *omophagia*, the desire to eat raw flesh. The most extreme form of *omophagia* is *allelophagia*, in which men devour one another, becoming like wild beasts and ferocious animals. Such behavior allows them to escape from the human condition: it is a way of getting outside oneself by imitating those animals least subject to domestication.

It is at Delphi, in the great pan-Hellenic sanctuary of the eighth century, that Dionysos presents the full extent of his influence. In partnership with Apollo, the most ambitious god in the pantheon, Semele's son dominates not only the assemblies of local gods but also the whole course of Greek religion. Although he is originally from Thebes, Dionysos can be found in two parts of Delphi: in the heights of Mount Parnassus, where the members of the Thyiads, "the agitated ones," gather every other year in the Corycian cavern to honor him in the secret liturgy of the *trietēris* ("triennial festival"); and in the sanctuary of the Pythia, in a tomb-cradle beside the golden statue of Apollo, where he waits in mortal slumber until his servants come to wake him and where the Pure Ones, the priests of Apollo, privately offer sacrifice to him. At Delphi, Dionysos holds himself aloof from the giving of oracles, whereas in other sanctuaries oracles are closely connected with him. But this is because at Delphi he forms, together with Apollo, one of a pair of forces who are alternative poles in a system open to all of the altars or sanctuaries they share. Apollo has his Dionysian side, just as Dionysos presents more than one Apollonian aspect. The close connection between them at Delphi is the culmination of all the alliances that link them together at other places and in other ways.

Dionysos and Apollo are particularly joined in Orphic thought and its theogonic discourse, which was wholly at variance with the official dogma of Hesiod's theology. The religious system of the city and of the world, Hesiod's theology categorically rejected the way of life advocated by followers of Orpheus, who renounced the world and sought to be saved by returning to the primordial unity that preceded diversity. In the succession of divine ages described in the Orphic theogony, Dionysos is at once the last ruler and the first. In the last age he appears in the guise of the child who is lured by the Titans with toys—a spinning top, a devilish rhombus, and a mirror—and then slaughtered and devoured after being first boiled and then roasted (in breach of the normal order of the sacrificial ceremony). In being torn apart, scattered abroad, and broken into seven pieces, Dionysos experiences for himself the effects of the utmost differentiation, in accord with the process that began after the first age under the aegis of Phanes-Metis, another name for Dionysos. The primordial god of the perfect Unity, Phanes-Metis comes back at the end in order to return things once again to the beginning. In this scenario Apollo, even at Delphi, plays a role in the odyssey of Dionysos. Apollo buries the remains of Dionysos's murdered body at the foot of Mount Parnassus; shares the sovereignty of the oracle with Night, the primordial power; and, finally, becomes the Sun, the greatest of the gods even to Orpheus himself, rising to the summit of Mount Pangaeus in Dionysos's Thracian kingdom.

The success of Dionysos in Orphic theology reveals more than his ability to appear as the youngest of the Olympians and the oldest of the ancient gods. It demonstrates too his mystical calling, his natural tendency to rule over mysteries. In Ephesus, in the late sixth century, the philosopher Heraclitus denounced those who prowl in the night, in particular "magi, Bacchants, and mystics." It is sacrilegious, according to Heraclitus, for people to be initiated into what they dare to call mysteries. From the discoveries at Olbia on the shores of the Black Sea, we now believe that Dionysos first appears as the initiator in the sixth century, long before a Scythian king had enrolled in the band of Bacchus (Gr., Bakchos) in this same city, where he was fond of going for the aesthetic pleasure of living *à la grecque*—even to the extent of becoming a follower of Dionysos. This initiation was already known to King Scylas (Herodotus, 4.79), who had already begun preparations for it when a prodigy occurred: his palace of white marble, struck by lightning, was reduced to ashes. Nonetheless Scylas went ahead with the initiation ceremony, during which he publicly played the Bacchant, staggering through the town with a band of revelers.

What Herodotus implies in his account of Scylas going through with the initiation *(teletē)* is stated clearly in Euripides' *The Bacchae* in the voice of Dionysos. To Pentheus, who has failed to recognize his divinity and who will remain firmly entrenched in a ridiculous error, Dionysos, appearing as a stranger, recounts how the god introduced him to his rites, during which Dionysos watched him while he himself looked upon the god. In this mirror image, the initiation seems to denote an experience in which the Bacchant comes face to face with his god: he becomes as much a Bacchus as is Dionysos. The lord of the Bacchanalia refuses to reveal this experience to Pentheus; these are unspeakable things *(arrēta)* that non-Bacchants may not know (1.472). At Cumae, in the fifth century, a similar formula prohibited entry to a Greek cemetery "save to those who have been initiated to Dionysos."

At Olbia and at Cumae, Dionysos obviously does not receive the official, public worship that so many cities practice during the winter months, when solemn processions are attended by the entire population. Sacred laws from Asia Minor clearly distinguish between regular sacrifices, in which a goat or even a large ox is offered to Dionysos in full view of the city, and more private ceremonies in which the priestess of Dionysos celebrates an initiation into the cult of the god who drives people mad, inciting men and women to raving lunacy. There is a difference between *thuein* and *telein.* The same holy law of the Miletians, in 276 BCE, specifies that the rites of consecration *(telestēria)* should be invested in the priestess, who can initiate people into Dionysos Bakcheios "in the city, in the country, or in the islands." These are the so-called trieteric mysteries, which take place every two years. At Miletus they were celebrated at the same time as the Feast of the Return, when the god, escorted by the priests and priestesses, came back and entered the town.

In more than 150 cities of Asia Minor and the islands, Dionysos appears in the guise of Bakcheios, the god of the bacchanals—those who, like him, have become *bakchoi.* "Many are those who carry thyrsi; few are the Bacchants," according to a saying of the initiation masters quoted by Plato in his *Phaedo* (69c). To the initiate is reserved the experience of frenzy and possession, seeing the god face-to-face and sharing his madness and delirium. In the last golden tablet, a book of the dead unearthed at Vibo Valentia in Calabria in 1974, the titles *mystic* and *bacchant* are given to the chosen ones who go to the right, under the sign of memory, and take the sacred path that leads to the gods. Dionysos follows the same direction, from the sixth century on, to enter, via Iacchos, into the system of Eleusinian gods—the mysteries founded by Demeter on the fringes of Athens.

In connection with Dionysos the Initiate—who, under the name of Mustes, has a temple between Tegea and Argos (Pausanias, 8.54.5)—we find esoteric practices and rules of secrecy. Near Mantinea, in a great ancient chamber known as the *megaron,* the honey companions *(meliastai)* worship Dionysos, a neighbor of Black Aphrodite (Pausanias, 8.6.4). At Brysai, on the slopes of Mount Taigetos in Laconia, only women are permitted to view the statue of Dionysos, ensconced in an open-air sanctuary, and the sacrifices they perform are carried out in the greatest secrecy (Pausanias, 3.20.3). Males are also excluded on Lesbos, at Aigai, and on the island on the shores of the Atlantic described by Posidonius. The privilege of experiencing a private, face-to-face encounter with Dionysos or of being truly possessed by him is restricted to women, notwithstanding the violent objections of some modern-day feminists, who condemn the Dionysian interest in women as another way of oppressing them. The most unfortunate effect of this misinterpretation is to obscure the Dionysian union and its fundamental aspect: it is an individual allegiance that rejects kinship or feudal ties and, in the fluid form of the private *thiasos,* creates associations and communities independent of authority and outside the control of the state. If the mystical and mysterious side of Dionysos appears less clearly in the Athenian city-state—no doubt because the mystical pole there is called Eleusis—still it is a major component of Dionysianism in very many cities from the earliest times. Whether he resides in the center of town or camps on its outskirts, Dionysos is always the lord of dementia and of the ability to get outside oneself.

The popular tales of his coming and his manifestations describe, often in explicit terms, the favored *modus operandi* of Dionysos. It has to do with what the Greeks call the god's *epidēmia:* the tendency of a power to take up residence in one sanctuary and then switch to another temple and another country. Thus Apollo likes to spend the winter in the company of the Hyperboreans, making it possible for Dionysos to be "woken" by his priestesses, who proclaim his return. This is *epidēmia* in the sense of appearance or presence *(parousia)* and not in the sense of contagion, which would suggest that Dionysos moves from one place to another like a contagious disease whose infectious source is located on foreign soil (in the country of the Thracians) and is responsible for the violent fevers that invade the healthy, vigorous body of the Hellenic nation. One need only peel the outer shell of legend from this picture, only recently revealed with the aid of a number of myths concerning Dionysian Thrace and the god's enemies, to uncover the reality of a very faithful history. The Dionysian *parousia,* as originally intended, presents two interlocking aspects. The god who comes is a foreigner and remains so, carrying within him the most unwavering strangeness.

Yet the opposite side of Dionysos, and his appearance vis-à-vis the other gods, is that he affirms through his disavowal that he is a god too strange, and too much a stranger, to be believable. In Greece, the stranger, as opposed to the "barbarian," belongs to the society of those who share the same blood, the same language, and the same gods, according to Herodotus's definition. Dionysos, indeed, is no barbarian god, even when his outrages smack of barbarism. Born in Thebes, in the town of Kadmos, he is a great god, the equal of Apollo, the oracular power known as Ismenios. Dionysos presents himself in his status as a foreigner in more than one of his Joyous Entrances. For example, at Patrae in Achaia (Pausanias, 7.19.7–9), Dionysos enters as an idol in a sealed chest, like a demon god classed as a foreigner, and is conveyed by an equally strange king, a prince stricken with madness for having looked at the face, the mask, of Dionysos. This strange team puts an end to an equally outlandish sacrifice in which the human blood of both sexes had to be shed, bringing forth a sickness *(nosos)* in the land; the earth is diseased with punishment imposed by a cruel Artemis.

But the stranger who comes with Dionysos, instead of making himself a host and returning the gracious generosity seen in a feast like the Xenia, appears ungrateful to those who find him. The strangeness of Dionysos seems to imply that he cannot be recognized as a god at first sight. Thus he is obliged to offer a public demonstration of his divine power so that all people can see what a great god they have failed to acknowledge.

The appearance of Dionysos requires the revelation of Otherness through its exacting violence. There are those who do not know him and still slight him, doubters and those who neglect, scorn, or refuse to believe in or accept him. And there are those who are called on to persecute him, whom he has chosen to be his tormenters and thus the most striking witnesses to his *parousia,* once they have become his rightful victims. In Boeotia, in the city of Orchomenus, the daughters of King Minyas, absorbed in household tasks, pay no heed to Dionysos. But then the god, in the guise of a young girl, carefully encourages them to join in his mysteries. Suddenly, all three are entranced by Dionysos's metamorphoses—the girl disappears, and the god is a bull, a lion, a leopard. They watch in fascination as milk and nectar flow along the weaver's loom. Already they are caught in the web; wishing to honor the unknown god by offering sacrifice, they draw lots to see who will have the privilege of providing the chosen victim. The tragically elected Leucippe falls upon her own son and, with the help of her sisters, tears him to pieces in front of Dionysos (Antoninus Liberalis, *Metamorphoses* 10).

In Thrace, where Dionysos is also treated as a stranger, Lykurgos embodies the irreconcilable foe whose blindness compels the god, despite himself, to unleash the cruelest of deeds. Like a madman, Lykurgos brandishes his double ax, the *pelekus,* to kill Dionysos, not knowing that in Thessaly, at Pagasai, Dionysos is called the god of the ax, Pelekus. Lykurgos, hallucinating in his *mania,* turns the weapon back upon his own flesh and blood: he strikes down his children, whose living limbs, arms, and lopped-off legs appear to him as so many branches on a vine. This happens before the Edonians, incited by Dionysos, attempt to put an end to the fatal barrenness of their land by handing over their king to wild horses. The king is to be torn apart on Mount Pangaeus, where the oracle of Dionysos, like that at Delphi, will be erected. On its peak, Orpheus, the worshiper of the greatest of the gods, whom he names Apollo, is torn to pieces by Thracian women with a violence borrowed from Dionysos.

The stranger-god finds the full measure of his *parousia* in murderous frenzy, in the *mania* that leads to killing and to the spilled blood of a son torn apart by his mother, to children who are cut down alive by their father, and to father and daughter, such as Icarus and Erigone, losing their lives for lack of pure wine. Dionysos is truly himself only in *unyielding* madness, when the *mania* creates, through murder, a taint, a *miasma*, a sickness or pestilence. One must be cleansed of this stain; it is urgent to escape the plague, for in it appears the contagious power of those who fall into madness, which affects an entire town or even a whole country. In the *mania* of Dionysos is a taint that the god himself experiences in the course of his life (Apollodorus, *Library* 3.5.1). When he discovers the vine, Hera, his stepmother, breathes madness into Dionysos, dooming him to the wanderings of all madmen. Dionysos goes to Proteus, then to Cybele in Phrygia; at last he finds Rhea, who eases and puts an end to his nomadic delirium. Dionysos is purified, delivered from the taint of his madness. While with Rhea he learns the rites of his cult, and he receives from her his raiment, his Bacchus outfit, which he gives to Pentheus in *The Bacchae.*

The tales of his epiphany thus show how the worship of Dionysos, with its formalized mythology, establishes itself within the sphere of the purification called for by the insanity that the stranger carries. Dionysos the Purificator (Lysios) is the opposite side of the Bacchanal, the god who leads men and women astray in his frenzy. That he is a dual god is shown by his pairs of neighboring temples, at Thebes, at Corinth, and at Sicyon. The unclean madness that forms the basis of his cult is always part of him, however disciplined and civilized Dionysos may seem in the pantheons of cities unmindful of his fundamental wildness.

BIBLIOGRAPHY

Detienne, Marcel. *Dionysus Slain.* Translated by Mireille Muellner and Leonard Muellner. Baltimore, 1979.

Detienne, Marcel. *Dionysos à ciel ouvert.* Paris, 1986.

Farnell, Lewis R. *The Cults of the Greek States,* vol. 5 (1909). Reprint, New Rochelle, N.Y., 1977. See pages 85–344.

Jeanmaire, Henri. *Dionysos: Histoire du culte de Bacchus.* Paris, 1970.

Kerényi, Károly. *Dionysos: Archetypal Image of the Indestructible Life.* Princeton, 1976.

Nilsson, Martin P. *The Dionysiac Mysteries of the Hellenistic and Roman Age* (1957). New York, 1975.

Otto, Walter F. *Dionysos: Myth and Cult.* Bloomington, Ind., 1965.

Segal, Charles. *Dionysiac Poetics and Euripides' Bacchae.* Princeton, 1982.

West, M. L. *The Orphic Poems.* Oxford, 1983.

Marcel Detienne
Translated from French by David M. Weeks

DIOSCURI. *See* Twins.

DISCIPLESHIP.

[*This entry focuses on Christian discipleship. For discussion of related notions in wider contexts, see* Leadership; Authority; *and* Tradition.]

In nearly all religions and in many philosophical schools the normative tradition is established, preserved, and transmitted by a process of discipleship. In this way the bearers of the tradition are formed under the personal supervision of accredited masters, who in turn become capable of instructing others by example and personal direction. In many professions and trades, the novice is apprenticed to a master. Discipleship in religious and quasi-religious societies differs from apprenticeship insofar as it involves a total way of life and a comprehensive system of values. Discipleship is a prominent feature of many Eastern religions, such as Hinduism and Buddhism, and of many Hellenistic schools, such as Pythagoreanism and Epicureanism. Apollonius of Tyana, a Neo-Pythagorean philosopher of the first century AD, was virtually divinized by his disciples.

Judaism. In comparison with other religious groups, the Israelites did not surround the bearers of their traditions with notable veneration. The Torah was seen as God's law rather than the wisdom of Moses; the messages of the prophets were viewed as the word of God rather than the prophets' own. Yet leaders such as Moses, Elijah, and Jeremiah had servants and assistants who in some cases (e.g., Joshua and Elisha) were divinely appointed to succeed their masters.

In rabbinic Judaism the master-disciple relation more nearly approximated that of the Hellenistic schools, as described above, except that the primary focus remained God's revealed law, not the person of the master. Rabbinic students learned the law under the guidance of a particular master, who taught by example and personal contact as well as by lecturing on sacred texts. The pupils were expected to revere and serve their master.

New Testament. Before Jesus, John the Baptist gathered disciples who entered into a stable relationship with him (*Mt.* 9:14, *Mk.* 2:18, *Jn.* 1:35). The disciples were mutually united by the rite of baptism, by fasting, and by special forms of prayer. They kept their identity after the death of John the Baptist (*Acts* 18:25, 19:3–4).

The New Testament alludes also to the disciples of the Pharisees (*Mt.* 22:16, *Lk.* 5:33). In one passage the adversaries of Jesus refer to themselves as disciples of Moses (*Jn.* 9:28). Paul, too, is said to have had disciples (*Acts* 9:25).

The public ministry. Jesus bound disciples to himself in a particularly close way, thanks to his filial consciousness (*Mt.* 11:25–27) and his urgent sense of mission (*Mk.* 1:14–15). He personally selected his disciples (*Mk.* 1:16–20 and parallels), and by acceptance of this call the disciples became specially attached to the person of Jesus. These intimate disciples made up a wandering band who shared common meals and a common way of life, including a prescribed form of prayer (*Lk.* 11:1). They not only heard the public preaching of Jesus but also received fuller explanations in private (*Mk.* 4:13–20 and parallels). Placing themselves totally at the disposal of the Kingdom, the disciples had to separate themselves from their wives, their family, their property, and their previous occupations. They were tested and trained by the experience of being sent on missions to preach the Kingdom, to heal, and to cast out demons (*Mk.* 6:7–13 and parallels).

As the career of Jesus unfolded, the accent was increasingly shifted from the proclamation of the Kingdom to sharing the lot of the master, including rejection, extreme suffering, and death (*Mk.* 8:34 and parallels; *Lk.* 14:27). According to one text, which probably reflects a post-Resurrection extension of the idea of discipleship, all who follow Jesus are expected to take up their own crosses daily (*Lk.* 9:23).

The term *disciple* as used in the Gospels admits of no precise definition. It applies in the first place to an inner group of men who shared the mission of Jesus and walked in his company, especially the Twelve who later came to be called apostles. There are indications that the group of disciples was narrowed toward the end of the ministry of Jesus (*Jn.* 6:66). In a wider sense, the group of disciples included such persons as Cleopas (*Lk.* 24:18) and Joseph of Arimathea (*Jn.* 19:38). Luke evidently intends the reader to understand that "the seventy" of chapter 10, verses 1–16, are disciples. The women of Galilee who follow Jesus and minister to him are not described as disciples (*Lk.* 8:2–3, *Mk.* 15:40–41).

After Easter. The community of the disciples, temporarily dispersed, was reconstituted by the risen Jesus. The twelve apostles in particular became the authorized witnesses to Jesus and had chief responsibility for controlling the traditions about his life and doctrine. In the early church the calling and ministry of the companions of Jesus were made paradigmatic for new converts, so that in some texts all Christians are called disciples. Already in passages such as *Matthew* 10:42, the synoptic Gospels seem to use *disciple* in this extended sense. In the last discourse of Jesus in the gospel of John, the mutual love and union of the disciples are seen as a permanent feature of the church. In *Acts* 6:1 to 21:16, Luke, presumably following his sources, uses *disciple* to mean simply a Christian. As virtual synonyms he also uses *brother* and *saint.* The feminine term *mathētria* is used in *Acts* 10:36 to refer to a woman disciple (Tabitha).

Outside the four Gospels and *Acts* the term *disciple* is not used in the New Testament, but other terms serve a similar function. In *1 Peter* the patient suffering of Jesus is held up as an example "that you should follow in his steps" (2:21). In *Hebrews,* Jesus is repeatedly described as a "pioneer" in suffering, obedience, and glorification. And in *Revelation* the 144,000 saints, who have been chaste and undefiled, are said to "follow the Lamb wherever he goes" (14:4).

Paul depicts the Christian as engrafted into the death and resurrection of Jesus. Dying to sin, the baptized are freed from slavery and brought into the glorious freedom of God's children. Paul sees the whole Christian life as a recapitulation of the existence of Jesus and hence as an exercise of what other authors call discipleship. The humility and obedience of Jesus in his incarnation and crucifixion, according to Paul, are a model for all Christians (*Phil.* 2:5–10). We are to imitate God as he gives himself to us in Christ (*Eph.* 5:1–2). Paul, who consciously imitates Christ, proposes himself, together with Christ, as an example to be imitated by his converts (*1 Cor.* 11:1; cf. *1 Thes.* 1:6; *2 Thes.* 3:7, 3:9; *1 Cor.* 4:16; *Phil.* 3:17).

The terms *following* and *imitation,* as used by Paul and others, have a shared meaning with *discipleship,* but they do not necessarily involve direct dealings with the person of Jesus as experienced in the present. The shift of terminology away from *discipleship* is no doubt connected with the change of situation caused by the death and ascension of Jesus. Yet perhaps this shift is not inevitable, for the Gospels and *Acts,* as we have seen, speak of discipleship in the post-Easter situation.

Postbiblical Christianity. The term *disciple* (Gr., *mathētēs*) remained important for some of the early church fathers, such as Ignatius of Antioch, who regarded the martyr as the "true disciple of Christ" (*Rom.* 4:2, 5:3). Origen and the authors of the Acts of the Martyrs stressed the spiritual value of participation in the atoning sufferings of Christ. In the fourth century, Antony and the Desert Fathers saw the monastic and eremitical life as an "unbloody martyrdom" and thus as perfect discipleship. Throughout the Middle Ages this theme was echoed by monastic writers such as Bernard of Clairvaux (1091–1153), who looked on the monastic life as an imitation of the poverty, humility, and charity of the earthly Jesus.

Evangelical poverty in the following of Jesus was urged by the leaders of radical reform movements of the high and late Middle Ages (Arnaldo da Brescia, Pierre Valdès, John Wyclif, and Jan Hus) and by the founders of the mendicant orders (Francis of Assisi, Dominic). In the fourteenth century the Brethren of the Common Life commended the following of Jesus to all Christians. Emanating from this movement, *Imitation of Christ*, a devotional book ascribed to Thomas à Kempis (d. 1471), advocates "the royal road of the Cross." In his *Spiritual Exercises*, Ignatius Loyola (d. 1556) sought to dispose the exercitant to hear and generously answer the call of Christ the King "to labor with me, that by following me in suffering, he may follow me in glory" (no. 95).

Trained in the pietism of his father, the Danish Lutheran Søren Kierkegaard (1813–1855) saw the essence of Christianity as a responsive patterning of one's life after that of Jesus. He attacked the church establishment of his day for putting obstacles in the way of authentic discipleship.

Early in the twentieth century the Roman Catholic moral theologian Fritz Tillmann tried to develop a total moral system based on the following of Christ as a fundamental principle. Shortly thereafter, the Lutheran Dietrich Bonhoeffer, in *The Cost of Discipleship* (German original, *Nachfolge*, 1937), protested against certain interpretations of "justification by faith alone" that would seem to dispense Christians from the rigorous demands of the Sermon on the Mount. Karl Barth (1886–1968), after praising Bonhoeffer, proposed his own doctrine of the Christian life as discipleship, contrasting it with the medieval ideal of the "imitation of Christ." For Barth, the copying of those who previously obeyed Christ might actually be a form of disobedience, if it prevents Christians from hearing what Jesus is asking of them as individuals today (*Church Dogmatics* 4.2.533–553).

The Second Vatican Council (1962–1965) introduced the vocabulary of discipleship into official Roman Catholicism. In twenty-seven cases the council documents use the term *disciple* as a virtual synonym for *Christian*. In his first encyclical, *Redemptor hominis* (1979), John Paul II described the church as the "community of disciples" in which Christ says to each and every member "Follow me" (no. 21). Several Catholic theologians (K. H. Schelkle, R. E. Brown) have seen priests as successors of the original disciples; others (H. Schürmann, J. B. Metz) depict discipleship as a paradigm of the vowed religious life.

Systematic Reflection. The idea of the Christian life as discipleship is often a deliberate effort to avoid overemphasis on the acceptance of abstract doctrines or the following of abstract rules. Discipleship emphasizes what is individual and brings the believer into personal relationship to Christ. The concept is one that inspires heroism in the service of the kingdom of God.

Christian discipleship in the post-Easter situation is admittedly problematical. Since Jesus is no longer visibly present, the attempt to respond to his personal direction can lead to illusions. It is not surprising, therefore, that the ideas of following or imitating Christ eclipsed, for many centuries, the concept of discipleship.

However, the recent revival of the category of discipleship has solid theological warrants. For the Christian, Jesus is not just a historical figure or a remote being beyond space and time. According to the New Testament, he has promised to be present with his followers in every age, as they go about their task of "making disciples" of all nations (*Mt.* 28:20). He identifies himself in a special way with the members of his church, so that when they are served he is served (*Mt.* 10:42, cf. *Mt.* 25:31–46) and when they are persecuted he is persecuted (*Acts* 9:5). The church, therefore, is not a self-enclosed, autonomous institution but a community constantly permeated by the "real presence" of the risen Lord. Through its scriptures, its institutional structures, and its public worship, the church, invoking the Holy Spirit, gives a new presence to Christ and thereby makes living discipleship, as contrasted with mere imitation or abstract conformity, possible. By putting its members in communion with the living Christ, the church allows the Lord-disciple relationship to continue.

In such a theology of discipleship the Gospels recover their value as documents through which Christ continues to address his community and to shape ideas and attitudes consonant with his own. Discipleship continues to make demands similar to those made in the first generation, so that the renunciation of family, that of wealth, and that of secular occupations become, at least for some, live options.

Discipleship applies in different forms and degrees to different individuals, each of whom lives out a personal relationship to Christ as Lord. In a particular way, those called to public ministry in the community must practice discipleship so that, with Paul, they may be able to say "Be imitators of me, as I am of Christ"

(*1 Cor.* 11:1). Although they never replace Christ as the "one Master" (*Mt.* 23:10), their personal assimilation of his outlook by study, prayer, and self-denial enables them to form others in the Christian life.

Although Christianity is distinctive in looking to the historical and living Jesus as Lord and Master, it resembles other religions in that faith is kept alive not simply through books and academic instruction but through the personal influence of those who are links in a chain of living discipleship.

[*See also* Jesus.]

BIBLIOGRAPHY

Bonhoeffer, Dietrich. *Nachfolge.* Munich, 1937. Translated by R. H. Fuller and Irmgard Booth as *The Cost of Discipleship,* 2d ed., rev. & unabr. (New York, 1959). A classic polemic against the advocacy of "cheap grace."

Dulles, Avery. *A Church to Believe In: Discipleship and the Dynamics of Freedom.* New York, 1982. The first chapter proposes the concept of the church as community of disciples.

Hahn, Ferdinand, August Strobel, and Eduard Schweizer, eds. *Die Anfänge der Kirche im Neuen Testament.* Göttingen, 1967. Translated by Iain Nicol and Ute Nicol as *The Beginnings of the Church in the New Testament* (Edinburgh and Minneapolis, 1970). Three sequential essays on discipleship before Easter, after Easter, and in the early church. Clear, well-informed, noncontroversial.

Hengel, Martin. *Nachfolge und Charisma.* Berlin, 1968. Translated by James Greig as *The Charismatic Leader and His Followers* (New York, 1981). Influenced by Weber's sociology, Hengel portrays Jesus as a charismatic leader and holds that institutionalization "petrifies" discipleship; criticizes A. Schulz and H. D. Betz for making analogies between Christian discipleship and the rabbinic schools.

Kittel, Gerhard, and Gerhard Friedrich, eds. *Theologisches Wörterbuch zum Neuen Testament.* 10 vols. in 11. Stuttgart, 1949–1978. Translated by Geoffrey W. Bromiley as *Theological Dictionary of the New Testament,* 10 vols. (Grand Rapids, Mich., 1964–1976). The articles in this collection are still fundamental for New Testament data. See especially "Akoloutheō" by Gerhard Kittel, "Manthanō" by K. L. Rengstorf, and "Mimeomai" by W. Michaelis.

Leeuw, Gerardus van der. *Phänomenologie der Religion.* Tübingen, 1933. Translated by J. E. Turner as *Religion in Essence and Manifestation* (London, 1938). At points indicated in the index, includes useful passages on discipleship as a general religious phenomenon.

Schelkle, Karl Hermann. *Jüngerschaft und Apostelamt: Eine biblische Auslegung des priesterlichen Dienstes.* Freiburg, 1957. Translated by Joseph Disselhorst as *Discipleship and Priesthood,* rev. ed. (New York, 1965). Seeks to harmonize the New Testament concept of discipleship with the priestly ministry in the church today, reflecting devotional and apologetic as well as exegetical concerns.

Theissen, Gerd. *Soziologie der Jesusbewegung.* Munich, 1977. Translated by John Bowden and published under two titles: *The First Followers of Jesus* (London, 1978) and *Sociology of Early Palestinian Christianity* (Philadelphia, 1978). Theissen holds that the primary bearers of early Christianity were wandering charismatics specially called by the Son of man to a life of ethical radicalism.

AVERY DULLES, S.J.

DISCIPLES OF CHRIST. The Disciples of Christ is an American-born religious group formed in 1832 by the merger of the Christian movement led by Barton Stone with the "Reforming Baptists," headed by Thomas and Alexander Campbell. Most of the early leaders of the movement, including Stone and the Campbells, had been Presbyterians, but they imbibed deeply of the spirit of religious freedom in the wake of the American Revolution. Stone was one of the leaders of the Kentucky revival at the turn of the nineteenth century. Distressed by Presbyterian opposition to the revival, in 1804 he and five other ministers left the church, announcing their plan to be "Christians only" in "The Last Will and Testament of the Springfield Presbytery."

Thomas Campbell came to America in 1807, having been a Presbyterian minister in Northern Ireland. Disturbed by the sectarian spirit of the American church, Campbell clashed with the synod, and in 1809 he was suspended from the ministry. Campbell and a few of his supporters almost immediately formed the Christian Association of Washington (Pennsylvania), and Campbell wrote a fifty-six page explanation of his views, called the *Declaration and Address.* Thomas Campbell's son, Alexander, arrived in America shortly after the publication of the *Declaration and Address.* Twenty-one years old at the time, Alexander Campbell had been influenced by the reforming ideas of Scottish evangelist Robert Haldane while spending a year in Glasgow, and he immediately embraced his father's independent position. He quickly rose to the leadership of the movement. The Campbells joined with Baptist associations from 1815 until 1830 and were known by the name Reformers.

Preaching similar pleas for Christian union and in frequent contact with one another in Kentucky, the Stone and Campbell movements sealed a remarkably successful union in 1832. Alexander Campbell and his followers generally favored the name Disciples of Christ, while the Stone churches continued to use the name Christian Church. Many local congregations were called Churches of Christ. All three names have been used throughout the movement's history. The new church spread rapidly with the westward migration of population; at the time of the union in 1832 it was estimated to have 22,000 members, and by 1860 that figure had grown to nearly 200,000.

Two ideas undergird Disciples thought, both of them highly attractive amid the optimism on the American frontier in the 1830s. First was an emphasis on Christian union. Second was an appeal for the "restoration of the ancient order of things" as a means of attaining unity. The battle cry of the movement, stated in 1809 by Thomas Campbell, was "Where the Scriptures speak, we speak; and where the Scriptures are silent, we are silent."

The Disciples were Arminian, believing in freedom of the will, and they were revivalistic, although never given to extreme enthusiasm. They held traditional views on most questions and were most visibly set apart by their restorationist views on the local church. They organized autonomous congregations presided over by elders and deacons and emphasized weekly observance of the Lord's Supper. In the early years of the movement, Alexander Campbell was caustically anti-institutional, but by the 1840s antimission sentiment abated. Most early Disciples were also strong postmillennialists, believing that the second coming of Christ would be ushered in by the world reformation begun by Luther and capped by their own restoration movement.

In addition to the Campbells and Stone, the most prominent early leader of the Disciples was another Scottish Presbyterian minister, Walter Scott, who is credited with formulating the "five-finger" plan of salvation—faith, repentance, baptism, forgiveness of sins, and gift of the Holy Spirit—which was preached by a generation of pioneer Disciples evangelists. The Disciples were slow in developing denominational institutions; consequently, the most powerful leaders of the movement were editors of religious journals. Alexander Campbell edited the *Christian Baptist* from 1823 to 1830 and the *Millennial Harbinger* from 1830 until 1864, just two years before his death. Stone, Scott, and scores of other preachers also published papers that tied the loose-knit movement together.

While conceiving of themselves as a protest against sectarian division, the Disciples quickly became a part of the denominational competition in the American Midwest and South. Alexander Campbell's influence among the Baptists was particularly strong, and in some parts of the West, the Disciples devastated Baptist associations. The church spread rapidly westward from Ohio and Kentucky and as far south as Tennessee and Texas.

The years after the Civil War form a second era in Disciples history. By 1866, all of the first generation leaders of the church were dead, and dramatic shifts in power occurred within the church. The Disciples continued to grow rapidly; the religious census of 1906 listed around 1,150,000 members in the movement. But the census also revealed that a major schism had taken place within the church. Deep sectional and sociological tensions had begun to appear shortly after the Civil War.

In spite of the facts that the Disciples were strongest in the border areas and that most of the church's leaders had urged moderation during the slavery controversy, Disciples were seriously divided by the Civil War. In 1863, northern Disciples passed a resolution of loyalty to the Union at the meeting of the American Christian Missionary Society, which had been formed in 1849. Southern Disciples were deeply angered. Although most Disciples argued that the church could not divide because it had no denominational apparatus, in the years after the Civil War northern and southern newspapers and other institutions became increasingly antagonistic. In the census of 1906 the most conservative wing of the movement (which was almost entirely southern) was identified separately and designated the Churches of Christ.

Although the tensions of the nineteenth century had clear sectional and sociological underpinnings, the debate also had a doctrinal focus. As it became ever more apparent that the hoped-for millennium of peace and unity was not imminent, conservative Disciples lost interest in Christian union as a practical goal, and liberal Disciples increasingly discarded legalistic restorationism as a means of attaining union. The most visible issues that divided churches were support for the missionary society that had been founded in 1849 and the scripturality of the use of instrumental music in worship. The founding of the society (which had Alexander Campbell's tacit approval) seemed to some an abandonment of the anti-institutional principles of the early movement; the society further alienated many southerners because of the passage of political resolutions during the Civil War; finally, the organization was attacked as "unscriptural" by rigid restorationists. The introduction of organs into the churches also rankled conservatives, who considered them symbols of decadence and found no evidence of their presence in the New Testament churches. By 1900, hundreds of conservative local congregations had separated from the movement as independent Churches of Christ.

The most powerful Disciples journal during the late nineteenth century was the *Christian Standard*, published in Cincinnati, Ohio, by Isaac Errett until his death in 1888. The most influential journal among the conservatives of the South was the *Gospel Advocate*, edited for over half a century by David Lipscomb in Nashville, Tennessee. By the end of the century, however, leadership of the movement had drifted toward James H. Garrison, who in 1874 became editor of the Saint Louis–based *Christian-Evangelist.* Garrison was grounded in the nuances of Disciples theology, but he was irenic in spirit and encouraged a new generation of Disciples leaders to take the mainstream of the movement into the center of liberal American Protestantism.

In the early twentieth century the Disciples suffered a second major division and a slowing growth rate. As a new generation of Disciples liberals, particularly a group associated with the University of Chicago, pressed for a more ecumenical view of the Disciples mission and a more liberal understanding of the scriptures, conservative opposition solidified around the *Christian Standard.* Finally, in the 1920s, the conservatives began withdrawing their support from Disciples organizations and in 1927 established the rival North American Christian Convention. These dissentient conservative congregations remained loosely associated in the Undenominational Fellowship of Christian Churches and Churches of Christ. The more liberal wing of the movement adopted the name Christian Church (Disciples of Christ).

A full body of boards and commissions developed in the twentieth century, headquartered mostly in Indianapolis and Saint Louis. In 1968 the church restructured into a representative and more centrally controlled organization, losing perhaps one-third of its listed congregations in the move and completing the second schism, which had been in progress since the 1920s.

Disciples have been important leaders in modern ecumenical activities. The *Christian Century* began as a Disciples journal (founded as the *Christian Oracle* in 1884), and its editorial corps was long dominated by Disciples. The Disciples have also been prolific builders of universities and colleges, perhaps the most widely known being Texas Christian University, Butler University, Drake University, and Bethany College.

[*See also the biography of Alexander Campbell.*]

BIBLIOGRAPHY

The best general summary of Disciples history is William E. Tucker and Lester G. McAllister's *Journey in Faith* (Saint Louis, 1975). A sociological interpretation of Disciples history in the nineteenth century can be found in my books *Quest for a Christian America* (Nashville, 1966) and *The Social Source of Division in the Disciples of Christ* (Atlanta, 1973). A survey of the movement written by a leader of the conservative Christian churches is James D. Murch's *Christians Only* (Cincinnati, 1962). A Churches of Christ perspective can be found in Earl I. West's *The Search for the Ancient Order*, 2 vols. (Indianapolis, 1950). Three older works that remain significant are William T. Moore's *A Comprehensive History of the Disciples of Christ* (New York, 1909), and two books by Winfred E. Garrison, *Religion Follows the Frontier* (New York, 1931) and *An American Religious Movement* (Saint Louis, 1945).

David E. Harrell, Jr.

DISCIPLINE, SPIRITUAL.

See Spiritual Discipline.

DISEASES AND CURES.

What resources offer a grip on the religious meaning of diseases and cures? Sociologists, anthropologists, psychologists, political economists, and historians of religions wrestle with this question by applying various and valuable interpretive approaches. Without imposing false consensus on these attempts, this article scans the subject matters that help them focus on the religious value of disease and cure. These include myths of the origins of disease and cure, descriptions of the powers of affliction and healing, systematic cosmologies and physiologies, the ritual scenarios of diagnosis and healing, and the social groups that take shape around outbreaks of disease and spectacles of cure.

Myths of Origin. The accounts of the origins of diseases and cures frequently provide the fundamental terms in which cultures understand these realities. The myths of origins of disease let healers and their cultures know what they are up against when they confront sickness. For example, in the northwest Amazon area of South America, in the upper Río Negro region, the Baniwa people know that many diseases originated when the culture hero Kuai was consumed by the fire that swept through the world at the beginning of time. From Kuai's mouth and other body orifices streamed saliva and fluids that became the poisons of this world. And from the fur on his body came the pathogenic darts and slivers that invade human beings. Only masters of fire, who are specialists in religious curing, can handle these toxins and draw them from the sufferers' bodies. Obviously, the accounts of disease origins can vary widely from culture to culture. In Sūkyō Mahikari, a popular new religion in Japan, for instance, diseases originated in primordial times when the earth was like a sea of mud. Deputy ruling gods, relatively unrighteous beings, forced Kuniyorozu Tsukurinushi no Ōmikamisama (whose divine power is beyond imagining) and the other righteous gods into retirement behind the rock door of heaven on Mount Fuji. In addition, the unrighteous deputies pierced the divine being's eyes with holly boughs, dismembered his body, and consumed everything, including his intestines. The world was plunged into pale light, and it reversed its course. Now, however, the divine being will return to reveal himself and thus restore to the world the full light needed to overcome the darkness that generates disease. The rock door of heaven has now opened. The saved are becoming children of the sun's light *(yokoshi no tomo)* who can heal the sick by projecting divine light through the palms of their hands.

The accounts of the origins of cure also open up the universe of meaning that binds a culture and stimulates its creativity in the face of sickness. Each category of *materia medica* has its own origin. For centuries, Qollahuaya healers in the Bolivian Andes, for example, have been remarkable herbal curers. They possess a pharmacopoeia of nearly nine hundred medicinal plants, carefully classified according to local symbolic orders (Girault, 1984). This extraordinary feat seems motivated and organized by the fact that the plants are vehicles for the fluids, especially fat, blood, and water, that come from the body of Pachamama, Mother Earth, who is a divine being. She gives life to the human offspring who dwell on her mountainside. Curative powers are transferred from the body of Mother Earth to the circulatory systems of her children through the various species of plants. They are gifts of Mother Earth, and their energies are released when the plant leaves are steeped in water as a tea and drunk by the patient (Bastien, 1985, p. 601).

Rattles, drums, costumes, songs, and the implements and techniques of cure may have mythic origins that account for their power. In Eurasia, for example, drums are a part of the religious healer's curing practice. The studies of L. P. Potapov, S. I. Vajnštejn, and M. Jankovics (Potapov, 1968; Vajnštejn, 1968; Jankovics, 1984) show that the myths of origins of these drums and the powers that fill them when they are played take concrete expression in their structural design and in the drawings depicted on the hides of the drumhead. The drums of Altaic peoples (such as the Shor, Teleut, and Kumandın) often depict mythic beings associated with constellations of the zodiac. Uralic peoples (such as the Selkup, Ket, Dolgans, Nganasani, Evenki, and Eveny) draw maps of the sky, centered often on the Milky Way, the supernatural path along which the healer travels to enter the original world of celestial powers. These skymaps illustrate a mythic geography and locate the principal powers pertinent to the ecstatic healer's practice. [*See* Drums.]

Powers of Affliction and Healing. Powers of affliction and healing can be extraordinary beings with a mythic history. Few investigators continue the tradition of wide-ranging comparisons of whole geographic areas, such as Otto Zerries did in his study of South American spirits of sickness (Zerries, 1955); fewer still study afflicting powers on a worldwide scale, as Forrest E. Clements did (Clements, 1932). Most contemporary investigations examine one locale, although they often conclude with broad theoretical statements based on particular cases. Powers of affliction and cure are fascinating because they draw attention to fantastic existences that transcend ordinary experience. [*See* Affliction.] Throughout the Muslim world, for example, there exist three levels of living beings more exalted than humans: angels, satanic beings, and *jinn*. These last are demonic spirits. The word *jinn* derives from the Arabic *jann*, a word that denotes the hiddenness of something veiled, especially a partially formed entity that lurks in the womb. From deep within and under cover of the darkness constituted by the very limits of human form and knowledge, *jinn* insert disease and confusion into human life. They seek to take up residence in a victim's body, where they stay invisible and where their motive and mode of knowledge remain inaccessible to their suffering human host. This typifies the predicament of sickness wherein the human being houses the unfamiliar and the strange; and it demonstrates why medicine is often a culturally privileged way of extending knowledge into the realm of the unknown. Frequently, music and dance are the medical means by which patients negotiate compromises with the *jinn* who afflict them (Crapanzano, 1973). Beyond the Muslim world, music is a key medical instrument, and therefore it is a rich resource for the student of religion. In a broad comparative study, Rouget demonstrated how music, instruments, and dance reveal the presence of pathogenic and curative powers when they are performed in the rituals of cure (Rouget, 1977).

The powers of healing are often exemplary beings who serve as models for medical practice and may include the most supreme forms of divine being, as is the case, for example, in the biblical tradition of the Hebrews (*Ex.* 15:26) and among the Akan peoples of Ghana (Appiah-Kubi, 1981). [*See* Healing.] Myths of primordial healers and culture heroes who taught medical techniques and conquered diseases in the beginning, the biographies of saviors who rescued humanity from sickening evil, the hagiographies of saints renowned for cure, the canonical descriptions of founders, and the anecdotes and lore that surround prophets and teachers famed for healing are all sources that describe the basic powers of healing. Thus, for example, the Christian Gospels amply describe the miraculous cures of Jesus, the divine physician who, through signs and wonders, such as the casting out of the unclean spirits, announces the dawning of a new and purified kingdom. In the Pali canon, Śākyamuni Buddha heals through his teachings on impermanence and through his instructions on therapeutic meditations that release individuals from the psychic states that bind them to suffering existence. Frequently religious healers model themselves on the first beings to overcome the disease that they confront in the operating theater and in the clinical arena.

Cosmic and Corporeal Systems. Cosmologies and physiologies are cultural constructs that offer systematic appraisals of the order in which disease insinuates itself to inspire disorder. By locating the powers and processes of sickness and health in relation to the cosmic forces in the space of the world or the body, cosmology and physiology offer a systematic source for understanding the religious meaning of disease and cure. These systems are not merely spatial. The cosmos experiences the rhythms of time: the seasons, the cycles of stars, the diurnal pulse of day and night. And the body manifests its tempos in the rhythms of sleeping and waking, work and rest, hunger and satiety, youth and old age, as well as in the periodic expressions of menstrual blood, urine, feces, sounds of speech, and festive song. In explaining how these diverse experiences inhere as a single whole (whether it be the universe or the body), cultures present organized symbolic systems that can be a resource for understanding the religious meaning of disease and cure.

In circumstances where systematic cosmologies are known to medical specialists, they often diagnose disease by examining the intercalibrated movements of seasons, stars, day and night, male and female, the basic elements of matter, the cardinal directions, and the zenith and nadir of the universe as well as the underlying forces that cause them to relate to one another. By carefully tracing such symbolic expressions, Porkert outlined the religious cosmology that serves as a theoretical foundation for many kinds of Chinese medicine (Porkert, 1974).

Physiology similarly systematizes the arrangement of forces that constitute life and well-being. A large range of elements, with complicated histories, compose the human person. Thus, blood, fat, body fluids, bone, orifices, souls, sounds, shadows, and other life-principles and dynamisms have a history. Knowledge of this constitutional history can be quite systematic and lead the investigator toward forces that transcend individual life and go beyond humanity as a whole. The human constitution takes root in primordial and supernatural forces that converge in a reproductive life-process marked by the stages of the life cycle and of human generations. Joseph W. Bastien's studies disclose how physiology in the Bolivian Andes, for example, is a circulatory system that centers on the heart *(sonco)* that regulates respiration, reproduction, and digestion. Fat *(wira)*, blood *(yawar)*, and air *(wayra)* converge on the heart in the form of food and breath. It breaks down these primary fluids into secondary ones (phlegm, gas, bile, milk, semen) and by-products (feces, urine, sweat), and then disperses them throughout the body. Each fluid and product possesses a discernible cognitive and emotional quality. This physiology, used by diagnosticians and healers, also grounds the communal acts that govern social reproduction. Thus, spiral choreographic patterns danced at certain seasons of the year promote the well-being of the corporate ritual community because they imitate the centripetal and centrifugal actions of the heart as it gathers in nutrients and redistributes them to the entire body. The work of R. Devisch in Africa and of Francis Zimmermann and Sudhir Kakar on South Asian materials shows that such applications of systematic physiologies are widespread and that their religious meanings vary widely (Devisch, 1984; Zimmermann, 1982; Kakar, 1982, pp. 219–251). The body serves as a microcosm where the powers of disease can be located, contested, pacified, eliminated, or accommodated. With extraordinary clarity, Alfredo López Austin has illustrated the extent to which Mesoamericans used ritual physiologies to organize and motivate whole empires (López Austin, 1980). In any case, the cultural rendering of the dynamics of the body fan outward to relate patients and doctors to the organized processes of the world.

Texts and Doctrines. Texts and doctrines also give explicit and systematic treatment of the themes of disease and cure. The *Huang-ti nei-ching su-wen* represents a classic medical text with a long history in China. Its systematization of disease, diagnosis, and cure became a focus for reinterpretation through the centuries (Veith, 1966). Because they are closed symbolic systems and taxonomies, canonical texts not only record the lists of available medicines and techniques but disclose the meaning of disease and cure by permitting tradition, formed around the text, to probe to their fundaments the seams between the contradictary readings that accumulate over time. In this way, as William R. Bascom made clear for Yoruba divination, diagnostic texts open onto doctrinal statements about human and cosmic nature (Bascom, 1969, 1980). But, as Robert D. Pelton pointed out (Pelton, 1980), the nearly two thousand song-poems used in West African divinatory systems are presented as so many puzzles and are, in turn, subjected to criticism each time that a patient's experience of physical disorder calls metaphysical order into question. Examples of doctrinal texts not primarily composed as documents for the clinical setting prove worthwhile. Such are the Mahāyāna *sūtra*s and treatises dedicated to the power of the Healing Buddha, as studied by Raoul Birnbaum (Birnbaum, 1979), and the

Aztec administrative descriptions of health care systems and medical divisions of labor, as presented by López Austin (López Austin, 1974, 1975).

Rites of Medical Practice. Most rewarding is a close study of the rites of medical practice, taken in their full, symbolic expression. [*See* Medicine.] The rituals of cure are diverse and fascinating. They often consist of distinct ritual episodes whose ensemble creates a shifting rhythm of performance. Some outstanding cultural studies of medical practices, such as the works of Victor Turner, who reoriented the study of medical anthropology toward religious symbolism, reveal how powerful symbolic actions can be conveyors of meaning (Turner, 1968). Ritual acts of cure include dramatic speech-acts of noises, songs, blessings, and curses. Analyses of curative ritual formulas, such as those found in the Mongolian texts of exorcism studied by Sárközi (Sárközi, 1984), and of the accompanying ritual paraphernalia, such as the effigies analyzed by Walther Heissig (Heissig, 1986), can illustrate underlying cultural values. Even the gestures that prepare and consecrate ritual medicines before the curing event begins can be extremely revealing of religious meanings. Herbert Fischer has shown how sigificant even subtle movements of the fingers can be in transmitting religious powers and meanings (Fischer, 1965). Fischer points to many cultural traditions where tiny, stylized movements of the fingers become means of uncovering and dislodging pathogenic matter and of revealing the supernatural body latent in the human body. On close analysis, even apparently simple ceremonies of healing prove incredibly complicated. This seems to be the case with *pirit,* Buddhist ceremonies of healing celebrated in Sri Lanka and other countries where Theravāda Buddhism holds sway. Although *pirit* is a popular rite, commonly celebrated for the sick in folk culture, Lily de Sylva has outlined at least four main types of *pirit* ceremony in Sri Lanka. Furthermore, the rite may be broken down into at least thirty-two component parts and features, many of which have their own history and can be further subdivided into scores of formulae or prescribed ritual gestures (de Sylva, 1981).

Perhaps it is because of the elaborate symbolism, so multivalent and far-reaching, that is at work in rites of diagnosis and cure that the processes and spectacles of cure provide individuals and cultures with new opportunities for acquisition of religious powers and new forms of knowledge. Disease and cure open the horizons of knowledge and the experience of humanity to new realms. Illness frequently awakens people to their communal and individual past, to the meaning of their intentions, ideas, and emotions, and to the wider horizons of their physical and spiritual world. The knowledge gained from illness may not be ordered into a unitary system. Since illness comes unexpectedly, the way it expands the cultural horizon of knowledge may be piecemeal and uneven. Furthermore, evaluations of individual instances of sickness and cure may be given selective attention, depending upon the needs and opportunity for reflection afforded the community during that situation. Such is the case among the Gnau people of New Guinea, who, like many peoples the world over when faced with urgent sickness, bow to the pressure to know its cause, how to behave toward it, and how to achieve healing. Illness plays a role in shaping their cosmology and their identity, based as it is on a collection of ancestors and spirits active in disease and cure. But the Gnau recognize that the causes of disease are myriad and the issues that account for a particular instance of sickness are complicated enough to blunt the drive toward consistency, predictability, or certainty of diagnosis and cure (Lewis, 1975, pp. 338ff.). Nonetheless, the staging of Gnau rites of cure involves entire villages, and the experience is generally reckoned to expand communal knowledge of a universe composed of many principles, powers, and concerns.

Once the symbolic processes of specific ceremonies of cure have been analyzed and interpreted, it is possible to trace their comparative history. The changes that such rites undergo as they are passed down through time or as they are diffused through geographic space via trade or war become themselves a resource for understanding what is religiously important about the rites. Thus, in an illuminating study, John M. Janzen delineated the history and diffusion of Kongo rites of cure in central Africa over nearly three hundred years. Such a treatment allows Janzen to focus on the fixtures that the historical tradition preserved as well as on the spontaneous innovations brought by each creative community that enacted the rites (Janzen, 1981).

Disease and Society. The role of disease and cure in reorganizing personal and social experience often is exploited to reshape worldviews and recast social orders. Since sickness is regarded as an adverse form of change, resulting from the ambivalent presence of a new or unwelcome mode of being, the language of disease and cure frequently inserts itself into attempts at innovation or reappraisal of tradition. That is why investigators such as Oskar Köhler can demonstrate that configurations of symptoms can become peculiar to subgroups in society and why the religious language of sickness, pollution, purification, and cure often mark movements of rebellion, reaction, utopian efforts, and revolutions (Köhler, 1978).

Countless numbers of millenarian cults report the epidemic outbreak of dancing sicknesses. In the 1560s, for example, local divinities in the Peruvian Andes swept down from the sky or rose out of their earthen shrines to enter the native population and afflict them with uncontrollable dancing diseases. The frenzied dance would bring on the end of the world, overthrow Spanish overlordship, and restore power to local people and gods. By the thousands, Andean Indians became savior-gods incarnate and danced the Taqui Oncoy, "the dance of the Pleiades." After nearly a decade, Spanish authorities crushed the movement and condemned some eight thousand leaders to corporal punishment or exile.

Since powers of affliction strike their victims without their consent, disease becomes a vehicle of social change, resistance, and unrest for which the restless cannot be held accountable, for they are victims themselves (Lewis, 1971). In this way, symptomatology and epidemiology can indicate far-reaching social stirrings and help pinpoint latent motives for them. Conversely, cults of disease can be ways of carrying forward ancient religious traditions or sociopolitical structures in the face of the overwhelming power of a dominant religion or political authority. This is the light in which Ernesto de Martino interprets certain folk diseases and rites of musical cure in rural Italy (de Martino, 1957).

At times, the language of disease and cure appears to be a vehicle for the creation of new religious forms and experiences. The spontaneity of disease, circumventing the process of institutional permissions, prompts laypeople to experiment with new religious forms and combine elements of traditions that appear to be quite disparate. Many of the so-called independent Christian churches of Africa provide an important forum for the religious interpretation of disease and rites of cure. It appears that these churches maintain long-standing traditions of African religiosity while, at the same time, they give new life and meaning to the Christianity brought by European missionaries. In Douala, Cameroon, a growing group of devotees follow two prophetic women leaders. The two prophetesses call their disciples the "sick ones of the Father" and divide them into groups, according to the categories of the sick mentioned in the Gospels: the blind, the paralyzed, the epileptic, the deaf, and the dumb. The disciples do not actually manifest these symptoms. Eric de Rosny points out that many of them do not appear to be sick at all, but, deep within themselves, they must identify with these diseases in their inner being in order to qualify for participation in the group of the elect (de Rosny, 1986). The two prophetesses deliver lengthy discourses that reweave the imagery and understanding of traditional African and Christian belief. It is the experience of their peculiar illnesses that provides the basis for this social reshaping and rethinking. Finally, the religious power of diseases and cures is explored by self-conscious attempts to institute new religions. By offering a new analysis and providing a new meaning for sickness *(mijō)* and illuminating its relationship to personal difficulties *(jijō)*, and by showing how they both involve accumulations of *hokori*, acts of the mind that deviate from the will of God the Parent, the popular new Japanese religion called Tenrikyō hopes to inspire people to make a transformation from reason to faith. This complete change of heart will be achieved through the constant guidance *(tebiki)* and warnings *(teire)* given the world by God through the Tenrikyō religious movement. In this manner, illnesses become stepping stones toward a new faith in a newly revealed divine order (Tenrikyō, 1966).

The mythic origins of disease and cure indicate to what extent the experience of sickness and healing reach into the depths of culture, the human condition. It is not surprising, therefore, to find the significant imagery of disease and cure appearing at all levels of personal and social life. These symbols, beliefs, and ritual acts then serve as resources for understanding particular historical situations and for reflecting on human nature.

BIBLIOGRAPHY

Appiah-Kubi, Kofi. *Man Cures, God Heals: Religion and Medical Practice among the Akans of Ghana.* Totowa, N.J., 1981.

Bascom, William R. *Ifa Divination: Communication between Gods and Men in West Africa.* Bloomington, Ind., 1969.

Bascom, William R. *Sixteen Cowries: Yoruba Divination from Africa to the New World.* Bloomington, Ind., 1980.

Bastien, Joseph W. "Qollahuaya-Andean Body Concepts: A Topographical-Hydraulic Model of Physiology." *American Anthropologist* 87 (September 1985): 595–611.

Birnbaum, Raoul. *The Healing Buddha.* Boulder, Colo., 1979.

Clements, Forrest E. "Primitive Concepts of Disease." *American Archaeology and Ethnology* 32 (1932): 185–252.

Crapanzano, Vincent. *The Hamadsha: An Essay in Moroccan Ethnopsychiatry.* Berkeley, 1973.

Devisch, R. *Se recréer femme: Manipulation sémantique d'une situation d'infécondité chez les Yaka du Zaire.* Berlin, 1984.

Fischer, Herbert. "The Use of Gesture in Preparing Medicaments and in Healing." *History of Religions* 5 (1965): 18–53.

Girault, Louis. *Kallawaya: Guérisseurs itinérants des Andes.* Mémoires de l'Institut Français de Recherches Scientifiques pour le Développement en Coopération, vol. 107. Paris, 1984.

Heissig, Walther. "Banishing of Illnesses into Effigies in Mongolia." *Asian Folklore Studies* 45 (1986): 33–43.

Jankovics, M. "Cosmic Models and Siberian Shaman Drums."

In *Shamanism in Eurasia,* vol. 1, edited by Mihály Hoppál, pp. 149–173. Göttingen, 1984.

Janzen, John M. *Lemba 1650–1930: A Drum of Affliction in Africa and the New World.* New York, 1981.

Kakar, Sudhir. *Shamans, Mystics, and Doctors: A Psychological Inquiry into India and Its Healing Traditions.* New York, 1982.

Köhler, Oskar. "Die Utopie der absoluten Gesundheit." In *Krankheit, Heilkunst, Heilung,* edited by H. Schipperges, E. Seidler, and P. U. Unschuld. Munich, 1978.

Lewis, Gilbert. *Knowledge of Illness in a Sepik Society: A Study of the Gnau, New Guinea.* London School of Economics Monographs on Social Anthropology, no. 52. London, 1975.

Lewis, I. M. *Ecstatic Religion.* London, 1971.

López Austin, Alfredo. "Sahagún's Work and the Medicine of the Ancient Nahuas: Possibilities for Study." In *Sixteenth-Century Mexico: The Work of Sahagún,* edited by Munro S. Edmonson. Albuquerque, 1974.

López Austin, Alfredo. *Textos de medicina nahuatl.* Mexico City, 1975.

López Austin, Alfredo. *Cuerpo humano e ideología.* 2 vols. Mexico City, 1980.

Martino, Ernesto de. *La terra del rimorso.* Milan, 1957.

Pelton, Robert D. *The Trickster in West Africa.* Berkeley, 1980.

Porkert, Manfred. *The Theoretical Foundations of Chinese Medicine: Systems of Correspondence.* Cambridge, Mass., 1974.

Potapov, L. P. "Shaman's Drums of Altaic Ethnic Groups." In *Popular Beliefs and Folklore Tradition in Siberia,* edited by Vilmos Diószegi. Budapest, 1968.

Rosny, Eric de. "Mallah et Marie-Lumière, guérisseuses africaines." *Études* (Paris) 364 (April 1986): 473–488.

Rouget, Gilbert. "Music and Possession Trance." In *The Anthropology of the Body,* edited by John Blacking. New York, 1977.

Sárközi, A. "A Mongolian Text of Exorcism." In *Shamanism in Eurasia,* edited by Mihály Hoppál, vol. 1, pp. 325–343. Göttingen, 1984.

Sylva, Lily de. *Paritta: The Buddhist Ceremony for Peace and Prosperity in Sri Lanka.* Spolia Zeylanica: Bulletins of the National Museum of Sri Lanka, vol. 36. Colombo, 1981.

Tenrikyō Church Headquarters. *Tenrikyō: Its History and Teachings.* Tenri, Japan, 1966.

Turner, Victor. *The Drums of Affliction: A Study of Religious Processes among the Ndembu of Zambia.* London, 1968.

Vajnštejn, S. I. "The Tuvan (Soyot) Shaman's Drum and the Ceremony of its 'Enlivening.'" In *Popular Beliefs and Folklore Tradition in Siberia,* edited by Vilmos Diószegi. Budapest, 1968.

Veith, Ilza, trans. *Huang-ti nei ching su wen: The Yellow Emperor's Classic of Internal Medicine.* New ed. Berkeley, 1966.

Zerries, Otto. "Krankheitsdämonen und Hilfsgeister des Medizinmannes in Südamerika." *Proceedings of the International Congress of Americanists* 30 (1955): 162–178.

Zimmermann, Francis. *La jungle et le fumet des viandes: Un thème écologique dans la médecine hindoue.* Paris, 1982.

LAWRENCE E. SULLIVAN

DISMEMBERMENT. Among the many procedures that are carried out in sacrificial ritual, dismemberment and distribution of the victim's body figure prominently. Moreover, beyond its physical dimension, dismemberment also possesses complex and highly significant social, symbolic, and intellectual dimensions, as has been shown, for instance, in Jean-Pierre Vernant's analysis of the primordial sacrifice performed by Prometheus, according to Hesiod's *Theogony*. For, as Vernant has argued, the division of the victim's body in effect establishes the difference between gods, who are immortal and have no need of food (since they receive only the victim's bones and fat) and humans, who receive portions of bloody meat wrapped in an ox's stomach and whose lives are thus characterized by hunger, death, and ultimate bodily decay. [*See* Greek Religion.]

Whereas the Promethean model of sacrificial division (evident also in the sacrifices of the Greek city-states) served to discuss and establish the distinction between human and divine, other sacrificial patterns are more attuned to gradations of social hierarchy. Such is the case in Dinka sacrifice, as described by Godfrey Lienhardt, who presents what appears to be a "butcher's chart" detailing the assignment of different cuts of meat to different social groups, the prestige of group and cut being directly correlated. That the butcher's chart is, in effect, a diagram of social hierarchy is not lost on the Dinka themselves, who observe: "The people are put together, as a bull is put together." Lienhardt (1961) goes on to elaborate: "Since every bull or ox is destined ultimately for sacrifice, each one demonstrates, potentially, the ordered social relationships of the sacrificing group, the members of which are indeed "put together" in each beast and represented in their precise relations to each other in the meat which it provides."

A similar pattern is also evident in one of the most ancient Italic sacrifices, the Feriae Latinae, a ritual that dates to the period prior to Roman domination of central Italy but subsequently was taken over by the Romans and adapted to their purposes. Thus, according to Dionysius of Halicarnassus (4.49), all forty-seven cities that were members of the Rome-dominated Latin League were called upon to send representatives each year to the Alban Mount "to congregate, feast together, and take part in common rituals." Within the Feriae Latinae, however, were celebrated both the cohesion of the Latin League and the unequal status of its members, themes that found expression in the sacrificial banquet at the center of the rite. Thus, each city was assigned to contribute a different, carefully graded portion of food to the celebration ("some lambs, some cheeses, some a portion of milk"), while hierarchically ranked portions of meat taken from the sacrificial bull were distributed to all the participants. Given its sociopolitical importance, the distribution of meat was carefully scrutinized, and any mistake in the assignment of portions could force the repetition of the entire ritual, as could the failure of any participant to pray for the welfare of the whole Roman people. The latter offense would mark a failure of social solidarity; the former, of proper hierarchy.

A similar case is found in one of the best-documented sacrifices performed by the ancient Germanic peoples, that of the Semnones, as reported in chapter 39 of Tacitus's *Germania*:

> They say that the Semnones are the oldest and most renowned of the Suebi. This belief is confirmed in a religious ceremony of ancient times. At a fixed time, all the people of the same blood come together by legations in a wood that is consecrated by the signs of their ancestors and by an ancient dread. Barbaric rites celebrate the horrific origins, through the dismemberment of a man for the public good. . . .
>
> There the belief of all looks back [to the primordial past], as if from that spot there were the origins of the race. The god who is ruler of all things is there. Others are inferior and subservient.
>
> The good fortune of the Semnones adds to their authority. One hundred cantons are inhabited for them, and this great body causes them to believe themselves to be the head of the Suebi.

Several points must be made regarding the logic and intent of this grisly rite in which the public dismemberment of a human victim was the central feature. First, this was done in repetition or re-presentation of creation, insofar as the sacrifice celebrating the "horrific origins" *(horrenda primordia)* was performed at the very place where the "origins of the race" *(initia gentis)* were believed to be. This comes as little surprise, however, given the well-known Germanic myths that describe creation as resulting from the bodily dismemberment of a primordial giant by the gods themselves. (For the fullest account, see Snorri Sturluson's *Gylfaginning* 6–8.) [*See also* Cosmogony.] Second, the sacrifice was performed to confirm the Semnones' claim to primacy within the Suebian confederation, of which they considered themselves the "oldest and most renowned" *(vetustissimos se nobilissimosque)* members. This claim was also expressed in bodily terms: the Semnones regarded themselves as the "head of the Suebi" *(Sueborum caput)*, something that was perhaps no idle metaphor, but one reflected—and justified—in the formal distribution of the dismembered remains of sacrificial victims.

The theme of creation as the result of a primordial act of sacrificial dismemberment is also common in ancient India. [*See* Puruṣa.] As one celebrated text relates:

> When they divided Man [Skt., Puruṣa], how
> many pieces did they prepare?
> What are his mouth, arms, thighs, and feet
> called?
> The priest was his mouth, the warrior was made
> from his arms;
> His thighs were the commoner, and the servant
> was born from his feet.
> The moon was born of his mind; of his eye, the
> sun was born;
> From his mouth, Indra and fire; from his breath,
> wind was born.
> From his navel there was the atmosphere; from
> his head, heaven was rolled together;
> From his feet, the earth; from his ear, the
> cardinal points. Thus the gods caused the
> worlds to be created. *(Ṛgveda 10.90.11–14)*

The text is remarkable for the way in which it describes society and the cosmos alike as having both been formed from the bodily members of the first sacrificial victim. Thus, we are first presented with a set of social homologues to the human body, wherein four differentially ranked classes—priests (Skt., *brāhmaṇa*), warriors (*kṣatriya*), commoners (*vaiśya*), and servants (*śūdra*)—derive their respective hierarchic positions and characteristic modes of action (speech, force of arms, production and reproduction, and running of errands) from that bodily part with which they are associated (mouth, arms, thighs, and feet). Similarly, a second set homologizes parts of the cosmos to bodily members or faculties: moon to mind, sun to eyes, wind to breath, and so on. Moreover, the social and the cosmic sets themselves are implicitly correlated through the mediation of the body, for the cosmos—like the body and society—is organized into hierarchically ranked vertical strata: heaven (including the celestial bodies), atmosphere (including the wind), and earth. The overall pattern that thus emerges may be graphed as shown in table 1.

The logic of dismemberment thus establishes the priestly class as concerned with heavenly matters, such as sacred speech and the ritual fire, by their very nature, for priests and fire alike have their origin from the mouth (fire being thus the "eater" of whatever is placed into it, the sacrificial fire being called the "mouth of the gods"). The lower classes, in contrast, are relegated to more lowly, mundane pursuits; warriors occupy an intermediate status.

The model that is established within this myth (as also within the practice of Vedic sacrifice) is, quite lit-

TABLE 1. *Cosmic, Social, and Bodily Homologies according to Ṛgveda 10.90*

SOCIAL SET	BODILY SET	COSMIC SET
	UPPER REGION	
	Head	Heaven
	Mouth	Fire
Priest	Eyes	Sun
	Mind	Moon
	Ears	Cardinal points
	MID-REGION	
	Arms	
Warrior	Navel	Atmosphere
	Breath	Wind
	LOWER REGION	
Commoners	Thighs	
Servants	Feet	Earth

erally, that of an "organic" cosmos and a "corporate" society, the parts of which are ordinarily unified but are also analytically detachable, whereupon their hierarchic interrelations become fully evident. Moreover, the corporate nature of society also finds expression within the very rhythms of sacrificial ritual. Lienhardt's observations regarding Dinka sacrifice are, once again, most instructive:

> It is at the moment immediately preceding the physical death of the beast, as the last invocation reaches its climax with more vigorous thrusts of the spear, that those attending the ceremony are most palpably members of a single undifferentiated body, looking towards a single common end. After the victim has been killed, their individual characters, their private and family differences, and various claims and rights according to their status, become apparent once more.
>
> In the account of the role of cattle, I mentioned the Dinkas' way of figuring the unity and diversity of kin-groups in the unity of the bull or ox and in the customary division of its flesh. Similarly in a sacrifice, whilst the victim is still a living whole, all members of a gathering are least differentiated from each other in their common interest in that whole victim. With its death, interest turns towards the customary rights of different participating groups in the division of its flesh. . . . Sacrifice thus includes a re-creation of the basis of local corporate life, in the full sense of those words. The whole victim corresponds to the unitary solidarity of human beings in their common relationship to the divine, while the division of the flesh corresponds to the social differentiation of the groups taking part.
>
> (Lienhardt, 1961, pp. 233–234)

Although he does not use these terms, Lienhardt here masterfully describes the phases of aggregation and segmentation that mark most rituals. As is clear in the accounts of the Feriae Latinae and the Semnones' sacrifice, individuals and groups gather for the performance of a ritual in which they gradually surrender their sense of separate identity as they come to feel part of a broader social totality, united by bonds of kinship, polity, commensality, and/or common purpose. Then, toward the end of the proceedings, this social totality breaks into its constituent parts once again, only to be reunited at the next sacrifice. Further, as Lienhardt recognized, the moment at which the phase of aggregation ends and that of segmentation begins is that moment in which the victim is killed and its flesh divided.

Social segmentation thus coincides with sacrificial dismemberment, while aggregation corresponds to a victim that is whole. That victim, like society, contains within its body the potential to be cut into hierarchically differentiated pieces, but its life depends upon the preserved unity and cooperation of those pieces within an organic whole. These same processes also find abstract, philosophical expression at times, as in the thought of Empedocles (fifth century BCE), who describes the entire cosmos as being ruled by two competing processes: Strife, which tears things apart and finds its representation *par excellence* in sacrificial dismemberment (see, for example, his fragments numbered B128, B137, and B20 in the Diels-Kranz collection), and Love, the force that reunites those things rent asunder by Strife. For that matter, things are not so dissimilar when it comes to the celebrated Aristotelian tools of analysis (i.e., separating a whole into its constituent parts) and synthesis (i.e., reassembling the parts into an organic whole), whereby thought is dismembered and put back together, after the fashion of a sacrificial ox.

[*See also* Sacrifice.]

BIBLIOGRAPHY

An important collection of essays on the general theme of dismemberment within sacrificial ritual has appeared under the editorship of Christiano Grottanelli, Nicola F. Parise, and Pier Giorgio Solinas: "Sacrificio, Organizzazione del cosmo, dinamica sociale," *Studi storici* 25 (October–December 1984): 829–956. Further studies on the same theme, organized by the same editors, will be forthcoming in *L'Uomo*. Also of great interest are the essays that appear in *La cuisine du sacrifice en pays grec*, edited by Marcel Detienne and Jean-Pierre Vernant (Paris, 1980). Discussion of the Dinka materials is found in Godfrey Lienhardt's *Divinity and Experience: The Religion of the Dinka* (Oxford, 1961). On the Feriae Latinae (and its possible connection to myths of creation by sacrificial dismemberment), see Walter Burkert's "Caesar und Romulus-Quirinus," *Historia* 11 (1962): 356–376; on the Semnones, see L. L. Hammerich's "Horrenda Primordia: Zur 'Germania' c. 39," *Germanisch-Romanische Monatsschrift* 33 (May 1952): 228-233, and Alfred Ebenbauer's "Ursprungsglaube, Herrschergott und Menschenopfer: Beobachtungen zum Semnonenkult (Germania c. 39)," in *Antiquitates Indogermanicae: Gedenkschrift für Hermann Güntert*, edited by Manfred Mayrhofer et al. (Innsbruck, 1974), pp. 233–249. I have also discussed many of these materials at greater length in *Myth, Cosmos, and Society: Indo-European Themes of Creation and Destruction* (Cambridge, Mass., 1986).

BRUCE LINCOLN

DĪVĀLĪ, also known as Dīpāvalī, is an important renewal festival celebrated all over India in October–November at the time of the autumn equinox. Dīvālī marks the end of the rainy season and the harvest of the summer crops. The name *Dīvālī* can be translated as "row of lights," in reference to lights lit on the nights of the transition from the waning to the waxing moon. These lights stand for the hope kindled by the new season that comes at the end of the dangerous monsoon. In many ways the festival is a celebration of a new year. Accordingly, debts are paid off, and merchants close their accounts in anticipation of new wealth.

Dīvālī is a three-night festival, the last night of which is the first night of the waxing moon. The celebrations incorporate a number of mythic elements, many of which find colorful regional variations. As in any renewal rite, care is taken to cleanse and purify homes and shops, and people make certain to perform special ablutions in a ritual bath. The festival is most obviously characterized by the seemingly infinite number of oil lamps that are lit everywhere, as well as by the noise of exploding firecrackers that are said to frighten away evil spirits and to welcome the arrival of Lakṣmī, goddess of prosperity. In some regional practices the lamps are said to light the darkness for departed ancestors or to welcome the demon king Bali.

It is to Lakṣmī, however, that the people offer jewels and money, delicate foods, and special new clothes made for the occasion. Much importance is placed on the giving of gifts to all members of the family and to the neighborhood servants who help people throughout the year. Men gamble at various games in a ritual reenactment of the dice tournaments played by the gods to determine the fate of human beings. [*See also* Gambling.]

The festival is associated with several Puranic myths. Their underlying idea calls forth what was at issue during the rainy season and centers on the notion, which holds true for ancestors as well, that underworld creatures play a crucial role in the acquisition of wealth. A well-known myth relates how the dwarf Vāmana (an incarnation of Viṣṇu) asked Bali to grant him as much land as he could cover in three steps. The generous demon king agreed. To his amazement, two of the dwarf's steps covered the earth and the sky; the third, planted on Bali's head, sent the demon to the underworld, a region that became his domain. For his generosity, Bali was then allowed to come to the surface of the earth during Dīvālī in order to bestow wealth on human beings.

Another myth, one in which the god Kṛṣṇa is said to slay Naraka (or Narakāsura, the "demon of hell"), similarly marks the momentary halt of evil underworld powers. Naraka is the son of Bhūdevī, the earth goddess, and Varāha, the incarnation of Viṣṇu as a boar, who had rescued the goddess when she lay buried under the waters of the sea. Although he was ultimately killed by Kṛṣṇa—as all demons must eventually be killed by a god—Naraka, like Bali, is nevertheless paid homage when the question of wealth is at stake.

In North India the second day of Dīvālī is reserved for the worship of the hill Govardhana, near the town of Mathurā, a site of deep religious significance for devotees of Kṛṣṇa. Once Indra had captured all of the world's cattle. Kṛṣṇa freed the cows, but the enraged Indra flooded the earth with a downpour of rain to drown the valuable animals. Kṛṣṇa then raised Govardhana so that the cows would be saved. The importance of the myth is clear in the context of Dīvālī, for in Hindu thought the cow is a powerful and evocative symbol of prosperity. The ritual here primarily involves worship of cattle, but—in a play on the word *govardhana* (lit., "cow-increasing")—offerings are made to mounds of cow dung *(govar)* to ensure continued prosperity and wealth *(dhana)*.

One final ritual marks the celebration of Dīvālī. Girls and women, who at the onset of the rainy season had tied protective threads around their brothers' wrists, now invite the boys and men for delicacies in exchange for gifts. This rite is accompanied by the worship of Yama, lord of the dead, and his twin sister, Yamī. [*See also* Yama.] Yama is also known as Dharmarāja ("king of the social and cosmic order"), for that very order is then restored with the return of prosperity, which is dependent upon women and on controlled underworld powers.

[*See also* Hindu Religious Year.]

BIBLIOGRAPHY

For textual details on the festival, see P. V. Kane's *History of Dharmaśāstra*, 2d ed. (Poona, 1958), vol. 5, pt. 1, pp. 194–210. Some interesting regional variations are given in Lawrence A. Babb's *The Divine Hierarchy: Popular Hinduism in Central India* (New York, 1975) and in Oscar Lewis's *Village Life in Northern India* (Urbana, Ill., 1958).

MARIE-LOUISE REINICHE

DIVINATION is the art or practice of discovering the personal, human significance of future or, more commonly, present or past events. A preoccupation with the import of events and specific methods to discover it are found in almost all cultures. The culture possibly least interested in divination is that of the traditional Australian Aborigines, yet even they hold divinatory "inquests" at funerals to discover the identity of the sorcerers responsible for the deaths.

Much of science itself has evolved from forms of divination and may be said to continue certain aspects of it. Astronomy, for example, is deeply indebted to ancient Near Eastern and Hellenistic astrological researches; mathematics and physics were advanced by Indian, Pythagorean, and Arabic divinatory cosmological speculations; and several leading Renaissance scientists were inspired by the divinatory schemes of Qabbalah and Hermetism in their search for the moral harmonies and direction of the universe. Yet it would be incorrect to label divination a mere infantile science or pseudoscientific magic, for modern science and traditional divination are concerned with essentially distinct goals. This helps to explain the continuing fascination with divination even today on the part of well-educated people, notably in regard to astrology, the *I ching*, and spiritualism or necromancy (séances with the dead). Divination involves communication with personally binding realities and seeks to discover the "ought" addressed specifically to the personal self or to a group. Science, however, if faithful to its own axioms, cannot enunciate any "oughts" because of its methodological, cognitive, and moral neutrality: it only offers hypotheses about reality and is concerned with general statistical regularities, not with unique persons or events. The existential situation and binding transcendental realities are beyond its concern. It may be argued that, precisely to the degree that such modern disciplines as psychotherapy and Marxist theory leave science behind, they take on divinatory (and therefore religious) functions, and represent modern contributions to the history of divination.

Basic Forms. Anything can be used to divine the meaning of events. It is very common to assign spontaneous and arbitrary meaning to signs or omens when one is deeply anxious about the outcome of a personal situation. But the cultural form of divinatory methods and signs is seldom entirely random: each one expresses a specific logic.

A full list of divinatory agents, therefore, would amount to a catalog of both nature and culture. H. J. Rose, in his article "Divination, Introductory and Primitive," in volume 4 of the *Encyclopaedia of Religion and Ethics* (Edinburgh, 1911), classifies the most common means used to obtain insight as follows: dreams (oneiromancy); hunches and presentiments; involuntary body actions (twinges, sneezes, etc.); ordeals; mediumistic possession; consulting the dead (necromancy); observing animal behavior (e.g., ornithomancy, interpreting the flight of birds); noting the form of entrails of sacrificial victims (extaspicy or haruspicy), or the victims' last movements before death; making mechanical manipulations with small objects such as dice, drawing long or short stalks from a bundle, and so on (sortilege); reading tea leaves (tasseography), or using playing cards (cartography), etc.; decoding natural phenomena (as in geomancy, palmistry, phrenology, or astrology); and—of course—"miscellaneous." Plato—in an analysis that still forms the basis of most modern treatments (as in the world survey of divination edited by Caquot and Leibovici, 1968)—distinguished "ecstatic" and "nonecstatic" types, with the latter including all inductive and empirical systems of noting portents, studying entrails, and so forth. But ecstatic states and inductive methods can be mingled confusingly; indigenous interpretations of so-called objective omens often assume spirit possession of the omens and/or ecstatic insight in the diviner, while some mediums appear quite normal when "possessed."

It would be more useful to establish what the indigenous theory of divination is, rather than to attempt to assay the states of mind actually experienced by diviners in different cultures and periods. The same conscious experience of heightened awareness can be interpreted in one culture as deep wisdom and in another as spirit possession. Under the influence of such interpretations, in fact, an individual diviner might permit himself to drift into a deeper mediumistic trance, or on the contrary strive toward a more intense lucidity. How a condition is interpreted influences the way it unfolds and realizes itself.

Stressing the indigenous theory of divination also directs us to the cosmological assumptions and the attitudes toward the self that unit various seemingly unrelated methods. For example, cultures that stress mediumistic interpretations of trance usually also explain the casting of lots or the conformations of entrails in terms of spirit possession: divination, according to this overarching viewpoint, consists of the forms of communication developed by invisible beings to instruct humanity on the meaning of events. But cultures that have developed a concept of a decodable impersonal and elemental divine order would see the entrails or the sortilege in terms of microcosmic echoes of vaster harmonies. In general, then, we may distinguish three general types of divination, based on indigenous meanings: those based on the immediate context when interpreted by the spiritual insight of the diviner (intuitive divination); those based on spirit manipulation (possession divination); and those reflecting the operation of impersonal laws within a coherent divine order (wisdom divination). See figure 1 for subcategories and examples of these three general types.

FIGURE 1. *A Typology of Divination*

I. INTUITIVE DIVINATION (in which the diviner spontaneously "sees" or "knows" reality or the future)

   A. Hunches and Presentiments

   B. Insights of Spiritual Masters, Saints, Gurus

II. POSSESSION DIVINATION (in which spiritual beings are said to communicate through intermediary agents)

   A. Possession of Nonhuman Agents (augury)

   Examples: Divination by arbitrary movements of heavenly bodies (meterology)

   Divination by fire (pyromancy); divination by water (hydromancy); divination by stones, as in throwing dice (lithomancy)

   Divination by observation of the flight of birds (ornithomancy); divination by observation of quadrupeds, fish, insects, or reptiles

   Divination by lots (sortilege or cleromancy)

   B. Possession of Human Agents

   Examples: Divination by body twitches or pains

   Divination by judicial ordeal

   Divination by dreams (oneiromancy)

   Divination by glossolalia (speaking in tongues), spiritualistic séances, and prophecy (varying forms of possession in which the medium's general awareness of the world and of the self is preserved)

   Divination by full mediumism or oracular trance (in which self-awareness and world-awareness are said to be lost, as the spiritual being takes over the medium completely)

III. WISDOM DIVINATION (in which the diviner decodes impersonal patterns of reality)

   Examples: Divination by temporal patterns in movements of heavenly bodies (astrology)

   Divination by patterns in earth formations (geomancy)

   Divination by body forms, often said to be influenced by astrological forces (morphoscopy): in the hand (palmistry or chiromancy); in the liver (hepatoscopy) or entrails (extaspicy or haruspicy); in the head shape (phrenology)

   Divination through mathematical correspondences (numerology; *I ching; hati*)

Intuitive divination. The Shona of Zimbabwe esteem their *hombahomba* diviners above all other kinds because these remarkable men, consulted by strangers who travel from far off to seek their help, can spontaneously tell their visitors' names, family connections, urgent problems, and even minor experiences encountered on the journey. People speak in awe of the piercing eyes and aura of penetrating awareness of these diviners, whose fame can spread over great distances. And yet—an example of how types of divination can run into one another—the *hombahomba* may attune himself to the consultation by casting *hakata* dice (a form of wisdom divination), after which, in one reported case, the diviner became possessed before returning to a state of mind in which he could begin the inquiry.

Intuitive divination is perhaps the elementary form out of which, through various interpretations, the other two developed. It is seldom much stressed, although its distribution as hunches and presentiments is universal. The reliability of amateur intuitions is not usually considered very great, yet in many cultures extraordinary spiritual masters are often credited with this type of divinatory insight, which then has more prestige and credence than any other. For example, disciples of a *tsaddiq* or saintly master in Hasidic Judaism frequently claim that their master can look into a person's soul at first meeting and determine not only the past lives but also the future course of that person. Precisely the same claims are made for many Hindu gurus. These insights by the guru are regarded as far more reliable and authoritative than the various forms of wisdom divination common to India, and these in turn are more esteemed than folk mediumistic and possession divination methods.

Possession divination. There are many varieties of possession divination. The most common is augury: divining the message sent by spiritual beings through nonhuman creatures or things. The classic form of augury, much used in ancient Greece and Rome, consisted of attending to the flight of birds, which were thought to be seized by the gods or spirits and directed according to a code known to the diviner. But all other forms of interpreting supposedly objective spirit messages were also included in the Latin term *augurium.*

Even when human agents are seized by the spiritual beings, this does not always imply trance: a popular form of divination in ancient Near Eastern, medieval European, and even modern societies such as Mexico, is to pose a question and then attend to the first chance words one overhears from passing strangers on the street. Another almost universal method whereby spirits or divinities communicate with a person is to induce twitches or sudden pains in the body. Quite explicit meanings can be derived from this, depending on the part of the body affected and other indications, and of course varying according to the specific cultural context. The theory behind the contemporary use of the Ouija board is explicitly spiritualistic, yet all that one must do to use it is put oneself in a receptive mood: ordinary awareness remains. A very similar state is apparently involved in some cases of glossolalia, according to American Pentacostals I have interviewed, but full mediumistic trance is reported in many studies (see, for example, Felicitas Goodman, *Speaking in Tongues,* Chicago, 1979). The divinatory interpretation of dreams is another very widely used method; here manipulation by spiritual beings begins to require outright alteration of consciousness, although only when the ego has already dimmed its awareness.

Full divinatory possession of human beings may be of several theoretical forms: prophetic inspiration, shamanistic ecstasy, mystical illuminations and visions, and mediumistic or oracular trance. They differ according to the degree of ego awareness and lucidity, awareness of the ordinary world, and the theoretical recipient of the divinatory message. The prophets of the Bible seem to retain a lucid sense of themselves and the world as they exhort their audience, although they are gripped by an overmastering sense of the integral meaning of events as illuminated by God's presence. The recipient of this revelation of temporal meaning is both the prophet and the human community. In shamanistic trance the struggle between ego awareness and the spirits is often portrayed as being so intense that it forces a displacement of the shaman from this world: the shaman may fly far away to interrogate the spirits or God, and may have to struggle with bad spirits and force them to confess their role in human events. As recipient of the divinatory communications, the shaman may later report on his conversations to an assembled audience, or may permit the audience to eavesdrop on the actual interviews or even to be directly addressed by the spirits through his mouth, but in any case he remains self-possessed and afterward can recall everything that occurred. For the mystical visionary, on the other hand, the entire ordinary world is eclipsed by the ecstatic revelations, and the mystic is the sole direct recipient of the communications. The oracular medium, however, loses all awareness, it is said, and therefore often remains ignorant of the message that is communicated directly from the spiritual being to the audience.

The dependency in particular cultures or subgroups of a culture on "objective" augury methods, or on methods that progressively encroach on or even obliterate ego awareness, suggest differing views of the self, society, and the world. Satisfactory cross-cultural studies of divinatory theories from this point of view have not yet been made, but some points may be tentatively suggested. All kinds of possession divination assume a mysterious, arbitrary world governed by personal powers who are involved with a vulnerable humanity. The human self must learn how to submit to or cajole these capricious and often dangerous spirits. However, in loosely organized, relatively egalitarian societies with an emphasis on personal initiative, we can expect more confidence in the ability of the human ego to sustain its integrity when faced with the spiritual powers. This is what we find, for example, in circumpolar and related cultures in Europe, Siberia, and North America. A study by H. Barry, I. L. Child, and M. K. Bacon (cited by Erika Bourguignon, *Possession,* San Francisco, 1976) shows that hunting-fishing cultures generally depend on short-term risks and personal initiative, so that individuals are trained from childhood to be self-reliant and self-sufficient: each adult can master all the cultural skills necessary to survive, and ego alertness is highly valued. In such societies mediumistic divination is not found; instead, individuals possess an encyclopedic knowledge of portents, and of methods for obtaining auguries of the capricious spirits' intentions. The autonomous ego can negotiate its way through a mysterious cosmos, while the shaman, able to retain ego awareness and control even in the most intimate relationship with the spirits, is the group guide.

The same cross-cultural study indicates that children in agricultural societies are trained to be obedient, reliable, cooperative, and patient—qualities needed for ceaseless cultivation of crops and for interaction with fixed communities. The social group, not the individual, is the survival unit; personal success is obtained through accommodation to others. Even the powerful must submit to the more powerful and the spirits, while the weak survive only through self-effacement. Here, mediumistic trance expresses the natural state of things. A survey of African cultures by Lenora Greenbaum (in *Religion, Altered States of Consciousness, and Social Change,* edited by Erika Bourguignon, Columbus Ohio, 1973) has shown that mediumistic divinatory trance is most common in societies having slaves and two or more hereditary (i.e., fixed) classes, such as commoners and nobility, and possessing populations over one hundred thousand. I might add that in such societies a sense of relative deprivation and ego diminution must be common, since individuals meet people every day who enjoy other roles in life. Less advantaged groups (the poor, women, and so on) might well seek transcendental release from the resultant frustrations through mediumistic trance more often than more privileged sectors of society (see I. M. Lewis, *Ecstatic Religion*, Baltimore, 1971). In any case, here one obtains power only through radical self-effacement; even kings become divine only through being possessed. This is the opposite view from that underlying shamanism.

It is perhaps inevitable that, at the center of social power, attempts are made in such cultures to master all that can be known of the arbitrary will of the gods. The court diviners frequently compile mountainous records of precedents of monster births or other omens, the results of centuries of haruspicy, and so forth, as in Babylonia, where we see the fruit of intense efforts to maintain clarity as far as is possible. The Babylonian priests noted every heavenly sign over many centuries, identifying each celestial body with a god. But no system emerged from this, for the classical Babylonian worldview was polytheistic and predicated on power, passion, and personal whims of the divinities. Yet the result was a hierarchy of divination methods: present at the courts were alert, learned priests who interpreted the will of the gods in elaborate augury ceremonials, while among the lower classes mediumism and a much more random and confused use of omens indicated the insecurity of ego control.

When the entire social structure and even the cosmos is felt to be inauthentic, as in late antiquity, mediumistic ecstasy may tend to apocalyptic predictions of the end of the age: the muted protest becomes radical and explicit. Or mystical visions may teach the negation of the entire world. In such cases, divination merges with salvation cults.

Wisdom divination. The elaboration of divination systems based on a unified field of impersonal and universal processes that can be studied, harmonized with, and above all internalized by nonecstatic sages, is an important but rare development in the history of religion. It is most often found in complex civilizations that have been defeated by equally powerful cultures and therefore must integrate their own indigenous views with other perspectives. Wisdom divination is a syncretistic movement beyond specific cults, approaching the elemental ground from which all personal spirits and cultic gods as well as cultural groups arise. But the speculative effort must usually begin in court and priestly circles, for it depends on a cumulative effort of generations and a specialized learning of which, in most early civilizations, only centralized priesthoods are capable. Only after literacy and education become general can the sagelike diviner detach himself from court circles and apply himself to individual and nonpolitical concerns.

Thus it was only after Babylonia fell to Persian conquest in the sixth century BCE that its priestly thinkers were challenged by a view that placed "Truth" (the Zoroastrian *artha*) and a cosmic order founded in a supreme being above the capricious gods. The new empire embraced many cultures, making possible as a real option personal conversion to such missionizing, universal monotheisms as those espoused by the Jews and the Persians. The old social boundaries—and their gods—now became part of a vaster order, and an attempt was begun to link individual lives directly to a single cosmic pattern rather than to any intermediate hierarchies. Inevitably, the effort was eventually to lead to a kind of pagan monotheism, but it began as an attempt to confirm the polytheistic view. With the new radical improvements in mathematics and astronomy, the first personal horoscope known to us was made of a ruler in 410 BCE. The new cities and academies of the Hellenistic world spurred the fusion of Zoroastrian, Babylonian, Jewish, Syrian, and Greek currents; as Franz Cumont (1912) has made clear, astrology came to function as nothing less than a universal and syncretistic religious perspective that underlay or influenced all the religions of late antiquity. Even synagogues, as we know from recent excavations, commonly traced the zodiac on their sanctuary floors or walls.

The growing separation of divination and wisdom from the central institutions of power was resented by many kings and emperors. One of Augustus's first acts as emperor was the burning of about two thousand collections of pseudo-Sibylline oracles circulating among the people, since some of the oracles favored rival figures or criticized Roman policies, while others, by Jewish proselytizers, predicted the impending messianic era. Several Roman emperors outlawed all nonofficial divination; Constantine the Great and his successors used Christianity as an excuse to roast to death any astrologer and client caught in private consultation (see Cramer, 1954, and D. Grodzynski's article in Vernant et al., 1974). Even in modern times astrology can have political aspects: the Nazis directed certain agents to gain reputations in the United States and England as astrologers, and then to predict the success of Nazi endeavors or otherwise demoralize Western efforts. Within Nazi Germany itself, astrology was strictly an instrument of state.

Today, however, astrology serves usually as a muted protest against everyday social identity or generally accepted scientific values and cosmology. While interest in astrology is widespread, it has been especially favored by the so-called counterculture, and by many in the lower and lower-middle classes, particularly women, since it desubstantializes oppressive personal relationships, offering instead an exotic alternative identity in which faults are erased or elevated into association with a "star family" embracing strangers. In an increasingly fluid, anonymous, and heterogeneous society, pattern and typological identities are discovered within a larger cosmic harmony, and a sense of control is restored to personal life through the aesthetic and probabilistic terms in which predictions are couched. The power of such a vision is seen in the fact that it persists, even though the zodiac houses and their stellar correlates, fixed as they were during the hellenistic period, are now literally two thousand years out of congruence, making the system obsolete even in its own terms.

A quite similar history of a wisdom divinatory system is that of the *I ching* in China. It was the practice in court circles of the Shang dynasty to consult the nature spirits and royal ancestors—and especially the celestial supreme being—concerning all significant state decisions. Scapulimancy was the favored technique—in the late Shang period tortoise shells were generally substituted, supplemented by sortilege with long and short yarrow stalks. These methods had their roots, respectively, in hunting-fishing cultures to the north and in agricultural tribes to the south. Although these methods already involved a conception of heavenly and earthly polarities, it was apparently only after the Shang were overthrown by the Chou, and after the Chou had expanded rapidly in succeeding centuries to embrace cultures throughout northern, central, and even southern China, that an elemental metaphysics arose that transcended all gods and spirits and was encapsulated in the *I ching* as such. There is no reference to personal spirits or gods anywhere in the text of the *I ching* in its present form, which stems from the late Chou and Former Han dynasties. Instead, all of reality is regarded as woven out of a dialectic of *yin* and *yang* forces (contracting and expanding, respectively): all things and persons are composites in the process of transformation. Using the elaborate binary code of this method, one can discover what the transformations imply, but only if one has attained true nobility and tranquility of character. Confucian mandarins and philosophers through the ages ruled their lives by this text, but only in the Ming dynasty did its use become widespread among the general populace, reflecting the growth of literacy and the escalating complexity of Chinese civilization. The *I ching* had come to serve as a quiet intellectual aid to personal transcendence and mastery of immediate social pressures. This function—the same one it serves today in the West—differed from its earlier Confucian use as a guide in official life and in social activity often associated with the court. [*See* Yin-yang Wu-hsing.]

The Chinese had a number of other forms of wisdom divination, in particular a distinctive form of astrology and an elaborate geomancy. The latter offered detailed instructions on the cosmic forces affecting any specific site, and professional geomancers were consulted whenever a house was to be built, a road laid, or a grave site chosen. Astrology too governed all aspects of village life by the later medieval period, despite the general folk use of many possession divination methods, ranging from countless omens and portents to outright mediumistic séances.

Hindu astrology combined some elements of the Chinese system and more of the Middle Eastern system into its own configuration. Other significant forms of wisdom divination include the Islamic *hati* system *(al-khaṭṭ bi-raml)* and the several derivations of it in West Africa (especially the Yoruba and Fon Ifa systems), Zimbabwe, and Madagascar.

Divination in Western Religions. The Jewish and Christian traditions are markedly ambivalent about divination. For example, the rabbis criticized the use of folk methods found in surrounding cultures, just as the Torah itself forbids all appeals to local nature spirits or to the dead. While the efficacy of such appeals is not necessarily denied (*1 Sm.* 28), such acts were thought to suggest that God is not the one source of all events and of all truly reliable knowledge. (See *Dt.* 18:10–22; *Lv.* 19:26, 19:31, 20:6–7, 20:27; *Jer.* 10:2; and the tractates *Pes.* 113a and *Ned.* 32a from the Talmud. For a full discussion, see Cohen, 1949.) Thus prophetic inspiration directly from God, the use of Urim and Tummim in the Temple, certain kinds of omens, and even dream divination by Joseph in Egypt and at local shrines in ancient Israel were certainly acceptable. So most Talmudic rabbis permitted dream divination, water gazing, and the use of omens; contradictory views were expressed concerning astrology, but by the Middle Ages most rabbis accepted what was in effect the science of the day. Moses Maimonides, however, made a scathing attack upon it: freedom of will, he said, is fundamental to Torah spirituality; those who follow God cannot in any case by subject to the stars (see, e.g., *Dt.* 4:19–20), while a close analysis of astrology shows it to be based on poor reasoning and worse science. Necromancy was explicitly condemned in the Torah (*Dt.* 18:11), and there is very little reference to any kind of spirit possession in the Talmud; the late medieval dybbuk possession chiefly involved tormented but not malicious spirits who sought expiation for sins. Yet qabbalistic meditations resulted in a wide variety of wisdom divinatory methods based on the divine image sustaining the whole of creation, and prophetic ecstatic visions were sought by mystics from the Talmudic age on.

In Christianity some of the same themes and ambiguities reappear, but now the antithesis between good and bad divination is understood as part of a war between Christ and Satan. For example spirit possession, mediumistic and otherwise, is a frequent phenomenon and is generally viewed as demonic and requiring exorcism. However, astrological signs can be good, for they marked Jesus' birth. Dream divination by Joseph or Pilate's wife, casting lots, and mediumistic glossolalia are all approved (*Mt.* 1:20, 2:2, 2:12, 27:19; *Acts* 1:26, 10:10), unless performed by non-Christians like Simon Magus or by sorcerers (*Acts* 8:9, 13:6, 16:16). Folk methods used in the Roman empire and afterward were readily incorporated into Christian and official usage, although the fourth-century Synod of Laodicia and the contemporaneous Theodosian Code outlawed divination (drawing on earlier precedents in Roman legislation). Thus divinatory invocation of pagan deities or spirits, schismatic prophetic movements within Christianity, and even oracular attempts to criticize or delegitimize the ruling regime were all stamped as "Satanism."

Similar attitudes continued into later European cultures, but a rich and highly varied regional folk practice of divination persisted. From Islamic civilization—itself the inheritor of Middle Eastern, Persian, and even Indian methods of divination—came scholarly catalogs of divinatory significances of dreams, omens, and studies of specialized systems such as palmistry, astrology, and crystal gazing. Astrology—despite the rejection of it in the late Roman empire by church leaders who often cited critical analyses by earlier pagan philosophers—came to be regarded as a universal science in the Middle Ages. The Renaissance renewed acquaintance with classical criticisms (permitting astronomy to develop as an independent science), but the increasing literacy of later generations spread knowledge of these systems and encouraged devotees to elaborate their own methods further and publish studies of them. Cartomancy (including the use of tarot cards), phrenology (divination by head conformations), graphology (handwriting analysis), and many other novel systems or elaborations of earlier systems developed at this time. Pietists of the Reformation heartily condemned these alternative systems of wisdom, but continued to use dreams, omens, and even scriptures opened at random to comprehend events.

In the modern period, devotees of such systems as astrology or water witching often feel constrained to offer "scientific" explanations for the claimed success of their methods—explanations often extrinsic to the methods themselves. Extrasensory perceptions (precognition, etc.), for example, have been cited, or the "synchronicity" invoked by C. G. Jung for the power of the *I ching:* with the mind tuned in by the divinatory apparatus and method, the diviner may notice the minute evidences of interconnections and processes in the environment that are usually ignored, or the diviner may in this heightened state even comprehend vaster elemental wholes leading inevitably to certain outcomes. It is even suggested that divinatory consciousness may be able to pick up unobservable rhythms in events, in somewhat the same way that a radio picks up invisible transmission. These hypotheses may describe real processes; unfortunately, they are at present untestable.

Sacrificial Motifs. In any case, divination is fundamentally directed by religious, not scientific, concerns. Its basic curiosity is not about how the world is constructed apart from the pulsing heart of the observer, but about the existential meaning of particular human lives. Above all, divination illuminates suffering and alleviates doubt. It restores value and significance to lives in crisis. But to achieve this, all systems of divination demand the submission of the inquirer to transcendental realities, whether these be divine persons (possession divination) or the underlying divine order (wisdom divination). The inquirer is made to achieve spiritual distance from the self and the immediate crisis.

This recentering of the self is usually directed by sacrificial motifs and rituals. Almost all African divination, for example, ends in sacrifice to the spirits named in the consultations as responsible for the crisis, and many rites also begin with sacrifice. Very often the act of divination is simply a sacrificial rite: in Nilotic and Bantu cultures, the answer is "read" from the entrails of victims. Often the actions of the sacrificed victim give the spirit's answer. In Zaire and nearby culture areas, chickens may be fed a partially toxic substance: if the bird dies, God has accepted it and signified "yes" to the question; if not, the answer is "no." A similar logic directs witch ordeals. As in Africa, so also in Europe is the observation of the last convulsive movements of a sacrificial victim a divination practice. Strabo tells us that the ancient Gauls often killed a slave or captive by a sword stroke in the back: the future was then told from the way he fell, his movements, and the way the blood flowed. Even wisdom divination is frequently given a mythical source in a primal sacrifice (as in the case of the African Dogon and Bambara rites, and also the Yoruba and Fon systems of divination, called Ifa and Fa, respectively. The oracle bone divination of Shang dynasty China had a sacrificial context, and the actual procedure by which one consults the *I ching* is basically structured by sacrificial ideas. Mediums perhaps most dramatically embody a sacrificial logic: those initiated in the spiritualistic religions of Nigeria and Dahomey, for example, and in their perpetuations in recent centuries in the Caribbean, must undergo a symbolic and psychic death and resurrection—one so experiential that occasionally the offering to the spirits, the medium-candidate, does not rise again from the ground.

All this expresses a deeper truth, that divination requires the radical submission of the diviner and indeed the client to the transcendental sources of truth, before their lives can be transformed and set straight, before they can be reincorporated harmoniously into the world. In short, divinatory rites follow the pattern of all rites of passage. The client, having learned in the course of the rite to offer up to the divine all egocentric resistance, ends the session reoriented to the world and able to take positive and confident action in it.

G. K. Park (in Lessa and Vogt, 1965) has suggested that divination assists in political and personal decision making precisely by removing the decision from contesting parties and giving it an objective legitimacy, both through its spiritual source and its convincing ritual drama. O. K. Moore (ibid.) has added that even the "randomizing" of decision outcomes in divination is actually adaptive in situations where egoistically obvious or socially customary decisions might end up limiting personal or group survival chances. By hunting in accord with the cracks that appear on heated deer shoulder blades, the Naskapi Indians of Labrador are prevented from overhunting favorite areas and are therefore more likely to find game year-round.

Wisdom divination also often works in this way: by freeing the inquirer from customary ways of thought, it frequently reveals fresh insight into problems. Thus the cryptic proverbs or aphorisms (as in the Ifa system or the *I ching*), or the nonbinding details and universalizable generalities (as in astrology), open up a cosmic perspective that in itself bestows tranquility and a renewed ability to cope effectively with crises. One learns to see behind appearances and to cultivate a continual attitude of tranquil self-offering. The momentum of wisdom divination, in short, is to internalize the basic attitude operating in all divination; it does this by rendering the structures of the transcendent into a form in which they can be grasped consciously and autonomously. The very vagueness of the answers in most forms of wisdom divination aid in this personal appropriation, making the client participate in shaping meaning out of the session.

[*For further discussion of this topic, see* Oracles; *see also* Geomancy; Necromancy; *and* Dreams.]

BIBLIOGRAPHY

Useful historical surveys of divination and related topics in world cultures include Lynn Thorndike's monumental *A History of Magic and Experimental Science*, 3 vols. (New York, 1923–1958), and Auguste Bouché-Leclerq's still very useful *Histoire de la divination dans l'antiquité*, 4 vols. in 2 (1879–1889; reprint, New York, 1975). Thorndike's history is chiefly oriented to Western culture, but the first two volumes deal with antiquity. Bouché-Leclerq focuses on classical Greco-Roman cultures. A total of seventeen learned articles on divination in particular cultures, and an additional twelve articles on astrology and other religious aspects of heavenly phenomena in world cultures, can be found in the *Encyclopaedia of Religion and Ethics*, 13 vols., edited by James Hastings (Edinburgh, 1908–1926), under "Divination" (vol. 4, 1911) and "Sun, Moon, and Stars" (vol. 12, 1921). More up to date is the excellent survey edited by André Caquot and Marcel Leibovici, *La divination: Études recueillies*, 2 vols., (Paris, 1968), which, in addition to the expected essays on the major ancient Near Eastern, classical, and Asian cultures, contains numerous essays on pre-Christian European cultures; the ancient civilizations of the Americas; native or tribal cultures in Siberia, Africa, and elsewhere; and modern folk and urban Western societies—all with helpful bibliographies. The most recent English symposium is Michael Loewe and Carmen Blacker's *Divination and Oracles* (London, 1981), with nine authoritative essays ranging from Tibetan culture to Islam.

An anthropological symposium on divination that refers to political aspects as well is *Divination et rationalité*, by Jean-Pierre Vernant and others (Paris, 1974). A useful selection of important theoretical anthropological essays on divination is included in *Reader in Comparative Religion: An Anthropological Approach*, 2d ed., edited by William A. Lessa and Evon Z. Vogt (New York, 1965); later editions include some more recent studies but omit much from the second edition. Mediumship has evoked the greatest attention from anthropologists; see, for example, *Spirit Mediumship and Society in Africa*, edited by John Beattie and John Middleton (New York, 1969), in addition to the studies mentioned in the text of the foregoing article.

For an authorative summary of what we know about ancient Mesopotamian divination, see A. Leo Oppenheim's *Ancient Mesopotamia* (Chicago, 1964), pp. 198–227, or W. H. P. Römer's "Religion of Ancient Mesopotamia," in *Historia Religionum*, edited by C. Jouco Bleeker and Geo Widengren, vol. 1 (Leiden, 1969), especially pp. 172–178. H. W. Parke has summarized his many authoritative studies on Greek mediumship in his brief *Greek Oracles* (London, 1967); he does not ignore social and political implications. Still outstanding is Franz Cumont's *Astrology and Religion among the Greeks and Romans* (1912; reprint, New York, 1960). More recent are Hans Lewy's *Chaldaean Oracles and Theurgy: Mysticism, Magic and Platonism in the Later Roman Empire*, new edition by Michel Tardieu (Paris, 1978), and Frederick Henry Cramer's *Astrology in Roman Law and Politics* (Philadelphia, 1954).

Talmudic views of divination are well discussed by Abraham Cohen in his *Everyman's Talmud*, new ed. (New York, 1949), pp. 274–297; further information is available in the article "Divination" by Shmuel Aḥituv and others in the *Encyclopaedia Judaica*, 16 vols. (Jerusalem, 1971). A general survey of Muslim divination is available in Toufic Fahd's *La divination arabe* (Leiden, 1966), and in the various symposia mentioned above. On *hati* geomancy, see the article by Robert Jaulin in the collection by André Caquot and Marcel Leibovici, cited above, and Robert Jaulin's *La géomancie: Analyse formelle* (Paris, 1966).

For a penetrating study of the Yoruba Ifa system, see Wande Abimbola's *Ifa: An Exposition of Ifa Literary Corpus* (London, 1976).

Any study of Chinese divination should begin with Joseph Needham's brilliant study *Science and Civilisation in China*, vol. 2 (Cambridge, 1956), pp. 216–395; an excellent bibliography is appended. Among the many perceptive studies of the *I ching* is Hellmut Wilhelm's *Heaven, Earth and Man in the Book of Changes: Seven Eranos Lectures* (Seattle, 1977). A useful survey of other forms of Chinese wisdom divination as well as of allied forms of the *I ching* is Wallace A. Sherrill and Wen Kuan Chu's *An Anthology of I Ching* (London, 1977). Also see Stephan D. R. Feuchtwang's *An Anthropological Analysis of Chinese Geomancy* (Vientiane, Laos, 1974).

EVAN M. ZUESSE

DIVINE, THE. *See* Holy, Idea of the; Sacred and the Profane, The; *and* Transcendence and Immanence.

DIVINE CHILD. *See* Child.

DIVINE PRESENCE. *For discussion of the Jewish concept of divine presence, see* Shekhinah.

DIVINITY. *See* Deity; *see also* Gods and Goddesses *and* Supreme Beings.

DIVINIZATION. *See* Apotheosis; Deification; *and* Heroes.

DJANGGAWUL (also called Djanggau) is a collective name for Dua-moiety mythic beings who figure prominently in the religious life of northeastern and north-central Arnhem Land. In northeastern (Yirrkalla) perspective, they are two sisters—the elder is Bildjiwuraroyu, the younger Miralaidji—and their brother, simply called Djanggau. At the beginning of their adventures, they are accompanied by Bralbral, their *mari* (mother's mother's brother or mother's mother's brother's son's son). In the north-central (Milingimbi) version, the elder sister is called Djanggau, the younger Ganyudingu; they have no companions, but during their travels they meet other *wongar* (Dreaming) characters.

In the Milingimbi cycle the two sisters are daughters of the Sun Woman. In the Yirikalla version, although their are many references to the Sun, the linkage is less explicit. In both, the Djanggawul move from east to west, from the mythical island of Bralgu, the Dua-moiety land of the dead (one of the moiety homes of the immortals and of spirits of Dua-moiety dead), to their final disappearance in the sunset.

The Djanggawul sisters are creators, responsible for populating the Arnhem Land region with the first human beings. They also shaped the topography of the country and instituted customs, including ritual. They are simultaneously fertility mothers and goddesses and are identified separately from the Wawalag mythic constellation on one hand and the Kunapipi mother on the other. [*See* Wawalag *and* Gadjeri, *respectively.*] The following is a brief summary of the Yirrkalla myth.

The two sisters and their brother come to the island of Bralgu, somewhere in the Gulf of Carpentaria, from an unknown land. The sisters have elongated clitorises, their brother a long penis; these are later transformed into sacred *rangga* posts. They live together, but from the mythic standpoint this is not technically regarded as an incestuous relationship. (In the creative era, marriage rules, constraint between brothers and sisters, and moiety divisions had not been formulated.) With Bralbral, they prepare a seagoing bark canoe (sometimes noted as a raft) and load it with sacred emblems, kept in a *ngainmara* (conical mat).

During their journey across the sea, the Djanggawul name various marine creatures and birds, and their sacred emblems are stained with foam and spray from the waves. Once they reach the mainland, they beach their canoe and unload the emblems. Holding sacred *rangga* in each hand and using them as walking sticks, with the emblem-filled *ngainmara* and woven bags slung across the backs of the two sisters, they move across the country. Their dragging genitals make grooves in the ground; the brother's waistband forms a long sand hill. By plunging *rangga* into the earth, they make water holes. A special *djuda* (tree) *rangga*, stood upright in the ground, springs into life as a fully leafed tree, complete with birds. *Djanda* (goannas) become sacred *rangga*, especially identified with Djanggau, the brother.

When they reach Arnhem Bay, the elder sister gives birth to the first human children. Boys are placed in coarse grass to encourage the growth of body hair. Girls are put under a *ngainmara* mat to keep them smooth and soft. From this time onward, the sisters remain pregnant, and the children they produce grow up to become the progenitors of present-day eastern Arnhem Landers.

At Marabai the sisters leave their sacred possessions in a shelter while they go to collect shellfish. On their return, they find these have been taken by their brother and his companions (presumably their own male children). Going in search of them, they hear clapping sticks and find the men performing a secret-sacred ritual. (Before this incident, men had no sacred ritual or emblems. Everything belonged to the two sisters.) The sisters relinquish their right to control these, but they emphasize that they retain their own power and sacredness. The brother cuts the clitorises of his sisters and his own penis; the segments removed become sacred *rangga*.

The Djanggawul meet a *wongar* man named Buralindjingu, and sing of their travels, telling their story. Then the two sisters are, like circumcision novices, decorated with sacred clan designs, because their clitorises have been cut. Buralindjingu gives them cycad nut "bread," which they eat sacramentally. When they reach Galiwinku (Elcho Island), two boys, sons of the Djanggawul, become the first to undergo circumcision. The brother carries out this rite to ensure that their penises do not grow too long, as his did; however, although he shortens his, he is not circumcised.

The Djanggawul continue to move from place to place, "into the setting sun." The sisters give birth to many children, and their brother performs rituals and leaves sacred emblems for the new people.

Comparing William Lloyd Warner's (1937) Milingimbi versions of the Djanggawul (*Djunkgao* in Warner's spelling) with this outline of the Yirrkalla myth reveals a number of differences. For instance, the sisters' procreative ability receives little mention in the Milingimbi versions; there are references to the "incestuous rape" of the younger sister; and the Yulunggul and Wawalag myth is said to overlap with the Djanggawul sequence. [*See* Yulunggul.] This is not the case in either the Yirrkalla myth or in the Milingimbi versions I recorded in 1950. But Warner's reference to Yulunggul has led Chris Knight (1983, pp. 34-35) to suggest that " 'the serpent' takes the form of the [Djunkgao] Sisters themselves." According to Djanggawul ideology, this suggestion is out of context, as is the statement (by Warner, accepted by Knight) that the loss to the men of the sisters' bags (containing the sacred objects) and of their right to perform life-giving ritual is symbolically connected with their supposed "incestuous rape." The only "incest"—not rape—that takes place, outside Warner's version, is the brother's sexual association with his two sisters, and that was not regarded as incest. On the other hand, all known versions include the section on the sisters' loss. One interpretation holds that a contrast is being drawn between the natural act of childbirth and the simulated ritual symbolism of childbirth by the men.

The Djanggawul is a basic mythic and ritual cycle in this region, and it is directly connected with the important Dua-moiety *nara* ("nest" or "womb") rituals. It not only reflects basic principles inherent in all Aboriginal religious systems but also expresses a unique way of treating them. As fertility mothers, the two sisters, in conjunction with their brother, are responsible for peopling the country. Their procreative powers are also brought to bear on the growth of all natural species. They are, indeed, replenishers of the earth. Clearly associated with this theme, and more obvious in the Milingimbi versions, is the Sun, who is the mother of the two sisters. The two sisters' travels across the land replicate the movement of the Sun across the sky. Originally, it is said, the sisters accompanied their mother on her daily journey, but the heat generated by three suns was too much for natural species and human beings. Consequently, they returned to Bralgu, where they joined their brother and their companion to begin their travels. The spirit people at Bralgu sent out the Morning Star to guide them on their way, and the Sun came up for them, driving away the darkness and lighting up the land, sending its glowing rays in every direction and warming all it touched (Berndt, 1952, p. 304).

A central symbol throughout the cycle is the *ngainmara*, which represents the sisters' uteruses, as well as other cognate images. This mat, sometimes in connection with baskets, is usually referred to in conjunction with *rangga* poles. In that case, they represent female and male attributes. However, the children within the pregnant sisters, like the emblems within the *ngainmara*, are male *and* female children, and they are called *rangga*. In a ritual context, postulants enter the *nara* ground (entering the mothers) and on leaving it are reborn spiritually. In this respect the myth and its symbolism exemplify the essential complementarity of male and female and underline both the natural and the symbolic consequences of the sexual act, the importance of both its material and its spiritual dimensions. This has corresponding relevance for the whole of the natural world.

BIBLIOGRAPHY

Berndt, Ronald M. *Djanggawul: An Aboriginal Religious Cult of North-Eastern Arnhem Land.* Melbourne, 1952. A detailed study of the Djanggawul (Djanggau) religious system. It includes, in translation, 188 songs from the Yirrkalla (northeastern Arnhem Land) perspective.

Knight, Chris. "Lévi-Strauss and the Dragon: *Mythologiques* Reconsidered in the Light of an Australian Aboriginal Myth." *Man* 18 (March 1983): 21–50. An unsuccessful attempt to examine some Australian Aboriginal materials in relation to Claude Lévi-Strauss's work. Unfortunately, the choice of data is not carefully made, and consequently a number of Knight's interpretations are open to criticism.

Warner, William Lloyd. *A Black Civilization: A Study of an Australian Tribe* (1937). New York, 1958. This classic study of an Australian Aboriginal society in Arnhem Land contains the first account, with analysis, of the Djanggawul (Djanggau) myth and ritual.

RONALD M. BERNDT

DOCETISM. Derived from the Greek word *dokēsis* ("appearance"), the term *docetist* is used to refer to those who denied the reality of Christ's physical incarnation. The expression "docetist" first appears in Eusebius's *History of the Church* (6.12.6) in reference to those who circulated the *Gospel of Peter*, an apocryphal gospel written around the middle of the second century. There is no evidence for a single sect of "docetists." Clement of Alexandria attributes it to Julius Cassianus, who was thought by some to be the author of the Nag Hammadi tractate *Testimony of Truth*. Hippolytus refers to docetism as a many-sided heresy based on gnostic speculation about Christ. Tertullian rejects all accounts of the birth and incarnation of Jesus that made Jesus' humanity appear "unreal" (*Against Marcion* 4.21; *Flesh of Christ* 23). Insistence on the incarnation, that is, the Son becoming flesh, was directed against such speculation by the Council of Nicaea (325).

Docetic speculation found it difficult to unite the divine Son, or Logos, with a human being subject to suffering and death. The Johannine letters (*1 Jn.* 4:2, 5:6; *2 Jn.* 7) condemn those who will not confess that Jesus came in the flesh. These persons apparently did not advocate a theory of docetism, but they seem to have rejected the role of a suffering and dying Son of God in salvation. At the beginning of the second century, Ignatius of Antioch and Polycarp referred to those who denied the fleshly reality of the birth, life, and death of Jesus and who claimed that Christ's suffering was only apparent and not real.

The Nag Hammadi writings provide a variety of explanations of the Savior's incarnation and suffering. Some accept the incarnation but reject the suffering and death, believing that the heavenly (immortal) Christ left the body before the crucifixion. The *Gospel of Truth* states that Christ "stripped himself of the perishable rags and put on imperishability." Similar explanations are found in *Trimorphic Protennoia* and the *Apocalypse of Peter*. In the *First Apocalypse of James* the risen Lord says, "I am he who was within me." Such explanations of Jesus' crucifixion have yet to develop a systematic docetism that denies the reality of the incarnation.

Disputes over the nature of Jesus' incarnation divided Valentinian teachers. For some, the Savior was only spiritual, for others he was spiritual and psychic but not fleshly. Images of Christ as a polymorphous divine being were common in the second century. He was said to appear in different forms, according to a person's ability to perceive him. This motif is attached to the transfiguration and the resurrection. The conclusion drawn from such images in the *Second Apocalypse of James* was that the Savior's body was not like that of other humans. This discovery led James to believe that the Christ is the Holy Spirit and the Invisible One who did not take on flesh.

According to Irenaeus, some gnostics divided the Christ so that the Word never left the pleroma. Therefore, an image was crucified. Other gnostics spoke of Christ as possessing a "nonbodily body." For many gnostics, the inner, spiritual reality of the Savior represents the true, inner self of the gnostic.

The images and concerns that generated docetic speculation emerge from the level of popular piety. They were a consequence of identifying Jesus as the incarnation of a divine being. Not surprisingly, they appeared first in circles influenced by the Johannine vision of Christ as the divine Logos. The polymorphous Christ represents a widespread archetype of the divine. The opponents of these docetic developments saw a danger in losing the significance of Jesus' humanity and in denying the soteriological power of his death. The gnostic teachers had no single explanation of Christ. The christological debates of the third century clarified the issues. Against docetic tendencies rooted in an aversion to a suffering divinity and to the flesh, these debates insisted that the Savior had become flesh. Later Christians, such as Jerome (c. 347–420) and Theodoret (c. 393–c. 458), used "docetism" to refer to explicit denial of the whole humanity of Jesus. At the level of imagination, docetism is still a common way of picturing Jesus as a divine being.

BIBLIOGRAPHY

Excellent accounts of docetism occur in histories of Christian doctrine. See, for example, Aloys Grillmeier's *Christ in Christian Tradition*, vol. 1, *From the Apostolic Age to Chalcedon (451)* (New York, 1965), which continues to be a standard summary of the christological debates of the first five centuries. Jaroslav Pelikan's *The Christian Tradition*, vol. 1, *The Emergence of the Catholic Tradition, 100–600 A.D.* (Chicago, 1971), is a readable general account of the history of Christian doctrine in this period which makes illuminating use of original sources. See also *The Nag Hammadi Library* (San Francisco, 1977) for English-language translations of primary sources.

Pheme Perkins

DOCTRINE. Most dictionaries record two related senses of the term *doctrine:* according to the first, it is the affirmation of a truth; according to the second, it is a teaching. The two are not mutually exclusive: to affirm something as true is a way of teaching it, and that which is taught is usually held to be true.

The denotation of the term is thus reasonably clear. However, the connotations (i.e., the feelings and attitudes associated with it), differ according to where the emphasis is placed in a given instance. As the statement of a truth, doctrine has a philosophical cast; as a teaching, it suggests something more practical. The first connotation prevails among the secular sciences. The doctrine of evolution, for example, comprises a body of knowledge that is appropriately characterized as a theory, but not a teaching. Philosophical discourse reveals more variation: according to the context, "the doctrine of the equality of man" may be taken either as a precise axiom belonging to a political theory, or as a practical maxim designed to guide political action.

Religious doctrines tend to be characterized by their practical intent. Even when a doctrine appears in the shape of an abstruse theoretical disquisition, it is usually the case that any speculative interest is strictly subordinated to the spiritual, which is the dominant concern. For example, the orientation of Judaism is toward practical obedience to the law of God, not speculative knowledge of his being. [*See* Torah.] The doctrinal element in Judaism thus reveals an intimate connection with the notion of teaching. The most important figure is the rabbi ("teacher"); the most important word is *torah* ("instruction"), which refers to God's revelation in the Hebrew scriptures and, more specifically, to his law as presented in the five books of the Pentateuch. In a broader sense, *torah* encompasses the oral as well as the written law, together with the continuing tradition of rabbinical interpretations. The Talmud ("study") is an authoritative compilation of expositions of the law and applications of it to particular circumstances. It has been observed that the phrase "to read the Talmud," while grammatically correct, is a violation of the text's religious character, since the only appropriate response to the Talmud is to study it.

In Islam, the *sharī'ah*, or study of God's law, is of paramount importance. [*See* Kalām.] Here the doctrinal element is subordinated, of course, to judgments about moral and ritual behavior. The term *kalām*, however, indicates a kind of thought very close to that indicated by the English terms *doctrine* and *theology*. *Kalām* literally means "word" or "speech," and the Qur'ān is deemed *kalām Allāh*, the word of God. In the course of time, *kalām* has come to mean both a single truth and a system of truth (as is the case with the English term *doctrine*), and has played an important role in the history of the Islamic tradition.

Christianity uses the terms *doctrine* and *dogma* to designate the teachings through which salvation is offered to all those who hear and respond. [*See* Dogma.] An early example of such a doctrinal affirmation is Paul's claim that Christians have been "reconciled to God by the death of his Son" and that "much more, being reconciled, [they are] saved by his life" (*Rom.* 5:10).

The development of Christian doctrine is closely allied with the task of instructing catechumens who are being prepared to receive the sacrament or rite of baptism. As late as the third century, Augustine, in *De magistro* (Concerning the Teacher), reveals a major concern with doctrine in this sense. His specific tractate on Christian doctrine, *De doctrina christiana*, is not an exposition of the content of Christian doctrine but a discussion of the most effective way to teach it. Indeed, the immense Augustinian corpus contains no speculative overview of Christian knowledge; his most memorable works in the field of doctrine are devoted to specific themes that troubled the faith of Christians in his time: free will *(De libero arbitrio)*; divine providence *(City of God)*; the Trinity *(De Trinitate)*. Even the great disquisitions on doctrine by Thomas Aquinas (the *Summa theologiae* and *Summa contra gentiles*) are in the form of questions and answers that reveal an obvious affinity for the method of catechetical instruction. Luther's most important contribution to the area of doctrine is his *Longer Catechism* and *Short Catechism*; Calvin's *Institutes of the Christian Religion* is an expanded version of a small handbook he originally produced to assist Christians in understanding the teachings presented in Luther's catechisms.

The examples of such major Catholic and Protestant figures are evidence of the dominant focus of Christian doctrine on spiritual instruction. The teaching focus of doctrine has both a constructive and defensive thrust. It is, in part, an attempt to refute heresies within the church and false teachings without, as many historians of doctrine have pointed out. This polemical aspect offers a partial explanation for the greater emphasis on certain themes and the neglect of others at a particular time and place. Still, the refutation of error is not an end in itself, but a means through which to enhance the efficacy of the soteriological aspect of the teaching, which remains the paramount concern.

A Category of Comparative Religion. Doctrine is not restricted to Christianity. There are examples in each of the world's major religious traditions of affirmations that possess the same kind of authority and intent: in Judaism, the Shema' ("Hear!") with its admonition "Hear, O Israel! The Lord is our God, the Lord is one"; in Islam, the testimony of the Shahādah that "there is no god but God, and Muḥammad is his prophet." Examples of doctrine central to other religions include the doctrine of the permanent self, or *ātman*, in Hinduism; the doctrine of nonself, or *anātman* (Pali, *anatta*), in Buddhism; the Confucian doctrine of "humanity" or *jen;* the Taoist doctrine of the efficacy of nonaction, or *wuwei;* and the Shintō belief in *kami*, the presence of sacred power in things.

It is even more significant that each religion makes use of words that, though not exact synonyms for the terms *doctrine* or *teaching*, are very close to them in meaning: *torah* ("instruction") in Judaism and *kalām* ("doctrine, theology") in Islam; *darśana* ("school, viewpoint") in Hinduism; Dharma ("teaching") in Buddhism; *chiao* ("teaching") in Confucianism and Taoism; *Butsudō* ("way of the Buddha") in Japanese Buddhism; *kami no michi* ("way of the Japanese divinities") in Shintō. [*See also* Chiao.]

The prevalence of a doctrinal factor in all of the world's major religions suggests that it ought to be treated as a general category in the academic study of religion. This has, at times, not been recognized with sufficient clarity because of a romantic bias that exalts feeling over thought and deems "doctrine" an alien intrusion into a religious form of existence that is essentially nonrational in character.

However, the notion of a dichotomy between thought and feeling in the religious life is not tenable. Feelings, perceptions, and emotions require form and structure to become the content of human experience. By the same token, mysticism and rationalism reveal an intimate affinity, since most mystics become known to us through the discursive accounts of their ineffable experiences that they produce. Even the symbol systems of nonliterate societies have a doctrinal or rational aspect that gives religious shape to communal life.

Doctrine, then, is a category in the comparative study of religion that belongs with ritual, sacrament, mystical experience, and other factors whose importance has been recognized for some time. Like them, doctrine is designed to focus the mind, emotions, and will on the religious goal that the community has accepted as its ultimate concern.

Buddhism. Buddhism provides a striking example of the role played by doctrine in the realization of a religious goal. According to the Buddhist Dharma, or teaching, the existence of man is determined by limitless craving *(tṛṣṇā)* that produces anguish *(duḥkha)* and a fundamental distortion of one's thoughts and feelings about the world. The teaching offers release from the tyranny of those disordered perceptions and a path of deliverance from the endless cycle of birth and rebirth *(saṃsāra)* to which man's obsessive desires have bound him. The teaching consists of training in the control of thoughts and feelings, conscientious ethical behavior, and an intensive discipline of inner concentration and meditation. The doctrinal component supports the posture of mind and heart that is to be assumed throughout the various stages of the training. [*See* Dharma.]

However, in his present state of illusion, the seeker is never able to discern the true difference between the theoretical and the practical. He does not know what is a mere palliative and what truly heals. In this state he perceives Buddhist teachings as paradoxical: metaphysical reticence is advised in meditations that seem endlessly speculative; simplicity is advocated in arcane terms. These paradoxes are themselves symptoms of the ignorance of the seeker, who does not even know what constitutes the simplicity and healing that he seeks. The doctrine or teaching leads him along a path that, by both wakening and frustrating his speculative curiosity, brings about a transformation of thought and feeling that is the prerequisite for the authentic liberation that is his goal.

The doctrine of *nirvāṇa* (Pali, *nibbāna*) is a striking case in point. The term literally means "blowing out," as when a candle is extinguished. It is used to indicate the final end of man. But what is it? Four possibilities have been suggested: (1) it is absolute nonexistence; (2) it is a positive state of bliss and tranquillity; (3) it is a state that can only be indicated in terms of what it is not; and (4) it is something ineffable, incapable of being rendered in either positive or negative terms. Depending upon the Buddhist text or school that is consulted, each of these options receives some sort of support. On what basis is one to choose among them?

The scholar-observer who, as a speculative venture, examines the doctrine from without, will probably make a choice based on historical grounds (which option is closest to the original teachings of the historical Buddha?) or on systematic considerations (which is most consistent with Buddhist thought as a totality?). On the other hand, a Buddhist will judge them according to their efficacy as religious vehicles. From this perspective, it may appear that each option makes a contribution according to changes in circumstance as the Buddhist seeker proceeds along his religious path.

The notion of *nirvāṇa* as extinction is as austere and forbidding to the average member of a Buddhist society as it is to a nonbeliever. Still, it may be effective as a means to separate the seeker from some of the distorted perceptions of "existence" that are one cause of his anguish. In different circumstances, the prospect of an end that includes bliss and tranquillity may be more therapeutic; at other times, the way of negations, or an even more intricate path of "spiritual agnosticism," eschewing both negations and affirmations, may be efficacious. While man remains in a state of bondage to his anguish and illusions, a definitive description of his final end is of little value. The authority of the doctrine of *nirvāṇa* lies rather in the therapeutic role it plays in the attainment of a goal that will only be truly known in the process of its concrete realization. When this takes place, it will become apparent that the "goal" was in the seeker's possession all the time. The doctrine has led him on an arduous journey to a destination that, once reached, coincides with the place of departure that he never left.

Theology and Doctrinal Form. At the present time, doctrine is frequently associated with systematic theology. [*See* Theology.] For over a thousand years of church history, theology had diverse meanings, some of which were remote from those of Christian doctrine. Plato used the word *theology* to describe the stories about the gods told by poets; Aristotle used it to describe his doctrine of immutable substance. Augustine distinguished three senses: the theology of the poets, a civic theology based on public ceremonies, and a theology of nature. Sometimes the term was used in a narrow sense by Christian thinkers, who restricted it to the doctrine of God.

Muslim theologians such as al-Ghazālī (1058–1111 CE) participated in a golden age of theology devoted to the task of reconciling Greek philosophy with the faith of Islam. During the same period, Maimonides (Mosheh ben Maimon, 1135/8–1204) worked on the reconciliation of Greek thought with Judaism; Thomas Aquinas (1225–1274) undertook a similar task in respect to the Roman Catholic faith. Even more important is the fact that during the twelfth and thirteenth centuries revisions in medieval education were made that, among other things, introduced the notion of doctrinal theology as an academic discipline with a status similar to that of the secular subjects taught in the university curriculum.

Hugh of Saint-Victor (c. 1096–1141) developed an approach to theology that subsumed the two senses of the term *theory* (i.e., both intellectual endeavor and contemplation of God) under the complex notion of "speculation," which had previously been applied, for the most part, to religious meditation. Hugh characterized the method of theology as a kind of thought that is theoretical, both in the rational sense of submission to the norms of logic and in the contemplative sense of religious aspiration and vision. However, the delicate balance that he proposed is the prescription of an ideal and not what most works of systematic theology are, in fact, like. Theologians readily acknowledge that the norms of rational adequacy as a rule take precedence over a devotional focus. They deem it sufficient that theology provides rational support for the spiritual life without functioning as a direct expression of it.

The institutionalization of systematic and doctrinal theology in universities and seminaries has guaranteed for it a place of continuing importance in the history of the church from the time of the Renaissance to the present. However, it is evident that in the course of its long history the church has also made use of other forms (e.g., epistles, catechisms, creeds, tractates, and biblical commentaries) to express the concerns of doctrine. At the present time, there is some evidence that the essay is replacing the systematic tome as the preferred means for doctrinal discussions among both Catholic and Protestant thinkers. [*See* Creeds.]

The fourth book of Augustine's *Christian Doctrine* offers comments about doctrine that are still relevant to the contemporary scene. Augustine suggests that rhetoric is as important as logic in the communication of doctrine, though, like Plato in his attack on the Sophists, he is aware that the eloquence of rhetoric may deceive rather than enlighten. Augustine accepts, however, Aristotle's defense of the notion of a viable rhetoric that deals with the distinction between probative arguments and those based on a misuse of eloquence analogous to a formal logic that distinguishes between valid and invalid syllogisms. Augustine makes use of the rhetorical tradition derived from Aristotle to explore the capacity of Christian doctrine to teach, delight, and persuade. He recommends a subdued style for the task of careful instruction, a moderate style for condemnation and praise, and a grand style, forceful with the emotions and the spirit, for those moments when the need emerges to move the reader to action.

Contemporary experiments in the communication of doctrine through literature and other media are thus not unprecedented; they are, in fact, the continuation of a classical tradition of rhetoric toward which many thinkers, in both religious and secular disciplines, are at present showing a renewed respect.

[*See also* Truth.]

BIBLIOGRAPHY

The most up-to-date extended history of doctrine from a Protestant perspective is Jaroslav Pelikan's *The Christian Tradition: A History of the Development of Doctrine*, 4 vols. (Chicago, 1971–1984). A final volume is projected to cover the period since 1700. The work provides many revaluations of conventional historical judgments and includes an extensive bibliographical apparatus of primary and secondary sources. Nineteenth-century studies like Adolf von Harnack's *History of Dogma*, 7 vols. translated by Neil Buchanan (London, 1895–1900), and Reinhold Seeberg's *Text-Book of the History of Doctrines*, 2 vols. translated by Charles E. Hay (Grand Rapids, 1952), among others, remain indispensable in spite of inadequacies of interpretation corrected by later historians. Bernhard Lohse's *A Short History of Christian Doctrine: From the First Century to the Present*, translated by F. Ernest Stoeffer (Philadelphia, 1978) is a brief summary that is also a helpful essay of interpretation; George A. Lindbeck's *The Nature of Doctrine: Religion and Theology in a Postliberal Age* (Philadelphia, 1984) offers an approach to doctrine that makes use of the categories developed by philosophers of language. The *Dictionnaire de theologie catholique*, 15 vols, edited by Jean-Michel-Alfred Vacant et al. (Paris, 1903–1950), is important for an understanding of doctrine from a Catholic perspective. Also useful is the *Encyclopedia of Theology: The Concise Sacramen-*

tum Mundi, edited by Karl Rahner (New York, 1975). "Dogma," an essay by Rahner in this encyclopedia, together with his "Considerations on the Development of Dogma," in his *Theological Investigations,* translated by Kevin Smyth, vol. 4 (Baltimore, 1966), pp. 3–35, offer a sophisticated statement of the standard approach to Catholic doctrine and dogma. An informative account of the emergence of doctrinal theology as an academic discipline is G. R. Evans's *Old Arts and New Technology: The Beginnings of Theology as an Academic Discipline* (Oxford, 1980).

The following works offer useful discussions of rhetorical and literary genres other than systematic theology appropriate for contemporary statements of doctrine: Giles B. Gunn, *The Interpretation of Otherness: Literature, Religion, and the American Imagination* (Oxford, 1979); David Tracy, *The Analogical Imagination: Christian Theology and the Culture of Pluralism* (New York, 1981); Nathan A. Scott, Jr., ed., *The New Orpheus: Essays toward a Christian Poetic* (New York, 1964).

The following are useful studies of the role of doctrine in religions other than Christianity. For Judaism: Judah Goldin, ed. *The Living Talmud* (New York, 1957); Jacob Neusner, *The Way of Torah: An Introduction to Judaism* (Belmont, Calif., 1970); Leo Trepp, *Judaism: Development and Life* (Belmont, Calif., 1982). For Islam: Charles J. Adams, "The Islamic Religious Tradition," in *Religion and Man,* edited by W. Richard Comstock (New York, 1971), pp. 553–617; Fazlur Rahman, *Islam,* 2d ed. (Chicago, 1979). For the religions of India: Robert Baird, "Indian Religious Traditions," in *Religion and Man* (cited above), pp. 115–250; Ninian Smart, *Doctrine and Argument in Indian Philosophy* (London, 1964). For Buddhism: Edward Conze, *Buddhism: Its Essence and Development* (Oxford, 1951); Melford E. Spiro, *Buddhism and Society: A Great Tradition and Its Burmese Vicissitudes,* 2d ed., exp. (Berkeley, 1982). For the religions of China: Tu Wei-ming, *Humanity and Self-Cultivation: Essays in Confucian Thought* (Berkeley, 1978); C. K. Yang, *Religion in Chinese Society* (Berkeley, 1961). For the religions of Japan: Alfred Bloom, "Far Eastern Religious Traditions," in *Religion and Man* (cited above), pp. 254–396; H. Byron Earhart, *Japanese Religion: Unity and Diversity,* 3d rev. ed. (Belmont, Calif., 1982). For the religions of preliterate societies: W. Richard Comstock, *The Study of Religion and Primitive Religions* (New York, 1972); Mary Douglas, *Natural Symbols: Explorations in Cosmology* (New York, 1970); Clifford Geertz, "Religion as a Cultural System," in *Anthropological Approaches to the Study of Religion,* edited by Michael Banton (New York, 1966), pp. 1–46.

W. Richard Comstock

DŌGEN (1200–1253), more fully Dōgen Kigen; Zen master and founder of the Sōtō Zen school in Japan. Of noble birth, Dōgen entered the priesthood at the age of thirteen, following the deaths of his parents. He studied Buddhism, especially Tendai Buddhism, at Mount Hiei, one of the two main Buddhist centers in Japan at that time. In his studies, he faced a serious question concerning the basic Tendai Buddhist doctrine of *hongaku* ("original awakening")—the question of why practice is necessary if everyone is originally awakened to the Buddha nature, as Tendai Buddhism maintains. After studying Zen in Kyoto, Dōgen sailed in 1223 to China, where he finally attained awakening under the Zen master T'ien-t'ung Ju-ching (1164–1228). In 1227 he returned to Japan and began to propagate the *buddhadharma* he had realized in China and to promote *zazen* ("sitting meditation") as the right path to the *buddhadharma.* Until his death in 1253, Dōgen devoted himself in Kyoto and then in Echizen (modern Fukui Prefecture) to practicing *zazen,* training his disciples, and setting forth his thought in writing in order to introduce to Japan the "Right Dharma" that he considered on the basis of his awakening to be the essence of the Buddha's teaching.

Among the voluminous works by Dōgen, *Fukanzazengi* (The Universal Promotion of the Principles of *Zazen*) is the first, while the most important is *Shōbōgenzō* (The Treasury of the Right Dharma Eye), a collection of discourses and sermons currently compiled in ninety-five fascicles. Regarded as a monumental work of unique and profound religious thought, *Shōbōgenzō* occupies a central position in Japanese intellectual history. The ten-volume work *Eiheikōroku* (An Extensive Record of Eihei Dōgen's Dharma Talks), another collection of his discourses and sermons, is written in Chinese.

Dōgen's religious thought may be summarized in the following five points.

1. *Oneness of practice and attainment.* Attainment here indicates enlightenment, *satori,* or Zen awakening. This identity of practice and attainment is the solution to Dōgen's initial question, "Why is practice necessary if everyone is originally awakened to the Buddha nature?" Through his own awakening, which he called "casting off body and mind," Dōgen came to see that practice lies within attainment and attainment within practice. They are not two different matters, but one. He also stresses the importance of everyday activity for Buddhists.
2. *An emphasis on shikantaza, or zazen only.* In light of Dōgen's teaching of the oneness of practice and attainment, the practice of *zazen* in the authentic form is not considered as a means toward attainment. It in itself is attainment. And conversely, attainment is fully present in practice if one devotes oneself completely to practice.
3. *All beings are Buddha nature.* The *Nirvāṇa Sūtra,* one of the most important Mahāyāna Buddhist scriptures, states, "All sentient beings without exception have the Buddha nature." Rejecting this traditional

understanding of Buddha nature, which implies that the Buddha nature is a potentiality to be actualized sometime in the future through practice, Dōgen teaches that the Buddha nature is not a potentiality but an actuality that is fully realized in sitting meditation *(shikantaza)*. Further, this actuality of Buddha nature is applicable not only to sentient beings but to all beings, nonsentient as well as sentient. For the Buddha nature is understood by Dōgen not as an unchanging, substantial entity but as an ever changing, nonsubstantial reality that is realized inseparably from the transiency common to all beings. Hence "*all* beings *are* (rather than *have*) Buddha nature."

4. *Impermanence is Buddha nature.* In contrast to the traditional understanding of the Buddha nature as something beyond impermanence, Dōgen insists that impermanence, the undeniable reality common to all beings, is Buddha nature. He thus takes the Mahāyāna Buddhist notion that *saṃsāra* is *nirvāṇa* to its ultimate conclusion.
5. *Uji, or being-time.* For Dōgen being and time are completely inseparable. Being is time and time is being. Each particular thing, such as a pine tree or a mountain, and each particular person, such as Huang-po or Ma-tsu (Zen masters of T'ang China), is time. Furthermore, spring does not become summer. Spring is spring; summer is summer. Time does not fly away. Events are disconnected in the now. Yet as a continuous occurrence of "nows," time is a discontinuous continuity. This dynamic structure of being-time is realized in the true Self, which awakens to the impermanence–Buddha nature.

On the basis of these five ideas, Dōgen rejected the then prevailing notion that *mappō*, the decadent period of the latter Dharma during which enlightenment was impossible, had already arrived. Instead, he emphasized *shōbō*, the Right Dharma, which is realized here and now regardless of time and space. Dōgen also stressed the importance of the direct person-to-person transmission of the Buddha Dharma and advocated the priesthood as its bearer.

After Dōgen's death, Keizan Jōkin (1268–1325) propagated Dōgen's Zen to large numbers of people and developed the religious order. Today, that order, the Sōtō sect, is one of the largest Buddhist orders in Japan.

In the last few decades Dōgen's religious thought has attracted the interest of many thinkers in Japan and the West. In particular, the ontological bases of his thought as seen in the realization that "all beings are the Buddha nature" and his emphasis on "being-time" have attracted attention. Comparative studies of Dōgen and Western thinkers such as Martin Heidegger and Jean-Paul Sartre have elicited much discussion. One cannot overlook recent studies of Dōgen in relation to modern biology, psychology, and linguistic philosophy. With the recent growth of interest in *zazen* in the West, Dōgen's *shikantaza* has been gaining in influence in spiritual practices of Europe and America.

[*For further discussion of the role of Dōgen in the development of Zen Buddhism, and an elaboration of Dōgen's thought, see* Zen.]

BIBLIOGRAPHY

Works by Dōgen in Translation

Fukanzazengi. An English translation by Norman Waddell and Masao Abe appears in the *Eastern Buddhist,* n.s. 6 (October 1973): 115–128.

Shōbōgenzō. English translations of various fascicles are available in the following books: Yūhō Yokoi with Daizen Victoria, *Zen Master Dōgen: An Introduction with Selected Writings* (New York, 1976), and Francis D. Cook, *How to Raise an Ox: Zen Practice as Taught in Zen Master Dōgen's Shōbōgenzō* (Los Angeles, 1978). See also the translations by Norman Waddell with Masao Abe in the *Eastern Buddhist,* n.s. 4 (May 1971): 124–157, n.s. 5 (May 1972): 70–80, n.s. 5 (October 1972): 129–140, n.s. 8 (October 1975): 94–112, n.s. 9 (May 1976): 87–105, and n.s. 9 (October 1976): 71–87.

Works about Dōgen

Abe, Masao. "Dōgen on Buddha Nature." *Eastern Buddhist,* n.s. 4 (May 1971): 28–71. A comprehensive elucidation of Dōgen's view of the Buddha nature.

Kim, Hee-Jin. *Dōgen Kigen, Mystical Realist.* Tucson, 1975. The first systematic study of Dōgen in a Western language.

Kodera, T. James. *Dōgen's Formative Years in China.* Boulder, 1980. A careful historical study of Dōgen's early life. Includes an annotated translation of the *Hōkyō-ki,* a record of dialogues between Dōgen and his Chinese Zen teacher Ju-ching.

Viallet, François-Albert. *Zen, l'autre versant.* 2d ed., rev. & enl. Paris, 1971. Raised as a Roman Catholic, Viallet converted and became a Sōtō Zen priest. This book is a record of his Zen experience through a confrontation with his former faith.

MASAO ABE

DOGMA. [*This entry provides a technical discussion of the definition, function, and development of dogma in the Christian tradition, especially in Roman Catholicism. For wider discussion of religious beliefs, see* Theology *and* Creeds. *For a comparative discussion of the formulation of religious truths and teachings, see* Doctrine.]

Dogma, in the strictest sense, whether embodied in the sacred scripture of the Old and New Testaments or in tradition, is understood by the Roman Catholic church to be a truth revealed by God (directly and formally), which is presented by the church for belief, as revealed by God, either through a solemn decision of the extraordinary magisterium (pope or council) or through the ordinary and general magisterium of the church (episcopacy). It is to be accepted by the same faith that is due to the divine word itself *(fides divina)* or to the church's tradition *(fides catholica)*.

This magisterial definition, as it was given by the First Vatican Council, has the following historical antecedents: (1) the ancient philosophical (Platonic-Stoic) use of the word *dogma* to designate that which seems right to all, as opinion or teaching, as foundation or decision, as decree or edict, as a rational judgment that is identical to a moral decision, or as a decree of a legitimate authority; (2) the New Testament use, in which Old Testament law is said to be the dogma of God and the decisions of the apostolic council are designated as dogmas in *Acts* 16:4; and (3) the patristic and medieval transmission of both these strains, the dogma of God in distinction to the teachings of human beings or of the philosophers. The close connection between the "dogmas of the Lord" and the "fidelity to the church" is already asserted in the *regula fidei,* the canon of truth. Finally, synodal decrees are also considered dogmas in opposition to the dogmas of the heretics. The content referred to by *dogma* also occurs in the patristic and scholastic tradition under equivalent designations, for instance, *professio* and *confessio,* or (Catholic) truth in general; *fides,* the correct doctrine handed down by the church; and, in Thomas Aquinas, over against the concept of dogma, the narrowed concept of *articulus fidei.* What led to an emphasis on the formal authority of dogma was, finally, the emphasis on the claim to the limitless autonomy of human reason in the eighteenth and nineteenth centuries.

The definition of the concept and function of dogma in the Eastern Orthodox churches, in spite of the multiplicity and differing historical development of these churches, can begin with their formal unity in terms of doctrine, law, and liturgy. Faith is based upon the dogmas that have been transmitted in part through scripture and in part through the oral *paradosis* ("handing down" of tradition) of the apostles and have then been interpreted by the councils and church fathers. Because and to the extent that the church speaks with the authority of the Holy Spirit, it is infallible in the same way as scripture. The believing acceptance of the revealed truth of faith is necessary for salvation. The dogma of the church is present and closed in the doctrinal decisions of the first seven ecumenical councils (325–787), whose formulations are considered the embodiment of dogma and the summary of the teachings of scripture. The further dogmatic development of the Latin church is rejected. Dogma in the Orthodox churches has not so much a doctrinaire-intellectual function as it does a doxological and life-defining one.

The relationship to dogma of the churches and communities produced by the Reformation is defined by the theology of the reformers, which, on the one hand, does not dispute that the church may have to make obligatory statements and that the truth of scripture may only be able to be revealed through a painstaking process. It therefore accepts at least the trinitarian-christological dogma of the old church as an appropriate expression of the matter of the gospel. But, on the other hand, through the principle of *sola scriptura* (over against an association of scripture and tradition), the theology of the reformers takes up a different position, scripture being for them no longer merely the source and norm of all Christian speech, teaching, and preaching, but, rather, the single final authority. All confessions and dogmas are to be measured against it. In this sense, dogmatic statements (even the trinitarian-christological) are only secondarily binding for Protestant theology, and then only when it has been demonstrated whether and to what extent dogmas open up an access to direct biblical instruction, where it is presupposed that scripture, on the basis of its transparency, is its own interpreter. In spite of all confessional-theological discussions among the churches and communities growing out of the Reformation, and in spite of the changing theological positions and the change in the functional definition of dogma connected with them (from orthodoxy through rationalism and Pietism and from the purely ethical and practical interpretation to dialectical and existential theology), they agree both negatively and positively. Negatively, they agree in their rejection of the Roman Catholic understanding of dogma and its function for faith and church as "doctrinal law." Positively, they agree in the conviction that God's word must not only be existentially recognized but also known as objective truth and reproduced in statements and doctrinal teachings, however these may then be interpreted and qualified with regard to their binding character.

In the question of the development of dogma, Roman Catholic theology must proceed from the fact that the church defines statements as revealed by God if they satisfy one of the following conditions. (1) Even if previously stated, they were not always expressly defined or bindingly taught as revealed. (2) They articulate the express contents of statements of the earlier tradition in very different or newly developed conceptual terms (by defending the always known meaning of the revealed statement more expressly against heretical misinterpretations, by setting off more clearly individual aspects of these statements, or by placing these aspects in a dialectical interplay of faith and reason or in a more explicit relationship to other truths of faith and of reason). (3) They refer to statements in the tradition that may not be immediately equivalent to them or explicitly capable of being traced back to the apostles or that cannot even be supposed with historical probability to have been once previously available. Thus not only theology but also revelation (to the extent that it is only present in proclamation, acceptance of faith, and practice) has a history, a "development," and a "progress" after Christ, even if this history is essentially different from the development of revelation before Christ.

The problem of the development of dogma and its solution consists in the task of demonstrating the fundamental possibility and the actuality, in individual cases, of the identity of the later, "developed" matter of faith with the apostolic matter given in Christ. The difficulty of the problem lies in the fact that, according to church doctrine, the entire "public" revelation, entrusted to the church and its teaching office and involving an obligation of belief, was closed with the death of the apostles, that is, that the church can only continue to bear witness to what it has heard about Christ in the apostolic generation and has recognized as belonging to the deposit of faith. Therefore an additional, later, ecclesial revelation is not possible, does not expand the old Christian revelation, and cannot undergo an epigenetic transformation in the sense that might be implied by modernism. Because the solution to the problem (formally speaking and in general) must be sought in the fact that a new dogma is contained "implicitly" in an old dogma or in the whole of what was previously believed, the problem and its solution may be formulated in the following way.

1. What is the status of implicitness and what is the process of explication such that these can be recognized as factually given in the development of dogma? That is, how can the identity of faith, as expressed in an actual history of faith, and revelation after Christ be explained?
2. What implications are sufficient so that the explicated can be considered as revealed by God (and not simply taught by the church with infallible authority)? Such an implication is obviously to be applied, however, in such a way that it can be said not only that the new dogma, as derivative in its truth and certainty upon the original revelation, could thus legitimately appeal to the witness of God (purely objective implication) but also that it, of itself (even if in a different form), has always been witnessed to by God's self and has always been believed by the church (subjective implication).

The problem, precisely posed, has only been clearly present since the nineteenth century, that is, since there has existed a history of dogma that not only (as still in the post-Tridentine period) doxographically collects the proofs from an earlier time for the doctrine of the present and thereby considers these proofs to be only different from the contemporary doctrine in their external form but also sees that the recognition of revelational truth has a real history after Christ.

The problem is stated differently in Protestant theology, because there is in evangelical theology no faith statement of the church that could be an absolutely binding norm for the private understanding of scripture, and thus there can actually be, from the start, only a history of theology, not really a history of dogma and faith after scripture. Behind this problem is, as its natural presupposition, the problem of the historicity of the (ever the same) recognition of truth in general and that of reconciling a present continuing immediacy of the divine revelation in the church (which is necessarily historically new) with the relegation of the present proclamation back to an earlier historical past, that is to say, back to the apostolic period.

The first three centuries of Christianity and perhaps the following one and a half centuries, which saw the development and culmination of the first three, present a history of Christian belief and dogma in a confrontational struggle with the simultaneous assimilation of a non-Christian spiritual and cultural (Hellenistic-Roman) environment. However, the second long period after the waning of antiquity, that is, from the early Middle Ages to the Enlightenment, was a time of unfolding and differentiation of the substance of faith from within its own center outward into even more systematized distinctions that, because of their one point of departure from within, could be considered without really major confrontation with external contradictions and as a more or less homogeneous abstraction presupposed by all to be self-evident. (This was so in spite of the continuing influence of Platonism and the medieval reception of Aristotelianism, and in spite of the crises that occurred with the split between the Eastern and Western churches and with the Reformation of the sixteenth century.) This was, therefore, a time for summae and simultaneously and for the same reasons a time (because the whole was taken for granted) when one threw oneself into theological questions with enormous passion and almost became lost in them. It was a time the effects of which are reflected in the great catechisms of the modern period. It was a time in which one could take for granted long papal encyclicals over relatively small questions of detail of the Christian faith; in which the magisterium reacted carefully and quickly to real or imagined attacks against individual doctrines of this detailed system; and in which one had the impression that the entire system was clear and could hardly be further developed, except in the case of individual questions, so that the major work of theology had to be turned backward upon its own history.

Today (after a long preparation since the Enlightenment, from which time also dates the defensive dialogue with liberalism and modernism) we have doubtless entered upon a new, third phase in the history of faith and thus also in the history of dogma and of theology. Today it is no longer a question of an ever more detailed unfolding of the basic substance of faith within a homogeneous environment that has a common horizon of understanding with the church. It is much more a question of winning a new understanding (naturally preserving the substance of faith which has been handed down) of the one totality of faith in a non-Christian environment, in a new epoch of a global world civilization in which world cultures that were never Christian have appeared. It is also a question of a history of faith and dogma in a new diaspora, with confrontation and assimilation to be simultaneously carried out in a radically new way that includes even the most divergent belief, that of atheism and the doubt as to whether religion in general will survive. To that extent, there is a formal similarity between the period of the history of dogma now beginning and the first period, even if the matter and the tasks of the first and the third periods are radically different.

The history of faith and dogma will probably develop in the future not in the style of the second period, as an evolutionary unfolding and systematizing differentiation of the basic substance of faith, but rather as the transposition of this lasting faith into new and pluralistic horizons of understanding. Because of the incommensurable and not synthesizable pluralism of contemporary and future horizons of understanding, transpositions of faith will have to occur by means of a plurality of theologies that, despite the necessary readiness for dialogue of these theologies among themselves, will not be able to be synthesized adequately for the preservation and rediscovery of the one faith.

The task of the magisterium in this incipient period will, therefore, hardly consist any more in the definition of "new" individual dogmas, no longer so much in the anxious monitoring of supposed or real deviations from individual traditional doctrines, but rather in the preservation of the one entirety of the faith in its basic substance and, in fact, not so much through a "censuring," but rather through the positive, constructive, collaborative work on this new interpretation of the old faith that is demanded today in a new and not necessarily Christian environment.

The history of faith and dogma will continue, but it will have a different character, not so much the history of individual, newly articulated statements of faith and of the theology that reflects upon them, but rather the history of the restatement of the old basic substance of faith in the confrontation with and assimilation of the future horizon of understanding. It is self-evident that this history will be then no longer merely the history of the formulation of early Christian and Western dogmas and their theology (including their export to other countries) but rather the history of the faith and dogma of a universal church, however little we can concretely imagine today what is materially and formally meant by that. This naturally does not exclude but rather includes the fact that the changing new conception of the one entirety of the Christian substance of faith will also have consequences for the interpretation of many or all individual doctrines.

BIBLIOGRAPHY

A summary introduction to the history of the concept of dogma and the history of the problem of the development of dogma from a Catholic point of view can be found in Georg Söll's "Dogma und Dogmenentwicklung," in *Handbuch der Dogmengeschichte,* vol. 1, fasc. 5 (Freiburg, 1971), which includes an extensive bibliography. From the Protestant perspective the following articles in *Theologische Realenzyklopädie,* vol. 9 (Berlin and New York, 1982), pp. 26–125, should be consulted: "Dogma" by Ulrich Wickert and Carl H. Ratschow, "Dogmatik" by Gerhard Sauter, Anders Jeffner, Alasdair Heron, and Frederick Herzog, and "Dogmengeschichtsschreibung" by Wolf-Dieter Hauschild. See also Karlmann Beyschlag's *Grundriss der Dogmengeschichte,* vol. 1 (Darmstadt, 1982), pp. 1–54.

The relationship between kerygma and dogma (also in conversation with Protestant positions) is analyzed in Karl Rahner and Karl Lehmann's *Kerygma and Dogma* (New York, 1969), Walter Kasper's *Dogma unter dem Wort Gottes* (Mainz, 1965), and Karl Rahner and Joseph Ratzinger's *Offenbarung und Überlieferung* (Freiburg, 1965).

The problem of the development of dogma from a theological-systematic perspective is treated by Karl Rahner and Karl Lehmann in *Das Problem der Vermittlung,* "Mysterium Salutis," vol. 1 (Einsiedeln, 1965), pp. 727–787; by Karl Rahner in "The Development of Dogma," in *Theological Investigations,* vol. 1 (New York, 1961), pp. 39–77; by Karl Rahner in "Considerations on the Development of Dogma," in *Theological Investigations,* vol. 4 (New York, 1966), pp. 3–35; by Joseph Ratzinger in *Das Problem der Dogmengeschichte in der Sicht der katholischen Theologie* (Cologne, 1966); and from an evangelical point of view by Gerhard Ebeling in *Die Geschichtlichkeit der Kirche und ihrer Verkündigung als theologisches Problem* (Tübingen, 1954). An instructive analysis of the more recent Catholic models of the development of dogma can be found in Herbert Hammans's *Die neueren katholischen Erklärungen der Dogmenentwicklung* (Essen, 1965). For the modernist theological-critical approach, the broadly based source study by Émile Poulat, *Histoire, dogme et critique dans la crise moderniste*, 2d ed., rev. (Paris, 1979), should be consulted. It is written, however, from a somewhat sociological perspective.

With regard to the theory and the history of the development of dogma (as well as of the historiography of dogma), the prolegomena of the classic handbooks and manuals of dogmatic history are to be consulted: for example, those by Harnack, Seeberg, Ritschl, Köhler, Schwane, Tixeront, et al. In addition, see, for Catholic theology, *Handbuch der Dogmengeschichte*, edited by Michael Schmaus et al. (Freiburg, 1971–), which is arranged according to treatises; for the Protestant perspective, see Alfred Adam's *Lehrbuch der Dogmengeschichte*, 2 vols. (Gütersloh, 1965–1968), and *Handbuch der Dogmen- und Theologiegeschichte*, 3 vols., edited by Carl Andresen (Göttingen, 1980–1984). Recent positions can also be found in Avery Dulles's *The Survival of Dogma* (New York, 1971) and Gerald O'Collins's *The Case against Dogma* (New York, 1975).

KARL RAHNER and ADOLF DARLAP
Translated from German by Charlotte Prather

DOGON RELIGION. The Dogon inhabit the cliffs of Bandiagara, an area located in the southwestern region of the bend of the Niger River in Mali. This area consists of a vast, rocky plateau that ends in its southern part in a 200-kilometer-long cliff overlooking a vast plain. Numbering approximately 225,000, the Dogon are cultivators of millet and other cereals and breeders of small livestock; owing to the scarcity of permanent water sources on the plateau and on the cliffs, they have had to exploit all resources available to them. Onion and pepper gardens and plantations of large trees (ficus, baobab) surround the villages whose clay houses picturesquely conform to the jagged contours of the rock.

The Dogon are well known in ethnographical literature. Since 1931 they have been the subject of numerous publications by the French ethnologist Marcel Griaule (1898–1956) and by other researchers schooled in his methods. The Dogon are perhaps best known for their art, whose consummate form is sculpture in wood (masks, statuettes, locks).

The traditional religion of the Dogon is complex and involves, among other things, a rich myth of origin, belief in a unique god, and an intricate cult of the ancestors. Christianity has had little impact on their culture, but Islam, during the late twentieth century, has made significant inroads, without, however, destroying the vitality of long-standing religious beliefs and practices.

The Creation Myth. The Dogon myth of origin provides both an explanation of the world and a justification of Dogon social organization. The creation of the world was the deed of the god Amma, the one god and image of the father who existed before all things. [*See* Amma.] He traced the plan of the universe using 266 signs (a number corresponding to the gestation period for human beings). The design (the preliminary act of creation) corresponds to thought, which "conceives" before action or speech. Following an unsuccessful initial attempt, from which he salvaged only the four elements (water, earth, fire, and air), Amma placed in the "egg of the world," or the original placenta, two pairs of androgynous twins in the form of fish (to Sudanese peoples the catfish *Clarias senegalensis* represents the human fetus). Their gestation inside the egg was interrupted by an act of rebellion: one of the male beings prematurely left the "mother" (the placenta), deserting both "her" and his female counterpart, thus prefiguring the birth of single beings even though Amma had envisaged twin births. The solitary being descended into space and primordial darkness, taking with him a piece of the placenta that became Earth. Aware of his solitude, he traveled through space, attempted to reascend to heaven to join his female twin again, and even sought her out in the bowels of Earth, an incestuous act that brought to a climax the disorder he had already introduced into the world by leaving the placenta. The piece of placenta rotted and thus death appeared on earth.

Amma put an end to the male being's disorderly acts by transforming him into a fox, an animal that occupies a very important position in Dogon ideology. This small, wild creature, which is known more properly as *Vulpes pallida*, goes about only at night and never drinks water from ponds near the village—which, for the Dogon, explains why the fox was chosen to symbolize this enemy of light, water, fertility, and civilization.

The mythical fox Yurugu (also known as Ogo) was condemned to an eternal search for his lost twin. Moreover, he lost the ability to speak when Amma, from whom he had stolen speech, punished him by cutting off his tongue (indeed, actual foxes emit only a brief, almost clipped cry); but he still retained the power to foretell the future by "speaking" with his paws.

Unable to restore total order to his universe, Amma sought to mitigate the disorder let loose by the fox; he sacrificed Nommo, the other male twin who had stayed in the egg. Nommo's dismembered body purified the four cardinal points of the universe, and the blood that flowed forth gave birth to various heavenly bodies, edible plants, and animals.

Amma then burst the *Digitaria exilis*, a minuscule

grain into which he had "rolled" all the elements of creation; these elements emptied into an ark of pure earth (the remains of the placenta). In that ark Amma also placed Nommo, whom he had already resuscitated, and his other "sons," the four pairs of heterosexual twins who are the ancestors of the human race. He lowered the ark from the heavens by means of a copper chain; the ark crashed onto Yurugu's earth at the time of the first rainfall, which formed the first pool of water. The sun also rose for the first time. Nommo went to live in the pool while the eight ancestors settled on the spot where they had landed. Using the pure earth from their ark, these ancestors created the first cultivated field, and cultivation then spread throughout Yurugu's impure earth (the bush).

The ancestors initially communicated by means of cries and grunts until one of the Nommo twins, the master of water, life, speech, and fertility, taught them language at the same time that he instructed them in the art of weaving. He then revealed to the ancestors such other fundamental techniques as agriculture, blacksmithing, dance, and music. The first human society was thus founded; marriage was introduced when the ancestors exchanged sisters.

The descent of the ark is analogous to birth. The ancestors of humanity who began their life on earth can be seen as newborns emerging from the maternal womb; the ark is the placenta, and its chain is the umbilical cord; the rains are the fetal waters.

Cults and Social Organization. The four male ancestors founded the four major religious cults, which are also the pillars of social organization; among the Dogon, social order cannot be dissociated from religion. The eldest of the ancestors, Amma Seru ("witness of Amma"), is associated with the creator god and with air (sky). The patriarch of the extended family is Amma Seru's representative in the human community. His residence, known as the "big house," is the focal point of the paternal lineage, and this is where the altar to the ancestors is situated. The altar is composed of pottery bowls (deposited there whenever a family member dies) into which the patriarch pours libations in honor of the ancestors.

Paternal lineages combine to form a totemic clan; all members of a particular clan must respect the same taboo, be it animal or vegetable. The clan is headed by a priest whose vocation is revealed through trances that incite him to seek an object hidden by dignitaries of the clan at the death of the priest he will succeed. He remains subject to these trances, which force him to wander through the countryside prophesying; he is said to be possessed by Nommo. As the representative of the ancestor Binu Seru ("witness of the *binu*"), the priest is responsible for the cult of the *binu,* the ancestors associated with the various animal and vegetable species. According to the custodians of profound knowledge, the *binu* are also symbols of the different parts of Nommo's dismembered body; the ensemble of these *binu* represents the body resuscitated in its entirety. The cult itself is associated with water, and its ritual is celebrated in sanctuaries whose façades are periodically redecorated with paintings done in thin millet paste; each transformation favors a specific event—the coming of the rains, the harvesting of various crops.

The cult of Lébé is dedicated to the ancestor Lébé Seru ("witness of Lébé") who, having died, was subsequently brought back to life in the form of a large snake; this ancestor is associated with Earth (the planet and soil, as well as the mythic archetype Earth), and with vegetation that periodically dies and comes back to life. His priest is the *hogon,* the most senior of the region, whose authority once had political impact, since it was he who administered justice and controlled the marketplaces. The *hogon* and the totemic priest together celebrate the feast of sowing *(bulu)* before the coming of the rains; they distribute to the villagers the millet seeds that have been stored in the preceding year. These seeds are thought to contain the spiritual essence of this cereal. The mythical snake Lébé is said to visit the *hogon* every night to lick his body and thus revitalize him.

The fourth ancestor, Dyongu Seru ("witness of healing"), has a different status. He was in effect the first human to die, following the breach of an interdiction. His cult is celebrated by the mask society (which exists only on the cliff and on the plateau). It is an exclusively male association, which all boys enter after their circumcision; each one must carve his own mask and must learn the society's secret language. The dance of the masks takes place as part of funeral ceremonies for men. Objects of death, the masks are strictly forbidden to women, who are associated with fertility and the forces of life. Women can only observe the dances from far away.

The death and resurrection of Dyongu Seru are commemorated through the Sigi, a spectacular ceremony that takes place every sixty years; the last one was held between 1967 and 1974. This feast also marks, on the human plane, the renewing of the generations (sixty years is thought to be the average human lifespan) and, on the celestial plane, the revolution of the "star of *Digitaria exilis*" around the "star of Sigi," or Sirius. The Dogon's longstanding knowledge of this Sirius satellite, which was only recently discovered by astronomers, is a mystery that science has not yet uncovered. The ceremony, celebrated from village to village over a period of eight years, includes dances executed by men in single file (each generation is ranked according to age-group). Their costumes and paraphernalia refer to both maleness and femaleness: for example, the cowrie shells that decorate the dancers' costumes and the fish-head design of their embroidered bonnets are symbols of fertility; when they drink the ritual beer, they sit on a ceremonial seat, which is a masculine symbol. Another important component of the Sigi ceremony is the erection of the "great mask," a single tree trunk or log carved in the shape of a snake to represent the resurrected ancestor.

Dyongu Seru is associated with fire, death, the wilderness (in his role as hunter and healer), and, consequently, disorder—connections that, in turn, link his cult with the mythical fox Yurugu who, on a more mundane level, is commemorated in divination rites. Diviners trace framed grids in the sand, and during the night small foxes come to eat the food offerings placed on these "tables"; the configuration of spoors left by the animals are then interpreted as responses to questions about the future. Yurugu, however much decried for being the source of disorder, is respected for his ability to foretell the future, a gift that even Amma could not take away from him. In effect, by liberating himself from all rules through his act of rebellion, Yurugu placed himself beyond time. Ultimately he incarnates individual liberty, in opposition to the group solidarity essential for the survival of traditional societies, and therein lies his ambiguity.

The Dogon religious universe is also peopled by various categories of spirits who haunt the wilderness, the trees, and inhabited sites; these spirits are the outcome of Yurugu's incestuous coupling with Earth. They represent natural forces and the original proprietors of the soil, with whom men had to ally themselves in order to gain possession of cultivable land. Offerings presented to these spirits on different occasions propitiate them and renew the original alliance.

Speech and Being. A human being is viewed as a whole composed of a body and the eight spiritual principles of both sexes. A vital life force *(nyama)* animates the entire being. The ambivalence of the human condition (that is, its simultaneous maleness and femaleness), which recalls the law of twin births ordained by Amma but later destroyed by Yurugu, is mediated by circumcision and clitoridectomy; these procedures free the child from the influence of the opposite sex (located in the prepuce and the clitoris) and thus have an equilibrating function. Death destroys the tie that holds together the various components of a person's being; funeral ceremonies assure that each component is restored to its place and facilitate the transference of the vital force from the deceased to an unborn child, who will establish a cult for that ancestor.

Speech is fundamental in Dogon thought. It forms itself in the body, all of whose organs contribute to its "birth," and like human beings, it possesses vital energy and spiritual principles. The four basic elements enter into its composition, but water is the most essential component. In symbolic rapport with all technological processes, especially the art of weaving (the organs of the mouth are said to "weave" sounds), speech is both creative (on the divine plane) and fertilizing (on the human plane); in fact, intercourse between spouses is successful only if "good words" make the woman fertile. Speech is also the cement that holds together all social relationships and facilitates the advance of society, its progress and survival.

If ancestor worship and the belief in Amma dominate the religious beliefs of the Dogon, the mythical figures who command their worldview are Nommo and Yurugu: the two incarnate opposed and complementary principles (order/disorder, life/death, humidity/dryness, fertility/sterility) that wrangle over possession of the universe. That struggle, which is constantly rekindled, assures both the equilibrium and progress of the world.

BIBLIOGRAPHY

The most complete and most detailed version of the Dogon origin myth is given in Marcel Griaule and Germaine Dieterlen's *Le renard pâle* (Paris, 1965), an English translation of which is forthcoming. The first published version of the myth can be found in *Dieu d'eau: Entretiens avec Ogotemmêli* (Paris, 1948), Griaule's very popular book translated into English by Robert Redfield as *Conversations with Ogotemmêli* (London, 1965). Griaule's *Masques dogon* (Paris, 1938) still remains the definitive reference work on the mask society and on funerary ceremonies, as does that by Michel Leiris, *La langue secrète des Dogons de Sanga* (Paris, 1948), on the society's secret language. For information on perceptions of the person in Dogon society, one can consult Dieterlen's *Les âmes des Dogons* (Paris, 1941), even though our understanding of this question has been considerably enriched since that book's publication. Speech and its utilization at different levels of social life is analyzed in my own study *Ethnologie et langage: La parole chez les Dogon* (Paris, 1965), which has been translated into English by Dierdre La Pin as *Words and the Dogon World* (Philadelphia, 1986).

GENEVIÈVE CALAME-GRIAULE
Translated from French by Brunhilde Biebuyck

DOGS. The role played in the beliefs of various peoples by what is probably the oldest of domestic animals is generally an ambivalent one. As the companion of hunters and herders, the dog became a symbol of fidelity and vigilance. As a predator and scavenger, however, it has been seen as greedy, dangerous, and impure. For this reason, the Roman *flamen dialis* (priest of Jupiter) was not allowed to touch a dog, and Jews and Muslims have traditionally regarded the dog as an unclean animal. Although many peoples—the Inca of the Andes and the Dahomeans of West Africa, for instance—have prohibited the eating of dog's flesh, other peoples—Polynesians and some American Indian tribes (e.g., the Tsimshian of western Canada)—have regarded this practice as a cultic act.

The ambivalent symbolism of the dog is apparent in the Islamic tradition. On the one hand, black dogs are regarded as symbols of the devil or the carnal soul, and it is said that "angels do not enter a house where there is a dog." On the other hand, the dog of the Seven Sleepers, called *qitmīr,* is regarded as sanctified by constant faithful contact with the saints, like the human soul that can be purified by keeping company with saintly people.

In myth, the dog has been connected with both the sun and the moon. The idea of a dog on the moon, sometimes together with a man, is found, for instance, among the Central Inuit (Eskimo) of the Arctic and in Bengal, India. At the time of the Spanish Conquest, the Muisca of the highlands of central Colombia had the notion of a dog that was "daughter of the moon." On the other hand, the dog is the animal that accompanies Lugh, the ancient Irish deity who is considered to have been a sun god. Among the Aztec the dog-god Xolotl guides the sun safely through the lower world. The "dog days" associated with the ascension of Sirius—in the constellation Canis Major (the Great Dog)—are also connected with the sun. The dog may serve as protector against evil spirits (as in ancient Iran), but it may also itself be demonic in nature. In an ancient Mesopotamian text the female demon Lamashtu is petitioned to muzzle her hound. Many European sagas, some of them brought to the United States by settlers, tell of bewitched souls, sorcerers, and even the Devil appearing as dogs. The demonic *rākṣasas* of Indian mythology manifest themselves in this form.

The various functions assigned to the dog link it with a variety of divinities. A cuneiform inscription gives the names of four dogs belonging to Marduk, the supreme Babylonian deity. The dog served the Vedic god Indra as watchdog, and dogs accompanied the Greek goddess Artemis on the hunt and the Chinese Erh-lang in his struggle against demons; in Dahomey the dog is regarded as a sacred animal, and is the messenger of the demigod Legba, the trickster. Among the Norse, the wolves Geri and Freki were called "hounds of Óðinn." In Rome the *lares,* gods that protected the home, had a dog for companion or were represented as clad in dogskins. The dog was frequently connected with creation; among the Kato Indians (California), it was the companion of the creator; according to a tradition among the Songe (of the Kongo), a dog brought the first human pair to earth in a calabash. The Pima (Arizona) placed the moon and the dog at the beginning of the world. The origin of vegetation is linked to the sacrifice of a bull by Mithra, who is assisted by a dog. According to a Greek myth, it was a female dog that gave birth to the first vine.

The dog becomes in some societies a culture hero: in Maya manuscripts it brings maize to mankind; in tales of southern China human beings are indebted to the dog for rice; and in extensive areas of Africa, it imparts knowledge of edible plants. A female dog teaches the Bambuti Pygmies how to hunt. To peoples in Indonesia and New Guinea, in Africa (the Kuba), and among some North American Indians (Achomawi, Shoshoni), the dog or coyote is the mythical firebringer. Also widespread is the belief in the dog as ancestor of man. In Indonesia, Indochina, and South China (among the Yao), there is a tradition that the marriage of a princess and a dog produced a people or a dynasty. Among the Mongolians a yellow dog, representing the moon, was regarded as the first ancestor of Temujin. From the coasts of the southwestern Pacific to as far as North America there are myths in which the ancestress of a tribe married a dog. The Aleut believe they are descended from a dog that fell from heaven.

Sacrifices of dogs have been offered for a wide variety of purposes. In antiquity, the sacrifices were connected with the idea of purification: thus, Macedonian warriors were led between the two parts of a dog that had been cut in half in order that they might gain ritual purity. Among the Romans a dog was frequently sacrificed to mark entrance into a special office. African peoples too are familiar with the sacrifice of a dog in expiation—in connection with adultery (Yoruba), incest (Fang), or responsibility for the death of a human being (Senufo). But the sacrifice of a dog may also be offered to a divinity to spare the life of a human being (as in northern Togo) or to ward off some disaster. At the ancient Roman festival of Robigalia the dog was slain as a symbolic carrier of grain blight. The dogs sacrificed in the New Year festival of the Iroquois were considered messengers of the gods.

In Europe there is evidence as far back as the age of the megaliths of the custom of placing a dog in a dead man's grave. A parallel is the account of Patroclus's burial (*Iliad* 23.174). Among the Aztec and Maya, dogs were ceremonially slain and buried with the dead in order to accompany them on their journey across the river into the next world. Among the Chamba (northern

Nigeria) a black dog is sacrificed to conduct the dead chief to his ancestors. The belief that a dog leads the souls of the dead to the mountain resting places of their ancestors is found in Inner Asia among the Tunguz and Manchu. The Chinese formerly provided their dead with paper dogs as protectors. Remnants of the belief in the dog as a guide of the dead are also to be seen where the dog appears as companion to a war god such as the Mongolian Dayichin Tengri and the Tibetan Beg-tse; further, a dog is often portrayed on the helmet of Ares, the Greek god of war. Charon, the Greek ferryman of the underworld, is occasionally depicted as a dog, and in the Hellenistic period a dog is companion to Hermes in his role as *psuchopompos* (conductor of souls to the netherworld). Among the Parsis, it is customary even today for a dog to be brought into the presence of a person who has just died; this Zoroastrian custom is called *sag-did*, or "dog-view."

The dog is not only a guide into the world of the dead but also the guardian of that world. It was a widespread custom among the Greeks to put a honey cake in the grave: the dead person was to throw this to Kerberos, hound of the underworld, and thus pass by him unharmed into Hades. In India, two kidneys were put into a dead person's hands as a means of avoiding harm from the dogs of Yama, god of the dead. Indonesian literature tells of Asu Gamplong, the hound of Hell. According to the tradition of the Rama (Nicaragua), Tausun Tara, the dog of the underworld, eats evil souls but allows the good to pass by. Some Indian tribes of North America (Ojibwa, Iroquois) are familiar with the dog that guards the realm of the dead or the bridge into the next world. In a widespread Indo-European tradition, the soul may assume the shape of a dog before being permitted to enter the next world; the souls of criminals and suicides, in particular, wander about restlessly. In ancient Greece these souls were identified with the dogs who accompanied Hekate, the goddess of sorcery, while among the Germans, as dogs and wolves, they formed part of the retinue of Wodan, who in midwinter roamed the countryside as a savage hunter.

Gods and demons of death often take the form of members of the dog family. Anubis, the Egyptian god of the dead, is usually depicted with the head of a dog or jackal; in the form of a reclining black animal, it guards the mummy against evil powers. The Maya god Hunhau rules the underworld and is associated with a dog. In Hinduism, Śiva, the great destroyer, is "lord of the dogs"; his wife, the bloodthirsty Durgā, is called "the wolf-faced one" in the older literature. In Etruscan tomb paintings, Aita, demon of the underworld, wears a wolfskin cap. According to the *Kalevala*, the Finnish national epic, Ilmarinen, the smith with magical powers, must chain the wolf in the world of the dead before he wins the maiden. Among the Mansi and Khanty (Siberia), the demon of death is a dog, and on the Kamchatka Peninsula there is a saying: "One is most certain of entering paradise if one has been eaten by fine dogs." Just as corpse-eating dogs (part of the mortuary customs of the Tibetans and Parsis) become an image of death, so animals that lick wounds become an image of healing and life. The dog is one form taken by Gula, the Babylonian goddess of healing, and it is connected also with Asklepios, the Greek god of healing. Anubis, the Egyptian god of the dead, lends his assistance at the ritual opening of the mouth in order that the dead person's senses may once again be conduits of life. Among the Celts, the dog is not only connected with death but also plays a role in cults of healing and fertility. Finally, in the Hellenistic mysteries of Isis, the goddess's dog was supposed to show the way to eternal life.

BIBLIOGRAPHY

In older literature, special mention must be made of Maurice Bloomfield's *Cerberus, the Dog of Hades: The History of an Idea* (Chicago, 1905). Important basic material for evaluating the importance of the dog in the worship and popular customs of Asia, America, Europe, and Africa is provided in Freda Kretschmar's *Hundestammvater und Kerberos*, 2 vols. (1938; New York, 1968). The place of the dog in the intellectual life of Africa south of the Sahara is investigated in Barbara Frank's *Die Rolle des Hundes in den afrikanischen Kulturen unter besonderer Berücksichtigung seiner religiösen Bedeutung* (Wiesbaden, 1965). For specific studies of Indo-European cultures, see Frank Jenkins's article "The Role of the Dog in the Romano-Gaulish Religion," *Latomus* 16 (1957): 60–76, and Bernfried Schlerath's "Der Hund bei den Indogermanen," *Paideuma* 6 (1954–1958): 25–40. For the dog as demon, compare Barbara Allen Woods's treatment in *The Devil in Dog Form: A Partial Type-Index of Devil Legends* (Berkeley, 1959). The manifold connections between the dog and death are the subject of my article "Der Hund als Symboltier für den Übergang vom Diesseits in das Jenseits," *Zeitschrift für Religions- und Geistesgeschichte* 35 (1983): 132–144. The best comprehensive study of the dog in mythology and popular traditions, together with extensive bibliographies, is provided by Maria Leach in *God Had a Dog: Folklore of the Dog* (New Brunswick, N.J., 1961). Mary Oldfield Howey's *The Cults of the Dog* (Rochford, England, 1972) also provides many examples from a wide variety of cultures and religions.

Manfred Lurker

Translated from German by Matthew J. O'Connell

DOLGAN RELIGION. The Dolgans are a small, Turkic-speaking nationality living on the Taimyr Peninsula in northern Siberia. Their primary occupations are hunting and fishing; they also breed a small number of domesticated reindeer, which are utilized as means of transport during nomadic migration. During the winter season the Dolgans live in the forest-tundra zone, and toward summer they migrate northward into the tundra in pursuit of wild reindeer herds. In 1979, there were five thousand Dolgans, 90 percent of whom spoke their native tongue, which is derived from the Yakut language. The Dolgans appeared as a distinct nationality during the last three hundred years and are largely descended from the Tunguz and the Yakuts; their religion had its origin in the culture area of their formation. [*See map accompanying* Southern Siberian Religions.]

The Dolgans are converts to Christianity, and they bear Russian names. Their calendar—a six-sided small stick carved from mammoth bone—is known as the *paskaal* (from Russian *paskhal'nyi,* "relating to Easter"); the basic Russian Orthodox holidays are marked on the sides of the *paskaal.* The old men who can calculate time by this calendar are called *paskaalcit* and are deemed to be sages. Icons are found in each Dolgan dwelling, but the Russian Orthodox saints represented on them are no more revered than are the other spirits of the Dolgan pantheon.

In their mobile dwellings *(urasa),* special sanctity is attached to the four foundation poles *(suona)* in which the spirits who protect the people living in the *urasa* dwell. After a successful hunt, these poles are smeared with the blood of a wild reindeer and purified by the smoke of burning fat. When a dwelling's owner dies, the weeping of the *suona* is heard. The cover of the *urasa* is sewn out of reindeer chamois, on which are drawn the sun, moon, reindeer, or *urasa,* according to a shaman's instructions. The *urasa* functions as a barrier impenetrable to evil spirits. In building a permanent dwelling, the Dolgans leave two tall trees by the side of the entrance, so that the souls of the dwellers may live in their branches. The trees are termed *serge* ("post") in Yakut.

The Dolgans call all supernatural beings *saĭtaan,* a word of Arabic origin brought to the Dolgans by the Russians, who borrowed it from Turkic-speaking Muslims. In practice, small stones and anthropomorphic and zoomorphic images carved from wood or reindeer antler, as well as certain household objects, figure as *saĭtaans.*

All these objects are revered because they are bearers of spirits, either independently or by means of the shaman. A *saĭtaan* may be a personal helper of its owner or the protector of an entire family or nomadic group; it may, for example, be the hook used to hang the caldron in the *urasa.* Facing the hook, the Dolgans smear it with the blood or fat of a slaughtered animal and address it, saying, "May the caldron hung on thee be full lifelong!" One type of *saĭtaan,* with human form, is called the *baĭanaĭ.* The idea of the *baĭanaĭ* and the term itself are borrowed from the Yakuts, among whom Baĭ-baĭanaĭ is master of the forest. But among the Dolgans a *baĭanaĭ* becomes the personal helper of the hunter who made its image. However, the *baĭanaĭ* acquires power only after the shaman animates the figurine by placing his breath within it. Before going on a hunt, the hunter smears his *baĭanaĭ* with the fat of a wild reindeer and tosses it into the air in order to divine his chances of catching game. If the figurine falls on its back, there will be success; if it falls on its belly, there will be failure. Wooden images of birds and animals, called *singken,* also belong to the category of *saĭtaans* that assist hunters. Hunters carry them along on the hunt, together with the *baĭanaĭ.*

At the beginning of each winter month, the hunter purifies his *baĭanaĭ* with the smoke of burning fat. Upon killing a wild reindeer, he cuts the fat from the animal's knee and suspends it from the figurine. After a particularly successful hunt, the Dolgans feed not only the *baĭanaĭ* but all their *saĭtaans.* They hang them on poles over the hearth, into which they throw small pieces of fatty food. Then they arrange a low table near the hearth and place on it pieces of the heart and lungs of slain animals. Afterward, the *saĭtaans* are smeared with blood and placed in a box, where they remain.

During nomadic treks, white or piebald reindeer carry the boxes containing *saĭtaans* and icons in cases. Such a reindeer is decorated with a beaded, embroidered headband and a bell is hung on its neck. This reindeer is always placed just before the end of the animal train; the reindeer transporting the dwelling poles is tied to it. When they arrive at a new place, the Dolgans avoid setting up their *urasa* where another stood earlier, since strange *saĭtaans* might prove powerful and feel wrathful toward the newcomers.

The activities of the Dolgans are accompanied by many religious rites. After killing a reindeer, the hunter smears his rifle with its blood. The bones of a reindeer that has been eaten are buried in the ground, and a tripod of poles is placed above them so that other reindeer will not go near that place. Upon killing an arctic fox, the hunter cuts off its nose so as not to give away his luck with its skin. The Dolgans rarely hunt bears, which they fear and which they regard as women transformed into beasts. The hunter who has killed a bear lies on its back imitating sexual intercourse. Then the participants in the hunt take out the bear's heart, eat it, and caw like ravens. While fishing, the Dolgans present to the Master of the River or Lake beads or scraps of red wool tied to nets. Near the body of water they hang a fox skin from a rope attached to the ends of two sticks thrust into the ground. Some Dolgans throw small, flat pieces of dough into the water; impressions of crosses worn on the body are made on these.

Shamans play such a large role among the Dolgans that the emergence of each new shaman is met by his kinsmen with great joy. According to Dolgan tradition, a shaman owns one to three Tuuruu trees, the term designating the "world tree" among the Tunguz, and he sets the souls of the persons under his protection on their branches. Signs of a shaman's power are the number, height, and extent of branching of his trees. A weak shaman's tree will be sickly, and the people in his charge may die. On the second day after death, the shaman must accompany the dead person's soul into the netherworld.

Among the Dolgans, as among the Yakuts, shamans are called *oĭun*; a female shaman is called *udaghan*, as among the Yakuts, Buriats, and Mongols. The Dolgans divide shamans into several categories according to their ability. The strongest shamans, *ulakan oĭun*, can cure diseases, divine events, and generally know all that happens on earth. In the past, the frequent wars between groups of Dolgans were decided by shamanic duels, with each shaman trying to increase the *ilbis* or power of the war spirit of his group. He sheltered the *kut*, or soul, of his leader on a cloud and killed the soul of the opposing leader. The shamanic séance, which in some cases continued for several days and nights, is called *kyyryy* by the Dolgans, from the Yakut word *kyyr*, "to hop."

In the spring, when the first grass appeared, the shaman performed the annual shamanic ritual Djilga Kyyryy, by which he would divine what awaited his nomadic group. This ritual, the greatest religious festival of the year, is also called D'yly Oduuluur. To conduct this rite a new *urasa* was made, and seven or nine images of birds with heads turned toward the sun were fastened on top of the poles making up the *urasa*'s frame. The shaman departed on these birds to meet the chief of the upper world in order to secure his support for the forthcoming year. During this festival, the Dolgans and their shaman performed the ritual dance Kisi Kaamy Gynan ("people's step-by-step procession"). They circled the hearth three times clockwise, then exited from the tent and continued the same movement around it. This festival probably came to the Dolgans from their neighbors the Nganasani, who called it Any'o Dialy ("big day") and conducted it on the summer solstice. However, the dance is Yakut in origin.

[*See also* Yakut Religion *and* Shamanism, *article on* Siberian and Inner Asian Shamanism.]

BIBLIOGRAPHY

Dolgikh, B. O. "Proiskhozhdenie dolgan." *Sibirskii etnograficheskii sbornik* (1963), fasc. 5, pp. 92–141.

Popov, A. A. "Materialy po rodovomu stroiu dolgan." *Sovetskaia etnografiia* (1934), fasc. 6, pp. 116–139.

Popov, A. A. "Okhota i rybolovstvo u dolgan." In *Sbornik statei "Pamiati B. G. Bogoraza,"* pp. 146–206. Moscow, 1937.

Popov, A. A. "Kochevaia zhizn' i tipy zhilishch u dolgan." *Sibirskii etnograficheskii sbornik* (1952), fasc. 1, pp. 143–172.

Popov, A. A. "Perezhitki doreligioznykh vozzrenii dolganov na prirody." *Sovetskaia etnografiia* (1958), fasc. 2, pp. 77–99.

Popov, A. A. "The Dolgan Sajtāns." In *Shamanism in Siberia*, edited by Vilmos Diószegi and Mihály Hoppál, pp. 449–456. Budapest, 1979.

Popov, A. A. "Shamanstvo u dolgan." In *Problemy istorii obshchestvennogo soznaniia aborigenov Sibiri*, pp. 258–264. Moscow, 1981.

Boris Chichlo
Translated from Russian by Demitri B. Shimkim

DÖLLINGER, JOHANN (1799–1890), more fully Johann Joseph Ignaz von Döllinger; Roman Catholic professor of dogmatics and church history at the University of Munich (1826–1872), who became the controversial center of scholarly liberal Catholicism in Europe. Son of a pious Catholic mother and an educated, anticlerical father, he was ordained at age twenty-three and served briefly as a curate before finishing his doctoral dissertation and being appointed to Munich. There he was somewhat novel among Roman Catholics, though not unprecedented, in his emphasis upon the scholarly study of church history.

The key principle in Döllinger's thought, "organic growth," or "consistent development," gave not only approval but also limits to changes in the Catholic church. Early in his career, defending established developments in Catholicism, he denounced mixed marriages, affirmed the authority of the pope (1836), and favored the policy that Protestant soldiers be required to kneel at the consecration when they were present at a Catholic mass (1843). Likewise, in his works on Luther (1851) and the Reformation (1846–1848), he denounced the break in historical continuity effected by the Protestant schism. Later in his career, however, he came to oppose as "inconsistent with tradition" new prerogatives of the papacy, such as the opposition to modern scholarship and the assertion of infallibility. In 1863, Döllinger organized, without ecclesiastical permission, a meeting of one hundred Catholic theologians in Munich, to evaluate the scientific study of history. In his opening address he denounced scholasticism and called boldly for a thorough use of critical tools in examining church history, independent of Roman authority. Although hailed by liberal Catholics throughout Europe, such principles were soon condemned by Pope Pius IX, in his 1864 *Syllabus of Errors* and in his encyclical *Quanta cura.* Such disagreements intensified as rumors grew that unrestricted papal infallibility was to be affirmed at the First Vatican Council (1869–1870). For his opposition to infallibility, Döllinger was excommunicated, with both haste and publicity, in March 1871, by Archbishop Scherr of Munich. Some have seen the excommunication as gratuitous. Döllinger's opposition resulted partially from conciliar secrecy, which kept him from learning until too late the restrictions placed on infallibility. Because of the enforced ignorance, some of his arguments (1869–1871) sound more rhetorical than relevant.

Döllinger provided a rallying cry for the development in Germany of the "Old Catholic" church (which denied papal infallibility). He admitted he belonged to this church "by conviction," but he never formally joined. His refusal of an offer to become the first German Old Catholic bishop hampered that church's growth. Even after excommunication, he continued to attend Roman Catholic services, even though he was denied the sacraments by his excommunication. Despite political ability sufficient to hold national office under Ludwig I of Bavaria, neither his scholarship nor his statecraft was adequate to reconcile Catholicism with modernity. As important to Germany as Cardinal Newman was to England, Döllinger influenced Lord Acton and widened the ambit of historical consciousness in the Roman Catholic church. He has not yet found his definitive place in that church's history. Extolled in a book by his close friend the Old Catholic priest Johannes Friedrich (*Ignaz von Döllinger,* 3 vols., 1899–1901), he also was castigated by the Jesuit Émile Michael (*Ignaz von Döllinger,* 1892), whose criticism was so severe that Döllinger was repudiated even by the usually nonjudgmental modernist Friedrich von Hügel. The definitive Döllinger biography has not yet been written.

BIBLIOGRAPHY

For an interesting survey of Döllinger's development, from apologist for Rome to staunchly pre–Vatican I Roman Catholic, see Peter Neuner's *Döllinger als Theologe der Ökumene* (Paderborn, 1979). Showing similarities and differences between Newman and Döllinger, though with surprisingly superficial analysis of some materials, is Wolfgang Klausnitzer's *Päpstliche Unfehlbarkeit bei Newman und Döllinger* (Innsbruck, 1980). Lacking in details, but with an evenhanded treatment of the Vatican I infallibility controversy, is Walter Brandmüller's *Ignaz v. Döllinger am Vorabend des I. Vatikanums* (Saint Ottilien, 1977). Important correspondence is included in the work edited by Victor Conzemius, *Ignaz von Döllinger: Briefwechsel 1820–90,* 3 vols. (Munich, 1963–1971). An unsurpassed bibliography of Döllinger's writings, including translations, is in Stephan Lösch's *Döllinger und Frankreich* (Munich, 1955).

RONALD BURKE

DOMESTIC OBSERVANCES. [*This entry focuses on forms and practices of religious life in the home. It consists of six articles:*

Jewish Practices
Christian Practices
Muslim Practices
Hindu Practices
Chinese Practices
Japanese Practices

Where applicable, these articles give particular attention to women's religious responsibilities, which often govern religious life in the home in ways not common in other dimensions of religious life.]

Jewish Practices

Besides the synagogue, the home has traditionally been a main focus of religiosity both for the Jewish family as a unit and especially for women. Women were traditionally excluded from the duty of Torah study, which for men was, and to some extent remains, a major focus of spirituality. Moreover, women were not obligated to observe many of the religious practices that bound men. In particular, their place in public synagogue ritual was minimal. Consequently, domestic rituals, and especially those governed by women, are important focuses of their spirituality. For all Jews, certain ritual customs *(minhagim)* and rabbinic laws *(halakhot)* actually require a domestic setting. These rituals may be divided into those that are held on specific occasions of the Jewish calendar and those that are a constant presence in daily life.

Periodic Domestic Observances. The annual festival cycle begins in the spring with Passover, which focuses on two major domestic activities: the thorough cleaning of the home to remove leavened food, and then the Seder, the Passover eve feast, which has traditionally been led by the father and requires the participation of the children. Shavu'ot, in early summer, is accompanied by only minor domestic customs, such as decorating the home with greenery and partaking of dairy foods. The period of mourning for the destroyed Temple, which follows in midsummer, affects the home in a fashion opposite to that of the festivals: enjoyment of music, food, new clothing, and vacations, and joyfulness in general, are restricted. The fall holy days start with Ro'sh ha-Shanah and Yom Kippur, which are primarily synagogue-centered occasions but which include secondary domestic activities. On Ro'sh ha-Shanah, foods symbolizing good fortune are served at the family meal, and on Yom Kippur, family elders bless the young. During the week-long Sukkot festival the domestic focus is again pronounced. Temporary booths or huts *(sukkot)* are erected near or adjacent to each family home. Meals are eaten there, and some males follow the rabbinic tradition of sleeping in the booths at night. People entertain guests and generally pass time in the family *sukkah.* Ḥanukkah, in early winter, is focused domestically as well. Lights are ritually kindled in the home, and special holiday foods are prepared. Ḥanukkah also has indoor child-centered activities (gift-giving and living-room games). In late winter, Purim requires a formal feast at home, and women and children become particularly involved in the traditional sending of gifts of food to friends.

Perennial Domestic Observances. Besides seasonal events, the Jewish home also has perennial ritual activities, primarily on the Sabbath, when the routine of the home is transformed. Domestic rituals are observed on the Sabbath: candles are lit by the housewife on Sabbath eve; the *Qiddush* ("sanctification of the day") is chanted at the first of the three mandatory festive meals; families sing Sabbath songs *(zemirot)* and sometimes study Torah together. Of these customs, candle-lighting is a major rite for women, a virtual symbol of female religious identity. In recent times, with the attenuation of many more-burdensome Jewish customs, candle-lighting has remained vital and thus has become more prominent. According to some traditions, parents formally bless their children on Sabbath eve, and Sabbath night is a preferred time for conjugal relations. In the home the Sabbath ends with the ceremony of *havdalah* ("separation" of the Sabbath from the week), which involves the use of wine, spices, and a special braided candle, and at which a new fire is lit. Another perennial domestic ritual element is the display of religious artifacts. Foremost of these is the mandatory *mezuzah* inscription of biblical verses, encased on all doorposts. Brass or silver candelabra, wine goblets, and collections of Judaica books are common in the more prosperous homes. It is a custom to leave a section of wall in the home (about one square foot) unpainted, as a symbol of pain over the destruction of ancient Jerusalem *(zekher le-ḥurban).*

The celebration of rites of passage spills over into the home through the holding of festive meals. Domestically, the most marked rites of passage are mourning rites, which restrict the bereaved to their homes and require them to receive condolence visits. Memorial candles for the dead are lit at home. In the past, marriages in Mediterranean countries were patrilocal and some marriage observances paralleled mourning rites. The bridal couple were restricted to their new home for seven days of festivity, and daily rites were held in the presence of visitors. In our time, owing to the attenuation of patrilocality, the practice among many young Orthodox bridal couples, both in Israel and elsewhere, is to travel distances to visit their kin, and to be hosted in different homes where rites are held for the duration of seven days.

In Orthodox and traditionally observant families, the home is the scene of innumerable daily acts of individual piety: the ritual washing of hands upon arising, before meals and after voiding; the uttering of grace after meals, and of shorter benedictions before and after the partaking of any food. Prayers are recited upon waking and upon retiring at night, and three daily prayer services (*shaḥarit,* in the morning, *minḥah,* in the afternoon, *ma'ariv,* in the evening) are required of all adult males. In recent times, because of the weaker hold of the community, weekday prayers are frequently said at home rather than at the synagogue; hence, the role of the home in daily prayer has increased.

The most pervasive home observances are those that concern food and conjugal relations. Observance of the rules of *kashrut* (maintaining a ritually pure, kosher kitchen), is dependent upon the foods introduced into the home, and on the separation of various categories of foods in the kitchen and dining area. *Kashrut* also requires the services of extra-domestic agents, such as a *shoḥet* (ritual slaughterer), and of manufacturers of kosher foods. The maintenance of "family purity" *(ṭaharat ha-mishpaḥah)* depends to a greater extent on the privacy of domestic practice. "Family purity" consists of the maintenance of a monthly schedule of conjugal separation and reunion based on the menstrual cycle, and on the woman's periodic immersion in a *miqveh* (ritual bath). While the availability of an external agent, the *miqveh,* is required here as well, the element of domestic autonomy in this area of intimacy is nonetheless very strong. The autonomy of the home in this area was curtailed in traditional times (in Northern Europe roughly until the mid-nineteenth century, in Mediterranean lands until close to the mid-twentieth century). Decisions concerning the proper timing of immersion were not handled exclusively by the woman then, but rather in conjunction with a circle of elder females, family and neighbors. If there was any physiological irregularity, male rabbis were consulted. In contemporary Orthodoxy, middle-class sensitivities concerning the privacy of sexual matters have eliminated the role of the outside female circle; rabbis are consulted only in the most unusual cases. But it is in the maintenance of *kashrut* that the role of the home has increased most in contemporary times, and has assumed a novel symbolic weight. The affective term "kosher home" is now commonly used in reference to *kashrut* observance, which has gained much greater prominence in relation to its historical place in Jewish practice and thought. Over time, additional domestic practices have become more prominent (contemporary domestic Sabbath practices are innovations of the late sixteenth century). Most recently in the West, the pressure of Christmastime commercialism has encouraged Jewish families to elaborate the observance of Ḥanukkah, especially with parties, gift giving, and the decoration of the home, as an ethnic counterpoint to Christian symbols such as the tree and Santa Claus.

There are two major exceptions to this development (i.e., the increasing emphasis on Jewish domestic ritual). One is the virtual disappearance of the *ḥallah*-separation rite. Married women baking their bread used to separate and burn a small portion of the dough, as a symbol of the tithe that was due the priests in Temple times. *Ḥallah*-separation used to be a major female responsibility, similar to Sabbath candle-lighting and to the maintenance of family purity *(niddah)*. But as bread production has shifted from a domestic to a commercial setting, the rite has become uncommon. Another exception is in practices of the Hasidic movement, which encourages male groups to congregate by themselves, or at the court of the *rebbe,* the sect leader. In these congregations, adult males eat the third of the three required meals together, away from their families, on the Sabbath afternoon. Hasidism also encourages men to spend some of the holy days and Sabbaths at the distant court of the *rebe,* again separating them from their families.

[*See also* Kashrut *and entries on individual Jewish holy days and festivals.*]

BIBLIOGRAPHY

For a masterly, though brief, overview of the position of formal *halakhah,* see Aaron Lichtenstein's "Ha-mishpaḥah be-halakhah" in *Mishpeḥot Yisra'el: Divrei ha-kinus ha-shemonah-'asar le-maḥshavah Yehudit* (Jerusalem, 1976), pp. 13–30. On Ashkenazic Jewry, Jacob Katz's *Tradition and Crisis: Jewish Society at the End of the Middle Ages* (New York, 1961) provides a fine sociological overview; much pertinent information is scattered in the chapters on the family, religion, and Hasidism. In a shorter monograph, *Tsibbur ve-yiḥidim be-Maroqo: Sidrei ḥevra ba-kehillot ha-Yehudiyot ba-me'ot ha-18–19* (Tel Aviv, 1983), I describe eighteenth- and nineteenth-century Moroccan Jewry and thereby provide documentation for a section of Sefardic Jewry; some of this material appears in English in "Women in the Jewish Family in Pre-Colonial Morocco," *Anthropological Quarterly* 56 (July 1983): 134–144. A comprehensive ethnographic survey of religious and other home feasts in a village of Moroccan immigrants in Israel is given in Moshe Shokeid's "Conviviality versus Strife: Peacemaking at Parties among Atlas Mountains Immigrants in Israel," in *Freedom and Constraint: A Memorial Tribute to Max Gluckman,* edited by Myron J. Aronoff (Assen, Netherlands, 1976). One such feast is described in detail in my *Immigrant Voters in Israel: Parties and Congregations in a Local Election Campaign* (Manchester, 1970), pp. 140–147. The qabbalistic sources for some of the comparatively recent domestic Sabbath customs are cited in Gershom Scholem's *On the Kabbalah and Its Symbolism,* translated by Ralph Manheim (New York, 1965), pp. 142–146. In an overview of United States suburban Jewry, *Jewish Identity on the Suburban Frontier* (Chicago, 1979), Marshall Sklare and Joseph Greenblum analyze the novel weight of Ḥanukkah child-centered activities.

SHLOMO DESHEN

Christian Practices

Contemporary forms and practices of Christian religious life in the home vary widely among the various denominations and branches of Christianity, as well as among ethnic and socioeconomic groups within those broader divisions. The usual division of Western Christians into Roman Catholic and Protestant is, for the purpose of the present discussion, more suitably replaced by a distinction between those denominations, such as Roman Catholic, Episcopalian, and Lutheran, with strong liturgical traditions, and those, such as Baptists and Pentecostals, that have a less fully developed ritual heritage.

Western Christians often adorn their homes with religious images such as crucifixes and holy pictures, and Eastern Christian homes traditionally contain an icon corner where images of Christ and the saints are honored and where family prayers are said. A lighted candle or oil lamp usually burns before these icons. In the homes of families of the Eastern churches and the Western churches with more developed liturgies, palm or other branches blessed in church on Palm Sunday may be placed behind these images.

Traditional Roman Catholics sometimes provide small fonts for holy water at the doors of bedrooms, and during the month of May a Marian shrine may be set up in a corner of the home. The blessing of a new home, usually conducted by a priest, is practiced by some liturgically oriented Christian families of both East and West, with Eastern Christians observing an annual renewal of the house blessing during the period following the Feast of Theophany (Epiphany) on 6 January.

Some form of grace, said daily at the main meal or at each meal, is common among Christians, at least on special occasions. Also common among most denominations is the practice of an adult or older member of the family hearing a child's bedtime prayers.

Christian families observe the Lord's Day (Sunday) in various ways. A festive meal is often part of the day, which may be honored as a day of rest. Among some families of the nonliturgical traditions, family gatherings for prayer, often held early in the morning and consisting of Bible readings, hymn singing, and prayers by a leader, are customary.

Devout Christian families often say prayers for sick family members. These prayer services can include the laying on of hands and anointing with oil by a priest (in the liturgical traditions) or by a lay person (in the nonliturgical traditions). These rites of anointing are usually reserved for the seriously ill and dying in more conservative religious families. In the Eastern tradition, a priest, or, among Western Christians, a lay person or priest sometimes brings the Eucharist from the church to the sick person; in the less liturgically oriented churches the Lord's Supper may be celebrated by an ordained person in the sickroom.

Families of different denominations observe anniversaries of the deaths of family members and friends in various ways. Not uncommon among Eastern Christians, especially those of Slavic extraction, is the custom of burning a lighted candle before a picture of the deceased person during the day of the anniversary. A festive dinner, with gifts for the honored person, is commonly given on the saints' name days of family members, and various national groups enjoy festive meals featuring traditional ethnic foods on the feast days of their important saints.

The cycle of feasts and seasons of the Christian calendar provides many occasions for religious observances in the home, especially among Christians with strong liturgical traditions. During the pre-Lenten Carnival season, doughnut making and pancake suppers are common, such customs originating from earlier times when lard and other meat products had to be consumed before the beginning of Lent. While Lenten fasting and abstinence have become merely token or even nonexistent among many Western Christians, Eastern Christians commonly abstain from meat, butter, eggs, milk, and other animal products throughout this period, as well as during other penitential times. Some families in the nonliturgical churches are returning to the ancient practice of fasting twice weekly, usually on Tuesday and Friday. In the West during Lent, families often give money saved by having simple meals to charitable organizations. Also, soft pretzels continue to be served in some homes, a practice that originated in the Middle Ages when the shape of the pretzel was thought to resemble the crossed arms of a person at prayer. Hot cross buns, another customary food of medieval origin, are served in some Christian homes on the Fridays of Lent and during the last days of Holy Week.

Eastern Christian families continue their tradition of creating intricately decorated Easter eggs to be included in a basket of foods (with sausage, butter, cakes, and other foods proscribed during Lent), which is taken to the church and blessed at the all-night Easter service and eaten at a holy breakfast following that service on Easter morning. A similar breakfast has become popular among some Western Christian families in recent years following the restoration of the Easter Vigil service to its original time in the middle of the night. Two unique Eastern Christian family customs practiced during this season should be noted: (1) the bringing home of a lighted flame from the matins service of Holy Saturday (held on Holy Friday evening) and the marking of the form of a cross on the underside of every door lintel with smoke from this flame; and (2) the blessing of and picnicking at the graves of departed relatives and friends on the Sunday following Easter Day.

Many Western Christian families observe a similar memorial custom, but in the autumn season rather than at Easter. Picknicking at the graves of the departed on 2 November (All Souls Day) is common especially among Hispanic Christians; visits to cemeteries on that day, or the following Sunday, are also made by members of various denominations.

Eastern Christians continue the ancient practice of preparing fruit on the Feast of the Transfiguration of Christ (6 August) and flowers on the Feast of the Dormition of Mary (15 August) to be taken to the church for a special blessing. Some Western Christians have renewed a similar practice of bringing freshly baked bread to the church to be blessed at Lammastide (the first two weeks of August).

The Advent season encompasses immensely rich and varied family observances. The custom of the Advent wreath enjoys widespread popularity in the West. On the Advent wreath, constructed from a circle of evergreens surmounted by four candles (usually three purple and one rose colored), Christians light one additional candle each week during the four weeks of Advent. In some families the wreath is lighted before the evening meal to the accompaniment of brief prayers and often the singing of the Advent carol *O Come, O Come, Emmanuel.* Among Western Christians three traditional feasts during Advent are regaining the popularity they had in earlier centuries: Saint Barbara's Day (4 December), when a dormant branch of flowering cherry, known as the Barbara branch, is brought indoors and blooms on or near Christmas Day; the Feast of Saint Nicholas (6 December), which is often celebrated with small gifts placed in the children's shoes left outside bedroom doors on the eve of the feast; and the Feast of Santa Lucia (13 December, usually the date of the earliest sunset of the year), which is observed with customs dating from pre-Christian times and features saffron-yellow yeast buns, known as Lucia cakes, baked in the form of a spiral sun.

Among Hispanic people the last nine days of Advent are known as Posadas ("lodgings"). Children, portraying Mary and Joseph seeking shelter on their way to Bethlehem, go from door to door and are turned away repeatedly. Finally, the last home welcomes them, which then becomes the site of a joyful service and feast.

Some families honor the religious significance of the traditional Christmas tree by a ritual blessing of the tree. Often they place a crêche or nativity scene under or near the tree and adorn it with other traditional decorations, such as candles and glittering tinsel.

A festive family dinner on Christmas Eve is common among many ethnic groups, often with a prescribed number of courses (usually seven, nine, eleven, or twelve) limited to fish or vegetable dishes. The fact that the day before Christmas was one of strict fast and abstinence in previous centuries accounts for the tradition of a meatless festive meal. Ethnic variations abound at this Christmas Eve meal; among the better known is the Polish custom of the distribution by the head of the family of portions of a waferlike rectangle of unleavened bread, known as *oplatek,* with prayers and good wishes for the holy season and the coming year.

The Feast of the Epiphany (traditionally celebrated on 6 January but observed by some denominations on a Sunday near that date) is little observed in most Western Christian homes, although Twelfth Night parties on the eve of the feast, a custom dating from the Middle Ages, continue to be held or are being revived. In Hispanic cultures, 6 January, known as the Day of the Three Kings, is a major feast, and families of Slavic extraction continue the centuries-old custom of using blessed chalk to mark the doorways of their homes with the numerals of the current year and the initials of the Three Kings. Known as the Feast of Theophany among Eastern Christians, 6 January celebrates the manifestation of God's presence in the world that was given at the baptism of Jesus. Water, as the primal element representing all creation, is blessed in the churches and preserved by families at home; the custom of the reverent drinking of some of this blessed water by members of the family persists, and the priest uses the same water to bless the home on the traditional annual visit during this season.

Recent developments in Christian domestic religious observance include the adoption by some Christian families of Jewish feasts. These include Ḥanukkah near the winter solstice, with its custom of lighting the menorah (an eight-branched candelabrum), and the feast of Purim in the spring, when the story of Queen Esther is read aloud to the accompaniment of joyous noisemaking by children. Christian families celebrating these festivals serve traditional foods, such as potato pancakes for Ḥanukkah and prune-filled three-cornered pastries for Purim. Of particular interest is the celebration of the Seder (the Jewish Passover meal) in some Christian homes during Holy Week. As Christians rediscover the centrality of Jewish Passover imagery to their own beliefs and practices, especially its relevance to the Eucharist, they have begun to extend invitations to family and friends to celebrate a Seder with them annually; some families follow the Jewish ritual strictly, while others adapt it in various ways.

[*See also* Christmas; Easter; Epiphany; Popular Christian Religiosity; Carnival; *and* Halloween.]

BIBLIOGRAPHY

Much information on the domestic practice of European Catholics up until recent times can be found in Pius Parsch's *The Church's Year of Grace,* 5 vols. (Collegeville, Minn., 1953–1959). Francis X. Weiser's *Handbook of Christian Feasts and Customs: The Year of the Lord in Liturgy and Folklore* (New York, 1958) deals more directly with domestic practices among Catholics of European heritage prior to the Second Vatican Council. No comparable texts exist on domestic practices among families of the nonliturgical traditions or of those of the Eastern Christian tradition, although Constance J. Tarasar's *The Season of Christmas* (Syosset, N.Y., 1980) provides much information on family practices among Eastern Christians for the period between 15 November and 2 February.

The more recent contemporary trend toward self- or family-generated ritual is discussed by Virginia H. Hine in "Self-Generated Ritual: Trend or Fad?" in *Worship* 55 (September 1981): 404–419. My book *Passover Seder for Christian Families* (San Jose, Calif., 1984) provides an example of the adaptation of Jewish traditions among contemporary Christians. The bimonthly periodical *Family Festivals* (San Jose, Calif., 1981–) offers numerous examples of contemporary adaptations by Christian families of observances from diverse non-Christian religious traditions.

SAM MACKINTOSH

Muslim Practices

Owing to the segregation of the sexes and the belief that a woman's primary roles are as wife, mother, and manager of domestic affairs, the traditional Muslim home is largely the domain of women. Accordingly, many religious practices that occur within the home are performed exclusively by or facilitiated by women; these tend to be less formal and are often placed in the realm of folk practice. None of the five obligatory Muslim religious observances—the profession of faith, daily prayers, fasting, the pilgrimage, and almsgiving—is fundamentally bound up with the home. Indeed, public religious institutions and performances are generally the provinces of men. Women may attend the mosque and public religious gatherings, but their presence is seldom essential and frequently discouraged. They often remain onlookers or are relegated to separate areas where it is difficult to follow the central activity, such as a sermon, in any detail. Thus women's religious activities tend to take place in the home, where they can exercise some control and express their religiosity with a degree of freedom.

The Home Environment. Even within the home, a woman's behavior reflects on her family's reputation in the Muslim community. It is expected that she will be modest and circumspect in her dress and behavior, keep a good home, and be careful in performing her religious duties. Women are responsible for the protection of family health and well-being, which is achieved in part through vows and procedures to ward off the evil eye; both practices are popularly regarded as Islamic. Women are also charged with the care of young children and must see to their religious upbringing.

As managers of the home, women are responsible for creating and maintaining an environment conducive to proper Muslim behavior for all family members. Consequently, conventional domestic tasks take on religious significance. Ritual purity *(ṭahārah)* is an essential precondition for acts of worship. Things such as blood, certain bodily fluids, wine, pigs, and dogs are regarded as ritually unclean *(najis)*. A person, place, or object that comes into contact with any of these must be properly cleansed in order to be ritually pure *(ṭāhir)*. The state of ritual purity may be achieved by ritual washing *(wuḍū', ghasl)* for personal cleanliness and by washing in running water or a sufficiently large body of water for objects. Women are themselves often considered ritually unclean because of menstruation, childbirth, and childcare and must work hard at keeping themselves and their families, as well as their homes, appropriately clean. Clothes to be worn for prayer and other religious observances must be ritually pure. The vessels in which food and drink are cooked and served should be scrupulously clean as well. Some women devote a great deal of time and energy to these tasks: cleanliness is indeed next to godliness and often a prerequisite for it. In two *ḥadīths* (traditional accounts), the Prophet is reported to have drawn attention to the importance of ritual purity, saying "Purification is half of faith," and "The key to Paradise is worship [*ṣalāt*]: the key to worship is purification" (M. M. Ali, *A Manual of Hadith*, Lahore, 1944, pp. 41–42).

The preparation and consumption of food also have religious overtones. Bread, the archetypical food, is regarded as a symbol of God's generosity and must be treated with respect. Housewives take care not to dispose of uneaten bread with other scraps; rather, it is fed to beggars or animals or transformed into breadcrumbs for later cooking. Because certain foods are said to have been preferred or recommended by the prophet Muḥammad, their preparation has religious merit. In Iran dates are said to have been recommended by the Prophet as the first food to eat upon breaking the Ramaḍān fast. Other dishes are prepared as the result of vows to particular saints or, for Shī'ī Muslims, to the imams; their distribution is regarded as a praiseworthy religious act. In addition, entire meals are prepared for religious reasons and served at home. These include evening meals during the fasting month of Ramaḍān, to which the poor may be invited, or ritual meals served in consequence of vows, such as the *sufrah*s in Iran. Women are expected to know when and how to prepare dishes that have religious significance: some Iranian women, for example, recognize a different dish as appropriate for each night of the month of Ramaḍān. The exact round of meals is a matter of local tradition, known to the women of a particular town or region. The careful avoidance of prohibited foods in cooking is equally important. As the primary guardians of their families' Muslim identity, Chinese Muslim women go to great lengths to avoid cooking with pork and pork products in the midst of the non-Muslim, pork-eating Chinese majority.

Hospitality is considered one of the hallmarks of a good Muslim, and the burden of caring for guests falls chiefly on the shoulders of the host family's women. Here too, this responsibility takes on particular importance in areas where Muslims are a minority and proper accommodations and food are hard to find.

Rituals and Ceremonies. Specifically religious domestic observances for which time is set aside and special preparations are made include Qur'anic readings during Ramaḍān and special sermons at which women may officiate. In Iran and Iraq, Shī'ī Muslim women attend sermons combined with mourning for the martyred imams, particularly on 'Āshūrā' (10 Muḥarram), which commemorates the seventh-century CE martyrdom of Imam Ḥusayn and other men in his family along with the imprisonment and mistreatment of the women. The rituals may be sponsored by and for women; if sponsored by families and attended by men as well, separate areas are set off for the women. [*See* ʿĀshūrāʾ *and* Islamic Religious Year.]

Observances to mark regained health and answered vows may take place at any time of the ritual year. Auspicious days, such as the Prophet's birthday, are preferred. In Iran, ritual dinners (*sufrahs*) are often held on such occasions. A sermon commemorating the martyrdom of the imam or saint who answered the vow is followed by a dinner at which foods associated with the holy figure are served. Friends and family join in preparation of the dinner, then celebrate the answered vow and take home some of the remaining blessed food for their menfolk and children.

Many ceremonies marking rites of passage are held at home, and women play a major role in preparing for them. Among the ceremonies marking important stages in Muslim life are the formal naming of a child, circumcision, wedding contract ceremonies, and the reading of the Qurʾān over a body before it is taken away for washing and burial. [*See also* Rites of Passage, *article on* Muslim Rites.]

In Ethiopia, Egypt, the Sudan, and the Arabian Peninsula women participate in *zār* ceremonies. *Zār* refers to both the belief in possession by spirits (*jinn;* sg., *jinnī*) and ceremonies designed to alleviate illness caused by spirits. The ceremonies, which involve dancing and trance, often take place at the homes of afflicted women. Women who attend do not feel that belief in the *zār* and its effectiveness conflicts with Islam. *Jinn* are mentioned in the Qurʾān and are popularly identified with the spirits that can possess and trouble people. [*See* Folk Religion, *article on* Folk Islam.]

The extent to which a woman is willing and able to participate in group religious activities depends on her socioeconomic status, her education, the attitudes of senior men and women in her family, and her stage of life. For more observant and less traditional women, legitimate religious activity is determined by formal interpretations of religious law and includes formal religious education. Highly educated or strictly observant Muslim women may regard certain rituals, such as the *sufrah* or *zār*, as non-Islamic and avoid them. Denigrated practices are often viewed as vestiges of pre-Islamic rituals. Iranian Shīʿī *sufrahs*, for example, somewhat resemble *sufrahs* displayed in Zoroastrian ritual contexts. Women bearing heavy responsibility for the care of young children, food preparation, and housework have little time to attend religious gatherings.

Women perform essential services to their families and define themselves as good women in discharging their duties as Muslims, but the opportunity to socialize with other women in preparing for and celebrating religious occasions doubtless constitutes part of the rituals' attraction as well. By participating in individual and group religious observances at home, women are able to express their religious sentiments in ways that suit them personally and are socially acceptable. As women move into the public world of education, paid employment, and politics, circumspect behavior at school and in the workplace is added to their responsibilities as representatives of their families and their faith.

[*See also* Worship and Cultic Life, *article on* Muslim Worship.]

BIBLIOGRAPHY

An excellent introduction to the religious practices of Muslim women, with particular attention paid to women in Iraq, can be found in Robert A. Fernea and Elizabeth W. Fernea's "Variation in Religious Observance among Islamic Women," in *Scholars, Saints, and Sufis*, edited by Nikki R. Keddie (Berkeley, 1972), pp. 385–401. *Women in the Muslim World*, edited by Lois Beck and Nikki R. Keddie (Cambridge, Mass., 1978), is a useful collection of articles; part 4, "Ideology, Religion, and Ritual," includes information on women in Algeria, Morocco, Egypt, Iran, and China. Further material on the status, responsibilities, and views of women in contemporary Muslim societies is presented in *Women and the Family in the Middle East: New Voices of Change*, edited by Elizabeth W. Fernea (Austin, 1985).

A detailed explanation of ritual purity is provided under "Ṭahārah" in the *Shorter Encyclopaedia of Islam*, edited by H. A. R. Gibb and J. J. Kramers (Leiden, 1953). For information on food preparation and hospitality, see Aida Sami Kanafani's *Aesthetics and Ritual in the United Arab Emirates: The Anthropology of Food and Personal Adornment among Arabian Women* (Beirut 1983), esp. chap. 2, "Food Rituals," and chap. 10, "Islam, Rites of Hospitality and Aesthetics." See also Bess Ann Donaldson's *The Wild Rue: A Study of Muhammadan Magic and Folklore in Iran* (1938; reprint, New York, 1973). Women's religious practices in Iran are discussed in two articles in *Unspoken Worlds: Women's Religious Lives in Non-Western Cultures*, edited by Nancy Auer Falk and Rita M. Gross (San Francisco, 1980). Erika Friedl's "Islam and Tribal Women in a Village in Iran" (pp. 159–173) provides an interesting contrast to the material on urban women in my article on *sufrahs*, "The Controversial Vows of Urban Muslim Women in Iran" (pp. 141–155).

Lucie Wood Saunders describes the involvement of two Egyptian village women in *zār* ceremonies and includes references to other articles on the *zār* in "Variants in Zar Experience in an Egyptian Village," in *Case Studies in Spirit Possession*, edited by Vincent Crapanzano and Vivian Garrison (New York, 1977), pp. 177–191. Fatimah Mernissi's "Women, Saints and Sanctuaries," *Signs* 3 (1977): 101–112, offers a compelling discussion of women's visits to local shrines in Morocco. Patricia

Jeffery's *Frogs in a Well: Indian Women in Purdah* (London, 1979), one of the few works on Muslim women outside the Middle East, studies the domestic life and religious responsibilities of the women of *sayyid* families who administer a shrine south of Old Delhi.

Elizabeth Fernea has also worked on a number of films that vividly present the role of religion in Muslim women's lives. In particular, *A Veiled Revolution*, by Fernea and Marilyn Gaunt (1982, distributed by Icarus Films, New York), addresses the issue of veiling in contemporary Egypt, and *Saints and Spirits*, by Fernea and Melissa Llewelyn-Davies (1979, distributed by Icarus Films, New York), portrays personal dimensions of religious experience among Moroccan women. *Some Women of Marrakesh*, by Llewelyn-Davies and Fernea (1977, Granada Films, London) provides a finely detailed look at the lives of traditional women in Morocco.

Anne H. Betteridge

Hindu Practices

The Hindu home provides a necessary center for all social and religious life. A man has not fulfilled his duties and obligations to his ancestors unless he has been a householder. A woman is considered to be auspicious and blessed while she is married, and incomplete if she is not. Indeed, neither men nor women in Hindu society normally perform calendrical or life-cycle rituals unless they are wedded and their spouses are still alive. The home is where the major turning points in the life cycle (birth, marriage, and death) occur. Although practical considerations now make the hospital and the temple possible alternative locales, Hindus still associate such major occasions with the family living quarters. Traditional domestic architecture, wherever possible, anticipates the celebration of these periodic and grand events at home.

Household Observances. At a symbolic level, the household of a couple serves as a miniature of cosmic principles. Ideally, a home should be laid out as a series of rooms surrounding a single, larger courtyard. This is the same plan that astrologers use to depict the organization and movement of planetary deities and that priests use in laying out a sacred space for ritual purposes. Because of physical constraints, a shortage of proper building materials, and other economic and social concerns, contemporary Hindu homes in South Asia frequently deviate from the traditional ideal. Nonetheless, life in a modern house can still be linked, in several symbolic ways, to this basic design.

Where Viṣṇu is the prime deity it is common to have a tulasi plant growing in the family courtyard. This plant, treated as sacred, will always be tenderly cared for. Even when the tulasi itself is missing, a distinctively shaped pedestal intended for it often forms part of the basic household layout. No exact parallel exists for homes where Śiva is the foremost god. Nonetheless, there are other ways to mark off the symbolic center of family living space for special occasions. One common practice is to erect a square canopy made of bamboo stakes, mats, cloths, and vegetable greenery. This structure will generally be tied to one or more green branches, which serve symbolically as ritual center posts. Often these are further festooned with small pouches of grain, suggestive either of household fertility or simply of abundance. Like the tulasi plant, the ritual post functions as the *axis mundi.* Alternative expressions of the same idea take form through elaborate floor designs, complete with a pleasing vertical centerpiece. During the month of October–November, Hindus in Bengal traditionally put an oil lamp on a pole tied to the roof. Now often replaced by an electric bulb, this light helps the ancestors see their way in an annual journey made across the sky. In South India similar lights are placed on the central pillar of the temple for the same period. These folk concepts utilize a pillar-of-heaven concept. In this way, Hindu homes symbolically link family and temple life to ordered energy in the cosmos at large.

The Hindu home also shares its form with cosmic space by its customary orientation to the four cardinal points. Walls, doors, and even sleeping or eating locations inside are often identified in this manner. In Tamil-speaking areas people say that, ideally, the main door of the house should face the rising sun. The building's interior lines will then presumably allow the passage of morning air and light through the house in straight lines. Some orthodox homes in the South actually have a large mirror that faces the eastern entry, where a hall leading through the whole is not possible. This way the same effect is achieved in an illusory but still highly visual manner. Similar cosmic overtones govern other aspects of house layout. The family hearth, for example, recalls the sacred fire used in many Hindu rituals, just as a domestic well (if there is one) symbolically leads to the underworld. A typical Hindu residence also reserves space for the gods. The household shrine can be as grand as a separate room or as simple as a small picture or wall niche. Often a family's favorite gods are pictured in poster form, but they can also be represented in other, more traditional ways, such as by lamps, pots of water, or measures of grain.

No verbal terminology explicitly associates the parts of the house with parts of the body, yet the two are intimately linked. Indeed, the human body is considered by many Hindus to be a temple of the Lord, just as the household living space is a shrine. Hence daily bathing is a key part of the Hindu toilet, and the body should be internally cleansed by fasting in preparation for important events. Similarly, daily sweeping is essential to the maintenance of the house, as is the regular white-washing or repainting of interior walls. The use of a medicinal cow-dung wash on the floors is also part of traditional preparations for many ceremonial events. After such preliminaries, homes in many parts of India are further decorated with powdered floor designs, ritual wall paintings, bunches of specially tied leaves, or strings of flowers. These adornments help protect a dwelling against evil spirits and serve, as well, to beautify personal space. Similarly, a Hindu's own body is frequently beautified with scented powders after bathing. Protective strings or amulets, and black eye paste, can be added to ward off various unwelcome forces.

In a striking way, images of fire and cooking further link these two forms—the human body and the "body" of the home—within Hindu religious life. On the domestic hearth each day, foodstuffs are transformed through water and heat into consumable meals. Human digestion also provides a fire that refines and transforms food internally. Fire, for a Hindu, is itself a god (Agni), yet it is also the vehicle through which offerings at domestic rituals are carried to other gods via an open flame and rising smoke. Food consumption is often seen as a parallel process that makes offerings to an internal god. Thus all eating, but especially the partaking of full meals, is a semisacred activity. Orthodox Hindus bathe and change into clean clothes before meals, and prefer not to talk while seated for any significant feeding purpose. Many Hindus are also sensitive about having maximum privacy at this time. No one but an approved cook should tend the domestic hearth, and no one but the eater should look at the meal set before him. Because of the presence of an internal fire, the period reserved for food consumption is also a time of transformation. The threat of mismanaging this process, and hence of subsequent spiritual and physical disorder, is always present at such moments. Careful controls surround the eating process for this reason.

Firm rules also govern body movements in the home. Because personal or household space should be respected and kept clean, shoes or sandals must always be left at the door. Furthermore, Hindus are very aware of the symbolism of vertical placement. The lowest floor of a house is reserved for unclean visitors. Washermen or itinerant merchants sit or stand there. Higher levels are reserved for honored guests and for family members, while the very highest spots are used for sacred shrines and for valued photos of deceased relatives. One always sits and lies at a level lower than that allocated to these revered symbols. Similarly, much family etiquette revolves around bowing to senior members, often touching their feet. Women generally cover their shoulders (and in the North, their heads) in the presence of certain relatives. Such gestures indicate an attitude of special respect. Correct male behavior is similar. Men partially uncover themselves (legs, head, chest) when performing services for pay, thus acknowledging inferior status, but cover up (at least their legs) to express deference to senior relatives and to gods.

It is difficult to delineate male roles from female roles in discussing domestic observances. In wealthy homes male servants often cook, but among close relatives it is usually women who tend the family hearth. An exception arises when women in the house are menstruating, at which time they are not supposed to touch anything in the kitchen, or indeed to even enter that room. If no other female relatives are available, men may temporarily assume the task of food preparation at this time. Hindus can also be quite particular about taking cooked food from strangers, since in such a case they know little about the caste and pollution restrictions that were observed during its preparation. Many Hindu men who travel, or who live alone for other reasons, learn to cook for themselves.

A somewhat similar division of labor by gender governs worship at domestic shrines. Many Hindu women regularly tend a family altar, laying or hanging fresh flowers around the gods and saying prayers. In homes where elaborate daily rituals are performed, however, these are usually left to a senior male. Such intensive worship is by personal preference and is generally associated with individual orthodoxy. It is also common for families to conduct day-to-day rituals themselves but to hire a priest-specialist for the more elaborate work associated with honoring family gods during special festivals or at key domestic events.

Relation to Nondomestic Observances. It would be incorrect to draw any sharp division between Hindu household rites and nondomestic observances. The human body, the domestic living space, and the public temple, as pointed out earlier, are ritually similar. Worship relating to one, for a Hindu, is often equivalent to worship at another.

Hospitality, another key theme, also runs through both temple and domestic events. The reception accorded special household visitors has its own rituals of greeting, seating, and feeding. Gods are treated as household guests, while human visitors may be treated like gods. Foods appropriately offered a guest, as well as the sequence in which they are presented, have been codified in detail. In traditional circles even the serving dishes used to welcome guests are made of special metals and molded into special shapes. Details of gesture and posture are also important when one is receiving visitors. Such gestures are sometimes carefully described in folktales. Details of such hospitality rules, but not the principles, vary by region and by a family's social or community status.

For any Hindu, the house guest *par excellence* is the religious mendicant. Many devout, well-to-do people make a point of feeding ascetic wanderers daily. Family honor and personal merit both increase with the generous giving of food to one who has renounced the world. Popular religious legends tell of gods who become beggars in order to test a devout householder. These holy persons challenge the donor, testing to see if he or she is willing to sacrifice personal abundance for religious devotion. In all such encounters divine grace enters the household with the guest's presence, just as a deity is thought to enter the household shrine during worship. It is not uncommon, furthermore, to give foods that were first offered at the family shrine to strangers who later appear at the door.

Public and domestic elements also come together in other Hindu observances. One tradition, becoming more and more popular at present, is the hymn-singing evening among friends. This event can be held in a public temple, but it is also commonly organized in private. The participants either seat themselves facing a household shrine or use an image taken from that altar as a centerpiece. Such gatherings redefine space in a personal home, so that it becomes more like the space of the public temple.

Hindu domestic rituals spill into the wider world in other ways. A good illustration is provided by the popular southern rite called Poṅkal. This is the special boiling of raw rice *(poṅkal)* on a festive occasion, and its subsequent offering to one or more divinities. The symbolism of Poṅkal carries with it many of the associations between body, home, shrine, and cosmos already mentioned. At an overt level, Poṅkal transforms raw rice into a milky, mushy gruel that is then offered to a god or goddess with a short ceremonial *pūjā*. In a third step, the same food is later distributed among the key participants and eaten. At a deeper level Poṅkal is symbolically associated with the harvest of rice or the birth of a child. In each of these three transformations there is both careful control and the application of heat. In Poṅkal the cooking is confined by a pot; in a field rice is ripened or cooked by the sun, there held to the earth in which it was planted; in gestation a child matures or "cooks" inside the mother's belly while still confined to her womb. The Poṅkal ceremony is also linked to key calendrical festivals such as the Tamil New Year, where yet a further temporal transition is celebrated.

The *poṅkal* is generally cooked in new pots, often on a new stove. Normally it is prepared in the open, on a house threshold, or at the border of a temple compound. In this sense cooking *poṅkal* is a little like cooking at a picnic. The place is unusual and the method of preparation slightly different from normal. There is also a special ritual involved in the cooking, whereby each pot must boil up and spill out in an auspicious direction, but not substantially overflow. This rice-cooking ritual may be performed at home and the product directly offered to deities there, or it may be prepared in an open temple yard by women from separate households. It will then be offered to a publically enshrined god or goddess. The rite of Poṅkal thus moves a key domestic activity out of the inner sanctum of the kitchen and into more marginal and more open spaces. The preparation of this most vulnerable of food substances, boiled rice, is also opened up on such occasions to an unusual degree of public view. Both these changes suggest the temporary merger of domestic with wider human domains.

If the cooking of *poṅkal* involves a relaxation of the distinction between household and temple, it is also a key ritual in events that mark the overlap of a household social grouping with other key dimensions of community structure. A share of Poṅkal rice, for example, is often offered to immediate family ancestors. Furthermore, cooking *poṅkal* is a common ritual ingredient of festivals celebrated by much larger groupings of kinfolk, such as whole lineages, clans, or subcastes. The preparation of *poṅkal* is also a big event at calendrical celebrations for the village goddess. Here members of many different castes participate overtly. By joining in such an event, they define their common membership in a unit larger than the hamlet or single community.

Pollution. Hindu men and women both contract ritual pollution upon the death of close relatives. Complex rules govern how long one is disqualified from participating in festival events after a family funeral has taken place. Both sexes also suffer from temporary pollution after sexual intercourse (requiring a bath) and after eating foods cooked by persons of low caste (traditionally requiring additional acts of expiation). Hindu women acquire pollution during childbirth and menstruation as well. The rules vary by caste, region, and the general orthodoxy of the household as to the action and precautions necessary in such circumstances. Most urban or educated Hindus now consider some or all of these pollution ideas outdated. The enforcement of such restrictions persists, however, in many rural areas.

The Hindu concept of pollution is still imprecisely and incompletely understood by theorists, but it is known that this idea interweaves, in complex ways, such elements as domestic precautions, detailed rules for social intercourse, and several concepts of danger. Pollution, for the Hindu householder, involves a social misalignment, the loss of bodily substances, or a lapse in key biological functions. Either matter is out of place or primal energies have been misaligned. Pollution-linked restrictions serve to prevent such disorders from spreading. As in the Poṅkal ceremony, unusual admixtures and the heat that they generate are a necessary force in transformation. Such processes, though necessary, must be properly contained and monitored in order to confine the chaos produced as their by-product. Hindu domestic ceremonies symbolize the need for regulation and control. They thus ensure a fruitful channeling of vitalizing and heating forces of many kinds.

[*For discussion of the specific obligatory rites* (saṃskāras) *of the householder, see* Rites of Passage, *article on* Hindu Rites.]

BIBLIOGRAPHY

Two classical sources of great importance on domestic matters are *The Dharmaśāstras,* best summarized by P. V. Kane in *History of Dharmaśāstra,* 5 vols., 2d ed., rev. & enl. (Poona, 1968–1975); and *The Laws of Manu,* translated by Georg Bühler, "Sacred Books of the East," vol. 25 (1886; reprint, Delhi, 1964). No recent sourcebook provides a reader with the same colorful detail on a full range of Hindu domestic practices and at the same time charts an overview of first principles. Current works, however, do give a better idea of day-to-day household observances. An in-depth discussion of cooking, gastronomy, and food exchange, for example, can be found in Ravindra S. Khare's *The Hindu Hearth and Home* (Durham, N.C., 1976). A more technical treatment of a broad range of domestic and temple ritual is provided by Carl Gustav Diehl in *Instrument and Purpose: Studies on Rites and Rituals in South India* (Lund, 1956). Another excellent description of household ceremonies, especially those celebrating the life cycle of individuals, is to be found in Margaret S. Stevenson's *Rites of the Twice Born* (London, 1920). A still earlier work by Abbé Jean Antoine Dubois, *Hindu Manners, Customs and Ceremonies,* translated by Henry K. Beauchamp (Oxford, 1906), describes the whole range of Hindu ceremonials he encountered between 1792 and 1823, during his sojourn in southern India as a Catholic missionary. Though highly judgmental in places, the ethnographic detail he includes retains its value to this day. Much contemporary information about rural domestic practices in the North is contained in Ruth S. Freed and Stanley A. Freed's *Rites of Passage in Shanti Nagar* (New York, 1980). Information on central India can be found in Lawrence A. Babb's *The Divine Hierarchy: Popular Hinduism in Central India* (New York, 1975), and traditions in the Tamil-speaking area of South India (especially those surrounding the Poṅkal ceremony) are discussed by Louis Dumont in *Une sous-caste de l'Inde du Sud: Organization sociale et religion des Pramalai Kallar* (Paris, 1957).

Brenda E. F. Beck

Chinese Practices

Chinese domestic rituals are rich and varied, differing from place to place and over time. We know most about the observances of the southeastern provinces (Kwangtung, Fukien, and Taiwan) in the nineteenth and twentieth centuries; what follows reflects this imbalance in our knowledge. Widespread hints and a few fuller accounts of other provinces and other periods, however, give us confidence that, despite considerable variation in specific rituals, the same basic themes shaped domestic ritual throughout China for several hundred years prior to the establishment of the People's Republic in 1949, and continue to do so in places outside Communist control in the late twentieth century. Which of these rituals are still being performed in the People's Republic today, how widely and how openly, we can only guess; however, there is some evidence to suggest that while most have been severely curtailed, none of the major types of rituals has died out entirely.

The Chinese word *chia* means both "house" and "family," and everywhere in China there exists a close ritual connection between the building and its inhabitants. It is convenient to divide Chinese domestic rituals into three types: those concerning the house itself, those dealing with the life cycle of the family and its members, and those calendrical rites that are ordinarily performed by the household corporately, or by one or more household members for the benefit of the family as a whole.

Rites of the House. The placement and spatial proportions of a house are believed to affect greatly the fortunes and well-being of its inhabitants. Before building, then, care is taken to site and orient a house in a way favorable to those who will live in it. This is done by selecting a site, if possible, with the advice of a geomancer, a specialist in the technique of *feng-shui* ("wind and water"). A geomancer can tell from the topography of a potential site and its surroundings how well the "cosmic breaths" or "natural forces" *(ch'i)* set up by building the house will harmonize with those of the natural environment and the potential inhabitants. Geomantic siting and orientation are particularly important in a farmhouse, which can be built without regard to streets or nearby structures.

An urban house, of course, must be built on an empty lot and must face a street, so the opportunities for geomantic siting and orientation are correspondingly restricted. But in both urban and farm houses, the internal proportions of construction are another important consideration in assuring a harmonious dwelling. Such measurements as the size and placement of gates and doors, the arrangement of rooms, and, in particular, the placement of the ritual altar are deemed to affect the relations between a house and its inhabitants. Accordingly, not only geomancers but also carpenters must be familiar with correct proportions; carpenters' manuals contain both explicit instructions for the proper proportioning of a house and an occasional hint at how to cause discord in an enemy's family by purposefully building the house incorrectly.

Disharmony in family relations is sometimes attributed to bad geomantic siting or improper proportioning or layout of a house. To correct such spatial dissonance, it is not uncommon for people to erect a screen to prevent the direct entry of certain undesirable forces or spirits, reorient a door so it will face the domestic altar at a different angle, or perhaps build or take down a wall in order to restore harmonious relations between a house and neighboring structures. In extreme cases, houses geomantically diagnosed as incurable may be abandoned in favor of more salubrious sites.

Not only must a house harmonize with its spatial surroundings, it must also be occupied at a harmonious, and thus auspicious, time. A family moves into a new house during a two-hour period selected by a horoscope reader (who may double as a geomancer) to harmonize with the hours, days, months, and years of birth of as many of the family members as possible. The actual act of moving is marked by lighting incense to the household gods and ancestors on the new altar. The full celebration of moving into a new house is an elaborate one, often complete with major ritual sacrifices, officiated by Taoist or other priests, and including a large feast for relatives, friends, and neighbors.

Even after taking all prudent geomantic and horoscopic precautions, a family may still find its house a source of domestic disharmony. Certain rituals are designed to protect against this or to remedy it should it occur. Families who have moved into a previously occupied house will protect themselves against the spirit of the original owner, who is thought to reside in the house: on certain calendrical holidays this spirit, Ti-chi-chu ("lord of the foundation"), is worshiped with a small offering. In many areas, exorcisms, performed by Taoist or other priests, are employed either as precautions against possible haunting or in order to banish a ghost or spirit thought to be causing trouble.

In addition to such malevolent spirits, more benevolent or protective spirits also reside in the Chinese house. The local gods and family ancestors are enshrined on an altar, usually a prominent feature of a central parlor or another auspiciously located room in the house. They are the object of many of the calendrical and life-cycle rituals described below. Besides these, the house also plays host to some lesser spirits, the most important of which is Tsao-chün, the so-called kitchen god or, more accurately, "lord of the stove." The stove god is a low-ranking divinity, but many people consider him important because he is a sort of spy, sent by the Jade Emperor in Heaven to report on the activities of household members. As there is one stove for each household, even if there is more than one household in a dwelling, each household also has its own stove god, represented either by a picture or by his title written on red paper and pasted on the wall near the stove. This provides the stove itself with a certain sanctity. Thus, polluting substances (such as laundry, which is presumed to contain menstrual blood) cannot be placed on or hung in front of the stove, any more than these substances can come in contact with the altar. In addition, in some areas people ritually send the stove god back to Heaven to make his report on one of the last days of each lunar year; sometimes they place a bit of sticky candy on his lips so that his report will be brief and inarticulate, or alternatively, a bit of opium to soften his mood. Some families occasionally offer incense to a minor divinity associated with the household pigs or other livestock; rituals and stories surrounding this spirit are not as important or as elaborated as those concerning the stove god.

Life-Cycle Rituals. Domestic rites and celebrations accompany almost every stage in the life cycle of family members, including pregnancy, birth, early childhood, marriage, family division, death, and the passage to ancestral status. At each stage, both the family as a social unit and the house as a ritually charged space play an important part.

When a woman becomes pregnant, a spirit known as the "fetus spirit" *(t'ai-shen)* comes into being. This spirit, thought by some to be the soul of the unborn child, is not yet firmly attached to the fetus, but migrates around the house, changing its position from day to day. By reading a ritual calendar, people can discern, for example, that the fetus spirit will be in the bedroom today, on the roof tomorrow, in the front door the day after, and so on. No one worships or propitiates the fetus spirit, but all must be careful not to offend it for fear of harming the unborn child. Thoughtlessly driving a nail into a wall where the fetus spirit is staying, for example, may cause the child to be born with a harelip; sawing or cutting cloth in the fetus spirit's current room can cause missing limbs or digits; moving things that have long lain still at a time when the fetus spirit is in that room can cause spontaneous abortion.

Aside from such considerations, the pregnant woman has but few ritual restrictions placed on her. Birth ordinarily occurs in the woman's bedroom. The blood of birth, like the blood of menstruation, is polluting, and thus offensive to the gods. For one month following the birth, a new mother is treated as being in a state of ritual pollution, and is confined to the house. During that month, the room where the birth took place is also considered polluted, as is anyone who enters it. For a first son, a first-month feast often marks both the lifting of the state of pollution and the introduction of the child to the community; for subsequent sons and for daughters the ritual is often omitted.

A mother with young children has special ritual duties incumbent on no one else; she makes daily prayers and offerings to Ch'uang-mu ("bed mother"), a low-ranking spirit whose special concern is the health and growth of young children. Closely associated with the bed, the bedroom, and motherhood, the Bed Mother is ignored by other members of the household; she is also, unlike such domestic spirits as the Lord of the Stove, unaffected by pollution. After a woman's children are all of school age or older, she will no longer need the special protection of the Bed Mother, and will cease the prayers and offerings to her.

Since no rituals have marked puberty or other coming of age for Chinese boys or girls in late traditional or modern times, the next ritually important event in the life cycle of the family is marriage. Marriage, like the other life-cycle rituals mentioned above, is closely connected with both the family group and the house itself. After the initial negotiations and matching of horoscopes of the prospective spouses, the first major ritual is the engagement, in which members of the groom's family (but in most areas, excluding the groom himself) deliver the betrothal payment *(p'in-chin)* and other gifts to the bride's family, and the groom's mother places a ring on the bride's hand. A few weeks or months later, at a horoscopically determined day and time, the marriage itself takes place. The day before the wedding, members of the groom's family go to the bride's house to exchange some ritual presents for the bride's dowry, which they then proceed to take home with them. Part of the dowry—the clothing, jewelry, cosmetics, and bedroom furniture—is installed in the "new room" *(hsin-fang)*, ideally a newly built room, but minimally a newly outfitted one, in which the new couple will sleep. The next visit of the groom's relatives fetches the bride herself, who comes in splendor in a red sedan chair, and at a ritually auspicious moment is carried into the bedroom, the act marking the actual wedding. Later, she and her new husband worship the ancestors of his house, symbolizing the incorporation of the bride into her marital family. A feast follows, introducing the family's bride to relatives and neighbors.

With all sons bringing their brides to live as part of a joint family, the household will, inevitably, grow too large and its conflicts too intense to remain together as a joint corporation. The eventual establishment of separate household groups involves not only the equal division of property and residential space among the brothers but also the division of ritual responsibilities. After the households are divided, brothers may continue to share an altar for household gods and ancestors, but they can no longer share a stove or a stove god. A simple ritual of division involves a final common meal, followed by division of the ashes from the original stove and the consecration of a new stove, with a new stove god, for each of the newly independent households.

Death, like other phases in the life cycle, is an affair both of the family and of the house. A person's death places all family members, as well as the house (whether or not the person died at home), in a state of ritual pollution for a month, and initiates the most elaborate and sustained series of life-cycle rituals. At a ritually auspicious time, a priest or monk, depending on local tradition, places the body in its elaborately painted wooden coffin, which remains in the family's parlor until the burial. A paper soul-tablet with its own incense burner is set up on a special table adjacent to the family's altar. Copious offerings of food and incense are made night and day until the funeral, which must occur at a ritually opportune time, and thus may be delayed several weeks. The funeral involves the participation of many people besides the family members, and as such, is not a purely domestic observance. But the connection to the house remains strong; the two ritually crucial acts of the funeral, those that must be performed at proper times on pain of severe illness for family members, are carrying the coffin out of the house and lowering it into the grave. The family pays all funeral expenses, including a modest feast for a large gathering of relatives, neighbors, and friends. Those who come to pay their respects help offset the cost by bringing the family gifts of money.

After the funeral the temporary, paper spirit-tablet remains on its table for a few weeks, after which it is moved to the family altar, where it is still worshiped separately from the wooden tablets of previously deceased ancestors. After one or two years, a carved wooden tablet replaces the paper one, and the deceased takes a place among the ancestors of the household, to be worshiped as part of the domestic ritual calendar.

Calendrical Rituals of the Family. Calendrical rituals center around the altar, which is usually divided into two halves. The left-hand part (which stands at the observer's right when facing the altar) is the ritually superior half, and enshrines the household gods. These may include deities of Buddhist origin such as Kuan-yin or one of the Buddhas; historical heroes, such as the

Three-Kingdoms-era fighter Kuan-kung or one of the more local heroes; or purely traditional gods of the folk religion, such as T'u-ti-kung ("earth spirit"). There is usually a scroll hanging on the wall behind the gods' half of the altar, depicting whatever gods are popular locally. Families who feel particular devotion to an individual god may in addition place that god's carved wooden image on the altar in front of the scroll. A single incense pot serves for offerings to all the gods or, if need be, to a particular god on his or her birthday or other special occasions, such as the anniversary of the day when the god saved a family member's life or aided in some other extraordinary way.

The subordinate side of the altar, the right side (which stands at the observer's left), is the seat of the family's ancestral tablets. Depending on region and on individual preference, there may be a separate tablet for each ancestor or married pair of ancestors, there may be a single tablet-cabinet, containing rectangular wooden strips, one for each ancestor or pair, or the names of all the ancestors may be written on a broad, rectangular wooden board. In any case, the names of individual ancestors are always written on the tablets, together with their birth and death dates, and often the number of sons erecting the tablet. Exactly which deceased forebears are worshiped as ancestors varies from household to household, but the general rule is that a family should worship the household head's father and mother, father's father and father's mother, and so on back three to five generations from the current head. In fact, however, other ancestors are often included. For example, if a woman with no brothers marries into the family, she will bring her ancestors' tablets with her, and if a man marries into his wife's family, he may also bring his parents' tablets, or more if he has no brothers to take care of the tablets at home. Ancestors with surnames other than that of the primary ancestral line of the household cannot be worshiped together with the primary ancestors; they must have their own incense burner, and may be relegated to a separate, subordinate altar.

Daily devotions at the altar include incense offered morning and evening, first to the gods and then to the ancestors. Often, a third stick of incense is placed in a burner just outside the front door of the house and offered to dangerous ghosts. Any family member may perform these simple rites; in practice the duty most often falls to the senior woman.

More complex offerings to various spirits may come on the first and fifteenth days of each lunar month, corresponding roughly to the dates of the new and full moon, respectively. These offerings may include presentation of food and burning of ritual money as well as the customary lighting of incense. But the truly elaborate domestic offerings are reserved for special occasions of three kinds. First are the holidays, which are dispersed differently through the Chinese lunar and solar years from one region to the next; only the New Year and the Mid-Autumn festival, celebrated the fifteenth day of the eighth lunar month, approach universality. Second are the birthdays of individual gods, on which occasions households may worship individually or as part of a larger, community celebration. Finally, there are the death-day anniversaries of the family's individual ancestors; these are of course different for each family.

For any of these three sorts of calendrical occasions, each family will prepare and present its own offerings, which always include incense, food, and paper money, and may also include other paper offerings, such as clothing for the ancestors, and on some occasions firecrackers. Offerings always differ according to the particular occasion and according to which spirits are being worshiped. As a general rule, gods receive large, symbolic offerings, such as whole fowl or meat cuts and "gold" paper money. Ancestors receive smaller and more intimate presentations, including food cooked, chopped, and ready to eat, along with silver spirit money and in some places clothes or other practical goods, burnt in paper form. Ghosts, worshiped in many places in the seventh lunar month, receive massive and impersonal offerings, such as uncooked foods, and always the lowest denomination of paper money.

A calendrical ritual of any sort represents the discharge of a family's ritual obligations, either alone or along with other households in the community. At the same time, ritual occasions of this sort provide families with the opportunity to socialize and to strengthen ties with other families. All food offerings are eventually eaten, and all but the simplest are elaborate and expensive enough to be suitable for entertaining guests. Even on the private occasion of an ancestor's death-day, a family will invite a few relatives or neighbors to a ritual meal, and on a major community holiday or god's birthday every house in a village or a city street will be full of guests from outside the local community. On these holidays, as on so many other private and public occasions, the Chinese family affirms its good standing and its unity through ritual.

[*See also* Chinese Religion, *article on* Popular Religion, *and* Chinese Religious Year.]

BIBLIOGRAPHY

The best single source of modern analyses of Chinese domestic observances is Arthur P. Wolf's edited collection *Religion and Ritual in Chinese Society* (Stanford, Calif., 1974). Particularly informative for domestic rites are Wolf's "Gods, Ghosts, and Ancestors," pp. 131–182; Stephan Feuchtwang's "Domestic and Communal Worship in Taiwan," pp. 105–129; and Wang Sung-hsing's "Taiwanese Architecture and the Supernatural," pp. 183–192. A good general account, including interesting descriptions of exorcistic rituals, is David K. Jordan's *Gods, Ghosts, and Ancestors* (Berkeley, 1972). Maurice Freedman's writings are notable for their comprehensiveness and wealth of ideas, particularly those concerning ancestor worship and geomancy. See particularly his *Lineage Organization in Southeastern China* (London, 1958), *Chinese Lineage and Society: Fukien and Kwangtung* (London, 1966), and many of the articles collected and reprinted in *The Study of Chinese Society: Essays by Maurice Freedman,* edited by G. William Skinner (Stanford, Calif., 1979). These latter include not only treatments of ancestor worship and geomancy but rich accounts of marriage rituals as well. The most detailed and satisfying study of ancestral rites, including those in the home, is Emily M. Ahern's *The Cult of the Dead in a Chinese Village* (Stanford, Calif., 1973).

All the above sources concern the three southeastern provinces of Taiwan, Kwangtung, and Fukien; accounts of domestic rites in other areas of China consist primarily of descriptions of festivals and of life-crisis rituals, with little analysis. Good descriptions for Shantung can be found in Martin C. Yang's *A Chinese Village: Taitou, Shantung Province* (New York, 1945) and Reginald F. Johnston's *Lion and Dragon in Northern China* (New York, 1910); for Hopei, there is much useful material in Sidney Gamble's *Ting Hsien; A North China Rural Community* (New York, 1954; reprint ed., Stanford, Calif., 1968).

STEVAN HARRELL

Japanese Practices

The Japanese dwelling once was a sacred place in which images and symbols of numerous deities and spirits were the object of purely domestic ritual. Over the past century, and with increasing acceleration since the end of World War II in 1945, both the number of objects of veneration and the frequency of the rituals directed toward them have declined precipitously. Despite the decline, there nevertheless remain ceremonies and practices that speak directly to the notion that the dwelling and its occupants will enjoy the protection of an array of tutelary deities and spirits so long as they are fittingly propitiated.

In analyses of Japanese religious behavior it is common to distinguish three general domains: Buddhism, Shintō, and folk beliefs and practices. Although the categories are by no means exclusive, this tripartite division affords a useful way of organizing a discussion of change. The postwar period has seen the near eclipse of domestic practices belonging to the realms of folk religion and Shintō. Both were closely bound up in the annual cycle of agricultural and fishing communities, whose way of life has been irreversibly altered by the massive social and economic transformation of the past forty years. Shintō, furthermore, has long been deprived of its privileged position as the vehicle for the government's efforts to construct a national cult centered on emperor worship. Rites in the Buddhist idiom alone survive as the chief focus of domestic religious observances.

Before turning to these Buddhist rites, however, it is appropriate to survey briefly the rapidly vanishing world of household deities and spirits, for only a generation or two ago their benign presence was thought essential to the well-being of the domestic unit. Few dwellings would have contained all of them, given the very great regional variation in these matters, but it is safe to say that most would have had at least one.

Known by many names, the *yashikigami* (house deity) was found in one form or another throughout the country. Customarily enshrined in the corner of the house yard or on other land owned by the family, it served as the tutelary deity of the household or the community and in some places was thought to represent the spirits of the ancestors of the contemporary population. The rites associated with the house deity were essentially Shintō in character, but lacked any connection with the state cult. Equally common, perhaps, was the *toshi no kami* or *toshigami* (year deity), enshrined in the Shintō style on a shelf set high on the wall of the main room of the house. As the name implies, it was venerated chiefly at the New Year, at which time its vaguely tutelary powers were invoked to see the family safely through the coming year.

Once almost universal but quite rare since the disestablishment of state Shintō was the practice at the New Year and on some other festival occasions of hanging a scroll in the *tokonoma* (alcove) of the main room of the house bearing the characters *Tenshō kōtaijin* (i.e., the name Amaterasu Ōmikami, the sun goddess, founder of the imperial line). Offerings to this premier deity of the Shintō pantheon consisted of rice or glutinous rice cake and branches of the *sakaki* tree. Less ordinarily enshrined in homes than in places of business, Inari, usually referred to as the fox god but in reality the goddess of rice, was found in some house yards. In other areas, an image of the *bodhisattva* Jizō (Skt., Kṣitigarbha), the protector of children, was installed somewhere outside the house and, like Inari, was made the object of occasional offerings.

Many houses contained a pair of images of two other deities thought to bring good fortune. Ebisu, usually depicted with a large fish under his arm, and Daikoku, shown standing or sitting astride bales of rice and holding a hammer from which money and other valuables flow, were placed together on a separate shelf, and offerings of food were made to them periodically. Daikoku appeared in another form as well, as the largest of the four main pillars supporting the roof of the house. Called *daikoku bashira,* this post was the central point of the geomantic diagram from which all auspicious and inauspicious directions were calculated. Although no offerings were made to it, care was taken that the pillar was not defaced and that no one leaned disrespectfully on it.

Ritual of a combined folk and Shintō character is also a feature of the construction of the house itself. The site itself is protected by the placing of emblems of purity and sanctity called *shimenawa* (twisted straw rope) and *gohei* (folded white paper streamers). When the ridgepole is raised, a priest or the head carpenter, accompanied by the head of the house and his sons, performs rites designed to secure the good fortune of the family and from atop the structure throws down rice cakes to family members, helpers, and neighbors. The ceremony is followed by a feast featuring numerous dishes symbolizing prosperity, longevity, and felicity. Less widely practiced in cities than in the countryside, both the sanctification of the house site and the ridgepole ceremony are still widely observed.

There remain three other major domestic deities associated directly with the dwelling itself, *kama no kami* (deity of the stove), *suijin* (deity of the well), and *benjōgami* (deity of the toilet), all of whom received offerings primarily at the New Year. The first was enshrined on a shelf, where offerings of rice, tea, *sakaki* branches, candles, and incense were made. The well god, represented by a stone image or a small clay shrine set near the well or pump, received offerings of flowers. The toilet god has been of little importance in most areas for a long time, but was given a little rice at the New Year. Of the minor household deities, many were worshiped in limited areas or by certain kinds of households. It would be impossible to enumerate them here.

Until the end of World War II, which ended in a defeat so catastrophic that the carefully crafted structure of national Shintō was totally discredited, most houses had a shelf for Shintō deities called the *kamidana.* Made of plain wood and bearing unglazed pottery vessels for offerings, it held a miscellany of amulets *(fuda* or *omamori),* souvenirs from Shintō shrines, and most particularly a talisman from the imperial shrine at Ise, seat of the imperial ancestors. At the end of the war many people took down the *kamidana* or failed to incorporate one into new dwellings built in the postwar period. Nonetheless, the practice of collecting amulets from both Shintō shrines and Buddhist temples remains a vigorous one, and almost anyone on a visit or pilgrimage will purchase them to bring back to keep in the house, on his or her person, or, more recently, in the family automobile. These amulets are for easy childbirth, traffic safety, curing alcoholism, success in school examinations, and a host of other mundane concerns. Never the object of veneration or offerings, they are thought to serve a generally protective function.

Most of the rites associated with the household deities so far discussed are performed rather casually. An offering may be made by anyone who thinks of it, although the wife of the family head or the grandmother of the house is most likely to discharge this function as part of her domestic duties. Very different are the rites associated with veneration of the spirits of the deceased members of the household, for in this context the family coalesces as a worshiping unit. These rites center on the *butsudan* (Buddhist domestic altar), a cabinet with doors that normally stands in the main room of the dwelling. The altar doors are opened only when a ceremony is held or someone wishes to speak to the ancestral spirits. Although the altar may contain certain Buddhist paraphernalia, perhaps an image of a bodhisattva or scroll bearing a picture or sacred text, it is first and foremost the repository for the memorial tablets of deceased family members. For this reason it is called the ancestor shelf *(senzodana)* in many parts of the country.

On major occasions of worship, priests may be called to the home to conduct the services, but all the other ceremonies for the ancestral spirits are performed by members of the family. They may assemble as a collectivity or approach the altar individually, but on such occasions the presence of a ritual specialist is not required. Because the matter is rather complicated, it will be well at this juncture to lay out the variety and kinds of circumstances that lead the living members of the household to interact ritually with the spirits of their dead kin.

Particular attention is given the ancestral spirits on four occasions in the annual ritual cycle: New Year, the vernal and autumnal equinoxes, and Obon (Festival of the Dead) in the middle of July or August by the Western calendar. By far the most important of these is Obon, when the spirits are welcomed back to the house and given a feast by the members of the family. They remain for three days and are sent off again with gifts of food and flowers. On all four of these calendrically determined occasions, the collectivity of the ancestors is worshiped by the collectivity of the family. Other occasions for domestic worship center on the deceased individual. Special offerings and *sūtra* reading mark every seventh day of the first forty-nine days after death. Memorial services are held at the altar in a sequence of anniversaries of the person's death *(nenki* or *shūki),* generally the first, third, seventh, thirteenth, seventeenth, twenty-third, twenty-seventh, thirty-third, fiftieth, and one-hundredth. Depending on the family's sectarian affiliation and preferences, one of the last three anniversaries may terminate the series of observances for the deceased as an individual. In addition to these prescribed rites, rice, tea, and other foods are placed in the altar daily, usually at the time of the morning meal. For the more elaborate and formal rites, most people deem it appropriate that the family head officiate, but at all others any member may make the offerings. Inasmuch as responsibility for care of the ancestors is conceived as an extension of a woman's domestic role, it is not surprising to find that adult female members of the family are heavily involved in the daily offering of food and drink to the ancestral spirits, who are clearly thought to remain in need of care and sustenance.

More casual, less routinized contact between the living and the domestically enshrined ancestors is also common. Individuals may petition the ancestors for assistance in some endeavor, report successes to them and apologize for failures, seek their advice rhetorically by raising problems and expressing doubts about the best course of action in some matter, and offering them a portion of gifts of food brought to the family by visitors. At such times no formal offerings are made, but such interaction, in which conventional rather than ritual speech is used, clearly supports the contention that, as David W. Plath (1964) has put it, the Family of God is the family and the dwelling the site of the most intense religious activity in which most Japanese ever engage.

Until recent times the house was also the site of births, weddings, and funerals, as well as a number of other events marking stages in the life cycles of its members. Each was marked by the preparation of ceremonial foods and the display of ritual objects. Auspicious and festive occasions, as well as somber and inauspicious ones, were observed in the context of a concern for the continuity of the domestic unit, celebrating the addition of new members through birth or marriage, changes in their social position, and transition to the realm of ancestorhood. Today, however, women give birth in hospitals and weddings are held in commercial establishments. Only the funeral service remains a household event.

The annual round is punctuated by the observance of a combination of secular and religious occasions on which, as in the life cycle events, special foods are prepared by the women of the house and ritual objects specific to the event are displayed. There is still considerable variation in the scheduling of these rites and practices, but the establishment of a series of national holidays and adoption of the Western calendar in rural and urban areas alike have served to encourage standardization of the annual cycle. Many official holidays and not a few informal practices retain some vestiges of religious elements, although for the most part these have become much attenuated in recent years.

The annual ceremonial calendar begins with the great three-day celebration of Oshōgatsu, the New Year, which is essentially a family-centered holiday. Decorations are placed in and around the dwelling and offerings made to the ancestors and the deities. In many rural areas 15 January is marked as Koshōgatsu, Little New Year, by the preparation of special foods and other observances. On 3 March families with daughters celebrate Momo no Sekku or Hina Matsuri, Girls' Day, by setting up displays of dolls and making or purchasing special cakes and preparing a meal of auspicious dishes. The vernal equinox, Shūbun no Hi, today observed on 21 March, is a religious occasion for cleaning the family graves and venerating the ancestors. On 5 May families with sons mark Boys' Day, Tango no Sekku or Shōbu no Sekku, by flying cloth banners and carp streamers over the house, displaying objects such as miniature helmets, spears, swords, and masculine dolls, and as on Girls' Day, preparing or purchasing special cakes. Since the end of World War II, both these days have been combined into Children's Day, 5 May, but the old distinction is still widely observed.

Tanabata, the Star Festival, now held on 7 July for the most part, is the occasion for practicing calligraphy and setting up branches of living bamboo festooned with decorations in the yard of the house. The Festival of the Dead, Obon, is the paramount religious holiday. Formerly held on the thirteenth to the fifteenth days of the seventh lunar month, it is now observed in July in some areas and in August in others. The autumnal equinox, Shūbun no Hi, like the vernal, is an occasion for veneration of the ancestral spirits. The annual cycle formerly concluded with Setsubun, the eve of Risshun, first day of the old solar year. Today it falls out of sequence about 3 February. Each family member eats a number of boiled beans equal to his or her age in years and tosses roasted beans outside the house with the cry "Oni wa soto, fuku wa uchi" ("Devils out, good fortune in"). Like many of the formerly religious occasions, Setsubun increasingly is regarded as an observance children will particularly enjoy.

With the passage of time, many of these festive occasions, which formerly played such a significant role in the life of the household, will continue to fade in importance, and their meaning will be lost. Already most young Japanese have seen them performed in the traditional manner only in costume dramas on television or read about them in accounts of life before World War II. Nonetheless, the core of domestic ritual concerned with the care of the ancestors of the house remains the bedrock on which rests what is left of the sacred character of the domestic unit in Japanese society.

BIBLIOGRAPHY

In the interest of encouraging further reading, only sources in English are cited here. For treatments of the annual ceremonial cycle, household deities and spirits, and other religious practices centering on the family dwelling and its residents, see Richard K. Beardsley, John W. Hall, and Robert E. Ward's *Village Japan* (Chicago, 1959); Ronald P. Dore's *City Life in Japan: A Study of a Tokyo Ward* (Berkeley, 1958); John F. Embree's *Suye Mura: A Japanese Village* (Chicago, 1939); Edward Norbeck's *Takashima: A Japanese Fishing Community* (Salt Lake City, Utah, 1954); and Robert J. Smith's *Kurusu: The Price of Progress in a Japanese Village, 1951–1975* (Stanford, Calif., 1978). These topics are also dealt with in two important articles: Hiroji Naoe's "A Study of *Yashiki-gami,* the Deity of House and Grounds," in *Studies in Japanese Folklore,* edited by Richard M. Dorson (Bloomington, Ind., 1963) and Michio Suenari's "Yearly Rituals within the Household: A Case Study from a Hamlet in Northeastern Japan," *East Asian Cultural Studies* 11 (1972): 77–82. Domestic veneration of the ancestors is discussed in detail in my study *Ancestor Worship in Contemporary Japan* (Stanford, Calif., 1974), which includes an exhaustive bibliography on the subject. An excellent succinct statement concerning the meaning of the ancestral rites is David W. Plath's "Where the Family of God Is the Family: The Role of the Dead in Japanese Households," *American Anthropologist* 66 (April 1964); 300–317.

ROBERT J. SMITH

DOMINIC (1170–1221), Christian saint and founder of the Order of Friars Preachers, popularly known as the Dominicans. Born at Caleruega in Old Castile, Spain, of parents of the lesser nobility, Domingo de Guzmán received his early education for the clerical state from his archpriest uncle before going to Palencia to study arts and theology from 1186 until 1196. In the latter year he became a canon regular of the reformed cathedral chapter of his home diocese of Osma, where he was ordained to the priesthood and spent the next seven years. A diplomatic mission to Denmark in 1203 brought Dominic, as the traveling companion of his bishop, Diego d'Acebes, into contact with the Albigensian, or Catharist, movement in Languedoc.

This dualist heresy, which had its origin in the teachings of the Persian religious thinker Mani (216–276), had come to western Europe from the Bogomils of Bulgaria, spreading along medieval trade routes in the eleventh and twelfth centuries. The Albigensians (the name derives from the city of Albi, near Toulouse) offered a viable religious alternative for many men and women in southern France who were disenchanted with the institutional church, and the austere lives of the Albigensian teachers, known as the perfect, often stood in marked contrast to the wealth and immoral behavior of the Roman Catholic clergy.

Confronted with a profound challenge to Catholic teaching and authority, Innocent III (1198–1216) had enlisted the services of the Cistercians as preachers among the Albigensians. When Dominic and Diego arrived at the papal court in 1205 on their way home to Spain, after the unsuccessful completion of their Danish mission, Innocent sent them to join the Cistercian preaching mission. The nine years of Dominic's preaching among the Albigensians (1206–1215) constituted the germinating period for his understanding that the ecclesial crisis represented by the Albigensian movement could be met only by a group of doctrinal preachers who would proclaim the gospel and live in apostolic poverty. While in Languedoc, Dominic established a form of religious life for a group of converted Albigensian women at Prouille. This first community of Dominican nuns marked the beginning of countless ways in which women over the centuries would come to share in and help create the Dominican vision.

In 1215 Dominic gathered his first companions in Toulouse, and with the approval of Bishop Fulk they began to preach and live a communal religious life within the diocese. Dominic's vision, however, extended far beyond the confines of Languedoc. Hence he accompanied Fulk to the Fourth Lateran Council in 1215 to obtain papal approval for his dream of a band of doctrinal preachers available to serve the universal church wherever there was need. Innocent III approved of Dominic's idea in principle, but since the council had just forbidden the establishment of any new religious orders, the pope told him to return when he and his companions had selected an already approved rule under which they would live.

Dominic and the first friars chose the rule of Augustine, the rule under which Dominic had already lived as a canon regular, supplemented with legislation borrowed from the Premonstratensians and modified in ways appropriate to their new circumstances. In a series of three bulls between December 1216 and February 1217, Honorius III (1216–1227) officially approved Dominic's plan for a universal preaching brotherhood and addressed its members as "the Order of Preachers."

In 1217 only four years remained of Dominic's life, but they were to be years of intense activity in which he set forth the basic design for the Order of Preachers with bold strokes. Since Dominic believed that doctrinal preaching was required to meet the spiritual needs of men and women in an increasingly urban and academic culture, he saw study as essential to a universal preaching mission. Upon his return from Rome in 1217, Dominic dispersed the first sixteen friars gathered in Toulouse throughout Europe, sending seven of them to establish a religious house at the University of Paris. From the dispersal in 1217 until the spring of 1220, Dominic was on the road, preaching, visiting the friars he had sent out, gathering new members for the order, founding new houses, and seeking continued papal support for the work of the preachers.

Dominic's thought has survived not in his writings, for only a few of his letters are extant, but rather in the formative guidance that he gave to the first two general chapters of the order in 1220 and 1221. The idea of a general chapter was not unique to Dominic; begun by the Cistercians in the previous century, it had become the common form of unifying and promoting the life of a religious order. Dominic, however, saw the general chapter not as a gathering of abbots but as an assembly of brothers elected by their peers who would legislate for the common good. In Dominic's vision the master of the order was to be the center of unity on the universal level, the provincial on the regional level, and the prior on the local level. But the friars themselves, functioning through the general, provincial, and local chapters, were to assume responsibility for carrying on the life and mission of the order.

Under Dominic's dynamic leadership, the chapters of 1220 and 1221 established the basic constitutional framework that would ensure constant flexibility in adapting the order's preaching mission to diverse situations. They gave a primary place to study as essential to doctrinal preaching, embraced mendicant poverty, provided for dispensations from the constitutions when necessary so as not to impede preaching or study, and universalized the mission of the order by establishing eight provinces in western Europe. The chapters of 1220 and 1221 brought Dominic's vision to life: an order of preachers whose preaching would flow from a life of study and common prayer, lived in a community of brothers professing the vows and being jointly responsible, through a chapter system of representative government, for a universal preaching mission in cooperation with the bishops and with the papacy's protection and support.

Dominic fell ill during a preaching tour in Lombardy after the meeting of the general chapter of 1221, and he died in Bologna (where he is buried) on 6 August 1221. In 1234 he was canonized by Gregory IX (1227–1241), and he is commemorated in the Roman calendar on 8 August. The influence of Dominic perdures in the shared vision of a religious family of men and women dedicated to preaching the gospel to all people while living in a community that is committed to common prayer and simplicity and whose members are jointly responsible for their life and mission.

[*See also* Dominicans.]

BIBLIOGRAPHY

The most scholarly and reliable biography of Dominic is the work by M.-H. Vicaire, O.P., *Saint Dominic and His Times*, translated by Kathleen Pond (London, 1964). The documents that constitute the primary sources for Dominic's life have been collected by Francis C. Lehner, O.P., in *Saint Dominic: Biographical Documents* (Washington, D.C., 1964).

THOMAS MCGONIGLE, O.P.

DOMINICANS.

The popular name of the Order of Friars Preachers (Ordo Praedicatorum, abbreviated O.P.) was derived from the name of the order's founder, Domingo de Guzmán (1170-1221), generally called Dominic. In France the Dominicans were once known as Jacobins, from their priory of Saint Jacques at the University of Paris, and in England they were known as Black Friars, from the black mantles that they wore over their white habits.

Along with the Franciscans, the Dominicans constitute the heart of the mendicant friar movement of the thirteenth century. After the renaissance of the twelfth century, the presence within medieval society of a growing number of urban-dwelling and literate laypeople, critical of and often alienated from the institutional church, posed a great pastoral problem. The secular and religious clergy at the beginning of the thirteenth century seemed ill equipped to meet the spiritual needs of an urbanized laity and unable to cope with the rapid spread of the Albigensian and Waldensian heresies in the cities of southern France and northern Italy.

Between 1215 and 1221, Dominic with papal approval founded a religious order whose members would not be bound by monastic stability but would be itinerant doctrinal preachers, living a life of poverty in community and educated to minister to the spiritual needs of a literate urban laity. The presence of the Dominicans at the burgeoning universities of Europe established a mutual relationship that would have profound consequences for the history of European thought. From the local priory, which was seen as an ongoing theological school for preachers, to the great centers of study at Paris, Oxford, Bologna, and Cologne, the houses of the order constituted a vast educational network. Albertus Magnus (1200–1280) and Thomas Aquinas (1225–1274), with their monumental achievements of utilizing the insights of Aristotelian thought in the formulation of a new Christian philosophical and theological synthesis, represent the best of the Dominican tradition of study at the service of preaching the gospel in ever new and challenging milieus.

The same creative élan that marked the Dominican presence at the great university centers of Europe was also manifest in missionary activity. Within the first hundred years of their existence, the Dominicans had established missions in Scandinavia, the Baltic area, eastern Europe, Greece, Persia, the Holy Land, and North Africa.

Dominican emphasis on doctrinal preaching led popes and bishops to use the order in the work of the Inquisition. This darker aspect of Dominican history is somewhat counterbalanced by the positive impact that the order's model of government by elected representatives had upon the emerging parliamentary system of Europe.

From its earliest days the Order of Preachers embraced not only priests, student brothers, novices, and lay brothers, all of whom constituted what came to be called the first order, but also contemplative nuns (the second order) and women religious and laypeople living in the world (the third order). The first order grew rapidly in the first hundred years of the order's existence. In 1277 there were 12 provinces and 404 priories with about thirteen thousand friars whereas in 1303 there were 18 provinces and 590 priories with about twenty thousand friars. Because the Black Death took a great toll in the middle of the fourteenth century, the number of Dominican friars probably never exceeded thirty thousand at any one time during the Middle Ages.

The monasteries of Dominican second-order nuns, which numbered 4 during the last years of Dominic's life, increased to 58 in 1277, 141 in 1303, and 157 in 1358. Munio of Zamora, seventh master of the order (1285–1291), drew up a rule in 1285 for lay men and women who wished to be Dominicans while continuing to live in the world. It is impossible to estimate how many men and women shared the Dominican life and mission as members of the third order, but Catherine of Siena (1347–1380), mystic and doctor of the church, stands as an eloquent witness to the third order's profound influence upon medieval society.

The German Dominicans Meister Eckhart (1260–1327), Johannes Tauler (1300–1361), and Heinrich Suese (1300–1366) were leaders in the fourteenth-century mystical movement, but like all other religious orders the Dominicans experienced a considerable loss of members and a marked decline in observance and morale as a result of the Black Death. Raymond of Capua, twenty-third master of the order (1380–1400), inaugurated a reform movement in the last decades of the fourteenth century that resulted in the renewed life of the order in the fifteenth century, exemplified by Antoninus of Florence (1389–1459), Fra Angelico (1387–1455), and Girolamo Savonarola (1452–1498).

The Dominicans Johann Tetzel (1465–1519) and Tommaso de Vio Cajetan (1469–1534) played key roles in the events that inaugurated the Reformation, and Dominicans were to be found both joining the ranks of the Reformation preachers and defending the old faith before and after the Council of Trent (1545–1563). Although religious changes in Europe caused the disappearance or decline of the Dominican provinces in northern Europe, seven new provinces were founded in Central and South America. Dominican missionary activity in the New World was rendered illustrious by the preaching of Louis Bertrand (1526–1581), by the charitable work of Martín de Porres (1579–1639) and Juan Macias (1585–1645), and by the struggles of Bartolomé de Las Casas (1474–1566) to protect the Indians from the exploitation of Spanish colonial officials.

Although the order numbered between thirty and forty thousand friars and nuns in forty-five provinces in the seventeenth century, and Thomism flourished under such distinguished commentators as John of Saint Thomas (1589–1644), much of the outward structure of the order was swept away during the difficult period from 1789 to 1848. Under the impulse of the French Dominican preacher Jean-Baptiste-Henri Lacordaire (1802–1861) and the outstanding leadership of Vincent Jandel, seventy-third master of the order (1855–1872), the Dominicans entered upon a new spring in the mid-nineteenth century that ultimately produced in the early decades of the twentieth century the biblical scholar Marie-Joseph Lagrange (1855–1938) and the Thomistic theologians Reginald Garrigou-Lagrange (1877–1964) and Juan Arintero (1860–1928).

Dominican theologians Yves Congar, Dominic Chenu, and Edward Schillebeeckx were leaders in the new theological movement that flourished after World War II in Europe and culminated in Vatican II. The renewal of the order in accordance with the norms of the council began with the publication of the new constitutions written at the general chapter held at River Forest, Illinois, in 1968. The four subsequent general chapters have continued the renewal process and given special emphasis to new forms of preaching and to the modern media of communication, the ministry of social justice, and the development of the order in South America, Africa, and Asia. In 1974 the concept of the first, second, and third orders was replaced by that of the Dominican family. New emphasis was given to the common mission of the men and women of the order to preach the gospel, while recognizing the diverse ways in which the ministry of preaching is carried out by the clerical, religious, and lay members of the order.

Over the past seven centuries 18 Dominican men and women have been canonized, and 334 members of the Dominican family have been beatified. Furthermore, 4 popes, 69 cardinals, and several thousand bishops have been drawn from the Dominican order to the service of the universal church. In 1983 the Dominican family throughout the world included 7,200 friars in 42 provinces, 4,775 nuns in 225 cloistered monasteries, 40,816 women religious in 140 congregations, and 70,431 laity or secular Dominicans.

[*See also the biographies of Dominic, Albertus Magnus, Thomas Aquinas, Catherine of Siena, Eckhart, Tauler, Savonarola, and Las Casas.*]

BIBLIOGRAPHY

The most scholarly history of the Dominican order from its beginnings to the Reformation is *The History of the Dominican Order*, 2 vols., by William A. Hinnebusch, O.P. Volume 1 is entitled *Origins and Growth to 1500* (New York, 1966); volume 2, *Intellectual and Cultural Life to 1500* (New York, 1973). Hinnebusch's untimely death in 1981 prevented his completing two further volumes that would have taken the history of the order from the Reformation to the present. However, a concise summary of the material planned for the two final volumes can be found in his work *The Dominicans: A Short History* (New York, 1975).

The publication of two works edited and translated by Simon Tugwell, O.P.—*Early Dominicans* (New York, 1982) and *On the Beginnings of the Order of Preachers by Jordan of Saxony* (Oak Park, Ill., 1982)—have provided excellent selections of primary documents necessary for an understanding of the early history of the Dominican family. Both works also contain superb introductions to the sources of Dominican spirituality.

THOMAS MCGONIGLE, O.P.

DONATISM is the name given to the schism that divided the North African church from around at least 311 until the end of the sixth century. The immediate cause was the refusal of part of the clergy and congregations of Carthage, supported by bishops from Numidia, to accept the election of the archdeacon Caecilian as bishop of Carthage in succession to Mensurius. It was claimed that one of Caecilian's consecrators, Felix of Apthungi, had been a *traditor* (i.e., one who had handed the scriptures to the authorities during the Great Persecution of 303–305) and was therefore unworthy. It was also claimed that Caecilian had maltreated confessors in prison at Carthage by preventing food supplied by well-wishers from reaching them.

In the background of the schism, however, were important theological and nontheological issues. Since its emergence into history in 180, the North African church had been a church of martyrs. Its members believed themselves to be under the continuous guidance of the Holy Spirit. For many, the ideals of purity, integrity, and zeal for martyrdom took precedence over that of universality. Under Cyprian's guidance, the church had decided that a valid sacrament could not be administered by a cleric in a state of sin or to one who was outside the church. Congregations should separate themselves from a priest who was a sinner. In addition, in the latter part of the third century, the less romanized province of Numidia had become a separate province of the church, and its primate had acquired the right of consecrating each new bishop of Carthage. Now the bishops of Numidia were eager to assert the claim of their province in the government of the North African church.

These factors helped to consolidate opposition to Caecilian, and in 312 he was condemned to deposition by a council presided over by the primate of Numidia. The emperor Constantine, however, supported Caecilian, put a considerable sum of money at his disposal, and exempted from municipal levies clergy loyal to him. In April 313, the opposition appealed to Constantine, outlining their complaints against Caecilian and requesting arbitration from bishops in Gaul, as Gaul, they claimed, had not suffered in the persecution.

Long-drawn-out legal processes ensued. Constantine first delegated the opposition's complaint to Pope Miltiades, himself an African, but on the rejection of the pope's decision in favor of Caecilian (5 October 313) by the opposition, summoned a full council of Western bishops at Arles on 1 August 314 to decide the issue. The opposition, now led by Donatus of Casae Nigrae in southern Numidia, rejected this decision also. Only after the acquittal of Felix of Apthungi in February 315, another appeal, and the dispatch of a commission of bishops to Carthage did Constantine conclude that Caecilian was innocent; he pronounced judgment in that sense on 10 November 316.

Persecution (317–321) failed to destroy the Donatists, as they were now known. Under Donatus's leadership they became the majority party among North African Christians, and this predominance was only threatened temporarily by the exiling of Donatus by the emperor Constans in 347/8. Under the emperor Julian the Donatist leaders returned in strength. Their leader was now a cleric named Parmenian who was not a North African but described as a "Gaul or Spaniard." As bishop of Carthage, until his death in 391/2, he witnessed Donatism at the height of its power in North Africa. His death, however, was followed by schism between his followers. The new bishop of Carthage, Primian, was supported by the Numidians but opposed by Maximian, a descendant of Donatus who represented more moderate tendencies within the church.

The Maximianist schism was contained and unity within the Donatist church restored at the Council of Bagai on 24 April 394. Four years later, however, one of the principal Donatist leaders was implicated in the revolt against Emperor Honorius by the native chieftain, Count Gildo. On its failure, the Donatist church faced attack by the North African catholics, now ably led by Aurelius, bishop of Carthage, and Augustine of Hippo. Augustine took advantage of the fact that nearly all Christendom had remained loyal to Caecilian and hence regarded his catholic successors as the true bishops of Carthage. In addition, by their practice of rebaptizing converts the Donatists rendered themselves liable to the antiheretical laws of the emperor Theodosius. Moreover, the extremist Donatists and social revolutionaries known as Circumcellions, who since 340 had been terrorizing the landowners of the day and the catholic population in general, were considered a menace to civil authority. Augustine persuaded the government of the emperor Honorius to promulgate edicts banning the Donatists in February and March 405 and finally in May 411 maneuvered them into a conference with the catholics under an imperial commissioner, Marcellinus, to decide what party was the "catholic church" in North Africa.

In the previous twelve years Augustine had written a series of tracts designed to show that there was no historical justification for the schism and that rejection of universality as the standard of catholicism as well as erroneous teaching on the church and sacraments made the Donatists heretics. In addition, Bishop Aurelius's yearly conferences of catholic bishops of Carthage had revitalized the organization and sense of purpose of the catholics. When the conference met, all the advantages lay with them, although the Donatists still managed to match the catholics in number of bishops, namely 284. After three session of debate Marcellinus gave his decision against the Donatists. This was followed on 30 January 412 by an edict that effectively banned Donatism, confiscated Donatist property, and ordered the exile of Donatist leaders.

This time the repressive measures succeeded. Augustine provides evidence for the conversion of Donatist congregations and surrender of Donatist church property. The Circumcellions, however, remained active and eventually contributed to the downfall of Roman Africa when the Vandals invaded from Spain in 429. In the Vandal occupation (429–534) little is heard of the Donatists, but at the end of the sixth century, after the Byzantine reconquest, Donatism emerged again in southern Numidia. Descriptions of the progressive advance of the movement are found in a series of letters from Pope Gregory to his representatives in North Africa, to imperial officials, and to the emperor Maurice. After 601 nothing more is heard of the movement. Only further archaeological investigation of Numidian rural sites is likely to add to our information about the final phase of the sect.

Donatism demonstrates the continuance in the West of the biblical rigorist and individualist pattern of early Christianity that placed individual holiness under the guidance of the spirit as its highest ideal. The Donatists were the true successors of Tertullian and Cyprian in the African church, and they were protesters. Church and state must always be separate. Martyrdom must be accepted as a Christian duty. As far as the Donatist was concerned, the conversion of Constantine might never have taken place. In addition, Donatism, unlike any other Christian movement in the Roman empire, gave scope for revolutionary stirrings among the peasantry, for it expressed the peasants' hopes for the great reversal of material fortunes that would presage the millennium. Its forceful repression by church and secular authorities also provided precedents for the persecution of heresy in the Middle Ages and in the Reformation and Counter-Reformation periods.

Material remains of Donatism are still to be seen in North Africa, especially in Numidia, where the great church of Bishop Optatus of Timgad (388–398) is an outstanding monument to Donatism at the height of its power. Many Donatist chapels have been found in rural sites of Roman and Byzantine date in Numidia. Some Donatist literature has survived, notably the circular letter written by Bishop Petilian of Constantine to his clergy about 400; it is preserved in Augustine's *Contra litteras Petiliani.* Tyconius was a Donatist biblical exegete of first caliber whose work was used extensively in the early Middle Ages by orthodox writers such as Bede. Finally, Donatism found expression in peasant art forms, especially in woodcarving. These art forms often incorporated a biblical text or the watchword used by the Circumcellions, "Deo laudes."

[*See also* Christianity, *article on* Christianity in North Africa, *and the biographies of Cyprian, Augustine, and Constantine.*]

BIBLIOGRAPHY

Bonner, Gerald. *St. Augustine of Hippo: Life and Controversies.* London, 1963.

Brisson, Jean-Paul. *Autonomisme et christianisme dans l'Afrique romaine.* Paris, 1958.

Brown, Peter. *Religion and Society in the Age of Saint Augustine.* London, 1972.

Diesner, Hans-Joachim. "Die Circumcellionen von Hippo Regius." *Theologische Literaturzeitung* 85 (1960): 497–508.

Frend, W. H. C. *The Donatist Church: A Movement of Protest in Roman North Africa* (1952). Reprint, Oxford, 1971. Includes bibliography and a list of Donatist writers.

Frend, W. H. C. *Town and Countryside in the Early Christian Centuries.* London, 1980.

Lancel, Serge, trans. and ed. *Actes de la conférence de Carthage en 411.* Sources chrétiennes, vols. 194, 195, and 224. Paris, 1972–1975.

Mandouze, André. "Encore le Donatisme." *L'antiquité classique* 29 (1960): 61–107.

Monceaux, Paul. *Histoire littéraire de l'Afrique chrétienne,* vols. 4–6 (1901–1923). Reprint, Brussels, 1966.

Saumagne, Charles. "Ouvriers agricoles ou rôdeurs de celliers? Les Circoncellions d'Afrique." *Annales d'histoire économique et sociale* 6 (1934): 351–364.

Simpson, W. J. Sparrow. *St. Augustine and African Church Divisions.* London, 1910.

Tengström, Emin. *Donatisten und Katholiken.* Göteborg, 1964. Includes a bibliography.

W. H. C. Frend

DOORWAYS. *See* Portals.

DOSTOEVSKII, FEDOR (1821–1881), Russian novelist. Fedor Mikhailovich Dostoevskii's childhood was spent in the constrained atmosphere of a Muscovite charity hospital, where his father served as a doctor. It was the murder of his father (1838) which was alleged by Freud to have determined the course of Dostoevskii's epilepsy. This theory is usually discounted, but there is no doubt about the epilepsy itself, nor about its capacity to inspire in its victim something of a "higher awareness." Early symptoms of the condition were experienced in 1849 during his first period of imprisonment. By this time the young Dostoevskii, a graduate of the Academy of Military Engineering in Saint Petersburg, had already established a reputation with some works of fiction, the earliest and most acclaimed of which was *Poor Folk* (1846).

But it was not for his writings that Dostoevskii had been arrested. His crime was having participated in a utopian-socialist discussion group. At a time of repression in the aftermath of the European revolutions of 1848, Dostoevskii and his fellow "conspirators" found themselves arbitrarily sentenced to death. Only minutes before the execution was the sentence commuted. The years of penal exile in Siberia that followed (four years of hard labor and four of military service in the ranks) could not efface the memory of the cynically contrived mock execution, and Dostoevskii was to return to this near experience of death more than once in his later fiction.

The penal exile itself provided ample material for a semidocumentary study of it, *Notes from the House of the Dead* (1860–1861), which was to be published on Dostoevskii's return to European Russia. Part of the book was to be serialized in the short-lived journal *Vremia,* which Dostoevskii founded with his brother (1861). Despite the suppression of this journal, Dostoevskii was to revert to journalism throughout the years to come in order to ensure a modest income. But the greater part of his rarely adequate income was derived from the serial publication of his novels and novellas in the well-established literary periodicals of the day.

It was in the second of Dostoevskii's own periodicals, *Epokha,* that the first of his major works appeared, *Notes from the Underground* (1864). This anguished work ushered in the period (and introduced some of the thematics) of the great novels. The majority of these novels were composed in western Europe, to which Dostoevskii withdrew to escape his creditors. He found it necessary to mortgage his writings for some time, much to his disadvantage. Only after completing abroad much of *Crime and Punishment* (1866), all of *The Idiot* (1868), and *The Possessed* (1871–1872) was Dostoevskii in a position to return to his homeland. *A Raw Youth* (1875) and the unfinished *The Brothers Karamazov* (1879–1880) were thus exceptional in being composed on Russian soil by this most Europhobic of Russian patriots. Even so, with rare exceptions (such as *The Gambler,* 1867) all the novels have a Russian setting.

This is not to say that the novels are restricted by their time and place, deeply rooted though they are in each. In the dismal byways of Dostoevskii's Saint Petersburg or his provincial towns, problems and myths with universal implications are encountered. The significance of suffering, the limitations of reason, and the importance of free will are debated as early as *Notes from the Underground.* Each of the major novels has moral and religious problems at its center. Yet answers to these problems are not necessarily to be expected. Rather (as one of Dostoevskii's characters urges in *The Idiot*), "it is the continuous and perpetual process of discovery [which is important], not the discovery itself." Dostoevskii does not set himself up as an arbitrator between the characters engaged in this process. Indeed, in *The Possessed* and *The Brothers Karamazov* he even abandons his role as narrator to "independent" surrogates.

It is one of these surrogates who notes that "reality strives toward fragmentation." The world of the novels is replete with disorientation and disorder. Yet in the privacy of his notebooks Dostoevskii still insists that there is or ought to be some "moral center" or "central idea." However eroded such a central idea may be, however obscured in the contemporary mind, merely to depict its erosion should not be sufficient for someone like himself who has progressed to his "hosanna" through what he describes as "a great crucible of doubt."

After his second marriage (1867), and especially in the last decade of his life, Dostoevskii gradually reverted to the Orthodox Christianity of his youth. Indeed, even in the darkest days of his exile, he had never abjured his residual loyalty to "the image of Christ," regardless (as he wrote in 1854) of whether it corresponded to the truth or not. Nor had he abandoned a certain faith in some kind of golden age, yet to be recaptured. But none of this was enough to overcome a deep-seated reluctance, an organic inability, to proceed with a didactic novel. The creative process inevitably involved him in the production of works that are multicentered and polyphonic in both their philosophical and psychological concerns.

Nevertheless, he continued to nurture the hope that he might one day "compel people to admit that a pure and ideal Christianity is not an abstraction, but a vivid reality, possibly near at hand; and that Christianity is the sole refuge of the Russian land from all its evils." Toward the end of his life it seemed that *The Brothers Karamazov* might prove the appropriate vehicle for such a demonstration. The saintly figure of the elder Zosima would be called upon to act as the principal spokesman of faith in the work. Thus, the spokesman was required to perform a task to which his author was ill-suited. Equally important, the faith which Dostoevskii invokes was curiously diluted, even secularized. Not that it fails to reflect a "process of discovery"—but necessarily a part of that process are the incisive arguments presented by Ivan Karamazov and his Grand Inquisitor, critics of the divine dispensation.

The Dostoevskii whom one emperor had seemingly sought to execute was to be offered a state funeral by another. The didacticism which had little opportunity to flourish in the novels had found an outlet in the brash and chauvinistic journalism of the writer's later years—hence at least some of the acclaim which accompanied him to his grave. But it was the reputation of a novelist who had given his readers an insight into his crucible of doubt which was to live on. Had he not taken pride in the fact that he "alone had brought out the tragedy of the underground"? It was a tragedy, he had noted in 1875, "which consists of suffering and immolation; of the awareness of that which is better, and of the inability to attain it."

BIBLIOGRAPHY

Generally recognized as an outstanding survey of Dostoevskii, and one written with considerable insight into his development as a religious thinker, is Konstantin Mochul'skii's *Dostoevsky: His Life and Work* (Princeton, 1967). Another wide-ranging survey is provided by Richard Peace, *Dostoyevsky: An Examination of the Major Novels* (Cambridge, 1971). This contains interesting material on the novelist's treatment of religious sectarians. Robert L. Jackson's *Dostoevsky's Quest for Form* (New Haven, 1966) is concerned with the subject's idealism and his reluctance to confine himself merely to the phenomena of everyday life. Malcolm V. Jones, in his *Dostoyevsky: The Novel of Discord* (London, 1976), discusses the centrifugal forces in the fiction with erudition and tact. The classic treatment of the novelist's polyphonic technique is Mikhail Bakhtin's *Problems of Dostoevsky's Poetics* (Ann Arbor, 1973). By contrast, L. A. Zander in *Dostoevsky* (London, 1948) argues that his subject is essentially a proponent of Orthodox Christianity. Less partisan is the useful study of *The Religion of Dostoevsky* by A. Boyce Gibson (London, 1973). The symposium *New Essays on Dostoyevsky*, edited by Malcolm V. Jones and Garth M. Terry (Cambridge, 1983), contains my analysis of the teachings attributed to the elder Zosima, "The Religious Dimension: Vision or Evasion? Zosima's Discourse in *The Brothers Karamazov*," pp. 139–168.

SERGEI HACKEL

DOUBLENESS. The prehistoric cultures of Europe used images of doubles to indicate potency or abundance. This can be seen in the frequent use of double images of caterpillars, crescents, eggs, seeds, spirals, snakes, phalli, and even goddesses. Dualism is also expressed by two lines on a figurine, or in the center of an egg, vulva, or seed, and by a double-fruit symbol resembling two acorns.

The exaggerated buttocks of Upper Paleolithic and Neolithic figurines (called "steatopygous" in the archaeological literature) are probably a metaphor of the double egg or breasts, that is, of intensified fertility or pregnancy. Such figurines usually have no indication of other anatomical details; the upper part of the body is totally neglected. An intensification of the meaning can be seen in whirls, snake coils, spirals, and lozenges engraved on the buttocks of figurines created during the Copper Age of east-central Europe (5500–3500 BCE). Obviously, the fat female posteriors that appear on prehistoric figurines had other than erotic significance or simple aesthetic purpose. They were, in fact, the actualization of a cosmogonic concept. (See figure 1.) Egg symbolism made manifest certain basic beliefs, hopes,

FIGURE 1. *Doubleness.* Abundant fertility is symbolized by twin embryos in the womb of this figurine (c. 4600–4500 BCE) from the Cucateni culture, found at Novye Ruseshty, Moldavian S.S.R. In (1) front, (2) side, and (3) back views, the glyph of doubleness is evident on buttocks and thighs.

and understandings concerning creation, life origins, and the birth process as well as reverence for supernatural potency, expressed by the doubling device, the "power of two."

A glyph formed by two ellipses connected at one end—a double grain or double fruit—appears on ceramics, seals, and megaliths throughout the duration of Old Europe (6500–3500 BCE). The sign may have been retained from the Upper Paleolithic period: a sign of two connected ovals that look much like buttocks can be seen in Magdalenian parietal art. Similar signs are engraved on Irish megaliths. [*See* Prehistoric Religions, *article on* Old Europe.] The double-fruit glyph continued to be significant in Minoan ceramic art. By the Middle Minoan period, it can be seen in association with a tree and a sprouting bud, incorporated in the hieroglyphic inscription on seals.

The mystique of the power of two lingers in European folk tradition, especially in the East Baltic countries, which have remained a repository of ancient beliefs and traditions. Latvians have preserved to this day the word *jumis* and the deity of the same name. The meaning of the word is "two things grown together into one unit," such as apples, potatoes, and so on. *Jumis* and *jumm,* Finnish and Estonian words considered to be ancient borrowings from the Baltic, mean "two things or beings joined together," "bundle of flax," and "divinity who gives wedding luck." [*See* Baltic Religion.]

Twin ears of rye, barley, or wheat—a relatively rare phenomenon in nature—are a manifestation of *jumis.* When a double ear is found at harvestime, it is brought home by the reaper and put in a place of honor on the wall beside the table. In the following planting season, the *jumis* is mixed with the seed grain and sown in the field. *Jumis* is a force that increases wealth and prosperity, signified by double ears, double fruit, and double vegetables.

Neolithic images of the great goddess are frequently marked with two dashes over the hips, arm stumps, between the breasts, or on the pubic triangle. Often two horizontal or vertical lines are painted or incised across the face or a mask of the goddess. The double line also typically appears on mother and child figurines, which suggests that these lines may have connotations of resurgence and new life.

Double-headed goddesses convey the idea of twin birth on a cosmic plane. Figurines of "Siamese twins" are known throughout the Neolithic period and the Copper Age. The heads of these figurines are beaked and masked; the bodies are marked by chevrons, meanders, and crossbands. These attributes identify the image as a bird goddess. In Anatolia and the Agean area, two-headed figurines continue into the Archaic period of Greece. The twin aspect of the great goddess is also expressed by double-bodied or double-necked vessels from the Early Bronze Age in the Aegean, Crete, and Malta.

[*See also* Twins; Numbers; *and, for a broader perspective,* Dualism.]

BIBLIOGRAPHY

Butler, Michael. *Number Symbolism.* London, 1970.

Crawley, A. E. "Doubles." In *Encyclopaedia of Religion and Ethics,* edited by James Hastings, vol. 4. Edinburgh, 1911.

Gimbutas, Marija. *Sacred Images and Symbols of Old Europe.* Forthcoming.

Schimmel, Annemarie. *Das Mysterium der Zahl: Zahlensymbolik im Kultur-Vergleich.* Cologne, 1984.

MARIJA GIMBUTAS

DOUBT AND BELIEF. [*This entry is a philosophical discussion of the interrelation of doubt and belief in the Western tradition. For discussion of related issues in transreligional perspective, see* Faith; Knowledge; *and* Truth.]

Doubt and skepticism, although popularly accounted antithetical to religious belief and alien to the religious attitude, are in fact inseparable from every deeply religious disposition. The fact that twentieth-century philosophical critique of religion has focused on questions of meaning rather than on questions of truth (the usual preoccupation in the nineteenth century, when T. H. Huxley coined the term *agnostic*) does not at all diminish the importance of doubt as part of the intellectual process of religious belief. All authentic religious faith, indeed, may be viewed as a descant on doubt.

The Meaning of Doubt. The word *doubt,* although often regarded as the opposite of *belief,* signifies primarily vacillation, perplexity, irresolution. These primary meanings are discoverable in the Latin word from which *doubt* is derived: *dubito,* which is grammatically the frequentative of the Old Latin *dubo,* from *duo* ("two"). To doubt means, therefore, to be of two minds, to stand at the crossroads of the mind. The regular German word for doubt (*Zweifel,* from *zwei,* "two") brings out the vacillating connotation more obviously than does the English word. In German, *Zweifelgeist* means "skepticism, the spirit of doubt," and *Er zweifelte was er tun sollte* means "He was in doubt what he should do"—that is, he was of two minds about it. The Greek *doiazō* ("I doubt") also exhibits this two-mindedness.

Doubt, therefore, is not to be equated with unbelief or disbelief but rather with a vacillation between the two opposites: unbelief and belief. In doubt there are always two propositions or theses between which the mind oscillates without resting completely in either. To the extent that religious people deprecate doubt, what they are deprecating must be indecision rather than unbelief, and what skeptics find praiseworthy in it must be not unbelief but a willingness to recognize two sides to a question. Doubt is the attitude of mind proper to the skeptic, who is by no means necessarily an unbeliever any more than a believer. The only serious reproach that either believer or unbeliever may justly direct to the skeptic is that of declining to make up his mind in one direction or the other—that is, a moral rather than an intellectual reproach.

Modes of Doubt. Doubt may be considered in three modes: an attitude of mind, a philosophical method, and a necessary ingredient in or component of belief.

1. The characteristic attitude both of the ancient Greek thinkers and of the Renaissance men who admired and followed them has doubt as one of its fundamental inspirations. (By *attitude* is meant here an inclination of the will.) That is, rather than conceiving philosophy as a way of showing this or that proposition or thesis to be such as to lead logically to a settled conviction, thinkers in this tradition insist upon an openness of mind sustained by an ongoing attitude of questioning. Even when inclining to one view or another, such thinkers will always not only pay homage to doubt as a methodological principle but will endeavor in practice to keep their minds constantly alert to the claims of both sides of every question: they will show a judicial rather than a prosecuting or defensive attitude. Such an attitude, to the extent that it is successful in terms of its own aims, is creative, engendering openness of the will as well as of the mind. Like all attitudes it is, of course, susceptible to deformity. It may be feigned, for instance, to disguise a moral unwillingness to reach a decision because of the implications of making such a commitment. That the attitude of doubt can lead to such a moral deformity or perversity is of itself, however, no argument against its salutariness or its integrity. It is an attitude that has sustained the greatest minds of all ages in human history; a notable exemplar is Socrates.

2. Doubt as a philosophical method is exhibited in the thought of many important thinkers. Celebrated instances include Augustine and Descartes. In Augustine's dictum "Si fallor, sum" ("If I doubt, I exist") and in the well-known Cartesian formula "Cogito, ergo sum" ("I think, therefore I am") are to be found intellectual assurances that in the act of doubting one's own existence is an awareness of that existence, since if one can catch oneself doubting, one cannot be doubting that one exists and so at least one can be certain of the proposition "I exist," whatever that proposition be taken to mean. Doubt, then, is a methodological point of departure as well as an implicate of all thought. Thinking, in the sense in which it is understood in this intellectual tradition, which goes far beyond any computerlike function of the human brain, entails doubting.

3. While both of the foregoing modes of doubt are relevant to questions of religious belief, that which most sharply illuminates an understanding of the nature of religious belief is the notion that doubt is an implicate of religious faith and therefore of the religious belief that formulates that faith. By taking the view that authentic religious faith does not entail blind, thoughtless belief but must always be accompanied by an element of doubt, we recognize that such faith and the belief that formulates it are in some way sustained by doubt, making doubt and belief as inseparable from each other as are, in the human body, the arteries and the veins. If one hopes to preserve the vigor and vivacity of one's thought, one must conserve in it the element of doubt that sustains it. Authentic religious faith, whatever it is, can never be as the schoolboy is said to have defined it: believing steadfastly what you know isn't true; instead, it must always entail doubt. Some religious philosophers in the modern existentialist tradition, such as Kierkegaard, Unamuno, and Marcel, have emphasized that a faith unshaken by doubt cannot be authentic faith at all but is a mere blind nodding without either intellectual content or moral decision. I have called faith a descant on doubt, by which I mean, of course, that it rises beyond the doubt that is at the same time its necessary presupposition: one cannot have a descant with nothing to descant upon, nor can a descant ever leave the rest of the music permanently behind it.

Contemporary religious thinkers in the tradition of Kierkegaard talk of the "leap of faith," a phrase that sometimes exasperates their hearers. How does one jump from doubt to belief without injuring, not to say destroying, the integrity of the belief? Before dealing with this vital question, we must first clarify the relation between faith and belief, more particularly as these terms arise in religious contexts.

Faith and Belief. In religious literature faith and belief often have been identified with each other. In medieval usage the Latin *fides* ("faith") generally means both. Even in the New Testament the distinction between the two is not entirely clear, for the Greek word *pistis* ("faith") often has the older connotation of intellectual conviction alongside the notion of trust, the bending of one's whole being to God in complete confidence in his infinite goodness and in his ability to guard and to guide one's entire life in the best possible way. The thirteenth-century Thomas Aquinas, who became a quasi-official spokesman of the Roman Catholic church, and even Martin Luther, leader of the sixteenth-century Reformation, when they wrote of *fides,* often meant intellectual assent as much as an act of the will. The classic Lutheran dogmatic treatises usually distinguished three elements in *fides: notitia* ("knowledge"), *assensus* ("assent"), and *fiducia* ("trust"). By this they implied that both intellect and will are involved in *fides;* nevertheless, following Luther himself, they recognized *fiducia* as the principal element and the others as subordinate to it.

In much Christian literature, however, not least among heirs of the Reformation, the term *faith* is invested with a volitional connotation and *belief* with an intellectual one. The distinction is useful, for faith has an ethical content, with implicates of courage and perseverance that are irrelevant to intellectual assent to any proposition or thesis, religious or otherwise. Nevertheless, faith also entails a metaphysical stance. The object of faith is an "is," not merely an "ought to be." It is the postulated real, so that no matter to what extent authentic faith may be called volitional rather than cognitive, an act of the will rather than an intellectual affirmation, it must be somehow connected with the intellectual activity by which it comes to be formulated. Since, as we have seen, thought itself implies doubt, every assertion of belief that is not to be dubbed mere credulity presupposes an intellectual choice between two alternative possibilities. And since, as we have seen, doubt is an implicate of belief and all authentic faith has in it an intellectual element of belief, then doubt must be called an implicate of faith, no matter how much the volitional element in faith be emphasized.

Beliefs, moreover, cannot be held in isolation: they are part of a creedal system that may be called authentic only to the extent that they are not mere uninformed opinions or thoughtless presuppositions. As soon, therefore, as we start developing either faith or reason, the question of accepting this belief and rejecting that one inevitably arises. Without the coherence that is thereby achieved, one would soon be in a position like that parodied in apothegms such as "I believe there is no God and Our Lady is his mother." So although faith is an act of the will, it must be expressed not only in a particular belief but by a whole system of beliefs, each of which is believed to illumine the others. Hence there is in the mainstream of Western theological tradition the tendency to set forth creedal statements that call for believers' assent, as does, for example, the Nicene Creed. In Indian thought and practice, by contrast, one may hold one's own view *(darśana)* without repudiating that of another that seems logically incompatible with it. That attitude, however, arises from an emphasis on the inadequacy of all formulations of truth *(dharma).* The West, except in the more philosophical types of religious literature and in the more mystical varieties of religious experience, has been less skeptical about the capacity of religious symbols to portray the realities of the spiritual dimension of being.

Faith, although it entails an intellectual element of belief, plays a special and often misunderstood role in the Bible and therefore in all biblically oriented Jewish and Christian thought. A classic series of illustrations of the fundamental religious significance of faith is provided by the author of the *Letter to the Hebrews* (*Heb.* 11), who points to the actions of Abraham, Noah, and other biblical figures, upholding them as exemplars of the courage of those who have lived by faith. Such faith is typified in Abraham's going out "not knowing whither he went" (*Heb.* 11:8). It is closely akin to trust. We should note carefully, however, that although Abraham's courage may have been boundless, his ignorance was by no means absolute. He was not totally uninformed. He did not wander forth haphazardly as in a game of blindman's buff. Yet, considerable as his knowledge presumably was, his act entailed both great personal courage and a firm personal conviction that he could rely on the guidance and guardianship of God, in whom he reposed his trust and to whom he dedicated both his courage and his intelligence, using all the willpower and the knowledge at his disposal.

The "knight of faith," whom Kierkegaard depicts in *Fear and Trembling,* engages in a paradoxical movement that presupposes and transcends the "purely human" courage that mere renunciation of the world demands. His is a uniquely humble courage that makes him perfectly obedient to God. Faith is "the greatest and hardest" enterprise in which one can engage, entailing as it does a leap beyond even the highest ethical decisions of which anyone is capable. From all rational standpoints the leap is absurd, running counter to everything to which human wisdom directs our attention as reliable guideposts to right decision and noble action: common sense, logic, and experience. In his journals, Kierkegaard expressly asserts that "faith's conflict with the world is a battle of character. . . . The man of faith is a person of character who, unconditionally obedient to God, grasps it as a character-task that one is not to insist upon comprehending" *(Journals and Papers,* vol. 2, pp. 13–14). Kierkegaard was by no means an enemy of either the aesthetic or the intellectual or of the ethical life of man; his concern was to show the uniqueness of faith as a category transcending all other modes of human consciousness.

This distinctiveness that Kierkegaard saw in faith has warranty in the New Testament, from which he drew his principal inspiration. Through such faith the Christian is saved (*Eph.* 2:8) and made righteous in the sight of God (*Rom.* 5:1). Inseparable though faith is from belief, it is not to be equated with it. It has a quality that distinguishes it from every other activity of mind and will. Nevertheless, having recognized that distinctiveness, we must now explore further the relation of faith to whatever cognitive status can be assigned to belief.

Prevalent but erroneous is the notion that faith, especially in the tradition of the Protestant reformers, excludes claim to knowledge of God. Hence faith is often contrasted with sight. In the teaching of the Christian school at Alexandria, faith tended to be treated as a vestibule to knowledge, a prolegomenon to a Christian gnosis. By contrast, the reformers glorified living by faith. Yet the French reformer Calvin expressly states: "Faith consists in the knowledge of God [*cognitio Dei*] and of Christ" (*Institutes* 3.2.5). He is not claiming knowledge of God as God is in himself *(apud se)*; he does mean that we know him as he is in his dealings with us *(erga nos)*. Faith, then, even for so doughty a champion of its volitional character, has a cognitive element in it. Indeed, as good theologians no less than great mystics have always seen, faith yields a kind of knowledge, a gradual unfolding of awareness of God in human experience, apart from which awareness faith could not be indefinitely sustained. This awareness of that to which the name God is given is formulated in a set of beliefs that express in one way or another the stance to which faith leads the person who exercises it. Faith, practical and volitional as it is, is the means by which the "knight of faith" actually arrives at what he comes to call communion with (that is, entailing knowledge of) God. Just as we learn to drive or skate or play the piano less from books than by doing the thing, so through faith we arrive at the cognitive element to which it leads and is expressed in a set of beliefs.

Human knowledge is always limited and subject to revision, except in the case of mathematics, which is a closed system, a vast tautology that is indispensable as an instrument in scientific inquiry yet incapable by itself of yielding new information. Knowledge of the empirical world, based on observation and experiment, can never yield certainty. As Kant showed, we cannot know the "thing-in-itself." Doubt is therefore inseparable from all inquiry into and discoveries about the empirical world. Yet through advancement in the sciences we do have a better grasp of the world around us than did our primitive ancestors. We would not propose to go back to our forebears' view that the earth is flat with a blue dome of sky above it, but we must be prepared to doubt that our present knowledge of astronomy is irreformable and to recognize that a thousand years hence it, too, may seem primitivistic. When the "knight of faith," whose adventures take him to a dimension beyond the empirical world as commonly understood, expresses his faith in a creedal statement, he can claim only a kind of knowledge. Many philosophical objections attend his claim. For instance, has he merely experienced a psychological state within himself, or has he in any sense encountered the ground of existence, the ultimate reality? Or, again, might he have encountered God through the superego of his own psyche? He can never be consistently and constantly sure; yet his faith, ever challenged by such questions, survives the challenges. When the authentic believer goes on to proclaim his belief "in" God, he is speaking from experience, as is the swimmer who says he believes "in" swimming and knows that he knows what he is talking about.

Since the "knight of faith" is engaged in a practical, not a theoretical, inquiry, his method, like the method of the sciences, is inductive. The inductive method used so habitually and extensively in modern science entails making hypotheses and subjecting them to tests that result in their verification or falsification. While the "knight of faith" cannot verify or falsify the beliefs that express his faith in the same way that the scientist tests his hypotheses, his procedure is in some important respects analogous. As the creative scientist invests his time and may stake his reputation on the eventual verification of his hypothesis, so the "knight of faith" stakes his life and his final destiny on his. Although he cannot hope to provide a definitive, assent-compelling verification of his faith here and now, the claim implicit in his faith is verifiable or falsifiable in the long run. Such faith entails risk. It is, as Pascal saw, a gamble; yet it is by no means a mere idle gamble, for it is informed by one's whole interpretation of life, as the scientist's hypothesis is no mere guess, but is founded on the whole range of his scientific experience and inquiry.

We have seen that in the thought of the Middle Ages faith *(fides)* was generally equated with belief. The great thinkers of the thirteenth century were much more familiar with deductive methods of reasoning than with inductive ones. Despite the foundations for inductive methods that were laid by original medieval minds such as Robert Grosseteste, Roger Bacon, and Johannes Duns Scotus, medieval science did not advance as physics, chemistry, and biology have advanced in recent times. The medieval men certainly did not lack powers of observation. They made astonishingly perceptive discoveries and invented many ingenious technological tools. They were hampered, however, by not taking seriously enough those inductive methods by which modern science has made its advances. For the same reason they tended to underestimate the meaning and power of faith as the volitional, practical, risk-taking catalyst of authentic awareness of God, apart from which both the beliefs and the doubts that spring from it must lack authenticity. This peculiar role of faith was expressed in the nineteenth century by John Henry Newman. In his *Apologia pro vita sua* he reports that it was not logic that carried him on any more than it is the mercury in the barometer that changes the weather: "The whole man moves; paper logic is but the record of it."

The difference between the medieval and the post-Renaissance understanding of the nature of faith may be due also, at least in part, to a general change of outlook that the Renaissance brought about in respect to the nature of man. In medieval thought the will was treated as but one of several "faculties," or powers of the soul. Such was the change wrought by the Renaissance that a tendency developed to see the will as virtually synonymous with the whole person. In this view the whole person is the agent; hence the act of faith comes to be seen more and more as an act of the will.

Belief and Knowledge. The twentieth-century philosopher Bertrand Russell, in one of his best books, *Human Knowledge* (London, 1948), reminds us that "all knowledge is in some degree doubtful, and we cannot say what degree of doubtfulness makes it cease to be knowledge, any more than we can say how much loss of hair makes a man bald" (p. 516). He goes on to say that all words outside mathematics and logic are vague. After pointing out that empiricism as a theory of knowledge is inadequate, though less so than any previous one, he concludes that "all human knowledge is uncertain, inexact, and partial" (p. 527).

Russell's thought on this subject represents a development of the empiricist view championed in the eighteenth century by David Hume. According to Hume all human knowledge is reducible to more or less strong beliefs. Although some modern philosophers have argued for a clear distinction between knowledge and belief, they show only that it may be convenient to dub certain very strong beliefs knowledge in order to distinguish them from other beliefs that are weak. While I may feel so certain about some beliefs that I wish to assign to them a special place among my beliefs and so call them knowledge, I can never claim to be entirely certain that I have examined all possible alternatives, if only because I cannot know all the possible alternatives. When belief in a geocentric universe was fashionable, many must have felt confident that such a universe was demonstrable beyond a shadow of a doubt. If anyone doubted it, he could be asked to follow the movement of the sun from its rising to its setting and so be shown conclusively that the sun moved; yet that conclusion would be wrong according to today's reckoning.

For practical purposes one may choose to call one's strongest beliefs knowledge, but it can never be knowledge in the sense of an infallible grasp of truth or an acquaintance with reality. Even to say "I know I am in pain" is not an exception since it adds nothing to saying "I am in pain." If I did not know myself to be in pain, I could not be in pain; and if I were in pain, I could not have neglected to notice it. Of course I feel pain; but to say "I know" is to claim knowledge of what pain is, and this I cannot properly claim. Nor could such a claim to know result in any objective knowledge at all. As my friend you would presumably trust my word; nevertheless, you would be entitled to disbelieve me. John Austin in his essay "Other Minds" (*Proceedings of the Aristotelian Society*, supp. vol. 20, 1946) recognized this by pointing out that saying "I know" registers the highest possible cognitive claim in a form that authorizes someone to rely on the statement, so that it functions in a way similar to "I promise." Thus the claim to know is no more than a strident way of asserting a particular belief.

It is one thing to contend that everyone has the right to be sure of his beliefs; it is another thing to affirm that the beliefs are justified as claims to knowledge. By claiming to know, I would claim—judiciously or rashly—to have no doubt. If I affirm that something is a known fact, I am contending that no one has any need or any right to doubt it. No alleged facts, however, can be said to be so indubitable, and none, therefore, is so indisputable. When in creedal statements such as the Nicene Creed or the so-called Apostles' Creed we use the traditional "I believe" or "We believe," we exhibit the characteristically religious disposition of openness and its implication of the possibility of doubt. This doubt may be transcended by faith, yet the faith is meaningless apart from it. Perceptive, then, was the poet Alfred Tennyson's observation that more faith lives in honest doubt than "in half the creeds"; for unless the believer's affirmation recognizes the possibility of doubt, his faith has no vitality. The absence of doubt is the height of irreligion. Both the will to believe, which the psychologist and philosopher William James popularized in the late nineteenth century, and the will to doubt, which Bertrand Russell said he would prefer to preach, are necessary for a lively faith. When the authentic believer says "I believe," he omits a hidden qualifier—"*Nevertheless,* I believe." For if there can be nothing (outside the tautologies of logic and mathematics) that justifies a claim to certainty, then doubt is proper to every belief. Authentic belief does not sidestep doubt. On the contrary, when one seriously intends to live by faith, one does not at all claim that the formulation of that faith is adequate or irreformable.

Nihilism and Certainty. The role of doubt in belief can be clarified by a glance at two extremes: nihilism and certainty. Nihilism (from the Latin *nihil,* "nothing") consists in the dogmatic tendency to deny not only the existence of God but the permanence of any entity. According to such a view one can therefore say nothing that is absolutely true of anything since no claims to truth have any objective grounds. A classical exponent of nihilism in its intellectual aspect is Gorgias in Plato's dialogue of that name. In contrast to the earlier philosopher Protagoras, who held that "man is the measure of all things" (i.e., truth is relative to persons and circumstances), Plato's Gorgias taught that there can be no truth at all. On the practical or ethical side the nihilist denies all "higher" and "objective" values. In the nineteenth century the German philosopher Friedrich Nietzsche held that the interpretation of existence that Christianity bequeathed to Europe was fundamentally a life-negating pessimism. A particular form of nihilism emerged in Russia. Mikhail Bakunin (1814–1876) taught that society's only hope lies in its destruction, while, even more radically, Dmitrii Pisarev (1840–1868) taught that society is so evil that its destruction is a good in itself. Existentialism, by contrast, is not necessarily nihilistic, although some forms of it (e.g., those of Jean-Paul Sartre and Albert Camus) have nihilistic elements in them.

Certainty is a peculiarly difficult concept. After the Renaissance, John Locke, George Berkeley, and David Hume all paved the way for Kant's demonstration that we can have no certain knowledge of the "thing-in-itself." Noteworthy is the fact that down to the present century the papal index of prohibited books included these writers only in respect to those of their works that cast doubt on the possibility of certain knowledge. Although from Augustine to Thomas the medieval thinkers had discussed the conditions of certain knowledge, all of them held that at least some kind of knowledge is possible. Otherwise, how else could one know, for instance, that God exists? Modern thinkers, however, have generally been reluctant to recognize the possibility of absolute certainty except in the realm of logical and mathematical relationships that are (as we have seen) tautologies. Russell distinguished three kinds of claims to certainty: (1) logical, or mathematical, certainty—for example, if we grant that man is a rational animal, we may be certain that by implication man is an animal; (2) epistemological certainty, according to which a proposition is credible in the highest degree as a result of the abundance of evidence adduced for it—for example, we can be certain that the earth moves around the sun; and (3) psychological certainty, which occurs when a person merely feels no doubt about the truth of a proposition—for example, if after having known you for two minutes I were to say, "I am an excellent judge of people, and I know for certain that you are not to be trusted."

The Role of Doubt in Authentic Faith and Belief. Superficial critics of religion tend to ask, "How genuine is the believer's belief?" Such a question never yields—nor could it ever yield—any satisfactory answer. The questioner, having taken care to steer between the Scylla of nihilism and the Charybdis of a claim to certainty, would more fruitfully formulate the question by asking, "How genuine is the doubt behind the belief?" For when a believer says, "In spite of x, I believe y," that which is most likely to determine the significance of y is knowledge of the content to be assigned to x.

Doubt is a profound expression of humility. Without the humility that is and always has been at the root of all creative philosophical and scientific inquiry from Socrates onward, pretensions to religious faith are shown for what they are: at best a caricature, at worst a mockery, of religion. For humility is not only the virtue that corresponds to the vice of pride—which according to the teachings of all the great religions of the world is the fundamental obstacle to spiritual perceptivity; it is also closely connected with love, which is in Christian teaching the spring of all virtues. So faith and love respectively have as their implicates doubt and humility. If humility be radical enough it can become the best means of access to God, who "resisteth the proud, but giveth grace unto the humble" (*Jas.* 4:6). We may also say with E.-Alexis Preyre that "the man whom doubt, pushed to its extreme consequences, has led to total indetermination may 'find' God or not. But if he find God, the faith of that man is immovable" (*À l'extrême du scepticisme,* Paris, 1947, p. 168).

Laughter is likewise relevant to the spirit of humility and doubt. To be able to laugh at oneself is surely the hallmark of humility. Neither the religious fanatic nor the antireligious propagandist is likely to be able to do so, and so neither can ever laugh lovingly about religion. The mirth that springs from self-forgetfulness is a potent instrument in the attainment of religious insight, for it springs from deep humility and a childlike love that have matured into intellectual openness and awe before the mystery of being. That is impossible apart from doubt.

Faith, to have any value at all, emerges in personal encounter with divine being: "Scio cui credidi" ("I know whom I have believed"; *2 Tm.* 1:12). In childhood we learn to trust those who surround us with love. In due course we discover that, like all human beings, they, too, have their limitations. The deeply religious person, however, claims to have encountered the being in whom alone such trust may be placed without reserve, and so such a person sets no limits on the faith that issues from the encounter. What such a person may and should question is what precisely the encounter signifies and how it is to be interpreted. If the faith does not entail any doubt at all, surely it is a straw in the wind.

Moreover, without a willingness to doubt, religious tolerance is impossible. True, religious tolerance is not in itself the mark of authentic faith, for it may spring from mere indifference to or ignorance of the cardinal issues of the religious consciousness; but a faith that is fundamentally intolerant of any expressions of religion other than its own merely reveals its lack of confidence and the trivial nature of its thrust. Genuinely religious persons, whatever their beliefs, are always thoroughly impressed by the mystery of faith. The tendency to explain rather than to contemplate mystery is the vice of much popular, institutional religion and has immensely contributed to the disunity of Christendom as well as to the maintenance of barriers between one religion and another. The apocalyptic literature of religion unfolds the presence of mystery; it does not purport to explain it. Genuine religion is always full of wonder and therefore full of doubt, while irreligion is wonderless. With wonderless belief the devotee can offer only wonderless love, which is tantamount to blasphemy since it entails a casualness such as one might properly express in saying, for instance, "Of course I love candy, doesn't everyone?" Such religion, shorn of doubt, lacking humility, and therefore loveless, surely reveals its own ignorance and depravity, for it expresses a mere narcissistic looking at oneself in a mirror rather than an outpouring of love to the source and ground of being, apart from which religion is indeed vain.

[*For further discussion of doubt and belief in Western philosophy and religion, see* Philosophy and Religion; Philosophy of Religion; Epistemology; Intuition; Skeptics and Skepticism; Enlightenment, The; Existentialism; Logical Positivism; *and the biographies of numerous theologians and philosophers mentioned in the foregoing article.*]

BIBLIOGRAPHY

The classic source on doubt as a philosophical method is René Descartes's *Discourse on Method* (especially part 3). For a discussion of a "doubtful faith" that can partake of rational checks and balances yet allow beliefs that go beyond theoretical knowledge, see Immanuel Kant's *Critique of Judgment* (especially section 91). Another classical treatment of the nature of belief is Blaise Pascal's *Pensées*. Søren Kierkegaard's singularly important perceptions on doubt and belief are scattered throughout his works, but especially important are his *Journals and Papers*, 7 vols., edited and translated by Howard V. Hong and Edna H. Hong, assisted by Gregor Malantschuk (Bloomington, Ind., 1967–1978) and his *Either/Or*, 2 vols., translated by David F. Swenson, Lillian M. Swenson, and Walter Lowrie, with revisions and foreword by Howard A. Johnson (Princeton, 1959). John Henry Newman discusses belief in terms of an "illative" sense in *An Essay in Aid of a Grammar of Assent* (1870; reprint, with an introduction by Étienne Gilson, New York, 1955) and in his *Apologia pro vita sua*, 2d ed. (1865; reprint, New York, 1964). On the meaninglessness of "radical" doubt, see G. E. Moore's "The Refutation of Idealism," reprinted in *Philosophical Studies* (London, 1922); "A Defence of Common Sense," in *Philosophical Papers* (New York, 1959); and *Some Main Problems of Philosophy* (New York, 1953), especially chapter 1. Frederick R. Tennant's theory of belief and faith is expounded in his *Philosophical Theology*, 2 vols. (Cambridge, 1928), especially volume 1, chapter 11, and in his *The Nature of Belief* (London, 1943), especially chapter 6. Martin C. D'Arcy, S.J., in *The Nature of Belief* (London, 1931), gives an account consonant with the Thomist tradition. Also important are Dorothy Emmet's *The Nature of Metaphysical Thinking* (London, 1945) and John Hick's *Faith and Knowledge*, 2d ed. (Ithaca, N.Y., 1966). In several of my books, notably *Christian Doubt* (London, 1951) and *God beyond Doubt* (Philadelphia, 1966), I have discussed faith as a descant on doubt.

GEDDES MACGREGOR

DOV BER OF MEZHIRICH (c. 1704–1772), Hasidic teacher and leader of the movement from 1760. A scholar and an ascetic qabbalist from his youth, Dov Ber sensed a lack in the rigorous routine of study, fasting, and self-mortification that provided the standards for intense Jewish spirituality in his day. Tradition has it that he was a physically frail man, rendered so in part by the voluntary self-denial of his early years.

Toward the middle of the eighteenth century, Dov Ber came under the influence of Yisra'el ben Eli'ezer (1700–1760), the Besht, a wandering healer and folk teacher and the central figure of a spiritual revival movement that had met with some modest success among Jews in

Podolia. The Besht, though a person of significantly less rabbinic learning than Dov Ber, was a natural mystic and a charismatic personality who probably had mastered the supranormal powers of perception. Their meeting transformed Dov Ber's life. The Besht taught a religion of divine immanence, of the palpable presence of God in each place, each moment, and every human soul. In this teaching Dov Ber felt his own religious life come alive, and he was liberated by it from the excessive demands of his earlier asceticism.

While the death of the Besht occasioned a struggle for leadership in the nascent movement, most of the master's disciples followed Dov Ber as he moved the center of Hasidic teaching westward to Volhynian Mezhirich, where he served as preacher *(maggid)*. In the twelve years of his leadership, he attracted to Hasidism a dazzling group of young seekers, many of whom were to become important teachers, leaders, and authors in their own right. These include such well-known Hasidic figures as Menaḥem Mendel of Vitebsk, Shne'ur Zalman of Lyady, Levi Yitsḥaq of Berdichev, Elimelekh of Lizhensk, and Aharon of Karlin. It was Dov Ber who sent them forth to spread the Hasidic message throughout the Jewish communities of eastern Europe, and it is largely due to his impact that Hasidism became a far-flung and important force in Jewish history. His death in 1772 occurred just as the controversy and bans against the Ḥasidim were first being issued by the rabbinical authorities.

Dov Ber was a mystic intoxicated by the single idea of *devequt* ("attachment to God") as a return to the state of primal nothingness. He taught a panentheistic doctrine that bordered on acosmism: the transcendent God also fills all the worlds; his life-force is the only true vitality in all of being. The outer human self as well as the exterior appearance of all reality are the infinitely varied garb of God. As the devotee learns to transcend such externals, he will find only the One, that no thing that is in fact the only Being. Paradoxically, this highly abstract immanentism was combined frequently with entirely personalistic religious metaphors. God is often described by Dov Ber as a father who reduces the intensity of his presence in the world, a process called *tsimtsum,* the way a patient parent lessens the complexity of a concept while trying to impart it to a beloved child.

Much of Dov Ber's work focuses on issues of devotion. He taught that proper prayer must be for the sake of the Shekhinah (the exiled divine presence) and that supplication for one's own sake was selfish. Prayer as practiced in the Mezhirich circle was an ecstatic ascent to *devequt,* with the externals of worship successively cast aside as the worshiper, even while continuing to recite the prescribed liturgy, basked in the glow of God's presence. The heights of such prayer bordered on the prophetic; moments passed in which the worshiper's own voice was silenced as "the Shekhinah spoke from his mouth."

Unlike earlier Jewish mystics, who seemed to shy away from unitive formulations in discussing their experiences, Dov Ber freely advocated union with the divine. The human soul, wholly identified with *shekhinah,* the lowest of the ten divine emanations, had to return to *ḥokhmah,* or primordial wisdom, the highest of the ten and often called by the name *Ein,* representing the divine *nihil.* In this act of mystical self-annihilation, man served as a channel by which all the divine energy released in creation was reunited with its source, effecting a foretaste of ultimate redemption.

In Dov Ber's teaching, the messianic urgency that characterizes much of the earlier Qabbalah is set aside or "neutralized"; the immediate and highly individual act of *devequt* seems to mitigate the need for the long-range and collective striving for *tiqqun,* or cosmic redemption. This neutralization was also made possible by a vision that denied the ultimate reality of evil, considered an illusion that stood as a temporary barrier to our sight of the good.

Dov Ber's teachings were edited by his students and published after his death in *Maggid devarav le-Ya'aqov* (1784), *Or Torah* (1804), and *Or ha-emet* (1899). He is also frequently quoted throughout the many writings of his disciples, and his dominant influence is felt throughout the later Hasidic literature.

BIBLIOGRAPHY

Dov Ber's *Maggid devarav le-Ya'aqov* has been published in a critical edition by Rivka Schatz Uffenheimer (Jerusalem, 1976). His other works are available in reprinted traditional editions. While no work of Dov Ber's as such has been translated into English, the reader can obtain an idea of his teachings from the works of his disciple Menaḥem Naḥum of Chernobyl, *Upright Practices* and *The Light of the Eyes,* translated by me (both, New York, 1982). Dov Ber's thought is the chief subject of Rivka Schatz Uffenheimer's important study *Ha-Ḥasidut ke-mistiqah* (Jerusalem, 1968). For biography, see volume 1 of Samuel A. Horodetzky's *Ha-Ḥasidut ve-ha-ḥasidim* (Tel Aviv, 1951), pp. 75ff.

ARTHUR GREEN

DOVES. *See* Birds.

DRAGONS. The etymology of the term *dragon* (from the ancient Greek *drakōn* and the Latin *draco, -onis*) points to serpents, for the Greek term means "serpent," and it refers to real snakes as well as to mythical snakes or snakelike figures; the Latin term may also refer to actual serpents. By dragons we mean mythical creatures shaped like serpents or with serpent features, and often endowed with features or parts belonging to various animals (a body like a lizard's or a crocodile's, with a feline's or a reptile's head, a bat's wings, an eagle's or a lion's paws and claws, and a mouth endowed with many tongues and pointed fangs). Dragons are often presented as fierce, devouring monsters; according to many traditions, they spit fire; they may be chthonic, aquatic, or aerial beings.

Even though the specific shape of the dragon's monstrous body becomes increasingly standardized in time and assumes a heraldic fixity in the art of many cultures, as in the European or in the Chinese and Japanese, the dragon is better defined by its meaning and function in mythical thought than by that shape. Dragons are the symbols of elements, forces, or principles present, or active, in the cosmic (or precosmic) world. They thus express, in mythical language, aspects of the natural setting of the various societies, and the dangerous or positive qualities of those aspects, such as drought or rain, flood, and so on. Beyond this "natural" meaning they possess a more complex value on the cosmic level, being forces of stability or of disorder, of staticity or of dynamism, of death or of life. Again, they may have a similar meaning on a "social" or "political" level, symbolizing the enemies, or, in some cases, the champions, of a given culture, society, group, or class. In this case also, however, the symbolism of this first level expresses a second-level, "cosmic" symbolism of evil, disorder, and injustice, or of protection and strength.

The main Old World traditions about dragons can be classified in two different groups. A tradition belonging to cultures located in the western part of Eurasia and in some parts of East Africa presents dragons as chaotic beings, responsible for death and disorder, and vanquished by gods or heroes. This tradition has its roots in the ancient mythologies of the Near East, and of the Indian, Iranian, and European world, and it continues into the Christian culture of the European Middle Ages as well as into the Christian mythology of Egypt and Ethiopia. A second tradition is typical of East Asia (notably China, Japan, and Indonesia) and presents dragons as powerful and helpful beings. The distinction, however, is not a totally simple and straightforward one, for "positive" aspects are present in the dragon lore of the western area, notably in India (where myths present dragonlike beings that are similar to the dragons of East Asia), and dragon-slaying myths are not unknown to the East Asian cultures. In order to respect the complexity of the material, a more detailed treatment is required, based upon specific aspects and motifs of the dragon lore of the Old World, rather than upon the usual twofold classification.

Dragons in Cosmogonies and Eschatologies. The most ancient traditions about dragons go back to the Sumerian, Akkadian, and Egyptian mythologies of the first three millennia BCE. In these contexts dragons (often clearly serpentine; in some cases, as in that of Tiamat, of different, though unclear, shapes) represent forces or elements that interfere with the correct order or functioning of the world, and they are vanquished by gods who shape and organize the cosmos and, through their victory, acquire authority and power over the newly ordered world. The god Enlil defeats a monstrous being, the Labbu, in a Sumerian text. The god Marduk vanquishes the monsters Tiamat and Kingu in the Akkadian text *Enuma elish* of Babylon. In the mythology of the Syrian city of Ugarit (end of the second millennium BCE) the god Baal defeats the monsters Yamm ("sea") and Mot ("death"). The dragon Apopis is slain by the god Seth in Egyptian mythology. In similar mythical traditions the serpentine Vṛtra is killed by the warrior god Indra (or by the hero Trita) in Indic mythical narratives that go back to the *Ṛgveda*. In the Hittite texts of Bogazköy, the serpent Illuyanka is killed by the storm god. In Greek mythology, Zeus slays the monster Typhon, who had a hundred snake heads, and Apollo kills the female serpent *(drakaina)* at Delphi, and then builds his own sanctuary on the spot where the monstrous being has been slain.

In some cases, these myths have been interpreted as myths of fertility and of the seasonal pattern, because the victorious deity is often a storm god, and drought, rain, and the life of vegetation are often at stake. But the cosmogonic quality of these myths is clear in all cases: in order to construct, or to defend, the world order, the god has to destroy the primeval, chaotic dragon. In some cases (as in that of Apsu and the female Tiamat, who represent two parts of the original watery chaos, and of the younger monster Kingu) the dragonlike monster represents the preexisting, static, chaotic matter that must be broken, divided, and restructured to build the cosmos. In other cases (as in the myths about Apopis, the serpent who tries to stop the sun from rising and setting, or of Vṛtra, the "withholder" who blocks the cows symbolizing water and dawn) the serpentine monsters are beings that cause staticity and death by stopping the correct functioning of the world, and they must be eliminated.

The Hebrew Bible contains many traces of an ancient mythology, wherein Yahveh, in primeval times, defeats monsters that are extremely similar to the dragonlike beings dispatched by the various Near Eastern gods: to names already present in the more ancient Ugaritic texts *(Yamm, Mavet,* or *Mot)* one can add names such as *Peten, Naḥash, Rahab, Leviathan, Tannin, Behemoth.* Indeed, this seems to have been an ancient Israelite myth connecting creation to the fight against one or more primeval monsters, and thus a cosmogonical motif alternative to the one(s) contained in the first chapter of the *Book of Genesis.*

Given the structural correspondence between cosmogonies and eschatologies, it is not surprising to find that eschatological myths of various societies show a dragon as the being (or as one of the beings) responsible for the lapse into chaos and death that is to take place at the end of time. Thus in late biblical texts (e.g., *Dn.* 7, *Jb.* 7:12), as well as in Judaic and Christian texts of "apocalyptic" content (e.g., *Rv.* 12–13, 20), the primeval dragon is said to have been defeated but not totally destroyed, and to return at the end to wreak havoc, only to be finally annihilated. Other religious traditions also present dragonlike beings as eschatological enemies: thus the Germanic mythology (the Miðgarðr serpent of the *Prose Edda*) and the Iranian (the serpentine Azhi Dahaka, later called Zohak, who is chained to Mount Demavend by the hero Thraetaona/Feridun and who returns at the end of time).

Dragons as Abductors and Devourers. To the above themes one should connect the similar mythical complex that presents dragons as robbers who steal wealth or abduct women, and the theme of the devouring dragon. In some of the "cosmogonical" myths listed above (e.g., in the Ugaritic myth of Baal, Mot, and Yamm) the"chaotic" enemy is also presented as a devourer, or as a tyrant levying tribute; in other cases, such as the ancient Egyptian myth about Astarte and the sea (nineteenth dynasty), a goddess is sent (as "tribute"?) to the monster by the gods it terrorizes. But a more precise motif of this type has recently been reconstructed and called the Indo-European cattle-raiding myth. In the mythologies of many Indo-European-speaking societies (Indic, Iranian, Hittite, Greek, Roman, Germanic, and Armenian) versions or traces of a type of myth have been found, wherein a monstrous, serpentine, three-headed being steals cattle from a hero or a community; a god or hero retrieves the cattle and dispatches the monster. The Indic example is the very myth of Indra (and/or Trita) mentioned above, that is clearly cosmogonic; the Hittite example is the myth, also cited above, of Illuyanka and the storm god. This overlapping, and the eschatological developments of the Germanic and Iranian myths of this group (see above), point to a typological and historical connection between the theme in question and the cosmogonical myths mentioned in the preceding section, though there is no consensus among scholars on the original cosmogonic value of the cattle-raiding myths.

In the Iranian myth belonging to this group, the monster Azhi Dahaka/Zohak steals not cattle (though an interpretation of the stolen female as cattle has been proposed for the most ancient versions) but royal women, and his opponent Thraetaona/Feridun regains the young women (and, in the later versions, the usurped throne) by defeating the dragon. This theme of a dragon who steals women and is defeated by a hero who thus regains them is no less widespread than the theme of the devouring or greedy dragon. It is attested in ancient Greek mythology (e.g., the hero Perseus saves Andromeda from the dragon), and it is a central theme in medieval and modern dragon lore in Europe and Asia, appearing in folk tales collected from the oral tradition of European peasants down to the nineteenth and twentieth centuries, in which a "princess" is stolen by a dragon (or by some other monstrous enemy) and recovered by a young man of the lower social strata, who kills the monster and is promoted, often by gaining the hand of the "princess." In other folk tales of the same traditions, the dragon steals or devours vital elements such as light or water, or pollutes the soil or the air of whole regions.

Dragons as Withholders and Custodians. The tradition of the dragon as a greedy usurper, robber, devourer, or withholder may be combined with two other widespread motifs: the theme of the serpent who in primeval times deprived humankind of immortality—a theme attested, for example, in the biblical *Book of Genesis* (3:1–15) and in the Mesopotamian *Epic of Gilgamesh*—and the widespread theme, which is especially important in many Asian mythologies, of the snake that resides at the foot of the tree of life or the cosmic tree. Such combinations probably gave rise to the theme of the dragon as a custodian of the tree of life or of other sources of immortality or longevity: one should quote the ancient Greek myth of the dragon that guarded the golden apples of the Hesperides, killed by Herakles when the hero conquered the apples, or the *nāgas* of Indic tradition, that guarded the White Mountain and its wonder-tree Mahāsankha, "tall as Mount Meru," that produced a special fruit. In other cases the dragon is shown not guarding but attacking the holy tree: thus, in Iranian mythology (*Bundahishn* 18.2) the reptile created by Ahriman that damages the miraculous plant Gayo-kerena, or, in Germanic traditions, the serpent Niðhǫggr that attacks the roots of the cosmic tree Yggdrasill.

The theme of the dragon as guardian of the tree of life or cosmic tree is connected typologically to the theme of the dragon who guards treasures, widely attested in

China, India, and Europe. See, for instance, the ancient Greek tradition about the dragon that guarded the Golden Fleece and was killed by the hero Jason, who thus obtained the precious token of kingship; the serpents guarding the gold of Apollo among the Scythians (Herodotus, 3.116); and the Germanic myth of the snake Fafnir who guards the gold coveted by Regin and is killed by the hero Sigurd. The theme of the dragon guarding the tree of life became an important iconographical motif in ancient and medieval art of Asia and Europe: it is found, in a rigid heraldic scheme, even in the reliefs of the Baptistery of Parma and of other medieval churches.

Dragons as Enemies and Devils. In other traditions, dragons are ever-active, menacing symbols of evil. In some cases, their symbolic value is drastically "historicized," and they are identified by various societies or groups with real, external enemies such as foreign nations or oppressive powers and rulers. It has been shown that in many traditions of the cattle-raiding myth type the serpentine cattle raider (or abductor of women) is seen as the representative of an enemy (often non-Indo-European) group, against which the society that created the myths was engaged in a continuous warfare; in the Hebrew Bible and in the most ancient Christian texts the various monsters listed above are quoted to indicate neighboring nations (Egypt, Assyria, Babylon, etc.) or tyrannical rulers that oppressed Israel or persecuted the believers.

In later Judaic and in other religious and magical texts of the eastern Mediterranean of Hellenistic and Roman times, dragons and serpents are increasingly presented as symbols and instruments of the evil forces, and from this background, as well as from the eschatological value of dragons in biblical and other traditions (see above), the identification of the dragon with the enemy of God, Satan, arose. This interpretation was already explicit in the "canonical" Christian apocalypse (*Rv.* 20:2; see above), and it became the most generally accepted in the Christian world. In the new Christian context, numerous hagiographic and other traditions contained a restructured version of the ancient mythical theme of the battle against the dragon or monster, in which the dragon was an embodiment or an emissary of Satan. The best-known type of battle between a holy being and the devilish dragon in Christian traditions opposes the satanic enemy to a warrior figure. One might mention Saint George, a saintly knight of Anatolian origin, who often replaced the "pagan" dragon slayers of local, pre-Christian traditions; or Michael, the Archangel, an important figure of Christian angelology that is presented as a dragon slayer already in the earliest texts (*Rv.* 12:7–9). These two figures are extremely popular in Christian iconography from the earliest times; they are usually shown dispatching the satanic dragon with a lance or sword, clad in full armor, and Saint George is often depicted on horseback.

Saints George and Michael are not, however, the only Christian dragon-slayers. The Virgin Mary, mother of Jesus, for example, is often depicted as trampling a serpent, as the Second Eve who defeats the forces of evil, in fulfillment of the verse of the *Book of Genesis* (3:15) that announced an eternal enmity between the seed of Eve and the serpent; the iconographical type continues, today still, in Catholic sacred art. Finally, other dragon-fighters of Christian tradition, such as Saint Marcellus of Paris (fifth century) or Saint Hilary of Poitiers, appear not as warriors, but as bishops, their weapon against the dragon being not the sword or lance but the bishop's pastoral staff. The connection established by the hagiographic sources between their victory over the dragon and their role as culture heroes and as peaceful leaders of their communities shows that their treatment of dragons (often not slain, but tamed or chased away) has specific meanings, different from those of the other Christian narratives about dragons, and probably less concerned with a theological symbolism: we are told of Hilary that "he gave more land to humankind, for colonists migrated to the place that had been held by the beast" ("addidit terra hominibus, quia in loco beluae incola transmigravit").

Dragons as Givers of Fecundity and Life. In spite of the systematic "demonization" of dragon figures in the Christian Middle Ages, specialists of European folklore and medieval culture have shown that many aspects of the dragon lore of Europe point to a more complex symbolic and mythical value of dragons. It will suffice here to quote the heraldic use of dragons in crests, banners, and insignia, from late antiquity to modern times; the identification (that has been compared to "totemic" practices of tribal societies) of nations and lineages with dragons; the presence of dragons (often as symbols of fecundity and prosperity) in liturgical processions (such as the Rogations of western Europe) or in folkloric festivals (such as Carnival).

The "positive" traits of dragons in European traditions show the dragon lore of Europe to be polysemous. They may be usefully compared to the "positive" traits of dragons in East Asia, and especially in China, where dragon figures are no less polysemous than in the Western tradition. In China, the theme of dragons as forces or beings that have to be controlled and confirmed in order to "create" the cosmic order is well attested by, for example, the Confucian *Shu ching* (Book of Stories). That text recounts how the mythical emperor Yü, the founder of the Hsia dynasty, who gave the world its correct order, built the first canals, freed the land from the chaotic waters, and chased away the serpents and dragons, forcing them to reside in the marshes.

To this tradition one could add many others, such as the deeds of the dragon-slaying emperor Chuan-hin. However, one should note that Nü-kua (the goddess who ordered the world in primeval times according to another ancient text, the *Lieh-tzu,* and killed the black dragon) and her spouse, the mythical emperor Fu-hsi, are represented as dragonlike beings in sculptures of the first centuries CE. This paradox of the dragonlike dragon-slayer is emblematic of the complexity of Chinese dragon lore. Chinese dragons embodied the fertilizing qualities of water, and the importance of rain in the agricultural life of that region explains the increasingly ouranic traits of dragons, their wings, their connections with lightning.

Far from being a mere symbolic expression of the natural elements, however, Chinese dragons represent the rhythmic forces that rule the life of the cosmos. This is explicitly stated by the Taoist Chuang-tzu, who writes that the dragon is a symbol of rhythmic life because it embodies the waters that guarantee the living order of the cosmos by their harmonious movement. The cosmic value of dragons as symbols of rhythm and flux is not distinguished, in this text, from their value on the level of the material elements of nature.

The connection of Chinese dragons with rain is well exemplified by the ritual practices of ancient China; during droughts, images of the Ying dragon, a water figure, were made, to propitiate rainfall. Yet dragons are also important in rituals of cosmic renewal, as is shown by the presence of dragon masks during the lamplit, nightly festivities that close the Chinese New Year feast; and many traditions and practices point to the other value of dragons as symbols of cosmic rhythm. In particular, this is clear in the symbolic correspondences and ties between dragons and the Chinese emperors or Sons of Heaven who were also representative of cosmic rhythms and givers of fecundity. Thus we are told that an emperor of the Hsia dynasty ate dragons in order to ensure magically the welfare of his kingdom, and that when that same dynasty underwent a crisis and lost its vital force, dragons appeared to reestablish the correct rhythmic flux in various ways. Finally, mythical dragons were responsible for the ascension of monarchs to the heavenly regions, as happened, we are told, when Huang-ti, the Yellow Emperor, was abducted with several members of his court by a bearded dragon and carried to the sky.

Throughout Southeast Asia, in South India, Indochina, and Indonesia, dragons are water figures and symbols of fertility. This is attested not only by narrative traditions but also by ritual practices. Thus, in modern Cambodian weddings the bride is identified with the moon, her teeth are treated as if to deprive them of serpent venom, and the rituals are explicitly connected with myths about a dragonlike royal ancestress (see below); in Tenasserim (Burma), to stop the rainy season and to bring in the dry weather, a statue of Upagutta, a mythical serpent king, is plunged in water and offered sacrificial gifts, in a ritual that is a symmetrical reversal of the Chinese dragon rite mentioned above.

Dragons as Parents and Ancestors. Many traditions of Asia and Europe present dragons as the parents of heroes and holy men and as the mythical ancestors of kingly dynasties. The ancient Greek myth of the origin of the Boeotian city Thebes combines this theme with the theme of the serpent as guardian and withholder: the hero Kadmos kills the dragon that barred the way to the site of the future city and then sows the dragon's teeth in the earth, thus giving rise to the Spartoi ("sown men"), who become the first Thebans. Alexander the Great (r. 336–323 BCE) was believed by some to be born from his mother's encounter with a god in the shape of a serpent, and a similar legend was told of the Roman emperor Augustus. According to a Chinese tradition, the princess Liu was resting by a pond with her husband, when she was raped by a dragon and conceived thus the future emperor Kao-tsu; and the culture hero Fu-hsi (see above) was said to have been born from a pond that was famous for its dragons. Similar traditions are attested in Annam and Indonesia; and the Indian kings of Chota Nagpur were believed to have descended from a *nāga,* or serpentlike spirit, named Puṇḍarīka.

A series of Asian traditions recount the birth of a famous kingly ancestor or holy man from a prince or priest and a *nāgī* (female counterpart to the male *nāga*). Thus, according to a Palaung myth, the *nāgī* Thusandi and the son of the solar deity, Prince Thuryia, gave birth to three sons who became the kings of three lands (China, the land of the Palaung, and Pagan). Similar traditions about the origins of royal dynasties from female dragon figures exist in South India, Indochina, and Indonesia. In India the birth of the sage Agastya from the *apsara* Urvaśī is recounted in a comparable fashion.

In the legends, the dragon-woman is often recognized as such suddenly, because she smells strongly of fish, or because she is spied upon while she takes a bath and plays in the water with a *nāga.* In modern traditions of this kind from Cambodia, the female dragon is a moon figure, and her mythical marriage with a solar prince is the prototype of today's marriage rituals (see above), as well as a symbol of cosmic union between opposites.

Similarly, the traditions about the birth of a dynasty from the union of a watery, dragonlike female and a fiery solar male are symbolic of a primeval unity of opposites that prepares the new cosmos represented by the new dynastic order.

A comparable symbolic interpretation has not been offered by scholars for the European traditions of the same type, that also derive princely dynasties from dragonlike females, and are known both from medieval chronicles and other texts, and from modern folklore. In the best-known of these European narrative traditions (the story of the extrahuman female Mélusine or Mélusigne, often classified as a fairy by its medieval redactors) the female protagonist is spied upon by her husband, who discovers that she turns into a snake when taking a bath. The Mélusine stories have been compared to the myth told by Herodotus (4.8–10) about the birth of the ancestors of the three Scythian "tribes" from the hero Herakles and a powerful female being, who was half woman, half serpent, but decidedly chthonic rather than watery.

[*See also* Snakes; Monsters; *and* Chaos.]

BIBLIOGRAPHY

G. Elliot Smith's *The Evolution of the Dragon* (New York, 1919), although outdated, is still useful as a general study. The best discussion of dragons and their symbolic meaning is in Mircea Eliade's *Patterns in Comparative Religion* (New York, 1958), chaps. 5 and 8. This book has an excellent bibliographical appendix. On dragons as chaotic beings of primeval times and on the theme of the cosmogonic battle against such monsters in the ancient Near East, Indic, and Greek worlds, see Mary K. Wakeman's *God's Battle with the Monster: A Study in Biblical Imagery* (Leiden, 1973). For still wider comparative material, see Joseph Fontenrose's *Python: A Study of the Delphic Myth and Its Origins* (Berkeley, 1959).

On the "cattle-raiding myth," see Bruce Lincoln's *Priests, Warriors, and Cattle: A Study in the Ecology of Religions* (Berkeley, 1981), esp. pp. 103–122. On the Indo-European myths about the fight against the dragon, consult Viacheslav Ivanov and V. N. Toporov's "Le mythe indo-européen du dieu de l'orage poursuivant le serpent: Réconstitution du schéma," in *Échanges et communications: Mélanges offerts à Claude Lévi-Strauss*, edited by Jean Pouillon and Pierre Maranda, vol. 2 (The Hague, 1968), pp. 1180–1206.

A good source for medieval European dragon lore, especially the theme of the bishop as a dragon tamer, and an important critical study is Jacques Le Goff's "Culture ecclésiastique et culture folklorique au Moyen-Âge: Saint Marcel de Paris et le dragon," in *Richerche storiche ed economiche in memoria di Corrado Barbagallo*, edited by Luigi De Rosa, vol. 2 (Naples, 1970), pp. 53–90. This essay has been translated as "Ecclesiastical Culture and Folklore in the Middle Ages: Saint Marcellus of Paris and the Dragon," in Le Goff's *Time, Work and Culture in the Middle Ages* (Chicago, 1980), pp. 159–188. Le Goff and Emmanuel Le Roy Ladurie's "Mélusine maternelle et défricheuse," *Annales: Économies, sociétés, civilisations* 26 (1971): 587–622, offers a source on Mélusine.

Bibliography for East Asian dragons can be found in Eliade's *Patterns in Comparative Religion* (cited above), Barbara Renz's *Der orientalische Schlangendrache* (Augsburg, 1930), and Hampden C. Du Bose's *The Dragon, Image, and Demon, or The Three Religions of China* (London, 1886). On the mythical serpentine ancestress in Southeast Asia, see the bibliography provided by Eliade (cited above), adding Éveline Porée-Maspéro's "Nouvelle étude sur la nāgī Somā," *Journal asiatique* 236 (1950): 237–267.

CRISTIANO GROTTANELLI

DRAMA. [*This entry comprises eleven articles, a theoretical overview that examines varieties of performance activities and their components in connection with religion, and ten articles on particular cultural phenomena:*

Performance and Ritual
Ancient Near Eastern Ritual Drama
Middle Eastern Narrative Traditions
Indian Dance and Dance Drama
Balinese Dance and Dance Drama
Javanese Wayang
East Asian Dance and Theater
African Religious Drama
Native American Religious Drama
European Religious Drama
Modern Western Theater

For further discussion of performance traditions, see Dance.]

Performance and Ritual

Phenomena called "performance," "theater," "dance," "drama," "dance drama," or "dance theater" occur among all the world's peoples and date back at least to Paleolithic times. The terms themselves can be confusing because they vary according to who is using them. *Performance* is an inclusive term meaning the activities of actors, dancers, musicians, and their spectators and audiences. *Theater, dance,* and *music* are equivalent terms each referring to a specific genre of performance. *Theater* emphasizes narrative, *dance* emphasizes movement, and *music* emphasizes sound. *Drama* is written narrative dialogue.

Dancing, singing, wearing masks and costumes; impersonating other people, animals, or supernaturals (or being possessed by these others); acting stories, retelling the hunt; presenting time one at time two; rehearsing and preparing special places and times for these presentations—all are coexistent with the human condition. Even as scholars argue which came first, "entertainment" or "ritual," evidence abounds that the two are indissolubly braided together. For most, if not all, of human history, people have assembled both to be entertained and to achieve certain results by means of performance. Only recently have performances been treated as a commodity. This bias is possibly temporary. At present it is far from universal even within those cultures, like Western Europe and North America, that are most addicted to consumerism.

What do we know of the Paleolithic dancers-musicians-shamans-actors who used the caves of southwest Europe such as Tuc d'Audoubert? A modern spelunker follows a sunken river to a steep shaft and then must "crawl through claustrophobic low passages to reach the startling footprints of ancient dancers in bare feet and the models of copulating bisons, in clay on the floor beyond" (La Barre, 1970, p. 397). What was going on in the recesses of Tuc d'Audoubert? The footprints tell us that there was circular movement of people. Surviving bone and ivory "instruments" indicate that percussion, or even bull-roarers, may have been used in those remote times (Pfeiffer, 1982). The cave at Rocadel Moros near Lerida, Spain, contains markings and inscriptions indicating continuous use over a duration of two to three hundred generations (La Barre, 1970, p. 399). Caves and rock shelters in every habitable continent attest to the ancient, worldwide, and persistent presence of human ritual art.

These performance spaces—shall I call them theaters, shrines, or temples?—hidden in the earth and lit by torch, probably housed ceremonies concerning hunting and fertility. It is clear why the two are associated. Even today, among the hunters of the Kalahari Desert, when a large animal is taken, a brief ritual entreats the gods to replenish the game. As with animals, so with humans. The erotic temple sculptures at Konarak (Orissa, India, thirteenth century) are but one example among many joining fertility, dancing, and music. This ancient and abiding association of the performing arts with sexuality is one of the reasons churches and governments have tried to repress performers: there is a fine line, often crossed, between licit and illicit celebrations of fertility. Perhaps the illicit suggests the dangerous, the concealed, the difficult of access.

The secrecy that seems to have been part of the Paleolithic performances continues to this day. Ritual performance specialists ration and guard not only what they do but how they do it. Secret techniques are passed on within a family, as in Japanese *nō*, or they are kept within a special group or limited to one gender, as in the case of many initiation rites. This secrecy may partly explain the continuity of basic performance conventions from Paleolithic times to our own. Such conservatism needs to be understood, especially as we note that ritual, as Victor Turner emphasized, can also be the leading edge of change, even revolutionary change. What is conservative procedurally can be radical in terms of consciousness, individual behavior, and social structure.

Varieties of Performance. Performance and ritual interrelate in myriad combinations: in initiations and shamanic healing and exorcism; in the Mass, the Hindu temple service, and many other religious ceremonies; in great cycle plays, parades, and public celebrations of power both sacred and secular; in constructing and presenting the self in everyday life and in social role playing. There are ritual performances, rituals in performances, the ritual frames separating performance reality from the ordinary, and the ritual process underlying how performances are made. There is even performance as ritual—a postmodern attempt to resacralize experience by means of performance. Each of these circumstances must be understood separately before one can grasp the overall relationship between ritual and performance.

Even as the codifiers of the Judaic, Christian, and Islamic traditions often, and bitterly, opposed the theater of characterization and mimesis, they encouraged singing and certain forms of dancing. And despite interdictions and punishments, the most "dangerous" kind of performance—sexual mime, political and anticlerical satire, and farce—thrive always. The Mass is not only a source of medieval and Renaissance theater, but is itself inherently theatrical; ritual is a "doing," and therefore performative. To circumambulate a shrine, to light candles, to offer food, to sing orchant prayers, to "fall out" in the aisles, to be "ridden" by Ogun—all are ritual performances, as are the nearly silent meditations of a group of Buddhist monks assembled in a Kyoto shrine.

Frequently, worship, theater, dance, music, and healing overlap. Many secular performances incude a sacral dimension, and almost all sacred activities involve performing. In India this connection is rooted in the fundamental religious-aesthetic belief that performing is an offering to the gods. Traditionally, *devadāsīs* ("servants of God") danced to please the deities. Performances are often offered in temples as fulfillment of vows, thanksgiving, prayer, and celebrations of specific holidays. Masked dancing and theater in many parts of Africa and *kachina* dancing among the Hopi and Zuni of the American Southwest are further examples of worship that is consciously and fully theatrical. Anyone who has attended a church where gospel singing is part of the service has experienced the same thing. Among peoples who practice shamanism, performance is not only religious but medical. The shaman's singing, dancing, and theatrical storytelling relate her or his journey to, and adventures in, another world where the shaman battles malevolent or angry demons. Through this performacne, in which the audience often participates, a sick person is healed or lost.

The Ḥasidim, among the most fervent of Jews, sing and dance to ecstasy. Ḥasidim are deeply attached to their Simḥat Torah dances, their Purim plays (Yi., *Purimshpiln)* and masquerades. During Purim 1982 the Felt Forum of Manhattan's Madison Square Garden was filled with more than eighteen hundred Ḥasidim attending a production in Yiddish of *The Golem of Prague.* Like the traditional Purim plays, *The Golem* can be regarded either as worship or as a fabulous popular entertainment. It is in fact both.

No religion contains teachings more hostile to theater than Islam, yet the popular theater of the Middle East—Turkey and Iran in particular—is rich in a variety of both human and puppet forms. The *ta'ziyah* of the Shīʿī Muslims is an intense religious ritual and passion play that retells the martyrdom of Ḥusayn, the grandson of the prophet Muḥammad. So involved is the *ta'ziyah* audience that many spectators weep and flail themselves in sympathy with Ḥusayn's fate. Among Muslim mystics, the legendary dancing of the Mevlevīs (known in the West as the "Whirling Dervishes") arose in Anatolia under the inspiration of the poetic-religious philosophy of the thirteenth-century Ṣūfī sage Jalāl al-Dīn Rūmī (known also as Mawlānā). The intentions and mood of Mevlevī dancing is something like that of the Shakers, a Christian religious sect of the nineteenth and twentieth centuries. [*See* Taʿziyah; Darwīsh; Shakers; *and the biography of Rūmī.*]

Not all performances in the Islamic world are sacred. Alongside *ta'ziyah* is *rū-ḥūẓī*, an Iranian slapstick folk theater with connections to both *commedia dell'arte* and the popular theater of North India. And the Muslims of Indonesia—the nation with the world's largest Muslim population—delight in shadow puppets, live theater and dance (with stories from Hindu religious literature), and music.

Apparently, no amount of opposition can make people give up theater, dance, or music. Performance finds ways either in the interstices of the very doctrines that seek to stop it or it goes outside, "to the people," who cherish their entertainments, especially those that bring the mighty low and are often scatological, off-color, and sexy.

In India itself the prejudice against theater voiced by the *Manusmṛti* (second century CE) is more than overcome by the immensely influential *Nāṭya Śāstra* (second century BCE to second century CE). If anything, Hinduism is biased in favor of performance. Religious-cosmic theories of *līlā* and *māyā* (terms meaning performance, play, sport, illusion) posit a world that is a theatrical event on a cosmic scale. Thus India, like Africa, enjoys a profusion of dance, music, and theater.

The situation in the West is fraught with irony. The antitheatrical prejudice was articulated in Athens by Plato in the fifth century BCE at the close of the first great age of theater: all artists, but theater people especially, were to be chased from Plato's republic. Plato's arguments were later elaborated and ingrained into church doctrine by Tertullian and Augustine. But both Plato and Augustine were passionately involved in theater: Plato's dialogues are philosophical dramas, while Augustine the saint repented Augustine the avid theatergoer.

Why have Western and Islamic religious leaders been uncomfortable with theater, ambivalent about dance, but friendly to music? Theater is censored because it is dangerous, that is, subversive; dance is condemned because it is immoral, that is, sexual. Music, because it is abstract, can most easily be made to suit the ceremony at hand. The Puritans closed the theaters in England in the seventeenth century; in the twentieth century, Archbishop Twardowski of Poland ordered his priests to refuse absolution to women who danced the Charleston. Yet theater in the twentieth century has been censored more by the state than the church.

Still, despite all suspicions and condemnations, Western churches have used theater and dance. The great cycle plays of medieval England were ritual theater on a grand scale. One show was the complete history of humankind from the Creation through the Fall, the Flood, and the Crucifixion, then on to the Last Judgment. The performances—replete with angels, devils, hellmouth, and Eden—often ran from dawn to dusk for many days. Cycles consisted of a number of individual plays staged in different locations throughout a town. For example, at York in 1554, fifty-seven plays were put on at twelve to sixteen locations. These extraordinary cycles arose out of a confluence of the Mass, the *Quem quaeritis* trope, and popular entertainments that never died out from Roman times and whose shamanistic origins date back to prehistory. The cycles peaked in the fourteenth through sixteenth centuries. Although most were extinguished by the Renaissance, some remnants persist today, not so much in the famed Oberammergau performances as among Native American and Hispanic peoples.

The Yaqui Waehma begins at Lent and intensifies week by week, climaxing on Good Friday and Holy Saturday. Waehma retells the Passion, joining indigenous performance techniques to the religious theater brought from Europe by the Jesuits in the seventeenth and eighteenth centuries. Much of what the Yaqui do today took shape during the decades after 1767, when the Jesuits were withdrawn from the New World. Waehma consists of thirty to forty episodes and observances. The story focuses on the actions of masked figures called Chapayekas who join the Soldiers of Rome in the pursuit and crucifixion of Jesus. Waehma takes place everywhere in a Yaqui town or settlement: in the church, in various households, and along the Way of the Cross, which the Yaqui call the *konti vo'o.* Although the Chapayekas are successful in capturing and killing Jesus, they are not able to impose their rule permanently on the church. Three times the Chapayekas and the Soldiers of Rome storm the church on Holy Saturday morning. Inside the church are many children, "little angels," armed with small sticks. Close by are sacred Matachin dancers, Pascola ritual clowns, and a Deer dancer. Each time the Chapayekas and the Soldiers assault the church, they are driven back by little angels and by the flowers and leaves that the Pascolas and the Deer throw at them. The Matachinis dance, the church bell peals in alarm and celebration. The flowers and leaves represent both Christ's blood and the sacred *huya aniya,* the "flower world," of the Yaqui. Once pelted by such strong, good forces, the Chapayekas are defeated and transformed. They cast off their masks, soon to be burned along with an effigy of Judas, and rush into the church to kneel there in thanks. Not until Easter Sunday, after the biggest fiesta of the Yaqui year is over, is an official representative of the Roman Catholic church welcome.

The symbolism of the Yaqui ritual is so dense because it is a dynamic system of conscious oppositions and interpenetrations. In *The Yaquis* (Tucson, 1980), Edward H. Spicer notes that

> Waehma is many things . . . but its various facets constitute a unity of religious expression. Its action brings together most, or even all of the persons of a Yaqui community . . . it is therefore to be regarded as the most inclusive cooperative enterprise Yaquis engage in as Yaquis. . . . The ceremonial also makes explicit, in fact acted out for all to see, the most highly valued principles of human conduct; in this respect it is an elaborate morality play devoted to the allegory of the triumph of Yaqui social, political, and ecclesiastical institutions over evil made visible by the actors. (p. 71)

The Rāmlīlās (Skt., Rāmalīlā) of North India (see Schechner, 1985, pp. 151–212), performed annually in thousands of villages and cities, are much like Waehma. They are cycle plays dramatizing the acts of Rāma, the seventh incarnation of Viṣṇu. Rāmlīlās last anywhere from one to thirty-one days, depending upon where they are performed and under what circumstances. The greatest Rāmlīlā is that of Rāmnagar, patronized by the maharaja of Banaras. On big days (such as when Śiva's bow is broken by Rāma or when Rāma slays Rāvaṇa) Rāmnagar Rāmlīlā attracts crowds of up to eighty thousand. Among the crowds at Rāmnagar "spending a month with Rāma" are workers, farmers, professionals, and many *sadhus*, or holy people.

Rāma's story, as well known in India as the story of Jesus is in the West, is the subject of Vālmīki's Sanskrit epic *Rāmāyaṇa* and Tulsīdās's sixteenth-century Hindi version, *Rāmcaritmanas.* It is Tulsī's poem that is sung in the Rāmlīlā. Rāmlīlā is environmental theater; in other words, different sites are dedicated to key scenes: Ayodhyā is the site of Rāma's birthplace; Janakpur, the residence of Rāma's bride, Sītā; Chitrakut, the place where Rāma, Sītā, and Rāma's brother, Lakṣmana, begin their twelve-year exile; Pañcāvatī, where Sītā is kidnapped by the ten-headed demon king of Laṅka, Rāvaṇa; Rameṣvaram, where Rāma and the monkey general Hanuman lead their armies across a great bridge into Laṅka; and Laṅka, where the final battles against Rāvaṇa are fought. Spectators follow the action from place to place. Rāma, Sītā, Lakṣmana, Bharata, and Śatrughna are played by five young boys called *swarūps* or "forms," of the gods. While these boys wear their costumes and crowns, they are thought by many actually to be the gods a theater-minded person would say they are "representing."

Rāmlīlā deploys a complex of performance activities: theater, music, recitation and chanting, procession, and temple service. At Rāmnagar, the maharaja, often seated atop his royal elephant, is himself part of the performance. His attendance at each day's *līlā* is watched closely by the crowds. On special days the maharaja enters into the drama, attending Rāma's coronation, listening to Rāma's teachings, welcoming Rāma to the palace where the maharaja and his family attend Sītā, Rāma, and his brothers as they feast. The action of Rāmlīlā is simultaneously physical, narrative, and symbolic. Many believe the month of Rāmlīlā is when "God dwells among the people." It is a season of high festivity.

Great ritual cycles also persisted until the 1930s among the Elema of Irian Barat (Indonesian New Guinea). The Elema *hevehe* cycle of dances, festivities, and ritual observances sometimes took more than thirty years to finish. This extreme extension of time is characteristic of ritual cycles. Such performances are not mimetic: they symbolize and actualize simultaneously. In doing so they mesh the ordinary lives of the performers with the extraordinary activities of culture heroes. Far from being a "leisure activity"—as much modern theater and dance is—the medieval Christian cycles, the Waehma, the Rāmlīlās of North India, and the *hevehe* are "works of the gods," obligatory as well as celebratory. They demand a big share of the community's attention, energy, and wealth. Such a price is paid because these performances are the dynamic constructions of reality by means of which the whole community knows itself.

Ritual Frames. All performances, sacred and secular, are ritually framed. Frames mark and modulate transformations of time, space, and/or consciousness, signaling that a performance is about to begin or that a return to the ordinary is imminent. Sometimes frames are so "conventional" they are all but forgotten: the dimming of houselights, the lighting of candles, the final applause, the sprinkling of holy water. There is a continuum between religious frames and aesthetic ones, with many intermediate cases.

In the Ẹfẹ-Gẹlẹdẹ performances of the Yoruba, Ogbagba ("the divine mediator") and Arabi Ajigbale ("the sweeper") are "always invoked first to 'clear the way.' . . . They mediate the transition between everyday, ordinary activity . . . and spiritual activity. . . . [They] carry the festival into the world" (Drewal and Drewal, 1983, pp. 64–65). Ẹfẹ's closing dance is performed by "a special masquerader representing the deified ancestress of the community. Her appearance reassures the crowd of the mother's blessings and signals the conclusion of a successful festival as all reluctantly disperse to their compounds" (ibid., p. 37).

In the *kathakali* of India, even when danced as a tourist entertainment, performances begin by the lighting of the *kalivilakku,* a bronze oil lamp identical to that used in Hindu temple services. The *kalivilakku* burns throughout the performance, reminding all that *kathakali* is an offering to the gods, who are the first and most important spectators. Every performance closes with the *dhanasi,* a short prayer-dance. *Kathakali* developed in the seventeenth century from antecedents reaching back to the Sanskrit theater of the fifth to tenth centuries. One form of Sanskrit theater, *kutiyattam,* is still performed in temples. *Kathakali's* other roots are the martial art *kalarippayatt* and *teyyam* folk ritual. Most of a *kathakali* performance, which can last from less than an hour at a tourist hotel to all night in a Kerala village, is made of stories taken from the Hindu epics, *Rāmāyaṇa* and *Mahābhārata,* or from the Purāṇas. During a *kathakali* performance in a village, it is common enough to see people rise with hands clasped in front of them in the devotional pose, worshipfully honoring the performer playing, say, Śiva, as the god himself. Thus the theater and the temple meet.

The ritual frames of *nō* are as much aesthetic as they are religious. *Nō* arose in Japan during the fourteenth and fifteenth centuries out of shamanism, Shintō, Buddhism, and *sarugaku,* a popular entertainment that included magic, songs, and dances performed at shrines by troupes attached to Buddhist monasteries. The monasteries themselves mixed religious, political, and military elements. *Nō* today preserves its origins, and popular entertainment is continued by *kyōgen,* the comic plays that always alternate with *nō.* In *nō,* elements of shamanism are present in the great earthen jugs that resound under the polished wooden floor of the stage, in the procedures for entering and leaving the stage, and in the exorcistic action of many *nō* dramas. *Nō* theater architecture retains many qualities of a Shintō shrine.

Entering the *nō* stage is a two-part process. In the *kagami no ma* ("mirror room") the *shite* ("masked actor") gazes at himself in the mirror. He simultaneously merges with his mask and distances himself from it. The *shite* seeks an incomplete transformation, a dialectical tension between the power of the mask and his skills as an actor. But even when the *shite* achieves a proper state of mind he cannot enter the stage directly. He must first cross the *hashigakari* (literally, "suspension bridge") that links the mirror room to the stage. When the play is over the *shite* returns to the mirror room via the *hashigakari,* removes his mask, and carefully studies it before putting it away. This double framing—in the mirror room, on the *hashigakari*—reminds performers and spectators alike of the aesthetic ritual quality of *nō.*

How different are the ritual frames of Ẹfẹ-Gẹlẹdẹ or *kathakali* from what the *shite* does? And how far is what the *shite* does from what Konstantin Stanislavsky told the actors he trained? "You must prepare yourself for your first entrance on the stage while you are still at home." A performance day ought to be "uncluttered." Upon arrival at the theater, there is to be no gossip. "You must forget about life as a whole except that slice of it which is resounding in your heart as the life of the stage." As with the *shite* in the mirror room, the Stanislavsky-trained actor concentrates on the being into which he or she is transforming. Stanislavsky emphasized techniques of "concentration" to help the actor become the character. Techniques of ritual framing are thoroughly embedded in modern theater. These function just like sacred ritual frames, separating the ordinary from the nonordinary, marking the temporal, spatial, and psychosocial boundaries of the performance. Failure to establish the proper frames not only ruins the performance but spoils its fruits, what it is meant to accomplish.

Ritual Process: Ethological and Neurological. In *On Aggression* (New York, 1967), Konrad Lorenz relates how, just before World War I, Julian Huxley

> discovered the remarkable fact that certain movement patterns lose, in the course of phylogeny, their specific function and become purely "symbolic" ceremonies. He called this process ritualization and used this term without quotation marks; in other words, he equated the cultural processes leading to the development of human rites with the phylogenetic processes giving rise to such remarkable "ceremonies" in animals. (pp. 54–55)

All animals, including humans, exist within the same ecological web, but not all animals are alike: analogies must be put forward cautiously. The "dances" of bees are not dances in the human sense. Where everything is genetically determined, there is no art. To ethologists a ritual is a behavior sequence genetically transformed over the course of aeons. Behavior is rearranged, condensed, sped up or slowed down; functions change so that, for example, threat behavior becomes part of a "mating dance." Movements are exaggerated or simplified, becoming rhythmical and repetitive, often freezing into postures. Along with behavioral changes, conspicuous body structures develop such as a peacock's feathers or a moose's antlers.

Rituals in nonhuman animals do not occur haphazardly. They are associated with troublesome encounters: definitions of territory, hierarchy, mating, and access to food. Human rituals, which develop their particular details individually and socially rather than genetically, also cluster around the troublesome "mysteries" and "crises" of birth, puberty, marriage; sickness, healing, and death; war; hunting; the cycle of the seasons with their planting, harvest and fallow times, their times of rain and drought; the predictability or unpredictability of natural disasters and upheavals. Animal ritual deals with these on a strictly nonideological basis, through action rather than through thought. Most humans also deal with these mysteries and crises through ritual action. Ritual is the thought of the people. Anxieties are relieved and solidarity celebrated by ritual performances, the formal qualities of which are repetition, exaggeration, condensation, simplification, and spectacle. Human love of group singing and dancing, marching, mass displays, flag waving, cheering, clapping, and stamping may be individually or socially constructed even while being ethologically based.

In short, human rituals use sacrifice, violence, and celebration to express the plea, explicit or implicit, for "success" in living and dying. The integration of music, dance, and theater; the rhythmic sound-making and group movement; the display of masks and costumes; the processions, food sharing, fire burning, and bell ringing; the smell of incense: together all these give the audience, the congregation, or the entranced a deep, animal satisfaction.

In *The Spectrum of Ritual* (1979), d'Aquili, Laughlin, and McManus write: "One may trace the evolutionary progression of ritual behavior from the emergence of formalization through the coordination of formalized communicative behavior and sequences of ritual behavior to the conceptualization of such sequences and the assignment of symbols to them by man" (p. 37). Based on studies of brain structure and function, they propose a "cognitive imperative"—a peculiar human need to explain experience. Linking this cognitive imperative to ethological ritual yields the need to perform the relationships connecting immediate, individual experience to larger, even absolute, categories. There is a unique human need not only to explain things but to perform the explanations. Human rituals are theatrical, conceptual, and intellectual. "Human beings have no choice but to construct myths to explain their world. The mythic material may be social, or they may appear individually in dreams, daydreams, or fantasies" (ibid., p. 171).

The powerful feelings sometimes aroused by performances can be understood in terms of brain lateralization. The left side of the brain is "ergotropic" (energy-expending) and the right side is "trophotropic" (energy-conserving). D'Aquili and Laughlin propose that when one side is extremely stimulated a "spillover" arouses the other side "so that, briefly at least, both systems are intensely stimulated" (ibid., p. 175). This spillover can occur in shamanizing, trance dancing, yogic *samādhi*, and aesthetic performances.

The ethological and neurological theories answer some very important questions. They help explain not only the extraordinary persistence of performance conventions and the need for ritual frames to manage such powerful forces but also the apparently identical experiences of performers and their audience-spectator-participants down through many epochs and across cultures, genres, ideologies, and religous systems. The universality of trance—whether associated with dancing, singing, speaking in tongues, shamanizing, meditation, or hypnosis and whether individual or collective—is at least partly explained by the spillover theory.

What the ethologists and neurologists do not explain are the unique, creative qualities of ritual performance. For ritual is not just a conservator of evolutionary and species-specific behavior and thought; it is important also as a generator of new images, ideas, and practices. As Victor Turner put it in "Body, Brain, and Culture" (*Zygon* 18, 1983), one of his last writings:

> If ritualization, as discussed by Huxley, Lorenz, and other ethologists, has a biogenetic foundation, while meaning has a neocortical learned base, does this mean that creative pro-

> cesses, those which generate new cultural knowledge, might result from a coadaptation perhaps in the ritual process itself, of genetic and cultural information? (p. 228)

Ritual Process: Anthropological. Turner was among the first to emphasize the generative, creative, "antistructural" qualities of ritual. In examining these, he uncovered deep connections linking ritual, theatrical, and social processes. Turner elaborated on ideas implicit in Arnold van Gennep's *Les rites de passage* (1908). According to van Gennep, rites of passage—whether individual or collective, life-crisis or calendrical—follow a three-phase pattern: separation, transition or liminal phase, and reincorporation. Turner saw that the liminal phase—"betwixt and between" personal and social categories—was full of "positive and active qualities." As he wrote in *From Ritual to Theatre* (1982, p. 41), " 'Meaning' in culture tends to be generated at the interfaces between established cultural subsystems, though meanings are then institutionalized and consolidated at the centers of such systems."

These interfaces are dynamic hotbeds of "anti-structure" and "spontaneous communitas." By *communitas* Turner means

> the liberation of human capacities of cognition, affect, volition, creativity, etc., from the normative constraints incumbent upon occupying a sequence of social statuses, enacting a multiplicity of social roles, and being acutely conscious of membership in some corporate group. . . . Sociocultural systems drive so steadily towards consistency that human individuals only get off these normative hooks in rare situations. (Turner, 1982, p. 44)

An individual's experience of spontaneous *communitas* is the spillover phenomenon discussed above.

Thus two seemingly contradictory results are achieved during the liminal phase of a ritual: individuals are liberated from prior constraints on creativity and socially deviant behaviors, and, when this period of license ends, new statuses or norms are established or older ones reestablished. This describes perfectly the actions and importance of the Chapayekas among the Yaqui. This process Turner saw as channeling the living magma upwelling in all human societies: a periodic, temporary, molten creativity. It is also analogous to the training-workshop-rehearsal process of many if not all performance genres. Through this process all the "givens" or "ready-mades"—accepted texts, accepted ways of using the body, accepted feelings—are deconstructed, broken down into malleable bits of behavior, feeling, thought, and text. These bits are later reconstructed into a new order: the performance.

In traditional genres such as *kathakali*, *nō*, or ballet, neophytes begin training early in life. Training involves learning new ways of speaking, gesturing, and moving and maybe even new ways of thinking and feeling. New for the trainee, that is, but traditional for the genre. An important feature of *kathakali* training is the deep massage that actually reorients muscles and bones to the extreme turn-out and arched back necessary to perform *kathakali*. A no less radical reconstruction of the body is required for ballet. As in initiation rites, the mind and body are made ready to be written on in the language of the form being learned. Training enables the performer to speak *nō*, *kathakali*, or ballet: he or she is incorporated into the tradition, no longer a neophyte but an initiated member.

Turner went far beyond van Gennep in suggesting that the rites of tribal, agrarian, and traditional societies were like the artworks and leisure activities of industrial and postindustrial societies. These Turner called "liminoid," meaning they were like but not identical to liminal rites. Liminal rites are obligatory while liminoid activities are voluntary. Thus the workshops of experimental theater and dance are liminoid means of psychophysical retraining. While in liminal rites traditional behavior is inscribed, in liminoid arts new behaviors are created. But if the liminoid "initiations" called workshops are examined in detail one sees that "readymade," or old behaviors are deconstructed into flexible bits so that when reconstructed in different combinations they are experienced as new. Thus the avant-garde always appears to be advancing. Taking a longer view, say from 1875 to 1985, it is clear that elements of earlier avant-garde movements are recycled. And taking the very long view—from Paleolithic times to now—art does not advance at all in the ways science and technology do.

Resacralizing Performance. Orthodox scholarship says that theater "comes from" ritual, but the opposite is also true. In modern and postmodern societies, many people alienated from conventional religious ritual are turning to theater and dance, the "human potential" movement, and various forms of psychophysical therapy. In traditional societies, and in pockets of traditionalism in modern societies, there has been a resurgence of "fundamentalism." These movements within Hinduism, Judaism, Islam, Christianity, and other religions have their counterparts in the performing arts.

Since around 1960 theater and dance directors like Jerzy Grotowski, Anna Halprin, Tadashi Suzuki, Peter Brook, and Eugenio Barba have run workshops that are more "models for living" than preparations for performances. They have used, and transformed, rituals from Asia, Europe, Native America, and Africa. Their work is at the core of a thriving intercultural performance movement. Grotowski has been especially instrumental.

From 1959 to 1969 he developed and propagated his ideas of the "holy actor." This actor "works in public with his body, offering it publicly [as] a spiritual act." In *Towards a Poor Theatre* (Holstebro, Denmark, 1968), Grotowski insists the "holy actor" is not religious in the ordinary sense:

> I speak about "holiness" as an unbeliever. I mean a "secular holiness." If the actor, by setting himself a challenge publicly challenges others, and through excess, profanation and outrageous sacrilege reveals himself by casting off his everyday mask, he makes it possible for the spectator to undertake a similar process of self-penetration. If he does not exhibit his body, but annihilates it, burns it, frees it from every resistance to any psychic impulse, then he does not sell his body but sacrifices it. He repeats the atonement; he is close to holiness. (p. 34)

Grotowski's methods include not only rigorous exercises derived from Russian, Chinese, and Indian disciplines but also investigations "into the latest results in sciences such as psychology, anthropology, myth interpretation, and the history of religion" (ibid., p. 48). After 1967 Grotowski moved away from "theatre in the theatre." He undertook a series of "paratheatrical" experiments in Europe, the Caribbean, North and South America, and Asia. Trance dancing, Haitian Voodoo, Bengali Baul singing, and classical Asian dances were used as well as Grotowski's own techniques perhaps adapted from the human potential movement: face-to-face encounters and "vigils," improvised chanting and movement, running in total darkness through the woods, "passing fire" from person to person. What knit these experiments together was their seeking for the "authentic" or "genuine" in person-to-person interactions. Grotowski seemed to want spontaneous *communitas* detached from any specific religion. In 1983 Grotowski began his "objective drama" project, synthesizing elements of rituals of various cultures. Grotowski believes these have an "objective" impact on participants separate from their theological or symbolic significance.

Ritual Mythos. But what about meaning? Is it true that many rituals mean nothing, that what is sustaining about them is their ethological and neurological functions of group solidarity and individual release? Should scholars focus on ritual structure, as Frits Staal has demanded? ("The Search for Meaning: Mathematics, Music, and Ritual," *American Journal of Semiotics* 2, 1984, pp. 1–57). Or is there a thematic dimension to ritual that cannot be ignored?

From the end of the nineteenth century into the first decades of the twentieth, the "Cambridge anthropologists," working under the influence of James G. Frazer, developed a theory of ritual—especially the relationship between ritual and ancient Greek dance-drama-theater—that profoundly influenced all subsequent considerations. The work of Jane Ellen Harrison, Francis M. Cornford, and Gilbert Murray joined with the archetype theory of C. G. Jung to set the stage for the theories of Joseph Campbell, Susanne K. Langer, and Northrop Frye. The tendency of this thinking is the assertion that certain "ritual patterns" underlay Greek theater in particular and all theater in general. Although many of the historical details of the Cambridge theory have been discredited, the basic idea remains very attractive: Tragedy is a subspecies of comedy, and both are subsumed in an overall ritual pattern of struggle, sacrificial death, dismemberment, and resurrection. In Frye's words,

> Romance, tragedy, irony and comedy are all episodes in a total quest-myth. . . . The ritual pattern behind the catharsis of comedy is the resurrection that follows the death, the epiphany or manifestation of the risen hero. . . . Christianity, too, sees tragedy as an episode in the divine comedy, the larger scheme of redemption and resurrection. (Frye, 1957, p. 215)

Frye's references are Christian, but his description suits the classic Sanskrit dramas of Kālidāsa better than it does the wrenching violence of the Jacobeans, not to mention Shakespeare's more grisly pieces. Is Frye on to something universal? Does the theory work interculturally?

The other major attempt to specify ritual universality is Turner's notion of "social drama." A social drama follows a four-part sequence: breach, crisis, redressive action, and reintegration (or schism). A breach is an underlying fault in social life (the Montague-Capulet feud in *Romeo and Juliet*, the Cold War); a crisis is a precipitating event that cannot be overlooked (Romeo and Juliet falling in love, the blockade of Berlin by the Russians); redressive action is what is done to resolve, or attempt to resolve, the crisis; reintegration or schism are the two outcomes of the whole process. Characteristics of this four-phase process are the sudden eruptions of crisis out of a more or less quiescent breach and the often very complicated and drawn out redressive action. Aesthetic drama condenses this whole process, religious ritual condenses and repeats it, and social life extenuates it.

Turner himself sees things slightly differently. He links social drama, aesthetic theater, and the ritual process by asserting that

> the world of theater, as we know it both in Asia and America, and the immense variety of theatrical sub-genres derive not from imitation, conscious or unconscious, of the processual form of the complete or "satiated" social drama—

> breach, crisis, redress, reintegration, or schism—but specifically from its third phase, the one I call redress, especially from redress as ritual process. (Turner, 1985, p. 294)

This third phase Turner sees as a transformation and elaboration of the liminal stage of the ritual process.

If universality is the advantage, reductivism is the weakness of both the Cambridge and Turner theories. Turner's "social drama" theory is stronger than the Cambridge theory because it is not tied to a particular (Christian) narrative. But it is tied to Western aesthetics, with its appetite for conflict, crisis, and resolution. The themes of *nō*, Yoruba masked dances, *kathakali*, Siberian or Korean shamanism, Voodoo, or for that matter, of the syncretic Christian-Yaqui Waehma are not all satisfactorily explainable in terms of crisis and crisis-resolution. Sometimes, "redress" or "reintegration" are not wanted. Birth, death, sickness, puberty, marriage, conflict, wars, storms, earthquakes, droughts, and volcanic eruptions are not the monopoly of any culture. But the performance responses to these life events are wildly different. There is such a contradictory diversity of cultures that the "universal" themes and structures of comedy and tragedy as understood from the Greco-Christian religious or Western aesthetic perspectives are not clearly discernible outside their habitats.

Nō would seem to be a good test of Frye's and Turner's theses. On the surface there are plenty of resemblances between *nō* and classic Greek theater. A traditional program alternates the serious *nō* with the comic *kyōgen;* and *nō* itself contains both protagonist and chorus. But these resemblances are superficial. Neither *nō* nor *kyōgen* (or the two together) works out the basic "ritual action" of struggle, dismemberment, and resurrection that the Cambridge school sees at the heart of tragedy and comedy. Nor is the resolution of conflict arising out of crisis the goal of *nō*. In fact, the opposite is true. *Nō* invokes souls who can find no rest—a world populated by ghosts of Hamlet's father. These beings do not seek revenge but an audience: a chance to make themselves present again and again. They extenuate and elaborate their performances, rather than strive to conclude them. *Nō* plays end with the *shite* simply exiting, her or his story displayed but unresolved, the restless spirit at best temporarily relieved. The underlying action of many *nō* plays is not the resolution of a conflict nor a quest for resurrection, a Christian eternal life, but a shaman's exorcism or the seeking (but not finding) of Buddhist extinction.

The *shite* actually plays a double role. In the first part of a *nō*, he is often a caretaker, a recluse, or a person tied to a place where "something happened." In the second part, the *shite*—transformed into the true or essential form of the one associated with this spot—a defeated warrior, a betrayed wife, a grieving mother, a red-crested crane, the pine trees Sumiyoshi and Takasago, a god or goddess, the female demon Yamamba—dances and sings the story of his character's passion. The *waki*, the second actor, is both shaman and witness; he inquires, evokes, looks, and listens. A chorus of six to ten men, present on stage for the whole performance, chants parts of the story, adds descriptive passages, and even sometimes speaks with and for the *shite*, sharing his consciousness. Some believe the chorus originated as men chanting Buddhist *sūtras*. In addition to the chorus are four musicians playing drums and flute. Their music is percussive not melodic: it echoes the *shite*'s mood while driving him on. *Nō* plays are short—thirty to forty minutes each—but the cumulative effect of a program of five *nō* and four *kyōgen* is powerful. Maybe no exorcism occurs, but the ghosts have had their chance to tell their stories and show their dances. The *kyōgen* that alternate with *nō* are about bridegrooms or henpecked husbands, foolish feudal lords, animals, wrestlers, sly or drunk servants who outwit their masters, or *yamabushi*, "mountain priests" regarded by some as demigods, by others as demons. In *Kusabira* the *yamabushi* is more like the sorcerer's apprentice. In attempting to rid a gentleman of the pesky mushrooms ruining his garden, the *yamabushi* casts spells that only increase the number of fungi. In brief, *nō* makes present the dead and demonic, while *kyōgen* laughs at the foibles, superstitions, and hypocrisies of this world.

Conclusions. The varieties of ritual performances are uncountable. And ritual as such is part of the warp and woof of every kind of performance, religious and secular. There are no universal performative themes, actions, or patterns other than the ethological and neurological processes that shape the formal qualities and special experiences of the performer and spectator. All performances are ritually framed, but what these frames are and what they signify varies from culture to culture, even from performance to performance. Individual performances do not tell universal stories so much as provide observers with ways of understanding particular cultural and subcultural circumstances. Performers give participants a concrete, sensuous, and sometimes overwhelmingly powerful experience of cultural values. The similarity of the initiation-ritual process to the training-workshop-rehearsal process makes it probable that not only will religious ritual be secularized but that aesthetic performances will be sacralized: a very complicated two-way system.

What is it that makes a person human? A nexus of circumstances: speech, bipedal locomotion, brain size and complexity, social organization. But more too: when a certain primate learned to "re-actualize"—to dance, sing, and act out what was dreamed and remembered—a definite threshold was crossed. A performance of a nightmare, of yesterday's hunt or encounter with a strange band, of a sound heard in the forest—each are "second actualities" that when performed well rival the first in detail and presence. This second actuality has additional qualities that make it even superior to the first: it can be based on what is not, as easily as on what is: the "recalled" or "restored" dream, hunt, encounter, or sound may be imaginary. And it can be elaborated on and improved through repetition. What counts is how well it is performed and how neatly it fits, or adds to, an existing or emerging worldview. Thus three classes of performance events are possible: what was, what is imagined, and what falls between history and imagination. This third class of events, which shares both in the authority of recollection and the creativity of the imagination, is most powerful. Moreover, once such a realm of virtual actuality is given concrete existence in performance, it can lead to a third, a fourth, . . ., an *n*th.

In these ways performance has always and everywhere been "in relation to" religion. Sometimes this relationship has been mutually supportive and sometimes hostile. There is nothing in performance that is intrinsically proreligious or antireligious. Archaeological and anthropological evidence indicates a coexistence of performance and religion at least since Paleolithic times. And the ethological and neurological evidence suggests that among humans ritual and performance are identical: repetitive, condensed, intense, communicative displays and doings. Articulated religious beliefs, aesthetic enjoyment and theories, political ideologies and manipulations: these are some of the uses people have found for ritual-performance behavior. As Victor Turner was fond of saying, "to make believe is to make belief."

[*See also* Ritual *and* Ritual Studies.]

BIBLIOGRAPHY

Aristotle was the first to propose an intimate connection between ritual, dance, music, and theater. In his *Poetics* he declared that Greek tragedy arose "as an improvisation (both tragedy and comedy are similar in this respect) on the part of those who led the dithyrambs, just as comedy arose from those who led the phallic songs" (chap. 4). E. R. Dodds in *The Greeks and the Irrational* (Berkeley, 1951) investigates the relationship between shamanism and the Greeks—thereby linking the sources of European culture with Asia. E. T. Kirby in *Ur-Drama: The Origins of Theatre* (New York, 1975) theorizes that all theater is originally shamanistic. The ancient Sanskrit *Nāṭyaśāstra,* edited and translated in two volumes by Manomohan Ghosh (Calcutta, 1961–1967), not only details how, what, where, and when to perform but also demonstrates the connection between performing and ancient Vedic-Hindu practices. For a detailed consideration of these connections, see M. Christopher Byrski's *Concept of Ancient Indian Theatre* (New Delhi, 1973). Discussions of the even earlier ritual performances of Paleolithic Europe are found in John E. Pfeiffer's *The Creative Explosion: An Inquiry into the Origins of Art and Religion* (New York, 1982) and in Weston La Barre's *The Ghost Dance* (Garden City, N.Y., 1970).

Perhaps the first modern attempt to make a systematic and comprehensive survey of the links among performance, mythology, and religion was James G. Frazer's *The Golden Bough,* 2 vols. (London, 1890), which he eventually expanded to twelve volumes and a supplement. Frazer's approach—encyclopedic, intercultural, comparative—stimulated much research and speculation. Among the most important of these investigations were those of Jane Ellen Harrison, Gilbert Murray, and Francis M. Cornford. These scholars felt they had discovered an ancient "primal ritual"—a seasonal death-rebirth drama common to the ancient Near East. See Harrison's *Themis* (Cambridge, 1912), which includes Murray, "Excursus on the Ritual Forms Preserved in Greek Tragedy," Harrison's *Ancient Art and Ritual* (London, 1913), and Cornford's *The Origin of Attic Comedy* (London, 1914). As provocative and suggestive as the ideas of these scholars are, they are open to strong criticism because the existence of the "primal ritual" cannot be proved; therefore, the relationship between it and succeeding Western theater (Greek, Elizabethan, modern) is at best tenuous. A. W. Pickard-Cambridge, in *Dithyramb, Tragedy and Comedy,* 2d rev. ed. (Oxford, 1962), convincingly critiques the Cambridge school. Regardless, Theodor H. Gaster in *Thespis,* 2d ed. (Garden City, N.Y., 1961), discusses traces of seasonal myths and rituals in the ancient Near East that might prefigure secular performance. And the ideas of Harrison et al. are popular among philosophers and literary theorists eager to specify the genres of "tragedy" and "comedy." Among the most notable works of this kind are Susanne Langer's *Feeling and Form* (New York, 1953) and Northrop Frye's *Anatomy of Criticism* (Princeton, 1957).

The relationship between ritual and performance has also been most fruitfully investigated by anthropologists and performance theorists, many of whom have fieldwork experience among living cultures. Such material has been gathered since the end of the nineteenth century. Under the anthropological aegis the discussion shifts to eyewitness and even participatory accounts of actual performances. These data form the basis for theories of ritual process. Anthropologists propose dynamic ongoing relationships between aesthetic, religious, and social performances. Among notable works in this area are the following: Mircea Eliade, *Rites and Symbols of Initiation* (New York, 1958) and *Shamanism: Archaic Techniques of Ecstasy,* rev. & enl. ed. (New York, 1964); Erving Goffman, *The Presentation of Self in Everyday Life* (Garden City, N.Y., 1959); Victor Turner, *The Ritual Process* (Chicago, 1969), *Dramas, Fields, and Metaphors* (Ithaca, N.Y., 1974), *From Ritual to Theatre* (New York, 1982), and *On the Edge of the Bush* (Tucson, 1985); Clifford Geertz, *The Interpretation of Cultures* (New York, 1973); Richard Schechner, *Essays on Performance Theory,* (New York, 1977;

new edition in progress) and *Between Theater and Anthropology* (Philadelphia, 1985); Sally F. Moore and Barbara G. Myerhoff, eds., *Secular Ritual* (Assen, 1977); Roy A. Rappaport, *Ecology, Meaning, and Religion* (Berkeley, 1979); Robert P. Armstrong, *The Powers of Presence: Consciousness, Myth, and Affecting Presence* (Philadelphia, 1981); and John J. MacAloon, ed., *Rite, Drama, Festival, Spectacle* (Philadelphia, 1984). A collection of studies relating ritual and drama is *Drama and Religion*, edited by James Redmond (Cambridge, 1983).

Ethologists and psychologists have also contributed to the discussion, focusing especially on the continuities between animal and human behavior and the relation of brain structure-function to ritual action and felt experience. See *Human Ethology*, edited by Mario von Cranach, Klaus Foppa, Wolf Lepenies, and Detlev Ploog (Cambridge, 1979), and *The Spectrum of Ritual* (New York, 1979) by Eugene G. d'Aquili, Charles D. Laughlin, Jr., and John McManus.

In addition to comprehensive and intercultural works, there are many studies of ritual performances in individual cultures. Only a few can be cited here: Baldwin Spencer and F. J. Gillen, *The Native Tribes of Central Australia* (London, 1899); Gregory Bateson, *Naven*, 2d ed. (Stanford, Calif., 1958); Raymond Firth, *Tikopia Ritual and Belief* (London, 1967); Victor Turner, *The Forest of Symbols* (Ithaca, N.Y., 1967); Richard A. Gould, *Yiwara: Foragers of the Australian Desert* (New York, 1969); F. E. Williams, *The Drama of the Oroko* (London, 1940); Edward L. Schieffelin, *The Sorrow of the Lonely and the Burning of the Dancers* (New York, 1976); Simon Ottenberg, *Masked Rituals of Afikpo* (Seattle, 1975); Charlotte J. Frisbie, ed., *Southwestern Indian Ritual Drama* (Albuquerque, 1980); Henry John Drewal and Margaret T. Drewal, *Gèlèdé: Art and Female Power among the Yoruba* (Bloomington, Ind., 1983); Frits Staal, ed., *Agni: The Vedic Ritual of the Fire Altar*, 2 vols. (Berkeley, 1983); and Bruce Kapferer, *A Celebration of Demons: Exorcism and the Aesthetics of Healing in Sri Lanka* (Bloomington, Ind., 1983).

RICHARD SCHECHNER

Ancient Near Eastern Ritual Drama

It is now commonly recognized that drama in the ancient Near East originated as a program of ritual acts performed at seasonal festivals, especially at the New Year festival. The central theme of this program was "off with the old, on with the new"; it was designed to mark the end of one lease of communal life and to ensure the next. The program is attested in many parts of the world and survives—albeit in attenuated form—in folk plays still performed in northern Greece and in such popular diversions as the English mummers' play.

The principal components of this ritual program are as follows:

1. The deposition (or even execution) of the reigning king, regarded as the embodiment of communal life momentarily ended, followed by the installation of a successor, regarded as a new avatar (or incarnation) of the ideal, perpetual kingship ("Le roi est mort; vive le roi!"). Often a temporary king is appointed during the interval.
2. The ceremonial "marriage" of the new king to a chosen bride in order to ensure the continued fecundity of the people. This epitomizes a brief period of sexual license observed by the community as a whole to the same end.
3. A combat between principals or teams symbolizing, respectively, new year and old, summer and winter, rainfall and drought, or simply life and death. When waged by principals, the victor (necessarily the embodiment of regeneration) becomes the king. Often the defeated antagonist is identified as a dragon who has impounded the subterranean waters and caused drought, or who has embroiled the sea and rivers and brought floods. His discomfiture ensures the irrigation of the soil in proper measure, and the power to control it is then formally vested in the victorious new king.
4. A communal feast, whereby members of the community recement their bonds of kinship by commensality, thus becoming companions in the literal sense of the word. The community's gods are thought to be present either as guests or as hosts. The ancestral dead are likewise in attendance, since the ongoing existence of the community necessarily involves the past as well as the present and future ("Our founders are with us in spirit").

Often the ritual program takes the form of the burial and subsequent disinterment of a puppet representing the temporary death and subsequent revival (resurrection) of vegetation and fertility.

Six factors turn this ritual program into drama in the modern sense of the term:

1. It comes to be interpreted as the representation in present time of a situation or process that essentially transcends the particular moment when it is performed—that is, as the punctualization of something essentially transtemporal. This is accomplished by representing the successive functional acts as incidents (or episodes) in a myth or story, the actors then impersonating supernatural beings, such as deities, or demons.
2. There is shift of focus from the ritual plot to the interplay of characters. The actors are no longer cardboard figures representing such abstractions as old year and new, life and death; the combat becomes one of conflicting personalities.
3. The action comes to be performed by a professional class (e.g., priests) rather than by the community as a whole. The broad masses then constitute an audi-

ence. This converts drama in the original sense of the term, namely, something done (Gr., *draō,* "do"), into theater, something watched (Gr., *theaomai,* "watch"), that is, into a spectacle.

4. Subsidiary elements are introduced in order to enhance popular interest and attention. Familiar songs are inserted in which the audience may join; messages are repeated verbatim when delivered, so that latecomers to the performance may catch up with the preceding action; the several incidents are tricked out with details drawn from traditional folklore; things are done abortively twice and successfully only at the third try, thereby increasing momentum and excitement.
5. The ritual combat is sometimes rationalized as the commemorative reenactment of a historical event, the actors being identified with traditional heroes and their adversaries. In certain parts of Greece, for instance, the opposing teams were portrayed as the followers of Alexander and Darius respectively, and in the English mummers' play they become at times King George and Napoleon. Indeed, by this process the ritual purport may be obscured altogether, as when the folk play develops into the enactment of an incident from scripture (e.g., the Flood, the Annunciation, or the Crucifixion in the medieval mystery plays or the story of Esther in Jewish plays staged at Purim). [*See* Purim Play.]
6. In the course of time, when the original function of the performance has been forgotten, the action may degenerate into burlesque, farce, or masquerade, as is often the case in the modern survivals. This development eventually gives rise to comedy.

The earliest examples of ritual drama come from the ancient Near East. They are preserved in hieroglyphic and cuneiform texts emanating from the civilizations of the Egyptians, the Babylonians and Assyrians, the Hittites of Asia Minor, and the Canaanites of ancient Syria. These texts date in general from the second and third millennia BCE, although their contents in several cases represent traditions older than the documents themselves. Most of them are explicitly associated with seasonal ceremonies, either being accompanied by a formal "order of service," or else containing interspersed liturgical rubrics. It should be observed, however, that since the ritual drama was (and still is) often performed in pantomime, the dialogues being recited and the story narrated by a "lector," some of the texts appear to be scripts for these "presenters" rather than libretti for the actors. [*See* New Year Festivals.]

Egypt. The Egyptian texts are the oldest. The *Ramesseum Coronation Drama* is inscribed on a papyrus unearthed in 1896 in the precincts of the Ramesseum at Thebes. The manuscript dates from the reign of Sen-Wosret (Sesotris) I (c. 1970 BCE), but it is believed that the contents go back some thirteen centuries earlier to the time of the first dynasty. The text was designed for the ceremony of installing (or reinstalling) the pharaoh at a New Year festival. It includes such elements of the ritual pattern as the combat, the death of the old king and the lamentation over him, the investiture and enthronement of the new king, a communal feast attended by the governors of the several provinces (nomes) of Egypt, and various acts (for example, the threshing of grain and the milking of goats) designed to promote fertility.

The successive ritual acts are construed as an enactment of the mythic discomfiture of the god Osiris by his evil brother Seth. The combat is taken to represent the fight between them. The new king is identified with Horus, son of Osiris, who avenged his father and defeated Seth. The two sacred women who bewail the slain king are the goddesses Isis and Nephthys, who bewailed Osiris. The official who invests the new king is the god Thoth, who adjudicated the contest between the gods. The various regalia are explained symbolically: the maces handed to the new king are the testicles of Seth wrested from him by Horus and then grafted upon himself to increase his vigor. The threshing of the grain represents the belaboring of Osiris by his rival. Interspersed rubrics identify the actors with their mythic counterparts and list props for the various scenes.

The *Edfu Drama* is engraved, with illustrative reliefs, on one of the walls of the temple at Edfu (Idfu; ancient Bekhdet); this text was composed for a ritual performance at a spring festival. Its central theme is the reinvigoration of the king as the epitome of communal life. It consists of a prologue, three acts (subdivided into scenes), and an epilogue. At one point, there is mention of a "chief lector," and since there is no indication of separate speakers, it is probable that the action was performed in pantomime and that what we have before us is simply the script for that "reciter."

The contents include such ingredients of the ritual pattern as the combat, the installation of the victor as king, and a "sacred marriage" at which he is the bridegroom. The action is interpreted mythically: the king is the local god, Horus of Bekhdet; his adversary, termed "the Caitiff," or "Monster," is identified as a hippopotamus (analogous to the dragon elsewhere), and the bride is the goddess Hathor of Dendera.

The *Memphite Theology* (or *Memphis Drama*), inserted on a slab of black granite now in the British Museum, was written in the reign of Shabaka (c. 712–697 BCE), but a preamble states expressly that it was copied from an original, which has been dated by modern scholars some eighteen centuries earlier. It was designed to be performed at a festival.

The theme is, once again, the death or discomfiture of the old king, the ritual lament over him, the combat, and the installation of the victor as the new king in the city of Memphis. The king is again identified with Horus, his defunct predecessor with Osiris, the wailing women with Isis and Nephthys, and the combat as that between Horus and Seth. The action, however, is not only mythified, but also historicized; the upshot of the combat is that the god Geb awards Upper Egypt to Seth and lower Egypt to Horus, but both areas are eventually united in a single country whose capital is Memphis. The text concludes, in fact, with a hymn to Ptah, patron god of that city.

It has been suggested also that certain mythico-magical texts engraved on plaques and stelae depicting Horus treading triumphantly on snakes, crocodiles, and scorpions were copied from ritual drama. There is, however, no indication that these myths were associated with seasonal festivals, nor do they include several of the typical elements of the ritual pattern. [*See also* Egyptian Religion, *article on* The Literature.]

Babylonia and Assyria. The evidence for drama among the Babylonians and Assyrians is inferential and indirect but nonetheless persuasive. First, we have a long mythological poem, the *Enuma elish* (wrongly called an epic of creation), which was recited by a priest as part of the liturgy of the New Year festival. This relates how Marduk, the primary god of Babylon, vanquished a rebellious marine monster named Tiamat and her cohorts, how he thereby acquired sovereignty over the gods, was installed in a newly built palace, and, at a banquet, determined the world order. Although this text is a literary composition and not a scenario, it clearly conforms to the ritual pattern of combat, enthronment, and renewal, and it is therefore reasonable to conclude that it is based on some more ancient seasonal drama. [*See* Enuma Elish.]

Second, we have a series of texts—albeit fragmentary—in which what seem to be successive acts in a seasonal ritual are interpreted mythologically as representing incidents in a story concerning Marduk. This has suggested that these texts accompanied a dramatic performance. It has been proposed alternatively, however, that they refer rather to historical events that learned academicians explained as exemplifications of a traditional myth.

From the Hittites comes a text that describes how the weather god, with the aid of a mortal, defeated a marine dragon named Illuyanka, how this was followed by a desired precipitation of rain, and (apparently) how control of the suberranean waters was thereafter vested in the king. The story is tricked out with folkloric motifs and was designed for recitation at an annual festival. It is prefaced by a petition for rain and is accompanied by a description of the festival ceremonies. Hence, although it is once again a liturgical recitation rather than the actual text of a play, it clearly derives, like its Mesopotamian counterpart, from some earlier dramatic performance. Another Hittite text describes a ritual combat, in which the antagonists are historicized respectively as the Hittites themselves and a neighboring people called the Masa (possibly the Maeonians of Lydia).

That sacred drama was known also to the Canaanites in the second millenium BCE may be confidently deduced from a lengthy mythological poem discovered at Ras Shamra (ancient Ugarit) on the north coast of Syria. This relates how Baal, god of rainfall and fertility, successively vanquished Yamm, lord of seas and rivers, and Mot, genius of aridity and death. By virtue of defeating the former, he acquired sovereignty over the gods and was installed in a newly built palace. At an inaugural banquet tendered to the gods, he deliberately excluded Mot, whereupon his offended rival lured him down to the netherworld. During his sojourn there, all fertility failed on earth. An interrex was appointed in the person of a young god named Athtar—probably the genius of artificial irrigation—but he was too small to "make the grade," and the languishing earth was revived only when Baal's sister Anat, aided by the Lady Sun, descended into the lower regions, retrieved him and gave him burial, as a necessary prelude to his eventual resurrection. Thus revived, Baal finally discomfited Mot in combat and made known his return by an impressive display of sheet lightning.

Clearly a myth of the alternation of wet and dry seasons in the Syrian year, this poem reflects unmistakably in its contents and sequence the characteristic features of the standard seasonal ritual—the combat, interrex, enthronement, and banquet. A colophon states expressly that it was redacted (or recited?) by a disciple of the high priest. It was therefore a liturgical chant, probably recited at an autumnal festival that inaugurated the rainy season after that of the winter squalls and the dry summer months.

A burlesque version of the primitive seasonal drama may be seen to underlie another composition from Ras Shamra, conventionally known as the *Poem of Dawn and Sunset.* This consists of two sections: the first gives the rubrics for a ritual ceremony at the time when grapes ripen, and the second an accompanying mythological narrative. Two women encounter the aged supreme god El at the seashore while he is shooting down a bird and boiling it for his dinner. They make ribald remarks about his senility and seeming sexual impotence. Thereupon he gives forthright proof to the contrary. The ladies bear a pair of siblings. Someone—apparently the cuckolded husband of each—reports to the god that the children (of whose true parentage he is evidently unaware) glow like dawn and sunset—a common trait of divine offspring—whereupon El cynically suggests that their proper place would be up in the sky alongside the sun, moon, and fixed stars. Subsequently, further children, called "the gracious gods," are born. El is informed that these have insatiable appetities—another common folkloric trait of divinely begotten children. He thereupon consigns them to the desert, there to forage for their food. After a time, they fall in with the official custodian of grain and beg food and drink. Although he has only a meager supply to meet his own needs, he apparently feeds them, or they break into his silo. The rest of the story is missing, but a few fragmentary words at the end may be interpreted to mean that as a reward for his generosity, the gods annually bestow a due measure of crops and fruits. The text would thus be a more or less comic version of the ritual drama acted out at a festival of renewal in June, when vines are preliminarily trimmed. The seduction of the two women would then reflect the sacred marriage, and the children would be the gods subsequently astralized as the Heavenly Twins (Dioscuri), the regnant constellation of that month.

Hebrew Scriptures. Literary echoes of the sacred drama have also been recognized by several modern scholars in certain of the biblical psalms. Those, for instance, that begin with the words, "The Lord reigneth" (or "hath become king"), Psalms 97 and 99, for example, would have been patterned after a traditional type of hymn composed for the annual enthronement of the god at the New Year festival (even though the ceremony itself may have been discarded); while Psalm 93, which acclaims the Lord as having acquired sovereignty by subduing "the mighty waters," as occupying a gorgeous temple, and as issuing eternal decrees for the government of the world, would reflect the same myth as the Mesopotamian and Hittite texts, based on the seasonal pattern. [*See* Psalms.]

Some scholars have also suggested that the *Song of Songs* is really a pastoral drama, in which a country maiden (the Shulammite) abducted by the king (Solomon) for his harem, is won back by her shepherd lover. There is, however, no evidence of such secular drama in the ancient Near East. Moreover, this view depends very largely on dubious interpretations of certain passages, and the assumed scenes of the drama sometimes consist of a single verse! It is therefore more probable that the biblical book is simply a repertoire of love songs.

Ritual Patterns in Greek and Other Literature. Much of the same ritual pattern that underlies the ancient Near Eastern texts may be recognized also as one of the main sources of classical Greek drama, for Gilbert Murray (1912) has pointed out that in several of the classical Greek tragedies that have come down to us, notably in those of Euripides, it is possible to discern—albeit through a glass darkly—such standard elements of the primitive ritual pattern as the combat (usually attenuated to a mere verbal altercation), the discomfiture of the loser (e.g., Pentheus or Hippolytus), the ceremonial lament, and sometimes also the resurrection of the fertility spirit (modified, to be sure, into a mere final theophany, like that of Dionysos in *The Bacchae*). On this theory, the prologue, which came eventually to summarize the background of the play, would have developed out of a more primitive ritual formula that served originally not to introduce the characters but to inaugurate the religious ceremony at which the play was performed. (Such a prologue indeed occurs in the aforementioned Canaanite *Poem of Dawn and Sunset.*) So, too, the division of the chorus into two halves would be a survival of the two opposing teams in the ritual combat.

A striking example of how the primitive ritual drama survived in literary form has been detected by Murray in *The Bacchae* of Euripides. Here he finds a mythified version of the combat, the dismemberment (in this case, of Pentheus), the lament, the retrieval of the scattered members, and, as "by a sort of doubling," the resurrection, attenuated into the final epiphany of the true god Dionysos instead of the revivification of the slaughtered victim.

Some twenty years later, Francis Cornford (1934, 1961), an eminent British classicist, applied this theory to Greek comedy, arguing that traces of the combat, the death-and-resurrection, the sacred marriage, and the banquet could be recognized in each of the extant plays of Aristophanes. It must be noted, however, that other scholars have questioned this assumption.

Nor is it only in Greek drama that survivals of the ritual pattern may be recognized. Equally impressive is the evidence afforded by the so-called Homeric *Hymn to Demeter.* This describes the rape of Demeter's daughter Persephone and the search for her by her mother and the goddess Hekate. But the successive incidents in the narrative reproduce to a nicety certain features of the ritual associated with the festival of Thesmophoria and with the Eleusinian mysteries. Thus, the search by torchlight reproduces the torchlight procession by female worshipers; the fast observed by Demeter reproduces the period of abstinence and mortification characteristic of seasonal ceremonies; the emphasis on her glum abstention from mirth and laughter finds its explanation in the statement of Plutarch and other writers that the festival was observed in a grim, lugubrious mood and that all merriment was forbidden; while the obscene gestures and jokes of the crone Iambe correspond to the chanting of ribald songs couched in iambic meter as a means of stimulating fertility.

It is not, however, in the seasonal pattern alone that the origin of Greek drama may be recognized. Other scholars—notably William Ridgeway (1915) and even Murray himself—have suggested that an alternative source lay in some cases in the commemorative stories of ancient heroes recited on the anniversaries of their births or deaths or at annual festivals when their shades were believed temporarily to rejoin their kinsmen (this would be like the reenactment of historical incidents in modern pageants, for example, on President Washington's birthday).

Finally, survivals of the primitive ritual pattern have been recognized by several modern scholars not only in drama but also in other forms of literature. It has been claimed, for instance, that some of the hymns of the Hindu *Ṛgveda* were chanted in seasonal masquerades and that some of the odes in the Chinese *Shih ching* were the libretti of crude harvest pantomimes. The Scandinavian *Elder Edda* and the legend of the Holy Grail have likewise been derived from ritual archetypes. Doubtless in certain cases, enthusiasm has outrun sobriety, but this can scarcely detract from the fact that a set of usages so constant and recurrent in ancient communities may be expected to have left its impress on their literature and art.

[*See also* Literature, *article on* Literature and Religion; Poetry, *article on* Poetry and Religion; *and* Epics.]

BIBLIOGRAPHY

The most comprehensive account of standard seasonal rites, ancient and primitive, and of their survival in popular usages is still James G. Frazer's monumental *The Golden Bough*, 3d ed., rev. & enl., 12 vols. (London, 1911–1915). Of several condensed editions, my abridgement, with notes, is the most recent: *The New Golden Bough* (1959; New York, 1977). Highly stimulating also, though sometimes exaggerated, is Jane Ellen Harrison's general treatment of the subject in her *Ancient Art and Ritual* (London, 1913).

Translations and discussions of the ancient Near Eastern texts can be found in my *Thespis: Ritual, Myth, and Drama in the Ancient Near East*, 2d ed. (1961; New York, 1977); translations alone appear in *Ancient Near Eastern Texts relating to the Old Testament*, 3d ed., edited by James B. Pritchard (Princeton, 1969). For a translation and discussion of the Egyptian Edfu drama, see A. M. Blackman and H. W. Fairman's "The Myth of Horus at Edfu I–II," *Journal of Egyptian Archaeology* 21 (1935): 26–36, 28 (1942): 32–38, and 29 (1943): 2–36. On the relations of the seasonal patterns to classical Greek tragedy, see Gilbert Murray's "Excursus on the Ritual Forms Preserved in Greek Tragedy," in Harrison's *Themis* (Cambridge, 1912), pp. 341–363, and on their assumed relation to Greek comedy, see Francis M. Cornford's *The Origin of Attic Comedy*, 2d ed. (1934; New York, 1961). On traces of the pattern in Euripides' *The Bacchae*, see E. R. Dodds's edition, *Bacchae* (Oxford, 1944), and on the ritual background of the Homeric *Hymn to Demeter*, see N. J. Richardson's *The Homeric Hymn to Demeter* (Oxford, 1974). Survivals in modern Greek folk plays are described by R. M. Dawkins in "The Modern Carnival in Thrace and the Cult of Dionysus," *Journal of Hellenic Studies* 26 (1906): 191–206, and by A. J. B. Wace in "North Greek Festivals," *Annual of the British School at Athens* 16 (1910): 232ff. The alternative view that Greek drama developed out of recitations at the annual or periodic commemoration of heroes is best presented in William Ridgeway's *The Origin of Tragedy* (London, 1910).

On the medieval mystery and miracle plays, the best source is E. K. Chambers's *The Mediaeval Stage*, 2 vols. (Oxford, 1903), but the older collection of texts in William Hone's *Ancient Mysteries Described, Especially in English Miracle Plays* (London, 1823) is still useful. The standard work on the English mummers' play is R. J. E. Tiddy's posthumous *The Mummers' Play*, edited by Rupert S. Thompson (Oxford, 1923), where some twenty-three specimens are collected.

Regarding literary forms of the ritual pattern, see, for the odes in the Chinese *Shih ching*, Bruno Schindler's essay in *Occident and Orient*, edited by Schindler (London, 1936), pp. 498–502; for the *Elder Edda*, Bertha S. Phillpotts's *The Elder Edda and Ancient Scandinavian Drama* (Cambridge, 1920); and for the legend of the Holy Grail, Jesse L. Weston's ingenious, but much controverted work *From Ritual to Romance* (Cambridge, 1920). For possible echoes of the pattern in the Psalter, see my *Thespis*, 2d ed. (1961; New York, 1977), pp. 442–452, and Aubrey R. Johnson's "The Role of the King in the Jerusalem Cultus," in *The Labyrinth*, edited by S. H. Hooke (London, 1934), pp. 73–111. For a skeptical critique of this view, however, see S. G. F. Brandon's essay "The Myth Ritual and Position Critically Considered," in *Myth, Ritual and Kingship*, edited by S. H. Hooks (Oxford, 1958), pp. 261–291.

THEODOR H. GASTER

Middle Eastern Narrative Traditions

Popular religious storytelling has been widespread in the Islamic Middle East since the earliest times, and its forms have varied considerably according to time, place, and branch or sect of Islam. For the period before 1500, sources for religious storytelling are few and widely scattered; nevertheless, some idea of the situation can be gained. With the establishment of Shiism as the state religion in Persia in about 1500, important new forms of religious oral narrative appeared, some of which are still practiced in the twentieth century.

Religious storytelling on the popular level has its roots in formal preaching in the mosque. In its broadest sense, it attempts to interpret the religion and meet the spiritual needs of the common people in a manner more accessible to them than that of a preacher representing the religious establishment. This kind of storytelling quickly came to reflect the values and beliefs of popular Islam and in doing so widened the gap between the Islam of the theologians and jurisprudents and that of the common people. The sources for the study of popular religious storytelling reflect, by and large, the views of the small educated class, including the religious class, and deplore the existence and influence of popular oral narrators.

In the first century of Islam it became the practice of governing authorities to appoint a preacher for the local mosque and pay him a stipend from the state treasury. At the same time, unofficial preachers (*qāṣṣ*, lit. "storyteller"; pl., *quṣṣāṣ*) began delivering sermons in mosques and elsewhere. While the official preachers represented the views of the religious establishment, the free preachers were not so restricted. Enlightenment mixed with entertainment in their sermons, and edifying tales slowly developed into entertaining ones, always within the framework of transmitting and interpreting the tradition of the Prophet. Some popular preachers were highly respected men of great learning, and al-Jāḥiẓ (d. 868/9) included Ḥasan al-Baṣrī (d. 728/9) in his list of learned popular preachers. Most, however, were bent on impressing their audiences, and since it is easy to pass from edifying tales to profane ones, they began to enjoy great success among the uneducated. By about 892, popular preaching was considered a problem in the Muslim community, and the government announced that storytellers, astrologers, and fortune-tellers were not to appear in the streets and mosques of Baghdad. In Spain in the twelfth century, religious storytellers were banned from performing in cemeteries and from telling tales in which the Prophet's name was mentioned, and municipal authorities were charged with preventing women from attending their sessions in tents.

Because of the bias of the sources in favor of the religious establishment, most accounts of popular preachers and storytellers after the ninth century describe them as charlatans and often associate them with beggars and confidence men. They were accused of mixing edifying narratives from the Qur'ān with fanciful biblical legends, stories from pre-Islamic Arabia and Persia, eschatological and cosmological tales based on invented chains of authorities, romances with religious associations, and popular etymologies, leaving no questions unanswered. Among the public, they became more highly regarded than the theologians, who condemned them for falsifying the religious tradition. They were also opposed by the Ṣūfīs, who maintained that they did not transmit true mystical experiences. More than one source describes their practices used to impress their audiences, which included painting their faces, artificially stimulating the flow of tears, making histrionic gestures, pounding on the pulpit, running up and down its stairs, and even throwing themselves off it. These storytellers flourished in Iraq, Persia, and Central Asia but were relatively scarce in the Hejaz and in Muslim North Africa. Whatever the accuracy of these accounts may be, it is clear that the popular religious storytellers, like the friars of medieval Christianity, bridged the gulf between an intellectual and distant religious establishment and an illiterate populace needing spiritual guidance and education in terms they could comprehend.

When the Safavids (1500–1732) were establishing Shiism as the official religion in Persia, one of the means they used to spread their message was the oral storyteller. This appears to have stimulated the development and specialization of oral narration, and to judge from the sources, religious storytelling flourished in Persia from the sixteenth to the early twentieth century. I shall describe here the three most important forms.

Rawẓah-khvānī began with public readings from *Ruwẓat al-shuhadā* (The Garden of Martyrs), a collection of stories by Ḥusayn Vā'iẓ Kāshifī (d. 910 AH/1504–1505 CE) about the Shī'ī imams. Soon moving out of the mosque and into public places and private houses, *rawẓah-khvānī* became an integral part of religious life. It is still practiced widely in Iran. Another form of oral religious narrative, rarer today, is a variety of picture storytelling called *pardah-dārī*. Working in pairs, narrators make use of a large canvas on which are painted pictures of the imams in their struggles with the opponents of Shiism. The canvas is slowly unrolled or unveiled as the story is related in a mixture of prose and verse. Finally, there is *sukhanvarī*, which began in Safavid times and is all but extinct in Iran today. Probably deriving from an older rivalry between Shī'ī and Sunnī religious storytellers, *sukhanvarī* was a contest in which two narrators attempted to outdo each other in improvising verses praising the imams and condemning the Sunnīs. The contests would usually take place in coffeehouses and were most popular during the nights of Ramaḍān.

Among the Sunnīs of Ottoman Turkey and the Turkic peoples of Central Asia, religious storytelling was practiced to a modest extent. It is believed that the *meddah*s (dramatic storytellers) of Turkey were originally religious storytellers, and nineteenth-century travelers report hearing popular religious narratives in Kabul and Bukhara. Today the practice has almost disappeared from Sunnī Islam, but it is still popular among the Shīʿī communities of Iraq and Anatolia, in addition to Iran. There a variant of *rawẓah-khvānī* is common: passages from *maqtals*, books that relate the martyrdom of the imams, are recited, most often during the first ten days of Muḥarram (the first month of the Muslim lunar year).

[*See also* Taʿziyah.]

BIBLIOGRAPHY

Because references to religious storytelling are so widely scattered, the following sources have been chosen for their bibliographical references as well as their information on the subject. Charles Pellat's "Ḳāṣṣ," in *The Encyclopaedia of Islam*, new ed., vol. 4 (Leiden, 1978), gives a basic introduction to the subject but focuses on Arabic sources. Ignácz Goldziher in his *Muslim Studies*, edited by S. M. Stern, vol. 2 (New York, 1973), pp. 149–159, discusses the early preachers of Islam and the rise of popular preaching. This was originally published as *Muhammedanische Studien*, 2 vols. (Halle, 1889–1890). The scandalous side of popular religious storytelling is depicted vividly by C. E. Bosworth in his *The Mediaeval Islamic Underworld*, vol. 1 (Leiden, 1976), pp. 15, 24–29. The various forms of dramatic religious storytelling in Iran are described by Bahrām Bayẓāʾī in his *Namāyish dar Irān* (The Theater in Iran; Tehran, 1965), pp. 71–76. Metin And describes Shīʿī religious practices and storytelling in his "The Muharram Observances in Anatolian Turkey," in *Taʿziyeh: Ritual and Drama in Iran*, edited by Peter Chelkowski (New York, 1979), pp. 238–254.

WILLIAM L. HANAWAY, JR.

Indian Dance and Dance Drama

In the cultures of the Indian subcontinent, drama and ritual have been integral parts of a single whole from earliest recorded history. The first evidences of ritual dance drama performances occur in the rock paintings of Mirzapur, Bhimbetka, and in other sites, which are variously dated 20,000 to 5000 BCE. The ancient remains of Mohenjo-Daro and Harappa (2500 to 2000 BCE) are more definitive. Here archaeological remains clearly point to the prevalence of ritual performance involving populace and patrons. The Mohenjo-Daro seals, bronze figurines, and images of priests and broken torsos are all clear indications of dance as ritual.

The aspect of Vedic ritual tradition closest to dance and drama was a rigorous system called *yajña*. Various types of sacrifices called *yajña*s were held at different astronomical confluences and lasted for five, seven, fifteen, or twenty-one days. These rituals were dramatic performances presented in a sacred enclosure. Usually three altars symbolized the celestial, terrestrial, and mundane worlds. The altars were in the shape of a square, a circle, and a semicircle. The performance included incantation, verses recited in different meters in specific intonation, movement in eight directions along a circumambulatory path in the sacred enclosure, and offerings of sixteen auspicious objects. Combined, these activities constituted a comprehensive ritual drama. Participating were the priests and the *yajamāna*, the person desiring the performance of the sacrifice. Roles were clearly defined: the patron, his wife, the priest, his assistants, and members of the society representing the various vocations.

The ritual's movement pattern was dramatic from inception to conclusion. The cosmos was symbolically recreated for the duration of the performance, and the movement of the universe in its process of involution, evolution, and devolution was suggested. The ritual's ultimate conclusion was the ritual burning of the sacred enclosure.

The concern of the Vedic poet was also focused on images of dance and drama, as evidenced by the inumerable textual references to these arts. Some members of the Vedic pantheon were dancers: Ūṣa, the goddess of the dawn; Indra, the god of the thunderbolt; and the two sets of twin gods, the Māruts and the Aśvins.

Archaeological remains from the Mauryan period provide evidence of the prevalence of ritual dance and dance drama. The terra-cotta figures of the dancing girls, the drummer, and others of this period suggest preoccupation with ritual dance. The tradition continues in the Sunga, Stavahana, and Kushan periods (second century BCE to second century CE), culminating with the great Buddhist stupas, Jain monuments, and early Hindu temples of the Gupta period (fourth to sixth centuries CE). The frequency of ritual performance is evident from the architectural remains of sacrificial enclosures, sculptural reliefs, and literary evidence.

The Nāṭya Śāstra. Attributed to Bhārata, the *Nāṭya Śāstra* (second century BCE to second century CE) enunciates a theory of aesthetics and the techniques of dramaturgy in thirty-six chapters. These chapters discuss dramatic evolution, theatrical and stage construction, and the presentation of drama. Drama is viewed as a reenactment of the cosmos, which is composed of celestial, terrestrial, and mundane worlds. It is compared to a ritual performance *(yajña)* and aims at emancipation or release *(mokṣa)* gained through the purification of emotion *(rāsa)*.

Like the stupa and temple, the theater is a sacred enclosure, and the stage is the sacred altar. A center is established, and all else radiates from it. The stage center is demarcated. The performance is a ritual that begins with offerings to the sacred center and the deities of the eight directions. The *Nāṭya Śāstra* devotes a full chapter to the preliminary rituals *(pūrvaraṅga).* These comprise various entries and exits of three principal dancer-actors who establish the ritual space through song and mime. Drama proper follows. The *Nāṭya Śāstra* clearly draws upon Vedic ritual drama to create the edifice for dramatic ritual. It extracts elements from the four Vedas: intonation, recitation, gesture, language, music, and the internalized states of emotion, to create a fifth whole that Bhārata called the fifth Veda of drama. With speech, movement, music, and costumery, the performance is early multimedia. The *Nāṭya Śāstra* recognizes regional variations and can be presented in either stylized or natural modes.

Enunciated in oral tradition two thousand years ago, the precepts of the *Nāṭya Śāstra* are still followed in India in many dance and drama forms in whole or in part. The preliminaries invariably invoke principal deities; the sacred enclosure is demarcated. Whether the performance is in open space or in a closed theater, a center is established. Offerings are made of eight auspicious things, such as coconut, water, turmeric, and so forth. Once the director and his companions have established the consecrated space, the audience is invited to participate in the mythical, consecrated time of the drama.

The architectural plans of many stupas and temples built between the second and thirteenth century provide evidence of adhering to a sacred geometry of the square and circle. In each instance, a center is fundamental. Many rituals were performed in different areas of the temple, from the inner sanctum to outer enclosure. By the eighth century and particularly between the tenth and thirteenth century, special structures called *naṭamaṇḍapa* were built for ritual dance and dance drama.

Music and dance were included as part of temple offerings (*sevas*) involving flowers and incense. A solo dancer performed before the deity. Hereditary dancers called *devadāsīs* also performed in the temple sanctum. This practice was prevalent in all parts of India. Many other ritual dance dramas were performed in the courtyard, a tradition that continued and developed in many parts of India.

Ritual Dance Drama. The ritual dance-drama form with the longest continuity, called *kuttiyattam,* is performed today in special theaters (*kuttambalamas*) in Kerala. The spectacle held in these special theaters within the temple precincts is performed by professional acting families called *chakyars*. Such families can trace their genealogies back to the tenth century of the common era.

The play starts with the sounding of a large, pitcher-shaped drum, the *mizhavu.* The director and his companions enter, almost exactly as described in the *Nāṭya Śāstra,* carrying a brimming vase and a pole. In the central area of the stage, eight auspicious gifts, *aṣṭamaṅgala,* are offered; these offerings almost replicate the offerings within the temple sanctum. The actors then circumambulate the stage, establishing the eight directions and the three spaces of the universe—nether, terrestial, and celestial.

A single play takes from seven to nine nights to complete. Each act is elaborated upon in minutest detail. A repertoire of ten plays is extant, although today only excerpts are presented. Night after night audiences witness these performances in rapt attention. Participation in the performance is a ritual act comparable to the daily worship the devotee offers to the deity inside the temple.

In the Guruvayur Temple (c. fifteenth century CE), the dance drama called *Kṛṣṇattam* is presented in the temple courtyard rather than in a *kuttambalama.* The life of Kṛṣṇa is enacted by a totally male cast of actors over a period of eight nights. The performance is based on the *Kṛṣṇagiti,* a text composed by King Manavedan. The favorite episodes of Kṛṣṇa's life—his birth in a dark prison, his childhood pranks, his conquest of the snake demon Kaliya, his destruction of the demonness Pūtanā and the demons hidden in tree trunks, his playful sport with the cowherdesses (*gopīs*), and his final journey to heaven *(svargarśana)*—are all re-created in a charming spectacle full of lyricism and fluidity. The faces of some actors are painted in green or red, symbolizing good and evil characters, respectively; other characters wear large masks.

The *kathakali* dance drama form was inspired by *kuttiyattam.* By some accounts it developed as a reaction to *kṛṣṇattam.* Eclectic in character, it is a highly sophisticated art form utilizing the preliminary rituals of *kuttiyattam* and presenting dance dramas based on the Indian epics, the *Rāmāyaṇa* and *Mahābhārata.* While *kathakali*'s ritualistic origins are not immediately clear, it draws essentially upon the rituals held in the temple sanctum.

The countless ritual dance drama forms of several village communities in Kerala are fundamental to the evolution of all temple dance drama forms. The preserve of the socioeconomically deprived and backward classes, these forms are known as *teyyams*, a name derived from the word *daivam* ("to be god"). Many different forms of *teyyam* and *teriyattam* continue to be performed in Kerala. In these performances, the spirit of the deity enters the actor so that the ritual enactment invariably culminates in magic and trance. These forms characteristically feature elaborate makeup, high headgears, and oversize costumery, all designed to create an otherworldly vision. In the form called *mudiyettu,* an enclosure is made, and the image of the goddess Kālī is traced on the ground with the powders of different cereal grains. Another person, who many be considered devotee or priest, worships the image. Then this priest/devotee dances in a trance state and obliterates the image. A second enclosure is made, and the action of the dance drama shifts to this second space. A lamp, which had accompanied the first part of the performance, is moved to the second enclosure, symbolizing continuity. The story of Kālī vanquishing the demon Darika is enacted in the second enclosure. Until about the mid-twentieth century, the role of Kālī was performed by the same actor who worshiped and obliterated the image in the first enclosure; today they are different actors. At the end of the performance, the actors who take the roles of Kālī and Darika become possessed.

It is important to remember that for those forms drawing inspiration from the temple, the ritual precedes the dramatic spectacle, and the actors always are narrators and performers of the myth. In village dance drama rituals, however, the performer is not an actor but is transformed for the duration into the deity. The performance, therefore, invariably ends in trance with the actor possessed.

Similar dance-drama forms are known elsewhere in India. The patterns of chanting *mantra*s in the temple sanctum; singing inside the temple; and performing dances in the dance hall *(manadappam),* dance drama in the temple courtyard, and dance drama in the village field or open spaces are pan-Indian.

One can identify three major systems of dance as ritual process and ritualistic dance drama from the thousands of distinctly regional or local forms. The first is an offering of music and dance, usually performed by a solo female dancer or a group of dancers. This genre owes its repertoire in varying degrees to the traditions followed by *devadāsī*s, *māhari*s, and others, and includes the *bhāratanāṭyam* of South India, the *orissi* of Orissa, and the *ardhananṛtyam* of Andhra Pradesh.

The second system includes the dance dramas within and without the temple courtyard. Here the performers are largely male dancer-actors, not devotee-narrators as in the solo offering. The medieval cycle plays concerning the life of Kṛṣṇa or Rāma emerged within this broad category. While known throughout India, they are special to the North and East. The third system is characterized by the presentation of themes from the *Mahābhārata* and *Rāmāyaṇa.*

Performances of Rāmalīlā are pervasive throughout India. The life cycle of Rāma, hero and god, is also presented during early autumn in Java, Bali, Thailand, and Malaysia. Commencing with ritual preliminaries—invoking gods of the water, earth, and sky and the deities of the quarters, and seeking benediction—the life of Rāma is enacted nightly in episodes about his birth, his ultimate coronation, the banishing of Sītā, and, in some versions, his immersion in the waters of the river Saryu. The Rāmnagar Rāmalīlā and the Tulsīghāṭa Rāmalīlā are held in different parts of the city of Banaras. These ritual dance-drama performances take on a special quality because the locale itself is transformed into the situs of the story. Each episode is performed in a different place. The singer-director recites verses from the *Rāmacaritamānas,* a sixteenth-century work by Tulsīdās. Young boys, especially trained for the annual performance, act their roles in the changing locales; the audience identifies them with the mythical heroes. During the performance of the Rāmalīlā, a period of over twenty days, the actors who play the main role of Rāma and his brothers are considered deified. They are consecrated through ritual before the beginning of the dance drama; from that time on the human is icon come to life. Only after their final performance when they remove their headgear do the actors return to mundane life. Until that time, the audience worships them as they would an icon, the sacred and the profane are concurrent without tension, and actual time and place become mythical while also retaining their own ordinary identities.

Ritual and dance drama around the Kṛṣṇa theme constitute another performance system throughout India. Inspired by the early life of Kṛṣṇa, especially that narrated in the *Bhāgavata Purāṇa* (c. ninth century), the cycle of Kṛṣṇalīlā plays is performed two weeks before the Janmāṣṭamī, the day of Kṛṣṇa's birth on the eighth day of the waning moon of July–August. The most important of these is the *Vṛndāvana Kṛṣṇalīlā.* Again, as in the case of Rāmalīlā, young boys are trained for their roles, initiated, and consecrated. For the duration of the cycle plays, these young boys, as Kṛṣṇa, his consort Radha, and other cowherdesses (*gopī*s), are considered deified. Beginning with Kṛṣṇa's birth, a new episode in his life is presented each day. This is known as *līlā.* [*See* Līlā.] The enactment of the stories in the early life of Kṛṣṇa culminates in the *rāsa,* the circular dance of great antiquity in which Kṛṣṇa stands in the center with the *gopī*s surrounding him. During the dance, Kṛṣṇa creates the illusion in which each *gopī* believes her partner to be Kṛṣṇa. In the *Vṛndāvana Kṛṣṇalīlā* the one young Kṛṣṇa suddenly is multiplied, leading to complex circle dancing until Kṛṣṇa and his consort Rādhā finally stand in the center. All others pay obeisance to the icon *(mūrti)* of Kṛṣṇa and Rādhā as they would within the temple. Ecstatic cries fill the arena. Devotees prostrate themselves before the young dancers who are, for that time and space, deities.

In Manipur, the same Kṛṣṇalīlā becomes Rāsalīlā and is performed five times yearly to coincide with the full moon of spring, the monsoons, late autumn, and so forth. Instead of young boys, young girls before puberty take the principal roles. The *gopīs* can be women of any age, from ten to more than sixty. The enactment of Kṛṣṇa's early life is a moving spectacle, but the presentation of *rāsa* provides the most heightened ecstatic experience. The *rāsa* is held in the Govindjī Temple precincts in Manipur in springtime; the *mahārāsa*, or grand *rāsa*, in the November full moon. The *gopīs* arrive in two files of twenty to forty dancers each, dressed in glittering skirts and transparent veils. They sing verses from the tenth section of the *Bhāgavata Purāṇa*, each *gopī* vying with the others to communicate her yearning for the Dark Lord. Tears flow effortlessly. Singing in falsetto, with minimal restrained gestures, also occurs. Always played by a young girl, Kṛṣṇa appears, dances, and looks for the *gopīs*. *Rādhā*, dressed in a green skirt to distinguish her from the red-skirted *gopīs*, then appears. This provides an opportunity for a solo dance of great beauty. A dialogue through music and dance takes place between the two, followed by estrangement and then reunion. As in the *Vṛndāvana Kṛṣṇalīlā* the dance ends with a circular movement but without a number of Kṛṣṇas appearing.

The atmosphere is charged with devotion *(bhakti)*. Members of the audience enter the arena and bow down or prostrate themselves before the dancer-deities, offer gifts, and then retreat. The dance can last all night until early in the morning, when the *gopīs* and the audience worship the child actors portraying Kṛṣṇa and Rādhā as they would the icons inside the temple sanctum.

BIBLIOGRAPHY

Bhattacharya, D. H. *Origin and Development of the Assamese Drama and Stage.* New Delhi, 1964.

Blank, Judith. *The History, Cultural Context and Religious Meaning of the Chau Dance.* Chicago, 1972.

Desai, Sudha. *Bhavai: A Medieval Form of Ancient Indian Dramatic Art.* Ahmedabad, 1972.

Ghosh, Manomohan, ed. and trans. *Nāṭyaśāstra.* 2 vols. 2d rev. ed. Calcutta, 1967.

Guha, Thakurta P. *The Bengali Drama.* London, 1930.

Hawley, John Stratton. *At Play with Krishna: Pilgrimage Dramas from Brindavan.* Princeton, 1981.

Hein, Norvin. *The Miracle Plays of Mathura.* New Haven, 1972.

Jones, Clifford, and Betty True Jones. *Kathakali: An Introduction to the Dance-Drama of Kerala.* San Francisco, 1970.

Raju, P. T. *Telugu Literature: Andhra Literature.* Bombay, 1944.

Ranganath, H. K. *The Karnataka Theatre.* Dharwar, 1960.

Shekhar, Indu. *Sanskrit Drama: Its Origin and Decline.* Leiden, 1960.

Vatsyayan, Kapila. *Traditional Indian Theater: Multiple Streams.* New Delhi, 1980. Includes extensive bibliography.

Kapila Vatsyayan

Balinese Dance and Dance Drama

Balinese dance and dance drama are integral to the distinctive Hindu-Buddhist religious practices found in Bali, Lombok, and parts of East Java, Sumatra, and Celebes recently converted to Bali-Hindu religion or settled by Balinese under Indonesia's national program to relocate population. Many sourcebooks for Balinese drama derive from the pre-Muslim period of Javanese civilization. Beginning in the fourteenth century, Java's hinduized courts confronted first Islamic, then Western forces of trade, political authority, and religious instruction; the ritual and drama apparently central to Javanese statecraft altered accordingly. Neighboring Bali, in part isolated from these developments and from the more intensive style of Dutch colonialism, provided a context for the continuing cultivation of both scribal and performing arts tied to rites of ancestor commemoration and a cult of kingship, to wet-rice agricultural cycles, and to intricate temple systems that organize productive lands, civic units, domestic space, and funerary areas into networks of shrines. Hindu deities and local ancestors make periodic visitations to these shrines to be entertained. Moreover, demonic agents both regularly and occasionally upset the social and cosmic equilibrium and must be appeased at places vulnerable to their influence, such as the ground, the sea, and all crossroads.

Balinese temple celebrations always include the playing of gongs and metallophones (*gamelan*, the instruments for which the percussion orchestra is named) and specific dances in ritual processions; they may also include shadow puppet theater *(wayang)*, masked dance drama *(topeng)*, or many unmasked dance dramas. Performances may be used to upgrade life-crisis rites, such as tooth filings, weddings, and cremations. A specific orchestral ensemble accompanies each variety of dance and drama. Important genres include *gambuh*, *topeng*, *parwa*, and *wayang*. In *gambuh*, unmasked courtly dramas dating back at least four hundred years, the orchestra adds haunting flutes to its percussions. *Gambuh* tales come from the indigenous cycle of love and political intrigue called Malat in Bali and Panji in Java. Masked *topeng*, performed either by a soloist or by multiple actor-dancers, stages narratives from dynastic chronicles. *Parwa*, probably originating around 1885, is similar to *wayang wong*, in which masked dancers replace the famous leather puppets of *wayang kulit;* but *parwa* contents are restricted to episodes from the *Mahābhārata*. Bali's versions of the *Rāmāyaṇa* remain the basic source for *wayang*, both the renowned nighttime varieties that project puppet shadows onto a screen and the daytime version without shadows, regarded as a more potent message to ancestral shades. Myriad additional genres represent one of the fullest flowerings of dramatic dance in the history of civilizations.

Complex rules delimit which episodes in what performance mode are suited to which rituals; variations reflect Bali's history of shifting sponsorships by courts, ancestor groups, localities, and now national and commercial agencies. Several types of dance involve divine or demonic possession (for example, the prepubescent trance dancers of *Sanghyang Dedari*). Trance occurs frequently in Balinese ritual, most spectacularly among the participants in the famous exorcist battles based on the Tantric tale of *Calonarang*, in which the witch Rangda (whose dread masks belong to village-area temples) engages the friendlier force of lionlike Barong (whose costumes are usually owned by hamlets). The end is inevitably a standoff. Most Balinese dance dramas, however, are thought to be given not by deities or demons, but for them. Bali's traditional concept of "audience" includes the ordinarily remote deities, lured to their "seats" for the show; partisan ancestors, to whom descendants may have "promised in their hearts" a particular performance; human spectators of all social ranks; and outsiders as well, including foreigners and tourists. Indeed commoners, called "outsiders" to noble courts *(puri)*, are essential spectators. That ritual and drama are seldom designed for a closed public, despite the culture's exclusivistic hierarchies, helps explain the resilience of Bali's semiprofessionalized dance and drama organizations: talented peasants moonlighting in troops for hire.

Any Balinese ritual mobilizes an array of specialists, some restricted by caste or social position, others not. Brahmana priests *(pedanda)* specialize in Sanskrit and esoteric manuals that prescribe rituals for purifying water *(tīrtha)* required by their clients for ceremonies. Puppeteers *(dhalang)*, not restricted to a particular caste but sometimes concentrated in certain ancestral lines, are highly respected virtuosi: a *dhalang* is the actors, propmen, screenwriter, director, and conductor rolled into one. Young dancers are intensively exercised in choreographic codes that replicate in gestures what a *dhalang* depicts through puppets. A temple celebration, cremation, wedding, or other ritual may be elaborated into a bustling, muted circus, with multiple rings of performers and onlookers, perhaps including a priest intoning *mantras*, a reading group reciting select texts, a *wayang*, various phases of the ritual itself, extra attractions, and several *gamelan*. Historically transforming genres of dance and drama have combined and recombined select channels of refined versus agitated form: sound (in phased periodicities of percussion), voice (in chant and prayer, individual and choral song, and spoken dialogues), languages (Sanskrit; Old Javanese, or Kawi; High Balinese; vernacular Balinese; Indonesian), styles of movement, and levels of gesture. Certain performers—the puppeteer, the *topeng* soloist, the translating and paraphrasing servant-clowns of *wayang wong*—must master all codes.

Dance and drama in Bali portray stock types of conventional characters, ordered into cosmically opposed sets, right-hand ("mountainward") and left-hand ("seaward"). The familiar panoply from Hindu myth and epic includes gods; heroes; adventurous knights; ladies; prime ministers; ladies-in-waiting; servants; ogres; demons; animals (some anthropomorphic); and clowns, the most popular figures, marked by specifically Balinese characteristics. Stage layouts, the situation of performances in and around temples, and the punctuation of ritual by dance and drama help articulate such conceptually opposite attributes as refined and crude and divine and demonic implicit in all spatial arrangements, interactions, and temporal flow. Styles of offerings and priestly functions, too, activate complementary cycles of patterned sound, gesture, story, and ritual regalia: from the esoteric *mantras* and *mudrās* (hand postures) of *pedanda* (high priests of the right-hand powers) or *sengguhu* (high priests of the left-hand powers), to the charms, tokens, and homey icons of the many *balian* ("curers") dealing in sorcery and love magic. The realms of health and disease, activities of allure and cure, and the values of aesthetics and exorcism remain intertwined in Bali-Hinduism, where any analytic separation of the theatrical, the political, and the religious arts is difficult to sustain.

Recent studies of Balinese dance and drama adopt helpful, although conscientiously rationalized, schemes advanced by I G. Sugriwa, R. Moerdowo, and other Indonesian scholars. They distinguish four types of dances. There are dances indispensable to ritual sacrifice, performed in the inner temple by the deities' female attendants and male guardians, drawn from the community concerned. There are optional dance dramas of the middle courtyard that heighten a temple ceremony or a crisis rite; masks and costumes and the performers themselves, perhaps hired from outside, are ritually consecrated. A third type encompasses "secular" dances performed in conjunction with a temple ceremony, but outside the walls, along with cockfights and games of chance; one example is the flirtatious Joged, a dance that recalls precolonial royal involvement in prostitution and other service monopolies. Finally, commercial dances, casually performed with unconsecrated masks, have flourished in tourist shows; the consummate example is the picturesque monkey dance (the Cak), which has become the trademark of Balinese culture in Indonesia under the regime of President Suharto.

The rich interplay among dance, drama, and religious practice and belief in Bali pertains to many important issues. Balinese Hinduism's stress on dance in popular ritual sets it off vividly from Islamic values of neighboring islands and of the Indonesian nation. Although many dramatic texts in Bali originated in India, its dance is very different from South Asian varieties, as are its temples. The rituals garnished with Balinese dance drama have counterparts among non-Hindu Indonesians, particularly wet-rice growers and societies organized into rival centers of authority marked by competitive displays during rituals of death, reburial, marriage, circumcision (not practiced by Balinese), or other passage rites. A major problem in interpreting Balinese arts concerns their place in rivalries among rajas, among localities, and among other sponsors. The manufacture of sacred objects—gongs, masks, daggers, written texts, and the like—and expertise in rituals necessary to maintain and periodically cleanse and reconsecrate them remain important in Balinese notions of status and prestige. Moreover, dramas often contain stories of their own origins and credit different social segments, dynasties, and ancestors with instituting distinct arts and performances. Contrary claims in these matters still vitalize Balinese social and political processes and introduce complications into the historiography of Balinese religion, dance, and drama.

Explicit Bali-Hindu philosophies of religion correlate action, word, and thought, thus orchestrating ritual deed, spoken syllables, and mental images in a theory of the interrelation of visual, verbal, spatial, and sonic arts. Some Balinese experts make fine distinctions between trance and "inspiration" *(taksu)* as well as other conditions of dramatic and religious awareness. Although several modern institutes and schools for the preservation and advancement of Balinese arts have promoted new experiments in training and documentation (including musical notation systems), traditional court-based or village-centered training techniques persist for music, dance, drama, sculpture, painting, and so forth. Certain principles of Balinese religion seem manifest less in popular creed than in ideals of transmitting from masters to novices complex aesthetic skills, such as musically structured muscular coordination of postures plus pulsations of eyes, limbs, feet, and fingers. Performers achieve exemplary concentration, self-control, and personal effacement; their poise seems to exist in dynamic tension with the risk of demonic abandon. Judging from Balinese culture, a religion can be danced as much as believed.

BIBLIOGRAPHY

A recent, insightful general description of Balinese dance is I M. Bandem and Fredrik De Boer's *Kaja and Kelod: Balinese Dance in Transition* (Oxford, 1981). The classic account, which accentuates dramatic narrative, remains the splendid volume by Beryl de Zoete and Walter Spies, *Dance and Drama in Bali* (1938; reprint, Oxford, 1973). There are fine illustrations with concise descriptions and case studies in Urs Ramseyer's *The Art and Culture of Bali* (Oxford, 1977). The abundant philological work on Balinese texts, many involved in dance drama, can be surveyed, beginning with Christiaan Hooykaas's *Religion in Bali* (Leiden, 1973) and *Drawings of Balinese Sorcery* (Leiden, 1980); Hooykaas alone produced a score of major books of translation and commentary. On performance contexts for right-hand and left-hand magic, see Marie-Thérèse Berthier and John-Thomas Sweeney's *Bali: L'art de la magie* (Paris, 1976). For a guide to the intriguing collection of work done by assorted artists, musicologists, anthropologists, and performers in the 1920–1930s, see *Traditional Balinese Culture*, compiled by Jane Belo (New York, 1970). Still vivid and relevant are many parts of Miguel Covarrubias's *Island of Bali* (New York, 1937). Background on social and historical processes at work in religion and dramatic arts is reviewed in my book *The Anthropological Romance of Bali, 1597–1972* (New York, 1977) and Clifford Geertz's *Negara: The Theater State in Nineteenth-Century Bali* (Princeton, 1980). All of the works listed include extensive bibliographies with copious relevant literature in Dutch, Indonesian, and Balinese.

James A. Boon

Javanese Wayang

Wayang kulit, also known as *wayang purwa* ("shadow play"), is a type of puppet theater that is indigenous primarily to Java, the most populous island of Indonesia, but that flourishes also on the Indonesian islands of Bali and Lombok and in the state of Kelantan on the Malay Peninsula. *Wayang kulit* is performed by a sacral puppeteer *(dalang),* who, accompanied by the percussive yet flowing music of the *gamelan* orchestra, moves intricately crafted leather figures in front of an oil lamp to cast flickering shadows on a white screen as he chants mythological narrative in old sanskritized Javanese or other languages. Variants of *wayang kulit* include the wooden-rod puppet form *wayang golek* among the Sundanese of West Java and a human dance drama *(wayang wong)* patterned after the puppet plays.

Wayang kulit traditionally lasts all night—from 9 PM to 7 AM—and is a rite as well as a drama. It is performed at weddings and circumcisions, to exorcise evil spirits, and to cure. *Wayang kulit* also embodies an elaborate mythology and philosophy. The two great Hindu epics, the *Māhābharata* and the *Rāmāyaṇa,* are the mythological sources for some of the *wayang kulit* narrations. The *Rāmāyaṇa* depicts the quest of Prince Rāma, aided by the white monkey god Hanuman, for Princess Sītā, who is abducted by the monster king Rāvaṇa. The *Māhābharata* portrays the battle between the five knightly brothers, the Pandavas, and the hundred rival princes, the Kurawas. But these plots are only a skeleton for a vast cycle of interlocking episodes developed by the Indonesians. In addition to the Hindu epics, variants of *wayang kulit* draw on stories from Arab, Javanese, and other traditions, as well as contemporary plays, including some addressing such topical matters as family planning or national ideology.

Wayang kulit characters are categorized according to their status, temperament, and manner, and their interrelationships are plotted through intricate genealogies that trace them to the origins of the world. The refined characters tend to appear on the puppeteer's right, the crude ones on his left. The refined princes, epitomized by Arjuna of the Pandavas, have narrow, almond-shaped eyes, down-turned noses, slightly bowed heads, no chin whiskers, and delicate physiques. Crude monsters, typified by Buriswawa, are fat, with heavy, bristling eyebrows, round eyes, bulbous noses, and red faces. Battles between refined heroes and crude monsters carry psychological as well as political meanings, symbolizing the tension between fleshly desire and spiritual tranquillity. Related themes include the hero's search for his origin and destiny as he passes through temptations represented by forest nymphs, and his search for the self, symbolized by his climbing inside the ear of his own miniature replica to discover the universe inside the person. For Javanese, to experience the symbolism of a *wayang* play is vicariously to struggle through the life cycle and to undergo mystical exercises, and they have composed meditations and treatises on the plays that explicate their meanings in relation to Javanese philosophies and theologies, as well as world religions.

A central role is played by Semar, the short-legged, stout, hermaphroditic, and misshapen clown. Brother to Batara Guru (Śiva), Semar was of pre-Hindu, local Javanese origin (c. 600 CE), and he combines the earthly role of lowly servant with the powers and wisdom of the highest god. It is he who appears on the screen at midnight, when the elements rage, to restore order. Having a relation to the princes somewhat like that of Shakespeare's Falstaff to Prince Hal, Semar balances their extreme refinement, heroism, and nobility with his earthiness and buffoonery (a buffoonery that, when necessary, is transformed into awesome might).

If the clown-servant Semar represents, as some have suggested, the earthy Javanese substance beneath the courtly Hindu glaze, Prince Arjuna is the consummate Satriya, the cultured and noble knight. Before a great battle, Arjuna is troubled by the need to kill his cousins and boyhood playmates, the Kurava. In his distress he turns to his divine mentor, Kṛṣṇa, who is driving Arjuna's chariot. Kṛṣṇa explains that Arjuna must fulfill the code of his knightly caste and follow the predetermined path of his life: he must slay the enemy. He should perform that deed, however, while maintaining an inner detachment from it. Spiritual tranquillity in the midst of worldly conflict is a core ideal of hinduized Javanese philosophy.

Wayang kulit has been part of Javanese experience for perhaps a thousand years, dating back at least to the time of King Airlangga in the eleventh century CE. Yet *wayang kulit* remains very much a living tradition, influencing the political and secular as well as the religious life of Indonesians. The late President Sukarno once wrote a newspaper column under the penname Bima, the blunt and strong Pandava brother, and he named a regiment after the female warrior Srikandi. Sukarno also referred to his relation to Indonesia as analogous to that of a *dalang* to his puppets, and in other ways he and others have drawn on the imagery of *wayang* in interpreting political life. Comic books on newsstands depict the adventures of Semar's sons Petruck and Gareng in contemporary costumes and situations. Pedicabs are painted with the image of Semar, and he is the guardian figure for a contemporary mystical cult. Classical performances of *wayang kulit* abound, not only in palaces and schools but also as part of community life—at weddings and village festivals, amid the laughter of children and the gossip and meditative conversation of their elders.

BIBLIOGRAPHY

A standard source on *wayang kulit* is J. Kats's *Het Javaansche tooneel,* pt. 1, *Wajang poerwa* (Weltevreden, 1923), which describes principal characters and some stories. *Sedjarah wajang purwa,* edited by Raden Hardjowirogo (Djakarta, 1955), provides descriptions of a larger number of characters. For Balinese dance and drama, the classic source is Beryl de Zoete and Walter Spies's *Dance and Drama in Bali* (New York, 1938). Regarding *wayang kulit* in Malaya, see Jeanne Cuisinier's *Le théâtre d'ombres à Kelantan,* 2d ed. (Paris, 1957). An excellent brief introduction is Mantle Hood's "The Enduring Tradition: Music and Theater in Java and Bali," in *Indonesia,* edited by Ruth T. McVey (New Haven, 1963).

Translated texts of the Javanese plays, together with helpful interpretations, appear in *On Thrones of Gold: Three Javanese Shadow Plays* (Cambridge, Mass., 1970), edited by James R. Brandon. A profound comment on the meaning and worldview of the *wayang* is provided in A. L. Becker's "Textbuilding, Epistemology, and Aesthetics in Javanese Shadow Theater," in *The Imagination of Reality: Essays in Southeast Asian Coherence Systems*, edited by A. L. Becker and Aram A. Yengoyan (Norwood, N.J., 1979). A fascinating interpretation of mystical meanings of the *wayang kulit* is provided by Mangkunegara VII of the court of Surakarta in his *On the Wajang Kulit and Its Symbolic and Mystical Elements*, translated by Claire Holt (Ithaca, N.Y., 1957). A provocative sociological interpretation is given in Benedict R. O'G. Anderson's *Mythology and the Tolerance of the Javanese* (Ithaca, N.Y., 1965), and a useful ethnographic view is Clifford Geertz's *Religion of Java* (Glencoe, Ill., 1960), chap. 18.

Concerning ritual aspects of Balinese shadow plays, see Christian Hooykaas's *Kama and Kala: Materials of the Study of Shadow Theatre in Bali* (Amsterdam, 1973).

JAMES L. PEACOCK

East Asian Dance and Theater

From ancient times, theater and religion have had a close, often symbiotic, relationship in East Asia. Theatrical performance is an integral part of certain animistic, Confucian, and Buddhist rites in China, Korea, and Japan. Priests have been performers, and even today temples and shrines provide places for performance. Play cycles based on religious myth and legend are numerous. Aesthetic systems reflect religious worldviews. Although drama is increasingly secularized in the contemporary world, religious values and beliefs continue to be projected to audiences through masked plays *(sandae* in Korea, *satokagura* and *nō* in Japan), popular dramas (*kabuki* in Japan and *ching-hsi* and other forms of Chinese opera), and puppet plays (*gogdu gagsi* in Korea and *bunraku* in Japan).

Shamanism and Animism. Since prehistoric times people in northeast Asia have communicated with animistic spirits for the benefit of the living through songs and dances. In the fourth millennium BCE, the inscription on a Chinese oracle bone mentions a dance of sympathetic magic performed to induce the spirits to bring rain. Before the time of Confucius (or K'ung-tzu, c. 551–479 BCE), songs and dances dedicated to the Eight Deities and supervised by the royal steward constituted an important state ritual of the Chinese court. Performing a masked play is a folk ritual in northwest Korea, intended to repulse evil spirits at the beginning of summer. Dances of demon exorcism (*namahage* and *emburi* for example) are central features of lunar New Year festivals in scores of villages in Japan. The Lion Dance, familiar through East Asia, may have derived from totem worship in prehistoric times.

The three-part structure of the rituals of Shintō, containing many animistic elements, reveals one reason performing arts in Japan are naturally linked to the practice of animism: the god (or *kami*) is summoned into this world, entertained, and sent away. Because deities had to be entertained, a large number of religious dances developed. In Japan many dances enact, often in attenuated, symbolic form, myths of the islands' founding gods and goddesses. The god remains enshrined in his or her god-house during court or shrine dances *(mikagura)*, hence the dancer and the god are separate. At agricultural festivals, village actors wear the costumes and masks of ferocious demons *(oni)*. In these folkloric dance dramas *(satokagura)*, the spirit moves freely into the world of humans by possessing the performer.

From these primal traditions has come the concept of a sanctified stage area. A sacred playing space, often on the ground, is set apart from the mundane world by the placement of tree branches at the four corners. This idea, in developed form, can be seen in the Japanese *nō* stage. A plain square platform is marked off by four pillars and covered by a roof in the style indicating the dwelling of a god. The bridgeway *(hashigakari)*, on which the spirit-protagonist of a *nō* play enters, mirrors the sacred passageway marked out on a shrine ground along which a god would make his or her journey from the other world to a temporary home at festival time.

In shamanistic traditions, the shaman is a professional communicator with the spirits. Throughout East Asia and from earliest times, dance and song have been essential shamanic skills. The Chinese *Li chi* (Book of Rites; fourth century BCE) tells of shamans wearing animal skins who drive out evil spirits, and *The Elegies of Ch'u* of the first century BCE describes elegantly dressed male and female shamans singing and dancing seductively to woo deities to make the passage down into this world. Contemporary shamans continue the tradition of being skilled singers and dancers. Dances of Japanese shamans are relatively simple, while seances *(kut)* of present-day Korean shamans contain complex dances designed to please the god being invoked. The purely theatrical skill of juggling can be part of the shaman's repertory in Korea. In Japan, juggling and acrobatics were associated with Shintō agricultural festivals in medieval times as "field music" *(dengaku)*, and they are still performed today during Shintō festivals such as the New Year celebration.

The origin of theater in Japan is described in the *Kojiki* (Records of Ancient Matters; 712) and the *Nihongi* (Chronicles of Japan; 720) in a myth that has the shape of a shamanistic performance. The sun goddess, Amaterasu, has withdrawn in anger from the community of fellow deities into a rock cave, thus plunging Japan into darkness. Another goddess, Ama no Uzume, tries to lure her from the cave by showing her breasts, lowering her skirt, and dancing joyfully on an overturned tub. The assembled gods and goddesses cry out and clap with delight. Hearing their laughter, Amaterasu leaves the cave to see what is causing so much merriment—thus light is restored to the world. Like a shaman, Ama no Uzume entices a goddess to leave her private world and join the community on whose behalf she is performing. Like a shaman, she entices the goddess with joyful singing and dancing. And like a shaman, she uses a mirror and holds a sprig of a tree, two favorite shamanic implements.

Links between shaman and performing artist are not difficult to identify. The Chinese ideograph for shaman represents two people practicing a skill, by inference, the skill of performance. The same ideograph is used in Japan for a Shintō priestess *(miko)*, who serves at a shrine as a *kagura* dancer. The old Korean term *kwangdae* meant shaman or popular performer interchangeably. In Korea the husbands of female shamans performed masked plays *(sandae)* and puppet plays *(gogdu gagsi)*. One of the standard roles in plays of both genres is the female shaman, usually depicted as a young and alluring prostitute. It is also believed that *pan'sori* narrative singing was developed into a Korean national art by these same low-status performers in the eighteenth and nineteenth centuries. (Confucian and Buddhist teaching equally hold the shaman in contempt.) A Japanese myth says that the spreading pine tree painted on the back wall of a *nō* stage symbolizes the Yogo Pine, the tree through which the god descended to earth during performance. Stamping at the conclusion of a *nō* play and the earth-stamping dance sequences in village *kagura* are contemporary examples of Ama no Uzume's stamping steps described twelve hundred years ago. The four flags worn on the back of a Chinese opera general are averred to derive from the Chinese shaman's flags of exorcism.

It has been theorized that acting originated in East Asia in the shamanic act of possession. There are difficulties with such an argument. The village actor in Japan who wears the mask and costume of a demon may or may not be possessed by the mask's spirit; in neither case, however, is he functioning as a trained shaman. Conversely, the shaman, possessed by a deity and speaking the deity's words, rarely enacts past events in that deity's life as the actor would do. Rather, the shaman's function, at least as we know it today, is to bring the god's knowledge and power into the mundane world in the service of practical needs (curing sickness, assuring prosperity, et al.). The art of mimesis (acting) and especially the enactment of a story about a character (drama) are not essential to this function. Similarly, the action of a *nō* drama has been likened to a shamanistic seance because in the typical play an intermediary, usually a Shintō priest, summons a dead spirit or deity to enter this world. But the parallel is inexact: the enticed spirit does not possess the intermediary but becomes independently manifest on stage. Finally, and in a more general sense, the performing arts may have had their origin in shamanism. If so, we must imagine ancient man waiting for a shaman professional to create the first songs and dances. What is more likely is that after song and dance existed, shamans utilized these theatrical arts for religious purposes.

Confucianism. While less influential perhaps than primal traditions, Confucianism has affected the performing arts in three main ways. First, according to Confucian doctrine, the performance of appropriate music and dance helped assure the harmonious working of the universe. Confucian rulers supported court performance as a ritual function, often co-opting preexisting animistic rituals. During the T'ang dynasty (618–907) in China, the Koryŏ dynasty in Korea (from c. the eleventh century), and at the Japanese imperial court during the Nara and Heian periods (710–1191), rulers patronized large contingents of palace performers, and they established official schools to preserve the ritually correct forms. The Pear Garden school, founded by the emperor Hsüan-tsung (712–754), was the most famous of these in China. The Japanese form of court dance, *bugaku*, continues to be patronized by the emperor in modern Japan and thus represents an unbroken tradition of some thirteen hundred years. Second, Confucian ideals of proportion, moderation, and symmetry set the aesthetic tone of court performance. *Bugaku* is an excellent reflection of Confucian ideals in its sedateness, repeated patterns, and geometric symmetry of form.

Third, the ethical norms of Confucianism—social duties as expressed in the "five human relationships"—set the standards of morality for dramatic characters, especially in popular theater. Filial piety is celebrated in Chinese operas such as *The Lute Song* (c. 1358), and duty to one's lord in scores of Japanese *kabuki* and *bunraku* plays such as *The Forty-seven Loyal Retainers* (1749) and *The Subscription List* (1841). Korean *sandae* present a peasant's view of Confucian morality: unfilial sons and unfaithful wives are mockingly satirized. Domestic plays *(sewamono)* in eighteenth-century *kabuki* and *bunraku* use the conflict between human feelings *(ninjō)* and social duties *(giri)* as a major plot device. Chikamatsu Monzaemon (1653–1724) wrote a score of domestic plays in which young lovers, unable to meet the heavy demands of duty—to spouse, parents, children, employer—choose to die together rather than live under Confucian restrictions.

Buddhism. Between the seventh and the eleventh centuries, Buddhism was widely propagandized in East Asia by popular forms of masked drama. *Giak*, the Buddhist masked dance drama of Korea, was brought to Japan in 612 by the Korean immigrant, Mimaji (Jpn., Mimashi), who had learned the art in China. Called *gigaku* ("elegant entertainment") in Japan, it was supported by the imperial court as a means to spread the new state religion. *Gigaku* is described in a fourteenth-century book on music, *A Short Manual of Instruction*, as a procession that passed through the city streets in which masked performers enacted comic scenes ridiculing the evils of drunkenness, lechery, and lewdness. Court-supported performances died out, but village masked plays, such as the widespread *sandae* in Korea, and the Lion Dance (Jpn., *shishimai*) that is seen everywhere in East Asia, are believed to be their descendants. Remnants can also be seen in contemporary *gyōdō* processions in Japan, in which monks wearing masks of *bodhisattva*s circle a statue of the Buddha. Popular, anticlerical views of Buddhism can be seen in contemporary Korean *sandae*. Buddhist monks are ridiculed for being venal and lustful.

The origin of *nō* in Japan can be traced back to ninth-century performances of sorcerers *(jushi* or *noroji)* who would impersonate a guardian deity of Buddhism such as Bishamon at the New Year exorcism ceremony, and of temple sextons who would play his *oni* (demon) antagonists. In the twelfth and thirteenth centuries, Buddhist priests enacted teachings and legends of Buddha in *ennen nō* and *sarugaku nō*. Even after professional actors took over in the thirteenth and fourteenth centuries, troupes lived at Buddhist temples. The troupe organized by Kan'ami Kiyotsugu (1333–1384), the nominal founder of *nō*, was attached to the Kōfukuji in Nara, and most of Kan'ami's life was spent performing at Buddhist temple festivals around the country. A dozen *nō* plays out of the repertory of 240 concern Shintō deities. *Ōkina*, a ceremonial piece commemorating felicitous longevity, is the most ancient and sacred. The majority, however, are deeply imbued with Buddhist teachings. By the time of the great actor Zeami Motokiyo (1363–1443), the protagonist *(shite)* of a typical *nō* play was the ghost of a famous man or woman who was suffering torment in Buddhist hell. At the conclusion of such a play, the spirit abandons the sinful human ties binding him or her to this world and, through the mercy of Amida Buddha, attains salvation in Western Paradise. While Zen philosophy is expressed by characters in some *nō* plays, the Pure Land salvation of Amida is far more pervasive (as it is in *kabuki* and *bunraku* plays).

Early puppet plays in Japan emphasized Buddhist miracles and legends. *The Chest-Splitting of Amida*, showing the Buddha saving a dying girl by placing his heart in her chest, was a sixteenth-century favorite. Buddhist ghosts of the dead and reincarnated spirits are standard characters in Chinese opera, *nō*, *bunraku*, and *kabuki*, becoming, in the latter, objects of parody in the nineteenth century. Buddhist concepts underlie several features of playwriting. Coincidence abounds, not because playwrights were careless, but because of the belief in reincarnation: people whose paths had crossed in previous lives were fated to meet again in later incarnations. The Buddhist idea that the world is transient and in constant flux finds its parallel in the episodic structure of Chinese operas, Korean *sandae*, and Japanese *kabuki* and *bunraku* dramas. The relative unimportance of climax, so noticeable to the Western theatergoer, is a reflection of the belief that each moment is equal to any other, that life is a stream constantly flowing. Zen concepts of intuitive apprehension—as opposed to explicit statement—underlie the *nō* aesthetics of restraint, suggestion, and abhorrence of realistic detail in staging. A practical man of theater, Zeami nonetheless formulated a particularly Buddhist vision of the ideal *nō* performance. It should express *yūgen*, a quiet beauty tinged with dark, melancholy emotion. The *nō* actor and theoretician Komparu Zenchiku (d. between 1468 and 1471) carried Zen aesthetics to its furthest when he spoke of the art of *nō* passing through "six wheels," an image relating to the Buddhist duality of illusion-reality, and leading to ultimate enlightenment, symbolized by the wheel of emptiness and the sword.

For the sake of convenience, the contribution of each religion to the performing arts has been discussed separately here. Yet such a division is necessarily arbitrary and perhaps misleading. One aspect of dance or theater may reflect several East Asian religions. To cite but one example, the annual cycle of full-moon festivals that is celebrated by performances in all parts of East Asia relates to local traditions, Confucianism, Buddhism, and, indeed, Taoism as well.

[*See also* Music, *articles on* Music and Religion in China, Korea, and Tibet *and* Music and Religion in Japan.]

BIBLIOGRAPHY

No single book adequately addresses the topic of this article. Halla Pai Huhm describes the unique role of shamanism in the performing arts of one country in *Kut: Korean Shamanist Rituals* (Elizabeth, N.J., and Seoul, 1980), while the classic study of shamanism in East Asia remains Mircea Eliade's *Shamanism:*

Archaic Techniques of Ecstasy, rev. & enl. ed. (Princeton, 1964). There are interesting chapters on Shintō ritual and myth in performance in Fred Mayer and Thomas Immoos's *Japanese Theatre* (New York, 1977). Buddhist contributions to *nō* are covered in detail in Inoura Yoshinobu's *A History of Japanese Theater*, vol. 1, *Noh and Kyogen* (Tokyo, 1971), and in Patrick Geoffrey O'Neill's *Early Nō Drama* (London, 1958). Oh Kon Cho's *Korean Puppet Theatre: Kkoktu Kaksi* (East Lansing, Mich., 1979) discusses Buddhism and shamanism as butts of satire. In *Major Plays of Chikamatsu* (New York, 1961), Donald Keene offers an analysis of Confucian and Buddhist values in Japanese popular drama. The most complete accounts of early religious influences on Chinese theater are still those of A. E. Zucker, *The Chinese Theatre* (Boston, 1925), and Cecilia S. L. Zung, *Secrets of Chinese Drama* (1937; New York, 1964.)

James R. Brandon

African Religious Drama

In traditional Africa, everyday life, blending profane and sacred activities, is permeated with music, dance, rhythmic movement, symbolic gestures, song, and verbal artistry. Body adornment—costuming, painting, tattooing, decorating, and masking—is not only a mark of status, age, and sex differentiations but also serves as an element of beautification, play, imitation, impersonation, and visual communication of religious values.

Dramatic performances by soloists and groups of actors interacting with active spectators originate from the combination of these features in recurring formal settings. Simple routine activities as well as momentous events—the hoeing of a field, the telling of a tale, the recitation of an epic, the coming out ceremony of a newborn child, the celebration of a marriage, the initiation of young men and women, the enthronement of a chief, or the burial rites of a headman—are accompanied by dramatic performances, all with more or less explicit religious content. Groups of interacting participants (protagonists, preceptors, experts, attendants, musicians, singers, active audience), in specific settings and at prescribed moments, portray characters and enact events through the combined use of words, songs, gestures, rhythms, dances, mimicry, music, and artifacts. The narration of a tale, for example, becomes a performance event in which narrator and audience may enhance the presentation of a text through phonic, verbal, and mimetic features, including dialogue, choral singing, handclapping, gestures, and sometimes music and special costumes (Ben-Amos, 1977, pp. 13–16; Finnegan, 1970, pp. 500–502).

In the performance of an epic, Nyanga bards of Zaire identify with the central hero by acting out select passages before an audience that responds with encouragements and sung refrains (Biebuyck and Mateene, 1969). Accompanied by song and music, Pygmy hunters among the Bembe of Zaire perform spectacular solo and duo dances. Painted and dressed in animal hides and feather hats, the hunters imitate the behavior of certain animals and the techniques used to spear them in a display of skill and prowess that placates the deities presiding over the hunt. The Khomani of southern Africa stage plays in which men and boys act out, with appropriate sound effects, the hunting of a gemsbok or a fight between baboons and dogs, or plays in which women and girls imitate the movements and habits of turtles (Doke, 1936, pp. 465–469). After harvest time among the Malinke and Bamana of West Africa, disguised men, accompanied by a female chorus, present nocturnal comical and satirical sketches that portray characters such as a thief, a braggart, or an adulterous woman. Each performance is a structured entity that starts with a ballet with male and female participants. A prologue, which is both sung and acted, follows, introducing the individual actors. Last are the actual plays in which the actors also engage in dialogue with the musicians (Labouret and Travélé, 1928). Countless other examples could be given of such performances where dramatic action offers an opportunity for entertainment, display of artistic skill, social prestige, and reward. Broad religious conceptions are implicit in the overall purposes of such performances, which show the close bond between animals and humans or the disastrous consequences of not living in conformity with standards set by the ancestors.

The elements of religious drama emerge more directly in activities linked with hunting, planting, harvesting, and other seasonal events. These performances not only ensure a successful hunt or abundant crops but also placate the supernatural beings that are responsible for order in nature, appease the spirits of the animals, attract and neutralize evil beings, purify humans of their sinful interference with natural forces, and protect against witchcraft.

In dances preceding an actual expedition, elephant hunters among the Baasa of eastern Zaire are painted and specially dressed to present the village audience with a sequence of realistic skits in which elephants are praised and appeased before being symbolically killed (to increase the chances for a safe and successful hunt). The movements of the elephant are vividly recreated by a disguised hunter who carries two small elephant tusks. At the same time, actors painted to portray marauding leopards symbolically evoke the dangers of the deep forest, while others brandish spears and display medicines to depict the power, tribulations, and joys of the specialist hunters. The song texts are specifically addressed to famed ancestors, divinities, and elephant spirits to protect and purify the hunters.

Divination and therapeutic sessions may be simple events in which a diviner or healer submits the patient to private consultation and treatment. If masks, figurines, and other sculptures are used, the sessions develop into a sequence of dramas in which mystic powers are captured, controlled, and released for the benefit of the patient.

Among the Kongo of southwestern Zaire, when a person is diagnosed by a diviner to be suffering from a sickness or misfortune caused by *nkosi*, the patient must be treated by a ritual expert who holds complete control over this mysterious power. *Nkosi* is contained in a secret mixture of mineral, vegetal, and animal ingredients placed in the cavity of a wooden figurine and consecrated by the sacred words and deeds of a healer initiated to this power.

The treatment consists of an ordered sequence of dramatic events. The invited healer, accompanied by attendants playing small slit-drums, carries the figurine to the outskirts of the village. Dialogue and action including the patient's relatives follows. After receiving gifts, healers and assistants proceed to the patient's house. The figurine is placed on a mat while the patient, surrounded by many relatives, is seated outside. There follows a series of dramatic actions, accompanied by songs, imprecations, gestures, music, and rhythmic movements. The figurine is manipulated like a puppet while the power contained in it is exhorted, conjured, and appeased with words, gestures, and sacrificial blood; the patient and relatives are aspersed with lustral liquid; the patient is rubbed successively with white clay, oil, and the medicines contained in the figurine; and the rules and prohibitions linked with *nkosi* are interpreted (Van Wing, 1941, pp. 89–90).

Funerary ceremonies are sometimes accompanied by a spectacular dramatic finale intended to honor the deceased and their families. An elaborate example is the Bobongo of the Ekonda of west-central Africa. Organized *équipes* of men or women rehearse for several weeks before presenting the theatrical spectacle three to fifteen months after the death of an important man. The performance includes a combination of special body ornamentation, dance, acrobatics, pantomime, song, panegyrics, tales, lessons in ethics, and invocations of nature spirits and dead quasi-divinized twins. It also involves the construction of special decors, platforms, fences, and litters in which solo dancers are brought to the village (Iyandza-Lopoloko, 1961; Vangroenweghe, 1977).

Dramatic forms of expression climax in those rituals and festivities in which masked, painted, and costumed actors, sometimes carrying artifacts (clubs, whips, scepters, staffs, swords, axes, rattles, phalli, figurines), engage in prescribed and staged performances. The intricate action involves a combination of sung and spoken texts, vocal signals, music, dance, gestures, and mimicry by specially disguised performers who interact with one another and with the participating audience. These maskers represent ancestors, divinities, nature spirits, monsters, and mythological or undefinable *sui generis* creatures. In many ethnic groups these total performances, incorporating elements of what is conventionally called drama, sacred opera, and ballet, form an intrinsic part of men's initiations (for example, puberty rites, induction into voluntary associations and cult groups, enthronement rites for chiefs and headmen, and initiation schools for ritual experts). The numerous activities of these initiations—which may extend over a considerable period of time and may be staged in several prescribed settings—are interspersed with performances in which the actors embody supernatural beings and human prototypes.

Outstanding examples of traditional African dramatic art are found in the young men's Mukanda rites, held periodically by a large number of related ethnic groups in southern Zaire, northeastern Angola, and northern Zambia. Novices are circumcised at an early stage of the rites as part of the transition from boyhood to manhood, but the overall aims of the Mukanda institution are social, didactic, moral, and aesthetic. Living in prolonged seclusion, the young men are not only trained in vital economic activities but are thoroughly educated in values and beliefs. They spend a large part of their secluded life learning how to perform dances, music, and songs and how to manufacture costumes, masks, and other paraphernalia. Throughout the Mukanda, the elders and ritual experts who organize and direct the rites, and even the women and noninitiated males who are excluded from their secret activities, are involved in a series of celebrations in which choreographic and musical performances are as essential as the material and social aspects. Masked and costumed male performers, singly and in groups, participate in the secret and public events.

Among the Chokwe, who have the most highly developed mask institution, maskers appear in all major stages of the Mukanda rites and in the public festivities that follow. The masks, hierarchically organized, fall into distinctive semantic, morphological, and functional groups. They also differ in the materials used (some are sculptured in wood; others are constructed of fibers, beaten bark, and resin), in size and volume, in the ornamental designs, and in the related accessories, costumes, and paraphernalia. Each fully outfitted masker impersonates a unique character and refers symbolically to a range of religious, cosmological, moral, philosophical, and social concepts.

Masks may represent an ancestor of a chief or a lineage founder, a nature spirit, a mythological being, or some *sui generis* creature that exists only through the mask, as well as social and psychological types. All maskers are thought to be *ikishi*, beings who rise from the dead for the Mukanda through the intercession of ritual experts and devotees. For both insiders and outsiders, masks and maskers are always surrounded with an aura of sacredness, mystical power, danger, and mystery. The maskers have distinctive roles as impersonators of "others." Those that directly embody specific ancestors or nature spirits perform in situations of social control: they lend authority, dignity, integrity, and conformity to the proceedings; they protect against witchcraft or interference by noninitiates; they supervise and sanction the fermentation of corn, the brewing of the sacred corn beer, and the preparation of medicines; they sanction the secrecy and accuracy of the rites; they discipline and test moral and physical strength. Others that depict prototypical characters in the guise of legendary figures assume the roles of entertainers, comedians, and social critics to underscore basic social and moral values. All maskers stir strong emotions among novices and initiates as well as among noninitiates: they spread terror and anxiety; they create an atmosphere of severity and restraint; they engage in the burlesque, the libidinous, the satirical.

The danced and masked dramas of the Mukanda rituals alternate between reality and fiction, tragedy and comedy, and combine the performing arts to convey deep religious, moral, philosophical, and sociopolitical messages. Moreover, in several ethnic groups, the closing of the Mukanda period is followed by dance tours. Organized by previous and recent novices and their tutors, these masked dances function as displays of individual artistic talent and skill and as sources of prestige and material reward. These dance tours have gradually become independent dramatic performances in which the secular element of entertainment and fun overshadows the lingering sacredness attributed to the masks (Bastin, 1982; Lima, 1967).

In numerous festivals imbued with religious meanings among West African peoples (e.g., the Yoruba, Igbo, Abua, Urhobo, and Ijo of Nigeria), the central actors are maskers, often recruited from the members of secret societies, cult groups, and certain age groups. The spectacles performed at designated times by Yoruba Gẹlẹdẹ maskers follow a precise plot pattern in danced sketches that include social comments, satires, caricatures of strangers, and scenes honoring important persons and depicting hunters and women at markets. Artistic competition and the search for prestige in such performances are keen (Drewal, 1975, pp. 142–146). Their overall purposes, however, are the propitiation of witches through prayers, offerings of food, and sacrifices. Typical Yoruba masquerades linked with the Egungun cult start with a sequence of songs and invocations to divinities, ancestors, and elders along with acrobatics and dances; next are plays in which mythical themes are enacted together with satirical and burlesque sketches of characters; the performance ends with a procession to collect gifts (Drewal, 1975, pp. 46–48). Among the northwestern Igbo of Nigeria, some of the maskers in plays produced by males of the same age group represent women. These plays are performed at feasts held soon after harvest or at celebrations for the earth spirit. The forms of the masks depict ideal feminine beauty and character; the male maskers imitate female dancing style and portray women at work or at leisure (Boston, 1960). In the Afikpo-Igbo Okumkpa play, which is part of a calendar of seasonal festivals, as many as one hundred maskers (always thought to be personifications of ancestral and nature spirits) present danced and sung satirical and topical scenes that are conceived as commentaries on the lives of real persons (Ottenberg, 1975, pp. 87–127).

Dramatic impersonations of supernatural beings and mythological, legendary, and prototypical characters are accomplished not only through masks but also by simpler methods of mimicry, dance, word, object, and gesture. A case in point is the initiation of men and women into the hierarchically graded Bwami association of the Lega in eastern Zaire. Most phases of these initiations consist of structured dramatic sequences. Stereotypical characters are depicted in pantomimes by expert dancers and preceptors or are represented by natural objects and artifacts (including masks and figurines) that are displayed and manipulated in song and dance contexts. The characters are ancestors, legendary persons, illustrious initiates of the past, personified animals and objects, or social, physical, and psychological types. All of them positively or negatively illustrate the association's code of values.

In one episode, for example, an initiate represents Kyamunyungu za Baitindi ("big arrogant one of the passionate dice players"). The sickly old man, stumbling, irascible, and loaded with bags containing valuables, arrives uninvited in a village to play the dice game. In highly dramatic action that involves a cast of other initiates, the old man provokes the villagers by quarreling with the headman, interfering with the dice throwing, and challenging his opponents to a fight; unwilling to listen to advice, he is chased away. This scene refers to the novice who must passively listen to the advice of his tutors and show respect and restraint in all his actions.

The countless episodes in which ancestors (generalized or specifically named), stereotypical characters (e.g., Great Old One or Beautiful One), personified animals (e.g., pangolin or turtle), objects (e.g., a bark pounder or a shell), and activities (e.g., poison ordeal or divination) are enacted are always performed with dance, music, and song and with appropriate objects and paraphernalia. In many instances the dramatic effects are enhanced by light and dark contrasts (some of the action takes place at night, at dawn, or in a closed initiation house lighted with burning resin torches), special vocal features (dialogues, orations, praises, name shouting) and musical features (imitation of nature sounds; use of mirlitons, bull-roarers, and other unusual and sacred musical instruments; message drumming), and by alternating solo dances and ballets by initiated men or women (Biebuyck, 1973).

Theater in the modern Western sense may be a fairly recent development in Africa, but from immemorial times drama has been an intrinsic part of narrative sessions, rituals, and other celebrations (Schipper-de Leeuw, 1977, pp. 7–38). Moreover, the dramatic enactment of characters and events may become the most important feature in initiations and cult activities and as a result may be established as a partly independent form. The dramatic performances—short, self-contained sketches, longer, conceptually interrelated scenes, or elaborate plays—are multifunctional. They are total aesthetic expressions in which the participants, using a multimedia system of communication, display individual and collective skills in the arts of dance, song, music, sculpture, design, and costume to emphasize beauty, pageantry, inventiveness, harmony, and perfection. They are sources of entertainment for the actors and for the audience, which often actively participates as part of a chorus or an orchestra or by responding with its own dance, song, hand clapping, and dramatic action. They provide means of gaining prestige and reward and of reaffirming status, rank, and authority not only of the participants but also of the ancestors and supernatural beings. They incorporate multifaceted messsages on religious, moral, social, and political themes. Finally, those performances in particular that involve maskers are thought to be sacred occasions during which divinities, ancestors, nature spirits, and mythical beings return to the human world to be honored and placated, to bring communal well-being, and to sanction the rules and practices of initiations and rituals.

BIBLIOGRAPHY

Bastin, Marie-Louise. *La sculpture tshokwe*. Meudon, 1982.

Ben-Amos, Dan. "Introduction: Folklore in African Society." In *Forms of Folklore in Africa: Narrative, Poetic, Gnomic, Dramatic*, edited by Bernth Lindfors, pp. 1–34. Austin, 1977.

Biebuyck, Daniel P. *Lega Culture: Art, Initiation, and Moral Philosophy among a Central African People*. Berkeley, 1973.

Biebuyck, Daniel P., and Kohombo C. Mateene. *The Mwindo Epic from the Banyanga*. Berkeley, 1969.

Boston, J. S. "Some Northern Ibo Masquerades." *Journal of the Royal Anthropological Institute* 90 (1960): 54–65.

Doke, C. M. "Games, Plays and Dances of the ≠Khomani Bushmen." *Bantu Studies* 10 (1936): 461–471.

Drewal, Henry John. "African Masked Theatre." *Mime Journal* 2 (1975): 36–53.

Finnegan, Ruth. *Oral Literature in Africa*. London, 1970.

Graham-White, Anthony. *The Drama of Black Africa*. New York, 1974.

Hanna, Judith Lynne. *To Dance Is Human: A Theory of Nonverbal Communication*. Austin, 1979.

Iyandza-Lopoloko, Joseph. *Bobongo, danse renommée des Ekonda*. Tervuren, 1961.

Labouret, Henri, and Moussa Travélé. "Le théâtre mandingue (Soudan français)." *Africa* 1 (1928): 73–97.

Lima, Mesquitela. *Os "akixi" (mascarados) do Nordeste de Angola*. Lisbon, 1967.

Ottenberg, Simon. *Masked Rituals of Afikpo: The Context of an African Art*. Seattle, 1975.

Schipper-de Leeuw, Mineke. *Toneel en Maatschappij in Afrika*. Assen, 1977.

Traoré, Bakary. *The Black African Theatre and Its Social Functions*. Ibadan, 1972.

Vangroenweghe, Daniel. "Oorsprong en verspreiding van Bobongo en Iyaya bij de Ekonda." *Africa-Tervuren* 23 (1977): 106–128.

Van Wing, J. "Bakongo Magic." *Journal of the Royal Anthropological Institute* 71 (1941): 85–97.

DANIEL P. BIEBUYCK

Native American Religious Drama

In all regions of North America, indigenous peoples practiced various public rituals for the purpose of communicating with the supernatural spirits and powers that controlled their universe. The most ubiquitous and theatrical form of the dramatic performance was dance in which actors wore elaborate costumes and masks representing the supernatural beings they sought to appease. These dance dramas often involved a special performance area that included entrances and exits for the performers; a chorus of singers and dancers; principal dancers; scenic backdrops; special lighting effects; and, most importantly, plots revolving around myths of creation and supernatural beings and powers who were perceived to inhabit the everyday world. These dance dramas were characterized by masquerade, imitation, role reversal, burlesque, and reenactments of myths and personal visions.

American Indians relied greatly on their ability to mime the behaviors of those animals and birds that were important to their religious life. The environment played a great role in ritual performance, which was grounded empirically in knowledge of the seasons, flora, and fauna. As might be expected, hunters chose to emulate in their dances those animals that were important to their survival, while farmers performed rituals that focused on the agricultural cycle.

Dance drama was performed to the accompaniment of vocal music sung by an individual or chorus. The songs might contain meaningful text, sometimes short phrases that poetically captured the theme of the dance, or meaningless vocables that despite their lack of semantics were highly structured both melodically and rhythmically. The range of native musical instruments in North America was comparatively limited. Various sizes and shapes of drums served as the major accompaniment to song in all regions. Rhythmic patterns were characterized mainly by single unaccented beats, duple accented beats, and accented triplets. Only in the Pueblo Southwest do we find a highly structured sense of rhythm, particularly in some of the mimetic animal and bird dances, in which there is a perfect correspondence between song, drum, and dance steps without benefit of measured beats in the strict Western sense of time. [*See* Music, *article on* Music and Religion in the Americas.]

Costumes were both realistic and stylized. On the Plains, a Buffalo dancer would dress in the hides of a bull, complete with a headdress of horns, a robe over his shoulders, leggings made from the hairless part of the hide, and a buffalo tail hanging conspicuously from his waist. Similarly, Eagle dancers of the Pueblo Southwest soared gracefully in the dance plaza wearing costumes made from eagle feathers topped with a headdress representing the bald eagle's crown and golden beak. But in the Northwest Coast region, where wood sculpture reached its highest aesthetic form in all of North America, intricately carved masks, made to be manipulated by strings revealing masks within masks, and carved and painted dance houses and scenery frequently featured stylized representations of ravens, whales, bears, and other animals and birds significant to the coastal culture. [*See also* Iconography, *article on* Native American Iconography.]

All ritual performances were for the benefit of the general public as well as the principal performers, and all performances required a specially constructed performance area. Frequently, the public part of the performance represented only a small part of a longer ritual that sometimes took several days or weeks. For example, among the Lakota on the Great Plains, the vision quest was regarded as a personal and private form of mediation and propitiation. However, it was necessary for a medicine man to interpret the candidates' visions. Frequently, in order to legitimate the experiences, the supplicants were directed to reenact their visions before the entire village. This reenactment took the form of imitation of various animals or birds that had informed them, and appropriate costumes representing the buffalo, wolf, elk, bear, or eagle were worn.

On a larger scale, Plains Indians performed the Sun Dance collectively, after individual dancers had participated in private vision quests. An integral part of the ceremony, the elements of which were widely diffused to nearly all Plains tribes, was the erection of the medicine lodge, or sacred arbor, in which the performance occurred. Dancers wore special costumes including long kilts, necklaces representing sunflowers, and wreaths of sage around their wrists, ankles, and forehead. The segments of the dance in which the Sun was propitiated were directed by the Sun Dance leader. The performance lasted for several days and was accompanied by other intrusive dances prior to going on the buffalo hunt. [*For further discussion, see* Sun Dance.]

The Kwakiutl of the Northwest Coast were unsurpassed as dramatists with a full sense of lighting, scenery, costumes, and plot. The dance dramas were presented in cycles and depicted the kidnapping of the hero by a spirit who bestowed supernatural power upon him before returning the hero to the village. The hero was most frequently possessed by a "cannibal spirit" and therefore craved human flesh. In the reenactment, a frenzied hero was led back into the dance house by villagers and fed flesh believed to have been taken from a human corpse, although more likely it was animal meat. The dance house was replete with trap doors and tunnels, and performers could quickly appear and disappear magically. The dancers wore huge masks with movable parts, some representing the large beak of a bird, through which the dancers cried out "Eat! Eat!" Hollow stems hidden beneath the floor were used as microphones through which the voices of the actors could emanate from any part of the house. Dolls strung on ropes partly obscured by the dim firelight flew through the air for dramatic effect. Finally, the principal dancer, believing he had consumed human flesh, calmed down to end the event gracefully.

In the Northeast, the best-known Iroquoian sodality

was the False Faces. The society was formed when a supernatural being called False Face appeared to the Iroquois in the form of detached faces and taught them the art of curing. The elaborate masks were carved and painted in grotesque ways, and when worn by the society, members were believed to frighten away malevolent spirits that caused sickness. The mask was carved from a living tree and was painted red or black depending on whether the carver began work in the morning or afternoon. Noses, mouths, and eye holes were twisted and contorted, and long shocks of horsehair fell over the wearer's shoulders. The False Faces performed during the midwinter festivals on the New York and Canadian reservations. Additionally, they visited every Iroquois house in fall and spring in order to exorcise evil spirits. Wearing the masks and tattered clothing, the False Faces carried turtle shell rattles and hickory sticks. When someone had contracted a disease over which the False Faces had power, the leader of the society was informed, and the troop of False Faces appeared at the patient's house, striking and rubbing their rattles against the house as they entered. Once inside they sang and danced, accompanied by the shaking of rattles. Some of the dancers would scoop up hot embers from the fire and blow them on the patient in order to cure him.

In the Great Lakes area the ritual of the Midewiwin was enacted by the Ojibwa and other central Algonquians. Translated as "Great Medicine Society," the Mide (the shortened form of the name) held its meetings once a year in a special lodge resembling a large wigwam varying in length from one hundred to two hundred feet and in width from thirteen to thirty feet. In height it was seven to ten feet with an open apex that was covered with cattail mats and birchbark during inclement weather.

The Midewiwin was a membership organization, and people were admitted on the basis of application, of having a suitable dream, or by replacing a deceased relative who had been a member. Both men and women could join, and the religious leaders of the Mide were elected by its membership. The main annual functions were initiatory, and curing rites were conducted by carefully trained Mide shamans.

The Mide priests determined which candidates would be accepted into the society, and candidates were expected to pay for the rites of initiation, which included knowledge of the myths, rituals, songs, and remedies of the society. All ceremonies had originated in revelations and were carefully transcribed on birchbark scrolls with a bone stylus and handed down pictographically from generation to generation.

The initiation rite was the most dramatic. The candidates knelt on mats surrounded by four posts inside the medicine lodge. Two members held the candidates' shoulders, while four others thrust their medicine bags at them. As the four leaders approached, the candidates were overcome by the power of the leaders' spirits and fell lifeless to the ground. When revived, each candidate spat out a small cowrie shell called *migis*, which was the sacred emblem of the Mide. The initiator then offered the shell to the four directions and sky after which it magically disappeared again into the candidate's body, and the candidate was fully resuscitated. All members were required to attend meetings once a year for the renewal of their spiritual powers, but smaller gatherings could be held for the treatment of the sick, singing songs, and strengthening their belief in the power of the Mide. A feast was an inseparable part of all Mide functions.

One of the most important ceremonies of the Southeast was the Green Corn Dance, a celebration of the harvesting of one of the major food staples of North America. Known among the Creek as the Busk (from the Creek word *puskita*, "to fast"), the ceremony of first fruits took place in August. The Busk was actually an aggregation of different ceremonies, including the drinking of *Ilex cassine*, or "black drink," used as an emetic to purge the participants and purify themselves. A sacred fire was built, and young initiates had their flesh scratched to make them brave. Both men and women performed various dances including the Stomp dance, which was performed in a serpentine pattern by a line of alternating men and women. The women wore turtle-shell shakers around their knees that accompanied the antiphonal singing of the group. At the end of the Busk, the various clans participated in a stickball game that marked the conclusion of the ceremony. Variations of the Green Corn Dance were found also among the Seminole, Cherokee, Choctaw, Chickasaw, and Yuchi of the Southeast, as well as among other tribes where corn was cultivated.

The Southwest is where the highest concentration of dance drama is found not only with the elaborate agricultural rituals of the Pueblos, but with the various curing rituals, puberty ceremonies, and mimetic animal dances. Literally hundreds of these rituals were performed by the Navajo, Apache, and Pueblo peoples each year. In many cases native rituals are still held in conjunction with feasts of the Catholic church. All provide colorful spectacles equal to any of the religious pageants of North America and Europe.

The Hopi of Arizona perform a number of masked dances on their mesas. The *kachina* dances, named after the spirits of the dead, are the most intriguing. The Hopi believe that in mythological times the *kachinas* came from their homes in the West to bring them rain and to ensure them long and happy lives. Later, the *kachinas* showed the people how to make masks and costumes and taught them their songs and dances with the understanding that if the people performed the ceremonies correctly, the supernaturals would continue to bring prosperity to the villages. There are over 250 named *kachina* spirits among the Hopi, each represented by a different mask and costume. It is believed that the men who impersonate the spirits at the *kachina* performances become the spirits they represent. Women and uninitiated youth are not supposed to know that the *kachina* dancers are really their clansmen. At each performance the *kachinas* bring gifts for the children and place them in the center of the village plaza. The *kachina* dances are performed during the first half of the year, when their appearance is supposed to ensure the successful planting of crops. The ceremonies represent intense periods of ritual performance in which all men and women in the village undergo instruction in their faith. It is also a time when the people entertain their spiritual benefactors.

At the time of the summer solstice, the Niman dance is performed in which all the *kachinas* appear en masse before the villagers who thank the supernaturals for the gift of a good harvest. It is believed that the *kachinas* then leave to return to their homes. When they return to their homes, they visit the dead, who are performing rituals of the winter solstice while similar ceremonies are being performed by the living during the summer.

In New Mexico among the Zuni the Shalako ceremony is held in November or December each year. Six dancers are dressed to represent giant birds, the messengers of the rain gods, with conical costumes attached to their waists measuring in height from ten to twelve feet. They have birdlike faces complete with beaks that are movable, protruding eyes, and upcurved tapered horns. At midnight, they enter special houses that have been built for their performance. They utter birdlike calls and clack their beaks in rapid succession. They dance and make speeches telling the people to pray for an abundant harvest and long lives for the villagers.

The Shalako dancers are joined in their ritual by the ten Koyemshi, or "Mudheads," the children of a legendary incestuous union. These impersonators are appointed by the Zuni priests to serve for one year and are then free from further duties for another four years. The Koyemshi entertain at all public rituals when the *kachinas* are away from the village by providing comic, and sometimes obscene, interludes between the more serious dances. Sometimes they play Euroamerican games such as beanbag. The jokes, puns, and riddles that they cry out to the villagers are filled with scatalogical references, and they play pranks and make obscene jokes about the most respected and sacred aspects of Zuni religion. In this manner they make moral and ethical points by burlesquing those institutions and individuals with whom people come in contact every day. They also burlesque their most sacred beliefs through vulgar references that strongly constrast with appropriate Zuni behavior. For the duration of the ritual, the onlookers participate vicariously in what is temporarily socially approved behavior.

The Koyemshi appear as ludicrous figures. They wear formless baglike cotton masks that have bumps or knobs protruding from them. The knobs are filled with raw cotton seeds and earth or dust taken from the footprints made by the people in the streets around the village. Sometimes feathers are tied to the knobs, and the lower part of the mask is tied to the knobs with black cotton in scarflike fashion. Under the scarf they wear a small bag containing squash, corn, and gourd seeds. Their masks and bodies are painted with pink clay that comes from the sacred lake. These clowns also wear black homespun kilts, and the leader adds to his kilt a black tunic worn over his right shoulder. As is true with the Hopi, the Zuni dancers and clowns serve to underscore the religious values of the society by occasionally emphasizing the absurd. [*See* Clowns.]

Nearby in Arizona and parts of New Mexico and Oklahoma, numerous bands of Apache perform a ceremony used variously as a puberty ceremony, or to cure illness and avert catastrophe. The Mountain Spirits dance, or Gahan, as it is properly known, is an essential feature of the female puberty ceremony, in which the young initiate ritually represents White Painted Woman, the divine mother of the Apache culture hero, or in some cases, Mother Earth. The Apache believe that performance of the ritual brings good fortune to the initiate, her family, and to the entire tribe.

In this ceremony four male dancers represent the four directions, or Mountain Spirits, powerful supernatural beings who act as intermediaries between humans and the Great Spirit. The initiate is secluded in a special lodge. She is painted and dressed by a woman of impeccable reputation who also has received a vision from the White Painted Woman. Each day a male singer sings appropriate songs for her. Each night the masked dancers appear in spectacular and grotesque costumes. They are dressed and painted by a shaman in a special brush arbor before the evening ceremonies begin. The shaman paints their bodies with designs representing the sun, moon, lightning, planets, rain, and rainbow. After being painted and instructed, the dancers line up facing east. They then spin clockwise, spit four times into their headdresses, and put them on after feigning this action three times. A fire is made in the ceremonial lodge by rubbing sticks together, and each night the masked dancers enter the lodge and dance around the lodge in a prescribed manner. They wear wooden headdresses shaped like huge rainbows projecting from their black-hooded faces. Yellow buckskin kilts are tied from their waist, cuffed by long fringed boots. They carry wooden swords in each hand, and as they dance in rigid, angular patterns, bending and crouching in near-balletic movements, they slap their swords vigorously against their thighs and legs. On the fourth night, the candidate joins the dancers dressed in a yellow buckskin fringed dress with designs like those of the masked dancers. At the end of the four days, the young woman scatters pollen over the people who were brought to her to receive her blessings.

The Apache regard the dance as particularly powerful, and each of the aspects of the dance must be done properly lest harm befall the tribe. If the dance is not executed properly, it is believed that the dancers may have trouble with their eyes and noses, their faces will swell, or paralysis will set in.

Among one of the most vivid ritual performances of the Navajo of the Four Corners region of the Southwest is the Yeibichai, also known as Night Chant. The word *yeibichai* is partly a corruption of the Zuni word for "spirit" plus the Navajo term for "maternal grandfather," hence it literally means "grandfather of the gods." The ceremony was handed down by supernaturals and was thought to be particularly efficacious in curing both psychosomatic and somatic disorders, especially insanity, deafness, or paralysis.

The ritual is sponsored by one man and his clan relatives in winter and is performed outdoors on a barren plateau. A sacred hogan is built at the west and a brush arbor shelter for the dancers at the east. Between the two a row of bonfires is built.

The ceremony takes nine days, the first eight being composed of secret ceremonies, and the last day, a public performance. In the dance the Grandfather of the Gods is personified by the lead dancer, who wears buckskin hunting clothes. The other dancers wear masks and kilts and resemble Pueblo *kachinas*.

The ritual specialist in charge of the Yeibichai is the chanter, a person who has chosen to learn the sacred ritual. He pays to be taught and studies for many years learning by rote every detail. During this time he collects sacred objects such as prayer sticks, herbs, turquoise, white shell, abalone, and jet, which he will use in his ceremonies. The specialist also may learn a few lesser rites plus the Blessingway, a ritual that must follow every other ritual to atone for any possible mistakes in them.

During the first four days, the patient and his relatives purify themselves by sweating and taking emetics. The patient and the chanter pray to the supernaturals to aid them in the ceremony. Each supernatural must be named in the proper order lest misfortune befall them. The chanter sings sacred songs and administers potions and sacred pollen to help rid the patient of evil forces.

During the next four days, the chanter and helpers coax the supernaturals into the ritual area by constructing sand paintings of them. The final power will arrive when pollen has been sprinkled on the sand painting. In these paintings, male divinities are represented as having round heads, while females have square heads. The *yeis*, as these male and female divinities are called, are pictured as standing on clouds or lightning and guarded by rainbows. The completed painting forms an altar sometimes ranging in width from four to eighteen feet.

Next, the patients are bathed and dried with cornmeal and painted with the symbols of the supernaturals. They are then brought into the hogan to receive power from the supernaturals represented in the sand painting. Sand from various parts of the painted figures is pressed against their ailing parts, and they are made one with the supernaturals and share their power. Finally the sand is swept up so that it may not be contaminated. The Navajo word for the design means the "going away of the group" and the design itself is regarded as a temporary visit from the supernaturals. On the ninth night, both the chanter and the patient must stay awake until dawn while the power increases in them. The Yeibichai impersonators are dressed in grotesque masks and decorated kilts with as many turquoise and silver necklaces, bracelets, and bow guards as they can put on. They spend the night publicly dancing and singing. The patients must not sleep until sunset, when they enter the sacred hogan and stay there for four nights. The rite is ceremonially concluded with the Bluebird Song, sung in honor of the bird of the dawn that brings promise and happiness.

Although most dance dramas were performed by groups of singers and dancers, the Deer Dance of the Yaqui of the Southwest is a unique solo performance. The Yaqui believed that the deer had the power to cure or cause illness and also to bring thunder, lightning, and rain. Dancing to the deer deity also ensured food and fecundity for the people and animals.

A religious pageant announcing the Deer Dance, which took place just before Easter, was suddenly interrupted by the presence of four to six dancers and four singers striking gourds with sticks to create a rasping sound. All dancers were naked from the waist up and wore grotesque masks representing human faces. The lead dancer, however, wore small deer antlers attached to his head and a cocoon rattle, six to eight feet in length and filled with pebbles, wrapped around one leg.

The lead dancer performed most of the Deer Dance alone. His movements mimicked that of the deer with great realism, his head moving quickly and erratically from side to side as if he had picked up the scent of danger. His feet scratched the earth before he quickly bolted upward, leaping gracefully over some imaginary barrier. Then, as the dance came to a close, the dancer became hunter and hunted, imitating the actions of a man with bow and arrow carefully stalking his prey. Letting fly the arrow that mortally wounded him, he fell to the ground quivering as he breathed his last.

BIBLIOGRAPHY

Densmore, Frances. *Chippewa Music.* Bulletin of the Bureau of American Ethnology, no. 45. Washington, D.C., 1910. A classic work on the Chippewa with detailed discussion of the Midewiwin.

Densmore, Frances. *Yuman and Yaqui Music.* Bulletin of the Bureau of American Ethnology, no. 110. Washington, D.C., 1932. A good description of the Yaqui Deer Dance.

Drucker, Philip. *Indians of the Northwest Coast.* Garden City, N.Y., 1955. A discussion of various tribes of the Pacific Northwest with some emphasis on material culture and ritual drama.

Kurath, Gertrude P. *Iroquois Music and Dance: Ceremonial Arts of Two Seneca Longhouses.* Bulletin of the Bureau of American Ethnology, no. 187. Washington, D.C., 1964. A description of music and choreographic patterns of numerous Iroquoian rituals including the False Face society.

Ortiz, Alfonso, ed. *New Perspectives on the Pueblos.* Albuquerque, 1972. The section entitled "Ritual Drama and Pueblo World View," by Ortiz, himself an anthropologist and Pueblo, is one of the best theoretical introductions to ritual drama.

Powers, William K. *Oglala Religion.* Lincoln, Nebr., 1977. Includes a description and analysis of the vision quest, sweat lodge, and Sun Dance of the Lakota Indians of the Great Plains.

Powers, William K. *Sacred Language: The Nature of Supernatural Discourse in Lakota.* Norman, Okla., 1986. Contains descriptions and illustrations of various animal impersonators among the Lakota.

Reichard, Gladys A. *Navaho Religion.* New York, 1950. Perhaps the best work ever done on Navajo symbolism.

Roediger, Virginia More. *Ceremonial Costumes of the Pueblo Indians.* Berkeley, 1941. An excellent illustrated book of ceremonial costumes, including those described for the Hopi and Zuni.

Tyler, Hamilton A. *Pueblo Gods and Myths.* Norman, Okla., 1964. A good historical background to the Pueblo with an emphasis on cosmology and worldview.

Underhill, Ruth M. *Red Man's Religion.* Chicago, 1965. Although stylistically dated and somewhat patronizing, there are excellent descriptions of ritual drama from most parts of native North America.

WILLIAM K. POWERS

European Religious Drama

Ancient drama ceased to be performed at the beginning of the Middle Ages. Christian authors like Tertullian (third century) complained that it was cruel, obscene, and idolatrous. Whatever the justification for such complaints, by the fifth century it was no longer relevant to the dominant Christian culture. Performances in the ancient manner may have been offered in Byzantium as late as the seventh century, but they were sporadic and culturally insignificant. A Christian imitation of classical Greek tragedy, *Christos paschon* (fifth century?), may or may not have been performed. Curiously, in spite of the memories of ancient drama that lingered in Byzantium, European religious drama was created in the Latin West rather than the East.

Ancient dramatic texts were copied and read in the West throughout the Middle Ages. The tenth-century nun Hrosvitha of Gandersheim wrote attractive Christian comedies imitating the comedies of Plautus, but it is unlikely that they were performed. In the later Middle Ages, the terms *tragedy* and *comedy* referred to narrative works like Dante's *Commedia*. The mimes, folk plays, and quasi-dramatic entertainments performed sporadically during the Middle Ages did not establish a significant dramatic tradition, and they have disappeared almost without a trace.

In the tenth century several brief plays appeared that were written for performance. These plays were not imitations of ancient drama but original compositions. They all depict the visit of the Marys to the sepulcher of Christ on the morning of the Resurrection. They are to be sung rather than spoken, and they begin with the Angel's question: "Quem quaeritis in sepulcher?" ("Whom do you seek in the sepulcher?"). Since they are attached to the Easter liturgy they are called liturgical dramas.

Liturgical dramas of the nativity of Christ appeared in the eleventh century. By the twelfth century there were dramas of the postresurrection appearances of Christ, the Ascension, Pentecost, the Slaughter of the Innocents, and the Prophets of Christ. There were also dramas on less explicitly liturgical subjects: Lazarus, the apostle Paul, Joseph and his brothers, Saint Nicholas, and the Antichrist. Two long vernacular plays survive from this period: *Le mystère d'Adam* and *La seinte Resurreccion*. Both are spoken rather than sung, and they require more sophisticated acting and staging than the liturgical plays. By the fifteenth century vernacular religious drama was flourishing throughout Europe. In addition to plays on biblical subjects there were saints' plays, miracle plays, and morality plays. Some of the plays were gigantic by modern Western standards, requiring a whole day or even several days for performance and using huge casts and elaborate stage machinery.

During the Renaissance, Protestant and Roman Catholic authorities discouraged the performance of medieval religious drama, and it was gradually supplanted by the secular theater. Only one medieval play has survived to the present in more or less continuous performance: *The Mystery of Elche* (c. 1420), which is presented annually in the town of Elche in Spain on the Feast of the Assumption. The well-known *Oberammergau Passion* is of later origin (seventeenth century) and is performed only at ten-year intervals. A few medieval plays have occasionally been revived in the twentieth century. Of these, the fifteenth-century morality play *Everyman* is the most enduringly popular.

There has been much speculation about the origins of the tenth-century Resurrection play. Historical scholarship has sought a specific "source" and located this source in a ninth-century lyric composition (trope) that was used to ornament the regular liturgy. In *The Drama of the Medieval Church* (1933) Karl Young argues that the Resurrection play began as a trope of the Introit of the first mass of Easter day. This trope was eventually separated from the Introit and attached to Easter matins. In the new position its dramatic quality could be exploited, and it began to be acted.

The possibility of a deeper relationship between the Resurrection play and the liturgy of the church is suggested by the fact that in every culture in which drama is an indigenous form, the earliest examples are closely associated with religious rituals. The rituals are dramatic in quality and the dramas have obvious ritual elements and themes. The relationship between Greek religious ritual and Greek drama was apparent to Aristotle, and the lingering influence of this relationship can be seen in several of the extant Greek tragedies. Both the form and the theme of the Resurrection play point to a similar relationship with Christian ritual.

Baptism is the Christian rite of initiation. The sequence of events in a liturgical ceremony is described in what the Middle Ages called an *ordo*, an order of procedure. As performed in the early centuries, the *ordo* of baptism required the candidate to descend naked into the font, to be immersed three times, and, on emersion, to be signed in holy oil and blessed by a bishop. This sequence is itself a generalized drama in which immersion in water is the visible expression, or "imitation," of cleansing from sin.

In elaborating Paul's ideas of baptism and resurrection (*Rom.* 6:3–4) Cyril of Jerusalem (fourth century) uses the terminology of Greek dramatic criticism: "O Paradox! We did not really die, we were not really buried, we were not really crucified and raised again; but our imitation [*mimēsis*] was a likeness [*en eikoni*], and our salvation a reality" (*Catechesis mystagogica* 2.5).

Cyril understands baptism in two ways. The ritual occupies the foreground. It is a real action because it produces "a reality," namely, the rebirth and salvation of the candidate. This reality is absolute. It is caused by the intervention of the divine—the Holy Spirit—in the world of time. Baptism is also a stylized enactment by imitation *(mimēsis)* of the death and resurrection of Christ. This historical drama defines the ritual by giving it a specific meaning that is true, rather than conjectural, as far as Christianity is concerned.

Throughout the earlier Middle Ages the Easter Vigil was the preferred time for baptism. The candidates prepared for their initiation during Lent. They were baptized at around midnight on Holy Saturday. Dressed in white robes, they then proceeded to their first Communion, which occurred early on Easter morning, a time roughly coincident with the moment of Jesus' resurrection, which baptism enacts.

Like baptism, the Mass is a real action. By means of consecration, bread and wine are transformed into the body and blood of Christ. The change is a transubstantiation, a change of substance, not a symbolic change or a commemoration.

The Mass *ordo* is a sequence of discrete ritual moments arranged in the form of prologue, rising action, climax, and denouement. This structure took shape over centuries and with innumerable variants. It was regarded, however, as divinely ordained, which means that the arrangement of the ritual moments follows the will of God rather than natural causality. The structure cannot be explained, but it must be observed if the ritual is to produce its miracle.

The initial tone of the Mass is solemn and the concluding tone is joyful. The climax is the miracle of the real presence. It is both a recognition *(anagnōrisis)* of Christ and a reversal *(peripeteia)* of the tone of the ritual. Medieval liturgists described the reversal as a change from sorrows *(tristia)* to rejoicing *(gaudium)*. The Mass, in the Classical Greek sense, is therefore comic rather than tragic in structure.

Bits of scriptural history are embedded in the structure of the Mass. When the celebrant repeats the words of Christ at the Last Supper during the consecration he is, for the moment, representing the historical Christ. Representation also occurs during the celebrant's "extension of hands" *(extensio manuum)* in imitation of the arms of Christ on the cross.

In the ninth century these and related historical elements led to a full-scale interpretation of the Mass in which each ritual moment was equated with an event in the life of Christ. The most elaborate description of the Mass from this point of view is the *Liber officialis* of Amalarius of Metz. According to Amalarius the climax of the Mass is the commingling. Because Christ's body and blood are united in the commingling, it corresponds to the Resurrection. The two subdeacons who assist represent the two Marys who visited the sepulcher on Easter morning. At the moment of the commingling, their solemnity is changed to joy, as though through the announcement of the angel to the historical Marys.

In this interpretation the Mass is both a ritual and an elaborate historical drama. The ritual provides the absolute reality on which the drama rests. It is, however, a generalized reality, a sacramental ground. The drama gives this sacramental reality a specific narrative meaning that allows it to be "understood." It seems probable that the Amalarian interpretation was popular in the ninth and later centuries precisely because the laity no longer understood the Mass on its own terms and welcomed the assistance that the interpretation provided. At any rate, for the reasons outlined above, ninth-century Easter liturgy was dominated by the theme of the Resurrection.

The Resurrection play of the tenth century was performed at Easter. Its structure reproduces in little the structure of the Mass: a movement from sorrow, through a climax which is a recognition and a reversal, to rejoicing. And the historical moment that is its subject, namely the Resurrection, is the moment Amalarius equated with the climax of the Mass. Liturgy also provides the stage on which the play is performed, the clerics who act its roles, and vestments that serve as its costumes.

In the Mass generalized ritual action is primary and narrative drama secondary. In the transition from ritual to drama this relationship is inverted. The Resurrection play makes the story primary and ritual action secondary, secondary in the sense of being a submerged sacramental ground, an *a priori* shaping principle that must be deduced *a posteriori* from the materials it has shaped. The sequence of ritual moments is not a plot. It is, rather, a form that can be the shaping principle of many different plots, both historical and fictional. It provides the absolute reality on which medieval religious drama builds it appearances.

When the ritual structure of the Mass becomes the ground for a play about the Resurrection, this structure seems to be replaced by a plot, a story with characters. The clerics who perform the actions of the ritual become actors. Their ceremonial gestures become mimetic gestures expressing human motives. Their prayers and chants become stylized dialogue, still sung, but dialogue in which questions produce replies and commands are visibly obeyed. Meanwhile, because the congregation no longer participates, as it does in the ritual, it becomes a group of spectators, an audience.

Underlying these visible changes there is a movement from ritual sequence to natural causality. The ritual moments in the Mass follow one another in a given order because they must be in that order. Natural causality is not so much absent from the *ordo* as irrelevant to it. On the other hand, because the events of a plot occur in natural time, they are subject to causality. If scriptural history says they occurred, they are necessary; if not, they are only probable. Scripture, for example, states that when the Marys came to the sepulcher they encountered an angel. The angel is thus a necessary element of the Resurrection play, even though outside of the sphere of natural causality. Scripture is vague, however, about the gestures of the Marys when they encountered the angel. The actors performing the roles of the Marys must decide what gestures the Marys probably used. In several extended versions of the Resurrection play the Marys report their experience to the apostles. The Bible says that such a report occurred but does not provide the dialogue. Several plays therefore use a well-known lyric composition (sequence) that begins "Dic mihi Maria" ("Tell me, Mary") for the dialogue. The popularity of this composition demonstrates that it was widely considered an acceptable—therefore probable—version of the dialogue. Hence its appropriateness for the play.

Unlike ritual reality, the reality of drama is contingent. Scriptural history is true in a special sense, and, therefore, necessary; but other kinds of history can err, and elaborations based on probability are contingent by definition. The reality of medieval religious drama is therefore a hypothetical reality, "reality in appearance," in which the reality of the appearance is sustained by the absolute reality of the sacramental ground on which it rests.

Ritual reality is an *ordo*, absolutely determined. "Reality in appearance," however, is plastic and can be manipulated. Three kinds of manipulation are common in medieval religious drama: extension, invention, and imitation.

Extension is the addition of historical episodes to an already existing drama. The visit of Mary Magdalene to the cross can be added, for example, at the beginning of the Resurrection play, and the appearance of Christ at Emmaus at the end, without changing the play's structure. The limit of extension for scriptural drama is shown by the English Corpus Christi plays; they begin with the Fall of Lucifer and end with the Last Judgment, but they retain the comic structure, including the visit to the sepulcher as the climax, of the Resurrection play. For religious drama based on historical sources other than scripture (the *Legenda Aurea*, for example) the limit of extension is the limit of the historical narrative.

Invention is the creation of episodes that are not found in history. As is evident from the problem of the gestures of the Marys confronting the angel, even the briefest historical drama uses extension because history never provides all of the details that drama requires. Whenever extension occurs it moves the drama from history toward fiction. The report of the Marys to the apostles is scripture, but the dialogue beginning "Dic mihi Maria" is fiction. Scripture states that the Marys brought ointment to the sepulcher. Where did the ointment come from? Probably from a spice merchant. How was the ointment obtained? Probably by bargaining. Bargaining has its humorous as well as its serious aspects, so an invented spice-merchant episode, freed of the restrictions of the biblical narrative, has the potential of becoming amusing or satirical. One of the earliest episodes invented for the Resurrection play is the "spice merchant" *(unguentarius)* scene. It is mildly satiric. It is also anachronistic. Historical research might have produced something like a Palestinian merchant of the first century, but the result would have baffled the audience. Therefore the dramatist produced a character who is "probable" in the sense of resembling the sort of merchant with whom his audience was familiar. This means also that the character has the quality of "realism."

A brilliant instance of realistic invention is provided by the *Second Shepherds' Play* of the Wakefield Cycle (fifteenth century). Scripture states that shepherds visited the infant Jesus. What were the shepherds like? The Wakefield dramatist creates a comic vignette of medieval English shepherds that is so effective that it all but eclipses the Nativity scene that is the play's subject. A similar impulse toward free invention is evident in the gigantic French *mystères* of the late Middle Ages, which are based on saints' lives rather than scripture. This playful impulse is made possible by the fact that, as long as the sacramental ground is respected, it will sustain—that is, make acceptable—almost any kind of invention. The playfulness is expressed in passages that are alternately humorous, grotesque, satirical, serious, and intensely devout, and in abrupt juxtapositions of the comic and the ploddingly didactic, the realistic and the miraculous.

The late medieval morality play is entirely fictional, being made up out of the probabilities of theories of religious psychology. Because it is fictional it is more cautious—more rationalistic—than the plays based on scriptural history and saints' lives. Its characters are more consistent, its dialogue more restrained, and its use of digressive, comic, and realistic materials and abrupt juxtapositions more conservative. Its reliance on the sacramental ground of ritual is evident in its comic plot, which regularly hinges on the miraculous conversion or salvation of its protagonist, and in its use of religious themes and characters from the invisible world: good and bad angels, departed souls, demons, and comic "vices" who reappear in Renaissance drama rationalized as villains, like Iago, or as comic embodiments of the principle of disorder, like Falstaff.

Imitation is simply the use of models. The Resurrection play embodies the concept of a "reality in appearance" resting on a sacramental ground. Once the original form of the play became widely known, it could be a model for other Resurrection plays and for plays using the same techniques but different subject matter. As the dramas became more complex through extension and invention, the possibilities for imitation multiplied. By the fifteenth century (and probably much earlier) medieval religious drama had institutionalized itself, and its authors drew their techniques primarily from other dramas. Because the "reality in appearance" of religious drama is explicit and the sacramental ground is *a priori* and invisible, the surface eventually came to seem real— that is, autonomous—while the sacramental ground came to seem a corollary of subject matter and hence either an accident of history or a liability, rather than the foundation on which the drama rests.

During the Renaissance, French and Italian drama rejected the medieval tradition. At first the alternative was direct imitation of the tragedies of Seneca and the comedies of Plautus and Terence. Since ancient drama rests on a ground entirely different from, and alien to, the ground of medieval drama, it is not surprising that most of the direct imitations were stillborn. In seventeenth-century France direct imitation gave way to a neoclassicism that paid homage to ancient models but was based on rationalist principles of verisimilitude, decorum, and the norm of nature. The dramas of Molière and Racine assume that appearance is autonomous and seek to create the illusion of reality by subjecting all of their materials to the rule of probability.

Their plays resemble thought-experiments arising from the question, "Given this situation and these characters, what would be the probable result?" The comic plots are pure fiction. The myth and legend that provide the subject matter of the tragic plots are drained of their ancient religious import: myth and legend provide a means of distancing the thought-experiment, or drama, from immediate experience and thus of emphasizing its status as "autonomous appearance."

Spanish and English drama of the Renaissance took an opposite path. As neoclassic critics rightly observed, Shakespeare's plays ignore verisimilitude and decorum and are filled with extravagant language, improbable inventions and characters, and astonishing juxtapositions of the serious and the comic. They may be considered in this regard a final flowering in a secular context of the traditions of religious drama. Shakespeare's enormous history cycle, extending from the "fall" of England through the murder of Richard II to its miraculous "salvation" following the defeat of Richard III, is a secular equivalent of the Corpus Christi play. Several of his tragedies end on a note emphasizing the redemptive quality of suffering: *Romeo and Juliet*, *Hamlet*, and *Macbeth*. The motif of salvation by miracle is rationalized by the "unrealistic" devices of coincidence and disguise in comedies like *The Comedy of Errors*, *Twelfth Night*, and *Measure for Measure*; it becomes explicit in *The Winter's Tale* and *The Tempest*. The medieval tradition also appears in characters influenced by medieval conventions (Falstaff as comic vice), in ritualistic scenes (Othello kneeling to pledge allegiance to Iago), in magic and miracles (*Midsummer Night's Dream*, the rebirth of Hermione), and in the emphasis at the end of many of the plays on reestablishment of community *(As You Like It, Hamlet, Measure for Measure, The Tempest)*. According to later, neoclassic (eighteenth-century) criticism, Shakespeare's plays should be failures. They are sprawling, loosely constructed, improbable, and indecorous. The fact that they succeed is evidence of their reliance on a reality deeper than the "autonomous appearance" of neoclassic drama and of the continuing importance of this deeper reality for the modern audiences who respond to them.

Liturgical drama is emphatically not an antiquarian subject, and its reemergence in extremely popular vernacular forms in the twentieth century is significant. Paul Claudel and T. S. Eliot, among others, have attempted to revive religious drama in the twentieth century; their efforts have not been fully successful. Perhaps this is because their plays are concerned primarily with subject matter, that is, with appearance. A few twentieth-century plays have begun with ritual rather than subject matter, and these seem moderately effective: Timothy Rice and Andrew Lloyd Webber's *Jesus Christ Superstar* and Leonard Bernstein's *Mass*. Popular movie and television entertainments—Westerns, thrillers, science fantasies—retain the comic structure of ritual and its convention of "salvation by miracle," although the miracles are always rationalized as coincidence, luck, or "intervention from beyond." Popular entertainment, however, is limited by its dependence on stereotypes and formulas. Its "reality in appearance" is thin and predictable when compared to the "reality in appearance" observable in medieval religious drama and in English and Spanish drama of the Renaissance.

BIBLIOGRAPHY

The standard bibliography of medieval drama is Carl J. Stratman's *Bibliography of Medieval Drama*, 2d ed. (New York, 1972). Supplements are provided by C. Clifford Flanigan in *Research Opportunities in Renaissance Drama* 18 (1975): 81–102 and 19 (1976): 109–136. The best history of the Roman Mass is Josef A. Jungmann's *The Mass of the Roman Rite*, rev. ed., 2 vols. (New York, 1959). E. K. Chambers's *The Mediaeval Stage*, 2 vols. (1903; reprint, Oxford, 1925) is dated but has interesting material on medieval folk drama. Karl Young's *The Drama of the Medieval Church*, 2 vols. (1933; reprint, London, 1967), remains the standard treatment of the subject from the historical point of view and reprints most of the texts of the surviving liturgical plays. The most complete collection of texts of Latin liturgical dramas is Walther Lipphardt's *Lateinische Osterfeiern und Osterspiele*, 7 vols. (Berlin, 1975–1981). An analysis of medieval religious drama emphasizing its reliance on liturgy is offered in my *Christian Rite and Christian Drama in the Middle Ages* (Baltimore, 1965). See also J. D. A. Ogilvy's "*Mimi, Scurrae, Histriones*: Entertainers of the Middle Ages," *Speculum* 38 (1963): 603–619; George La Piana's "The Byzantine Theatre," *Speculum* 11 (1936): 171–211; and H. A. Kelly's *The Devil at Baptism: Ritual, Theology, and Drama* (Ithaca, 1985). European vernacular drama is surveyed in Richard Axton's *European Drama of the Early Middle Ages* (London, 1974), and the English cycle plays are reviewed in V. A. Kolve's *The Play Called Corpus Christi* (Stanford, Calif., 1966). Very suggestive general discussion of ritual and drama is found in Northrop Frye's *Anatomy of Criticism* (Princeton, 1957). C. L. Barber's *Shakespeare's Festive Comedies: A Study of Dramatic Form and Its Relation to Social Custom* (Princeton, 1959) and E. M. W. Tillyard's *Shakespeare's History Plays* (1944; reprint, New York, 1964) are representative of discussions of Shakespeare from a ritual and generally Christian point of view.

O. B. Hardison, Jr.

Modern Western Theater

Where religion has kept alive its affinity with dance, drum, and the dramatic appearance of the gods, it has remained vital. Where drama has kept alive its quality of magic disclosure, it has remained indispensable. These legacies have proved difficult to maintain in Western society, but they contain the heart of the expectations people bring to theater and to religious ceremony alike.

The ancient and persistent link between religion and drama may be viewed as the result of several factors, including the following:

1. a probable common ancestry in the ritualized behavior of prehistoric human beings (from this point of view, ritual, or at least the ritualization of behavior, provides a matrix in which both drama and religion grow);
2. the known development of theater and drama in historical times from within, or at least in association with, specific religious traditions and festivals (examples, in the West, are to be found in ancient Greece, where drama began as part of festivals dedicated to the god Dionysos, and in medieval Europe, where it took root in both Christian and non-Christian religious ceremonies);
3. the quasi-priestly or shamanic characteristics of theatrical performers and, conversely, the theatrical qualities of religious liturgies;
4. the necessity of drama and religion alike to employ means of acting out stories, in the former case primarily for the sake of entertainment (along with whatever instructional and/or propagandist aims may be present) and in the latter case primarily for the sake of actualizing in the present the stories and myths that are vital to a given religious tradition;
5. the influences exerted by drama and religion upon each other indirectly through the media of culture—schooling, publishing, and (nowadays) broadcasting.

Specific aspects of the general connections between religion and drama are discussed elsewhere in this encyclopedia. Here attention will be confined to drama and religion in the Western world (Europe and the Americas) from the sixteenth century onward.

It is often supposed that the theater in modern Europe and America, like Western civilization in general, has steadily become more secular, which is to say, less and less concerned with religion. The truth of this assumption, with respect to theater and modern society alike, is debatable. To the extent that it may be true, it is balanced by the fact that Western religion itself has undergone a kind of secularization: it has, in many quarters, undergone demythologizing, the "death of God," and a radical turn toward political action in "this world," all without losing its identity as religion. More significant than the phenomenon of secularization is the fact that, in most European and American societies in modern times, the professional theater and institutional religion have both become culturally marginal—perhaps for similar reasons.

Before 1700, the principal places for public storytelling were theaters and churches. The advent of novelistic fiction in the eighteenth century meant that stories could be told to a wide audience without people having to gather in a public place. Even so, theater remained a popular institution throughout the nineteenth century while revivalistic religion, if not regular church attendance, was also vigorous, especially in America. The immense success of motion pictures and television in the twentieth century reduced the audience for live theater to a very small portion of the population. Although, compared to this, the number of churchgoers remains very large, perhaps twenty to twenty-five times as great in America, it too has shrunk as the audience for film and television has grown. The electronic age, vastly increasing a trend already begun by popular publishing, has brought about a change in social patterns that affects the way people gather in public—or do not so gather—to participate at the performance of stories, rituals, and myths.

The change in patterns of assemblage has not been quite the same for all social classes. The popularity of religious gatherings continues more vigorously among the poor than among the affluent. One might even argue that religion serves as a theater of the poor, although it would be more accurate to say that among them the bifurcation between religion and drama is not as deep as among those with higher incomes.

Insofar as religion and theater are middle-class institutions, they are, ironically, of less and less importance to the middle class. The social bracketing of the two institutions leads to a kind of aesthetic bracketing as well: theater becomes pictorial (and hence no significant competition for film and television), while religious rituals become archaic, not to say quaint. In this situation, theater and religion often look to each other for some lost component to help restore their immediacy. The fundamental link between them is their performance of "magic" to make what is unseen seen and what is absent present, and this in the immediacy of a specific time and place.

Although European Christianity was much indebted to classical Greek and Roman civilization, it also inherited the Bible's view of history as fulfillment of divine promise and of Christ as a redeemer who did not fit either the tragic or the comic prototypes of antiquity. Hence, Christianity brought into European culture many sensibilities concerning human character, experience, and historical existence that were significantly different from those upon which the drama of Greece and Rome had been based. It is likely that these sensibilities became mixed with those of the religions that were already practiced in Europe when Christianity arrived. In any case, some very unclassical ideas emerged, and these proved to be of much importance to drama: for example, that human nature is not divided into a limited number of fixed character types; that some individuals are subject to marked changes in character as a result of experiences they undergo; and that human history in general is capable of genuine novelty and surprise. As they worked their way into dramatic expression on stage, these ideas led to a mode of drama concerned with processes of history, the dynamics of class interaction, and the confrontation of the human soul with temptation, with conscience, and with God.

An unprecedented, and subsequently unexcelled, outburst of dramatic genius occurred in the sixteenth century. The greatest talents were those of William Shakespeare in England and Lope de Vega in Spain. Their writing for the stage was based upon very different ideas of dramatic form from the Greek and Roman classics. These ideas led to a form more loose, more episodic, more open to variety in human characterization, more concerned with reflective consciousness, more open to depictions of the grotesque and the ugly. The immediate sources of the new sensibility, with its profound effect upon dramatic form, theater design, and modes of acting, are thought to lie in the medieval Christian dramas known as mystery plays, in popular religious festivals whether Christian or not (some of which gave rise to mummers' plays, concerned with death and resurrection), in biblical literature, and in Christian homilies.

In England, the new dramatic sensibilities were expressed by Shakespeare and most of his contemporary dramatists, using themes much indebted to the humanists and to Protestant (mostly Puritan) reformers of that age and showing the strong influence of a rising middle class. In Spain, the new sensibilities were expressed by Lope de Vega and Pedro Calderón de la Barca, using ideas more congenial to feudalism and to Roman Catholicism. The Renaissance, with its ambivalent attitude toward Christianity, the church, and dogma, empowered dramatists not only to express their own religious ambivalence but also, in the process, to fashion a new dramatic form.

Puritan influence on drama, noticeable during the reign of Elizabeth I in England, soon changed to hostility toward theatergoing. By the early seventeenth century, most Puritans would have been startled to know that John Calvin had spent many Sunday afternoons watching the performance of plays, even if those were indeed plays on scriptural subjects by Theodore Beza. In 1642, English Puritans who had achieved municipal power in London closed all theaters, partly because the stage was thought conducive to loose morals but also because it was associated with the royal court, the nobility, and Roman Catholicism. Although the theaters were allowed to reopen in 1660 with the accession of Charles II to the throne, this forced closing left its mark on all subsequent relations between church and theater throughout the Western world, relations that are sometimes intense but most often strained.

With some exceptions, the seventeenth and eighteenth centuries were not periods of important interaction between religion and drama. In the Counter-Reformation, Jesuits throughout Europe made widespread use of dramas to propagate the faith, producing a legacy of post-medieval didactic theater that has had widespread influence, for example on the twentieth-century Marxist playwright Bertolt Brecht. The neoclassic dramas of France in the seventeenth century, especially those of Jean Racine and Thomas Corneille, and also the comic dramas of Molière, are not well understood without knowledge of Christian doctrine and ethics in that age: such as, for example, Jansenist theology, which was important to the work of Racine. The anticlericalism that spread during the Enlightenment, especially in France and Germany, exacerbated ancient tensions between religion and theater, with the result that the rift between them was at its widest in the Age of Reason. Whether that has anything to do with the fact that this was not an especially creative period of playwriting, as compared to epochs before and after, is a matter for speculation. The theater of the eighteenth century went in for extraordinary scenic effects and allied itself with experiments being made by painters and architects. It tended more toward the pictorial than the performance aspect of theater and hence was very distant from any deep religious sensibility.

The Romantic movement that began in the late eighteenth century was quite a different matter. It stimulated the use of religious themes in drama, often in unorthodox forms. Goethe's *Faust* is perhaps the most famous example; but it is difficult to think of a Romantic playwright from England or the continent in whose dramas religious ideas or experiences do not make an appearance, whether in a positive manner (as in *Faust*), a negative manner (as in much of Ibsen), or a highly charged ambivalent manner (as in the works of Wilhelm von Kleist, Georg Büchner, and others).

During the nineteenth century, European drama began to display two major interests: the effect of social conditions upon human existence (leading to a style usually known as Realism) and the quest for meaning in life amid the uncertainties occasioned by the French Revolution, the industrial revolution, and the emerging evolutionary view of nature. Depictions of the quest for meaning, more than the positivistic concern for social realism, led frequently to plays depicting a search for God or for the protagonist's soul. Henrik Ibsen's *Brand* (1866) and *Peer Gynt* (1867) fall into this category, as do many plays by August Strindberg, such as *Advent* (1898), *To Damascus* (1898–1904), *Easter* (1900), and *The Ghost Sonata* (1907). At the same time, there was also a tendency for the more realistic or "secular" plays to develop a symbolic mode that verges on myth and confronts an audience with quasi-religious mystery. Ibsen's *The Wild Duck* (1884) and *The Master Builder* (1892) are of this kind, as well as Strindberg's horrifying plays about marriage, *The Father* (1887) and *The Dance of Death* (1901). It is worth noting that Ibsen was interested in the religious existentialism and anticlericalism of Søren Kierkegaard, and that Strindberg was at one time a practitioner of alchemy and at another a disciple of Emanuel Swedenborg.

To this tendency among major nineteenth-century playwrights to evince an interest in religious themes, the most notable exception is Anton Chekhov. In him the heavens are closed. The symbolism of plays like *The Seagull* (1896) and *The Cherry Orchard* (1904), strong and beautiful as it is, does not hint of transcendent mystery. The closing speech of Sonya in *Uncle Vanya* (1897), with its vision of an eventual heavenly peace, is moving precisely because the audience recognizes that her words are only wistful.

George Bernard Shaw, a fourth luminary among playwrights at the turn of the century, was a severe critic of contemporary Christianity, mostly because of what he saw as its moral hypocrisy and its alliance with capitalism; yet he introduced religious motifs in almost all his plays, and it may be said of him, as of William Butler Yeats, that he invented a religion of his own. Made up of ideas taken from Christianity, from the philosophers Friedrich Nietzsche and Henri Bergson, and from Fabian socialism, Shaw's faith amounted to a divination of the creative force of life. While concern for life as both rational and holy is never absent from Shaw's work, the plays in which it is most prominent are *Man and Superman* (1903), *Major Barbara* (1905), *Back to Methuselah* (1922), and *Saint Joan* (1923). Meanwhile, Shaw's Irish compatriot, the poet Yeats, was making use of theater to communicate not only the legends of Irish patriotism but also poetic religious visions, especially in plays written late in his life, such as *Calvary* (1921), *The Resurrection* (1927), and *Purgatory* (1938).

World War I put an end, not to romanticism in the arts, as used to be said, but to its nineteenth-century phase. Following the catastrophe of 1914–1918, the theatrical motifs and styles of the preceding century continued but in a deeper, more tortured form. The quest for meaning became more desperate. One result in the theater was a form known as expressionism, which used theatrical resources—decor, costuming, lighting, music, scene construction, performance technique—to achieve effects more like painting, cartooning, clowning, and poetry than like the narrative art that most Western theater has been. Indeed, from Yeats onward the experimental Western theater has reached out to Eastern (mostly Japanese) stylistic conventions, which are themselves firmly rooted in religious tradition.

In the work of German expressionist playwrights such as Ernst Toller, Ernst Barlach, and Oskar Kokoschka (better known as a painter) is found an outrage against existence that is at once moral and religious, the latter with varying degrees of explicitness. Art of this kind, in the theater as well as in other forms, was employed by the theologian Paul Tillich to depict the religious situation in Germany in the late 1920s. He wrote of such art as engaged in a religious protest against "bourgeois self-sufficient finitude," as he termed the attitude that had infiltrated both the churches and other social institutions and against which much serious theater of the time protested.

Such a theater of antireligious religious protest (to use a very dialectical expression for it) was also brought forth by the first playwright of the American theater to achieve an international reputation—Eugene O'Neill, whose plays often depict "the creative pagan acceptance of life," as he put it, "fighting eternal war with the masochistic, life-denying spirit of Christianity" (quoted from *Playwrights on Playwriting*, ed. Toby Cole, New York, 1961, pp. 237ff.). The plays of O'Neill that treat specifically of this religious theme include *Desire under the Elms* (1924), *The Great God Brown* (1926), *Lazarus Laughed* (1928), *Dynamo* (1929), and *Mourning Becomes Electra* (1931).

In O'Neill's works there is also another, slightly different understanding of the modern religious situation, one closer to the views of Tillich mentioned above. O'Neill articulated this in a letter to the critic George Jean Nathan. Here he wrote of his desire to dig at "the roots of the sickness today," which he went on to describe as "the death of an old God and the failure of science and materialism to give any satisfying new one for the surviving primitive religious instinct to find a meaning for life in, and to comfort its fears of death with" (quoted in *A History of Modern Drama*, ed. Barrett H. Clark and George Freedley, New York, 1947, p.

690). Such a sense of the loss of God, of meaning, of satisfaction and comfort, may be called post-Nietzschean, after the German philosopher who was the first among modern intellectuals to write of the "death of God." This view of the modern human situation, when held with passion, gives rise to a conviction known as existentialist, of which O'Neill was the first and remains the foremost exponent in American theater. His deepest expressions of this attitude are to be found in his late plays, particularly *The Iceman Cometh* (1939) and *Long Day's Journey into Night* (1940), but it is anticipated much earlier in his expressionist plays, such as *The Emperor Jones* (1920) and *The Hairy Ape* (1922).

In Europe, too, one can discern a line of development from the pre-expressionist, anarchist outcry of Alfred Jarry's *Ubu roi* (1896) through the expressionist drama—including many examples from Russia, France, and Italy not mentioned here—continuing in specifically existentialist dramas such as *No Exit* (1944) by Jean-Paul Sartre and *Caligula* (1944) by Albert Camus, thence into the post-1945 "theater of the absurd" (including the work of Eugène Ionesco, Arthur Adamov, Jean Genet, and Fernando Arrabal; in America, Edward Albee and others) and culminating in the plays of Samuel Beckett, most famously in his first published play, *Waiting for Godot* (1952).

Crucial to this development, as also to the experimental theater of the 1960s and 1970s, were the ideas put forward by Antonin Artaud in a book of essays entitled *Le théâtre et son double* (1938, translated as *The Theater and Its Double,* 1958). Artaud's "theater of cruelty," as he called it, is actually a theater of pure gesture in which words and ideas are "cruelly" subordinated to actions performed for their own sake *(l'acte gratuit).* This concentration upon the theatrical gesture per se would return theater to the domain of ritual. Theologically speaking, an *acte gratuit* is the action of a divinity that is answerable only to itself. Avant-garde theater in the twentieth century has been an attempt to return theater to its religious roots without necessarily adopting—indeed, often opposing—religious faith.

There was, however, a movement in midcentury to restore religious faith to the theater by way of a return to poetic drama. The movement's most prominent figure was the poet T. S. Eliot, who in 1934 was asked by E. Martin Browne, a theater director working for the Anglican diocese of London, to compose some verses (later known as "Choruses from *The Rock*") for a diocesan stage production. This was followed by a commission from Browne and Canterbury Cathedral that resulted in the play *Murder in the Cathedral* (1935), which made Eliot famous as a playwright and which is arguably the best poetic religious drama written in modern times. Later Eliot aspired to the writing of religious plays composed in verse about people in modern circumstances, partly because of the aesthetic challenge such a task presented, partly for the sake of propagating Christian faith in the modern world, and partly as an answer to existentialist playwrights. He wrote five of these, of which the most popular has been *The Cocktail Party* (1949). Others active in the revival of poetic religious drama have been Christopher Fry, Ronald Duncan, Henri Ghéon, and André Obey. However, the Belgian Michel de Ghelderode, who wrote perhaps the most forceful religious dramas of the century, chose not to use verse. Instead, he adopted a theatrical style somewhere between that of expressionism and absurdism, yielding works of strong religious and theatrical interest such as *Barabbas* (1929), *Chronicles of Hell* (1929), *The Women at the Tomb* (1928), and many more.

An important result of the competition given to theater by film and television has been the recognition by the more innovative theorists and practitioners that theater is not necessarily an art of representation. Instead, the leading innovators have viewed it as an art of *performance,* which means that interest focuses upon the actuality of the performer's existence and the interaction between the performer, the other performers, and the spectators. There have been attempts to work from an aesthetic of actuality rather than one of imitation. As was noted above in connection with Antonin Artaud, this awareness, and the techniques of performance associated with it, tend to move theater in the direction of ritualization and thus bring to the surface one of its more important yet hidden connections with religion.

For this reason, it may be argued that there has been no more significant development in the relation between theater and religion in the twentieth century than the experimental theater movement of the 1960s and 1970s. Its most influential exponent has been Jerzy Grotowski, founder of the Polish Laboratory Theater. Other groups of note are the Odin Teatret of Eugenio Barba (Sweden), The Living Theater of Julian Beck and Judith Malina (founded in New York but resident in Brazil and in Europe for many years), the Performance Group of Richard Schechner (New York), and the Open Theater of Joseph Chaikin (New York). Of these groups, only Odin Teatret and The Living Theater are still intact in the mid-1980s, and only the former remains artistically significant. The movement is in abeyance, but its influence upon serious thinking about theater and its relation to religion is likely to endure.

Black religion in North America, unlike most white religion, has made very direct artistic contribution to the theater. The general reason for this is that worship in the black church has retained, far more than in the white, a vigorous and emphatic performance tradition. Narrative recitation in black preaching, for example, is theatrical in the deepest sense of the word; music and rhythm provide the structure of the service; dancing (sometimes known as "shouting") is often practiced. The service of worship aims at a visible experiential encounter between the suppliants and a God who provides security, dignity, and freedom. Specifically, there has been a close connection between black church music and music performed for entertainment in clubs and theaters. In the commercial theater, this connection has been manifest in many productions, among them Langston Hughes's *Tambourines to Glory*, with gospel music by Jobe Huntley (1949), Hughes's *Black Nativity*, directed by Vinette Carroll (1961), and Carroll's own *Your Arms Too Short to Box with God* (1975). A work of great power was *The Gospel at Colonus* (1983), conceived and directed by Lee Breuer, with music by Bob Telson and a "book" drawn from Sophocles' *Oedipus at Colonus* plus a few passages from his *Oedipus Rex* and *Antigone* in translations by Robert Fitzgerald and Dudley Fitts. This text was sung, orated, danced, and preached as if it were scripture in a service of black church worship. Here gospel music, black tradition in preaching, an avant-garde approach to theater practice, and the ritual basis of Greek theater as echoed in the Sophoclean text all joined to provide a glimpse of the ecstasy that a living tradition of religious theater can provide.

BIBLIOGRAPHY

On the ancient connections between religious rituals and drama, see Theodor H. Gaster's *Thespis: Ritual, Myth, and Drama in the Ancient Near East* (New York, 1950) and A. W. Pickard-Cambridge's *The Dramatic Festivals of Athens*, 2d ed., revised by John Gould and D. M. Lewis (Oxford, 1968). These well-known authorities should be supplemented by *Ritual, Play, and Performance*, a collection of readings edited by Richard Schechner and Mady Schuman (New York, 1976), and by Schechner's *Essays on Performance Theory, 1970–1976* (New York, 1977), both of which cast the subject in broader light. The rise of European drama from liturgy has been documented by Karl Young in his two-volume study, *The Drama of the Medieval Church* (1933; reprint, London, 1967), but the standard view of the growth of European drama solely from Christian origins has been challenged in *The Origin of the Theater: An Essay*, by Benjamin Hunningher (New York, 1961).

Indispensable for understanding how Western drama has been structured to represent changing views of reality, some religious and some not, is *The Idea of a Theater*, by Francis Fergusson (Princeton, 1949). For the influence of biblical thought on Renaissance drama, see my book *The Sense of History in Greek and Shakespearean Drama* (New York, 1960) and also Juliet Dusinberre's *Shakespeare and the Nature of Women* (London, 1975). An analysis of developments in nineteenth- and twentieth-century drama as they pertain to modern consciousness and its search for meaning is to be found in my *Romantic Quest and Modern Query: A History of the Modern Theatre* (New York, 1970). The views of Paul Tillich cited in the article above are from his book *The Religious Situation*, translated by H. Richard Niebuhr (New York, 1932). *European Theories of the Drama*, edited by Barrett H. Clark (New York, 1947), is the standard sourcebook for theoretical writings about the whole of Western drama, both ancient and modern.

There is no book dealing comprehensively with religion and modern drama. A good book of limited scope is *The Great Pendulum of Becoming: Images in Modern Drama*, by Nelvin Vos (Grand Rapids, Mich., 1980). See also *The Making of T. S. Eliot's Plays*, by E. Martin Browne (London, 1969). Among reference works on modern drama as a whole, Myron Matlaw's *Modern World Drama: An Encyclopedia* (New York, 1972) is particularly useful.

TOM F. DRIVER

DREAMING, THE. Throughout the Australian continent, with few exceptions, Aborigines traditionally believed that at the beginning of time powerful characters (deities) arose from or appeared in the land. They shaped the land, preparing it for the human populations that were to follow them. They created or gave birth to people, allocating particular territories to them (and vice versa) and linking them, by divine decree, with particular languages and codes of behavior. Generally, the deities were credited with establishing the bases of Aboriginal society in the various regions for which they were responsible. Once that part of their task was completed, they did not disappear from the face of the earth but remained spiritually immortal in their own land, in full possession of a life essence which ensured that human beings and all aspects of the natural environment would continue uninterrupted.

The concept of the Dreaming encompasses all of this and a great deal more, including what has been called "totemism." The basic indicator of what is (or was traditionally) regarded as sacred, the Dreaming serves to articulate the main components of Aboriginal religion. Variously defined, this concept has its own identifying terms among differing Aboriginal groups: *alcheringa* (Aranda), *djugurba* (Western Desert), *bugari* (La Grange), *ungud* (Ungarinyin), *djumanggani* (eastern Kimberley), *wongar* (northeastern Arnhem Land), and so on. Such words are not necessarily translatable, but nearly all of them refer in one sense to a category of actions and things, mythic beings, natural species and elements, and human or human-type characters of the far distant past, the creative era, or the beginning. In addition, however, they imply a condition of timelessness. They do not refer only to the past as such, but to the past in the present and into the future—a past that is believed to be eternally relevant to all living things, including human beings.

Baldwin Spencer and F. J. Gillen (1904, p. 745) were probably the first observers to use the expression "dream times" for the past in which mythic ancestors lived. Émile Durkheim (1915) did not specifically use this term, but like Spencer and Gillen, he did link the concept with the idea of "conception totemism," which involves revelation through a dream of the mythic association of a child to be born. A. R. Radcliffe-Brown (1952, p. 166), writing in 1945, spoke of a "World Dawn" and of mythic characters as "Dawn Beings." However, the use of such terms to conceptualize the Dreaming overemphasizes the aspect of the past.

A. P. Elkin (1933, pp. 11–12ff.) stated that, where cult totemism is concerned, the question to be asked of an Aborigine is "What is your dreaming?" The answer, Elkin suggested, would point to a "totem" creature or some other mythic representation. (Cult totemism, in Elkin's terms, refers to rituals relating to mythic characters in either human or nonhuman manifestations: such rituals were owned by particular persons by virtue of their being spiritually associated with such characters.) Elkin, however, drew a distinction between a personal "totem" (as a "dreaming") and its broader religious frame (as the "dream-time," that is, "the eternal dream-time of spiritual reality"). Among the Karadjeri of the northwestern Kimberley, *bugari,* like a number of other such terms from other areas, includes both the "dreaming" and the "dream-time," as Elkin defines these. But it can also mean an ordinary dream. Such usage can be confusing, although Elkin made it clear that he was referring to what he called "the great dreaming," or "dream-time"—"the age of the mighty heroes and ancestors, who indeed still exist." Justification for the use of the term *dream* in this connection rests on the Aboriginal belief that, prior to a child's birth, his or her "totem" makes itself known to the child's parents or certain other close relatives in a special dream. But it is useful to distinguish the Dreaming from ordinary dreams and dreaming, by spelling it with a capital *D.*

In regard to what is believed to be conveyed at such a time, Durkheim (1915, pp. 247, 250–251) noted that a "life-power" was inherent in what he called the "first ancestors." Here he was following Spencer and Gillen, who had reported that when a spirit child "of the same totem as the corresponding ancestor" entered an appropriate woman, she would become aware that she was pregnant. The assumption was that there had been a transference of part of the life power possessed by a mythic being. Radcliffe-Brown (1952, p. 167) also referred to totem centers, associated with mythic beings and containing within them a "life-spirit" or "life-force" that could be released to revitalize natural species. Theodor G. H. Strehlow (1947, p. 17) wrote of "life-cells": "every cell in the body of a particular mythic being is potentially either a separate living creature or a living human being." Thus, a sacred linkage between a human being and a particular mythic character is revealed through some peculiar or special event prior to his or her birth—not necessarily in a dream. Nevertheless, there is abundant evidence from many different Aboriginal areas to substantiate the belief that a dream, in this connection, is a vital medium for establishing a person's association with the Dreaming (as Elkin demonstrated). However, it is only in specific circumstances that a dream is directly connected with the Dreaming in a religious sense; ordinary dreams are quite a different matter. Failure to recognize this distinction has, in the past, led to a distortion of the concept of the Dreaming. Géza Róheim's study (1945, pp. 210ff.) is an example.

While the term *Dreamtime(s)* continues to be used by some writers (for example, Stanner, 1965, p. 214), it has become more common to refer to *the Dreaming,* which implies a much wider context. The concept of the Dreaming is also often taken to include what has been called "totemism." Lévi-Strauss (1969) has drawn attention to the confusion which can result when totemism is regarded as a separate phenomenon.

The Dreaming, then, includes a mythological period located "long ago," in "time long past," when deities moved over the country, getting it ready for the emergence of human beings. These mythic beings were not necessarily in human form. Despite their suprahuman qualities or potentialities, they behaved in a very human way, much as traditionally oriented Aborigines were to do in the human era. Wherever they went in their travels through the land, these mythic characters left some evidence of their presence: for instance, a watercourse formed from their tracks, a rocky outcrop that came about through the weapons or other objects they left, a deposit of red ocher from the blood they spilled, a depression left by the mark of their buttocks as they sat or an indentation as they slept, water holes or soaks where they had urinated or that they dug or made by using their sacred emblems, and so on. There are thousands of such examples all over the continent, each holding part of the spiritual substance, the life essence, of the characters concerned. Moreover, in the formative era of the Dreaming, some of these mythic characters were killed or died "naturally" or were metamorphosed as features of the landscape or as natural species; some went into the sky or disappeared beyond the confines of a particular territorial group. Whatever they did, they remain eternally alive spiritually.

In identifying totemism, one clue is the ability of mythic characters to change shape and/or to be symbolically represented by some visible, living natural species. For example, the mythic character may have mythic associations with a member of that species and may be manifested in that form. If the mythic character is symbolized by a particular creature, then all creatures of that genus are believed (generally, though with some exceptions) to have within them the same life force as that being—that is, they contain the same Dreaming essence. Where human beings are concerned, the Dreaming spells out in a broad sense a relationship between them and nature, including the natural species, in which all are within the same universe of life and meaning and are bound together by strong emotional ties (Berndt, 1970, p. 1041). The pivotal binding forces, the vital linkages, are the deities themselves. Both humans and animals share a common, sacred life force derived from the Dreaming and inherent in the deities.

A critical issue in this connection is *how* they come to share this. On the one hand, most natural species and elements are representations or symbols of particular mythic beings. However, their continued existence within the physical world depends on species-renewal rites performed by human beings. On the other hand, insofar as human beings are concerned, a totem, in the form of a particular natural species, serves as an intermediary, or an agent, which transfers part of a mythic being's spirit to a potentially pregnant woman.

In Australian totemism, social and personal symbols are couched in the images of natural species that link men and women with the nonempirical world of the Dreaming. This is a world that, according to traditional Aboriginal belief, was not only established by the deities but is also spiritually maintained by them (in the eternal sense of the Dreaming). But the Dreaming has to be constantly re-created through ritual performances if the world is to be regenerated in a physical sense. That regeneration is possible only through the aid of the Dreaming deities, who must be persuaded through ritual to release their life-giving power.

It is not simply that human beings have the imprint of a particular deity upon them or within them. Nor is it really a question of their being descendants of a deity, for in physical terms, Aborigines may well claim that the mythic beings are their ancestors. However, many Aborigines believe, in a traditional context, that they do have spiritually within them part of a deity's own life force. In effect, they are living representatives of particular deities, and in identifying with these deities, an Aboriginal person is assured of a place in the divine plan expressed through the concept of the Dreaming.

BIBLIOGRAPHY

Berndt, Ronald M. "Two in One, and More in Two." In *Échanges et communications: Mélanges offerts à Claude Lévi-Strauss,* edited by Jean Pouillon and Pierre Maranda, vol. 2, pp. 1040–1068. The Hague, 1970. Discusses several aspects of Lévi-Strauss's view of totemism, with regional examples.

Durkheim, Émile. *The Elementary Forms of the Religious Life* (1915). Translated by Joseph Ward Swain. New York, 1965. This insightful classic study concerns many aspects of totemism and the Dreaming. While Durkheim was, of course, unable to utilize more recent anthropological materials on these topics, many current studies have been strongly influenced by his work.

Elkin, A. P. *Studies in Australian Totemism* (1933). New York, 1978. A detailed report of some of Elkin's fieldwork in the northwestern Kimberley area of Western Australia, covering a wide range of totemic phenomena. It was on this basis that his later views of Aboriginal religious life were elaborated.

Lévi-Strauss, Claude. *Le totémisme aujourd'hui.* Paris 1962. Translated as *Totemism* (Harmondsworth, 1969). A penetrating study of totemism which stimulated a revival of interest in this direction. In putting forward his own theory of totemism within a broad setting, Lévi-Strauss critically reviews a number of other sources.

Radcliffe-Brown, A. R. *Religion and Society.* London, 1945. Reprinted in his *Structure, and Function in Primitive Society* (London, 1952), pp. 153–177. A general study of religion that brings in some Aboriginal material, including a critique of Durkheim (1915).

Róheim, Géza. *The Eternal Ones of the Dream.* New York, 1945. In many ways this is an interesting study, since it includes firsthand field material, but the author's psychoanalytic interpretative frame dominates his analysis.

Spencer, Baldwin, and F. J. Gillen. *The Northern Tribes of Central Australia.* London, 1904. While this classic study can be criticized in terms of its incompleteness in many respects, and its empirical as well as conceptual shortcomings, it remains an important source book.

Stanner, W. E. H. "Religion, Totemism, and Symbolism." In *Aboriginal Man in Australia,* edited by Ronald M. Berndt and Catherine H. Berndt, pp. 207–237. Sydney, 1965. Although Stanner wrote several articles on Aboriginal religion, this particular contribution is probably the best since it encapsulates his theoretical approach as well as his specific views on the topic.

Strehlow, T. G. H. *Aranda Traditions.* Melbourne, 1947. A detailed study of Aranda religion in terms of myths and rituals. It contains some of the best material on these central Australian people.

RONALD M. BERNDT

DREAMS. As a category, "dreams" can designate not only dream states and the waking reports of these states but a variety of other experiences that might also be called "visions," "waking dreams," "hypnogogic fantasies," or "hallucinations." [*See also* Visions.] A mere catalog of dream types or a description of sleeping states is distinct from and, insufficient for understanding the kinds of knowledge associated with dreams. To grasp cultural theories of dreams as theories of thinking, it is necessary to analyze patterns in the perception of dreams. While these social and cultural patterns are, of course, perceived by individuals who make them meaningful in terms of their own psychodynamics, in this article we shall concentrate on the socio-cultural meanings of such patterns. Furthermore, cultural and religious theories of knowlege expressed in ideas about dreams are analytically distinct from what today we might or might not be able to know about the actual *content* of the experiences so categorized.

For these reasons, therefore, in this article I shall emphasize patterns in the perception of dreams as reflected in dream classification, attitudes toward dreams, and behaviors that dreams are perceived to influence, determine, or explain. By so doing, I shall delineate principles for understanding the religious and cultural functions and meanings of dreams across time and space.

Royal Message and Apocalyptic Dreams. An outside observer may recognize at least two types of dreams in the Hebrew scripture (Old Testament). The first is a "message" dream, a communication from God to a king or prophet in which the dreamer is no more than a medium. "Hear now my words," God says to Moses, "if there be a prophet among you, I the Lord will make myself known unto him in a vision and will speak to him in a dream" (*Nm.* 12:6ff.). Political divination dreams, closely related to message dreams, include the dream of Pharaoh that was interpreted by Joseph: "The seven good kine are seven years and the seven good ears are seven years. The dream is one" (*Gn.* 41:1ff.). Through Joseph's interpretation, Pharaoh secures his political power by storing away sufficient supplies to get through a lean period. Joseph notes the prophetic value of repeated dreams: "And for that the dream was doubled unto Pharaoh twice; it is because the thing is estabished by God, and God will shortly bring it to pass" (*Gn.* 41:32). The more directly the dream or the vision is an expression of divinity, the sooner it will be realized; this rule of thumb also applies to divination in general.

Joseph himself, in *Genesis*, has a political divination dream: "For behold, we were binding sheaves in the field and lo, my sheaf arose and also stood upright; and behold, your sheaf stood around about, and made obeisance to my sheaf" (37:5). The dream came to pass, and Joseph became much more powerful than his brothers, who did in fact bow to him. In another such dream, Daniel sees a figure with a head of gold, breast and arms of silver, belly and thighs of brass, legs of iron, and feet of iron and clay. And a stone "smote the image upon his feet," presumably a shattering experience. In Daniel's interpretation, the head was Nebuchadrezzar; the breast and arms were the second kingdom; the belly the third kingdom, and the legs the fourth. The dream illustrates royal succession and kingship.

The second type of dream, the "apocalyptic" dream, while also a communication from God, differs from the political divination dreams in that it is imaginary. Whereas the dream image of Jacob's ladder (*Gn.* 28:12) makes it clear that there is a link between heaven and earth and the angels are able to go up and come down the ladder, apocalyptic dreams are set in a world startlingly distinct from that of everyday life. Take, for instance, Ezekiel's description of a whirlwind that comes out of the north in a great cloud and a fire of amber. Out of the midst of the fire emerged the likeness of four living creatures "and every one had four faces, every one had four wings, and their feet were straight feet;" and "they had the hands of a man under their wings on their four sides; and the four had their faces and their wings," and their wings were joined one to the other "and they appeared like wheels . . ." (*Ez.* 1:4–28). Here, too, a difference can be noted from the relatively straightforward dream of Joseph, in which his brothers are sheaves doing obeisance before him.

God speaks not through symbols of ordinary daily life, but through powerful, imaginary, divinely-inspired symbols. Elisha sees a chariot and horses of fire, and is whisked off to heaven by a whirlwind (*2 Kgs.* 2:9). Daniel, in a dream, sees four beasts: the first, a lion with the wings of an eagle, walking upright like a man; the second, a bear with three ribs in its teeth, who is told to "devour much flesh"; the third, a leopard with four wings of a fowl and four heads; the fourth, with "great iron teeth" and ten horns (*Dn.* 7:3–7). In another vision, Daniel sees a man clothed in linen, his face of lightning, his eyes "lamps of fire," his voice "like the voice of a multitude" (*Dn.* 10:5–6).

Apocalyptic dreams, like apocalyptic literature in general, reflect withdrawal from the present social and political world and from the realm of sense impressions to an imaginary, internal universe where, as in Blake, we can see truly only with the eyes of the soul.

Ancient Mesopotamia (dreams and divine kingship). Most of the available sources from ancient Mesopotamia deal with divination as related to kings or persons of unquestionable political authority. In his study of the dream books discovered in the library of Ashurbanipal, A. Leo Oppenheim (1956) identifies three kinds of dreams: message dreams (divine messages revealed to kings and other important political figures); "symptomatic" dreams, which relate directy to the spiritual and physical health of the dreamer; and mantic (prophetic) dreams. As we have seen, apocalyptic literature stresses dreams of the third type. Certain ancient authors even went to the trouble of burying their texts with instructions that they should be unearthed at a time several generations in the future, when their contents would be understood. The dreams analyzed by Oppenheim, however, are predominantly message dreams. (Oppenheim's choice is understandable, as these are the best documented dreams and as he emphasizes dream and interpretation as one unit.) He distinguishes three steps in the interpretative process: (1) the protasis (description of the phenomenon or symbols to be understood), (2) the apodasis (prognosis of events to come), and (3) the solution or ritual act to be carried out. In that they encompass experiences, ideas, and actions, dreams and their interpretations are, according to Oppenheim, at once psychological, social, and religious.

One of the earliest known message dreams is that of Gudea, king of Lagash, who ruled about 2000 BCE. An enormous figure whose head touched the skies appeared in a dream and instructed Gudea to build him a dwelling. Gudea then saw what he interpreted as the first stone of the edifice being lowered from heaven in a basket. The dream was understood as an order from the god Ningirsu instructing Gudea to build him a temple. Upon awakening, Gudea did as he had been told. In a similar example, the son of the Egyptian king Amunhotep II, Thothmose IV, went to sleep between the paws of the monumental Sphinx of Giza. In his dream, the sphinx granted him protection and assured his succession to the throne.

Greece and Rome. Although dreams certainly did not mean the same things to Greeks of the Homeric period as they did to contemporaries of Sophocles or to the early Christian writers, there are, nonetheless, certain common themes that make it possible to talk about attitudes toward dreams and religion in the classical traditions. One of the most basic themes, which can be recognized in other contexts as well, is that knowledge in dreams comes from a reality outside the rational, empirical self, beyond the reach of the senses. This reality is perceived as an external force. At times (in Old Testament message dreams), the dream can be uncommonly clear and forceful because of its clarity; at other times (as in Old Testament apocalyptic dreams), it is more an ecstatic experience of overpowering feelings. At all times dreams perceived to be religious are known in a different mode from that of the waking senses.

In Homer, the external quality of the dream is represented by the image of a dream figure who visits the dreamer; this figure is the dream itself. As E. R. Dodds points out (1951, p. 104), the word *oneiros* in Homer nearly always means a dream figure rather than a dream experience. Moreover, the external origin of the dream is accentuated by the emphasis on *seeing* a dream rather than merely *having* it. In Herodotus and in the Epidaurian and Lydian temple records (about which I shall say more shortly), the dream is said "to stand over" the dreamer. As in the Old Testament and Mesopotamian materials, dreams of certain types are obeyed as messages from the deity, although nearly all inscriptional evidence is of Hellenistic or Roman date (ibid., p. 108). However, the divine-message dream seems to decline in frequency and importance after the fifth century BCE, as one might expect, considering how intimately it was associated with the institution of divine kingship. However, other kinds of dreams believed to be communications from deities did not decline in importance. Indeed, author of the *Epinomis* (attributed to Plato) notes that "many cults of many gods have been founded, and will continue to be founded, because of dream-encounters with supernatural beings, omens, oracles and deathbed visions."

That dreams were not simply associated with what is called "the irrational" is demonstrated by the frequency with which they are sent by Apollo. This may at first seem surprising, since Nietzsche (*The Birth of Tragedy*, 1871), Benedict (1922), and others associate the term *Apollonian* with rationality and oppose it to the term *Dionysian*, associated with ecstasy; in Homer, however, Apollo was a god of prophecy and sender of plagues who later acquired other attributes. He was also associated with the Delphic oracle and worshiped on this account. Though theories of divination are linked with science and religion, encompassing both knowledge and belief, they cannot in our context be used in any way to dichotomize the two. Those who suppose that knowledge is unitary, or, at the very least, that ignorance is monolithic, cannot understand how beliefs in dreams and oracles could express a theory of knowledge.

The Greeks referred to a knowledge of the future as "mantic," and the Romans referred to the same as "divination." Both terms apply to knowledge derived from the outside that is added to human understanding. Divination was an important social force: instead of being ridiculed as a superstition, it was professed by governments, represented by venerable institutions, boasted of by poets, demonstrated by philosophers, and practiced by nearly everyone. Significantly, the Stoics, who had such a profound effect on the social sciences (as moral sciences), were particularly emphatic about what they called the "mantic science," believing that it represented extrarational knowledge.

But if divination, generally speaking, designates a particular kind of knowledge as well as particular faculties of the knower, it is nonetheless also inseparable from practice. Attempts to forge the idea of divination as knowledge (or foreknowledge) and that of magic as rite into a conceptual unity led to one of the most profound of philosophical problems: the conflict between foreknowledge and freedom. For it is logically impossible to wish to know the future in order to change it. Clearly, in the Greek world (and Greek tragedy in particular), one of the primary functions of dreams is to reveal the logic of destiny, conceived as an irrational sense of the ineluctable. As Aeschylus (525–426 BCE) says in *The Persians*, "When man runs toward his ruin, the gods speed his fall" (l. 1732). One dimension of Greek tragedy, then, is the conflict between the logic of destiny and individual free will. Dreams are used to great effect, in a variety of ways, to express this confict.

According to the Cynics, divination (and dreams) were no more than a subterfuge, of interest only to sick minds. But attempts to discredit divination did not come only from the atheists: one can speak of a Judeo-Christian tradition that discredits beliefs in the divinatory and prophetic functions of dreams (see *Dt.* 12:1; *Eccl.* 5:2; *Jer.* 23:32; *Zec.* 10:2). The matter hinges on what kinds of divination are acceptable, and why.

Plato notes that medicine and mantics are of the same blood, since the two arts have the same father, Apollo (*Phaedra* 244h). As practitioners of medicine saw and read the signs of the body, so practitioners of mantic science saw and read the signs of the soul. However, Plato did not uncritically accept knowledge obtained from divination. Neither mantics nor hermeneutics can ever be enough for the wise man, he remarked, because one can know through either of them what was said but not whether in fact this thing was true. Moreover, for Plato, knowledge of the supernatural was of various kinds, each corresponding to a particular state of mind. There were four types of mania: (1) that of Apollo (prophetic delirium), (2) that of Bacchus (mystical drunkenness), (3) that of the Muses (poetic inspiration), and (4) that of Eros (philosophical contemplation) (Bouché-Leclercq, 1975, p. 51). The sequence proceeds from instrumental (the prophetic delirium in which the prophet is the mouthpiece of a deity) to voluntaristic (the philosopher who contemplates).

By contrast, for Aristotle (384–322 BCE), divination and dreams are natural, not supernatural. Thus he denies that dreams ever come from outside the dreamer's physical sensations and memories, and he flatly refutes the claim that they establish relationships with the supernatural *(de divinatione per somnum)*. In this respect Aristotle aligns himself with Hippocrates and the medical tradition, about which I shall have more to say shortly. For Plotinus, too, divination acts by natural signs, as it is "a reading of natural letters."

The ideas of Aristotle and the medical profession did not hold sway, however, for the Stoics (including Marcus Aurelius) derived their proofs for the existence of gods from the existence of oracles. If oracles exist and divination is practiced, they held, then *ipso facto* the gods exist. The early Christians could not, of course, deny the existence of oracles. Rather they attacked divination and oracles as devices used by demons or evil genius over which Jesus Christ would eventually reign, having laid siege to such forces of evil in the world.

It was not until Augustine (352–430 CE) that the Christian church determined the orthodox stance toward the entire question of oracles. In his treatise *De divinatione daemon,* Augustine states explicitly that supernatural knowledge can only come from one of two clearly defined sources: God or the demons. Generally speaking, Christianity eliminated external magical rites of divination and substituted prayer, thus leaving room for dreams, visions, and prophetic inspirations, provided these were God-sent. Even in Christianity, however, the possibility of doubt remained: was the dream sent by God or not? Indeed, Luther prayed to God not to send him any dreams whatever, so he would not have to deal with the question.

The matter of deceitful dreams is very old indeed. In the *Odyssey* there are true and false dreams that not even the gods can tell apart with any certainty. For Homer, deception is a fact of existence; gods deceive mortals as they deceive one another. Zeus, for example, sends Agamemnon a divine drama that incites him to fight the Greeks in a battle he is destined to lose. It is Penelope who explains that dreams escape by two doors, one of horn, the other of ivory (*Odyssey* 19.560ff.). Dreams passing through the gate of ivory are deceptive and vain; those by the gate of horn, veridical. All this is well and good, but the question remains: how does one tell what sort of dream one has had? These difficulties increased when God was given the attributes of omniscience and omnipotence, for this meant that by definition God could not deceive. Indeed, these questions did not go away; in his *Discourse on Method* (1637) Descartes wrestled valliantly with the implications of the issue of dreams and doubt and the existence of God.

Medicine and religion (ancient Greece and Rome). In the works of Greek and Roman authors, there is no very clear or satisfactory correlation between veridical, religious dreams, on the one hand, and deceitful, profane dreams, on the other. This should perhaps come as no surprise, since the various sciences of divination all depend upon chance, over which no man has rational control. [*See* Chance.] There is a sort of principle of uncertainty guiding diviners, not to be confused with deceit.

This is especially true of dreams for two reasons. First, dream interpretation is the encyclopedic divinatory art and science in which all others are included. For not only do all other techniques of divination appear as symbols in dreams to be decoded; dream interpretation also links body and mind as no other divinatory technique can. Birds, bones, cadavers, livers, left hands, stars, tortoise shells, and palms can all be dreamed, and when they are the dream interpreter is expected to know at least as much about reading such signs as the dreamer. Second, all these can be interpreted as it were on a double clavier: with respect to the state of the body, or with respect to the mind-soul, or both.

Ancient writers on dream interpretation tended to specialize in certain kinds of dreams and/or certain kinds of dreamed knowledge. Hippocrates (c. 460–377 BCE), for example, concentrated only on dreams that concerned bodily states, leaving the rest to divination. Thus his very "science of dreams" selected certain kinds of dreams for interpretation and ignored others. Another doctor, Herophilus, distinguished three types of dreams: those sent by God, those that come from the soul itself, and those that are of a mixed type, such as erotic dreams; the latter enter the dreamer from the outside but are called upon by a wish or preoccupation of the soul (Bouché-Leclercq, p. 297). The dream books and materials examined by Oppenheim in the library of Ashurbanipal concentrated chiefly on message dreams and dreams of kings, whereas the dream book of Artemidorus Daldianus (second century CE) did not even consider message dreams but rather focused on the dreams of the common folk, the interpretation of which did not require supernatural assistance.

There is yet another feature of dream interpretation as divination that must be mentioned, namely, ideas about the supernatural character of instinct. Instinctive acts of animate beings—human beings included—were themselves used in divination. If for Socrates nature is demonic and man is part of nature, then man is demonic in some respects. And indeed Socrates had his demon. Such notions about divination and the natural world appear to have been accompanied by a certain mistrust of reason, which could be a faculty of deception as well as of knowledge. As Artemidorus notes in the *Oneirocritica*, animals tell the truth precisely because they lack reason and cannot lie. This principle that only sentient beings lie serves as the basis for his theory of enthusiasm, which considers the flight patterns, calls, and movements of birds of prey, along with the movements of heavenly bodies, as sources of knowledge. Similarly, divination could be applied not only to the behavior of other animals but also to man himself; it could be "anthropological."

Human divination was composed of two categories; intellectual acts and involuntary physical acts. In intellectual acts, the divine instruments were language, activities, and signs; in physical acts, they were the science of shivers, including convulsions or palpitations *(salissatio memorum)*, sneezes *(sternutatio)*, and humming in the ears *(tinnitus aurium)*.

In addition to helping us understand how epilepsy could have been seen as a divine illness, the concept of using man for divination also illuminates how ambiguous was the idea of a mind-body dichotomy. For if one said that dreams came from the body, for example, such a position did not preclude the possibility of using symptoms as divine symbols, and vice versa.

Divination, then, designates a kind of knowledge outside rational control, generally attributed to supernatural beings, natural forces, or some combination of powers which reason cannot know. Unlike prophecy, divination is analytically, but not factually, separable from magical rites and practices. Furthermore, it refers to a knowledge of the past and future that is ordinarily hidden and contained in signs. Because it links internal, feeling states with social representations and rituals, divination in dreams is an extremely potent cultural force. Through the Greco-Roman tradition it has influenced Western concepts of reason, science, religion, and knowledge.

Certainly, dream interpretation as a social event is directly related to divination throughout the Mediterranean and in many other parts of the world. As Victor Turner notes, in addition to revealing the future by means of signs, divination refers " 'to the analysis of past events,' especially untoward events; this analysis often includes the detection of guilt. Where such untoward events are attributed (as they are in most preliterate and some literate societies) to sorcery and witchcraft, the diviner has great freedom of judgment in detecting and determining guilt" (Turner, 1964, p. 205). Thus, divination-as-dream-interpretation often deals with painful feelings of guilt, conflictual social relationships, jealousies, and various other relations between individual motives and group values.

Dreaming cures. The very close relations between dreams, misfortune, suffering, and illness are represented by the Mediterranean practice of incubation, the sleeping in a sacred place in order to dream a cure to ailments of body and soul, and to seek guidance, fortune, and knowledge of the future from a divine being. [*See* Asklepios.] Incubation provides us with a fine example of a process for acquiring knowledge, assuaging suffering, and seeking divine assistance through an individual rite that relies on social practices. As it is often physical suffering that prompts the individual to use dreams to effect a cure, and as the dreamer who encounters the divinity often obeys divine counsel, there is no way of dividing incubation into knowledge on the one hand and action on the other. Nor can the dream be analyzed as a rationalization for actions in the way myths are sometimes construed as relating to rites. Incubation, then, encompasses individual suffering, individual rites, and social categories precisely because dreams reveal a source of external assistance in dealing with internal suffering and pain.

Although generally associated with the cult of Asklepios and, more specifically, with his temple at Epidaurus, incubation as an institution is still widespread throughout the Mediterranean, as I have pointed out elsewhere (1981). Moreover, the cult itself treats mind and body as a unit, despite the fact that the use of medicine (which supported the idea of a mind-body dichotomy) was growing in the Hellenistic and Roman worlds. In the early Roman empire, all major cities had temples to the god of medicine, and there were at least as many Asclepia as sanctuaries of other great Greek gods. Alexander the Great (356–323 BCE) was a devotee of Asklepios and of the Epidaurian god in particular, and even Galen (b. 130 CE) was quite willing to perform an operation as he was instructed in a dream (Dodds, 1951, p. 121). At the height of the cult in the late second century, Christians considered it their most formidable rival, for parallels with Asklepios—half man and half god, savior and healer—had to be dealt with seriously by Christians who made similar claims for Christ. Arthur Darby Nock, Stanley Frederick Bonner and others have emphasized the similarity between the cult of Asklepios and Christianity in terms of religious feelings toward a divine healer.

Asklepios had a variety of distinguished dreaming patients, from Pausanias (fl. c. 150 CE) to the well-known orator Aelius Aristides (b. 117?). The number of extant votive offerings to Asklepios consisted of representations of ailing organs (ears and eyes), or of other kinds of representations, and is indeed impressive. In many cases the god, appearing with his snakes, actually effected cures upon the dreamers, either by taking out his knife and operating, or by instructing his serpents to lick the afflicted body parts (Edelstein, 1945). Some dreams left "rapports," or earthly tokens, behind, such as leeches found by the dreamer upon awakening. A severe operation was performed in dream by Cosmos and Damian upon a patient so reluctant that Damian had to hold him while Cosmos operated with a knife; another operation was performed in dream by a certain saint, who put on a leg the wrong way, so that the toes pointed backward.

Aelius Aristides. More than three hundred thousand lines and two hundred dreams are left to us in an extraordinary testament of religious devotion to the god of healing, make the journal of Aelius Aristides one of the most important documents for our subject. Aristides was horribly afflicted by shortness of breath, deafness, intestinal pains and gastric disorders, tumors, chronic headaches, and miscellaneous ailments. His suffering prompted him to make contact with Asklepios in dreams, and the god responded by commanding Aristides to keep a journal to be dedicated to him: "Straight from the beginning the God ordered me to write down my dreams. And this was the first of his commands." In return for these directives, Aristides became a "priest of the god," obeying dreamed dictates and submitting to Asklepios truly "as to a doctor" (Behr, 1968, p. 206). Asklepios instructed him to bathe, induce vomiting, take enemas, bleed himself profusely, and make pilgrimages to various sanctuaries such as the one at Epidaurus. Once, when doctors predicted death if he did not agree to surgery for a tumor in his groin, Aristides put his faith in Asklepios, who instructed him not to listen to these "gardeners," but rather to "hold firm" and "bear up." In the course of a few months he did in fact rid himself of the tumor, although other ailments continued for years.

The effect of conflicting religions. Pagans and early Christians alike found convincing links between their own pains and dreams. Indeed, as second-century Roman society was characterized by what E. R. Dodds (1951) has called a crisis of identity, it is not surprising that the Christian attitude toward dreams was rather like that of the devotees of Asklepios, except for the substitution of a shrine of a martyr or saint for a pagan temple.

In keeping with the pervasive doubt and uncertainties of the period, one finds an emphasis on contemplation in which dreams play a major part. In his *Meditations*, Marcus Aurelius (121–180 CE) talks about the need for withdrawal into the self and for contemplation, a notion elaborated much earlier by Plato and others who held that the unexamined life is not worth living. "Know thyself" became a refrain. True, the attitude is not yet fully mystical, and Marcus does not advocate with the Neoplatonist Plotinus the notion that "all things are within," yet his disenchantment with the political, social, and sensual orientation of his society is clear. Montanists like Tertullian (c. 155–c. 222 CE) recommended rather severe asceticism in an effort to bridle bodily desires; intellectualists like Plotinus placed desires inside the psyche itself, burying these unconscious forces within. Maximus (d. 370 CE) advocated the supression of the physical senses in order to allow deeper truths to be perceived: "Strip away the outer garments, abolish in thought the preoccupation of the eyes, and in what remains you will see the true objects of your longing" (quoted in E. R. Dodds, *Pagan and Christian in an Age of Anxiety,* Cambridge, 1965, p. 93). "True" dreams were thought to be those in which the senses have been silenced, and God speaks; conversely, dreams from the body drown out God's voice.

Some writers stress how essential a state of ritual and bodily purity is for communication with God in dreams; this idea has carried over into Islam, which prescribes ablutions both in order to obtain God-sent "message dreams" and in order to rid oneself of the impurity of sexual dreams. However, the basic preoccupation with dreamed knowledge of unseen and essential realities persists universally in ideas about dreams. This idea has deep roots in our concept of human tragedy. Aeschylus writes: "In slumber the eye of the soul waxes bright, but in the daytime man's doom goes unforeseen" (*Eumenides* 104–105). Knowledge of fate is essential but does not come through rational use of sensual knowledge. Tireseus is a *blind* prophet; sight in dreams, sight as prophetic or divinatory "insight," and knowledge of the unseen (fate and the gods) being fundamentally related. In all societies dreams link the unseen world of feelings with the unseen world of the supernatural, relating knowledge of both and distinguishing it from knowledge of the daily world of rational experience derived from sense impressions and evaluated in terms of self-interest. Indeed, the theme of dreamed faculties as second sight and dreamed knowledge as insight will preoccupy us for the remainder of this article.

Christianity, Dreams, and Divination. Tertullian, a contemporary of Aelius Aristides, Pausanias, Galen, and Apuleius, adapted to Christian beliefs the categories of dreams commonly used in divination. He distinguished between dreams that come from God, dreams that come from demons, and dreams that are the products of bodily sensations. The third category is one in which sleep speaks instead of God, who is silent; when God is silent, the body is heard. Dreams "caused" by bodily needs are antithetical to dreams "caused" by God. It is worth noting that the same general classificatory pattern has been found in contemporary Morocco and indeed seems prevalent in the Islamic world.

Another second-century writer, Synesius, a Platonist who converted to Christianity and the author of a treatise on dreams, held that as a matter of principle all dreams are true. However, it is not given to everybody to perceive the truth. Individuals must acquire discipline and skill at decoding dreams for themselves; not being able to do so admits to a shameful dependence on interpreters, which itself belies inadequate understanding of divine revelation. Like Plotinus, Synesius held that all parts of the universe were mutually dependent, such that each phenomenon is a "legible writing of the future" and man himself is part of this universal natural semiology. If, therefore, the usual subject-object relationship were reversed and birds, for example, were assumed to have intelligence, it would logically follow that such birds would use men to tell their future. The result would be "anthroposcopy." Understanding consists in "reading" nature's inscriptions, whether in dreams, the movements of the stars, or the flight of birds of prey.

There is yet another way in which Christian beliefs drew on divinatory notions associated with dreams: through ideas about a soul, or life principle. Souls could be either healthy or sick, states that—as analyzed by the Pythagoreans—were defined not by the absence or presence of any particular quality, but by the balance of constitutive elements (i.e., an equilibrium of the four humors). According to Aristotle and other authors, Christian and non-Christian alike, true dreams do not come from good common sense or proper use of the senses so much as from an exceptional nature and a greatness of soul (see Aristotle's *Poetics*). Aristotle believed that poets need to experience directly the emotions felt by heroes, which he associated with ecstasy. Aristotle also held that such greatness was, in fact, an indication that outstanding men and poets were uncommonly vulnerable to melancholia, which was thought to be a disease of the soul, or, perhaps more accurately, of the liver, the seat of the emotions. Plutarch, however, opposed the prevailing opinion that all melancholics always had true dreams; instead he maintained that it was normal they should once in a while, since they dreamed so much anyway. Reasoning along the same lines, and holding, like Synesius, that all dreams are true, Tertullian remarked that "we receive dreams from God, there being no man so foolish as never to have known any dreams come true" *(De anima).* One of the authors of a treatise on melancholia much admired by Galen, a certain Ruphus of Ephesus, held that activities of the mind were the direct cause of melancholia.

An outstanding feature of dreams in the Greek and Roman worlds is the variety of ways they were used socially and psychologically. For the Skeptics, who opposed divination, and for whom *ataraxis* (freedom from mental perturbation and excitement) was an aim, dreams could be selected for their conformity to ideas about desirable knowledge, thereby allowing dreamers to remain unflappable. For the more socially minded Stoic, dreams reflected fortitude in the face of pain, as with Aristides. For others, they reflected ecstatic states and overpowering emotions. Sometimes this is rationalized in terms of the origin (cause) of each type of dream. Significant dreams, for Aristotle, must come from within, for there are no God-sent dreams. For Tertullian, by contrast, all dreams are God-sent. And Artemidorus claims that often the kind of dream cannot be judged until it has been realized and/or interpreted, thus emphasizing the contingent nature of its knowledge and the social relationships in terms of which it must be understood.

Artemidorus's Oneirocritica. The most important dream book from the entire Greek and Roman period is that of the Lydian dream-interpreter Artemidorus Daldianus (second century CE), who wrote his book as instructed in a dream. Dedicated to the emperor Hadrian and written for Artemidorus's son, the *Oneirocritica* (Interpretation of Dreams) is hardly original. Yet it is by far the most comprehensive and systematic treatment of dreams before Freud, and contains a rather extraordinary analysis of dreams in daily life, examined in terms of the specific social, physical, and psychological circumstances of the dreamer.

Generally speaking, Artemidorus can be grouped with the Skeptics because of his theory of knowledge and divination. Indeed, the very vocabulary he uses to describe the effects of dreams is paralleled most strikingly by astrological discussions (Claes Blum, *Studies in the Dream Book of Artemidoros*, Uppsala, 1936, p. 47). And the work is characterized by what Blum has referred to as "a special mantic style" (p. 50).

Divination was, however, not incompatible with science, at least not for Artemidorus and others of the period. Artemidorus's treatment of the subject of dreams and their interpretation is avowedly "scientific," by which he means it is based upon experience and careful observation. If in the natural world astrology and astronomy should have been rather closely linked, then it is perhaps not surprising that in the psychic world dreams and social interactions should also be closely associated. Indeed, divination for Artemidorus was an all-encompassing theory of knowledge in which dream interpretation occupied the central position as a science of all divinatory sciences. If Artemidorus has been called an empiricist, he is also a humanist in that his science of dream interpretation supposed an inclusive theory of knowledge and of thinking.

Sources for Artemidorus include Posidonius, Macrobius, and Cicero. Like Plato, who in the *Republic* propounds the theory that moderation and justness allow the soul in sleep to grasp the truth, Cicero (*On Divination* 1.60) notes that the freer a man is of passions, the more likely he is to have prophetic dreams. The idea that great men have prophetic dreams—and that prophetic dreams can be dreamed only when the passions are bridled—appears in the early Christian writers like Tertullian as well as in the writings of the Stoics who, like Plato, advocate the need for an elite of philosopher-statesmen. Such ideas again reflect the mind-body dualism, which during the early Christian period was a basic concern of all those who in that age of anxiety sought to define the realtionship between individuals and a society. For pagan and Christian alike, only the pure in mind and body could receive prophetic dreams.

According to Macrobius (395–423 CE), for example, there are four categories of dreams: (1) those caused by the body and its needs *(ventris plenitudo vel inanitas)*, (2) those caused by *illusio*, (3) prophetic dreams in which *cogitatio* is obscured by *illusio*, and (4) direct revelations from God in which there is cooperation between God and the soul *(revelatio* and *cogitatio)*. These direct revelations are of two kinds, *oraculum* and *visio; oraculum* are verbal messages from God, while *visio* are divinely sent images. Christian writers simply invert these categories placing God-sent messenger dreams at the head of the list and dreams derived from bodily passions at the bottom. For example, the classifications of the pagan Posidonius and the Christian Tertullian are essentially the same, save that Tertullian puts the devil in the place of immortal spirits of the air and Christ in the place of the pantheistic god. For the *immortales animi* of Cicero, Tertullian substitutes the demons.

As one would expect, Artemidorus aimed his book at the two intermediate categories, both because his "empirical" methods dictated that he concentrate on the kinds of dreams that he could interpret, and because his principles of understanding could not be programmatic. Rather, they are grounded in circumstances, like the dream-stuff itself. Indeed, for Artemidorus, external realities influence the kinds of dreams that he writes about in his dream book. As in Freud's definition of the dreamer's "day-residue," the "circumstances" include the dreamer's wealth, age, profession, nationality, and social class as well as the circumstances of the dream, and when and how it was dreamed. Yet individualization is also important to the interpretations of Artemidorus, who depends heavily on specific context to establish his claims to a scientific approach.

Artemidorus uses classificatory systems that cannot be clearly distinguished from their Christian counterparts as theories of knowledge. Indeed, all members of all societies can be said to have ideas about all kinds of dreams experienced, although their interpretative systems will inevitably focus on certain categories of dream reports to the exclusion of others. The two kinds of dream reports Artemidorus does *not* deal with are those that are clearly divinatory or clearly physical; contextual analysis and empirical methods of interpretation work for dreams of intermediate types but are not applied to dreams dealing either with pure soul or pure body.

The problem of dualism is reflected in the idealization of dreams believed to be the clearest, most desirable, most significant communications from divinities, (i.e., sacred), on the one hand, and the condemnation of dreams believed to be grounded in bodily needs and sensations (i.e., profane), on the other. In Christian belief this problem is exacerbated by a dichotomy between God-sent and demon-sent dreams. Such a dichotomy also exists in Islam but is mitigated there by the far greater variety of demons. Thus dualism may inculcate and individualize religious and cultural values by grounding them in personal belief and experience in dreams.

Initiatory Dreams: Siberian Shamanism. In Siberia and the Arctic, initiation dreams of shamans contain one or more of the following themes: dismemberment followed by replacement of internal organs and viscera; dialogue with supernatural beings or with spirits and souls of dead ancestors; and revelations in the form of dreamed knowledge, techniques, or secrets. Mircea Eliade (1964) writes of one candidate who dreams he is being thoroughly overhauled: his limbs are removed and disjointed with iron hooks, his bones are cleaned, his body fluids discarded and his eyes torn from their sockets. Thus dismantled, he is gathered up and fastened together with iron. The Buriats not only have "sickness-dreams" of the initiatory type but believe that in initiatory dreams shamans are frequently cooked as well as dismembered. Such intense anxiety dreams threatening the integrity of the body ego are reported to be of overwhelming power; there is little question of their voluntary acceptance or rejection. As if this were not enough, in a great many instances the shaman who has such an initiation dream does not decide to become a shaman, even though he knows his dream beckons him in that direction; he refuses, out of fear, and goes on about his own way, until he falls mortally ill. At that point there is what might resemble a pact with the terrifying forces: the individual promises to become a shaman in return for restored health.

Dreamed Myth, History, and Religion: North American Indian Religions. The concept of the body that lies sleeping, its senses inert, while the soul or life principle undergoes metamorphoses in religious experience, helps us understand the various functions of dreams in North American Indian religions. As Hallowell (1976) notes, the Ojibwa believe that to become acceptable social beings, adolescent males must undertake dream fasts in which they acquire powers from supernatural guardian spirits in exchange for promises from the neophytes to do, or not to do, certain things. We rejoin here Kant's concept of categorical and moral imperatives (*Critique of Pure Reason,* 1781). Obedience to moral injunctions that come into conflict with self-interest is universally expressed by dreams. Such moral imperatives are strong forces that have been explained logically (Kant), psychologically (Freud), and sociologically (Durkheim).

The dream fasts of the Ojibwa are sacred, religious experiences: the essential conditions for the experience are that the boy be pure and clean, that he never have engaged in sexual intercourse, and that he observe ritual avoidances prior to the fast. During the fast he is removed from contact with the earth and instructed to climb into a nest in a tree built for him alone; no food or drink must pass his lips. The dream quests are seen as the most important event in the life of the individual; from the quest is derived knowledge, power, strength, and good fortune. "You will have a long and good life if you dream well," said one grandfather to his grandson on the eve of his dream fast (Hallowell, 1976, p. 384). As we have seen in the case of shamanistic experiences, preparation for the dream involves deprivation and pain (in this case hunger) as well as isolation. As in the case of Roman, Greek, and early Christian beliefs, the body is mortified so that the soul, or life principle, can enter into contact with divine beings.

Among the Diegueño of North America, too, painful dreams are interpreted by a "dream doctor," who makes a distinction between significant and insignificant varieties, the latter including "love dreams."

The well-known vision quest of the Plains Indians likewise involves attempts to deal with dualism through immolation of the body; the vision quest relies upon knowledge and power acquired by the soul in the dream-vision. Whereas among the Winnebago and Central Algonquin, adolescent boys set out in search of dream-visions, among the Plains Indians, visions were sought by adult men who, in the west (e.g., among the Cheyenne), inflicted substantially more torture upon themselves. Some lopped off finger joints when seeking religious visions. In speaking of sun worship, Clark Wissler characterizes Plains torture as "feeding-the-sun-with-bits-of-one's-body."

The Mohave and the tribes of the southern Colorado River believe dreams to be the source of cultural knowledge and religion. The significant, power-bestowing dreams were here too distinguished from less significant, body-related (i.e., sexual) dreams. Power-bestowing dreams were by definition related to contact with mythical-historical gods and ancestors. Such dreams were often assessed in terms of myths. Since all knowledge of importance was believed to be social, and all such knowledge was believed to be dreamed, the Mohave theories of dreams are quite explicitly both social and epistemological. Magical powers, knowledge of myths, ritual skills, songs, and therapeutic techniques are all believed by the Mohave to originate in dreams. A. L. Kroeber has called the Mohave a "dream culture." George Devereux (1957) has compared their myths and their dreams, noting that the myths can only have been dreamed in a condensed or allusive form. Because the telling is inseparable from the fascination and pleasures of listening to good stories, narrative skills in reciting dreams and myths were not only important for dream learning, but also for the social acceptance of dreamed knowledge. Furthermore, it was believed that myths always had to be dreamed by shamans to be true. "Every shaman tells a different story of the creation," one Mohave told Devereux. "One may hear it told in several ways. All stories relate to the same event, but the way of telling it is different, as though different witnesses related it, remembering or forgetting different details. It is as though an Indian, a Negro and a Frenchman would tell it, or as though (several people) were describing a car accident we had witnessed" (Devereux, 1957, p. 1036).

Dreams, Pain, and Public Ritual: Australia and the South Pacific. As Roheim (1952) and others have noted, central Australian tribes frequently speak of history as "the Dreaming"; through dreams, the history of clans, places, and spirits can be known and made present, and the telling of dreams overlaps with myth, history, and totemic beliefs and rituals. As in North America, we find here the belief that essential knowledge (culture?) is dreamed.

Baldwin Spencer and F. J. Gillen (*The Northern Tribes of Central Australia,* London, 1899) have reported initiation dreams of folk doctors (shamans) that are astonishingly like those of Siberian shamans. There are three primary types of initiatory experiences. In the first type, the candidate goes to the mouth of a cave and falls asleep, a practice similar to Mediterranean incubation. In dream, a spirit comes to the candidate's soul-body, pierces his neck from behind with a lance, making a large hole in his tongue. A second lance severs his head. Thus beheaded, the candidate, not surprisingly, succumbs. He is carried into the cave, given new innards, and then returned to the world of men, where he spends the next year learning the secrets of his profession from other medicine men. In the second type of initiatory experience, the candidate goes to dream at the mouth of a cave and in dream is abducted to the underworld by the men of the Dreaming. In the third, he must spend a lengthy period in a deserted place where two old medicine men press rock crystals into his head, make a cut in his tongue, and pierce a hole under the fingernail of his right hand.

Without belaboring the point, it seems clear that initiation rites are painful and that candidates do not very willingly submit to the pain inflicted upon them. Furthermore, the mortification of the body and the pain inflicted in rites and dreams is believed to increase the "insight" of the medicine men, giving them more spiritual and cultural power. In these cases, dreamed powers and dreamed knowledge "make" the shaman.

Dreams also "make" patients, and by so doing "make" folk doctors who treat them. Derek Freeman (1967) vividly describes a therapeutic ritual among the Iban (Sea Dayaks of Borneo) based upon beliefs in incubus dreams. Infants who die are believed to be carried off by incubi, or evil spirits who have had sexual relations with the children's mothers in dreams. The shaman pursues and fights with incubi in a public ritual that is rather effective in dealing with the grief of the parents and family, and in asserting the power of the community over death and unseen forces. The example underscores how the experience of a nightmare can be held to cause the death of an infant, and how such beliefs can be represented by a terrifying public ritual in which the sorcerer or medicine man battles with the unseen forces of spirits and with death.

Demons, Possession, and Religion. As Ernest Jones has shown, beliefs in incubi and succubi are universal, as are night terrors and nightmares. In all societies, individuals dream of intercourse with spirits, seductive beings who through metamorphosis make themselves attractive and desired by the dreamer's sensual and earthly self, only to show themselves for what they really are after they have seduced the lascivious and unsuspecting dreamer. Jones adduces copious materials to illustrate the "admixture of erotic and apprehensive emotions" in nightmares (Jones, 1949, p. 77).

Such dreamed seductions frequently give rise to therapeutic measures, as in the case of the Iban mentioned earlier. Not infrequently, in North Africa, the Mediterranean, and other parts of the Islamic world, the dreamer awakens from his or her dreamed seduction "possessed" by the seductive spirit. Cases of hysteria (both individual and collective) together with various forms of *bouffé delirant* (acute, delusional psychosis) frequently focus around sexual anxieties and wishes. In fact, the union of demon and human is sometimes expressed by the idea of a "marriage" between a *jinn* and the possessed individual. Not only does such spirit marriage "explain" sexual impotency with human partners, it also plays a role in a variety of illnesses contracted "in dream." Therapy consists of persuading or obliging the spirit to leave the body of the patient. Hundreds of Moroccans make pilgrimages yearly to sanctuaries, incurring considerable expense to their families. Here they await the dream believed to cure them, like the pilgrims to the Asclepia described earlier. In the majority of cases of "pathological" possession, patients have dreamed of *jinn,* demons of Islam, whose existence is thus forcefully thrust upon them by the dreamed experience; the dreamers' families must also contend with the *jinn* possessing their afflicted relatives. In other parts of Africa, too, possession is associated with dreams.

Of course, not all possession takes place explicitly in dreams, nor is possession in dreams either inevitably associated with illness or uniformly religious. However, it is clear that dreams make *jinn* and other demons real to individuals; dreams as it were give blood to cultural beliefs and values. In dreams, elite and masses alike represent to themselves evil and suffering and their capacities to deal with them. As Melford E. Spiro and others have shown, these representations frequently take the form of demons, gods, and idealized states. Indeed, sexual desires and anxieties have spawned many a demon, and with demons religions are built.

Furthermore, as I. M. Lewis has noted in *Ecstatic Religions* (1971), cults of possession can be direct and major religious forces, establishing links in the minds of believers between individuals, public morality, ancestor cults, and cosmological and divinatory systems. It seems unlikely that possession could take place without dreams. Sharply differentiated from illness, ecstatic states are ones to go into and come out of; like dreams, they are transitory experiences out of which individuals necessarily "awaken."

Conclusion. In dreams, doctors and divinities heal, inform, and counsel; in dreams, demons and spirits acquire flesh and blood, religions come alive, shamans find powers, and kings make temples to the gods. Human nature requires that we represent and communicate ideas and emotions to ourselves and others and consequently, that we project inner feelings into the external world just as we internalize natural and social worlds within. This article has explored ways in which dreams and perceptions of dreams and their classificatory systems all manifest social representations and collectively held beliefs about knowledge. When, for example, we grant connections between time, memory, and dreams, Mohave notions of dreamed knowledge are not simply culturally relative ideas functional for members of Mohave society alone, and fanciful or absurd to those of other societies. Dreams for the Mohave are part of their theory of knowledge, as comprehensive as the Greco-Roman divinatory tradition to which we in the West own much of the framework of our own thought. In the second century, a variety of theories of knowledge were reflected in classifications of, attitudes toward, and theories about dreams. Indeed, in *all* societies we can expect to find relations between dreams and theories of knowledge, between human, subjective, social, natural and supernatural (divine) worlds. In ancient Rome, dreams were believed to give rise to knowledge of fate and the divinities as well as to knowledge of physical health, professional success, and spiritual well-being.

The various theories of dreaming examined here suggest that precisely because dreams break the bondage of natural time and space, they make palpable the dualism between the present, "natural" world of the senses, on the one hand, and the internal world of past experience, future hopes, and live-in gods, on the other. When we leave our bodies deep in slumber, we have access in dream to theaters of the mind where internal families play out conflicts, wishes, and fears, providing us with a variety of possibilities for understanding, play, and creation.

[*See also* States of Consciousness.]

BIBLIOGRAPHY

Behr, Charles A. *Aelius Aristides and the Sacred Tales.* Amsterdam, 1968. Because Aristides is an important source for those interested in religion, healing, and personal experience in the Roman world as these apply to dreams, this book is an extremely valuable resource. A thorough clinical analysis of the case of Aristides has yet to be written.

Benedict, Ruth. "The Vision in Plains Culture." *American Anthropologist* 24 (1922): 1–23. One of the best overviews of the cultural uses of dream-visions in a variety of cultural areas of North America.

Bouché-Leclercq, Auguste. *Histoire de la divination dans l'antiquité* (1879–1882). 4 vols. Reprint, New York, 1975. One of the most comprehensive and thorough treatments of divination in ancient Rome and pertinent to the study of dreams and epistemology.

Devereux, George. *Reality and Dream: The Psychotherapy of a Plains Indian.* New York, 1951. One of the only accounts of the psychotherapy of an American Indian that makes liberal use of the patient's culturally grounded beliefs in dreams and guardian spirits.

Devereux, George. "Dream Learning and Individual Ritual Differences in Mohave Shamanism." *American Anthropologist,* n.s. 59 (December 1957): 1036–1045. One of the best studies of dream learning, this article examines dreams as the source of Mohave myths and songs.

Dodds, E. R. *The Greeks and the Irrational.* Berkeley, 1951. The chapter on dreams, a classic, has yet to be superseded.

Edelstein, Emma J., and Ludwig Edelstein. *Asclepius.* 2 vols. Baltimore, 1945. The standard work on temple inscriptions to Asklepios.

Eliade, Mircea. *Shamanism: Archaic Techniques of Ecstasy.* Rev. & enl. ed. New York, 1964. An interesting account of shamanism and ecstasy containing striking material on dreams.

Fahd, Toufic. *La divination arabe: Étude religieuses, sociologiques et folkloriques sur le milieu natif de l'Islam.* Leiden, 1966. A mine of facts and information with relatively little interpretation, the volume is nonetheless essential.

Firth, Raymond. "The Meaning of Dreams in Tikopia." In *Essays Presented to C. G. Seligman,* edited by E. E. Evans-Pritchard et al., pp. 63–74. London, 1934. One of the most sophisticated treatments of dreams in an ethnographic context.

Freeman, Derek. "Shamman and Incubus." *Psychoanalytic Study of Society* 4 (1967): 315–343. Perhaps the best account available of a public, curative performance by an accomplished folk healer who proceeds on the basis of beliefs in dreams.

Freud, Sigmund. *The Interpretation of Dreams* (1900). 2 vols. New York, 1961. Freud's Herculean work on dreams and the irrational.

Hallowell, A. Irving. *Contributions to Anthropology.* Chicago, 1976. Contains several papers that are classics in the anthropological study of Ojibwa theories of dreams and knowledge.

Hamilton, Mary. *Incubation or the Cure of Diseases in Pagan Temples and Christian Churches.* London, 1906. The standard work on temple sleeping.

Jones, Ernest. *On the Nightmare.* London, 1949. An important resource, in spite of an overly dogmatic psychoanalytic focus, on the nightmare within the European tradition.

Kilborne, Benjamin. "Pattern, Structure, and Style in Anthropological Studies of Dreams." *Ethos* 9 (Summer 1981): 165–185. One of the few overviews of the anthropological literature on dreams.

Lincoln, Jackson S. *The Dream in Primitive Cultures.* London, 1935. The only book devoted to a comparative study of the cultural functions of dreams in various societies, primarily North America.

Oppenheim, A. Leo. "The Interpretation of Dreams in the Ancient Near East." *Transactions of the American Philosophical Society* 46 (1956): 179-373. The standard work on ancient Mesopotamian dream interpretation.

Róheim, Géza. *The Gates of the Dream.* New York, 1952. A valuable, if ungainly and excessive, compendium of fact and theory on dreams among central Australian tribes.

Les songes et leur interpretation. Sources orientales, vol. 2. Paris, 1959. A first-rate collection of articles on the question of dream interpretation in various written traditions.

Tedlock, Barbara, ed. *Dreams in Cross-cultural Perspective.* Santa Fe, 1984. A useful collection of papers by anthropologists and linguists.

Turner, Victor. "Divination." In *A Dictionary of the Social Sciences.* New York, 1964.

Tuzin, Donald. "The Breath of the Ghost: Dreams and the Fear of the Dead." *Ethos* 3 (Winter 1975): 555-578. An ethnographic treatment linking beliefs in ancestors and beliefs in dreams.

Vernant, Jean-Pierre, et al. *Divination et rationalité.* Paris, 1974. A highly interesting and scholarly collection of articles pertaining to divination in the ancient world, one of which includes some of the finest examinations of divination and theories of knowledge available.

Von Grunebaum, G. E., and Roger Caillois, eds. *The Dream and Human Societies.* Berkeley, 1966. An indispensable source for readers interested in dreams, religion, and culture, offering a range of perspectives from a variety of disciplines.

BENJAMIN KILBORNE

DRUGS. *See* Psychedelic Drugs.

DRUIDS. In his brief description of Gaulish society of the first century BCE, Caesar divides his text into three unequal parts dedicated to the druids, the knights, or *equites,* and the plebs (*Gallic Wars* 6.13). His account of the druids is concise and clear:

> In all of Gaul there are two classes of men who count and are honored, for the people are barely more than slaves: they dare do nothing on their own and are consulted on nothing. When most of them become overwhelmed with debt, overburdened by taxes, and are forced to submit to the violence of those more powerful, they put themselves in the service of noblemen who have the same rights over them as masters do over slaves. Of these two classes, one is the druids and the other the knights. The former watch over divine matters, administer public and private sacrifices, and rule all matters of religion. Many young people come to be taught by them and to benefit from their attention. It is they, in fact, who settle disputes, both public and private, and if any crime has been committed, if there has been a murder, or if any dispute arises in regard to an inheritance or boundaries, it is they who decide and assess the damages and fines; if some person or persons do not agree with their decision, that person or those persons are forbidden to participate in the sacrifices. This penalty is the most serious they know. Those who are thus forbidden are considered to be impious and criminal: people stay away from them and shun contact to avoid being stricken with a serious malady. Cases they wish to bring to trial are not admitted, and no honor is accorded them. A single leader commands all these druids, and he exercises supreme authority over them. Upon his death, he is succeeded by the preeminent druid; if there are several of equal status, they decide the title by a vote of the druids and sometimes by force of arms. At a certain time of the year, they assemble in a sacred place in the land of the Carnutes, which is thought to be the center of Gaul. To that place come

all those with disputes, and they submit to the druids' judgments and decisions. Their doctrine was developed in Britain, and from there, it is thought, it came to Gaul; even today, most of those who wish to learn more about this doctrine go there to learn it. The druids do not customarily go to war and pay taxes, as do the rest of the Gauls; they are exempt from military service and free of all types of obligations. Encouraged by such great privileges, many people of themselves seek instruction by the druids, and others are sent by their parents and relatives. It is said that there they learn a very large number of verses by heart: some of them stay at this school for twenty years. They are of the opinion that religion forbids these verses from being committed to writing, which can be done for public and private reports with the use of the Greek alphabet. It seems to me that they have established this custom for two reasons: because they do not want to spread their doctrine among the people, and because they do not want those who learn by trusting to writing to neglect their memories, since it is usually the case that the aid of texts results in less application to learning by heart and less memory. Above all they try to instill the conviction that souls do not perish, but pass after death from one body to another; this strikes them as being a particularly suitable way to inspire courage by suppressing the fear of death. They also have much to say about the stars and their movements, the greatness of the world and of the earth, the nature of things, and the strength and power of the immortal gods, and they convey these speculations to youth.

Organization of the Priestly Class. The functional tripartition of Gaulish society is clearly outlined by Caesar and corresponds to that of medieval Irish society as attested in epics of the high Middle Ages. (See table 1, part A.) Caesar incorrectly confounds artisan class and plebs under a single definition, but he gives the specific Gaulish name for servants *(ambacti)* in another context.

Caesar's definition appears different from that of later Greek writers Diodorus Siculus and Strabo, who list druids (philosophers), bards (poets), and *vates* (soothsayers and sacrificers). But in fact there is no contradiction or difference. Caesar defines the priestly class as a whole in relation to the rest of society, while the Greeks describe its internal structure.

TABLE 1. *Correspondences between Gaulish and Irish Social Distinctions*

FUNCTION	GAUL	IRELAND
A. *Function within the larger society*		
priest	*druids*	*druid*
warrior	*equites*	*flatha* ("nobility")
craftsman and cultivator	*plebs*	*aes dana* ("people of art")
B. *Function within the priestly class*		
"philosopher"	*druids*	*druid*
"poet"	*bards*	*bard* or *filidh*
diviner and sacrificer	*vates*	*faith*

The structural affinity of Gaulish and Irish society extends even to the names of the priestly functions. (See table 1, part B.) A single deviation in these Gaulish-Irish equivalences is the inferior position of the Irish bard, a specialist in songs of praise and reproach whose original functions were usurped by the substitution of the *filidh*, etymologically a "seer," who also possessed magic, writing *(ogham)*, and satire. Both reproach and satire were sung, and there came to be a confusion between the former and satire, a magical poetry with irreparable and mortal effects.

The *filidh* originally was involved with divination and prophecy, but medieval texts suggest a wide range of specializations, including historian, judge, storyteller, satirist, leech, harpist, and cupbearer. [*See* Filidh.] The soothsayer or *faith* was a technician of prediction. The *faith* was the one priestly function open to women, and this accounts for the existence of Irish terms for druidesses (Ir., *bandrui, banfile, banfaith*), which occur due to the assimilation of the title *faith* to *druid*, where the latter is used inclusively to designate the priestly functions. In Gaul, several inscriptions from the Roman era and a reference in Hirtius, a historian of the first century BCE, furnish us with the name of the *gutuater*. On the basis of etymology (Ir., *guth*, "voice"), the *gutuater* must have been a druid who made invocations. But whatever their place in the internal hierarchy and whatever their specialization, all members of the priestly class were druids, set off from the rest of society.

As the holder of spiritual authority, the druid took precedence over temporal power, represented by the king, with whom he formed a couple; the druid was the intermediary between the gods and the king, and the king played the same role between the druid and society. Thus, it was the king who rendered justice, but the druid who made law. The druid was not bound by any obligation, either fiscal or military, but he had the right to bear arms and to make war whenever he wished. The warrior druid is a common personage in Irish epic. Again it was the druid who pronounced the *geasa* ("injunctions, interdicts") that bound all individuals—especially the king—to a closed network of interdicts and obligations of all kinds. One of the most famous interdicts of Ulster was that the Ulates were not to speak before the king and that the king was not to speak before the druid. But the druid—who never courted royalty, save for aberrant and extremely rare cases—was in the service of the king, to whom he owed counsel, information, or prediction that would allow the king to rule his kingdom well.

The alliance between the king and the druid explains why the druid disappeared in Gaul after the Roman conquest: the Gauls' adoption of the Roman political system based on the *municipium* removed the druid's entire *raison d'être,* and it is likely that druidism, despite its initial vitality, declined slowly and became almost clandestine. The edicts of Tiberius and Claudius, which subjected the druids to the same censure as the *mathematici,* were not the only cause nor the preponderant reason for their disappearance. As to human sacrifice, which so often aroused the disparagement of the ancient authors, nothing proves that it was as frequent and widespread as was believed. In any case, sacrifice plays a part in the rituals of all religions.

It is also known that the druids were the Celtic representatives of an Indo-European priesthood. Their name is explained by the Celtic **dru-wid-es* ("the very wise ones") and not by the Greek *drus,* an etymology attributed to Pliny the Elder. The Greeks, Romans, and Germans had colleges of priests, but the Celts were the only ones besides the Indians to possess a hierarchized and structured priestly class. The druids were not pre-Celtic priests any more than they were mere philosophers; even less were they shamans or sorcerers.

BIBLIOGRAPHY

Guyonvarc'h, Christian-J., and Françoise Le Roux. *Textes mythologiques irlandais,* vol. 1. Rennes, 1980.

Le Roux, Françoise, and Christian-J. Guyonvarc'h. *La civilisation celtique.* 4th ed. Rennes, 1983.

Le Roux, Françoise, and Christian-J. Guyonvarc'h. *Les druides.* 3d ed. Rennes, 1982.

FRANCOISE LE ROUX AND CHRISTIAN-J. GUYONVARC'H
Translated from French by Erica Meltzer

DRUMS are instruments that produce sound through the striking, rubbing, or plucking of stretched membranes. The religious use of drums is historically and geographically extensive, but by no means universal. They are conspicuously lacking in many Christian and Islamic liturgical traditions, as well as in various African religions. Their absence from the oldest forms of religious music of such well-known hunter-gatherers as the African Pygmies and San (Bushmen), the Australian Aborigines, the Väddas of Sri Lanka, and others suggests that drums are not particularly archaic or "primitive" but rather are associated with the later cultural systems of sedentary agriculture and urban civilization. They are important in both local traditions and in the "great" intercultural, literate religious traditions.

Drums have relatively low value in Middle Eastern and European religious traditions, somewhat more in East Asia, Oceania, and Native America, and high value and variety of uses in South Asian, African, and Inner Asian and circumpolar shamanistic traditions. Where drums are used, they may have considerable symbolic or ritual value: E. Manker (in Diószegi, 1968, p. 32) describes how, when Christian missionaries burned the drums of Saami (Lapp) shamans, the Saami protested that the drums were their compasses; how could they find their way in the world without them?

Description. Drums belong to the organological class membranophones, instruments that produce sound by means of a stretched flexible membrane (skin, plastic, etc.). Instruments shaped or played like drums, but lacking membranes—the "slit-drums" or "log drums" of many tropical areas, the "bronze drums" of Southeast Asia, the "steel drums" of Trinidad, and so forth, are idiophones or solid instruments. Other mislabels, such as "tambourine" (correct only for frame drums with jingles) or "tom-tom" (corruption of a Sinhala/Tamil name for paired kettledrums), often have been indiscriminately applied by Westerners to non-Western drums in much the same way as labels like "witchcraft" and "voodoo" have been widely and derogatorily applied to non-Western religions.

Drums are described by number of membrane heads (one to five), by material composition (wood, earth/clay, metal, bone, etc.), by shape of body (shallow frame, round-bottomed kettle, straight-sided cylindrical, bulging barrel, narrow-waisted hourglass, etc.), and by playing technique (hands, sticks, suspended clappers), decorations, and other physical features. Although such features are the basis of scientifically accurate descriptions, religious traditions themselves often categorize and evaluate drums in terms of less tangible but religiously more significant factors.

Symbolism. Drums may carry a wide range of symbolic values, both positive and negative. The negative symbolism best known in the West, that of sensuality and licentiousness, is based on culture-specific associations of drums, rhythmic dance, and sexual abandon. Because this particular symbolism is not universal (for example, dance and sexuality may be seen as normal, as religiously beneficial, or as unrelated to drums), the negative symbolism of sensuality may be rarer than other negative associations. Another important one is the association of drums with pollution. In South Asia, for example, drums have sometimes been considered religiously polluting because the hands of those who touch or play them must come in contact with the skins of slaughtered animals, or because of associations with powerful, dangerous beings and forces; hence, both making and playing drums have been restricted to low castes. The negative association of drums with noise and chaos may be less widespread than is sometimes assumed: for example, drums were included only in a few scattered, atypical cases in the European Christian "Instruments of Darkness" complex described by Claude Lévi-Strauss in *From Honey to Ashes* (New York, 1973). Christian and Buddhist images of hells with sinners imprisoned in drums gain at least some of their negative impact from the demons shown beating them.

In their positive roles, drums may be associated with almost any aspect of religious experience, and may even themselves be considered deities. One common symbolic complex links them with elements of nature, biology, and cosmology. A drum may embody an *axis mundi* of the cosmic tree or mountain in its wooden or earthen body, the life force of a helping spirit in the form of the animal that supplied its skin, the voice of thunder or of an animal/spirit in its sound, and elements of hunting or pastoral lifestyles in its manufacture, treatment, and use. Another widespread symbolic complex derives from social relationships: drums may form "family" relationships with one another or with humans; sets of them may constitute hierarchies that parallel or are included within human and divine hierarchies; and they may play functional roles within society and the pantheon, ranging from invoking the deities to functions as practical as telecommunication. The "royal drums" of Africa and ancient South India were part of the property, symbols, and tools of divine kingship, considered so powerful and important in some cases that it might be more appropriate to speak of the king as a symbol of the royal drums than the reverse. The model of royal and divine proclamation is often central to the religious symbolism of drums, whether or not they are actually sounded for communication or musical purposes. Where the symbolic connection of drums, dance, and sensuality exists, it may become a positive symbol of divine enjoyment and celestial pleasures, with court and village dances serving as models for, or sacramental participations in, their heavenly counterparts.

It should be emphasized that the symbolism of drums does not support any unitary hypothesis of universal sexual symbolism. Drums may be seen as feminine because of their hollow bodies and soft skins; as masculine because of their intrusive sounds and the rigid sticks or hand tensions required to play them; or as neuter, androgynous, or symbolic of sexual union because of any of these or other reasons. The paired high/low-pitch kettledrums of Asia are often considered male/female; but if low is "male" in one culture, it is just as likely to be "female" in a neighboring culture. The multioctave drum sets of West African and Afro-American possession religions are often viewed as "families," with the largest and lowest drum acting as "mother," and with primary contrasts drawn across generational rather than gender lines. As with most instruments, drums are more widely played by men than by women; but for almost every case of a male-oriented drum tradition or practice, a corresponding female-oriented example can be found somewhere, occasionally even in the same culture or religious tradition.

Religious Use. Drums may be excluded from religious uses, used peripherally to demarcate the temporal, spatial, or structural boundaries of religious occasions, or integrated in positive, essential ways into religious thought and performances. If they are used religiously, their role is usually musical; but sometimes they function instead as signaling or communication devices, as silent cult objects or offerings, or in other capacities. Drums may or may not have special religious status compared with other musical instruments. For example, many Islamic traditions exclude all instruments equally from religious observances. Some Christian traditions have admitted other instruments while excluding drums. Many African and South Asian traditions assign special roles and status to a wide variety of drums. In most of Central and North Asia, drums were the prime focus of ritual, while other instruments were used for secular music. Generally, the great intercultural religious traditions of Near Eastern origin have shown more hostility or indifference to drums than have many others; but this ultimately may be due as much to the lack of early wide distribution and musical importance of drums in the area as to religious factors.

The vast range of religious valuations and uses of drums can be suggested by a few specific examples.

African and Afro-American traditions. Although images of a "dark continent" filled with compulsively throbbing, obsessively omnipresent drums, witch doctors, and similar colonialist missionary-in-the-cannibal-pot stereotypes have partially faded away in the post-independence period (1950s onward), the ideal pan-African perspective of many writings continues to mask a range of cultural, religious, and musical diversity as great as is found in Europe or in Asia. The use of drums in African religions is a typical example of this diversity, with cases ranging from drums playing central, essential religious roles to their total absence from a religious tradition.

Colin Turnbull, in *The Forest People* (New York, 1961) and *Wayward Servants* (New York, 1965), found the drums used occasionally by the Mbuti Pgymies to be a late import from contacts with sedentary non-Pygmy villagers. Drums were not suitable by reason of their heavy wooden construction to the traditional Mbuti nomadic-forager lifestyle and their associated religious observances—a point equally worth noting in regard to other hunter-gatherers who lead a nomadic life without the assistance of draft animals. Even the pastoralist Fulbe, distributed through nearly the entire sub-Saharan borderland, adopted drums only in ceremonial contexts arising from culture contact with neighboring sedentary agricultural peoples such as the Hausa. Agriculturalists, in turn, need not accord drums a significant place in religion: Maraire (n.d.) reports that the Shona of Zimbabwe assign a very high religious value and function to the plucked idiophone *mbira* used in Bira possession rituals, while considering drums and their music appropriate to less sacred contexts oriented around socializing and entertainment. In the last analysis, neither race, place of residence, nor ecological adaptation is an accurate predictor of the importance or unimportance of drums in African music and religion.

Against this background of diversity, of contrasting occurrences interspersed with significant blank spaces where no uses are found, the pattern of use of drums in African religions stands out clearly as one of remarkable religious and artistic richness. In some cases, drums and ritual are so closely associated with each other that the same term can be used to refer to both (Turner, 1968, p. 15). If drums are not universally present, they nevertheless occur throughout the continent in nearly every possible physical shape (beside those mentioned above, goblet-shaped, conical, cylindroconical, and footed varieties are widespread), musical function, and religious value, and application. Drums may be found in every position and role from that of peripheral accessories that signal the start of ceremonies to that of spirit beings in their own right, called to life through invocations and rituals, tended by priests and acolytes, and housed, unseen by profane eyes, in sacred dwellings. They are so widespread and important that even religious traditions of Near Eastern origin—those of the Falasha Jews and Coptic Christians of Ethiopia, as well as of the Islamic Ṣūfīs—overcome the reservations widespread among non-African branches of their respective religious traditions to the extent of allowing some liturgical drumming by cult members, leaders, or priests. Frequently, however, the drumming is less extensive and elaborate than that used by neighboring religious traditions of local African origin. The paired kettledrum apparently spread with Islamic conquests and conversions. Its most widespread ritual use, however, is in ceremonies of state, rather than in Islamic worship.

Although only extensive reading in the ethnographic, religious, and ethnomusicological literature would give an adequate sense of the religious uses of African drums, a few topics of broad interest are worth mention.

Talking drums. The widely mentioned "talking drums" that transmit verbal messages by playing tonal and rhythmic abridgments of stylized phrases are frequently slit-drums (i.e., wooden percussion tubes) or xylophones, rather than true drums with membranes; but drums may also be used for communication, as in the cases of the *atumpan* two-drum set of Ghana or the variable-tension hourglass drums widespread in West Africa. Most reported cases of religious use have involved announcements and communications among cult members (e.g., to invite guests to an initiation ceremony), a peripheral application sometimes combined or alternated with the widespread practice of using drums to accompany religious dance. However, there have also been reports (e.g., among the Ewe and Yoruba) of "talking drums" used for direct communication with gods or spirits, transmitting messages in the form of invocations or prayers—a function of greater apparent religious centrality and importance than announcing and signaling.

Royal drums. One especially characteristic function, best documented in East Africa but occurring in other regions as well, is the use of drums as royal emblems or regalia, a religious function insofar as it usually relates to concepts and cults of sacral kingship. Drums may be personalized spirits or ancestors, or conduits of power; in either case, they are the sacralizing and legitimizing emblems of royal rule, and as such receive honor, offerings, and ritual care that may be greater than that accorded the king himself. Royal drums are the prime example of drums that may be religious artifacts without necessarily being musical instruments as well: some royal drums are never played, and a few may exist entirely on a divine plane, invisible to all but the gods themselves (Lois A. M. Anderson, n.d.). Other royal drums may have a full range of musical uses while still enjoying a higher ritual status than their profane counterparts; such was the case with the *entenga* tuned-drum ensemble of the Buganda court. Often, as with the Buganda and Rwanda royal drums, several sets existed, each with its own kind and degree of religious, political, and musical function. Playing and/or priestly service of the royal drums might be restricted to male members of either hereditary noble or service classes. As was also the case with royal drums in ancient South India, some African royal drums were the recipients of ritual blood sacrifices.

Possession. Drums may not be used at all in possession cults (cf. the Shona Bira, mentioned above). But their importance in West African areas exploited by the slave trade led to their use in Afro-American possession religions such as Haitian Voodoo, Brazilian Candomblé, the Lucumi of Cuba, the Shango religion of Trinidad, and others. In keeping with their West African sources, these religions use drums in cross-generational "families" of three or more to accompany spirit-possession rituals and dances. There has been some controversy as to whether the sounds of the drums actually "cause" or induce possession, that is, whether their effects are best understood in physiological or cultural and religious terms.

Rhythm and time. The musical variety of African religious drumming extends from the austere patterns of widely spaced single beats used by the Falasha Jews, to elaborate polyrhythms (one rhythm played simultaneously with one or more contrasting rhythms) of the complex and compelling sort that most listeners associate with African styles. The question of possible conceptual relationships between musical rhythm and cosmological/calendrical time has been raised by Alan P. Merriam in his article "African Musical Rhythm and Concepts of Time-Reckoning" (in Thomas Noblitt, ed., *Music East and West,* New York, 1981, pp. 123–141) and by others. The unresolved issue is whether the perception by foreign observers of "time" and cyclicity in African music (or their being labeled as such in European languages) corresponds significantly to African conceptions, given the apparent lack in African languages of a "time" domain that extends to musical categories. J. H. Kwabena Nketia (n.d.) has suggested that music itself might constitute an extralinguistic, complementary system of conceptualization. We might hypothesize that musical rhythm is one fundamental human mode of perceiving and conceptualizing time, whether lexically labeled as such. If so, the apparent "polyrhythm" of simultaneous contrasting-length market weeks in West Africa may share an underlying conceptual unity with musical polyrhythms. On the other hand, we might equally hypothesize that musical polyrhythms result at least in part from the proliferation of conceptually multigenerational drum "families" that replicate socioreligious concepts of ancestor-descendant relationships. While research trends during most of the twentieth century have moved gradually away from consideration of such broad issues, favoring a view of music as an autonomous "art" intelligible only in terms of acoustic-structural principles peculiar to itself, new approaches in the century's final decades suggest a growing interest in the conceptual bases of the close links between music and religion that are so evident in African behavior and performance.

Buddhism. Buddhist traditions share a common symbolic valuation of drums but differ widely in patterns of use. The act of proclaiming the Buddhist teaching is traditionally known as "sounding the drum of the Dharma," either because of a proclamation by Śākyamuni Buddha (c. 560–480 BCE) after his enlightenment that he would sound the "drum of immortality" *(amatadundubhiḥ),* or because of an edict of the Indian emperor Aśoka (d. 232 BCE) that "the sound of the war drum [*bherighoṣa*] has now become the sound of *dharma* [*dharmaghoṣa*]." Both *dundubhiḥ* and *bherī* were royal/military drums. Perhaps because of the Buddha's *kṣatriya* (warrior/princely) caste origin, Buddhist drum symbolism relies heavily on the concepts of royal authority and invincibility. Drum sounds reach everywhere, filling earth and sky; they are clear and unmistakable; and they cannot be ignored or overwhelmed by lesser sounds. These are all characteristics both of the royal drums themselves and of the teaching proclaimed by the Buddha.

The use of drums in Buddhist ritual, derived from the stupa (reliquary mound) cult sanctioned in the *Mahāparinibbana Sutta,* is said to date back to the death of the Buddha (c. 480 BCE). They are pictured on the railings of the stupa in relief sculptures of the first century BCE–first century CE period. In Indian Buddhism up to the early second millennium CE, drums served the function of elaborating and ornamenting the *tāla* rhythmic cycle outlined by the cymbals, according to standard Indian musical practice of the time. Written drum notations were introduced before the mid-eighth century CE.

Sri Lanka. Modern practice varies with traditions and cultures. Generally, Theravāda Buddhism restricts the use of instruments to laymen, while Mahāyāna and Vajrayāna traditions allow monks to play them as well. In present-day Sri Lanka, Theravāda Buddhism exists in conjunction with a variety of indigenous *yakkha* (local spirit) cults whose priests are hereditary low-caste drummer-dancers using their ritual and artistic skills to control a variety of powerful forces. Just as their gods are admitted to the Buddhist pantheon in a subordinate role, so also their instruments and performances find a subordinate, boundary-marking role in some Buddhist ceremonies.

Two kinds of drums, the *dawula* (cylindrical drum) and the *tammätamma* (paired kettledrums), play a more central role in the orthodox Buddhist cult of stupas and other types of *cetiya* (relics), in the *pañcavādya,* or fivefold instrumental music that can be traced back to the first centuries of Indian Buddhism. The drums play auspicious music based on beat patterns conventionally associated with the Buddha, with acts of offering or circumambulation, and so on. The players are of the same caste and are often the very same persons as those who serve as priests of the *yakkha* religions. The primary drum of the *yakkha* cult, the *gäta bere* barrel drum, also finds an important place in Buddhist rituals as the *mangulbere,* or "auspicious drum." In the chief Buddhist temple of Kandy, even high-caste specialists play the hourglass *udäkki* drum to accompany secret songs of praise in the inner shrine.

Nepal. In the Vajrayāna Buddhism of the Newars of Nepal, drums find both more diverse and more central ritual roles. Parallels with Theravāda include the use of paired kettledrums in the fivefold offering music and the adoption of drums from local cults, such as the barrel drums adorned with ram's horns *(yakkakhiṃ)* embodying the indigenous god of dance (Nasadyaḥ) which accompany some dances with Buddhist contents. Specific drums are allocated to specific castes, from the small barrel drum *(naykhiṃ)* of the butchers to the deified barrel drums *(damaḥkhiṃ),* decorated with masks of the deities they embody and played by the highest castes of Buddhist Tantric priests. In processions farmers play the *dhimay,* which is made from an irregularly shaped cross section of tree trunk. They and the oilpresser caste play the *mākhiṃ* barrel drum to accompany songs of praise at Buddhist temples. Vajrācārya priests accompany some of their Tantric *cārya* songs and dances with the *kwotaḥ,* a three-headed drum set made by joining a large horizontal and small vertical barrel drum together. The drum becomes the embodiment of both the god of dance and the Buddha Vajrasattva during performance, and it plays musically structured, notated compositions of *mantra* syllables evoking the presence of Buddhas and gods. Drumming, singing, and dancing, along with meditation, become the technical means for generating the *maṇḍala* of Buddhas in the performers' own bodies, voices, and minds.

Central and East Asia. Outside the South Asian homeland of Buddhism, drums lose their caste associations and some of their practical musical importance, while retaining their symbolic value. In Tibetan Vajrayāna, the double-headed frame drum *(rnga)* is used in both vocal and instrumental performances, but in a role supporting the cymbals, which provide a primary musical structure based on elaborate mathematical sequences. The hourglass drum made from two human skulls (Skt., *kāpāla-ḍamaru*), adopted from the Indian *Kāpālika* yogic tradition, is also largely subordinate, often being replaced by a similar wooden drum. Nevertheless, such drums may symbolically embody the entire range of Buddhist concepts and teachings and enjoy greater practical importance in specialized ritual/meditational traditions. In East Asian Mahāyāna Buddhism, drums are often used, together with an assortment of metal and wooden idiophones, to mark off the subdivisions of musical structures. Japanese Buddhist practices range from the elaborate drumming in Zen temples to the greatly lessened use of drums in traditions such as Buzan-ha Shingi Shingon, in which idiophones such as the wooden fish-shaped *mokugyō* play beat patterns accompanying chants. Some traditions give drums a practical role to match their symbolic value, as with the Nichiren school Nihonzan Myōhonji pacifist monks who walk about chanting and beating a small single-headed frame drum, literally "sounding the drum of the Dharma" to call attention to their Buddhist teachings and way of life.

Shamanism. In the "classical" shamanism of Inner and North Asia, drums play central roles in religious belief and practice. The drum is the shaman's primary religious tool for attracting helper gods or spirits, for taming or inciting them to action, and for carrying the shaman away on spiritual flights to heavenly realms or to the underworld. The drum itself is part of the shaman's pantheon, a living spirit helper or a theriomorphic steed such as a horse or a deer. It may serve as object as well as agent of religious acts, being treated to life-cycle rituals, like those performed for humans, from its "birth" to its "death," as well as to cyclic or occasional ceremonies encouraging or exhorting it to perform its helping function. It may also serve the shaman as a tool for specialized ritual purposes, as in drum-divination ceremonies in which the upturned skin of the drum is sprinkled with small grains that move about through sympathetic vibration when a second drum is played nearby (or, if the drum has two playing heads, when the second head is beaten) to form divinatory patterns on the drumhead. The type of drum used may indicate the shaman's status in a graded hierarchy of initiatory rankings. In contrast to many religious drum traditions, shamanic drumming is frequently performed by women, as female shamans are fairly widespread.

The shaman's drum is usually a shallow frame drum with a wooden circular or ellipsoidal body and one skin head, played with a stick. Small jingling pieces of metal or bells may be mounted either on or inside the drum, or worn separately on the shaman's costume. Making the drum recapitulates a primordial cosmological quest, as in this song of the Tibetan Bon tradition:

> If I seek a drum, where do I seek?
> I seek in the four directions, and the eight between;
> On the Chief of Mountains, in the center of the world,

There, there is a tree growing;
A mighty sandalwood tree has grown.
Now, having cut a branch from it,
Bending, bending, forced in a coiled circle,
Knowing the method, hewn by an ax's blade,
With the hide of a black antelope covered over,
That amazing drum, that swastika-circle drum,
Sewn together with effort, by the pressure of a tendon,
Has a miraculous, melodious, sweet sound, full of meaning:
Beaten, it is beaten in the highest heaven;
Sounds, it sounds at the peak of the world-mountain;
The realm of demons trembles: *Shig shig!*
When I beat on that great drum, then
Even all the ocean, churned, clouds up with mud;
The massive Chief of Mountains, shaken, is thrown down;
The water-serpent children are uneasy in their minds;
E ma! How great this most superior of wonders!

The feeling of joyful mastery expressed here is the result of spirits, called and subjugated by the drum, entering the player's body and merging into a single identity under his control. Siberian ethnographic accounts are seldom detailed enough to show exactly what role the drumming plays in this course of events, but the process is quite clear for the related Himalayan shamanic traditions. The shaman begins by drumming at moderate speed in a dotted-rhythm beat pattern, singing an invocation of the "first shaman"; he then changes to a slightly slower, steady rhythm, as he sings an invitation song to the spirits who will come to help in the ritual. As he senses the approach of the spirits, his body begins to shake, sounding the metal bells on his costume or in the drum, and the beating grows louder. The drumming becomes irregular, suddenly breaking off into short periods when the drum is silent, and only the sound of the shaking bells carries on the emotional momentum of the performance. The singing is interspersed with special vocal effects: singing into the face of the drum, grunting, whistling, sneezing, and altered tones of voice. These events are signs of the entry of a spirit into the drummer's body, and of the struggle for control between him and the spirit. As the shaman asserts mastery over the spirit, the drum reenters with a strong, steady beat, the shaman begins a song of praise to the helping spirits, and the way is open for subsequent ritual stages of dancing, travel to spirit worlds, diagnosis, divination, curing, or whatever is required by the ritual.

The combination of heightened emotion and use of the drum to summon and control spirits, evident both in shamanic songs, as quoted above, and in the actual events of the ritual, is characteristic of the full geographic range of Asian shamanism. Use of the drum as a "steed" for a flight to the spirit world is a more limited phenomenon. Mircea Eliade (1964) argues that ecstatic flight is the historical and religious core of the shamanic complex, and that those traditions that lack it represent a degenerate stage; I suggest in "Musical Flight in Tibet" (in the journal *Asian Music* 5, 1974, pp. 3–44) that the practice of drumming to attract the tame theriomorphic spirits is a religious transformation of widespread use of music by Asian hunters and pastoralists to lure and control animals, and that the ideology of spiritual flight is a later and more localized superimposition on a conceptual basis of the shaman as a spiritual hunter-pastoralist. In some religious traditions outside the "classical" Asian/circumpolar area, broad similarities in ideology and practice seem to justify comparative extension of the term *shaman* (originally from the language of the Tunguz of Siberia); some of these traditions (e.g., the Mapuche of Chile) use drums in ways similar to Asian shamans, while many "shamanic" traditions of Latin America use hallucinogenic drugs and/or rattles whose symbolic and functional status so closely parallel that of the shaman drum as to suggest that they are local substitutes for it.

Other traditions. Drums have seen religious use on every inhabited continent, although in Aboriginal Australia they were characteristic only of coastal zones of contact with Melanesian cultures. They have been used throughout most of human history and found a place in the religions of ancient civilizations of both the Old and New Worlds.

Near East and Mediterranean. Drums appeared rather late in Mesopotamia. Clapper idiophones were shown in the artwork of the Mesilim and Ur I periods (c. twenty-eighth–twenty-fourth centuries BCE). Drums alone begin to appear in depictions of ritual dances in the neo-Sumerian period (twenty-second–nineteenth centuries BCE). Frame drums *(adapa?, balag?)* existed in sizes ranging from extremely large varieties played by two men down to small handheld types carried by dancers; the latter apparently spread to Egypt (sixteenth–eleventh centuries), Israel (*tof*, mentioned in *Exodus*, *Psalms*, etc.), Greece (*tumpanon*, sixth–fifth centuries?), Rome (*tympanum*, c. 200 BCE), and eventually throughout the Near East, where it is still widespread under the Arabic name *daff*.

In Sumeria, drums were ideographically linked with the god Enki and by ritual and symbolic attention to their skins with the bull, symbol of sacred strength. The small frame drum became associated (c. 2000 BCE) with women players and with revelry and has generally retained these associations throughout its geographical and historical range. Even today it is widely played by women at weddings. In Israel the small-frame drum was excluded from Temple ritual. Other drums may have been employed until the ban on instrumental music following the destruction of the Temple in 70 CE. The small-frame drum was associated in Egypt with the goddess Isis and in Greece with the imported Cybele and native Dionysos cults. Eventually it spread to Rome along with these three "orgiastic" religions.

Cultic associations with dance and sexual license helped to shape Judeo-Christian attitudes to drums up to the present day, but they may not be entirely responsible for the subsequent exclusion of drums from the Jewish, Christian, and Islamic liturgies. In fact, such associations applied only to one type of drum (the small-frame drum); but this was, perhaps significantly, in an area where few types were available as more "respectable" liturgical alternatives. Cylindrical drums, goblet-shaped or footed drums, and a few other types were known in Sumeria and Egypt. In Israel, Greece, and Rome frame drums may have been the only drums available. There is no evidence of musically important or elaborate rhythmic traditions that might have stimulated the importation or invention of other types. Even the drum perhaps most characteristic of the Near East, the paired kettledrum, did not appear until the beginning of the second millennium CE.

At any rate, we see the disappearance of drums and other instruments from the Jewish liturgy in the first century CE, after the destruction of the Temple and the rise of the less ritualistic synagogue tradition. Christianity, perhaps simply following the lead of its parent tradition and culture, seemed to mirror the synagogue in its apparently exclusively vocal musical practices. Islam, in its turn, excluded drums, instruments, and "music" from its worship, which nevertheless came to include melodically chanted "readings" from the Qur'ān and religious poetry; these in turn eventually came to embrace possible rhythmic accompaniment with drums, even the once-suspect frame drum. By the early second millennium CE the Ṣūfī movement began to develop, leading to ritual traditions that use drums along with other instruments to accompany inspirational dancing. Drums would likewise gradually reenter Christian religious music through the influence of European folk, military, and art music traditions.

India and China. Textual evidence indicates the presence of drums in India and China by at least the late second millennium BCE; they are probably considerably older in both regions. There is some evidence for the use of drums in the Indus Valley civilization of the third millennium BCE. The earliest Indian sacred texts, the Vedas, seem to regard drums as primarily military instruments used by the Central Asian Aryan tribes who migrated into India some time after the middle of the third millennium. Later Tamil (South Indian) literature, which may reflect a much earlier culture, describes a cult of sacred royal drums reminiscent of African traditions, including sacrifice and ritual care by priests who were avoided because of their association with powerful, dangerous beings. Such cults may have provided the initial impetus that led to the eventual high religious value of drums in Hinduism. Another stimulus was provided by the decline of Vedic sacrificial ritual and its supplanting by the performance of *pūjā* offerings, a development particularly stressed in Buddhist traditions, where we find the first evidence of musical *pūjā*. Hindu traditions parallel their Buddhist counterparts in variety and richness, incorporating drum music at every level; and one of the three supreme post-Vedic gods, Śiva, is identified with the hourglass-shaped *ḍamaru* drum, which he plays to accompany his own cosmic dance. The elaborate rhythms of Indian drumming were, at least until the growth of Islamic dominance in the second millennium CE, part of a tradition that was inseparably both aesthetic performance and religious offering, whether Hindu, Buddhist, or Jain, and hence a reflection of the same ideals of complexly multifaceted individuality that appear in Indian pantheons and ritual practices.

In China, by contrast, drums and their music were a balanced component in both a carefully orchestrated musical structure and the elemental cosmic structure it embodies. Drums were part of an ideal system of *pa yin* or "eight sounds" represented by the names of eight characteristic materials from which instruments are constructed: metal, stone, silk, bamboo, wood, skin, gourd, and earth. Each of the instrument groups corresponding to these materials in turn corresponds to a cardinal point of the compass, a season of the year, a natural element or phenomenon, and other cosmological features. Drums are classified under their most characteristic constituent material, skin, and they correspond to the north, to winter, and to water. In Confucian ceremonial music, they play a musical part that is slow and simple in terms of technique and rhythmic density but that, together with the other instruments of the ensemble, forms part of a restrained, carefully regulated, and balanced whole. Barrel drums, some very large, are the most characteristic type used.

Americas and Oceania. New World civilizations, like their Old World counterparts, made use of drums. Ritual applications included sacrifices that sometimes involved human victims and, among the Incas at least, used their skins as drumheads. However, reports of at least one "drum" used in sacrificial rituals are the result of misidentification: the Aztec *teponaztli* was a slit-drum, or wooden percussion tube, rather than a membranophone.

The drum most widely used in American music and

ritual is the frame drum, the form, ideology, and use of which in many regions show general parallels to that of the Asian shaman's drum. In addition to their shamanic use, frame drums were utilized in a wide variety of local religious contexts; among the best-known examples are the Plains Sun Dance and War Dance, as well as the late nineteenth-century Ghost Dance and other postcontact syncretistic and revitalization movements. Frame drums are played with sticks held in one hand only, a practice that links them with other unacculturated Native American drum traditions and distinguishes them from Euro-American and Afro-American traditions and styles.

Two relatively recent traditions show some unusual features. Thomas Vennum, in his *The Ojibwa Dance Drum* (Washington, D.C., 1982) and subsequent work, has examined the history of the "dream drum" revealed in a vision by the Great Spirit to Tailfeather Woman of the Sioux in the nineteenth century and passed on to the Ojibwa (Chippewa) and other Northeast Woodlands peoples through manufacturing and song-learning rituals ultimately intended as a way of creating intertribal peace. While the "dream drum" is a larger and more elaborate version of the widespread frame drum, other physical types of drums may also attain religious importance. The best-known example is the water drum used to accompany songs in the sacramental peyote rituals of the Native American Church. The drum consists of a solid-bottomed body that forms a vessel into which water is poured and with the single playing head covering it at the top. Using more or less water creates a higher or lower sound; the dampness also changes the tension of the drumhead (which can be tuned by making it wetter or dryer), and the sound has a characteristic wavering reverberation caused by the movement of the water inside.

In Oceania, the area richest in variety of musical instruments was Melanesia, where log slit-drums (percussion idiophones) generally enjoyed more religious and musical prominence than true drums with membranes. Oceanian drums tend to have only one playing head, often made from fish or shark skin and to be set or held in vertical position and played with the hands. Hourglass shapes are common in Melanesia, and cylindrical types are widespread in Polynesia.

Drums were accorded sacred status in Polynesia, kept and tended by priests in temples, and considered receptacles of *mana* (sacred power). Some were associated with sacrifice, including, in Tahiti, human sacrifice. Many were "royal drums," used to honor chiefs as well as gods; one Hawaiian king traveled with such a drum in his canoe. Important drums of chiefs or gods were often large, with smaller versions used in lesser contexts; ensembles of varying sizes were found in some areas. The Hawaiian ceremonial Mele Hula dances utilize two drums: the larger *pahu hula* of wood, played with the hands, and the smaller *pūniu* made from a coconut shell, played with a braided fiber "stick." Although other instruments are also used, the drums are reserved for the most important dances.

Drums and Possession. Afro-American religions, shamanism, and many other religious traditions employ drums in conjunction with, and apparently to induce, a kind of experience known in the research literature as "possession" or "altered states of consciousness." Behind such standard labels lie essential differences in both the experience itself and the process of achieving it: Haitian priestesses and Tibetan oracles, for example, are controlled by the beings who enter their bodies, while the Tamang shaman asserts control over the spirits who enter his. Both of the former rely on others to play drums for them during the ritual, but the shaman acts as his own drummer. What all these traditions have in common is a varied range of techniques for transformation of personal consciousness into a correspondingly varied range of experiences of identity with a god or spirit and, in many but not all cases, the use of drums with or without additional instruments. [*See* Spirit Possession *and* Shamanism.]

A famous and controversial hypothesis by Andrew Neher (1961, 1962) posits an automatically causal, physiological link between drumming and ritual experiences of consciousness-transformation. Neher cites laboratory experiments with photic driving (pulsating lights) and covariation of alpha rhythms in the brain to support a suggestion that rhythmic drumming, with its wide frequency spectrum and high energy content, would automatically affect a normal brain in such a way as to affect alpha rhythms and produce reactions similar to those reported by laboratory subjects: visual, tactile, kinesthetic, and emotional sensations for experiments with light, but only "unusual perceptions" and muscle twitching reported for actual tests with drums. He predicts (1962) that a beat frequency of 8–13 cycles per second (the range of normal alpha variation) will be found to predominate in "possession" rituals with drums.

Neher's hypothesis has been accepted without further examination by a number of ethnologists and scholars of religion (e.g., Siikala, 1978) but has been questioned or rejected by ethnomusicologists investigating actual drum usage in transformation rituals. Gilbert Rouget (1977, 1985) argues, based on extensive studies of African and Afro-American traditions, that the laboratory experiments differ greatly from the conditions and experiences of actual ceremonies; that automatic physiological causation is out of the question because most of those who hear the drumming (even the same individuals on different occasions) do not experience trance or possession; and that if Neher's quantitative predictions were correct, "then the whole of sub-Saharan Africa should be in trance from the beginning to the end of the year." But in fact, given the speeds that occur in drum music elsewhere, if Neher's (1961) dubious alternative of a lower limit of 4 beats per second were accepted, much of the world would be in perpetual trance.

While proponents and opponents of the hypothesis have tended to argue over its merits on the basis of logic and conviction, Neher's quantitative prediction has not been subjected to quantitative testing by comparison with measurements of drum rhythms in actual performances. Figure 1 shows a comparison of (A) Neher's (1962) predicted minimum tempo of 8 beats per second for "trance" rituals, with transcriptions of actual drumbeat tempos in (B) the "invitation" song to helping spirits sung by a Tamang shaman; (C) the instrumental "Invitation to the Protector of Religion" *(Chos skyoṅ Spyan 'dren)* played for the Tibetan state oracle *(Gnas-chuṅ chos skyoṅ)* before he sinks into a quiescent state to receive the god Pe-har; and (D) the "Song of Invitation" *(Spyan 'dren gyi dbyaṅs)* sung to the oracle just before he begins to show evidence of having been transformed into a state of conscious identity with the god.

Clearly, the minimum quantitative requirements of the hypothesis are not satisfied by two of the best-known Asian traditions that ought to fall within its intended scope. Example B of figure 1 is ⅝ of the required minimum speed, while Example C would have to be 280 times as fast to reach the minimum 8 beats per second. Other well-known Asian traditions (e.g., Tibetan and Newar Tantric *sādhanas*) likewise fail to satisfy the hypothesis; and, while one might expect to find more cases of African and Afro-American traditions that fall in the predicted quantitative range, there are also African cases that do not meet the requirements of the hypothesis (John Blacking, n.d.). In any case, the hypothesis in its given form must be rejected, as the occurrence of exceptions to its predictions show the operation of cross-cultural variables external to the species-universal mechanisms of human physiology. The possibility cannot be excluded that a more sophisticated reformulation of a physiological-causation theory will lead to verifiable, significant results. Current research on musical and religious practices show, however, such a wide range of variation as to render the search for causal universals progressively more difficult, and also greater apparent progress in the investigation of cultural and ideological factors that seem to underlie both religious and musical practices.

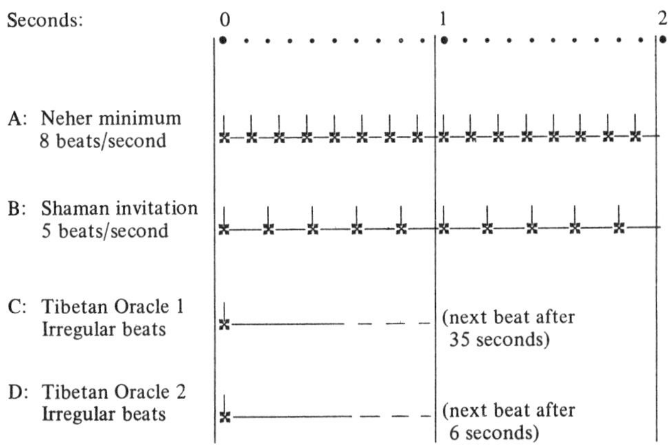

FIGURE 1. *Neher's Minimum Projected Tempo Figures Compared with Drum Tempos in Two Ritual Traditions*

BIBLIOGRAPHY

Although drums are both musical and religious instruments, it is difficult to find studies that do not ignore or misinterpret one of these two aspects. Information is scattered in journal articles and general religious and musical studies of particular areas; and many important findings of recent researchers are still unpublished, as indicated by the number of "n.d." (no date) citations for information used in this article.

The most extensive previous general study, A. E. Crawley's article "Drums and Cymbals," in the *Encyclopaedia of Religion and Ethics,* edited by James Hastings, vol. 5 (Edinburgh, 1912), is flawed by outdated and inaccurate ethnographic data and by discredited interpretive approaches. These faults are common to many nineteenth- and early twentieth-century ethnographies (and almost universal in travelers' and missionaries' accounts); while later studies have increasingly tended to treat music and religion as autonomous, mutually unintelligible domains. Thus, even such excellent ethnographic studies of drum-centered ritual traditions as Victor Turner's *The Drums of Affliction: A Study of Religious Processes among the Ndembu of Zambia* (Oxford, 1968) or Bruce Kapferer's *A Celebration of Demons: Exorcism and the Aesthetics of Healing in Sri Lanka* (Bloomington, Ind., 1983) exclude drums and their music from the depth of analytical attention paid to other components of ritual symbolism and performance.

The scientific, physical description of drums is given accurate and readable treatment in the "Terminology" section ("Membranophones," pp. 459–463) of Curt Sachs's *The History of Musical Instruments* (New York, 1940), an organological classic with a wealth of accurate information organized around partly outdated historical viewpoints. The most comprehensive and up-to-date organological information will be found in the *New Grove Dictionary of Musical Instruments,* 3 vols., edited by Stanley Sadie (New York, 1984).

The most ambitious recent effort to relate African drumming and ideology, criticized by some specialists for lack of methodological explicitness and generalization of localized West African experience to a pan-African scale, is John M. Chernoff's *African Rhythm and African Sensibility* (Chicago, 1979). A less exciting but perhaps more reliable ethnomusicological study, also from West Africa, is J. H. Kwabena Nketia's *Drumming in Akan Communities of Ghana* (Edinburgh, 1963). The classic work on "talking drums," with an old-fashioned perspective and pronounced missionary bias, is John Carrington's *Talking Drums of Africa* (London, 1949). Among the more technically oriented organological studies of specific regions, Olga Boone's *Les tambours du Congo Belge et du Ruanda-Urundi* (Tervuren, Belgium, 1951) is one of the more comprehensive. There are a number of good studies of religious and symbolic aspects of drumming-centered ritual traditions in Africa, among which Victor Turner's works (including the book already cited) are outstanding examples.

General works on Buddhist drums are unavailable; and on drum symbolism, only Rinjing Dorje and Ter Ellingson's article "Explanation of the Secret *Gcod Ḍa ma ru'*: An Exploration of Musical Instrument Symbolism," *Asian Music* (1979): 63–91, gives Buddhist primary source material, a text on the symbolism of a Tibetan drum. The standard work on shamanism, Mircea Eliade's *Shamanism: Archaic Techniques of Ecstasy*, rev. & enl. ed. (New York, 1964), contains valuable information on the ideology and use of drums, as do various articles in *Popular Beliefs and Folklore Tradition in Siberia*, edited by Vilmos Diószegi, (Bloomington, 1968); *Shamanism in Siberia*, edited by Vilmos Diószegi and Mihaly Hoppál (Budapest, 1978); and sections of Anna-Leena Siikala's *The Rite Technique of the Siberian Shaman* (Helsinki, 1978). The only detailed study of music and drumming in a "classic" Asian shaman tradition is Valerie Jill Poris's "Shamanistic Music in the Bhuji River Valley of Nepal" (M.A. thesis, University of Wisconsin, Madison, 1977). Andrew Neher describes his drum-possession hypothesis in two journal articles, "Auditory Driving Observed with Scalp Electrodes in Normal Subjects," *Electroencephalography and Clinical Neurophysiology* 13 (June 1961): 449–451, and "A Physiological Explanation of Unusual Behavior in Ceremonies Involving Drums," *Human Biology* 34 (February 1962): 151–160. The best counterarguments to Neher are given by Gilbert Rouget, in a short article, "Music and Possession Trance," in *The Anthropology of the Body*, edited by John Blacking (London, 1977), pp. 233–239, and in a book that is so far the most complete study of its subject, *Music and Trance: A Theory of the Relations between Music and Possession* (Chicago, 1985).

TER ELLINGSON

DRUZE. The Druze (Arab., Durūz), a closed, tightly knit, Arabic-speaking religious sect, number some 180,000 in Syria, 140,000 in Lebanon, and 50,000 in Israel, plus small communities in Jordan, the United States, Canada, and Latin America (1983 figures).

Formative Period. Three men played a central role in the foundation of the Druze sect in the early eleventh century. One was the Fatimid caliph of Egypt, Abū ʿAlī al-Manṣūr al-Ḥākim bi-Amr Allāh (985–1021), a manic-depressive who suffered from attacks of madness alternating with periods of humility, and whose divinity became an article of faith among his followers. He persecuted Jews, Christians, and Sunnī Muslims alike, burned Fusṭāṭ (Old Cairo), and demolished the Church of the Holy Sepulcher in Jerusalem and many other churches and synagogues, while actively promoting Ismāʿīlī propaganda as the recognized head of the Ismāʿīlī religious hierarchy. In 1017 al-Ḥākim began to favor a movement, led by the Ismāʿīlī missionary Ḥasan al-Akhram, that proclaimed his own divinity.

After the murder of al-Akhram in 1018, Ḥamzah ibn ʿAlī, a Persian felt maker, became the leader and, in fact, the major founder of the new sect. Ḥamzah gained the favor of al-Ḥākim and built up a missionary organization that made many converts, especially in Syria. His doctrine differed from Ismāʿīlī teachings in emphasizing the immediate presence of the cosmic one (God) and in playing down the importance of the subordinate emanations. He taught that al-Ḥākim was the embodiment of the ultimate One, the godhead himself, compared with whom ʿAlī and the Ismāʿīlī imams were but minor figures. In claiming that he himself was the imam, the cosmic intellect and principle, Ḥamzah went beyond even the most extreme Ismāʿīlī doctrine, and his teachings amounted to a new and independent religion. Ḥamzah taught that al-Ḥākim in his divine capacity had created five supreme cosmic leaders or ranks (*ḥudūd*)—ʿAql, the Intellect or Universal Mind (who was Ḥamzah himself); Nafs, the Universal Soul; al-Kalimah, the Word; al-Nūr al-Bāsiṭ, the Pervading Light; and al-Tālī, the Follower—each of which was embodied in an actual person. The dark side of the cosmos was represented by a number of false *ḥudūd*, likewise the creatures of al-Ḥākim and embodied in contemporary individuals. The cosmic drama between the true *ḥudūd*, with Ḥamzah at their head, and the false *ḥudūd* would be resolved when al-Ḥākim openly supported the former and abandoned the latter.

The third founding figure of the Druze sect, from whom it received its name, was Muḥammad ibn Ismāʿīl al-Darazī, an Ismāʿīlī teacher who was part Turkish and came from Bukhara to Egypt in 1017/18. He taught that the divine spirit embodied in Adam had been transmitted to ʿAlī and from him, through the imams, to al-Ḥākim. Not enough is known about the relationship between Ḥamzah and Darazī, who may have been at first Ḥamzah's disciple; however, there can be no doubt about the keen rivalry between them for the favors of al-Ḥākim and for followers, nor about their bloody conflicts, doctrinal disagreements, and mutual accusations. In 1019/20 Darazī died; he was probably executed on al-Ḥākim's orders following a denunciation by Ḥamzah, although Druze sources assert that he did not die but withdrew secretly to Syria. In 1021 al-Ḥākim "disappeared"—possibly assassinated at the instigation of his sister Sitt al-Mulūk, who had reason to fear for her life from him. This event was followed by a period of persecution of the adherents of the Ḥākim cult in Egypt. Ḥamzah went into hiding the same year but was soon killed, although his successor in the leadership of the sect, Bahā' al-Dīn al-Muqtanā, was, or pretended to be, in touch with him and as late as 1038 still predicted his return. The Druze concept of the *ghaybah* ("absence") of the founder figures parallels the Shī'ī doctrine according to which the last imam did not die but is merely absent, is still living on earth, and is to return at a preordained time as the Mahdi, or divinely "guided" messianic leader.

The Druze sect is remarkable for the brevity of its formative period: not more than three years passed between the arrival of the two Ismā'īlī teachers Ḥamzah and Darazī in Egypt and the death of both, as well as of the caliph al-Ḥākim, whom their teachings raised to the status of the sole divine figure. With these three founders dead (or in hiding, as the Druze teachings will have it), the period of canonization began, with al-Muqtanā issuing pastoral letters and laying down the laws of Druze orthodoxy. The collection of 111 letters (also including some by Ḥamzah and Ismā'īl al-Tamīmī, as well as some writings by al-Ḥākim himself) was to become the Druze scripture, called *Rasā'il al-ḥikmah* (Epistles of Wisdom). In 1034 al-Muqtanā, too, withdrew, but he continued to send out epistles until 1042/3.

At the time of al-Muqtanā's withdrawal most of the new sect's adherents were in Syria, where they had been proselytized by Darazī's emissaries. They became known as the community of Darazī, *durzī* in Arabic, whence the plural *durūz* (Druze). With al-Muqtanā's withdrawal Druze proselytizing ceased, and the doctrine was adopted that there could be no further admission into the ranks of the *muwaḥḥidūn* ("declarers of oneness"), as the Druze call themselves, nor conversion to the *dīn al-tawḥīd* (monotheism), as they term their religion.

Social Organization. Internally, the spiritual hierarchy of the Druze underwent a gradual change that resulted in the division of the community into two classes: the *'uqqāl* ("knowers," i.e., sages) and the *juhhāl* ("ignorant"). The *'uqqāl* (sg., *'āqil*) are those initiated into the doctrines of the Druze religion, knowledgeable about the gnostic-cosmological-moralistic writings produced by the Druze sages in the course of their history. The external signs of their status are their special garb and white turbans. The most learned and pious among them have the title "shaykh" and are recognized as the leaders. In preparation for their high office the shaykhs are trained in special schools, and the more zealous among them spend time in spiritual retreats, or *khalwahs*. In each district one of the shaykhs, usually a member of a leading family, is chosen as the *ra'īs* ("head"), the supreme religious authority. All the *'uqqāl* must behave with utter decorum, be peacemakers, lead a morally impeccable life, and abstain from stimulants, lying, stealing, and revenge. They attend the Friday eve services in the *majlis* ("place of gathering"), which corresponds to the Muslim *masjid*, or mosque. Only the *'uqqāl* are allowed to read the Druze secret books and to know of, and participate in, the secret ritual.

The *juhhāl*, the uninitiated majority of the community, are held to a less strict code of behavior and, unless they are strongly motivated to make efforts toward attaining *'āqil* status, remain in their "ignorant" position and must find comfort in the hope that in a future rebirth they may manage to achieve the *'āqil* rank.

Laws and Doctrines. The laws prescribed by Ḥamzah are considered binding by the Druze to this day. Among them are those insisting on equality in marriage between husband and wife—a notable departure from the traditional Muslim *sharī'ah* law—and restricting divorce to weighty, stated reasons. As a result, the position of women among the Druze is much better than that in traditional Muslim society.

Ḥamzah and Muqtanā instituted seven commandments that replace the well-known "Five Pillars" of the faith of Islam; these can be summarized as follows:

1. The Druze must speak the truth among themselves (but lying to outsiders is permitted).
2. They must defend and help each other to the point of carrying arms for this purpose.
3. They must renounce all former belief leading to a negation of the oneness of God.
4. They must dissociate themselves from unbelievers.
5. They must recognize the absolute oneness of the Lord, who was incarnated in al-Ḥākim.
6. They must be content with whatever the Lord does.
7. They must submit to the Lord's will and orders.

Druze tenets also include the belief that in the end al-Ḥākim and Ḥamzah will reappear, conquer the world, and establish justice, and that the Druze living at that time will be the universal rulers. An important Druze belief concerns the fixity of the number of souls and instant rebirth after death, which means that the number of the living Druze is believed to remain always the same. Another doctrine, that of *taqīyah* ("dissimulation"), shared with the Shī'ah, requires that in order to preserve the secrecy of their faith the Druze must pretend that they accept the faith of the ruling majority, which, in most areas inhabited by the Druze, was Sunnī Islam.

Some principles of Druze religion, through the Ismāʿīlīyah, go back to Neoplatonism and are common to several gnostic sects. These include a belief in periodic human incarnation or manifestation of the deity and a specific interpretation of the revealed religions, whose founders, such as Moses, Jesus, and Muḥammad, it considers teachers of esoteric truths only. Despite their doctrine of separation between themselves and other religions, the Druze do participate in the veneration of certain saints ("prophets"), whose tombs are places of pilgrimage for members of other religions as well. They hold in especially high esteem Nabī Shuʿayb (Jethro), the father-in-law of Moses, whom they believe to have been one of the incarnations of the first cosmic principle, the Intellect or Universal Mind, and they visit his grave near Ḥiṭṭīn in the Galilee, also venerated by the Jews.

Later History. In Ottoman times the Druze enjoyed considerable independence and were governed by their own local ruling houses, headed by emirs. Periodically they attacked the Turks (as in 1584) and, when suffering defeat, retreated to their almost impregnable mountain villages.

One of the most outstanding Lebanese Druze leaders was the emir Fakhr al-Dīn al-Maʿanī II (1572–1635), an enlightened ruler who, carrying out the doctrine of *taqīyah,* professed the Druze religion before his own people and Islam before the Ottoman authorities and, in addition, showed much sympathy for Christianity. He spent several years as a refugee in Florence and was reported to have been baptized. In 1624 the Porte recognized him as the lord of Arabistan, from Aleppo to the frontiers of Egypt. Ultimately the Turks became suspicious of his loyalty, took him captive, and beheaded him.

Despite their commandment to help and defend one another, the Druze, too, were caught up in the struggle between the Qaysī and Yamanī factions that fought bitterly all over the area in the seventeenth and eighteenth centuries. In the bloody conflict, the "red" or northern Qaysī faction was comprised of Muslim Arabs, Christian Arabs, and Druze, and so was their enemy, the "white" or southern Yamanī faction. At the same time, however, the Druze maintained armed resistance against the Turks and were engaged in bloody wars with the Maronite Christian Arabs.

In the eighteenth and nineteenth centuries there was a movement of the Druze from southern Lebanon to Jabal Ḥawrān in southwestern Syria. They drove out the original inhabitants and after 1860 remained the only population of the Ḥawrān, which acquired the name of Jabal Druze. There they enjoyed quasi-independence.

Occasionally the Druze helped the Turks against the latter's enemies, for example, against the Wahhabīs who threatened Damascus in 1810. Throughout the nineteenth century and until the end of World War I the Druze were involved in clashes almost constantly, mainly with the Maronite Christians, but occasionally also with the Turks. These fights tended to degenerate into massacres, such as that of the Christians by the Druze in Jabal Druze in 1825, and of the Druze of Matn, Lebanon, by the Maronites in 1845. In the same year the Druze also attacked the monasteries of Abī and Sulimah. In 1860 the Druze burned 150 villages and massacred some 11,000 Christians, mostly Maronites. These events led to armed European intervention and to the occupation of Lebanon by French troops. In 1879 the Druze raided Suwaydah, the capital of Jabal Druze, the response to which was a Turkish punitive expedition. In 1893 they fought the great bedouin tribe of the Ruwalā. As late as 1920 and 1925 they staged major uprisings against the French authorities in Syria.

This enumeration, which includes only the major conflicts involving the Druze, indicates the extent to which, conditioned by their religious tenets, they have insisted on self-determination and independence and considered all outsiders, whether Muslim or Christian, their enemies. With their fierce participation in the Lebanese civil war that began in the mid-1970s, the Druze remained true to this old-established pattern. In Israel the Druze have been recognized as a religious community of the same rank as that of the Muslim and Christian Arabs, have requested and been granted the right to serve in the armed forces, and have either remained neutral or sided with the Jews in the Arab-Israeli conflict.

BIBLIOGRAPHY

Alamuddin, Nura S., and Paul D. Starr. *Crucial Bonds: Marriage among the Lebanese Druze.* Delmar, N.Y., 1980.

Ayoub, Victor F. "Political Structure of a Middle Eastern Community: A Druze Village in Mount Lebanon." Ph.D. diss., Harvard University, 1955.

Ben-Dor, Gabriel. *The Druzes in Israel: A Political Study.* Jerusalem, 1979.

Bouron, Narcisse. *Druze History.* Translated, annotated, and edited by Fred Massey. Detroit, 1952.

Dana, Nissim. *The Druse: A Religious Community in Transition.* Jerusalem, 1980.

Guys, Henri, trans. and ed. *Théogonie des Druses.* Paris, 1863.

Halabi, Rafik. *The West Bank Story.* Translated by Ina Friedman. New York, 1982.

Hitti, Philip K. *The Origins of the Druze People and Religion.* New York, 1928.

Makarem, Sami. *The Druze Faith.* Delmar, N.Y., 1974.

Patai, Raphael. *The Druze: "Enfants Terribles" of the Middle*

East. Institute of Jewish Affairs, Research Report, no. 3. London, 1984.

Silvestre de Sacy, Antoine Isaac. *Exposé de la religion des Druzes.* 2 vols. Paris, 1838.

Touma, Toufic. *Paysans et institutions féodales chez les Druses et les Maronites du Liban du XVIIe siècle à 1914.* 2 vols. Beirut, 1971–1972.

RAPHAEL PATAI

DUALISM. As a category within the history and phenomenology of religion, dualism may be defined as a doctrine that posits the existence of two fundamental causal principles underlying the existence (or, as in the case of the Indian notion of *māyā* as opposed to *ātman,* the painful appearance of existence) of the world. In addition, dualistic doctrines, worldviews, or myths represent the basic components of the world or of man as participating in the ontological opposition and disparity of value that characterize their dual principles. In this specific religio-historical sense, dualism is to be distinguished from the more general philosophical doctrines of transcendence and metaphysical irreducibility, which are opposed to monistic or pantheistic doctrines of immanence. This article will examine dualism only in the former sense, as a religio-historical phenomenon. I will begin with a systematic overview of the nature and types of dualism and then proceed to a closer examination of some specific historical instances.

As as religio-historical phenomenon, dualism is more specific than either simple duality or polarity. Not every duality or polarity is dualistic, but only those that involve the duality or polarity of causal principles. Thus not every pair of opposites (such as male and female, right and left, light and darkness, good and bad, spirit and matter, sacred and profane) can be labeled as dualistic, even when their opposition is emphasized. They are dualistic only when they are understood as principles or causes of the world and its constitutive elements. In addition, in order for pairs of opposites to be dualistic, it is not necessary that they be mutually irreducible or coeternal. Indeed, one may be the creation of the other, as in the dualistic doctrine of the Bogomils, where Satan, created by God, is in turn the creator of the human body. In short, there is no dualism where there is no question of cosmogony or anthropogony, where there is no account of the principles responsible for bringing the world and man into existence. This means that a concept of mere ethical dualism, stressing the moral opposition between good and evil and their respective protagonists (as in the Christian concepts of God and the Devil), is not properly dualistic in the religio-historical and phenomenological sense unless good and evil are also connected with opposite ontological principles, as in Zoroastrianism and in Manichaeism. The simple contrasting of good and evil, life and death, light and darkness, and so on is in fact coextensive with religion itself and cannot be equated with the much more specific phenomenon of dualism.

Role in Monotheism, Polytheism, and Monism. In the historical phenomenology of religion, dualism need not be opposed necessarily to either monotheism, polytheism, or monism. Dualistic manifestations of monotheism can be found in the *Gāthās* of the Zoroastrian Avesta and in Christian gnosticism. Here one finds an ontologically inferior and often demonic figure, such as Ahriman (Angra Mainyu) in the Avesta or the Prince of Darkness in Manichaeism or the psychic demiurge in gnosticism, all of which exist as a second principle along with the supreme God. Only in Marcionism does this dualism lead beyond monotheism to a properly ditheistic doctrine (the supreme god of perfect goodness as opposed to the inferior god of "justice"). In addition some forms of non-gnostic Christian speculation deeply influenced by Platonism can be regarded as dualistic. Rather than a gnostic belief in two irreducible agencies that account for the existence of man and the universe, there is in the speculation a belief in the fundamental opposition of the immaterial human soul and the material (i.e., physical) body. Although here it is the same God who creates both the soul and the body, the occasion for the creation of the latter is the primordial sin of the originally "incorporeal" (i.e., not bound to a material body) rational souls. This primordial sin can accordingly be viewed as a second principle or cause that motivates God to create the human body in its present constitution and the visible world in which man must live until the final apocatastasis, or restoration of his primordial, "immaterial" condition.

Such is the picture presented by the platonizing anthropology of Origen. In this case one can speak of an anthropological dualism, which implies not only the dual constituents of soul and body, but more importantly a duality of causes: the omnipotent will of God and the sin of a created soul, the latter motivating the creation of the human physiological body and the material world. Clearly, sin is not to be understood here as the efficient cause of this "second creation"; it merely motivates the subsequent ("second") creative act of God. Sin is here to be understood as "previous sin," as distinct from the original sin of Adam. While the latter was committed by Adam as a fully corporeal man, this "previous sin" was committed by the preexisting souls in a kind of "prologue in heaven." Elements of this Origenian tradition of anthropological dualism are also found in Gregory of Nyssa, who thought that God created the human (sexual) body because of his foreknowledge of the (not sexual) sin of Adam and his fall from paradise.

One finds a somewhat different form of non-gnostic, dualistic monotheism in certain Jewish thinkers who admit the existence of angelic agents who cooperate with God the creator. In Philo Judaeus, for instance, these angels are particularly concerned with the creation of man or his lower constituents. Philo shows here the clear influence of Plato, who in his *Timaeus* had opposed the great Demiurge, creator of the immortal part of the soul, and the "generated gods," whom the Demiurge appoints to create the lower, mortal parts of the soul and the human body.

Needless to say, dualistic formulations of monotheism were criticized by Christian theologians, who sought to avoid any limitation of the absolute creativity of God. Nevertheless, it should be noted that some of the abovementioned conceptions (those of Philo and Plato) were originally intended to safeguard God's innocence in relation to evil. Thus the Platonists attributed human evil not to God but to the freedom of the will and to man's corporeal nature.

Dualistic conceptions can also be found in polytheism. In some polytheistic cosmogonies there is an opposition between two distinct causal principles, represented on the one hand by the older, semipersonal *archai,* or principles of an elementary character, and on the other by a new race of youthful and energetic gods. Thus Ouranus, in the cosmogony of Hesiod, and Apsu, in the Mesopotamian *Enuma elish,* are each violently opposed in their egocentrism and ontological passivity by new gods, among whom figures a wise and energetic demiurge who creates or sets in order the world, apportions lots, and fixes destinies. It should be noted that in this type of cosmogony the vanquished primordial entities do not completely lose their sacredness. Ouranus, for instance, retains a prophetic function, Apsu remains pure, and Vṛtra (an analogous figure in Vedic cosmogony) remains a brahman. In other words, the character of these primordial entities, fated to a final defeat and transformed substantially into the elements of the universe, is far from demonic; they remain quite different from the aggressive beings that characterize the Zoroastrian and gnostic worldviews.

Finally, even monism can be expressed in dualistic terms. This is the case, paradoxically enough, in the classical *advaita* doctrine of Śaṇkara, and in other systems that reduce the multiplicity of the material world to illusion, that is, to metaphysical nonexistence. These systems in fact correspond to my definition of dualism, inasmuch as *māyā* (illusion), though ontologically insubstantial, nevertheless gives rise to the phenomenal world and its suffering. Instances of dualistic monism can be found outside India as well. In Greece the monistic doctrine of Parmenides is not without dualistic overtones, with its opposition between truth and opinion *(doxa),* a distinction that was also proper to Plato. More profoundly intermingled and at the same time opposed are the coeternal principles of Love and Discord in the ontology and cosmology of Empedocles. One also thinks of Heraclitus's essentially dualistic doctrine of "war" *(polemos),* where the "way downward" and the "way upward" oppose each other, all within the context of the axiological preeminence attributed to the principle of Logos, which has as its material aspect fire.

Types of Dualism. We may now move on to a more systematic examination of dualism by presenting a typology of its basic forms. It must be kept in mind that the following typology will require verification through comparative historical research. From the systematic point of view, every form of dualism may be classified by type as either radical or moderate, either dialectical or eschatological, and as either cosmic or anticosmic. I shall examine each of these pairs in turn.

Radical versus moderate. Radical dualism and moderate dualism may be distinguished from each other on the basis of their respective views of the two fundamental principles. Radical dualism admits two coequal and coeternal principles (in the sense that both of them exist and act from the very beginning, whatever may be their final destiny; see below). Late Avestan and medieval Zoroastrianism, as well as the early Gathic doctrine of the two primordial spirits, are examples of such radical dualism. In particular, the two Gathic spirits are to be understood as existing independently from the very beginning of the world with their perfectly contrary natures: notwithstanding the interpretation given by most Iranologists, their choice means merely the declaration of their inborn natures, and the bad spirit has nothing in common with Ahura Mazdā, the high god. Their mention as "twins" (*Yashts* 30.3) does not imply more than their being symmetrical and contrary in essence to each other. [*See* Twins.] Manichaeism and some varieties of medieval Catharism also belong here. Among the Greeks there exists a radical dualism in Orphism, with its conception of the *kuklos tēs geneseōs* ("the cycle of birth") and the dualistic implications of its metaphysics; in Empedocles' theory of the two opposed principles of Love and Discord; in Heraclitus; and in Plato's doctrines of the two alternating revolutions of the world, mentioned in the *Statesman,* and of the coeternity of the Ideas and the "receptacle" *(chōra).* There are also several forms of radical dualism in India, particularly in the Sāṃkhya system, with its opposed principles of *puruṣa* and *prakṛti.*

Unlike the radical dualism, moderate (or "monarchian") dualism exhibits only one primordial principle, while a second principle somehow derives from the first, often through an incident that took place in a kind of prologue in heaven. This second principle then plays a central role in bringing the world into existence. Many of the gnostic systems provide examples of moderate dualism, in particular the systems of Valentinus, where the very structure of the divine, pneumatic world (the *plērōma*) allows for the possibility of a fall in heaven. The fall of Sophia, the last *aiōn,* is a result of her location on the periphery of the divine *plērōma.* This dangerous position amounts to a kind of predestination. Although this does not destroy the moderate, or monarchian, character of Valentinianism, it does show that gnostic metaphysics here includes a concept of crisis or instability in the divine that is fundamentally dualistic. It also provides evidence of gnosticism's connections with other speculative trends during the Hellenistic period, such as the Orphic, Pythagorean, and Platonic traditions. Other examples of moderate dualism are the anthropogony of Plato's *Timaeus,* and medieval sects (some of the Cathari and the Bogomils).

Evidence of radical or moderate dualism among nonliterate cultures is ambiguous, and this very fact may be significant for our understanding of the formation process of dualistic ideologies and creeds. Thus while the Algonquin myth of the two brothers Ioskeha and Tawiskaron, born of Ataentsic (a primordial female being) can be traced to a type of radical dualism, since the brothers have, respectively, a positive and negative relation to creation from the very beginning, other American myths of a dualistic character are quite different. They may present a supreme being who in the beginning is unopposed but is later joined by a second figure of unknown origin who begins to interfere in the creation process. The unknown origin of the rival, who is often characterized as a demiurgic trickster, may be intended to indicate that his earlier absence was really an unmanifested presence, and that he is in fact an integral part of a single, all-inclusive scenario. The same seems to be true of the North American myth of Nih'asa (or Napiwa), the "hard man" who arrives late, origin unknown. He succeeds in taking control of the earth with the creator god's permission, but then immediately acts against the latter's purposes. The less tragic Chukchi myth of the primordial times conveys the same impression. The supreme being creates everything, but forgets to create Raven (who in other Northeast Asian myths is a trickster and a secondary demiurge). The supreme being's forgetfulness points to the fact that Raven is implicitly, even before his birth, a constituent element of the universe. In fact, the myth tells us that he comes into being in darkness, during the night following creation, born of a creator god's abandoned garment. Thus the creator is, in one way or another, responsible for the totality of existence, and Raven owes his existence to a kind of inborn necessity.

It would seem, therefore, that the most ancient formulations (or at least the simplest) did not choose between the two possibilities of radical and moderate dualism. Perhaps such an alternative was not recognized. Such may also have been the case with what we have called the moderate dualism of the Valentinians and of other gnostics and sectarians, whose mythologies not infrequently remind us of the dualistic scenarios of archaic cultures.

In this connection one may also mention the mythologies of the Yazīdīs, the Ahl-i Ḥaqq, and the dualistic myths and legends found in the folklore of eastern Europe. The latter have been influenced both by the doctrines of the Bogomils, who themselves drew upon certain Christian apocryphal writings; but they have also some features in common with the dualistic mythologies found among the Tatars of the Altai and among other Turkish and Mongolian populations of Central Asia.

Dialectical versus eschatological dualism. Dialectical dualism may be distinguished from eschatological dualism by the fact that the two irreducible principles recognized by the former function eternally, whereas in the latter case they do not. In dialectical dualism the two principles are often conceived of as good and evil, respectively, both in the ethical and metaphysical sense. Samples are to be found in Orphic speculation on the one and the many, in Empedocles and Heraclitus, and in Platonism. The Hindu opposition of *ātman* and *māyā* also represents this type of dualism, as does the Chinese ideology of *yin* and *yang,* and various theosophical speculations.

The distinctive feature of eschatological dualism is the belief that the evil principle will be overcome at the end of history. Examples of this type of belief can be found in Zoroastrianism, Manichaeism, gnosticism, Bogomilism, and Catharism. As can be seen from this list, many forms of eschatological dualism are historically dependent on doctrines within Christianity, where soteriology is strongly eschatological (though nondualistic). Similarly, some forms of dialectical dualism are connected with monistic speculations. It should also be noted that whereas dialectical dualism is always radical dualism, eschatological dualism can be grounded on either radical dualism, as in the case of Zoroastrianism and the Manichaeism influenced by it, or on moderate dualism, such as one finds in most gnostic traditions, in Bogomilism, and in Catharism.

Cosmic versus anticosmic dualism. Cosmic and anticosmic forms of dualism are distinguished by their attitudes towards the world. Cosmic dualism contends that creation is fundamentally good, and evil comes to it from the outside. Zoroastrianism can be named as a typical example. Anticosmic dualism contends to the contrary that evil is intrinsic to the world, present in an essentially negative or delusive principle or substance such as matter, the body, or the inferior soul. Examples here include Orphism, gnosticism, Manichaeism, Bogomilism, Catharism, and certain forms of Hinduism. In Manichaeism, for instance, we find the notion of the world as being made out of the dark, material substance of demons, molded by a divine demiurge, the Spiritus Vivens. The cosmos is created as a providential engine in order to permit the progressive liberation of the souls trapped within it, which are eventually guided to the heavenly paradise.

Relative Importance of Types. A general consideration of the typology that has just been presented permits one to make several interesting observations. First of all, the first opposition, that between radical and moderate forms of dualism, seems to be the least significant. This calls into question the frequent assumption that dualism in its genuine form implies the coeternity of the two principles. The fact that this particular alternative caused important clashes in the Catharist churches of the Western Middle Ages should not lead us to overestimate its importance. The fundamental ambiguity involved in the question of the origin of the rival of God, the demiurge-trickster, in the dualistic mythologies of a number of nonliterate cultures points rather to the relative unimportance of this opposition. From the metaphysical point of view, it is rather the second form of typological opposition, that between dialectical and eschatological dualism, which is the most important. Finally, in relation to the actual conception and practice of life, it is the third opposition, that between dialectical and eschatological dualism, which is the most important. Finally, in relation to the actual conception and practice of life, it is the third opposition, that between cosmic and anticosmic dualism, that is central.

This final point enables us to recognize the specific character of Zoroastrianism in relation to the other types. As an outstanding form of cosmic dualism, Zoroastrianism is to be distinguished sharply from anticosmic Manichaeism, in spite of their similarities as both radical and eschatological. The fact that Manichaeism, which is generally gnostic and Western in character, nevertheless shares in the radical and eschatological form of Zoroastrian dualism suggests the conceptual and iconographic influence of the Iranian religious milieu.

The opposition of cosmic and anticosmic is less helpful for arriving at a specific characterization of Platonic and Hermetic forms of dualism. Both Plato and Plotinus strongly affirmed the beauty and order of the cosmos (something that sets Plotinus apart from the gnostics). Nevertheless, they occasionally expressed less optimistic views. In the *Laws,* for example, Plato formulated an opposition between two souls, one good and the other evil. Furthermore, both he and Plotinus shared the Orphic doctrine of the body as the tomb or prison of the soul and the view of life as a kind of death. In the end, it is impossible to describe the thought of either as consistently cosmic or anticosmic.

Dualism in History. Up to this point my approach to dualism has been systematic. But the history of religions entails more than a purely phenomenological or systematic outlook. Employing a comparative-historical method raises the question of possible historical connections between different forms of religious dualism, and engages one in analyzing the historical milieus in which these phenomena arise. A historical-comparative treatment of dualism as a specific category of religious thought and experience need not revert to diffusionist explanations that presuppose a single historical origin of dualism and explain its subsequent geographical extension as a consequence of cultural diffusion and adaptation. The diverse historical forms of dualism can be better explained on the basis of parallel development, provided this approach avoids the presuppositions of evolution and physiological development. Yet it is not less historical in character than the diffusionist approach. I have in mind here a historical typology that would explain the independent development of analogous religious phenomena such as dualism on the basis of comparable religious and historical circumstances or presuppositions. In any case, in the present state of our knowledge it would be hard to support a diffusionist explanation of the widespread presence of dualism in different cultures, times and religions. Given the presence of forms of dualism in the archaic cultures of North America, it is clearly impossible to view all forms of dualism as having a single geographical point of origin, such as Iran. Here it is best to focus only on those connections that can be historically documented.

As was pointed out above, such connections can be found between some forms of Manichaean and Zoroastrian dualism. Similar comparative-historical conclusions could be drawn concerning the relationship between the dualistic conceptions found in eastern European folklore and in such western Asian sects as the Yazīdīs. One could possibly speak of a certain dualistic propensity in the ethnological background of these areas without losing sight of the opposite possibility, namely, the direct influence of the great dualistic religions and the active dualistic sectarian movements such as the Bogomils. Similar possibilities exist in the case of the well-established dualistic mythologies of the Inner Asian Turks and Tatars (see, for example, the dark figure of Erlik, an antigod particularly connected with the realm of death). These may have been influenced not only by Iran but also by the dualistic folklore traditions of eastern Europe.

Even in Iran, there have occasionally been peripheral formulations of dualism that cannot be explained on the basis of Zoroastrian ideology alone. The characterization of Ahriman as a kind of demiurge-trickster, for instance, is not unlike the characterization of similar figures in the nonliterate cultures of Asia. Ultimately we are led to question the origins of Zoroastrian dualism itself: to what extent was it influenced or predetermined by the figure of Zarathushtra? To what extent, and in which ways, was Iranian religion characterized by dualistic tendencies prior to Zarathushtra? Which were more important for this, those elements that were paralleled in the Vedic literature of India (such as the parallel figures of Indra-Vṛtrahari and Verethraghna), or those that recall Inner Asian folklore?

However these questions are to be answered, one possibility deserves special mention, namely that of what one might call a "dualistic imperialism." What I have in mind may be illustrated by considering the historical fate of the so-called earth diver, the mythical theme of a bird or animal that dives into the primordial sea in order to bring up some mud for the creator, who then spreads it on the surface of the waters to create the earth. This motif is quite widespread, being found in Inner Asia, eastern Europe, and North America. What is interesting is that it has dualistic implications only in the Old World, which seems particularly significant in view of the fact that other dualistic myths are far from rare in the New World. It may mean that the originally nondualistic motif of the diver was first given a dualistic interpretation in Asia, some time after versions of it had spread to North America. The reasons for such an insistence on a dualistic interpretation of the motif in Asia can only be guessed at, but once it had taken hold it could have modified the earlier situation and led to the appropriation of themes previously extraneous to dualism. Thus one would have a kind of "dualistic imperialism" whose more peculiar manifestations would have appeared in Iran or at its borders. Such a hypothesis need not have anything to do with the theory that dualism as such originated in these regions.

It is now time to turn our attention to other territories and cultures in which dualism, in forms very different from those found in Inner Asia and North America, was once widespread. These territories extend from the border of the Achaemenid empire in the East to Sicily and Magna Graecia in the West. Here Orphism and Pythagoreanism, both typical forms of dualism, took forms quite different from those found in Iran, Inner Asia, and North America. Rather than a supreme being opposed by a devilish or tricksterlike demiurge, we find a form of anthropological dualism that is at the same time ontological and cosmological. The doctrines of *sōma-sēma* (body-tomb), *metensōmatōsis*, and purification from "previous sin" characterize this mysteriosophical, anthropological dualism, which is rooted in a metaphysics that opposes oneness and multiplicity in the context of an eternally recurring cycle. The term *mysteriosophical* is intended to refer to the tendency of Orphism and Pythagoreanism, and later Plato and Platonism, to adapt elements from the theology of the mystery religions to their own philosophies. The mystery religions themselves seem to have been free from the antisomatic attitudes typical to Orphism and Pythagoreanism.

The anticosmic and antisomatic doctrines of Greek mysteriosophy are comparable in some respects to the monistic-dualistic speculation found in the Indian Upaniṣads, some of which were roughly contemporary with the mysteriosophic currents of the West. Greek mysteriosophy no doubt contributed to the development of similar trends in the West, for example, in the form of gnostic, Hermetic, Neoplatonic, and Neo-Pythagorean dualism and in gnostic antisomatism, which connected death with *erōs* and *genesis* ("birth") with *phthora* ("corruption, death"). Although gnosticism, and in particular Christian gnosticism, was undoubtedly heir to the eschatological setting of non-gnostic Christianity, these objective historical and phenomenological connections with pagan mysteriosophy should not be overlooked.

Also not to be overlooked is the question of the influence of North Asian, northeast European, and Balkan forms of animism and shamanism on the development of dualism in the Mediterranean area, as well as in Iran and Central Asia. The problem of the relation between such non-Greek forms of animism and shamanism and some of the "irrational" aspects of Archaic and Classical Greek culture is well known. Although the issue is certainly of primary importance, it should not be forgotten that important differences separate the *metensōmatōsis* and asceticism of Orphism and Pythagoreanism from the animistic creeds and practices of northeast European shamanistic cultures. In particular, the ethical and ontological motivations of the Greek mysteriosophic traditions are conspicuously absent in such cultures. The same is true of those Balkan personages, such as Zalmoxis, who are connected in Thrace with practices and beliefs of "immortalization" that are quite different from the Orphic conception of death and reincarnation in the context of ethical and ontological purification. Nevertheless, these so-called barbarian elements may form an essential part of the history of European dualism.

The "Pythagorean" abstention from meat was also attributed to Zalmoxis. Moreover, for the celibate sect of the Ktistai, and also the pagan sect of the Pious Ones (Eusebeis) of Balkan antiquity, abstaining from meat (Strabo, 7.3.3.5) may recall some corresponding aspects of the medieval Balkan sect of the Bogomils, founded by a priest named Bogomil ("he who prays to God," or perhaps "he who loves God"). The dualistic folklore of the Balkans and eastern Europe, as well as the more or less dualistic apocrypha popular there, are also a part of this history. These oral and literary instances are particularly interesting in that they may show the influence of gnostic motifs drawn from literary texts and oral legends originating in the East. Generally speaking, one can say that "Oriental" dualism, derived from both literary and oral traditions and characterized by the opposition of a creator and an inferior demiurge (the lower god of gnosticism, or the demiurge-trickster of ethnology and folklore), was influential in those Balkan and eastern European regions where dualistic trends were already in evidence. The di-theism of those imported mythologies may have been prepared for by indigenous conceptions of a duality of gods, such as the white god and the black god mentioned by a medieval (not authoritative) text (Helmold's *Chronica Slavorum*, twelfth century).

Plutarch's View. We have considered some of the more important historical and systematic forms of dualism as found in different religious contexts. We may now consider briefly a type of dualistic thought that, far from being limited to the expression of a particular creed, was a key to the interpretation of different religious systems and of religion in itself. This type of dualistic thought is exemplified in Plutarch's treatise *Isis and Osiris*. The aim of the philosopher and theologian of Chaeronea is to show, on the basis of Platonic or Middle Platonic hermeneutics, that dualism, as the idea of two opposing forces manifesting themselves in the universe, is a notion common to most of the religions of his time.

In the course of developing his thesis, Plutarch provides us with precious information concerning the Persian, Mesopotamian, and especially the Egyptian religions. The information he gives concerning the Osiris-Seth opposition in Egypt is the sole ancient literary document containing a complete form of that basic myth. His interpretation of the different characters of the myth and of the different forms of relationship that link them together is clearly Platonic and heavily speculative. He goes so far as to introduce different kinds of opposition, a hostile opposition between Osiris/Horus and Seth and an opposition of cooperation and transcendence between Osiris and Isis, a married couple. Osiris is interpreted as the ideal world, or the transcendent model that informs matter, that is, Isis, the female, nourishing agency of all beings in the visible world. It is important to note that Plutarchian hermeneutics synthesizes these two different kinds of dualistic opposition into a unitary structure. As a result, in Plutarch's interpretation, Isis does not totally eliminate the evil figure of Seth from the world after the victory of Horus over him. Despite his inborn malignity, Seth is clearly conceived of as a presence necessary for the equilibrium of the world. Thus, despite his acceptance of the Platonic notion expressed in *Theaetetus* 176ab that evil is intrinsic to the lower world, Plutarch's speculative Platonism actually goes beyond Plato. Plato had never managed to unite the two different forms of dualism found in the *Laws* (the two opposing souls of the universe, one good and one bad) and in the *Timaeus* (the invisible and the visible as necessary constituents of being).

Would it be too much to suspect that Plutarch, though aided by the use of Platonic speculation, did not himself purely invent this complex, yet unitary, "Egyptian" structure? Egyptian documentation lends support to the idea that Seth, god of deficiency, sterility, and loneliness, god of the desert and of hostile countries, was explicitly acknowledged as a constituent element of the Egyptian pantheon and universe. He has, for instance, a positive role in the daily struggle against the serpent Apophis, the enemy of the sun. That is not all. Recent studies of the Egyptian Seth have demonstrated that he possesses traits characteristic of a trickster. Moreover, the comparative study of the Egyptian mythology of Seth and that of Yurugu (Ogo) among the Dogon of West Africa has shown considerable structural affinities between the two. In the Dogon myths, Yurugu is a sterile, lonely, adversarial character; yet at the same time he is an indispensable element in the universe. He is furthermore a trickster; he is "pale fox" (the name refers to *Vulpes pallida*, an African fox). It is remarkable, having made peregrinations among the many forms of dualism, to come across something reminiscent of that pedantic, aggressive, unhappy, and inescapable dualistic figure, the demiurge-trickster (Raven, Coyote, and others) typical of quite a number of preliterate mythologies. Could this mean that, far from being a protest against monotheism, a protest intended as an option in favor of the innocence of God over his omnipotence, dualism may be interpreted (in at least some of its forms) as rather an insufficient actualization of God's omnipotence? And that the most extreme and irreconcilable form of dualism, namely dialectical dualism, both in its quietistic and combative forms, was fated to present monotheism with its most radical challenge? This can be seen also in the dialectics of Hegel, Nietzsche, Marx, and Freud, all of which are samples of "dualism" in the modern world.

[*See also* Tricksters *and* Demiurge.]

BIBLIOGRAPHY

For a vast exposition of the problems concerning the forms and the diffusion of dualism in the nonliterate and literate religions, see my *Il dualismo religioso*, 2d ed. (Rome, 1983). Also see my study *Selected Essays on Gnosticism, Dualism and Mysteriosophy* (Leiden, 1978), which makes reference to dualism in gnosticism and the Iranian traditions. Jacques Duchesne-Guillemin offers a comparative perspective on Iranian dualism in his study *La religion de l'Iran ancien* (Paris, 1962). The role of Zurvanism is somewhat exaggerated in Robert C. Zaehner's *Zurvan: A Zoroastrian Dilemma* (Oxford, 1955). Iranian dualism is also the subject of Mary Boyce's text *A History of Zoroastrianism*, 2 vols. (Leiden, 1975–1982) and my *Zamān i Ohrmazd: Lo zoroastrismo nelle sue origini e nella sua essenze* (Turin, 1958). On dualism in different religions and cultures, consult Mircea Eliade's "Prolegomenon to Religious Dualism," in his study *The Quest: History and Meaning in Religion* (Chicago, 1969), and his *Zalmoxis, the Vanishing God* (Chicago, 1972), especially chapters 2 and 3. Simone Pétrement's *Le dualisme dans l'histoire de la philosophie et des religion* (Paris, 1946) and *Le dualisme chez Platon, les gnostiques et les manichéens* (Paris, 1946) do not distinguish enough between the uses of the term *dualism* in philosophical-historical and religio-historical studies. The following sources treat particular aspects of dualism: *The Origins of Gnosticism* (1967; Leiden, 1970), which I edited; Hans Jonas's *The Gnostic Religion*, 2d ed., rev. (Boston, 1963); Marcel Griaule and Germaine Dieterlen's *Le renard pâle*, vol. 1 (Paris, 1965); Kurt Rudolph's *Gnosis* (San Francisco, 1983); and Jacques Duchesne-Guillemin's study *The Western Response to Zoroaster* (Oxford, 1958). Geo Widengren's *"Der Iranische Hintergrund der Gnosis," Zeitschrift für Religions- und Geistesgeschichte* 4 (1952): 97–114, discusses dualism in relation to the Upaniṣads. Franz Kiichi Numazawa makes a comparative approach to the Chinese Yin-yang ideology in his study *Die Weltanfänge in der japanischen Mythologie* (Fribourg, 1946). Oskar Dähnhardt includes precious information on dualistic folklore through eastern Europe and Asia in his book *Natursagen*, vol. 1 (Leipzig, 1907). Wilhelm Schmidt treats Asian dualistic mythologies in his *Der Ursprung der Gottesidee*, vols. 9–12 (Münster, 1948–1955). For a discussion of "second creation" and "previous sin," which is distinct from "original sin," see my *Selected Essays*, cited above, and the volume that I edited titled *La Doppia creazione dell'uomo* (Rome, 1978). As for dualism in the modern currents of thought and praxis mentioned at the end of the present article, see my *Selected Essays*, pp. 177–186.

UGO BIANCHI

DUMUZI was an ancient Sumerian god whose cult is attested from as early as 3500 BCE to as late as the Middle Ages; his Akkadian name is Tammuz. A month was named after him, and its Akkadian form was borrowed with other month names into the Jewish calendar. Dumuzi may rightly be considered a type of dying god of fertility, for into him merged over the course of time a very great number of originally independent fertility deities. Most of these did not develop along sociomorphic lines into powers in social and political life but remained gods of natural, economically important phenomena. The syncretistic nature of Dumuzi shows particularly clearly in litanies that formed part of the laments for him: they list as names for him those of deities such as Ninazu, Damu, Ningishzida, Alla, Lugalshudi, Ishtaran, Lusiranna, and Amaushumgalana. Even included are the names of all the kings of the third dynasty of Ur and of Isin, who in the rite of the Sacred Marriage had, while performing the relevant cult acts, become the god, embodying him.

The cultic and mythological pattern, all or part of which was characteristic for Dumuzi as the power in and for some specific seasonal kind of fertility, was one of wooing and wedding, celebrating the community's joy at having the god present among them. But it was also one of death and lament, sometimes combined with a search to bring the god back, expressing the community's grief at the vanishing of the power as its season passed, and its intense longing to have the god back. The pattern was undoubtedly a very early one and one generally conformed to. Of major deities who show traces of having once followed it but who then moved away from it to more sociopolitically oriented roles, one may mention Nanna and Ningirsu, for both of whom a Sacred Marriage rite is attested; to An (as Gugalana), Enlil, Ishkur, and Inanna are devoted myths that deal with their disappearing into the realm of the dead.

Dumuzi was generally visualized as a young man or boy. Under some of his aspects he is of marriageable age; in others he is younger, a mere child. He is dearly loved by the women who surround him—his mother, sister, and later, his young bride—and there is reason to assume that his cult was predominantly a women's cult.

The love songs of his wooing and wedding are all love songs to him or are self-praise of the bride hoping her body will please him; there are no love songs of his to Inanna. Correspondingly, the laments for him are by his mother, sister, and widowed bride, never by a father. One may also cite here *Ezekiel* 8:14: "There sat women weeping for Tammuz."

The love for Dumuzi as it finds expression in the texts is a love for what he is rather than for anything he might have done or achieved. This gives his image a characteristic passivity. He is being married, pursued, killed; he does not influence others by action, only by what he is—beloved or prey.

In trying to distinguish in the image of Dumuzi at least the major aspects under which the god could appear, one may single out the following.

1. *Dumuzi as Amaushumgalana.* This name means "the one great source of the date clusters," and refers to the single, huge bud the date palm sprouts annually, from which come leaves and fruit. The cult of this aspect of Dumuzi had its center in Uruk, whose region is still noted for its dates. It was a happy cult, knowing only the Sacred Marriage rite, not death and lament. The rite is pictured on the famous Uruk Vase, which shows Amaushumgalana approaching the door to the storehouse with his wedding gifts. At the door stands Inanna, ready to lead him in. A later text describing the ritual tells how Inanna dresses for the wedding in date clusters—the appropriate ornaments for her as numen of the date storehouse—and then goes to the storehouse gate to open it to Amaushumgalana. This act of the bride opening the door to the groom formally concluded a Sumerian wedding.

2. *Dumuzi the shepherd.* The name *Dumuzi* means "producer of healthy young ones," and characterizes Dumuzi as the power to produce healthy, well-formed offspring—specifically, as his title "the shepherd" suggests, healthy lambs. An earlier form of his name, *Damuzi,* was borrowed into Akkadian as *Tammuz.* Dumuzi's mother was the deified ewe Duttur; at times, perhaps from his cult among cowherds, the cow goddess Ninsuna took her place. Dumuzi's sister was Geshtinanna, also called Amageshtin, goddess of the grapevine. His cult and mythology comprised his wedding feast but also his death and the lament for him. His death was seen as caused by mountain bandits attacking his camp. Secondarily, a motif that has him flee from evil recruiters was borrowed from his aspect as Damu the conscript (see below).

3. *Dumuzi of the beer.* No separate name or epithet seems to mark off this particular aspect of the god, nor is it clear whether it belongs more nearly with Dumuzi or with Damu. In the relevant myths, Geshtinanna seeks her brother and is told that he is being readied for a festival or is in the brewery with wise masters. In one text his ghost asks that beer be brewed with certain red tubers into which Dumuzi's blood had turned when it spilled on the ground as he was killed. Ostensibly this beer will revive him.

4. *Damu the child.* The name *Damu* preserves the earlier form of the word *dumu* ("child"). Damu was envisaged as a young child who had escaped from his nurse and was sought by his mother. He was eventually found coming down the river. He represents the power making the sap rise in plants and trees in spring with the coming of the flood in the river. His nurse was a tree; his mother, a cedar goddess. His cult had its home in Uruk.

5. *Damu the conscript.* A different concept of the god existed in Girsu (Tello) on the lower Euphrates, originally a settlement of prisoners of war conscripted into the army as soldiers or labor troops. This Damu is a young boy, unmarried, the sole support of his mother and sister. His death occurs when a detachment of recruiters take him away—possibly for having dodged service—and he attempts to escape, only to be eventually caught for good or killed. The motif, with its dramatic chase, made its way into many of the myths dealing with Dumuzi the shepherd, where it does not belong. The Sumerian shepherd was an aristocrat with a large retinue of servants helping out with the work in the fold. The chase of a conscript by military police belongs on a much lower social level, in the world of serfs of the crown, not in that of free citizens. The name of Damu's sister in this aspect of him is Gunur ("thread spinner"); that of his mother is not clear. One tradition has him as son of Ningishzida and Ninazimua. A different deity called Damu, a goddess, was daughter of Nininsina in Isin (Ishan Bahriyāt).

[*See also* Dying and Rising Gods *and* Mesopotamian Religions, *overview article.*]

BIBLIOGRAPHY

Alster, Bendt. *Dumuzi's Dream: Aspects of Oral Poetry in a Sumerian Myth.* Copenhagen, 1972.

Jacobsen, Thorkild. "Toward the Image of Tammuz." *History of Religions* 1 (Winter 1962): 189–213. Reprinted in *Toward the Image of Tammuz,* edited by William L. Moran, pp. 73–101. Cambridge, Mass., 1970.

THORKILD JACOBSEN

DUNS SCOTUS, JOHN

DUNS SCOTUS, JOHN (c. 1266–1308), Franciscan philosopher and theologian, and founder of the school of Scotism. Born in Scotland and trained by his paternal uncle at the Franciscan friary at Dumfries, Scotland, Duns Scotus entered the Franciscan order at an early age and was ordained a priest. As a bachelor of theology he studied and taught at Oxford, completing his lectures on Peter Lombard's *Sentences,* which he began revising as the *Ordinatio* in 1300. When in 1302 the turn came for the English province to provide a talented candidate for the prestigious University of Paris, Duns Scotus was sent. During the demonstrations against Boniface VIII initiated by Philip the Fair, Duns Scotus sided with the pope and, as a consequence, was exiled from France. Just where he spent his exile is unknown, but with the death of Boniface and the accession to the papacy of Benedict XI, the church's ban against the king and the university was lifted, and Duns Scotus returned to complete his Paris lectures on the *Sentences.* He became regent master probably in 1305.

During his regency Duns Scotus conducted quodlibetic disputations covering a wide variety of theological and philosophical questions about God and creatures proposed by his audience. His later version of these questions *(Quaestiones quodlibetales),* like his *Ordinatio* (begun at Oxford, and hence referred to as the *Opus oxoniense*), was not finished at the time of his untimely death, yet these two works were widely copied for distribution and are largely responsible for his fame as a philosopher and theologian. In addition he left a number of important philosophical works on logic, psychology, and metaphysics, presented in the form of questions suggested by the works of Porphyry and Aristotle. Like *Collationes oxoniense et parisienses* (shorter questions on specific philosophical and theological topics), these were probably the result of disputations Duns Scotus conducted for the Franciscan students at Oxford and Paris. The most extensive and influential of these philosophical works are the *Quaestiones subtilissime super libros Metaphysicorum Aristoteles* and the important *Tractatus de Primo Principio,* a compendium of what reason can prove about God. Duns Scotus left Paris in the fall of 1307 to teach at the Franciscan house of studies in Cologne, where he died the following year. His remains rest in the nave of the Franciscan church near the Cologne cathedral, where he is venerated as blessed.

In his writings, Duns Scotus views theology as a practical science rather than a theoretical science, inasmuch as it gives human beings the necessary knowledge to reach their supernatural end. This end consists in sharing in the inner life of the Trinity in heaven. Developing Richard of Saint-Victor's insight that perfect love wants the beloved to be loved by others, Duns Scotus envisions the motive for creation as follows. God first loved himself, then he freely decided to create co-lovers of his infinitely lovable nature. Being orderly in his love, he next predestined Christ's human nature to share this glory and gave this nature the highest possible grace that could be bestowed upon a creature. Christ, the God-man, purchased grace for both angels and humanity. But because God foresaw Adam's sin and humanity's consequent fall from grace, Christ came as a suffering, rather than a triumphant, mediator. The most perfect form of mediation, however, would have been to preredeem, and Scotus proposes this as the rationale for Mary's immaculate conception, an argument that became basic for defenders of that doctrine until its declaration in 1854 as a dogma by Pius IX. Finally, God willed the sensible world to serve humanity.

As a philosopher, Duns Scotus modified the Aristotelian influence current in his day with insights of Augustine of Hippo, Anselm of Canterbury, Richard of Saint-Victor, and Ibn Sīnā (Avicenna). Developing Ibn Sīnā's conception of metaphysics, Duns Scotus provided a powerful rational proof for an infinite being, who he believed had revealed himself to Moses as the "I am who am."

In his philosophical system, Duns Scotus stressed the metaphysical primacy of the individual, each with its own unique "haecceity," which exists only because God's creative love wanted just "this" and not "that." On the other hand, he logically analyzed what individualized created natures must have in common, if scientific knowledge of them is to become possible.

Duns Scotus adopted the peculiar "Augustinian" tradition of the earlier Franciscan school, which stressed the "supersufficient potentiality" of the will for self-determination, and showed how it could be reconciled with the Aristotelian notion of an active potency, if one rejected the controversial principle that "whatever is moved is moved by another." In this and other ways he brought the earlier anti-Aristotelianism of his Franciscan predecessors into the mainstream of what contemporaries considered essential to Aristotle's philosophical system. For instance, he indicated how Aristotle's criteria for rational and nonrational faculties could be used to prove that the will, not the intellect, is the primary rational potency. Nonrational faculties are determined to act in one way, said Aristotle, all other conditions being the same; rational faculties are free to act in more than one way and thus are the basis of all creativity in the arts. If that be so, Duns Scotus argued, the intellect is nonrational, since it has but one mode of acting determined by the objective evidence. In this it resembles all active potencies that are collectively called "nature." The will alone has the basic freedom, when it acts with reason, for alternate modes of acting. Thus for Duns Scotus the distinction between nature and will represents the primary division of active potencies, corresponding roughly to the Aristotelian division of nonrational and rational.

Original also is Duns Scotus's development of Anselm of Canterbury's distinction of the will's twofold inclination, or "affection," namely, love of the advantageous on the one hand and love of what is right and just for its own sake on the other. As the seat of the former, the will is only an intellectual appetite that seeks happiness and self above all else. Only by reason of its affection for justice is the will free to moderate this self-seeking and, according to right reason, love what is good objectively for its intrinsic worth. Unlike Anselm, however, Duns Scotus understood justice not merely as a supernatural, infused gift, called "gratuitous grace" or "charity," but as a congenital or innate freedom of the will, free precisely because it liberates the will from that necessity Aristotle claimed was characteristic of all natural agents, namely, to seek happiness and the perfection of their nature above all else.

These two affections of the will are not volitions as such; though they incline the will, they do not necessitate it or cause it to act. The will itself determines how it will act, but when it does it acts in accord with one or the other of these affections. While the affection for the advantageous corresponds with Aristotle's conception of choice, the affection or bias for justice is an essentially Christian notion. This inclination, according to Duns Scotus, has a twofold effect: (1) it enables the will to love God above all else for God's own sake, and (2) it allows the will to moderate its natural inclination for happiness and self-actualization, either as an individual or as a species, and to love according to right reason. Thus the affection for justice provides the natural basis for a rational ethical philosophy. Both affections are essential to human nature, but they can be perfected supernaturally and directed to God as their object. Charity perfects the will's affection for justice, inclining it to love God for his own sake; hope perfects the will's affection for the advantageous, inclining it to love God because he has shown his love for us in this life and because he will be our ultimate happiness in the life to come.

Another important psychological notion of Duns Scotus' that influenced subsequent scholastics is his conception of intuitive intellectual cognition, or the simple, nonjudgmental awareness of a here-and-now existential situation. First developed as a necessary theological condition for the face-to-face vision of God in the afterlife, intellectual intuition is needed to explain our certainty of primary contingent truths such as "I think," "I choose," "I live," and to account for our awareness of existence. Duns Scotus never makes intellectual intuition the basis for his epistemology. Neither does he see it as putting persons into direct contact with the external sensible world, with any substance material or spiritual, or with an individual's haecceity, for in this life, at least, human intellect works through the sensory imagination. Intellectual intuition seems rather to be identified with the indistinct peripheral aura associated with all our direct sensory-intellectual cognition. We know of it explicitly only in retrospect when we consider the necessary conditions for intellectual memory.

The notion of intellectual intuition continued to be a topic of discussion and dispute down to the time of Calvin, who, influenced by the Scotist John Major, used an auditory rather than a visual sense model of intellectual intuition to explain our experience of God. Whereas Duns Scotus restricted intuition of God to the beatific vision in the afterlife or to the special mystical visions given to the prophets or to Paul of Tarsus, John Major explained that we may also experience God intuitively whenever he "speaks to our soul" through some special inspiration.

BIBLIOGRAPHY

The Scotistic Commission (Rome) began publishing a critical edition of the collected works of Duns Scotus in 1950. Only the first of four books of the *Ordinatio,* two of the three books of *Lectura* (begun in 1960), and the questions on Aristotle's *Metaphysics* (projected) are planned at present. Scholars still have to rely heavily on the Luke Wadding edition (Lyons, 1639), reprinted as *John Duns Scotus: Opera omnia,* edited by L. Vivès (Paris, 1891–1895), for the major portion of his writings. A critical edition of the *Tractatus de Primo Principio,* edited by Marianus Mueller (Freiburg im Breisgau, 1941), has been reprinted with translations in several languages. I have added to my earlier edition and translation an extensive commentary on this work in *A Treatise on God as First Principle* (Chicago, 1983). Selections from the *Ordinatio* are available in my *Duns Scotus: Philosophical Writings* (Edinburgh, 1962). The most recent edition of the *Quodlibetal Questions* (Latin text and Spanish translation) is by Felix Alluntis, *Obras del Doctor Sutil Juan Duns Escoto* (Madrid, 1968); an English translation by Felix Alluntis and myself is entitled *God and Creatures: The Quodlibetal Questions* (Princeton, 1975). An extensive bibliography by Odulfus Schaefer, *Bibliographia vita operibus et doctrina Iohannis Duns Scoti* (Rome, 1950), covers nineteenth- and twentieth-century secondary literature. This has been updated to 1965 by Odulfus Schaefer in the *Acta ordinis Fratrum Minorum* (Florence) 85 (1966) and by Servus Gieben in *Laurentianum* 6 (1965). Contemporary interest in Duns Scotus's thought is apparent from the international Scotistic Congresses held every five years (Oxford-Edinburgh, 1965; Vienna, 1970; Padua, 1975; Madrid, 1980), the proceedings of which are published under special titles in the general series "Studia Scholastico-Scotistica" (Rome, 1968–) by the Societas Internationalis Scotistica. *Duns Scotus on the Will and Morality* (Washington, D.C., 1986) contains a large selection of Latin texts that I have translated into English.

ALLAN B. WOLTER, O.F.M.

DURGĀ HINDUISM. In classical Hindu mythology the goddess Durgā is one of the principal forms of the wife of the great god Śiva. She is particularly celebrated for her victory over the buffalo demon Mahiṣāsura. At a higher level of abstraction she is considered to be the energy *(śakti)* of Śiva. Ultimately she is Devī, the Goddess, whose myriad names and forms are merely transient and adventitious disguises that overlay a unitary spiritual reality.

Most modern scholars have sought to find the ultimate origin of the goddess worship of Hinduism in the prehistoric Indus Valley civilization centered in what is now Pakistan. This theory is plausible, but the evidence for an important goddess cult in the Indus civilization is inconclusive, and the historical links of such a cult with classical Hinduism are impossible to document. Preclassical Vedic literature mentions numerous goddesses, but they are clearly of secondary importance. The earliest Vedic text, the *Ṛgveda,* praises several river goddesses, most notably Sarasvatī; the goddess Uṣas, the Dawn; Aditi, a rather vague mother of several gods; and the goddess Vāc, Speech. An ancillary Vedic text, the *Bṛhaddevatā* (2.77), includes Durgā among the many names of Vāc, but this is considered to be a late interpolation. The *Taittirīya Saṃhitā* (1.8.6.1) of the *Yajurveda* mentions Ambikā, later one of the common alternate names of Durgā, as the sister of Śiva. In the later *Taittirīya Āraṇyaka* (10.18), Śiva is said to be "the husband of Ambikā, the husband of Umā." Umā appears in the *Kena Upaniṣad* (3.12) as Haimavatī, the daughter of Himavat, the Himalaya.

It is not until the early centuries of the Christian era, however, that either Durgā in particular or the Goddess as a unitary concept become important figures in Hindu religious texts. Hymns in praise of Durgā as the Goddess appear in the *Virāṭaparvan* (6) and the *Bhīṣmaparvan* (23) of the epic *Mahābhārata,* the critical edition of which considers them to be late interpolations. In the *Harivaṃśa,* the "appendix" to the *Mahābhārata,* the Goddess consents to be born as Yaśodā's child, who is exchanged for Kṛṣṇa and killed by Kaṃsa. There follows another long hymn dedicated to her, but the critical edition considers this also to be an interpolation. The three hymns provide lists of her names and forms and praises of her greatness, but they do not narrate her mythological exploits. These appear in great detail in the classical texts known as the Purāṇas, dated between the third and fifteenth centuries CE.

Most important in this context is the section of the *Mārkaṇḍeya Purāṇa* known as the *Devīmāhātmya,* also called the *Caṇḍīmāhātmya* and *Durgāsaptaśatī.* This text celebrates the Goddess's victory over the buffalo demon Mahiṣāsura and over the demons Śumbha and Niśumbha. The great prevalence of Durgā's buffalo-killer form, known as Mahiṣamardinī, in iconography shows this to be her most important exploit. The *Devīmāhātmya* tells how the gods are oppressed for a century by the demons led by Mahiṣāsura. Finally they appeal to the great gods Viṣṇu and Śiva to rescue them. The anger of Viṣṇu and Śiva, joined with the anger of all the other gods, produces a mass of luminous energy. This then takes the form of a woman, the Goddess. Each god gives her his principal weapon. The god Himavat gives her the lion, which becomes her "vehicle." During a great battle she destroys the armies of Mahiṣāsura and finally beheads the demon himself.

In classical mythology many of the forms assumed by the wife of Śiva can be divided into those that are terrifying and those that are benevolent. Durgā Mahiṣamardinī belongs among the former, together with Caṇḍikā, Kālī, Vindhyavāsinī, Cāmuṇḍā, and many others. Her benevolent forms include Satī, Umā, Pārvatī, Śivā, and Gaurī. These benevolent forms have their own distinct cycle of myths, recorded in the Purāṇas and other works, such as Kālidāsa's *Kumārasaṃbhava.* She also appears as Yoganidrā ("cosmic sleep"); as Viṣṇumāyā ("world illusion"); as Ambikā ("the mother"); as Śakti ("divine energy"); and as simply Devī ("the goddess"). Since she is Śakti, those who worship her above all other gods are frequently called Śāktas. Śākta worship tends to blend into the somewhat heterodox current of Hinduism known as Tantrism, after the religious texts called the Tantras. Durgā as the one Devī, on the other hand, is one of the five great gods of the nonsectarian, orthodox Brahmanic cult known as Pañcāyatana.

As Hindu thinkers tend to conflate all her forms into a single great goddess, many modern scholars similarly consider these forms to be manifestations of a single archetypal mother-goddess concept. However this may be, it is also clear that most of these forms have distinct historical origins. They derive from a variety of goddesses from specific regions and localities, each associated with specific social or ethnic groups and fulfilling specific cultural functions. Many of the major terrifying forms of the Goddess, such as Durgā, seem to have arisen among semi-hinduized tribes such as the Śabaras and Pulindas and retain these associations in classical texts. Local forms of goddesses of disease, such as the goddesses of smallpox, may also have contributed to the evolution of these terrifying forms.

Durgā Mahiṣamardinī is popular especially in Bengal and Bihar in the east and in Tamil Nadu in the south. Her great festival is the Durgotsava, or Durgā Pūjā, also called Navarātra, celebrated during the first ten days of the waxing fortnight of the autumn month Āśvina. Clay images of Durgā are made and presented with varied offerings. Formerly many buffalo and goats were sacrificed to her, but this practice has been gradually dying out. Recitations of the *Devīmāhātmya* also play an important part in the festival. On the "Victorious Tenth Day" (Vijayadaśamī) the images are paraded to a river or tank. Now considered lifeless, they are deposited in the water.

[*See also* Goddess Worship, *article on* The Hindu Goddess.]

BIBLIOGRAPHY

The best work on the historical evolution of the Goddess is J. N. Tiwari's *Studies in Goddess Cults in Northern India* (Canberra, 1971). Also useful is M. C. P. Srivastava's *Mother Goddess in Indian Art, Archaeology and Literature* (Delhi, 1979). Translations of the basic myths from Sanskrit sources are easily found in Wendy Doniger O'Flaherty's *Hindu Myths: A Sourcebook* (Baltimore, 1975). Tamil myths are discussed in David Shulman's "The Murderous Bride: Tamil Versions of the Myth of Devī and the Buffalo-Demon," *History of Religions* 16 (1976): 120–146. A detailed description of the Durgā Pūjā festival appears in P. V. Kane's *History of Dharmaśāstra*, 2d ed., rev. & enl., vol. 5 (Poona, 1975).

DAVID N. LORENZEN

DURKHEIM, ÉMILE (1858–1917), French sociologist. Durkheim, a rabbi's son, was born in Épinal, Lorraine, and studied at the École Normale Supérieure. He taught from 1887 to 1902 at the University of Bordeaux and thereafter at the University of Paris, where he became an extremely influential figure. As a full professor from 1906, he was responsible for the training of schoolteachers, and he saw sociology as central to establishing a secular moral foundation for the Third Republic; to this end his sociological teaching was introduced into France's *écoles normales.* Within the university system, his influence as patron and prophet was great. Durkheimian sociology prevailed until the 1930s and has had much influence over historians, ethnologists, and other specialists. His ideas have had a shaping influence on sociology and social anthropology, and his later work on the sociology of religion has been of particular importance.

From his first major work, *De la division du travail social: Étude sur l'organisation des sociétés supérieures* (1893), he wrote and lectured on a wide range of subjects, including suicide, the family, crime and punishment, legal and political sociology, the history of socialism, the history of education, primitive classification, and the sociology of morality, knowledge, and religion. He also founded and edited the remarkable journal *L'année sociologique,* of which twelve fat volumes appeared between 1898 and 1913. He and his collaborators contributed monographs to the journal in which they critically surveyed relevant writings in many languages and disciplines with the aim of establishing sociology as a synthetic and systematic field with its own distinctive subject matter—the social—and its own methods. Sociology would transform existing specialisms and imbue them with a new spirit. The Durkheimian enterprise was the systematic exploration of the limits of social determination. The sociology of religion both exemplified and was central to this enterprise: religion contained "from the very beginning, even if in an indistinct state, all the elements which . . . have given rise to the various manifestations of collective life" (preface to vol. 2 of *L'année sociologique*).

Durkheim's earlier works treated religion only incidentally, seeing it as typifying earlier stages of social development and "mechanical solidarity." By his own account, it was in 1895 that he achieved a clear view of the central role of religion in social life and saw how to study religion sociologically. This reorientation resulted from his studies of religious history, notably the works of W. Robertson Smith and his school (which in turn was influenced by Durkheim's early mentor, N. D. Fustel de Coulanges). From these studies he drew both an overall perspective on religion (as consisting of institutions and practices, relating it to social integration and contrasting it with magic as secondary and derivative) and particular theses (concerning the clan cult of totemism as the earliest and most elementary form of religion, the social functions of totemic rituals, and the central idea of the divinization of the community). To Durkheim all this was a revelation when set beside the illusionist and psychological theories of the time. His first work in this field, "De la définition des phénomènes religieux" (1899), set out an agenda for the sociology of religion: since religious beliefs and practices involve conformity to society's moral power, the sociology of religion must study the social forces that dominate the believer and the conditions of existence that evoke religious sentiments, determine their form of expression, and are in turn affected by them.

Durkheim's theory of religion reached full maturity with his immersion in English and American ethnographic studies of Australian Aborigines and North American Indians. The material on Australian totemism seemed to offer evidence of the most primitive and simple religion that it is possible to find, with the American material allegedly providing evidence of its evolutionary development.

Durkheim thought he was dealing with the "most primitive" form of religion, but he failed to distinguish between cultural and structural simplicity and evolutionary priority. However, his interest was not in the question of origins but rather in discovering the "ever-present causes on which the most essential forms of religious thought and practice depend," using the Australian material as a "crucial experiment" to validate a general theory of religion. He assumed that here the constituent elements of religion would be especially visible, thereby revealing the "most essential elements" of the religious life. He further assumed that religion, though illusory, was not purely so, but was based on reality and expressed it: the task of the sociology of religion was to explain whence these realities expressed by religion "come and what has been able to make men represent them under this singular form which is peculiar to religious thought." In his masterpiece, *Les formes élémentaires de la vie religieuse: Le système totémique en Australie* (1912; translated into English as *The Elementary Forms of the Religious Life*, 1915), he developed this view of religion and advanced a number of claims.

Religion he defined as "a unified system of beliefs and practices relative to sacred things, that is, things set apart and forbidden—beliefs and practices which unite into one single moral community . . . all those who adhere to them" (*Elementary Forms*, p. 47). About religion, thus defined, he made three distinguishable claims.

1. The first was causal: religious beliefs, ritual practices, and sacred beings, the creations of collective thought, are generated and recreated in periods of intense collective effervescence. More generally, they are socially determined, reflecting the social structures within which they arise—as are the fundamental categories of thought itself (space, time, cause, class, totality, and so on), which are themselves of religious origin.

2. The second claim was interpretative: religion is a special way of representing social realities. This claim took two forms, cognitive and expressive. According to the first, religion is a way of comprehending reality (especially social reality), a "first explanation of the world," a kind of mythological sociology. According to the second, it is a way of symbolizing and dramatizing social relationships, so that the totem is the "flag" or "rallying sign" of the clan, and religious ritual and imagery a medium of mutual awareness.

3. The third claim was functional: religion perpetually makes and remakes the collectivity, by strengthening the bonds attaching the individual to society. It maintains the indispensable conditions of social, and therefore individual, life. It was thus that Durkheim could both assert the universal, indispensable integrative functions of religion, as cult and faith, and foresee its cognitive supersession by the scientific understanding of the world (and especially the human world, under the aegis of sociology).

This theory of religion has been subjected to many criticisms, many of them compelling—ethnographic, methodological, logical, and theoretical. Yet *Les formes élémentaires* remains a classic—not so much as a study in Australian ethnology or even as an exposition of a general theory of religion, but rather as a rich mine of ideas, not all fully exploited as yet by those engaged in the sociology of religion and of thought.

BIBLIOGRAPHY

Works by Durkheim

"De la définition des phénomènes religieux." *L'année sociologique* 2 (1897–1898): 1–28. Durkheim's first, rather formal, attempt to define the scope of the sociology of religion. Available in English translation in *Durkheim on Religion*, cited below.

"De quelques formes primitives de classification: Contribution à l'étude des représentations collectives." *L'année sociologique* 6 (1901–1902): 1–72. The classic statement of Durkheim's sociology of knowledge, later incorporated into *The Elementary Forms*. Translated by Rodney Needham as *Primitive Classification* (Chicago, 1963), with an introduction by Needham.

Les formes élémentaires de la vie religieuse: Le système totémique en Australie. Paris, 1912. The most systematic and mature statement of Durkheim's sociology of religion. Translated by Joseph Ward Swain as *The Elementary Forms of the Religious Life: A Study in Religious Sociology* (New York, 1915).

Durkheim on Religion: A Selection of Readings with Bibliographies and Introductory Remarks. Edited by W. S. F. Pickering. Boston, 1975. A most useful collection of articles and extracts by Durkheim and critical pieces by other authors.

Works about Durkheim

Evans-Pritchard, E. E. *Theories of Primitive Religion.* Oxford, 1965. Contains a magisterial, if rather negative, evaluation of Durkheim by the great British social anthropologist upon whom his influence was considerable.

Gennep, Arnold van. *L'état actuel du problème totémique.* Paris, 1920. A splendid, ethnographically informed critique by the great folklorist.

Lukes, Steven. *Emile Durkheim, His Life and Work: A Historical and Critical Study* (1972). Reprint, Stanford, 1985. Contains an extensive discussion of Durkheim's sociology of religion and the criticisms to which it has been subject; the reprinted edition contains a new preface by the author.

Parsons, Talcott. "Durkheim on Religion Revisited: Another Look at *The Elementary Forms of the Religious Life*." In *Beyond the Classics? Essays in the Scientific Study of Religion*, edited by Charles Y. Glock and Phillip E. Hammond. New York, 1973. An interesting, late statement of Parsons's influential and controversial view of Durkheim.

Stanner, W. E. H. "Reflections on Durkheim and Aboriginal Religion." In *Social Organisation: Essays Presented to Raymond Firth,* edited by Maurice Freedman. London, 1967. An admirable critique, both theoretical and empirical. Reprinted in *Durkheim on Religion,* cited above.

Tiryakian, Edward A. "Durkheim's 'Elementary Forms' as 'Revelation.'" In *The Future of the Sociological Classics,* edited by Buford Rhea. London, 1981. An interesting and provocative interpretation.

STEVEN LUKES

DUṬṬHAGĀMAṆĪ ("Gāmaṇī the wicked"), prince of a minor Sinhala kingdom who unified Sri Lanka as a Buddhist polity and ruled the island as overlord for twenty-four years (c. 161–137 BCE). In a manner characteristic of the rulers of classical India, Duṭṭhagāmaṇī marked his position as overload by constructing numerous religious monuments and with great donative ceremonies (*mahādānas*) for the Buddhist monastic order.

Duṭṭhagāmaṇī established his polity through a series of military campaigns against the Sinhala and Tamil rulers of other minor kingdoms. His polity was fragile, however, maintained more by an ability to coerce than by administrative institutions; it collapsed soon after his death. The image of Duṭṭhagāmaṇī was more enduring. It provided a model of the ideal Buddhist king and the ideal layman, who have the responsibility to protect and promote Buddhist institutions materially, for which spiritual benefits accrue.

The image of Duṭṭhagāmaṇī was embellished in a folk epic tradition that extolled his virtues as a pious king and his exploits as a warrior. This epic tradition was the source for the many versions of the Duṭṭhagāmaṇī story found in the Sri Lankan monastic chronicles and in later Sinhala literature. The classic version is found in the *Mahāvaṃsa,* the most important of the chronicles.

The qualities of piety and violence—antithetical in canonical Buddhist ethics—are woven together in the *Mahāvaṃsa*'s account of Duṭṭhagāmaṇī's military campaign to become overlord. He declares that his battles are "for the sake of the *sāsana* [i.e., Buddhism]" and "not for the pleasures of sovereignty." He goes into battle with monks in his army and a relic of the Buddha on his spear. The dramatic climax comes with Duṭṭhagāmaṇī's single combat with the Tamil king Eḷāra, who, while described as a just and righteous ruler, is judged by the *Mahāvaṃsa* as unfit to be overlord because he was not a Buddhist.

All versions of the story give prominence to the pious deeds done by Duṭṭhagāmaṇī after he became overlord. The *Mahāvaṃsa* says that, in addition to his construction of monuments (including the Great Stupa at Anuradhapura) and his many donations to the monastic order, he gifted sovereignty over the island to the relics of the Buddha, a sign of Sri Lanka's identity as a Buddhist polity. As a result of these meritorious deeds, we are told, he has been reborn in the Tusita (Skt., Tuṣita) heaven, and in the future will be reborn as a chief disciple of the next Buddha, Metteyya.

A crucial element in the story is Duṭṭhagāmaṇī's remorse over the killing done in battle, a motif that recalls Aśoka, the first Buddhist imperial ruler. A delegation of enlightened monks (*arahants*) counsels the king that he has no reason to feel remorse. In different versions of the story, various explanations for this counsel are suggested, an indication perhaps that the counsel itself troubled Buddhists: Duṭṭhagāmaṇī's victims were not Buddhist, and thus killing them was somehow not equivalent to taking human life; his intentions to protect the *sāsana* were good, and would outweigh the evil of his actions; there would be no opportunity for the fruits of these evil deeds to mature, since his rebirth in heaven was assured by his good deeds, and this counsel was given only to comfort his mind.

The folk epic tradition assumed a strong communalist character—specifically anti-Tamil—which became increasingly visible in the later literature. This communalist character has made the Duṭṭhagāmaṇī story a vitriolic element in the political and religious rhetoric of modern Sri Lanka.

The story was an important part of the *dhammadīpa* ("island of truth") tradition, which viewed Sri Lanka as the repository of the Buddha's teaching. It emphasized the necessity of political unity for the island to fulfill its religious destiny, as well as the special and exclusive relationship its rulers were to have with Buddhism.

The Duṭṭhagāmaṇī story has also had a continuing significance in Sinhala Buddhism as a background for interpretation. It has provided a context for resolving conflicts about ethical issues (e.g., whether violence is ever permissible), for elucidating points of Buddhist doctrine, and for legitimizing social and religious charters.

[*See also* Theravāda.]

BIBLIOGRAPHY

The *Mahāvaṃsa* version of the Duṭṭhagāmaṇī story has been translated by Wilhelm Geiger in chapters 22–32 of *The Mahāvaṃsa, or the Great Chronicle of Ceylon* (London, 1912). This classic version should be compared with the later versions found in the *Thūpavaṃsa,* translated from Pali by N. A. Jayawickrama (London, 1971), and in the *Saddharmālaṅkaraya,* a medieval Sinhala prose work, a translation of which is found in *An Anthology of Sinhalese Literature up to 1815,* edited by Christopher Reynolds (London, 1970). A classic discussion of the epic tradition is provided by Wilhelm Geiger in *The Dīpavaṁsa and Mahāvaṁsa and Their Historical Development in Ceylon,* translated by Ethel M. Coomaraswamy (Colombo, 1908). Many of the articles in the collection *Religion and Legitimation of Power in Sri Lanka,* edited by Bardwell L. Smith (Chambersburg, Pa., 1978), consider the place of the Duṭṭhagāmaṇī story in Sinhala "religio-nationalism"; related folk traditions are discussed by Marguerite S. Robinson in "'The House of the Mighty Hero' or 'The House of Enough Paddy'? Some Implications of a Sinhalese Myth," in *Dialectic in Practical Religion,* edited by Edmund R. Leach (Cambridge, 1968), pp. 122–152. An idea of how widely the story has functioned as a background for interpretation in Sinhala Buddhism can be gathered from the many references to Duṭugämunu (the Sinhala cognate of Duṭṭhagāmaṇī) in Richard F. Gombrich's *Precept and Practice: Traditional Buddhism in the Rural Highlands of Ceylon* (Oxford, 1971).

FRANK E. REYNOLDS and CHARLES HALLISEY

DVERGAR ("dwarfs") are an all-male race of superhuman beings in northern Germanic mythology. *Dvergar* invariably live in stones and in the earth. They are artisans in wood and metal and are gifted with magical creativity. To them the gods owe their most precious possessions, such as Þórr's hammer, Óðinn's spear, and Freyr's boat. *Dvergar* were the creators of the sacred mead, the drink of wisdom and poetic inspiration, and they themselves are endowed with wisdom and know the secret names of the elements. *Dvergar* originated asexually, molded from earth or quickened in the blood of giants, and they themselves do not engage in fruitful sexual encounters. In their possession of secret knowledge and their power of the magic chant they show a priestly aspect. *Dvergar* also serve as pillars of the sky.

Dvergar appear also in literature; in these contexts they are depicted as living in earth and stones, to which they may be passionately attached. They provide human heroes with magical weapons and possess powers of healing and enchantment. Only in fiction do we find descriptions of their appearance as stunted and deformed.

Both in myth and in fiction, *dvergar* are shown as servants of a more powerful order, offering their gifts willingly or, sometimes, under duress. Often insulted and mistreated, they sometimes exact revenge. In spite of their skills and their generosity, they are held in low esteem. The Old Norse word *dvergr* ("dwarf") has counterparts in the Anglo-Saxon term *dweorg* and the Middle High German word *getwërc;* but the creatures identified by these terms are less clearly drawn.

Depicted principally in the exercise of their craft, *dvergar* are the mythical representatives of their profession, that is, they represent the mysterious craftsman-priests of early civilizations. They show affinity with the earth-dwelling forces of magical creativity of the Mediterranean regions, such as Ptah of Egypt, Hephaistos of Lemnos, or the Daktyls of Crete.

BIBLIOGRAPHY

The pertinence of the *dvergar* to literature and faith is discussed by Helmut de Boor in "Der Zwerg in Skandinavien," published in *Festschrift Eugen Mogk zum 70. Geburtstag* (Halle, 1924), pp. 536–537. A number of de Boor's conclusions were refuted by I. Reichborn-Kjennerud in "Den gamle dvergetro," in *Studia Germanica tillägnade Ernst Albin Kock,* edited by Erik Roth (Lund, 1934), pp. 278–288. The meanings of the many dwarf names are probed in Chester Nathan Gould's "Dwarf-Names in Old Icelandic," *Publications of the Modern Language Association of America* 44 (1929): 939–967, and in my article "New Thoughts on Dwarf-Names in Old Icelandic," *Frühmittelalterliche Studien* 7 (1973): 100–117. The ritual significance of the artisan in early societies is discussed in Mircea Eliade's *The Forge and the Crucible,* 2d ed. (Chicago, 1978). I have interpreted the Norse figures in relation to the status of human artisans in "The Craftsman in the Mound," *Folklore* 88 (1977): 46–60.

LOTTE MOTZ

DWIGHT, TIMOTHY (1752–1817), president of Yale College and leader of Connecticut orthodoxy. A grandson of Jonathan Edwards, Dwight viewed himself as within the Edwardsean "New Divinity" tradition. But by Dwight's time the Edwardsean "consistent Calvinism" had become an arid scholasticism that denigrated all human activity, or "means," used in the process of attaining salvation. As Harriet Beecher Stowe later commented, the high Calvinistic system as expounded by Edwards's intellectual followers was like a "rungless ladder" with piety at the top and no human way to ascend. "Consistent Calvinist" ministers of early national America alienated their parishioners and dampened religious fervor. On the other hand, liberal moralists of the time were compromising the historic doctrines of the reformed faith and veering toward Unitarianism. Dwight, an important transitional figure in the development of a nineteenth-century American evangelical consensus, devised a practical theology with the avowed purpose of countering America's late-eighteenth-century slide into secularism.

As president of Yale College between 1795 and 1817, Dwight forged his system of theology, which he preached in sermon form, exerting profound influence on a multitude of students who later entered the ministry. With his pragmatic approach, Dwight did not abjure such Calvinist doctrines as depravity, election, or absolute divine sovereignty, but he avoided giving them the effect of rendering humanity powerless in the process of salvation. He laid emphasis on the means by which one can attain piety, accentuating the spiritual potency of an environment saturated in "true religion." In many an emotion-laden sermon Dwight exhorted his students to repent and receive the Savior. In his revivalistic preaching and his enhancement of Christian nurture, Dwight influenced such important divines as Nathaniel W. Taylor and Lyman Beecher, both of whom studied under him at Yale. These men devised the practical, evangelistic orthodoxy that spawned the interdenominational "benevolent societies" and played a major part in spreading the Second Great Awakening. Dwight's emphasis on nurture was later picked up and expanded by the influential Hartford theologian Horace Bushnell, a forerunner of the Social Gospel.

BIBLIOGRAPHY

Dwight's best-known work is his *Travels in New England and New York* (1823; reprint, Cambridge, Mass., 1969). In this four-volume compendium, he comments editorially on the religion, culture, and politics, as well as the geographical features of his region. Republished, the *Travels* has been edited and given an excellent introduction by Barbara Miller Solomon. Dwight's *Theology Explained and Defended in a Series of Sermons*, 4 vols. (New Haven, 1823), went through a number of nineteenth-century editions. It is the best and most comprehensive exposition of his theology. There are three modern biographical studies of Dwight, each of which views his life from a different perspective. Charles E. Cunningham's *Timothy Dwight 1752–1817* (New York, 1942) concentrates on his attainments as educator. It is the most complete biography of Dwight. Kenneth Silverman's work, *Timothy Dwight* (New York, 1969) focuses on the development of his social and political views as expounded in his narrative and epic poetry. Stephen E. Berk's *Calvinism versus Democracy: Timothy Dwight and the Origins of American Evangelical Orthodoxy* (Hamden, Conn., 1974) considers Dwight as theologian and ecclesiastical politician, relating his career to the broader social and religious currents of his time. It contains the only detailed appraisal of Dwight's theology.

STEPHEN E. BERK

DYING AND RISING GODS. The category of dying and rising gods, once a major topic of scholarly investigation, must now be understood to have been largely a misnomer based on imaginative reconstructions and exceedingly late or highly ambiguous texts.

Definition. As applied in the scholarly literature, "dying and rising gods" is a generic appellation for a group of male deities found in agrarian Mediterranean societies who serve as the focus of myths and rituals that allegedly narrate and annually represent their death and resurrection.

Beyond this sufficient criterion, dying and rising deities were often held by scholars to have a number of cultic associations, sometimes thought to form a "pattern." They were young male figures of fertility; the drama of their lives was often associated with mother or virgin goddesses; in some areas, they were related to the institution of sacred kingship, often expressed through rituals of sacred marriage; there were dramatic reenactments of their life, death, and putative resurrection, often accompanied by a ritual identification of either the society or given individuals with their fate.

The category of dying and rising gods, as well as the pattern of its mythic and ritual associations, received its earliest full formulation in the influential work of James G. Frazer *The Golden Bough*, especially in its two central volumes, *The Dying God* and *Adonis, Attis, Osiris*. Frazer offered two interpretations, one euhemerist, the other naturist. In the former, which focused on the figure of the dying god, it was held that a (sacred) king would be slain when his fertility waned. This practice, it was suggested, would be later mythologized, giving rise to a dying god. The naturist explanation, which covered the full cycle of dying and rising, held the deities to be personifications of the seasonal cycle of vegetation. The two interpretations were linked by the notion that death followed upon a loss of fertility, with a period of sterility being followed by one of rejuvenation, either in the transfer of the kingship to a successor or by the rebirth or resurrection of the deity.

There are empirical problems with the euhemerist theory. The evidence for sacral regicide is limited and ambiguous; where it appears to occur, there are no instances of a dying god figure. The naturist explanation is flawed at the level of theory. Modern scholarship has largely rejected, for good reasons, an interpretation of deities as projections of natural phenomena.

Nevertheless, the figure of the dying and rising deity has continued to be employed, largely as a preoccupation of biblical scholarship, among those working on ancient Near Eastern sacred kingship in relation to the Hebrew Bible and among those concerned with the Hellenistic mystery cults in relation to the New Testament.

Broader Categories. Despite the shock this fact may deal to modern Western religious sensibilities, it is a commonplace within the history of religions that immortality is not a prime characteristic of divinity: gods die. Nor is the concomitant of omnipresence a widespread requisite: gods disappear. The putative category of dying and rising deities thus takes its place within the larger category of dying gods and the even larger category of disappearing deities. Some of these divine figures simply disappear; some disappear only to return again in the near or distant future; some disappear and reappear with monotonous frequency. All the deities that have been identified as belonging to the class of dying and rising deities can be subsumed under the two larger classes of disappearing deities or dying deities. In the first case, the deities return but have not died; in the second case, the gods die but do not return. There is no unambiguous instance in the history of religions of a dying and rising deity.

The Deities. The list of specific deities to whom the appellation "dying and rising" has been attached varies. In most cases, the decipherment and interpretation of texts in the language native to the deity's cult has led to questions as to the applicability of the category. The majority of evidence for Near Eastern dying and rising deities occurs in Greek and Latin texts of late antiquity, usually post-Christian in date.

Adonis. Despite the original Semitic provenance of Adonis, there is no native mythology. What we know depends on later Greek, Roman, and Christian interpretations.

There are two major forms of the Adonis myth, only brought together in late mythographical tradition (e.g., the second-century CE *Bibliotheca,* falsely attributed to Apollodorus of Athens). The first, which may be termed the Panyasisian form, knows only of a quarrel between two goddesses (Aphrodite and Persephone) for the affections of the infant Adonis. Zeus or Calliope decrees that Adonis should spend part of the year in the upperworld with the one, and part of the year in the lowerworld with the other. This tradition of bilocation (similar to that connected with Persephone and, perhaps, Dumuzi) has no suggestion of death and rebirth. The second, more familiar Ovidian form narrates Adonis's death by a boar and his commemoration by Aphrodite in a flower. There is no suggestion of Adonis rising. The first version lacks an account of Adonis's death; the second emphasizes the goddess's mourning and the fragility of the flower that perpetuates his memory. Even when the two versions are combined, Adonis' alternation between the upper and lower worlds precedes his death.

The rituals of Adonis, held during the summer months, are everywhere described as periods of intense mourning. Only late texts, largely influenced by or written by Christians, claim that there is a subsequent day of celebration for Adonis having been raised from the dead. The earliest of these is alleged to be the second-century account of Lucian (*Syrian Goddess* 6–7) that, on the third day of the ritual, a statue of Adonis is "brought out into the light" and "addressed as if alive"; but this is an ambiguous report. Lucian goes on to say that some think the ritual is not for Adonis but rather for some Egyptian deity. The practice of addressing a statue "as if alive" is no proof of belief in resurrection; rather it is the common presupposition of any cultic activity in the Mediterranean world that uses images. Besides, Lucian reports that after the "address" women cut their hair as a sign of mourning.

Considerably later, the Christian writers Origen and Jerome, commenting on *Ezekiel* 8:14, and Cyril of Alexandria and Procopius of Gaza, commenting on *Isaiah* 18:1, clearly report joyous festivities on the third day to celebrate Adonis (identified with Tammuz) having been "raised from the dead." Whether this represents an *interpretatio Christiana* or whether late third- and fourth-century forms of the Adonis cult themselves developed a dying and rising mythology (possibility in imitation of the Christian myth) cannot be determined. This pattern will recur for many of the figures considered: an indigenous mythology and ritual focusing on the deity's death and rituals of lamentation, followed by a later Christian report adding the element nowhere found in the earlier native sources, that the god was resurrected.

The frequently cited "gardens of Adonis" (the *kēpoi*) were proverbial illustrations of the brief, transitory nature of life and contain no hint of rebirth. The point is that the young plant shoots rapidly wither and die, not that the seeds have been "reborn" when they sprout.

Finally, despite scholarly fantasies, there is no evidence for the existence of any mysteries of Adonis whereby the member was identified with Adonis or his fate.

Aliyan Baal. The Ras Shamra texts (late Bronze Age) narrate the descent into the underworld of the puissant deity Aliyan Baal ("the one who prevails; the lord") and his apparent return. Unfortunately, the order of the incidents in the several different texts that have been held to form a Baal cycle is uncertain. The texts that are of greatest relevance to the question of whether Aliyan Baal is correctly to be classified as a dying and rising deity have major lacunae at the most crucial points. Although these texts have been reconstructed by some scholars using the dying and rising pattern, whether these texts are an independent witness to that pattern remains an open question.

In the major narrative cycle, Baal, having won the rulership by vanquishing the dangerous waters, is challenged by Mot, ruler of the underworld, to descend into his realm. After some initial hesitation, and after copulating with a cow, Baal accepts the challenge and goes down to the lower realm, whence it will be said of him that he is as if dead. After a gap of some forty lines, Baal is reported to have died. Anat descends and recovers his corpse, which is properly buried; a successor to Baal is then appointed, and Anat seeks out and kills Mot. After the narrative is interrupted by another forty-line gap, El declares, on the basis of a symbolic dream, that Baal still lives. After another gap of similar length, Baal is described as being in combat with a group of deities. As is apparent from this brief summary, much depends on the order of incidents. As it stands, the text appears to be one of a descent to the underworld and return—a pattern not necessarily equivalent to dying and rising. Baal is "as if he is dead"; he then appears to be alive.

In another, even more fragmentary Hadad cycle (Hadad being identified with Baal), Hadad goes off to capture a group of monsters, but they, in turn, pursue him. In order to escape he hides in a bog, where he lays sick for seven years while the earth is parched and without growth. Hadad's brothers eventually find him and he is rescued. This is a disappearing-reappearing narrative. There is no suggestion of death and resurrection.

There is no evidence that any of the events narrated in these distressingly fragmentary texts were ritually reenacted. Nor is there any suggestion of an annual cycle of death and rebirth. The question whether Aliyan Baal is a dying and rising deity must remain *sub judice*.

Attis. The complex mythology of Attis is largely irrelevant to the question of dying and rising deities. In the old, Phrygian version, Attis is killed by being castrated, either by himself or by another [*see* Castration]; in the old Lydian version, he is killed by a boar. In neither case is there any question of his returning to life. There is a second series of later traditions that deny that Attis died of his wounds but do not narrate his subsequent death or, for that matter, his rebirth. Finally, two late, post-Christian theological reflections on the myth hint at rebirth: the complex allegory in the *Naassene Sermon* and the euhemerist account in Firmacus Maternus, in which a pretended resurrection is mentioned. Attis is not, in his mythology, a dying and rising deity; indeed, he is not a deity at all.

All of the attempts in the scholarly literature to identify Attis as a dying and rising deity depend not on the mythology but rather on the ritual, in particular a questionable interpretation of the five-day festival of Cybele on 22–27 March. The question of the relationship between the Day of Blood (24 March) and the Day of Joy (25 March) caught the attention of some scholars, who, employing the analogy of the relationship of Good Friday to Easter Sunday, reasoned that if among other activities on the Day of Blood there was mourning for Attis, then the object of the "joy" on the following day must be Attis's resurrection. Unfortunately, there is no evidence that this was the case. The Day of Joy is a late addition to what was once a three-day ritual in which the Day of Blood was followed by a purificatory ritual and the return of the statue of the goddess to the temple. Within the cult, the new feast of the Day of Joy celebrates Cybele. The sole text that connects the Day of Joy with Attis is a fifth-century biography of Isidore the Dialectician by the Neoplatonic philosopher Damascius, who reports that Isidore once had a dream in which he was Attis and the Day of Joy was celebrated in his honor!

Scholars have frequently cited a text in Firmacus Maternus (22.3) as referring to Attis and his resurrection on the Day of Joy: "Be of good cheer, you of the mysteries, your god is saved!" However, the god is unidentified, and the notion of "cheer" is insufficient to link this utterance to Attis and the Day of Joy. The text most probably reflects a late antique Osirian ritual.

Neither myth nor ritual offers any warrant for classifying Attis as a dying and rising deity.

Marduk. The figure of the king-god of Babylon, Marduk, has been crucial to those scholars associated with the Myth and Ritual school as applied to the religions of the ancient Near East. For here, as in no other figure, the central elements of their proposed pattern appear to be brought together: the correlation of myth and ritual, the annual celebration of the dying and rising of a deity, paralleled by an annual ritual death and rebirth of the king. Marduk is the canonical instance of the Myth and Ritual pattern.

In 1921, F. Thureau-Dangin published the text, transcription, and translation of a Seleucid era text, preserved in two copies, presenting a part of the ritual for the New Year festival (the Akitu) in Babylon. Despite a large number of references to the performance of the ritual in Babylonian texts (although not always to the Akitu associated with Marduk or Babylon) and scattered mentions of individual items in the ritual, this exceedingly late cuneiform text is the only detailed description of the ritual program in Babylon to survive. It enjoins twenty-six ritual actions for the first five days of the twelve-day ceremony, including a double reading of a text entitled *Enuma elish.* Assuming that this reference is to some form of the text now known by that name, the "Babylonian creation epic" as reconstructed by contemporary scholarship, the ritual suggests a close link to the myth. However, not one of the twenty-six ritual actions bears the slightest resemblance to any narrative element in the myth. Whatever the significance of the recitation of the text during the Akitu festival, the myth is not reenacted in that portion of the ceremonies that has survived.

Realizing this, some proponents of the Myth and Ritual approach have argued that the first five days of the ritual were only purificatory in nature, and go on to speculate that the next three days of the festival featured a dramatic reenactment of a myth of the death and resurrection of Marduk. This sort of imaginative speculation gave rise to a new set of problems. There is no hint of Marduk's death in the triumphant account of his cosmic kingship in *Enuma elish.* If some such myth was enacted, it was not the one stipulated in the ritual program. Nevertheless, scholars turned to a cuneiform text that they entitled *The Death and Resurrection of Bel-Marduk.* The title is somewhat misleading. There are sixteen episodes in the text, which appears to narrate Marduk's imprisonment. The text is fragmentary and difficult to interpret, but it appears to be in the form of a ritual commentary in which a set of ritual gestures are correlated to events in a subtextual narrative of Marduk's capture.

For an older generation of scholars, Marduk's imprisonment was equivalent to his death, and his presumed ultimate release represented his resurrection. More recent interpretations have minimized the cosmic symbolism: Marduk has been arrested and is being held for trial. By either reading, such a narrative of the king-god's weakness or crime would appear odd in a Babylonian setting. This caution is strengthened by the fact that the text is of Assyrian provenance and is written in the Assyrian dialect. It is not a native Babylonian text and could have played no role in the central festival of Babylon.

The so-called *Death and Resurrection of Bel-Marduk* is most likely an Assyrian political parody of some now unrecoverable Babylonian ritual composed after the Assyrians conquered Babylon in 691/689 BCE. At that time, the statue of Marduk was carried off into Assyrian captivity. From one point of view, the text has a simple, propagandistic message: compared to the gods of Ashur, Marduk is a weak deity. More subtly, for those Assyrians who held Marduk in some reverence, the notion of his crimes would provide religious justification for his capture.

The notion that the king undergoes an annual ritual of mimetic dying and rising is predicated on the fact that the deity, whose chief representative is the king, is believed to undergo a similar fate. If it is doubtful that Marduk was understood as a dying and rising deity, it is also doubtful that such a ritual was required of the king. Some scholars have held that the so-called ritual humiliation of the king on the fifth day of the New Year festival, with its startling portrayal of the king being dethroned, slapped, pulled by the ears, and reenthroned, is symbolic of his death and resurrection. But such an interpretation ignores both the manifest content of the ritual text and its date. During the humiliation ceremony, the king is required to recite a negative confession: that he did not overthrow his capital city of Babylon or tear down its walls, that he did not insult its protected citizens, that he did not neglect or destroy its central temple.

From one point of view, such a negative confession is ludicruous. What native Babylonian king ever contemplated, much less carried out, such actions? These were the actions of foreign kings (Assyrian, Persian, Seleucid) who gained the throne of Babylon by conquest and desecrated the native cult. However, as with Cyrus among the Israelites, so too for the Babylonians, foreign kings could be named who restored Babylon and its temple. Read in this light, the ritual humiliation of the king appears to be a piece of Babylonian nationalistic ritual rectification: good fortune and continued kingship comes to the (foreign) king if he acts as a pious (native) king would act. If not, he will be stripped of his kingship.

This understanding is made more plausible by the date of the only surviving texts of the ritual. They are all from the Hellenistic Seleucid period, that is to say, from a period after the ending of native kingship and the installing of foreign kings on the throne. The pattern may be earlier, dating back, perhaps, to the time of Sargon II (r. 721–705 BCE), the earliest conqueror of Babylon to adopt consciously the Babylonian etiquette of kingship and during whose rule, for the first time, one finds legal texts guaranteeing Assyrian recognition of the rights and privileges of the "protected citizens" of Babylon. In the present text of the New Year ritual, a set of actions designed to deal with the more proximate Assyrian conquerors has been reapplied to the relatively more foreign Seleucid rulers.

There is no evidence that the Babylonian Marduk was ever understood to be a dying and rising deity, that such a myth was reenacted during the new Year festival, or that the king was believed to undergo a similar fate.

Osiris. In contrast to the other deities considered above, Osiris has a thick textual dossier stretching over millennia. Although the full, connected myth is only to be found in Greek, in Plutarch's *Isis and Osiris* from the early second century CE, the Osirian myth can be reconstructed from the Pyramid Texts of the fifth and sixth dynasties. While the names of the actors and details of the incidents vary, this record is remarkably consistent over twenty-five hundred years. Osiris was murdered and his body dismembered and scattered. The pieces of his body were recovered and rejoined, and the god was rejuvenated. However, he did not return to his former mode of existence but rather journeyed to the underworld, where he became the powerful lord of the dead. In no sense can Osiris be said to have "risen" in the sense required by the dying and rising pattern; most certainly it was never conceived as an annual event.

The repeated formula "Rise up, you have not died," whether applied to Osiris or a citizen of Egypt, signaled a new, permanent life in the realm of the dead.

Osiris was considered to be the mythical prototype for the distinctive Egyptian process of mummification. Iconographically, Osiris is always depicted in mummified form. The descriptions of the recovery and rejoining of the pieces of his body are all elaborate parallels to funerary rituals: the vigil over his corpse, the hymns of lamentation, the embalmment (usually performed by Anubis), the washing and purification of the corpse, the undertaking of the elaborate ritual of the "opening of the mouth" with its 107 separate operations, as well as other procedures for reanimation, the dressing of the body, and the pouring out of libations. Through these parallels, the individual Egyptian dead became identified with, and addressed as, Osiris (perhaps earliest in Pyramid Texts 167a–168a). The myth and ritual of Osiris emphasizes the message that there is life for the dead, although it is of a different character than that of the living. What is to be feared is "dying a second time in the realm of the dead" (*Book of Going Forth by Day* 175–176).

Osiris is a powerful god of the potent dead. In no sense can the dramatic myth of his death and reanimation be harmonized to the pattern of dying and rising gods.

Tammuz/Dumuzi. The assessment of the figure of Tammuz (Sumerian, Dumuzi) as a dying and rising deity in the scholarly literature has varied more than any other deity placed in this class. For example, within a thirty-year period, one of the most significant scholars in the field, the Sumeriologist Samuel Noah Kramer, has revised his judgment regarding this question several times. Before 1950, Kramer thought it possible that Dumuzi was freed from death; between 1950 and 1965, he considered Dumuzi to be solely a dying god; since 1966, he has been willing to speak again of the "death and resurrection" of Dumuzi.

The ritual evidence is unambiguously negative. During the summer month of Tammuz, there was a period of wailing and lamentation for the dead deity. A substantial number of cultic hymns of mourning, going back to the second millennium BCE, have been recovered; by the sixth century BCE, the ritual was practiced in Jerusalem (*Ez.* 8:14); in Syria, it is witnessed to as late as the fifth century CE and, in variations, persisted through medieval times. If third-century Christian authors are to be trusted, the figure of Tammuz interacted with that of Adonis in Asia Minor. In all of these varied reports, the character of the ritual is the same. It is a relentlessly funereal cult. The young Tammuz is dead, and he is mourned. His life was life that of the shoot of a tender plant. It grows quickly and then withers away. It was a life which is "no more"—a persistent refrain in the lamentations. There is no evidence for any cultic celebration of a rebirth of Tammuz apart from late Christian texts where he is identified with Adonis.

Given the predilection of scholars concerned with Christian origins for a pre-Christian pattern of dying and rising deities, it comes as no surprise that, despite the lack of cultic evidence, it was widely supposed that the period of mourning for Tammuz must have been followed by a festival of rejoicing. This speculative conclusion seemed to gain support with the publication of the Akkadian *Descent of Ishtar* from the library of Ashurbanipal in Nineveh. The text narrates the descent of the goddess into the underworld and her return. However, the concluding nine lines of the text contain a series of enigmatic references to Tammuz, Ishtar's youthful lover, in the land of the dead. Although the text nowhere mentions it, scholars supposed that the purpose of Ishtar's descent was to bring Tammuz up. If so, this would place Tammuz securely within the dying and rising pattern.

Even on the basis of the Akkadian text alone, such an interpretation is unlikely. There is no connection stated in the text between Ishtar's descent and Tammuz. (Indeed, some scholars have suggested that the last lines referring to Tammuz were originally independent and added to the *Descent* as a scribal gloss). Even more detrimental to the dying and rising hypothesis, the actions performed on Tammuz in these three strophes are elements from the funeral ritual. Ishtar is treating Tammuz as a corpse. Finally, the line rendered in the earlier translations as "on the day when Tammuz comes up" has been shown to be a mistranslation. It either refers to Tammuz greeting Ishtar (i.e., coming up to her) in the underworld, or it is a reference to the month Tammuz. In the Akkadian version, Tammuz is dead and remains so. Such an understanding is witnessed to in other Akkadian texts. For example, in the *Epic of Gilgamesh* (6.46–50), the hero insults and scorns Ishtar, reminding her that all her previous lovers—Tammuz heads the list—have died as a result of their relationship to her.

Such considerations seemed to become purely academic with the publication of the Sumerian prototype of the Akkadian text, *Inanna's Descent to the Netherworld* (Inanna is the Sumerian form of Ishtar) and the closely related *Death of Dumuzi*. These early texts made clear that the goddess did not descend to the realm of the dead to rescue her consort. Rather it was her descent that was responsible for his death.

Inanna, the queen of heaven, sought to extend her power over the underworld, ruled by her sister, Ereshkigal. As in the Akkadian text, Inanna descends through seven gates, at each removing an article of clothing or royal regalia until, after passing through the seventh gate, she is naked and powerless. She is killed and her corpse hung on a hook. Through a stratagem planned before her descent, she is revived, but she may not return above unless she can find a substitute to take her place. She reascends, accompanied by a force of demons who will return her to the land of the dead if she fails. After allowing two possible candidates to escape, she comes to Erech, where Dumuzi, the shepherd king who is her consort, appears to be rejoicing over her fate. She sets the demons on him, and after he escapes several times, he is captured, killed, and carried off to the underworld to replace Inanna. In this narrative, Dumuzi is a dying god.

In 1963 a new portion of the *Descent of Inanna* was announced. Here, it would appear, there is yet a further episode. Inanna, in response to Dumuzi's weeping, decrees an arrangement whereby Dumuzi will take her place for half the year in the underworld and then return to the realm of the living; his sister, Geshtinanna, will then take Dumuzi's place in the underworld for the other half of the year, and, likewise, return.

For some scholars, this new conclusion to *Inanna's Descent* was sufficient to restore Dumuzi/Tammuz to the class of dying and rising gods. Such an understanding is unlikely. The myth emphasizes the inalterable power of the realm of the dead, not triumph over it. No one ascends from the land of the dead unless someone takes his or her place. The pattern of alternation—half a year below, half a year above—is familiar from other myths of the underworld in which there is no question of the presence of a dying and rising deity (e.g., Persephone, as in Ovid, *Fasti* 4.613–4, or the youthful Adonis as described above), and is related, as well, to wider folkloristic themes of death delayed if a substitute can be found (e.g., Stith Thompson, *Motif-Index* A 316; D 1855.2; P 316). Such alternation is not what is usually meant in the literature when speaking of a deity's "rising."

As the above examples make plain, the category of dying and rising deities is exceedingly dubious. It has been based largely on Christian interest and tenuous evidence. As such, the category is of more interest to the history of scholarship than to the history of religions.

[*See also the entries on the specific deities mentioned herein.*]

BIBLIOGRAPHY

The classic formulation of the dying and rising pattern was made by James G. Frazer in *The Golden Bough*, 3d ed., 12 vols. (London, 1911–1915), esp. vol. 4, *The Dying God* (1912), p. 6. Frazer cites a representative sample of the older scholarly literature. A full bibliography, from the perspective of Old Testament scholarship, is supplied in Karl-Heinz Bernhardt's *Das Problem der altorientalischen Königsideologie im Alten Testament* (Leiden, 1961). Günter Wagner's *Pauline Baptism and the Pagan Mysteries*, translated by J. P. Smith (Edinburgh, 1967), offers not only a full bibliography from the perspective of New Testament research but also a brilliant critique of the notion of dying and rising deities.

For Adonis, the old collection of all the relevant texts and testimonia by W. W. Baudissin, *Adonis und Esmun* (Leipzig, 1911), has been partially superseded by Wahib Atallah's *Adonis dans la littérature et l'art grecs* (Paris, 1966). The most consistently critical position toward Adonis as a "rising god" is in Pierre Lambrechts's "La 'résurrection' d'Adonis," in *Mélanges I. Lévy* (Brussels, 1955), pp. 207–240; compare Lambrecht's *Over Griekse en Oosterse mysteriogodsdiensten: De zogenannte Adonismysteries* (Brussels, 1954).

The relevant texts on Aliyan Baal are collected and translated in Cyrus H. Gordon's *Ugaritic Literature* (Rome, 1949) and Godfrey R. Driver's *Canaanite Myths and Legends* (Edinburgh, 1956), both of which reject the dying and rising pattern. Theodor H. Gaster is thoroughly convinced of its applicability; see his *Thespis: Ritual, Myth, and Drama in the Ancient Near East*, 2d rev. ed. (1961; reprint, New York, 1977). Arvid S. Kapelrud is more cautious; see his *Baal in the Ras Shamra Texts* (Copenhagen, 1952).

Hugo Hepding's old collection and typology of sources for Attis, *Attis: Seine Mythen und sein Kulte* (1903; reprint, Berlin, 1967), remains standard. The fundamental work on Attis as a dying and rising god is a series of publications by Lambrechts: "Les fêtes phrygiennes de Cybèle et d'Attis," *Bulletin de l'Institut Historique Belge de Rome* 27 (1952): 141–170; *Attis: Van herdersknaap tot god* (Brussels, 1962); and *Attis en het feest der Hilariën* (Amsterdam, 1967).

For Marduk, the text of the New Year ritual is available in English translation by A. Sachs as "Temple Program for the New Year's Festival at Babylon," in *Ancient Near Eastern Texts relating to the Old Testament*, 2d ed., edited by J. B. Pritchard (Princeton, 1955), pp. 331–334. The *Death and Resurrection of Bel-Marduk* is available in a less adequate translation by Stephen H. Langdon: *The Babylonian Epic of Creation* (Oxford, 1923), pp. 34–49. A shorter recension, with an important essay that challenges the parodic interpretation, has been translated by Tikva Frymer-Kensky: "The Tribulations of Marduk: The So-Called 'Marduk Ordeal Text,' " *Journal of the American Oriental Society* 103 (January–March 1983): 131–141. The major critical treatment of Marduk as a dying and rising god is Wolfram von Soden's "Gibt es ein Zeugnis dafür das die Babylonier an die Wiederauferstehung Marduks geglaubt haben?" *Zeitschrift für Assyriologie* 51 (May 1955): 130–166.

The most useful treatment of Osiris, with full critical bibliography, is contained in the notes and commentary of J. Gwyn Griffiths's *Plutarch's De Iside et Osiride* (Cardiff, 1970). The newest material on Dumuzi and Inanna, with bibliography for the older, is found in Samuel Noah Kramer's *The Sacred Mar-*

riage Rite: Aspects of Faith, Myth, and Ritual in Ancient Sumer (Bloomington, Ind., 1969). Kramer and Diane Wolkstein's *Inanna* (New York, 1983) provides a highly literary translation.

JONATHAN Z. SMITH

DYNAMISM. In philosophy, dynamism is "the system, theory, or doctrine which seeks to explain the phenomena of the universe by some immanent force or energy" *(Oxford English Dictionary)*. In the study of religion, dynamism is the theoretical viewpoint that finds a universal, immanent force or energy underlying—either logically or chronologically—all religious (and/or magical) beliefs, practices, and forms of association. This viewpoint has also been known as animatism, preanimism, dynamistic preanimism, and, very occasionally, predeism.

Religious dynamism received its most precise theoretical formulation at the beginning of the twentieth century, especially in the writings of R. R. Marett, Konrad T. Preuss, and Marcel Mauss. It contributed to the waning of the evolutionistic animism then prevalent and exerted a great deal of influence on both the study of religions generally and the study of certain cultural areas, but in the end it succumbed to criticism. In its classic form it finds no advocates today. Some of its elements, however, persist with varying degrees of vitality.

Before Preanimism. Dynamism was formulated as a theoretical alternative to other proposed theories on the origin of religion. Its conceptual configurations took shape from contemporary general attitudes toward religion and other human cultural phenomena, from current theories against which it reacted, and from ethnographic data that had surfaced in the nineteenth century.

Nineteenth-century thought on religion was dominated, by and large, by the idea of evolution, its procedures by a historical, generally noncontextual comparison of surface features arranged in logical progression. [*See* Evolutionism.] Each of the several theories advanced along these lines took its name from the stage of religion it posited as earliest: fetishism, naturism, totemism, manism, animism, and so forth.

Dynamism reacted most directly to the view that at its earliest, religion comprised a belief in a multitude of supernatural, personal beings with whom human beings interacted. The most popular such theory, first formulated by the British ethnologist E. B. Tylor in *Primitive Culture* (1873), counted both human souls and independent spirits among those beings, and was called animism (from the Latin *anima;* hence "preanimism"). In developing his theory, Tylor deliberately neglected emotion in favor of intellect. In his view, animistic beliefs were originally explanatory: the belief in souls explained phenomena such as life and death, dreams, and apparitions; spirits formed elements in a full-blown theory of personal causation. A similar theory, manism, proposed by the British social thinker Herbert Spencer (*Principles of Sociology,* 1876), derived all higher religious forms from a belief in ghosts *(manes)*. [*See* Animism and Animatism *and* Manism.]

The work of James G. Frazer stood in a more ambiguous relation to dynamism. On the one hand, R. R. Marett called *The Golden Bough* the greatest compendium of preanimistic phenomena ever compiled. On the other, many of Frazer's interpretations were held suspect. Frazer conceived a stepwise development between religion and magic. In discussing magic, he emphasized external, immutable, and mechanical sequences of events, or laws, disregarding any possible efficient cause. Taboo he saw as a form of negative magic, while religion developed in the wake of magic's failure and posited the existence of potent superhuman beings whose wills one had to propitiate.

Principles of evolution and the common identification of modern nonliterate civilizations with prehistoric culture made the wealth of ethnographic material then becoming available to Western thinkers essential to all middle to late nineteenth-century theories of religion. Frazer's "magical stage" showed that not all ethnographic material fit an animistic or manistic model. For the dynamistic theories, the most important single ethnographic datum was the Melanesian word *mana*, bequeathed to the Western scholarly world by R. H. Codrington's *The Melanesians* (1891). Codrington spoke of *mana* as "a force altogether distinct from physical power, which acts in all kinds of ways for good or evil, and which it is of the greatest advantage to possess and control" (p. 118, n. 1). The American ethnologist Alice C. Fletcher had already spoken of "Sioux" religion in similar terms.

Some writers surpassed ethnography to anticipate features of the dynamistic theories. Apparently writing in ignorance of Marett's proposed animatism, J. N. B. Hewitt noted that a notion of magical potency was common among North American Indians. He suggested that the Iroquois word *orenda* was suited to denote this notion, and on it he based a definition of religion. Hewitt did not openly oppose other theories, nor did he set his definition in the context of further reflections on religion. Nonetheless, his article significantly influenced the development of dynamism on the European continent.

By contrast, John H. King's earlier work, *The Supernatural* (1892), lay in obscurity until Wilhelm Schmidt brought it to scholarly attention. King derived all religion from a sense of luck or chance. But he posited an intervening stage between this initial period and a later, more manistic one, an era of religion centered on nonpersonal, all-pervasive power, such as *mana, wakan* (Lakota), or *boylya* (Australia).

Classic Dynamistic Theories. Evolutionary thought can integrate evidence incompatible with previously formulated developmental schemes very economically by postulating further, formerly unrecognized developmental stages. These stages assume their preferred places at the beginning of developmental series. Insertion at the initial position allows the rest of the series to remain relatively undisturbed and at the same time claims the greatest possible significance for the newly posited stage or stages.

At the end of the nineteenth century, two new theories sought to redress the inadequacies of evolutionistic animism by assigning it a derivative position. One theory, first voiced by Andrew Lang in 1898, argued, mostly on historical-ethnographic grounds, that religion originally centered not on a multitude of spirits but on a supreme creator invoked to explain the existence of the cosmos. The other, dynamism, first enunciated by Marett, combined logic with certain ethnographic data to postulate not a preanimistic superpersonal deity but a preanimistic, nonpersonal power or, as it was commonly called, *mana.* Nevertheless, some dynamists, Marett among them, advanced only cautious evolutionary claims. They saw *mana* as logically primitive but not necessarily as temporally prior to the idea of deity.

In addition to the common emphasis on power as constitutive of religion, dynamistic theories shared several other characteristics. First, they denigrated the mental abilities of peoples at the dynamistic stage (the primitives). On the one hand, most abandoned the intellectualist orientation and considered religion a matter not so much of individual belief as of collective processes and actions prompted by collective emotion. Whether emotionalist or not, they generally denied that primitives were capable of, or interested in, the causal thought that Tylor and Frazer required of them. On the other hand, those who spoke of a universally pervasive power were forced to admit that primitives did not clearly conceive of power as such. These scholars often claimed to work out logically the notion of power implicit in primitive speech and action.

Second, dynamistic theories softened the sharp distinction between religion and magic that Frazer, among others, had postulated. The force underlying religious and magical practices was identical. In addition, dynamists usually balked when others based the separation of religion and magic on a distinction between coercion and propitiation. In their view, religious and magical acts alike could be coercive, propitiatory, or both simultaneously. When a distinction was made, dynamists tended instead to distinguish magic from religion—not altogether satisfactorily—on grounds of the agent's moral or social position (good versus bad intent, communal versus individual acts). Third, dynamistic theories envisioned taboos not as the result of cognitive imaginings about causal processes but as a reaction to immanent but fearful power.

By definition, dynamistic theories equate power with the beginning or most elementary form of religion. But the classic dynamistic theories did not all conceive of power in identical terms. For Marett, power was an aspect of the supernatural, manifested as the extraordinary and inexplicable. It evoked emotions, especially awe, that impelled those who encountered it to attempt to establish relations with it. Marett distinguished positive and negative modes of the supernatural: *mana* (the supernatural has power) and *taboo* (power may be harmful; be heedful of it). He imagined development proceeding from the undifferentiated and indistinct to the differentiated and distinct, and for him it made sense to distinguish magic and religion only on a more developed, moral level.

A second view was expressed by Preuss, in his highly influential article "Der Ursprung der Religion und Kunst." For Preuss, "supernatural" and "mystical" carried connotations of the spiritual, the animistic. As a result, unlike Marett, he posited at the initial stage of human development a distinctly nonmystical, efficacious power believed to reside in all objects, both animate and inanimate, and to operate in all activities, both those we consider magical and those we consider natural. Human actions with regard to this power were prompted by the intellect, or rather, by the so-called *Urdummheit* ("primal stupidity") of humanity transcending the bounds of instinct. In Preuss's view, this power was originally differentiated; the idea of a universal, indwelling power such as *orenda* developed late. The gods, Preuss thought, were in origin only natural objects of special magical efficacy. Thus, he derived religion (which he identified with a concern for gods) from the era of magic.

A third view was expressed by Mauss in his *General Theory of Magic.* Unlike Marett's and Preuss's notions, Mauss's power (he called it *mana*) was neither supernatural nor natural, but social and unconscious. Originating in collective emotions and impulses, *mana* consisted of society's relative values and differences in potential. It undergirded both religious and magical practices, which Mauss distinguished only with difficulty, and at the unconscious level it was universal and undifferentiated. But it was not opposed to differentiated representations. It called them into existence and provided a field for their operation. In the realm of magic (on which Mauss's work focused), differentiated representations occurred in three forms: the abstractly impersonal (laws of sympathy), the concretely impersonal (differentiated potentials), and the personal (demons).

Elaboration and Application. In the ensuing years, several writers expressed and expounded dynamistic views. Differences between various notions of power persisted, inherited in part along national lines, but no new major, theoretical positions developed. In England, for example, E. Sidney Hartland synthesized and refined a variety of positions but made no significant theoretical contributions of his own. Alfred Vierkandt sought to refine Preuss's views by prefacing his initial era of magic with a premagical stage and by supplementing the intellectual confusion of subjectivity and objectivity that Preuss saw underlying magic with a similar practical and affective confusion. But these were essentially modifications in detail.

In general, those with dynamistic leanings seemed bent on (rather superficially) conciliating rather than adjudicating differing views of power. For example, Émile Durkheim and Lucien Lévy-Bruhl maintained that Preuss's magical and intellectualist orientations, respectively, differed more in language than in substance from religious or magico-religious and emotionalist views. At heart, dynamism remained the simple assertion that in origin or in essence religion was a complex of acts and beliefs centering on a reified, autonomous, efficacious, quasi-substantive power residing in all objects, whether that power was differentiated or universal, and whether or not the practitioners themselves formed any clear ideas about it.

Dynamistic views influenced many areas of the study of religion outside theoretical ethnology. In these areas, too, different dynamistic heritages were displayed clearly. But in general writers did not appreciate and often did not discuss the different possible notions of power. In attempts to increase dynamism's scope and adequacy, some even took the movement toward conciliation one step further, combining dynamistic views with other theories.

In the human studies, for example, Durkheim linked dynamism above all with totemism. For him, *mana* was the imperative force of society manifested (more or less) as the totemic principle, while the soul was *mana* individualized. Thus, the soul was conceptually, though probably not temporally, posterior to *mana.* Not surprisingly, the philosopher Lévy-Bruhl developed his notion of "primitive mentality" in what came to be a clearly dynamistic context. Lévy-Bruhl thought that the primitive felt rather than represented (i.e., conceived) an all-pervasive, ever-dynamic "essential reality, both one and multiple, both material and spiritual" (Lévy-Bruhl, 1966, pp. 16–17). In the history of religions proper, Nathan Söderblom outlined three constituents of primitive religion: animism, *mana,* and a belief in a primitive "originator" *(Urheber).* Rather more exclusively dynamistic, Gerardus van der Leeuw made power the center of his phenomenology of religion.

Those who reflected more concretely on religion also applied dynamistic insights. Somewhat like Söderblom, Marett's student E. O. James discovered in his study of Australia that the impersonal power at the center of religion was manifested in animatistic, animistic, and anthropomorphic forms even at the primitive level. Summarizing a decade of intense dynamistic influence on North American ethnology, Franz Boas's article on religion in the *Handbook of American Indians* made the belief in magical power, with varying degrees of individualization and personification, "one of the fundamental [religious] concepts that occur among all Indian tribes" (Boas, 1910, p. 366).

Descriptions of literate cultures also found dynamistic formulations useful. John Abbott, a bachelor of Oxford in the British civil service, wrote a lengthy description of Indian practices that interpreted *śakti* as the Indian equivalent of *mana,* manifested in the positive and negative forms of *puṇya* ("merit") and *pāpa* ("evil"). In the second quarter of the twentieth century, H. J. Rose refused to assign priority to either dynamism or animism in discussing the earliest religion of the Greeks, but his treatment of early Roman religion was thoroughly dynamistic, equating the Latin *numen* with *mana* and Latin *sacer* with *tabu.* [*See* Numen.]

On the Wane. The combination of the dynamist viewpoint with others could not forestall criticism. Because awareness of developments in anthropology and the history of religions has always varied, dynamism waned more slowly in some areas than in others. Eventually, however, several critiques devastated the classic dynamistic formulations.

The ethnographic and linguistic critique not only opposed dynamism's genetic or essential universality; it questioned whether the notion of an impersonal, fluid power was at all appropriate to the cultures to which it had been ascribed. For both major areas supplying dynamists with ethnographic material, this critique began in 1914. Paul Radin, reviewing the writings of the Americanists Hewitt, Fletcher, William Jones, John R. Swanton, and Boas, noted the common appearance of personal beings in their accounts and suggested that they had been misled by the North American Indians' lack of concern for a supernatural being's precise form.

After surveying the cultures of several Polynesian islands—*mana* is as much a Polynesian as a Melanesian concept—Arthur M. Hocart contradicted not Codrington's accounts so much as the theorists' allegations that *mana* was nonpersonal and constantly evoked an emotional response. Radin characterized North American religions as "Tylorian animism"; Hocart declared *mana* to be "out and out spiritualistic." Later scholars would modify both characterizations.

A second critique, the historical, did not question dynamistic interpretations of *mana* but did doubt *mana*'s place as the foundation of all religion. Nineteenth-century evolutionary thought had been content to establish developmental stages from a logic of forms. The early twentieth century witnessed efforts to establish the connections among nonliterate societies historically. When applied to Oceania, both Schmidt's culture-historical approach and A. Capell's historical linguistics led to the conclusion that, far from being primary, *mana* actually belonged to the youngest cultural stratum.

A third critique addressed the presupposed orientation of religious beliefs and practices that underlay dynamistic views. This took two forms, structural-functional and semantic-symbolic. With Preuss, many dynamists held that all behavior was actual and effective, directly aimed at fostering life. Symbolism arose only when acts that had been conservatively preserved were no longer believed to be actually efficacious. Structural functionalists rejected the dynamists' assimilation of religious acts to technical acts and looked not to purpose but to hidden function in explaining ritual's preservation. Bronislaw Malinowski conceived of religious observances as the "cement of the social fabric" (Malinowski, 1948, p. 50), magic as the result of a psychophysiological mechanism to allay anxieties in the face of dangerous human impotence. Because magical power resided in human beings, Malinowski felt that any theory seeking the essence of magic in a power of nature *(mana)* was totally misdirected. A. R. Radcliffe-Brown sought to avoid the distinction between magic and religion and saw rituals as expressions of common sentiments essential to an orderly social life, but he felt no compulsion to reduce common social values and sentiments to a reified, efficacious power.

The roots of the semantic-symbolic critique lay in the aftermath of World War I. Europe's search for meaning revitalized the symbol, first among theologians, philosophers, and litterateurs, later among historians of religions, anthropologists, and other students of humanity. In a critique of preanimism and certain animistic and theistic notions, the German anthropologist Adolf E. Jensen completely reversed Preuss's notion. In Jensen's view, practices arise as semantically full expressions. Over time, symbolic contexts change and a state of application sets in. Practices then become semantically depleted. They are conceived as some variety of purposive act. Thus, both structural-functional and semantic-symbolic critiques relegated to the interpretive sidelines the purposive orientation on which dynamistic notions were based.

Dynamism lingered longest, it seems, in discussions of Roman religion. In contrast to the situation at the turn of the century, classics and anthropology were not closely related after World War I. In a critique of H. J. Rose, Georges Dumézil employed each of the three arguments leveled at classic dynamism. Citing the practice of baptism, Dumézil warned scholars not to mistake symbolic acts for efficacious ones. He intensively examined rituals, sayings, and terms such as *numen* to show the extent to which dynamistic interpretations strain the evidence. Finally, he noted that personal gods were inherited from the time of the Indo-European migrations; hence it made no historical sense to posit a strictly Roman predeistic period.

Dispersed Remnants. Today, classic theories of dynamism exert virtually no influence in the study of religion or anthropology. Descriptive failures and the results and limits of historical work have contributed to the disregard not only of dynamism but of all evolutionary theories. Furthermore, the semantic-symbolic view of religion that dominates at present, again in combination with descriptive failings, has made dynamism's nonevolutionary side unappealing. Nonetheless, several dynamistic elements, now removed from their former theoretical context, float dispersed throughout the study of religion.

Of these, the least important is probably the name about which the theories congealed. *Dynamism* (often used in the plural, *dynamisms*) now refers blandly to the changes characteristic of religious phenomena. In this usage, change has lost its purposive, effective character and arouses no desire to identify an efficient cause. Some scholars, such as Ugo Bianchi, use the term in combating what they see as a falsely static view of religion, promoted particularly by phenomenological investigations (*The History of Religions*, Leiden, 1975). But in such a case, the term *dynamism(s)* refers to a characteristic of the metaphysical background against which all religious phenomena necessarily stand forth. It says little about religion itself.

More important are the continuing investigations of the original ethnographic materials upon which the dynamists built. Some phenomena still seem actually to permit a quasidynamistic interpretation. Of impersonal power, Åke Hultkrantz writes, "*Orenda* is one of the most convincing proofs of such a conception that can be found" (Hultkrantz, 1983, p. 39). But later dynamists, such as Hartland, had already recognized that *mana* could not be adequately described as impersonal. More recently, Julian Pitt-Rivers has built especially on fieldwork by Raymond Firth in interpreting *mana* in the light of political anthropology, as exemplifying the sacred dimension that must be included in any comparative study of political power.

Perhaps most important, however, is the notion of power in the study of religion. Even such a convinced symbolist as Mircea Eliade has stated that "every hierophany is a kratophany" (Eliade, 1960, p. 126). Eliade interprets power ontologically. For him it refers to what is real (sacred) and "therefore efficacious, fecund, fertile" (p. 129). Eliade also cautions students of religion to keep several points in mind: the particular conception of power denoted by *mana* is not universal; power is not the whole of religion; and kratophanies exhibit differences in degree and frequency. [*See* Power.]

The analysis of religious power requires a more subtle approach than the dynamists ever developed, an approach that abandons the evolutionistic and narrowly essentialistic concerns of classic dynamism and that does not treat power monolithically, as an impersonal, all-pervading, efficacious essence. For years the problem lay dormant, apart from rather isolated comments such as Eliade's. Today, there are signs of an inchoate resurgence of interest in questions of religious power as found in both literate cultures, such as India, and nonliterate cultures. The new interest derives in part from a general reaction to radically synchronic and semantic structuralist interpretations. In time it may gain strength, if a general concern with praxis and power replaces the current widespread concern with meaning, as it has to some extent done already. At present, discussions of religious power are limited to particularist accounts of varying scope, usually informed by some degree of theoretical reflection in anthropology or similar fields. It is impossible to predict whether these discussions will continue to flourish, to what extent they will contribute to a new, general vision of religion, and what insights, if any, such a general vision might share with classical dynamism.

BIBLIOGRAPHY

Surveys of dynamism or of the views of individual dynamistic theorists, more or less extensive, are available in a large number of works written from a great variety of perspectives. The following are, perhaps, most useful or most readily available. Henri Pinard de la Boullaye's *L'étude comparée des religions*, vol. 1, *Son histoire dans le monde occidental*, 4th ed. (Paris, 1929), is an early work but a good bibliographical source that sets "dynamistic preanimism" in a detailed context. Wilhelm Schmidt's *The Origin and Growth of Religion: Facts and Theories*, translated by H. J. Rose (1931; reprint, New York, 1972), is a detailed critique but is limited by subsuming dynamism under the category of "magism," by too facile a distinction between intellectual, emotional, and volitional theories, and by the author's thoroughly polemical concerns. Robert H. Lowie's *The History of Ethnological Theory* (New York, 1937) is sensitive to issues of historical ethnology and "primitive rationality," sympathetic to both Tylor and Marett, but scathing in its attacks upon Frazer. E. E. Evans-Pritchard's *Theories of Primitive Religion* (Oxford, 1965), a more recent account, discusses its subject in terms of psychological theories, both intellectualist and emotionalist, and sociological theories. Jan de Vries's *Perspectives in the History of Religions*, translated by Kees W. Bolle (Berkeley, 1977), is readily available but annoying because it dismisses many theories simply on the grounds that they are "arbitrary." Eric J. Sharpe's *Comparative Religion: A History* (London, 1975) is a useful survey that highlights personal biography as much as theoretical reflection.

Standard works by dynamistic theorists include R. R. Marett's *The Threshold of Religion* (London, 1909), a collection of his most important articles on dynamism; Konrad T. Preuss's "Der Ursprung der Religion und Kunst," *Globus* 86 (1904): 321–327, 355–363, 375–379, 388–392 and 87 (1905): 333–337, 347–350, 380–384, 394–400, 413–419, which builds especially on the author's fieldwork in Mexico; Marcel Mauss's *A General Theory of Magic*, translated by Robert Brain (London, 1972); E. Sidney Hartland's *Ritual and Belief: Studies in the History of Religion* (London, 1914); Alfred Vierkandt's "Die Anfänge der Religion und Zauberei," *Globus* 92 (1907): 21–25, 40–45, 61–65; and E. O. James's *Primitive Ritual and Belief: An Anthropological Essay* (London, 1917). John H. King's *The Supernatural: Its Origin, Nature and Evolution*, 2 vols. (London, 1892), is as interested in modern occultism as in the history of religions.

R. H. Codrington's definition of *mana* cited in the text was quoted already by F. Max Müller in the Hibbert Lectures of 1878 (from a letter by Codrington to Müller). Codrington's views on *mana* were most widely dispersed by his *The Melanesians* (1891; reprint, New Haven, 1957). Subsequently, *mana* has evoked a large critical literature, including Arthur M. Hocart's "Mana," *Man* 14 (June 1914): 46–47; Julius Röhr's "Das Wesen des Mana," *Anthropos* 14/15 (1919–1920): 97–124; F. R. Lehmann's *Mana, der Begriff des "ausserordentlich wirkungsvollen" bei Südseevölkern* (Leipzig, 1922); Ian Hogbin's "Mana," *Oceania* 6 (March 1936): 241–274; A. Capell's "The Word 'Mana': A Linguistic Study," *Oceania* 9 (September 1938): 89–96; Raymond Firth's "An Analysis of *Mana*: An Empirical Approach, *Journal of the Polynesian Society* 49 (1940): 483–510, reprinted in his *Tikopia Ritual and Belief* (Boston, 1967), pp. 174–194 (*mana* as the ability to succeed, and, at the same time, successful results in areas of vital human interest beyond the capabilities of normal human effort and by divine gift); and, of more comparative than ethnographic interest, Julian Pitt-Rivers's *Mana: An Inaugural Lecture* (London, 1974), which discusses *mana* in connection with Mediterranean notions of honor and grace.

Early comments of a dynamistic flavor by Alice C. Fletcher are quoted in J. Owen Dorsey's "A Study of Siouan Cults," *Bureau of American Ethnology, Annual Report* 11 (1889–1890): 434–435; see also Fletcher's article "Wakonda" in the *Handbook of American Indians,* part 2, edited by Frederick W. Hodge (Washington, D.C., 1910). J. N. B. Hewitt's influential views on *orenda* were expounded in "Orenda and a Definition of Religion," *American Anthropologist,* n.s. 4 (1902): 33–46. Other works that interpreted North American religions in terms of impersonal power include William Jones's "The Algonkin Manitou," *Journal of American Folk-Lore* 18 (1905): 183–190; John R. Swanton's *Social Condition, Beliefs, and Linguistic Relationship of the Tlingit Indians,* "Bureau of American Ethnology, Annual Report," vol. 26 (Washington, D.C., 1907), see especially page 451, note c; and Franz Boas's "Religion," in the *Handbook of American Indians,* part 2, edited by Frederick W. Hodge (Washington, D.C., 1910), pp. 365–371. Paul Radin takes these theorists to task in his "Religion of the North American Indians," *Journal of American Folk-Lore* 27 (1914): 335–373. For an assessment of Radin's views, and for a survey of this interpretation of American Indian religions in a broader context, see Åke Hultkrantz's *The Study of American Indian Religions,* edited by Christopher Vecsey, (New York, 1983); see especially "Indian Religious Concepts," pp. 39–46.

Émile Durkheim discusses *mana* and the totemic principle in *The Elementary Forms of the Religious Life,* translated by Joseph Ward Swain (1915; reprint, New York, 1965). Lucien Lévy-Bruhl's notion of the primitive's prelogical participation in a homogeneous world is perhaps most easily accessible in his *Primitive Mentality,* translated by Lilian A. Clare (New York, 1923); his introduction to *The 'Soul' of the Primitive,* translated by Lilian A. Clare (1928; reprint, New York, 1966) quite clearly endows his views on prelogical mentality with a dynamistic slant. For the other authors cited as applying dynamistic insights, see Nathan Söderblom's *Das Werden des Gottesglaubens: Untersuchungen über die Anfänge der Religion,* 2d rev. ed., edited by Heinrich Karl Stübe (Leipzig, 1926); Gerardus van der Leeuw's *Religion in Essence and Manifestation,* 2 vols., translated by J. E. Turner (1938; reprint, Gloucester, Mass., 1967); John Abbott's *The Keys of Power: A Study of Indian Ritual and Belief* (1932; reprint, Secaucus, N.J., 1974); and H. J. Rose's *Ancient Greek Religion* (London, 1946) and *Ancient Roman Religion* (London, 1948).

Critiques of dynamistic views may be found in the later studies of Oceania and North America cited above. In the well-known *Argonauts of the Western Pacific* (1922; reprint, New York, 1953), Bronislaw Malinowski speaks of *mana* as figuring largely in all magical practices and beliefs. Only a few years later, however, in the title essay (1925) of *Magic, Science, and Religion and Other Essays* (New York, 1948), he finds dynamistic theories to be "pointing altogether in the wrong direction." A. R. Radcliffe-Brown discusses clearly his rejection of the search for origins and of culture-history in favor of "meaning" and "function" in the preface to the 1933 edition of his *The Andaman Islanders* (1922; Glencoe, Ill., 1948); for his interpretation of religion and magic, see especially *Structure and Function in Primitive Society: Essays and Addresses* (London, 1952), chapter 7, "Taboo" (1939), and chapter 8, "Religion and Society" (1945). The other critiques of dynamism mentioned in the text may be found in Adolf E. Jensen's *Myth and Cult among Primitive Peoples,* translated by Marianna Tax Choldin and Wolfgang Weissleder (Chicago, 1963), and Georges Dumézil's *Archaic Roman Religion,* 2 vols., translated by Philip Krapp (Chicago, 1970), especially the preliminary remarks and chapter 3, "The Most Ancient Roman Religion: *Numen* or *Deus?,*" pp. 18–31.

For Mircea Eliade's views on power, see especially *Myths, Dreams and Mysteries: The Encounter between Contemporary Faiths and Archaic Realities,* translated by Philip Mairet (New York, 1960), especially chapter 4, "Power and Holiness in the History of Religions," pp. 123–154. Scholars interested in Indian religions are today devoting a good deal of attention to religious power, usually conceived in terms of interaction. Among writings by Wendy Doniger O'Flaherty, see, for example, *Women, Androgynes, and Other Mythical Beasts* (Chicago, 1980). Recent anthropological writings that display an interest in power include Jay Miller's "Numic Religion: An Overview of Power in the Great Basin of Native North America," *Anthropos* 78 (1983): 337–354, and Adrian Campion Edwards's "Seeing, Believing, Doing: The Tiv Understanding of Power," *Anthropos* 78 (1983): 459–480.

GREGORY D. ALLES

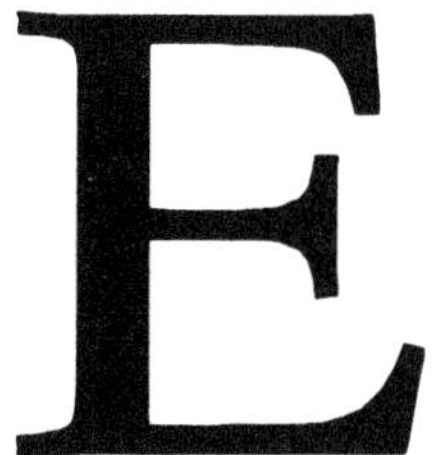

EA. *See* Enki.

EAGLES AND HAWKS. The terms *eagle* and *hawk* can be taken to refer generally to birds of prey, although there is much confusion as to the particular species (eagle, hawk, falcon, vulture, osprey, etc.) in bird symbolism and its description. Eagles and hawks seem to gather their symbolic value from their swiftness, soaring ability, and fierceness; through these qualities they are equated and associated with various religious principles and with deities of all kinds.

The sacred roles of the eagle and hawk in many religions derive from their association with the life-giving and life-sustaining powers of various deities who represent the forces of nature. The Aztec god of sun and war, Huitzilopochtli, is symbolized by an eagle. The sun's efforts to regain the sky from its daily rising in the east symbolize the struggle between the principles of the celestial, or spiritual, spheres and those of the lower world. The sun gods Re and Horus of ancient Egypt, who share similar attributes, are depicted as hawks or hawk-headed men.

A myth of the Iroquois describes how Oshadage, the Big Eagle of the Dew, bears a lake of dew on his back, which brings water and life to the earth after forces of fire have parched all plant life. Assyro-Babylonian religion provides a similar example: the divine lion-headed eagle Imdugud spread his wings after a drought, shrouding the skies in rain-bearing clouds. An Olmec deity, the dragon monster, is a composite of caiman, eagle, jaguar, serpent, and human, a figure that fuses sun, water, earth, and fertility symbolism.

Eagle and hawk symbolism is also associated with death, for the birds often act as the bearers of souls "heavenward." This is true of the hawk in California Indian religions as well as in the religious system of ancient Egypt, where the hawk was itself the emblem of the soul. In ancient Rome an eagle was released from an emperor's funeral pyre to signify the soul departing for the afterlife.

Because of their swiftness, eagles and hawks are the messengers and bearers of the gods. The *Iliad* and *Odyssey* of ancient Greek culture make reference to the gods' use of eagles as messengers. In Eddic mythology, both Freyja and Odin possessed a hawk's plumage that gave them the capacity for swift flight. The swiftness of the eagle Garuda is noted in the Hindu *Mahābhārata.* It was Garuda who stole the soma for Viṣṇu and so became Viṣṇu's mount. In Christianity the swiftness of the eagle's flight associates the bird with prayer rising to the Lord and with his grace descending to man.

As birds of prey, the eagle and hawk are often identified with gods of war and with supernatural malice in general. The eagle was the weapon bearer of the Roman gods and was often shown clutching a thunderbolt in its talons. According to the *Mahābhārata,* hawks are unlucky omens except when they precede a warrior into battle. As Jupiter's bird in Roman religion, the eagle was also a "storm bird," just as the hawk was among the ancient Greeks; both were identified with violent winds associated with the earth's malignant forces.

Eagles and hawks represent divine majesty, the superiority of the intellect over the physical and of the spiritual over the material. Thus the opposition of eagle (or hawk) and serpent represents the domination of baser forces by higher spiritual forces; so also, more generally, does the symbolic equation of eagle and thunderbolt. This principle is found also in such mythical creatures as the Christian griffin, the Olmec jaguar-monster deities, and the Assyro-Babylonian god Imdugud; in Greek imagery depicting a hawk ripping apart a hare; and, similarly, in Hindu imagery of the eagle Garuda and a serpent.

BIBLIOGRAPHY

An early work comparing themes and symbols that are found repeatedly in the myths and practices of many religions worldwide is Ellen R. Emerson's *Indian Myths, or Legends, Traditions and Symbols of the Aborigines of America Compared with Those of Other Countries, Including Hindostan, Egypt, Persia, Assyria, and China* (1884; Minneapolis, 1965). A more detailed study of Semitic symbolism is to be found in Maurice H. Farbridge's *Studies in Biblical and Semitic Symbolism* (New York, 1970). This is a rich historical discussion of Semitic religious and cultural symbols, including a brief but interesting discussion of the use of animal imagery. A very useful collection (with index) of myths representing cultures and religious traditions worldwide can be found in *The Mythology of All Races*, 13 vols., edited by Louis H. Gray (Boston, 1916–1932). E. Washburn Hopkins's *Epic Mythology* (1915; New York, 1969) and William J. Wilkins's *Hindu Mythology: Vedic and Purānic*, 2d ed. (London, 1973), offer extensive discussions of the Hindu epics, with detailed accounts of the various roles played by eagles and hawks. An authoritative discussion of the use of animal imagery in religious and cultural contexts is Jocelyn Toynbee's *Animals in Roman Life and Art* (London, 1973). This work makes extensive use of historical accounts and of the described behavior of animals in explaining their symbolic roles.

S. J. M. GRAY

EARTH. "May the rain-maker water the Earth-Mother that she may be made beautiful to look upon." Thus opens a prayer to Awitelin Tsita, the earth divinity of the Zuni of New Mexico. The chant continues, "May the rain-makers water the Earth-Mother that she may become fruitful and give to her children and to all the world the fruits of her being that they may have food in abundance. May the Sun-Father embrace our Earth-Mother that she may become fruitful, that food may be bountiful, and that our children may live the span of life, not die, but sleep to awake with their gods" (Matilda Coxe Stevenson, "Ethnobotany of the Zuñi Indians," in *Annual Report of the Bureau of Ethnology*, Washington, D.C., 1915, p. 37). Many North American peoples revered the earth and remained deeply impressed by its sacredness. In the first years of the twentieth century, a Cheyenne explained to a visitor, "It is by the earth that we live. Without it we could not exist. It nourishes and supports us. From it grow the fruits that we eat, and the grass that sustains the animals whose flesh we live on; from it come forth, and over its surface run, the waters which we drink. We walk on it and unless it is firm and steadfast we cannot live" (George Bird Grinnell, "Tenure of Land among the Indians," *American Anthropologist* 9, 1907, p. 3).

Native Americans are not the only people to speak of the earth with intimacy and emotion. Throughout history and across cultures, people have clung to their images of the sacred earth. It is worthwhile and necessary to come to grips with these images. In the first place, they reveal a reality that remains veiled in any other terms. Furthermore, the study of the images of the earth bears directly on our understanding of the human condition as it has been plumbed by so much of the human family. In this article we review several important aspects of the earth, seen as a religious condition: earth as the source of life, earth as it appears at the beginning of time, the image of earth as the primal mother, and earth as the locus of regenerative life.

Source of Life. The cosmos is a reservoir of sacred forces. From a religious perspective, the earth is the clearest epiphany of an ensemble of sacred apparitions: soil, stones, trees, water, shadows, vegetation, and the jumbled landscape of the world. These form a single, living, cosmic unity. The soil, the earth, signifies this tangle of concrete vitalities. The earth is the foundation, the generative source, of every expression of existence. From the earliest records we possess of religious history, the earth, united with everything else that is, supports and contains all the life forms that reveal themselves to human beings. Earth is a tireless fount of existence. The lesson that the Cheyenne man taught his visitor is that the religious meaning of the earth remains indistinguishable from all the life that takes manifest form through the powers of the earth: mountains, forests, water, vegetation, and so on.

The Creative Role of Earth in the Beginning. A great number of myths describe a distant time when the earth produced or helped create life in the world. Among the many mythic themes, we call attention to five: androgyny, parthenogenesis, hierogamy, sacrifice, and emergence.

Androgyny: fullness of being. Androgyny is an ancient and widespread image of wholeness. Myths make clear that the meaning of androgyny goes beyond its overtly sexual manifestation to symbolize the perfection of a primordial, nonconditioned state of being. [*See* Androgynes.] In fact, every beginning must start in the wholeness of being. Gods who manifested powerful aspects of the earth, especially divinities of vegetation and fertility, reveal traces of androgyny (cf. Nyberg, 1931, pp. 230ff., for bisexual earth divinities). These sources of holiness and power, such as Attis, Adonis, and Cybele in the Mediterranean world, portray the over-fullness from which life springs. In cosmogonic myths, chaos often represents the perfect totality, the undifferentiated unity, on which all subsequent existence bases itself. In such circumstances, the creative role of the earth is obscure but discernible. The earth exists "in germ."

Such is the case in the Japanese texts recorded in the *Kojiki* and *Nihongi.* In the beginning, heaven and earth were inseparably mingled together. These male and female principles formed a perfect and androgynous totality within an egglike chaos. Eventually a tiny, amorphous island was precipitated out of the chaos. In this island was a reed, a development of the germ that first existed in the center of the cosmic egg. The reed was the first articulate transformation undertaken by the earth; it generated a number of gods. Later, when heaven and earth separated definitively from one another, they took on the human forms of a man and a woman, Izanagi and Izanami. The union of the two separate principles generated the world. When the woman died giving birth to the fire god, the deities of local places, hearths, and vegetation arose from her body. For the moment we focus our attention on the first stage of creation and on the incipient, androgynous being that embraces the sacred powers of the earth. These are not yet clearly defined, but they include all possibilities of life. As such, the divine androgyny in which the earth shares at the most primordial stage of creation is the ultimate ground of the realities that follow.

Parthenogenesis. According to Hesiod, "Earth [Gaia] herself first of all gave birth to a being equal to herself who could overspread her completely, the starry heaven [Ouranos] who was to present the blessed gods a secure throne forever" (*Theogony* 5126f.). This divine couple procreated the gods, the cyclopes, and a slew of mythical monsters, arrogant children with a hundred arms and fifty heads. Although Gaia finds no prominent place in the Homeric Hymns, one of them is addressed to her: "It is the earth I sing, securely enthroned, the mother of all things, venerable ancestress feeding upon her soil all that exists. . . . To thee it belongs to give life to mortals and to take it from them" (*Hymn to Earth* 1ff.).

Ancient Greek traditions affirm that the earth existed before heaven, to whom the earth gave birth by parthenogenesis (i.e., without any male assistance or insemination; for treatment of parthenogenesis among Greek and other Mediterranean goddesses, see Uberto Pestalozza, *Pagine di religione mediterranea,* Milan, 1942, vol. 1, pp. 191ff.). Through such myths the power of the creative possibilities of the earth are portrayed as limitless. The motif of parthenogenesis by the primordial earth reappears in myths that account for all the species of animals and plants as having been born from the body of a primordial being, as well as in myths of virgin birth such as the Greek accounts of Hera who, alone and unaided by men, gave birth to Typhon, Hephaistos, and Ares. Izanami, the Japanese goddess of the earth, gave birth to a number of gods who issued from her own substance.

Hierogamy. Perhaps the most lavish and numerous myths depicting the role of the earth in creation are those that describe a marriage between heaven and earth, a hierogamy. [*See* Hieros Gamos.] Myths of this sort are reported from Oceania, Indonesia, Micronesia, Asia, Africa, Europe, and the Americas. When heaven encounters earth, life flows forth in innumerable forms. The union of heaven and earth is a fundamental act of creation; it generates life on a cosmic and biological scale. The Greek accounts about Gaia and the Japanese myths concerning Izanami show that the views of androgyny, parthenogenesis, and hierogamy are related and, on occasion, even overlap one another. All of these images, which are expressions of a coincidence of opposites, struggle to express the notion of creativity and of the cosmic fecundity of the earth. In the beginning of time, according to the Maori tradition, the sky, Rangi, and the earth, Papa, were locked together in a sexual union. Their children longed for the light of day. In the eternal darkness of their earthen womb, they plotted a way to separate their parents. Eventually, the children severed the bonds that tied heaven to earth and shoved their father into the air until light appeared.

According to Zuni accounts, the creator, Awonawilono, contained all being within himself. At first he existed alone in the universe, but then changed himself into the sun and produced two seeds from his own substance. With these he inseminated the waters. Under his warmth, the sea turned green and grew in size until it became the earth mother (Awatelin Tsita, the "fourfold-containing mother earth"), on the one hand, and the sky father (Apoyan Táchu, "all-covering father sky"), on the other. These cosmic twins embraced in union to produce the countless numbers of creatures. After many complications, the sun and the first ancestors he created managed to free the creatures germinating in the dark womb of the earth. Previously they had crawled over one another like reptiles, hissing and spitting out indecent words. Eventually, when the sky was lifted off the earth, these children escaped along a ladder to freedom and light (Frank Hamilton Cushing, "Outlines of Zuñi Creation Myths," in *Annual Report of the Bureau of American Ethnology,* Washington, D.C., 1896, pp. 379–384).

In myths of hierogamy, a sacred union with heaven, often symbolized by lightning, hail, or rain, is indispensable to the fruitfulness of the earth. It also serves as the model of fruitful human marriage. Hierogamy explains creation from some primordial whole that precedes it. The separation of heaven from earth is the first cosmogonic act, a fundamental shearing of primordial unity. In this widely known mythic drama, the fecundity of the earth with heaven is noticeably absent or sparsely distributed among the peoples of Australia, the Arctic, Tierra del Fuego, and the hunters and herders of North and Central Asia.

Sacrifice. In some myths of creation, the earth appears as a primordial victim of destruction (e.g., through conflagration, deluge, earthquake, petrification), especially through sacrifice, or even self-sacrifice. In such circumstances the fertility of the earth is never suppressed, for from the immolated or dismembered remains spring the species of plants, animals, linguistic groups, or races of humankind. The mystery of the creation of edible plants through the sacrifice of a goddess of the soil or earth was reenacted through agrarian rituals.

Most often, ritual sacrifices associated with the fertility of the soil were symbolic. In some cases, however, we possess reports of the actual sacrifice of living human victims. Such was the case, for example, among the Khonds of early nineteenth-century India. The Khond community, a Dravidian tribe inhabiting the hills of Orissa, a province of southern Bengal, bought a *meriah*, a voluntary victim who lived in the community for years, married, and fathered children. In the days preceding his sacrifice the *meriah* was ritually identified with the sacrificed divinity. The community danced in reverence around him. The victim was led in procession from the village to the virgin forest, the location of sacrifice. Participants anointed him and decorated him with flowers. They called upon the earth god, Tari Pennu (or Bera Pennu): "O God! We offer the sacrifice to you. Give us good crops, seasons, and health" (Frazer, 1926, p. 389). In front of representatives from every village in the vicinity, the *meriah* was slain, and a priest distributed fragments of the sacrificed body. These pieces were brought to the villages and ceremonially buried in the fields. The remains were burned so that the ashes could be spread over plowed fields to guarantee a good harvest.

In connection with the sacredness of the earth, the Aztec of central Mexico also performed acts of ritual sacrifice and dismemberment. When plants first sprouted, people sought the "god of the maize," a new shoot that was brought home, revered, and furnished with food offerings. That evening the new sprout was carried to a temple. The goddess of maize was honored by three different female age-groups. When the crop was ripe, the community celebrated a sacrifice in which a young girl represented Xilonen, the goddess of the new maize. After the young woman was sacrificed, the new crop could be consumed as food. Two months later, at the end of the harvest, another woman, representing the goddess Toci, was beheaded in sacrifice. A priest wore the flayed skin of the victim; another ritual specialist fashioned a mask from the victim's thigh. The masked participant played the role of a woman in childbirth in the harvest ritual.

These sacrifices ritually repeat the creation scenario in which the violent death of a primordial earth (e.g., through flood, fire, or violent self-sacrifice) gave rise to new forms, especially plants. Cut to pieces, the victim's body is identified with the mythic being whose death gave life to the cereal grain. [*See also* Dismemberment.]

Emergence. We have seen how the earth figures largely in the creation of cosmic structures, as well as plant and animal life. A large number of myths emphasize the role of the earth in the origins of human life. As mentioned above in the opening scenes of the Zuni creation account reported by Cushing, the solitary creator became the sun and impregnated the great waters with two seeds from his own substance. These germs of men and of other creatures eventually hatched in the darkness. Pośhayank'ya, the great sage (who perhaps represents the nocturnal sun), then emerged from the foamy body of the earth mother, who possessed four wombs, one on top of another. It was in the deepest of these womb-caverns that all creatures dwelled in the beginning. For the first time, Pośhayank'ya pleaded with the sun father to liberate humanity from the dank and crowded bowels of the earth. In order to deliver the forms of life from the obscure and indistinct conditions of its fertile matrix, the sun father began another round of creation, but this time he aimed to produce intelligent beings who could find their way out of the dark, uterine hold of life-engendering earth. These beings would have the freedom that comes from the knowledge of magical power and ritual.

For a second time the sun father inseminated the foamy earth mother to produce twins. The twins sliced open the mountains and slipped into the subterranean darkness. With their warm breath they hastened the growth of a climbing plant, enabling it to break through to the light above. They then fashioned a ladder from its stalk, thus permitting the creatures to ascend from the lowest cavern into the second chamber. The beings who stayed behind or fell along the way became terrible monsters, creatures of the deep. Step by step, the twins provided the plant-ladder to grow and led the earthly pilgrims toward open space and heavenly light. At each stage, the people grew in wisdom, and humanity multiplied along the way, filling up whatever space was made available in the earth by the twins. Eventually, the twins led out, one after another, six distinct groups of people, the ancestors of the six human races. They emerged on the surface of the earth still bearing signs of their fetal existence in the ground: their toes were webbed and their ears, like those of bats and other creatures of the night, were attached to their heads by large membranes. They could not yet stand erect but crawled on their bellies like lizards or hopped like frogs.

The Caniengas Mohawk, an Iroquois group, also reported that humans once dwelled in the dark womb of the earth, without sunlight and in strange form. One day, during a hunt, one of the intraterrestrials accidentally discovered a hole that led to the surface of the earth. On the surface, this huntsman captured a deer. Drawn by the good-tasting game and the fine countryside, the subterranean creatures decided to emerge into the light of day. Only the groundhog remained in the earth.

Similarly, referring to the Lenni Lenape or Delaware Indians, the nineteenth-century scholar John Heckewelder remarked that "Indian mythologists are not agreed as to the form in which they existed while in the bowels of the earth. Some assert that they lived there in a human shape, while others, with greater consistency, maintain that their existence was in the form of certain terrestrial animals, such as the groundhog, the rabbit, and the tortoise" (cited in Frazer, 1926, p. 427).

These myths of emergence from the earth illustrate to what extent the earth is seen as a mother. In fact, the gestation of the fetus and the act of parturition are viewed as recapitulations of the cosmic birth of humankind and the creation of life in general, when humans emerged from the deepest chambers of the earth. Within the earth humanity lived an embryonic existence; for that matter, all the forms of creation existed as embryos within the earth. All living beings passed through the various stages of development in a "ripening" process that has not yet come to completion. For that reason the fruits of the earth reflect many different degrees of transmutation. Some Indian minerological tracts, for example, describe the diamond as "ripe" *(pakka)*, whereas crystal is "unripe" *(kacca)*, and the emerald, still wrapped in its stone womb, is only an embryo. In the same way, base metals and unrefined ores are not yet fully "ripe," but human smiths and alchemists may imitate, hasten, and complete the powerful functions of the earth mother. [*See* Alchemy.]

This passage from the darkness of unconscious and preformal life to articulate form through emergence becomes a model for many human activities. When cultures wish to create something new, restore something worn, or regenerate a being, they reenact the pattern that was powerful enough to produce life in the first place. The act of procreation and birth of individual human beings in a culture is considered a reenactment of the primordial drama of emergence. The condition of the unborn child parallels the preexistence of humanity in the womb of the earth. Every fetal child relives the primal experience of humanity though its signs (darkness, water, enclosure, larval form, etc.). In other words, because the emergence myth is known, cultures recognize that every individual possesses a firsthand experience of the entire significant history of humanity. The human mother and her fertile powers are brought completely within the compass and sacredness of the great earth mother.

Mother Earth. Across the face of the globe, people cling to the belief that human beings were born from the earth. In some cases, human maternity is believed to result from the direct insertion of a child, an earthling, into a human woman's womb (whether in the form of a seed, an ancestral soul, or a miniature fetus). Up until the moment of its translocation into the human womb, the child had lived an embryological existence in the earth—in a cave, well, fissure, or tree. In Lithuania, for example, children were said to come from springs, lakes, or hills intimately associated with Žemýna, the earth mother, for she alone was responsible for the creation of new beings (Haralds Biezais, *Die Hauptgöttinnen der alten Letten,* Uppsala, 1955, pp. 338–342).

In many societies, the presence of a child in a mother's womb is attribued to her contact with some animal, stone, or other object. Whatever role the father and his sexual union with the mother might play, the fertility of the earth as the primordial mother is directly responsible for human motherhood and offspring. In such a setting of beliefs, human beings are, in a profound sense, people of their native land. Like the first humans in the earth, each new generation of children first lives among the rocks or in chasms. Aquatic animals such as frogs, crocodiles, fish, swans, or storks then bring them and place them magically in their mothers' wombs. Here again, fecund earth, the fertility of cosmic being, is represented by specific fruits or forms that take life from her (e.g., mountains, fertility stones, the waters of grottoes or springs, animals). A human mother simply receives children in their embryonic state. She is a container that helps the larval life of the earth attain a specifically human form. The belief is that the subterranean womb is the true *fons et origo* of embryological life, and once that is understood, the religious beliefs and practices described below make sense.

Memories of life in the womb. The experiences of mystics and shamans may be compared with prenatal existence in the womb of the earth. The primordial dark night of the soul portrays the opacity of subterranean life before emergence onto the surface of the earth. The power of North American shamans, for example, sometimes depends on their extraordinary abilities to remember their prenatal life. The images they recall from life in the womb bear striking similarity to the chambers, fixtures, sounds, and sensations of the subterranean world. [*See also* Caves.] The Guayaki of Paraguay often consult pregnant women as diviners, since their unborn children reveal secrets and truths to them. Fetal children possess the power to know obscure facts because they relive the primordial experience of the divine twins. These, in the first utter darkness of chaos, knew the germinal possibilities of all subsequent life forms and experienced them at first hand, in the darkness, before they pursued their diverse historical destinies.

At times the cultural community longs to return to the womb of the earth mother. The Yaruro people of Venezuela revered their great mother, who lived in the remote area of Kuma in the east, where the dead go. In the late 1930s, the Yaruro expressed the desire to reenter the realm of their mother in order to be reborn into the paradisal existence that preceded life and the arrival of colonial invaders (Vicenco Petrullo, *The Yaruros of the Capanaparo River, Venezuela,* Bureau of American Ethnology Bulletin 123, Washington, D.C., 1939, pp. 226ff.).

Labyrinths. The image of the earth as mother (with openings to the world in the form of galleries, mines, grottoes, and caves) and the desire to return to the embryonic stage of existence in the womb explain why the labyrinth can be an image of the body of the earth mother. The labyrinth, or meandering underground cavern, was an initiatory arena as well as a place to bury the dead. Entering a labyrinth (among other religious motivations for doing so) amounted to a ritual return to the womb of the mother. Labyrinthine caves were the sites of initiation, funerals, and marriages. It is in the fruitful womb of the earth that new forms of life first quicken. The labyrinth dramatizes the difficulty of discovering the past back to the sources of limitless creativity. [*See* Labyrinth.]

Malekula funeral symbolism, for example, describes Tenes (or Le-he-he), a frightening female being who lies in wait for dead men's souls. She stands at the entrance to a cavern; in front of her, outlined on the ground, is the sketch of a labyrinth. As the dead soul approaches, she rubs out half of the design. If the deceased has been properly initiated, he will know the entire outline of the labyrinth and find his road easily to the afterlife; otherwise the woman will swallow him. The labyrinths that one finds drawn on the earth in Malekula teach the living the road to the land of the dead. That is, they provide the living with the initiatory key that enables them to return into the bowels of the earth mother (A. Bernard Deacon, "Geometrical Drawings from Malekula and the Other Islands of the New Hebrides," *Journal of the Royal Anthropological Institute* 64, 1934, pp. 132ff.; John Layard, "Totenfahrt auf Malekula," *Eranos-Jahrbuch* 5, 1937, pp. 242–292).

Agrarian rites. Rites that mark significant moments in the agricultural calendar repeat what happened to the earth in mythical times. The mysteries of how life emerged from a germ hidden in an undifferentiated chaos, or was engendered in the sacred union between heaven and earth, or resulted from the violent death of divinities associated with the soil are reenacted in the rituals of the earth. Agricultural operations in the Andes, for example, are scheduled around the menstrual periods of Pachamama, Mother Earth. Special restrictions are observed at the times when Pachamama is "open," for the life of the community and the cosmos depend on her fertility.

Women usually play crucial roles in the rites associated with earthly fecundity. Insofar as women are symbolically assimilated with the land and insofar as agricultural work is homologous with the sexual act (so that the plow or spade is an emblem of the phallus, for example), women become epiphanies of the sacred power of the earth. The acts of women have worldly significance, for they channel the effects of the earth's ability to bear fruit and modulate its intensity. The Qur'ān declares, "Your wives are to you as fields" (2:223). The *Śatapatha Brāhmaṇa* (7.2.2.5) identifies the furrows of a plowed field with a vulva and the seeds sown in the furrow with semen. These ideas are widespread; they account for the prominent ritual role of women in agriculture. Many communities consider it auspicious if a pregnant woman sows the new seed; it augurs a good harvest, for the crops will grow apace with the fetus. Often women put the seed in the ground cleared by men, or women choose and store reservoirs of the fertile powers of the earth. Agricultural labor keeps one cognizant of the sacred origins of gardening; labor is the vehicle of meaning as well as the vehicle of its transmission from one generation to another.

For example, after the Canelos Quechua women of Ecuador have set a new field, they remain in it with their children and recount episodes from ancient myths about Nungui, the goddess of garden soil, whose power underlies all fertility. The neighboring women of the Jivaroan community also sing to Nungui at the time of planting. Nungui is short, fat, and black (characteristic features of many "dark virgins" or black madonnas associated with the soil). She forces crops to break through the surface of the earth by making them grow. Nungui dances at night in gardens that are well maintained; the new shoots of manioc are her dancing partners. Since plants tend to shrink during the daylight hours, Jivaroan women harvest them in the morning.

In a related ritual Jivaroan women ask Nungui for "babies," three red jasper stones *(nantara)* whose hidden location in the earth is revealed to them by the goddess in dreams. The *nantara* contain the female souls of manioc plants. Women hide the stones in the earth and keep them dark with an overturned food bowl placed in the center of the garden. The stones carry out the role of Nungui's mystical child who, in the primordial past, helped women accomplish all the tasks of farming with a single magical word. The prescribed layout of the contemporary Jivaroan garden and the red "children-stones" hidden there remain as signs of the perfect garden that existed at the beginning of time. When the time arrives to plant manioc seedlings, Jivaroan women gather to sing to Nungui while squatting over the new slips. The woman gardener places the first manioc cutting against her vaginal opening and paints the plant red before placing it in the ground. The identification of the fertility of women with the fertility of the soil is thus complete and direct. When they finish planting the fields, women dance for five nights in a row in honor of Nungui and request that her presence spur on the growth of the plants (Michael J. Harner, *The Jívaro: People of the Sacred Waterfalls*, Garden City, N.Y., 1973, pp. 70–76; Julian H. Steward and Alfred Métraux, "Tribes of the Peruvian and Ecuadorian Montaña," in *Handbook of South American Indians*, vol. 3, New York, 1948, p. 620).

The religious role of women, who are identified with the land, appears dramatically in ritual sexual unions performed in fields or in orgies with which the entire community punctuates the agricultural calendar. With these sacred acts, women and their partners commemorate the union of heaven and earth in order to stimulate the fruitfulness of the virgin soil. Communal sexual frenzy evokes the image of the divine couple during the confusion of the long cosmic night in the period before creation, or in their primal state within the cosmogonic egg. During orgies, the whole community celebrates this return to the undifferentiated state of the earth at the beginning of time. The custom of streaking naked across the earth to provoke the virility of the sky or of the fertilizing rains shows how rites associated with the earth break down the barriers between individuals, society, cosmic nature, and divine forms. The experience of society during orgy is that of seeds and primordial embryos. The community as a whole loses its articulate shape during the period of subterranean merging and disintegration that is an integral part or the process of germination. Individuality dissolves in the orgy, for neither law nor social form is maintained in the total fusion of sexes and emotions. As in the ritual of immersion in water, orgy undoes the structures of the community and identifies human life with the formless, precosmic chaos in the bowels of the earth before creation. Even when orgies are not literally carried out but are only staged as performances (e.g., phallic dances or parades, dancing between series of unmarried partners), the fruitfulness of life derived from the earth depends on the symbolic dissolution of norms through carousing, obscenity, debauchery, insult, or choreographic and choral union of bodies and voices normally held separate from one another. For example, it is in connection with the fertility of the earth that many of the so-called *hadaka matsuri* (literally, "naked festivals") celebrated throughout Japan find their meaning.

Lying on the soil. We have already seen that the conception and birth of human individuals are scaled-down versions of the creative process performed by the earth since the beginning of time. Human mothers repeat that sucessful first act by which life first appeared in the womb of the earth mother. For that reason, at the moment of birth, women from many cultures put themselves directly in touch with the earth and mimic her actions. In this way they partake as fully as possible of her powers and remain under her protection. In numerous societies women give birth in such a way as to deposit the child onto the earth, or else place the child on the soil immediately after birth. In some cases women in childbirth lie prostrate on the ground or move into the forest or fields. "To sit on the ground" was a common expression in ancient Egypt meaning to give birth (Nyberg, 1931, p. 133). Every authentic birth of an Aché of Paraguay repeats the first act of standing upright upon the primordial earth. The Aché birth rites include two moments: *waa*, a "falling" from the womb onto the soil, and *upi*, a "lifting up." The act of touching the earth introduces the child to the biotic condition shared by all animals and plants. By lifting him up from the earth, the mother repeats his transition from amorphous biological form to fully human stature—just as it was obtained by the primordial ancestors when they first emerged from the earth and stood upright upon it (Pierre Clastres, *Chronique des Indiens Guayaki*, Paris, 1972, pp. 14–16). The earth must be the mother who gives birth to every true human being.

Placement on the soil was also an integral part of healing rites. Sick persons were restored to health when they were created anew, remade in the image of the ancestral beings in their primordial situation within the earth. The Huichol of Mexico, for example, when on pilgrimage to Wirikuta, their place of mythic origins, stop by pools of water that open into the creative depths of the earth. The healer asks his patients, especially barren women, to stretch out full-length on the ground, which is the powerful body of the primal mother. The rite of placing a newborn child on the earth existed in ancient China, where a dying person was also set on the soil. The earth represents the powers both of birth and of rebirth to a new existence. The powers of the earth determine whether the transitions of birth and death are valid and well accomplished (Granet, 1953, pp. 192–198).

Death and Regeneration. As a form of regenerative darkness, the earth, in its sacredness and fertility, includes the reality of death. This was clear already in the myths of the sacrifice of a primordial divinity associated with the soil. The death of the god gives rise to life in new forms, especially that of plants. Life and death are simply two phases in the career of Mother Earth. In fact, "life" in the light of day consists of a hiatus, a brief period of detachment from the earth's womb. It is death that returns one to the primordial or eternal condition that existed before the cycle of life began.

Many of the terrifying aspects of the earth mother, in the form of the goddess of death or the recipient of violent sacrifices, are rooted in her status as the univeral womb, the source of all life. Death itself is not annihilation, but rather the state of the seed in the bosom of the earth. This helps explain why the bodies of the dead are buried in fetal positions in so many cultures. These "embryos" are expected to come back to life. In some cases, as stated above, the dead reenact the experience of the earth mother herself, who was the first person to die (e.g., Izanami of Japanese mythology, who died giving birth to fire). In such circumstances, the negative depictions of the earth mother as the goddess of death portray her role in the sacrificial mode of existence that makes passage from one form to another possible. The ubiquitous sacrificial dimension of symbolic existence guarantees the unending circulation of life. "Crawl to the earth, your mother," proclaims the *Ṛgveda* (10.18.10). "You, who are earth I place you in the earth," is a funerary formula from the *Atharvaveda* (12.1.11, 12.1.14). The Kraho of Brazil make every attempt to transport a dying man back to the soil of his maternal village. The inscriptions on ancient Roman tombs illustrate the same desire to rest in one's native earth. The vitality and fecundity of the earth, its sacred power to generate life without end, assures the reappearance of the dead in a new living form.

The rich symbolism of the earth is not exhausted by the cosmogonies, agricultural feasts, or burial practices of archaic peoples or tribal societies. The earth remains a powerful image of the possibility of new life and radically new social existence. In contemporary religious movements of rebellion or revolution prompted by desperate and oppressive circumstances, the earth becomes a focal image of renewal (Bruce Lincoln, "'The Earth Becomes Flat': A Study of Apocalyptic Imagery," *Comparative Studies in Society and History* 25, 1983, pp. 136–153; see also Werner Müller, *Geliebte Erde: Naturfrömmigkeit und Naturhass im indianischen und europäischen Nordamerika*, Bonn, 1972). In the eschatological or utopian visions of new regimes or revolutionary kingdoms the face of the earth will be renewed or the end of the world will intervene to impose a new and just order, symbolized by the leveling of mountains and the filling of valleys. All forms of life, without discrimination, will obtain easy and equal access to the plenteous vitality of the earth.

Cosmic Solidarity of Life. The religious imagery of the earth engenders a kinship among all forms of life, for they are all generated in the same matrix. The intimate relationship between earth and the human, animal, and vegetal life forms inheres in the religious realization that the life force is the same in all of them. They are united on the biological plane; their fates, consequently, are intertwined. Pollution or sterility on one level of existence affects all other modes of life. Because of their common origin, all life-forms constitute a whole. Unlike the sacredness of the sky, which appears vividly in the myths of the separation of the sky from the creaturely forms dependent on it, there is no rupture between the earth and the forms it engenders.

Furthermore, earth protects the existence of life in myriad forms, and safeguards against abuses (e.g., incest or murder) that threaten the good order of reproductive life. Ritual union between sexual partners and orgies celebrated in ceremony are restricted to decisive moments of the agricultural calendar. During the rest of the time, the earth mother is often a patroness of morality and a guardian of the norms conducive to fruitful existence. The earth punishes certain categories of criminals, especially adulterers, murderers, and sexual miscreants. In some cases, as in ancient Greece, the shedding of blood on the earth and incest could render the earth barren, with catastrophic consequences. Thus, in the opening of Sophocles' *Oedipus Rex,* a priest bewails the fate of Thebes because women suffer birth pangs without living issue and the fruits of the earth and the oxen in the fields are dying, as is the city itself.

Conclusion. The earth reveals the meaning and sacredness of life's ceaseless ability to bear fruit. This point comes home strongly in all the images we have examined. There is a tendency for agricultural divinities, active and dramatic, to draw attention from the primordial divinities of the soil. But in all the great goddesses who represent the capacities of agriculture and the fruitfulness of the tilled soil there exists the underlying presence of the earth as a whole, the sacredness of the physical place of life. It is true that the earth often appears in cosmogonic myths as a figure vaguer in outline than the more clearly delineated goddesses of specific crops or particular rites in the agricultural cycle. However, the role of the earth in the earliest stages of mythic history testifies to the abiding sacredness of life itself, regardless of the distinct forms that it may include. The myths of parthenogenesis, of the androgyny of the earth, of hierogamy, of the sacrifice of the primordial earth, and of emergence from the dark womb of the first times affirm the sacredness of the soil. That is, they disclose the meaning of its tireless creativity. That manifestation of the sacred in the form of the soil, whether as a general presence or divine figure, helps make sense of rituals and symbolic forms linked to the earth.

Descents into caves and grottoes, the imagery of subterranean embryos, scenarios of return to a prenatal existence, labyrinths, rites of swearing by the earth, deposition of the newborn on the earth or interment of the dead in earthen graves, the iconographic tradition of black madonnas, and the terrifying figures of great goddesses, as well as the stylized sexual orgies of agricultural feasts return the attention of the religious imagination to one of its most important sources: the inexhaustible powers of the universal procreator of life. Few images have generated such power within the religious imagination or held such a command over it throughout the course of human history. It is possible that the rise of the earth to primacy as a sacred form in the religious imagination was stunted by her sacred marriage with the sky and other male divinities (e.g., storm gods) who are important in agriculture. Nevertheless, the earth, especially in the image of the great mother, has never forfeited her role as the locus of life, the source of all forms, the guardian of children, and the womb where the dead await their rebirth.

[*See also* Nature.]

BIBLIOGRAPHY

Several fundamental works recommend themselves for their comprehensive coverage of the phenomenon, as well as for their insight. Although dated, these studies are still important and valuable: Albrecht Dieterich's *Mutter Erde* (Berlin, 1905); Theodor Nöldeke's "Mutter-Erde und Verwandtes bei den Semiten," *Archiv für Religionswissenschaft* 8 (1905): 161–166; Ernst Samter's *Geburt, Hochzeit und Tod* (Berlin, 1911), pp. 1–20; Wolf Wilhelm Baudissin's *Adonis und Esmun* (Leipzig, 1911), esp. pp. 443ff. and 505ff.; James G. Frazer's *The Worship of Nature* (London, 1926), pp. 316–440; Marcel Granet's "Le dépôt de l'enfant sur le sol," in his *Études sociologiques sur la Chine* (Paris, 1953), pp. 159–202; Henri Théodore Fischer's *Het heilig huwelik van hemel en aarde* (Utrecht, 1929); Bertel Nyberg's *Kind und Erde* (Helsinki, 1931); Willibald Staudacher's *Die Trennung von Himmel und Erde* (Tübingen, 1942); Vittore Pisani's "La donna e la terra," *Anthropos* 37–40 (1942–1945): 241–253; Uberto Pestalozza's *Religione mediterranea: Vecchi e nuovi studi* (Milan, 1951), esp. pp. 191ff.; and Gerardus van der Leeuw's "Das sogenannte Hockerbegräbnis und der ägyptische Tjknw," *Studi e materiali di storia delle religioni* 14 (1938): 151–167.

Mircea Eliade's *Myths, Dreams, and Mysteries: The Encounter between Contemporary Faiths and Archaic Realities* (New York, 1960), pp. 155–189, and *Patterns in Comparative Religion* (New York, 1958), chaps. 7 and 9, deal with earth and agriculture and offer ample bibliograpies. For a discussion of the images of the goddess in relation to the sacredness of the earth, see Andrew Fleming's article "The Myth of the Mother-Goddess," *World Archaeology* 1 (October 1969): 247–261, and *The Book of the Goddess: Past and Present,* edited by Carl Olson (New York, 1983), which deals with the role of the goddess in prehistory, Mesopotamia, Egypt, Greece, Rome, Canaanite-Hebrew culture, in Christianity, gnosticism, Hinduism, Buddhism, Japanese religion, Afro-American culture, Amerindian religions, and in contemporary thought and practice. Bibliographies for these topics are included on pages 251–259. *Mother Worship: Theme and Variations,* edited by James J. Preston (Chapel Hill, N.C., 1982), presents several cases from the New World, Europe, South Asia, and Africa.

Jürgen Zwernemann's *Die Erde in der Vorstellungswelt und Kultpraktiken der sudanischen Völker* (Berlin, 1968) is an example of a study of the full range of earth symbolism in a single culture. A most thorough and penetrating study of the earth is Ana Maria Mariscotti de Görlitz's *Pachamama Santa Tierra* (Berlin, 1978), which examines the history of belief and practice surrounding the earth mother in the South American Andes. Olof Pettersson's *Mother Earth: An Analysis of the Mother Earth Concepts according to Albert Dieterich* (Lund, 1967) redresses some of the hasty generalizations of Dieterich.

MIRCEA ELIADE AND LAWRENCE E. SULLIVAN

EAST AFRICAN RELIGIONS. [*This entry comprises three articles. The first,* An Overview, *explores ideas and practices basic to the traditional religions of East Af-*

rica. The second, Ethiopian Religions, *discusses the religions of particular Ethiopian peoples. The third,* Northeastern Bantu Religions, *surveys the religions of Bantu-speaking peoples in this region. For discussion of the religions of Bantu-speaking peoples in other parts of Africa, see* Central Bantu Religions *and* Southern African Religions.]

An Overview

East African religions do not form a single coherent body of beliefs and practices. They show great diversity in myths and cosmologies and in beliefs about the nature of spiritual powers; in kinds and authority of ritual experts; in the situations when ritual is performed; and in responses to the advent of Islam and Christianity. This diversity is consistent with the ethnic, geographical, and historical diversity of the region. Our knowledge of East African religions is very uneven, and this may also contribute to the seeming diversity.

The total population of East Africa in 1985 was in the order of some 100 million people. The population comprises some two hundred more or less distinct societies, each defined by its own language and sense of identity, its own traditional territory and political structure, and its own system of family relations, marriage, and religious belief and practice. These groups are distributed very unevenly in areas of high and low population densities.

East Africa contains several clearly defined geographical and cultural areas, with an immense variety of societies, languages, and religions. It has been the meeting place of several main language groupings, and its peoples are remarkably diverse in their cultures and forms of economic, political, and familial organizations.

In the northern part of the region live peoples representing several main language families and groups: Semitic and Hamitic (Cushitic), mainly in Ethiopia and Somalia, and three subgroups of the Chari-Nile group of the Nilo-Saharan family—Sudanic, in the far northwest corner, Nilotic in the upper Nile Valley, and Para-Nilotic (Eastern Nilotic or Nilo-Hamitic) mainly in the Rift Valley region. To the south are many people speaking Bantu languages (of the Niger-Congo family). There are small pockets of speakers of other language families (such as Khoisan, or "click," languages in northern Tanzania), and there are of course speakers of intrusive languages such as Arabic and English. In most parts of the region Swahili has long been used as a lingua franca, although in a debased form rather than in its proper form as spoken along the Indian Ocean coast. However, there appears to be no direct relationship between language and religious belief and practice.

The situation is different as regards economic, political, and familial types, and belief and practice are more obviously linked to them. Although there are a few hunting and gathering peoples, such as the Hadza of Tanzania and the Okiek of Kenya, the vast majority of the population consists of mixed farmers, growing grains and keeping some livestock, and pastoralist livestock herders.

A century of European colonial rule over the entire region and the long Arab colonial overrule along the coast have brought about degrees of unity and interaction. Trade and wars have also often linked peoples together in varying ways and degrees. Although East African peoples are traditionally farmers and livestock herders, large towns and urban centers exist throughout the region, from the ancient cities of Mombasa, Mogadishu, and Zanzibar on the coast to the modern cities of Nairobi, Addis Ababa, Kampala, and Dar-es-Salaam. Scattered are many lesser towns that have attracted mixed immigrant populations from the countryside and from which modern Christian and syncretist movements have spread out into the rural areas. Today there are virtually no peoples in the region who are unaffected by Christianity or Islam (although the depth of influence of these faiths varies widely); but traditional local religions remain active in almost every part of the area.

Divinity and Myth. All East African religions have a belief in a high god, the creator. Perhaps the most accurate term to translate this concept here is *Deity.* As would be expected, even though there are variations, in all of them the Deity is attributed broadly similar characteristics: omnipotence, everlastingness, ubiquity, and being beyond the comprehension and control of ordinary living people. The variations lie in the idioms and symbols used to express these features and abilities. These general characteristics are found in the high gods representing all the cosmologies of the region: Kwoth (Nuer; the name also means "breath" or "spirit"), Juok (Shilluk), Nhialic (Dinka), Mbori (Azande), Adroa (Lugbara; the name also means "power"), Ngai (Kikuyu), Kyala (Nyakyusa), Mungu (Swahili), and so on. The names are different, but the divine nature is the same. Usually the Deity is considered to be spatially unlocalized, but in some religions it is thought to be associated with mountains and other terrestrial features, as among the Kikuyu, who state that Ngai dwells on Mount Kenya and on lesser mountains of the Rift Valley area.

The Deity is usually considered remote and otiose: after creating the world it retired, leaving men and women on earth ultimately dependent upon it but pursuing their own ways cut off from divine truth and perfection and with a memory of a primeval paradise that

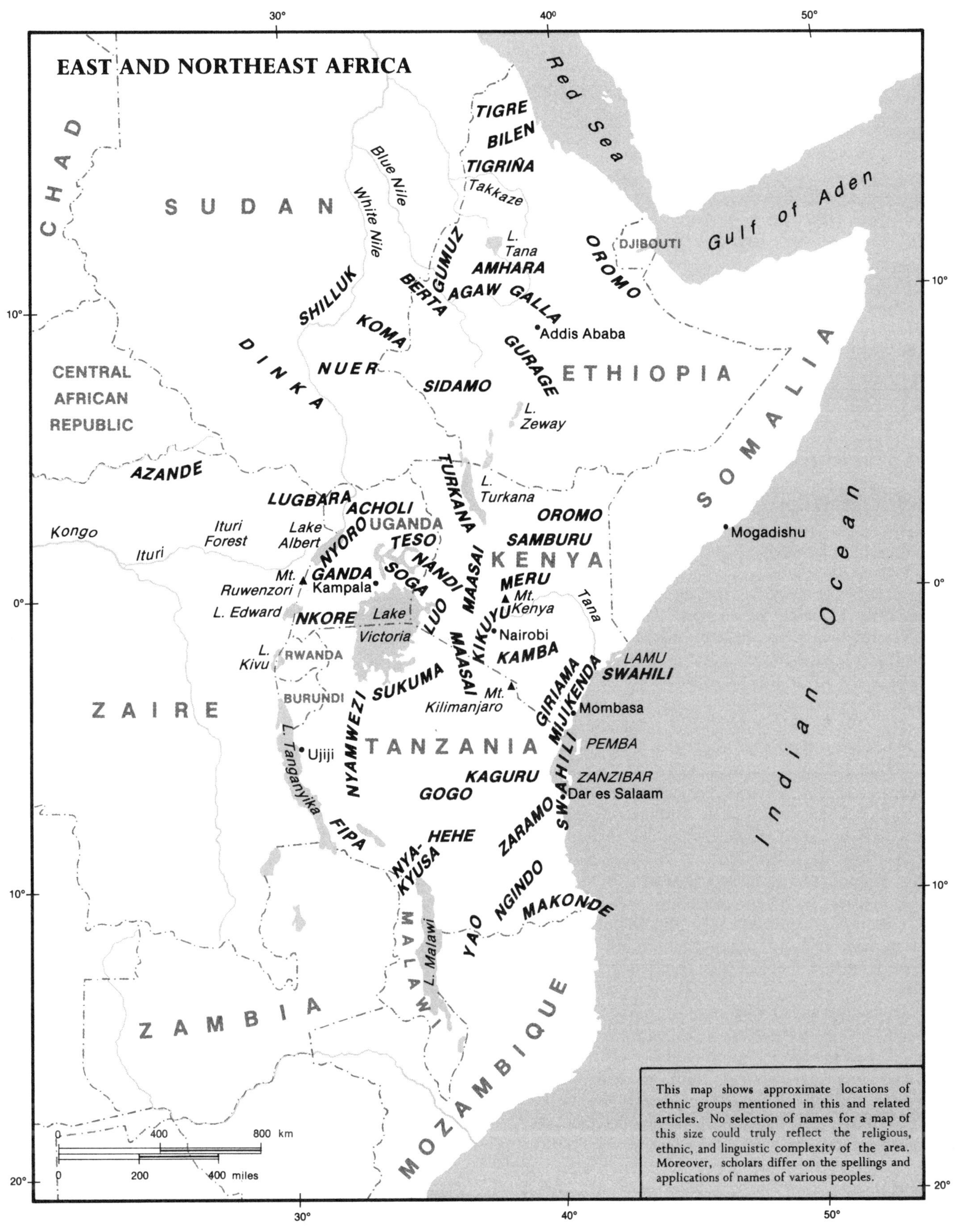

This map shows approximate locations of ethnic groups mentioned in this and related articles. No selection of names for a map of this size could truly reflect the religious, ethnic, and linguistic complexity of the area. Moreover, scholars differ on the spellings and applications of names of various peoples.

might one day be reached again with the help of prophetic leaders. Perhaps all peoples of the region have myths to explain the separation, often couched in terms of a Tower of Babel story in which a rope or a tree between heaven and earth was destroyed either by human foolishness or divine displeasure. (There is not the least reason to suppose that these separation myths are in any way due to diffusion from Christian sources.) There is considerable variation in the degree to which it is held that the Deity interferes in the everyday affairs of the living, beyond being responsible for death, and in beliefs held about the relationship between its creation of the world and the later formation of human societies. There is also much variation in its relationships with the many lesser deities that are found in all East African cosmologies.

These aspects and relations are stated in myth, each society having its own corpus of myth that tells of the creation of the world, the relationship between humankind and the Deity, and the formation of society. A typical example is that of the cosmogony of the Nilotic Shilluk of the upper Nile. Their myths tell of the creation of the world by Juok and of the later formation of the Shilluk kingdom by the culture hero or mediator, Nyikang. The mythical cooperation of creator and hero is a feature of many East African myths, their two activities being distinct in time and usually in place also. Nyikang, whose parentage is usually given as a father of heavenly provenance and a mother who was a creature of the River Nile with the attributes of the crocodile, is thus associated with sky, river, and earth; he separated the Shilluk from their neighbors and united his people as their first king. All later kings have been embodiments of Nyikang, and the installation of a new king is a dramatic representation of both the social diversity and the unity of the Shilluk as well as their mystical link with the Nile, on which they are ecologically dependent. The king, as Nyikang in immanent form, represents the ideal and true order of the world within himself. Godfrey Lienhardt has written about the Shilluk proverb that says "the Shilluk only believe what they see," pointing out that it is through their human king that they are also able to see what they believe.

Other than the distinction between the creation of the world and the formation of the particular society, the most widespread mythopoeic feature of the many and varied myths of the region would seem to be the attribution of reverse or inverted characteristics and behavior to the originally created inhabitants. They may be portrayed as incestuous or as being ignorant of kinship, the idiom used by most East African societies to express and validate everyday social relationships; they may be given close identification with animal species, the natural and the social thereby being brought into a single conceptual system; they may be said to have dwelt outside the present homeland in a state of primeval timelessness, their travels and adventures representing those of past migrations and final settlement into the present habitat; they construct a cosmic topography in which the particular society is set in both space and time as a moral community within an asocial and amoral wilderness.

With creation myths are found myths that tell of such matters as the relationships between people and wild and domesticated animals, between men and women, and between peoples of different societies and races; the origins of and reasons for death; the origins of fire and cooking, linked with the making of settlements and the exchange of primeval hunting for farming; and the nature and validation of the ties, rights, and obligations of descent, age, sex, and rank. It is frequently difficult to draw any meaningful distinction between what may be considered by outside observers to be myths and folk tales that tell of these and similar problems. As with myths, most folk tales are concerned with paradoxes and logical contradictions in the experience of the particular culture concerned. Perhaps the great majority of East African folk tales are told about agents who are animals or humans in the guise of animals; their adventures refer essentially and by implication to human behavior. Proverbs and riddles, many with similar implications, are found throughout the region.

In Ethiopia and the Swahili and Somali coasts, the areas with long-standing literacy and forms of writing, accounts of the formation of the world and society and their history may also be in written forms. They may profess to be historical chronicles of particular towns, peoples, or dynasties, but nonetheless they partake of the general nature of mythopoeic statements, using the same idioms as spoken myth. [*See* African Religions, *article on* Mythic Themes.]

Lesser Deities and their Relations with the Living. The Deity usually communicates with the living only indirectly, through refractions of its power in the forms of lesser deities, spirits, gods, powers, and ancestors, ghosts, or shades (almost every writer has his or her own terminology, which has led to a good deal of definitional confusion). These mystical entities may "float" freely or they may be attached to social groups (lineages, clans, neighborhoods, and others) by having localized shrines established for them. The relations of communication are complex, but essentially the deities may control or constrain the living by possessing them and making them sick, and the living may contact the deities by sacrifice, prayer, and self-induced trance.

Both parties are seen as interdependent, even if the living may not understand the full nature and motivation of the deities; but if contact ceases, the deities cease to have power and to "exist" in the awareness of the living at all.

There are many kinds of these deities found in East African religions, but they may conveniently be divided into the categories of spirits and ancestors, each comprising many subtypes. Spirits are considered as different from the transcendent and otiose Deity (even though the same word may be used for both, as is *kwoth* among the Nuer). They are immanent, more dynamic, and more immediately demanding; they are usually regarded as so numerous as to be beyond counting. Whereas the Deity is only rarely localized in shrines (as among the Kikuyu, who recognize certain fig trees as shrines for Ngai), many kinds of shrines, temples, and images are built for the spirits where they may be contacted by the living. Since spirits are invisible and unknowable, being of a different order than human beings, they need some locus where the living may contact them.

A spirit may be considered as a representation of some aspect of human experience whose power is thought to be outside the immediate community and beyond the everyday knowledge or control of ordinary people, until it exercises some form of power over a living person by possession or sickness. This experience may be that of nature, as with the smallpox and other disease "gods" of the Ganda or the earthquake and lightning spirits of the Lugbara; it may be experience of outside historical events, as with the "airplane" and "Polish" (refugee) spirits of the Nyoro; or it may be the individual experience of inner psychological states such as guilt and fear, as with the sky divinities of the Dinka. The possession of a living person by a spirit places him or her into direct and palpable contact with the particular experience: divination identifies the spirit, and sacrifice removes it from the possessed victim and restores the proper status quo.

Another aspect of spirit possession is that the victim is thereby singled out and acquires a new or additional mystical and personal status. In East Africa women appear more usually to be possessed by spirits; it has been suggested that this is so because women suffer from a greater sense of cultural deprivation and ambiguity of role than do men. Women's roles are less clearly defined than those of men, with the exception of the role of mother. When a woman is barren, therefore, her role is wanting and ambiguous: she may acquire a more definite one, largely independent and less under the control of husband or brother, by becoming the adherent and communicant of a spirit and so linking herself to other women who have been possessed. In some societies, for example the Lugbara, these women acquire a degree of personal independence and clearly defined identity but no more. In others, such as the Swahili, they become members of spirit cults and so of socially recognized groupings that stress their joint identity as against that of the men, who are seen as affiliated to a particular mosque in which women are never full members. The Swahili spirits are localized in particular places, each of which is associated with a particular cult group under the control of a spirit priest who has the powers of mediumship and divination. The women thus form a kind of mirror organization to that of the men. Something very similar is found in the *zār* cult of much of Ethiopia, Somalia, and the Muslim Sudan. Women are possessed, healed by an exorcist-medium, and then considered as cult adherents. The high incidence of this possession would seem to be linked to the particular problems, both social and psychological, of women in these largely Muslim societies.

The other main category of deity in East African religions is that of the dead, who, unlike spirits, are of the same order of existence as the living and so more easily understood and approached. There are many kinds and levels of ancestral worship, corresponding to the various kinds of ancestors: those of the direct line of descent, those of submerged descent lines, and those of other kin. They may be considered as individual ancestors, remembered by their personal names, or as collectivities of unnamed ancestral kin who are of less importance in living memory. As they are like the living, they may easily be worshiped by sacrifice in which they are given food, which is shared between them and the living as it is among kin, each category of ancestors representing a particular group or constellation of living kin that comes into contact with the dead on particular occasions. Also, as might be expected, the ancestors may themselves act as senior kin and initiate communication by sending sickness or trouble to the living and so draw attention to themselves.

Sacrifice is made typically to remove sickness or as a response of gratitude for removal of sickness, to avoid sickness and other troubles, and at times on regular occasions of group or individual purification. Each kin or lineage group makes its own sacrifices (since ancestors of other groups are of no interest to it). In centralized societies the royal ancestors may be offered sacrifice on state occasions by the ruler and his priests on behalf of the entire kingdom.

An example of lineage sacrifice is that of the Lugbara of Uganda. Here the most important and frequent sacrifices are made to the ghosts, those dead of the patrilineal lineage who have left sons behind them. They are believed to send sickness to their living descendants to "teach" them if the latter have denied respect to the living elders, who may invoke the dead to do this as part of an elder's duty. When the sickness has gone, the lineage elder sacrifices an animal to "thank" the dead and so "cleanse the home" of sin. People may also sacrifice to their matrilateral ghosts for broadly similar reasons and to the collectivity of dead who left no children. Similar sacrifices are reported from the Nyakyusa of southern Tanzania, but besides their being made by lineages to their own ancestors they are also made on behalf of all the members of neighborhoods and chiefdoms.

The relationship between ancestor and spirit worship is essentially that ancestors are linked to, and typically localized in, a shrine established by their descendants, whereas spirits are freer and if localized are tied to neighborhoods and wider settlements instead of to descent groups. The identity of the group concerned is clearly of central importance.

Sacrifice is typically made by ritual representatives of living groups. They are of two kinds: priests who are regarded as having special spiritual characteristics and skills, and ordinary senior people (elders) who sacrifice by virtue of genealogical position rather than special skills as such (although by being "nearer" to the dead than juniors they do have greater spiritual authority). It is true that in most East African societies priests may also be appointed on genealogical grounds, but in those cases they come from priestly lines, as the office is not open to members of other groups. Priests are repositories of divine knowledge and power that are usually considered to be vested in a descent line, so that there are myths that explain how this line was originally selected by the Deity for this task. Examples are the Masters of the Fishing Spear among the Dinka, the Nuer Leopard-skin priests, the Mugwe of the Meru of Kenya, the rainmakers of the Lugbara, the *laibon*s of the Maasai and their Para-Nilotic neighbors, the members of the most senior age-sets among the Kikuyu.

The priests who have these specialized duties are uniformly given aspects of sacredness and so set apart from ordinary people. For example, the Dinka Masters of the Fishing Spear carry life within themselves for their people and so may not die a "natural" death; when they feel their powers wane they ask to be buried alive so that the life remains for the community. At a politically higher level, the king of the Shilluk is smothered for the same reasons. The Lugbara rainmakers are considered almost as living ancestors, being symbolically "buried" at their initation as rainmakers, and they are buried at their real death later in ways that are the exact opposite of those of ordinary funerals.

Another universally found ritual expert is the diviner, a person, male or female, believed able to discover the mystical causes of sickness and other misfortunes in the everyday world of the living. Methods of divination used in East Africa are many, including the use of oracles (more or less mechanical devices believed to be beyond the physical control of the operators), trance and mediumship (often while possessed by a spirit associated with mediumship), the consultation of omens, and formerly, before colonial rule stopped the practices, the administration of ordeals and oaths. Diviners are usually also healers, treating both the material and the mystical aspects of sickness by the use of medicines and by divination.

In brief, sacrifice to spirits and ancestors removes sickness and guilt for the commission of sin (defined variously but essentially as an act against the will of the Deity and the proper order of authority within social groups) by the immolation of a victim identified with the sick person, thereby removing the "experience" that has disturbed or affected the local group and the moral role of the guilty person within it. Other rites are found throughout the region: those of tradition or transformation of status. The most widespread are rites of initiation at puberty and at death.

Initiation rites, more generally for boys than for girls, although these take place, are most elaborate in those societies in which age-sets and generation-sets provide the basis for political and military action and also regulate marriage. The best-known examples are the Para-Nilotic pastoralist societies such as the Maasai, Samburu, Nandi, Karamojong, and their related neighbors; some southern Ethiopian groups such as the Galla; and others such as the Nyakyusa of southern Tanzania, who also have age systems of political importance and complex initiation rites. These rites, as with all rites of transition, begin with a rite in which the initiates are separated symbolically (and often physically) from their families and is followed by a series of rites that takes place in seclusion or secret from the remainder of society. Finally there are the rites of reaggregation of the "new" person into society with his or her new role as an adult able to have sexual relations, marry, act as a warrior, and so on. In some cases, as traditionally among the Kikuyu, the period of seclusion might take many months and would finish with the elaborate symbolic rebirth of the "new" young man. But today initiation rites have lost much of their former importance and are performed somewhat perfunctorily in most of the region.

In those societies where ancestral cults are important, mortuary rites are likewise important; an example comes from the Lugbara of Uganda, where mortuary rites, especially for senior men, are long, drawn out affairs that involve the participation of kin over great distances. The disposal of the corpse is of little moment, but the symbolic destruction of the deceased's social identity, the restructuring of kin ties that were centered on him, and the rites of redomestication of the soul as a ghost in its new shrine are all of the greatest importance and elaboration. In societies where ancestral cults are lacking, such as the technologically simple hunting and gathering Hadza of Tanzania, these rites are of virtually no importance.

Explanations of and Responses to Evil and Misfortune. All East African religions have a concept of evil. Explanations of evil and responses to it are typically expressed in beliefs in witchcraft and sorcery, which are thus integral parts of any system of religion. The first fully adequate study of witchcraft—one which has not as yet been surpassed—concerns witchcraft beliefs among the Azande people of southwestern Sudan. The Azande distinguish between witchcraft (an innate mystical ability to harm others merely by wishing or thinking to do so) and sorcery (the use of material substances to do the same). Although this distinction is widespread in East Africa, it is not universal, and many societies refer merely to evildoers who use either or both means of harming others. [*See* Witchcraft.]

These beliefs are found throughout the region, although each culture has its own peculiarities of idiom in which to express the ideology of evil; in all of them, however, the ideology of a witch is that he or she is in some way a reverse of a full and properly behaving member of a community. The basic principles of the system of explaining coincidence, unexpected failure, disaster, or sickness are similar everywhere. It is consistent with the basic, small-scale, and personal relationships of everyday life in these societies that explanations of the unexpected and immediately inexplicable in technical terms should be sought in personal relations, as the activities of evil-intentioned persons. Their motivation is held to be hatred, envy, and jealousy against those who are more fortunate or successful. These emotions are felt toward others who are already known; it is extremely rare that such feelings are provoked by strangers. Their identity depends largely on the composition of the more important groups whose members should regard themselves as a community. Witchcraft is a kind of treachery, a perversion for ignoble ends of proper authority, obligation, and affection. Thus where the basic local group is a kinship one, witches are held to be kin of their victims and sorcerers thought to harm unrelated persons. Where such kin groups are unimportant, the distinction between witches and sorcerers may not be made.

These beliefs are linked to knowledge of technical causation. A belief in witchcraft regards the activities of witches as "the second spear," in the Zande phrase. It is clear that a man is gored by a buffalo: the belief in witchcraft is used to explain not that he was gored as such but why he was gored by a particular animal at that particular time and place. The identity of the witch is discovered by divination, and demands for reparation, vengeance, punishment, or other socially approved action can be taken by the community so as to restore proper relations between the concerned parties. The whole is an effective jural process once the premises are accepted.

Radical social change has occurred in almost all parts of East Africa during and since colonial times. Change leads to increases in disputes and tensions as traditional social roles break down and alter, and this is often expressed in terms of suspicions and fears of witchcraft and sorcery. These evildoers are traitors, coming symbolically from the outside of the community, and efforts are made to cleanse whole communities of them by mass purificatory religious movements led by prophets and healers, both Christian and non-Christian.

Religious Change and Prophetic Movements. East African societies have never been static, and at times in their history change has been rapid and radical. A usual response to the sense of confusion about the present, uncertainty about the future, and in some cases virtual breakdown of the social order has been and is the recourse to prophetic leaders. It is often held that East African prophets are a modern phenomena, but this is extremely unlikely; although historical records are few it may be safely assumed that they have always been a feature of the region.

If we omit here the famous Sudanese Mahdi Muḥammad Aḥmad who led his adherents to capture Khartoum in 1885 and established a theocracy there, the earliest cases for which reasonably reliable records are available include those from the southern Sudan and from what is now Tanzania (earlier prophets have been recorded from the Lake Nyasa region to the south). [*See the biography of Muḥammad Aḥmad.*]

Prophets have been a marked feature of the Nuer and Dinka of the Nilotic Sudan. At the end of the nineteenth century the Nuer prophet Ngundeng, claiming inspiration from a Dinka sky divinity and spending much time fasting and living in the wilderness, was able to bring together large, normally autonomous groupings to raid neighboring peoples and to stand together against Arab slavers and, later, British colonial rule. He built an earthen pyramid from which he would prophesy. After his death his son Gwek succeeded him, refusing cooperation with the government. A deformed man, Gwek would stand on top of the pyramid in a state of possession, uttering prophecies that foretold the end of colonial rule. He was killed and the pyramid destroyed some years later. Among the neighboring Dinka, Arianhdit was perhaps the greatest prophet, flourishing at the time of the First World War; he died in 1948. Dinka prophets were Masters of the Fishing Spear as well as Men of Divinity, thus being both priests and prophets with powers additional to those of ordinary priests. The main Dinka prophets may well have influenced the prophetic water cults that arose in Uganda at the time of the Uganda Mutiny, marked by the drinking of divine water that would remove the Europeans and their weapons.

Among the Lugbara, to the south, a water cult known as Yakan emerged about the turn of the century in response to human and cattle epidemics and to the intrusion of Arabs and Europeans, which seriously affected local life. The disturbance of a traditionally ordered society led the people to seek a famed prophet, Rembe, from the Kakwa people to the north. At first they obtained sacred water from him; later they invited him to enter their country to restore their damaged society. Rembe dispensed water that was imbued with divine power to his adherents, promising that drinking it would ensure the return of dead livestock and people (and so destroy the traditional ancestral cult), drive away disease and foreign newcomers, and make the drinkers immune to bullets. Adherents were regarded as equal, men and women, old and young, irrespective of clan differences, thereby symbolizing a primeval egalitarian society as portrayed in myth. The cult collapsed at his arrest in 1917, although the spirit Yakan who inspired him is to this day believed to be a wandering spirit. Like almost all prophets, Rembe tried to reconstruct society as it was thought to have been at the beginning of time, the utopia of the future being the same as the paradise of the mythical past.

The communal drinking of divine water was also found in southeastern and central Tanganyika during the Maji Maji rebellion (*maji* is Swahili for "water") against the German colonial government in 1905–1907. It was begun by a diviner or prophet called Kinjikitile, who was possessed by a local spirit as well as by a panethnic deity called Hongo. Those who drank Kinjikitile's water would be immune to bullets and would drive the Germans into the sea. The movement turned beyond his control politically; he was hanged, but the revolt was put down only after as many as a quarter of a million Africans had died. [*See the biography of Kinjikitile.*]

There were many other prophet-led movements of the time, such as the Giriama (a Mijikenda group of the Kenya coast) movement of 1914, led by prophetesses, and the Nyabingi movement in southwestern Uganda during the first quarter of the century and later, also led largely by women. Both of these began as religious responses to colonial rule and later became increasingly political in aim until they were put down by the colonial governments.

Many accounts of recent changes in East Africa have set conversion to Christianity apart from more traditional and pre-Christian prophetic movements (except in Ethiopia, the political center of which has been Christian since the fourth century—but Ethiopian Christianity has had no influence on other parts of the region, being physically so separate). This reflects the outsiders' distinction between "true" and "false" religions, but from the point of view of the local societies themselves the distinction is largely meaningless. Outside observers also distinguish between "traditional" and "world" religions, but here the differences are more significant. Christianity and Islam are parts of international networks of economic and political as well as religious relations, so that their adherents may become part of extrasocietal and extra-African groupings that are significant in the lives of educated and elite people. They are also literate religions and as such open up temporal and spatial visions and areas of knowledge of a wider world that are less accessible to traditional worldviews based upon particular local societies.

It may well and sensibly be argued that a person adopts a new faith both because he or she accepts, in an intellectual or emotional measure, its theological arguments and because he or she accepts it as a better way of dealing with the tribulations of everyday life than had been offered by the traditional faith. In all traditional East African religions the factor of healing is, and has probably always been, a central one. To this must be added a related factor: when fears and accusations of witchcraft and sorcery reach a critical stage, people turn to prophets who promise to cleanse the land of these evils. East Africa has had many new Christian and Islamic prophetic movements whose leaders promise a new society free of witchcraft, sickness, and poverty; in addition, the Christian message as expressed by missionaries refers, to a large extent, to the problems of physical and moral health and sickness. Another factor has been that of education. Until independence a high proportion of educational services were controlled by mission organizations; thus to acquire a Western education and enter the modern world one had to join a mission and become at least a nominal Christian. This kind of conversion has nothing to do with the individual sincerity of conversion and belief, which is a matter quite outside the competence of any outsider to evaluate.

Breakaway, or separatist, churches and sects have long been a feature of East Africa. They began largely as responses to what were seen (justifiably or not is not the immediate question at issue) as overbearing colonialist attitudes on the part of the mission churches. These separatist churches in East Africa seem to have developed rather later than those in other parts of the continent. They have been marked particularly in areas of very high population density, which have been those where, for obvious reasons, colonial efforts and influences were first directed and where the effects of "external" change and of land shortage and overcrowding have been the most severely felt. The Kikuyu, the Luhya, and the Luo of Kenya, the Chagga of Tanzania, and the Ganda of Uganda are among the most striking examples, and all of them have educated Christian elites and separatist churches. These areas also, as a not unrelated consequence, have produced most of the members of modern political and social elites.

Islam has been a feature of East Africa for many centuries. It has been a part of the religious situation in northern Ethiopia, the Sudan, and the Somali and Swahili coasts since the Middle Ages. The advent of Omani colonial rule based on Zanzibar in the eighteenth and nineteenth centuries revitalized it, and from the coast Islam penetrated into the interior along the trading and slave routes based on Zanzibar. In some cases whole groups near the coast became Muslim, as did the Yao, for example (often largely to prevent their being enslaved, often to enable them to participate in the slave trade as partners with Arabs and Swahili); in others, individual members of the trading settlements inland, such as Tabora and Ujiji in Tanganyika (now Tanzania), became Muslims. In addition, Muslims from the Indian subcontinent have been in the coastal towns for centuries and spread inland to the more modern colonial towns. In general, however, Islam has had relatively little religious impact on most of East Africa, and once the power of the Zanzibar sultanate was weakened it almost ceased to spread.

If we consider traditional Christian and Muslim prophetic leaders as members of a single category of religious experts, we may see that there are certain clearly defined phases of these movements in East Africa since the latter part of the nineteenth century. The first phase was that of the earlier effects of colonial rule, with which a link was seen with epidemics and other disasters; here the prophets were ultimately unsuccessful as religious or political leaders (although their inspirational spirits have usually lingered on as free spirits of one kind or another). The second phase was during the second quarter of this century, when the political aspects were less in evidence and more importance was given to missionization, missionaries being seen as colonial agents and even as betrayers of the Christian message as it affected Africans. The third and fourth phases have been contemporary but should be distinguished. One comprised the movements led by Christian prophets to reform mission churches and to found syncretist or reformed sects and churches; these continued the process mentioned in the second phase. The other has been the rise of more overtly political leaders during the period of gaining political independence from the colonial powers. The leaders' authority has usually had aspects of messianic and charismatic authority, but no more need to be said about them here. The third phase, however, is distinctly relevant and provides a main link between the histories and followings of traditional and world religions, especially Christianity in this particular region of Africa. The acceptance of new faiths, with either the abandonment of the old or a syncretism of the two, does not happen in a historical or social vacuum and cannot be considered in isolation from the traditional religious past. The same people, as individuals, move from traditional to world religions (and often back again): they are not members of separate communities.

[*See also* African Religions, *article on* Modern Movements. *For further discussion of particular East African religions, see* Interlacustrine Bantu Religions; Lugbara Religion; Nuer and Dinka Religion; *and* Nyakyusa Religion. *See also* Kwoth; Mulungu; Ngai; *and* Nhialic.]

BIBLIOGRAPHY

The basic accounts of East African religions are in the form of monographs on the religious systems of particular societies. Most, although by no means all, are by anthropologists, each of whom has lived among the people in question, has learned their language and ways of life, and can set the beliefs and rites firmly into their social, cultural, and historical contexts. They include two books by E. E. Evans-Pritchard. In *Nuer Religion* (Oxford, 1956), on the Nilotic Nuer of the southern Sudan, he discusses the complex Nuer beliefs of the soul, divinity, sin, sacrifice, and religious symbolism and relates them to the social structure. The other, *Witchcraft, Oracles and Magic among the Azande*, 2d ed. (Oxford, 1950), is essentially on notions of spiritual causation among a "pre-scientific" people of the southwestern Sudan. Both these books are classics in the study of African religions. The Dinka, neighbors of the Nuer and closely related to them, are the subject of Godfrey Lienhardt's *Divinity and Experience: The Religion of the Dinka* (Oxford, 1961), in which the relationships of belief and sacrifice to

Dinka efforts to understand and control their experience of the "outside" world are discussed with insight and subtlety. John Middleton's *Lugbara Religion* (London, 1960) deals in a more strictly sociological manner with the use made by the Lugbara of Uganda, who are related to the Azande, of ritual in everyday social and political affairs. The two books on the Nyakyusa, a Bantu-speaking people of southern Tanzania, by Monica Wilson, *Rituals of Kinship among the Nyakyusa* (Oxford, 1957) and *Communal Rituals of the Nyakyusa* (Oxford, 1959), deal in great detail with rituals of many kinds, set in their social context. Bernardo Bernardi's *The Mugwe: A Failing Prophet* (Oxford, 1959) deals with a particular priestly office among the Meru, an offshoot of the Kikuyu of central Kenya. Abdul Hamid M. el-Zein's *The Sacred Meadows* (Evanston, Ill., 1974) is concerned with the elaborate beliefs and rites of the Swahili town of Lamu, on the Kenya coast, which has nominally been Muslim for many centuries. F. B. Welbourn's *East African Rebels* (London, 1961) and F. B. Welbourn and B. A. Ogot's *A Place to Feel at Home* (Oxford, 1966) deal in detail and with sympathy with separatist church movements in southern Uganda and western Kenya respectively.

The other main category of writings on East African religions are surveys of various kinds in which comparisons are made between several local religions. Benjamin C. Ray's *African Religions* (Englewood Cliffs, N.J., 1976) is an excellent introduction to African religions in which those of East Africa feature prominently, in particular the Nuer, Dinka, Shilluk, Ganda, Lugbara, and Kikuyu. *Witchcraft and Sorcery in East Africa*, edited by John Middleton and E. H. Winter (London, 1963), and *Spirit Mediumship and Society in Africa*, edited by John Beattie and John Middleton (New York, 1969), contain essays by various authors on these matters among several different peoples. J. Spencer Trimingham's *Islam in East Africa* (Oxford, 1964) is a useful survey, and John V. Taylor's *The Primal Vision* (London, 1963) is a valuable short introduction to East African religion from a Christian viewpoint.

JOHN MIDDLETON

Ethiopian Religions

Situated in the northeasternmost part of the Horn of Africa, Ethiopia is populated by three major groupings of people. These groups speak languages classified as being related to three branches of Afro-Asiatic: Cushitic (e.g., Agaw, Bilen, Sidama, Oromo), Semitic (e.g., Amhara, Tigriña, Tigre, Gurage), and Nilo-Saharan (e.g., Majangir, Berta, Gumuz, Koma). Linguistic affiliations roughly correspond with religious observances. Centuries ago Cushitic- and Semitic-speaking Ethiopians were converted to Christianity and Islam but they still retain some traditional beliefs and practices. The traditional religious observances of the Nilo-Saharan peoples have been among the least influenced by Christianity and Islam. Cushitic religious traditions, principally those of the Agaw, profoundly affected the beliefs and practices of Ethiopians on the central plateau.

Agaw. Inhabiting the northern and central plateaus in the region of Gonder province, the Agaw form the linguistic and cultural substrate population of the Semitic-speaking Amhara and Tigriña. Their most northerly relatives, the mainly Islamic Bilen, are sedentary and engage in agriculture, as nearly all Agaw do. Three Agaw groups—the Qemant, Kwara, and Falasha (the last sometimes called Ethiopian Jews, who practice a pre-Talmudic form of Judaism)—live west of the Takkaze River and north of Lake Tana. Other Agaw groups live south of Lake Tana in Agawmeder and Damot. In 1964, Fredrick Gamst estimated the Agaw to number about 250,000.

The approximately 25,000 Qemant, who have a mixture of traditional and Hebraic religious beliefs, live in dispersed settlements that are defined by sacred groves, the abodes of culture heroes called *qedus*. Sacred groves, a feature widespread among other central Ethiopians, are the loci of all major religious ceremonies. Among the Qemant, these ceremonies are conducted by "officiates" *(wambar)* who hold the highest political and religious offices and belong to the Keber, or superior moiety. Keber moiety members trace their ancestry to the "pure" Qemant; all other Qemant belong to the Yetanti moiety. Both groups disdain manual labor other than agriculture. At the apex of the priesthood, the *wambar* are assisted on ceremonial occasions by higher and lower priests, who ritually sacrifice on behalf of the community a white bull or white sheep as an offering to the male high god, Mezgana, who is believed to reside in the sky. After performing purification rites, priests and laymen fast from the eve of the ceremony until the sacrifice the following morning. Worship of *jinn* at their natural abodes is also held to regulate rain, restore fertility, and rid the community of pests and disease.

Oromo. The eight to ten million Oromo, representative of the southern Cushitic, stretch from the southern tip of Tigre to Harar, then south to the Tana River in Kenya, and as far west as the tributaries of the Blue Nile. Their cultural life is varied, ranging from the seminomadic pastoralism practiced by the southern Boran, who have resisted conversion to Christianity or Islam, to the sedentary agricultural life of the Macha of western Shoa province. Shoan and Wollo Oromo long ago abandoned their traditional dependence upon cattle, a cultural transformation coinciding with their gradual acceptance of the religious beliefs and practices of the agricultural and Christian Amhara and Tigriña near whom they settled. Today, few traces of indigenous

Cushitic rites exist among the Muslim Jimma Oromo, who by this century had become devout followers of the Tijānīyah order of Islam.

Macha, Boran, and Guji Oromo, with slight variation, all share in common the Kallu institution, which Karl Knutsson describes as a social bridge between humanity and divinity. Through the figure of the Kallu, a ritual expert, a man's wishes are carried to divinity; this dignitary also constitutes the channel through which divinity's will is passed down to humanity. Moral rules of conduct are made manifest in the Kallu's daily behavioral and ritual performances associated with divinity. Macha manifestations of divinity find expression in the belief in Waka ("sky" or "god"); Atete, a female deity; and *ayana*, or divine agents. Kallu rituals, performed in groves of tall trees, incorporate sacrifices for rainmaking or ceremonies in honor of Waka. Possession by *ayana* spirits at regular intervals gives the Kallu man or woman a wider sphere of influence and power as a ritual clan leader.

Amhara-Tigriña. Inheritors of the monophysite doctrine of Christianity, which became the official religion of the old Aksumite kingdom in about 350 CE, the Semitic-speaking Amhara and Tigriña inhabit large areas of central Ethiopia. [*See* Aksumite Religion.] The provinces of Gonder, Shoa, and Gojam, and the district of Lasta in Wollo province are the traditional homelands of the Amhara, whom Ullendorff estimates to number from three to five million. Tigriña mainly inhabit the province of Tigre, their homeland, and approximately 500,000 are dispersed throughout several districts in highland Eritrea.

The Amhara-Tigriña have no cult associated with their supreme being and creator god, Egziabher ("the god from across the sea"). Predating the transplantation of Christianity, the Amhara-Tigriña worshiped good and evil spirits who were associated with trees, fountains, and animate and inanimate objects. Nowadays, extreme devotion is expressed to the Virgin Mary (Maryam), who is believed to dwell in such sacred natural areas as high mountains, springs, and groves of sycamore trees. Sacrifices and cult activities take place in sacred groves, though the "church" *(bet kristyan)* is the principal seat of religious worship. Dedicated in the name of a patron saint, the church is the focal point of the parish, the largest local, social, and political subdivision. At services, only the priest, deacons, and formerly the king may enter the sanctuary, which is completely hidden from the view of the communicants. Priests and laymen alike observe strict fasting laws throughout the year and always before major religious festivals. Before a modern system of taxation was introduced in this century, church and state administration was supported by an elaborate system of tithing in labor and kind, made possible by a surplus economy based on extensive agricultural production.

Gurage. The southernmost speakers of Semitic Afro-Asiatic, the Gurage inhabit the region in Shoa province where Lake Zeway and the middle course of the Gibbie River form, respectively, the general east and west boundaries. The Shoan Oromo live to the north, and Sidama groups stretch across the southern flanks of Gurage territory. Language and dialectical differences sharply demarcate the largely Christian and Muslim eastern Gurage from the adherents of traditional religion, which is still strongly observed among the western Gurage, who numbered about 50,000 in 1966. The cultural life of the western group is dominated by the cultivation of *Ensete ventricosum,* more commonly known as "false banana," a food staple consumed in great quantities on all religious or ritual occasions.

The remote supreme god of the western Gurage figures less prominently in religious beliefs and practices than do lesser deities, on whom major cult activities center. Guardians of the shrines dedicated to the lesser deities—Wak, the male sky god; Dämwamwit, the female deity; and Božä, the thunder god (all of whom reside in sacred groves where the great annual festivals are held)—exercise quasi-political and judicial roles in their spiritual capacity and sanction the authority of secular leaders. The annual festival of the female deity gives women ritual license to shed their customary subservient role and abuse menfolk verbally.

Majangir. Nilo-Saharan peoples, such as the Majangir, Anuak, and Nuer, occupy western Ethiopia, mainly along the Sudan border. In 1966, Stauder estimated the hunting and trapping Majangir to number fewer than 20,000 people. They live on the southwestern edge of the Ethiopian plateau in dispersed homesteads adjacent to forest areas, which they exploit for game. The material culture of the Majangir is as simple as their political and religious organization; the ritual expert *(tapat)* possesses characteristics of both shaman and priest, exercising quasi-political, "chiefly" duties. He derives his power mainly by control over spiritual sanctions, the threat of which is sufficient to maintain peace and order.

BIBLIOGRAPHY

Gamst, Fredrick C. *The Qemant: A Pagan-Hebraic Peasantry of Ethiopia.* New York, 1969. A brief, informative ethnographic account of social organization and religious ritual life of modern-day descendants of the proto-Ethiopians.

Knutsson, Karl Eric. *Authority and Change: A Study of the Kallu*

Institution among the Macha Galla of Ethiopia. Göteborg, 1967. An analysis of ritual and cosmology in the political organization of sedentary Oromo. A comparison is made of form and variation of the Kallu among other Oromo groups.

Legesse, Asmarom. *Gada: Three Approaches to the Study of African Society.* New York, 1973. A detailed analysis of the cyclical Gada age-grade system of the pastoral Boran Oromo of southern Ethiopia.

Levine, Donald N. *Greater Ethiopia: The Evolution of a Multiethnic Society.* Chicago, 1974. A bold, imaginative examination of the principal linguistic and sociocultural factors accounting for the shaping of modern Ethiopia.

Shack, William A. *The Gurage: A People of the Ensete Culture.* London, 1966. A comprehensive analysis of social and religious organization set against the cultural background of the food quest.

Stauder, Jack. *The Majangir: Ecology and Society of a Southwest Ethiopian People.* Cambridge, 1971. A model study of small-scale social organization of a hunting and gathering people.

Trimingham, J. Spencer. *Islam in Ethiopia.* Oxford, 1952. Repint, Totowa, N.J., 1965. The definitive study of the history and institutions of the Islamic peoples of the Horn of Africa.

WILLIAM A. SHACK

Northeastern Bantu Religions

The northeastern Bantu-speaking peoples of East Africa include the Ganda, Nyoro, Nkore, Soga, and Gisu of Uganda; the Kikuyu and Kamba of Kenya; and the Gogo and Kaguru of Tanzania. Although these societies are united by their common usage of Bantu languages, they differ considerably in political, social, and economic organization and in religious ideas and practices.

In most of these societies the creator god is regarded as a remote and distant figure, except among the Kikuyu where he is thought to be involved in the major events of personal and community life and is the object of ritual activity. The Nyoro and Nkore say that the creator god, Ruhanga, made the world and everything needed for human life on earth. He also established the three classes of Nyoro and Nkore society: the agriculturalists, the rulers (or royal clan), and the cattle herders. Each class is descended from one of Ruhanga's sons, whom Ruhanga tested before assigning them their social role. The Nyoro say that Ruhanga disinherited his fourth son, Kantu, and that he became the source of evil in the world and eventually corrupted the people. For this reason, say the Nyoro, Ruhanga withdrew to the sky and later sent disease and death into the world to punish the people. Because of his remoteness, Ruhanga does not play any role in Nyoro and Nkore ritual.

Among the Ganda, the creator god, Katonda, had a small temple and a medium who gave oracles at night. Katonda was known as the Owner of Heaven and the Master of Life, and it is said that every morning the heads of families would pray to him for the protection of their households. Although Katonda was important to everyone's personal destiny, offerings were not often made to him, and he appears to have had less ritual significance than most of the other gods; today he has no shrine or medium. According to Ganda mythology, it was the culture hero, Kintu, who established the world, populated the country, and founded the kingdom of Buganda. Death also came into the world as a result of the misdeeds of Kintu and his wife, Nambi, and their children, who allowed Nambi's brother, Death (Walumbe), to come to earth with them. After Death started killing people and was chased into the underworld, Kintu solemnly declared that Death would never kill all the people.

The Gisu say that the creator, Were, is a distant deity who allots each person his life span. Were has no shrines, and no sacrifices are made directly to him, although there is a vague belief that he is the recipient of sacrifices made to the ancestors and nature spirits. Were is regarded as being invisible and present everywhere "like the wind."

The Kikuyu say that the creator, Ngai, dwells on certain prominent mountains in western Kenya, including Mount Kenya. His presence is also said to be manifested in such natural phenomena as the sun, moon, stars, rain, rainbows, lightning, and thunder; he is also present in sacred fig trees, where sacrifices are made to him. According to Kikuyu tradition, Ngai gave the land to the ancestors, Kikuyu and Muumbi, and he told them to call upon him in times of need. Sacrifices are offered to Ngai in times of drought, famine, and epidemic and also during the agricultural cycle. The Kikuyu also pray to Ngai at the major stages of life: at birth, initiation, marriage, and death. On less important occasions, offerings and prayers are made to the ancestors.

The relationship between Ngai and the people is unilateral, while their relationship with the ancestors is reciprocal. People "beseech" Ngai for his blessings, which he may choose to give or to withhold, whereas they "pour out" beer and "slaughter" animals for the ancestors, who are expected to respond favorably. The shrines to Ngai are fig trees that are both publicly and privately owned. A diviner communicates with Ngai in his dreams and determines when it is appropriate to offer sacrifice. After a sheep is killed, its intestines are tied around a tree and a portion of meat is placed at the foot. Prayers are offered to Ngai while facing Mount Kenya and the other mountains at each of the cardinal points. Two days later a solemn beer-drinking ceremony may be held and prayers offered again to Ngai for rain, health, prosperity, and children. [*See* Ngai.]

The Kamba, who are neighbors of the Kikuyu, say that the creator god, Molungu, made all things, including men and animals; and thus the Kamba call him Mombi, "the molder" of all creatures. First, Molungu created the ancestors, then he made man and woman and sent them down from heaven. Later, another couple came up through the ant holes in the earth, and their children married those of the sky couple. As time passed, the people multiplied and their livestock increased and their crops prospered. However, one year the people failed to offer sacrifice to Molungu and he became angry and refused to send the rains, and there was great famine. Many of the original clans migrated to distant places, and these people are now the neighbors of the Kamba: the Kikuyu, Maasai, Meru, and others.

Originally, Molungu intended to endow human beings with immortality. He sent a chameleon with a message of eternal life to the people. When the slow-moving chameleon finally arrived, he began to deliver his message, saying, "I was ordered to . . . I was ordered to. . . ." But before he could finish, he was interrupted by the swift-flying weaverbird that had been sent by Molungu with a new message that the people would die. The bird delivered his message quickly and concisely, and since that day mankind has been mortal. According to another version, the chameleon was interrupted by a clever and agile hare who had overheard the message that Molungu gave to the chameleon, only he heard incorrectly and delivered the message that people would die.

Molungu is said to dwell beyond the skies and to observe mankind from the tops of Mount Kilimanjaro and Mount Kenya. He is thought to be well disposed to human beings and to intervene in human affairs when people act against the moral principles of society, but no sacrifices are offered directly to him. His dealings with the Kamba are mediated entirely by the spirits of the ancestors. In times of drought, flood, or epidemic, women gather and a goat is sacrificed. The women ask the ancestors to intercede with Molungu on behalf of the people. The sacrifice is intended to remove the ills and sins committed by the people during the year. The sacrificial animal is burned and the women call out all the offenses done by people in the community in order to purify it and to ward off Molungu's punishment. Occasionally, the Kamba pray to Molungu at other times, for example, to give thanks for the birth of a child or to ask that initiated children turn out well. The prayers to Molungu are brief and general in nature, reflecting his distance and impersonal character.

Among the Ganda, Soga, Nyoro, and Nkore, the primary focus of the traditional religion is upon the hero gods, the *lubaale* (Ganda), *misimbwa* (Soga), and *cwezi* (Nyoro and Nkore). These deities are thought to have been human beings who died and became gods. Some of the *cwezi*, for example, are said to have been ancient kings while others are described as having once been their royal servants. Each god has several shrines and priests throughout the country. In Buganda the most important gods were also in the service of the kingship. In precolonial times the king consulted them about matters of state, while the common people consulted them about personal misfortunes. These gods are still active today, and they are consulted about a variety of personal troubles, such as illness, crop failure, loss of money, barrenness, and loss of employment. To discover the cause of the problem, a person goes to a medium and pays a token fee (often described as a kind of gift) and, under probing by the diviner, states the nature of the problem. The medium then goes into a trance and tells the client (in the voice of the god) the remedy for the difficulty and also the additional cost involved in order to make the remedy effective. The diviner may tell his client to use certain medicines, usually obtained at the marketplace, and/or to make a sacrifice. The diviner usually gives some practical advice about the client's behavior as well. Sometimes the remedy requires the client to become initiated into the cult of the god so that persistent troubles will cease. This entails some expense and a lifelong relationship with the deity and his shrine.

Ghosts of the dead may also be diagnosed as the cause of personal misfortune, though not as frequently as the gods. Like the gods, the ghosts are communicated with through spirit possession and mediumship. But unlike the gods, the ghosts may be destroyed or rendered harmless by being placed in a pot that is then burned or buried in the ground.

The Gisu place shrines for the spirits of the dead in the compounds of important men or in special groves. These groves, which contain a number of fig trees, are sacred to the ancestors. The shrines in the homesteads are shaped like small huts, with forked branches extending through the roof so that offerings of meat may be hung upon them. Sacrifices take place at these shrines on important family occasions, such as the naming of a child, the circumcision of a boy, or personal misfortune. The central act is the offering of beer and an animal (e.g., cow, goat, or fowl) with an invocation. During the invocation, all the names of the dead must be recited lest a spirit feel slighted and cause trouble. Beer is sprayed over the participants as a blessing; red clay, signifying the renewal of health, may also be rubbed on them.

The matrilineal Kaguru offer annual beer and animal

sacrifices to the ghosts of the dead at clan ritual sites. These sites contain the graves of the founding female ancestor of the clan and those of her closest descendants. The graves are cleared of growth, and beer and flour are poured onto the gravestones. The blood of animal victims is also poured out. Often a miniature shelter for the ghosts is built on the site. The dead are said to gain nourishment from the offerings and to be made "cool" and "quiet" and therefore unlikely to bother the living. The fertility of the land depends upon such annual rites, for the spirits of the dead guarantee the productivity of the land. Cultivation and other work on the land is thought mystically to wear down the earth; and the misdeeds of the people, especially of the clan elders who live near the site, are also thought to disturb the ghost ancestors. The Kaguru believe that if such rituals were not performed, the land would be less fertile, the annual rains less favorable, and illness and misfortune more frequent.

Although the Kaguru do not believe in reincarnation, they say that newborn children come from the land of the dead, where, it is said, the ghosts have villages and live as do people on earth. The difference is that life and death in the land of the ghosts is the reverse of that on earth. The ghosts mourn when one of their number "dies" and is born on earth, and they rejoice when a person dies on earth and is "born" in their land. Hence, an infant's hold on life is precarious because the jealous ghosts wish to take it back, and many rites are performed for the ghosts in order to protect the child's life.

Gogo rituals are also concerned primarily with the ancestors, for they are believed to control the fertility of the land and the welfare of the clans who live on it. Cattle and beer are the chief offerings. These bridge the gap between human beings and the spirits because they belong both to the world of men and to the world of nature, as do the ancestor spirits themselves. The semi-pastoralist Gogo sacrifice cattle, their most valuable possession, to the ancestors for rain and good crops and to obtain their blessings at crucial stages in the life cycle. Beer is poured out around a post that is considered to be the architectural and ritual center of the household. Called the "nose of the homestead," the post is the locus of contact between the world of the living and the world of the dead in the domestic rituals. Beer may also be poured onto the gravestones of the dead, which also link the living to the world of the spirits.

Among the northeastern Bantu-speaking peoples, certain rites, or aspects of rites, are not aimed at the gods or spirits but at impersonal mystical forces that affect the welfare of human society. By means of ritual action bad forces may be removed and society purified and thereby spiritually renewed. The Gogo distinguish between good and bad "ritual states." For things to go well, a good or auspicious ritual state must be created. When things do not go well (for instance, if a woman miscarries or has a difficult childbirth or if cattle become diseased), a bad ritual state is said to prevail. In these circumstances it is assumed that the male ritual leaders have failed. Women must take over and act and dress like men and effect a ritual cure through dancing. The women's violent, masculine dancing is a reversal of normal female domesticity and a parody of the male's violent role in Gogo society. In this reversal of sex roles, the ritual state of society is "turned around." The inauspicious ritual state is taken to the boundary of the ritual area and "thrown down" into a swamp or pool, and the area is thus purified and a good ritual state regained.

Divination is central to all East African religions. The Kikuyu say that a diviner, called a "man of God" *(mundu mugu)*, is chosen by Ngai through dreams. "A father may teach, but it is God [Ngai] who chooses the [diviner]. He talks to him in the night: it comes into his head." Divination is performed by spilling out small counters (beans and stones) from a gourd that reveals the will of Ngai or, more frequently, the will of the ancestor spirits. The result of the inquiry is determined by the odd or even number of counters that are spilled out together with other small objects that have symbolic significance. Kamba diviners use the same technique. A few Kikuyu diviners are also inspired in dreams directed by the creator god, who gives long-range prophecies about future events. During the colonial period in Kenya, such prophecies about colonial intrusion helped to legitimate the Mau Mau revolt against British rule.

The Gisu diviner diagnoses his clients' problems by using a small wooden dish with pebbles in it. After invoking his ancestors for assistance, he swings the dish in an arc over his head, calling out the names of spirits who might be responsible for the problem or of people who might be causing it through sorcery or witchcraft. If the pebbles shake and rattle, then the wrong cause has been identified. When the pebbles form a mass and do not move, the correct diagnosis has been reached. The questions that the diviner puts to the test in this fashion are based upon his local knowledge and upon information gained from his client.

In the lacustrine kingdoms of Bunyoro, Nkore, and Buganda, the death, burial, and installation of kings were major ritual events that affected the whole kingdom. The kings were symbolically identified with the country as a whole, and hence their well-being was essential to the well-being of the kingdom. Thus they were surrounded by ritual prohibitions that were intended to keep them in a state of health and ritual purity. In Bunyoro the king's life was also strengthened periodically by the killing of human beings, sometimes in his stead as a mock king. Although the kings were not regarded as divine beings, in Bunyoro and Nkore it was said that the kings were killed when they grew old or ill or were wounded in battle, although there is no evidence that this actually occurred. That the kingship was thought of in this way, however, indicates the symbolic significance of the king as the source of life, peace, and order in his kingdom. In Bunyoro and Buganda there were also shrines for the spirits of the royal ancestors, and in Buganda these shrines were major ritual centers of the kingship. The mediums at the royal shrines conveyed advice from the royal ancestors to the king regarding matters of state, and all of the king's officials went to the shrines to be confirmed in office.

Fundamental to the social systems of the Gisu, Kikuyu, Kamba, Kaguru, and Gogo are rites of puberty and of initiation into adulthood. Their purpose is to transform young boys and girls into adult men and women. In these societies circumcision and clitoridectomy (or labiadectomy) are practiced. These physical operations are regarded as the outward signs of a new social position and of an inner moral change. Among the Gisu and Kikuyu, circumcision is thought of as a form of ordeal that testifies to the strength of character necessary for the change from childhood to adulthood. During the seclusion period, the initiated boys and girls are taught the rules governing sexual relations and the moral principles of society. For the Gisu, such rites are transformational, not merely transitional, "for it is in your heart," and the newly initiated person is said to be "like another person." The emphasis upon self-determination is also important, for a boy chooses when he shall be circumcised. When he does, he presents himself as a fully responsible agent to bear the ordeal and to stick to his resolution. Of the Kikuyu initiation rites, Jomo Kenyatta has said that "the moral code of the tribe is bound up with this custom and. . . it symbolizes the unification of the whole tribal organization." The rites mark the beginning of participation in the various governing groups in Kikuyu society, because age-group membership begins at this time. The history and legends are explained, as are the moral rules of society. Ngai and the ancestors are invoked, the misdeeds of childhood are symbolically cast away, and the initiates take an oath of loyalty and service to the Kikuyu commununity. Elements of these rites were also used during the Mau Mau oathing ceremonies. The Kaguru say that initiation into adulthood is the most important and impressive experience of their lives, and they conduct themselves in a noticeably different manner after going through it. Afterward, the fully initiated boys and girls can marry and have children, and the boys can own livestock and become warriors and elders in their society.

In precolonial times belief in witchcraft and sorcery was fundamental to East African societies. Although witchcraft and sorcery accusations are illegal under present law, in the past belief in witchcraft and sorcery functioned as an explanation of misfortunes that were not attributed to the gods or ancestors, and the process of finding and punishing witches functioned as a means of controlling socially deviant behavior and of resolving tensions within the local community. Belief in witchcraft and sorcery is based upon the assumption that many of the ills of life, including death, are caused by the evil intentions of human beings: hence the portrayal of witches as human beings whose behavior is the reverse of what is normal for humans. Witches and sorcerers are supposed to walk and dance upside down, to commit incest, to work at night, to travel at fantastic speeds, to go about naked, and to practice cannibalism. In short, witches and sorcerers are thought to confound the rules of society because they are bent upon destroying it. For the most part, witches were thought to be relatives of the people they attacked. The powers of witchcraft were also thought to be inherited and to be operative without a person's being aware of it. Sorcery, by contrast, was regarded as a conscious and deliberate action in which specific magical techniques were used to destroy other people. Witchcraft accusations were generally directed against people who exhibited antisocial characteristics—jealousy, spite, deceitfulness; even physical ugliness and unaccounted wealth were grounds for suspicion. In the past, diviners were employed to identify witches and sorcerers, and the accused were forced to confess and were often executed. Despite the illegality of witchcraft and sorcery accusations in the late twentieth century, belief in witchcraft and sorcery still exists in most of these societies as a way of explaining misfortune, and accusations may still be covertly made and acted upon.

Throughout the region of the northeastern Bantu-speaking peoples, the modern era has been marked by the increasing interaction of the traditional religions with Islam and Christianity. Although Islam and Christianity had long been present in certain areas of East Africa, it was not until the implementation of colonial rule with its new economic, educational, social, and religious order (or, in the case of Islam, the establishment in 1832 of the Omani Sultanate on Zanzibar and the subsequent development of extensive trading networks) that the introduced religions gained widespread influence.

By the late thirteenth century Islam had spread to the

trading ports along the East African coast, and in the fifteenth century Mombasa and Zanzibar had become important centers of Arabic influence; despite this, however, Islam did not penetrate beyond the coastal area until the early nineteenth century. In the nineteenth and early twentieth centuries Muslim teachers and religious leaders followed the Zanzibari traders along the inland routes that conveyed ivory and slaves from Buganda and northern Tanganyika. Through the agency of the kings of Buganda, notably Mutesa I, Islam took hold in Buganda, and Arabic literacy developed among the chiefly class. Despite the fact that Mutesa once martyred several dozen Muslim converts because of the zealousness of their faith and the threat it posed to the exercise of his authority, Buganda became the center of Muslim expansion and later the home of a community of Sudanese Muslims from the north.

Although the Portuguese established Christianity in Mombasa in the early sixteenth century, it vanished when the Portuguese were expelled in 1631. Christians were forced to convert to Islam. In 1844 missionary work began again in the Mombasa area, and in the 1860s missionary activity entered the inland, Bantu-speaking areas with the arrival of the Anglican Church Missionary Society and the French Catholic White Fathers at Mutesa's capital in Buganda. Several years later Mutesa's successor, Mwanga II, killed a number of royal pages for placing their Christian faith above their allegiance to the throne. After a prolonged struggle for power in the kingdom between adherents of Christianity and Islam, the Christian faction (with the support of British forces) was victorious, and Christianity became the established religion of Buganda. Thereafter, Buganda became the center of Christian expansion in the Bantu-speaking areas. One of the aims of missionary work was the supression of the Arab slave trade, and this motive also contributed to the establishment of colonial governments in Uganda, Kenya, and Tanganyika. During the colonial period, Islam made little headway in the Bantu-speaking areas, especially in parts formerly affected by the slave raids. The original Protestant and Catholic missions in Uganda spread into neighboring Kenya and Tanganyika, and colonial authorities rapidly opened these areas to other missions, such as the African Inland Mission and the missions of the Salvation Army, Scottish Presbyterians, Baptists, German and Swedish Lutherans, Seventh-day Adventists, American Mennonites, Moravians, and the Brethren.

While the European missionaries were primarily motivated by the teaching of the gospel, they also acted, consciously or unconsciously, as agents of colonialism, racism, and westernization. The establishment of mission schools and hospitals did much to break down African traditional culture, and the missionaries joined colonial officials in attempting to abolish many indigenous practices, such as circumcision rites (especially among girls), polygamy, bridewealth, mourning rites, twin ceremonies, and ancestor rituals. In this fashion the missionaries set about to educate and westernize the next generation of African leaders. The missionaries also taught about human equality and the importance of individuals and thereby helped to foster the seeds of anticolonialism among Africans who were later to take over the governments, schools, and churches of East Africa in the postcolonial period. From the beginning, African preachers and catechists assisted the European missionaries, and they played a major role in spreading Christianity outside the mission stations and in founding new churches. Sometimes the frustrations of European control and the upheavals of colonial and postcolonial life caused African religious leaders to found their own churches, especially in Kenya, where over 150 such churches were established before and after the independence period. These churches combined African and Christian beliefs and rites into indigenized Christian expressions; but many were short-lived, and a few had elements of political protest, such as the Dini ya Msambwa (Religion of the Ancestors) in western Kenya. After independence in the 1960s leadership in the mission churches gradually passed into African hands, and this was accompanied by a significant growth in church membership. At the same time there was a resurgence in traditional religion, especially in the practice of divination and healing, due largely to the absence of colonial repression and to the need for culturally suitable therapeutic techniques not found in Christianity, Islam, or Western hospitals. With the establishment of political parties and nationalist governments, the churches, which had originally shaped the leadership of the new nations, were effectively reduced to a marginal role in the politics of East Africa.

[*For further discussion of Ganda, Nyoro, and Nkore religions, see* Interlacustrine Bantu Religions.]

BIBLIOGRAPHY

Beattie, John. "Spirit Possession in Bunyoro." In *Spirit Mediumship and Society in Africa,* edited by John Beattie and John Middleton. New York, 1969. An excellent ethnographic survey.

Beidelman, T. O. *The Kaguru.* New York, 1971. Contains a brief but comprehensive account of Kaguru religion.

Heald, Suzette. "The Making of Men." *Africa* 52 (1982): 15–36. A perceptive psychological study of Gisu boys' initiation ceremonies.

Kenyatta, Jomo. *Facing Mount Kenya* (1938). New York, 1978.

An important interpretation from a Kikuyu point of view.

Lindblom, Gerhard. *The Akamba in British East Africa.* 2d ed. Uppsala, 1920. A classic ethnography.

Middleton, John, and Greet Kershaw. *The Central Tribes of the Northeastern Bantu.* Rev. ed. London, 1965. A comprehensive survey and bibliography that includes ethnic groups not covered in the present article.

Ndeti, Kivuto. *Elements of Ákámbá Life.* Ann Arbor, 1971. Contains an important interpretation of some Akamba religious ideas and practices.

Oded, Arye. *Islam in Uganda.* Jerusalem, 1974.

Ray, Benjamin C. "Sacred Space and Royal Shrines in Buganda." *History of Religions* 16 (May 1977): 363–373.

Rigby, Peter. "Some Gogo Rituals of 'Purification.'" In *Dialectic in Practical Religion,* edited by Edmund Leach, pp. 153–179. Cambridge, 1968.

Rigby, Peter. "The Symbolic Role of Cattle in Gogo Ritual." In *The Translation of Culture,* edited by T. O. Beidelman, pp. 257–292. New York, 1973. Both of Rigby's articles present substantive interpretations of Gogo rituals.

Roscoe, John. *The Baganda* (1910). London, 1965. A classic ethnography.

Routledge, W. S., and Katherine Routledge. *With a Prehistoric People* (1910). London, 1968. A well-informed account of the Kikuyu in the early twentieth century.

Welbourn, F. B. "The Impact of Christianity on East Africa." In *History of East Africa,* edited by D. A. Low and Alison Smith, vol 3. Oxford, 1976.

BENJAMIN C. RAY

EASTER, the most important of all Christian feasts, celebrates the passion, the death, and especially the resurrection of Jesus Christ. The English name *Easter,* like the German *Ostern,* probably derives from *Eostur,* the Norse word for the spring season, and not from *Eostre,* the name of an Anglo-Saxon goddess. In Romance languages the name for Easter is taken from the Greek *Pascha,* which in turn is derived from the Hebrew *Pesaḥ* (Passover). Thus Easter is the Christian equivalent of the Jewish Passover, a spring feast of both harvest and deliverance from bondage. [*See* Passover.] The Eastern Slavs call Easter "the great day" and greet one another, as do the Greeks, with the words "Christ is risen," receiving the response "He is risen indeed."

Easter is the earliest of all annual Christian feasts. It may originally have been observed in conjunction with the Jewish Passover on the fourteenth day of the month Nisan. Gradually, however, it was observed everywhere on Sunday, the day of Christ's resurrection. The Council of Nicaea (325) prescribed that Easter should always be celebrated on the first Sunday after the first full moon following the spring equinox.

Easter was fundamentally a nocturnal feast preceded by a fast of at least one day. The celebration took place from Saturday evening until the early morning hours of Sunday. In the fifth century Augustine of Hippo called this "the mother of all vigils." From at least the time of Tertullian (third century) the Easter Vigil (also called the Paschal Vigil) was the favored time for baptism, since the candidates for initiation mirrored the new life won by Christ from the darkness of death. [*See* Baptism.]

The symbolism of light became an important feature of this nocturnal festival. It was customary on the Saturday evening of the Easter Vigil to illuminate not only churches but entire towns and villages with lamps and torches; thus the night was called "the night of illumination." From at least the end of the fourth century in Jerusalem the lighting of lamps at vespers took on a special character at this feast. In Northern European countries the use of special lights at Easter coincided with the custom of lighting bonfires on hilltops to celebrate the coming of spring; this is the origin of the Easter fire later kindled in Western Christian Easter Vigils. Large Easter candles also became the rule, and poems were composed in honor of them and thus of Christ the light, whom they symbolized. Such poems stem from as early as the fourth century; the most famous, still employed in various versions, is the *Exultet,* which originated in the seventh or eighth century. In the East, among the Orthodox, Holy Saturday night is celebrated with a candlelight procession outside the church building. After a solemn entrance into the church, bells peal and the Great Matins or Morning Prayer of Easter begins. It is followed by a solemn celebration of the Eucharist according to the liturgy of Saint Basil.

The Easter Vigil also contains a number of biblical readings. In the East the baptisms took place during the long readings of the vigil, whereas in the West a procession to the baptistery took place after the readings had been completed. In both cases the celebration of the Eucharist followed the baptisms. With the decline in adult conversions and, hence, in Easter baptisms during the Middle Ages, the time for the vigil service (and thus the end to fasting) was moved up to Saturday morning; however, the Roman Catholic church restored the nocturnal character of the service in 1952 and other rites relating to Holy Week in 1956. In the current Roman Catholic, Lutheran, and Episcopalian rites the Paschal Vigil is the high point of a *triduum,* or three days of services, celebrating the death and resurrection of Christ.

From at least the end of the fourth century, Easter was provided in Jerusalem with an octave, eight days of celebration. With the medieval decline in the octave celebration, Monday and Tuesday of Easter week nevertheless retained the character of holidays. In a larger context the whole of the fifty days from Easter Sunday to Pentecost was properly called Easter, and so constituted a feast in its own right; the eight-day octave, however, was a time of special recognition of the newly baptized. The Sunday after Easter was called the "Sunday in white" because the newly baptized wore their baptismal garments for the last time on that day, and among the Orthodox the octave of Easter is still called "the week of new garments." [*See* Christian Liturgical Year.]

Devotions tied to the liturgy of Easter are the origins of liturgical drama. In the Middle Ages it was customary to bury the consecrated host and a cross, or simply a cross, in an Easter sepulcher on Holy Thursday or Good Friday. The host or cross was retrieved on Easter Sunday morning and brought to the altar in procession. From this practice developed a brief Easter play called the *Visitatio sepulchri* (Visit to the Tomb), which enacted the visit of the two women to Christ's empty tomb. The same dramatic dialogue can be seen in the eleventh-century poetic sequence *Victimae paschali laudes* (Praise to the Paschal Victim), which became part of the Western liturgy. [*See* Drama, *article on* European Religious Drama.]

A number of popular customs mark Easter Sunday and the rest of Easter week. One such custom, allied to the coming of spring with its earlier sunrise, is an outdoor sunrise service celebrating the resurrection. Such celebrations are especially popular among American Protestants. Since Easter was a time in which the newly baptized wore shining white garments, it became customary to wear new clothes on Easter Sunday and to show them off by walking around town and countryside; thus originated the Easter promenade or Easter parade, popular in many places.

Among the most familiar Easter symbols are the egg and rabbit. The egg symbolizes new life breaking through the apparent death (hardness) of the eggshell. Probably a pre-Christian symbol, it was adapted by Christians to denote Christ's coming forth from the tomb. In many countries the exchange of colored or decorated eggs at Easter has become customary. [*See* Egg.] The Easter bunny or rabbit is also most likely of pre-Christian origin. The rabbit was known as an extraordinarily fertile creature, and hence it symbolized the coming of spring. Although adopted in a number of Christian cultures, the Easter bunny has never received any specific Christian interpretation. [*See* Rabbits.]

Among Easter foods the most significant is the Easter lamb, which is in many places the main dish of the Easter Sunday meal. Corresponding to the Passover lamb and to Christ, the Lamb of God, this dish has become a central symbol of Easter. Also popular among Europeans and Americans on Easter is ham, because the pig was considered a symbol of luck in pre-Christian European culture. [*See* Pigs.]

BIBLIOGRAPHY

For a comprehensive survey of the Western liturgical development of Easter, see Ildephonso Schuster's *The Sacramentary* (New York, 1925). Good treatments of Easter and associated popular customs can be found in Francis X. Weiser's *Handbook of Christian Feasts and Customs* (New York, 1958) and in the same author's *The Easter Book* (New York, 1954). For discussion from the point of view of the history of religions, see E. O. James's *Seasonal Feasts and Festivals* (New York, 1961).

JOHN F. BALDOVIN, S.J.

EASTERN CHRISTIANITY.

[*This entry provides a historical survey and general introduction to the Orthodox branch of Christian religion. Particular Orthodox churches and numerous Eastern Christian church leaders mentioned herein are subjects of separate entries.*]

In its origins Christianity is Eastern rather than Western. Jesus was a Palestinian Jew, and during the early, formative centuries of the church's life the Greek and Syriac East was both numerically stronger and intellectually more creative than the Latin West. From around the year 1000 onward the balance has shifted, with Western Christendom assuming the more dominant role and the Christian East shrinking under social and economic pressure and, at times, active persecution. Yet the Eastern churches, with their continuing witness to an understanding of Christian faith and life radically different from that of either Roman Catholicism or Protestantism, have a vital part to play in the current movement toward Christian unity.

General Survey

In language and culture, early Christianity falls into three major areas: the Latin West, with its chief center at Rome; the Greek-speaking East, with its chief center at Constantinople from the fourth and fifth centuries onward; and the Syriac East, with its chief center at Edessa (modern-day Urfa, in southeastern Turkey). Despite minor schisms, all three areas initially constituted a single, undivided Christian communion. Separation occurred in three stages, at intervals of approximately five hundred years.

In the fifth and sixth centuries, the Syriac Christian world became separated from Greek and Latin Christendom. At the same time the Syriac Christians were themselves divided into two groups, the Nestorians and the non-Chalcedonians. The non-Chalcedonians also included other non-Greek Christians: the Copts (in Egypt), the Ethiopians, and the Armenians. Around the eleventh century (according to the usual view, in 1054), Greek

Orthodoxy became separated from Roman Catholicism, and in the sixteenth century Western Christendom became divided between Catholics and Protestants. This last division did not directly affect the Christian East, although in the nineteenth century Protestant missions were established in areas that had traditionally been associated with Eastern churches.

Eastern Christendom is thus subdivided at present into three main bodies: the Eastern Orthodox church, the "separated" Eastern churches, and the Uniate churches (see figure 1). The Eastern Orthodox church, often described simply as the Orthodox church, is also termed the Greco-Russian church and, by its own members, the Orthodox Catholic church (but this does not mean that it is part of the Roman Catholic church). The "separated" Eastern churches include the East Syrian church, also called the Nestorian, Chaldean, or Assyrian church (but by its own adherents usually termed the Church of the East), and the non-Chalcedonian Orthodox churches, often called "monophysite," although its own members prefer to avoid that name. The members of Uniate churches, who are also known as Eastern Catholics, are groups from the Eastern Orthodox church and the "separated" Eastern churches who on different occasions since the twelfth century have united with Rome. [*See also* Greek Orthodox Church; Russian Orthodox Church; Armenian Church; Coptic Church; Ethiopian Church; Syrian Orthodox Church of Antioch; Nestorian Church; *and* Uniate Churches.]

Eastern Orthodox Church. The Eastern Orthodox church is the second largest church in the contemporary Christian world, next to—but much smaller than—the Roman Catholic church. It developed from the Greek-speaking church of the eastern Roman or Byzantine empire, but numerically its main strength now lies in the Slavic countries (Russia, Yugoslavia, Bulgaria) and in Romania. It is a fellowship of some fifteen sister churches, all of them agreed in faith, using the same forms of worship, and joined with the others in sacramental communion, but each administratively independent. All acknowledge the honorary primacy of the ecumenical patriarch at Constantinople (Istanbul). The patriarch does not lay claim to a supremacy of universal jurisdiction such as is ascribed to the pope in Roman Catholicism. His position is more similar to that of the archbishop of Canterbury within the worldwide Anglican communion.

The Eastern Orthodox church today comprises various jurisdictions, named here according to the traditional order of precedence. The figures given are at best approximate and indicate numbers of baptized (as of the early 1980s) rather than actively practicing members. Of first importance are the four ancient patriarchates: Constantinople (5,000,000 baptized members), Alexandria (350,000), Antioch (600,000), and Jerusalem (80,000). The heads of these four jurisdictions are called patriarchs. The patriarchate of Constantinople consists mainly of Greeks living in Crete or Greeks who emigrated to the United States, Australia, and Western Europe. In the patriarchate of Alexandria, embracing the whole African continent, the episcopate is predominantly Greek, but about half the faithful are Africans in Kenya, Uganda, and Tanzania. The head of this church bears the formal title "Pope and Patriarch." The episcopate and faithful of the patriarchate of Antioch, which has its main centers in Syria and Lebanon, are Arabic-speaking. At Jerusalem the episcopate is Greek, but the flock is almost entirely Arab. The patriarchate of Jerusalem includes within its sphere of influence the semi-independent Church of Sinai.

Second in order of precedence are other patriarchates and the autocephalous (i.e., self-governing) churches of the Eastern Orthodox church: Russia (50,000,000?), Serbia (in Yugoslavia; 8,000,000), Romania (15,000,000), Bulgaria (8,000,000), Cyprus (440,000), Greece (8,000,000), Poland (450,000), Albania (250,000 in 1945), Georgia (500,000?), Czechoslovakia (100,000), and America (1,000,000). The heads of the churches of Russia, Serbia, Romania, and Bulgaria bear the title Patriarch. The head of the Georgian church (the position of which in the order of precedence has not been agreed on) is styled Catholicos-Patriarch. The heads of the other churches are known either as Archbishop (Cyprus, Greece, Albania) or as Metropolitan (Poland,

FIGURE 1. *Eastern Christian Churches*

1. EASTERN ORTHODOX CHURCH

   Ancient patriarchates: Constantinople, Alexandria, Antioch, and Jerusalem

   Other patriarchates and autocephalous churches: Russia, Serbia, Romania, Bulgaria, Cyprus, Greece, Poland, Albania, Georgia, Czechoslovakia, and America

   Autonomous churches: Finland and Japan

2. "SEPARATED" CHURCHES

   Nestorian Church (also known as East Syrian Church, Chaldean Church, and Church of the East)

   Non-Chalcedonian Orthodox Churches (also known as Oriental Orthodox Churches and often called "Monophysite" Churches): Syrian Church of Antioch, Syrian Church of India, Coptic Church, Armenian Church, and Ethiopian Church

3. UNIATE CHURCHES (also known as Eastern Catholic Churches): Ruthenians, Malabar Church of India, Melchites, Maronites, and others

Czechoslovakia, America). The autocephalous status of the last three churches—Georgia, Czechoslovakia, and, more particularly, the Orthodox Church in America—is called into question by some of the other Orthodox churches. Two of the above churches, Cyprus and Greece, are Greek in language and culture; five of them—Russia, Serbia, Bulgaria, Poland, and Czechoslovakia—are Slav, while Romania is predominantly Latin in culture. Georgia (within the Soviet Union) and Albania stand apart, each with its own linguistic and cultural tradition, but many of the Albanian Orthodox are Greek-speaking. Most of the parishes belonging to the Orthodox Church in America were originally Russian, but the greater part are now English-speaking.

Third in order of precedence are two churches, not as yet fully self-governing, that are termed "autonomous" rather than autocephalous. These are the churches of Finland (66,000) and Japan (25,000). The first of these, depending on Constantinople, is headed by an archbishop; the second, depending on Russia, is headed by a metropolitan. The small Orthodox Church of China, granted autonomy by the church of Russia in 1957, seems to have disappeared almost completely in the Cultural Revolution of the later 1960s.

"Separated" Eastern Churches. One of the "separated" Eastern churches, the East Syrian church (the Nestorian church), developed historically from the bishops and dioceses that refused to accept the Council of Ephesus (431), regarded by other Christians as the third ecumenical council. Theologically the East Syrian church has been influenced above all by the school of Antioch, and especially by Theodore of Mopsuestia (c. 350–428). It does not use the title *theotokos* ("God-bearer" or "Mother of God"), assigned to the Blessed Virgin Mary by the Council of Ephesus, and it rejects the condemnation passed on Nestorius, patriarch of Constantinople, by that council. With its main centers from the fifth century onward inside the Persian empire, the Nestorian church was largely cut off from Christians under Byzantine rule, and still more from Christians in the West. Nestorian missionaries traveled widely, founding communities in Arabia, India, and across eastern Asia as far as China. Now greatly reduced, the Nestorian church numbers no more than 200,000, living in Iraq, Iran, India, and above all the United States. Its head is known as "Catholicos-Patriarch of the East."

Also among the "separated" Eastern churches are the non-Chalcedonian Orthodox churches, which like the Eastern (Chalcedonian) Orthodox church represent a communion of sister churches, although in the case of the non-Chalcedonians there is a wider variety in the forms of liturgical worship. The non-Chalcedonians, also known as the Oriental Orthodox, are so called because they reject the Council of Chalcedon (451), accepted by Eastern Orthodox and Western Christians as the fourth ecumenical council. Thus, whereas Eastern Orthodoxy recognizes seven ecumenical councils, the most recent of them Nicaea II (787), and Roman Catholicism recognizes twenty-one, the most recent Vatican II (1962–1965), the non-Chalcedonians recognize only three: Nicaea I (325), Constantinople I (381), and Ephesus (431). Often called "monophysites" because they ascribe to Christ only one nature *(phusis)* and not two, the non-Chalcedonian churches have been chiefly influenced in their theology by Cyril of Alexandria (375–444). There are five independent non-Chalcedonian churches: the Syrian Orthodox Church of Antioch (200,000), also known as the West Syrian or Jacobite church, headed by a patriarch resident in Damascus, and with members mainly in Syria and Lebanon; the Syrian Orthodox Church of India (1,800,000), closely connected with the Syrian Orthodox Church of Antioch, under the leadership of a patriarch resident in Kottayam, Kerala, South India; the Coptic Orthodox church (4,000,000) in Egypt, headed by a patriarch; the Armenian Orthodox church (2,500,000), with a catholicos resident in Echmiadzin, Soviet Armenia, a second catholicos resident in Antelias, Lebanon, and two patriarchs, at Jerusalem and Constantinople (in the Armenian tradition a patriarch ranks lower than a catholicos); and the Ethiopian Orthodox church (16,000,000), which until 1950 was partially dependent on the Coptic church but since then has been fully self-governing, and whose head is known as the patriarch.

Uniate Churches. While accepting the primacy of the pope and the other doctrines of the Roman Catholic church, the Uniate churches (Eastern Catholics) have retained their own ritual and distinctive practices, such as allowing the clergy to marry. There are Uniate churches parallel to the great majority of the Orthodox churches mentioned above, whether Eastern Orthodox or Oriental. The largest groups among the Uniate churches are the Ruthenians (including the Ukrainians and the Byelorussians, or White Russians), who within the Soviet Union exist only as an underground church but who have over a million members outside the U.S.S.R.; the Malabar Church in India (2,000,000); the Melchites (500,000), mainly in Syria and Lebanon; and the Maronites (1,400,000), also in Lebanon, who alone among the Uniate churches have no parallel within the Eastern Orthodox or Oriental Orthodox churches. In total, outside the Soviet Union and Romania, there were in the early 1980s some 6,500,000 members of the Uniate churches.

Historical Development

The history of Christianity in the Balkans, and more especially of Greek-speaking Christianity, falls into four primary periods: the early period, prior to the conversion of Emperor Constantine (312) and the establishment of the Christian empire; the Byzantine period, extending from the establishment of Constantinople as the "new Rome" and Christian capital (330) to its capture by the Ottoman Turks (1453); the Turkish period (the *Turcocratia*), from 1453 to the outbreak of the Greek War of Independence (1821); and the modern period, from the early nineteenth century onward. [*For discussion of the regional dispersion of Orthodox Christianity, see* Christianity, *especially article on* Christianity in Eastern Europe.]

Slavic and Romanian Christianity follows this basic structure, with the Roman period (in Romania only), the period of Byzantine influence, the Turkish period, and the modern period. But in the case of Russia, which never passed under Ottoman rule, the main periods are Kievan Christianity (tenth to thirteenth century), the Moscow period (fourteenth to seventeenth century), the Saint Petersburg period (eighteenth century to 1917), and the modern period (since 1917). The evolution of the "separated" Eastern churches has followed a different pattern. Some of these churches (e.g., the Nestorian church and the Ethiopian church) were at all times largely or entirely outside the Byzantine empire, while others (e.g., the Syrian Orthodox Church of Antioch and the Coptic church) passed outside its control with the rapid expansion of Islamic power following the death of Muḥammad (632).

The First Three Centuries. The Jewish church, established at Jerusalem on the day of Pentecost and headed initially by James, "the Lord's brother" (*Mk.* 6:3), remained small, and after the fall of Jerusalem (AD 70) it ceased to maintain a distinctive identity. Semitic thought-patterns persisted to some extent within Syriac Christianity, but in the Greek-speaking churches from the second century onward the Christian message was presented to an increasing degree in Hellenic form. This assimilation of Greek thought is evident in Justin Martyr (c. 100–163/5) and the other second-century apologists, and also in the great third-century Alexandrian theologians Clement (150?–215?) and Origen (c. 185–c. 254).

Whereas Christ himself came from a rural background, Greek Christianity was from the start predominantly urban. The basic unit was the çity congregation, worshiping initially under the collegial leadership of a group of presbyter-*episkopoi*, but from the second century onward under the presidency of a single bishop. The bishop's authority extended also to the surrounding countryside, but until the fourth century or even later, Christian influence in many rural areas continued to be limited.

Before the conversion of Constantine, Christianity enjoyed no legal recognition from the Roman state. Persecution was intermittent, with long periods of toleration, especially during the third century. Yet the call to martyrdom was an ever-present possibility, looming large in the spiritual imagination of the first Christians. [*See* Persecution, *article on* Christian Experience.] With the establishment of the Christian empire in the fourth century, literal "martyrdom of blood" was largely replaced by the inner "martyrdom of conscience," attained through the ascetic self-denial of the monastic life. But in more recent times outer martyrdom has become once again an immediate prospect. During the Turkish period there were many "new martyrs" among the Greeks, Slavs, and Romanians, while in Soviet Russia during the thirty years following the Bolshevik Revolution (1917) far more Christians suffered death for their beliefs than in the entire three hundred years following Christ's crucifixion. In the history of the "separated" Eastern churches, both Nestorian and non-Chalcedonian, under Islamic rule there have also been many martyrdoms, and some of the most severe massacres have occurred in the twentieth century. The prayer of Ignatius of Antioch, martyred at Rome around 107, "Suffer me to be an imitator of the Passion of my God," has been lived out by countless Eastern Christians in modern times.

In the inner life of the pre-Constantinian church a decisive choice was made during the second century with the rejection of gnosticism. [*See* Gnosticism.] Reacting against gnostic dualism, Irenaeus of Lyons (c. 130–c. 200) and others insisted upon the Christian value of history, upon the true reality of Christ's human body and his physical suffering, and upon the intrinsic goodness of the material creation. Jesus, it was affirmed, does not save us from the world but with the world; the "God and Father of our Lord Jesus Christ" is also the creator of the universe. An emphasis upon the cosmic dimensions of salvation, and a high estimate of the spirit-bearing potentialities of material things, have always been features of Eastern Christian theology at its best. This is evident, at a later date, in the Orthodox defense of icons against iconoclasm (eighth and ninth centuries) and in the hesychastic teaching concerning Christ's transfiguration on Mount Tabor (fourteenth century).

The Byzantine Period. The outward position of Christianity was dramatically altered by the conversion of Emperor Constantine (d. 337) to the Christian faith around 312. This led in particular to two further events, which were of lasting importance for the evolution of Eastern Orthodoxy. [*See* Constantinianism.]

The founding of Constantinople. In 330, Constantine inaugurated the city of Constantinople as his capital, on the site of the Greek city of Byzantium. As the "new Rome" it became the chief center of Greek Christendom, gradually supplanting Alexandria, which hitherto had held the first place in the East. In the heart of Constantinople, beside the imperial palace, stood the "Great Church" of the Holy Wisdom (Hagia Sophia), built by Constantine and rebuilt on an enlarged scale by Emperor Justinian (d. 565). This church served as a visible symbol of God's blessing on the Christian empire, and it had a profound influence upon the development of the Byzantine liturgy.

The seven ecumenical councils. In 325, Constantine summoned the Council of Nicaea, the first in a series of seven general or ecumenical councils, all of them held in the eastern part of the Roman empire. The doctrinal decrees of these seven councils, together with holy scripture, embody in the eyes of Eastern Orthodoxy the basic truths of the Christian faith, accepted by all members of the church. (The term *ecumenical,* i.e., "universal," is derived from the Greek *oikoumenē,* "the inhabited world.") [*See* Councils, *article on* Christian Councils, *and* Creeds, *article on* Christian Creeds.]

The first two of these seven councils, Nicaea I (325) and Constantinople I (381), defined the church's faith in God as Trinity. Christians believe in one God who is at the same time three: Father, Son, and Holy Spirit. The Son is equal and coeternal with the Father, "true God from true God . . . one in essence [*homoousios*] with the Father" (Nicaea I), and the same is to be affirmed also of the Holy Spirit, who is "together worshiped and together glorified" with the Father and the Son (Constantinople I). The definitions were directed against the Arians, who denied the full divinity of the Son, and the Macedonians, who questioned the full divinity of the Holy Spirit.

The next four councils, Ephesus (431), Chalcedon (451), Constantinople II (553), and Constantinople III (680), were concerned more particularly with the doctrine of Christ's person. Christ is God and man at once, a single and undivided person. Because of this personal unity, his mother, the Blessed Virgin Mary, is styled *theotokos,* "God-bearer" (Ephesus), and it is also legitimate to say, with reference to the crucifixion, that "one of the Trinity suffered in the flesh" (Constantinople II). Moreover, since Christ is both entirely divine and genuinely human—not just half of each but totally God and totally one of us—he exists "in two natures," the one divine and the other human, both of them complete (Chalcedon), and he likewise has two "natural energies" and two wills (Constantinople III).

The christological definitions of these four councils, while accepted by the Eastern Orthodox church, are contested by other Eastern Christians. Members of the East Syrian, or Nestorian, church repudiate the decisions of Ephesus, and consequently those of Constantinople II. They believe that to speak, as these councils do, of God's being born or suffering death, even with the qualifying clause "according to the flesh," introduces an unacceptable confusion between Christ's godhead and his manhood and undermines the divine transcendence.

Standing in the christological tradition of Antioch, the Nestorians insist upon a clear distinction between the two natures in Christ. Even though they do not reckon Chalcedon as an ecumenical council, they have no objection in principle to its definition concerning the duality of natures. After the end of the fifth century there were few direct contacts between the Nestorians, living within the Persian empire, and the Greeks under Byzantine rule. But the mystical writings of Isaac the Syrian (d. about 700), Nestorian bishop of Nineveh, were soon translated into Greek, and have deeply influenced Byzantine and Russian spirituality. [*See* Nestorianism.]

The non-Chalcedonian or Oriental Orthodox Christians, standing in the christological tradition of Alexandria, occupy a place at the opposite theological extreme from the Nestorians. They accept the ecumenicity of Ephesus and strongly emphasize the title *theotokos,* but they reject the phrase "in two natures," affirmed at Chalcedon, seeing in this a "Nestorian" division of the one Savior into two. They prefer to speak of "one incarnate nature of God the Word," and when referring to Christ's "natures" in the plural, they are willing to affirm only that he is "from two" *(ek duo),* not that he is "in two" *(en duo),* a position that has led others to call them "monophysite." [*See* Monophysitism.]

Difficulties between the Nestorians, the Chalcedonians, and the non-Chalcedonians were aggravated by terminological misunderstandings. Trouble was caused above all by the word *phusis:* in Nestorius and the Chalcedonian definition this word signifies "nature" or "set of distinctive characteristics," while in non-Chalcedonian authors it tends to mean much the same as "person," for which Chalcedon uses the terms *prosōpon* and *hupostasis.* Cultural differences and the growth of national separatism among the non-Greek subjects of the

Byzantine empire also contributed to the split, although this did not become an important factor until the later sixth century.

In addition to defining doctrine, the ecumenical councils were also concerned with the administrative organization of the church. Their disciplinary regulations continue to form the basis of Eastern Orthodox canon law. In the canons adopted at Nicaea I, Constantinople I, and Chalcedon, the Christian world is subdivided into five patriarchates. In order of precedence these are Rome, Constantinople, Alexandria, Antioch, and Jerusalem. Two criteria determined the selection of these five: importance in the civil structure of the empire, and apostolic foundation. The first four were chosen as the leading urban centers in the ancient world, the fifth as the place where Christ died and rose again. All except Constantinople had a clear claim to apostolic foundation.

Behind the conciliar definitions lay the work of individual church fathers. Athanasius of Alexandria (c. 298–373) defended the full divinity of Christ against the Arians and did much to establish the theological sense of the key term in the Nicene definition, *consubstantial*, or "one in essence" *(homoousios)*. His word was complemented by that of the three Cappadocian church fathers—Basil of Caesarea (c. 329–379), his friend Gregory of Nazianzus (c. 329–391), known in Orthodoxy as Gregory the Theologian, and Basil's younger brother Gregory of Nyssa (c. 335–c. 395)—who stressed the threeness of the persons, or *hupostasis*, alongside the unity of essence. The Cappadocian formulation of trinitarian faith continues to this day to be normative in Eastern Orthodoxy, whereas the West has been deeply marked by the different, but not necessarily incompatible, approach of Augustine of Hippo (354–430). Basil and Gregory of Nazianzus, together with John Chrysostom (c. 354–407), are honored in the Orthodox tradition as the "three great hierarchs."

Arianism was also opposed by Ephraem of Syria (c. 306–373), the greatest of the Syriac church fathers, remembered both as an exponent of scripture and as a theologian-poet. For Chalcedonians as well as non-Chalcedonians, Cyril of Alexandria is the outstanding authority on the doctrine of Christ's person. Among later Fathers, Eastern Orthodoxy assigns a preeminent place to Maximos the Confessor (580–662), important both for his understanding of the human freedom and human will in Christ and for his teaching on prayer; and to John of Damascus (c. 675–c. 749), author of *On the Orthodox Faith*, which is regarded as an authoritative summary of doctrine. In the realm of spirituality, along with Maximos, the most influential writers are Evagrios of Pontus (345–399), disciple of the Cappadocians; Dionysius the Areopagite (c. 500); and John Climacus (c. 570–c. 649), abbot of the monastery of Sinai. [*See also* Arianism *and* Free Will and Predestination, *article on* Christian Concepts.]

The rise of Islam. The outward aspect of Eastern Christendom was drastically altered by the expansion of Islam in the 630s and 640s. The Arabs swiftly gained control of Syria, Palestine, and Egypt, so that the three patriarchates of Alexandria, Antioch, and Jerusalem came under non-Christian rule. The schism between Chalcedonians and non-Chalcedonians hardened, and efforts at reconciliation were abandoned. Henceforward the Greek patriarchates of Alexandria, Antioch, and Jerusalem played only a peripheral role in Eastern Orthodox history; the first two of these had in any case been greatly reduced in membership through the separation of the non-Chalcedonians. Within the Eastern Roman Empire the patriarchate of Constantinople was now left as the only major center.

Iconoclasm. During 726–843 the Byzantine church was preoccupied with a prolonged conflict concerning the holy icons, attacked by the iconoclasts ("icon smashers") but defended by the iconodules ("icon venerators"). The dispute involved not simply the theology of Christian art but also the nature of Christ's person, and so it may be seen in part as a continuation of earlier christological debates. Meeting under Patriarch Tarasios (d. 806), Nicaea II (787), the last of the seven ecumenical councils recognized by Eastern Orthodoxy, declared that it is legitimate not merely to paint icons and to place them in churches, but also to show to these icons veneration and liturgical honor. The faithful may make prostrations in front of them and kiss them, and candles may be lit and incense offered before them. Icons are to be valued not just for aesthetic and decorative reasons but also as a means of grace, as a "door" or point of encounter, bringing the worshiper into existential communion with the person or mystery depicted. The decisions of Nicaea II were reaffirmed in the Triumph of Orthodoxy (843), when the icons were restored definitively to the churches. The chief theological spokesman on the iconodule side were John of Damascus, Theodore of Studios (759–826), and Nikephoros (758–828), patriarch of Constantinople. Icons continue to occupy a central role in Eastern Orthodox worship; in the "separated" Eastern churches they are allowed, but their cult is less emphasized. [*For further discussion, see* Icons *and* Iconoclasm.]

The schism between Orthodoxy and Rome. The later Byzantine period, from 843 until the fall of Constantinople to the Turks (1453), is marked by three main developments. Negatively, there was an increasing alienation between the Greek Orthodox East and the Roman Catholic West; positively, there was a major missionary expansion northward into the Slavic lands and a deepened understanding of mystical theology.

The schism between Greek and Latin Christendom is conventionally dated to the year 1054, but it was not so much a single event as a gradual, fluctuating, disjointed process that cannot be precisely dated. The root causes of the division extend back far earlier than the eleventh century, while its final completion did not occur until long after, perhaps not until the schism at Antioch in 1724. The original unity of the Mediterranean Christian world became seriously weakened during the fourth to the eighth centuries. While it would be anachronistic to speak of a definite schism in this early period between the Greek East and the Latin West, there was a growing alienation between them. It is in this long-extended process of estrangement that the roots of the later schism lie.

First, the founding of Constantinople, the "new Rome" (330), displacing the "old Rome" as imperial capital, sowed the seeds of a future ecclesiastical rivalry between the Greek East and the Latin West. Second, during the early fifth century the barbarian invasions and the subsequent collapse of the Western Empire led the papacy, as the one enduring center of unity in the West, to assume a dominant political role not exercised by the patriarch of Constantinople in the East, where there was a strong secular head in the person of the emperor. Such learning as survived the Dark Ages in the West was almost exclusively by the clergy and for the clergy, whereas in the Byzantine East there was always a highly educated lay civil service. The laity never became a purely passive element in the Byzantine church community, and this provides a vital clue to church-state relations in the East.

Third, the Slav and Avar invasions in the Balkans in the late sixth and seventh centuries, and the rise of Islam in the seventh century, rendered travel more hazardous and contacts between East and West more infrequent. Mutual isolation was increased by linguistic difficulties: up to the year 400 there were many Westerners who knew Greek, and many Greeks who knew Latin, but after the fifth century very few on either side were bilingual. Finally, the papacy underwent a significant shift in orientation during the eighth century. Cut off from the Byzantine empire during the period when it was officially iconoclast, the popes began to look northward to the rising kingdom of the Franks instead of looking eastward to Constantinople. Two decisive moments marking this changed alignment were Pope Stephen II's visit to Pépin in 754 and the coronation of Charlemagne at Rome by Pope Leo III on Christmas Day 800.

In this way the unity of Christian tradition and civilization, which despite variations of emphasis had existed as a firm reality between East and West during the fourth or fifth century, had by 800 been gravely eroded. Greeks and Latins still belonged to one church, but they were becoming strangers to each other. More and more they were losing a common universe of discourse. [*See also* Schism, *article on* Christian Schism.]

The Photian schism. During 861–867 a grave conflict, leading to mutual excommunications, occurred between Pope Nicholas I of Rome and Patriarch Photios of Constantinople. Both sought to assert control over the newly emerging church in Bulgaria. Questions of church order and liturgical practice, such as the manner of administering confirmation, the observance of the Lenten fast, and clerical celibacy (not required in the East), also entered into the dispute.

More serious, however, were two doctrinal differences. First, Photios attacked the West for adding the word *filioque* ("and from the Son") to the text of the creed. The Orthodox church continues to recite the Nicene-Constantinopolitan Creed (381) in its original form, affirming that the Holy Spirit "proceeds from the Father," but the West has expanded the wording to read "proceeds from the Father and the Son." The exact date of this addition is difficult to determine, but it seems to have been made originally in Spain during the sixth century as a safeguard against Arianism. Behind the addition lies the trinitarian theology of Augustine, who nowhere suggested altering the text of the creed but in his own teaching advocated the doctrine of the "double procession" of the Spirit—in a form, however, that many Orthodox would not consider heretical. The addition was adopted by the Frankish church under Charlemagne at the Council of Frankfort (794), but was not immediately welcomed at Rome; in 808 Leo III wrote to Charlemagne that, while the doctrine implied by the *filioque* was theologically sound, the text of the creed should be kept unchanged. In the 860s, however, Nicholas I supported the use of the *filioque* by German missionaries in Bulgaria. Photios and the Byzantines considered that the West had acted wrongly in altering unilaterally the creed that is the common heritage of the whole church. Photios also thought that the doctrine of the "double procession" involved grave errors of theology in the doctrine of the Trinity, but here not all Orthodox take as severe a view as he did.

The second serious doctrinal difference concerned papal primacy. Nicholas I claimed for the Roman see a universal supremacy of jurisdiction, over the East as well as the West. Photios and the Byzantines were not prepared to allow this. The Greeks considered that the pope, as senior among the five patriarchs, possesses a primacy of honor within the worldwide church, but not universal power of jurisdiction; he is the first, but the first among equals. They believed that while appeals can legitimately be made to the pope from the East, he does not have the right to intervene unasked in the internal affairs of the Eastern patriarchates. According to the Byzantine view, the pope's authority is less than that of an ecumenical council, and he cannot by himself decide questions of doctrine.

Communion between Rome and Constantinople was restored after 867, but no real solution was found for the two basic issues brought into the open by the conflict, the *filioque* and papal primacy. These continued to cause trouble in the future.

The anathemas of 1054. The breach between East and West was widened by new developments in the eleventh century. First, it seems that in 1004 the church in Constantinople had ceased to include the name of the pope in the diptychs. (Diptychs are lists, kept by each hierarch, of the bishops with whom he considers himself to be in communion, and they serve in this way as a visible sign of church unity.) But the precise circumstances under which the omission occurred remain unclear. Then from 1014 onward it became the practice at Rome to sing the creed with the *filioque.* In the middle of the eleventh century, after a prolonged struggle between the Byzantine and the German, or Frankish, faction at Rome, the German party eventually gained control. There followed a series of popes who, influenced by the reform movements of Lorraine and Cluny, adopted a strong doctrine of papal authority, reasserting the claim to universal jurisdiction over the East as well as the West. During 1011–1071, the gradual conquest by the Normans of the Byzantine possessions in Sicily and South Italy destroyed a significant bridge between East and West.

Matters came to a head in 1054, when Cardinal Humbert, sent to Constantinople by Pope Leo IX on a mission of conciliation, grew exasperated by the intransigence of Patriarch Michael Cerularios and issued an anathema, or bull of excommunication, against him. Cerularios retaliated with a similar excommunication against Humbert. The chief point of contention in 1054 was the use of azymes, or unleavened bread: should the bread at the Eucharist be leavened, as in the Orthodox practice, or unleavened, as in the West? But also involved were the *filioque,* the papal claims, and clerical celibacy. The mutual anathemas of 1054 have often been treated as the final consummation of the schism between East and West, but they were actually limited in scope. Humbert excommunicated Cerularios, not the emperor or the Eastern church; Cerularios excommunicated Humbert, not the pope. The incident was quickly forgotten. In many areas regular sacramental communion between Roman Catholics and Eastern Orthodox existed long after 1054, especially in the patriarchate of Antioch. The incident of Humbert and Cerularios is not so much a cause of the growing alienation as a symptom of it.

The Crusades. The Crusaders increased the tension between Eastern and Western Christendom, although that was in no way their original intention. [*See* Crusades.] By replacing the Greek hierarchy with Latin bishops in the cities they captured, they brought the schism down to the local level. In the patriarchate of Antioch from 1100, and in the Holy Land at least from 1187, there were two rival patriarchs claiming the same throne and dividing the allegiance of the Christian people. The Fourth Crusade, diverted to Constantinople in 1204, sacked the city and set up a Latin patriarch there as well. The pillage of Constantinople by the Crusaders is something that the Orthodox East has never forgotten or forgiven. If any single date is to be cited for the firm establishment of the schism, the most appropriate—at any rate from a psychological standpoint—is the year 1204.

Scholasticism. The gulf between East and West was further increased by the rise of Scholasticism in the Latin world during the twelfth and thirteenth centuries. [*See* Scholasticism.] The Greeks continued to theologize in a patristic manner, making use of reasoned argument, but at the same time constantly invoking the authority of the church fathers and appealing to the mystical, apophatic (negative) approach. Meanwhile in the West, within the intellectual climate of the universities, a new style of theology came to prevail, more systematic and analytical, more dependent on logical proofs, and employing a terminology that the Greeks found unfamiliar. With the translation of much of Thomas Aquinas's (c. 1225–1274) work into Greek in the fourteenth century, a number of Byzantines became warm admirers of his scholastic method, which they sought to make their own. Two of the leading Byzantine Thomists were the humanist scholar Demetrios Kydones (c. 1324–c. 1398), who favored ecclesiastical union with Rome, and Gennadios Scholarios (c. 1405–c. 1478), the first patriarch after the Turkish conquest, who in later life led the antiunionist party at Constantinople yet never ceased to be a Thomist. But most Greeks found the scholastic spirit alien and preferred the older, patristic approach. The common universe of discourse was in this way yet further eroded.

The quest for reunion. From 1204 until the fall of Constantinople in 1453, the Byzantine emperors sought persistently to reestablish ecclesiastical union with Rome. Their motives, though in part religious, were primarily political: they needed papal support against their enemies in the West, and still more they needed Western help against the advancing Turks.

There were two major attempts at reunion. At the Council of Lyons (1274), a small Greek delegation, commissioned by Emperor Michael VIII Palaeologus (d. 1282), not by the Greek hierarchy as a whole, accepted the terms of union laid down by Pope Gregory X. At the council itself there was no discussion of the doctrinal points at issue, and the Greeks were given no opportunity to explain the Orthodox viewpoint to the assembled Latin bishops. At the Council of Ferrara-Florence (1438–1439) there was a genuinely representative Greek delegation, including Emperor John VIII and Patriarch Joseph II. Doctrinal questions were fully debated. Eventually the Greeks agreed to accept as legitimate the Latin teaching on the "double procession" of the Holy Spirit, but they were not themselves required to add the *filioque* clause to the text of the creed. It was decided that the use of unleavened bread in the Eucharist by the Latins and the use of leavened bread by the Greeks were equally legitimate. Each side was to continue following its own customs. The Greeks assented to the Latin doctrine of purgatory and to the Roman understanding of the papal claims, although over this last there was a certain ambiguity in the phrasing. Almost all the Orthodox delegates signed the act of union, with the one notable exception of Mark Eugenikos (c. 1394–1445), archbishop of Ephesus, who was later canonized by the Orthodox church.

So far as the Christian East is concerned, both these acts of union proved to be no more than agreements on paper. They were rejected almost at once by the vast majority of the Orthodox people. But the union of Florence has been used more recently by the Roman Catholic church as the basis for the establishment of Uniate churches in the Ukraine, Romania, Antioch, and elsewhere.

The Slav missions. Limited first on the East through the separation of the Nestorian and the non-Chalcedonian churches and then on the West through the schism with Rome, the Byzantine church expanded into the north from the ninth century onward. Around 863 the first mission to the Slavs was sent by Photios to Moravia (corresponding approximately to present-day Czechoslovakia), under the leadership of two brothers from Thessalonica, Cyril (Constantine) (c. 826–869) and Methodius (c. 815–c. 884), known as the apostles of the Slavs. A basic principle of the Slav missions outside the boundaries of the Byzantine empire, adopted from the start by Cyril and Methodius, was the employment of the native vernacular. In contrast to the medieval West, with its unvarying use of Latin as the language of the church, the Byzantine missionaries saw it as their first task to translate the Bible and service books into Slavonic. This greatly assisted the growth of a distinctively national Orthodoxy in the various Slav domains. [*See also* Missions, *article on* Christian Missions.]

The Moravian mission of Cyril and Methodius failed to take permanent root and was displaced by the Latin form of Christianity. But in Bulgaria, Serbia, and Russia, Byzantine missionaries achieved lasting results. In Bulgaria, Tsar Boris, baptized by Greek clergy around 865, wavered for a time between East and West but finally accepted the jurisdiction of Constantinople. An independent Bulgarian patriarchate was created around 927, with its seat at Preslav and then at Ohrid. Suppressed in 1018, it was revived during 1235–1393, with its seat at Trnovo. Under Tsar Simeon (893–927) the Bulgarian kingdom attained outstanding cultural brilliance, with a rich Christian literature in Slavonic (largely translations from Greek).

Christianity was established in Serbia under Byzantine auspices in 867–874. Despite many links with the West up to the thirteenth century, the Serbian church became firmly incorporated in the Orthodox world. In 1219, during the archbishopric of Sava, it was granted autocephaly; a Serbian patriarchate was created at Peć in 1346. Medieval Serbian Orthodoxy attained its greatest brilliance in the reign of Stephen Dušan (1331–1355).

Great Prince Vladimir of Kiev was baptized by Byzantine missionaries around the year 988, and under his leadership a flourishing national church was established in Russia with its center at Kiev. In the fourteenth century the chief center, civil and religious, was transferred to Moscow. The Russian church became independent of Constantinople in 1448, and in 1589 the metropolitan of Moscow was raised to the rank of patriarch, coming first in honor after the four ancient patriarchates of the East.

Romania occupies a place apart among the Orthodox nations in the Balkans, since in ethnic character the Romanians are predominantly Latin, not Greek or Slav, and speak a Romance language. Their Christian history extends back to the period 106–271, when Dacia, corresponding to part of modern Romania, was a Roman province. How far Christianity survived after the collapse of the Roman empire in this area is unclear. Bulgarian missionaries were at work in Romania during the ninth and tenth centuries, and the Romanian principalities of Moldavia and Walachia came under the influence of the church of Constantinople from the fourteenth century onward. But despite external influences, whether Greek or Slav, Romanian Orthodoxy has retained its distinctive national character.

Hesychasm. The period of the seven ecumenical councils, from the fourth to the seventh century, laid down the main foundations of the Orthodox faith concerning the Trinity and the person of Christ. In the later period, from the ninth to the fifteenth century, the Byzantine church explored the implications of this faith for the salvation of the human person. What are the effects upon humans of the vision of God "face to face," of transforming union with the divine glory?

Byzantine mystical theology assigns a central place to the vision of divine light. This vision is particularly prominent in the experience of Symeon the New Theologian (949–1022), who believed the divine light to be not a physical and material light but the uncreated glory of the Deity, the very presence of God himself. Another feature marking the spirituality of this period, especially in the fourteenth century, is the practice of the Jesus Prayer, a short invocation usually taking the form "Lord Jesus Christ, Son of God, have mercy on me." Its origins date back to the fifth and sixth centuries, but its use was by no means universal in the Orthodox East, and it is not mentioned by Symeon. The aim of the Jesus Prayer was to produce *hēsuchia* ("quiet") in the sense of inner stillness and silence of heart, and those who practice it are therefore known as Hesychasts. By the thirteenth century, if not before, the Jesus Prayer was often accompanied by a psychosomatic technique involving control of breathing and concentration of attention upon the place of the heart (there are some striking parallels here with Yoga and Sufism). The technique was taught on Mount Athos by Nikephoros the Solitary (or Hesychast, late thirteenth century) and by Gregory of Sinai (d. 1347). They and other hesychasts believed that the constant use of the Jesus Prayer leads, by God's grace, to a vision of divine light such as Symeon experienced.

During 1337–1341 the hesychastic tradition was vigorously attacked by a learned Greek from southern Italy, Barlaam of Calabria (1290–c. 1350). Dismissing the psychosomatic technique as superstitious and materialistic, Barlaam argued that the light seen by the hesychasts was not divine but created and physical. He was answered by a monk from Mount Athos, Gregory Palamas (1296–1359), later to be archbishop of Thessalonica. Distinguishing between the essence and the energies of God, Palamas maintained that, while the divine essence remains always beyond created human understanding, the saints have direct union with the divine energies, which are God himself. These energies are identical with uncreated grace. The light seen by the hesychasts, then, is not material and created, but is a manifestation of the divine energies. It is the same as the light that shone from Christ at his transfiguration on Mount Tabor and that will shine from his person likewise at the glorious second coming. The psychosomatic technique, Palamas argued, while only an optional aid and not an essential part of the Jesus Prayer, rests upon a sound theological principle: the human person is an integrated whole of body and soul together, and the body should therefore play a positive part in the act of praying. Faithful to the same holistic view of human nature, Palamas also held that the body shares in the vision of the light of Tabor; although the light is not physical but uncreated, it can be perceived through the bodily senses when these are transformed by the power of the Holy Spirit. The Palamite teaching on the essence and energies of God and on the divine light was confirmed by three councils held at Constantinople (1341, 1347, 1351). The lay theologian Nicholas Cabasilas (c. 1322–1395), a friend and supporter of Palamas, expounded the hesychastic theology in sacramental terms, with particular reference to baptism and the Eucharist.

Hesychastic teaching was revived through the publication in 1782 of the vast collection of spiritual texts known as the *Philokalia,* edited by Makarios of Corinth (1731–1805) and Nikodimos of the Holy Mountain (c. 1749–1809). Translated into Slavonic and Russian, and more recently into Romanian and many Western languages, this book has had a profound effect upon modern Orthodoxy. In the opinion of many, the hesychastic and Philokalic element constitutes the most dynamic aspect of contemporary Orthodox life. [*See also* Monasticism, *article on* Christian Monasticism.]

The Turkish Period. From the collapse of the Byzantine empire (1453) until the early nineteenth century, the Greek Orthodox world, together with the Romanian principalities and most of the Slav Orthodox territories apart from Russia, lay under the rule of the Ottoman Turks. The ecumenical patriarch of Constantinople was regarded by the Muslim authorities as "ethnarch," head of the Orthodox Christian *ethnos,* or nation, with both religious and civil responsibility for all Orthodox in the Turkish empire, Greek or otherwise. This resulted in a wide extension of the patriarch's sphere of influence, but with the liberation of the subject Orthodox peoples from Turkish rule in the nineteenth century, the jurisdiction of the patriarchate contracted and a succession of autocephalous churches was set up: Greece (1833), Romania (1864), Bulgaria (1871), Serbia (1879), and Albania (1937). Although diminished in size, the ecumenical patriarchate still retains its honorary primacy within the Orthodox church as a whole.

The Turcocratia was a period of deep conservatism

within Eastern Orthodoxy. Tolerated by their Muslim masters but treated as second-class citizens, with few opportunities for study and little scope for publishing books, the Orthodox adopted a defensive stance. They strove to hold fast to their Byzantine inheritance but failed on the whole to develop it in a creative manner, remaining largely content with a "theology of repetition."

But alongside this loyalty to tradition, Orthodox theology of the Turkish period is also marked by westernization. In search of the higher education denied them within Ottoman dominions, Orthodox Christians went to study at Western universities under Protestant or, more frequently, Roman Catholic professors, and they were inevitably shaped by the non-Orthodox instruction they imbibed. At the same time, Protestants and Roman Catholics both sought to enlist the Orthodox as allies in the controversies of the Reformation, and so the Orthodox were challenged to reflect more deeply on such questions as the authority of scripture, predestination, the infallibility of the church, the real presence in the Eucharist, and the state of the departed.

The first significant contact between Orthodoxy and the world of the Reformation came in 1573–1581, when a group of Lutheran theologians from Tübingen embarked on discussions with Jeremias II (c. 1530–1595), patriarch of Constantinople. In his *Answers* the patriarch adhered carefully to the traditional Orthodox teaching, inclining neither to a Protestant nor to a Latin viewpoint. But a later patriarch of Constantinople, Cyril I (1572–1638), adopted Calvinist teachings in his *Confession* of 1629. He gained few adherents, however, since the majority of Greek theologians in the seventeenth century favored Latin rather than Protestant categories. The Greek bishop in Venice, Gabriel Severus (1541–1616), came close to adopting the Roman Catholic doctrine of purgatory and interpreted the eucharistic consecration in terms of the scholastic distinction between substance and accidents, employing the word *transubstantiation.* Dosítheos (1641–1707), patriarch of Jerusalem, spoke also of transubstantiation in his *Confession of Faith,* adopted at the Council of Jerusalem (1672), which condemned Cyril; he also advocated the Latin doctrine of purgatory in his *Confession,* but later modified his position. The most constructive exchange between Orthodox and Western Christians in this period was the correspondence between the Eastern patriarchs and the Anglican Nonjurors in 1716–1725, but this did not in the end lead to any specific agreement.

Outside the Greek world, Petr Moghila (1596–1646), metropolitan of Kiev, established a strongly Latin style of theology within the Orthodox church of the Ukraine. This Latinizing fashion spread from Kiev to Moscow later in the seventeenth century, but in the next century Russian theology became increasingly dominated by Protestant models, particularly through the influence of Feofan Prokopovich (1681–1736). But Metropolitan Filaret of Moscow (1782–1867) inspired a return to the patristic sources, and this had been continued from the 1930s onward by members of the Russian emigration such as Vladimir Lossky (1903–1958) and, above all, Georges Florovsky (1893–1979), who adopted as his theological motto the slogan "neo-patristic synthesis."

In Greek theology a westernizing manner has persisted up to the present century in the works of such writers as Christos Androutsos (1869–1935) and Panagiotis Trembelas (1886–1977). But the younger generation of Greek religious thinkers, including Christos Yannaras, John Zizioulas, and Panayiotis Nellas, while eager to learn from the West, have at the same time sought to clarify the distinctively Orthodox criteria that should guide the theologian. Like Lossky and Florovsky, they have striven to recover a more patristic understanding of the Christian faith.

Care should be taken not to exaggerate the degree of westernization in Orthodox theology during the Turcocratia and in more recent times. Most of those Orthodox who adopted Western categories and terminology still remained fundamentally Orthodox in the substance of their thought and continued to uphold the traditional Orthodox standpoint on such matters as the *filioque* or the papal claims.

The Modern Period. At the start of the present century, except in Turkish dominions, almost all Orthodox were living outwardly in the situation of a state church, supported financially by the government, with a wide control over education and closely affiliated with every aspect of national life. Even within the Ottoman empire the Orthodox church enjoyed official recognition and specific privileges. The position was drastically changed by two events occurring within five years of each other: the Bolshevik revolution in Russia (1917) and the defeat of the Greek armies in Asia Minor (1922), followed by the exchange of populations between Greece and Turkey (1923). Both events accelerated the movement of Orthodox Christians to the West, although large-scale emigration had already begun before World War I. As a result, Orthodoxy is becoming more and more a Western church as well as an Eastern church.

The 1923 exchange of populations between Greece and Turkey meant that the patriarchate of Constantinople lost the greater part of its flock in Asia Minor. The Greek Orthodox of Constantinople (Istanbul) itself were exempted from the exchange, but subsequent pressures have caused their numbers to dwindle to little more than three thousand. The bulk of the patriarchate's membership is now in Crete (c. 550,000) and in the emigration (three to five million), particularly in North America. In Greece the church-state alliance has been weakened since the fall of the military regime in 1974, and since 1982 civil marriage has been allowed by the state as an alternative to an ecclesiastical ceremony. In Cyprus, however, the bond between church and state remains closer, and civil marriage is still not permitted for Orthodox Christians.

In Russia the privileged status of the Orthodox church came abruptly to an end at the 1917 revolution. The church was disendowed, deprived of its role in education, and even denied recognition as a legal entity. There was a massive closure of churches and monasteries, and during the 1920s and 1930s vast numbers of Christians were executed or died in prison. Persecution was relaxed after 1943, but renewed in the early 1960s. Interference continues in all aspects of church life. Despite tragic losses the Russian church has survived, reduced in outward scale but inwardly purified.

With the spread of communism elsewhere in Eastern Europe after World War II, the Orthodox churches of Serbia, Romania, Bulgaria, Poland, Czechoslovakia, and Albania have also passed under militantly anti-Christian governments. The severity of repression varies. In Albania the Orthodox church, along with all other religious groups, has been entirely eliminated; there are no functioning places of worship and no visible expressions of church life. But elsewhere the persecution has been less heavy than in the Soviet Union. Conditions appear to be least oppressive in Yugoslavia, although the government permits scarcely any new Orthodox churches to be opened and has sought to debilitate the Serbian church by encouraging the formation of a schismatic Macedonian Orthodox church (1967), which is not recognized by the rest of the Orthodox world. Among the Orthodox churches in socialist countries, it is the Romanian church that exhibits the most vigorous religious life, with a growing number of priests, an ambitious program of church-building, and many active monasteries, but the hierarchy is obliged to collaborate in all spheres with the state authorities. In almost all the Orthodox churches under communism, the state makes it virtually impossible for the clergy to organize religious instruction of children and other forms of youth work.

The Orthodox diaspora in the Western world is organized predominantly on national lines, with different ethnic dioceses coexisting on the same territory, but there is a growing desire for local unity. At present all the Greeks belong to the ecumenical patriarchate, and the Arabs belong to the patriarchate of Antioch. The Russians are divided into four jurisdictions. A few parishes depend directly upon the Moscow patriarchate in Russia. Another relatively small group, mainly in France, comes under the ecumenical patriarchate. There is an independent synod of bishops known as the Russian Orthodox Church Outside Russia, with its center in New York, and the fourth and numerically largest group is the Russian Metropolia in North America. In 1970 this last became the autocephalous Orthodox Church in America. A number of Romanian, Bulgarian, and Albanian parishes in the United States have also joined this newly constituted church, but it does not yet include the Greeks, who are the largest single group of Orthodox in the United States, or the Arabs and the Serbs. When the Orthodox in the United States, and also in other Western countries, eventually unite to form in each place a single local church, both their own inner life and their witness within Western society will be markedly strengthened.

At the end of the twentieth century Orthodox Christianity exists, therefore, in four different circumstances. (1) As a state church it enjoys official government support; this is the position in Cyprus and to a diminishing extent in Greece. (2) Under communist rule, the government is actively hostile to religion; this is the position of the Orthodox in Eastern Europe and above all in the Soviet Union. Churches in communist lands today comprise nearly 85 percent of the Orthodox communion. (3) Orthodoxy also exists as a minority in predominantly Islamic environments, which is the situation of the ancient patriarchates of Alexandria, Antioch, and Jerusalem. (4) Finally, we also find Orthodoxy as a minority in the Western world, settled in lands traditionally associated with Roman Catholicism or Protestantism.

The Oriental Orthodox churches are mostly in the third of these four situations, that is, a minority in a predominantly Islamic environment. The Ethiopian church, however, was until 1974 a state church, but in that year it came under communist rule, suffering fierce persecution. The Armenian Orthodox in the Soviet Union are also under communist rule, although in their case the repression is less stringent. In common with the Eastern Orthodox, the "separated" Eastern churches also have a growing diaspora in the West.

The Eastern Orthodox church, while active in preaching Christianity to the Slavs during the middle Byzantine period, has played little part in the missionary outreach of more recent times. For this there are several historical reasons, in particular the situation of oppression that the Greeks had to endure in the Turkish period and to which the Russians and other Orthodox in eastern Europe have been subject in the twentieth century. In both cases this has precluded organized missionary work. Nationalism, so the Orthodox must also in honesty admit, has often made them inward-looking and deficient in missionary vision. In the nineteenth century, however, the Russian church maintained missions in China, Japan, Korea, and Alaska, and in the last fifty years a lively African Orthodox church has grown up in Kenya, Uganda, and Tanzania, with native bishops and clergy.

The great majority of the Orthodox churches, both Eastern and Oriental, participate in the ecumenical movement and are full members of the World Council of Churches. [*See* Ecumenical Movement.] In addition, most are involved in bilateral dialogues with other Christians. The Eastern Orthodox began official doctrinal discussions, on a worldwide level, with Roman Catholics in 1980, with Old Catholics in 1975, with Anglicans in 1973, and with Lutherans in 1981. During 1964–1971 there were four positive meetings between the Eastern and the non-Chalcedonian Orthodox, at which both parties were able to agree that, despite differences in terminology, there was no essential discrepancy in christological faith, and a promising solution was proposed for the old dispute concerning the number of the natures and wills in Christ. Even though no formal act of union has as yet been effected, there appears to be no fundamental obstacle on the doctrinal level.

Orthodox believe that Christian unity should be founded not upon an agreed minimum but upon the integral fullness of the Christian faith. Yet even within a reunited Christendom there will always be room for wide, continuing diversity. There is a distinction to be made between the one essential faith and theological opinions: unity in faith does not entail uniformity in theological opinions. Orthodox also believe that, until unity in faith is attained, it is not right for divided Christians to share together in the sacraments. In situations of pastoral emergency, Holy Communion may be offered to non-Orthodox, but in principle eucharistic communion is to be seen as the conclusion and final end of the journey to unity, not as a stage on the way.

To many Western Christians, the prospect of unity with the Orthodox seems remote. But others in the West are convinced that Catholics and Protestants will never succeed in overcoming the divisions of the sixteenth century unless they take into account the prior separation between East and West. Standing as they do largely outside the circle of ideas in which the West has moved since the early Middle Ages, the Orthodox are called to serve as catalysts within the Western theological debate, suggesting long-forgotten solutions to familiar difficulties.

Doctrine, Worship, and Life

The term *orthodox*, from *orthos* ("right") and *doxa* ("belief"), means primarily "rightly believing" but has also the sense "giving right glory and worship to God." Although this section on doctrine, worship, and life deals largely with the Eastern Orthodox church, most of what is said applies also to the Nestorian and the non-Chalcedonian churches. These latter churches are discussed in more detail in other articles. [*For survey discussions of Christian doctrine and worship, see* Theology, *article on* Christian Theology; Church; Christian Spirituality; Worship, *article on* Christian Worship; *and* Pilgrimage, *article on* Eastern Christian Pilgrimage.]

General Spirit of Orthodox Theology. The bond between theology and prayer is heavily emphasized in Orthodoxy. Theology is seen not merely as an academic or scholarly pursuit but as preeminently mystical and liturgical. "Far from being mutually opposed, theology and mysticism support and complete each other. One is impossible without the other. . . . Mysticism is . . . the perfecting and crown of all theology . . . theology *par excellence*" (Vladimir Lossky). To safeguard the mystical dimension of theology, use is made of the negative or "apophatic" approach: as a mystery beyond our human understanding, God cannot be fully described in words but only apprehended, on a level beyond language, images, and intellectual concepts, in a union of love.

To express the double truth that God is both unknown and yet well known, both transcendent and yet immanent, many Orthodox thinkers employ the distinction made by Gregory Palamas, on the basis of earlier Greek fathers, between the essence and the energies of God. The divine essence, unknowable to created beings, signifies God's radical transcendence and otherness; the divine energies, in which we humans can participate, express his immanence and nearness. According to Basil of Caesarea, "We know our God from his energies, but we do not claim that we can draw near to his essence. For his energies come down to us, but his essence remains unapproachable."

Holy Tradition: Source of the Orthodox Faith. From the seventeenth century on, Orthodox have often spoken as if they accepted two sources of the faith, scripture and tradition. Today, however, most Orthodox repudiate this "two source" language, insisting rather that scripture and tradition form a single whole. Tradition also includes the creed, the decrees of the seven ecumenical councils, the writings of the Fathers, the liturgical service books, and the icons, yet it is not exhausted by any of these things, or by all of them together. Holy tradition is not just a collection of statements contained in written documents; it is to be understood as the "lived experience . . . the uninterrupted life of the Church," according to the Romanian theologian Dumitru Staniloae (b. 1903). It is "the life of the Holy Spirit in the Church . . . the critical spirit of the Church" (Vladimir Lossky). "Tradition is not only a protective, conservative principle; it is primarily the principle of growth and regeneration" (Georges Florovsky). When tradition is understood in this wide-ranging and dynamic sense, it becomes clear that scripture is to be understood as existing within tradition. Tradition is the context in which scripture comes alive, the process whereby the truth of scripture is reexperienced by the church in every generation. [*For discussion of the role of tradition in broad religious perspective, see* Tradition.]

The Orthodox church is not opposed to the critical study of the Bible in its historical setting. Even though many individual Orthodox incline toward a fundamentalist attitude, Orthodoxy as such is not committed to this approach. But while taking account of the findings of scholarly research, the church tests them in the light of its experience of the faith as a whole. Personal judgment is not excluded, but always the individual Orthodox reads scripture as a member of the ecclesial community, and so the decisive criterion for interpreting scripture is the "mind of the church." The crucial question is always how the Bible is interpreted by the saints and the Fathers and how it is understood in the church's liturgical worship.

God in Trinity. The Orthodox church continues to accept in its full integrity the teaching of the early councils on God as trinity-in-unity, one essence in three persons who are "united yet not confused, distinct yet not divided" (John of Damascus). The three persons are equal and coeternal; each is fully God and truly personal, and yet together they form not three Gods but one. The doctrine of the Trinity is not merely a theme for abstract speculation by specialists; it has practical and indeed revolutionary consequences for our understanding of human personhood and society. The human person is made in the image of God, that is to say, of God the Trinity, and the doctrine of the Trinity affirms that God is not just a monad, the One loving himself, but a triad of divine persons loving each other. Formed in the trinitarian image, the human person is thus created for relationship, sharing, and reciprocity. Cut off from others, isolated, unloving and unloved, no one is a true person, but only a bare individual. Our human vocation is therefore to reproduce on earth at every level, in the church and in society, the movement of mutual love that exists from all eternity within God the Trinity. In the words of the Russian thinker Nikolai Feodorov (c. 1828–1903), "Our social program is the dogma of the Trinity." [*See also* Trinity.]

Jesus Christ. In its teaching on Jesus Christ Orthodoxy continues to uphold in their fullness the christological affirmations of the early councils. Christ is fully and completely divine, fully and completely human, and yet not two persons but one. In the Incarnation the second person of the Trinity took not only a human body but also a human soul. He has human impulses and feelings such as we have, and "is tempted in everything just as we are, only without sinning" (*Heb.* 4:15). Yet he does not cease to be true God. He is both our God and our brother. Orthodoxy accepts as literally true the statements in the Bible about the virgin birth of Christ, his miracles, and his bodily resurrection. But while God is truly revealed to us through Christ's incarnate life, he is never exhaustively revealed; there is in all the events from Christ's conception to his ascension an aspect that surpasses our comprehension.

In its understanding of atonement, Orthodoxy links the crucifixion of Christ closely with the incarnation that precedes it and with the resurrection that follows it; these are all part of a single action, or drama. While notions of sacrifice and penal substitution are sometimes employed, the dominant model preferred by Orthodox theologians is that proposed by Irenaeus: Christ the Victor, triumphing on the cross over the powers of evil. Christ is our victorious king, not in spite of the crucifixion but because of it: "I call him king, because I see him crucified" (John Chrysostom). [*See* Jesus *and* Atonement, *article on* Christian Concepts.]

The Holy Spirit. Following the teaching of the early church, Orthodoxy regards the Holy Spirit not simply as a quality of God or an impersonal force but as fully personal, the third member of the Trinity, equal to the Father and the Son. It is the vocation of every Christian to become a Spirit-bearer: in the words of the Russian monk Serafim of Sarov (1759–1833), "The true aim of the Christian life is to acquire the Holy Spirit of God." The presence of the Spirit is particularly important for a proper appreciation of the eucharistic consecration. Following the narrative of the Last Supper, the culminating moment in the anaphora of the Eastern liturgies is the invocation, or epiclesis of the Holy Spirit upon the holy gifts; it is through the power of the Spirit that the bread and wine become the body and blood of Christ.

The Orthodox sense of the Holy Spirit's activity can be seen also in the significance attached to the spiritual father, or "elder" (Gr., *gerōn;* Rus., *starets*). He is someone who, through the direct inspiration of the Spirit, has been granted the gift of discerning the secrets in human hearts and of offering personal guidance. Although only a few Orthodox would claim to have a *starets* of their own, and almost all would say that genuine elders are rare and hard to find, the influence of such elders upon modern Orthodoxy has been far-reaching. The elder is commonly a priest-monk, but not invariably so; he may be a married priest, or else a nonordained person—a lay monk, or an ordinary layman. The same ministry is also sometimes exercised by "spiritual mothers," who are nuns or laywomen.

Despite the central place that the Christian East assigns to the Holy Spirit, most contemporary Orthodox are reserved in their attitude to the Pentecostal or charismatic movement. They feel uneasy about what they see as the emotional subjectivism and lack of sobriety evident in certain charismatic groups, and they insist, as indeed do many within the charismatic movement, upon the need to "test the spirits, whether they are from God" (*1 Jn.* 4:1). Although the gift of tears has an important place in Orthodox spirituality, little or nothing is said about glossolalia.

Salvation. Salvation is generally envisaged in terms of *theōsis*, "deification" or "ingodding": "God became human, that we might become god" (Athanasius of Alexandria). This does not mean that the distinction between creator and creature is abolished, or that we humans lose our characteristic personal identity and are "absorbed" in the "abyss" of godhead. On the contrary, even in the glory of heaven the differentiation between God and humanity continues; the beatific vision "face to face" is a union without confusion.

Salvation comes about through the convergence or cooperation *(sunergeia)* between divine grace and human freedom. Without God's grace, salvation is impossible; we humans cannot save ourselves. But at the same time Orthodoxy insists upon the vital significance of free will. In the words of the *Spiritual Homilies* (late fourth century?), attributed to Makarios of Egypt, "The will of man is an essential condition, for without it God does nothing." Our freedom has been restricted as a result of the Fall, but not obliterated. Western authors occasionally describe the Orthodox standpoint as "semi-Pelagian," but this is a misrepresentation. The Pelagian controversy was specifically a Western dispute; the Eastern teaching on grace and human effort is neither Pelagian nor Augustinian in its criteria, but differs from both.

Humans are saved by faith, in the sense of personal and loving trust in Christ the Savior. But at the same time faith is not to be isolated from works, since a living faith cannot but express itself in acts of love. Our works, however, do not earn us "merit." We humans can never have claims upon God, for salvation remains always his free gift. [*See* Grace; Justification; *and* Merit, *article on* Christian Concepts.]

The Church, the Communion of Saints. Orthodoxy has a strong sense of the unity of the living and departed. In "The Church Is One," an essay included in *Russia and the English Church during the Last Fifty Years* (edited by W. J. Birkbeck, 1895), the Russian religious thinker Aleksei Khomiakov (1804–1860) says:

> It is only in relation to man that it is possible to recognize a division of the Church into visible and invisible; her unity is in reality true and absolute. Those who are alive on earth, those who have finished their earthly course, those who, like the angels, were not created for a life on earth, those in future generations who have not yet begun their earthly course—all are united together in one Church, in one and the same grace of God. (pp. 193–194)

The total church, visible and invisible, is maintained in unity by the bond of mutual love and mutual intercession. Prayer for the departed occurs regularly in Orthodox worship, but most Orthodox prefer not to attempt any formulation of the way in which such prayer assists the dead, and they avoid the term purgatory. The invocation of the saints, and especially of the Virgin Mary, is likewise seen not as an optional extra but as an essential element in all Christian prayer, and such invocation occurs in every service. The participation of the unseen church in earthly worship is continually emphasized: "Now the powers of heaven worship with us invisibly" (Liturgy of the Presanctified Gifts). The Divine Liturgy is seen in this way as heaven on earth. The presence of the communion of saints is enhanced by the icons found in all parts of the church building as well as in Orthodox homes.

The Blessed Virgin Mary. A unique place in Orthodox devotion is assigned to the Holy Virgin. [*See* Mary.] The Russian theologian and ex-Marxist Sergei Bulgakov (1871–1944) writes, "A faith in Christ which does not include his Virgin Birth and the veneration of his Mother is another faith, another Christianity, from that of the Orthodox Church." In Orthodox services, Mary is addressed as "the joy of all creation," "more honored than the cherubim and incomparably more glorious than the seraphim." In this Orthodox reverence for her, combined with a sense of profound awe, there is also a spontaneous warmth, an affection that is homely as well as respectful.

The Blessed Virgin is regarded as *theotokos*, "God-bearer" or "Mother of God" (Council of Ephesus, 431), in the sense that she bore not just a man close to God but a single and indivisible person who is at once God and man. She is also called "Ever-Virgin," a title given to her by the Council of Constantinople (553). While Orthodox look on Mary as all-pure and all-holy, totally free from actual sin, they do not usually hold that she was free from the effects of original sin. In the past, Eastern Christians have sometimes inclined toward the Roman Catholic doctrine of the Immaculate Conception, but today it is generally rejected. On the other hand, the bodily assumption of Mary is an accepted part of Orthodox belief, but it is not considered desirable or even possible for this to be defined as a dogma necessary for salvation.

Councils. The Orthodox view the church as infallible, in the sense that there has never been a time when the totality of the church on earth has fallen into error. Nor can this ever happen. Infallibility is not the property of an individual person within the church, whether the pope or anyone else; it belongs only to the entire church as body of Christ. Even though truth will prove invincible within the church, at times of controversy it is often far from clear where the truth lies. The supreme visible expression of the church's authority is an ecumenical council, attended in principle by bishops from all parts of the Christian world. At a true ecumenical council the mystery of Pentecost is renewed: the Holy Spirit descends upon the episcopate, as it once did upon the apostles, and so the doctrinal decisions that the bishops make are irrevocable. But in defining doctrine, the bishops do not act in isolation from the rest of the faithful, on whom the Spirit has also been conferred through the sacraments of Baptism and Chrismation. One of the marks of a council's ecumenicity is therefore its acceptance by the whole body of the church.

Sacraments. Orthodox since the seventeenth century have usually recognized seven sacraments, basically the same as those in Roman Catholicism. The sacrament of Baptism, bestowing forgiveness of sins on the new Christian and admitting him or her to the church, is normally conferred in infancy. It is performed by immersion, except in cases of emergency or sickness, when it is sufficient to pour water over the forehead. [*See also* Sacrament, *article on* Christian Sacraments.]

The sacrament of Chrismation is equivalent to Western Confirmation. Chrismation takes the form of an anointing on the forehead and other parts of the body with the words "the seal of the gift of the Holy Spirit." It usually follows immediately after Baptism and may be conferred by a priest, but the chrism (ointment) that the priest uses has been blessed by a patriarch or head of an autocephalous church. Baptized Christians of other churches are generally received into the Orthodox church through the sacrament of Chrismation.

Babies receive the sacrament of Communion at the earliest opportunity after Baptism and Chrismation, and thereafter they communicate regularly. Communion is administered to the laity in a spoon, with both the bread and wine together. In the past Orthodox laypeople tended to receive Communion infrequently, only three or four times a year, following careful preparation through prayer, fasting, and perhaps the sacrament of Confession. In the twentieth century, however, Communion has become more frequent in many parishes, whether Greek, Russian, or Romanian. The Eucharist, or Divine Liturgy, is the main act of worship on Sunday, but except in certain cathedrals and monasteries it is not normally celebrated daily. The service lasts for about an hour and a quarter (often longer) and is always sung, with the use of incense and full ceremonial. As at all Orthodox services, there is traditionally no instrumental accompaniment during the Divine Liturgy (in the West, however, especially in Greek parishes, an organ is sometimes used). The normal eucharistic service is the Liturgy of Saint John Chrysostom. The somewhat longer Liturgy of Saint Basil is used ten times a year, mainly in Lent, while the Liturgy of the Presanctified Gifts is prescribed in Lent for weekdays and more particularly for Wednesdays and Fridays. The Liturgy of Saint James is used in a few places for his feast day, 23 October. In the Orthodox diaspora a small number of parishes follow a Western rite.

At the eucharistic consecration, it is believed, the bread and wine become the true body and blood of Christ. Some Orthodox writers since the seventeenth century have adopted the Roman Catholic term *transubstantiation*, but many deliberately avoid it. The eucharistic presence is understood to be objective and permanent. The sacrament is reserved for the purpose of giving Communion to the sick, but it is not carried in procession or used for blessing outside the actual service of the Divine Liturgy; Orthodox have no office equivalent to the Roman Catholic benediction.

The Eucharist is understood in sacrificial terms, as a "mystical sacrifice" or a "sacrifice without shedding of blood." It is not merely a commemoration of Christ's sacrifice on the cross, yet neither is it a new sacrifice or a repetition of the oblation on Calvary, since Christ died once for all. It is a sacrifice in the sense that, through the eucharistic consecration, Christ's unique redemptive self-offering is "re-presented," made directly present. At every Eucharist it is Christ himself who is the true celebrant, at once both priest and victim: "Thou art he who offers and he who is offered" (Liturgy of Saint John Crysostom). [*See also* Eucharist.]

In the Greek tradition the sacrament of Confession, conferring forgiveness of sins and absolution, is regarded as voluntary, and it is left to the conscience of the individual to decide how often he or she goes to

Confession. In the Slav Orthodox churches in the past it was the practice to go to Confession before each Communion, but this rule is now relaxed in many places.

The sacrament of the Anointing of the Sick (Gr., *euchelaion,* "oil of prayer") has never been restricted to those in danger of death; it is conferred on any who ask for it. It is seen as closely related to Confession. Both are sacraments of healing, and like Confession, the Anointing of the Sick transmits forgiveness of sins. The human person is a unity of body and soul, and so the sicknesses of both are healed together.

In the sacrament of Priesthood, or Holy Orders, men are ordained to serve the church in specific ministries. The sacrament functions on two levels: there are two "minor orders" in use at present in the Orthodox church, reader and subdeacon, and there are three "major orders," deacon, priest, and bishop. The diaconate is often a lifelong position, not merely a step on the way to the priesthood. The order of deaconesses, to which women were once ordained, has long been defunct in the Orthodox church, but many today would like to see it revived; almost all Orthodox, however, are opposed to the ordination of women priests. Married men may be ordained as deacons and priests, but marriage is not allowed after ordination to the diaconate. Bishops are required to be in monastic vows. [*See also* Priesthood, *article on* Christian Priesthood.]

The sacrament of Marriage begins with the blessing of rings, as in the West, but the culminating moment is the placing of crowns on the heads of bridegroom and bride. These are seen as crowns of joy and victory, but equally as crowns of martyrdom, since there can be no true marriage without loving self-sacrifice on both sides and the readiness to renounce self-will for the sake of the other. For certain reasons, particularly adultery, divorce may be granted and a second or even a third marriage allowed in church, but the service of remarriage after divorce differs from that of the first marriage. No one is permitted to enter into more than three successive marriages, whether after divorce or after the death of the other partner. In the past, recourse to contraceptives and other devices for birth control was forbidden, but contraception is now widely tolerated, especially among Orthodox in the West. Artificially procured abortions are regarded as a grave sin.

Alongside the seven sacraments, and not to be sharply distinguished from them, are many other blessings and sacramental actions, such as the Great Blessing of the Waters at Epiphany (6 January), the burial rites, the anointing of a monarch, and monastic profession. Monasticism has exercised a profound influence upon the Christian East since the fourth century. From the tenth century onward the chief center of Orthodox monastic life has been Mount Athos, a peninsula in northeastern Greece. Here, following a half-century of decline, there has been a notable renewal since 1970.

Prayer in the Home. The practice of family prayers, although less general than in the past, still continues within the contemporary Orthodox world. In each Orthodox household there is traditionally an icon corner or shelf, before which a lamp is lit, incense is offered, and the family prayers are said; here, as in church, the Orthodox worshiper feels a sense of "heaven on earth." Through special blessings of houses, fields, crops, cattle, and flocks, the liturgical sequence of the church's year has become integrally linked with the life of the household and with the agricultural cycle of the farm. The *Euchologion* (Book of Prayers) contains prayers for sowing, threshing, and wine-making, for new fishing-nets, and even for cleansing a jar into which a rat has fallen. Orthodox worship is otherworldly, but at the same time popular and practical.

General Spirit of Worship. At its best, Orthodox worship is marked by a double spirit of mystery and homeliness. There is at the services a sense of awe and wonder in the face of God's immediate presence, accompanied by a feeling of informality and freedom. The worshiper behaves like a child in his Father's house, not like a soldier on parade. Although in some places pews are being introduced, there is normally no fixed seating in the main body of the church. Members of the congregation may arrive late or leave early, and they may move about venerating icons during the service without disturbing the prayer of others. Not everyone stands or kneels simultaneously. Yet despite this variety in the manner of participation, and even though the singing is usually by the choir alone, Orthodox liturgical worship has never ceased to be corporate in character. Throughout the history of Eastern Christendom it has been usual to celebrate the services in the language of the people, albeit sometimes in an archaic form.

The climax of the church year is Pascha (Easter), not Christmas. [*See* Christian Liturgical Year; Easter; Christmas; *and* Epiphany.] The celebration of Christ's resurrection also dominates the worship on each Saturday evening and Sunday morning; doxological in spirit, Eastern liturgical prayer is marked by a sense of resurrection joy. Fasting and abstinence continue to be far stricter than they have been in the West since the Middle Ages. Most Orthodox churches have adopted the new, or Gregorian, calendar that is observed in the West, but the churches of Jerusalem, Russia, Serbia, and Poland, together with Athos, still adhere to the old, or Julian, calendar, which is thirteen days in retard of the Gregorian.

Through the use of material symbols and symbolic gestures involving the body, full scope is given by the Orthodox to the physical aspect of worship. The faithful participate in prayer with their bodies through frequent use of the sign of the cross, deep bows or prostrations to the ground, and fasting. At Confession the priest lays his hand on the penitent's head; at the funeral service the dead body lies in an open coffin and all approach to give the "last kiss" to the departed. The materiality of the sacramental signs is emphasized through, for instance, the plentiful use of water in the immersion at baptism. The eucharistic bread is always leavened, and the wine is always red. Hot water, known in Greek as *zeon,* is added immediately before Communion, and Communion itself is given to all under both kinds. Oil is blessed at the vigils of great feasts and used for anointing, rivers and the sea are blessed at Epiphany, and grapes are blessed at the Feast of the Transfiguration (6 August). Worship is not only with the mind or through the ear.

The apostle Paul's injunction "Pray without ceasing" (*1 Thes.* 5:17) has deeply impressed the Christian East. Prayer is to be understood not merely as a series of acts performed corporately in church or privately at home, but also in a deeper sense as a state that is to be continuous—not so much something that we do from time to time as something that we are all the time, not an occasional activity but an integral part of our very self. The Jesus Prayer, largely restricted in the past to monastic circles but now more and more widely diffused among the laity, has as its purpose precisely to bring about such a continuous state. Our aim in praying, as Basil Caesarea expresses it, is that "our whole life should become one constant and uninterrupted prayer."

The Last Things. In its theology and worship the Christian East is strongly eschatological. The age to come is repeatedly called to mind not merely as an event in the future but as a present reality in which we share by anticipation here and now. At the end of the world, Christ will return in glory, the dead will be raised, and the Last Judgment will follow. While the exact relation between our body in its present state and our resurrection body is not something that at this juncture we can clearly understand, according to the Christian view the true human person is not the soul alone but the soul embodied; the separation of soul and body at death is therefore no more than temporary, and on the Last Day the two will be reunited. Because human beings are endowed with free will, hell—understood as the continuing rejection of God—exists as an ultimate possibility, Universalism, the belief that in the end all must inevitably be saved, was rejected as a heresy by the Council of Constantinople (553). But since God is inexhaustible in his love and is infinitely patient, it is legitimate to hope that in the end all will freely choose to accept him, so that he will indeed be "all in all" (*1 Cor.* 15:28). However, the final consummation of the end remains a mystery beyond our present understanding.

BIBLIOGRAPHY

Surveys. Two introductory surveys covering history and doctrine, both by Orthodox authors, are John Meyendorff's *The Orthodox Church: Its Past and Its Role in the World Today,* rev. ed. (New York, 1981), and my *The Orthodox Church,* (1964; reprint, New York, 1983). Neither of these deals with the "separated" Eastern churches; for a general historical introduction to these, see A. S. Atiya's *A History of Eastern Christianity,* (1968; Millwood, N.Y., 1980).

Historical Development. On the evolution of theology in the Byzantine period, the best summary is John Meyendorff's *Byzantine Theology: Historical Trends and Doctrinal Themes,* 2d ed. (New York, 1979); consult also Jaroslav Pelikan's *The Christian Tradition: A History of the Development of Doctrine,* vol. 2, *The Spirit of Eastern Christendom, 600–1700* (Chicago, 1974). On Christology after 451, see John Meyendorff's *Christ in Eastern Christian Thought* (New York, 1975). Dimitri Obolensky's *The Byzantine Commonwealth: Eastern Europe, 500–1453* (London, 1974) provides a clear and authoritative picture of Byzantine-Slav relations, both cultural and religious.

On the schism between Orthodoxy and Rome, Steven Runciman's *The Eastern Schism: A Study of the Papacy and the Eastern Churches during the Eleventh and Twelfth Centuries* (Oxford, 1955) supplies a well-documented factual narrative. For an Orthodox treatment of the underlying issues, challenging but at times one-sided, see Philip Sherrard's *The Greek East and the Latin West: A Study in the Christian Tradition* (London, 1959). Yves Congar's *After Nine Hundred Years: The Background of the Schism between the Eastern and Western Churches* (New York, 1959) is a perceptive analysis by a sympathetic Roman Catholic. For a full treatment of the hesychastic controversy, see John Meyendorff's *A Study of Gregory Palamas* (London, 1964).

A well-written account of the Turkish period, but one that makes only limited use of Eastern Christian sources, is provided in Steven Runciman's *The Great Church in Captivity: A Study of the Patriarchate of Constantinople from the Eve of the Turkish Conquest to the Greek War of Independence* (Cambridge, 1968). On the Catholic communities, see Charles A. Frazee's *Catholics and Sultans: The Church and the Ottoman Empire, 1453–1923* (Cambridge, 1983).

On the contemporary Orthodox world, consult Peter Hammond's *The Waters of Marah: The Present State of the Greek Church* (New York, 1956), which conveys vividly the atmosphere of Orthodox worship; Mario Rinvolucri's *Anatomy of a Church: Greek Orthodoxy Today* (London, 1966); Christel Lane's *Christian Religion in the Soviet Union: A Sociological Study* (Albany, N.Y., 1978); and Stella Alexander's *Church and State in Yugoslavia since 1945* (Cambridge, 1979).

Doctrine and Worship. The best general treatments of Orthodox theology are by Russians of the emigration; see especially

Vladimir Lossky's *The Mystical Theology of the Eastern Church* (London, 1957) and Georges Florovsky's *Collected Works,* 5 vols. to date (Belmont, Mass., 1972–). Sergei Bulgakov's *The Orthodox Church* (London, 1935) deals in detail with the doctrine of the church. For Greek academic theology in the twentieth century, see Frank Gavin's *Some Aspects of Contemporary Greek Orthodox Thought* (Milwaukee, 1923) and Panagiotis N. Trembelas's *Dogmatique de l'église orthodoxe catholique,* 3 vols. (Chevetogne, Belgium, 1966–1968). For a less "scholastic" and more creative approach by younger Greek theologians, see Christos Yannaras's *The Freedom of Morality* (Crestwood, N.Y., 1984), John D. Zizioulas's *Being as Communion: Studies in Personhood and the Church* (Crestwood, N.Y., 1985), and Panayiotis Nellas's *Deification in Christ: Orthodox Perspectives on the Nature of the Human Person.* (Crestwood, N.Y., forthcoming.)

On biblical criticism, consult Veselin Kesich's *The Gospel Image of Christ: The Church and Modern Criticism* (Crestwood, N.Y., 1972). On sacramental theology, see Alexander Schmemann's *Sacraments and Orthodoxy* (New York, 1965) and Paul Evdokimov's *The Sacrament of Love: The Nuptial Mystery in the Light of the Orthodox Tradition* (Crestwood, N.Y., 1985). The services for nine of the twelve Great Feasts are given in *The Festal Menaion* (London, 1969), and the services for Lent in *The Lenten Triodion* (Boston, 1978), both translated by Mother Mary and myself.

Basic texts on the spiritual life, and especially on the Jesus Prayer, can be found in Nikodimos of the Holy Mountain and Makarios of Corinth's *The Philokalia,* translated and edited by G. E. H. Palmer, Philip Sherrard, and myself, 3 vols. to date (London and Boston, 1979–). For a less monastically oriented approach, by a married parish priest, read Alexander El'chaninov's *The Diary of a Russian Priest,* edited by myself (London, 1967). On the early history of the Jesus Prayer, see Irénée Hausherr's *The Name of Jesus,* "Cistercian Studies," no. 44 (Kalamazoo, Mich., 1978); for its influence in Russia, see the anonymously written *The Way of a Pilgrim, and The Pilgrim Continues His Way,* new ed. (London, 1954). The ministry of spiritual fatherhood is well discussed in Irénée Hausherr's *Direction spirituelle en Orient autrefois,* "Orientalia Christiana Analecta," no. 144 (Rome, 1955). For the different grades in monasticism and the profession rites, consult Nalbro' Frazier Robinson's *Monasticism in the Orthodox Churches* (London and Milwaukee, 1916).

The best interpretation of the icon in its theological and liturgical context is Leonid Ouspensky and Vladimir Lossky's *The Meaning of Icons,* rev. ed. (New York, 1982).

KALLISTOS WARE

EAST SYRIAN CHURCH. *See* Nestorian Church.

EBIONITES is the name given to a Jewish Christian sect that flourished during the early history of the Christian church. The origin of the term, a Hebrew word meaning "poor persons," is obscure. It may have been an honorific title given to an original group of Christians who were Jews living in Jerusalem that needed assistance from Christians elsewhere in the Roman empire (*Rom.* 15:25, *2 Cor.* 9:12). It was first used by the Christian bishop Irenaeus of Lyons (Gaul) in the late second century to designate a Jewish Christian sect. Some later writers used it ironically to refer to the "poverty of understanding" of the members of the sect, who did not believe that Jesus Christ was the divine Son of God. There is no evidence to support the claim of some Christian writers that it derived from a person named Ebion, the supposed founder of the sect.

The origin, history, and distinct character of the Ebionites has been a subject of intense debate in recent years. It is possible that the Ebionites go back to the earliest period of Christian history, when most Christians were Jews and some continued to observe the Jewish law. If so, they would be the earliest example of a Christian movement within Judaism that was eventually left behind as Christianity adapted to the influx of gentile converts. These Christians eventually became a distinct group that, along with other groups (e.g., the gnostics), was rejected as heretical by the emerging "great" church. They are sometimes identified with the *minim* ("heretics"), mentioned in the Talmud.

The Ebionites were Jews who accepted Jesus of Nazareth as the Messiah (Christ) while continuing to maintain their identity as Jews. They cultivated relations with Jews as well as Christians though they were welcomed by neither. They followed the Jewish law, insisting on circumcision, keeping the Sabbath and celebrating the Jewish festivals (Yom Kippur, Passover, etc.), and observing the dietary laws (e.g., abstention from pork) and other Jewish customs. They repudiated the apostle Paul because of his denigration of the Jewish law. They saw Jesus as a prophet, an exceptional man in the line of Jewish prophets (as described in *Deuteronomy* 18:15), and denied the virgin birth. They justified their way of life by appealing to the example of Jesus' life: he was circumcised, observed the Sabbath and celebrated the Jewish festivals, and taught that all the precepts of the law should be observed. They celebrated Easter on the same day that the Jews celebrated the Passover, and they held the city of Jerusalem in high esteem.

Besides the Ebionites there were other Jewish Christian sects, such as the Nazarenes, the Symmachians, and the Elkasites, but it is difficult to distinguish one from the other, and the names are not used with any consistency. *Ebionite* is the most common designation, and it may simply have been a term used to characterize any form of Jewish Christianity with a stress on the observance of Jewish law. Although early Christian writings directed against heresy sometimes linked the Ebionites with other heretical groups, such as the gnostics, the distinctiveness of the Ebionites lies less in their doctrines than in their attitude toward the Jewish law.

The Ebionites had their own gospel, but it is not possible to reconstruct its content in any detail. Ancient writers mention three Jewish Christian gospels, but because of the fragmentary nature of our information, it is difficult to distinguish these works clearly. The *Gospel of the Ebionites* (a modern designation) may have been similar to the *Gospel of Matthew*, but it did not include the narrative of the virgin birth and Jesus' infancy.

Information on the Ebionites is scattered over three centuries, from the middle of the second to the middle of the fifth, suggesting that the sect had a continuous history as a distinct group from the earliest period. A continuous history cannot be documented, however, and it is more likely that the persistence of people called by the name Ebionites is evidence that within Christianity, in spite of the break with Judaism and the bitter polemic against Jewish practices, there continued to spring up groups of Christians who believed that one could be a Christian and still observe the Jewish law.

The greatest strength of the Ebionites was in Palestine and Syria, areas where Judaism flourished. One community of Ebionites lived in Pella, east of the Jordan River, and claimed to be descended from the original group of Christians, who were thought to have fled Jerusalem at the time of the war with the Romans in 70 CE. There was a resurgence of Jewish Christianity in the late fourth century, encouraged by Jewish messianism and the emperor Julian's attempt to rebuild the Temple in Jerusalem. Jews began to hope for their return to Jerusalem and Judaea, a rebuilding of the Temple, and restoration of sacrifices—the beginning of a messianic age. After this period little is known of the Ebionites.

BIBLIOGRAPHY

Klijn, A. F. J., and G. J. Reinink. *Patristic Evidence for Jewish-Christian Sects.* Leiden, 1973.

Schoeps, Hans J. *Theologie und Geschichte des Judenchristentums.* Tübingen, 1949.

Simon, Marcel. *Verus Israel: Étude sur les relations entre chrétiens et juifs dans l'empire romain, 135–425.* Paris, 1964.

Strecker, Georg. "Ebioniten." In *Reallexikon für Antike und Christentum.* Stuttgart, 1959.

ROBERT L. WILKEN

ECCLESIASTES. One of the Five Scrolls used on the Jewish festivals, *Ecclesiastes* is read at Sukkot (Tabernacles). Jewish editions of the Hebrew Bible place it within the Writings (Ketuvim); Christian editions of the Old Testament place it among the Poetic Books. The English title, *Ecclesiastes*, follows the Greek name of the book in the Septuagint and means "one who addresses an assembly." The Hebrew title, *Qohelet*, also the name of the man to whom authorship is ascribed, is a feminine active participle of a verb meaning "to assemble," and might be translated "female speaker in the assembly [Heb., *qahal*]." However, it is constructed with masculine verbs (1:2, 12:8–10) and may be compared to the name *Soferet* (i.e., "female scribe"), listed among the descendants of Solomon's servants following the Babylonian exile (*Neh.* 7:57).

Author, Language, and Date. The name *Qohelet* is probably a pseudonym. The author presented himself as a son of David (1:1) and a king in Jerusalem (1:2). He may have wished, not without irony, to impersonate Solomon, the reputed master of wisdom (*1 Kgs.* 5:12 [Eng. version 4:32], 10:23f.). He lived in Hellenistic times during the late fourth or the early third century BCE. The Hebrew in which he wrote is quite different from that of the *Prophets*, *Proverbs*, and *Job*, and is closer to the language of the rabbinic period. It also contains a number of Aramaisms and shows affinities with the Phoenician.

Qohelet was a sage of the Israelite and early Jewish tradition. Unlike *Job* and *Proverbs*, his book shows at least indirect acquaintance with various schools of Hellenistic philosophy (Stoics, Epicureans, Cynics, and Cyrenaics). Because he knew nothing of the Seleucid persecutions or of the Maccabean Revolt, he probably wrote before 168 BCE. Ben Sira (Ecclesiasticus; c. 220–190 BCE) appears to have borrowed from him. The date of *Ecclesiastes* thus may be placed at least a generation before the *Book of Ben Sira*.

Literary Composition. Because the book abounds in non sequiturs and contradictions, scholars of past generations suggested that it was an anthology of reflections upon existence written by different hands. A general uniformity of language, style, and even tone has led others to consider the book as the intellectual diary of a lay teacher who reacted to the trends of a rising cosmopolitan culture. At an advanced age, which he described with sardonic realism (12:1–8), he wrote out these reflections, peppered with quotations from traditional wisdom. A disciple published the notebook with his own touches (1:2a, 1:12, 1:15; 12:11–13). According to another hypothesis, Qohelet argued with the opinions of his predecessors and also debated his own; the book represents classnotes by one of his students.

The rhythmic prose of Qohelet was suitable to sapiential pedagogy. It included a number of poetic maxims similar to those found in *Proverbs*, *Job*, and *Ben Sira*, and in short essays and pious exhortations. A modest doubt concerning the worth of existence "under the sun" pervades the counsel to fear God.

Literary Genre and Ancient Parallels. The book has no exact model in the ancient Near East or in Greece, but several writings of international wisdom from the second and first millennia BCE present similar views. In Egypt, the *Song of the Harper*, the *Man Who Was Tired of Life*, the *Lamentations of Khakheperreseneb*, and several tomb inscriptions mourned the evils of self-righteous piety, individual, and social corruption; the attraction of death; and the emptiness of life on earth. In Mesopotamia, the advice of Siduri in the *Epic of Gilgamesh* and the *Dialogue of the Blasé Master with His Cunning Slave* lamented the boredom of occupations but humorously refrained from recommending suicide. In Greece, pre-Classical rhapsodists and gnomists, especially Hesiod, Theognis, and Phocylides, maintained a delicate balance between belief in a supreme deity and the injustices of individual retribution. These themes were treated anew by Hellenistic philosophers. One cannot demonstrate a direct influence from any of these parallels.

Beliefs and Message of Qohelet. The book, as we have seen, is not so much a proof or doctrine as a redaction of the teacher's thought. Nonetheless, his major beliefs may be outlined.

Theocentric premise. Qohelet looked at both sides of every question. Yet, his approach to life must be viewed as that of a man of faith. He was soberly aware of the presence of a God who "has made it so that men shall be in awe before him" (3:14). The cultic expression for "before" God, *millefanav* (lit., "from at his face"), came to designate a psychological awareness of divine intimacy. For Qohelet as well as for the earlier sages, the fear of God was neither the dread of the unknown nor the unadulterated terror of divine judgment but implied a response to holy love. Ecclesiastes did not accept a philosophy of impersonal determinism but resolutely acknowledged the will of the omnipotent Sovereign. Like the poet of *Job*, he was bold enough to reject the orthodox doctrine of individual retribution. His sense of transcendence, together with his revulsion against cosmic and moral evil, led him to temper his trust in God with a reverent agnosticism.

Critique of self-sufficient humanism. From his theological vantage, Qohelet was able to offer a satire of Solomon's experiments in the pursuit of pleasure and of his political ambition (1:12–2:26). It is in the context of this satire that the motto of the book, "empty gusts of empty winds, all is emptiness" (1:2), is to be understood. There is no enjoyment of mortal existence, not even happiness in work, unless one sees in all things "a gift of God" (3:13).

In spite of his God-centered humanism, Qohelet was obsessed by cyclical time, which he depicted in a series of fourteen antitheses (3:1–8). While he admitted that "God made every thing beautiful in its own time" and had given the sons of Adam the awareness of historical duration (3:11; a notoriously difficult passage), they are unable to discern the purpose of creation "from beginning to end." Qohelet ignored the main themes of Hebraic faith, such as chosen people, covenant, revealed law, Zion, messianism, or any form of eschatology.

Social conscience and moderation. His mind wavering on the worth of existence (4:1–11:10), Qohelet examined the plight of the oppressed, the curse of solitariness, the risks of political involvement, the ambiguities of cultic conformism, the corruptibility of state officials, the vanity of wealth, the uselessness of longevity, the relativity of wisdom, and the unreliability of woman. Nevertheless, he reaffirmed the enjoyment of life in the company of his beloved wife (9:9). He preferred sapiential meditation to worldly power (9:16) and warned against the excesses of prudence (11:1–6). His final advice was moderation in all things (11:7–10).

Qohelet in the Jewish and Christian Traditions. Because *Ecclesiastes* differed dramatically from the rest of the Hebrew Bible (with the exception of the "words of Agur" in *Proverbs* 30:1–4), the canonicity of the book was disputed. The Tosefta, the Talmud, and the *midrashim* contain protracted rabbinical discussions on its value and sanctity. The church fathers quoted from it liberally. Medieval Schoolmen and Protestant reformers used it to support their views on the depravity of man, and Romanticists liked to admire its "elegant skepticism." Modern critics have called the Jerusalem sage "a gentle cynic." Contemporary exegetes compare him to religious existentialists.

[*See also* Wisdom Literature, *article on* Biblical Books.]

BIBLIOGRAPHY

Hundreds of commentaries and monographs have appeared on *Ecclesiastes* in the past two centuries alone. The following list suggests contemporary trends.

Braun, Rainer. *Kohelet und die frühhellenistische Popularphilosophie*. Berlin and New York, 1973. A thorough analysis of the relevant texts.

Crenshaw, James L. "The Eternal Gospel (Eccl. 3:11)." In *Essays in Old Testament Ethics*, edited by James L. Crenshaw and John T. Willis, pp. 15–55. New York, 1974. Discussion of an obscure passage, crucial for the interpretation of the whole book.

Crenshaw, James L. "The Shadow of Death in Qoheleth." In *Israelite Wisdom*, edited by John G. Gammie et al., pp. 205–216. Missoula, Mont., 1978. Examines the relation between the fear of death and the love of living.

Glasser, Étienne. *Le procès du bonheur par Qohelet*. Paris, 1970. A novel approach to the meaning of happiness.

Gordis, Robert. *Koheleth: The Man and His World* (1951). Reprint, New York, 1968. An original translation and a stimulating elucidation of many unclear passages.

Rad, Gerhard von. *Weisheit in Israel*. Neukirchen-Vluyn, 1970. Translated by James D. Martin as *Wisdom in Israel* (Nashville, 1972). A mature appraisal of Qohelet's quarrel with the priestly Judaism of his day.

Scott, R. B. Y. *Proverbs, Ecclesiastes*. Anchor Bible, vol. 18. Garden City, N.Y., 1965. A modern translation with introduction and notes.

Terrien, Samuel. *The Elusive Presence: Toward a New Biblical Theology*. New York, 1978. Contains an extensive bibliography on pages 373–389.

Whybray, R. N. "Qoheleth the Immoralist?" In *Israelite Wisdom*, edited by John G. Gammie et al., pp. 191–204. Missoula, Mont., 1978. A perceptive interpretation of Qohelet's irony concerning self-righteousness.

SAMUEL TERRIEN

ECCLESIOLOGY. *See under* Church.

ECK, JOHANN (1486–1543), German Roman Catholic theologian known for his opposition to the Protestant reformers. Born Johann Maier in the Swabian village of Eck, he entered the University of Heidelberg at age eleven. Thereafter he studied at Tübingen (Master of Arts, 1501), Cologne, and Freiburg (Doctor of Theology, 1510). In 1510 he began studies at Ingolstadt, where he received a second doctorate and assumed a position on the theological faculty. He quickly became the dominant theological force at Ingolstadt and retained his position and his dominance there until his death. Eck was ordained to the secular priesthood in 1508 and preached regularly during the years he spent in Ingolstadt.

Eck's early years revealed broad intellectual interests. He published on logic (*Bursa pavonis*, 1507; *In summulas Petri Hispani*, 1516; *Elementarius dialectice*, 1517) and on Aristotle (1517, 1519, 1520). He read geography and canon law, and his affinities for the humanists were reflected in his study of Greek and Hebrew and his fondness for classical sources. In theology, his most significant early work was the *Chrysopassus* (1514), a treatise on predestination. In it Eck declared his preference for the Franciscans Bonaventure and Duns Scotus but asserted that he would not be bound to any theological party—a notable declaration in view of his attachment to the nominalists during his years in Freiburg. The *Chrysopassus* expounded doctrines of merit and free will that would soon be under attack by Luther and other Protestants.

Luther's Ninety-five Theses (1517) changed Eck's life. At his bishop's request Eck responded to the theses, and ensuing exchanges led to the Leipzig Disputation (1519) between Eck and the Wittenbergers Luther and Karlstadt. Shortly thereafter Eck went to Rome and helped secure papal condemnation of Wittenberg theology. He was commissioned (1520) to publicize in Germany the papal bull *Exsurge Domine*, which condemned forty-one propositions attributed to Luther, and which Luther publicly burned.

The rest of Eck's life was devoted largely to combatting Protestants in Germany and Switzerland. Although he had no confidence that disputation would convince his Protestant opponents, he engaged in debate when he thought public policy might be influenced—notably in Baden in 1524. He was the most important Catholic participant in discussions with Protestants at Augsburg (1530) and Ratisbon (1541). His anti-Protestant publications included the following: defenses of papal authority (*De primatu Petri*, 1520), the doctrine of purgatory (*De purgatorio*, 1523), the sacrament of penance (*De satisfactione* and *De initio poenitentiae*, both 1523), and the sacrifice of the Mass (*De sacrificio missae*, 1526); the *Enchiridion* (1525), a manual intended to refute common Protestant errors; cycles of sermons (German and Latin, 1530); and a German translation of the Bible (1537). Two memoirs (*Schutz red*, 1540, and *Replica*, 1543) are polemical tracts that also provide biographical details.

Eck's writings were the most widely distributed anti-Protestant theological works of his generation. He played a major role in convincing Roman Catholic authorities that Luther's teachings were novelties dangerous to the security of the faith. He helped shape the strategy widely used against the Protestants: to take positions representing a medieval consensus and, in defending them, to anticipate possible Protestant objections, avoid scholastic demonstration, and emphasize scriptural arguments.

BIBLIOGRAPHY

Despite its age and some serious flaws, the most satisfactory biography of Eck is still Theodor Wiedemann's *Dr. Johann Eck, Professor der Theologie an der Universität Ingolstadt* (Regensburg, 1865). For a thorough modern treatment of one aspect of Eck's theology, see Erwin Iserloh's *Die Eucharistie in der Darstellung des Johannes Eck* (Münster, 1950). Two exemplary critical editions of works by Eck are *Enchiridion locorum communium adversus Lutherum et alios hostes ecclesiae, 1525–1543*, edited by Pierre Fraenkel (Münster, 1979), and *De sacrificio missae libri tres, 1526*, edited by Erwin Iserloh, Vinzenz Pfnür, and Peter Fabisch (Münster, 1982).

WALTER L. MOORE

ECKHART, JOHANNES (c. 1260–1327?), called Meister Eckhart; German theologian and mystic. Eckhart was born at Hochheim in Thuringia (in present-day East Germany). After entering the Order of Preachers (Dominicans) at Erfurt, he began theological studies in Cologne about 1280, possibly being among the last students of Albertus Magnus. In 1293 Eckhart was in Paris as a young lecturer and in 1302 he held the chair once held by Thomas Aquinas. A versatile personality, Eckhart was chosen in 1303 and in 1307 to be the religious superior of a province of numerous Dominican houses and institutions. During his second teaching period in Paris, after 1311, Eckhart laid the foundations for what he intended to be his great work, the *Opus tripartitum,* a synthesis of commentaries on the Bible, philosophical-theological treatises, and sermons on the Christian life.

In 1314 Eckhart was active in Strassburg, a city rich in theological schools and centers of preaching and mystical prayer. Eckhart, without neglecting his theological teaching (among his students were the famous mystical writers Johannes Tauler and Heinrich Süse), traveled widely to Dominican and Cistercian houses as preacher and spiritual director. By 1322 this demanding apostolate had been transferred up the Rhine to Cologne.

By 1326 Eckhart was under attack for his theology by the archbishop of Cologne. Rivalry between Franciscans and Dominicans; the heated atmosphere of the excesses in piety, as well as the genius of Rhenish mysticism; Eckhart's preaching about God and human personality in a vivid, colloquial German—all contributed to Eckhart's difficulties. Mindful of the accusations leveled previously against Thomas Aquinas, and insulted by a local inquisition presuming to evaluate the Dominicans who stood under papal protection, Eckhart appealed to the papacy, then at Avignon. He spent the remaining months of his life traveling the roads to and from southern France, appealing his case before the papal Curia. In 1329 John XXII concluded formally that seventeen of the articles ascribed to Eckhart (only a sample of the longer list) were to be construed as heretical or supportive of heresy, but the papal document observed that Eckhart, prior to his death, had rejected error. Eckhart's place and time of death remain unknown.

Eckhart's professorial works in Latin together with his popular German sermons develop a single system that is a religious metaphysics of spirit-in-process. Spirit here has a twofold significance. In a daring appropriation of apophatic mysticism, Eckhart defends the otherness of the divine being, that "wilderness" that to us is no-thing. For Eckhart, the Trinity exists only on the surface of the absolute, for the three persons display activity. The ultimate reality of the absolute is "the silent godhead" from which in love enormous processes come forth from transcendent peace. The second manifestation of spirit is human personality. Eckhart, whom some have called the greatest depth psychologist before Freud, describes human life both theoretically and practically as a birth. The true self that is being born in each person is a word of God, just as Jesus, the divine Logos, is a word of God. This birth happens in the midst of a metaphysics of psychological praxis: only by letting the world of finite being and desires be can the individual prepare for the birth at the center of his or her personality (in the "spark" of the psyche) of that new self that is the fulfillment of God's personalized love and of our individualized personality.

Eckhart exercised an extraordinary influence not only upon Tauler and Süse and other Rhenish mystics but also upon Nicholas of Cusa. Martin Luther too admired these and other mystics of the German school from the fourteenth century, but, because of the papal condemnation, he knew them only from anonymous collections. After 1800 the German thinker Franz von Baader rehabilitated a number of mystics, including Eckhart, who then influenced Hegel and, more extensively, Schelling. In the twentieth century, scholarship has discovered more writings of Eckhart, has employed critical methods to verify and comprehend them, and has filled in the picture of a genius of extraordinary depth. Martin Heidegger, both Jungian and Freudian psychologists, and Asian scholars have found Eckhart to be an inescapable voice in philosophy, theology, and personal life. Since 1965 a significant renaissance of interest in Eckhart's work has been taking place in Europe, North America, and Asia.

BIBLIOGRAPHY

Texts of Eckhart's works, in Latin and medieval German, are available in *Die lateinischen Werke* (Stuttgart, 1956–1964) and *Die deutschen Werke* (Stuttgart, 1958–). On Eckhart's life, see Josef Koch's "Kritische Studien zum Leben Meister Eckharts," *Archivum Fratrum Praedicatorum* 29 (1959): 5–15. A bibliography of writings on Eckhart is available in my "An Eckhart Bibliography," *The Thomist* 42 (April 1978): 313–336. There are three new, worthwhile collections of Eckhart in English: Mathew Fox's *Breakthrough: Meister Eckhart's Creation Spirituality* (New York, 1980) offers numerous sermons with commentary and bibliography; Edmund Colledge and Bernard McGinn's *Meister Eckhart: The Essential Sermons, Commentaries, Treatises and Defense* (New York, 1981) offers selections from the Latin and German works, with bibliography; Maurice O. Walshe, in *Sermons and Treatises*, 3 vols. (London, 1980–), presents particularly fine translations. See also *Master Eckhart:*

Parisian Questions and Prologues, translated by Alfred A. Maurer (Toronto, 1974).

THOMAS F. O'MEARA, O.P.

ECOLOGY. The concept of ecology was developed in the study of religion from the 1960s onward. The word *ecology* (from the Greek *oikos,* "house, habitat," and *logos,* "doctrine") is adopted of course from the biological study of the interdependence between organism and natural environment. It later became a methodological tool in geography, sociology (human ecology), and anthropology (cultural ecology). In reference to religious studies, ecology enters as a central concept in two major ways: in a movement for the preservation of nature, that is, religious ecological conservationism; and as a perspective and a method in the study of religion, or ecology of religion. In addition there are different ecological analyses in anthropology and folklore bearing on religion.

Religious Ecological Conservationism

This is a movement among religious groups and thinkers who are concerned about the defilement of nature in modern civilization, calling for man to take responsibility for preserving the ecological balance. It has found its interpretation in some theological works.

Most so-called primitive peoples try to establish a harmonious relationship with their environments. The depreciation of nature in early Western culture had some of its roots in the Hebraic (Semitic) divorce between divinity and nature and in gnostic ascetic tendencies in Near Eastern religions and early Christianity. This negative attitude was given theological and philosophical basis in the works of Thomas Aquinas, Francis Bacon, and René Descartes. The Black Death as well as the great geographical discoveries of the time may have aggravated this indifference to nature. During the Romantic period there was a new inclination toward geopiety among some thinkers and authors, but industrialism, with its efficient, materialistic use of nature, overrode it and stimulated continued alienation. Still, in 1864 George P. Marsh published the first book on the conservation of nature, *Man and Nature,* and a growing feeling for nature and its beauty began to spread.

After World War II, the modern ecological movement burst forth on the scene. As expressed by one writer, John E. Smith, there is now an awareness in the Western world that the view of nature as a resource is destroying nature as a human environment. Models for a new appreciation of the environment have been found in reponses to nature among some non-Western peoples, such as the North American Indians. It has escaped many of these nature lovers, however, that the basic motive behind American Indian environmentalism is the conception of nature as a manifestation of the supernatural or the divine. On the other hand, some theologians (Johannes Aagaard, Gorden D. Kaufman, and others) are convinced that the knowledge of ecological connections and man's place in nature demands a reorientation of modern theology, and a new kind of theological argument has surfaced, sometimes referred to as religious ecological conservatism.

Ecology of Religion

Ecology of religion is the investigation of the relationship between religion and nature conducted through the disciplines of religious studies, history of religion, and anthropology of religion. Other studies, which do not primarily concentrate on religion but affect it secondarily, such as anthropological and folkloristic analyses, will be discussed below.

Development of an Ecological Perspective on Religion. There are two main sources of the modern studies of ecology of religion: geography of religions and cultural ecology.

Geography of religions. The relationship between environment and religion has preoccupied some geographers and culture historians since the eighteenth century. Of particular interest here is Friedrich Ratzel's "anthropogeography," which, at the end of the nineteenth century, sought environmental impact on culture and religion. Sometimes religio-geographical studies led to extreme environmentalism, as for instance with Ellsworth Huntington's analyses of cultural dependence on climatic conditions.

The modern geography of religions, guided by Manfred Büttner, David E. Sopher, and others, is primarily engaged in investigating the influence of religion on environment—in this case, social groups as well as the man-made landscape (sacred groves, temple towns, and so on). For a long time the old task of observing environmental influence on religion was abandoned until cultural ecology opened up new horizons.

Cultural ecology. The historicism and cultural relativism prevalent in the period between the two world wars stimulated the general opinion among anthropologists that environment had a constraining, not a creative influence on culture (the "possibilistic" theory). Environment could allow certain cultural developments, but it could not further them. This attitude slowly changed after World War II, particularly after the American anthropologist Julian H. Steward published a series of articles on what he called cultural ecology. He studied the cultural and economic conditions of the Great Basin Indians of North America, noted for their cultural poverty and exposure to an inhospitable environment, and he found clear correlations between their cultural matrix and environment. The environmental impact seemed primarily to concern the economic and technological aspects of culture, with the social organization affected only indirectly. By extension he discovered similar relationships between nature and culture among other peoples and on other continents. Moreover, he observed cross-cultural regularities among peoples who shared the same basic type of natural habitat, and he was able to state that similar cultural adaptations to environment constituted creative processes of the same cultural type.

This is no simplistic environmental theory. "Cultural adaptation" involves a process in which the cultural heritage plays a major role that indeed grows as environmental dependence diminishes. The closer the cultural is to the environmental, the less important the historical factor will be, and vice versa. In practice this means that religion is a prevailing part of a less adaptable historical heritage. Consequently, there are few references to religion in Steward's methodology.

Steward called his program "cultural ecology," a term chosen to pinpoint the scientific character of the method and its proximity to the social and natural sciences. The culture-ecological model served to explain the process of evolution in cultures ("multilinear evolution"), which actually was his primary concern. In order to realize this goal he established cross-cultural types and investigated the possible transitions between these types through changed environmental integrations.

It may seem that structural operations of the kind indicated here have little meaning for the study of religion. This is a misconception, for, in fact, a religio-ecological model can easily be formed on Steward's culture-ecological model provided that certain changes and shifts of emphasis are made.

The Model of the Ecology of Religion. The ecological debate has proceeded on the foundation laid by Steward in the 1950s. Methodological innovations launched during the intervening years have scarcely improved on his approach to religion through ecology. Steward's model remains the best basis for the development of a method in the ecology of religion.

The rationale for such a method is simple. In its formal aspects every religion is part of culture and thereby subject to the methodological approaches that characterize cultural research, including the ecological approach. The gains are a deeper understanding of the process through which religions are formed and a general knowledge of the sequence of ecologically classifiable types of religion. At the same time, there are two important limitations to religio-ecological studies. First, they are applicable only to so-called primitive cultures, or cultures with a low technological capacity where the environment's impact on culture outweighs technology's (the old German dichotomy of *Naturvölker* versus *Kulturvölker* in part applies here). Second, the ecology of religion cannot replace the history of religion in the discernment of religious content, the formation of religious beliefs, the development of individual myths and rites. It is the organization of religious elements and the structure of religion and its contents that are susceptible to an ecological treatment, and here is where the ecology of religion can achieve real importance.

It stands to reason that any model of the ecology of religion can be used for a materialistic conception of the religious process. The model presented here, first presented in 1965, has been interpreted in this light by some scholars. It need not be used that way, however, and it certainly was not designed to be so interpreted. Ecology of religion presents a broad framework that justifies the operation and intrinsic value of religion, emphasizing not just economy but the total natural environment. The goal is to assess the impact of environment on religion both directly and indirectly; that is, through technological, economic, and material culture, and through the social structure. The methodological model needs to be structured so that it weighs the religio-ecological integration against important historical factors. Indeed, it should allow for the possibility that man's religious life springs from autonomous psychic factors.

Viewed in this way, ecology of religion is a valuable aid in the study of religion. It stresses the creative role of environmental adaptation, for a long time overlooked in religious studies, and at the same time it supplements but does not supplant historical and phenomenological studies of religion. In particular it helps explain some of the basic forms of religion found in primitive or primal cultures.

The strategies of ecological method may be divided into two kinds of operations: studies of particular religions, and comparative ecological studies.

Studies of particular religions. These are ecological studies of particular religions known to the specialist scholar. The aim is to interpret the religion in the light of its ecological relationship with its environment. The investigator will find that the prevailing environmental impact operates indirectly, through a cultural filter of traditional religious ideas. Direct influence is seen in the use of animals and plants as forms of spirits, talismans, and ritual attributes. However, their selection is basically determined by religious value patterns, and they therefore constitute only superficial proof of the direct influence of nature.

It is possible to grade the influence of environment on religion according to the level of integration. In "primary integration" religious elements or complexes are ecologically adapted to basic traits of sustenance and technology—these traits constitute what Steward calls the "cultural core." For instance, in a hunting culture, religious traits associated with hunting demonstrate a primary integration. With "secondary integration" there is an adaptation of religious beliefs and rituals to the social structure, which, in turn, has already been modeled on the ecological adaptation of the cultural core. In other words, ecology first contributes to the formation of the social structure and then, through the social, influences religion. Both primary and secondary integration refer to the structure and organization of religion. "Morphological integration," on the other hand, concerns the particular traits of a given religion: beliefs and rituals are modeled on natural phenomena, and parts of the physical environment are used as ritual paraphernalia.

In observing these changes the scholar should also be aware of a religion's capacity to form the environment (for instance, by an injunction against the killing of animals, as in Jainism and later Indian culture), which actively complicates the religio-ecological process.

Comparative studies of religions. Each ecologically analyzed religion is a manifestation of a cross-cultural, ecological "type of religion," a concept corresponding to Steward's cultural type. The type of religion is determined by religious features that figure in the primary ecological integration, and that are present wherever we find the same economic, technological, and social levels of integration, and the same general ecological setting. Such types of religion are, for instance, the Arctic hunting religion and the semidesert hunting and gathering religion (see below). These types of religion appear without necessary culture-historical connections. Thus, the semidesert hunting and gathering religion may be found in independently originating enclaves in the Great Basin of North America, in Australia, and in the Kalahari Desert. In general profile, organization, and structure, the religions of the Great Basin Shoshoni and Paiute Indians, the Australian Aborigines, and the San are very similar.

Cross-cultural arrangements of ecological types of religion are often related to particular forms of civilization. On the basis of these coordinations it is sometimes possible to follow the shifting types of religion through prehistoric times. The study of cross-cultural types also allows the scholar to closely observe the historical-ecological processes of change involved.

Selected Ecological Types of Religion. As yet there is no index available of the types of religion that have been diffused over the world or succeeded each other historically with changed ecological integrations. (Such changes may proceed from changes in environmental conditions, cultural and social forms, religious structure, and so forth). In general, however, the types appear as specialized religious forms coordinated with the pursuits of hunting, collecting, fishing, agriculture (horticulture), and pastoral nomadism. Here we are not dealing with hypotheses about some kind of economic determinism, but with real integrational processes where the general patterns correlate with environment and ecological conditions, including economic processes. (Even strong idealists like Wilhelm Schmidt and Adolf E. Jensen have proceeded from similar correlations in their culture-historical interpretations.)

The establishment of religio-ecological types presupposes identification at four levels: environmental setting; cultural core and cultural type; religious features associated with the cultural core; and similar ecological, cultural, and religious systems in several places, independent of possible historical relationships. The recurrence of such similarities indicates a common type of religion.

It is impossible here to give more than a summary description of the more fully researched types of religion. Our goal is a general impression of the interplay between environment and religion in primitive cultures, that is, those where the technological basis is too weak to resist the forming pressure of nature in the environmental adaptation process.

Arctic hunting religion. This is a type of religion that is found in the Arctic and sub-Arctic zones from Eurasia to North America. The Arctic is known for its tundra (barren, frozen plains), and the sub-Arctic for its *taiga* (the broad, coniferous belt stretching south of the tundra). Although there are cultural differences, and some religious differences as well, it is possible to view the ethnic groups in the two zones as continuous within the one circumpolar area. The basic cultural core is that of a hunting and fishing culture adapted to climate and fauna (with the aid of skis, snowshoes, dresses, and habitations made from animal skins). The reindeer nomadism of northern Europe and Asia represents a modification of this hunting culture, so recent that it has not considerably changed the hunting structure. [*See* Arctic Religions.]

As for religious features associated with the cultural core, there are the belief and ritual complexes associated with game animals, known as animal ceremonialism—the respect for and veneration of killed animals. This includes the ceremonial killing, eating, and burial of game animals, particularly the bear. Another expression of religious "animalism" is the idea of a master of the animals who protects, withholds, or allows game to be killed. Here also could be mentioned the concept of man's guardian spirit in animal disguise, who helps individuals in times of need. To the Arctic hunting religion also belong cults dedicated to landmarks, mountains, stones, and trees (or wooden pillars), mostly to secure luck in hunting; furthermore, it holds an uranian world view with three to nine cosmic levels, and professes an intense kind of shamanism, presumably encouraged to no small degree by the extreme environment and climate.

Since Arctic hunting religions appear continuously throughout the northernmost areas of the world, they offer unusual opportunities to study the crosscutting influences of historical events and ecological adaptations. Some religious elements, such as the bear cult with its attendant ideas, myths and tales, and rituals, are obviously products of historical diffusion; others, like the stone cult, seem modeled primarily on religio-ecological preconditions. In many cases one cannot tell what the motivating powers could have been while in others it is possible to establish that similar ecological adaptations paved the way for the diffusion of religious features.

Hunting and gathering religions of the semideserts. This type of religion is represented, among other places, in the Great Basin of North America, the Kalahari Desert, and the interior of Australia. It is possible that the nineteenth-century parallels among aboriginal lifestyles in these three regions are the results of convergent developments from lifestyles originally more divergent.

Although there are differences in climate and natural environment, the areas indicated are similar in being very dry with little precipitation, with grass, scattered plants, and lone trees in most places, occasionally yielding to desert. Roots, herbs, berries, nuts, and mostly smaller game make up the food resources. The summer rains in the Kalahari, providing temporary access to herds of large game, constitute an exception to the climatic and environmental monotony. The basic cultural core is a strict adaptation to the gathering of wild seeds, nuts, and berries, and the hunting and collecting of smaller animals. [*See* Khoi and San Religion.]

These religions conform to their culture-ecological situations, except that in Australia there exists a highly developed totemism. Archaeological data suggests that the latter may be a leftover from an earlier, more complex cultural structure. Otherwise the basic religious picture is rather similar among these semidesert peoples: there are group rituals concentrating on gaining food, such as thanksgiving rites or increase rites; supernatural security is sought in the difficult desert existence through the acquisition of guardian spirits, appeals to a supreme being, propitiation of hunting spirits, or initiation into mythical tribal secrets; individual or collective trance experiences are induced in order to gain insight or power to cure the sick; and men have a religiously meaningful relationship to the landscape and its supernatural resources (such as local spirits and totems). [*See* Australian Religions.]

This description fits the Basin Indians and the Australian Aborigines particularly well; since our knowledge of San religion is less complete, some deviations from the general picture are possible.

Pastoral nomadic religion. This type of religion, principally represented in the Old World, once was prevalent in wide areas of Eurasia and Africa. Viewed historically, pastoral nomadism appeared as a concomitant to agricultural development; ecologically it belongs to the steppes, where domesticated animals could graze and migrate between pastoral lands. The horse nomads of the central Asian plateaus offer an excellent example of true pastoral nomadism: their cultural core is characterized by such features as an economy based on horses, sheep, cattle, and camels, the use of portable, felt dwellings, and a collective working organization. Patrilinearity and strong tendencies toward patriarchalism accompany this nuclear structure. [*See* Inner Asian Religions; *see also* Horses.]

Within pastoral nomadic religion there is a close connection with the environmental pattern and its reflections in culture: the significant role of the herd animal (in this case the horse) in the cult, the protection of these animals by a supernatural being, the importance of increase rituals with offerings to the supreme being, and the veneration of stars and landmarks. It is a picture that coincides with ancient Mongol religion, for instance, and it once had a counterpart in the culture of pre-Islamic pastoralists. It is interesting to find parallels among nonnomadic cattle-raising tribes such as those in East Africa: Bruce Lincoln has convincingly shown how their religion closely corresponds to the ancient religion of Indo-Aryan cattle pastoralists. [*See* Indo-European Religions; *see also* Cattle.]

Other Ecological Approaches to Religion

While the religio-ecological approach just described is the methodological key that best serves the ecological interests and ambitions of the historian of religion, there are other approaches that also could seriously attract attention. Two are described here.

Ecological Anthropology. This approach, also labeled "new ecology," was introduced by Andrew B. Vayda and Roy A. Rappaport in the late 1960s. It is a more thoroughly biological view wherein environment, man, culture, and society supposedly constitute one ecosystem. Human populations are part and parcel of this system, just as animal populations are in biological ecology. Religion is represented as a natural part of man's ritual behavior in adjusting to the environment. The importance of tradition is played down, the role of environment is emphasized. Indeed, to the environment is assigned a selective importance that in other ecological approaches belongs to culture. Although Rappaport presents his method as nonreductionist, it is really ecological materialism. However, he can claim that it is meaningless to separate environment from culture (religion) since both are joined together into one unit within the ecosystem.

Whatever the reactions of the student of religion, it is quite certain that Rappaport's works on ecology and religion, mostly regarding the inhabitants of New Guinea, belong to the most astute and intellectually rewarding literature on the subject.

Ecology of Tradition. This approach was launched by Lauri Honko, whose aim is to investigate the adjustment of popular tradition to the milieu in the broadest sense of the word. In contrast to other ecological programs, Honko emphasizes man's role as producer and as carrier of tradition within the ecosystem. This approach is feasible since the subject of the ecology of tradition is not the cultural system as a whole but just tradition itself, of which religious beliefs and rituals may be a part.

[*See also* Geography.]

BIBLIOGRAPHY

The environmentalist approach may be characterized by two works, Friedrich Ratzel's *Anthropogeographie*, 2 vols. (Stuttgart, 1882–1891), and Ellsworth Huntington's *Civilization and Climate*, 3d ed., rev. (1924; Hamden, Conn., 1971).

The conservationist attitude as a theological issue has been dealt with in Gordon D. Kaufman's "A Problem for Theology: The Concept of Nature," *Harvard Theological Review* 65 (1972): 337–366. An interesting discussion of the connections between environment, conservation, and religion in primal culture will be found in *American Indian Environments: Ecological Issues in Native American History*, edited by Christopher Vecsey and Robert W. Venables (Syracuse, N.Y., 1980), particularly in the first chapter on environmental religions by Vecsey.

The geography of religions is well described in David E. Sopher's *Geography of Religions* (Englewood Cliffs, N.J., 1967) and in Manfred Büttner's "On the History and Philosophy of the Geography of Religion in Germany," *Religion* 10 (Spring 1980): 86–119. There is a huge German literature on the subject, by Büttner and others.

The culture-ecological approach was first delineated in Julian H. Steward's *Theory of Culture Change: The Methodology of Multilinear Evolution* (Urbana, Ill., 1955). This is the classic book on which most later approaches are more or less based. It is also the work from which the elaboration of the ecology of religion has proceeded. For the latter approach, see my "Type of Religion in the Arctic Hunting Cultures," in *Hunting and Fishing*, edited by Harald Hvarfner (Luleå, Sweden, 1965). Introductions to the methodology of the ecology of religion with contributions by myself, Svein Bjerke, C. G. Oosthuizen, and others will be found in the section "Religio-ecological Approach," in *Science of Religion: Studies in Methodology*, edited by Lauri Honko (The Hague, 1979), and *Temenos* 21 (1985). A major contribution to a religio-ecological perspective is Bruce Lincoln's *Priests, Warriors, and Cattle: A Study in the Ecology of Religions* (Berkeley, 1981).

The systematic ecological approach where religion functions within an ecological framework (ecological anthropology) is best represented by Roy A. Rappaport's *Ecology, Meaning, and Religion* (Richmond, Calif., 1979), a highly sophisticated but very reductionistic piece of work.

Religion is subsumed under the perspective of ecology of tradition (folklore) in Lauri Honko's "Traditionsekologi: En introduktion," in *Tradition och miljö*, edited by Lauri Honko and Orvar Löfgren (Lund, Sweden, 1981).

Åke Hultkrantz